General Insurance

The Irwin Series in
Insurance and Economic Security

Davis W. Gregg   *Consulting Editor*

Tenth Edition

GENERAL INSURANCE

David L. Bickelhaupt
Professor of Insurance and Finance
College of Administrative Science
The Ohio State University

1979 **RICHARD D. IRWIN, INC.** Homewood, Illinois 60430
Irwin-Dorsey Limited Georgetown, Ontario L7G 4B3

To all the "consumers" of this book—
teachers, their students, and others who
used the first nine editions—and especially
to all those who read this edition.

© BUSINESS PUBLICATIONS, INC., 1936

© RICHARD D. IRWIN, INC., 1942, 1947, 1953, 1957, 1961, 1964, 1970, 1974, and 1979

ISBN 0-256-02150-3
Library of Congress Catalog Card No. 78–72058

Printed in the United States of America

1 2 3 4 5 6 7 8 9 0 A 6 5 4 3 2 1 0 9

One of our young daughters once described my writing work as that of a "book doctor." The analogy is appropriate, especially if the late night hours are compared to those of an obstetrician. The birth of a book is not unlike that of a baby—the conception often easy; the pregnancy long; motherhood sometimes overdue; a subsequent edition somewhat easier (but not much); and actually seeing a healthy final product always appears as a miracle. This pretty much sums up my feelings as I complete this Tenth Edition.

Purpose and uses. *General Insurance* is designed primarily as a text for students who have had no other college course on insurance and risk. As such, it combines basic terminology, principles, and contracts. It is also comprehensive in presenting all-lines insurance, including life, health, property, and liability coverages. Its occasional usefulness for second-level courses in insurance is also expected. After all, courses vary greatly in the class time or credit hours allowed, from perhaps as little as 30 classroom hours in a 10-week quarter to as much as 75 hours in a 15-week semester. (See the suggested assignment schedule for different course lengths, that follows this preface.)

Students, too, vary considerably in their reasons for taking insurance courses. Most are business students who are required (or choose) to take one such course while in college. Increasingly, however, other students are taking these introductory courses, including (1) nonbusiness students who desire only to learn about insurance by becoming more knowledgeable buyers of personal insurance; (2) business students who will be making significant insurance and risk-management decisions as executives or personnel of large and small organizations; and (3) students who are interested in pursuing a wide variety of insurance careers on a professional basis, including those who are studying this book for examinations of the Insurance Institute of America (college credit has been approved for these courses by the American Council on Education) and the Casualty Actuarial Society, and for agents' license examinations in many states.

This text adopts a reasonable approach for the average classroom having many such students together for a normal time of 40–50 hours of instruction. It intentionally avoids being so brief that the student is left with merely a description of *what is,* rather than the better educational objective of understanding *why* things are the way they are. The overall objective is one of *breadth with sufficient depth* of knowledge and understanding.

v

Organization. In Part I Risk, Insurance, and Risk Management, risk is introduced as the foundation for insurance, which is one of the major alternatives used to treat uncertainties in regard to financial losses. The economic significance of insurance in our society is described in Chapter 2, which is followed by a reasonably concise chapter on risk-management decision making, an important consumer trend and viewpoint.

The insurer's viewpoint is stressed in Part II, where the overall relationships among the major functions of insurance organizations are explained in chapters on contract fundamentals, marketing, underwriting and rating, and loss payment. A separate chapter discusses why and how insurance is regulated, which has widespread effects on all insurance operations.

With the background provided by (1) the risk-management consumer and (2) the insurer approaches to the study of insurance, the next two parts provide more specific analysis of the individual kinds of life-health insurance (Part III) and property-liability insurance (Part IV). Separate chapters treat each of the major types of insurance and contracts, primarily for better understanding of the insurance needs and solutions in individual, family, and business consumer situations.

The concluding Part V looks at the future of insurance, reappraising selected examples of the most significant consumer, business, and social uses for the continuing and challenging changes ahead in insurance during the 1980s.

Changes. The process of change is seldom easy, but it *is* necessary. Since the death some 18 years ago of the original author, John F. Magee, I have added and deleted, organized and reorganized, and written and rewritten in order to recognize the many new developments in the business of insurance and its teaching.

Authors are often asked, "Is this a major revision?" and the usual answer is a hearty yes. However, because this revision retains its basic organization of major parts, students and reviewers may see less change than has actually occurred. Part I chapters have been reorganized and consolidated, and the chapters on liability risk and general liability insurance separated. "Change for the mere sake of change" in chapter titles and sequencing has been avoided, but within many chapters the headings and discussion of topics have been changed to clarify relationships and promote understandability.

New sections have been added on such topics as the risk control and risk financing aspects of risk management, cost comparisons in life insurance, variable and adjustable life insurance, the impact of the Pension Reform Act (ERISA), the growth of group dental and vision care insurance, health maintenance organizations (HMOs), national health insurance proposals, the effects of federal tax reform acts on estate planning, product and malpractice liability problems, automobile insurance residual market systems, current auto no-fault insurance laws, the 1978 changes in flood insurance, and the Overseas Private Investment Corporation (OPIC) coverages.

New contracts emphasized include the new readable-type personal auto policy (PAP), the Homeowners' 76 program, and the businessowner's policy (BOP). New issues considered include international insurance, arson problems, the free-trade insurance exchange in New York City, kidnap-ransom, and legal expense insurance.

Tables and figures are frequently used to summarize and condense information and concepts. Newly added, for example, are those which explain the differences among legal types of insurers, illustrate the use of reinsurance, explain the methods of insurance regulation, analyze the fire insurance contract, compare the costs of various homeowners' policies, differentiate among indirect loss coverages, and compare laws which increase payment to auto accident victims.

Teaching aids.   To supplement the insurance contracts illustrated in the text many teachers may wish to obtain sample insurance contracts for their classes from such sources as the Insurance Information Institute (111 William Street, New York, N.Y. 10038) and the American Council of Life Insurance (1850 K St. NW, Washington, D.C. 20006). The use of the annotated outlines at the beginning of each chapter, both before and after reading the text material, has been pointed out as helpful by many readers. Teachers may obtain from the publisher, free of charge, a solutions manual including complete answers to all the essay and objective questions at the end of each chapter. This also includes new visual aids prepared by Michael M. Delaney of the University of Nebraska at Omaha.

Acknowledgments.   Special thanks are due to Eleanor B. Sapp, whose excellent typing enabled me to meet many deadlines during the past year. In addition to many friends who provided information and ideas, I want particularly to thank George L. Head, CPCU, CLU, Director of Risk Management for the Insurance Institute of America, who provided without payment review of each of the chapters in Parts I, II, IV, and V. This was the most valuable and thorough review I have ever seen of any book. It encouraged literally hundreds of changes for which credit properly belongs to him. The responsibility for the final product remains mine, however, and I shall always appreciate hearing from readers who wish to send me other general or specific reactions.

March 1979   **David L. Bickelhaupt**

Suggested assignment schedule
for different course lengths

For 30 class sessions*	For 45 class sessions*	Topic	Chapter
1	1	Risk and risk-treatment alternatives	1
2	2	Insurance and its significance	2
3	3–4	Risk-management decision making	3
4	5	Insurance contract fundamentals	4
5	6–7	Insurance marketing	5
6	8–9	Insurance underwriting, rating, reinsurance, and other functions	6
7	10	Insurance loss payment	7
8	11–12	Insurance regulation	8
9	13–14	Life insurance principles	9
10	15–16	Individual life insurance contracts	10
11	17–18	Life insurance contract features	11
12	19	Annuities and pensions	12
13	20–21	Individual health insurance	13
14	22	Group life and health insurance	14
15	23–24	Government life and health insurance	15
16	25–26	Coordinating life and health insurance	16
17	27–28	Fire insurance	17
18	29	Indirect loss insurance	18
19	30	Transportation insurance	19
20	31	The liability risk	20
21	32	General liability insurance	21

(continued)

---

*The length and number of class sessions are based on the assumption that the normal course will contain either 30 or 45 individual classes of about one hour each, with outside reading assignments in preparation for the classes averaging about two hours each. Some variation of the suggested timing is natural, depending upon the interests of students and teachers, and the desire to use other supplementary materials. Several of the assignments may be easily shortened, if necessary, by omitting a portion of some chapters. In some survey or introductory courses, the teacher may wish to consider omitting Chapters 18, 19, 21, 25, 26, and increasing emphasis on the other chapters.

Contents

PART I
RISK, INSURANCE, AND RISK MANAGEMENT

PART II
THE STRUCTURE AND OPERATIONS OF THE INSURANCE BUSINESS

PART III
LIFE AND HEALTH INSURANCE

PART IV
PROPERTY AND LIABILITY INSURANCE

PART V
THE FUTURE OF INSURANCE

APPENDIXES

List of figures

List of tables

PART I

RISK, INSURANCE, AND RISK MANAGEMENT

Students may wonder why this book, and many other insurance texts, emphasize the concept of risk in early chapters. The reasoning is that without risk there would be no insurance. Thus, a good understanding of risk is essential to the study of insurance, before more extensive discussion of insurance companies and contracts.

The rationale in Part I is first to establish a foundation of knowledge about risk, a basic characteristic of life resulting from uncertainty or variation in regard to financial losses. Chapter 1 explains what *risk* is, classifies the major types of risk, and outlines the major alternatives that are useful in treating risk. Insurance becomes significant because it is a major alternative helping to solve many of the problems that risk creates. Chapter 2 brings this idea into focus, as it reviews how *insurance* works, and the importance of insurance in terms of its history, its various fields, its benefits, and its place in our economic society. Chapter 3 presents the broader and increasingly popular concept of *risk management* as a decision-making process. It includes the place and functions of the risk manager within an organization, the steps in the risk-management process, and examples of coordinated risk treatment.

With the background of Part I, the relevance and organization of the other major parts of this text are clarified. The text proceeds to concentrate on the insurer viewpoint (Part II), to emphasize the consumer viewpoint in the more specific analysis by types of insurance (Parts III and IV), and to look ahead to the future of insurance (Part V).

Chapter 1

Concepts considered in Chapter 1—Risk and risk-treatment alternatives

Risk is *uncertainty of financial loss,* in brief, but there are many kinds.

  Values with which risk is concerned are based on human needs.

  Different reactions to risk and insurance (which reduces risk) occur.

  What risk is becomes the foundation for insurance: differentiated on the basis of *objective* (measurable) and *subjective qualities,* and *variation* between expected and actual results.

  Risk-related terms often confused with risk include: *perils* (causes), *hazards* (acts or conditions which increase loss), and *losses* (decreases in value).

  Classifications of risk are needed in order to study risk properly.

  Speculative and pure risks are distinguished by *loss or gain* versus *loss or no loss* situations (to which insurance applies).

  Personal, property, and liability risks are major types of pure risk.

  Insurable risks must, in total, be substantially *important, accidental, calculable,* and *definite,* and *not excessively catastrophic.*

Why treat risk is a basic question, answered by the facts that *security* is a natural goal, that *direct and indirect losses* are high, and that *other costs* (inefficiency, misestimates, worry) are also great.

Basic methods of treating risk are two: (1) *risk control* (minimizing losses) and (2) *risk financing* (paying for losses that do occur).

  Risk control methods are four:

  Risk avoidance is helpful but limited in application.

  Combination, segregation, and diversification, often used together.

  Loss prevention and reduction, often the first consideration.

  Noninsurance transfers, such as subcontracting and licensing.

  Risk financing methods include two types: (1) *risk retention* and (2) *risk transfer.*

  Risk-retention methods are four:

  Absorption in current operating expense, which is common.

  Funding and reserves, which help meet some perils.

  Deductibles and excess plans, a form of partial retention.

  Self-insurance, sometimes used, but often a misnomer.

  Risk transfer methods include three:

  Credit arrangements, difficult for unpredictable losses.

  Noninsurance transfers, such as hold-harmless agreements.

  Insurance, the predominant method of treating pure risk, is described by *economic* definition as a method of reducing risk by transfer and combination, but also as a *legal* contract, a *business* institution, a *social* device, and a *mathematical* technique.

Risk and risk-treatment alternatives

An understanding of *risk* is the basis of insurance. Thus an insurance book should begin with the concept of risk, an idea familiar to all. Risk is an everyday thing to every person, business, or organization. Generally, risk has to do with the uncertainty of losing, or not gaining, something of value. Risk occurs because of the variation in outcomes or results. Insurance emphasizes the variable results of financial losses. Uncertainty rather than certainty characterizes risk; unpredictability rather than predictability; not knowing rather than knowing.

THE VALUES WITH WHICH RISK IS CONCERNED

What values does risk concern? Many different kinds, including all the goals of life and life itself. These goals begin the complex explanation of human motivation. A well-known psychologist, Abraham Maslow, states a theory of motivation that views behavior as dominated by five levels of needs or wants: (1) survival, (2) safety and security, (3) love and belongingness, (4) esteem, and (5) self-actualization.[1] Once the physiological drives for survival, such as hunger and thirst, are met, decisions are based upon a quest for the other goals. Note that the second level of needs, which is very closely related to the idea of risk, centers on safety and security. A reasonable level of security, including economic, emotional, and other types of stability, is a very common need. Often, attaining this goal in life helps reduce the risk of losing happiness or success.

The third level of needs emphasizes that "no man [or woman] is an island." A successful life, whether measured in dollars or happiness or inner peace, is rarely complete without approval by, or relationship to, other persons or groups. Here love is an excellent example of risk. Like risk, love is all around us, tremendously important, yet difficult to define or predict and hard to get along with—or without. Too much love is bad, and too little is worse. Love can miraculously inspire, or hopelessly frustrate. Risk is much the same in its uncertainty.

---

[1] Abraham H. Maslow, *Motivation and Personality,* 2d ed. (New York: Harper and Row, 1970).

3

Esteem, the fourth level of needs, requires an ego built upon respect, from yourself as well as others. It involves prestige and recognition for achievement, which are difficult goals in the face of natural fears and feelings of inferiority. Self-actualization, the final level in this hierarchy of needs explaining motivation, is the most elusive of all. Trying to change and grow as a person toward personal satisfaction, fulfilling one's highest potential, is perhaps life's most uncertain goal.

All of these motivational needs determine the values with which risk is concerned. The many uncertainties surrounding such goals are the essence of numerous risks. Sometimes these many risks seem contradictory in nature.

DIFFERENT REACTIONS TO RISK

Risk represents both the desirable and the undesirable. Linus, in the famous *Peanuts* comic strip, doesn't want risk. He drags his "security blanket" around continuously in order to have the comfort of something he knows and avoid the unknown real world. His friend Charlie Brown has a perplexing risk, too, as he never knows whether or not the unpredictable Lucy will pull the ball away from him as he attempts to kick off the new football season. Even Charles Schulz as the creator of these successful cartoon characters has risks, as he found out recently when a Russian paper pirated his cartoons.[2] The paper claimed to have no obligation under international law to pay a single kopeck for Charlie's ideas. These examples illustrate the undesirable features of risk—unpredictability or not knowing, insecurity, and some resulting discontent or loss.

But ask business persons about risk! They want it, and it is important to them. They like risk and live by the creed of "nothing ventured, nothing gained." They invest their time, effort, and money for the uncertain profits which may result from their entrepreneurship. Business persons buy and sell, hire and fire, with the hope of profit and the threat of loss in mind. They are risk seekers rather than risk dodgers, with an attitude oftentimes of "What a dull world this would be if everything were known and there were no risks." The feeling is not limited to the business field. The skydiver, the astronaut, and the dragracer have a similar idea. Sir Walter Scott did, too, when he said: "One hour of life ... filled with noble risks, is worth whole years of paltry decorum."[3]

Why is risk so important, yet different, to business persons and to Linus or Charlie? The influence of risk is apparent in the many attitudes toward it, varying from negative to positive reactions. It may result in substantial losses,

---

[2] "Reds Nab Charlie Brown," *Columbus* (Ohio) *Dispatch,* September 13, 1973, p. 15B.

[3] Sir Walter Scott, *Count Robert of Paris,* chap. 25.

worry, and inefficiency. The difference is briefly stated in differentiating between *speculative* risk (uncertainty about *profit or loss* situations) and *pure* risk (uncertainty about *loss or no loss* situations). These are discussed further on later pages in this chapter.

The above examples illustrate the problem of using such a word as *risk* without first finding out what it is. That difficulty describes *insurance*, too, because a tremendous variety of ideas emerges in our everyday use of the term. Basically, it is a system for *reducing risk.* The surprising thing is that insurance is almost hated by some persons, yet highly desired by others. One person thinks of insurance as a tricky legal contract, while to another it is a valuable business, and to still another an important and necessary part of the family budget. The many different connotations suggest that further definitions should be deferred until a basis for understanding has been established.

WHAT RISK IS

A logical basis for such understanding is the concept of *risk,* which is the foundation for insurance. Without risk, there would be no need for insurance. Basically, risk is *uncertainty, or lack of predictability.* It concerns values (usually monetary ones) which may be lost or not gained, and it is the *variation in possible results* which causes risk to occur in so many situations. And what widespread risks do exist! No one ever reaches the state of absolute certainty. From the moment of birth until life has ceased, every individual constantly faces the possibility of unexpected and unwanted happenings.

Examples of risk are everywhere, ranging from the unavoidable to those assumed by choice. Human existence itself creates such risks as not knowing when death, ill health, injury, or unemployment will occur. Examples of risk by choice would be the formation of any form of business enterprise, drilling a new oil well, or investing money in real estate. Indeed, anyone who owns property automatically assumes the risk of such perils as fire, windstorm, theft, or liability lawsuits. The inability to predict[4] when or if these perils may cause losses is a risk that property owners acquire with their ownership.

Persons in the insurance business often use the word *risk* in a different manner to describe the object of potential loss. Thus, a building may be referred to as "the risk" in a fire insurance contract. This is a technical use of the term which should not be confused with the more important general description of what risk is.

---

[4] This aspect of risk, predictability, is emphasized in some definitions. See Davis T. Ratcliffe, "Risk," *Journal of Insurance,* vol. 30, no. 2 (June 1963), pp. 269–70; and "Teaching the Meaning of Risk," *Journal of Risk and Insurance,* vol. 38, no. 3 (September 1971), p. 455. For more thorough discussion of the definition of risk, see *Essays in the Theory of Risk and Insurance,* ed. J. D. Hammond (Glenview, Ill.: Scott, Foresman and Co., 1968).

Uncertainty and risk

Risk concerns *variations* in possible outcomes in a situation. *Uncertainty* is often used as a synonym for risk, although when so used it usually refers to *objective* (measurable or quantified) uncertainty.[5] Economists and statisticians use this concept when they measure variation in occurrences. One such measure of variation called the standard deviation helps predict expected variations from a norm. The predictability of an expected probability actually occurring is increased as the number of events is increased, as will be seen later in the discussion of the principle of large numbers.

Insurance is closely related to variations in losses. Note that risk is *not* merely chance of loss, for anything that is absolutely certain not to happen (0 percent chance of loss) or absolutely certain to happen (100 percent chance of loss) does not involve objective risk. Anywhere between the points of certainty, 0 percent and 100 percent probability of loss, involves some uncertainty and thus risk. For example, the chance of loss may be 10 percent, or one out of ten, that a person will be in the hospital in a given year. Risk exists in this situation because some variation from the one-in-ten probability will occur.

The *degree* of risk is measured by variation between the expected (probable) results and the actual results. In the above example, there is a greater degree of risk when the percentage of variation is high. If one employer has ten employees, he cannot be very certain that only one will be in the hospital that year. However, an employer with 100,000 employees can reasonably predict that 10,000, or very close to this number, will be in the hospital. The actual variation from the expected number hospitalized will be slight (a lower percentage than in the case of only ten employees), and the degree of risk will be low.

Subjective uncertainty, which involves a feeling or state of mind as to expected results, differs from the above concept of objective uncertainty. Lack of knowledge as to the real facts, prejudices, unwarranted high hopes, and other factors can cause different predictions. Therefore different subjective risks occur, and these often deviate from the underlying objective risk. This kind of uncertainty is not readily measurable and is not usually what is meant when the term *risk* is used.

Economic risk

Are all risks economic? One might rush to answer yes, but a second thought would suggest that although most risks have financial consequences,

---

[5] The classic treatment of this subject is found in Alan H. Willett, *The Economic Theory of Risk and Insurance* (Philadelphia: University of Pennsylvania Press, 1951), pp. 5–6; and Frank H. Knight, *Risk, Uncertainty, and Profit* (Boston: Houghton Mifflin Co., 1921), pp. 233–34.

not all necessarily do. Moral, spiritual, and other risks could be identified, as well as the more obvious loss of economic values. Many definitions of risk refer to it as uncertainty *of financial loss*. For insurance, this is the major concern about risk.

RISK-RELATED TERMS

Terminology becomes important in the serious study of any subject. It is the basis for communication and understanding. Terms that are loosely used in a general or colloquial sense can lead only to misunderstanding in a specialized study area such as insurance. See Figure 1–1, showing the relationship among these terms and risk.

Perils

In contrast to risk, which is the uncertainty of loss (or results or happenings), the word *peril* should be used to identify the *cause* of risk. Examples of perils are commonplace and include fires, automobile accidents, thefts, earthquakes, windstorms, forgeries, water, illness, and hundreds of other causes of uncertainty.

A classic use of the word is that in the *"Perils* of Pauline," the hair-raising silent movie melodramas in which poor Pauline was caused great uncertainty as to her life and limb.

The law has coined the term *acts of God* to describe perils operating without human agency or intervention and not preventable by human foresight or care. Fires caused by lightning are often so considered, as are storms, extraordinary floods, and other forces of nature.

Hazards

The various *acts or conditions which increase the likelihood or severity of a loss* are termed *hazards*. Ordinarily, many separate hazards attach to any particular object or person. The sum total of the hazards constitutes the perils which cause the risk.

A practice of the insurance business divides hazards into two major classifications. The first of these is termed *physical hazards,* and this classification includes everything relating to location, structure, occupancy, exposure, and the like. The term *moral hazards* is applied to those factors that have their inception in mental attitudes. Included in this second group are the hazards created by dishonesty, insanity, carelessness, indifference, and other causes that are psychological in nature.

Physical hazards. Physical hazards include conditions such as these: wastepaper piled under a staircase, gasoline stored on the premises, weak

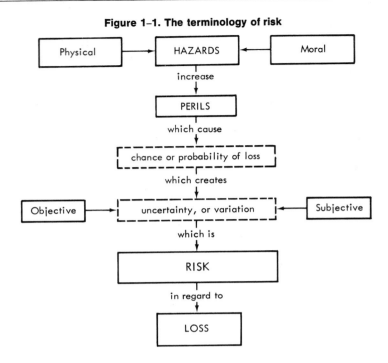

Figure 1-1. The terminology of risk

construction which may fail in a heavy wind, unsafe brakes on a car, holes in a sidewalk, inadequate inventory checks in a store, and improper water drainage systems. Each of these conditions, as well as many others, would increase the chance of a loss occurring in regard to a specific peril such as fire, wind, water, theft, or other accident.

Insurance involves an evaluation of all the hazards and of the loss-prevention facilities for minimizing the loss in the event of the happening of the peril insured against. Measuring the hazard is the task of insurance rating or pricing.

Moral hazards.   The term *moral* is applied to that group of hazards which grows out of the *mental attitudes* of individuals. Carelessness or mental instability most decidedly contribute to a risk. While the term *psychological* might be more apt, a reason for the term *moral* is found in the fact that particular emphasis is given to dishonest acts and to fraud through the deliberate destruction of insured property. The term *moral hazard* is in no way limited, however, to cases involving moral instability but includes in its scope all factors contributing to risk that are mental in their nature.

Appraisal of moral hazard requires the study of the character and reputation of the person under consideration for insurance. Evidence pointing to the fact that an insured ever defrauded any other person, or had a previous bankruptcy record, is an indication of possible moral hazard in regard to insurance. Investigators also concern themselves with insureds' reputation in trade, their rating with the banks, their standing with competitors, and finally the regard in which they are held by those with whom they transact business. Individuals who have a reputation for taking unfair advantage of legal technicalities or who have repudiated contracts in the face of possible financial loss are regarded as likely to resort to other unethical methods. Finally, in the moral hazard category are to be found those abnormal mental cases known as "pyromaniacs," individuals who act under an irresistible impulse to set fires.

A distinction is sometimes made between *moral* and *morale* hazards, including as examples of increasing chance of loss such morale conditions as carelessness and indifference. Laziness, disorderliness, and lack of concern for others are termed morale problems rather than moral problems (problems involving dishonesty). Leaving car doors unlocked increases automobile thefts; bad smoking habits increase fire losses; and hurried, unthinking action can cause many personal injuries.

Losses

An economic *loss* is the undesirable end result of risk. It is the *decrease or disappearance of value,* usually in an unexpected or at least relatively unpredictable manner. In general terms, not all losses are related to risk; some losses are the result of intentional actions, as for example the gift of property to someone. Other losses may be expected because they are known always to occur, such as depreciation of physical properties which can be expected as well as predicted fairly accurately. Many losses, however, cannot be predicted and become the result of risks. Illustrations include loss of property due to fire or theft or other perils, loss of income due to property destruction or personal perils of death or disability, increased expenses such as medical costs, and loss of assets due to legal liability for losses affecting other persons.

An example of the relationship among the terms discussed in this section is as follows: Mr. Rich owns a Chris-Craft cabin cruiser. He knows that some (1) *hazards* (contributing factors) such as the captain's negligence or structural faults of the ship contribute to (2) *perils* (causes of risk) such as fire, collision, or sinking, which cause (3) *risk* (uncertainty of financial loss), which may result in (4) *loss* (decrease in value). The hazard of the captain's inattention to rocks and shallow water may contribute to the peril of collision and the risk or uncertainty of having a financial loss or repair bill of $5,000 to the ship.

Figure 1-2. The classifications of risk

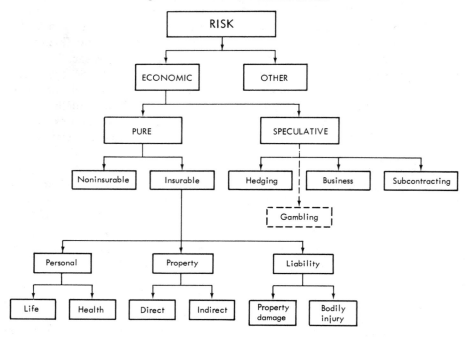

CLASSIFICATIONS OF RISK

Speculative and pure risks

Two basic kinds of economic risks are (*a*) speculative risks and (*b*) pure risks.[6] See Figure 1–2 for a diagram of the classifications of risk in this section. *Speculative* risks involve the chance of *loss or gain,* whereas in *pure* risks there is only the chance of *loss or no loss.*

Pure risks are "pure" in the sense that they do not mix both profits and losses. The business of insurance is concerned with the economic problems created by pure risk. The introduction to this chapter contrasted the businessperson's attitude toward risk with that of Linus and Charlie Brown in the comic strip *Peanuts.* The risk seeking by businesspersons is for speculative risk, with the purpose being the prospect of gain if the business venture is successful. The risk aversion by the comic strip characters is for pure risk,

---

[6] Basic types of risk are also differentiated as "fundamental" (those universal and impersonal) and "particular" (those individual and personal). Another distinction is sometimes made between "dynamic" and "static" risks, but an understanding of "speculative" and "pure" risks is more meaningful in most discussions about risk.

with the prospect of loss being the unhappy result of the giving up of Linus' "security blanket" or Charlie's football-kicking episodes. A more common example of pure risk is that found in ownership of property. In regard to such a peril as windstorm, the owner may either suffer a loss or not have a loss. There cannot be a gain from having the loss (if insurance is involved, it is assumed that payment is *not* for more than actual loss).

Because *speculative risk* involves an element of both profit and loss, it may sometimes be nullified by a process known as *hedging*. Hedging is a procedure by which two compensating or offsetting transactions are used to assure a position of "breaking even." For example, a manufacturer who buys raw material may suffer a loss if the price of the raw material falls before the finished product is offered on the market. If the price of the raw material rises, a speculative profit will result, but a manufacturer is in business to make a profit on production and not on cost changes. The speculative risk may be avoided by "selling short" a commodity contract for delivery of an equal amount of raw material at a stated price at about market time for the finished product. The manufacturer will lose on the short sale if prices for raw materials advance, but gain if prices of raw materials decline. The net result of the hedging contract of short sale is to eliminate speculative risk on the cost of raw material when the goods are sold.

The hedging process is not always available, for it depends on the existence of an active commodity futures market. The futures market is well developed for some goods within certain time limits, but unavailable for many other goods. The result of hedging is similar to a "hedged" bet, where after a bet is made, the bettor doesn't want to keep the risk and makes an opposite bet for exactly the same amount and odds.

Subcontracting is another example of avoiding speculative risk, in which a general contractor obtains contracts at fixed prices for parts of the total job to be completed in the future.

The presence of a risk as an *existing* condition is the factor that removes insurance from the category of a *gambling* risk, a special type of speculation. Insurance does not create risk, but transfers and reduces risk already in existence. Contrasted to this is a bet; no risk exists before, but one is *created* at the time of the gambling transaction, putting values at risk that were not in jeopardy before the bet.

Gambling operations may involve many of the attributes of insurance, such as large numbers, spread and homogeneity of risk, and predictability. Probably this is the reason so many uninformed persons think of insurance as gambling and sometimes even feel that they have "lost the bet" if they fail to have a loss equal to the cost of insurance. The distinction is not in the method of operation, which may appear similar, but in the fact that insurance concerns itself with an existing risk. Speculation and insurance are both based upon socially and economically useful risks, too, while gambling is generally regarded as a less desirable method of speculation.

Personal, property, and liability risks

The risks confronting human beings are ordinarily divided into three classifications: (*a*) risks involving the person, (*b*) risks involving loss or damage to property (including indirect loss of income), and (*c*) risks involving liability for the injury to the person or property of others. Figure 1–2 shows this relationship.

The first of these classifications of risk is ordinarily termed *personal* and is chiefly concerned with the time of death or disability. Of death there is no uncertainty; but the time of its occurrence is uncertain. And aside from death, there is the risk of incapacity through accidental injury, illness, or old age. Personal risks are often divided into *life* and *health* risks. Sometimes they are called "personnel" exposures.

The second classification of risk is that which arises from the destruction of *property*. The possible loss of a cargo or ship at sea is considered a risk to those engaged in maritime operations. *Direct* losses by fire, lightning, windstorm, flood, and other forces of nature offer a constant threat of loss to real estate, as well as all kinds of personal property and property involved in any form of transportation. *Indirect* losses also may occur, including the loss of profits, rents, or favorable leases.

The third classification of risk is occasioned by the operation of the law of *liability*. An individual may be legally liable for an injury to another, as, for instance, through an accident when the driver of an automobile is negligent and injures a pedestrian, or when a person is injured on someone's property. Such a risk is termed a "third-party" risk because when insurance is used to shift the burden of responsibility, the insurer and the insured person have agreed that a "third party" (the injured person) will be paid for injuries for which the insured is legally liable. The liability risk includes both *bodily injury* and *property damage* risks.

Insurable risks

Not all risks are *insurable*. In order to be considered insurable, a risk must substantially meet the five requirements outlined below: (1) importance, (2) accidental in nature, (3) calculability, (4) definiteness of loss, and (5) no excessively catastrophic loss. Many insured risks do not meet each of the requirements perfectly, but when considered as a whole they may meet the requisites adequately.

Importance.   Because of the element of expense in carrying on the business of insurance, premiums include a charge to provide for this cost. In the case of small risks that involve a threat of no great consequence, the cost of handling the business would make the rate prohibitive. For example, a pen may be lost or eyeglasses broken. To make a risk insurable, the amount of loss must be of such *importance* as to make the cost element a minor factor in the premium charged.

Accidental nature. Insurable risks must also normally be *accidental* in nature. Insurance is intended to cover fortuitous or unexpected losses. The loss need only be accidental *from the standpoint of the insured.* (It could, for example, be intentionally caused by someone else, such as a thief or a vandal.) Intentional losses caused by the insured are usually uninsurable because they cannot be reasonably predicted, and payment for them would violate public policy by encouraging such actions as fraud or arson. Other losses are so common as to be expected rather than unexpected. Wear and tear and depreciation are examples.

Calculability. A third requisite of an insurable risk is that it be *calculable.* It must permit a reasonable statistical estimate of the chance of loss and possible variations from the estimate. Losses may sometimes be unpredictable to an individual, but be predictable in the aggregate and thus become insurable for a group. As a corollary to this requirement, the risk must be one of which there are a *large number* in existence, though insurers occasionally cover isolated risks concerning which there is no previous experience. For example, aviation insurers are faced with the necessity of providing insurance that will keep pace with the rapid advances in the field. The advent of jet- and rocket-propelled aircraft created a need for insurance in a field where statistical data were entirely lacking. The same is now true for the supersonic (SST) aircraft, where $50 million or more may be the cost of each plane. Most insurance is written, however, to cover risks where losses may reasonably be expected and where mathematical treatment or judgment based upon experience permits an estimate of losses sufficiently exact to make possible a workable estimate of their probable cost. When experience extends over a number of years and the number of risks is great enough, a premium can be computed that will assure a sum sufficient to pay losses and compensate the insurer, and provide stability and permanence in the business. When new insurance forms are instituted, it becomes necessary to make rates that are dependent upon what is sometimes called "underwriting judgment," and in some instances this is nothing more than an approximation or guess to be adjusted with the accumulation of experience.

Other requirements for an insurable risk also relate to the prime requisite that the risk must be reasonably calculable. The need for large numbers applies not only for total risks accepted by an insurer but must also be met within each class of risks. Thus a large number of *homogeneous,* or similar, exposures to loss must be present to make a risk insurable. The exposures must also be *independent* of one another, so that reasonable estimates of loss can be made.

Definiteness of loss. The losses should be *definite,* for otherwise estimates of possible loss are difficult. Many insurance contract provisions have the objective of making the insured losses as clear and definite as possible. The perils as well as the losses must be clarified in the contract. Whether or not the loss actually occurred, and if so how many dollars of loss were involved, must be discernible.

No excessively catastrophic loss. Ordinarily, no excessive *catastrophe* (very large) possibility of loss should be associated with an insurable risk. Accepting a few such risks together with smaller risks would make accurate predictions of loss impossible and could destroy the financial stability of an insurer. Today many losses are called catastrophic if they exceed $1 million, but for most insurers losses are not excessively catastrophic unless many millions of dollars are involved. Nuclear and war risks are examples. What size loss is deemed catastrophic depends upon the financial resources available.

In total. The student should note that these requirements for an insurable risk are not absolute. Insurability is best described as a relative matter in which the insurable quality of the risk is determined by appraisal of all the requirements together. The size and ability of the insurer are also important. Many common kinds of insurance do not meet each of the requirements perfectly. Consider, for example, the following: Is theft insurance "definite" (that is, was the item really stolen, or just lost)? Are all drivers "similar" in regard to risk of automobile accidents? (Obviously not, though they may be relatively similar within age, type of car, and other classifications.) Is a fire caused by carelessness always "accidental"? Aren't windstorms such as hurricanes and tornadoes "catastrophic" in nature?

Careful analysis in applying each of the requirements for an insurable risk to a particular peril shows that few, if any, are "perfect" insurable risks. Most are only relatively good ones, and some are fine examples of bad ones. Many contract and insurer underwriting restrictions deal with this problem, trying to improve the insurability of a peril by such methods as limitations on the amount of coverage and locations, prohibited types, specific contract definitions, deductibles, and reinsurance. What is "insurable" may change over time and with the use of such limitations. Flood damage, for example, was considered uninsurable for many years, but it may now be insured in many areas through a federal government insurance program.

WHY TREAT RISK?

Studying risk and insurance is suggested in Part I to answer the following questions: *What* is risk, *why* treat risk, and *how* may risk be treated? (Chapter 1). *How* significant is insurance in this process? (Chapter 2). *What* is risk management, and *how* are risk-management decisions made? (Chapter 3).

In classifying the types of risk, some possible answers to these questions have already been suggested. Speculative and pure risk were distinguished, so that the emphasis was placed upon pure risks, involving chance of loss or no loss, but not those risks having profit as a predominant feature. Hedging was explained as one example of a method for dealing with speculative risk. Gambling risks were excluded from consideration because they involve the creation of risk rather than the treatment of existing economic risk. The concept of insurable risks was emphasized. One might think that an insurance text could stop right there and conclude that insurance is *the* answer to the problem of handling risk. No such easy, pat answer is intended, for no risk in theory or in practice should be handled with insurance as a perfunctory solution. A proper solution should include full consideration of all the available alternatives for dealing with risk, after an understanding of why treating risk is so often necessary.

Security a natural goal

The quest for security, or reasonable certainty, is a basic human drive. The concern is natural—a desire for knowing that the future will provide the necessities of life (and perhaps some luxuries, too).

Risk, or uncertainty of financial loss, is a threat to those future needs and wants. The values with which risk is concerned were discussed at the beginning of this chapter. Perils can destroy or damage assets and interrupt or terminate income. Such losses can decrease the future enjoyment of life, and this is why most persons prefer to do something about risk rather than merely accept it as is.

Losses from pure risk

This reaction to risk is particularly appropriate in regard to pure risk. The future result is either loss or no loss. The loss may be serious, crippling a business or causing an individual or family great financial hardship. One type of loss is *direct* physical loss, such as fire damage, which results in almost $4 billion of *property* loss each year in the United States. *Indirect* loss is also considerable, such as lost profits following a direct loss. Billions of dollars are lost, too, because of the loss of human *life* values due to such perils as death and disability.

Other costs of pure risk

In addition to actual losses, other undesirable results stem from risk. At least three factors add to the cost of risk: (1) *inefficient investment of assets* held to meet uncertainties, (2) *misestimates of chance of loss,* and (3) *worry.*

Uncertainty itself is a costly thing, *even if no losses ever occur* as anticipated. That amount of money "put away for a rainy day" may have to be put in very safe investments in order to be readily available if and when it does rain (or some other peril causes loss). Without such uncertainty, perhaps the money could be invested in a much more productive capacity with consequent greater return.

Uncertainty involves many situations where estimates of the probability of loss are necessary. Most persons will not predict the chance of loss correctly: some will be pessimistic and overestimate; others will be optimistic and underestimate. The result is either wasteful preparations for losses that are not as likely as expected or lack of preparation for unexpected losses that may have serious financial consequences.

Worry is also a very costly item. The time spent in thinking about real or imagined chances of loss is expensive. The "opportunity cost" of worry time and effort is probably staggering when one considers the many other things that could be done if there were no fear of loss. "If we only could work as hard as we worry" is an expression that indicates the cost of lost peace of mind.

In total, the cost of risk is high and interest in the methods by which risk can be treated is logical.

BASIC METHODS OF TREATING RISK

Two basic methods of treating risk are: (1) *risk control,* in order to minimize losses, and (2) *risk financing,* in order to reduce the costs of those losses which do occur.[7] In almost all cases it is not merely a choice of using risk control *or* risk financing, but good risk management requires the use of some of *both* methods of treating risk.

Risk *control* involves a number of alternatives, and here again the choice is not limited to just one of them. The goal is the proper *choices,* using all the methods which result in benefits that exceed the costs. Many organizations use all or many of the techniques in order to best handle the diverse types of risk that have been discussed in this chapter. The alternatives include: (1) *risk avoidance*; (2) *separation, diversification,* or *combination* of loss exposures; (3) *loss prevention and reduction*; and (4) some *noninsurance transfer of loss.*

Risk *financing* also includes many alternatives which can be used separately or in conjunction with one another and with the previously identified risk control measures. Financing methods are subdivided into two categories: *risk retention* and *risk transfer.* Risk retention helps provide different types of funding when paying for losses: absorption in expenses, special reserves,

---

[7] The development of this classification of methods for treating risk is credited to Dr. George L. Head. It has been adopted by the Insurance Institute of America for its RM 54, 55, and 56 courses leading to the Associate in Risk Management national professional designation. For a thorough treatment of these concepts, see Dr. Head's *The Risk Management Process* (New York: Risk and Insurance Management Society, 1978).

"self-insurance," (and "captive" insurers), and deductibles. The most common technique of risk transfer is *insurance,* but some *noninsurance transfers* of risk and *credit* mechanisms are also useful.

The following sections discuss each of the methods of risk control and risk financing separately. Chapter 3 emphasizes these methods of treating risk in the broader context of the process of *risk management,* a decision-making process by which risks are identified and measured, and then the choices among risk control and risk financing methods are made and carried out. Figure 3–3 there summarizes these alternatives in relation to the four steps in risk management.

Risk control methods

Different ways of subdividing the major methods of risk control are possible. A four-fold subdivision is discussed within this section of the chapter. The emphasis of each method is on achieving the purpose of minimizing losses which might occur to assets and income.

Risk avoidance.   One of the most obvious methods of handling risk is to *avoid* as many risks as possible. If one does not want to have to try to predict economic losses, *some* losses can be avoided by various decisions in everyday life. A family can decide to rent rather than buy a home, thereby avoiding the risk of losing the home value through the peril of fire. A business may lease its automobiles and avoid assuming the risk of losing those values (even though it may be accepting in the lease another risk—that of legal liability for returning the automobiles in good condition). A person who is worried about poisonous snakebites or heat exhaustion can live in the Arctic, or at least locate in areas with a minimum of risk from such perils. The risk of airplane accidents, drownings, and sports injuries can be avoided largely by keeping away from airplanes, water, and sport events, respectively.

However, avoidance of risk is no practical solution to the many risks that are involved in normal activities. True, some unusual risks with high chance of loss can be avoided, but realistically the avoidance of risk is only an alternative in regard to a restricted number of economic risks. For all the other risks other solutions must be considered.

Combination, segregation, and diversification.   *Combination,* or pooling, of exposures to loss is a common method of risk control. This method broadens the units of exposure and may aid in predicting future losses. It may "spread the risk" and create more stability in loss experience. Combination is a basic principle of insurance and "self-insurance," and it may also be used in many other business situations. For example, the corporation as a typical form of doing business combines the assets of many stockholders and spreads exposure to loss from a few individuals to thousands of investors. Also, mergers of companies combine many different exposures to loss. Growth within a business firm also combines and extends the scope of loss exposures, when, for example, a business expands its marketing by adding new sales outlets. Employees, too, use combination as a method of reducing risk when they join to practice collective bargaining through unions.

The examples are numerous, but usually the combination process has to be used in conjunction with other methods described here. For example, in order to be most effective, combination of exposures is used *with* segregation and diversification or with other methods of risk financing. The mere combining of exposures is not effective in reducing risk. In fact, it may increase more than it decreases risk if the added exposures are more concentrated or variable than the previous exposures.

Among the simplest but most important methods of risk control are segregation and diversification. *Segregation,* the separation or dispersion of loss exposures, is often an effective way of limiting the severity of loss by reducing the concentration of exposures. It may also increase the number of exposure units. *Diversification* uses different types of loss exposures, as opposed to having only one type, in order to improve on predictability (usually frequency). When assets or activities are duplicated at different locations, the diversification technique is being used.

Common business examples of segregation and diversification (in parentheses) are:

1. Physically separating buildings (and using masonry as well as wood buildings).
2. Using fireproof interior building construction, such fire walls and incombustible and smokeproof stairwells and elevators.
3. Storing inventory in several locations (and types of buildings).
4. Maintaining duplicate records to reduce accounts receivable losses (and using paper as well as microfilm records).
5. Transporting goods in separate vehicles instead of concentrating high values in single shipments (and shipping by truck, railroad, and air).
6. Limiting money exposures at any one location.
7. Prohibiting key employees from traveling together (and using different transportation conveyances).
8. Limiting legal liability by forming several separate corporations.

Classic examples of the *failure* to use segregation and diversification are found in catastrophic fires, such as those that took place at a Linden, New Jersey, oil refinery (1970—$50 million), a New York telephone central office (1975—$70 million), and in Santa Barbara, California, where 200 homes were destroyed by fire in 1977. The Tokyo airplane crash which killed over 70 key employees and agents of one sales firm a number of years ago and explosions in large grain elevators in 1976–78 are also examples of catastrophic losses due to the lack of segregation and diversification.

Loss prevention and reduction. Two methods of risk control, loss prevention and loss reduction, could be discussed separately, but they are combined in this section because they are so closely related to each other. Techniques which help prevent or reduce loss are often logical and important, for losses are seldom completely taken care of by any one method of treating risk. The total effects of loss are usually much greater than the indemnification available through insurance or any other alternative; thus, preventing or reducing the loss is just good common sense if it can be done with reasonable cost in relation to its potential benefits. In some cases, such as saving lives or preventing human injury and suffering, cost may be a secondary factor.

Loss prevention may involve the elimination of the chance of loss and thus *risk*; more often, a reduction in the *probability* of loss is accomplished. *Loss reduction* has the goal of reducing the severity of loss, and it includes steps taken to accomplish this either before or after loss.

Loss prevention and loss reduction are not the same thing as *risk* reduction. The uncertainty (risk) of variable losses may still be the same, even though the chance of decreasing value (loss) is reduced or there is a reduction of the conditions increasing the ratio of the likelihood of loss (hazards) to the cause of loss (peril). For example, reducing the probability of loss from 10 percent to 5 percent does not necessarily reduce either risk or the variation in expected as compared with actual results at these two loss probabilities.

The topic of loss prevention and reduction is so large that only a brief mention can be made here of the many techniques available to agents, brokers, consultants, insurers, and insureds. Fire-resistive structures are built. Protective devices are installed in boilers. Lightning rods are installed. Safety devices guard much industrial machinery. Such firms as Underwriters' Laboratories inspect most electrical appliances. Construction is aimed at the reduction or elimination of tornado, earthquake, and hurricane losses. Most of these activities take place *before* losses occur. Loss reduction methods that are used after losses happen include the prompt investigation, reporting, and settlement of claims. Another method is the use of salvage companies to sell damaged goods.

Steps to prevent and reduce losses are the result of both private and community undertakings. Some of the larger projects, such as those involving flood control, are carried on by the federal government. Public measures for loss prevention and reduction also include police and fire protection and municipal building codes. An important question in regard to these activities is to determine who should be *responsible* for them. In total, it becomes in most cases a joint responsibility of (1) government, (2) insurers, (3) private organizations, and (4) the insureds themselves.

The sources of information on loss prevention and reduction are myriad: hundreds of booklets on specific problems in loss prevention are available through the National Fire Protection Association, the Insurance Institute for Highway Safety, engineering journals, and many other sources. A new government source is the National Highway Traffic Safety Administration. Another is the Occupational Safety and Health Administration, which has made thousands of inspections of employers since its inception in 1971. Given sufficient funds and ingenuity, the extent of loss prevention and reduction can be almost limitless. Insurers, agents, and specialized loss prevention businesses can aid their clients considerably in this process.

Noninsurance transfers. The final method of risk control involves *noninsurance transfers*. Such transfers are effected by means of a contract, other than insurance, in which one party transfers to another *legal responsibility* for losses. A later section will discuss other noninsurance transfers which are methods of risk financing rather than risk control. These transfer the *financial burden* of the transferor. The transferor receives payment for losses from the transferee (or they are paid on behalf of the transferor), but the ultimate responsibility for the losses remains with the original party to the contract. *Subcontracting* is one important example. As an illustration, a contractor may wish to transfer the possibility of injury to the contractor's employees in a particularly dangerous part of a construction project. This may be done by hiring subcontractors to do that work, under contracts in which the subcontractors hire their own employees. The responsibility for these employees is, by contract, transferred to the subcontractors, who would be obligated to pay workers' compensation losses. (Some responsibility for losses to members of the public as a result of the construction might also be transferred, but the transfer is seldom complete.)

A manufacturer could use another method of noninsurance transfer, that of *licensing*. If the manufacturer does not want to produce or sell certain goods, and wishes to transfer some of the responsibilities of these tasks to someone else, this may be done in licensing contracts. Under these arrangements, the manufacturer would receive only a royalty or fee for licensing others to do the work. The licensees would have the responsibility for injuries to their own employees. In addition, some protection might be achieved in reducing the exposure to liability losses from the public, either in the manufacturing or the distribution of the product.

Risk financing methods

In most cases, losses are only lessened by the methods of risk control just discussed. The one exception is risk avoidance, in which the probability of loss, and thus risk, is eliminated. Under all the other techniques, losses still occur—and some additional choices are necessary in deciding how to pay for them. These alternatives are the methods of *risk financing,* explained in the following sections.

Most losses of any importance require a combination of these alternative financing methods, often in conjunction with risk control measures as well. Risk financing may be divided into two major types: (1) risk retention and (2) risk transfer. In each of these major areas, several significant methods of risk financing are recognized.

Risk retention.   If risk has not been avoided, you may decide to keep it. Sometimes this is called "risk assumption," but *risk retention* seems the better term because you retain rather than newly assume the many risks which you already have. The residual risks must in some way be paid for, or financed.

Probably more pure risks are retained due to *lack* of planning than due to any rational process of planning. Some risks are retained because the existence or significance of the risks is not known. Lack of knowledge or inability to reach the right decision (even with adequate knowledge) may result in retention of risks. Information may be available and not used, or perhaps the necessary information is unavailable. An illustration is retaining the risk of loss to property by falling meteors (or perhaps flying saucers?) because of (1) not knowing anything about meteors, or that a possibility of loss from this source exists, or (2) not knowing that insurance could be obtained for such a peril. *Unplanned* retention of risk might also result from unintentional or irrational action or from passive behavior due to lack of thought, laziness, or lack of interest in discovering uncertainties of loss.

Some *unimportant* risks may be intentionally ignored. This is not considered a method of treating risk but instead a method of *not* treating it. For example, the loss of a glove or pen may cause no financial hardship to an individual, so the risk of loss is ignored and no plan for occurrence of the loss is made. Similarly, a business may decide that smaller buildings or properties are of relative unimportance and knowingly ignore any payment plans for such insignificant risks.

Important risks regarding those losses that could cause financial hardship for a family or business must be paid for in some appropriate manner. *Planned* risk retention is one method, occurring when it is the result of purposeful, conscious, intentional, and active behavior.

The *why* of risk retention is based upon this fundamental question: "What reasons are there for using retention?" These include (1) necessity, where other alternatives are not possible; (2) control or convenience; and (3) cost. The first reason is that risk retention must be used; the second and third should result from a conscious effort to analyze the benefits of retention in terms of control, convenience, or cost, and the ability of individuals or business firms to handle their own risks effectively.

Some pure risks can only be financed by retention. They are knowingly retained by *necessity,* or default, as it is impossible to transfer them. Typical examples of such risks are responsibility for criminal acts and unusual obsolescence of property. Occasionally, a peril that is normally insured against may be uninsurable because of high probability of loss or bad loss experience. This category of retained risks is relatively small, for the transfer of most risks (at some price, even if very high) is usually possible. Sometimes markets for insurance are temporarily unavailable, and retention is necessary until the competitive world markets make adjustments permitting risk transfer. Examples are offshore oil drilling equipment in recent years and extremely poor substandard housing in blighted urban areas.

Retention of risk may be practiced by some individuals or business firms because they wish to have the *control or convenience* of paying their own losses. Regardless of cost comparison, some firms may wish to have the benefits of direct and complete control. Hospital expenses of employees, for example, may be paid directly by the employer in order to obtain the most rapid payment possible and employee goodwill. Or, a manufacturer in a competitive technical field might decide to retain both property and products liability exposures in connection with highly secret inventions of a research laboratory.

The economics of alternative risk treatment are a major consideration in most decisions to retain risk. A comparison of the *cost* involved in each alternative method of financing losses is necessary. If insurance against earthquake damage is available, how much will it cost? If earthquake damage could be prevented by extra-strong building construction, how much would this cost? Would a "self-insurance" program with a reserve fund be feasible, and what would its cost be? In each of these comparisons the need for complete evaluation is obvious. Not only loss frequency and severity but *all* costs of the various alternatives, including indirect[8] as well as direct costs, are needed for fair comparisons.

The time, effort, and cost required to make a reasonable cost comparison among alternatives is an important factor. Unfortunately, many businesses do not try to make such a comparison. The process is not necessarily a complex one; with experience, the *idea* can be put into effect with relatively little trouble or expense. Chapter 3 includes a comparison table to illustrate how this can be done as part of risk-management decision making. Exact comparison for larger business exposures and numerous perils may be more complicated in practice.

Almost everyone may use each of these methods of financing losses to some extent. For a business firm, many factors are often important, such as the firm's size; its overall objectives; its philosophy; its capacity to absorb losses from assets, operating funds, or credit expansion; and its ability to predict losses.

Does a small firm face the same problems of risk that a larger firm does? Basically, yes, for the small firm probably has the same major perils which may cause loss, such as fire, windstorm, negligence, liability, crime, and so on. (A few exceptions exist, such as on-location steam boiler exposure and radioactive isotopes.) A larger firm, however, may be able to use risk-retention plans to a greater degree because it *may* be able to (1) better predict its

---

[8] The principle of "indirect" costs often exceeding the "direct" loss by as much as four or five times was pioneered by H. W. Heinrich in his book *Industrial Accident Prevention* (New York: McGraw-Hill Book Co., 1931).

larger number of diversified losses, and (2) if it does err in prediction, it *may* have larger reserves or surplus to absorb unexpected losses.

Absorption in current operating expense. Looking more closely at each of the methods of risk financing used by business firms, one finds that the most common method is to absorb losses as a part of regular operating expense. In a highly recommended research study, *Corporate Self-Insurance and Risk Retention Plans,* Goshay found that of 156 risk-retention plans by large corporations (most with assets of between $25 million and $300 million) for fire, liability, and workers' compensation perils, almost half maintained no reserves, all losses being paid as a current expense when the occasion demanded.[9]

In smaller firms, it is less likely that current operating expenses can withstand the potential losses. Some other perils which might be considered for absorption in current operating expenses are glass breakage, transportation shipment damage, and automobile physical damage. Many other exposures might be added to this list in particular situations. It is essential that the potential loss severity be low in relation to the assets, surplus, or working capital of the business firm, and that loss frequency be high in order to achieve some measure of predictability of future losses. These same attributes should be carefully considered in any of the risks retained, even where reserves are maintained, as discussed in the next section.

Funding and reserves. Irregular drains of substantial amounts of assets, surplus, or working capital are not desirable or practical for business. A fund (of actual segregated assets) or a reserve (usually a bookkeeping entry of earmarked surplus) may be used to offset some irregular losses which are too large to be absorbed in current operating expenses but not so large that the business firm can reasonably retain them.

There are many difficulties in connection with funds or reserves maintained for risk-retention plans. Funds in particular usually represent an ideal rather than actual practice. Most businesses use a bookkeeping reserve rather than an actual cash fund. The problems include: (1) How large should the fund be? (2) How can it be accumulated without intervening losses that might be disastrous? and (3) How can the fund be maintained, without the temptation to use it for other emergencies or in regular operations of the business? If liability or earmarked surplus reserves are used, the general tendency is to find the assets representing the reserves tied up in nonliquid assets, and oftentimes there is little chance that cash will be available to meet the irregular, larger losses for which the reserves are intended. The income tax laws are another disadvantage, for a current business deduction is not allowed (except in some workers' compensation "self-insured" plans and bad debt reserves) for the formation of a reserve to meet most losses.

---

[9] Robert C. Goshay, *Corporate Self-Insurance and Risk Retention Plans* (Homewood, Ill.: Richard D. Irwin, 1964), p. 112.

In all, funding and reserves, although better than not having them at all, have limited application to most of the perils faced by individuals, families, and small businesses. It is only for *some* type of losses of *some* situations, *with* careful and continuing efforts to maintain the objectives of the plan, that full risk retention with reserves is a satisfactory solution.

Deductibles and excess plans. It is in the area of *deductibles,* a form of *partial* risk retention, that many of the most exciting current applications of risk retention are being considered and practiced. The principle of having the policyholder receive payment only for losses over a stated amount (or percentage figure) has been accepted for many years in certain types of insurance, such as marine, credit, collision, and windstorm coverages. It has been widely adopted for many personal lines, such as automobile collision, homeowners, and disability income.

The large commercial buyers of insurance, too, have had access to large deductibles for some years. The growth of interest in, and availability of, detuctibles in the $1,000 to $10,000 or more per loss range had been one of the most significant changes in the insurance market during the past decade. One special type, called an *excess plan,* usually has a deductible of more than $100,000. The deductible amount is chosen to approximate the maximum probable loss, and insureds usually provide their own loss-prevention services. The Fire Insurance Research and Actuarial Association publishes tables of recommended fire and windstorm insurance rate credits for $10,000, $25,000, $50,000, and $100,000. The Industrial Risk Insurers and the Factory Mutuals use deductibles of some kind in almost all of their plans.

The size of the deductible to be chosen varies according to a number of factors: the nature of the perils, including the frequency and severity of loss patterns; the financial ability of the insured to withstand losses; the existence of reserves or funds; the desire for claims handling by the insured or the insurer; the need for loss-prevention services; and many other criteria. The total circumstances and objectives must be appraised: a deductible of $500 may be too large for some situations, while one of $50,000 may be too small for others. Oil companies and other large companies with diversified exposures often use deductibles of $1 million or more.

A review of the reasons for using deductibles given by insureds might include:

1. *Cost* economies
    a. Precluding small claims and maintenance expenses.
    b. Omitting regular, expected normal losses that can be handled effectively by other means.
    c. Avoiding state premium taxes.
    d. Avoiding regulated rates or excessive class rates.
    e. Not "trading dollars" with the insurer.

2. *Control* purposes
   a. Of claims payment, for speed and convenience.
   b. Of loss-prevention activities.
   c. To encourage safety consciousness of employees.
   d. To help employee relations.
3. *Coverage*
   a. To obtain coverage by meeting underwriting requirements.
   b. To separate primary and excess insurance.
   c. To improve loss experience and relations with the insurer.
   d. To meet legislative requirements.
   e. To help management realize its stake in loss prevention, and the value of insurance for catastrophic losses.
   f. To supplement self-insurance plans.

"Self-insurance."   Only the most complete and formal plans for financing risk are properly described as *self-insurance* plans. Such plans are sometimes used by business firms. In most cases, these plans are only partial methods of keeping risk within the firm. Briefly, to deserve the designation of self-insurance, a plan must include certain requisites which apply similarly for sound insurance company operation.

Some of these requirements have already been discussed under the heading of *insurable* risks. To be self-insurable, the same characteristics are necessary. These include the need for large numbers of important, homogeneous, accidental risks, which have the quality of being definite and calculable and do not involve the chance of too large a catastrophic loss. *High frequency* and *low severity of losses* in order to have reasonable *predictability* are essential. For the most part, large organizations are the only ones that can meet these requirements properly. Self-insurance is not realistic for individual or family risk problems.

Self-insurance also requires attention to other points. The plan must have *management's full support* and understanding; it should provide essential *loss-prevention activities* whenever economically feasible; it should normally involve a *savings fund* (not just a "reserve" on the balance sheet) to meet unanticipated losses; and it should provide important recordkeeping and *loss-analysis data*. The size of the funds necessary depends on many factors, including the financial stability of the firm, the maximum probable losses expected, the possible repetition of losses within a certain period, and tax considerations.

The main consideration is care in setting up and administering the self-insurance plan, not beguiling oneself into a feeling of security when the plan is not adequate. This solution can be used successfully by larger firms when judicious steps are taken to assure that the plan is really one of self-insurance. The most common example of self-insurance is in the field of workers' compensation (for industrial injuries and diseases), while some of the largest businesses also use this method for meeting part of their automobile, fire, or health insurance risks.[10]

A relatively new and popular method of retaining risk, closely related to self-insurance, is the use of "captive" insurers owned by an organization with the purpose of insuring its own risks. This development is discussed in Chapter 3.

Risk transfer. Some of the most important risks and losses which must be financed by individuals and businesses cannot be retained. The sole method left for consideration is the transfer of as much as possible of the unpredictability, or the losses, to someone else. Three methods are possible: (1) credit arrangements, (2) some noninsurance transfers, and (3) insurance.

Credit arrangements. The use of credit contracts to pay for losses may be considered as one method of risk transfer. However, borrowing money usually has other primary purposes, such as financing homes or business expansion. Since credit is always limited, depending upon the financial situation and capabilities of the borrower ("When you need it most is when it's hardest to get"), it seems generally unwise to use credit for relatively unpredictable needs. Pure risks, especially for larger and infrequent types of losses, are difficult to handle by borrowing *after* the need arises. Unless prior arrangements are made (such as letters of credit from banks), you may be adding the additional risk of not being able to obtain credit instead of actually transferring these losses to others.

Other noninsurance transfers. Risks may be shifted to others by several other types of noninsurance transfers. In a risk financing method, it is the *financial burden* of loss that is transferred, not the ultimate legal responsibility (which is transferred in the noninsurance methods of risk control discussed previously).

A *hedging contract* has been shown to be a method of transferring some speculative (loss *or* gain) risks. Sometimes this balancing of possible profit and loss through two offsetting contracts is called "neutralization." The method cannot be used for pure risk, which involves no possibility of gain.

The best example of noninsurance transfers for risk financing is the *hold-harmless agreement*. In this contract clause, the transferee agrees to hold the transferor harmless in the case of legal liability to others. The transferee agrees to pay claimants (or the defense costs of claims or lawsuits), or to repay such losses if they fall on the transferor. If the transferee is unable to pay the losses, the ultimate responsibility remains with the transferor.

Several types of legal contracts commonly use hold-harmless agreements. In *lease contracts* a wide variety of legal responsibilities are transferred from

---

[10] A recent monograph analyzing many of the self-insurance techniques is *Self-Insurance: A Risk Management Alternative* (Malvern, Pa.: Society of CPCU, March 1978).

one party to another in this manner. For example, proper maintenance is often stated in a lease to be under the care of the transferee (lessee) who rents property from an owner. Homes, apartments, automobiles, and many other types of leased property are common today.

Construction contracts also often use hold-harmless agreements to transfer the financial burden of some (but seldom all) of the legal liability losses from the owner to the contractor. *Supply* contracts are a further example, with the supplier usually agreeing to hold the manufacturer or distributor harmless in claims resulting from the supplier's negligence. The extent of the transfer of risk may occasionally extend further to include all of the manufacturer's negligence as well.

Bailees, or persons holding property of others temporarily, often accept by *bailment contract* or common law some risks from the property owners. Liability for damage to goods is shifted from owner to bailee in hundreds of everyday business situations, such as railroad or airline tickets, truck shipments, laundries, warehouses, parking lots, and repair shops.

Most risk transfer methods are far from complete. The uncertainty in regard to *some* perils in *some* circumstances for a *limited* length of *time* for a *limited amount* may be transferred to others. Still, the major risks of families and businesses remain with them unless the final method of risk transfer, *insurance,* is used.

Insurance.   Most important to insurance as a method of treating risk is an understanding of (1) what it is, (2) how it works, and (3) its significance. The first concept is developed here, while the second and third concepts are covered in Chapter 2.

A definition of *insurance* may be developed from several viewpoints: economic, legal, business, social, or mathematical. Regardless of which viewpoint is taken, a full interpretation should include both a statement of its objective as well as the technique by which the purpose is achieved.

There is no one brief definition that does justice to the many important viewpoints of insurance. It may be an economic system for reducing risk through transfer and pooling of losses; a legal method of transferring risk in a contract of indemnity; a business institution providing many jobs in a free enterprise economy; a social device in which the losses of few are paid by many; or an actuarial system of applied mathematics. It is all of these and more, depending upon how one views the major purposes, methods, and results of insurance. Table 1–1 summarizes the five viewpoints from which insurance can be defined.

Probably the most widely used definition of insurance is an *economic* one. In this sense, insurance is a method which *reduces risk* by a *transfer* and *combination* (or "pooling") of uncertainty in regard to financial loss. Depending on whether the viewpoint is that of the insured or the insurer, it may be that only transfer is needed in order to have an insurance plan (transfer of risk reduces the *insured's* risk), or only combination (as in the "self-

Table 1-1. Definitions of insurance

Viewpoint	Objective	Technique
Economic	Reduction of uncertainty	By transfer and combination
Legal	Transfer of risk	Through payment of a premium by insured to insurer in a contract of indemnity
Business	Sharing of risk	By transfer from individuals and businesses to a financial institution specializing in risk
Social	Collective bearing of losses	By all members of a group contributing to pay losses suffered by unfortunate ones
Mathematical	Predicting and distributing losses	By actuarial estimates based upon principles of probability

insurance" plans discussed previously). Usually, however, the economic concept of insurance involves both transfer and combination of risk.

From a *legal* standpoint, an insurance *contract* or *policy* is used to transfer risk for a *premium* (price) from one party known as the *insured* or *policyholder* to another party known as the *insurer.* By virtue of a legally binding contract, the insured exchanges the possibility of an unknown large loss for a comparatively small certain payment. It is not really a guarantee against losses occurring, but a method of assuring that repayment, or *indemnity,* will be received for losses that do occur as the result of risk.

Why is it important whether or not a plan is determined legally to be insurance? It is significant because many types of regulation and taxation apply specifically to insurance. Warranty service contracts, for example, are commonplace today for automobiles,[11] tires, and appliances. If such warranties are not legally defined as insurance because of the all-loss (not merely risk) nature of their promises, the companies offering the warranties need not organize an insurance company, hold reserves, or pay state insurance premium taxes. Variable annuity contracts, if not defined by the courts as exclusively insurance contracts, become subject both to state insurance laws and to the federal securities legislation of the Securities Exchange Commission. These legal decisions, and others in regard to such contracts as employee benefit plans and hospital and medical benefit plans, have become very important in insurance.

As a *business* institution, insurance has been defined as a plan by which large numbers of people associate themselves and transfer risks that attach to individuals to the shoulders of all. Insurance may also be looked upon as an important part of the financial world, where insurance serves as a basis for

---

[11] An interesting development is that of warranty contracts that extend automobile warranties past the usual 12 months or 12,000 miles covered by auto makers. By the late 1970s about 250 concerns were offering such warranties, including the Big Three auto makers themselves.

credit and a mechanism for savings and investments. Insurance as a business is a common way of thinking about what insurance is, for many persons have contact with the thousands of insurance organizations and their more than a million employees. It has become a major part of the free enterprise economy.

An adequate *social* definition giving recognition both to the end of insurance and to the means for effecting it has been admirably stated thus: "We should define insurance, then, as that social device for making accumulations to meet uncertain losses of capital which is carried out through the transfer of the risks of many individuals to one person or to a group of persons. Wherever there is accumulation for uncertain losses or wherever there is a transfer of risk, there is one element of insurance; only where these are joined with the combination of risks in a group is the insurance complete."[12]

To effect insurance, persons who are exposed to loss agree to contribute to indemnify or repay whichever member of the group shall suffer loss. All members contribute to a common fund, and payments are made out of this fund to those who have suffered loss. Thus, a person owns a house valued at $50,000 which may be totally destroyed by fire. For the payment of a definite sum (the insurance premium) the financial consequences of a $50,000 loss are eliminated by exchanging an uncertain large loss for a certain small cost. The sum total of such individual transactions makes insurance a social method by which unfortunates (those having losses) are compensated by the whole group.

In the strictest interpretation of the term, contributions to a fund are not essential. It is conceivable for private groups to rely entirely upon assessments after losses to indemnify the sufferers, and in such instances no funds may be accumulated in advance. In the case of the government functioning as the insurer, a fund may be accumulated, or the beneficiaries may depend for their insurance payments upon the taxing power.

In a *mathematical* sense, insurance is the application of certain *actuarial* (insurance mathematics) principles. Laws of probability and statistical techniques are used to achieve predictable results. The details of how this is done are covered in Chapter 2.

Note to students: It is hoped that you will follow the advice given in the Preface, which recommended as a regular procedure in reading this text: (1) First read the outline of "concepts considered in the chapter" on the left-hand page at the beginning of the chapter; (2) Read the chapter; and then (3) *Go back to reread the outline* in order to review how the basic parts and subparts fit together.

---

[12] A. H. Willett, *The Economic Theory of Risk and Insurance,* Columbia University Studies in History, Economics, and Public Law, vol. 14 (New York: Columbia University Press, 1901), p. 388. See also reprinted edition published under the auspices of the S. S. Huebner Foundation for Insurance Education (Philadelphia: University of Pennsylvania Press, 1951), p. 72.

FOR REVIEW AND DISCUSSION

1. Why is an understanding of risk important to the study of insurance?
2. Risk often has a different meaning to different persons or to the same person in different situations. Illustrate this statement with the three examples, and explain why this paradox is so common.
3. Explain why you agree or disagree that "chance of loss is an inadequate description of risk."
4. Paul states: "Speculative risk is what I want." Carol says: "Not me, I'd rather have pure risk because . . ." How do you think Carol would finish her sentence, and what might be Paul's reasoning?
5. Distinguish between the use of the term *risk, uncertainty, peril, hazard,* and *loss.* Why should they be differentiated?
6. An author has said: "The *risks* which families and businesses face are all pervasive. For the study of insurance it is meaningful to *classify risks* in several *different* ways. By doing so, one can learn for *which* risks the insurance techniques is best adapted to provide a *solution* to the important *problems* of risk." How would you explain the reasons why each of these statements is true, with particular reference to each of the italicized terms?
7. Why is it necessary to distinguish between:
   a. "Pure" and "speculative" risks?
   b. "Preventable" and "insurable" risks?
   c. "Gambling" and other risks?
   d. "Personal," "property," and "liability" risks?
8. Are all risks insurable? Why or why not?
9. Mr. I. M. Secure is purchasing a home and knows he will acquire several new risks. Classify and describe these risks.
10. Both physical and moral hazards may be involved in many risks. What are the purposes and problems of identifying these types of hazards?
11. Are each of the requisites for an insurable risk met by risks that are insured? Why or why not? Explain each of the requirements briefly, and give an example of a risk which is sometimes insured that does *not* satisfy each requirement very well.
12. Do you think a risk such as traveling to and from the moon will ever be insurable? Upon what rationale do you base your answer?
13. *Insurance Facts* says that last year (*a*) "aggregate property loss in the United States from fire was $3.6 billion" and (*b*) "total dollar cost of traffic accidents was $41 billion." Explain whether or not you feel that these figures are the complete cost of fire and automobile accidents.
14. Explain the two basic alternatives for treating risks.
15. What factors *should* determine the method of risk treatment that is chosen in order to take care of a particular peril?
16. Can an *insurer* use both of the basic methods of risk treatment? Illustrate each basic method.

17. *a.* Why is *planned* risk retention a common practice?
    b. Under what circumstances can it be used?
18. Whose responsibility is loss prevention and loss reduction, and why?
19. An adequate description of "insurance" requires an explanation of *what it is, its purpose,* and *how it accomplishes its goal.* Explain.
20. *Why* is the legal definition of insurance important in our society?
21. Explain how risks are transferred by means other than insurance.
22. Under what circumstances, and from whom, is "self-insurance" advantageous?
23. Several different definitions of insurance are not only possible but also necessary to really understand insurance. Explain this statement.

Chapter 2

Concepts considered in Chapter 2—Insurance and its significance

The significance of insurance is seen in understanding *how it works*, its *history*, its many *fields*, its numerous *benefits*, and its *statistical evidences*.

 How it works can be explained by the *insurance equation*, by the concept of *probability and uncertainty*, and by the *principle of large numbers*.

 A brief history of insurance reviews its growth.

  Ancient insurance ideas of loan-risk contracts and risk sharing.

  The Middle Ages and the merchant era of fire-marine risks.

  The 18th century and early America, when U.S. insurers began.

  The expanding 1800s, which saw catastrophic fires in many cities.

  Twentieth-century growth, paralleling industrial expansion in the automobile, aircraft, and space ages.

 The fields of insurance are classified for better understanding:

  General divisions contrast the gigantic *social* and *voluntary* fields:

  Social (government) insurance is *compulsory*, is either *federal* (such as OASDHI) or *state*, encompasses *large groups,* and aims at providing *minimum benefits* for economic security from *some universal perils* such as old age, injury, sickness, death, and unemployment.

  Voluntary (private) insurance includes:

   Commercial insurance, the "insurance business," which is:

    Personal insurance, for loss of *earning power* and added *expenses* of death or disability, in *life* and *health* insurance,

    Property insurance, for loss of ownership use or value of assets, insured in *fire, marine, casualty,* and *surety* insurance.

    Multiple-line and all-lines insurance, *important trends.*

   Cooperative insurance, such as *nonprofit* Blue Cross–Blue Shield.

   Voluntary government insurance, which is government administered but *not* compulsory, such as FHA and FCIC.

The benefits and costs of insurance are reviewed with the inquiry as to what our society would be like *without* insurance.

 General benefits of insurance are seen as *peace of mind, keeping families and businesses together, increasing marginal utility* of assets, providing a *basis for credit, stimulating saving,* providing *investment capital,* the *advantages of specialization, loss prevention,* and many special benefits of individual kinds of insurance.

 Costs of insurance should be evaluated, too.

 Statistical evidences of employment, assets, sales, and other figures show the powerful force of insurance in our free enterprise economy.

Insurance and its significance

Risk and its treatment have purposely been the primary subjects of the first chapter of this book. In the broad picture *insurance* is only one method of solving some of the problems of risk, but its place is a *substantial* one. By all measures—assets, income, investments, insurers, employees, insureds, direct and indirect benefits—insurance looms as a giant in our society today.

A brief look at how insurance works is presented first in this chapter. Next, to see how insurance has grown, its history is reviewed. Then an overview of the fields of insurance is given, indicating the immense scope of the entire subject. In the final section of the chapter, the general and specific benefits of insurance are summarized.

HOW INSURANCE WORKS

How can any organization assume a large risk for a comparatively small premium and then soon thereafter make a large loss payment? For example, life insurance pays losses for death claims on policies issued and in force for less than a year. Fire insurance on buildings may result in the payment of thousands of dollars in return for the payment of a few dollars in premium.

The insurance equation. Insurers deal primarily with groups. In the case of the life insurer, it is not concerned with when one person will die but with how many will die each year out of a large group. Knowing this within reasonable limits, the life insurer sets its premium charges so that it will take in enough money to be able to carry on the business and to pay all claims. In the case of other forms of insurance, the procedure is the same. The fire insurer is interested not in whether specific buildings will burn but in what the ratio of losses to premiums will be when a large group of buildings is insured. The equality between the receipts taken in and what is paid out constitutes what may be termed the "insurance equation."

In addition to securing sufficient funds to meet all losses, insurers must collect enough money to carry on the business. There are expenses such as salaries, rentals, supplies, taxes, and agents' commissions—all of which form a part of the cost of doing business. Certain insurers also provide special services in engineering, rate making, and loss prevention that are designed to save property and lives.

There must also be some source to take care of any deficiency as a result of losses or expenses beyond the normal expectation of the insurer. Surplus is one means by which these unexpected losses or expenses are paid. Capital put up by the stockholders of an insurer is another source for stock insurers. Stockholders who invest funds in insurance do so for a profit, and, accordingly, in the computation of the premium some provision must be made to compensate the owner of the capital invested in the enterprise. An alternative to using stockholders' capital to assure financial solvency is an assessment on policyholders (used by some smaller mutual insurers).

In addition, insurers make an additional charge to set up specific reserves required by state laws, and also reserves for catastrophes. Losses are based upon average expected losses, but from time to time abnormal losses occur. For example, various fires have from time to time destroyed large areas in our important cities, windstorms have damaged wide areas, and accidents have caused the death of a large number of people at one time. Catastrophes of this sort must be taken into consideration by insurers in computing the premium.

Summarizing, the factors that enter into the computation of a premium may be listed as follows: (1) the cost of *losses*; (2) the cost of doing business or *expenses;* and (3) the cost of capital, or *profits*.

These costs vary with the different kinds of insurance contracts written. The loss cost may be as much as or more than 90 percent of total premiums (as it is for hospitalization insurance), or about 65 percent (as for automobile insurance). It may be as little as 5 percent in such kinds of insurance as title, steam boiler explosion, or fidelity bonds, in which loss-prevention services are more feasible and important than payment of losses. The cost of doing business is affected greatly by the marketing system used and the services rendered to the policyholder by the agents of insurers. Capital and assessment costs are also variable according to the legal type of insurer and the state laws.

Stated in more complete terms than just that premiums and costs must be equal, the insurance equation is a revision of a basic accounting concept that total outgo and income must be equal. For an insurance business, total income (that is, premiums, interest earnings, and miscellaneous income) must in the long run equal total payments (that is, losses, expenses, and profits). Reserves and surplus are items that temporarily restrict outgo. Figure 2–1 illustrates this relationship.

Probability and uncertainty.   Another explanation of how insurance works centers on the application of the essential concepts of probability and uncertainty. The function of insurance is to assume the burden of the risks which individuals are unwilling to carry. The insurer is able to reduce the sum total of all the uncertainties (risk) to a reasonable degree of certainty. Within calculable limits the insurer is able to foresee the normal losses and estimate the catastrophe losses so that the premium charge to pay all losses as well as to cover expenses and profits can be computed.

Figure 2-1. The insurance equation

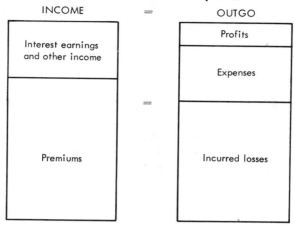

The ability to do this places the insurer on a footing quite different from the insured. Were it not for this ability, insurance would be nothing more than the accumulation of many small chances into one enormous chance. While in each individual case the element of uncertainty is extreme, in total a reasonably definite loss may be predicted. The uncertainty element is not entirely eliminated. Some insurers are more successful than others. Although every insurer endeavors to achieve reasonable predictability, some companies will err and suffer losses and expenses beyond what they take in.

Probability measures the chance of occurrence of a particular event. In the field of insurance, the theory has proved to be of great importance in measuring (predicting) losses. The probability of loss (p) is expressed algebraically by means of a fraction whose numerator is the number of unfavorable possibilities and whose denominator is the total number of all possible events.

If we let:

n = Total number of units, or separate events (favorable and unfavorable)
a = Number of ways considered unfavorable (loss)
b = Number of ways considered favorable (no loss)
p = Probability of an unfavorable outcome (loss)
p_1 = Probability of a favorable outcome (no loss)

Then:

$p = a/n$

and

$p_1 = b/n$

A simple illustration of another probability formula is found in the experiment of tossing a coin. There are but two ways in which a coin may fall: either heads up or tails up. The probability that it will fall heads up is found by using the number of possible successful chances as the numerator of the fraction and the total number of chances as the denominator. Thus, given a large enough number of tosses, we have the probability of tossing a head as ½.

With relation to any given event, the two extremes are certainty and impossibility. Between the two there are varying degrees of probability. It will be recognized, however, that the degree of uncertainty (risk) and the degree of probability do not represent similar concepts. If a thing is certain to happen, then its probability is represented by unity, or 1. If it is impossible that it should happen, there is no probability, or probability is represented by 0. Impossibility, then, is negative certainty. The event is certain not to happen.

Uncertainty of loss (risk) is a more difficult concept. Basically, however, the idea is that of *variability* of the chance (probability) of loss. A number of statistical methods are helpful in measuring the variability of expected losses, which is what insurers must do when they issue insurance contracts promising to pay for future losses. Most students who have had a basic course in statistics should recall concepts such as normal distribution and standard deviation, which are used to measure objective risk.

The principle of large numbers.   In addition, one principle in particular is of great importance to insurance. This is the *principle of large numbers,* or "law of averages," which briefly states that, relatively, *actual results tend to equal expected (probable) results* as the number of independent events increases. In other words, as a larger number of such events are included, the difference between actual and expected results becomes a smaller percentage (though not in absolute numbers) of the expected results.

Insurance is concerned with the number of times an event, or loss, may be expected to happen over a series of occasions. Certain happenings occur with surprising regularity when a large number of instances are observed. The regularity of the happenings increases as the observed instances become more numerous. The concept is that of "credibility," which indicates the degree of reliability that one can place upon the use of past experience to predict what will happen in the future.

Applying these conclusions to insurance in a hypothetical case, assume that we are considering the predictability of automobile accidents in a given city for a group of Toyota car owners. From data gathered on all cars in a city over the past several years, we can construct a "probability distribution" such as Case 1 in Figure 2–2. This shows the relative likelihood (percentage probability) of each possible outcome in terms of the accidents occurring, expressed as a percentage of all the cars in the city which are involved in an accident during a year. Case 1 distribution shows that experience to have varied from 8 to 16 percent of all the cars. From other data, suppose we learn that the Case 2 distribution depicts the experience of Toyota car owners, with accidents ranging from 4 to 26 percent in different years. From Figure 2–2 we can observe that the smaller group of Toyota owners exhibits wide variation in results. If we were using these data to predict future accidents for this

Figure 2–2. Probability of losses (hypothetical)

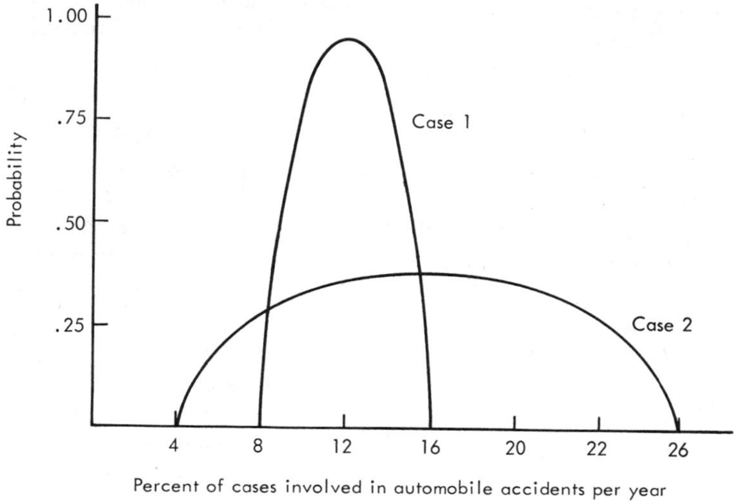

Case 1: 10,000 cars (entire group of car owners in the city).
Case 2: 100 cars (Toyota car owners only).

group, we could only predict within a wide range of percentages, with relatively low probability of actual experience being equal to expected experience. Case 1 shows that the variation of results is much less for the entire group of car owners in the city, and our predictions for the future could be made with greater likelihood of the accidents occurring within a smaller range of percentages. With the use of the principle of large numbers, Figure 2–2 shows that the reliability of our predictions increases for the larger group.

This is the "magic" of insurance, increasing predictability and reducing risk through the use of the principle of large numbers. Insurers have learned the wisdom of insuring the largest number of similar risks possible. A great number ensures more regular and more accurately predictable losses.

Adequate statistical data.   In using the mathematical laws of probability, uncertainty, and large numbers, frequent reference has been made to the need for adequate statistical data. Unless accurate statistical information is available, predictions in the form of probabilities will be defective. Therefore, in each of the fields of insurance, carefully compiled statistics are assembled to accumulate experience as a basis for rate making. For example, the statistical data used in estimating the number of deaths for life insurance purposes are arranged in a "mortality" table showing how many persons at a given age will probably die during each year. In fire insurance, statistics are developed on details of construction, occupancy, protection, and exposure pertaining to different types of buildings. For automobile insurance, data for many classifications of type and use of car, territory, age of driver, and other factors are collected. The proper classifications and use of trend factors to anticipate changing loss factors help to achieve equity or fairness in the rates charged to many insureds with different loss probabilities.

It is the constant aim to reduce judgment factors to a minimum, and to predicate rates as far as it is possible upon a purely scientific basis which rests on the use of statistical data in applying known laws of probability, uncertainty, and large numbers. This, then, is how insurance works. It applies mathematical tools in using statistical data on groups, in order to achieve better predictions than can be made by individuals. The success of insurers in doing this explains why insurance, among the several alternatives discussed in Chapter 1, has become the predominant method of treating risks.

The student should note that the explanation of how insurance works could apply either to private insurance or to social insurance. Consideration of the differences between these two major fields of insurance is presented later in this chapter. Social, or government, insurance could have been discussed as a separate alternative method for treating risk, but the broader concept of insurance is explained here as a single risk-treatment method.

A BRIEF HISTORY OF INSURANCE

In the light of the common lack of understanding about insurance, an appropriate title for this section might be "the mystery with a history." Will and Ariel Durant in their provocative book *The Lessons of History*[1] have observed, with words that are surprisingly appropriate to the field of risk and insurance, that

> most history is guessing; the rest is prejudice. . . . we must operate with partial knowledge, and be content with *probabilities*. . . . perhaps, within these *limits,* we may ask what history has to say. . . . It is a *precarious* enterprise, and only a fool would try to compress a hundred centuries into a few pages of *hazardous* conclusions. We proceed.

We proceed to *insurance,* where history is important in obtaining proper perspective because the roots of the insurance idea go far back in the pages of history. This section merely serves as an introduction to the wealth of knowledge which history contains about insurance. By learning more about the past, one can better understand the present and appraise the future of insurance.

Ancient insurance ideas

Insurance has a rich and colorful history. It is a part of many ancient civilizations, and almost any economic history contains references to practices which can be identified as the forerunners of modern insurance techniques.

---

[1] New York: Simon & Schuster, 1968, pp. 12–13. Emphasis by italics added here.

The evolution of insurance is not so precise that one can point with confidence at a single civilization, or year, or transaction, and say: "That was the beginning of insurance." Certainly, however, the origins were present in biblical times. Some authors even describe insurance arrangements thousands of years before the Christian calendar began (perhaps not as it is known today, but, nevertheless, with similarities of purpose and method).

The Babylonians and Hindus used contracts known as "bottomry" loans to shift the burden of risk from owners of ships and cargoes to moneylenders who agreed to cancel the loan if the ship or cargo were lost during a voyage. If the venture was successful, the charge for the bottomry loan was a high one which combined both interest and the cost of risk. Insurance has been called "the handmaiden of commerce," for it was with early commercial activities and the great dangers of travel and trade that such contracts appeared. The Phoenicians, Greeks, and Romans developed agreements that correspond in most essentials to written contracts used 2,000 years later in marine ventures to the New World. Moneylenders and traders used these loan-insurance agreements in their vast negotiations throughout the ports of the Old World.

Not only were risks shifted from one party to another in ancient times, but the idea of sharing and pooling risks was also used. Chinese merchants divided their cargoes among several ships for perilous voyages on the rivers of ancient China, for the purpose of not having any one merchant suffer a total loss of cargo because of one disaster. The famed storage of grain during the "Seven Fat Years" in preparation for the "Seven Lean Years" is adequately explained in the Bible to denote a clear recognition of the principle of community and group sharing of risk.

Life insurance, too, can be traced to ancient civilizations such as Rome. Burial funds were common in those days. In Greece religious organizations collected and dispersed funds for burial costs of members. The Egyptians left many evidences in the tombs of the pyramids that burial societies were then in existence. Feudal guilds included burial costs in their system of dues, although documentation is difficult in the tracing of their use through the Dark Ages.

The Middle Ages and the merchant era

Perhaps the real origins of insurance stem from the advances made in commerce during the Middle Ages. Venetian decrees in the 15th century regulated marine insurance contracts, and the Hanseatic League used indemnity contracts for trade with all of Europe. The Mediterranean trade with Europe and the Near East rapidly expanded the need for specialized services in the guaranteeing of financial solvency in the face of navigation disasters.

New financial specialists known as "underwriters," appeared. They wrote their names under contracts of insurance as they accepted maritime risks. In the coffeehouses of England, particularly, the individual insurer grew in significance as England and France forged to the peak of their naval supremacy. Lloyd's of London became the best-known center of marine insurance and remains today as an important source of worldwide insurance on ships and cargoes.

Fire insurance appeared in the 17th century, prompted by a disastrous fire which destroyed 85 percent of London in 1666. The failure of several insurance schemes in this period led to increased desire by the public for stronger insurance plans. One famous plan by Nicholas Barbon, a dentist turned builder who guaranteed to repair houses he built if they were later damaged by fire, was doomed to early failure because of lack of recognition of the substantial risks assumed in the agreement.

The 18th century and insurance in early America

The beginnings of corporate insurance, as opposed to individual insurers whose guarantees were limited to their personal fortunes, appeared in 1720. The "Bubble Period," during which speculators and insurers alike failed in a financial panic of widespread repercussions, brought forth restricted charters from Parliament for two insurance companies, the London Assurance Corporation and the Royal Exchange Assurance Corporation. These companies had a monopoly on corporate insurance, and perhaps the wisdom of the royal charters is evidenced by the fact that these two insurers are still strong companies today.

Colonial America naturally took ideas from England for the first companies in the United States. Much of the early insurance was written by branch offices of English insurers. But new American companies sprang up to meet the needs of a growing America. Benjamin Franklin organized the first incorporated fire insurance company, the Philadelphia Contributionship, in 1752. The Mutual Assurance Company (1784) was known as the "Green Tree" because of the emblem on its "fire mark," a plaque fastened to the outside of insured houses to identify them for the fire-fighting companies maintained by the insurance company. The oldest joint stock company was formed in 1794 to do a fire and marine business (and for a few years, life insurance, too) under the name of the Insurance Company of North America. In life insurance, other companies were started but remained small until after 1800: the Presbyterian Ministers' Fund in 1759 and the Episcopal Corporation in 1769.

The expanding 1800s

Economic expansion in the 1800s found more life insurance companies ready for business: the Pennsylvania Company for the Insurance on Lives (1809), the New York Life Insurance and Trust Company (1830), the New England Mutual Life Insurance Company (1836), and the Mutual Life Insurance Company of New York (1843). The beginnings of scientific actuarial mortality tables appeared, and life insurance quadrupled in the decade following the Civil War.

The fire insurance business prospered also, while growing pains developed in the form of concentrated city construction and expanding market problems as the first agency systems were developed. Disastrous city fires tested the strength of the fire insurance companies and pointed toward crucial needs for improved building codes and fire fighting equipment. The Chicago Fire in 1871 is famous as it resulted in a property loss of over $150 million, which was an especially huge loss for that time. Almost $100 million of the losses was insured. Numerous other fire disasters were almost as important, however, as each tried the resources and services of the insurance companies: fires in New York in 1835; New Orleans in 1854; New York in 1862; Portland, Maine, in 1866; and Boston in 1872 ($75 million property loss, just one year after the Chicago fire!).

State regulation of insurance began about 1850 as several states established boards or commissions for the supervision of the business. Solvency and tax revenues were the prime objectives of the new laws, through deposit, investment, reserve, and premium tax requirements. The first separate insurance departments were established in 1855 (Massachusetts) and 1859 (New York). Men such as Elizur Wright became the stalwart proponents of better insurance regulation as abuses were corrected and mathematical standards improved in many phases of the insurance business.

20th-century growth

The development of insurance in the 1900s has paralleled the major economic changes of the times. The expansion of the railroads, the advent of the automobile age, the mass production techniques of modern industry, the wars, the introduction of the airplane, and the changing social consciousness of an affluent society—all of these factors and many more closely affected the rise of insurance as a major business of the 20th century.[2]

Some of the landmarks in fire and windstorm insurance were the San Francisco fire of 1906 (property loss of $350 million), the New England hurricane of 1938, the Texas City ship explosion of 1947 (3,500 killed or

---

[2] Some excellent insurance company biographies are available which clearly show how insurance reacted to the major events of the 19th and 20th centuries. The author has seen nearly a hundred such historical works which tell much about insurance history. Representative of these publications are: Nicholas B. Wainwright, *A Philadelphia Story* (New York: Frederick Fell, 1952); Thomas C. Chubb, *And There Were No Losses* (New York: John B. Watkins Co., 1957); Hawthorne Daniel, *The Hartford of Hartford* (New York: Random House, 1960); R. Carlyle Buley, *A Study of the History of Life Insurance: The Equitable Life Assurance Society of the United States,* vols. 1 and 2 (New York: Appleton-Century-Crofts Co., 1953 and 1967); William Cahn, *A Matter of Life and Death* (New York: Random House, 1970); Humbert O. Nelli, *A Bibliography of Insurance History* (Atlanta: Georgia State University, 1971); and Donald J. Cannon, ed., *Heritage of Flames* (Garden City, N.Y.: Doubleday and Co., 1977).

injured) and the East Coast windstorm of 1950 (over 1.5 million separate insurance claims). In more recent years there have been a number of windstorm catastrophes, such as Hurricanes Betsy ($715 million insured loss in 1965), Celia ($30 million, 1970), and Agnes ($100 million, 1972) and tornadoes through 17 Southern and Central states ($430 million, 1974).

Transportation risks changed as the railroads encountered competition from the motortruck and airline industries. New chemicals, radioactive materials, and industrial processes have caused continual risk analysis innovations for property insurance. Riot insurance coverage assumed major importance as part of the fire insurance contract with the multimillion-dollar losses at Watts in 1965 and hundreds of other cities in the late 1960s.

Major developments in casualty insurance have been the rise of workers' compensation insurance since the early 1900s and the growth of automobile insurance to insure more than 110 million drivers today at a cost of $25 billion per year. Negligence laws have increased the need for many other forms of liability insurance. Modification in liability laws, such as non-fault automobile insurance, appeared in the 1970s. Concentrated valuable properties have expanded crime insurance needs. High medical costs and loss of income have skyrocketed health insurance to a multibillion-dollar part of the insurance field. Multiple-line insurance, combining property and casualty coverages in homeowners' and business contracts, was a major change for the current generation of policyholders.

Life insurance, too, has undergone significant change since 1900. Many new companies have competed for the growing needs of a prosperous economy until today almost 1,800 life insurers are in business. Group insurance through employers for their employees has shown rapid growth, and today group pension, life, and health insurance play an important part in labor negotiations. New mortality tables have been adopted and merchandising methods changed to encompass family plans and complete estate programming. The life insurers had a most remarkable record for a financial institution during the Great Depression of the 1930s, with less than one tenth of 1 percent of policyholder funds lost during that period. Life insurance amounts in force have grown tenfold in the past 20 years, to over $2.5 *trillion* today in 380 million contracts with 144 million insureds. Many insurers in the late 1970s were expanding their corporate structures to include mutual funds, variable annuities, and life insurance, as well as broadened financial services.

THE FIELDS OF INSURANCE

General

The *total* field of insurance is described briefly in this section. The basic classification emphasizes the difference between *social* and *voluntary* insurance. In essence, this is the distinction between compulsory *government* insurance and voluntary *private* insurance. Voluntary insurance includes the major category of commercial insurance, which is what persons usually have in mind when they refer to *the insurance business.*

Commercial insurance is divided into personal (life and health) and property types of protection, and traditionally in property insurance the major groupings of fire-marine and casualty-surety insurance have been important. With recent trends toward broader insurance operations and contracts, the terms *multiple-line insurance* and *all-lines insurance* have become significant.

Another useful method of studying the fields of insurance is to analyze the legal types of insurers and their organization. Chapter 5 will use this approach in studying the marketing of commercial insurance.

Figure 2–3 shows the relationship among the fields of insurance discussed in this section. In terms of taxes or premiums, the total sales volume is more than $300 *billion* a year.[3] The relative sizes of the parts of this gigantic total field should be noted. A current perspective is needed, as well as the historical one presented in the preceding section of this chapter.

Social (government) insurance

Social insurance is compulsory and is designed to provide a minimum of economic security for large groups of persons. It concerns itself primarily with the unfavorable losses (income and costs) resulting from the perils of accidental injury, sickness, old age, unemployment, and the premature death of the family wage earners. In total, social insurance is about 45 percent of all insurance in the United States, as measured by combining social insurance contributions (taxes) and voluntary insurance premiums.

The term *social insurance* could conceivably include all insurance, since all insurance possesses widespread social implications and involves large groups. However, the concept is limited here to those insurance plans which are required by government, are usually administered by federal or state governments, and have as their object the provision of a minimum standard of living. The element of compulsion is predicated upon the experience that some persons cannot or will not voluntarily purchase insurance, and the obligation of the government derives from its duty to protect the general welfare of its citizens.

Social insurance is designed to provide an answer to dependency problems of society. It embraces large groups of citizens, and the cost is sometimes distributed among those who participate and sometimes among all citizens. The plan undertakes to furnish for each insured and his or her family a layer of protection adequate for their basic needs in the event of universal types of losses.

---

[3] We see figures in billions so often today that comprehension of just how large an amount a "thousand million" is becomes difficult. An example may help: if you spent $1 million at the rate of $1,000 a day, it would take nearly three years to spend it all. How long would it take to spend $1 *billion* at the same rate? (Answer: More than 2,700 years!)

Figure 2–3. The fields of insurance, and premium (or tax) volume

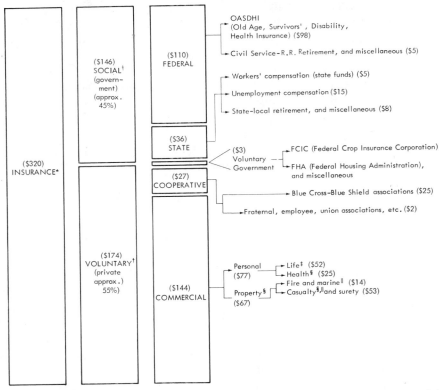

* All figures are in *billions* of dollars for the year 1977. Complete data were not available at press time, so some estimates are included.

† Social insurance figures are "taxes"; voluntary insurance figures are "premiums."

‡ Life insurance includes *insured* annuities with about $17 billion of premiums, but intentionally excludes uninsured private pension contributions.

§ Casualty premiums excludes about $2 billion of health insurance premiums written by property insurers. This amount is included in health total. Workers' compensation (about $8 billion written by casualty insurers) is included in casualty total but could be classified as health insurance. Note also that BC-BS premiums are separately noted above.

|| Homeowners' and commercial multiple-peril premiums apportioned one half to fire, one half to casualty.

¶ Another method of dividing the property field (including liability) is on the basis of who pays the premium dollar. *Business* consumers purchased approximately one half and *individual or family* consumers purchased one half of the $53 billion total.

Sources: The 1977 publications of *Insurance Facts, Best's Aggregates and Averages, Life Insurance Fact Book, Source Book of Health Insurance Data,* and *Budget of the U.S. Government.*

Social security legislation provides for programs of insurances and assistances. There are at present ten programs embraced by the general term *social security.* They comprise five forms of social insurance and five public assistances.

The *social insurance* plans include (1) federal Old-Age, Survivors, Disability, and Health Insurance (OASDHI); (2) state workers' compensation systems (and several federal); (3) federal-state systems of unemployment compensation; (4) state-sponsored (in five states) temporary disability insurance, or "cash sickness" insurance; and (5) health insurance, added to the OASDHI in 1966 with the Medicare program for the elderly. A rationale for including automobile liability insurance as a sixth category can be developed, especially in several states where it is compulsory before obtaining a license plate. It is excluded here, however, because the compulsion is not universal in the United States and because private insurers are the primary source of the liability protection.

In contrast to social insurance, *public assistance* includes no contributions or payments directly from the individuals or employers. It is financed by general tax revenues, and recipients of social assistance programs must meet certain standards of "need" to become eligible for benefits. Examples include the federal-state programs for (1) old-age assistance, (2) aid to the blind, (3) aid to dependent children, (4) Medicaid for medical care to the needy, and (5) institutional care for the aged, destitute, and other groups.

Contributions for social insurance benefits are compulsory for covered groups. Social insurance thus limits the freedom of the individual. In a strict sense, it is not an undemocratic process; rather, it changes the method of reaching a desirable objective. It reverts to earlier group methods that required every individual not only to provide for himself and his family but also to contribute, if able, to the needy in the community.

Social insurance is treated separately in Chapters 15 (Government Life and Health Insurance) and 28 (Government Property and Liability Insurance). The remainder of this section stresses the kinds of voluntary insurance and especially commercial insurance, which is the basis of the private sector of insurance.

Voluntary (private) insurance

Voluntary insurance is not based primarily upon governmental compulsion and is sought by the insured to meet a recognized need for protection. Voluntary insurance divides itself into three groups: (1) *commercial* insurance, (2) *cooperative* insurance, and (3) *voluntary government* insurance.

Voluntary insurance includes a wide range of insurance protection. *Commercial* insurance represents that division of the field usually thought of as the "insurance business," including those privately formed insurers which are organized with profit as a normal business objective. In addition to the commercial insurers there are certain nonprofit organizations that offer insurance protection to members, such as those belonging to fraternal lodges or unions. These nonprofit organizations form a class known as *cooperative* insurance. They are not to be confused with mutual insurers which are in a sense cooperative but are operated like other commercial insurers. Only organizations that plan their operations strictly on a nonprofit basis fall logically into the cooperative group. Blue Cross-Blue Shield hospital and medical insurance associations are the largest examples of this type. Finally, the government appears in the voluntary field by making insurance available where the hazards are so great that private insurers cannot well assume the risk. Examples include the federal insurance program for crops (against droughts, floods, and other perils), riot, crime and flood insurance by the Federal Insurance Administration, and the mortgage guarantee insurance of such organizations as the FHA. These insurance functions have important social implications but are all classed as *voluntary government* insurance because there is no complete element of compulsion. The choice of whether or not insurance will be carried rests largely with the insureds.

Commercial insurance. The most important of the kinds of voluntary insurance and the most highly developed of all the forms of available insurance protection is called *commercial* insurance. A vast number of insurance forms have been developed to meet the needs of insureds for family protection and for the protection of business enterprises. When the term *insurance* is used, it is usually commercial insurance to which reference is made.

In contrast to the cooperative plans, commercial insurance receives its motivating force from the profit idea. Agents located throughout the country present their insurance plans to prospects and receive as their compensation a commission on the business they produce.

Two major classifications are parts of commercial insurance: (1) *personal* insurance and (2) *property* insurance. Partly as the outgrowth of historical development and partly as the result of legal restrictions, commercial insurers have specialized in particular kinds (lines) of insurance. Traditionally, many insurers wrote business only in such categories as life and health, fire and marine, or casualty and surety insurance. Today many insurers include several or all of the categories. These insurers have become known as multiple-line or all-lines insurers.

Personal insurance. Another classification of all kinds of insurance might contrast "individual or family" versus "business" insurance, depending on the nature of the *purchaser* (family as opposed to business firm purchases). The above division is based, instead, on the nature of the *perils*; that is, whether they are more directly concerned with losses due to loss of (1) earning power of a person or (2) values of a physical property.

The loss of earning power by persons results from their death, injury, illness, old age, or loss of employment. The branches of insurance covering some of these contingencies have not, it seems, acquired names in keeping with their purposes, so that death is a contingency covered by life insurance, injury and sickness are contingencies covered by health insurance, old age is insured by annuities or pensions, and unemployment insurance indemnifies for the loss of part of income and is a type of social insurance. Life insurance, including annuities, and health insurance are important parts of the personal category of commercial insurance.

Life insurance in its simplest form undertakes to protect the insured's family, creditors, or others against pecuniary loss which may be the outgrowth of the death of the insured. The loss occasioned by death, against which life insurance attempts to provide protection, is the cessation of the current earning power of the insured. Applying an economic interpretation to the concept of death, the permanent loss of current earning capacity amounts to an "economic death." From an economic standpoint, death may be (1) actual, (2) living, or (3) retirement. The first classification represents the so-called casket death. Permanent disability from the economic standpoint is "living death," while living beyond the period of earning capacity represents "retirement death."[4]

Health insurance provides benefits for medical expenses, or for time lost because of injury or illness. Although health insurance is written by life insurers, injury and illness are also viewed as casualties, and casualty and multiple-line insurers write some of this type of business. Some insurers limit their business only to forms of health coverages, including accident insurance.

Property insurance. Property,[5] used here as a synonym for *ownership,* is the right to use and dispose of an animal or thing for a legitimate end without the interference of any other person. *Property* insurance against loss arising from the ownership or use of property includes two general classifications. The first indemnifies the insured in the event of loss growing out of damages to, or destruction of, his or her *own* property. The second form pays damages for which the insured is legally *liable,* the consequence of negligent acts that result in injuries to *other* persons or damage to their property. This is known as "liability insurance."

Recently many writers and data have been using the separate categories of property and liability insurance, but the practice is not universal. In the general sense used here, property insurance protects both physical and financial assets. Traditionally, the more usual division of property insurance has been the major groupings of fire and marine, casualty and surety insurance. Most states have permitted insurers to write *multiple-line* insurance since the early 1950s, and now many insurers write all of these major kinds of property insurance.

Fire insurance in its simplest form provides indemnity for loss or damage caused by fire. It may be written to cover not only direct loss but consequen-

---

[4] These concepts of economic death were developed by one of the early academic pioneers of life insurance, Dr. Solomon S. Huebner.

[5] Although a sound argument can be made for including a person's earning power as one of his valuable "properties," the distinction here between personal and property insurance seems justified on the basis of more generally accepted use of the term *property.*

tial (indirect) loss as well, such as loss of profits resulting from a fire which closes a business for several months. The fire field has also been extended to include a number of perils closely allied to fire or from which fire may be expected to develop, such as windstorm, explosion, smoke, earthquake, and riot. Damage to property from these perils frequently results in serious injury to the property insured, with further damage caused by fire following the disaster. It is not always easy to establish a line of demarcation between one cause and the other, and it was a natural consequence that fire insurance should be extended to cover both classes of peril. Thus we have in the fire insurance business policies covering the so-called *allied lines*.

Marine insurance covers goods primarily while they are in the process of transportation. It includes protection against the perils of fire and allied lines and also many other perils of navigation and transportation, such as theft, sinking, and collision. Although often written by fire insurers, marine insurance and its contracts are quite unique in their flexible and broad protection. They may insure one's own property while in transit or one's legal liability for others' property (such as a railroad, airline, or trucking firm has for goods in its care).

Casualty insurance is not as easy to define. Such insurance started with accidental injury insurance (1850) and steam boiler explosions (1867). Accepting "casualty" to mean "accident"—that is, a violent mishap proceeding from an unknown or unexpected cause—casualty insurance might be presumed to include any loss or damage when an accident is the cause of the loss.

However, this could apply to almost any kind of insurance. The better explanation is to recognize the meaning of the term *casualty* (1) by a process of elimination (all insurance not classified as fire, marine, or life) or (2) by reference to statutes, in which the states define the kinds of insurance which a casualty insurer can write.

The major kinds of casualty insurance today are shown in Table 2–1. Automobile insurance is by far the most important category, including more than one half of the total premium volume. A wide variety of other kinds of insurance are also a part of casualty insurance.

Surety insurance, or surety bonds, are often included with casualty insurance. Many casualty insurers are licensed to write "fidelity" (employee dishonesty) bonds and many types of "surety" bonds. These contracts are basically guarantees of performance of an expressed obligation and cover not only dishonest acts but also negligence or lack of ability. Examples include contract, executor, and many kinds of judicial bonds.

Multiple-line and all-lines insurance. For many years, the business of property insurance was carried on chiefly by insurers that devoted their efforts to a single "line," or major kind, of insurance. A fire insurer wrote only fire insurance, and a casualty insurer only the various kinds of casualty insurance mentioned above. Monoline insurance companies were the normal

Table 2–1. Kinds of casualty insurance

Kind of insurance	1977 premiums (in billions)
Automobile	$30.5
Workers' compensation	9.3
Miscellaneous liability	7.1
Multiple-peril*	6.1
Accident and health	2.4
Fidelity and surety	1.0
Crop-hail	0.3
Boiler and machinery	0.2
Burglary and theft	0.1
Credit, glass, aircraft	0.3
Total	$573.3

* Not included in this figure are $6.1 billion of premiums apportioned as the property insurance part of multiple-peril contracts.
Source: *Insurance Facts,* (New York: Insurance Information Institute, 1978), p. 10.

method of operation in American insurance. The "American" system of separating insurance into compartments of fire and casualty lines was strengthened by state laws which licensed insurers for one or the other of these major fields of property insurance, but not both.

The separation of fire and casualty insurance has broken down since 1900 in what has been called the *multiple-line insurance trend.* The convenience of and the need for broader automobile, aircraft, and other contracts were two of the factors causing the breakdown of the legislative barriers. (See Chapter 27 for a more complete discussion of this change.) Gradually the restrictions disappeared, and today all states[6] permit a fire or marine insurer to write all casualty lines, or a casualty insurer to write all fire and marine kinds of business.

Many insurer *groups* have written some multiple-line insurance since the 1920s. *Individual* insurers have often been licensed for the broad fire-casualty market since legislation permitted them to do so (1950 in most states). Note that the term has been accepted to denote not just several kinds of insurance, but the combination of at least two kinds of insurance, specifically the traditional *fire* and *casualty* lines.

The real multiple-line insurance change has centered in the last two decades on combinations of coverages in a single multiple-line package *contract.* The homeowner's policy is the best example, combining fire, theft, and liability protection in one insurance contract for the family. Many new business

---

[6] By specific statute or by insurance department rulings in five states. See David L. Bickelhaupt, *Transition to Multiple-Line Insurance Companies* (Homewood, Ill.: Richard D. Irwin. 1961). p. 37.

multiple-line contracts for stores, industries, and service businesses have also evolved.

The newest trend in broader insurance organizations and contracts is the *all-lines* trend, which combines *personal* and *property* insurance. The term *all lines* should not be used in a technical sense, for few insurers or contracts do include every possible kind of insurance. In a general sense, however, the term is useful today to describe the broadening nature of insurance operations which combine at least most of the basic types of insurance, including the traditional fire, casualty, life, and health lines.

The all-lines trend so far has been evident mostly in the formation of many large all-lines insurer *groups*. Most major property insurers have formed or bought life insurance subsidiaries. Many of the larger life insurers in the 1970s became all-lines groups by adding property-liability affiliated companies. All-lines insurance *contracts* are not yet permitted in most states, though life and disability insurance for a homeowner's mortgage has been combined with the homeowner's policy in a few new contracts. Many states, however, still prohibit personal life insurance from being combined in the same contract with property insurance. The differences in purpose, duration, and form of the contracts are given as reasons. It appears, however, that the benefits of cost reduction, greater convenience, and better coverage will eventually be recognized in more flexible laws to permit more all-lines insurance contracts.

Cooperative insurance.   The term *cooperative* is usually applied to associations operating under hospital, medical, fraternal, employee, or trade-union auspices. The associations are organized without regard to the profit motive and represent, in fact, an effort to accomplish the ends of social insurance by private enterprise.

By far the most important example of cooperative insurance, comprising 90 percent of the total business of cooperatives, are the Blue Cross, Blue Shield, and other medical insurance plans (see Figure 2–3). These cooperatives are an interesting combination of social and private insurance. They emphasize the *nonprofit*, cooperative objective and are administered in most states under special state statutes which essentially remove them from the commercial category of voluntary insurance. The associations are not incorporated or licensed as insurance companies, and some of the usual state taxes and regulations do not apply to them. Such plans include representative membership in their boards of directors from medical groups and the public. They write more than half of all hospital insurance and a significant portion of other medical cost insurance in the United States.

Fraternal societies often provide life insurance benefits for their members. The associations are ordinarily small, to a large extent local in their operation and management, and they bring together persons having a common ethnic origin or religious belief. Employee mutual sick benefit associations provide cash payments to members when sick and sometimes at the time of death.

Voluntary government insurance. Insurance that falls into this category of voluntary insurance is principally distinguished from social insurance in that there is no complete element of compulsion. The various plans offered are designed to benefit the entire community but are used only by those persons who wish to use the available benefits.

In this category are to be found such plans as the insurance of mortgage loans by the Federal Housing Administration, the insurance of growing crops by the Federal Crop Insurance Corporation, and government life insurance, administered by the Veterans Administration, for members of the armed forces. Also, one state (Wisconsin) offers life insurance through a state fund.

Because the plans are required for most chartered banks, the Federal Deposit Insurance Corporation (FDIC) and a similar plan for savings and loan associations (FSLIC) are not included here as voluntary government insurance systems.

Voluntary government insurance usually provides protection in fields that private insurance cannot safely enter. This is because of lack of experience in the field or because of the catastrophic perils connected with the insurance. Coverage of such perils on a safe basis is beyond the capacity of private enterprise.

In some instances there is an overlapping of government voluntary insurance and insurance offered by commercial insurers. One example is crop insurance, which today is available through either the FCIC or commercial insurers. The crops and areas covered, however, may not be the same.

More recent examples have appeared with federal insurance programs for riot, flood, and crime insurance through the Department of Housing and Urban Development. The insured does not usually have to purchase the coverage and the federal insurance administrator is the administrator for these plans. (See also Chapter 28.)

THE BENEFITS AND COSTS OF INSURANCE

What would our society be like without insurance? If one ponders the answers to that provocative question, many of the benefits of insurance are highlighted.

Would banks loan money on homes or businesses if they were uncertain as to whether or not the collateral value could be lost due to fire, wind, or other perils? Would finance companies approve installment loans for automobiles or other household goods? Or would anyone *want* to own an automobile if liability for losses caused to others could not be insured? Or to own a home that could be destroyed in a few hours without any recovery for the loss? Would workers choose hazardous but important occupations if it were uncertain whether the employer could pay for a work injury? How could a young family man or woman provide an income for dependent children without life insurance? Or for payment of large medical bills?

The examples are many, and they range throughout the basic parts of our society, from agriculture to commerce, banking, manufacturing, transportation, and communication. The business of insurance provides the factor of protection now regarded as essential throughout our economic and business environment.

While there is scarcely anyone who does not at some point or other make contact with the business of insurance, there are few indeed who without some reflection and investigation have an adequate idea of the great size and importance of the total field. There is no business or individual that does not owe it substantial credit for daily comforts and conveniences.

General benefits of insurance

Some examples of the wide scope and benefits of insurance have already been presented in the first chapter. A summary of the most important general benefits of insurance would include:

1. *Peace of mind.* Almost everyone has a basic desire for some security or peace of mind. To the extent that insurance provides certainty or predictability, it helps an individual or business by improving the efficiency of actions by reducing anxieties. This is a psychological factor that is difficult to measure in terms of specific benefits. It is nonetheless important in our everyday life.

2. *Keeps families and businesses together.* The existence of insurance often supplies the financial aid which permits a family or business to continue despite serious adversities that have occurred. The death or disability of a "breadwinner" can bring financial disaster to a family. With family income stopped, the spouse or children may have to give up their home and accept undesirable alternatives such as foster homes, living with relatives, or accepting relief payments. A fire or a liability suit can cause the failure of a business. Such perils can be met through insurance, which provides money at the time of need in order to keep the family or business intact.

3. *Increases marginal utility of assets.* From an economic standpoint, insurance serves as an intermediary between those who have small need for a minor amount of capital or income (i.e., the cost of insurance) and those who have great needs for the immediate use of large sums to meet losses they have suffered. Marginal utility refers to the use value of the last (marginal) unit. Basically, insurance takes the least useful "last" dollar of low marginal utility from all policyholders and repays the important "first" dollars[7] of high marginal utility to those unfortunate persons who have suffered severe losses.

4. *Provides a basis for credit.* One finds it impossible to visualize the credit economy of today without insurance. Several kinds of insurance are in-

---

[7] An exception to this statement is the use of deductibles, which may not pay the policyholder until after the loss has exceeded a specified minimum.

valuable as the foundation for credit transactions. Personal and business bank loans of many kinds use life insurance (either face values or cash values) as a guarantee that the loan will be repaid in spite of uncertain contingencies such as the death or disability of the borrower. Fire insurance is invariably required by mortgagees who loan money with real or personal property as collateral. Creditors must know that their collateral will not disappear in a fire, windstorm, or other loss, and this security is accomplished by having debtors purchase proper amounts of insurance for their homes or automobiles.

5. *Stimulates saving.* Many kinds of insurance are important because they encourage thrift. An insurance premium, though small in relation to the possible loss it protects against, is basically a prepayment in advance of potential loss. All the payments are gathered together to form a fund from which those few who do suffer losses are paid. In essence, the plan of insurance encourages all to save so that unfortunates can be repaid for their losses. In addition, life insurance has special advantages in stimulating savings. The long-term contracts, often over a whole lifetime, build substantial cash, emergency, or retirement values. Policyholders treat their regular premium payments as an obligation to their families or beneficiaries, and greater savings result than in other good-intentioned but irregular savings programs.

6. *Provides investment capital.* The savings held as assets by insurance companies are not stagnant. They provide a gigantic source of important capital for our economy. The American Council of Life Insurance reviews the creative force of almost $352 billion of life insurer assets at the beginning of 1978 by showing how these funds are used: government and industrial *bonds,* $161 billion, or 46 percent; *mortgages,* $97 billion, or 27 percent; *stocks,* $34 billion, or 10 percent; *loans* to policyholders, $28 billion, or 8 percent; *real estate,* $11 billion, or 3 percent; and *cash and miscellaneous,* $21 billion, or 6 percent.

Another measure of life insurers' investments is provided by recent data which separate investments made for "socially desirable purposes." These include investments for environmental improvements, hospitals, family housing, and education. The life and health insurance business now publishes an annual breakdown of statistics on the more than $1 billion a year spent on such projects.[8]

In addition to the large sums invested by life insurers, property insurers had $120 billion in investments. These insurers have heavy investments in bonds and much greater investments in stocks than the life insurers. Not including the assets of social insurance programs, in 1978 the investments of private insurers in the United States totaled over $470 billion. Such assets and their investment have a tremendous impact on families and businesses through the money and capital markets of the United States.

---

[8] See *Social Report of the Life and Health Insurance Business* (Washington, D.C.: Clearinghouse on Corporate Social Responsibility, 1978), p. 31.

7. *Advantages of specialization.* It is common sense that an insurance organization that specializes in risk bearing can usually perform its services more efficiently than someone else. When a business transfers its risk to an insurer it says in effect: "Here, you take care of those bothersome unpredictable risks of loss, and we'll pay attention to the main purposes of our business." The productive aspect of insurance thus emerges as an incentive to businesses or individuals, relieving them of accidental losses so that more effort, personnel, and capital can be directed toward the work for which they are best suited. For example, a department store is normally better off to shift its pure risks to an insurer and then to concentrate its efforts on greater sales or other merchandising services. The alternative of "self-insurance" or do-it-yourself insurance is better only when a very large store with diversified risks can do a better job than the insurer. Even in such a case, the store must further consider the loss of profits it has in effect given up (the "opportunity costs" in an economic sense) because it is using time and personnel to provide its own insurance program.

8. *Loss prevention.* Insurance benefits society by fostering considerable effort to prevent losses (see Chapter 1). This result is a subsidiary goal for most kinds of insurance, but undoubtedly more loss-prevention work occurs because of insurance than would occur without it. The net effect is advantageous, as lives are saved or property values preserved. Examples are fire prevention campaigns, motor vehicle safety research, health education by life insurers, elevator and boiler inspections, and many others. Also important in this work are associations sponsored by insurers, such as the National Automobile Theft Bureau, Underwriters' Laboratories, and many others.

9. *Special benefits of individual kinds of insurance.* In addition to the above eight general benefits of many kinds of insurance, each particular kind has some special benefits which make it significant to our economy. For example, consider the special purposes and achievements of life insurance. Among the separate benefits of life insurance are: establishes an immediate and liquid estate, encourages gifts to charity, aids in planning for education costs, reduces mortgage worries, offers a safe and reasonable investment service, and provides retirement income. For each particular kind of insurance a supplementary list of special benefits might be developed. The student should think about such fields as transportation insurance, theft insurance, and health insurance to provide additional examples of such benefits.

Costs of insurance

It would be unfair to consider only the benefits of insurance without mentioning possible negative considerations. The institution of insurance is not maintained without costs to the policyholders. The total premium and tax volume shown in Figure 2–3 ($320 billion in 1977) less the payments received and savings credits of insureds and beneficiaries would be one rough measure of this cost. The expenses of operating an insurer and its agency system, which often take 20 to 40 percent of the insurance premium, must be balanced against the benefits enumerated above.

From an economic viewpoint, insurance personnel could be used elsewhere in providing useful products and services. If they were not employed in the insurance business, other productive contributions to our economy could be made.

Insurance, like other worthy institutions, occasionally has some direct adverse effects. The encouragement of fraud to collect dishonest claims and the increases in carelessness that occur when people feel completely insured are two such examples. It is hoped that such effects are relatively minor but some, such as fires caused by arson, are a major and increasing problem. Although the costs are difficult to measure precisely, constant effort to control these possible added costs of the insurance system is necessary.

Statistical evidences

The major contributions of insurance can be summarized concisely in sales, employment, asset, and other figures which show its size and diversification throughout our economy. The sales volume of the total fields of insurance, in terms of premiums and taxes, has already been noted.

More than 1½ million persons are employed in the voluntary sector of insurance in the United States. This means that about one out of every 50 *employed persons* directly receives a livelihood from insurance. Not all of these persons are in insurance sales work, either, for almost two thirds of insurance employment is nonsales work.[9] Many men and women are needed by insurance for such jobs as underwriters, claimspersons, accountants, secretaries, clerks, statisticians and actuaries, advertising experts, research specialists, investment counselors, and management positions from top executives to personnel managers to field managers of many types. Few people realize that insurance employment exceeds that found in many other major parts of our economy, such as banking or mining or chemical products.

Another measure of significance has already been introduced in referring to the *assets* controlled by insurance organizations and the *investments* which stem from the use of these assets. (See tables in Chapter 6 for life and property insurer investments) Few other institutions, even financial ones, can compare with the several hundred billion dollars of funds put to use by insurers. Virtually every area of our economy receives some capital from investments made by the insurance business. In the race into space in which the United States placed men on the moon, life insurance funds provided capital for the development and manufacture of jet spacecraft. Another major use of

---

[9] *Life Insurance Fact Book* (New York: American Council of Life Insurance, 1978), p. 92.

the assets held by insurers (in fact, their major purpose) is the payment of *losses*. Each year life insurers alone pay more than $25 billion to policy-holders and beneficiaries, including about 40 percent in death payments and 60 percent in "living benefits" such as annuities and policy dividends.

The conclusion is clear. By any measure of employment, assets (and their use), or premium volume, the institution of insurance is of major significance in the economic activity of the United States. The private sector alone employs 1.7 million persons, holds some $470 billion of assets, and has an annual income of more than $170 billion. The interests of everyone are closely affected by the giant size and scope of insurance. Insurance is the cornerstone of the private property system and an essential element of our free enterprise economy.

A warning is also pertinent. The insurance business can operate efficiently only in an environment in which it can effectively accumulate data on the whole range of risk problems, from risk probabilities and analysis to a system of total risk management which assures the solvency of insurers as well as the clients that insurance serves. This is the central topic of the next chapter.

FOR REVIEW AND DISCUSSION

1. Paul is explaining what insurance is to his friend Karen. Briefly describe several methods he might use to explain how insurance works and why you think one method might be better than another to do this.

2. A newspaper article recently concluded that if an insurer received $1,000 in premiums and paid out $600 in losses, it made a profit of $400. Does this seem reasonable? Is the conclusion correct?

3. Explain how predictability is achieved through the use of insurance.

4. How can the history of the "insurance idea" help you understand its current use? Cite several examples of early insurance ideas.

5. Divide the class into about seven groups. Let each group discuss for five minutes any examples which illustrate the significance of insurance. Then have each group, through one person chosen as the reporter, present to the class what it considers to be the two *best* examples.

6. Why is it of some importance *to the insured* whether a type of insurance is part of the *social* or the *private* field of insurance?

7. In terms of size, what is the approximate *relationship* of—
   a. Voluntary and social insurance?
   b. Federal insurance as a part of social insurance?
   c. Commercial insurance as a part of voluntary insurance?
   d. Personal and property insurance as a part of commercial insurance?
   e. Life insurance as a part of personal insurance?
   f. Automobile insurance as a part of casualty insurance?

8. "The development of social insurance is in fact a threat to the insurance business." Explain why you agree or disagree with this statement.

9. How do social and voluntary forms of insurance differ? Identify the basic kinds of each as to their purposes and methods of operation.

10. What kinds of perils (causes of loss) are included in fire insurance? Marine insurance? Casualty insurance? Personal insurance? Multiple-line insurance? All-lines insurance? Why are the last two types important?

11. How do cooperative types of insurance vary from commercial and voluntary government types? Give examples of each.

12. Why is the term *casualty insurance* misleading? How did casualty insurance evolve?

13. How does insurance differ from assistance? Why is this important?

14. How has the scope of social insurance changed over the years? Give examples of some of the changes of greatest significance.

15. What are some of the benefits, of insurance?
    a. To the individual?
    b. To the business economy?
    c. To society?

16. "Over-insurance leads to fraud, full insurance to carelessness, and even partial insurance to some diminution of watchfulness." This statement is made by Willett in *The Economic Theory of Risk and Insurance*. Justify insurance in light of the statement.

17. "Insurance is one of the most fundamental parts of our entire economy," said a well-known businessman recently. If he were speaking to a group of college seniors, how would you *outline* his talk on this subject?

18. Insurance is available throughout the world today. Why do you think insurance has become of tremendous significance in the United States, whereas in other countries its position varies greatly?

Chapter 3

Concepts considered in Chapter 3—Risk-management decision making

Risk-management decision making is explained in terms of

The scope of risk management, which briefly is coordinated risk treatment: systematically analyzing and deciding on the best alternatives.

Its *purpose* is to reduce the adverse effects of risk by conserving the assets and income of businesses, institutions, and individuals.

Its *method* is the use of the four risk-management steps, particularly by integrating the two basic risk-treatment methods of *risk control* and *risk financing*. It is *not* all management, nor all risks, but it is much more than mere *insurance* management.

The place of the risk manager is presented as a growing position of significance within the *organizational framework* of managerial decisions, with broad *responsibilities* and *qualifications* for performing tasks well in a professional manner.

The steps in risk management are the decisions made in regard to:

Risk identification, through the use of the *risk and insurance survey, loss-exposure charts, financial statements, flow charts,* and other methods.

Risk measurement, through applying mathematical tools and often new quantitative techniques to loss *frequency, severity,* and *variation.*

Choice and use of methods, reviewing the basic alternatives of risk treatment of Chapter 1, as well as other alternatives, such as *captive insurers.*

Risk administration, coordinating and implementing policy statements, and monitoring procedures in order to meet continually changing needs.

An example of risk-management decision making illustrates the four steps in risk management for a plastics manufacturer.

A case study for business risk management of a modern shopping center includes questions reviewing the total process of risk-management decision making.

Risk-management decision making

The whole understanding of risk and risk-treatment alternatives as presented in Chapter 1, and of insurance as discussed in Chapter 2, leads to the major decision-making process of the persons or businesses facing the problems of risk. There is a dilemma in deciding on the sequence of presenting ideas in regard to risk management: (1) Should the alternatives of risk treatment be discussed first, and then the process of risk management? or (2) Should the scope and steps in risk management be presented to the student first, and then the risk-treatment alternatives? This text has chosen the first sequence because risk-management decision making is an integrative process. As such, it becomes more meaningful to have a reasonable background of information about risk and alternatives in treating it before the coordinating steps of risk management are studied.

A danger exists in thinking of each of the methods of treating risk as a single and complete solution to the problem of risk. In practice, it is much more common to find all, or at least several, techniques used together to provide the best answers for meeting the financial problems of risk. How this is done through the process of risk management is the focus of this chapter.

THE SCOPE OF RISK MANAGEMENT

The two basic methods of treating risk—risk control and risk financing—are integrated in a process known as *risk management*.[1] In terms of *purpose,* risk management is described as the effective reduction of the adverse effects of risk. "The objective . . . is to preserve the ongoing ability of his organization to provide its goods and services to its customers, . . . to conserve assets, both human and physical, and to protect the earning power of the corporation."[2]

As to *method,* risk management is the use of the steps in risk management (see next section), and particularly concerns the use of the two basic risk-

---

[1] Robert I. Mehr and Bob A. Hedges, *Risk Management in the Business Enterprise* (Homewood, Ill.: Richard D. Irwin, 1963), p. vii. This is the first use of the term in the title of a textbook. The 1974 edition is titled *Risk Management: Concepts and Applications.*

[2] H. Felix Kloman, "Alternatives in Risk Management," *Risk Management,* June–July 1973, p. 42.

treatment methods of risk control and financing. In effect, it is *coordinated risk treatment.*

Risk management is basically a problem of decision making for either a *personal* or a *business* situation. Each situation is unique in the sense that none is exactly the same, even though some common characteristics may be identified. Both personal and business risks can be taken care of, or "managed," but most efforts and principles of risk management have centered on business risk. With increasing consumer education in family finance, it is expected that the personal consumer will increasingly use the risk-management technique.

The term *risk management* is a relatively new and popular one, though its exact meaning and scope are neither fully understood nor fully accepted.[3] It is not all management of a business. In fact, it does not concern all risk, and the term as it has evolved thus far is really "(pure) risk management," it being understood that the process does not deal with speculative risks. Management reluctance to accept the term *risk management* sometimes stems from executives not understanding that the field is limited to pure risks and primarily to protecting the organization's assets and income from accidental losses.

Management is the whole process of planning, organizing, and controlling people and things. Risk management is only a part of this process, but an extremely important one. It has been correlated with the "security" function, one of the six principal functions of businesses: (1) technical, (2) commercial, (3) financial, (4) security (protection of property and persons), (5) accounting, and (6) managerial.[4] Even in this limited concept, risk management is estimated to be 10 percent or more of all business activity of managers.

Risk management is clearly more than just *insurance management,* a concept which would be primarily limited to decisions of when, how much, how, and where to insure the uncertainties previously described as insurable-type risks. Certainly, insurance as *one* of the techniques of handling risk is needed. In fact, it may remain as the principal method of treating the many risks of business. But without careful study of *all* the alternatives in risk management in a coordinated decision-making process, insurance may oftentimes be used where it shouldn't be used, or not used where it should be used. Although some risks usually must be insured, to deserve the title of *risk manager* a person must do much more than merely be an "insurance buyer."

---

[3] The origin of the term is not precise. One of the earliest uses appeared in chap. 35 of the fourth edition of Albert H. Mowbray and Ralph H. Blanchard, *Insurance* (New York: McGraw-Hill Book Co., Inc., 1955). Newer editions give a fuller explanation of the functions and principles of risk management.

[4] Credit for this concept belongs to Henri Fayol, *General and Industrial Management* (New York: Pitman Publishing Corp., 1949); and to C. Arthur Williams, Jr., and Richard H. Heins, *Risk Management and Insurance* (New York: McGraw-Hill Book Co., 1964), table 2–1, pp. 13 and 77, who first used it in an insurance text. A third edition discusses this idea on p. 24.

THE PLACE OF THE RISK MANAGER

The changing function of *risk managers* toward the broader risk-management concept began to occur during the early 1960s.[5] Acceptance of this wider perspective was gradual, but the "risk-management trend" has escalated rapidly in the past decade. The only trade journal of the professional society of risk managers, now representing almost 3,000 of the larger U.S. businesses, institutions, and governmental bodies, was called *The National Insurance Buyer* until the early 1970s. Now it is titled *Risk Management,* and it is published monthly by the Risk and Insurance Management Society (RIMS).

RIMS has provided a strong impetus toward making risk managers key executives on the management team. An educational emphasis is providing opportunities for fundamental and advanced preparation for the expanding job of risk manager. The Insurance Institute of America has designed a series of courses in cooperation with RIMS, leading to the professional designations of Associate in Risk Management (ARM), and Loss Control Management (LCM). In addition, regular national and regional conferences, and publications and research grants sponsored by the RIMS Risk Studies Foundation, have aided the growth possibilities in this field considerably.

American businesses and institutions are rapidly recognizing the need for professional risk managers. Increasing insurance costs, the broadening scope of liability exposures, governmental legislation tightening safety standards, and other factors are creating a fuller appreciation for the value of risk-management activities. Major business publications have featured risk management as a need for small and medium-sized companies as well as the larger corporations.[6] Risk-management decision making may include much more than traditional tasks related to property and liability insurance. It now often comprises the whole spectrum of protection, including safety and employee benefit administration problems.[7]

To carry out risk-management decision making, many business firms and institutions have created the position of risk manager as a specialist performing this function for management. Only a few of these specialists have this exact title, and the majority are still known instead as "insurance manager," "corporate insurance director," or by other titles. Increasingly, the position is a full-time one, particularly in organizations with more than 1,000 employees. In many other firms (about one fourth of the RIMS members), the risk manager (by whatever the title held) is performing risk-management

---

[5] One of the earliest books that compiled articles describing the increasing duties of risk managers was *The Growing Job of Risk Management* (New York: American Management Association, 1962).

[6] See "The Risk Management Revolution," *Fortune,* July 1976, p. 36; and "Big Push in Risk Management," *Dun's Review,* June 1977, p. 62.

[7] Thomas B. Morehart and John J. O'Connell, "The Risk Manager's Role in Employee Benefits Administration," *Risk Management,* October 1977, p. 42.

functions as a part-time job in connection with other duties within the organization.

In a fairly large firm, the risk manager's *position within the organization* usually involves reporting to a top-level financial executive. In smaller firms, the risk manager probably operates more in a staff function, reporting directly to the president. Studies show that about one third of the risk managers consider themselves to be members of top management, while more of the others are part of middle management.[8] Almost 80 percent report to top managers—the president, vice president, controller, or secretary—of their organization. More than half of RIMS members were risk managers for organizations with more than 2,000 employees and $100 million annual gross sales. Figure 3–1 shows the place of the risk manager for a typical RIMS member. New corporate risk-management organization systems are also appearing, tying insurance and safety functions more closely together.[9]

The *responsibilities* and authority of the risk manager are quite broad. They cut across many phases of the activities of an organization, and often the risk manager shares the responsibility for certain functions with other executives. A recent study showed that the risk manager of larger firms had, in a majority of the cases, full responsibility for property and liability: (1) risk identification and evaluation, (2) selection of insurer, (3) approval of insurance renewals and amounts, (4) negotiation of insurance rates, (5) seeking competitive insurance bids, (6) insurance record keeping, (7) choosing deductibles, and (8) insurance claims handling.[10] The risk manager usually shared authority for: (1) deciding whether or not to insure or retain (including self-insurance) risks, (2) selection of insurance broker, (3) instituting safety expenditures, and (4) reviewing contracts other than insurance. Increasingly, the risk manager is also becoming involved in self-insurance administration; safety administration and compliance; working with the personnel manager on workers' compensation and in designing and arranging for employee benefit plans of group insurance and pensions; and coordination of the total risk-identification, analysis, and control functions of the organization. There are few areas, O'Connell concludes, in which the risk manager has not been acquiring a greater degree of control over the decision-making process.

---

[8] American Society of Insurance Management Study of the Risk Manager and ASIM (New York: Woodward and Fondiller, 1969). A January 1978 study prepared for RIMS, *The Risk and Insurance Manager: A Study of Responsibilities and Compensation* (Princeton, N.J.: Sission and Co.), compares changes and shows the risk manager's increasing importance.

[9] A series of three articles by Russell A. Drake, Jr., Richard S. Johnson, and James A. McCullough illustrates new organizational and administrative structures for risk management in the October 1977 issue of *Risk Management*.

[10] John J. O'Connell, "Changing Responsibilities and Activities of Risk Managers—1969 vs. 1975," *Risk Management*, January 1976, pp. 19-22. The data are from his 1975 Ohio State University dissertation, "Variables Related to Differences in the Risk Management Function in Large Organizations."

Figure 3–1. Organization chart showing the place of the risk manager

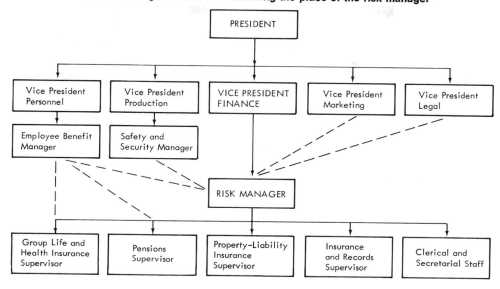

One other important role of the risk manager is to encourage and help management to formulate a *policy statement* on the objectives and responsibilities of risk management. Having such a written policy statement approved by the president and the board of directors can aid the risk manager greatly in defining the scope and limitations of the job. The objectives, responsibilities, authority, and general policies of his or her department should be clearly stated. Setting broad guidelines in this way improves the risk manager's relationships with other executives and departments, and in obtaining the cooperation of many persons within the organization who are crucial to a risk manager for information and for the supervision of risk management in the firm.

The *qualifications* for good risk managers are determined by the extent of their important and usually broad responsibilities. They usually have a college education, as well as insurance and other business experience of many years, and often technical background in accounting, engineering, or law. Personal characteristics which enhance their effectiveness are leadership abilities, initiative, tact in working with others, and sound decision-making judgment.

Risk managers should understand the particular insurance needs of their organizations, because of their day-to-day contact and experience in their own firms. They should be familiar with and well trained in analyzing insurance coverage, rates, and markets. They are *not,* however, substitutes for good insurance agents or brokers. Agents should be able to supplement the work of risk managers and to provide many essential services in aiding them

to locate insurance markets and loss-prevention services and to obtain fair
loss settlements. Other advisers may often be used by or in conjunction with
the insurance agent. Examples include safety engineers, accountants, attorneys, and trust experts.

Sometimes *the insurance agent,* particularly for small and medium-sized
firms, serves in effect as the risk manager for an organization which has no
one person assigned to these responsibilities. Larger agencies, especially,
offer to serve in this capacity. Care must be taken to see (1) that the services are much broader than mere insurance coverages, and include a real
risk-management scope of loss prevention and other risk-treatment alternatives, and (2) that the insurance agency knows the special individual needs
of the organization. The agent or broker cannot be expected to have a sufficiently accurate knowledge of all the ramifications of the insurance and risk
needs of a huge business organization on a continual basis. With a large organization, a very small rate differential may mean a difference of thousands
of dollars in premium. The expense of surveys to determine necessary improvements to secure even a minor adjustment in rate will pay where the
premium volume is large. With reference to coverages, the large concern may
quite safely eliminate certain risk from the insurance program and carry other
risks on a deductible or catastrophe basis. While the professional agent and
broker can cooperate with the insurance buyer in solving such problems—
in fact they are quite essential—it is nevertheless true that the final responsibility for the risk-management program rests with the concern itself. It is
because of this that the trained risk manager is coming to occupy an important position in the field of administration.

For international organizations the growing task of *international risk
management* is another area of great challenge for risk managers. Foreign
operations bring many new problems, including conflicts in corporate goals,
different legal and cultural environments, and communication difficulties.
A landmark study shows how risk management practices vary for multinational companies.[11]

THE STEPS IN RISK MANAGEMENT

The risk-management function is perhaps best described and understood
in terms of the decisions which are a part of it. The process begins with a
recognition of the existence of various risks. Basically this is the *identification or classification* of risks. Then the risks of loss must be *measured, analyzed, and evaluated* in terms of frequency, severity, and variability. Next
a decision must be made as to the *choice and use of the methods* for meeting
each specific risk identified. Some risks may be avoided, some retained under

[11] Norman A. Baglini, *Risk Management in International Corporations* (New
York: Risk Studies Foundation, RIMS, 1976).

planned programs, and some transferred by such a method as insurance. Once the methods of treatment are chosen, plans for *administration* of the program must be instituted.

The above decisions are summarized as the key steps in the total process of treating risk:

1. Identification.
2. Measurement.
3. Choice and use of methods of treatment.
4. Administration.

Risk identification

Chapter 1 has already presented the fundamental ideas of what risk is and the classifications of risk, which are the basis for risk identification. Closely akin to the life-health insurance programming process discussed in Chapter 16 is the *risk and insurance survey* made in regard to the property-liability risks for a given establishment. Although most often used in business situations, the term is also appropriate in the individual or personal area. The survey is not limited to property-liability risks, but can and often does include life-health risks as well, even though many of the forms and methods used emphasize the property-liability aspects of risks.

Nature.   Risk and insurance surveys are known under a variety of names. They are called *plans, abstracts, analyses, audits, fact-finders* and other such names.[12] In practice all are essentially designed to identify the risks and perils and then plan for providing methods (including insurance) for meeting them. They may also uncover points of weakness in existing insurance programs, suggesting rearrangements of amounts and coverages. The plans should indicate risks that the insured may carry, losses that may be prevented, and where insurance is, therefore, not needed.

The need.   The usual risk and insurance survey is basically designed for businesses, but nonprofit institutions, including government divisions, also need and can use the same principles to advantage.

In a specialized use, it also fits the needs of a trustee who often faces new and unfamiliar responsibilities and many perplexing problems. State and city officials, corporation directors, guardians, executors, and trustees subject themselves to grave criticism or direct personal liability if without verification they are satisfied that the risk and insurance programs of their predecessors are sufficient. Frequently such persons have but the vaguest idea of the risks that threaten the institutions under their care. Verbal recommendations

---

[12] For example, see the general "Risk Analysis" form published by the Insurance Division of the American Management Association. A new "Risk Analysis Guide," by A. E. Pfaffle and Sal Nicosia, has also been produced by the AMA. For specific industrial groups, see Bernard Daenzer, "Risk Discovery Guide" (New York: AMA, 1978).

or suggestions may be misunderstood or misinterpreted. The carefully prepared risk and insurance program, coordinated by professional life and property insurance counselors, presents a logical solution of the problem.

The risk and insurance plan, while of special interest and value to large
business undertakings and to institutions, is by no means limited in value to
large enterprises. Many small and medium-sized businesses need a good risk
and insurance survey as much as do the larger firms. It is the smaller businesses, in fact, that are particularly vulnerable to financial ruin as the result
of a mistake or an omission in good insurance protection. In a small business
it might be possible to follow the rule "When in doubt, insure." This practice
might prove to be less expensive and provide as much protection as would
result from an expensive program of insurance and risk administration within
the firm. However, small businesses must also plan to take advantage of all
insurance cost reductions that are economically advisable. Otherwise, small
profit margins can turn into business losses. The lack of full-time, or even
part-time, "risk managers" (such as might be found in the larger business
firms) also emphasizes the need for organized and systematic action by small
businesses.

The method.   The risk and insurance survey involves risk detection, identification, and classification. Sometimes it also includes estimates of the risk
or loss values, which are part of risk measurement. The insurance agent or
broker may help in the planning and may to a large degree be able to prepare
the survey. The work, however, will often require the close cooperation of
representatives of the business firm or institution.

All pure risk exposure will be carefully searched out. A chart may be
drawn, sometimes known as a *loss-exposure survey chart,* such as that shown
in Figure 3–2.

Elaborate survey charts have been prepared to met the needs of different
types of business establishments. Special survey forms have been prepared by
insurers, insurance consultants, and insurance agencies. Several different but
effective methods of risk identification are used, such as (1) *the financial
statement method,* (2) analyzing *flowcharts* of the firm's functions and
operations, (3) *systems analysis,* and (4) *personal inspections.*

In the *financial statement method,* each account title in the balance sheet,
the profit and loss statement, and other financial statements is listed separately and analyzed to determine the potential perils that might cause losses.
Real estate, cash, inventories, personal property, accounts receivable, income
accounts, and so on, each has special characteristics that affect loss. This can
be an effective and comprehensive method for identifying risks.

Using *flowcharts* is another systematic method for identifying losses for a
firm. Charts showing the entire operations in detail are prepared, and each
step in the production and distribution of goods and services is analyzed to
consider the potential losses that might occur at each point or location in the
process.

Figure 3–2. Loss-exposure chart accompanying risk and insurance survey

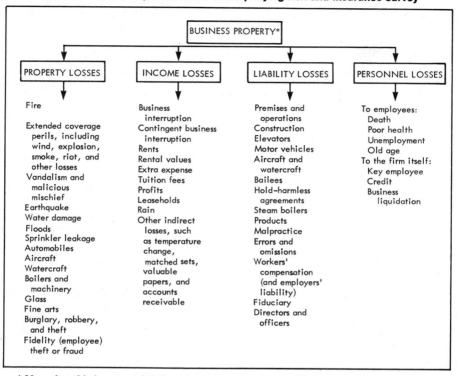

* Note that this is a *partial* listing of only some of the possible losses.

† The "personnel" classification was first developed in C. Arthur Williams, Jr., and Richard M. Heins, *Risk Management* (New York: McGraw-Hill Book Co.). The latest edition appeared in 1976.

The newer concept of *systems analysis* can also be applied in identifying risks, with financial management techniques (such as the careful prediction of cash flow) included, as the firm's total systems of responsibility and authority are evaluated.

All of these solutions are of value as checks against possible exposures, but none of them will replace the technical knowledge that is applied by the insurance agent, augmented by the specialized information that can be derived from the insured's own risk manager. *Personal inspections* of premises and operations remain a significant source of knowledge to the risk manager. Risk managers may also want to develop their own loss-exposure lists.

An organized risk and insurance survey is considerably more than the completion of a published checklist or the arbitrary insertion of recommendations in a set of blank forms. It includes (1) perils or loss identification and (2) diagnosing the particular firm's exposures. An impressive-looking survey delivered by a person who is not fully competent to make it can be a danger in that it may give a sense of security not warranted in the circumstances if it has not been tailored to the special needs of the individual organization.

Risk measurement

In Chapter 1 risk was examined as to basic speculative (loss or gain) and pure (loss or no loss) types. Degree of risk was shown to be measured by variation between expected and actual losses. In describing how insurance works, in Chapter 2, the concepts of probability and uncertainty of loss were described.

Probability of loss is measured in several ways: as to (1) *frequency*, (2) *severity*, and (3) *variation*. It is important for risk managers, on the basis of the past loss experience of their firms or that of similar classes of risk exposures, to estimate the future losses that may be expected. They must also try to predict variation in future losses, as to both frequency and severity, in order to help them decide what to do about various loss exposures. This is the task of risk measurement.

Some losses may be found to be so infrequent that it would be uneconomic to try to deal with them. Damage to property by "flying saucers" or "unidentified flying objects" (UFOs) may be an example of this type of loss probability. At the other extreme, some losses may be so frequent as to be regularly anticipated. If small in amount, relative to a firm's assets or income, then the situation may suggest that the risk manager take steps to retain them by absorption in normal expenses or by setting up a reserve to handle them as they occur. Not only must the frequency of loss be high and the severity low, but the variation of losses within a time period (such as one year) must be regular and predictable within ranges that the firm can handle. Chapter 2 illustrated how the principle of large numbers was used to help predict variation.

Measuring losses by using mathematical tools[13] and statistical data is the principal technique of risk measurement. Properly carried out by the risk manager, this step can aid the risk manager greatly in suggesting the risks and losses that it is most important to treat. For example, if an organization owns 100 automobiles that have averaged 25 losses a year, totaling $25,000, a loss "frequency" of 25/100 (or ¼) and an average loss "severity" of $1,000 can be calculated. With more data, the loss "variation" or risk could be estimated. The process can also be helpful in pointing toward the best choice of risk-treatment methods (discussed in the next section) and in analyzing loss retention and loss funding alternatives.[14]

---

[13] Jack E. Brucker and John J. O'Connell, "Quantitative Techniques and Risk Management," *Risk Management,* May 1975, p. 16.

[14] James V. Davis, "Moving toward Financial Quantification of Risk Management," *Risk Management,* November 1977, p. 25.

Sophisticated mathematical studies and models are not always necessary.[15] If data are lacking, or the cost of making more precise estimates is too high, then simpler methods of measuring risk may be advisable. For example, risk managers often divide potential losses into various categories of importance to their firm. Classifications of loss frequency, severity, and variability may be established, such as those losses which are of high, moderate, or slight importance. Estimates of "maximum possible loss," the worst that *could* happen, and "maximum probable loss," the worst that is *likely* to happen, are valuable measures. In this way the solutions for the most significant kinds of loss can be tackled first and others of minor importance can be disregarded in the process of risk management.

Computers are becoming both an important tool and a new source of information on potential loss problems for risk managers. They are a means by which a much improved risk-management information system can be developed to aid decision making, and a supplement to quantitative tools that can make risk and loss measurement feasible and practical. On the other hand, from a security and safety standpoint computers bring a whole new set of problems to an organization. The computer room is a concentrated area with extremely valuable equipment and with records that are vital to many organizations. New "Halon" and CO_2 fire extinguishing systems are needed, sabotage and vandalism must be prevented, tape erasure problems avoided, employee fraud and espionage by competitors checked, and loss of electric power to the computers anticipated with backup alternative power sources. A challenging specialized area for risk-management techniques has emerged in the 1970s.[16]

Choice and use of methods of risk treatment

The third step in risk management is taken after risks have been identified and measured. It is one of the most crucial and difficult phases, because it involves careful evaluation of both the suitability and the cost of various alternatives.

The most significant characteristic of the *risk-management concept* is that it is a *synthesis* of all methods of dealing with risk. Even the consideration of one peril, such as fire, usually requires that a risk manager integrate the two basic methods of *risk control* and *risk financing*. These alternatives have been discussed in Chapter 1, but a review is presented here and is summarized in Figure 3–3, together with the steps in the process of risk management.

---

[15] A recommended primer for measuring probability and risk, forecasting losses, and using present value and linear regression concepts and break-even models is Mark R. Greene, *Decision Analysis for Risk Management* (New York: Risk and Insurance Management Society, 1977).

[16] See "Risk Management and the Computer," *Risk Management*, August 1976, p. 7.

Figure 3–3. Risk-treatment alternatives and the steps in risk management

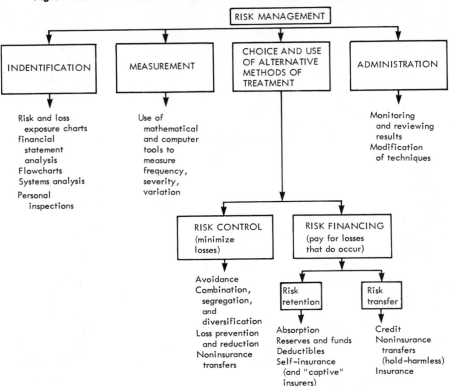

In addition to some forms of risk *avoidance, combination* (and its related methods) and *noninsurance transfers, loss prevention and reduction* are emphasized among the methods of *risk control.* Their purpose is to minimize losses. Examples of loss prevention and reduction include good building construction, adequate fire-fighting and protective equipment, burglar alarms, safety contests, the use of safes for valuable properties, duplicate records, and many other techniques. Cost is one of the major limitations, as well as the fact that very few situations exist in which loss is completely preventable.

Risk financing methods include many common and useful techniques of risk retention and risk transfer. *Risk-retention* plans include four methods under which risks are retained. *Absorption* of losses in operating expenses may be limited. *Reserves* have the major disadvantage of providing only a bookkeeping limitation on the use of assets; they do not guarantee that cash will be available for meeting losses. The use of maintenance, depreciation, or savings *funds* for meeting small, frequent, and normal losses may be appropriate, but such funds are often only partial solutions to the problems involved in most risks. There are a number of types of insurable risks that may, as a matter of policy, be retained without setting up a funded reserve. The nature and extent of such risk retention will depend upon the size of the business, its financial ability to absorb losses, the loss frequency, and whether or not there are any particular advantages to be derived from commercial insurance. Glass, for example, may be the subject for insurance with one concern because of the high value of the plate glass involved; with another firm, however, glass may be regarded as a routine maintenance item.

Deductibles and excess plans are closely related to the use of funds and reserves, because they involve risk retention, too. In fact, reserves and funds can be used to finance the deductible portion of losses that are retained when insurance is purchased. Many of the same factors used in choosing other types of risk retention plans would apply in deciding on the type and size of appropriate deductibles.

Self-insurance, as a risk financing method, is feasible where there is a sufficient risk spread, with a limited exposure at any one location. Funded reserves are established to pay losses. Regular payments are made to the fund, and losses charged to it. Loss evaluation is practiced by maintaining good records of loss amounts and causes. An adequate loss-prevention system is incorporated into the plan. It is essential in this respect to distinquish between self-insurance and no insurance. There can be self-insurance only if the risks are sufficiently spread and the amount of risk at each location is such that a severe loss will not adversely affect the company or the funds set up for the losses. Most of these funds come from current earnings and current cash flows, which become important considerations.[17]

If property values are concentrated, going without insurance (even with an adequate fund available to pay all losses) is simply placing the fund at risk. With a building valued at $1 million and $1 million on deposit to meet any fire loss, going without insurance means inviting the loss of $1 million in cash instead of the loss of the building. The property owner may have accumulated a substantial fund to pay losses, but such a situation cannot be said to be self-insurance. The insurance premium may be saved, but a serious loss might spell financial disaster. An example of the failure of what was purported to be a self-insurance fund is the state office building that was presumably covered under the Michigan state fire fund. It was destroyed with an estimated loss of $4.5 million. It is interesting to note that the state library located in the destroyed building was insured in private companies for a total of $2 million for a premium slightly in excess of $3,000. Other examples of the failure of pseudo "self-insurance" plans by business or government units have been observed. Although 22 states now have self-insurance funds for insuring fire and extended coverage perils, six states which once had them have abandoned them.[18]

---

[17] Ralph E. Gentry, "Assessing a Company's Ability to Self-Assume Risk," *Risk Management,* February 1977, p. 38.

[18] Mark R. Greene and Michael L. Murray, "Self-Insurance of State Property," *Journal of Risk and Insurance,* March 1978, p. 109.

One risk financing method, closely related to self-insurance, has gained in popularity in recent years as a method of obtaining some tax advantages and closer control of contract design and loss payment. This is the *captive insurer,* a legally separate insurance company that is organized by a firm primarily to write its own insurance. Special tax savings can be achieved by licensing the insurer in Bermuda or other foreign countries, and several hundred captive insurers were formed in the 1970s.[19] One state (Colorado) passed a law in 1972 specifically in order to permit and attract such insurers. The time and expense of such extra arrangements necessarily restricts this alternative of treating risks to the larger firms. Special requirements must be met to gain IRS tax approval.[20]

Among the methods of *risk transfer,* by far the most important is *insurance.* Credit arrangements and some limited use of *noninsurance transfers* (hold-harmless agreements, for example) are also possible.

Cost comparisons among *all* the methods of risk treatment have frequently been recommended in this text. In order to give a simple example of how this can be done as part of risk-management decision making, two of the most common methods of risk financing—*risk retention* and *insurance*—are contrasted here. An illustration might use a matrix table, such as that shown in Table 3–1, to compare alternative costs of insuring or retaining the risk of loss to a building by fire. In this table, some arbitrary judgment figures must be used, such as the cost of worry. However, if some attempt is made to predict reasonable amounts, the decision to insure or retain the risk becomes a more rational one as compared with a decision based on little or no attempt to compare costs. In the example, if the probability of fire is relatively high and the $50,000 loss to the firm is significant to the firm's financial position, the decision to insure rather than retain the risk is logical.

Retention of risks due to lower estimated costs than the costs of other alternatives does occur. Insurers cannot always be right in their estimate of losses, nor most economical in their expense of operation. Whenever they are wrong or inefficient, retention may be advisable.

Risk administration

Once the choice of risk-treatment alternatives has been made, and the plan has been put into effect, the risk manager must devise a system for implementing and periodically monitoring the details of risk management.[21]

---

[19] A concise summary of the definition, types, advantages, feasibility, expenses, and locations of captive insurers is found in *The John Liner Letter* (Wellesley Hills, Mass.: Shelby Publishing Corp.), vol. 14, nos. 10 and 11 (September and October 1977).

[20] J. Richard Barnes, "The Colorado Captive—An Answer to IRS Objections?" *Risk Management,* April 1977, p .40.

[21] Dr. George L. Head divides the administration step into two parts—the implementing of the techniques and the monitoring of the results. See *The Risk Management Process* (New York: Risk and Insurance Management Society, 1978).

Table 3-1. Comparison of the alternative cost of retention and insurance

Decision	Outcome*	
	Fire	*No fire*
1. Retention	Potentially insurable losses .... $50,000 Uninsured† losses .... 5,000 Worry .... 1,000 Total $56,000	Worry .... $1,000 Total $1,000
2. Insurance	Cost of insurance .... $ 1,000 Uninsured losses .... 5,000 Worry (uninsured losses) .... 100 Total .... $ 6,100	Cost of insurance ..... $1,000 Worry (uninsured losses) 100 $1,100

* To simplify the illustration, only two outcomes are assumed: total loss by fire or no fire.
† Uninsured losses are those losses that cannot be insured, such as inconvenience, loss of customers, and perhaps depreciation and credit costs for rebuilding.
Source: The first textbook to use such a comparison, from which this is adapted, is C. Arthur Williams, Jr., and Richard M. Heins, *Risk Management and Insurance* (New York: McGraw-Hill Book Co., 1964), pp. 62–63. In their 1971 edition (p. 228), these authors add the probabilities of losses, and the use of deductibles with various amounts of insurance. In their 1976 edition (p. 222), they evaluate tax factors, also evaluated for both insured and uninsured losses, and retention with and without the use of safety measures.

Actually, the process must be carried out in conjunction with each of the first three steps of risk management. The total process should be coordinated to agree with whatever written policy statement has been adopted. New risks must be continually identified, and all risks must be frequently remeasured. Treatment alternatives, too, must be reconsidered and reviewed for their effectiveness and their actual and potential costs. One example of new perspectives for risk management is summarized: "The challenge is simple. Ours is a waste society, one in which we have tolerated an appalling waste of human, natural, and financial resources. Can we change before we waste ourselves to extinction?"[22]

Procedures for obtaining continuous information from all executives and departments of the firm, and from outside agents or consultants, must be well established. Only by revising the formal organization and informal channels for overseeing the functions of risk identification, measurement, and choice of treatment alternatives to meet changing needs can the risk manager achieve success in his or her challenging task.

One important part of risk administration in regard to the choice of insurance is to arrange for the actual issue of the contracts of protection. Sometimes this requires the use of "binders" for temporary coverage, particularly of property-liability insurance. This makes insurance effective immediately, even though the complete written contract may be obtained weeks later.

[22] H. Felix Kloman, "Risk Management in a Waste Society," *Risk Management,* April 1973, p. 9.

Through cooperation among insurance underwriters, agents and brokers, and risk managers,[23] this procedure must be carried out carefully, by arriving at a clear understanding of when the protection is effective and what the scope of the coverage will be when the completed contract is written. Some binders may be given orally, but it is the best practice to have such agreements put into written binders as soon as possible. The administration of loss and prevention programs and of existing and continuing coverage is also important. The risk manager keeps precise renewal information on insurance contracts in order to check with the insurance agent and prevent any lapse in the needed coverage. The technique of risk-management administration involves the coordination of many persons and much information. It is the continual problem, and opportunity, of good risk management to put the whole process together in the most effective manner possible.[24]

An introductory text in the field of risk and insurance should not lose sight of its major premise, namely, that for most personal situations and for many business situations, insurance is the most effective method of meeting important risks. If this were not true, then the subject for study in this whole text might be called risk management. The predominant method of treating pure risk *is* insurance, however, and it is here that this book places its emphasis. Given a familiarity with the process of risk management, from which decisions to insure stem, the student needs most to discover and evaluate the wide scope, techniques, and benefits of insurance. It is on the insurance method that many of the following chapters concentrate, though the insurance choices made should be considered within the context of the risk-management process. Insurance should usually be the final consideration, after proper appraisal of the possible benefits of other risk-treatment alternatives through the risk-management process outlined in the preceding section.

AN EXAMPLE OF RISK-MANAGEMENT DECISION MAKING

In reviewing the above steps, an example may be helpful. Consider the problem of a small manufacturer of plastic toys. The risk manager for such a firm might put together a package of risk management that would include:

I. *Step 1—Risk identification*
   Fire and explosion are relatively obvious as two major risks of loss, and the answers below emphasize these. Other risks are classified by using a checklist of perils, and comparing these with financial statement accounts.

II. *Step 2—Risk measurement*
   By using past company records, the risk manager finds out that there has been extreme variation in both the number and amount of losses during the

---

[23] Edward J. Denari, "The Triad in Risk Management," *Risk Management,* November 1977, p. 11.

[24] A helpful source of current information is a loose-leaf service compiling risk-management subjects in Matthew Lenz, Jr., ed., *Risk Management Manual* (Santa Monica, Calif.: Merritt Co.).

past 20 years. The degree of risk is therefore high. Industry loss probability is also found to be higher than that for most manufacturers. Values of buildings, machinery, inventory, and other property are appraised.

III. *Step 3—Choice and use of method of treatment.*

    A. *Risk control methods* are used:

        1. *Avoiding some risks:* in order to conserve working capital and avoid risk, three trucks are *leased* by the firm, with the rental company taking care of the fire, theft, and collision coverage. The same technique is chosen in leasing a new computer to replace an outdated one.

        2. *Segregating* the storage of finished goods in a separate building, located away from the more hazardous production facilities, is decided upon.

        3. *Diversifying* the product line, so that destruction of one type of specialized machine would not shut down the production process, is adopted by management at the risk manager's recommendation.

        4. An intensive *loss-prevention and loss-reduction* program against the perils of fire and explosion is adopted. A sprinkler system, a fire patrol, night security guards, the training of employees in fire prevention habits and the use of fire-fighting equipment, regular inspections and proper building construction are each used to advantage.

        5. A *noninsurance control* of risk is accomplished by subcontracting with another firm to produce one of the more toxic plastics necessary in the company's research department.

    B. *Risk financing methods* are used:

        1. *Retaining* some risks by the following actions:

            a. A *reserve* is set up in the corporate accounts to take care of smaller losses up to $1,000. (Such losses might have been just absorbed in the operating expense account.)

            b. A *deductible* of $1,000 is purchased in connection with the fire insurance contract. Letting the supervisors know that this has been done may encourage the prevention of losses.

            c. *Self-insurance* is considered but decided against as a method of treatment because values are concentrated at one location.

        2. *Transferring* some risks is chosen for the following:

            a. The building and its contents are *insured,* including fire and explosion coverage, for $750,000, with a $1,000 deductible. Consultation with several different insurers and agents helps determine the proper perils and the amounts of coverage.

            b. A *noninsurance transfer* of risk is made by means of a hold-harmless agreement with the firm's major sales distributor, in which the distributor agrees to pay for any product liability losses caused by negligence in the distribution process.

IV. *Step 4—Risk administration*

    A. The above choices of risk-treatment alternatives are carefully checked for conformity with the written policy statement of the firm.

    B. The choices are implemented by notification and discussion with other departments of the firm: rental of the trucks through the purchasing department; segregating finished goods by consultation with the inventory control section; diversification of product line with the production department; reserve accounts with the accounting department and the treasurer's office; deductibles explained to the supervisors of various departments; loss-prevention program coordinated with the safety and security department; sale of the unneeded computer with the accounting and property departments. Fire insurance is also purchased through a carefully selected agent who will provide appraisal services for property values at stated time intervals.

C. An annual, or more frequent, review of the risk-management decisions in regard to choices of methods and values is scheduled for the future.

A CASE STUDY FOR BUSINESS RISK MANAGEMENT

The following final example[25] may be useful to the student in reviewing the technique of business risk management. From the facts given, a risk and insurance survey for the shopping center owner can be developed to aid in determining the answers to the kinds of questions which are raised at the end of the case study information.

The Riskee Shopping Center

The Facts:

Mr. I. M. Sure is the developer and chief financier of a new shopping center to be located on the outskirts of a fast-growing residential suburb near a major metropolitan city. He has organized the enterprise under the legal title of Success, Inc., and though construction has not yet begun, he is asking your advice in regard to the risks and insurance he should consider necessary during the developmental and operating stages of his business venture.

The center will provide 88,000 square feet of store space, and the purchase of the land has just been completed. An architect has been retained and has begun plans for a slanted L-shaped line of stores set at an angle to an important traffic route.

Preliminary arrangements have been made for leasing space to a large supermarket chain, a branch department store, a well-known national restaurant, a theater, a variety store, and several auxiliary service-type operations, including a barbershop, a dry cleaner, a branch bank, and an insurance agency.

Twenty-four tenants in all will occupy the premises under 15-year leases which stipulate a minimum rental plus a sliding percentage of sales agreement. The lease relieves the tenant of liability for rent if the premises are substantially damaged by fire.

---

[25] Other case study examples are available in William M. Howard, *Cases on Risk Management* (New York: McGraw-Hill Book Co., 1970); Jerry S. Rosenbloom, *A Case Study in Risk Management* (New York: Appleton-Century-Crofts Co., 1972), which provides an in-depth treatment of a large chemical company's risk-management programs; and Mark R. Greene and Oscar N. Serbein, *Risk Management: Text and Cases* (Reston, Va.: Reston Publishing Co., 1978).

The flat-roof building will be a "fire-resistive" construction. The largest section of the building will be the 18,000 square feet of open space for the supermarket. The heating equipment is designed to be placed at the rear of the building and will provide steam heat for all the stores in the center.

Eighty thousand square feet of macadam parking space are to be provided, with painted 45-degree parking stalls for about 400 cars. Floodlights on aluminum pylons and attendants for the parking lot were considered but decided against.

Storage space is to be kept at a minimum in order to provide maximum selling space. Each tenant is to be responsible under its lease for its own (1) snow removal; (2) trash removal; (3) repair of fire damage to the building; (4) air conditioners, if the tenant desires them; and (5) fire extinguishers.

A small rental and maintenance office is to be maintained in the shopping center, and ten office and service employees will be employed.

Some questions for case study:

1. What risks does Mr. I. M. Sure have at present, while he owns the vacant land that is to be used as the shopping center site? Are these "speculative" or "pure" risks? Should we have some form of insurance to meet these risks?

2. After construction is under way, what risks does Mr. Sure face? What insurance should he consider?

3. Assuming the shopping center to be complete, make a hypothetical risk analysis for Mr. Sure. What risks does the locational factor alone suggest? Are there any life and health risks?

4. Complete the risk and insurance survey that might be performed by a risk manager for Mr. Sure by outlining with brief explanations a business insurance survey for the Riskee Shopping Center. Include the following:

   a. Possible risks which Mr. Sure might *avoid*. Give specific examples.

   b. Possible losses which Mr. Sure might try to *prevent or reduce*. Give examples.

   c. Possible risks which Mr. Sure might *self-insure*.

   d. Possible risks which Mr. Sure might *transfer* by some method *other than* insurance.

   e. An insurance proposal as to the coverages you would recommend to Mr. Sure. Separate the essential, desirable, and available coverages.

5. Now, assuming that the shopping center is complete and that the tenants have moved in, discuss the exposures and special insurance problems which each of the following tenants might have:

   a. The department store.

   b. The supermarket.

   c. The restaurant.

   d. The branch bank.

   e. The dry cleaner.

   f. The insurance agency.

The coordination of insurance and risk programs for the Riskee Shopping Center is a modern example of the great need for extensive planning in the process of risk management. Only after alternatives to insurance have been carefully analyzed and integrated into the total system for meeting risk can the result deserve to be called risk management. The intelligent business (and personal) consumer of insurance will aim at achieving the many benefits of the risk-management process, through insurance purchased and coordinated with other alternatives included in the risk-management concept.

FOR REVIEW AND DISCUSSION

1. What is risk management, and how does it relate to insurance?
2. How have risk management and the risk manager's job changed in the past decade?
3. Suppose you are a merchant just beginning a new drive-in restaurant. You own the building and several vehicles and have 30 employees. What property and liability risks would you think it most important to insure? (Rank in order of importance along with brief reasons.)
4. In learning about risk and insurance, principles or basic ideas should be stressed. Explain two significant ideas which you believe will be of lasting value to you as a consumer in each of the following areas:
   a. The scope of risk management.
   b. Risk identification and measurement.
   c. The steps of risk management.
   d. The place of the risk manager.
5. Indicate some of the responsibilities and services which professional risk managers are able to render to their employers. How do risk managers usually fit into the organization of their firm?
6. There are several ways in which each of the different risks may be handled. One method is not adopted to the exclusion of others, but each method may be most useful for particular risks. Explain, differentiating between the methods of *risk control* and *risk financing*.
7. Describe, with at least two examples for each, how the risk-management concept might be applied by (a) a personal insurance consumer and (b) a business insurance consumer.
8. Refer to the "Case Study for Business Risk Management" near the end of this chapter, and have different groups of students consider Questions 1 through 5. Have the class as a whole discuss the proposed answers from each group.
9. How might the insurance and risk problems of a municipality differ from those of an individual? Of a business? Of a nonprofit organization?
10. If an insurance agent makes a survey for a client and the client adopts the program in its entirety, as recommended, what is the position of the agent if a loss develops that proves not to be fully covered by insurance?

11. Coordination is one of the desirable attributes of a good personal or business insurance and risk program. What have you learned about the *kinds* of coordination that are needed and *how* they can be achieved?

12. Suppose you are a new businesman just starting a new "Steak and Chips" drive-in restaurant. You own the building and several vehicles, and you have 20 employees. Estimated total assets of the corporation are $100,000; capital and surplus, $30,000; gross sales, $120,000; and estimated net profit per year, $12,000.

    a. .What steps would you take in order to make management decisions in regard to the risks that this firm faces?

    b. Give a separate example of each of the methods of risk treatment that might be used by the firm.

    c. In regard to one type of risk of loss, describe how a combination of methods of risk treatment might be used.

13. In what ways are risk managers important to the insurance business, and how would you predict their future?

14. Have separate groups of students discuss and report to the class how risk managers are becoming more involved in broadening responsibility for loss prevention, safety administration, and employee benefit plans.

15. Appoint different class members to answer questions about risk management by playing the roles of (*a*) President, (*b*) VP—Finance, (*c*) VP—Production, (*d*) VP—Personnel, (*e*) VP—Marketing, (*f*) VP—Legal, (*g*) VP—Accounting, (*h*) Risk Manager, (*i*) Employee Benefits Manager, (*j*) Safety Manager, (*k*) Insurance Agent, and (*l*) Risk Management Consultant. The role-playing can be aided by preparing identification signs that show the whole class which students have each of the above titles.

PART II

THE STRUCTURE AND OPERATIONS OF THE INSURANCE BUSINESS

The insurance business is analyzed in Part II on the basis of the major **functions** performed by the insurer, and how these are regulated. Chapters 4–7 present the *insurer* viewpoint, in contrast to the previously discussed risk-management concept, which is the insured's viewpoint of risk and insurance. Chapter 4 explains the fundamental legal nature of insurance *contracts,* which are the basic product of insurance. Chapter 5 discusses how this product and its accompanying services are *marketed* to the consumer through various insurers and agency systems. In Chapter 6, the unique task of *underwriting,* or the selection and pricing of insurance, is presented, together with several miscellaneous functions. The final function of major importance, *loss payment,* including types of insurance adjusters and procedures, is the subject of Chapter 7. The reasons and methods for the extensive *regulation* of the operations of the insurance business are the focus of Chapter 8. Regulation is so closely tied together with so many of the major functions of carrying out insurer operations that it is beneficial to discuss the regulatory process as the concluding chapter of Part II.

Chapter 4

Concepts considered in Chapter 4—Insurance contract fundamentals

Insurance contract fundamentals are the basis for the rights and obligations of the insurer and the insured, and are sometimes the source of perplexities and misunderstandings.

The relationship of insurer functions explains the *insurer* viewpoint of Part II in this text.

The insurance contract or policy is the tangible means by which private insurance is created.

The basic characteristics of being a *future, contingent, service, risk* contract describe the unique combination which is insurance.

General legal requirements must be met to establish valid and enforceable insurance contracts.

Special legal characteristics of the insurance contract are very important in understanding its purposes and the laws and legal interpretations which help achieve these goals:

Its personal nature, which affects its assignability.

Its conditional nature, the promises for one party's obligation being based upon the other party's actions.

Its strict compliance nature, resulting from the fact that the insurer usually prepares the contract. Even though the "benefit of the doubt" goes to insureds in case of the lack of clarity, insureds who do not read their policies are foolish, for oral evidence usually cannot contradict the written contract.

Its indemnity nature, for the purpose of repaying insureds as nearly as possible for the *actual losses* they have sustained—not more, not less. The contrast with *valued policies* is noted.

Insurable interest supports the concept of indemnity, although its requirements vary among the types of insurance.

Subrogation rights also maintain indemnity and hold wrongdoers responsible for the results of their actions.

Concealment, representations, and warranties show the insurance contract to be one of *utmost good faith* between the insurer and the insured, especially for *material* or important facts.

Fraud involves the *intent* to deceive, such as claims "padding."

Agency law principles assume importance in insurance, which is largely marketed through agency systems.

Insurance contract fundamentals

In your insurance contracts, should you read (*a*) every word, (*b*) only the important words, or (*c*) none of the words? A practical person, and those who know multiple-choice tests, would sensibly choose the middle-of-the-road answer (*b*). But what are the important words?

That's the goal of this chapter—to learn about the basic product of insurance, the insurance contract, and about some of the important legal words and fundamentals upon which it is based. Hopefully, you will then feel that you can and should read more of an insurance contract, without a dictionary and an insurance agent at your elbow.

THE RELATIONSHIP OF INSURER FUNCTIONS

In addition to recognizing the importance of your viewpoint as a consumer of insurance, which is often emphasized in this text, you should recognize the importance of the insurer viewpoint—you should understand how the insurance business is structured, and how its operations are carried out. The first step is to study some of the fundamentals of insurance contracts, which are the basic product designed by insurers. This explains the significance of this chapter.

However, it is in a broader perspective that insurance contracts become meaningful. The goal of insurers is to bring the contract and its services to the purchaser. Chapters 4 through 8 emphasize the overall *functional* viewpoint in the study of insurance by answering the question "What essential functions does the insurer carry out, and how does it do so?" Once the contract has been designed (Chapter 4), these functions include the marketing of insurance (Chapter 5; the underwriting, rating, reinsurance, and other functions (Chapter 6); the loss-payment function (Chapter 7); and the control or regulation of these activities (Chapter 8).

In diagram form these functions are related in the functional viewpoint of insurance as shown in Figure 4–1. This figure depicts the relationship among all topics covered in the chapters of Part II.

Figure 4–1. The functional viewpoint of insurance

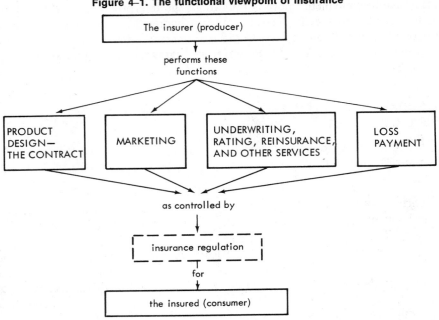

THE INSURANCE CONTRACT OR POLICY

Contract law is of extreme importance to the field of insurance. Private insurance is usually created by a written contract or *policy*. Sometimes insurance begins with an oral agreement between the insurer (or its agent) and the insured and later is completed by a written contract. The most tangible product resulting from the insurance system is the written contract which transfers the risk of financial loss from the insured to the insurer. Thus, insurance is fundamentally dependent upon the legal principles of contracts.

Many persons think of the physical piece of paper upon which the insurance contract is written as the whole of insurance. Since this document is what the insurance purchaser sees, he or she may unconsciously assume that this is all there is to it. One tends to forget that there are many other parts of insurance. The risk transfer, the application of the law of large numbers, the freedom from worry, the inspections and the loss-prevention services, the advisory functions—all of these services tend to be forgotten when only the contract of insurance is considered. Even the payment of losses in dollars of currency is neglected in such thoughts by insurance purchasers, that is, unless they happen to suffer losses for which reimbursement is paid!

The contract is significant in insurance, but the "service beyond the contract" is also of tremendous importance to the consumer. In Chapter 7, on insurance loss payment, more is said about the interpretation of the contract as it is applied to specific losses. Also, in Chapter 8 on insurance regulation, the relationship of contract law to the requirements of state laws is explained. Before studying more specifically the principles of insurance law in this chapter, other basic attributes of insurance are reviewed.

INSURANCE: A FUTURE, CONTINGENT, SERVICE, RISK CONTRACT

Is insurance an "intangible" product? Many writers characterize it as such, in contrast to such goods as clothing or automobiles, which can be seen, felt, and frequently used in everyday life. The description is not a sufficient answer as to why insurance is different from other economic products. Insurance *is* tangible in many ways, such as in the form of a contract or a loss payment check. It is more than a mere piece of paper, for it is also a promise to pay money. The real differences that characterize the insurance product and its marketing can be summarized by saying that the insurance contract is unique in that it is a *future, contingent, service, risk* contract.

Unlike most of the physical goods that one purchases for immediate enjoyment, insurance is usually thought of as providing *future* benefits when loss payments are made. The policyholder does not, however, realize that he or she is using the insurance by obtaining a significant benefit immediately and continually throughout the contract period of protection. The relief from anxieties and freedom from worry as to financial losses are real insurance benefits. The policyholder often forgets this, however, and contemplates only that the insurance is purchased to obtain a loss payment sometime well into the future. A fire, an automobile collision, a death, or a retirement are all future considerations to the insurance purchaser.

More than that, policyholders buy insurance with the conviction that such perils will not really cause losses to them. They buy it "just in case," but at the same time thinking that "it will never happen to me." This quality of insurance emphasizes its *contingent* nature. The feeling of contingency is supported by fact, too. Only the unfortunate minority who actually suffer loss need the services of loss payment. Families may continue insurance for many years without an automobile loss, or for a lifetime without a fire or theft loss to their home. A business may continue through millions of worker-hours without a disabling injury to any of its employees. The very nature of insurance is based on contingencies that may or may not occur and that normally occur only infrequently.

The preceding comments have suggested the need for considering insurance as a *service* contract rather than a single physical product. It is, in fact, a bundle of services. Insurance becomes a unique product because the policyholder needs help in understanding its varied benefits. That is why in the marketing of insurance the personal service of an agent is so often necessary.

Even though it is the ultimate responsibility of the insured to understand the contract, agents can be most helpful. Through them prospective insurance buyers learn about needs in regard to risks and how insurance prevents losses, transfers risks, and pays benefits in the case of losses. They learn how liability insurance pays the legal cost of defense in lawsuits. They find out how life insurance serves as a basis for credit, creates a liquid estate, and offers alternatives for using capital in the form of life income guarantees. In return for the cost of the contract, the policyholder receives many advisory services, some at the inception of the policy, others during the term of the contract or at the time of loss, and some at the end of the contract period. Many of the services of insurance are provided before the real needs for it are realized—at the time of loss.

The *risk* of financial loss is a final characteristic that differentiates insurance from other goods and services. The basis of the insurance contract is uncertainty about many perils which may cause accidental loss. Insurance transfers the risk of such losses to the insurer, a professional risk bearer. Other service contracts may be future and contingent, but they do not involve payment for perils such as fire, collision, and death.

GENERAL LEGAL REQUIREMENTS

The rights and obligations of the parties to an insurance agreement are determined largely by reference to the general laws which govern contracts. The agreement by which insurance is effected is a contract in which the insurer in consideration of the payment of a specified sum by the insured[1] agrees to make good the losses suffered through the happening of a designated unfavorable contingency. The insurance contract need not be in writing, but as a matter of business practice such agreements are ordinarily written. Even social insurances, such as workers' compensation, are written, though the terms appear in a state law rather than in a private agreement.

A contract has been defined as "an agreement enforceable by law." A more complete definition would include certain essentials which the law requires: (1) the *offer* and its *acceptance*; (2) the *object* of the agreement must be *legal*; (3) the *parties* must be *competent*; and (4) generally a *consideration,* or payment, is essential. A lack of any of the essential elements prevents the enforcement of the agreement. To be valid and enforceable, insurance contracts must meet these four general legal requirements.

Offer and acceptance.   A legally binding agreement, or contract, requires both an offer by one party and an acceptance by another party. In insurance

---

[1] Historically the term *insured* was distinguished from *assured* and *insurance* from *assurance*. Assurance concerned the duration of life where death either occurred or did not. Insurance related to uncertainties that could result in either whole, partial, or no losses at all, such as fires, collisions, and similar events. The distinction is no longer common, although the word *assurance* is used by a few companies in the United States and quite a number in Europe.

the *offer* is usually made in a request for coverage by the prospect, or applicant. The simplest method, used for many types of property and liability insurance, is an oral request to an agent, either in person or by telephone. In life and many forms of health insurance the offer must be made in a written application.

Before a contract is effective, *acceptance* of the offer is necessary. In property-liability insurance, the agent usually has authority to "bind" or accept the offer, even without receiving any payment from the applicant. The protection may commence immediately, if desired, based entirely on the oral request of the applicant and the oral acceptance by the agent. A written "binder," or temporary contract, may be issued by the agent, pending later writing of the actual contract (usually within 15–30 days), but this is not essential in order for the agreement to be effective.

In life insurance, the method and timing of legal acceptance are different. The written application and the first premium payment are usually submitted together to the agent, who issues a "conditional receipt." Acceptance is held by most courts in such cases to be as of the time when the applicant meets the underwriting standards of the insurer, including a medical examination if required. Then the coverage requested is made effective as of the time of the application and premium payment. If the premium is not paid with the application, the insurance does not become effective until the contract is delivered to the applicant while in good health and the premium is paid. If the applicant does not meet the underwriting standards of the insurer, the insurer may make a counteroffer with a different contract, which the prospect may accept or reject upon delivery by the agent.

Legal purpose. The second requirement of a legally binding contract is that it must have a *legal purpose* or object. The courts will not enforce an insurance contract, for example, if it has an illegal purpose or is contrary to public policy. Examples include a thief attempting to insure stolen property; life insurance taken out by the applicant with the proven intention of murdering the insured in order to collect payment; or fire insurance taken out by you on your neighbor's house in the hope that it will burn (this would lack an "insurance interest," as discussed later in this chapter, and it would be against public policy because it would be a gambling contract).

Competent parties. Valid contracts also require that the parties making the offer and those accepting the contract be legally *competent* to make the agreement. In insurance, the most common problem arises in connection with applicants who are minors (under age 18, or 21 in some states). Such applicants may have the option of repudiating contracts, up to the time they reach legal adulthood, unless the contracts are for necessities, such as food, shelter, or clothing. Some insurance contracts are thus voidable by applicants who are minors, and these applicants would receive a full return of the premiums paid. Some states have made exceptions for life and health insurance contracts by establishing special age limits of 14–16, beyond which age minors are considered to have the legal capacity to insure themselves and the contract is binding.

A similar problem may occur in insurance contracts written for insane or intoxicated persons, who cannot make legal contracts because they fail to understand the agreement.

Insurers, too, must be competent to enter into a legal contract by meeting charter and license requirements of the states (see Chapter 8). In cases where such legal capacity is lacking, many courts have nevertheless held the contracts binding on the insurer, or on its corporate officers personally.

Consideration.   The final requirement for a valid contract is some *consideration* exchanged by both parties to the agreement—a right or something of value given up, or an obligation assumed. In insurance, the applicant typically makes a premium payment, or the contract may become effective on the basis of the applicant's promise to pay and to meet other conditions of the contract. The insurer's consideration is its promise to pay for specified losses or to provide other services to the insured.

SPECIAL LEGAL CHARACTERISTICS

The remainder of this chapter concerns special legal characteristics of the insurance contract. These are not necessarily unique to insurance contracts, but in total they help describe the fundamental ideas upon which insurance contracts are based. A good understanding of the characteristics should aid the insurance consumer in reading insurance contracts and in comprehending the underlying legal concepts which are essential to most insurance contracts. Figure 4–2 summarizes the characteristics.

Personal nature

The insurance contract is *personal* and follows the person rather than the property concerned. We speak of "insuring property." Yet this is not technically the situation. Insurance actually provides repayment of a loss arising out of some undesired happening. It is impossible to guarantee to a person that possessions will not be lost, or even to guarantee to replace them with like and kind. It is possible, however, to provide for indemnification to the person who has incurred the loss. Hence, if an individual should pay for a fire insurance contract and subsequently sell the property without arranging with the insurer to transfer the insurance to the new owner, there would be no payment by the insurer in case of fire because there would be no loss on the part of the original insured. The measure of insurance payment is loss to the insured, not loss of specified property.

One result of the personal nature of insurance is that many insurance contracts are not freely assignable by the policyholder to other parties. Most insurance contracts (life insurance being an exception) represent a personal agreement between insurer and insured. To permit a fire or automobile in-

**Figure 4–2. Special legal characteristics of
insurance contracts**

surance contract to be assignable without the insurer's approval would be unfair to the insurer. Only by knowing and investigating each policyholder it insures can the insurance company correctly appraise the risk it is accepting. A parallel illustration of a personal contract in the entertainment field may help the student realize the value of this aspect of insurance. Bob Hope's manager could not fulfill a personal appearance contract by Bob Hope by sending someone else to appear for him.

Conditional nature

The obligation to perform on the part of one of the parties to an agreement may be conditioned upon the action of the second party. A clause in an insurance contract requiring such performance is usually referred to as a *condition.* Failure of one party to perform relieves the other party of obligation.

Where an insurance contract is subject to a condition, the condition is usually regarded as either precedent (before) or subsequent to (after) the time at which a promise becomes binding on the promisor. An illustration of a common *condition precedent,* which must take place before a promise becomes binding, is the requirement in many insurance contracts that an insured who suffers a loss must give proper notice and proof to the insurer before the claim is payable. Note that the insured does not have to file a claim but that the insurer is not obligated to pay unless the insured does so in the proper manner. An example of a *condition subsequent* is an insured's failure to cooperate with the insurer in defending a liability claim. Here the promise of the insured is not fulfilled, and that failure subsequently relieves the insurer of its earlier promise to pay.

Strict compliance nature

Contracts of adhesion.   The insurance contract is said to be a "contract of *adhesion*" in that it is ordinarily prepared in all its details by the insurer and the insured has no part in drawing up its clauses or determining its wording. In applying for insurance, the applicant either accepts the policy as prepared by the insurer, does not purchase the insurance, or contacts another insurer that may use some different contract wording. Contracts are sometimes modified to meet individual needs, but even when so modified, the contract with its amendments is prepared by the insurance company. A contract of adhesion is contrasted to a "bargaining contract" in which both parties contribute to the terms and conditions.

The insurer does not always draw up the contract. Sometimes legislation requires that specific wording be used. Other times the insured may be a large corporation that is in a position to ask for and obtain special contract provisions. In such cases, the intent of the entire contract and of both the insurer and the insured would probably be considered in interpretations of the contract by the courts.

Benefit of doubt to insured.   Since the insurer has the advantage in drawing up the agreement and is expected to represent clearly the intent of all the parties, it is generally enforced that where the terms of the policy are ambiguous, obscure, or susceptible of more than one interpretation, the construction most favorable to the insured must prevail.[2] The rule is based on the assumption that the insurer is under a duty to make its meaning clear. When the insurer has failed to be clear, the "benefit of the doubt" goes to the policyholder. This applies, however, *only* when the *court* decides the contract is unclear, not every time the insured misinterprets or does not understand a provision. Sometimes, however, this principle may help insureds, offsetting their lack of participation in drawing up the contract.

Insureds should read contract.   Where there is no ambiguity, the contract is to be enforced in accordance with its terms. If the contract is clear and understandable, its meaning may not be distorted by interpretations. Consideration must be given to the generally understood meaning of the terms used and to the entire context to determine the nature and extent of coverage.

A corollary to the strict compliance rule is that the law holds persons to be bound by the terms of a written contract which they sign or accept, regardless of whether or not they have taken the trouble to acquaint themselves with all

---

[2] *Knouse* v. *Equitable Life Insurance Company of Ohio*, 181 Pac. (2d) 310.

its terms and conditions.[3] Too many insurance contracts are complicated and difficult to understand. It is probably safe to state that regardless of the clarity or obscurity of the terminology, most people do not read their policies. Insureds assume that a policy meets their needs and let it go at that. It is no defense, however, when the loss occurs, to claim ignorance of the terms of the policy because of failure to read the agreement. The insured's failure to read the contract does not change or extend the rights of the insured as stated in the written policy. The advice to insurance buyers should be: "To avoid problems (and uncertainties!), *know* what is in your insurance policy by reading it, or having it explained, or both."

Oral evidence. In connection with the insurance contract, the rule of law applying to *parole* or oral evidence has been expressed in a leading case: "It is a fundamental rule, in courts both of law and equity, that parole contemporaneous evidence is inadmissible to contradict or vary the terms of a valid written instrument."[4] Thus, an insured cannot usually contradict the written contract by saying that the agent *said* the policy covered a specific type of loss.

Although the contract in the ordinary course is not subject to modification by parole evidence, the language of the policy is nevertheless not binding in clear cases of mutual mistake of fact or where there is a mistake on one side and fraud inducing it on the other. In such cases, the injured party has an equity right to ask that the contract be reformed to the true agreement. An example might be a contract which is written, with incorrect oral information from a prospective insured, for insurance on a wrong building.

Indemnity nature

Many property, liability, and health insurance contracts are essentially contracts of *indemnity* or repayment. By this it is meant that insurance provides reimbursement for actual damage sustained by the insured. This being the case, the total policy amount (face value) is not the amount payable in the event of a loss but rather represents a maximum limit to the liability of the insurer. Under the indemnity rule, if a property is valued at $5,000 and insured for $10,000, the insurance company would only pay $5,000 to the policyholder who suffers a total loss. If the insured receives reimbursement for part or all of the loss from any other source, the liability of the insurer is

---

[3] This is the general rule. See *Grace* v. *Adams,* 100 Mass. 505. However, some recent cases seem to say that the insured does *not* have to read his or her policy. Special situations sometimes occur, such as those in which the insured has reasonably relied upon advice of a professional agent, but it is unwise for policyholders to assume that courts will be lenient in excusing them from a contract's written terms.

[4] *Northern Assurance Co.* v. *Grand View Building Assn.,* 182 U.S. 308 (1902).

often reduced in the same amount.[5] An exception to the use of indemnity in property insurance is the "valued policy," where the full policy amount is paid for a total loss under certain circumstances described in a later section of this chapter.

Property insurance. The destruction or damage of the *property* described in the contract of insurance is not the contingency upon which the insurer promises to indemnify the insured; it is only when the insured has suffered a loss that the insurer may be called upon to make a payment under the contract.[6] In most cases of property insurance the approximate value of the property can be estimated before a loss, or determined after a loss, within reasonably narrow limits. Some cases present special problems, however, such as older buildings that are now used for different purposes than when they were built. For example, a large stable or coach house now used as a garage at the rear of a residence would probably never be replaced as it was if it were destroyed by fire. Here the functional value of the building is more important than the replacement value. The insurer would usually limit the insurance amount written to its functional value.

Liability insurance. *Liability* policies paying for damage to other persons or their property are a special example of indemnity. They were formerly written as contracts of indemnity. If insureds were declared bankrupt and therefore did not pay the injured parties to whom they were legally liable, then insurers were not obligated to pay. In such situations the insureds suffered no loss; therefore indemnification by the insurers could not be made.

The liability policies as now issued are regarded not as contracts of indemnity against loss but as contracts of indemnity against liability. The insurer pays if the insured is liable for damages within the scope of the contract, even if the insured is declared bankrupt and technically could not pay the injured party.

In setting the limits of insurance for liability policies, care must be taken to write the policy amount high enough to take into consideration the unknown nature of jury verdicts. In buying liability protection, the policyholder should often purchase higher limits than the minimum or standard limits available.

One of the most difficult applications of the idea of indemnity in liability situations is the determination of reasonable payment for such items in the claim as "pain and suffering," "mental anguish," and so on. Actual medical

---

[5] The U.S. Supreme Court has set forth the basic rule by stating that where there is a contract of indemnity, such as fire insurance, and a loss happens, anything that reduces or diminishes that loss reduces the amount which the indemnifier is bound to pay (*Chicago, St. Louis & New Orleans R.R. Co.* v. *Pullman Southern Car Co.,* 139 U.S. 79). Exceptions to this rule may be found, particularly in some indirect loss insurance and in many types of individual health insurance.

[6] *Draper* v. *Delaware State Grange Mutual Fire Ins. Co.,* 91 Atl. 206.

costs and loss of income are much easier to justify on the principle of indemnity.

Life and health insurance. *Life* insurance and many *health* insurance contracts are not based upon the indemnity principle. Here it is the difficulty of determining precise values that prevents the contract from being, strictly speaking, based upon indemnity. One cannot say that the life of a person is worth (or not worth) precisely $10,000 or $50,000 or $300,000. Thus the life insurance contract agrees to pay a certain stated amount rather than an amount determined after the loss to be a repayment for the loss. There can be no question raised by the insurer paying the loss as to whether or not the loss of life actually resulted in an equivalent economic loss to the insured or the beneficiaries of the life insurance contract.

Valued policies. A special case of the indemnity doctrine concerns the *valued policy* in property insurance. There are properties that are extremely difficult to appraise accurately. Thus, the valued policy is used, just as in life insurance. In this category fall works of art, antiques, rare collections, and family heirlooms. Because of the difficulty of arriving at any satisfactory agreement as to value following a loss, it is deemed advisable in this class of business that the insurer and the insured agree upon a value at the time the policy is issued.

The valuation agreed upon must be fair to both insurer and insured. It should not be so high as to create a desire by the insured to have a loss payment rather than the object insured, yet it should be high enough to compensate the insured reasonably if loss should occur.

Thus the Picasso monument in Chicago's Civic Center Plaza has reportedly been insured for $300,000. If total loss results, the policy amount will determine the amount of the insurance claim payment. Even if the 160-ton, 50-foot-high sculpture actually turns out to be worth only $200,000, at the time of loss the full amount of $300,000 would be paid. Another example is Leonardo da Vinci's famous painting *Mona Lisa*, which was recently insured for $40 million.

In writing a contract of this type, there is no violation of the indemnity idea. Rather, an agreement is made in advance as to the amount necessary to indemnify the insured in the event of loss or damage to the property. The use of the valued policy in such situations is regarded as sound practice because such articles of unique value may be subject to honest differences of opinion at any particular time. Many items worth several thousand dollars or more should be insured in this manner.

Valued policy laws. From time to time there develops a demand by the public for *valued policy laws* in connection with the insurance of other types of property, such as homes. The opportunity to use such policies to overinsure has caused insurance authorities to frown upon the general use of this contract. Nevertheless, several states have enacted statutes that make valued policies mandatory for insurance on homes or other *real estate* property. Such laws are limited to apply only when an insured property is *totally* destroyed, and usually only for certain perils, such as *fire or windstorm*. The amount of insurance in force is then taken as conclusive evidence of the true value of the property and the loss, regardless of the actual value. Property owners reason that it is unjust for them to pay for insurance over a number of years and then to get less than the face of the policy if their property is destroyed. The reasoning has its appeal. However, experience in the insurance business indicates that there is less injustice if the responsibility for fixing a reasonable amount of insurance is placed upon insureds than if insureds are permitted to make a profit through the destruction of their property. Valued policy laws are believed to invite carelessness and fraud, stimulate overinsurance, and violate the indemnity rule.

Insurable interest

Closely related to the concept of indemnity is the requirement that all insurance contracts contain an element of *insurable interest*. An insurable interest is a right or relationship in regard to the subject matter of the insurance contract such that the insured can suffer *financial* loss from damage, loss, or destruction to it. The subject matter might be a property, a life, or another interest.

Without an insurable interest, a contract is a wager or gambling contract. It also could be an undesirable incentive for some persons to cause losses or injuries on purpose. When an insurable interest exists, no profit results, for insureds merely receive repayment for the loss they have suffered.

A clear example of insurable interest is ownership of *property,* with a fire, windstorm, or other peril causing a financial loss. However, many other types of insurable interest are common. Mortgagees, bailees, and creditors may have insurable interests, and oftentimes there are several persons who have insurable interest in the same property. A homeowner may insure his or her interest in property, for example, while at the same time the policy insures the mortgagee's interest up to the value of the mortgage.

Liability creates many insurable interests. Either an automobile owner or driver may be held responsible for losses caused by the car; thus each has an insurable interest. Employers may also be liable for employees' automobiles. Tenants oftentimes are liable for injuries caused to the public on the premises. Property owners may be held responsible for the actions of contractors, and contractors for the actions of subcontractors. All such losses may be the basis of an insurable interest.

The continuance of *life and* good *health* serves as the basis for many other examples of insurable interest. Death, injury, or sickness may result in financial losses to the persons insured, or to their families, creditors, business partners, or employers. The right of persons to insure their own lives, as well as the right of close family members to insure blood relatives, is based on a presumed insurable interest. Other insurable interests for life or health insurance are based upon actual losses (either increased expenses or reduced income potential) resulting from the relationship to the insured. For example, a creditor can insure the life of a debtor, normally up to the amount of the loan, or a businessperson may insure a partner's life for the potential loss this would cause the partnership.

In later chapters, the question of when an insurable interest is required will be discussed. Generally, property insurance has the legal requirement that an insurable interest exist at the time of loss, whereas life insurance requires an insurable interest only at the time the contract is purchased.

Subrogation rights

In common law it is held that a person who causes a loss or who is primarily liable ought ultimately to be made responsible for the damages sustained. In connection with the law of insurance, it is a matter of equity that upon paying the insured the amount of the loss, the insurer has a right of action against the person responsible for the loss. In some cases, subrogation rights are limited or eliminated by law. In other cases, the insurer has subrogation rights because of a specific subrogation clause in the contract, rather than from equitable or common-law rules.

The right of the insurer against such persons does not rest upon any contractual relationship but arises out of the nature of the contract of insurance as one of indemnity. If the insured is indemnified, it would be inequitable for him or her also to try to collect from the parties responsible for the loss. If the insured were permitted to do this, a double collection of the loss, from both the insurer and the responsible party, might result in a profit to the insured. Subrogation is also a fair principle in that it holds wrongdoers responsible for the results of their wrongful actions instead of permitting them not to pay only because an insurance contract was in force. The overall cost of insurance to policyholders is also reduced in this manner.

The doctrine of *subrogation* gives the insurer whatever rights the insured possessed against responsible third parties. It is basically a process of substitution, the insurer taking over the rights of the insured that existed at the time of the loss.[7] From the time of the loss the insured may not release any rights that might prove beneficial to the insurer.

The right of subrogation by the insurer is limited in amount to the loss payment which has been made to the insured. The insurer cannot make a profit by subrogating against the person who caused the loss. In fact, oftentimes

---

[7] For an extensive treatment of the idea and use of the principle of subrogation, see Ronald C. Horn, *Subrogation in Insurance Theory and Practice* (Homewood, Ill.: Richard D. Irwin, 1964).

subrogation rights are of little value to the insurance company. There may be no doubt that someone else was responsible for the loss, but in order to re-coup its loss payment the insurer party must have the financial ability to pay for the loss he or she caused. In many cases the time, expense, or difficulty of legal proof may prevent the insurer from using its subrogation rights to re-cover the loss payment. If it appears that it might cost $1,000 to collect a $600 claim, the insurer logically may not use its subrogation rights.

The importance of subrogation varies greatly for the various types of insur-ance. In life insurance it is not used. Limited use is found in fire insurance, where proof of the cause of fire is often difficult. A common illustration of subrogation is in automobile insurance, where the insurer first pays under collision coverage for damage to the insured's car. Then the insurer takes over the rights of the policyholder by subrogation and brings suit against the other driver involved in the accident to receive reimbursement. If the insured did not receive full payment from the insurer because of a deductible in the policy, the insured would retain the right to sue the responsible party for the deductible amount. Sometimes a joint suit for the full amount is filed, but the insurer is not obligated to do this.

Effect of concealment, representations, and warranties

Concealment. Since the contract of insurance concerns itself with risk and uncertainty, it has been established as a fundamental doctrine of insur-ance law that neither party practice *concealment*. The contract is said to be one of "utmost good faith." Both parties to the agreement must stand on an equal footing. This doctrine makes mandatory the affirmative disclosure to the insurer of all *material* or important facts that are the exclusive knowledge of the insured. For example, if there is knowledge on the part of the owner that the property insured was in grave danger of destruction at the inception of the agreement and if this information is not disclosed to the insurer, an unbal-anced agreement will result.

The concealment of a material fact need not be intentional or fraudulent in order to make a policy voidable, and it is no defense to plead mistake or forgetfulness. If the insurer would have declined the risk or accepted the policy upon different terms if it had possessed all the facts, the policy is voidable.

The terms *void* and *voidable* are sometimes used interchangeably, but such use is not correct. A *void* agreement is one that is entirely without legal effect, and neither party can enforce it. For example, the law makes certain require-ments essential for the validity of a contract, and in the absence of these essentials the contract is void. Thus, a contract having an illegal object cannot be enforced at law by either party.

A *voidable* contract is one that may be affirmed or rejected at the option of one of the parties but is binding on the other. If the insured has failed to comply with a condition of the contract, the insurer may elect to fulfill its part of the agreement, or may choose to treat the contract as voidable. There are frequent instances in which the insurer has a technical right to claim a forfeiture but in the interests of equity and good public relations decides not to exercise that right. Only seldom does the insured have the right to treat a contract as voidable—perhaps in a case where the insurer has grossly misrepresented the contract benefits.

The concealment doctrine had an early start in ocean marine insurance, and due to the nature of the business a strict interpretation applies even today. A ship or cargo may be insured in London, yet the property may be located in some far corner of the globe. Since the property is beyond the possibility of inspection by the insurer, full reliance and dependence must be placed upon the insured for all pertinent facts.

In the case of other types of insurance, the property or persons insured are ordinarily convenient for inspection, and consequently the material facts essential for an appraisal of the risk are within the range of the insurer's observation. When it is not made the subject of express inquiry, the concealment must be intentional to make the policy voidable. The insured needs only to answer fully and in good faith all inquiries made by the insurers. One exception to the rule provides that when important facts bearing on the risk are so unusual that they would not ordinarily be inquired about or readily discovered by the insurer, the obligation of affirmative disclosure is present, whether or not express inquiry has been made.

Representations. A *representation* is a statement made by the insured to the insurer at the time of or prior to the formation of a contract. Since it is the right of the insurer to have full knowledge of the subject of insurance, it frequently becomes necessary to depend upon statements of the insured, from whom it is most convenient to ascertain the pertinent facts. A *misrepresentation* (false statement) on the part of the insured of any *material* (important) fact has the same effect as a concealment and affords a basis for making the contract voidable by the insurer.

The difference between concealment and misrepresentation is that the insured conceals if a silence is maintained when there is an obligation to speak, and misrepresents if a statement is made which is not true. The determination of what is material is based on the same ideas as apply in the cases of concealment illustrated earlier. Each set of facts must be evaluated in the given situation, by the courts if necessary. For example, a response of "No" by a businessperson applying for theft insurance to the question "Have you had any theft losses?" might be considered a material misrepresentation if, in fact, the applicant carelessly forgot a large loss that occurred two years earlier —but perhaps it would not be considered such if the only previous loss was a very small one which happened five years earlier.

Warranties. When the application for the insurance contract is made a part of the policy, the answers to specific questions on the application are deemed *warranties*. If false, they make the policy voidable by the insurer. Many warranties may also be included in the policy itself.

The difference between a warranty and a representation is that a warranty is a part of the contract itself and must therefore be strictly complied with, whereas a representation is usually an incidental statement preceding the contract and not actually a part of it, though it may be an inducement to it. The difference in effect is that in order to make the contract voidable a warranty need only be false, whereas a representation must be both false and material.

In order to constitute a warranty, a statement must not only be intended as such but must be definitely indicated as a warranty either through its incorporation into the policy or through being specifically referred to as such. Where there is any doubt as to whether a warranty was intended, the statement is to be regarded as a representation and must be shown to be material in order to defeat the policy.

Many states have modified by legislative act the strict application of the doctrine of warranties for most kinds of insurance except marine. Where the doctrine has been thus modified, the insurance is sometimes voidable only if a loss occurs during a breach of warranty, or is caused thereby, or if the breach materially increases the risk. This, in effect, causes *most warranties* in insurance contracts *today* to be *considered as representations*. It is wise, however, not to tamper with warranties incorporated into insurance policies, but to comply with them to the letter, for it is still the tendency of some courts to enforce the original strict rule, declaring the policy voidable when a warranty is breached, regardless of how trivial or immaterial to the loss it may be.

Effect of fraud

A false representation or the concealment of a material fact *with the intent and result* that it be acted upon by another party may constitute *fraud*. A concealment amounts to a false representation if active steps are taken to prevent discovery of the truth. This is the case if a representation is made that is in part true, but certain facts are suppressed.

To constitute fraud the representation must be of past or existing acts. It follows, therefore, that expressions of opinion, belief, expectation, or intention do not constitute fraudulent statements. The representation must be of material fact that would lead to reliance upon it by the party to whom it is made. Commendatory expressions of value or false representations made where the parties deal on an equal footing and have equal means of knowledge are not held to be fraudulent. For example, if an applicant for automobile insurance said, "I am a very good driver," there could be no fraud, as this was merely an expression of opinion. However, if an applicant said, "I have never had an accident," where in fact the applicant had several recent accidents and was making the statement with the idea of getting a lower insurance cost, fraud might be provable.

An active intent to deceive or the intentional misleading by one person of another is usually present. The person making the statement must know that it is false or make the statement in reckless disregard of whether it is true or false. Finally, in order to constitute fraud the misrepresentation must be relied upon by and injure the other party. In such cases a contract becomes voidable at the option of the injured party.

The requirements for proving fraud are difficult to meet. An insurer must prove intent to defraud on the part of the insured. Intent involves premeditation, and it is hard to show what a person thought before an action, unless intent is very clearly indicated by present or repeated past actions or statements. If proved, however, fraud is a serious matter. It may permit the insurer to rescind the contract. For example, if in order to obtain a lower rate the insured purposely misstates in an automobile insurance application that no young family members use the car, the coverage may be lost because of the fraudulent action of the insured. A more common but perhaps equally serious example is the intentional exaggeration of any insurance claim for the purpose of receiving overpayment for a loss.

Summary

In order to review the concepts of concealment, representations, warranties, and fraud, the requirements for making an insurance contract voidable by the insurer are shown in Table 4–1.

Table 4–1. The effects of concealment, representations, warranties, and fraud

Concept	Requirements for voidability	Example
Concealment	Must be silence which is material (or important)	Applicant for windstorm insurance fails to tell agent that a tornado is known to be approaching the property
Representations	Must be statement (oral or written) which is false *and* material	Applicant for theft insurance falsely states that no recent losses have been suffered, when in fact a loss occurred a few months previously
Warranties	Must be false, and incorporated and identified in the contract or application as a warranty	Applicant for marine insurance answers question in the application falsely, by stating that the ship is used on inland rather than ocean waters
Fraud	Must be false, with an intent to deceive, and be relied upon by and cause injury to the other party	Insured purposely overstates a claim in order to obtain a larger loss payment than is justified.

Agency law principles

The development of modern large-scale enterprises has made it necessary to entrust much business to representatives. In the case of corporations this is particularly true. Since the major part of the insurance business is in the hands of corporate insurers, the part played by the agent is important. Chapter 5, on insurance marketing, explains the predominance of agency systems in insurance. In this chapter the legal relationship is considered, and the term *agency* refers to this rather than to a specific corporation or business firm that calls itself an insurance agency.

Agency by agreement.   Agency involves a *principal* who authorizes a second party, an *agent*, to create, modify, or terminate a contract with a third party. The agent acts on behalf of the principal. An agency relationship could be created by an oral agreement, but most agency agreements are reduced to writing. In the business of insurance, a written document, the *agency contract,* or "commission of authority," usually designates the parties and outlines the specific authority of the agent to act for the principal, or insurer, in dealing with the insurance buyer. Most agency relationships are created in this manner.

Agency by other means.   By operation of law or court interpretation, other agency relationships may be created. A principal's conduct may prevent the principal from denying the existence of the agency. If the principal permits someone to act in such a way that third parties may reasonably believe that an agency relationship exists and if they rely upon the attitude of the principal, the principal cannot validly claim that there is no agency. The agency thus created is said to be an *agency by estoppel,* which means that the principal is precluded, or stopped, from using the right to deny that an agency relationship exists.

The application of this principle to insurance prevents an insurer from denying a fact which has been admitted by the insurer's previous action. For example, suppose an employee (who is not an agent) of an insurer were carelessly given some numbered and signed policies. Even though the insurer did not intend the employee to be an agent, if the contracts were filled in by the employee, the insurer might be estopped or prevented from later denying coverage.

Estoppel is closely connected with the principle of *waiver,* the intentional relinquishing or abandonment of a known right. Thus an insurer or an agent may accept a premium payment from the insured, knowing of a violation of a policy condition, such as the storage of large amounts of gasoline on the premises. The condition may be waived by the act of accepting the premium. A waiver may also occur after a loss. The insurer may waive such rights as the requirement for written proof of loss by the insured. Suppose the insurer denies liability for the loss. Then the insurer's right to receive proof within a specified number of days after the loss may be held to have been relinquished, or waived.

Sometimes a person may claim to have authority to act for a given principal without actually having such authority. If, however, the principal later ratifies the act of the unauthorized agent, the agreement becomes effective and binding upon the principal from the inception of the original agreement.

This situation creates an *agency by ratification*. Ratification may be either expressed or implied from any act, expression, or conduct which would definitely indicate the intent of the principal to adopt the transaction. Assume that an insurer tells an agent not to write a liability insurance contract for more than $100,000 but that later the agent does and the insurer accepts the payment of the premium. That acceptance would ratify the agency relationship for the transaction.

The scope of *apparent authority* assumes an extremely important place because the responsibility of the principal for acts of the agent often exceed the powers expressly conferred in definite instructions to the agent. Incidental powers for which the agency was created are often implied, and the general uses and customs of the community tend to expand or limit the agent's authority. An agent's actions bind the principal if they fall within this apparent authority.

For example, insurers issue to their agents lists of "prohibited risks" that the company will not write, such as amusement parks, nightclubs, sawmills, and bowling alleys. In addition to listing prohibited risks, some insurers list properties which may be insured only after specific referral to the company and special inspection. If the applicant is unaware of such limiting instructions given to the agent, and an agent writes a policy anyway, the insurer would have to pay the applicant for a loss unless it had canceled the policy. However, the insurer would have a right of action against the agent for violating his or her agency contract.

FOR REVIEW AND DISCUSSION

1. Lee, in frustration, states: "I'll never read all those legal words in my insurance contracts, but I always have the feeling I should do so." Is there a solution to this dilemma? Explain.

2. One person says that insurance is "intangible," while another states that it is "a future, contingent, service, risk contract." Which description do you prefer, and why?

3. Identify three special legal characteristics of insurance, and explain the reason for the importance of each to the policyholder.

4. From the insurer's standpoint, why are the following important in the insurance transaction:
   a. Its strict compliance nature?
   b. Its indemnity nature?
   c. Insurable interest?
   d. Subrogation?
   e. Agency law?

5. Must insurance contracts be in writing? Why or why not?

6. Why do you think the application of the concept of subrogation varies among the different types of insurance? Give examples from the property and life insurance fields.

7. The strict compliance rule is justified by the fact that the insurer has an advantage in drawing up the insurance agreement. In your opinion, are insurance contracts sufficiently complex to concede a real advantage on the part of the insurance company?

8. Disinguish between a "warranty," a "representation," a "concealment," and "fraud," and explain the importance of each to the insurer and the insured.

9. Mr. B. Scottfree is an agent.
   a. He is suspended by the Careful Insurance Company. The company takes its supplies from the agent's office. The agent reissues an expired policy, collecting and retaining the premium. Is there any liability on the part of the insurer, or must the policyholder suffer the loss?
   b. Suppose that after suspension but before the supplies are taken, Mr. Scottfree issues a policy. The company accepts the premium. Upon what theory is the agent's act validated?
   c. Suppose the agent is not suspended, but has instructions not to insure certain prohibited properties. Carelessly, he issues a policy on a prohibited risk. Before notice reaches the home office of the company, the property burns. Discuss the questions of liability involved.

10. What examples can you give of possible violations of the concept of indemnity in insurance? Indicate *how and why* they deviate from the indemnity approach.

11. Match the following description in column 2 with the most appropriate term from column 1, by pairing the letters with the correct numbers:

Column 1	*Column 2*
a. Insurable interest	1. Important in insurance marketing
b. Concealment	2. Thus, not all insurance is assignable
c. Subrogation	3. If material, may make contract voidable
d. Valued policy laws	4. Must include intent to deceive
e. Agency law	5. Insurance amount paid for total loss
f. Personal nature	6. Without it, insurance would be a profit
g. Fraud	7. Insurer takes over insured's rights
h. Ambiguity	8. Insured should read contract
i. Contract of adhesion	9. Insurer prepares the contract
j. Strict compliance rule	10. Benefit of doubt may go to insured

Chapter 5

Insurance marketing—the process of getting a "bundle of services" in connection with insurance contracts from the insurer to the insured—is a main part of the functional approach to the study of insurance. Although insurance agents are the best-known part of insurance, this chapter emphasizes the *who* and the *how* of the total process.

Comparisons of insurance and other marketing help in understanding *the insurance product and the insurance market.*

The legal types of insurer include *stock* and several types of *mutual* companies, as well as other relatively less important types such as *Lloyds, reciprocals, fraternals, savings bank life,* and *health associations.* Differences in purposes, ownership, pricing, financial security, assessment rights, price, incorporation, and policyholder services are distinguishing characteristics. A summary reviews these differences.

Criteria for choosing an insurer explain the factors which the insurance consumer should consider, including *financial strength, service,* and *cost.*

Types of insurer representatives are not limited to *agents* but also include *solicitors, brokers,* and *service representatives.* Their use and significance vary by type of insurance and territory.

The professional concept is growing in insurance, stressing the technical knowledge, educational requirements, advisory skills, integrity, and attitude of all insurance personnel in performing their marketing and other functions properly.

Criteria for choosing an agent or broker suggest that the insured should evaluate these factors: knowledge and ability, willingness, integrity and character, and representation.

Marketing methods in insurance include the alternatives among:

Agency versus direct-selling systems, with agency methods predominating in insurance;

Life insurance agency systems using *general agents* and *branch managers;*

Property insurance agency systems using *independent* and *exclusive* agents, with growing modifications of these methods; and

Group insurance systems, well established in life-health insurance, with various *mass merchandising* plans growing in property-liability insurance.

Insurance marketing

Insurance agents are the most visible and the best-known part of insurance marketing. Of 1.7 million persons employed in the insurance business, approximately one third are sales personnel and two thirds have nonsales jobs. About one half of the sales force derive 50 percent or more of their income, and the other half obtain less than 50 percent, from life insurance.[1] Selling insurance as a career is an important part of the insurance business, yet an understanding of the insurance marketing *process* includes much more than that. This chapter emphasizes the *total* insurance distribution system—its product, its insurers and their representatives, its marketing methods, and how its consumers make their choices within the different parts of the function of insurance marketing.

Why should insurance students care how the insurance business is organized to market its contracts and services? Several reasons may apply. First, some students may be considering career opportunities in insurance, and if so, there are thousands of marketing jobs available. Second, as consumers of insurance, students may gain a better understanding about the many choices and decisions among insurers and agents which purchasers must make in buying insurance. Finally, the marketing process is a key function in insurance operations, and the methods used by insurers to sell and service insurance contracts are significant in determining their costs and usefulness.

Insurance personnel, and consumers too, are often quoted as emphasizing that insurance is different from other products common to our everyday life. But is insurance *really* a "unique" product? If so, is this primarily because insurance is complex and "intangible," or is it because insurance is a future, contingent, service, risk contract with substantial legal characteristics, as explained in Chapter 4?

COMPARISONS OF INSURANCE AND OTHER MARKETING

The similarities *and* the differences can be enlightening. How well the comparison is made will determine the depth of understanding that one has about insurance and its marketing process. This chapter differentiates among

---

[1] *Insurance Facts* (New York: Insurance Information Institute, 1978, p. 3); and *Life Insurance Fact Book* (Washington, D.C.: American Council of Life Insurance, 1978, p. 92).

the various types of insurers, their marketing methods, and their representatives. It also explains the professional concept and the consumer viewpoint of insurance marketing. With this information, the most beneficial thinking can be that which asks: "Why is this so for insurance but not for the XYZ business?"

Marketing the insurance product

Marketing, the directing of the flow of goods and services from the producer to the consumer or user, is a particularly important business activity for insurance. In Chapter 4 the insurance product was described as a written legal contract *plus* the "bundle of services" included with it. The educational, motivational, advisory, and other services prior to, at the time of, and after the issuance of the contract make the purchase of insurance at least in some ways dissimilar from buying automobiles, restaurant meals, or clothing. The nature and characteristics of different products help determine the best sales appeals, procedures, pricing methods, and techniques to be used in the distribution process.

Sales personnel in our society are sometimes unfairly stereotyped as being like Willy Loman in the famous play *Death of a Salesman*. However, the essential nature of the marketing activity cannot be forgotten. The insurance agent is the basis of marketing for the insurer. Unissued contracts in the agent's file cabinets are as worthless as overstocked buggy whips in the warehouse of a misguided manufacturer a few decades ago. The insurer must develop the marketing system that becomes the link between the insurer (producer) and insured (consumer or "policyholder"). Other businesses can have small yet profitable operations. Relatively, there is more need for an insurer than for other businesses to have a reasonably large and diversified market, because predictability of losses is usually increased by larger numbers and spread of risk. Thus, the marketing of insurance assumes a predominant place among functions performed by insurers, as previously shown in Figure 4–1 of Chapter 4.

The insurance market

In one sense, a *market* is a meeting of people who have as their purpose the transaction of business. The term can mean either the region in which a commodity is sold, or the group of persons who might be expected to purchase, or the place of purchase. As examples, there are, respectively, the central West Coast market, the young marrieds' market, and the local market.

In insurance terminology, *market* is used to indicate both the area of distribution and the available source of the different coverages. In the first instance, persons in the middle salary brackets might be referred to as a market for retirement annuities, or large industrial organizations as a market for group pension plans. The second and more restricted use of the term applies it to the place or source for the purchase of different forms of coverage, such as the aviation, fire, or marine insurance markets. This concept of insurance marketing has already been discussed in Chapter 2, where the fields of insurance were classified into various personal and property lines of business. In addition to knowing *what* risks are the subject of insurance, one must know *who* distributes the insurance product and *how* the marketing is accomplished.

Insurance buyers or their agents have little difficulty in placing ordinary risks—that is, in "finding a market." As a risk tends to involve special features, the limitations of the market appear. Every company selects risks on the basis of underwriting judgment, and there are many classes that one company or another will not write at all. For example, some fire companies will not insure restaurants. In the liability field, motorcycle or drag car races are risks that some companies will not accept. In health insurance, many insurers would not write accident insurance for a scuba diver.

Local agents may limit their business to either life or property insurance, or they may embrace all forms of the insurance business. An all-lines agency represents companies that will afford facilities for all the classes of insurance that its customers require. Frequently, the limitations of local agents require that they seek outside facilities. In such instances, agents are said to "broker" the line, or as much of it as they are unable to handle. The transaction involves a division of commissions.

The risk manager for an organization selects agents and insurers, and must be familiar with the insurance market and its limitations. The usual coverages, such as fire and automobile insurance, are obtainable in every community through a local agency. For more hazardous lines that are not written in volume, the market is more limited. It is true that almost every measurable risk is insurable. It does not follow that every agent has the facilities for placing every insurable risk. Ability to place unusual lines is evidence that the agent or broker is well informed and keeping abreast of developments in the insurance field.

LEGAL TYPES OF PRIVATE INSURERS

The *insurer* that bears or carries the risk of insurance is sometimes referred to as a "risk bearer" or an "insurance carrier." The term *insurer* is more accurate than *insurance company* because some insurers are not incorporated.

Private insurers are divided broadly into three major groups by their *legal type* of organization, as follows: (1) *stock* companies, (2) *mutual* companies, and (3) *other* insurers. "Other" insurers include (*a*) reciprocal exchanges; (*b*) Lloyds associations; and (*c*) fraternal societies, mutual savings bank life systems, and health associations. These basic legal types also might be separated into those insurers that are *commercial* or proprietary in nature and those that are *cooperative* in nature. The first category has profit-seeking owners other than policyholders, such as in stock companies and Lloyds associations. Cooperatives are organized for the benefit of the policyholder-owners, such as in mutual companies, reciprocals, and fraternals.

Insurers may also be divided according to the *types of insurance* they write, as property, liability, life, and health insurers. Chapter 2 compared insurers in this way as it explained the fields of insurance.

According to *domicile,* U.S. insurers are considered *domestic* by the state in which they are organized, *foreign* by all other states, and *alien* if incorporated in another country.

Figure 5–1 summarizes the relationships among private insurers by legal type of organization. Observe that stock and mutual insurers are by far the most significant, both in terms of the number of insurers (about 85 percent of the total) and in terms of the sales volume (about 90 percent of the total). All "other" types of private insurers are relatively unimportant in regard to the total insurance business, but in particular types of insurance or geographic areas they may be more prominent. Examples are the fraternal life insurers in Wisconsin, the savings bank life insurers in Massachusetts, and the Blue Cross–Blue Shield plans in the hospital and surgical field.

Note that *government* insurers are excluded in the discussion of marketing in this chapter. These types, although part of the total marketing aspects of insurance, operate on principles quite different from those of private insurers. They are compulsory rather than voluntary for large segments of the market. Their growing importance, however, is a factor that should be considered in studying each of the private insurers included in this chapter.

Self-insurers are also excluded, since they are less a type of marketing for insurance than an alternative for treating risks (see Chapter 3).

Another meaningful way of classifying insurers, that of differentiating among the various insurance marketing *systems,* is emphasized in a later section of this chapter.

Stock companies

Stock insurance companies are incorporated business organizations organized as profit-making ventures and owned by stockholders. Sometimes they are termed "proprietary." Laws enacted by the various states govern their operation, and they are obliged to satisfy the designated authorities as to their capital, reserve fund, assets, and investment. The contracts they issue are usually written for a definitely stated consideration (premium). The insured receives no benefit (dividend) from the earnings of the company and pays no assessment or additional premium if losses exceed income. The insured's first cost is usually the final cost.

The capital subscribed by the *stockholders* serves as an extra amount in addition to premium payments out of which losses can be paid. Additions

Figure 5-1. Comparison of legal types of U.S. private insurers by number and sales (figure above each type is number of insurers; figure below each type is billions of dollars of premiums, 1977)

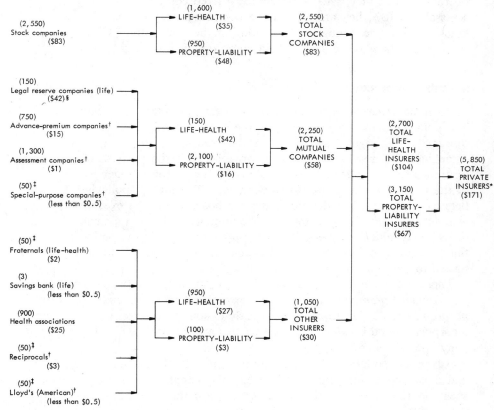

* Excludes "voluntary government" types as explained in Chapter 2, whose premiums are about $3 billion.
† Most or all of these types write *property-liability* insurance.
‡ This means 50 *or less*, wherever used in this figure.
§ Estimated at 55 percent of total stock and mutual life premiums combined.
Sources: *Life Insurance Fact Book, Insurance Facts, Best's Aggregates and Averages*, and *Source Book on Health Insurance Data*, 1977. Estimates included for some 1977 figures.

made to the surplus serve the same purpose. Stockholders are entitled to any of the residual profits after losses and expenses have been paid and proper reserves set up.

The facilities of stock companies are often national or even worldwide in their scope. In the United States, stock companies generally write their contracts through local agents, paying them a commission on the business. Approximately one third of them write business in all or most of the states. Some insurance is purchased through brokers who represent the policyholder.

Stock insurance companies thus have the following as their basic characteristics: (1) they are incorporated and owned by stockholders who supply capital funds serving as part of the financial security for the firm's operations; (2) they issue contracts for a fixed cost (the contracts are nonassessable); (3) they are often large companies that do business in many kinds of insurance throughout the nation or the world; and (4) they operate through agents who are usually paid on a commission basis.

Mutual companies

A mutual insurance company is a corporation owned by its *policyholders.* The policyholders also *participate* in the operations of the company, at least through voting rights, and share in the company's financial success and, sometimes, failure. The company is organized for the purpose of providing insurance for its policyholders at low cost. Every policyholder is a member of the company. There are no stockholders. The mutual policyholder-members elect the board of directors, and the board elects the executive officers who actually manage the company. The mutual corporation assumes the risks of its policyholder-members. When the premiums in a given period are more than adequate to meet losses and expenses, part or all of the excess is returned to the policyholder as a "dividend."

There are a number of different kinds of mutual insurers. These include (1) *advance-premium* mutuals, (2) *assessment* mutuals, and (3) *special-purpose* mutuals. They may differ greatly in some characteristics, but each is incorporated and is owned by policyholders who receive dividends if the company operations are successful.

Advance-premium mutuals. This type of mutual company is best known and most important, writing 98 percent of all mutual insurance. Practically speaking, the operations of advance-premium mutuals may be very similar to those of the stock companies. Legally, the advance-premium mutuals are different because they are owned by the policyholders, have no stockholders, and usually pay policyholder dividends. However, they are like the stock companies that also operate on an advance-premium basis, collecting most or all of the cost of the insurance at the time the contract is written. They usually do business in a wide variety of types of insurance and in a fairly large geographic area.

These advance-premium mutuals issue a nonassessable contract in which the maximum cost of the insurance is set when the policy is begun. Legal requirements for writing nonassessable policies require these mutuals to possess specified amounts of surplus to provide for the financial solvency of the company in case of temporary periods of heavier than normal losses or expenses. A few mutual companies in this category issue a partially assessable contract, but this is the exception.

Many of these advance-premium mutuals issue dividends to policyholders. The original price may be the same as the stock company rate. At the end of the policy period a return may be made as a dividend for any excess amount beyond the losses, expenses, and reasonable reserves and surplus of the company. The actual amount of the return is unknown to the policyholder until after the insurance contract expires, it being dependent upon the experience of the company for that policyholder classification. The actual net cost (original price less dividend) to the policyholder is thus uncertain until the dividend is paid.

In most states the advance-premium mutuals must comply with the same reserve, investment, policy form, and regulatory laws as apply to stock companies. Their organization requirements are somewhat different, as a minimum number of policyholders are required to start a company and the board of directors must be set up in the charter and bylaws as subject to the control of policyholders rather than stockholders.

Examples of the advance-premium mutual include companies writing only life and health insurance—(Northwestern Mutual Life and Connecticut Mutual Life) and companies writing nearly all lines of insurance—(State Farm and Nationwide). In the life insurance field, both stock and practically all mutual companies operate on an advance-premium basis. They are often referred to as *legal reserve* companies and do not permit assessments against the policyholders.

Assessment mutuals.   There are many small insurers writing primarily fire and windstorm insurance for farm and small-town dwellings on an assessment basis. They probably number more than 1,300, but account for less than 2 percent of the total premium writings of all mutual insurers. In some rural communities, these township or county farmers' mutuals are well known, however, and they may write a majority of the farm property risks in some small local areas.

Assessment contracts are written in two ways, either in a limited or an unlimited policy. Some require no advance premiums at all, relying entirely on assessments at the end of the policy period. A member who belongs to an insurer in which liability is unlimited is bound to pay a proportional share of all losses and legitimate expenses of the company. The unlimited liability for assessment has caused some concern to many who fear that a serious catastrophe might involve them in assessments greater than they could meet. On the other hand, because farm risks are so scattered, a farmers' mutual with a reasonable number of risks may be comparatively free from the catastrophe hazard, unless perhaps located where prairie or forest fires or widespread windstorms are a menace. Most of the farm mutuals operate with the unlimited assessment plan, but others may state a definite dollar limitation on the assessment or limit it to a certain multiple of the policyholder's premium.

Special-purpose mutuals.   Some mutual companies are considered a separate category because they were organized with a special purpose in mind. Usually these organizations limit their insurance to a definite type of business, such as milling or grain, lumber, or drug manufacture. In the past these insurers were known as "class mutuals," and they wrote insurance only for the occupational class in which they had specialized knowledge. Many were started on this basis, with the objective of special low rates or forms of coverage, but now write business for many types of firms, even though they retain the old class name for the insurance company.

An important group of small New England "factory mutuals" base their operations on the belief that prevention should be the first and basic aim in any effort to secure low-cost fire insurance. The Factory Mutual System developed in the 1800s to insure large manufacturing properties. A technical staff of trained engineers was organized, and a laboratory for research and testing was established. This group was largely responsible for the adoption of the automatic sprinkler system and many other fire safeguards. There are now about four companies organized together as the Associated Factory Mutual Insurance Companies, cooperating efficiently in engineering, inspection, research, and loss adjustment.

The Factory Mutuals require insureds to pay large deposit premiums, several times the yearly cost. At the end of the policy period, deductions are made for the substantial loss services, other expenses, and actual losses paid, and the balance is returned to the insured. The contracts are written using special representatives in the field but no agents. The purposes of the Factory Mutuals are to provide insurance for large and high-grade industrial and institutional properties and to emphasize loss prevention. Similar in regard to these purposes, about 100 stock insurance companies have organized an association known as the Industrial Risk Insurers, which operates through agents in writing these large exposures.

Other Insurers

Although stock and mutual insurers write almost nine tenths of the total private insurance business in the United States, there are other legal types that merit attention because (1) they represent the wide variety of insurers in the market, (2) they may be relatively significant in particular types of insurance, or (3) they help illustrate the principles of insurance in showing the student how insurance works, what problems it has, and what features the insurance consumers should be looking for in their choices of insurance contracts and services.

Lloyds.   In contrast to stock and mutual insurers that accept risks as corporations are the *Lloyds insurers,* whose basic characteristic is that they are *individual* insurers. Although this type of insurance accounts for less than 1 percent of the total insurance sales in the United States, the concept of insurance written by individuals is important. Historically Lloyds organizations are significant, too, and in the world market they are very predominant in reinsurance and in insuring unusual and difficult risks. Two types of Lloyds should be distinguished: "Lloyd's of London," which is by far the most important, and the "American Lloyds," which are small and few in number.

Sometimes called the world's most fascinating marketplace, Lloyd's of London is one of the most famous institutions for the insurance of risks. It still bears the name of the coffeehouse[2] in which it originated more than 300 years ago as a center of shipping news and financial information. Lloyd's as a corporation neither subscribes to policies of insurance nor directly issues them. Insurance is written by individual "underwriting members" who sign "each for himself and not for another." The insurer, then, is not Lloyd's but the underwriters at Lloyd's. A policyholder insures *at* Lloyd's but not *with* Lloyd's.

Membership in Lloyd's has been compared with membership in the New York Exchange. The exchange sets up standards with which its members must comply, yet purchases of insurance are transactions between members and their customers. Members are elected to membership. Individually, they are insurers; collectively, they are Lloyd's. Regulatory measures add formal requirements of substantial initial net worth (about $200,000 for Americans) for the carefully selected members, an annual audit of their accounts, and restriction of commitments in relation to their capital. Also, a reserve fund requirement states that all current premiums must be segregated under a deed of trust as a fund out of which claims may be paid. Every penny of a member's assets stands squarely behind any risks assumed. Corporations are not admitted to membership. There is a further element of protection in a central guarantee fund, and a separate trust fund is held in the United States for American policyholders.

There are more than 10,000 members from around the world (also called "names") at Lloyd's.[3] These members are organized into approximately 300 "syndicates," with a membership varying from a few to more than 500 in each. A syndicate is operated by an agent or "underwriter," who commits the members of that syndicate to the risks insured. A policy is written through a

---

[2] There have been some intriguing books and even movies about Lloyd's of London. For two classic books on the subject, see C. E. Golding and D. King-Page, *Lloyd's* (New York: McGraw-Hill Book Co., 1952); and Ralph Straus, *Lloyd's: The Gentlemen at the Coffeehouse* (New York: Carrick & Evans, 1938). For those addicted to the late, late TV shows, watch for reruns of Tyrone Power in *Lloyd's of London,* a swashbuckling movie of the 1940s. An excellent color film of the same title is available through Lloyd's representatives, showing the everyday operations of Lloyd's in London today. The traditions are preserved: the famous Lutine Bell is rung once for bad news and twice for good news; red-coated messengers are called "waiters"; and major losses are entered in a book with a quill pen! Current review of Lloyd's operations is contained in a monthly publication, *Lloyd's Log* (London: Lloyd's). *Rough Notes* magazine carried an interesting series by Roy C. McCormick in 1973, titled "Taking the Mystery out of Lloyd's."

[3] "Lloyd's of London: Is the Exclusive Club Now Open?" *Risk Management,* February, 1977, p. 29.

"broker." There are more than 200 firms of Lloyd's brokers. With an adequate description of the risk, the broker offers the insurance to the underwriters, and each underwriter who wishes signs a slip (underwrites his or her name to it, hence the term *underwriter*), indicating the amount of insurance accepted. When the broker has obtained enough signers so that the amounts they assume will total the required insurance, Lloyd's Policy Signing Office draws up the policy and affixes its official seal. This document, however, is not signed by the corporation but by individuals who must themselves pay their proportional share in the event of loss. The function of the corporation of Lloyd's is purely to supervise transactions and guard the reputation of the institution.[4]

The fame of Lloyd's of London is heightened by the unusual risks that have been insured there. Examples of this market's versatility include a prize of $2 million offered for the capture of the famous Loch Ness monster; Elizabeth Taylor's illness in the filming of *Cleopatra* (on which a $2 million loss was paid); Marlene Dietrich's legs and Jimmy Durante's nose against accidental injury; hole-in-one golf prizes of $50,000 or more; space missile launchings; and a wide variety of other unique risks.

Many of these spectacular risks obtain widespread publicity for Lloyd's of London. Although Lloyd's is not the biggest insurer in the world, its sales of insurance and reinsurance exceed $2 billion a year, and it is probably the best known of all insurers. Today, marine risks make up one third of its total business, and nonmarine, motor, and aviation risks make up the bulk of its business. Some large life insurance amounts are written. Excess liability risks involving millions of dollars are quite commonplace. Practically any large loss in the world—whether it is a multimillion-dollar fire, a big ship or airplane crash, or a major hurricane—involves Lloyd's of London, as either an insurer or a reinsurer.

Lloyd's of London is licensed directly only in two states, Illinois and Kentucky, though Lloyd's brokers and agents operate throughout the United States and the rest of the world. Although the usual United States family would have little need for directly insuring at Lloyd's of London, United States businesses often insure at Lloyd's to obtain needed high-liability limits, special coverages such as worldwide package policies, or hard-to-obtain protection for large exposures or unusual perils.

In the United States there are a few "American Lloyds" associations. About 30, including several in Texas, write primarily auto-physical-damage insurance. In the American Lloyds each member is ordinarily liable for only a specified maximum. The strict regulations of the London Lloyd's governing membership, deposits, and audits are not a requisite of the ordinary American Lloyds. Each organization depends upon the financial strength of its individ-

---

[4] "Insurance—Risky Business," *Time,* August 6, 1973, p. 67. More recently, the legs of TV's star Angie Dickinson were insured in 1977 for $1 million.

ual members within their limited liability. Some insureds have not understood that the American Lloyds and the original London organization have no connection. The American Lloyds form of insurer plays a relatively insignificant role in United States insurance. However, the concept of having individuals rather than corporations write insurance is important. (The reader is also referred to Chapter 29 for information on a new development in the U.S., the formation of an "insurance exchange" and "free trade zone" in New York City.)

Reciprocals

The *reciprocal* exchange or interinsurance association is a type of cooperative insurance. Each policyholder under this form of insurance contract is insured by all of the others. Each insured is also an insurer, as contracts are exchanged on a reciprocal basis.

The reciprocal exchange is not in the legal sense a mutual insurer because the individual subscribers assume their liability as individuals, not as a responsibility of the group as a whole. Another basic difference from mutual insurers is that reciprocals are not incorporated as companies but are formed under separate laws as associations. Reciprocals are contrasted with Lloyds because Lloyds are: (1) proprietary or profit seeking and (2) the Lloyds insurer is not also an insured, as is always the case in a reciprocal.

The funds held by a reciprocal are the sum total of individual credits held for the account of individual subscribers. These subscribers are required over a period of years to accumulate reserves representing a multiple ranging from two to five annual premiums before underwriting earnings, if any, are returned in cash. A separate account is maintained for each subscriber, and out of this is paid only a proportional share of each loss and expense. Beyond that, the reciprocal can usually levy an assessment of up to a multiple of premiums paid, such as ten times, but the liability of each subscriber is definitely limited. Reciprocal insurance is quite distinctly an American development.

The policyholders, or subscribers, appoint a manager to whom is entrusted the responsibility of carrying on the business. The manager derives authority from a power of attorney and is known as an "attorney-in-fact." An advisory committee has ultimate control over the manager. Reciprocals are not incorporated, so no capital assets are available to prevent insolvency.

The major characteristics of reciprocals are (1) the dual nature of each insured as an insurer (with stated limits of liability), (2) the system of individual accounts, and (3) the use of an attorney-in-fact under the control of an advisory committee.

Reciprocals are relatively unimportant in the total business of insurance (only about 50 writing a few percent of all property-liability insurance), but in certain areas and for specific lines such as automobile insurance they have acquired some significance. Although usually small, a few reciprocal exchanges have grown to substantial size. Examples are the Farmers Insurance Exchange (Los Angeles), the Inter-Insurance Exchange of the Automobile Club of Southern California, and the United Services Automobile Association (San Antonio, Texas).

Fraternals, savings bank life, and health associations

In the field of life and health insurance there are several special types of insurers formed under provisions in the state laws separate from the laws applying to stock, mutual, reciprocal, and Lloyds associations. They are often essentially mutual in their operations and have the goal of low-cost insurance for members. They differ, however, by not being incorporated as insurance companies under the state insurance laws.

A *fraternal* society is a special type of insurer providing insurance benefits, particularly life insurance, for its members. The operations of the fraternal are closely related to and controlled by the bylaws of a lodge or a nonprofit social organization. Many fraternals are church oriented, such as the Lutheran Brotherhood and the Knights of Columbus fraternal benefit societies. The fraternal orders have tax exemptions. A possible undesirable feature is the fact that the tax exemptions usually permit the fraternal order to assess the policyholder in case of financial difficulties. The popularity of the fraternals was high until the 1920s, after which they declined in importance. Since 1950 several of the larger fraternals have expanded on the basis of operations which closely parallel normal mutual insurer techniques and growth. Total life insurance in force is approximately $40 billion (1977), but this amount is only 2 percent of total life insurance in force in the United States.

Savings bank life insurance systems operate in three states: Connecticut, Massachusetts, and New York. A centralized agency in each of these states administers a plan through which participating mutual savings banks may issue limited amounts of life insurance. The limits vary by state from $10,000 to $53,000, and the policies are sold on an over-the-counter basis without the use of agents. The financial backing of the plans does not include the total assets of the banks, as only the insurance department assets of the bank and certain contingency funds of the state administrative agency are available to insureds. Although the life insurance in force is only about $10 billion, in these three states the amount represents approximately 3 percent of the total life insurance.

Health associations are important in the insurance of medical care expenses, especially in the prepayment of hospital and surgical expenses. More than 800 plans are in operation, but by far the largest and best known are the Blue Cross and Blue Shield associations. More than 100 of these plans write more than one half of the total U.S. hospital-surgical insurance. These are nonprofit, tax-exempt, unincorporated, voluntary organizations set up in most states under special enabling legislation. They are administered by trustees who represent the hospitals, the medical profession, and the communities involved in a particular geopraphic area, such as a part of or an entire state. A primary distinction from other insurers is that the objective of these associations is to provide health insurance for a very broad segment of the population. Impliedly, this aim includes such groups as the low-income classes and the aged and justifies the differences in taxation and regulation usually applied to Blue Cross–Blue Shield plans as compared with other insurers. Marketing distinctions also include the use of salaried representatives for enrollment in place of agents; contracts by the plans with hospitals and doctors to provide medical services rather than pay losses in dollars; and an emphasis on group enrollment through employers instead of individual contract sales, which enroll 10 percent of the subscribers.

Dental insurance has also adopted the service approach for prepayment plans, as dental service plans similar to those of Blue Shield have offered group dental insurance in many states since the mid-1960s. The Delta Dental Plans Association coordinates many of the nonprofit associations. More than 100 insurance companies, too, offer dental insurance as a part of regular group health insurance contracts. Dental insurance is said to be the fastest growing of all employee health insurance plans in the United States, with more than 30 million persons now covered (six times the number ten years ago). More than one of every five companies has dental insurance for its employees. Vision care insurance is expected to be the next most rapidly growing employee health insurance fringe benefit during the 1980s.

A wide variety of other health associations exist for the purpose of providing prepayment insurance plans for communities, unions, colleges, or clients of a group medical practice. Examples include the Health Insurance Plan of New York, the International Ladies' Garment Workers' Union plan, the Kaiser Foundation plans, and the Ross-Loop Medical Group (Los Angeles). In the 1970s, much attention was given to the formation of "health maintenance organizations," or HMOs, for meeting the rapidly expanding health care payable under the federal Medicare program. Some HMOs have been sponsored and financed by the larger life insurers (see Chapter 14).

Summary

The major differences among the primary legal types of insurers are presented in Table 5–1. Most consumers will purchase their insurance from stock and mutual insurers, so their differences are most important to note. However, in theory and for some insureds in some kinds of insurance, differences among the other types may also be meaningful.

The most significant reason for knowing these distinguishing characteristics is to understand *why* each may be important to the policyholder. Purpose and ownership of the insurer are determining factors in maintaining efficient con-

Table 5–1. Summary of differences among legal types of insurers

Distinguishing characteristic	Stock	Mutual	Lloyds	Reciprocals
Purpose	Profit to stockholders	Returns to policyholders (insurance at low cost)	Profit to individual members	Insurers are insureds
Ownership ..	Stockholders (incorporated)	Policyholders (incorporated)	Individual members	Individual subscribers (associations)
Financial strength ..	Based on capital and surplus	Based on surplus only (no capital)	Members' net worth and un-limited liability, reserves, trust funds	Individual accounts and reserves
Price	Fixed, known price	Net price not known	Fixed price	Possible returns on individual accounts
Assessment right	None	Some mutuals may assess policyholders, if needed	Entire personal assets of members	Limited assessment rights

trol of the enterprise, and for possible conflicts of interest between owners and insureds. Financial strength is crucial to overall solvency and continuity of insurance. Prices may be fixed, or the net cost to policyholders may depend upon possible returns, based upon the future costs and expenses of the organization. Potential liability of the policyholder may also vary according to limited or unlimited assessment rights against the insureds. Wise consumers should know how these characteristics may affect the insurance purchased and its cost.

CRITERIA FOR CHOOSING AN INSURER

How does the insurance consumer go about choosing an insurer that best meets his or her needs? With all the various legal types of insurers discussed in the previous sections, the selection is not easy. A good rationale must consider several major factors, plus some others which may overlap with the criteria for choosing an agent, discussed separately later.

Although Part II of this text emphasizes the insurer viewpoint, it is necessary to keep the insured's (consumer) viewpoint always in mind. This is particularly true for the marketing function, and essentially the professional attitude is one of agents advising their clients as if the risk problems were their own. The professional concept of insurance marketing and the agent's part in that concept are discussed in later sections of this chapter.

It might seem at first thought that the selection of the insurance company would be one of the first and most important decisions of the insurance buyer. Personal or business purchasers of insurance *may* select the insurer; however, often they do *not*, for most insurance is bought through agents. In *life and health* insurance, it is most common to have the agent represent only one insurer, so the selection process is a combination one. As the purchaser chooses the agent, the insurer is also automatically chosen. This may also be true in cases where the consumer selects the insurer (perhaps on the basis of the insurer's advertising or general reputation) and then looks for an agent who represents that insurer. The "exclusive," one-company representation, agency system in property and liability insurance (see later section of this chapter) is similar in its effects on the market selection process of the insurance buyer.

Although the purchaser is not always involved in choosing the insurer, the process of evaluating insurers may need to be understood. This is particularly important for the large business firm, with perhaps thousands or millions of dollars of coverage written by a few insurers, and in any of the (relatively) infrequent cases in which the purchaser does business directly with the insurer without the services of an agent.

Companies enjoying the best reputations ordinarily attract high-grade representatives. With state regulatory agencies scrutinizing the financial position of companies, the ability of companies to pay is rarely expected to become a problem. The attitude of companies with respect to claims may differ, however, and the insured is concerned with the company's attitude regarding technicalities and the reputation of the claim department for satisfactory dealings with insureds at a time of loss.

The insured is interested in knowing the scope of the contracts offered by an insurer and in whether or not the insurer is liberal with respect to underwriting. A company that is selective in choosing risks may prove unsatisfactory when a buyer has a more difficult type of risk to be insured. The insurer's facilities for rate analysis and for loss-prevention recommendations that may favorably influence insurance costs are also important to the consumer.

The size of an insurer is not always a controlling factor in its selection; financial strength and size are not necessarily equivalents. Growth over a period of years is significant. The buyer who limits purchases to well-known and recognized companies and places business with an agent or broker of outstanding reputation will probably have accomplished much in choosing the best possible insurer. If statistical data about the insurer are needed for further analysis, several readily available sources are useful. The state insurance departments can provide some current information. Financial history, ratings, and analyses on individual insurers are published in annual volumes of *Best's Insurance Reports*.

Here are some of the criteria to be considered in choosing an insurer:

1. *Financial strength.* Although surplus—or capital and surplus—is re-

quired by all states, the requirements vary considerably. The present net worth of the insurer is a starting point in the financial analysis of an insurer, but many other factors may need to be considered. The type of business written, the trends observed over a number of years, the underwriting and investment activities analyzed separately, the adequacy of reserves, and the ratios of policyholders' surplus to liabilities (and to net premiums written) are all significant considerations. Basic to all these factors is the general quality of the management, which over a period of time ultimately determines the financial strength of the company.

2. *Service.*   The ability of the insurer to provide proper protection for the insured is essential. Does the insurer specialize in a few lines of insurance contracts, or does it sell all coverages which the purchaser may need and want? Is the insurer experienced in offering all the contracts it will write? Will the insurer tailor-make contracts to meet individual needs of the insurance buyer? Does it have capacity and adequate reinsurance for the largest risks the buyer may require? Is it licensed in all states in which the buyer needs coverage? In addition to indemnification for losses, can the insurer provide the necessary engineering and loss-prevention services which the purchaser needs? What are the general attitude and reputation of the insurer with regard to prompt and fair settlement of all reasonable claims?

3. *Cost.*   Although often thought to be the most important criterion, cost should usually be considered and compared after the above two criteria are analyzed. Costs do vary,[5] and a too low cost can be just as bad as a too high cost. Lower costs are an obvious direct benefit to the purchaser of insurance, but *too* low costs can result in an unduly strict attitude toward claims payment, inadequate reserves or other financial weaknesses, or perhaps undesirable decreases in the number of quality of agents and representatives who provide services to the insurance buyer.

Initial costs are only part of the necessary analysis, for final costs over a longer period of protection must be considered, including possible rate changes, dividends, assessments, or premium adjustments under audit or retrospective rating plans. In life insurance (see Chapters 10–12), *net* cost comparisons over a period such as 20 or more years, considering dividends, cash values, and interest factors, may be needed. For large businesses, the insurance costs should be analyzed with other risk-management costs, such as loss prevention.

TYPES OF INSURER REPRESENTATIVES

The insurance buyer is often most concerned, and rightly so, with the representative of the insurer with whom direct contact is made. The legal type of

---

[5] See, for example, Joseph M. Belth, *Life Insurance: A Consumer's Handbook* (Bloomington: Indiana University Press, 1973); and *Life Insurance Rates and Data* (Cincinnati: National Underwriter Co., annual).

insurer or the marketing system used is often of secondary importance to the insured. The applicant for insurance makes contact with the insurer through one or more of the following: (*a*) agents, (*b*) solicitors, (*c*) brokers, and (*d*) service representatives.

Agents

The agent is a representative of the insurer, and the authority under which he or she operates is delegated through an agency contract. The agent is appointed by an insurance company to act as its representative with authority to solicit, negotiate, and effect contracts of insurance in its behalf.

The powers of the agent are governed by the "agency contract" with the insurer. The terms *general agent, local agent,* and *state agent,* among others, are frequently used in the insurance business. The local agent who makes contact with the applicant for insurance may be designated *general agent, regional agent,* or simply *agent.* All of these terms have a specialized significance within the business and may represent the nature of the agent's position with the company or the commission arrangement.

Legally, regardless of terminology, a property-liability agent is either a *general agent* or a *limited agent.* A general agent (other than in life insurance) can bind a risk and thereby make insurance effective immediately and prior to the actual delivery of the policy. Many such agents do not have to wait for the contract to be written by the insurer, as the agent or the agency office writes the contract for such usual coverages as fire, auto, or homeowners' policies. If the agent's powers are limited or restricted, the scope of the delegated authority determines what may be done or not done. It has been noted in Chapter 4 that secret limitations may not apply, and the principal may be bound if the action is within the agent's implied or apparent authority.

Life. In the strict legal sense, company officers act in the capacity of agents in issuing policies and otherwise conducting the affairs of the corporation. However, as the term *agent* is used here, regularly salaried officers of the company are by definition excluded. The life insurance business customarily limits the authority to issue or modify life insurance contracts to company officers. Life insurance agents are *limited* agents. Generally speaking, life insurance agents are authorized to solicit, receive, and forward applications for the contracts written by their companies. Agents are authorized to receive the first premiums due on applications, but not subsequent premiums. An exception is the "industrial" life insurance agent, who does collect renewal premiums regularly at the home of the policyholder and forwards them to the company.

The authority of the life insurance agent is limited not only in the matter of collections but also in the ability to accept risks or bind the coverage. The life insurer issues the contract after receiving the written, signed application and also usually a medical examination report. The agent cannot "cover" the policyholder immediately, nor can contract modifications be made later without the approval of the insurer.

Property. Agents appointed to represent property and liability insurers are as a rule granted the powers of a *general* agent. The limitations to their authority are set forth in the agency agreement. Such agents may *bind* their companies by oral contract as well as waive policy provisions. Among other responsibilities they inspect risks and often also collect initial and renewal premiums.

Many such agents write contracts in their own offices for fire, auto, or homeowners' policies. Special contracts for business liability, steam boiler explosion, glass breakage, or other perils may have to be issued by the insurer in the home office or the branch office. Few agents have authority to bind or issue bonds.

Solicitors

A *solicitor* is an individual authorized by an insurance agent or broker to solicit contracts of insurance, acting only on behalf of the agent or broker. The solicitor does not have the authority to bind the insurer with respect to risk, but is authorized to collect premiums. The solicitor is an employee of the agent. The agent is responsible for acts or omissions within the scope of the solicitor's employment. In some urban areas, the larger insurance agencies may employ numerous solicitors.

Brokers

Brokers, who represent the *policyholder* rather than the insured, may also be valuable in rendering service to the insurance purchaser. With widespread contacts and knowledge of many fields of insurance, many brokers offer significant advice and counsel to their clients. The larger insurance brokerage firms are especially well equipped to handle the problems of insurance for a buyer with individual and specialized requirements. Sometimes "excess" or "surplus line" brokers are needed to place unusual or large types of risks.

Unlike the agent, who legally represents the insurer, the broker acts on behalf of the insured. Thus, the broker, but sometimes not the agent, is an independent contractor. The broker serves the insured by assisting the applicant for insurance in placing risks, yet is paid by the insurer. By informing themselves of rates, forms, and markets, brokers are useful and recognized intermediaries between the insurer, or the agent, and the insured.

Insureds are sometimes confused because they do not differentiate between an insurance broker and an agent. The insurance agent is acting under specific and delegated authority from the insurer and is often authorized to bind coverage within delegated limits. The broker, on the other hand, has no such authority, and is usually recognized as the agent of the insured. Because the broker is held to represent the policyholder, the insured is bound by the acts of the broker with respect to all the negotiations between insurer and insured. Any misrepresentation, mistake, breach of warranty, or fraud perpetrated by the broker on the insured's behalf makes the insured responsible as if the insured had committed the acts.

It is important to understand clearly that the broker cannot make insurance effective. The broker is not a party to the insurance contract as an insurer. However, many insurance agents may be licensed as both agents and brokers. The simplest illustration is to be found in the case of an agent who commits the insurer for a part of a line and acts as a broker in placing any excess coverage.

There are brokers who specialize in writing insurance for lines that are otherwise difficult to place. These are called *excess line brokers* (or *surplus line brokers*).[6] In some classifications a market for coverage is difficult to find; for example, a category that has a high loss frequency or a severity potential so great that it would strain the facilities of the ordinary markets. Then there are lines fraught with great uncertainty, such as products liability coverage of new and untried cosmetics and drugs. Other examples of business done by excess line brokers include liability insurance for amusement parks and ski resorts.

In some instances the brokers are obliged to seek a market such as that afforded by Lloyd's of London or other international insurers. In other cases the business is placed for a premium higher than locally established rates with companies that have not been licensed to do business in a particular state and are known as "nonadmitted companies." The nonadmitted character of much of the market handling excess lines business should invite the careful scrutiny of the financial responsibility and reputation of the insurer by the prospective insured. The excess line broker may not always deal with the insured directly but may be sought out by the insured's broker. Many states require special licenses for excess line brokers.

While the major part of life insurance production is handled by company agents, there are a number of *life brokers* who place the business they produce with the company that they feel to be in a position to handle and service the line adequately. Group insurance has proved a fertile field for brokers. Since underwriting rules of companies differ so widely, the placing of a group risk may involve its submission to several companies. A significant volume of brokerage business also arises from life agents who fundamentally represent one life company but place business in another because clients want the par-

---

[6] The variety and complexity of these markets can be seen in the many markets discussed in publications such as the *Excess and Surplus Lines Manual* (Santa Monica, Calif.: Merritt Co.); and *Agents and Buyers Guide* (Cincinnati: National Underwriters Co.).

ticular plan it offers or because they may place the business on a more favorable basis. While this type of business is classed as brokerage, the life agent is
to be distinguished from the life broker who is attached to no particular company and originates business and places it where the best market is to be
found. Estate planning, group insurance, pension plans, and other fields in
which transactions are large and competition keen are fields in which the life
brokers are more and more making their influence felt.

Service representatives

Many companies and some large agencies employ specialists on a salaried
basis to work with and assist agents in writing the more complex lines. Such
employees are termed *service representatives,* and they may help an agent to
sell or service insurance. Company officers, managers, or general agents of
insurance companies employed on a salaried basis are not included in the
category of service representatives. A license is not usually required by the
state to act as a service representative.

Examples of service representatives are common in both the life and property insurance fields. In property insurance, "special agents" are used by
many companies to initiate agency contracts, help the agent on special sales
problems, and generally keep the agent informed of new contracts and services of the insurer. Engineering, appraisal, and loss-prevention services are
often provided by company specialists in conjunction with local agents. Company claims adjusters also work in cooperation with the agents on many of the
losses involving large amounts or special problems.

In life insurance the service representatives include advanced underwriting
specialists who aid the life agent in estate programming and pension or tax
planning. Many salaried training specialists are used by general agents to re-
cruit, supervise, and help the new life agent. Most companies writing group
life and health coverages provide salaried company representatives who aid
the life insurance agent in writing group contracts.

THE PROFESSIONAL CONCEPT OF INSURANCE MARKETING

The insurance business is placing increasing emphasis upon the value
of education and training, based upon the premise that the insurance agent is
no longer a mere canvasser for business. Instead, more agents are learning
to diagnose and treat the broad risk and insurance needs of their clients. With
the emphasis upon education and the focusing of insurance protection in such
a manner that the needs of the applicant are cared for on the most economical
basis possible, the *professional idea of personal service* was developed.

Emphasis on the professional status of the insurance agent has been a
source of misunderstanding in some instances. Reference to the professional
concept and professional ethics has led some to assume that the use of the

term *profession* carries an implied reflection upon the term *business*. This is not the case. The professional concept recognizes many forms of business negotiation in which representatives of differing interests meet on opposite sides of a bargaining table. Each knows that the other is "trading" to make the best possible deal, and there is nothing unethical in such transactions.

Professional insurance agents bring technical knowledge and experience to the service of their clients. In addition, they may call upon their company associates for assistance. These include highly trained specialists. The professional concept makes the agent the representative of the policyholder in working out an insurance program that will best meet the insured's needs. The agent and the client are on the same side of the bargaining table. Agents can be successful only to the extent that they satisfy the needs of their clients. The fact that the agent legally represents the insurer does not prevent the agent from being fair and professional in serving the policyholder. The professional concept does, however, require the agent to exercise extra care in seeing that all advice and actions are in keeping with the highest possible ethics.

The insurance business makes training and educational facilities[7] at all levels available. Correspondence courses and special home office training courses are offered. For those who wish to become specialized experts at the top of their profession, with evidence in recognition of their qualifications, there are the vigorous educational programs and the examinations of the American College and the American Institute for Property and Liability Underwriters.[8] With the objective of establishing higher educational standards in life and health insurance, the American College awards to properly qualified persons the professional designation CLU (Chartered Life Underwriter) upon completion of a series of ten national written examinations.

The American Association of University Teachers of Insurance (now the American Risk and Insurance Association) initiated a similar movement that resulted in the formation in 1942 of the American Institute for Property and Liability Underwriters. The term *underwriter* is used in a broad context, for not only do agents receive the professional designation of CPCU (Chartered Property Casualty Underwriter), but also many home office or branch offices persons who perform each of such insurer functions as product design, marketing, underwriting, rating, and loss payment. The designation is awarded to qualified persons who successfully pass a series of ten written examinations involving in addition to insurance knowledge the broad range

---

[7] See Mildred F. Stone, *The Teacher Who Changed an Industry,* and *A Calling and Its College* (Homewood, Ill.: Richard D. Irwin, 1960 and 1963, respectively), for the story of Dr. S. S. Huebner, a leader in the growth of insurance education in colleges and in the founding of The American College (its new name) in 1927.

[8] The student desiring further information about these programs can obtain bulletins and course study outlines by writing the American College at Bryn Mawr Avenue, Bryn Mawr, Pa. 19010, or the American Institute at Providence and Sugartown Roads, Malvern, Pa. 19355.

of related business subjects such as accounting, economics, law, management, and finance. The usual procedure of a successful candidate is to participate in two-hour class study groups meeting weekly during a five-year continuing education program.

More than 35,000 persons have now achieved the coveted CLU designation, and over 10,000 have the CPCU designation. In addition, tens of thousands of others have partial credit or are currently improving their capabilities through the CLU–CPCU programs. Also important are the certificate courses offered by the American College in the areas of management, taxes, financial counseling, estate planning, employee benefits, and pension planning; its new Master of Science in Financial Services degree; and its continuing education program for practicing CLUs, operated jointly with the American Society of Chartered Life Underwriters.

The Insurance Institute of America (IIA), which is closely associated with the CPCU program, has a study program leading toward an IIA certificate in general insurance, and specialized associate designations in claims, management, risk and loss control management, and underwriting. A sales training program in life and health insurance is offered by the Life Underwriter Training Council (LUTC), which each year enrolls more than 30,000 agents in its courses. The Life Office Management Association (LOMA) also has an extensive educational program of examinations for persons working in life insurance offices.

The professional concept assumes a client's reliance upon a person of particular skills or training. Professional ethics require conduct that will warrant implicit confidence on the part of a client. For example, the Society of CPCU has a Code of Ethics detailing ten unethical practices, such as misrepresentation, which could lead to a CPCU's expulsion, suspension, reprimand, or censure. The insurance agent is sometimes compared to the pastor, the doctor, or the family lawyer. To the extent that insurance persons are experts bringing specialized knowledge concerning the principles and uses of insurance unselfishly to clients, the analogy is good. It is, therefore, proper to emphasize the professional status of the insurance agent, recognizing that a public attitude of respect must be earned.

It is also well to indicate that not all insurance agents or brokers are fully qualified to render a professional service. There are many agents who are needed in the insurance business without the skill and educational requirements necessary to plan a life estate satisfactorily or to serve the needs of a complex business establishment. More and more, however, the broadening use of insurance to meet a wide variety of family and business financial needs suggests that the insurance personnel of the future will often have to be of professional caliber. The wider viewpoint of "risk management" is a good example of the growing need and opportunities for professionalism in insurance.

CRITERIA FOR CHOOSING AN AGENT OR BROKER

Since most insurance is written through the agency system, the choice of a competent and reliable insurance agent is often the most important decision for the purchaser of insurance. If an "exclusive" agent who represents one insurer only is chosen, this selection also determines the insurer with which business is conducted. If an "independent" agent is chosen, the insurance buyer often leaves the selection of the insurer up to the agent, or at least relies heavily on the agent's recommendations.

A substantial part of the insurance premium, often between 5 and 25 percent, represents commission or salary to the agent. In the event that no service or inadequate service is rendered for this part of the premium, the insured is paying for something not received. The purchaser of insurance must determine whether or not the agent or broker is only an order taker. If so, the insured is getting something less than full value.

Some insureds place insurance with a number of agents. Frequently this distribution is made on a reciprocity basis to create goodwill or on a patronage basis to distribute a line among a number of friends. Sounder practice today suggests selecting one agent or broker (or as few as possible) to handle an entire insurance account. Skilled agents as well as the insurance buyer should prefer this practice. They would rather have fewer accounts for which they are fully responsible than a wide participation in risks where they contribute little in the way of service. Sometimes an account may be split so that the property and liability lines are handled by one agent, and the life, health, and pension business by another agent. It is usually not wise to have too many agents, however, for the more that one agent knows about your total insurance account, the better he or she may be able to analyze the risk and recommend protection for your total needs.

The insurance consumer who allows friendship to be the dominant factor governing the selection of an agent may suffer lack of adequate protection or pay an exorbitant amount for excessive or duplicating coverages. Placing insurance only on the basis of personal friendship is as foolish as selecting a doctor, a lawyer, or an architect on that basis. It is becoming more and more a recognized fact that the arranging of an insurance and risk program to fit individual needs is work for trained technical experts. Because of the complex nature of various risks, insurance forms, coverages, and rates, it is essential that the insurance and risk adviser be selected with the same care and discrimination that are used in choosing other professional assistance.

Here are some of the criteria that might be used to evaluate insurance agents and brokers:

1. *Knowledge and ability.* The agent or broker must do a two-fold job of education: learn about your risk and insurance needs; and help you understand and appreciate the value of the services rendered to you as an insurance

buyer. The agent must have the background and experience necessary to identify, analyze, and treat risk properly; and to learn and teach, ask and answer. Many insureds need the ability of a truly professional insurance person—one who can detect and solve complex problems of varying markets, coverage, forms, and rates. One method of evaluating the agent's knowledge and ability is to ask questions such as these: "Are you a CLU or a CPCU? If not, are you working toward these or other educational program objectives on a regular basis? Are you a full-time agent?" Not all part-time agents, nor all agents who have not completed professional designations, are bad. However, agents who are fully committed to the insurance business are more likely to be able to do a really successful job for their clients by keeping abreast of rapidly changing knowledge requirements.

Normally the insurance consumer needs a competent agent who performs the wide variety of services essential to proper insurance protection. These include helping the policyholder in understanding needs, analyzing significant risks, finding markets, comparing alternative coverages and contracts, arranging for credit or installment payments, checking on the accuracy of classifications and the rates charged, providing loss-prevention or engineering services, making valuation appraisals, seeing that claims payments are made promptly, frequently reviewing changing needs, and many other important duties.

2. *Willingness.* If qualified, can and will the agent also take the time to *apply* his or her knowledge with an attitude of conscientiousness that will result in the full appraisal of all your needs and alternatives? Unless this is done, you won't receive any benefit from all that knowledge and ability. The agent must be able to do a good job and be willing to take the time and make the effort to see that services (including those of agency staff and companies) are performed in the most adequate way possible.

The agent must survey the buyer's risks and insurance and should offer to recommend additional legal, accounting, or consulting services when these are needed. Loss-prevention suggestions and help with filing claims for losses are important parts of the service provided to the insurance buyer. The best-qualified agent is no good for *you* unless the time and desire are present to perform these services regularly at the time you need them.

3. *Integrity and character.* Even willing and able agents or brokers lack an important requirement if they are unable to command the confidence and trust of the insured. An insurance purchaser who cannot believe and act on recommendations given is not receiving full value from the insurance dollar spent.

Since insurance advice is purchased in order to obtain certainty, agents or brokers must be able to give their clients both psychological and actual security. In other words, consumers need someone with whom they can identify closely in discussing their financial goals and needs. The values of agent and client, if similar, can aid them in establishing a good rapport with each other. The age of the agent in relation to that of the insured may be a factor in this regard, but differences in age are probably less important than differences in ideas and life-style. Confidential information from the purchaser is often required in order to provide good insurance counseling services; thus the agent or broker must respect the buyer's trust with as complete honesty as would a doctor, a lawyer, or an accountant.

4. *Representation.* Good agents do not represent poor insurers. They must represent or have contacts with one or many insurers that can provide the required protection and services for the insured. All the necessary coverages, including even special or unusual ones, must be available through the agents in a prompt and efficient manner at a reasonable cost. The insurer or insurers they represent should be capable of writing many different kinds of insurance, with a progressive attitude toward newer coverages and forms designed to meet the particular needs of individual buyers.

Whether to select an agent or broker as the intermediary in placing insurance in a given community will depend largely upon custom and the state law. In some large cities much of the insurance business is in the hands of brokers and very little contact with applicants for insurance is made directly by agents. In most areas opposite conditions prevail and business is handled largely through agents representing the insurers.

Insurance agencies and brokerage firms vary from the individual agent to organizations having a large staff and offering a wide degree of specialization. Some are one-person agencies, others have a half-dozen agents and office personnel, while still others have as many as a hundred employees and operate much like a small insurance company. These organizations differ in the services they are able to offer, their methods of doing business, and the types and kinds of insurance they handle. In the multiple-line (property and liability) agency, life insurance today is often included to make it an all-lines agency. Frequently, the members of the agency who handle the life business limit their activities to this field. Also, in the large multiple-line agency certain persons become recognized experts in such lines as fire, liability, workers' compensation, or fidelity and surety coverages. In selecting the agent or broker with whom to deal, it is therefore important for the insurance consumer to determine whether or not the particular agent and agency office have the needed experience and service facilities.

The suggestion has been made that large business accounts be offered for competition on an annual basis. This can sometimes achieve lower costs for insurance. However, some buyers have attempted to do this, with not too satisfactory results. Agents who secure an account in open competition will do the best they can to service the account, but if they do not regard the insured as a permanent client, they may provide less service. Insureds have found the method detrimental because in a period of unfavorable losses a business firm may have no assurance of continued coverage and competing insurers will be reluctant to participate. Thus, insurance buyers may seriously limit their market. This will not be the case if an insurer may expect over a period of years to recoup losses incurred in an unfavorable year. From the standpoint of the buyer as well as the agent, a long-term relationship on a professional basis seems to work out best in the long run.

Whatever choice of agent or broker is made by the applicant for insurance, the choice should be made carefully. For the businessperson or even for the family spending a substantial portion of income on insurance, this is not a selection to be made in a haphazard manner. Thoughtful evaluation of the representation offered by the agent or broker is required, including such factors as knowledge, ability, integrity, and attitude. Choosing an agent or broker is not an easy task, but for the insured it is an essential step toward a sound insurance and risk program.

MARKETING METHODS

Agency versus direct-selling systems

Insurance is distributed from insurers to policyholders in a variety of ways. The most important is the *agency system* of representatives who operate under the authority given them by insurers to make legal transactions with consumers of insurance. The complex nature of insurance and its usual significance to the insured make such personal contact through an intermediary essential to the sale of most insurance.

Insureds seldom come in contact with insurer officers. The contact between insured and insurer is usually made through an agent. The discussion of insurer representatives in this section assumes major importance when the widespread use of agency systems in marketing insurance is realized.

Direct-selling systems are the exception to the general rule that insurance is sold mainly through agents. Under these systems the insurer deals directly with the insured, without agents, through employees of the insurer. In specialized and limited lines in certain market segments of insurance, these systems may assume some importance. Airport vending machines for selling aviation accidental death protection are one example. Another common example is health insurers who operate by using direct-mail advertising. All correspondence is direct from the company to the prospect, and the insurance contract is written and serviced by mail or telephone without an agent. For another example, the Factory Mutuals deal directly with insureds in writing fire insurance for large businesses. A few automobile insurers have applied the direct-mail system successfully in writing automobile insurance, and some life insurance sales are also accomplished in this way. Direct-mail solicitation has been successful in recent years for books, records, clothing, and other products, and undoubtedly it will grow in insurance for qualified, carefully selected markets. Sales through credit cards are growing, too.

In life and health insurance the growth of *group insurance* (see Chapters 12 and 14) with sales through salaried employees in place of commissioned agents is evidence of a trend that might be called a compromise between direct and agency systems of marketing. The idea of selling through employers has also begun to be applied in the property-liability field, especially for automobile and homeowners insurance (see the last section of this chapter).

Life insurance agency systems

A distinction should be observed between the usual agency method of marketing life insurance as opposed to property insurance. In marketing life insurance, the insurers normally use agents who *represent only one insurer*. The agent sells life insurance for one company and therefore is closely related to the needs, rules, and policy forms of that insurer. A *general agent* often provides field supervision of the sales in a given territory for the insurer and is in a position similar to that of a wholesaler of manufactured products who distributes goods for one major producer. The general agent works under the authority of the insurer, and hires, trains, and directs the activities of the life agents working for a given general agency office. The general agent is paid a commission for the business written, but the actual acceptance of the life insurance contracts is performed at the home office of the life insurer. Many insurers have a *branch manager* instead of a general agent. The branch manager usually operates more as an employee of the insurer than as an individual entrepreneur and is likely to be paid largely by salary. The distinctions are not always maintained.

Life and health insurance is sometimes highly specialized, and many representatives of life and health insurers devote themselves exclusively to these lines. Within the field are specialists who devote themselves to a particular line, such as business life insurance, group insurance, or pension plans.

A development of the last decade has some life insurance agents selling mutual funds or other investments as well as life insurance contracts. This may be regarded as an important change in life insurance agency systems, as different licensing, training, compensation, and organization may evolve from these broadening financial counseling services in the future.

Property insurance agency systems

In property insurance two major agency systems of marketing are used to distribute the fire, automobile, and other casualty insurance contracts: (1) *the independent agency system* and (2) the *exclusive agency system*.[9] The

---

[9] The primary terms used to describe insurance marketing systems have caused much confusion in recent years. The Committee on Property and Liability Insurance Terminology of the American Risk and Insurance Association agreed upon the basic terms used above: (1) direct-selling, (2) independent agency, and (3) exclusive agency systems. See also David L. Bickelhaupt, "Trends and Innovations in the Marketing of Insurance," *Journal of Marketing*, vol. 31, no. 3 (July 1967), pp. 17–22.

distribution system for property insurance is different from that for life insurance for many reasons. Among them might be the historical fact that in the property business the ten largest companies have written a smaller share of the business; the need of property-liability agents to have several insurers in order to write large risks or varied types of insurance; and the short duration of the property-liability contract, which permits or requires property agents to change their clients' insurance from one insurer to another as needs and markets fluctuate.

The independent agency system. Traditionally the predominant method has been an agency system in which the agent *represents several* or *many insurers*. This is known as the *independent agency system*. The agent is independent in the sense that business is placed with any one of a number of insurers (perhaps as few as 3 or as many as 30) that the agent represents. The agent is not an employee of the insurers, and sells on a commission or fee basis as an independent contractor. The insurers recognize the agent's ownership, use, and control of policy and expiration records. The agent often has the authority to bind the insurer immediately for many of the kinds of insurance written for his or her policyholders. A branch office or general agency of each insurer may supervise the activities of the agent for a regional territory.

The exclusive agency system. The *exclusive agency system* of marketing property insurance has risen in recent decades with the growth of automobile insurance and simplified insurance coverages (nonbusiness) for the individual. Here the agent normally represents only *one company,* as in the case of the typical life insurance agent. The agent's contract limits representation to one insurer or to a few which are under common management. It reserves to the insurer the ownership, use, and control of policy and expiration data. The agent may have binding authority. The larger exclusive agency insurers, such as State Farm Mutual, Allstate, Liberty Mutual, and Nationwide Mutual, have made tremendous increases in their sales of automobile insurance in the last decade, and more recently they have been showing substantial gains in fire, homeowners', and even life and health insurance.

Comparisons. The advantages and disadvantages of these two marketing systems in property insurance are not easily seen by the policyholder. Certainly the terms are often misleading. Less desirable than the above contrast between independent and exclusive agency systems are the two terms *American Agency System* and *direct-writing system,*[10] which have been extensively used to describe, respectively, these two competing systems of marketing. Ob-

---

[10] A term unfortunately still in wide use. For detailed summaries of the methods of operation of these insurers, see George Nordhaus and Stephen Brown, *Marketing Property and Casualty Insurance* (Santa Monica, Calif.: Insurance Marketing Services, 1976), chap. 8. Note that some insurers, such as State Farm, use modifications of both systems: only established agents become, after about four years, "independent contractors," but only for that one insurer.

viously, the direct-writing system can be just as "American" as the American Agency System, and the American Agency System just as "direct" as the direct-writing system! Even with the newer suggested terms, one should point out that independent agents are dependent to a certain extent on the insurers they represent and that exclusive agents may have some measure of independence from their insurer. Also, the exclusive agency system is not automatically better or of higher caliber, as its name may imply. In fact, its critics call it the "captive" agency system!

The marketing changes of recent years have resulted in considerable competition. Benefits to the consumer in the form of lower costs through emphasis on reducing expenses and on increasing options for broader coverages have been a favorable result of the competitive era during the past several decades. Insureds must analyze their choices in terms of both *cost and service* from the individual agent, regardless of the name of the agency system. By some cost effectiveness measures, the use of exclusive agents appears to allow higher levels of sales at lower costs, but the quality of the service received by customers must also be compared. For example, duplication of activities by independent agents is greater, but it may help in the tailoring of service to their clients.[11]

The main advantage of the exclusive agents is lower cost, through reduced commissions or decreased expenses due to centralization of some functions, such as policy writing, record keeping, billing, training, advertising, and sales. The exclusive agent also has the potential advantage of receiving more education and training from an insurer that can design such programs specifically for the agent. The insurer has closer control over the education and the activities of the agent, and receives full and direct benefit from the success of the support it gives to the agent. Representing one insurer can simplify the agent's job but may narrow the help which the agent can give a client who, for example, needs to obtain a difficult type of coverage.

Independent agents have substantial advantages in representing more than one insurer and in their ownership of expirations. Since no one insurer is best in all lines and all territories, independent agents serve as experts in choosing the best companies to write insurance that will meet the individual needs of their clients. They thus have a wider choice and variety of coverages, prices, and services for their policyholders. Properly used, their position of "independence" can enable them to bring good benefits to clients by placing insurance with strong and reliable insurers at reasonable prices. This feature of being able to select from a wide variety of companies is emphasized in advertising by the agents who belong to Independent Insurance Agents of America (IIAA).

Trends. It is fair to predict that no one agency system will be destroyed

---

[11] Michael Etgar, "Cost Effectiveness in Insurance Distribution," *Journal of Risk and Insurance,* vol. 42, no. 2 (June 1977), p. 211.

by the other in the current era of changing distribution patterns of insurance. Each system has some merit, and each will retain and increase its share of the market to the extent that it meets the real services needed by the insurance consumer.[12] In striving to do this, both systems are increasing educational efforts for their agents, encouraging them to participate regularly in national and company professional programs of all kinds. Perhaps performance in this area will be the key to long-run changes.

The exclusive agency system has grown very rapidly in the automobile and homeowners' insurance market during the past two decades. The new property-liability affiliates of major life insurers (Prudential, Metropolitan, and Equitable, for example) have also used the exclusive, one-company representation, agency system successfully in the 1970s. The exclusive agency system has yet to show that it can adapt to the fields for business coverages, where the independent agency system still predominates.[13]

It seems that the two major agency systems, independent and exclusive, are becoming more similar each year. During the early 1970s several of the largest independent agency systems began to issue exclusive agency contracts for their regular agents. These include: Insurance Company of North America, for all lines; and the Chubb Insurance Group and Royal-Globe Group, for personal (nonbusiness) lines. Other independent agency companies have one-company agreements, but only for special classes of agents, such as those just beginning in the business. The agent agrees in these contracts to place virtually all insurance with the one company. Many independent agency companies have also adopted techniques of premium payments similar to those of exclusive agency companies. The "direct-billing" system of having bills sent to the policyholder directly from the insurer, instead of from the agent, has gained in popularity consistently for the past 20 years. Cost savings, especially with the use of computers, have hastened this trend. Under this method, the agent is relieved of the time-consuming and expensive task of extending credit to the consumer and then collecting the premiums.

Conversely, the exclusive agency insurers have adopted some of the successful methods of their competitors. For example, some of these companies have granted their larger and more successful agents certain rights that are similar to the ownership rights which independent agents have to renewals and records. Under these agreements, established exclusive agents are paid by the insurer for their book of business if they leave or retire from their exclusive agency company. The benefits might be larger if they sold the business of

---

[12] These services are evaluated in J. David Cummins and Stephen N. Weisbart, *The Impact of Consumer Services on Independent Insurance Agency Performance* (Glenmont, N.Y.: I.M.A. Educational and Research Foundation, 1977).

[13] The large independent agencies are particularly strong in business coverages, although one study does not show that larger size, by growth or merger, is necessarily the road to cost economies. See J. David Cummins, "Economies of Scale in Independent Insurance Agencies," *Journal of Risk and Insurance*, vol. 44, no. 4 (December 1977), p. 539.

their policyholders on the open market, but the sums or renewal commissions to which the agents are entitled under these contract provisions with the insurer may be substantial. Also, more of the exclusive agency insurers are gradually permitting their agents to "broker" business with other insurers. This is particularly important in insurance for businesses, where large exposures sometimes require insurance with several insurers in order to place the total protection correctly.

Group insurance systems

One example of how the changes in insurance marketing have accelerated is *group* insurance. Marketing to consumers in this system is usually done on a group basis through the employer, with payroll deductions as the convenient method of premium payment. Labor unions, credit unions, finance companies, professional associations, and other groups may also be used to obtain the primary desired result, which is the lowering of insurance costs to the members of the groups.

Group life-health insurance.   In *life* insurance the trend toward increased group insurance has been continuous since such plans began more than 50 years ago. Today almost one fourth of all life insurance premiums, and nearly one half of the total life insurance in force, is group insurance. *Health* insurance, with the major growth occurring during the past 20 years, has used the group method of marketing even more extensively. More than three fourths of all health insurance premiums written by U.S. life insurance companies is group insurance, and for the other primary health insurer (Blue Cross–Blue Shield) the proportion is higher. *Annuities* or insured pensions, too, have used the system widely, with three fourths of the total premium income coming from group plans. The group insurance trend is shown in further detail in Chapter 12, where group annuities are discussed, and in Chapter 14, where group life and health insurance are treated.

Maxi-style business trends.   The group phenomenon can be looked at as a part of the increased affinity for "big business," a move toward "maxi-style"[14] systems of marketing. Perhaps it is a reaction to the gargantuan billion-dollar business enterprises that there is also this increased tendency toward "big purchasers." Contracts of purchase of a whole new specialized type are appearing in many fields of business: automobile manufacturers sell in thousand-car lots to governmental agencies and international automobile leasing companies; institutional buyers of securities negotiate with special brokerage firms for millions of shares of stocks; discount department stores buy entire product lines of some producers; and realtors sell whole com-

---

[14] Portions of the following section are adapted from David L. Bickelhaupt, "Insurance Marketing: Maxi-Style for the 1970s," *Bulletin of Business Research* (Ohio State University), vol. 46, no. 3 (March 1971), p. 1.

munities of housing developments. The power of the group buyer is matched to that of the group seller.

Group property-liability insurance. What does mass buying and selling have to do with *property-liability* insurance? *Mass merchandising* is quite apparent in property-liability insurance today, as well as in the life-health fields. It is important to know *why* this trend has occurred. Most explanations center on the prospective efficiency of group coverage. However, the consumers emphasis on lower prices also helps explain why insurance mass merchandising exists.

Mass merchandising plans in property-liability insurance *are* different from group life-health insurance in some respects, particularly in that most such plans have individual selection, rating, and contracts instead of group underwriting. However, employer participation is involved in the arrangements for the plans, premiums are collected through payroll deduction, and the causes and objectives of the plans are similar to those of group life-health insurance. Although not technically group insurance, mass merchandising is a part of the trend. The terminology is neither well developed nor consistent. The term *mass merchandising* boils down to selling and servicing personal lines of insurance to large groups, usually with a common employer, through a payroll deduction plan. Other terms closely allied to mass merchandising are *mass marketing* (a broader term, denoting sales to much larger groups without any common ties such as employment), *group insurance* (a legal term, usually requiring group underwriting techniques and special legislation), *franchise merchandising* (payroll deduction), and *collective merchandising* (including some of all the preceding attributes).[15]

Mass merchandising plans for groups of several hundred or many thousands of persons naturally vary considerably in detail. Automobile insurance has been the primary coverage, but many also offer homeowners', personal excess liability, and, recently, even life and health insurance. Several plans incorporating the characteristics of group insurance (group selection and rating, guaranteed coverage, and employer payment of at least part of the premium) have appeared. A listing of the major efforts by insurers thus far encompasses many of the larger property-liability insurance company groups. Group plans aimed at trade associations instead of employers may be emphasized by these insurers in the decade ahead.

Future mass merchandising plans will grow in the personal lines. Almost all households have need for auto and home property and liability insurance. An insurance teacher[16] has pointed out that this is primarily because of the agency system, which has built the path to mass merchandising by convincing the public that insurance is a social necessity!

How far, how fast is the crucial question. Probably less than 10 percent of

---

[15] Bernard Webb, *Mass Merchandising of Automobile Insurance* (Santa Monica, Calif.: Insurors' Press, 1969).

[16] Robert Mehr, University of Illinois.

property-liability insurance premiums is collected today under mass merchandising plans. Some persons predict that more than 30 percent will be sold in these systems in the 1980s. The speed with which the plans grow will depend on many other developments, such as:

1. *Liability system changes.* The combination of no-fault auto insurance and mass merchandising trends might result in group auto compensation. Both systems emphasize cost savings as their most salable point.

2. *Union attitudes.* The United Auto Workers unions and other consider this an important new "fringe benefit" and a major area of negotiation.

3. *Costs—inflation trend.* This pushes insurance costs up (faster than rate changes) and causes clamor for change.

4. *Regulation changes.* With existing laws, public interest, and other factors, the prevailing attitude seems to be one of a "holding action" only. Many states permit such plans, while many others do not. It is increasingly apparent, however, that legislation is more and more geared to the consumer, and the trend is toward state laws that approve these plans. Another factor is possible tax law changes: Could these new plans become a tax-deductible, nonincome employee fringe benefit?

5. *Employer attitude.* Probably the most significant factor is what the *employer* decides about all this. That is the key. What reaction will the employer get from the employee, if take-out pay exceeds take-home pay? Will the employer be blamed for poor claims adjustment or rate increases or cancellations? Worse yet, will the employer have any legal liability if errors are made or coverage is not adequate? The payroll deduction plan sounds good, but what about the cost? How far should the employer go? Should banking, credit, gasoline purchases, and even auto purchases also be provided on a payroll deduction group plan? How does the employer make the vital choice as to who should do the employee counseling—agent or insurer (company) employee? This is the factor most discussed by agents with the implication that the employee may lose substantial benefits of individual personal service in the mass merchandising plans and that the agents may lose their ownership of expiration records.[17]

The estimates of savings are one of the problems of any such new type of distribution system. Some insurers have said that the costs will be lowered as much as 15 percent; others say that the costs will be lowered only 5 percent. Administrative savings may not be as much as expected, and perhaps will only be passed on to the employer in various hidden costs, such as the payroll deduction costs or the labor costs of having employees discuss insurance on "company time," either in formal counseling appointments or in informal discussions with other workers.

Coverage may be less than under individual plans, but will the employee recognize this and purchase an additional policy, or will the tendency be to

[17] John F. Neville, "Mass Merchandising and Ownership of Expirations," *Independent Agent,* September 1973, p. 17.

accept the group coverage? Discrimination is also raised as a potential problem, especially from a regulatory viewpoint. It seems difficult to try to appraise this aspect of the problem without knowing the details of a specific plan. Who is a plan being unfair to—the worker who doesn't own a car, or the better driver, perhaps? Is it a mandatory plan or a voluntary plan that the worker can accept or reject? How is the rate calculated?

There will be some benefits.[18] If mass merchandising is efficient for the insurer as a means for achieving volume and profit, then it may be for the agents, too (at least some of them). Safety and loss prevention are important potential benefits. About 2 percent of costs in most plans are allocated for such things as driver clinics and safety contests. Most deaths under age 40 are from automobile accidents, and savings in rehiring and retraining could be large.

Perhaps some of the goals of mass merchandising, if achieved in an orderly, meaningful way from the insurance consumer's standpoint, will help solve some other insurer problems, such as auto insurance costs and increasing government intervention. Pertinent is the observation that the United States is the only country in the world with group insurance as a major part of the private insurance business (about one fourth of life, three fourths or more of annuities and health insurance). Yet the United States is also the country with the largest private insurance business and the least social insurance encroachment into the private sector. Group insurance systems may have helped in preserving the private insurance business from the expansion of social insurance systems.

FOR REVIEW AND DISCUSSION

1. John says: "Insurance marketing means insurance *agents*." Marcia says: "Partially, yes, but the insurance marketing *process* means much more." Explain these statements.

2. "Insurance marketing is really quite different from the marketing of other products." Explain (*a*) whether or not you agree with this and (*b*) what difference it makes to the insurer.

3. Match the characteristic in column 2 with the type of insurer in column 1. Use each number only *once*, for the *most closely* related item.

Column 1	Column 2
a. Reciprocals	1. Emphasize loss prevention
b. Lloyds associations	2. Are often assessable
c. Stock companies	3. Mostly write life insurance
d. Mutual companies	4. Insure lumber, drug, etc., exposures
e. Health association	5. Interinsurance exchanges

---

[18] John R. Lewis reviews eight of these in "Observations on Mass Merchandising of Property and Liability Insurance," *CPCU Annals*, vol. 24, no. 2 (June 1971), p. 174, as he critiques Spencer Kimball and Herbert S. Denenberg, *Mass Marketing of Property Insurance* (Washington, D.C.: U.S. Government Printing Office, June 1970), p. 6.

f. Savings bank insurers
g. Fraternals
h. Farm mutuals
i. Factory mutuals
j. Class mutuals

6. Have capital and surplus
7. Individual insurers
8. Blue Cross–Blue Shield
9. Life insurance, in 3 states
10. Policyholder dividends

4. What are the basic characteristics of advance-premium, assessment, and special-purpose mutuals? Why is each type important in the insurance market?

5. Discuss points of similarity and differences among London Lloyd's and (a) the American Lloyds (b) mutual insurers, and (c) reciprocals.

6. Insurers may be differentiated on the basis of their ownership and their stated objectives. How do stock companies, mutuals, Factory Mutuals, fraternals, and health associations differ as to ownership and objectives?

7. How do stock companies, advance-premium mutuals, assessment mutuals, reciprocals, and Lloyds differ in their use of surpluses and their sources for deficits?

8. By what type of insurer is the major volume of each type of insurance business written? Can you explain some of the differences noted?

9. Divide the class into two groups, one defending and the other criticizing the proposition that "direct-selling systems in insurance are likely to increase."

10. Why do the agency systems in life and property insurance differ? Does the power of the typical agent in these fields differ, too?

11. Who owns the agent's records, and therefore the expirations, under the "independent agent system"? May a company withdrawing from an agency turn these records over to a competing agent? Would your answer be different for an "exclusive agent"?

12. Distinguish between an agent and a broker. May the same individual be both? What is an "excess line broker"?

13. Mr. I. M. Goodfellow operates a retail store and feels that for business purposes he should divide his insurance business so that as many customers as possible will participate. Can you see any dangers in this practice? What is the solution you recommend?

14. What does the "professional concept" of insurance marketing include? Does this explanation offer any reasons as to why agency systems are more important than direct-selling systems in marketing insurance?

15. Explain three criteria which a businesshead should follow in choosing an insurer and three other factors of importance in selecting an insurance agent or broker. Would you answer this question differently if the insured were an individual or a family rather than a business?

16. Which is more important to the ordinary insured, the choice of an insurer or the choice of an insurance agent? Why?

17. Explain what "mass merchandising" is, and two potential benefits and two problems for the (a) insurer, (b) insured, and (c) agent.

18. Who is the key to the future expansion of "mass merchandising" group insurance plans? Explain why you think so.

Chapter 6

Concepts considered in Chapter 6—Insurance underwriting, rating, reinsurance, and other functions

Underwriting, which is closely **related to other insurance functions,** includes the *selection* and *pricing* of insurance contracts.

Its purpose is to obtain a reasonable and *profitable* group of risks in spite of the tendency toward *adverse selection.*

Selection of risks is ultimately done by the *insurer,* but the *agent* and other sources of *underwriting information* are crucial in many lines.

Rating, or *pricing,* of insurance contracts is the field of *actuarial science.*

Fire insurance rates are used as a basic example, to show how insurance prices are determined.

Rating bureaus help insurers analyze the various *factors* affecting loss and set *class* rates for groups of like properties and *specific,* or *schedule,* rates for *larger* individual business properties.

The insured can lower insurance costs by decreasing the poor features and increasing the good features of the property insured.

Automobile insurance has rating factors different from those for fire insurance, and uses both class rates and individual rate modifications.

Special problems of underwriting are noted:

Deductibles, for reducing costs and loss payment problems.

Minimum premiums, to recoup expenses, prevent adverse selection.

Annual and term policies, to create fair prices for longer contracts.

Installment plans, to permit convenient regular payments.

Reinsurance is the transfer of insurance from one insurer to another.

Its purposes are to spread risks, especially large ones, and to permit growth of insurers.

Reinsurance organizations are of several types: *professional reinsurers* writing only reinsurance, *reinsurance departments* of insurers, and *reinsurance pools.*

Reinsurance agreements include *treaty,* or automatic, and *facultative,* or specific, types.

Reinsurance contracts are of the *share-of-risk* and the *excess-of-loss* types, which distribute the insurance or losses between insurer and reinsurer.

Retrocessions occur when reinsurers insure with other reinsurers.

International aspects are important in reinsurance competition.

Other functions of insurers are often overlooked but vital to success.

Investment departments are more common among life insurers, but of increasing significance for property-liability insurers.

Other departments include "auxiliary" services such as legal, educational, actuarial, research, public relations, and administrative.

Insurance underwriting, rating, reinsurance, and other functions

One of the most interesting features of insurance as a "business affected with a public interest," and as a business which provides a wide variety of coverages to almost everyone, is that the insurer is not usually required to write an insurance contract for each person who applies for one. Should an insurer as a service-oriented business firm be obligated to accept all applications for insurance? At first glance, there appears to be something wrong with a business that can refuse to do business with persons most likely to have losses (who perhaps need the product most), while continually striving to accept as clients those persons who are least likely to have losses. A few second thoughts are pertinent: in addition to the "public needs," doesn't the insurer also have a primary obligation to all its insureds and its owners to do business so that it remains financially solvent and obtains reasonable profits?

The dilemma is real, accentuated today by the growing importance of many social problems and by the recognition of insurance as a frequent and useful solution to the financial consequences of these problems.

The challenging nature of the underwriting, rating, and reinsurance topics emphasized in this chapter is illustrated by the following growing and gigantic problems of the insurance business:

1. *Riots and civil disorders.* Can the private insurance business continue to pay for the hundreds of millions of dollars of damage suffered in more than 100 U.S. cities in the past dozen years? Can the urban "blighted" areas continue to buy the fire, crime, and liability coverages needed in these high-risk locations? Will the energy shortages of the 1970s cause more potential losses of these types during "blackouts" in the future?

2. *Air transportation and space exploration.* Can the tremendous new exposures to loss be met by the private insurance business? With more than a $50 million cost for a single SST airplane, and multibillion-dollar spaceflights planned for the 1980s, what are the limits of capacity for private insurers? Is there a need for government insurance plans to supplement the private sector?

3. *Automobiles.* Can the private insurance business continue to provide protection for the "automobile economy" of today and at the same time aid in solving the pressing problems of increasing death and injury tolls on the highways, court congestion with liability lawsuits, rising jury awards, and some unpaid automobile accident victims?

4. *Products and professional liability.*   Will mounting losses from million-dollar lawsuits for medical malpractice and alleged faulty products drive insurers from these fields or endanger their total capacity to insure?

UNDERWRITING RELATED TO OTHER INSURANCE FUNCTIONS

Part II of this text has approached the study of insurance on a functional basis. The major activities of insurance organizations have been analyzed separately in previous chapters on the insurance product (contract fundamentals) and the marketing of insurance. The next major part of the process of insurance is *underwriting,* the selection and rating of the risks that are insured. Several other functions, including reinsurance, are also included in this chapter examining insurance from the viewpoint of the insurer.

The functions of an insurer are necessarily closely related to one another. No one activity exists alone, and each activity has many direct effects on the others. The student is advised to look again at Figure 4–1 to see these relationships. For example, the types of contracts offered by an insurer may determine how the contracts are distributed through an agency system to the policyholders. Agents are often important in helping to redesign insurance contracts to meet specific needs of the insurance market.

The interrelationship of the major insurance activities is nowhere more apparent than in the underwriting process. An insurer that has organized a good system of distributing a wide range of insurance contracts and has set up logical procedures for loss adjustments still cannot operate successfully without proper attention to the selection and pricing of its product. The *underwriters*[1] of a company are those who have the task of accepting, rejecting, or revising insurance contracts which the marketing system brings to the insurer. Whether or not the underwriting function is properly carried out, of course, has an important effect on the frequency and size of insurance losses. Unless contracts are properly *rated* or priced, the acceptance of risks can cause the financial insolvency of insurers and inequity among insureds.

Discussion of some of the specific methods and problems of insurance underwriting will be deferred until later, when a greater familiarity with the various insurance contracts has been achieved. In this chapter the student should strive for a basic knowledge of the general functions of selecting and rating risks in insurance. The process of *reinsurance,* or the purchase of in-

---

[1] The term is often used in a variety of other ways. In everyday insurance language it is frequently used to refer to the agent or salesperson. Even the professional designations CLU (Chartered Life Underwriter) and CPCU (Chartered Property Casualty Underwriter) use the word *underwriter* in a broad sense to mean one who writes or does business in insurance. Sometimes the underwriters are the actual insurers, as when one refers to the underwriters at Lloyd's of London. The term originated there, with the practice of underwriters signing their acceptance of part of the risk under the broker's description of the desired insurance.

surance by insurers, is so closely connected with underwriting that it is also discussed in this chapter.

Purposes

A general description of *underwriting* is simple: it is the selection and rating of risks which are offered to an insurer. The process is based on *selection,* so this part of the definition of underwriting is discussed first. *Rating* is so significant a part of the total process as to be explained in a separate section of this chapter.

Selection implies that there are some acceptances and some rejections, or that not all risks will be accepted for insurance. An understanding of why some risks must be selected by an insurer and some rejected will make clear that insurance underwriting is one of the major functions of an insurer. It is also an activity that is not found in most other businesses. A somewhat comparable activity exists in banks and savings and loan institutions, where the credit selection process assumes a similar major role.

Suppose an insurer were willing to write an insurance contract for every individual who asked for protection against loss. Or suppose it automatically accepted every person or business that the marketing force of the insurer had sold on completing an application for insurance. Would it be sound business practice for an insurer to operate in this manner? The student may answer: "Of course. The company needs large numbers of risks and a diversification or spread among various kinds of risks, geographic locations, and so on. Why shouldn't an insurer accept all the separate risks it can get?" After further consideration the student might add: "Naturally, the insurer won't want the bad risks, or those which seem to offer a high probability of loss, for it will lose money in writing such poor risks."

A more complete answer might then suggest itself. The insurer does not want bad risks, it is true; but even bad risks could be accepted if the price charged for the contract were high enough to pay for all losses and expenses and still permit the insurer a profit on the business. Here is the crux of the problem—the insurer must accept only policyholders who will in total be *profitable* risks. The purpose of underwriting is thus found to be the acquisition by the insurer of selected insureds who at least in the long run will return a profit to stockholders (or policyholders of a mutual-type insurer).

This point has been emphasized: "an insurer accepts risks precisely because it can find a set of terms on which the business can be written profitably. . . . these terms are of four general types: the premium rate, the policy provisions, the hazard presented in the risk, and the reinsurance arrangement."[2]

---

[2] George L. Head, "Underwriting—In Five Easy Lessons?" *Journal of Risk and Insurance,* vol. 35, no. 2 (June 1968), p. 308. The author advocates study of underwriting as a decision-making process, from profit objective to decision variables, processes, and constraints.

An important corollary to understanding the underwriting function is the fact that most insurance prices are based upon an *average* rate for an entire class or group. Some insureds within each class will be better than average and some worse than average. Which type of policyholders will an insurer that does no selection of risks tend to have? A moment's thought will indicate the extent of the problem: those persons who are better than average are most likely not to want or need the insurance, and conversely, those persons who know they are worse than average will be most likely to desire the insurance contract. This result is natural, for in everyday language the bad risks at the average rate are obtaining a bargain.

An example of how class rates are useful in achieving equity among similar exposures within each class is shown in Figure 6–1. All exposures with an indicated loss rate of between $1.00 and $2.20 are combined in one class (A) for an average rate of $1.60 per $100 of insurance. However, if the individual insureds are separable on the basis of underwriting information (potential loss characteristics, or past losses), it is fairer to establish two classes (B and C) with rates of $1.30 and $1.90, respectively. If the classes are large enough to retain predictability, a third choice is to establish four classes of averge rates (D, E, F, and G), with respective rates of $1.15, $1.45, $1.75, and $2.05. More equity is thus achieved, for the differences between exposures at the low end and the high end of each class are reduced. Within each class, no matter how large it is, remains the problem of the poorer risks being most likely to apply for insurance, but inequity in the rates is lessened as the classifications are refined by having more classes.

The tendency for insurance contract applications to include a preponderance of "poorer than average for the class" risks is found throughout the field of insurance. Whenever the applications result from free choice on the part of the individuals who wish to transfer their risks to an insurer, the

Figure 6–1. An illustration of class or average rates

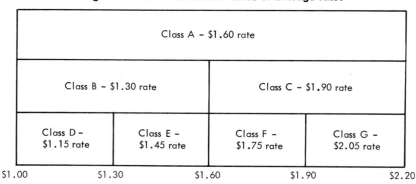

choice will be *against the insurer*. The worst risks will be most apt to apply for insurance, and the better risks most likely not to apply. This tendency is called *adverse selection,* and every insurer must be aware of its existence and results. The results of adverse selection can be financial disaster, as the insurer ends up with poor risks but obtains only an average price for the protection it provides. The result will be the opposite of the stated purpose of insurance underwriting—a large, safely diversified, profitable group of risks.

Two illustrations of adverse selection show why an insurer usually cannot just accept all insurance applications. In life insurance, the most likely persons to apply if no medical examinations or statements were required before the writing of the contract would be persons in poor health. In theft insurance, the typical application would tend to come from applicants who have had many thefts or from situations in which valuable properties lack proper burglary or robbery protection.

The major need for insurance underwriting thus stems from the tendency toward adverse selection which without underwriting would be ruinous to insurers. Even with selection by the insurer of the risks it will accept, some adverse selection always exists whenever a class or group rate is used. Profitable risks can only be achieved by careful selection of risks which reasonably offsets the adverse selection factors involved in insurance applications. The insurer also needs to know as much as possible about the policyholders it accepts, for only then can fair classifications and sufficient prices be determined.[3]

The process of underwriting is the means by which the insurer evaluates the potential risks it has been asked to accept. A compromise is often necessary between two objectives: (1) to obtain a *large number* of individual risks within each classification, so that reasonable predictability of losses is possible, and (2) to obtain *homogeneity* of risks within each classification, so that reasonable equity between the better and poorer individual risks is achieved. The care with which an insurer combines these objectives is vital to its underwriting success and thus the success of the whole operations of the insurer.

Consequently, underwriters may be looked upon as the backbone of the insurance business. Their job is essential. They must say no many times, but their function is also oftentimes to say yes by helping the consumer become insurable.[4] Proper rate classes and prices, with good loss-prevention practices, can help make insurance available to all persons who need it.

---

[3] Underwriting techniques vary by type of insurance. The Associate in Underwriting Program is providing new publications for study by underwriters, such as G. William Glendenning and Robert B. Holtom, *Personal Lines Underwriting,* and others in this series published by the Insurance Institute of America (Malvern, Pa.).

[4] The social and consumer responsibilities of the underwriting function are well emphasized in J. J. Launie, J. Finley Lee, and Norman A. Baglini, *Principles of Property and Liability Underwriting,* 2d ed. (Malvern, Pa.: Insurance Institute of America, 1977).

Selection of risks

The selection of risks and the pricing of the contracts which are to be issued are closely related. If an adequate price for a class of risks has been established, the insurer must underwrite to secure at least an average group of policyholders. Otherwise, losses paid will exceed the premium income for paying losses. If the pricing for an insurance contract is inadequate, then even normal underwriting methods will fail to produce a profitable group of insureds. The alternative in such a case is to increase prices or to practice severe risk selection, only accepting the best risks of each class. Despite the necessary interrelationship between pricing and selection in the underwriting process, pricing is separately treated here as a major part requiring a number of examples.

The agent and insurer as underwriters.   For most insurers the choice of policyholders begins with the underwriting done by the agent. Except for the relatively few applications which are initiated by the insured, there is substantial selection of risks by the agent in most lines of insurance. Each time an agent prepares a prospect list or, for example, telephones Mr. White instead of Mr. Green to sell insurance, the first step in underwriting is performed. If an insurer appoints high caliber and well-qualified agents, they will often try to choose their clients from good homes, reasonably high-income groups, good neighborhoods, less dangerous occupational groups, and so on.

Even though the agent does some underwriting for the insurer, much of the underwriting is performed by salaried employees in the home offices and branch offices. That is why underwriting must ultimately be considered an insurer function. This is true for a combination of reasons. Agents, though they should have their companies' interests in mind as they sell insurance, cannot perform all the needed underwriting services. Their position is not completely unbiased, either, for they are paid on a commission basis, regardless of the quality of the contracts they sell. Sometimes they may not be qualified to make the selection, as in life insurance, where medical examinations are usually essential. Again, the agent may not have all the necessary information to make proper underwriting choices, as in automobile insurance, where only preliminary underwriting information is secured by the agent. The insurer is in a much better position to check with the state motor vehicle department for the applicant's past accident record and with credit investigation companies for financial and moral faults. Agents' lack of data and their technical inability in specialized fields such as medicine or engineering place the prime responsibility for underwriting with the insurer. This is logical, for it is the insurer that is accepting the risks and the insurer that is obligated to pay the losses in the insurance contracts.

The general technique of the insurer is to provide underwriting rules to be carried out by its agents and company personnel in the underwriting departments. Agents receive instructions on what risks not to write as well as encouragement in the form of directives and sales contests which specify what types of contracts and what kinds of policyholders are particularly desired. In fire and liability insurance, *underwriting guides* are common. One insurer may specify bars and bowling alleys, for example, as generally unacceptable. Another insurer may prohibit insurance on lumberyards, seasonal hotels, and plastics factories.

Other types of applicants are often specified as insurable only after the insurer has detailed information and an opportunity to have a company representative investigate or inspect the applicant's property. Examples of such a referral situation, where the agent may not have authority to bind the coverage immediately, are steam boiler explosion risks and comprehensive liability risks for businesses. Automobile insurers may request referral of taxi firms, youthful or elderly drivers, long-haul truckdrivers, motorcycle risks, and others.

The *binding* authority which many agents possess for putting the contract into effect immediately is a good example of the fact that agents do perform important underwriting services for their insurers. Many property insurance contracts go into effect in this manner. The insurer receives the application and the contract which has been put into effect at the same time. It may then request cancellation under the contract terms, but this would be an unusual case after the agent has written the business. Even in somewhat doubtful cases, the insurer is more likely to continue the protection and perhaps ask for additional information prior to renewal of the contract. Underwriting by the insurer and the agent takes place not only at the time of the original application but also at each expiration and renewal of the insurance contract. Loss experience and other new information are significant in renewal underwriting.

Sources of underwriting information. Underwriting is not just the technique of saying no to all difficult or doubtful risks. Both the agent and the insurer must learn how to say "yes, but," and then in a tactful way explain how an applicant can become more acceptable by loss prevention or other methods. Good judgment and good information are needed in this process. The sources of underwriting information upon which insurers rely include: (1) the applicant, (2) the agent, (3) the insurer's own inspection or claim department, (4) insurer bureaus and associations, and (5) outside agencies.

The *applicant* for an insurance contract often makes both written and oral statements. Signed written statements are normal procedure in life and health insurance, and the applications become a part of the contract. Automobile and business risk applicants also frequently prepare written statements as a means of giving the company basic underwriting details. *Agents* for many kinds of insurance provide their companies with reports, opinions, and recommendations which are valuable aids to the insurers in selecting their policyholders. Many *insurers* maintain separate *inspection departments* to provide the underwriters with physical inspection and engineering reports on the properties of applicants. The insurer's claim department, too, may be a source of important underwriting data for renewal decisions.

Insurers also combine efforts to maintain *bureau or association* lists of undesirable insurance applicants. The Medical Information Bureau (MIB) for life insurance and the Index Bureau of the American Insurance Association for automobile and other insurance offer a centralized index service of applicants who have been refused insurance, had frequent losses, or had suspicious or fraudulent claims. Used by most of the major insurers, their files are an effective means of spotting claims repeaters and fraud attempts. Other bureaus representing many insurers are maintained for regular inspection and rating services such as are discussed in regard to fire insurance in the next section of this chapter.

Many kinds of insurance use *outside agencies* to supplement the information gathered from the applicants, agents, and insurer representatives. Physicians supply life insurance companies with medical reports after physical examination of the applicants. Standard financial reference services such as Dun & Bradstreet are used for many insurance applications from business. Life insurers have used credit investigations by outside firms for many years. Recently, automobile insurers have increasingly used such investigations as routine checks on new applications, especially for younger drivers. These are not just financial investigations for credit purposes but are also valuable in determining poor habits or moral problems of the prospect from such sources as employers, neighbors, or associates. The judgment of *moral hazard* is crucial, yet difficult, for many kinds of insurance. The mental attitudes which cause increased losses were discussed in Chapter 1. The aim of these investigations is not only to obtain negative information but to obtain positive character reports that will permit insurance to be written. The importance of independent investigative companies to insurers is apparent from the size of the largest firm, Equifax, Inc., which employs about 10,000 persons. Hooper-Holmes and other firms are also important in the field of providing underwriting information to insurers. They now have the increased challenge of performing their important tasks in compliance with the Fair Credit Reporting Act of 1970 and the Privacy Act of 1974.

RATING (OR PRICING)

General

The pricing of insurance contracts is a specialized part of underwriting which requires the services of experts. Basically, insurance rates are calculated by *actuaries* who apply sound principles of mathematics to the particular pricing problems of insurance. The manuals, rate charts, and formulas which actuaries develop for insurers and company bureaus are used by agents as they quote the contract price of insurance to policyholders. Underwriters, too, perform substantial parts of the rate-making process, including classification of risks and applying rates.

The fundamental basis for most insurance rates is the estimate of future losses. The task of making this estimate is complicated in some kinds of insurance, by the lack of data in regard to past loss experience. In life insurance, the job of setting correct prices is aided by a wealth of past experience but hampered by the need to make predictions that extend many years into the future. The scope of life insurance mortality data is amazing, and the techniques of analyzing and graduating the recorded data are part of the field of study known as *actuarial science*. The methods and calculations are sufficient to merit separate study of these procedures in later chapters of this text.

Fire insurance as an example

As an example of property insurance rating methods, the field of fire insurance offers a valuable insight into the many different factors that must be considered in setting the price to be charged for insurance. The problems involved are numerous, and it is through the cooperation of insurers in rating bureaus that many of the solutions are reached.

Rating bureaus.   The work of fire insurance rating is placed in the hands of specialized rating bureaus. There are about 40 such organizations handling the problems of fire rating in this country. Some operate only within one state, while others combine several states within their territorial jurisdiction.

Fire insurance rates are usually regulated by the state, although some states do not regulate them. Most states make provision for (1) rating organizations (2) advisory organizations, and (3) individual insurers to file rates. Insurers are obliged to file with state authorities all rates, plans, and rules that they propose to use, except inland marine risks, which by general custom of the business are not written according to manual rates or rating plans. An insurer may satisfy its obligation to make such filings by becoming a member of or a subscriber to a licensed rating organization which makes such filings on its behalf. The license issued authorizes the *rating organization* to promulgate rates, examine policies, and make reasonable rules for such procedures as the correction of any error or omission found by the rating organization. In contrast to a rating organization, the bill defines an *advisory organization* as an organization which assists insurers by collecting and furnishing loss or expense statistics or by submitting recommendations, but which does not make rate filings. In effect, these rating and advisory organizations are monopolies, permitted under state statutes in order to allow cooperation and limited price fixing for fire insurance, subject to regulation of their activities by the states. Reasonable uniformity and competition are achieved by permitting individual insurers to file separate rates.

It is the function of the rating bureau to apply the rating schedule in use in the territory to each property that is the subject of insurance. The task requires a huge staff of inspectors, engineers, and scores of experts highly trained in specialized fields. Rate manuals and prices are published, and corrections are furnished from time to time to insurers and their representatives. Application for a new rate or for rerating a building already rated may be filed with the rating organization either by the owner of the property, an insurance agency, or an insurer.

Rate analysis. Insureds who handle their affairs in a businesslike manner will not be content to be told that the rate on their buildings is 2 percent of value per year when they know that across the street a property owner pays one half of 1 percent. First, they will want the discrepancies justified, and second, they will want to know to what extent a downward revision of their own rates is within their control. All of this information is obtainable through an analysis of the makeup of the rate.

The effort to eliminate as far as possible the element of judgment in evaluating hazards makes the problem of rate determination for a sizable structure a complicated and technical procedure. The average insurance agent does not make a rate analysis. This work is assigned to the highly trained experts of the rating bureaus. The agent and the insured, however, may take the makeup of the rate and determine where it will be profitable to eliminate hazards for which charges are made in the rate.

The *perils* included in a fire insurance contract may be more than just fire damage. Although the rate analysis example here refers only to fire as a cause of loss, separate prices are developed by the fire rating bureaus for other perils commonly included with the basic fire insurance contract. These include "extended coverage" (for windstorm, smoke, explosion, riot, and other perils); "indirect losses," such as business interruption loss of income, rents, and extra expenses; water damage and sprinkler leakage; and earthquake.

The price of fire insurance also varies with the location or *territory* of the property, the structure or *construction* of the building, the use or *occupancy* of the property, the loss-prevention or *protection* facilities, and the proximity or *exposure* to other risks. For example, the factor of structure or construction class changes the price significantly. Standards for the classes are carefully defined by the rating bureaus, and a "frame" building pays a higher rate than a "brick" or a "fire-resistive" building.

Two types of fire insurance rates are set by the bureau: (1) *class* rates, or "tariff" rates, for groups of average properties; and (2) *specific* rates, or "schedule" rates, for individual properties. The idea of having some rates for groups of risks with similar characteristics and other, individual rates for risks that differ widely in their specific characteristics is common to many types of insurance. A further look at these two types of rates follows.

Class rates. Class rates are group rates, an average price applying to each similar category or classification. The outstanding example of class rating is to be found in separate *dwelling* houses or *residential* homes. Class rates are developed to apply to all dwellings not subject to some special hazard. Class-rated dwellings are subdivided into groups in accordance with construction, with a rate assigned to such classes as frame or brick and to combustible or noncombustible roof. The rate also varies as to the fire protection classification of the city or town and the number of families occupying the property. In addition to class-rated dwellings, many jurisdictions apply class rates to buildings where the elements of construction and occupancy are similar enough to permit a ready grouping into rate classes. New Insurance Services Office (ISO) filings in 1978 expanded class rating considerably, to most smaller buildings in "general" classes (mercantile, churches, schools, warehouses, offices) and to "habitational" classes (apartments, motels, boarding-houses).

The purposes of class rates are economy and simplicity, yet reasonable equity, so that the individual buildings within a given class do not vary too much with regard to potential loss-causing characteristics. Thus, for example, all one-family brick dwellings in a midwestern town of 200,000 population and with fire hydrants might have a one-year fire rate of $0.30 per $100 of insurance.

Specific or schedule rates.   When class rates do not apply, the rate is said to be "specific." *Specific rates* are set by the rating bureaus for larger mercantile and manufacturing properties, educational institutions, public buildings, and many types of *business* establishments. Specific rates are determined by the application to the particular risk of a schedule designed to measure the relative quantity of fire hazard with respect to the particular risk. The system is known as *schedule rating*. Specific rates are published for individual towns and cities and for each eligible individual building. The new ISO manual requires class rates to be used for properties to which such rates apply. Most larger buildings use specific rates developed after a physical inspection of the individual property. These include sprinklered, manufacturing, cleaners, hotel restaurant, and other risks.

Schedule rating is a plan by which differences in hazards with respect to different properties are measured. It undertakes to produce an equitable price for fire insurance. Schedule rating takes into consideration the various items that contribute to the peril of fire, including the construction of the building, its occupancy or use, its protection, and its exposure to nearby buildings. Credits and charges representing departures from standard conditions as to each of these items are incorporated into the schedules. Thus, a schedule rate is the sum of all charges less the sum of credits.

Schedule rating has not by any means solved the fire insurance rating problems. A schedule, of itself, is an arbitrary and empirical standard. However, among several or many insureds using the same schedule, equity and uniformity may be obtained.

Municipal grading schedule (Insurance Services Office).   In both class and schedule rating of properties, another factor to consider is the municipality in which the properties are located. ISO has helped in this process by evaluating cities of over 10,000 population. An engineering survey is done, grading many *physical conditions of the city* and *fire defenses.* For example, in cold climates there is a heating hazard as well as a hazard growing out of difficulty in getting fire apparatus to respond quickly and operate efficiently in cold weather. In hot, dry climates there is increased combustibility, and fires may be spread rapidly by high winds. Likewise, earthquakes, tornadoes, hurricanes, floods, forest fires, and other unusual conditions contribute to the conflagration hazard. The *municipal grading schedule* considers these factors, as well as water supplies, the adequacy and capability of police and fire department equipment and personnel, fire prevention programs, building laws, and other items. Deficiency points are assigned on the basis of regular inspections which grade areas into ten classes of protection from one (the best) to ten (the worst). Cities can obtain a higher classification and thus a lower basic insurance rate by making recommended improvements and having a new inspection survey performed. In many communities the control of the basic rate falls only indirectly within the control of individuals. However, to the extent that they can influence the city government to update fire department equipment or training programs, or to reduce or eliminate fire hazards, individuals can contribute to a lower community rate. (Recently, a new system of grading cities of more than 500,000 population considers only the *loss* experience of those cities.)

What the insured can do to lower rates.   The details of schedule rating are many, and they make the problem of rating seem complicated. The insured is primarily interested in knowing that it is possible to reduce the insurance premium through the elimination of chargeable construction defects or the installation of protective devices. Each of the following examples shows the wide range of what can be done by insureds to lower their costs of insurance.

One of the first points that the insured should consider is charges for features of *construction* classed as "other than standard." Here frequently the variation from the requirements may be only slight, and by means of some inexpensive modification the risk may be made standard and a substantial saving effected. In the case of such things as stairs, heating, lighting, and electrical wiring, slight alterations to correct defects frequently result in savings far in excess of the cost. Another factor to consider is the *exposure* from adjoining buildings. If a building of superior construction is exposed on any side by a high-rated risk, such as a small frame addition at the rear of a brick building, it is frequently possible to eliminate the exposure charge by removing the unneeded addition. A rate may also be materially lessened by entirely closing unprotected openings. Standard fire doors, fire shutters, wire-glass windows set in steel sash and frames—all contribute to the elimination of exposure charges, and their installation frequently proves to be profitable. It frequently happens that a hazardous *occupancy* or use of the property is eliminated, and through neglect or oversight no application is made for re-rating. Whenever there have been any changes in occupancy in either the insured property or an adjacent property, an investigation to ascertain their effect upon the rate is in order. Charges for hazards growing out of *faults of management* are usually the outgrowth of carelessness or indifference. Since such hazards are readily corrected, a charge is made which aims to make their elimination profitable to the insured. Charges are made for such hazards as broken plaster or windows, heating pipes improperly placed near combustible material, improper receptacles for oily or other waste, the accumulation of rubbish, and other indications of slack housekeeping. The insured will find it inexpensive as well as common sense to correct such faults.

Perhaps no single improvement to a property will have a greater effect on a rate reduction than the installation of an *automatic sprinkler system*. Sprinkler systems are now used in almost every type of structure. In buildings where the temperature is below the freezing point of water, a dry system is available. Instead of being filled with water, the pipes contain air under pressure up to the sprinkler head. When a sprinkler head is opened, the compressed air is released and water then flows through the system and through the opened valve to drench the fire. The cost of sprinkler installation is unreasonably high for risks involving small values. However, when large values are involved, over a term of years the savings on the insurance premium will pay for the sprinkler system. In addition, many fire losses can be avoided or substantially reduced by sprinkler systems, and both lives and property saved.

Credits on the rate are also allowed for *other protective features* designed to minimize the risks of fire. Among these are approved fire extinguishers, automatic fire alarms, and security guard service. When the installation of such equipment is contemplated, care should be exercised to see that it meets the standard of rating requirements. Considerable money might be spent for equipment that would receive no credit on the rate because of failure to meet the required specifications.

When *new building construction plans* are being considered, their submission to the fire insurance rating bureau will frequently bring forth suggestions to increase the safety of the property and lessen the insurance cost. A slight addition to the thickness of a floor or wall; a change in roof specifications; changes in floor openings, elevators, vents—all may become profitable investments by saving on insurance premiums. While much may be done in the way of correction after a building is completed, obviously the planning stage is the best time to catch and eliminate chargeable hazards. Moreover, at this stage, at a very small cost or even at no extra cost, improvements can be made that would be too expensive to consider in a completed building. Through submission of the plans and specifications to the rating bureau, a complete rate analysis may be obtained for study before final acceptance and approval of the plans.

The money saving that can be achieved by eliminating hazards is but one benefit, and perhaps the least important of a number that policyholders should consider. In spite of adequate fire insurance protection, insureds will suffer many indirect losses, some probably not insured, in the event of fire. They are, therefore, interested in taking steps to minimize all known hazards with a view to increasing the safety of their property entirely apart from the saving in insurance premium. The desire for the safety of human lives may also be an overwhelming factor in deciding to do all that is possible to prevent fire losses.

Automobile insurance as another example

All rating plans aim at obtaining enough (but not too much) money for the insurer to pay total claims and expenses, while at the same time providing reasonable equity among the prices charged the various insureds. Many of the same types of factors are used in pricing automobile insurance as are used in pricing fire insurance. Class rates are the usual rating method. The *location* and *use* of the property are the basic loss-causing characteristics classified. Because of higher loss frequency than in fire insurance, it is also common to develop individual rate modifications for insureds on the basis of their accident records.

Territorial differences in price are important in automobile insurance, as each rating territory, which may be as large as a whole state or as small as a part of an urban area, pays a rate based on the losses attributable to automobiles garaged in that territory. Thus, a New York automobile or driver causing a loss in Florida would affect New York liability rates, not those of Florida. Generally, rural areas pay lower prices for automobile insurance than do urban areas, but the actual losses of the area are also important. One city may have more than double the rate of another city of the same size because of poor loss experience. The loss-producing characteristics may be largely uncontrollable, such as snow, ice, fogs, and hills, or they may be partially controllable, such as poor road design, lenient juries, and lax police enforcement.

The *use* factor in automobile insurance rates is primarily related to classification of drivers. The principal and secondary drivers are grouped in hundreds of classifications based on age, sex, and marital status. Generally, married persons have lower rates than unmarried persons; persons over age 30 lower rates than persons under 30; and females lower rates than males. Separate classifications also apply to private passenger automobiles used primarily in a business, as opposed to those used mostly for pleasure and those used for transportation to and from work regularly more than a stated number of miles. Commercial vehicles, such as large trucks, have separate rating plans.

Experience of the drivers is also a significant factor in pricing. Many rating plans require higher rates if the driver (or family members using the automobile) have had recent automobile accident *losses*. The driving record thus influences the charges considerably. For example, being responsible for one accident within the past three years might increase the price of insurance by 20 percent, while two accidents could cause a 50 percent or more increase. These "demerit" plans of stock and mutual bureaus and independent insurers vary in the percentage additions to cost. Price discounts of about 15 percent are granted for driver education courses completed by drivers under age 21, and to owners of two or more automobiles if they insure them in the same policy. The system of individual rate modifications based upon loss experience is somewhat like the "schedule" rates for fire insurance on individual business properties. In place of estimating the prospective effect of good and bad features of the property through a physical inspection, the individual rates are developed by increasing the class rate by percentages on the basis of actual automobile insurance losses of the individual insured.

During the period 1974–78 a few states passed legislation banning the use of age and sex as rating factors in automobile insurers. Claiming unfair discrimination, Massachusetts, North Carolina, and Hawaii are requiring the use of other rating factors such as driving experience and mileage use, but these types of laws are being challenged by many insurers. (See also Chapter 24.)

Special problems

Deductible clauses.   A deductible clause in an insurance contract provides that the insurer will pay a loss only when the loss is in excess of a specified amount or percentage. The clause made its early appearance in marine contracts because marine insurers recognized that in the case of goods particularly susceptible to damage there would otherwise be many claims for insignificant losses. There seemed to be little point in adding to a rate the amount of a loss that could reasonably be anticipated. Thus, marine contracts usually provided that the insurer was to be relieved of all partial losses on certain types of goods and that in other classifications the loss must exceed a designated percentage of value in order to be collectible.

The percentage of value is sometimes called the "franchise," and thus the term *franchise* deductible. No loss is payable unless the loss equals or exceeds the percentage or franchise. If the loss reaches this figure it is paid in full. Another clause provides that a named percentage of the loss or a stated dollar amount is always deducted from the claim and the amount above this deductible is paid the insured. This is known as a *straight* deductible in many types of insurance.

The deductible principle has found an important place in other branches of insurance. In automobile insurance, for example, owners of automobiles might be perfectly satisfied to have small damages repaired themselves. If the insurer is liable for the repair of minor losses, the cost of handling the claims is entirely out of proportion to the damage sustained. For this reason, automobile insurance for the car of the insured is frequently written with a straight deductible clause providing that the company is not liable unless the loss exceeds an amount named in the clause, such as $50 or $100 or $250, and then the insurer pays only the amount by which the loss exceeds the specified deductible.

Small deductibles written in connection with property insurance are sound in theory. They effectively eliminate most of the small "nuisance" claims, and in the long run they make possible a lower insurance premium. The insured receives a reduced premium where a deductible is used. Adjustment expense in settling a small nuisance loss is often more than the amount of the loss. A $50 loss payment may often involve $100 or more in agents' and adjusters' time and completion of necessary forms. The loss records show that the adjustment and payment in full of such claims do increase insurance costs considerably because for many types of insurance the greatest number of losses are small ones. With rising loss costs, deductibles as a means of reducing insurance premiums are often increasingly advantageous to consumers in holding insurance costs down. (See Chapter 1 for other discussion on the reasons for using deductibles.)

It has not proved feasible in connection with most property insurance to provide a franchise type of deductible for payment in full if the loss exceeds the amount of the deductible. In the case of a $100 deductible there is a grave temptation to stretch an $80 or $90 loss to the point where it exceeds the deductible, if by so doing the full amount of the claim is to be paid. A combination of the straight and franchise deductibles is the so-called variable, diminishing, or *modified* deductible used in some homeowners' policies. For example, in the case of a $100 loss or less, the full amount of the deductible applies. The amount payable for loss between $100 and $500 may be 125 percent of the amount in excess of $100. When the loss is $500 or more, the loss deductible disappears. This is illustrated as follows:

Amount of loss	Deductible amount	Loss less deductible	Amount collectible	Franchise amount
$100	$100	0	0	$100.00
200	100	$100 × 125%	$125.00	75.00
400	100	300 × 125%	375.00	25.00
500	100	400 × 125%	500.00	0

The franchise amount in the right-hand column is the amount of loss not collected by the insured, and this disappears when the amount of the loss reaches $500.

The modified type of deductible has the advantage of not encouraging exaggerated claims by the insured in order to receive loss payment. In keeping with the theory that a deductible's purpose is to eliminate small losses but *not* to reduce a loss payment when the loss is *large*, it is an equitable method. Its disadvantage is greater complexity and possible lack of understanding by the insured. In fact, the major disadvantage of all deductibles is the practical problem of educating insureds to understand that the reduced cost and other benefits of deductibles more than offset the slightly lower loss payments they receive.

Sizable deductibles have been introduced recently in the field of fire insurance. Forms are offered that allow deductibles at the insured's option ranging from $5,000 up to $250,000. A schedule of rate credits is applicable according to the percentage of value represented by the deductible amount which the insured selects. The higher the percentage which the deductible bears to the basis of insurance, the greater is the credit allowed. Experience shows that the less the amount of the loss, the more frequent the occurrence. If insureds can handle losses up to a given point and eliminate such losses from their insurance coverage, the loss experience will be reflected in much lower rates. Consumers should not cling to traditional deductibles, and should periodically review their choices of deductible amounts.[5]

Newer types of deductibles are becoming more common, too. In addition to the straight, franchise and modified deductibles just discussed the *aggregate deductible* is increasing in popularity. This is applied to total losses in a year. Its use is appearing frequently in liability (particularly for product claims) and some forms of health insurance.

Minimum premiums. There are certain fixed costs that attach to the issuing of an insurance policy. For example, a fire insurance rate may call for $0.40 for each $100 of insurance written for a period of one year. Obviously, if one asked for $100 insurance, the insurer could not profitably issue a policy for $0.40. A certain amount of expense is involved in the office labor required in preparing the policy. That cost alone often exceeds $25 per contract written. For this reason it is customary to require a *minimum premium,* sometimes referred to as a "policy fee."

In some fields of insurance a large expense is caused by inspections or other such services. If the amount of insurance ordered does not bring the premium up to a specified minimum,the underwriting requirements indicate a charge that must be met regardless of the rate. Finally, there are short-term risks in which there is a tendency of applicants for insurance to apply for

---

[5] But choose the large deductibles carefully. A recent $1 million loss at First National Bank of Chicago involved the good news that the bank had insurance coverage but the bad news that its insurance contract had a deductible—for $1 million (*Newsweek,* October 24, 1977).

coverages for a period of 30 to 60 days when they sense peculiar circumstances that tend to increase the risk. Examples would include auto insurance only during winter driving months, or fire insurance only while the heating system is turned on. If such insurance were written at the proportional part of the annual rate, there would be a tendency to create a situation of adverse selection against the insurer. Hence, the minimum premium has to be set at an amount sufficiently large to reimburse the insurer for the risk.

Annual and term policies.   The time specified in the policy during which the coverage is effective is its *term*. A property insurance policy written for one year is called an *annual policy*; if written for a longer period, it is called a *term policy*. Certain types of risks are accepted on an annual basis only; others are written for a longer term, sometimes with a rate reduction; still others are written for less than one year at an increased short-term rate.

When policies are written on the term basis with a prepaid premium for the entire term, it is sometimes the rule in property insurance to charge for all years after the first year a premium equal to 85 percent of the annual premium rate. The usual terms are one and three years. The premium for three years is 2.7 times the annual rate, if the premium is paid in advance. However, most insurers now follow new Insurance Services Office rules which charge the *full* annual rate for each year beyond the first year.

Policies written for a period of less than a year are ordinarily written for a special purpose, such as to bring about an expiration date at a particular time or to add to insurance during the period of a temporary inventory increase. Policies written for less than a year are charged on what is termed the *short-rate basis*. Tables are prepared to show short-rate premium calculations, as if a regular contract were written and then canceled. For example, a 180-day contract would cost 60 percent of the annual premium. (ISO now applies a new method, charging 90 percent of the full unearned premium.)

In the early days of fire insurance *perpetual* policies were offered, and a few insurers continue the practice today. Perpetual policies are written under a continuous contract for a single premium. While the insurance is in force, the investment return on premium deposits is used to pay claims and operating expenses. The coverage may be terminated by either the insurer or the insured, and when so terminated the premium deposit is returned to the insured.

Installment plans.   Term rates for longer than a year with annual *installment payments* are allowed in some types of insurance. For example, in the casualty field 2.5 times the annual premium plus 5 percent is the charge for a three-year term policy if paid in installments of 50, 30, and 20 percent for the first, second, and third years, respectively. To permit taking advantage of term discounts with equal annual installment payments, the deferred premium plan (DPP) has been devised. The plan provides for an annual DPP rate which is 105 percent of the one-year regular rate whether the policy is written for three or five years. Conversion tables are provided for converting annual premiums to DPP plan premiums. Premium payments on a monthly basis are also increasingly common. An extra premium charge of about 3 percent is required.

A wide variety of premium payment plans have recently appeared in insurance. With automobile insurance costs rising and the concept of account selling (all insurance of a policyholder with one insurer) gaining favor, policyholders are often faced with the need to spread their insurance premiums over a number of payments. Some insurers have set up separate finance plans to permit the insured to do this on a quarterly, semiannual, or monthly basis. Larger agencies have also designed such finance plans to aid their clients. The trend appears to be toward monthly payments, which are especially suitable for the all-lines insurer groups that can offer the insured a plan with one convenient monthly premium for all types of insurance.

REINSURANCE

The underwriting process is closely related to reinsurance, and the underwriter must know how his or her ability to accept risks is both broadened and limited by reinsurance available to the insurer.

Purposes

How can an insurer accept large risks that today sometimes exceed $20 million in a single building, a ship, or an airplane? How can liability contracts for business firms be written that have policy limits of $50 million or more? How can a person now have in excess of $10 million of life insurance? Few, if any, insurers could absorb such loss payments without endangering their financial solvency.

In exposures affecting many insureds at one time, such as hurricanes, how can insurers avoid the concentration of loss that occurs? Gigantic losses do not occur frequently, but when they do they illustrate the "real why" of insurance —protection against losses which perhaps could only be met by the techniques of the insurance system. In recent years the examples of such losses are a review of the headlines throughout the world: "$750 Million Insured Loss in Hurricane Betsy," "Easter Tornadoes Result in over $400 Million Loss Payments," "Tanker Loss off English Coast May Exceed $40 Million" "Oil Refinery Loss Tops $36 Million," and "Canary Island Collision of Two 747s Causes $160 Million Loss."

The purpose of reinsurance is to provide at least part of the answers to the questions in the preceding paragraphs. In order to secure a large number of similar risks to permit prediction of losses with a reasonable degree of certainty, insurers have devised the practice of reinsurance. *Reinsurance* is the transfer of insurance business from one insurer to another. Its purpose is to shift risks from an insurer whose financial safety might be threatened by retaining too large an amount of risk to other *reinsurers* that will share in the risks of large losses. It may also have the purpose of stabilizing profits and losses of insurers and permitting more rapid growth by having the reinsurer take over from the insurer part of the requirements for maintaining reserves on expanding business. Profit, of course, is the normal motivation for the transaction from the reinsurer's standpoint.

If risk is concentrated in large amounts on a few properties, obviously the variation from the average may and probably will be great. For this reason, the insurer seeks to limit its lines and secure the widest possible dispersion of risks. For example, if statistics show that over a period of time one dwelling house in a thousand will be totally destroyed each year by fire, then the contribution of $40 by each of a thousand homeowners will make up a fund sufficient to pay the loss for the one $40,000 house. If in the group of houses there is a house valued at $200,000 and the owner of that house pays $200 into the fund, that is, $10 for each $10,000 coverage, the fund at the end of a year will total $40,160. If, however, the $200,000 dwelling should be destroyed, the fund would be inadequate to reimburse the owner. In order to enable an insurer to provide the full coverage for differing insurance values at the established rate, the practice of reinsurance has been devised.

Reinsurance organizations

Reinsurers are of two basic types: (1) *professional reinsurers* that do a reinsurance business only, and (2) *reinsurance departments* of insurers that write mostly insurance but also write some reinsurance. About three fourths of the market for reinsurance in the United States is written by the full-time professional reinsurers, numbering about 30. However, in the past two decades the number of U.S. insurers that have organized reinsurance departments has almost tripled to about 100.

A special type of reinsurer is the *reinsurance pool,* which is an association for the exchange of reinsurance among two or more insurers according to an automatic agreement. Each reinsurer receives a certain amount or proportion of the risks or losses of the other reinsurer or reinsurers, and each cedes or gives to all the others a predetermined part of its risks or losses. These pools are also used for spreading infrequent catastrophic types of risks among insurers of a company group or fleet. Examples of such reinsurance pools, sometimes called syndicates, are those found for such risks as nuclear fission, insurance in foreign countries, marine insurance, large industrial risks, aviation, oil refineries, and foreign credit insurance. Well known in these fields are the American Nuclear Insurers, the American Foreign Insurance Association, the American Hull Insurance Syndicate, the Factory Insurance Association, and the United States Aviation Underwriters.

Reinsurance agreements

There are two principal forms of reinsurance agreements in regard to the method by which the reinsurance goes into effect: (1) specific, or facultative, reinsurance; and (2) treaty, or automatic, reinsurance.

Specific, or facultative.   *Specific* reinsurance, also termed *facultative* reinsurance, is a form which concerns itself with a specific optional transaction. Each contract under specific reinsurance is written on its own merit and is a matter of individual bargaining between the original insurer and the reinsurer. This form is termed facultative because the reinsurer is under no obligation through previous agreement of reciprocal arrangement to accept the risk. Also, the insurer may or may not offer the risk to the reinsurer. Each party thus retains the faculty or privilege of accepting or rejecting the reinsurance agreement. Facultative reinsurance is still widely used because some risks will always fall outside the scope of the automatic arrangements discussed next.

Treaty, or automatic.   *Treaty,* or *automatic,* reinsurance exists when the insurer agrees in advance to offer some types of risks and the reinsurer agrees to accept those risks. The individual risks may be undetermined at the time of the agreement. The reinsurer agrees to insure an amount or a proportionate part of a designated class of past or future business written by the insurer. Treaties controlling the major part of the business today obligate the reinsurer to accept a specfic part (the ceded or reinsured amount) of each risk assumed by the original insurer, and the original insurer on its part is obligated to cede a like portion of the risk. The liability of the reinsurer attaches as soon as the original insurer assumes the risk. Automatic[6] protection is thus assured for the original insurer, as the reinsurer has agreed beforehand to accept all risks within the terms of the treaty.

Reinsurance contracts

Facultative and treaty reinsurance agreements may use either of two basic ideas in distributing the insurance risk between the original insurer and the reinsurer. The reinsurer agrees to accept either (1) *a share* of the *amounts of risk* which the insurer writes or (2) an *excess* of the *losses* beyond certain established limits.

A special type of contract which is not regularly used by an insurer is called "portfolio reinsurance." This occurs when the reinsurer takes over all the risks of certain lines of insurance from the original insurer, oftentimes when the insurer is discontinuing such business.

Share-of-risk contracts.   Reinsurance contracts that share risks may in-

---

[6] Sometimes the insurer retains the option of determining what it will reinsure, and the treaty is termed an "open treaty" or a "facultative treaty." Here the automatic part of the arrangements for reinsurance is limited to the general type of reinsurance contract and its provisions, but the actual risks and amounts to be ceded to the reinsurer are subject to negotiation.

volve two fundamental ways[7] of distributing the business written by the insurer. In one type, known as *quota or pro rata share,* the insurer cedes a proportional share of every insurance contract of a given kind. For example, in fire insurance the insurer might keep only one third of each risk and the reinsurer accept two thirds. In that case the reinsurer would receive two thirds of the premium (less commissions paid by the insurer to agents) and pay two thirds of any losses. This form of reinsurance contract enables the original insurer to write much larger amounts of insurance than it otherwise could, and it is particularly useful to smaller insurers that want to expand rapidly.

Another common type is the *surplus share,* in which the reinsurer does not participate in every risk of the original insurer but accepts only that part of the risk which goes over certain limits. Usually the limit is established in relation to the "line" retained by the original insurer, and the reinsurer may, for example, agree to take three lines above the retention. The reinsurer does not participate unless the insurance exceeds the net retention. Surplus treaties are one of the most common types of reinsurance arrangement in fire insurance. Often a second or third surplus treaty is used, involving several different reinsurers on the same risk for amounts up to five or ten times the amount of risk kept by the original insurer.

Excess-of-loss contracts.   The second basic type of reinsurance contract, *excess-of-loss,*[8] is designed to afford protection against large *losses* only. *Individual* coverage is used when protection is desired on a single, large exposure. *Catastrophe* coverage applies to classes of exposures, irrespective of the number of risks involved, or against an accumulation of losses in excess of a stipulated limit. The coverage may be limited to a certain area, such as a designated city, or it may be nationwide in scope. A special form of catastrophe coverage may be limited to a definite class where an insurer desires to protect underwriting profits by having the reinsurer pay all losses when the loss ratio exceeds an agreed percentage of the earned premiums. This is called "excess-of-loss ratio" reinsurance. There are many other variations.

Unlike the quota share cover, in the case of loss under excess-of-loss reinsurance there is no obligation on the part of the reinsurer until the gross claim is shown to be in excess of the amount payable by the ceding company. The reinsurer shares *only* a portion of *losses* in excess of the retention; it does not receive a full proportional share of the premium. Thus, this type is sometimes called "nonproportional" reinsurance. Sometimes, in order to hold the

---

[7] Reference here is primarily to property-liability reinsurance contracts. In the life insurance field two basic types are also used: the "coinsurance" type and the "yearly renewable term" type. Since life risks involve total losses only rather than total or partial losses, reinsurance contracts in the life and property fields are not completely analogous. Basically, however, the "coinsurance" type is closest to the share-of-risk contract and the "yearly renewable term" is most like an excess-of-loss contract.

[8] Excess-of-loss reinsurance is sometimes confused with "catastrophe covers," which have similar goals of protecting against large losses only but are written as direct insurance between policyholder and insurer.

ceding company interested in the gross amount of the loss settlement, the agreement is written so that the ceding company continues to participate in the excess loss in an agreed percentage.

Excess-of-loss contracts are the type of coverage by which many insurers, especially in automobile, liability, and other types of casualty insurance, cover the catastrophe risk. Fire and allied lines such as windstorm insurance have also used this type of reinsurance with increasing frequency. American and alien companies accepting reinsurance write the coverage, and London Lloyd's writes many of these increasingly popular reinsurance contracts.

A summary of the types and characteristics of reinsurance organizations, reinsurance agreements, and reinsurance contracts is presented for review in Table 6–1.

Table 6–1. Summary of types of reinsurers and reinsurance

Types	*Characteristics*
1. *Reinsurance organizations*	
a. Professional reinsurers	Write reinsurance only
b. Reinsurance departments	Write reinsurance, but are primarily insurers
c. Reinsurance pools	Associations of insurers writing or sharing reinsurance jointly
2. *Reinsurance agreements*	
a. Specific, or facultative*	Optional choice allowing ceding insurer to offer, and reinsurer to accept, individual insurance risks; neither party obligated in advance to do so
b. Treaty,* or automatic	Binding agreement in advance to have ceding insurer offer, and reinsurer accept, some proportion or amount of designated types of insurance
3. *Reinsurance contracts†*	
a. Share-of-risk	Reinsurer shares *risks* (premiums and losses) with insurer
a. Quota or pro rata share	Reinsurer and original insurer share part (or a percentage) of the entire premiums and claims on the risks insured
b. Surplus share	Reinsurer shares risk only above a net retention by insurer
b. Excess-of-loss	Reinsurer shares only *losses* proportionally with insurer
a. Individual contracts	Reinsurer agrees to pay losses on a single exposure above the retention amount paid by insurer
b. Catastrophe	Reinsurer agrees to pay catastrophic losses on classes of exposures above the amount, or a specified loss ratio, retained by insurer (generally liability insurance)

* A variation may combine these two types in a "facultative treaty," in which the agreement in advance is limited to the general terms that will apply for the reinsurance. The insurer is not required to reinsure nor the reinsurer to accept business, but if they do so, the terms of the reinsurance agreement automatically apply.

† Life insurance uses two other types not described here: "yearly renewable term" and "coinsurance" plans.

Retrocessions

Reinsurance enjoys no immunity from the operation of the principles governing sound practice for insurers. The reinsurer must also avoid a concentration in "conflagration" areas or catastrophe situations and must maintain a wide distribution of its risks. Since the reinsurer may have lines ceded from a number of different sources, it is easily possible that it might find itself with an unwarranted accumulation of risk in a single policyholder or a given locality or class. To relieve itself of this unsatisfactory accumulation, the reinsurer would itself have to resort to reinsurance. The act of reinsuring any part of a reinsurance contract is termed a *retrocession*. In compensation, liability, and life risks, the reinsurer sometimes finds the amount of reinsurance far greater than it is willing to carry. In such cases, it can accept the entire excess and in turn seek reinsurance through retrocession, retaining only as much of the risk as it deems prudent.

An example

The entire area of reinsurance is an example of the essential need to spread risk among many risk bearers. Much of the process goes on without policyholders being aware of its existence, since they are not a party to the reinsuring arrangements. Yet it is an important part of the security behind many insurance contracts. Without reinsurance, most insurers could accept only a limited amount of insurance on any one risk, perhaps only a few thousand dollars. With reinsurance, many insurers can accept millions of dollars of insurance from an insured and through reinsurance distribute a large share of the risk to many others. Greater financial solvency for all insurers and reinsurers is the result.

Consider the hypothetical illustration of an agent who sells $9 million of fire insurance on a manufacturer's plant. Three insurers may each take $3 million of coverage in separate policies. Perhaps Insurer A has a quota share treaty reinsurance agreement with Reinsurer W that takes two thirds of this $3 million policy. Insurer B may have a surplus share treaty with Reinsurer X to take five "lines" above a $300,000 retention by Insurer B, or $1.5 million. This would leave $1.2 million to be arranged by Insurer B in a facultative reinsurance agreement with Reinsurer Y in a second surplus agreement. The third $3 million policy may be spread to Reinsurer Z in an excess-of-loss contract, in which Insurer C agrees to take care of all losses up to $600,000 and Reinsurer Z will pay any loss exceeding that amount up to $3 million. Any of the reinsurers, or all of them, may decide that their total risk is too great, and through retrocession transfer some of their risk to other reinsurers. See Figure 6–2 for illustration of this example of the use of reinsurance contracts.

The example illustrates how one policyholder's risk may result in several

Figure 6-2. An example illustrating the use of reinsurance contracts

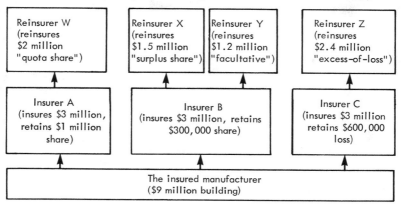

insurance contracts and many reinsurance and retrocession agreements. The relatively large dollar figures in the example should not be taken to mean that reinsurance is used only for large business risks. It is in everyday use by practically all insurers for many risks. Fire insurance on homes and automobile liability insurance of more than $25,000, as well as many other common types and sizes of insurance contracts, have reinsurance regularly involved. The "retention" by the original insurer, of course, may be larger where the insurer is large enough to absorb such losses.

International aspects

The reinsurance area is noted for several unusual characteristics: its *international* character, its extreme *flexibility* and freedom from insurance regulation as to forms and rates, and its high level of business *conduct* on a basis of good faith between the contracting parties. A substantial reinsurance business, about one third of all U.S. reinsurance, is conducted in the United States by reinsurers from other countries, including London Lloyd's. Branch companies of alien reinsurers are also active. These companies compete with the full-time professional U.S. reinsurers[9] and with the reinsurance departments of U.S. insurers, which have increased rapidly in recent years. The reinsurance premium that is exported from the United States is an item of some importance in the balance of payments.

The widespread market for reinsurance—a world spread that is needed by all countries—is partially responsible for the great flexibility which reinsurers

---

[9] Examples of the largest reinsurers are: U.S. professional—General Reinsurance Corporation and American Re-Insurance Company; alien professional reinsurers—North American Reassurance Company/Swiss Reinsurance Company, Skandia Reinsurance Company, and Munich Reinsurance Corporation.

have in designing new and special contracts for the individual needs of insurers. The large and sometimes complex nature of reinsurance arrangements
and the necessarily high caliber of reinsurance personnel for such contracts
make reinsurance a unique part of the insurance business. It is only on an
international basis that giant risks can be spread throughout the world, even
to the USSR in its "Ingosstrakh" reinsurance company, by the process of reinsurance. Risks of $10–50 million may be placed in the competitive rein-
surance market in only a few days. Increasing losses and increasing needs for
multimillion-dollar reinsurance coverages for fire, windstorm, riot, liability,
aircraft, shipping, and many other types of damages promise to make reinsurance of growing importance in the international marketplace.

OTHER FUNCTIONS OF INSURERS

Contract design, marketing, and underwriting have been reviewed in the
past three chapters as major functions of insurers. There are, however, other
activities of insurers that are necessary in carrying out the business of insurance. One of these, the investment function, is a particularly significant activity for insurers. Some of the minor functional areas would be found in any
sizable business firm. Many of them are "auxiliary" types of operations aimed
at providing services facilitating the major functions of insurers.

Some insurers perform the auxiliary functions under the supervision of the
marketing (or "production" or "agency") department, the claim department,
or the underwriting department. Other insurers accord separate status to these
activities in such departments as the legal department, the actuarial department, the accounting department, the statistical and research department, the
public relations department, the advertising department, and the education department. Also, a large number of other internal services may be grouped together under an administrative department that performs secretarial, purchasing, filing, printing, mailing, storage, employment, and employee benefit
functions. Only a few of these activities are unique enough to insurers to warrant separate treatment. Nevertheless, how such services are performed in an
insurance organization is significant in understanding their relation to the
major insurance functions.

The investment department

The *investment* department of insurers is of great importance in (1) providing financial strength for the insurers and (2) reducing the overall costs
of insurance by making effective use of the sizable assets that many insurers
have. The prepaid nature of many insurance payments by policyholders, especially in life insurance, creates funds which the insurer must invest pro-
ductively and wisely.

The prospective earnings of *life insurers* on total assets, which at the start of 1977 were $320 *billion,* are a major calculation in the pricing process of life insurance. More than 20 percent of the total income of life insurers comes from investments. The approximate holdings of life insurers by types of assets are summarized in Table 6–2.

Table 6–2. Investments of U.S. insurance companies, 1977 (beginning)

Type of asset	*Billions of $*	*Percent of total assets*
1. Mortgages	92	29
2. Bonds		
Government	20	6
Industrial and miscellaneous	121	37
Total bonds	141	43
3. Stocks	34	11
4. Real estate	10	3
5. Policy loans	26	8
6. Cash and miscellaneous	19	6
Total all assets	322	100

Source: *Life Insurance Fact Book* (Washington, D.C.: American Council of Life Insurance, 1977), p. 68.

Although 80 percent or more of these assets represent the "legal reserves" of the contracts for policyholders and must be invested largely in long-term secure investments such as bonds and mortgages, life insurers also have major choices to make among many other investment alternatives for the remainder of their assets. Millions of dollars are invested every day by life insurers in such varied areas as the aviation industry (which is said to be supported by insurers to the extent of more than 40 percent of its outstanding bonds), home mortgages, urban redevelopment housing projects, shopping centers, office buildings, and space exploration.

The impact of these assets is significant. Life insurers provide financial capital to the economy. Bonds and mortgages are the primary type of investments, totaling more than 70 percent of all assets. Mortgages held by life insurers represent one seventh of all mortgages in the United States. Stocks have been increasing in the overall portfolio and now are valued at $34 billion. They total only about 11 percent of assets, but a changing philosophy, a lessening of legal restrictions, and the growth of insured annuity funds are creating increased interest in stock market activity by life insurers.

In recent years the importance of investment income to *property-liability insurers* has become strikingly apparent. Although traditionally the insurers in these fields have stressed *underwriting* profits from insurance operations, for most insurers the past decade has seen a dwindling of this source of income to an uncertain amount in relation to the *investment* profits. Investments have served (1) to provide the primary source of stockholder dividends and

(2) to strengthen the surplus to protect policyholders. Investment income has not been a direct consideration in the pricing of property and liability insurance.[10] Today it appears to have taken on increased significance in the total activities of property-liability insurers. During the decade 1967–76, the stock property-liability insurers suffered an *underwriting loss* of $5 billion, whereas during the same period they had an *investment profit* of about $23 billion.[11] With this importance, the proper use of assets for investments attains a new perspective and the investment function or department may assume a much greater role in this field of insurance. The current picture is summarized in Table 6–3.

Almost 60 percent of the total assets of $108 billion of property-liability insurers is invested in bonds, while stocks account for one fourth of total assets. Less than 1 percent of assets is in mortgages, in contrast to almost 30 percent of the assets of life insurers. The short-run nature of the obligations of property-liability insurers and the greater need for liquidity to meet catastrophe losses explain some of the differences between life and property-liability investment holdings. Note the higher percentage of bonds held by property-liability insurers (58 percent, as opposed to 43 percent). The stock portfolio of 25 percent, in contrast to the life insurers' 11 percent, is partially the result of fewer legislative restrictions on investments by property-liability insurers. It is also caused by the need for investments which increase in value along with inflation, in order to meet the growing loss payments of property-liability contracts.

The table also shows distinct differences between stock and mutual company investments. Relatively more bonds and less stock holdings are found in mutual companies. One study indicates that during the past decades stock companies earned significantly more on their common stock portfolios than did mutual companies.[12] Tradition, the types of insurance contracts written, and the size of the insurers are major factors in these differences.

What do these figures in Tables 6–2 and 6–3 mean in regard to the investment function of insurers? The contrasts between life insurers and property-liability insurers have been pointed out, but more important to the evaluation of the function of investments for all types of insurers are the facts that in-

---

[10] This attitude is in sharp contrast to the life insurance situation. For example, note that the booklet *Insurance Facts, 1977* (New York: Insurance Information Institute), p. 30, contains no breakdown of the investment use of assets of the property-liability business. The *Life Insurance Fact Book, 1977*, pp. 67–87, has 20 pages of detailed information on investments! The volatility of property-liability investment profits or losses and the difficulty of determining the source of such income as due to policyholder or other assets have been advanced as the reasons for this contrast.

[11] *Best's Fire and Casualty Aggregates and Averages* (New York: A. M. Best Co., 1977), pp. 36 and 144.

[12] James S. Trieschmann and Robert J. Monroe, "Investment Performance of P-L Insurer's Common Stock Portfolios," *Journal of Risk and Insurance*, vol. 39, no. 4 (December 1972), p. 545. See also Stephen W. Forbes, "Profitability in the Nonlife Insurance Industry: 1954–74," *CPCU Annals*, vol. 30, no. 2 (June 1977), p. 126.

Table 6–3. Investments of property-liability insurers, 1977 (beginning)

Type of asset	Billions of $			Percent of total assets		
	Stock	Mutual	Total	Stock	Mutual	Total
1. Bonds						
Government	6.8	3.7	10.5	8.1	15.5	9.8
Other	39.7	12.2	51.9	47.6	50.7	48.2
Total bonds	46.5	15.9	62.4	55.7	66.2	58.0
2. Stocks						
Preferred	2.8	4.5	3.3	3.3	2.2	3.1
Common	19.4	4.3	23.7	23.2	17.7	22.0
Total stocks	22.2	4.8	27.0	26.5	19.9	25.1
3. Mortgages	.2	.1	.3	.2	.3	.3
4. Real estate	.9	.5	1.4	1.1	2.2	1.3
5. Premium balances	7.0	1.4	8.4	8.3	6.0	7.8
6. Cash and miscellaneous......	6.8	1.3	8.1	8.2	5.4	7.5
Total all assets	83.6	24.0	107.6	100.0	100.0	100.0

Source: *Best's Fire and Casualty Aggregates and Averages* (New York: A. M. Best Co., 1977), pp. 58, 10B. Data include 945 stock companies and 308 mutual companies, representing more than 95 percent of the total business written. Reciprocals and Lloyds associations are omitted in these figures.

surer assets are tremendous, totaling more than $400 *billion* in 1977, and that these assets need proper management. The assets are *not* automatically invested in certain types of holdings according to precise state laws, but are, within regulatory limits, the result of the decisions made by many financial committees and experts in the insurance business. For bonds and mortgages backing the reserve liabilities, much individual choice by the insurer is permitted in regard to the exact types of bonds or mortgages purchased. For other investments representing voluntary reserves or surplus of the insurer, a wide range of preferred and common stocks, real estate, and other holdings must be carefully considered.

The opportunities are bright for investment and financial management personnel in insurance companies. The size of their responsibility and the relative importance to the insurer of their activities promise to make their task of increasing significance in the future.[13]

Other departments

The following brief treatment of the auxiliary departments of insurers should not be taken to mean that the departments are unimportant. In fact, the success of many insurers can be traced to the excellent support given by these departments to the primary operating departments of marketing, underwriting, and claims and to the investment department.

The *legal* department, for example, often works closely with the claims department of property and liability insurers. It is generally also responsible for meeting general incorporation, licensing, and taxation laws of the many states in which insurers do business. Oftentimes it helps design insurance contracts, drafts agency agreements, and provides general legal counsel for the insurer. In life insurance it offers substantial aid to the sales and underwriting departments by reviewing estate tax problems and planning settlement options.

The *actuarial* department is most closely related to the rating or underwriting department of insurers. Life insurance companies, in particular, need a separate actuarial staff to diagnose mortality trends, determine costs for the various contracts, and provide research for many phases of their activities. Close cooperation is needed with the accounting, statistical, and computer areas in order to coordinate expense, loss cost, and other studies.

Separate *research* departments are not common for most insurers, but increasingly the need for economic and social research is being realized. Some companies now have substantial staffs to analyze economic trends, policyholder opinion surveys, market potentials, investment opportunities, and

---

[13] For further information on insurer investments, see Robert W. Cooper, *Investment Return and Property-Liability Insurance Ratemaking* Homewood, Ill.: Richard D. Irwin, (1974); and J. David Cummins, ed., *Investment Activities of Life Insurance Companies* Homewood, Ill.: Richard D. Irwin, (1977).

other factors important to insurer operations. An organization including many of the research directors, the Society of Insurance Research, was formed in 1971. A new Insurance Research Institute was started in 1978 by insurer-sponsored organizations.

A *public relations* department is maintained by some insurers. News releases, claim dissatisfactions, and general service to the community and public are part of its activities. Coordination with the claims, education, and advertising departments may be essential in many of its projects. Several major trade associations for public relations are supported by many insurers.

Education is another growing area of insurance organizations. Several hundred directors of educational activities for insurers are joined together nationally in a professional effort to improve insurance education through the Insurance Company Education Directors' Society. Many insurers today provide extensive programs of education for management development and the training of claimspersons and underwriters, as well as regular separate schools for agents and employees. They also support many professional educational organizations (see Chapter 5).

Many general *administrative* services are necessary for the efficient operation of an insurer. There are numerous jobs for personnel managers, purchasing experts, computer programmers, clerical and filing help, secretaries, and many other types of administrative personnel. The paperwork essential to insurance organizations creates employment for many thousands of persons, and a successful insurer must be well organized in the administrative areas to provide efficient results. Automation offers substantial help today for many problems in handling administrative services, but it is unlikely that the current ratio of two nonsales jobs for each sales job in insurance will change rapidly. The wide scope of employment in the insurance business is seen in this chapter to include personnel from practically all the fields of marketing, finance, management, and the information sciences.

FOR REVIEW AND DISCUSSION

1. After your study of the underwriting function, do you feel that insurers must write insurance for all applicants? Explain your position.

2. Why do rating and reinsurance topics pertain to underwriting? How is underwriting related to the other major functions of an insurer?

3. Why can't an insurer just accept all applicants for insurance when a "class" rate is used for the price of the contract?

4. What limitations does the insurer set in relying upon the agent to perform the selection of proper risks? What other sources of underwriting information are commonly used in various kinds of insurance?

5. What is "adverse selection," and how does the insurer overcome this problem? Give examples from life, health, fire, and automobile insurance.

6. What is a class fire rate, and how is it found? How does a specific fire rate differ from the class rate, and how is it determined? Give an example of each.

7. You are the risk manager for a large corporation that is planning the construction of 20 large brick warehouses with sprinkler systems. What arguments will you offer in support of this type of construction?

8. The Medical Office Building has just been completed, and application for a fire rate filed. A substantial charge is included in the rate because the building has wooden interior walls. Wherein did the owners fail concerning this rate? What other features of this risk would heavily influence the insurance rate that the building owners will have to pay?

9. Can a public interest campaign be used to make the classification of a city for its fire insurance rate a community affair and perhaps reduce the rate?

10. What is the purpose of a "schedule" fire insurance rate? How does this compare with the purpose of "merit" rates for automobile insurance?

11. How can individual business property owners lower fire insurance costs?

12. Substantial deductibles may encourage self-insurance. Why do deductibles of $10,000 or upward have a place in the insurance business?

13. What are the purposes of deductibles? term policies? installment plans?

14. Mr. Foster finds a "modified" deductible in his homeowner's contract. In what way is it modified? Is its purpose sound in theory and practice?

15. Explain the principal reasons for reinsurance, and distinguish between: (a) facultative and treaty reinsurance; (b) reinsurance and retrocession; and (c) share-of-risk and excess-of-loss reinsurance.

16. To what extent is reinsurance an international activity? Why?

17. If you were the manager of investments, how might your job vary if you worked for a life insurer instead of a property-liability insurer?

18. Contrast the investments of different insurers, indicating the possible reasons for the differences in the portfolios of the insurers you discuss.

19. Has the relative importance of the investment and underwriting operations of insurers changed in the past decade? If so, what might this mean for finance majors in a college of business?

Chapter 7

Concepts considered in Chapter 7—Insurance loss payment

Insurance loss payment is the primary reason for, and result of, many insurance contracts. Uncertainty about losses creates the need for insurance.

The significance of this function is widespread. The spectacular losses, such as multimillion-dollar fires, explosions, and windstorms, are the ones that get the headlines. However, the thousands of everyday smaller claims paid by insurers are those that benefit most policyholders.

The purpose of "loss adjusting" is *fair* and *prompt* payment of justified claims. The *reputation* of the insurer is greatly influenced by the manner in which loss payments are made.

Insurance adjusters are of *five types*. Which type is used for a particular loss depends on many factors, such as the kind of insurance, the volume of business written by the insurer, the frequency and difficulty of the claims, the ability of the agent, and the insured.

Agents often settle smaller losses and help in many other losses, depending on the type of insurance.

Staff adjusters are full-time, salaried employees of one insurer, and are active in such fields as automobile losses.

Independent adjusters represent various insurers on some losses.

Adjustment bureaus regularly represent many insurers and are especially useful in fire, windstorm and other property damage losses.

Public adjusters are hired by the insured in some difficult claims.

Claim procedures vary among the different kinds of insurance.

Fire insurance losses are based upon proper *notice* and *proof* of loss by the insured, and the insurer's payment of *actual cash value* follows certain *rights and conditions* stated in the contract.

Liability insurance losses are more difficult to settle because a third-party claimant is involved. Also, the responsibility for injury, its extent, and its future results must be determined. Personal injuries are more difficult to evaluate than property damages.

Life insurance losses are usually paid directly by the insurer through the agent to the beneficiaries. The payment is usually a *fixed-dollar* amount, with some *settlement option* choices available and relatively few legal problems except for the incontestable clause, suicide, and accidental death claims.

Insurance loss payment

Did you ever hear of a moose stomping a compact car?[1] A bull wrecking a swimming pool? A can of hair spray that exploded, after having been put in a toilet, blowing the user from the toilet seat into the bathtub? A patient who billed the insurance company for a seashore vacation because the doctor had prescribed salt water for an injured toe—and later sued the doctor for malpractice because the toe became infected? Well, insurance adjusters have had all of these claims—but most losses are *not* so funny.

The payment of losses is certainly the most obvious of the important functions of insurance. Without claims culminating in loss payments there would be no insurance business. To Joan and John Q. Public, insurance *is* losses— dollars of payment for unfortunate happenings. Not all "happenings" in the language of today's generation are losses, and not all losses are paid for by insurance—but many are.

Before you read this chapter, it is recommended that you first look back at Figure 4–1 to review the relationship of loss payment to all the other major functions of insurers. In the chapter, don't be overconcerned about the phrases and language of particular insurance contracts. Such references are necessary as examples of loss payment techniques and problems and as an introduction to later chapters which analyze insurance contracts in more detail. It is the purpose of this chapter to provide a broad picture of insurance in action, using specific illustrations from three major fields of insurance to show the scope of insurance losses and the methods for paying them.

SIGNIFICANCE

The basic function of loss payment is commonly referred to as *insurance adjusting*. The term is not very satisfactory, but it has become well fixed in the business of insurance. It is hoped that some better term may be adopted in the future, for "adjustment" connotes something that requires a compromise or change before settlement is reached. Since this is not always true, a

---

[1] Into a subcompact car, no doubt. The losses mentioned in the first paragraph of this page are among those noted in "Humor Found in Insurance Claims," *Columbus* (Ohio) *Dispatch,* April 8, 1977. To make things worse, or funnier at least, that person who landed in the bathtub told his story to the ambulance attendant, causing him to laugh so hard that he dropped the stretcher and broke both of the patient's wrists.

better phrase might be *claims payment,* with the persons who do this work referred to as *claimspersons.* However, since the more common reference today is to adjusting and adjusters, these terms will be used frequently in this chapter. Insurance adjusting does have the same objective as the perhaps more accurate terms *loss payment* and *claims payment.* A loss, a claim, and an adjustment may logically be three different amounts, though here the term *adjustment* is used to mean the final insurance payment by the insurer.

Loss payments are a daily part of the routine of the insurance business. Thousands of loss checks are delivered to insureds every day—for automobile accidents, hospital expenses, burglaries, explosions, deaths, and occupational injuries. Sometimes the routine becomes the spectacular, and losses such as Hurricane Betsy in 1965 can affect hundreds of thousands of persons. That loss was the largest national disaster for insurance ever to occur in the United States. Its 1 million claims and $715 million of insured losses were seven times the damage done by the San Francisco earthquake in the early 1900s. Hurricane Camille involved $225 million of insured losses, and Hurricane Agnes cost insurers almost $100 million. Single-building fires can sometimes be amazingly large, too, as was shown in the more than $50 million losses for a New Jersey oil refinery in 1970 and for a French plastics factory in 1977.[2]

The repayment for the values which have been lost is often the point at which policyholders have the strongest possible realization of why they purchased insurance contracts. Up to that time they may have had a feeling that there were a number of vague reasons why they purchased the protection. When they actually receive a loss check which makes it possible for them to rebuild their homes or replace their automobiles, they have specific and tangible knowledge of why they needed the insurance. They may often wonder what they would have done if they had not had the proper insurance coverage.

PURPOSE

Insureds who have honestly suffered loss or damage need approach the insurance company in no apologetic frame of mind. The claim settlement which they ask for is theirs by right of purchase. It should be the objective of both insurers and insureds to arrive at a fair and equitable measure of the loss. There will frequently be areas of disagreement. With both parties resolved to reach an equitable adjustment, disagreements are usually readily reconciled.[3]

Insurance adjusters today are an important contact between the insurer and the policyholder. It is incumbent upon them to deliver the goods which the agent has sold. The insurance business recognizes that years of insurance pro-

---

[2] For a detailed study of "Insurance Copes with Catastrophe: The Xenia Tornado," by the Columbus chapter of CPCU, see the *CPCU Annals* (now *Journal*), vol. 29, no. 20 (June 1976).

[3] See Willis Rokes, *Human Relations in Handling Insurance Claims* (Homewood, Ill.: Richard D. Irwin, 1967).

gramming and planning will come to nothing if the insured is faced with diffi-culty following a loss. New adjusters are taught at the outset that it is their function to settle claims equitably and not, as is sometimes believed, for the least sum to which they can get insureds to agree. Adjusters are further in-structed, when insureds do not know what is due them under their contracts, to take steps to explain what amounts should be included in their claims. By the same token, in the interest of equity in the business, adjusters are trained to recognize sharp practices and to resist padded claims or fraudulent de-mands. Fairness to the uninformed *and* resistance to wrongful claims are for the benefit of both the insurance business and the insureds, who in the long run must pay rates based upon loss experience.

From the point of view of the insurer, claims adjustments afford an attrac-tive area of competition, especially in types of insurance where premium rates are relatively similar and price competition is a minor factor. Although only a minority of all insureds have a loss in a given year, the reputation of the insurer rests not only on how satisfied the claimants are but also on how many other persons the claimants tell about their losses and payments. Ironically, dissatisfied policyholders will tell *everyone* why they believe they were un-fairly treated, whereas satisfied claimants will take their payment as a matter of course. If the insurer fails in effecting a prompt and equitable adjustment following loss, it will have failed in the most crucial of all competitive areas.

This is not to say that there should be competition among insurers by over-payment of claims, which only results in higher insurance costs for all. There is no one who recognizes prompt services and sound practices with respect to the settlement of claims more readily than does the agent or broker. If in-dependent agents become dissatisfied with the adjustment practices of a com-pany, they will direct their business to other insurers. Exclusive agents cannot change their business to another insurer, but because of the sizable business they write they can effectively criticize their insurer if it is being unfair or too reluctant in paying just claims. Likewise, experienced insurance buyers soon learn the reputation of insurers with regard to claim service.

Loss adjustments are set in motion when insureds file notices of loss with their insurers. The adjustment is the means for accomplishing the ultimate aim of insurance. Claims are filed under only comparatively few of the many thousands of insurance policies written. It is the purpose of the adjustment to determine the question of liability for a given loss and to reach an agreement with respect to the loss or damage payable under the insurance contract.

INSURANCE ADJUSTERS: TYPES AND ORGANIZATION

Since insurance policies are contracts, the terms and conditions are care-fully stated so that in the event of losses insureds have their contracts to follow in effecting an adjustment. As a matter of practice, a company repre-sentative approaches the insured, and if investigation shows the loss to be

Figure 7–1. Insurance adjusters*

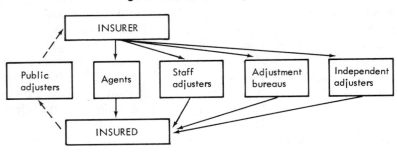

* A special type of adjuster is also noted for marine insurance, in Chapter 19.

legitimate, a settlement is attempted, sparing the insured as much technical detail as possible. All such persons who aid in the loss payment are termed *claimspersons,* or in more common language, *adjusters.* Adjusters fall into five categories: (1) agents as adjusters, (2) staff adjusters, (3) independent adjusters, (4) adjustment bureaus, and (5) public adjusters. The relationship of these five types of adjusters is illustrated in Figure 7–1.

Agents as adjusters

It is common sense on the part of the insurer to allow the agent whenever possible to pay the smaller losses to the policyholder. After all, the agent is usually closest to the client, is familiar with the insurance contracts which the insured has, and normally has the earliest facts on the occurrence of the loss. The agent has, too, a prime interest in seeing that the consumer receives prompt and fair treatment in the loss payment. Satisfaction of the policyholder is important to the agent in terms of goodwill and continued business with the insured and his or her friends.

In *property* insurance many agents have the authority of their companies to settle a claim with the policyholder immediately. For smaller and un-complicated losses this is the most expedient and efficient way to pay claims. For example, local agents may be given permission by their companies to settle all losses of certain kinds up to a stated dollar amount. For a new agent or a small agent this authority may only extend up to $100. For larger and more seasoned agents the authority may extend to $500 or more, and in addition agents may be given responsibility for actually issuing checks in the name of their companies. The custody of such a checkbook, of course, must be carefully controlled by the company. An abnormal number of losses would occasion a review by the insurer to be sure that the agent was not being overly liberal in paying claims. For agents it is a valuable right which enables them to render prompt service to their policyholders with a minimum of paperwork.

Some of the kinds of losses where this practice is becoming more and more prevalent are fire, windstorm, medical payments under home and automobile contracts, and automobile collision and miscellaneous damage (to the insured's car).

In larger losses or losses which involve more complex adjusting methods, such as in *liability* insurance, it is necessary to provide specialized help to the agent and the insured. One of the four other types of adjusters will be used in such cases. This is reasonable because it is the duty of the insurer to see that losses are equitably paid. An agent with little legal background should not be permitted to attempt to settle liability claims, nor should one with little experience in adjusting an infrequent business interruption loss be given sole authority to determine the company's liability and amount of loss payment. The funds for loss payment are the prime responsibility of the insurer. A wrongful claim payment would be improper for the insurer, for the agent, for the policyholder, and for other policyholders whose rates may be raised in the future by careless or exaggerated claims payment.

In *life* insurance the agent is often directly involved in loss payment. The claims procedure for smaller contracts is a simple one—notice to the company and a death certificate are often all that is required before the policy amount can be paid. The life agent usually forwards the death notice and certificate to the insurer, and the check is issued by the company for delivery to the policyholder's beneficiary by the agent. Life insurers do not have the problem of determining the extent of loss payment that is common in property insurance losses, for the contract itself states the amount to be paid upon loss. An exception would be the extra payments for accidental death, which require legal investigation and definition in some cases. For the larger policies, various installment payment options in place of a lump-sum cash payment may need to be explained by the agent. In health insurance contracts, life agents may need and be required by their companies to use special personnel from their claims departments.

One of the most rewarding feelings for an agent is the personal satisfaction received as a result of actually seeing "insurance in action." It may be the disabled husband thanking the agent for having included disability income protection in health insurance which provides the family with steady income during a long period in which he cannot work. Or perhaps it's a dream home that can be built again on the ashes of a fire that otherwise would have caused the loss of a lifetime of savings. Many life insurance agents can point with quiet pride to families whose sons and daughters have grown up to attend college without financial hardship in spite of the unexpected early death of family breadwinners. Because agents see firsthand the value of insurance in such circumstances, the almost missionary zeal of some agents can be understood—and appreciated. This aspect of an agent's work—being able to see the results of a job well done—can make it one of the most satisfying of all careers.

Staff adjusters

The contact between local agents of property-liability insurers and the home office is maintained through special agents, state agents, or general agents. Among other functions, these representatives of the insurer often have jurisdiction over loss adjustments. Other insurer representatives who make adjustments are known as company or *staff adjusters*. In the casualty field in particular, they are usually employees who devote their entire time to loss settlements. Automobile claims lend themselves to the services of staff adjusters since in most instances only one insurer is concerned with such claims. Also, the volume of claims is such that companies have found it to their advantage to maintain claims offices staffed by specialists in the various lines they write. Some automobile insurers in larger cities maintain "drive-in" claims locations where immediate estimates and payments for damages are made.

The use of staff adjusters depends on the volume and kinds of business written in the territory in which the loss occurs. To support a full-time staff adjuster in a given area the insurer must have enough claims to be adjusted. Some companies use staff adjusters almost exclusively, while others are more apt to use the services of the other types of adjusters available.

Independent adjusters

Independent adjusters are experts who have made loss adjusting a business. Some have specialized in particular fields. Others possess a general knowledge and understanding of adjustment procedure and handle losses when it is impossible or inconvenient for the company representatives to give prompt attention. Some independent adjusters operate as individuals within a limited area; others have built up sizable organizations and extend their operations over a wide area; and still others accept assignments on a national basis. For example, Crawford and Company (Atlanta) has more than 3,000 employees and 500 branch offices. Several thousand independent adjusters are members of the National Association of Independent Insurance Adjusters. Its members are encouraged to participate in the educational program of the Insurance Institute of America leading toward professional examinations for the Associate in Claims (AIC) designation.

Independent adjusters work for the insurers who request their services. A typical use would be in automobile insurance where the insurer has only a small volume of business in a given area or where the policyholder has an accident while traveling there. It would be expensive and inefficient to send a staff adjuster from the home or branch office to settle the occasional claim which occurs in such areas. Instead, the insurer hires an independent adjuster to do the job. The independent adjuster often builds up a continuing working relationship with particular insurers, in addition to accepting infrequent adjusting assignments, from a larger number of insurers. The tremendous variety of claims situations and the goal of reaching loss payments equitable to both insurer and insured make the career of an independent adjuster a challenging one.

Adjustment bureaus

Becoming more and more important as factors in all fields of claim adjustment except life insurance are the *adjustment bureaus*. These are separate corporations, supported by many insurers that regularly use their services. Their sole business is claim adjustment, and they often have many branch offices. Bureau adjusters are highly trained and experienced men who devote their entire time to adjusting losses. Insurers look with favor upon the trend toward bureau adjustment, feeling that it tends toward an equitable treatment of all insureds and eliminates competition among adjusters and agents in building a reputation for generosity by excessive claim payments. Bureau adjusters aim to effect prompt and satisfactory adjustments with a minimum of controversy or litigation; on the other hand, they are equipped to cope with fraud or false claims.

One of the largest and best-known adjustment bureaus is the General Adjustment Bureau, which is very active in settling fire and windstorm losses, and more recently, automobile physical damage and other claims. The organization has a national headquarters in New York City and regional offices in New York, Atlanta, Dallas, Chicago, San Francisco, and Denver. Annually over 2 million losses are adjusted with less than 1 in 100,000 going to court. The General Adjustment Bureau has over 700 branch offices with more than 8,000 employees. One other large organization, the Underwriters Adjustment Company, has headquarters in Chicago and provides adjustment facilities for 13 states in the Midwest. Such large-scale adjustment bureaus are especially important in coordinating loss adjusters for the tremendous burden of thousands of claims within a few days after a major disaster. Many hundreds, for example, were sent to Louisiana and Texas to help handle the thousands of losses caused by Hurricane Betsy. With the increasing frequency of southeastern windstorms in the early autumn, the GAB has on the basis of modern hurricane warning systems sent adjusters to the Southeast in advance of the actual storms.

Public adjusters

As the name implies, *public adjusters* represent the public, in contrast to the adjusters who represent insurers. The public adjuster is retained *by the insured* to negotiate the loss settlement. Public adjusters offer their services, usually on a fee basis, using their expert insurance knowledge in estimating damages and effecting loss settlements. It is sometimes assumed that a staff adjuster is biased and will make borderline decisions to the advantage of the insurer. Such situations are the exception, for most insurers strive toward fair loss payments. Insureds who feel inadequate to approach such a problem of adjustment without assistance in representing their interests can turn the loss over to a public adjuster. Sometimes attorneys will be retained by the insured to perform a similar function.

In some states public adjusters are required to obtain a license from the insurance department of the state. An examination may be required, and the state licensing authority exercises control over the practices of the adjusters to the end that their operations be ethical. One reason why this is important is that public adjusters acts as agents for the insureds within the scope of their employment. If the public adjuster perpetrates a fraud in an attempt to get a generous adjustment then the policy is voided quite as much as if the fraud were perpetrated by the insured. To permit any other holding regarding the operations of a public adjuster would open wide the door to fraud. All that would be necessary to perpetrate a fraud upon the insurer would be the insured's complete delegation of the responsibility for adjusting a loss to a public adjuster whose acts might be later disavowed.

CLAIMS PROCEDURES

A general insurance text cannot give consideration to all the aspects of claims and adjustment procedures for all types of insurance. The following major types of claims will be discussed here: (1) fire, (2) liability, and (3) life. The examples are selected because of the significant differences of one class from the others and because of the importance of these three types of insurance to the average insurance purchaser. The student will also find other claims procedures discussed in sections of many later chapters. For example, the chapters on transportation insurance, workers' compensation, automobile insurance, and health insurance will provide additional contrasts for the study of claims methods.

Fire insurance losses

Rights and conditions.   The fire insurance contract imposes definite conditions upon the insured immediately upon the occurrrence of a loss. (See Chapter 17 for specific contract wording on "loss provisions." All of the post-loss provisions are conditions on the insured, rather than duties or obligations. However, the insurer may deny loss payment if these conditions are not met.

The purpose of *notice of loss* to the insurer is to convey the information that a loss has occurred, so that the insurer may take whatever steps it deems necessary to investigate the loss. The policy specifies written notice, but usually companies waive this provision and proceed with the adjustment after the insured notifies the agent in any manner. What constitutes immediate notice is subject to interpretation and is dependent upon the circumstances surrounding each case. The insured should exercise due diligence and forward the notice without unnecessary delay. If there is no reason to prevent it, notice should be given the day the loss occurs, or at least the following day. In one case, the policy was in a safe in the building that was burned and could not be obtained until 53 days after the fire; yet the notice was held sufficient. In another case, a notice given 14 days after a fire, unaccompanied by any circumstance excusing the delay, was held not to be immediate notice, and payment was denied. The penalty to the insured for lack of proper notice is severe, for the insurer can treat the contract as voidable on the ground that the insured has failed to meet an important condition of the policy.

The submission by the insured of a *proof of loss* is the second condition for loss payment. This document has to do with the knowledge and belief of the insured as to the time and origin of the fire, title to the property, the cash value of each item and the amount of loss, loans outstanding, other insurance, and the like. The proof of loss, unless waived, should be furnished to the insurer or its agent within 60 days after the termination of the fire. Blank forms designed to meet the requirements of the insurer are often used.

The proof of loss is a statement of fact concerning the property, the loss, and the insurance. Information is first necessary to indicate compliance with the policy terms and conditions. The next concern is then with values, a point of the utmost importance to all parties to the contract. The insurer is usually obligated to indemnify the insured to the extent of the *actual cash value* of the property destroyed or damaged, with deductions for depreciation. A limit is fixed by the cost of repairing or replacing the destroyed or damaged property within a reasonable time with material of like kind and quality. Proving the loss rests upon the insured, and this requires the ability to demonstrate the values of the property.

A misconception of some insureds is that after a fire the damaged property should not be touched until it is examined by the fire insurance adjusters. Insureds are under no obligation to leave the property undisturbed; on the contrary, they should do everything reasonable to *prevent further damage*. Insureds who fail to protect their property adequately from further loss after a fire cannot collect for the additional loss thus occasioned. For example, they may need to dry machinery to prevent rusting, board up windows, or provide temporary roof repairs to avoid further damage to the contents of a building.

The insured should make a complete *inventory* stating the quantity and cost of each article and the amount claimed as a loss. If the goods destroyed have an established open-market value, the quotations on the day of the fire, plus freight and handling charges, less discounts, form the basis of the valuation for adjustment purposes. In the case of a manufacturer, the production or acquisition cost serves as a basis. It is the insured's job to prepare the inventory, although the agent or adjuster often gives advice or helps in other ways to see that the inventory is complete.

In the event that an agreement on values lost cannot be reached, provision is made in the policy for an *appraisal precedure* which either party may demand. The number of cases in which appraisal proceedings are actually used is infinitesimally small. Many adjusters who have spent a lifetime in adjusting have never had a loss go to appraisal procedure, but the procedure is still of potential value to both parties to the contract where an honest difference of opinion exists. The insurer and the insured each select an appraiser, and these two appraisers select a third appraiser. Awards signed by two or three of the appraisers determine the amount of the loss. The finding is conclusive, and neither party can appeal from it, except on the ground of irregularity in the appraisal, such as fraud, mistake, or willful misconduct on the part of the appraisers.

Besides appraisal, when insureds have complied with all the conditions of their policies and still fail to effect a settlement, they may have recourse to *lawsuit* in the courts. In order that questions of liability may not accumulate against insurers and be revived at indefinite dates, the usual policy provides that "no suit or action on this policy, for the recovery of any claim, shall be sustainable in any court of law or equity unless commenced within twelve months next after the fire."

The fire insurance contract provides for two *options of settlement by the company*: (1) replacing or restoring the subject matter of the insurance to its former condition, or (2) taking all or any part of the property at the agreed or appraised value. If a company feels that it may rebuild the damaged property with like kind and quality at less cost than would be required to make a payment for damages, it may elect to do so. If the insurer elects to rebuild, the amount of damage recoverable for a breach is not thereafter limited to the amount of insurance. The option to repair or replace involves the insurer in the business of building construction, and it is very uncommon to exercise the option. When at all possible, insurers prefer to settle losses by a cash payment.

Under the second option the insurer may sometimes settle a loss by taking all or part of the property and paying its agreed or appraised value to the insured. This method is fairly common for damaged merchandise property, which the insurer turns over to a professional *salvage* company to be sold. The amount realized is credited to the insurers, who, in turn, pay the insured a total loss. However, the insured has no right to ask the insurer to take the property and salvage it. The policy specifically says that there can be no abandonment of the property by the insured to the insurer. Several salvage companies have repair facilities for drying, airing, sorting, and auctioning goods damaged by fire, smoke, or water. An example is the Underwriters Salvage Company of New York, with offices in more than 20 major cities.

Special problems.   In the event of a *total loss of merchandise in a business,* a physical inventory is, of course, impossible. The value of the destroyed property must be determined by the books and accounts of the insured. If the books are properly kept and inventories are accurately taken at stated periods, it is comparatively simple to compute the value of goods on hand at the time of the fire. To accomplish this, one must take an inventory as a starting point, add to this purchases made, and deduct sales. Since purchases are recorded on the basis of cost and sales income is recorded on the basis of selling price, it is essential to reduce the item of income from sales to a figure that will represent the cost of the items sold and not the selling price. The normal margin of profit, as a percentage of sales, is used to determine the cost of goods sold. An example follows:

Inventory calculation for statement of loss

Inventory of stock on hand at beginning of year (cost)		$1,000,000
Adjustment for depreciation		40,000
Actual value of stock at beginning of year		$ 960,000
Subsequent purchases		500,000
Total goods to be accounted for		$1,460,000
Sales $800,000		
Less profit (30%) $240,000		
Cost of goods sold $560,000	Deduct	$ 560,000
Value of stock on hand at time of fire		$ 900,000

The problem of determining value and loss or damage is more difficult for *buildings* or *machinery*. Because such fixed assets are designed for use over a long period of years, the problems of depreciation and obsolescence become factors of major importance. In relation to a fixed asset, *depreciation* has been defined as the inevitable decrease in value resulting from wear, tear, and the lapse of time. When the decrease in value is the outgrowth of an improvement in a manufacturing process or a discontinuance in the demand for the product manufactured, the loss is due to *obsolescence*. Arbitrary accounting charge-offs on the straight-line basis often are not or do not attempt to be an accurate measure of the value. A property built during a period of low construction costs might actually be growing *more* valuable each year as building costs advance; yet a straight-line depreciation of some arbitrary percentage, say 5 percent, would furnish a book value of less than cost. The actual value would be greater than cost in this case.

In recent years, the availability and use of *replacement value coverage*, particularly for buildings, has grown rapidly. For properties not more than 20 or 30 years old, insurers will today often write insurance that will pay full replacement cost without any deduction for depreciation. This avoids any problems of estimating depreciation to be subtracted in the loss payment. Insurance consumers should consider this coverage when it is available. Several insurers are also beginning to offer such coverage for insurance on contents and personal property.

Because of the difficulties involved in fixing a building value, a satisfactory and competent *appraisal* (an expert estimate of valuation—not the loss appraisal procedure mentioned earlier) may be needed. For any building of substantial value, an appraisal made by a reputable appraisal firm is a cost which the insured should be willing to accept in return for its importance in the event of a serious loss. The American Appraisal Company is an example of a company providing specialized appraisal services. For smaller buildings, the agent or insurer may help the insured without separate cost to appraise the value of the property. Values may be brought up to date with a table of price index trends for various types of construction, such as brick, frame, or steel.

When an adequate appraisal of buildings has been made by competent appraisers and has subsequently been kept up to date, the problem of valuation for *total loss* is not a difficult one. When no appraisal has been made, blueprints covering original building plans and subsequent additions, photographs, or building permits will generally help to fix the date of construction, the estimated depreciation, and the replacement cost. Several methods are used for fixing value when neither appraisal nor plans are available as a guide: the "discount method," based upon computing future earnings of the building on the basis of past experience, and the "square-foot method," based upon the estimated cost of other buildings of like construction.

In the event of *partial loss* to a building, the customary procedure is to obtain from a reliable contractor or builder an estimate of the cost to repair and replace the damaged property. Frequently, a builder representing the insured and another representing the insurer work together in making the estimate of loss. The policy does not undertake to replace old with new. Depreciation is, therefore, usually to be deducted from the replacement figure. Different parts of the building will be subjected to different depreciation figures, depending upon the age and the state of repair. Architect's fees do not represent a proper claim in minor losses, but for larger losses the fees represent part of the cost to repair or replace and may properly be included in the loss claimed.

Several other special problems[4] of fire insurance losses are discussed in Chapter 17. Special limitations on the insurer's liability are treated there, including the important problems of *contribution and apportionment* (where several contracts insure the same property), *coinsurance* requirements (to encourage insurance amounts reasonably close to total values of the property), and *nonconcurrence* (which involves conflicting provisions in different policies).

---

[4] Further details of property loss adjustments can be studied in Paul I. Thomas, *How to Estimate Building Losses and Construction Costs* (Englewood Cliffs, N.J.: Prentice-Hall, 1976); and Paul I. Thomas and Prentiss B. Reed, *Adjustment of Property Losses* (New York: McGraw-Hill Book Co., 1977).

Liability insurance losses

Differences from other losses.   The adjustment of liability claims differs from the adjustment of direct damage claims in that the *claimant is not the insured*. In representing the insurer, the adjuster is not dealing with a customer of the insurer, as is the case in settling the usual direct damage property loss.

A liability claim carries with it a basic element of conflict with respect to the claim because one person has caused someone else either (1) property damages or (2) personal injuries. Mental attitudes frequently intensify the degree of conflict. Different individuals have different approaches and attitudes toward a given situation. The owner of a new Cadillac might want a scratch on a fender to be removed at considerable expense. To another individual such a scratch is incidental, and that person would neither spend a substantial sum to repair the scratch nor expect an insurer to do so. Finally, a difference in the attitude of a claimant from that of a defendant regarding the extent of a personal injury is natural. Persons injured in accidents tend to exaggerate the nature and extent of the injury, while it is natural for the defendant to discount or minimize its importance.

Property damages.   The extent of a claim for *damage to property* is measured by the amount of the loss occasioned the property owner. The measure of loss is the difference in value between the property undamaged and the property in its damaged condition. While the cost of repair may serve as a measure of damage, there is no obligation to restore a property to its original condition if the cost for repair exceeds the value of the property before the damage. For example, an old automobile virtually demolished is worth a claim only for the value of the car before the accident, less its salvage value. Property damage liability claims must be differentiated from direct-loss insurance claims. A fire claim, for example, usually includes only payment for the direct damage to the property unless additional coverage is purchased to provide for the indirect results of the loss of use of the property, such as loss of profits or rents. In property damage liability claims, however, the loss of use may be included. The rental cost of a similar automobile, for instance, would be included in a liability claim against the person causing damage serious enough to prevent the use of an automobile for some time.

Personal injuries.   Determining an adequate amount of compensation for a *personal injury* is not a simple process.[5] This statement is supported by the number of verdicts in widely different amounts for seemingly identical injuries. In no other area of loss adjustment will the measure of damages be influenced to such a large degree by the fallibilities and prejudices that are

---

[5] Many legal references would indicate this difficulty, and authors have written many pages on the subject. For example, see Corydon T. Johns, *An Introduction to Liability Claims Adjusting,* 2d ed. (Cincinnati: National Underwriter Co., 1972); and James H. Donaldson, *Casualty Claim Practice* (Homewood, Ill.: Richard D. Irwin, 1976).

characteristic of human nature. The difficulties increase when a jury or a judge attempts to assign a monetary value to a severe personal injury. A disabling injury is a more severe financial loss to a wage earner than to a housewife. Who can measure the loss of the housewife's love and care of small children? Who will differentiate with respect to the amount of pain suffered? What impact will social position, financial circumstances, and reputation of the claimant have upon the amount of the settlement? Finally, what will be the effect of the ability, resourcefulness, forensic talents, and persuasiveness of the claimant's attorney if the case goes to trial? All of these factors must be weighed by the adjuster in an attempt to reach a settlement that can be conscientiously recommended to the insurer.

Some liability contracts use the words *bodily injury* instead of *personal injury*. These terms are not identical in the coverage they may provide. The broader coverage is personal injury, which may include bodily harm to others, as well as other types of harm, such as psychic trauma. This may occur without any actual physical injury.

Minor injuries that involve primarily a loss of time are not too difficult to handle. The same is true with respect to medical bills and hospital expenses, if any. The area of uncertainty in such cases involves suffering and inconvenience. These cases are settled on the basis of consideration given to wages lost or expected to be lost because of the injury, the age of the injured person, the number of dependents, the amount of medical care expense, the nature of the injury, and the extent of pain suffered. For a person suffering from a broken leg, for example, medical expenses and income lost, plus a settlement for suffering, are the usual measures of damages.

The situation is quite different with more serious injuries. In the case of fatality some states limit recovery by statute. Where there is a statutory limitation for death, the law may specify "instantaneous death." If the injured party is not killed instantaneously, claim may be made for an additional amount for medical expenses, for loss of wages before death, and for "conscious suffering," depending upon the magnitude of the injury and the length of time. When the injured party lives and suffers permanent injury, the problem of damages becomes increasingly complex. In some low-verdict areas the judgments vary substantially from those of high-verdict areas.

In recent years, many insurers have adopted procedures to reduce the time and cost of personal injury cases. One such method is to make an "advance payment" to the claimant in situations where liability is quite evident. The amount is deducted from the final settlement. This method has the advantage of lessening financial hardship to the injured claimant and his or her family and of permitting the best medical and rehabilitation treatment immediately. It also enables better relations to be maintained between the claimant and the insurer during the sometimes long period of several years before final settlement.

Steps in the claim process. Following an accident that may involve a liability claim, *notice* should be given the insurance company as promptly as possible, whether insureds feel themselves to be liable or not. Insurers have printed forms indicating the nature of the data the insured will be expected to acquire. Whether or not injured persons received first aid or medical attention is significant information, and the name of the attending physician and hospital should appear in the report. The name and address of all witnesses are required. If an automobile is involved, the name and address of the owner and driver, the driver's license number, and the car license number should be taken. It is important to note the exact location of the accident and weather conditions. A detailed sketch should show the relative positions of the cars just before and after the collision. In complying with the state requirements for reporting accidents, insureds should make duplicate copies of any written forms or reports and hold them for the insurance adjuster.

Liability policies vest much control of claims and litigation arising out of them with the insurer. In very clear language it is provided that the insured shall not admit or voluntarily assume any liability, offer to settle any claim, or incur any expense without the written consent of the insurer. An exception to this requirement may permit the insured to provide immediate medical and surgical relief that appears to be imperative at the time of the accident. Even in such an instance, insureds must admit no liability. Although they believe themselves to be liable, the interpretation of the law may be different than they think. An admission of liability by insureds can jeopardize both insurers' right of "subrogation" against others and protection under the policy for the insureds. Basic control of settlement should remain with the party that has the most effective legal resources and that is to pay the indemnity—namely, the insurer. If the insurer entrusted the matter of making settlements to its numerous policyholders, it would have a precarious existence indeed.

When the report of an accident involving a claim reaches the insurer and coverage is verified, company representatives will conduct an *investigation* to determine whether there was, in fact, negligence and whether the negligence was the proximate cause of the damage. A police report, if available, will be obtained. All pertinent facts are secured promptly from the insured, and then contact with claimants is made immediately. Witnesses are interviewed, and oftentimes written or taped statements are taken. A factual statement in simple, straightforward terms is the goal.[6]

The summary report prepared by the adjuster will contain all pertinent information and reach a conclusion as to liability. It will then appraise the nature of the injuries or property damage. In the case of personal injuries a settlement value is assigned in an amount which in the adjuster's opinion

---

[6] Here are a few classic examples of policyholder statements that fell short of this objective: "To avoid a collision, I ran into the other car"; "I collided with a stationary bus coming the other way"; "I consider that neither vehicle was to blame, but if either was to blame, it was the other one"; and "I bumped into a lamppost which was obscured by a pedestrian."

would be a proper settlement from the point of view of the insurer and the insured. Such an evaluation does not undertake to establish a "bargain" figure for the insurer, but rather it establishes a reasonable figure that would enable payment without suit. Any points that will help to bring the case to a conclusion, such as the attitude of the claimants or their attorneys, are mentioned.

Although the insurer controls an adjustment by determining the action to be taken concerning an offer of compromise, the insurer is obligated to give as much consideration to the interests of the insured as it does to its own. The insuring agreement obligates the insurer to defend any suit against the insured with respect to the perils covered, even if such suit is groundless, false, or fraudulent. The insurer may elect to effect a settlement within the policy limits; otherwise it must assume the defense of the insured. A serious question occasionally develops when the insurer receives an *offer to settle within the policy limits* from the claimant. The position of the insurer becomes a precarious one when it refuses such an offer of settlement and elects to go to trial. If a judgment is then awarded against the insured in an amount in excess of the policy limits, the insured may argue that the loss should have been adjusted on the basis of the earlier favorable offer and may claim that the insurer should pay the full amount of the trial award. If the conduct of the insurer is such that the insured suffers (1) because of *negligence* or (2) *bad faith,* then the insurer may be held liable for the full amount of damages without regard to policy limits. These two rules are matters of grave concern to insurers because policy limits are virtually wiped out by their operation.[7] There is protection for the insured since the insurer cannot abandon or neglect a defense or deliberately settle a claim in its own interest at the expense of the insured except at its own peril. On the other hand, the insurer should, and can, resist any settlement that it feels is excessive. It must resist fraud, and it can be aided in this effort by organizations such as the Insurance Crime Prevention Institute.

Following an accident that results in a claim for damages, the responsibility of the insureds does not cease when they turn the adjustment over to the insurer. The *cooperation clause* obligates the insured to render full assistance in the settlement or adjustment of a suit and prohibits the insured from admitting or assuming liability. The clause is held to be a material condition,

---

[7] An interesting California case illustrates the potential problem. In *Crisci* v. *Security Insurance Co.* (266 A.C. 435; 58 Cal. Reptr. 13; 426 P. 2d 173 [1967]), an insured was sued under a liability contract for an injury on her premises. The claimant offered twice to settle for less than the $10,000 policy limit, but the insurer refused. Judgment after trial, was for $91,000! The insured sued the insurer and was awarded $91,000, plus $25,000 for mental distress and grief in losing her property to pay the judgment. The court viewed with favor the idea that any insurer refusing to settle within the policy limits should be absolutely liable for the final judgment. This extreme view is debatable, and contrary to the more common rules of liability by the insurer only if the larger verdict results from the insurer's negligence or bad faith. Normal mistakes of poor judgment by the insurer would not alone create liability.

and if the insured fails to comply with its requirements, the contract may be voidable. Insureds may feel that it is the responsibility of the insurer to make the investigation. They may feel sorry for the claimant. However, any willful obstruction on the part of insureds to the defense of the insurer violates the cooperation clause. Insureds must give full and truthful accounts of all the circumstances, and they must attend court and testify to these facts as witnesses if requested to do so.

When liability has been established and a value placed on a claim, insurers prefer to make a prompt *settlement*. Although an adjuster may refuse a claim that is unreasonable, litigation is avoided if possible. Nothing is to be gained by bringing a case to trial that can be settled reasonably in any other way, and the nearer a case comes to litigation, the more expensive it becomes. Much of the cost must be borne out of the insured's settlement, and in many cases the fees of the plaintiff's attorney are a percentage of the settlement. Thirty percent or more is very common. Court costs, assessed by the court on either or both parties, may be in addition to this figure. Most cases, therefore, are settled as a result of negotiations between the claimant and the insurance adjuster. For an increasing number of claims, *arbitration* may be used to settle losses under a few thousand dollars.

Not all liability claims are settled for their estimated value. Where there is definite liability and the amount of the claim does not seem to be too excessive, the insurer may elect to pay rather than assume the uncertainties of litigation and additional costs. There are other situations in which liability is doubtful and the insurer may be able to defeat the claimant's suit against the insured. Here again the question of cost presents itself. If a case of this kind can be settled for a reasonable sum, the insurer may prefer to close the case with such a settlement. Finally, there are cases of this kind that on the basis of the insurer's investigation would indicate no liability. However, because of the limitations of witnesses, the possibility of an unsympathetic jury or a persuasive opposing attorney, and the trend of verdicts in the jurisdiction, discretion may be the better part of valor. A reasonable settlement is to be preferred to the risk of an excessive verdict resulting from a trial.

It is apparent that a loss may be settled at any one of several stages. The claims adjuster may settle following the investigation. Failure to settle may result in suit. After a suit is filed, the case may be settled before trial, sometimes "on the courthouse steps." If the case goes to trial, which only a few percent of all claims do, settlement will be based upon the verdict except where an appeal is entered. Every effort should be made, and usually is, to effect a satisfactory adjustment at the earliest possible stage of the claim.

Life insurance losses

The settlement of life claims is usually taken care of by the life insurance agent. Unlike other fields of insurance, for life insurance there is no specialized claims adjuster. The definiteness of the death peril and the amount of insurance payable make it possible for the agent to arrange for the payment from the insurer. In the unusual situation where a claim is questioned, the law department and the claims department of the insurer will cooperate to provide the necessary legal advice.

Since life insurance in its simplest form pays a lump sum (called a "face value") upon the death of the insured, many claims are death claims. Endowment contracts and annuities may provide an income benefit upon the survival of the insured to a fixed date or age. The choice as to the method of payment may be made by the insured, or by the beneficiary if the insured has not made a choice. Technically, the life insurance policy does not provide for payment upon death but rather for payment upon submission of *proof of death* to the insurer. This notice may be given by a beneficiary or the legal representative of the insured. Many claims are paid within a few days or weeks.

Life insurance contracts provide that the policy shall be *incontestable* by the insurer after a certain designated period during the lifetime of the insured, usually two years. The clause gives the company time to investigate any factors bearing on the application, and at the same time it results in greater certainty to insured and beneficiary after the two-year period. There are some exceptions, but in most cases the insurer is prevented from raising defenses later that would be hard for policyholders or their beneficiaries to disprove, such as those based upon misrepresentation or fraud. For example, if any applicant for insurance secures a policy and dies a year later, and it can be shown that the applicant was suffering from cancer but sent a substitute to pass the medical examination, there would be no obligation to make payment. Misstatements of age are treated in a separate clause; the contract is not voidable in such cases, but is corrected to provide benefits for the true age of the insured.

In determining the liability of the insurer for a death claim under a life insurance policy, the question of whether or not the insured committed *suicide* may upon occasion become important. The policy provides for a return of premiums paid in the event of self-destruction within a period of a year or in some instances within two years. If suicide is suspected but cannot be proved, there is a presumption against it. This means that if the life insurance company contests the payment of a policy on the basis of suicide, it must establish the fact by a preponderance of evidence so that no other reasonable inference may be drawn from the circumstances.

In cases where policies provide that if the insured dies as a result of *accidental death,* double (or sometimes more) the face of the policy is to be paid the beneficiaries, proof must be submitted that the death was accidental. The question of accidental death is often surrounded by uncertainty, arising out of court decisions and the different wording of the various insurance contracts themselves.[8] Death by accidental means must usually be "independent of all other causes," with no liability if death is due directly or indirectly to disease or bodily or mental infirmities. The final resort for determination is a jury.

It is a simple matter if the policy provides for a distribution under lump-sum payment or one of the *settlement options*. If, however, the insured has not chosen a settlement option, then the beneficiary may choose the settlement option, and the settlement of the claim will take on additional complications. For larger policies, this may involve a completely planned settlement, utilizing the policy proceeds for cash, interest, installments, or life income payments. An agreement with the beneficiary following the death of the insured may utilize one or more of the settlement options to provide for differing needs, subject to the consent and approval of the insurance company. Not only may options be combined, but the agreement may include the power to change from one option to another, the privilege of increasing or decreasing installment payments, and withdrawal privileges. In making these choices in a planned settlement option, the life insurance agent can be of substantial service to the purchasers and beneficiaries of life insurance.

FOR REVIEW AND DISCUSSION

1. How would you describe the purposes which policyholder and insurer should have in effecting a loss payment under an insurance contract?

2. "Losses are the reason for insurance," says Percy Pessimist. "Perhaps true," says Oliver Optimist, "but that's not why I buy my insurance." With which of these persons would you side in an argument over the purposes of insurance, and why?

3. Who adjusts insurance losses? Why are different types of adjusters used in the various fields of insurance? Include reference to the major advantages of an insurer using different types of adjusters.

4. The agent's authority to settle losses directly with the insured varies greatly. What factors are involved in this disparity?

5. Mr. Rogers owns a warehouse in which musical instruments are stored. A fire occurs, burning a hole in the roof. He advises his employees to touch nothing until the adjusters arrive. Is this good advice? Explain.

6. In adjusting a fire insurance loss, it is necessary to determine "the actual cash value of the property at the time of loss." How is this done?

7. Compare the special problems of loss payment in fire, liability, and life insurance. Rank these three types of insurance in terms of the difficulty of loss adjustment, and explain your order of ranking.

---

[8] In *Landress* v. *Phoenix Mutual Life Insurance Company* (291 U.S. 491), Mr. Justice Cardozo referred to accident insurance law as the "Serbonium bog." The reference from Milton's *Paradise Lost* (book 2, line 592) reads, "A gulf profound as that Serbonium bog. Betwixt Domiata and Mount Casius old, Where armies whole have sunk."

8. Under the fire insurance contract, what conditions are placed on the insured after a loss has occurred?

9. Are valuation problems in a fire insurance loss different for buildings, merchandise, and other types of property? Explain how the insured can reduce these problems.

10. What options does an insurer have in settling a fire insurance loss? Explain any preferences that the insurer will usually have.

11. Why are loss payments under liability insurance contracts usually under the control of the insurer rather than the insured? Does this mean that the policyholder has nothing to do in regard to a liability claim?

12. X brought action against Y, an insured, for personal injuries. X offered to settle for a sum that was within the policy limits of $10,000. The insurer refused the offer, allowed the case to go to trial, and the claimant obtained a verdict of $15,000. Why might the insurer be liable for the amount in excess of the policy limits?

13. Why are liability insurance losses, as opposed to property insurance losses, more difficult to settle? As opposed to life insurance losses?

14. Assume that your friend Carl has had an automobile accident. He believes he was responsible, but he does not want to tell his insurer about it because he has a good driving record. The accident only involved a dented fender and a few minor bumps to the occupants of the other car. (*a*) What advice and procedure do you recommend? (*b*) If Carl was injured but not at fault for the accident, what advice do you offer him?

15. The loss payment function of insurers is carried out by many different persons. Discuss the various career opportunities that adjusting losses may provide for college students.

Chapter 8

Concepts considered in Chapter 8—Insurance regulation

Insurance regulation is more extensive than regulation for many other businesses, particularly regulation by the states.

Why insurance regulation is needed can be seen from its purpose of protecting the public and insureds in what is basically a *long-term, complex, future, financial promise* contract.

Methods of insurance regulation are *two*:

Self-regulation of insurance is considerable but sometimes ineffective.

Government regulation of insurance involves *three* types:

Government legislation, primarily *state laws,* is based upon Public Law 15 which followed the famous SEUA decision in 1944.

Administrative action is very important, with the *insurance commissioner* in each state exercising broad enforcement powers of licensing and examination of companies and agents in an *insurance department.*

Court action helps interpret the insurance laws or *codes.*

Kinds of insurance regulation by the states include the birth, life and death of an insurer.

Formation and licensing of insurers require *incorporation,* meeting minimum *financial requirements,* and other standards.

Insurer operations are supervised as to—

Contracts and forms, with *basic wording* approval for some (but not all) kinds of insurance required by the state insurance department.

Rates are controlled to some extent in *fire* and *auto* insurance.

Expense limitations are placed upon *life* insurance in some states.

Reserves are required: *legal* reserves for life insurance, and *unearned premium* and *loss* reserves for property-liability insurance.

Asset and surplus values are watched closely.

Investments are limited to the safest securities for most assets of life insurers; more lenient rules apply to property-liability insurers.

Agents' licensing and trade practices aim at qualified, honest, and fair treatment of policyholders.

Taxation of insurance is an important (more than $2 billion) revenue producer for the states through a special *premium tax.*

Rehabilitation and liquidation of insurers are supervised carefully.

Some current regulatory issues include: *insurer guaranty funds, rate regulation, federal versus state regulation,* and *other issues.*

Insurance regulation

If one looks at any of the major changes in business today—products, pricing, marketing methods, occupational safety, mergers, equal employment opportunities,—which one is *not* very closely related to regulation of how these changes are occurring? Practically none; and the same observation applies to insurance!

All forms of private business enterprise have some regulation of their activities, either by self-imposed rules and customs or by specific regulations of government. Sometimes the government provides extensive controls for business organizations, including almost every phase of the operations from creation to liquidation. For other businesses there is minimum government regulation, perhaps only for the purposes of providing necessary tax information. The purpose of this chapter is to explain *why* and *how* the business of insurance is regulated.

WHY INSURANCE REGULATION IS NEEDED

The general purpose of insurance regulation is to protect the public against insolvency or unfair treatment by insurers. From the state's viewpoint, regulation is also important as a revenue producer through state taxes on insurance premiums.

The insurance business is among the types of private enterprise subject to much government regulation. It is generally classed as a business which is "affected with a *public interest*." This characteristic is the reason why many forms of government supervision[1] of insurance are deemed necessary. Although competition is an effective regulator for some businesses, in insurance *uncontrolled* competition would work a hardship upon the buyers of insurance, most of whom do not understand insurance contracts. Much of the insurance written is to protect third parties who have not participated in making the contracts. The value of the contracts depends upon the ability of the insurers to fulfill their promises to the public, sometimes many years after the issuance of a policy. Ability to carry out the provisions of contracts depends upon many factors, including the efficient operation of the insurer, the selec-

---

[1] Used here as a synonym for regulation, which is sometimes thought to have a stronger connotation of active direction.

tion of satisfactory risks, the determination of proper premium rates, and the wise investment of adequate reserves. Consequently, the needed integrity and *long-range financial stability* of insurers place insurance in an area which has traditionally been considered appropriate for government regulation.

The question of how much regulation is necessary is a more difficult one. Insurance falls into the category of heavily regulated business but does not belong in the same class as banks and public utilities, which are examples of the most complete public regulation requirements. Many banks are subject to federal charters, whereas insurers are not.[2] Unlike insurance companies,[3] public utilities have close government control of their organization (under "certificates of necessity"), their complete rate schedules, and their maximum profit return in relation to invested capital. The extent of regulation of insurance is reviewed in succeeding sections of this chapter by descriptions of the major methods and kinds of insurance regulation.

METHODS OF INSURANCE REGULATION

The *state* government is undoubtedly most important in the regulation of insurance. Before considering this and other phases of government insurance regulation, however, it is logical to summarize the self-regulation of insurance.

Self-regulation of insurance

To the extent that a business provides adequate self-regulation for itself, government regulation is often unnecessary, or at least diminished in some degree. In insurance it is not realistic to think that the entire job of regulation can be done by internal, as opposed to external, methods of supervision. C. A. Kulp points out that the insurance business does discipline itself more than most persons realize:

> The extent of self-regulation is very considerable. No business has more incentive to cooperative effort or more to lose by failure to cooperate . . . insurers are given wider legal leeway in cooperative action than other businesses . . . The privilege and the responsibility of cooperative action do not preclude public regulation . . .[4]

---

[2] Though such charters have been advocated for parts of the business, such as interstate life insurer charters on a voluntary basis. Senate committees have also proposed mandatory federal charters for auto insurance several times since the late 1960s. The Brooke Bill in 1977 focused attention on such charters in insurance.

[3] All insurers are not technically "companies" or corporations, but the use here refers to all private insurers. *Social* insurance systems such as are discussed in Chapters 15 and 28 might be considered much closer to the concept of a public utility, and their regulation and administration are correspondingly more akin to government regulation of public utilities.

[4] C. A. Kulp, *Casualty Insurance* (New York: Ronald Press Co., 1956), pp. 533–34. This passage does not appear in the Kulp-Hall fourth edition of 1968.

There are many insurer and trade association groups that exercise considerable control or provide advice in regard to each of the major functions of insurance. For example, forms and rates for many fire, automobile, liability, and other types of insurance are filed by the Insurance Services Office on behalf of individual member companies for approval by the state insurance departments. This saves much duplication and reduces costs. In claims administration, the General Adjustment Bureau and other associations handle losses for insurers, so that several insurers involved in the same losses do not need to provide separate loss investigation and payment services. Many insurers cooperate with one another in coordinating loss prevention; examples include the Insurance Institute for Highway Safety, the National Auto Theft Bureau, the Insurance Crime Prevention Institute, and Underwriters' Laboratories. Marketing activities are regulated by rules applying to members of such organizations as the National Association of Insurance Brokers, the Independent Insurance Agents Association of America, and the National Association of Insurance Women. Research is enhanced by insurers' joint efforts in the Life Insurance Marketing and Research Association and the Society of Insurance Research. Better public relations and legislation are promoted by the American Council of Life Insurance, the Insurance Information Institute, and the Risk and Insurance Management Society.[5] In improving insurance education and setting standards for professional courses and designations the following organizations are important: the American Academy of Actuaries, the American College, the American Institute for Property and Liability Underwriters (and the related Insurance Institute of America), the Life Office Management Association, and the Life Underwriter Training Council. Teachers of insurance and other industry personnel exchange much valuable information through meetings and publications of the American Risk and Insurance Association and the Insurance Company Education Directors Society.

Many insurers and these types of organizations supply many representatives directly to industry committees that tackle the major problems of insurance. Oftentimes these industry committees work in conjunction with government regulatory bodies to draft legislation, coordinate programs, and offer constructive aid to the formulation of action designed to improve both self-regulation and public regulation of insurance. For example, the National Association of Life Underwriters (NALU) has sponsored legislation through its state organizations (for implementation in state legislative bodies) to control the practices of agents in replacing one life insurance contract with a new one. This legislation would prohibit "twisting" without adequate written comparisons of the new and old policies.

In evaluating the success of self-regulation in insurance, it is important to

---

[5] Some organizations function in several types of self-regulation activities. RIMS, for example, is active in education, research, public relations, and the promotion of legislation on behalf of its members.

mention that widespread differences exist between the United States and other countries. Extremely different methods and results may be found in particular lines or classes of insurance, or in the various states. Self-regulation is no panacea; it works extremely well in some parts of insurance, while in others it is disappointingly ineffective. Difficult areas for self-regulation include many aspects of insurance which are closely related to competition, such as regulation of production costs, commissions, advertising, and rates.

In some foreign countries, such as England and the Netherlands, self-regulation has worked well. So little government regulation exists in England that this general comment has been heard: "In England, insurers may do anything, the only requirement being that they publicize what they are doing!" Still, cooperative action of the insurers has succeeded in achieving high standards of financial solvency and fair treatment to policyholders. The reasons attributed to the excellent success of self-regulation in England include the philosophy, attitudes, and traditions of English insurers, as well as their smaller number and size. Even the Swiss, the epitome of democracy and freedom, have a proverb which says: "Anything that is not prohibited ought at least to be regulated!" Other countries, such as West Germany and the Scandinavian nations, follow the strictest patterns of governmental regulation of insurance, including approval procedures for most forms, commissions, and rates. The United States seems to fall between the extremes. Self-regulation is relied upon much more in the United States than in West Germany, but much less than in England.

As a review of this section on self-regulation and as an introduction to the next section on governmental regulation, see Figure 8–1, which summarizes the methods of insurance regulation.

Government regulation of insurance

Three basic methods of providing insurance regulation are available to government: (1) legislation, (2) administrative action, and (3) court action. Corresponding to the three main branches of the government, each of these methods is significant in the supervision of insurance. Legislation is the foundation of insurance regulations, for it creates the insurance laws. The insurance laws of each state are often combined in what is known as an *insurance code*,[6] and these codes are of primary importance. Administrative action is also very important, as the application and enforcement of insurance laws are left in the hands of the insurance *superintendent or commissioner* in each state. Court action is of lesser importance, but it has great value in regulation because of its ever-present potential effect in providing detailed interpretations of troublesome parts of the law.

---

[6] The insurance code for an individual state may be bound in a volume which today often exceeds several hundred pages.

Figure 8–1. Methods of insurance regulation

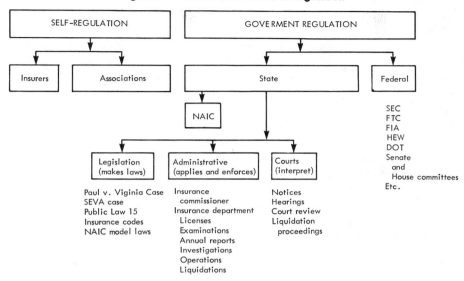

Government legislation. The regulation of the insurance business *by the states* was well established by the late 1800s and continues today as the predominant form of regulation. The practice is based upon a series of court decisions, and it has been continued in the face of some contention that because of the number of jurisdictions, insurance might better be regulated by the federal government. The classic case is *Paul* v. *Virginia,* in which the United States Supreme Court decided in 1868 that insurance "is *not* a transaction of commerce" and thus can be neither interstate commerce nor subject to federal regulation.[7] Until 1944, a period of 75 years, the Paul decision was upheld by the Supreme Court.

In 1941, complaints were made to the Department of Justice that certain insurance company practices were in violation of the Sherman Antitrust Act. As a result a momentous four-to-three decision was handed down in 1944 by the U.S. Supreme Court before one of its largest audiences in history. This case, *United States* v. *South-Eastern Underwriters Association et al.,*[8] now known to the legal profession and to the insurance business as the SEUA *case,* held that insurance *is* commerce. Thus, because of its interstate nature

---

[7] Today it is difficult to rationalize such a decision, but in 1868 it was understandable, as the now-famous decision stated: "Issuing a policy of insurance is not a transaction of commerce. They are not commodities to be shipped or forwarded from one state to another and then put up for sale. . . . Such contracts are not interstate transactions, though the parties may be domiciled in different states. They are, then, local transactions and are governed by local law" (*Paul* v. *Virginia,* 231 U.S. 495).

[8] 64 U.S. 1162.

it would often be subject to federal regulation. As a matter of practice, because of delegation of authority by Congress, the regulation of the business of insurance remains a state function.

The specific delegation to the states of the power to regulate insurance occurred with the passage of *Public Law 15* in 1945.[9] Congress made the Sherman Act, the Clayton Act, and the Federal Trade Commission Act applicable to the business of insurance after January 1, 1948, "to the extent that such business is not regulated by state law." In other words, jurisdiction for regulating interstate insurance was left with the individual states as it had been for many years, but the important proviso was added that would permit the federal government to take over insurance regulation whenever the state regulation became inadequate.

The specific implications of this rather general requirement have not been fully settled, though most cases indicate that federal jurisdiction will not usurp the states' powers as long as legislative action to provide insurance supervision has been taken.[10] Most states increased their insurance regulation heavily in laws passed as a result of the SEUA decision and Public Law 15, and they have continued their efforts to retain the power to supervise insurance. Investigations totaling thousands of pages of testimony have been carried out by the Senate Antitrust and Monopoly Subcommittee. Alleged inadequacies in state insurance laws have been pointed out, but federal legislation has not taken over any significant part of state regulation of insurance. Targets for Senate and House investigations have been automobile insurance (particularly substandard or high-risk insurers), the credit life insurance field, and insurance activities of bank holding companies. More recently, insurer solvency funds, product liability, and automobile no-fault plans have been topics for federal hearings.

Thus, the development of insurance regulation by the states has had a colorful history. Interesting details on some of its other landmarks, such as the Armstrong Investigation of 1905, the Merritt Committee Investigation of 1911, the Temporary National Economic Committee studies in 1939–41, and investigations of health insurance practices in 1910 and 1951–58, are contained in other volumes.[11]

In summary, the regulation of insurance by governmental legislation has been found to be almost completely a matter of insurance laws passed by the

---

[9] Also known as the McCarran-Ferguson Law, C 20, 79th Cong., 1st sess. For those students wishing to have an excuse for a birthday party in its honor, the law was passed on March 4, 1945. Members of the Ohio State University Alpha chapter of Gamma Iota Sigma (national insurance fraternity) ingeniously did so in 1977.

[10] *FTC* v. *National Casualty Company* (1958) and *FTC* v. *Travelers Health Association* (1959). The first serious effort in many years to advocate a repeal of the McCarran-Ferguson Law occurred in 1977, with hearings conducted by the House Judiciary Committee.

[11] Including appendix I of the classic reference: Edwin W. Patterson, *The Insurance Commissioner in the United States* (Cambridge, Mass.: Harvard University Press, 1927).

individual states. The state insurance codes have the distinct disadvantage of lacking uniformity. The critics of state regulation emphasize the duplication, complexity, and inefficiency that may result from nonuniformity. With increasing mobility, more uniformity of state laws is needed. However, advocates of federal regulation for insurance must provide much stronger arguments than just simplicity and economics, for today the political and social repercussions of any trend away from states' rights are overwhelming.[12] The taxes and fees (see later section on taxation) paid by insurers to the states in the annual amount of more than $2 *billion* in 1977 are stark evidence of the stakes involved. Legal precedent to date has firmly established for the individual states the regulatory responsibility for insurance and its benefits in tax revenue. (See later section of this chapter on regulatory issues.)

Administrative action. The broad powers which the *insurance commissioner*[13] of each state possesses are the key to the enforcement of insurance laws by the states. The administrative powers of the commissioners are derived from statutes which create the office. Usually these statutes are not very detailed in defining the authority and responsibility of the commissioner. The many thousands of bills and laws that today concern insurance matters and the general increased reliance on administrative law have made the position of commissioner increasingly important in state government. The commissioner's wide authority extends from the licensing of insurers and agents to requiring annual reports from the insurers to approving forms and rates (in some but not all lines of insurance) and investigating complaints of many kinds.

In most states the insurance commissioner is *appointed* by the governor and is a member of the governor's cabinet. The logic of this method of choosing the head insurance regulatory official is that the governor is ultimately responsible for the business success of his or her term of office and therefore should be able to appoint a person to carry out this responsibility. The prime disadvantage of this message is that political influence may be asserted on the commissioner's decisions. The short tenure of appointed commissioners, averaging two to three years, is also bad. In about ten states where the job of insurance commissioner is an *elective* office, the disadvantageous situation of a short term in authority is also complicated by the vagaries of voter appeal. One wonders whether the electorate could choose a person of the necessary high caliber and integrity with any better measure of success than appointments by the governors have produced. The dilemma of obtaining better commissioners and longer terms of office seems unavoidably tied to the political party system of our governmental system. Some observers, though criticizing

---

[12] Spencer L. Kimball, *Essays on Insurance Regulation* (Ann Arbor, Mich.: 1966), pp. 15 and 57.

[13] A large majority of the states use this title or "commissioner of insurance"; about eight "director of insurance"; and four "superintendent of insurance." *Best's Insurance Reports—Property-Liability—1977* (New York: A. M. Best Co.), p. viii.

the perhaps too broad powers and political selection of the insurance commissioner, marvel at the handicaps which are often overcome by generally
low-paid insurance commissioners. Others criticize the system as unworkable.

The insurance *department* with which most insurance commissioners carry
out their duties may vary from a few persons in some of the smaller states to
about 800 employees in such a state as New York. Approximately 15 states
each have more than 100 employees, including company examiners. Many
departments have existed since the 1850s. The New York Insurance Department has been in operation for over 100 years.

Its competent personnel have been responsible for an excellent record of
supervision in that state and for a vast influence upon insurance regulation in
many other states that have relied upon New York as a guide for their insurance legislation and administrative action. Also of importance is the fact
that many New York laws apply to *all* insurers licensed there, including those
domiciled in other states. This is important in creating uniformity in regulations among many states, and has become known as the *Appleton Rule*.

The major powers of the insurance commissioner have been mentioned as
licensing, examination, and investigation. After following the required incor-
portion procedure if it is a domestic organization, each insurer in the state
must be *licensed* for the lines of business it plans to write. The commissioner
has broad interpretative powers in deciding whether or not an insurer is qualified, financially and otherwise, to operate in the state. After issuance, licenses
are usually renewable on an annual basis. The insurance commissioner has
considerable power to refuse to issue a renewal license as well as the power
of suspension or revocation. Examinations are also conducted which determine the issuance of insurance agents' or brokers' licenses by the insurance
department.

The *examination of insurers* once they have been licensed is also an important task of the commissioner. The continued solvency of insurers is the
major objective of such detailed examinations, which are conducted according
to law at intervals of from three to five years. The checking of assets, liabilities, and reserves is part of this procedure, as is the review of almost all
underwriting, investment, and claim practices of the insurer. A zone system
is used in cooperation with the National Association of Insurance Commissioners (NAIC) to avoid unnecessary duplicate examination by many states.
In this way the examination of insurers licensed in many states is standardized
and simplified, and the results of the regular zone examination are accepted
by all states in which the insurer does business. In the intervening years between complete examinations of insurers, every state requires the filing of an
annual statement with the insurance commissioner. This is a report of current
financial conditions and of changes which have occurred during the year. A
standard NAIC form is used which for most details provides uniformity of
the information requested in the statement. These annual statements are
available to the public in the state insurance department offices.

The National Association of Insurance Commissioners, which celebrated its centennial in 1971, is a voluntary association of the top insurance administrator from each state. It is important not only for the zone examination procedures, but also for its influence through the commissioners on uniformity of insurance laws in the various states. Recommendations and *model laws* are studied by its committees and discussed at semiannual meetings. The position of the commissioners has aided to some extent in the adoption of such suggestions by the states. However, major criticism has been aimed at the NAIC for its inability to bring about greater uniformity in state insurance legislation. The last several years have seemed to bring about a revitalized NAIC and interest in increased cooperative action among the states.[14] Many model laws have been recommended for such areas as holding companies, variable contracts, guaranty funds, and unfair advertising and trade practices. Major research projects have been completed, covering automobile insurance, premium taxation, measurement of property-liability insurance profitability, credit life and health insurance, and mass marketing. Statistical reporting systems both for testing company solidity ("early warning tests") and for measuring profitability have been operational since the early 1970s.

In most states the *investigation* powers of the insurance commissioner extend to a wide variety of powers to determine whether or not insurers or their representatives are meeting the requirements of the statutes. Free access to records and books of insurers and hearings on such matters as rate violations or unfair trade practices are examples of this authority. As a result of such procedures, which are often informal, the commissioner may issue administrative rulings or advisory opinions in regard to the business conduct of insurers or their agents. In extreme cases the commissioner may declare the insolvency of an insurer in liquidation or rehabilitation proceedings. All such powers have as their major goal the protection of insurance policyholders and claimants. These parties should not treat the functions of an insurance commissioner as a guarantee against any and all possible loss, but the commissioner's insurance regulatory powers provide important means of preventing or reducing such losses and abuses.

Figure 8–2 shows the relationships of the company examination and audit, agent licensing, rating and forms approval, and policyholder service functions. Substantial statistical record keeping is a part of the insurance department's work. The warden aids in enforcing the laws passed by the legislature and interpreted by the courts, and in carrying out the administrative rulings of the department. The magnitude of the task is considerable. For example, in a recent year in Ohio there were more than 1,200 companies licensed; 50,000 agencies with 190,000 licenses for individual agents issued; 30,000 rate filings submitted; and in excess of 10,000 agents' license examinations ad-

---

[14] See Jon C. Hanson, "The NAIC: Its Nature and Scope," *CPCU Annals,* vol. 26, no. 1 (March 1973), p. 10. The addition of a research unit has been one of the best improvements during the 1970s.

Figure 8–2. The organization of a typical state insurance department

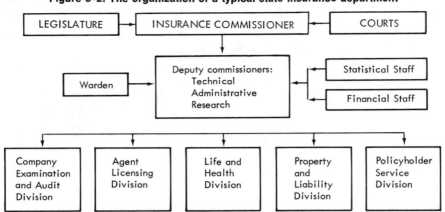

ministered. The spirit of consumerism has increased attention by insurance department personnel to their responsibilities for taking care of policyholder complaints. Some departments have installed consumer "hot lines" to accept toll-free telephone calls. Many calls are not complaints (which center on auto, health, and direct-mail insurance), but merely requests for information.

Court action. The extremely broad authority of insurance commissioners is subject to some measures of review and interpretation by the courts. The *notice* and *hearing* procedures which are conducted by commissioners in order to arrive at official rulings may be reviewed by the courts to determine whether the commissioner's duties have been in conformity with the statutes.

Examples are actions to compel the commissioner to issue a license to an insurer or to prevent its cancellation, and court review of decisions to permit rate increases or of refusals to do so. Not only may the courts be used in private actions (or by the attorney general of the state) against an insurance commissioner, but the reverse may also be true. The commissioner may, for example, petition the courts to enforce compliance with laws or rulings.

KINDS OF INSURANCE REGULATION BY THE STATES

The specfic state laws which regulate insurance cannot be discussed in detail in this chapter. The insurance codes, as well as the general business laws, of each of the 50 jurisdictions vary too much to permit a complete treatment of the subject. For specific insurance laws, administrative practices, and court decisions, the lawyer and the student of insurance must refer to the regulatory activities in a particular state. However, a general picture of the kinds of insurance regulation in the states is also necessary. This section of the chapter summarizes the regulation usually found in the more important insurance jurisdictions, such as New York State. Care must be taken to compare the specific state laws and rulings with the general review presented here.

Insurance regulation by the states is largely aimed at the insurers that conduct an insurance business within their jurisdiction. Some regulation is also provided for agents, brokers, and other persons who are part of the marketing of insurance contracts and services provided to insurance policyholders. The regulation of insurers falls into the following categories: (1) formation and licensing requirements, (2) supervision of operations, and (3) liquidation procedures. The second category includes a wide variety of regulatory controls, some extensive and some slight, over such activities as contract forms, rates, reserves, assets, and trade practices. Truly, the birth, life, and death of an insurer are in the hands of the state regulators.

Formation and licensing of insurers

Insurance companies are required to meet specific standards of organization, often higher ones than are set for general business organizations. The rationale for such higher standards has been discussed in the first section of the chapter. Basically, the need is for methods which have the objective of assuring the solvency, competence, and integrity of the insuring organization. The first step is *incorporation,*[15] an introductory process in which the state recognizes and approves the existence of a new legal identity. Today all but one state use this method of formation for insurance companies.[16] The New York Insurance Law, for example, outlines in detail the procedure to be followed under the incorporation statute, including written proposal to the superintendent of insurance, name to be used, territories and kinds of business in which operations are planned, and public notice in newspapers of intention to incorporate.[17]

The next step, *licensing,* is a check on the insurer's financial condition to ascertain that it has the required capital and surplus for the kinds of insurance permitted in the license. The statutory requirements for licensing must be met by *domestic* (domiciled or having their home office in the state), *foreign* (out of state), and *alien* (out of the United States) insurers. The requirements sometimes vary among these three types of insurers, but the laws usually specify at least as high standards for foreign and alien insurers as for domestic insurers. Standards also vary by legal type of insurer, with requirements for mutual insurers being somewhat different from those for stock insurers. For example, the financial requirements for mutual companies are stated in terms of surplus rather than capital plus surplus, and additional re-

[15] Reciprocals, Lloyds associations, fraternals, and some health insurance associations do not legally become incorporated by this process. They do, however, file similar statements of their present status and proposed activities as stated in their charter and bylaws.

[16] Rhode Island, where insurers must petition the General Assembly.

[17] *New York Insurance Law,* secs. 48–49.

quirements are set for the minimum number of policyholders with which to start a mutual company.

The financial standards that insurers must meet in order to obtain and retain a license vary tremendously in the different states. In some states as little as $25,000 of capital or surplus is required to write a specific kind of insurance, such as fire insurance. Each additional kind of insurance for which the company is to be licensed requires an additional amount of capital or surplus. For multiple-line insurance, including all kinds except life insurance, the states also exhibit wide variation: "The strictest state sets its requirement at $3,550,000. . . , which is over thirty-five times the standard of the most lenient state, which requires only $100,000."[18] About 15 states require less than $500,000, 20 between $500,000 and $1 million, and 15 jurisdictions set $1 million or more as the minimum standard for a new domestic multiple-line company.

The licensing procedure is not dependent on financial requirements alone. Many states give the insurance commissioner leeway to apply considerable judgment in acting, or refusing to act, upon a license application. The objective of licensing is ostensibly to assure a preliminary method of lessening the chance of the insurer's financial insolvency, particularly during the more difficult formative years. On the basis of the same objective, a license may be denied for many other reasons, including the bad faith or reputation of the proposed incorporators or management of an insurer. General managerial ability is undoubtedly as important as capital and surplus requirements in achieving sustained financial stability for an insurer. For that reason, the insurer's license is no more a guarantee against failure than an automobile driver's license is a guarantee against accident.

Insurer operations

As a protection against insolvency and unfair treatment of policyholders, insurance regulation continues after the formation and licensing of an insurer. The states exercise some control over many phases of the operations of insurers. The basic idea of continual regulation is that most obligations of insurers extend years into the future and that the state should provide supervision to see that the promises in the contracts are fulfilled. The ways in which insurer operations are supervised are strikingly different among the states and among the various kinds of insurance. Most states do provide some regulation of the following types: contracts and forms, rates, expense limitations, reserves, asset and surplus values, investments, agents' licensing and trade practices, and taxation.

---

[18] David L. Bickelhaupt, *Transition to Multiple-Line Insurance Companies* (Homewood, Ill.: Richard D. Irwin, 1961), p. 65. The requirements have only increased by relatively minor amounts in the 1970s.

Contracts and forms. The strictest regulation of contracts is applied to fire insurance, where each of the states stipulates the exact wording for the standard fire insurance contract. All states require a standard fire insurance contract, and almost all states use the New York form (see Chapter 17). Many differences in the wording of other contracts are found, however, and independent insurers and the various rating bureaus may have individualized contracts which vary in some important particulars. Life insurance contracts are not standard contracts in the sense that similar forms or benefits are required. Most states do, however, provide some uniformity by requiring a number of "standard provisions" in life contracts pertaining to such items as the grace period, loan and surrender values, and the like. The best examples of little regulation over contracts and forms are found in the marine and health fields. Except for a few required provisions, these contracts are the most nonuniform of insurance contracts and should be carefully studied by policyholders in order to determine what benefits, conditions, and exclusions they contain.

Rates. The price of insurance contracts is also controlled to a varying degree in the different lines of insurance. In some kinds of insurance, such as marine insurance, practically no regulation exists in the states. In other kinds, the supervision of rates is indirect, as in life insurance where regulation is aimed at maintaining minimum reserves (and thus affects the prices which must be charged in order to be able to pay losses and expenses).

Most other major kinds of insurance are subject to some direct-rate regulation. Every state has statutory standards set forth in an insurance rating law. Approximately one-half of the laws in the states have the same basic objectives as those set forth in the National Association of Insurance Commissioners "All-Industry Bill," which has served as a model during the past 30 years. (The bill's name does *not* mean that all states adopted it, merely that many insurers supported its provisions.)

The early attempts to establish rate making on a sound basis through various regional organizations generated a hostility on the part of the public. Opposition was voiced on the ground that cooperative action was monopolistic and contrary to the public interest. Various state legislators undertook to prohibit cooperative rate making by the enactment of bills (known as "anticompact laws") which prohibited combinations between insurers for the joint fixing of rates. It became apparent, however, that far from being in the public interest unlimited competition could also be injurious. It is much easier to set an inadequate price for insurance than for other products. Insurance costs, and thus prices, must be based upon estimated minimum costs of losses, expenses, and services to be provided for the years ahead. Insurance commissioners realized the importance of safeguarding the solvency of insurers, and it was found that the disastrous consequences of unrestricted competition could be avoided through the organization of rating bureaus. Rates could be predicated upon statistical information combining the loss experience of many insurers. Laws were then enacted authorizing the association of insurers for the purpose of making rates.

Basic standards recognized by rating laws required (1) that rates be *reasonable* and *adequate* for the class of risks to which they apply; (2) that no rate *discriminate unfairly* between risks involving essentially the same hazards and expense elements; (3) that consideration be given to the past and prospective loss *experience* (including the catastrophe hazards, if any) and to a reasonable underwriting profit. Rates are considered reasonable (not too high) and adequate (not too low) when they produce sufficient revenue to pay all losses and expenses of doing business, and in addition produce a reasonable profit.[19]

Rating laws provide specifically that there is no intent to prohibit or discourage reasonable competition, nor do they prohibit or discourage uniformity. The state insurance department passes upon the reasonableness of the rules and regulations of rating organizations. A rating bureau may not exclude or withhold its facilities from any insurers, each of which has the statutory right to become a bureau subscriber by paying reasonable fees. It is the intent of the laws to permit concerted rate making, but it is not their intent to require an insurer to participate in such rate making.

When rates have been promulgated (set), allowing any return of the insurance premium to an insured, except dividends to a class, is regarded as discrimination. A concession in rates is contrary to the law, whether it is made in the form of a direct payment or a credit on premium or by means of any subterfuge. The statutes do not prohibit the payment by one broker or agent of a part of his or her commission or other compensation to other licensed agents or brokers.

The proposed rates are not actually made by the states (except in a few states, for some lines, as in Texas and Louisiana) but by the rating bureaus or by individual insurers if their size and experience justify separate rates. The bureau method is used in fire insurance, workers' compensation, surety bonds, automobile insurance (by some but not all insurers), and other lines. Individual insurer rate making has increased in the past decade and has become an important factor in automobile insurance[20] and the new forms of multiple-line homeowners' and commercial policy contracts.

Approval of the proposed rates for some of these lines of insurance is required by the insurance commissioner. Three types of rating laws prevail for most states: (1) prior approval laws, (2) file-and-use laws, and (3) open competition laws. The fourth type, in which the state makes the rates, is less important because only a few states use it. About one-half of the states require

[19] Frederick G. Crane, "Insurance Rate Regulation: The Reasons Why," *Journal of Risk and Insurance,* vol. 39, no. 4 (December 1972), p. 511.

[20] One of the conclusions reached by the U.S. Department of Justice Task Force on Antitrust Immunities in *The Pricing and Marketing of Insurance* (Washington, D.C., U.S. Government Printing Office, January 1977) is that too rigid rate regulation reduces competition.

prior approval before the rates can be used. About ten permit the use of new rates immediately (so-called *file and use* laws), but the insurance commissioner may disapprove them within a certain time limit. About 16 states use a third method, *open competition* laws. These laws do not require the approval of most property and liability insurance rates at all, relying upon the insurance commissioner to disapprove rates used by insurers only if competition in the market place has been substantially threatened.

Rate approval is not required for all property and liability insurance. Most states do not apply the prior approval type of rating laws to special lines such as aviation and health insurance and reinsurance. (See later section on current issues in regulation.)

Expense limitations.   Other than direct regulation of insurance prices by required rate approval, some state laws supervise the cost of *life* insurance by limiting the expense portion of the premium. The New York law is most influential in this regard because all insurers doing business in that state must conform to its limitations for all insurance contracts that they write anywhere. Maximum commissions and allowances of 55 percent during the first year are set for business written by life insurers in New York State.

Reserves.   It is the practice of the states to require insurers to set up as a liability a reserve considered adequate to meet policy obligations as they mature. The only insurers excepted are certain types of mutual insurers operating on an intrastate basis and usually confining their operations within a small local area. In the case of these local mutuals, the reserve requirement may vary, depending upon the assessment liability provided in the policy.

In life insurance the *legal reserve* is an amount which augmented by premium payments under outstanding contracts and interest earnings will enable the life insurer to meet its policy obligations. These include death benefits and nonforfeiture benefits, such as policy loans and surrender values.

In the field of property insurance the *unearned premium reserve* must at all times be adequate to pay a full proportionate return premium to policyholders in the event of the cancellation of a policy before it expires. The reserve should be adequate to reinsure the business, if necessary. The basic purpose of the reserve is to meet all liabilities under the contract and to pay expenses of claim services *in the future.* At the same time, it accounts for income received but not yet earned and for repayment if the contract is discontinued.

A second type of reserve required of property insurers is the *loss reserve.* Since many contracts of this type do not involve immediate payment of all losses *that have occurred,* a reserve must be set up to assure their payment. For example, a workers' compensation claim may be made against the insurer today. In many cases the loss payments may be made gradually according to law during a long future period of disability. In automobile liability cases it may be several years after a loss before a court decides who is liable and for how much. In such cases, an estimate of the reserve that will be needed to pay the insurer's obligation is made and carried on its books as a loss reserve. In this way, losses and loss expense for claims that are known but not yet paid are provided for by the insurer under the loss reserve laws of the states.

Assets and surplus values. The value of assets appearing in the balance sheets of insurers must be correct in order that liabilities, reserves, and residual surplus items have true meaning. Nearly 50,000 individual securities held by insurers are valued according to practices adopted by a committee of the National Association of Insurance Commissioners. Stocks are usually given year-end market values, while some bonds (especially those which are nonamortizable) are given estimated or "Convention" values. The valuations are advisory only to the states, but the result is a good example of voluntary and state regulation working together. For some insurers, such as mutual insurers, both surplus accumulation and distribution are subject to regulation aimed at providing equitable treatment for all policyholders.

Investments. To protect the solvency of insurers, most states have laws governing the types of securities that may be purchased for investment. The strictest regulations apply to life insurers since they hold many billions of dollars of assets for many years for their policyholders.

Life insurers are subject to vigorous supervision of their investment portfolios. Each annual statement filed with the insurance department lists every individual investment with detailed information about its acquisition, costs, values, and earnings. The insurance laws require a high standard of investment quality. Mortgages and bonds are the prime investments in the portfolio of life insurers, involving a large majority of total assets. Most states grant some limited permission for other investments. Stocks may be limited, for example, to about 5 percent of assets or to a specified proportion of surplus, such as 50 percent. Real estate holdings, especially commercial properties and housing projects, are also limited to a maximum of between 10 and 20 percent in various states. The legality of all holdings of the insurer is checked carefully in periodic audits of the securities.

The investment of assets by *property and liability insurers* is also supervised, although the laws are more lenient and vary greatly among the states. The laws of each state must be consulted in order to determine the investment restrictions. The general practice aims at requiring the safest types of investments for all assets held as reserves (unearned premium and loss reserves) and other liabilities. Cash, bonds of high grade and specified experience, and perhaps preferred stocks of proven equality may be permitted for such assets. The remainder of assets (representing capital and surplus) may be invested in a wider range of securities, including common stocks meeting certain standards. Limitations on real estate holdings, on the size of single investments in relation to total assets or surplus, and on investments in out-of-state companies, as well as many other restrictions, are also common.

Many states prohibit insurers from financing debt by issuing their own bonds. Most other financial institutions are similarly restricted by state laws. This is an important difference that must be borne in mind when the investment portfolios and practices of insurers and other commercial enterprises are being compared.

Agents' licensing and trade practices. An important control on insurer operations is maintained through laws in all states which require insurance agents and brokers to be licensed. The insurance departments usually administer these laws, with the objective of permitting only competent and trustworthy representatives to be used by insurers. The standards vary tremendously, from mere payment of a license fee to a comprehensive written *examination* following required attendance in insurance courses approved by the department. New York's written examinations require 90 classroom hours of study. They have influenced some other states, such as Florida, to raise their licensing requirements for insurance agents. The examinations are often divided into separate tests for life insurance, health insurance, and multiple-line insurance. In states that license brokers, the examinations for insurance brokers are usually more difficult and extensive than those given to agents. Adjusters and consultants are licensed, also, in a few states.

Special laws in many states, called *countersignature laws,* require that all property insurance contracts written in a state must be signed by an agent who is a resident of that state. Such laws are often criticized because they may add to the cost of insurance without providing any real services to the consumer. Agents must also represent only insurers that are authorized and licensed in the state. An exception is made under some *surplus line laws* which in some states permit a special licensed agent to represent unauthorized insurers in cases where the risks cannot be fully protected by licensed insurers within the state.

Unfair trade practices in insurance are made illegal in all states under laws similar to the Federal Trade Commission Act. These laws aim at retaining jurisdiction for the states (under the provisions of Public Law 15) in preventing fraudulent and unethical acts of agents and brokers. They provide fines and, more important, suspension or revocation of licenses as penalties for violations. Examples of such unfair practices in insurance include (1) *rebating,* the returning of any part of the premium (except in dividends) to the policyholder by insurer or agent as a price-cutting sales inducement; (2) *twisting,* a special form of misrepresentation in which an agent may induce the policyholder to cancel disadvantageously the contract of another insurer in order to take out a new contract; (2) *misappropriation,* in which the agent unlawfully keeps funds belonging to others; (4) *commingling,* which some states prevent by requiring a separate bank account for the agent's premium funds; and (5) *misleading advertising,* which is restrained by many regulations for full and fair information in advertisements by insurers and agents. The insurance commissioner has broad powers to prevent the above unfair practices and exercises this authority by investigating complaints as well as initiating investigations of any questionable acts of insurers or their representatives.

Taxation. Revenue for the states has become an important reason for insurance regulation. The insurers pay what amounts to a sales tax on gross premiums received from all their policyholders. This *premium tax* is usually about 2 percent, although some states charge up to 4 percent of premiums. The tax is paid by insurers; its cost, of course, is included in the price of insurance contracts and thus is paid indirectly by the policyholders. Premium taxes, and other license and miscellaneous fees, exceeded $2 billion in 1977.

That the taxes are primarily for revenue purposes rather than to pay for the cost of insurance regulation is obvious from the statistics. The state premium tax goes into the general revenue fund of the state, with insurance department expenses being based on separate appropriations from that fund. Only about 5 percent of the above total tax revenue and fees is used for operation of the state insurance departments. Many states even use less than the amount of the separate license and miscellaneous fees (not the much larger premium tax) collected from insurers, in order to pay the costs of insurance department regulation. The range is quite diverse, from less than 50 percent of these fees, to more than 300 percent.[21] If public regulation of insurance is lacking in any respect, the state legislatures should first look to see whether the insurance departments are provided with adequate funds and personnel to carry out the necessary supervision of insurance in a consistent and equitable manner.

Federal *income* taxes also apply to insurers. Property-liability insurers pay regular corporate income taxes on statutory underwriting profits and on net investment income. Some of the smaller mutual insurers and reciprocals are exempted from these taxes (if their income is less than $75,000 a year), but only 2 or 3 percent of the total business is written by these insurers. For life insurers, a different situation exists. Prior to 1959, life insurers received very favorable tax treatment, but the Federal Income Tax Act of 1959 increased their taxes considerably. A complicated formula applies now, still somewhat favoring life insurers as savings institutions but taxing investment income and some of the underwriting gain above that necessary to keep reserves on a legal basis. There is debate as to whether stock or mutual insurers pay more income taxes in relation to the insurance business they do. No definitive answer appears possible on the basis of the available data, for the comparisons are often incomplete. Changes in the tax laws during the last decade have removed many of the former differences in tax burden upon the various types of insurers.

Rehabilitation and liquidation of insurers

The insurance commissioner of a state not only officiates at the birth and growth of an insurer but also at its demise if necessary. An insurer may be *liquidated* for a number of reasons, including financial insolvency. Some liquidations may be made voluntarily in order to effect a corporate reorgani-

---

[21] Compiled annually by the Insurance Industry Committee of Ohio (Columbus).

zation or merger. Reinsurance of all outstanding liabilities and contracts may be achieved, so that no loss results to policyholders. For example, since 1908 no life insurance policyholder of a New York–licensed insurer has suffered loss through an insurer failure. Such losses have been prevented in other states for periods of 30 or more years.

The insurance commissioner acts under the insurance laws as the official in charge of supervising rehabilitation (if the insurer can be restored to financial stability through reorganization) or liquidation if the insurer is dissolved. The purpose of both actions is to conserve as much of the insurer's assets as possible and to provide fair treatment for claimants, policyholders, and investors. A good example of how the collapse of an insurer can be averted short of liquidation proceedings, and of how an insurer can be rejuvenated (by restricting its expansion and imposing underwriting and expense limitations) occurred in 1976 for the Government Employees Insurance Company (GEICO). This was one of the largest insurers ever to undergo such rehabilitation proceedings.

Sometimes the license of an insurer is *suspended* temporarily, for not meeting financial solvency standards or for other noncompliance with department rulings on rates, advertising, and so on. This may be a prelude to liquidation proceedings or only a temporary situation to enforce changes in the insurer's operations. Nevertheless, it is a powerful tool of enforcement.

SOME CURRENT REGULATORY ISSUES

The increased interest in insurance regulation during recent years is a phenomenon of the times. Many factors are responsible, but perhaps the age of "consumerism" has created the environment for greater inquiry into insurance than has ever been made before.[22]

Insurer guaranty funds

One of the most shocking financial news items of the 1970s was the exposure of the Equity Funding Corporation of America fraud in California. Allegedly involving life insurance contract amounts of more than $2 billion, the scheme was perpetrated through the use of false computer records. Bogus policies were recorded for an affiliate, Equity Funding Life Insurance Company (an Illinois company), and resold to reinsurance companies. Twenty-two persons were indicted for taking part in the fraud, which saw Equity Funding Corporation stock soar from $7.50 to more than $80 in a few years. This was primarily a stock swindle in which 60,000 life insurance policy sales on nonexistent persons were recorded as the basis for showing false corporate

[22] The escalating popularity of insurance regulation topics can be seen in many journals and trade publications in the insurance field during the past decade.

growth. Most of the real 20,000 life insurance policyholders did not lose their investments. In contrast, most investors recovered only 15 to 20 percent of their dollars in a reorganization into a new company, Orion Capital Corporation, in 1977. National Investors (of Arkansas) assumed 1,000 policies that it had formerly coinsured; some contracts were reinsured; and others were protected by the real assets of Equity Funding Life. This case illustrates that life insurance solvency regulation by the states is needed. It also shows that insurance regulatory laws could be helpful to the consumer even in a most complicated ruse involving the Securities and Exchange Commission and many stockbrokers. The ability to perpetrate the fraud is not an indictment of state regulation of insurance, considering the freak nature of the occurrence. Life insurance reserve requirements created real assets for bona fide policyholders, and only the phony policies were backed by phantom assets.[23]

Some insurers do suffer liquidation because of financial difficulty. In some states the number of liquidations is a cause for concern, particularly in some kinds of insurance, such as automobile insurance (and mostly for high-risk, substandard, newer insurers). The result has been some support for a federal guaranty fund for insurers that would operate somewhat as the FDIC does for banks. State deposit laws and several special state workers' compensation security funds are already in use which are similar in principle to this idea. The need for a federal plan for all kinds of insurance has not yet been proved conclusively.

In recent years, all but a few states have adopted *guaranty fund plans* to protect consumers against the insolvency of property-liability insurers. Model legislation proposed by the NAIC encouraged states to adopt such laws, which do not include life insurance. The plans are administered on a state-by-state basis, but basically they assess solvent insurers in order to pay the unpaid claims of an insolvent company and to return unearned premiums to its policyholders. Although insolvency is a rare occurrence, involving less than 1 percent of property-liability insurers in the past several years, the funds have paid out approximately $150 million. Insurers each pay a proportional share of the losses, based on their premium volume in the state. The guaranty funds appear to be doing a good job of protecting the consumer, with several improvements being adopted in some states. These concern (1) giving the funds immediate access to assets of the insolvent insurer (rather than waiting until liquidation proceedings are completed), (2) giving the funds priority before general creditors to obtain assets of the insolvent insurer, and (3) permitting a tax offset against premium taxes to solvent insurers for money paid into the guaranty funds.[24]

---

[23] "Equity Funding Ruse a Freak—State Regulation Not Indicted," *National Underwriter* (Property and Casualty Edition), September 14, 1973, p. 1. See also Lee J. Seidler, Frederick Andrews, and Marc J. Epstein, *The Equity Funding Papers* (New York: John S. Wiley & Sons, 1977).

[24] "Insolvency Laws: Better Protection for the Insurance Comsumer," *Journal of American Insurance,* Winter 1976–77, p. 1.

Rate regulation

Another issue closely related to maintaining the financial strength of insurers is rate regulation. The issue has been of special significance to the property-liability sector of the business, where the prior approval type of rate regulatory law (see previous section) has been under strong fire for the past decade.

Many subissues are involved, such as:

1. The present extent of competition in the major fields of property-liability insurance (particularly automobile insurance).

2. The proper measurement of underwriting profits for business on an "adjusted" or "statutory" basis, whether or not investment profits should be included, and the appropriate asset or sales basis for calculating rates of return.

3. The relative effectiveness of the present prior approval rate regulatory laws of most states (rate bureau membership permitted, and rate filing and approval required) versus the "open competition" type of permissive regulation (no rate filing or bureaus required).

4. The relationship of the rate regulatory problem to the state versus federal regulation arguments (if present state rate regulation proves inadequate, a new strong argument for federal regulation of insurance emerges).

The pros and cons of many programs have been stressed. Sentiment seems stronger than ever for possible change away from the strict regulation of rates by prior approval laws which require affirmative action by the insurance commissioner before the rates can be used. About ten states employ the file-and-use method, which permits the immediate use of filed rates, without approval.

The open competition approach, which was pioneered in California, has also been adopted in 15 other states. It relies upon competition to set the price for property-liability insurance. Open competition between rating bureaus (membership not required) and independent insurers is permitted and encouraged by the lack of requirements for filing or obtaining approval of rates. These laws require the insurance commissioner to monitor competition (and disapprove rates) and to develop "share of market" and "workable competition" standards. The need for good definitions, and for enforcement of antitrust laws, in these states is stressed.[25] The goal is rate adequacy but not rate excessiveness, with sufficient markets for the needed coverages of insurance. New York has experimented with open competition since 1970. The experience of these states has been largely favorable in reducing rates.[26]

The danger that open competition, no-filing laws will become synonymous with *no* regulation is a factor of considerable importance. This could have the undesirable result of encouraging federal legislation to fill the possible gap

[25] "Monitoring Competition: A Means of Regulating the Property and Liability Insurance Business" (Milwaukee: NAIC, 1974).

[26] For Illinois, see David R. Klock, "Competitive Rating Laws and Insurer Conduct," *Journal of Risk and Insurance,* vol. 39, no. 4 (December 1972), p. 589. For New York, see *Competition in Property and Liability Insurance* (State of New York Insurance Department, March 1973).

in state regulation. The potential effects on overall competition, agency systems, rating bureau services, small and large insurers, and many other parts of the insurance business must also be considered.

A national opinion study conducted in 1977 may give some clues as to the future direction of insurance rate regulation. The open competition concept was favored by 47 percent, prior approval by 40 percent (13 percent had no opinion). The reasons given centered on keeping prices down, free enterprise, and government control of excessive prices.[27]

Federal versus state regulation

This issue has been discussed earlier in this chapter. It seems to be a perpetual favorite topic among armchair insurance critics, and even qualified observers can disagree on at least some aspects of the problem. Some point out that the state supervisory system is still predominant in almost all aspects of insurance. Others warn that growing federal involvement in some phases of insurance are apparent in advertising and mergers (FTC), variable life insurance and annuities (SEC), and pensions and occupational safety (Departments of Labor and HEW).

The most striking characteristic of the federal involvement in insurance is the fragmented authority over insurance matters among more than a dozen different agencies.[28] The only agency reaching out for overall control seems to be the Federal Insurance Administration, which since 1968 has been growing, with its federal insurance plans for flood, riot, and crime insurance (see also Chapter 28). Its interest has also extended into many other fields, such as products liability, no-fault hearings, and federal insolvency fund proposals. Currently it is undertaking a massive 18-month study of insurance and public policy, which will undoubtedly be significant to insurance regulation in the 1980s.

Other regulatory issues

The wide range of other current topics concerning regulation is symptomatic of the era of accelerated change in which we live. The social responsibility of insurance regulation is to recognize that changes in and out of insurance are constantly altering the social responsibility of insurance regulation. The goals of insurance regulation should change accordingly.[29]

---

[27] *Public Appraisal of Pricing, Profits, and Regulation in the Auto Insurance Business* (New York: Insurance Information Institute, June 1977).

[28] *Regulation of Insurance* (Chicago: Alliance of American Insurers, 1977), p. 5.

[29] Richard E. Stewart, "Ritual and Responsibility in Insurance Regulation" and "The Social Responsibility of Insurance Regulation," in Spencer Kimball and Herbert S. Denenberg, eds., *Insurance, Government, and Social Policy* (Homewood, Ill.: Richard D. Irwin, 1969).

It is hoped that this chapter has piqued the interest of the reader and will spur further inquiry into many of the other regulatory issues that might be included here. A partial listing would include: (1) group credit life insurance price regulation; (2) regulation and taxing of out-of-state transactions of insurers not licensed in the state;[30] (3) the requirements of the Securities and Exchange Commission for variable annuity and mutual fund sales; (4) the position of the Federal Trade Commission and the states in regulating out-of-state direct-mail advertising by insurers; (5) malpractice and products liability tax reform laws; (6) the burgeoning problems of corporate conglomerates and insurance mergers;[31] and (7) "truth-in-life insurance" and other more "readable" insurance contracts, which have been advocated as answers to the needs of insurance consumers. Some additional issues with regulatory aspects are considered in Chapter 29.

FOR REVIEW AND DISCUSSION

1. For each of the following statements that is *false,* explain *why* it is not true:
   a. Self-regulation of insurance by cooperative voluntary efforts of insurers is considerable, but it does not work for some insurance activities.
   b. Most insurance regulation is performed by the federal government.
   c. The insurance commissioner in the states is more of a figurehead than a powerful administrator.
2. Why might "uncontrolled competition work a hardship upon the buyers of insurance"?
3. Is self-regulation an effective means by which the insurance business can be regulated? Cite several examples, and contrast it with administrative action.
4. *Explain* the relationship among the three basic methods by which government regulates insurance, that is: (1) legislation, (2) administrative action, and (3) court action.
5. Does the federal government or do the state governments provide most of the regulation for insurance? Briefly explain the important parts that (1) the *Paul* v. *Virginia* case, (2) the South-Eastern Underwriters (SEUA) case, and (3) Public Law 15 played in the development of insurance regulation to its present situation.
6. The insurance commissioner (or superintendent) in each state has powerful regulatory duties. Discuss several of the major *functions* of this official. What are some of the principal *problems* in connection with proper insurance supervision by the commissioner?
7. Evaluate the need for state regulation of insurance in each of the areas of (*a*) incorporation and licensing, (*b*) operations, and (*c*) liquidation.

---

[30] *State Board of Insurance* v. *Todd Shipyards Co.* (1962), 370 U.S. 451; and Samuel H. Weese, *Non-Admitted Insurance in the U.S.* (Homewood, Ill.: Richard D. Irwin, 1971).

[31] Robert A. Marshall, *Life Insurance Mergers and Consolidations* (Homewood, Ill.: Richard D. Irwin, 1972).

8. Briefly discuss the extent of state regulation of insurance as to (a) contracts and forms, (b) rates, (c) reserves, and (d) investements. Include examples of how state regulation differs for some of the major fields of insurance.

9. In addition to income taxes and other taxes which may apply to many business enterprises, are insurers subject to any special forms of taxation? If so, explain the kind and extent of such taxation.

10. "Open competition" rate laws have recently been adopted by several states that have had "prior approval" laws for many years. Explain the difference, if any, in the (a) purposes and (b) the methods of these laws. Are there any other alternatives?

11. "It is better for state insurance regulation to concentrate on maintaining insurer *solvency* and *not* trying to regulate the *price* which insurers charge for their contracts." Do you agree or disagree, and why?

12. In your opinion, has insurance regulation improved or decreased in effectiveness during the past 20 years? Explain your rationale.

13. In the future, how can insurance regulation meet "the challenge of change" which its environment will undoubtedly bring? What part in this process will probably be taken by (a) insurers, (b) insureds, and (c) the regulators?

14. What lessons might be learned in regard to the Equity Funding Corporation fraud case by (a) insurers, (b) regulators, and (c) consumers?

15. The Department of Transportation decided to require air bags in automobiles starting in 1982. Discuss, on the basis of this chapter's reading, (a) what kind of government regulation this is, (b) whether it should be based on federal or state regulation, and (c) how such regulation might affect the insurance business.

PART III

LIFE AND HEALTH INSURANCE

Part III is "a matter of *life and death*" . . . and *health and disability* as well. The insurance systems that are used to protect families and businesses against *loss of income* or *increased expenses,* due to death or disability, are the subject of Chapters 9–16 on *life and health insurance.* Part I introduced the risk-management viewpoint. Part II looked at insurance from the functional viewpoint of the insurer. Part III is the first part of this book to emphasize the "by line" approach to insurance and risk.

Chapters 9–12 discuss the field of *life* insurance (and annuities), beginning with *general principles* underlying the protection and investment aspects of this important part of the insurance business. What a student and rational consumer should know is stressed in regard to actuarial base, legal doctrines, and cost. Basic *types of contracts* are analyzed to learn that all life insurance policies are fundamentally of these types: term, whole life, and endowment. *Contract features* provide considerable flexibility to meet changing consumer needs, and *annuities* and pensions protect the consumer against "living too long" instead of "dying too soon."

Health insurance in a wide variety of *individual* contracts is the subject of Chapter 13. The *group* insurance technique is discovered in Chapter 14 to be one of the fastest-growing parts of both life and health insurance.

Government insurance systems for life and health insurance (Chapter 15), including the extensive OASDHI, and workers' and unemployment compensation plans, are seen as a social insurance base in the U.S. insurance picture. The *coordination* of all government, group, and individual life-health insurance is the challenging task of Chapter 16.

Chapter 9

Concepts considered in Chapter 9—Life insurance principles

Life insurance principles include:
 Its nature is *protection* against the financial *loss of income* earning ability caused by death, or *investment* for similar loss in old age.
  Compared with other insurance contracts, it is *not indemnity;* it is *unique* in combining long-term protection and investment; and it has *insurable interests* based on relationships or financial losses.
 Fundamental concepts of life insurance include:
  The life insurance equation (Premium cost = Mortality + Expenses − Interest earnings).
  Actuarial basis from basic *term, whole life,* or *endowment* contracts.
  Development from assessment plans, often unsuccessful ventures.
  Level premium plan, which creates reserves and cash values.
  Investment functions, which offer immediate creation of estates; stable yield with high safety; managerial, tax, and other advantages.
  Legal doctrines of *divorce, common disaster, presumption of death, presumption against suicide, rights of creditors, murder, fraud,* and *legal execution.*
 The mortality table, including discussion of:
  What it is—a compilation of probable mortality at each age.
  Where it comes from and its purposes, as aided by *actuaries.*
  Its basic construction in which death rates are calculated.
  Different mortality tables for many different groups of insureds.
  Development of the 1958 CSO table, the most widely used today.
 Life insurance premium calculations:
  Advancing premiums as age increases, a basic characteristic.
  The interest factor, compounding of premium payments.
  The gross premium, net premiums plus loading expenses.
 Life insurance reserves:
  Origin, the level premium plan of overpayment in the early years.
  Definition, present value of future benefits less premiums.
  The reserve account, mostly "legal reserves."
 Underwriting of life insurance, which includes:
  Medical examinations for many applicants.
  Other factors and sources of information, such as inspection reports.
  Substandard or impaired risks, with occupational or physical ratings.
  Nonmedical life insurance, increasingly used today.
  War clauses, restricting payment for war deaths of military personnel.

Life insurance principles

Like riddles? Try this one. What field of insurance has grown in one generation during the last 20 years: (1) from $458 billion to $2,583 billion of "insurance in force" or total contract values; (2) from $13 billion to over $72 billion of "premiums" or annual sales; (3) from 260 million to 390 million contracts; and (4) from $90 billion to over $352 billion of assets?[1] The answer: *life insurance*. The reasons for such growth: See the next five chapters, beginning with this chapter on the basic principles and concepts upon which the field of life insurance is based.

THE NATURE OF LIFE INSURANCE

The basis for life insurance is *income earning ability*, the economic part of total "human life value." The potential earning power of the individual is one of the greatest assets that any family or business owns. It is worth many times more than the buildings, automobiles, or other assets that we think of as most valuable. Life insurance protects the insured's family, creditors, or others against financial loss growing out of the death of the insured.

Definition

Legal status was given long ago to the definition which indicates the life insurance agreement to be:

> A contract by which the insurer, for a certain sum of money or premium proportioned to the age, health, ... and other circumstances of the person whose life is insured, ... if such person shall die within the period limited in the policy, will pay the sum specified ... to the person in whose favor such policy is granted.[2]

Policies provide methods for payment of the proceeds in installments or in some manner other than a lump sum; the choice is made by the insured or by the beneficiary if the insured has not made a choice. The choices are termed "optional modes of settlement" or "settlement options."

---

[1] *Life Insurance Fact Book* (Washington, D.C.: American Council of Life Insurance, 1978), pp. (1) 18, (2) 56, (3) 18, and (4) 68.

[2] *Ritter* v. *Mutual Life Insurance Company*, 169 U.S. 139 [1898].

In addition to the life policy, which has as its purpose creating capital (payment in the event of a death), the life insurance business has developed another type of contract termed "the annuity." The annuity furnishes systematic liquidation of capital and is especially useful protection in the event of old age, when a guaranteed lifetime income is needed after earning capacity has decreased or stopped.

Compared with other insurance contracts

The essential difference between life insurance and other forms of insurance designed solely to protect against an uncertain peril is that life insurance has the added function of accumulation. (The type of life insurance known as "term insurance" is usually an exception to this.) A considerable part of the premiums paid for life insurance represents a payment on the part of the insureds to a fund for investment to be administered by the insurer. The dual role of creation and an estate *and* its management and investment in the interest of the insured are features peculiar to the business of life insurance.

Not a contract of indemnity. Strictly speaking, one cannot say that the life insurance contract is one of indemnity. In buying life insurance, an insured undertakes to compensate his or her estate, dependents, or others for the loss occasioned by untimely death. However, when settlement is made, the beneficiaries under the policy are under no obligation to demonstrate, as a condition precedent to collecting the insurance, a direct financial loss as a result of the death of the insured. The insured's value as a producer may have long since ceased, yet the beneficiaries have the right to participate fully in the policy in accordance with its terms.[3] Life insurance pays a specific amount of money, without regard to actual monetary loss.

Although the basic use of life insurance is the protection of life values, life insurance contracts have found additional uses. They are used for holding and accumulating assets, as a means for transferring business ownership, and in connection with the establishment of a trust. All these uses lend value to the services of the life insurance business. In many instances the secondary uses supplement and merge with the primary use.

A unique risk. In all forms of insurance except life insurance, the happening of the unfavorable contingency which gives rise to the loss is uncertain. In life insurance the contingency is death, which is universal and certain. Be-

---

[3] Life insurance in the early days was widely used as a vehicle for gambling, with policies taken out on the lives of important men in public life. Early opposition to life insurance included many who felt that insurance on the life of a person was a thing to be abhorred, and in some instances it was absolutely prohibited by law. A turning point was reached in 1774, with the enactment of the famous statute 14 Geo. III, c. 48, *An Act for Regulating Insurance upon Lives, and for Prohibiting all such Ins. except in cases where the Persons Insuring shall have an Interest in the Life or Death of the Person Insured.*

cause the happening of the contingency insured against is certain, life policies provide for certain payment, unless written only for a term. The uncertain element is the time when such payment must be made.

Insurable interest required. Although the life insurance contract is not one of indemnity, this fact does not preclude the requirement basic to all insurance of an *insurable interest*. This exists when the insured will actually suffer a loss if the contingency insured against happens. The requirement is not one that the insurer may waive; it is essential if the policy is to be enforceable.

The doctrine of insurable interest is considerably broader in the field of life insurance than in other fields of insurance. In most states this is governed by statute, and no uniform rule can be set forth. Generally, however, so far as a person's *own life* is concerned, there is no precise monetary value. The courts have held that any person has an insurable interest in his or her own life for any amount. Persons may, therefore, buy as much insurance as an insurer is willing to write and as they are willing and able to pay premiums on.

It has sometimes been held that to establish insurable interest in close relationships, there must be pecuniary (or financial) interest in the continuance of the life of the insured. In the case of *husband and wife,* pecuniary interest is presumed. Actual pecuniary loss growing out of the death of an insured, as well as an expectation or presumption of pecuniary advantage in the case of certain near relationships, will support an insurable interest. This is particularly the case where the policy has been obtained in good faith and not for the purpose of speculation, and where natural affection would normally operate to protect the life of the insured.

A *creditor* may have an insurable interest in the life of a debtor to the extent of the debt. Typical examples of such insured debts in today's "credit economy" are automobile loans; installment loans for television sets, furniture, and household appliances; and small personal loans. Credit life insurance is one of the fastest-growing areas of life insurance, with more than a 10 percent increase every year but one for the past 30 years.[4] If the policy is one taken out by a debtor and is used as collateral for a loan, it is generally held that the debtor may take out the policy for any amount and deliver it to the creditor. The right of the creditor to the benefits under the policy is limited to the amount of the indebtedness. If, however, the creditor takes the policy out, the amount of insurance must not be largely in excess of the amount of the debt. In any case, the debtor must consent to the issuance of the policy.

There are other relationships from which a pecuniary interest arises sufficient to establish an insurable interest under a life contract. A substantial amount of life insurance is written insuring the life of a *partner* in a business

---

[4] *Life Insurance Fact Book,* p. 33. See also Chapter 14 of this text.

venture for the benefit of the surviving partner or partners. Sometimes the proceeds of such a policy are payable to the firm, and in other instances the proceeds provide a fund with which the surviving partners buy the deceased partner's interest. A firm may also insure the life of a *key person*, such as an important officer upon whose life a substantial portion of the earnings of the firm depend. In the case of employees, insurable interest is dependent upon the value of the employee to the business. An employee who could be easily replaced would hardly be one in whom the employer could reasonably claim an insurable interest. However, a business usually has an interest in any employees occupying key positions, such as the president, executive officers, and department heads. In the event of doubt, however, valid insurance may be written if the employee (instead of the employer) applies for the policy and designates the employer as beneficiary. In the case of a small corporation where the stock is closely held, the lives of *primary stockholders* may be insured, the proceeds to be used to buy the stock of a deceased stockholder.

In summary, in the field of life insurance, in addition to the insurable interest every person has in his or her own life, there are both *monetary* and *nonmonetary* losses that will meet the requirement for an insurable interest. Some may be partially related to replacing financial losses, while others cover situations involving a presumed natural affection of a reasonable expectation of benefit.

FUNDAMENTAL LIFE INSURANCE CONCEPTS

The life insurance equation

In Chapter 2 the concept of how insurance works was explained in terms of an equation in which the incoming premiums and investment earnings of an insurer equal the outgoing payment of losses, expenses, and profits. For individuals, death is certain, but the time of death is uncertain. For large groups of persons, however, the insurer can predict accurately the number of deaths to be expected. The life insurer cannot predict *who* will die, but it can predict *how many* persons will die within a given time. The key to the insurer's ability to reduce uncertainty is that it uses the principle of large numbers to deal with many persons.

In its simplest form, here is the method of computing a life insurance premium, assuming that 10,000 individuals aged 58 wish to insure their lives for a period of one year for $1,000. Reference to a standard mortality table indicates that the death rate per 1,000 is 17. The life insurer, therefore, will count on 170 deaths during the year, or payments equal to $170,000. Since there are 10,000 in the group to pay the losses at the beginning, if a premium of $17 is collected from each of these and the death experience is exactly that of the expectation, the insurer will have $170,000 with which to pay claims, and the account will balance to a cent. In the interest of simplicity, the costs of doing business are not considered at this point.[5]

Since there is no assurance that the death rate will exactly follow the expectation in the given year, insurers collect somewhat more than they need to pay the expected claims. In addition to this, they must add a "loading" to the mortality cost in order to have enough to pay the operating expenses of the company. Finally, funds held for reserves or surplus are invested and the investment income is used to reduce the cost of insurance. If the insurer is able to operate at an expense less than it calculated, or if the death claims do not equal the expectations, the savings are accumulated and at the end of the business year they may be apportioned to policyholders as a dividend or to stockholders as profits. Thus, in the long run, the equation balances. Premiums collected and interest earned equal the total of death claims, expenses, and dividends or profits paid.

To summarize, the insurance premium is predicated upon the following assumptions: (a) mortality, (b) loading for expenses and contingencies, and (c) interest to be earned on reserves. The insurer expects the mortality experience to be less than the assumed tabular experience; an effort is made to keep expenses under the amount assumed in the rate calculations; and the interest rate is conservative. All of these margins provide safety factors.

Actuarial basis of basic contracts

The standard forms of term, whole life, endowment, and annuities are the bases of all calculations. The mathematical work is done by persons who are called *actuaries*.

When the insurance is for the whole life of the insured, the insurer pays a definite sum whenever death may occur. Because of this, such a contract is known as a *whole life policy*. Which insureds will die within a comparatively short time and which will live to very old age, no one knows. The actuary does, however, have a very close approximation of how many will die and how many will be paying premiums each year. Computing the annual premium payments and decreasing them by the amount of interest expected to be earned, the actuary is able to determine how much must be received in premiums to have on hand funds to pay the death benefits. The "limited-payment policy" is a whole life form, but it is distinguished from the "ordinary life" policy, which provides for premium payments for as long as the insured shall live, in that its premium payments are made only for a definite number of years or until a certain age. The usual premium payment periods are 10, 20,

---

[5] The mortality table used for this calculation is the Commissioners' 1958 Standard Ordinary Mortality Table, generally referred to as the "1958 CSO Table." This table appears in Table 9–1 in a later section of this chapter.

or 30 years, or to age 65. The policy does not mature (pay the face value) until death occurs.

The usual *endowment policy* differs from the whole life policy in that the face of the policy is paid if the insured is living at the end of the term indicated in the contract. If the insured dies during this term, the face of the policy is paid to the designated beneficiary. Thus, with a 20-year endowment contract for $1,000, if the insured lives to the end of the term, he will receive $1,000, but if the insured dies before the end of the term, $1,000 will be paid to whoever is designated as beneficiary.

The *term policy* promises to pay the face of the policy if the insured dies during the stated policy period, such as 5, 10, or 20 years, or perhaps before a certain age, such as 65 or 70. Whole life, endowment, and term policies carry different premium charges. The premium for the term policy is the lowest, and there are increasingly higher rates for other forms up to the highest cost short-term endowment. In every case the premium is computed upon the basis of the coverage afforded in the contract.

The *annuity* provides for a periodic payment for a number of years or for life. The annuity idea is the opposite of life insurance in that the annuity is concerned not with accumulation but with the liquidation of funds. Chapter 12 discusses annuities separately from other life insurance contracts.

The actuary is able to combine term insurance with whole life, whole life with an annuity, and so on, in order to work out in a single contract any needed combination of savings and protection. The special contracts are the actuarial sum of the combined basic contracts. It is evidence of the competitive nature of the insurance business that many combinations or special policies are made available to the insured.

Development from assessment plans

Life insurance in its simplest form provides for insurance written on a year-to-year basis. Based upon the mortality experience, a group of insureds of a given age may each be charged a premium sufficient to provide a sum that is adequate to meet death claims for a year. Each succeeding year the premium will be higher since the survivors will be older and the mortality experience will show a higher death rate.

In early life insurance associations, the *assessment plan* of life insurance usually made no provisions for a reserve out of which to pay death claims; rather, the plan was based upon the payment of all benefits out of current premiums. Proponents of this plan failed to recognize that as the years went by, there would be a natural increase in claims unless sufficient new younger members could be obtained to maintain the mortality rate of the group on an even basis. Because the death rate increases more rapidly for older persons, the average age of the group was very difficult to maintain. Another problem was that assessment companies usually collected equal annual assessments from each member, regardless of age. The lowest cost occurred when the majority of members were young, but young people began to drop out when the assessments became higher. The greater the average age of the group, the more difficult it became to secure new members. As the younger members dropped out, the inevitable result was an even higher rate of assessment and not infrequently a collapse of the organization. The loss to those old members who all their lives had contributed to the benefits of others was disheartening and often tragic.

The assessment method of writing life insurance has proved unworkable. The requirement of low premiums in the younger productive years and high premiums in the older years of lessening productive capacity tends (a) to defeat the purpose of life insurance and (b) to affect mortality experience adversely. As premium charges increase, many of those insured feel that they can no longer afford to carry the insurance. If the insurance is dropped at a time when the insured has real need of it, the plan has defeated its purpose. The second disadvantage is that policyholders drop their insurance because rates are high—only when they feel themselves to be in reasonably good health. Insureds suffering from some disease that may shorten their lives usually struggle to keep their insurance in force, regardless of increased cost. As the well members drop out and the ill remain, the mortality figures will soar and the premiums predicted on normal experience will not produce funds adequate to meet the claims. For both these reasons, assessment insurance no longer occupies an important place in the field of life insurance.

The level premium plan for permanent protection

One-year renewable term insurance policies are available with premiums calculated on the basis of the amount necessary to insure a person for one year. At younger ages, the premiums appear particularly attractive, but as permanent insurance the contracts manifest the same defects of increasing costs and adverse selection as assessment plans. To correct these defects, a plan that would not increase the premium with the age of the insured was devised and has become familiar to life insurance policyholders. The number of deaths still rises with increasing age, but the premium paid by the insured is constant throughout the premium-paying life of the contract. This disposes of the disadvantage of an increasing premium each year. The plan is one of averaging or leveling; hence the term *level premium*. Premiums substantially in excess of the cost of protection are collected in the earlier years of the policy. The excess is invested, and the accumulated sum reduces the amount of risk each year. (See Figure 9–2 in later section of this chapter.)

Reserves. The state law establishes a minimum amount that the insurer must have available to guarantee future obligations with respect to all policies. This amount is known as the *reserve*. It is sometimes called "reserves required to meet future claims," and it is quite often called the "legal reserve."

**Figure 9–1. Diagram showing decreasing amount at risk, first 20 years
of whole life policy issued at age 35**

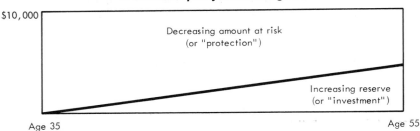

As the insured grows older, the reserve reduces the risk for the insurer so that a constantly increasing premium is not required to meet the increased mortality rate (see Figure 9–1). Under the level premium plan, the *net amount at risk* to the insurer is the face of the policy less the policyholder's reserve increased by interest earned from investments. Level premium plans, therefore, are a combination of protection and investment.

Combining protection and investment. Life insurance policies are classified as (*a*) temporary or "term" and (*b*) permanent or "whole life." Temporary life insurance provides protection only for the number of years designated in the contract, or to a specified age. If the policyholder outlives the term indicated in the policy, the coverage is terminated and no payment is made.

Permanent life insurance combines a saving or accumulation feature with the element of pure insurance. Basically the contract is composed of two elements: (*a*) the reserve and (*b*) pure life insurance. The reserve represents invested savings. Different forms of permanent insurance are designed to meet specific needs. The amount of the savings or investment account increases each year as premium payments are made. Since pure life insurance, that is the net amount at risk, is on a decreasing basis, if the insured lives long enough, the investment element would ultimately equal the face of the policy.

Cash values. Although the reserve is a group matter, parallel with it is a *cash value* allocated to each individual policy. The cash value, which also builds up from year to year, may be withdrawn by the policyholder or borrowed against.

Borrowing is quite different from withdrawal, and it sometimes occasions misunderstanding. A loan requires interest, and the question is frequently put: "Why should a policyholder pay interest on his or her own money?" The question points up a difference between the reserve and the cash value. The reserve is a group asset and must continually be increased at the rate of interest contemplated in rate calculations if the insurer is to meet future policy obligations. A policyholder loan is just another investment (at a fixed and guaranteed rate) to the insurer. Interest is required because of the interest-earning assumptions underlying the contract. If the cash value is withdrawn and the insurance terminated, that part of the reserve designed to meet the maturity of the policy is freed. Withdrawing the cash value, then, means the termination of insurance. Borrowing the cash value with a loan at interest keeps the insurance in force.

The investment functions of life insurance

Interest is one of the assumptions upon which the calculations of life insurance premiums are based. Hence, the investment of the reserve takes on importance. The continued accumulation of life insurance funds is inherent in the level premium system. The investment of these funds in a manner that will earn the necessary interest and assure payment of the principal on maturity is one of the major functions of the insurance business.

Life insurance replaces income lost in the death of policyholders, to dependents or others, or replaces income to policyholders in old age. To the extent that life insurance is purchased for *protection,* it is a contract of insurance. It provides a maximum income with security because life insurance may be planned to distribute both principal and income. To the extent that life insurance is purchased as a source of income, it becomes an *investment.* Annuities, discussed in Chapter 12, are also fundamentally investments.

To state that life insurance is a unique type of investment need not reflect unfavorably upon other types of securities. It is a particular type of investment carefully worked out to meet a particular need. Forms of life insurance having an element of investment give policyholders the benefit of investment skill and management. The insured has an ownership in a diversified cross section of the accumulated reserve of the life insurance company writing the contract.

The yield from cash-value types of life insurance is not the highest yield available to savers or investors. It is usually comparable with the yield from some banking accounts, savings and loan accounts, and government bonds and other high-grade securities, but it is often less than the yield from some other types of investments, such as stocks, real estate, or other investments were safety of principal is not the same. Valid comparisons of safety and yield are not easily done, for they must include careful analysis under proper assumptions, including the choice of investment goals, guaranteed and expected-but-not-guaranteed returns, the time periods for investment, the costs of investment, tax effects, and many other factors.

In evaluating the yield or return on life insurance as an investment, the net *aftertax* and *after-investment-expense* returns are important. Improper comparisons are often made which try to equate life insurance yield with returns on stock investments or mutual funds. Oftentimes the effect of income taxes, and the expenses of making these or other alternative kinds of investment, are neglected in the comparisons. For middle- and higher-income investors, the tax factor can mean 3 (or more) percent less on a net basis, with perhaps an additional 1 percent reduction from the gross return because of the expense element. Thus a gross return of 10 percent becomes 6 percent (or less) on a net basis. The substantial advantage of life insurance is that current income taxes are not payable on the interest buildup of the cash values, the so-called inside interest.

An interest rate of about 3.5 percent is guaranteed on the life insurance policy, but this is not the real rate of return on the savings portion of the contract. The policyholder usually receives a greater return through dividends. The guaranteed amounts are only minimums, used to calculate the basic reserves and cash values. In cash-value life insurance, the contract is a package of protection *and* savings. The *cost of protection* must be subtracted from the package, taking into consideration each year's cost of protection on the basis of the yearly renewable term insurance premium. This cost is relatively small at the younger ages, and for this reason a short-term (5–20 years, perhaps) comparison makes investments other than life insurance appear favorable. For longer investment periods of 20 years or more, the life insurance contracts show a better relative rate of return because the rapidly rising yearly cost of guaranteed protection at the older ages is built into the package contracts at a guaranteed price.

One authority flatly states that "there is no such thing as *the* rate of return on the savings element of a cash-life life insurance policy."[6] There are many ways of calculating the return, and many of the methods used by life insurance agents may be incorrect. An assumption of high cost for the protection element in the contract can make the savings return look very high, and an assumption of low cost can make it appear very low. Belth suggests that the rate of return be viewed as equal to the rate of return on comparable savings methods, such as the 5 or 6 percent paid by large mutual savings banks. A correct comparison of investment yield in life insurance contracts is a very technical and complicated matter. Improvements in the calculations used in past years are available from several sources now, including Belth's own suggested method.[7] For a discussion of term as opposed to permanent types of life insurance, which implicitly involves the investment alternatives to life insurance, see Chapter 10.

Another way of looking at life insurance earnings is to consider the net rate of return earned by life insurers on their total invested assets. In 1977 this was nearly 7 percent. Note that this is a return based upon investments

---

[6] Joseph M. Belth, *Life Insurance: A Consumer's Handbook* (Bloomington: Indiana University Press, 1973).

[7] See *Life Rates and Data* (Cincinnati: National Underwriter Co., 1977); and "Contract Cost and Benefit Comparisons," in *Life and Health Insurance Handbook,* ed. Davis W. Gregg and Vane B. Lucas, (Homewood, Ill.: Richard D. Irwin, 1973), chap. 16.

which are required to be placed largely in bonds and mortgages (approximately three fourths of the total assets in recent years) with high safety. The earnings rate has increased steadily from a low of about 3 percent 25 years ago to more than 6.8 percent today. For individual life insurers, of course, it varies. The earnings rate above the lower guaranteed rates upon which cash values are based has been a primary source of substantial returns to policyholders of "participating" contracts, upon which dividends are paid.

The usefulness of life insurance as an investment is dependent entirely upon the financial position, resources, and investment needs of the investor. However, for most investors the advantages of life insurance are:

1. *Safety* of principal and income.
2. Steady reasonable *yield.*
3. Ready marketability or *liquidity* (the cash values).
4. *Protection of assets from creditors.*
5. *Liquidation* options, especially lifetime annuity income.
6. Use of *loan values or* use as *collateral* for loans.
7. *Convenience* of purchase amounts, premiums, and investment management.
8. *Semicompulsory* nature, assuring *completion* of investment plans and an "instant estate."

Life insurance is always available as high-grade collateral for a loan. It may be purchased in face amounts that are convenient, and when used as an investment, it frees the owner from the responsibility for the selection of individual investments. Installment purchases are available to fit the convenience of the buyer. The investment is protected by the state regulation to which the life insurance business is subject. No other institution can equal the service of life insurance in providing protection against losses growing out of life risks. It creates many estates which, with or without the good intentions of the person insured, would otherwise never be accomplished. As soon as the life insurance contract is in force, an "instant estate" is created. The premium-payment plan encourages continuance of the contract, which in effect becomes a "self-completing" program over a long period of time. If investment is the primary need, life insurance may provide not only that the income will be regular and sure but that the period of income cannot be outlived by the recipient. For the inexperienced investor, life insurance eliminates reinvestment problems, expenses, and risks. Investments in life insurance may be arranged so that there will be freedom from seizure from the insured's creditors (see next section). It is the only form of investment that may be liquidated on installment plans that involve life contingencies, and the investment objective is protected against the failure of completions because of death.

Life insurance does not meet all investment needs, however, and increasingly it is being used by many persons in coordination with other investments in order to achieve the best investment results. For other persons the combined goals of protection *and* investment are reasonably achieved through the use of life insurance as the primary purchase. Many persons should consider a combination of investment media, using life insurance as a partial base for the total program. Including some high-yield and capital growth potential investments may help meet the need for accumulating large amounts of capital for retirement or other purposes and may help serve as a hedge against the erosion of dollar values through inflation.

Legal doctrines

Several legal doctrines are applied in the field of life insurance which are fundamental to an understanding of how life insurance works and how it is used by policyholders to accomplish certain goals.

Effects of divorce.   Where there is no statute covering the situation, the general rule is that a *divorce* does not deprive the irrevocable beneficiary of rights under a life insurance policy. In a few jurisdictions, however, the statutes make provision for terminating the interest of an irrevocable spouse-beneficiary following a divorce from the person whose life is insured, and a new beneficiary may be named. With a revocable beneficiary, which is very common, the spouse may, of course, change the beneficiary as he or she sees fit.

Common disaster.   In the event of a disaster in which both the insured and the beneficiary lose their lives, there is no common-law presumption as to the survivor. So far as the rights of the estate of each are concerned, much may depend upon establishing which of the two outlived the other. The courts have held that the burden of proof rests upon the representatives of the beneficiary. For example, if a husband insures his life naming his wife as beneficiary and both are killed in a disaster under such circumstances as to raise a doubt as to which died first, the benefits of the insurance will not go to the wife's estate unless it can be shown that she actually survived her husband. Because many insurance policies today, if they do not have a contingent beneficiary, provide for the reversion of the beneficiary's interest to the insured when the beneficiary dies first, proof of survivorship by the beneficiary is required. However, the need is taken care of in many policies by including a *common disaster clause.* This states that in case of death in a common accident (or within a specified number of days, such as 60) the insured shall be presumed to have survived the beneficiary. This prevents the payment of the insurance to the beneficiary's estate and permits the proceeds to be distributed through the insured's estate or as otherwise provided in the common disaster clause. This usually reduces estate taxes, because the amounts are not taxed in both estates.

In almost all states, legislation called the *Uniform Simultaneous Death*

Act[8] has been passed in order to reduce the problem of proving who died first. This provides that when the insured and the beneficiary have died and there is not sufficient evidence that they have died at different times, the proceeds of the policy shall be distributed as if the insured had survived the beneficiary.

Presumption of death.   The question arises as to the rights of a beneficiary under a life insurance policy *if the insured disappears* and is assumed to be dead but actual proof of death cannot be presented. Unexplained absence for seven years, with no communication with those who might be expected to hear from a person if the person were alive, raises the presumption of the death of the absent party. "The presumption of the duration of life with respect to persons of whom no account can be given ends at the expiration of seven years from the time when they were last known to be living."[9]

The presumption of death is prima facie; that is, it is rebuttable. Evidence may always be introduced to show that the person presumed to be dead was seen alive or that a reasonable explanation can be advanced for the absence. In most cases involving life insurance, therefore, the beneficiary must prove by a preponderance of evidence the time that such death took place. Insurers sometimes make voluntary payments before the seven-year period has passed, as for example they did to the beneficiaries of the Navy men who lost their lives in the disappearance of the submarine *Thresher* a number of years ago. Deaths in airline crashes and multiple drownings have been treated similarly.

Presumption against suicide.   Life insurance policies do not pay their full face value if the insured meets death as the result of *suicide* within a limited period, usually one or two years from the date of issue of the policy. Instead, in order not to encourage suicide (which is against public policy), only a return of premiums is paid if suicide occurs within the one- or two-year period. If the insurer writing a life insurance policy denies liability on this ground, the burden of proof rests upon the insurer to show that there was in fact a suicide. "The love of life is ordinarily sufficient inducement for its preservation, and, in the absence of proof that death resulted from other than natural causes, suicide will not be presumed."[10] When the evidence permits reasonable doubt as between the conclusion that death was caused by suicide and the conclusion

---

[8] This act has been enacted in 47 states and the District of Columbia. It has not been adopted in Georgia, Louisiana, or Ohio. However, Georgia and Louisiana have insurance law provisions which stipulate that in the case of simultaneous death the proceeds will be distributed as if the insured survived the beneficiary—unless the policy provides otherwise. Thus, although in form three states have not adopted the Uniform Law, as a practical matter the principle contained in this law has been enacted in all jurisdictions except Ohio. Ohio uses a set of presumptions as to who died first, such as older before younger persons, female before males, and other rules.

[9] *George* v. *Jesson,* 6 East. 80, 85; and *McCartee* v. *Camel,* 1 Barb., chap. 455.

[10] *Union Casualty and Surety Co.* v. *Goddard,* 75 S.W. 832.

that it was the result of an accidental or natural cause, the presumption operates against a finding of suicide.[11] Suicide is established when the evidence indicates that death was self-inflicted and permits no other reasonable inference. Drug overdoses and automobile carbon monoxide deaths are examples of situations in which difficulties arise in differentiating between accidental and intentional deaths.

Rights of creditors to life insurance values.   Since life insurance represents the accumulation of a fund for investment, the rights of *creditors* in the case of the insolvency of the insured are frequently perplexing. There is no fraud of creditors by the insured when reasonable insurance premiums are paid upon policies and the beneficiaries designated are such dependents as wife or children.[12] State statutes exempt the life insurance proceeds from the claims of creditors, and the tendency has been to liberalize exemptions.[13] In most states a third-party *beneficiary* under a policy effected by any person on his or her own life is entitled to the proceeds of the insurance against the creditors and representatives of the person whose life is insured.[14]

State exemption statutes vary greatly, but fall into one of several broad classifications: (*a*) statutes exempting close relatives, (*b*) statutes exempting all insurance from creditor claims if effected in favor of a person other than the insured, (*c*) statutes exempting a limited amount of protection, (*d*) unlimited exemption, and (*e*) special statutes. The most widely used exemption statute provides that the *beneficiary, other than the insured or the person effecting the insurance,* shall be entitled to the "proceeds and avails" of the policy without any limitation (based on the amount of premium or the face amount of the policy) against the creditors and representatives of the insured.[15] The law provides no protection against creditors of a beneficiary.

---

[11] *White* v. *Prudential Insurance Company,* 120 App. Div. 260.

[12] Under the terms of the Bankruptcy Act, in the case of bankruptcy the bankrupt is permitted to retain his or her insurance and keep it in force but is required to turn over an amount equal to the cash value to the trustee in bankruptcy. The United States Supreme Court has ruled that if the state statutes exempt a policy, it is exempt in bankruptcy proceedings.

[13] For complete analysis of the types, extent, and reasons for the protection of life insurance against creditors, as discussed in this section, see Stuart Schwarzschild, *Rights of Creditors in Life Insurance Policies* (Homewood, Ill.: Richard D. Irwin, published for the S. S. Huebner Foundation for Insurance Education, 1963).

[14] The exemption is justified upon the theory that an individual has definite obligations to wife, children, and dependents, as well as to creditors, and that there is as much justification in protecting dependents through insurance as there is in putting creditors in a preferred position. The protection of the interests of a beneficiary by statutory enactment is based upon the premise of an obligation to beneficiaries that may rightfully precede that of personal creditors.

[15] Laws of this type make an exception in protecting the proceeds of insurance against claims of creditors by providing that the amount of any premium paid to *defraud* creditors shall go to the benefit of the defrauded creditors from the proceeds of the policy. "Avails" includes cash value, dividends, and other values.

Special statutes may apply for: (*a*) group insurance, (*b*) fraternal insurance, (*c*) recipients of relief, (*d*) annuitants, and (*e*) recipients of disability income. Protection against creditors of beneficiaries is a characteristic of these statutes.

Fraud, murder by beneficiary, and death by execution. In case of *fraud by the insured misappropriating funds to pay premiums,* the defrauded person may usually obtain reimbursement from the proceeds of the policy. In the event of *murder of the insured by the beneficiary,* the courts have ruled that the beneficiary cannot collect the life insurance policy proceeds. The murderer should not profit from the criminal act, so the policy is paid instead to the estate of the insured. The insurer is exempted from payment only when there is no beneficiary who is free of the taint of crime or when the policy is obtained by the beneficiary with the intent of defrauding the insurer. In the past, life insurance policies often excluded payment for *death of the insured by execution.* Now practically all policies pay for death by legal execution just as they would for any other kind of death.[16]

THE MORTALITY TABLE

Life insurers must estimate the price of their insurance contracts in a safe and equitable manner. The goal requires analysis of *mortality* costs, *interest* earnings, and other *expense* factors. Because of a wealth of statistical information and of favorable mortality trends during the 20th century, the pricing of life insurance contracts is sometimes considered one of the easiest of all insurance rating tasks. However, accomplishing the safety of principal and fairness among all policy holders is not always simple. The long-range nature of the necessary predictions for life insurance contract spans 40 years or more. Very few businesses attempt to guarantee a fixed price for their product for such a long time into the future as life insurance does. Even most other insurance policies are based upon predictions of costs for only a limited period of one or a few years.

What it is

The basic obligation of life insurers is to pay death benefits, so they must know the expected life span of an insured group. The *mortality table* summarizes conveniently the probability of living or dying. It shows the probable death rate at each age, and by starting with a given number at a given age it shows how many persons will probably die during each succeeding year.

---

[16]*Weeks* v. *New York Life Insurance Company,* 122 S.E. 586–35 A.L.R. 1482.

Where it comes from and its purposes

Life insurance *actuaries*[17] construct tables showing the mortality experience of large groups of people. Applying the principles of probability and large numbers, they can predict rather closely the number of deaths and the time of their occurrence in any large group. The greater the number of cases under observation, the greater is the accuracy of predictions. Large numbers permit variations from the average to cancel one another, the actual results tending to equal the expected results.

Statutory enactments prescribe the table to be used for certain *purposes*. The actuary needs the mortality table (*a*) to calculate premium rates, (*b*) to calculate nonforfeiture benefits on lapse or surrender, (*c*) to value contract liabilities, (*d*) to calculate gains and losses from insurance operations, and (*e*) to calculate dividends on participating contracts.

A department known as the actuarial department is headed by the company actuary, who is frequently a company officer. The actuarial staff varies with the size of the organization, its needs, and the nature of the business. There may be an associate actuary or a number of assistant actuaries and mathematicians. The work of the actuarial department is closely allied with that of the medical department.

Basic construction

A completed mortality table seems to suggest that in its construction the actuary started with the number of lives indicated in the radix and then followed the history of that group from year to year until there were no survivors. Actually, the actuary determines the actual mortality rates for all the ages to be included in the table, and from these a table is built based upon such radix as is selected. The mortality table is an assemblage of data that show the probabilities of death and survival. The number of living at the youngest age is called the "radix" of the table. The radix is an arbitrary figure. (See Table 9–1, number living at age 0.) The completed table shows how many persons die at each age and how many survive out of a given number of persons under observation.

By knowing the number of persons in a group of a given age and the number of persons dying during the year, the probability that a person of a given age will live one year can be calculated. Applying the probability that a person of that age will live one year to the number living at any given age, the number who are expected to be alive at the beginning of the next succeeding year is determined. The process is repeated for each age.

---

[17] The title "actuary" within a company is one which may or may not indicate that the person has achieved the professional designation as a Fellow of the Society of Actuaries (FSA). Although many persons may perform actuarial functions, only those who have completed the rigorous examinations of the society are entitled to use the designation FSA following their names.

Table 9–1. 1958 CSO (Commissioners Standard Ordinary) Mortality Table

Age	Number Living	Number Dying	Death Rate Per 1,000	Expectancy, Years	Age	Number Living	Number Dying	Death Rate Per 1,000	Expectancy, Years
0	10,000,000	70,800	7.08	68.30	50	8,762,306	72,902	8.32	23.63
1	9,929,200	17,475	1.76	67.78	51	8,689,404	79,160	9.11	22.82
2	9,911,725	15,066	1.52	66.90	52	8,610,244	85,758	9.96	22.03
3	9,896,659	14,449	1.46	66.00	53	8,524,486	92,832	10.89	21.25
4	9,882,210	13,835	1.40	65.10	54	8,431,654	100,337	11.90	20.47
5	9,868,375	13,322	1.35	64.19	55	8,331,317	108,307	13.00	19.71
6	9,855,053	12,812	1.30	63.27	56	8,223,010	116,849	14.21	18.97
7	9,842,241	12,401	1.26	62.35	57	8,106,161	125,970	15.54	18.23
8	9,829,840	12,091	1.23	61.43	58	7,980,191	135,663	17.00	17.51
9	9,817,749	11,879	1.21	60.51	59	7,844,528	145,830	18.59	16.81
10	9,805,870	11,865	1.21	59.58	60	7,698,698	156,592	20.34	16.12
11	9,794,005	12,047	1.23	58.65	61	7,542,106	167,736	22.24	15.44
12	9,781,958	12,325	1.26	57.72	62	7,374,370	179,271	24.31	14.78
13	9,769,633	12,896	1.32	56.80	63	7,195,099	191,174	26.57	14.14
14	9,756,737	13,562	1.39	55.87	64	7,003,925	203,394	29.04	13.51
15	9,743,175	14,225	1.46	54.95	65	6,800,531	215,917	31.75	12.90
16	9,728,950	14,983	1.54	54.03	66	6,584,614	228,749	34.74	12.31
17	9,713,967	15,737	1.62	53.11	67	6,355,865	241,777	38.04	11.73
18	9,698,230	16,390	1.69	52.19	68	6,114,088	254,835	41.68	11.17
19	9,681,840	16,846	1.74	51.28	69	5,859,253	267,241	45.61	10.64
20	9,664,994	17,300	1.79	50.37	70	5,592,012	278,426	49.79	10.12
21	9,647,694	17,655	1.83	49.46	71	5,313,586	287,731	54.15	9.63
22	9,630,039	17,912	1.86	48.55	72	5,025,855	294,766	58.65	9.15
23	9,612,127	18,167	1.89	47.64	73	4,731,089	299,289	63.26	8.69
24	9,593,960	18,324	1.91	46.73	74	4,431,800	301,894	68.12	8.24
25	9,575,636	18,481	1.93	45.82	75	4,129,906	303,011	73.73	7.81
26	9,557,155	18,732	1.96	44.90	76	3,826,895	303,014	79.18	7.39
27	9,538,423	18,981	1.99	43.99	77	3,523,881	301,997	85.70	6.98
28	9,519,442	19,324	2.03	43.08	78	3,221,884	299,829	93.06	6.59
29	9,500,118	19,760	2.08	42.16	79	2,922,055	295,683	101.19	6.21
30	9,480,358	20,193	2.13	41.25	80	2,626,372	288,848	109.98	5.85
31	9,460,165	20,718	2.19	40.34	81	2,337,524	278,983	119.35	5.51
32	9,439,447	21,239	2.25	39.43	82	2,058,541	265,902	129.17	5.19
33	9,418,208	21,850	2.32	38.51	83	1,792,639	249,858	139.38	4.89
34	9,396,358	22,551	2.40	37.60	84	1,542,781	231,433	150.01	4.60
35	9,373,807	23,528	2.51	36.69	85	1,311,348	211,311	161.14	4.32
36	9,350,279	24,685	2.64	35.78	86	1,100,037	190,108	172.82	4.06
37	9,325,594	26,112	2.80	34.88	87	909,929	168,455	185.13	3.80
38	9,299,482	27,991	3.01	33.97	88	741,474	146,997	198.25	3.55
39	9,271,491	30,132	3.25	33.07	89	594,477	126,303	212.46	3.31
40	9,241,359	32,622	3.53	32.18	90	468,174	106,809	228.14	3.06
41	9,208,737	35,362	3.84	31.29	91	361,365	88,813	245.77	2.82
42	9,173,375	38,253	4.17	30.41	92	272,552	72,480	265.93	2.58
43	9,135,122	41,382	4.53	29.54	93	200,072	57,881	289.30	2.33
44	9,093,740	44,741	4.92	28.67	94	142,191	45,026	316.66	2.07
45	9,048,999	48,412	5.35	27.81	95	97,165	34,128	351.24	1.80
46	9,000,587	52,473	5.83	26.95	96	63,037	25,250	400.56	1.51
47	8,948,114	56,910	6.36	26.11	97	37,787	18,456	488.42	1.18
48	8,891,204	61,794	6.95	25.27	98	19,331	12,916	688.15	.83
49	8,829,410	67,104	7.60	24.45	99	6,415	6,415	1,000.00	.50

Since the radix of the table is arbitrary, the numbers in the columns headed "Number Living" and "Number Dying" are significant only as they serve as a basis for determining the proportion between the number living and the number dying. The column headed "Death Rate per 1,000" is the mortality rate, the basic feature of the table, and from it the other columns are derived. These columns are usually arranged under headings such as those appearing in the 1958 Commissioners Standard Ordinary Mortality Table, which appears in Table 9–1. The final column, "Expectancy, Years," is often included to show the expected number of years of life at each age.[18]

Different mortality tables for different needs

A difference in mortality tables does not mean that one is accurate and the other incorrect. Different tables are computed for different needs.

The rate that is important for life insurance premium calculations is the mortality rate of *insured* lives rather than the mortality rate of a mixture of insured and uninsured lives. It is also important that the group of insured lives be representative of the group to be insured. At first thought, it might seem reasonable to use the mortality ratios based upon insured lives to construct tables for both life insurance and *annuities*. Since, however, annuities provide for periodic payments from a given date throughout the lifetime of the annuitant, the longer the annuitant lives, the greater will be the cost of the insurer. In the case of life insurance on the other hand, the longer the insured lives, the greater will be the income in the form of premium payments for the life insurer. Hence, although a decreasing trend in mortality rates is a factor of safety for life insurance computations, it makes the table unsafe for annuity computations.

Annuity computations are essential in determining the value of optional settlements. The mortality data of insured lives prove inadequate for two reasons: (*a*) adverse selection of lives and (*b*) financial adverse selection. First, if the beneficiary in poor health has a choice, some form of settlement other than a life income will be selected. When impaired risks through self-selection are eliminated from the averages, the life expectancy of the remainder will be considerably longer than the average of the entire group. As to financial adverse selection, when investment yields are high, beneficiaries tend to elect a form that places policy yields within their own control. An upward trend in investment returns prompts the withdrawal of policy cash values. The tendency to leave funds with the insurer in a period of low yield causes an

---

[18] Don't be too discouraged by the life expectancy for your own age, for the trend is toward increasing longevity. To better the averages, consider the findings of one recent study: mortality rates seem to decrease if you are married, have many close friends and relatives, are a church member, and belong to many groups. "Longevity Linked to Social Contacts," *Columbus* (Ohio) *Dispatch,* February 2, 1978.

investment burden when it may be difficult to secure the required yield. The withdrawal of funds as interest rates increase may necessitate the sale of securities and thus disrupt a long-term investment program.

Annuity tables have been constructed based upon the experience of annuitants. The 1937 Standard Annuity Mortality Table found wide acceptance. Then a table called the Annuity Table for 1949 was published by the Society of Actuaries. Another annuity table, the 1955 American Annuity Table, is used by many companies. For group employee annuitants, the Group Annuity Table for 1951 is often used. For reserve calculations, new 1971 Individual, and Group, Annuity Tables are available. Projection scales to account for the declining mortality trends are used with many of these tables.

In the *group* insurance field, for life insurance contracts such as are written on employees through employers, the insurers use the Commissioners 1960 Standard Group Mortality Table. In the *industrial* life insurance field, for smaller policies, a 1941 table has been mostly replaced by the Commissioners 1961 Standard Industrial Table.

As indicated, there are more than a half-dozen mortality tables in current use for the differing needs of life insurers writing the various basic forms of life insurance (ordinary, group, industrial) and annuities (individual, group).

Development of the 1958 CSO Table

The life insurance business is highly competitive, and from year to year mortality improvement has been reflected in lower premium costs to the individual buyer. Since the turn of the century, life expectancy at birth has risen by more than 20 years. Most of the improvement occurred in the early 1900s with control of communicable diseases. Premium changes come about among mutual insurers through increased dividends and among stock insurers as a result of competitive rates. Both classes of insurers predicate their *rates* on *actual* mortality experience. In calculating *reserves and cash surrender values,* however, one of the *mortality tables* mentioned in the previous section is used, as recommended by the state insurance department and made mandatory by legislation of the states.

The American Experience Table appeared in 1867 and was adopted as an early standard. A new mortality table presented to the National Association of Insurance Commissioners became known as the Commissioners 1941 Standard Ordinary Mortality Table (1941 CSO Table). Mortality improvement sparked an interest in the development of a new table called the Commissioners 1958 Standard Ordinary Table (1958 CSO Table), based upon the mortality experience of 15 large companies for the years 1950–54. The model legislation accompanying the new table provides for the permissive use of lower mortality rates for women than for men. The 1958 table has been adopted for use by all states for policies issued after 1965, although the older table remains of importance for the many policies issued under the provisions of the 1941 table. The 1958 CSO Table is used in the text examples.

LIFE INSURANCE PREMIUM CALCULATIONS

The pricing of life insurance is an example of applied mathematics. The mortality tables, interest tables, and basic formulas are used to calculate the charge to be made for the life insurance contract.

Advancing premiums as age increases

The problem of computing the cost of insuring a group at any age for a period of a year is a matter of simple arithmetic. For example, reference to the 1958 mortality table shows that of 9,373,807 individuals living at the age of 35, 23,528 will die within a year. To insure all the members of the group at age 35 for $1,000 for one year will require a fund sufficient to pay $1,000 for each member dying during the year—$23,528,00 ($1,000 × 23,528). The premium each insured must pay to contribute his or her part to all the claims is $2.51 ($23,528,000 ÷ 9,373,807). To insure the survivors for another year, the charge must be higher since there are fewer members of the group (9,350,279) to pay the premiums and the number of deaths (24,685) will have increased the mortality rate. The 1958 CSO Table reflects a decreasing mortality rate for age zero through nine years and an increasing rate after age ten.

Thus insurance premiums, following the mortality rate for each year, advance each year. As the advanced ages are reached, the cost becomes prohibitive. For example, at the age of 85, of 1,311,348 survivors there will be 211,311 deaths. Hence, to pay the claims will require $211,311,000 ($1,000 × 211,311). Thus to insure a person at the age of 85 will cost $161.14 ($211,311,000 ÷ 1,311,348). While the pure premium charge for mortality is comparatively small when the insured is young, this charge increases sharply during the latter part of the life of the surviving members of a group.

The interest factor

All life insurance policies provide for the payment of the first premium before the insurance becomes effective. Since premium payments begin at the inception of the contract and benefits are payable at some future date, the element of interest must be introduced into the calculations to establish an equality between sums now due and sums to be due in the future.

Life insurance calculations are performed upon the basis of compound interest, that is, interest upon interest. The annual rate is expressed in simple interest. At the end of the first interest term, the amount of interest is added to the principal, and the interest rate is applied to the sum to find the interest due at the end of the succeeding term. Interest may be compounded annually or oftener.

For example, if $1,000 is invested at 2.5 percent for one year, $1,025 will be due at the end of the year. At compound interest, the amount due at the end of the first year is treated as a new principal, and the interest for the second year is $25.62, which added to $1,025, equals $1,050.62, the amount due at the end of the second year. *Interest earned* is the difference between an accumulated amount at interest and the principal invested. Continuing the process for a third year, the amount due is $1,076.89. The *principal,* or amount invested, is $1,000. The interest earned at the end of the three years is $76.89. Appendix A contains a compound interest table and is used to indicate the sum that a principal amount at compound interest will produce in a given number of years at 2.5 percent and other selected interest rates. For better understanding, the student should take a different interest factor (3.5 percent or 5 percent), for a longer period of years, and see how large a sum results.

The process of finding the *present value* of an amount due in the future is called *discounting.* The system is the opposite of that used in compound interest calculations. If, for example, A has $10,000 due him ten years hence, the debt is obviously worth something less than $10,000 because of the element of interest. We have just seen that $1,000 at 2.5 percent compound interest has a value of $1,076.89 at the end of three years. Applying the principle of compound discount, $1,076.89 at the end of three years has a present value of $1,000. As with compound interest, mathematicians have calculated compound discount tables which show the present value of $1 at the end of any number of years. Appendix A shows the present value of a sum payable years hence, at 2.5 percent and other selected interest rates.

Since life insurance benefits are sums payable at a future time, the premiums are due and payable at an earlier date than the due date of the benefits. In establishing the equivalence of benefits and premiums, the discount calculations are basic. The premium is adjusted to the benefit, and not the reverse. One buys, as a rule, a policy for a given number of dollars, say $10,000, rather than as much insurance as a given premium will buy. It becomes necessary, then, to know the present value of the benefits to establish the equivalence of premiums.

In computing the net premiums up to this point, only the actual mortality cost has been considered. By reducing the amount of the death claims to their value at the beginning of the policy year, the factor of interest is introduced and an accurate figure secured. Hence, at the age of 35 the actual cost of insuring all the members of the group for one year will be $2.44 ($23,528,000 × 0.975610 ÷ 9,373,807). This is the net premium for a $1,000 policy written for a term of one year at the age of 35.

To recapitulate:

One-year term, age 35 net premium

No interest			
Number living	Number dying	Amount of policy	With interest
9,373,807	23,528	$1,000	$23,528,000 × 0.97560976 = $22,954,146.43
$\dfrac{\$23,528,000}{9,373,807} = \$2.51$			$\dfrac{\$22,954,146.43}{9,373,807} = \$2.44$

The process of life insurance premium calculation is illustrated in its basic form in this example for a one-year term policy. In order to determine the price for other insurance contracts, a *net single premium* (NSP) that would pay for the duration of the entire policy, with interest earnings, is calculated. The technique of doing this for a five-year term policy and a whole life policy is shown in Appendix B. Also explained there is the process of converting the NSP to a net level premium (NLP), an annual premium cost figure which is needed because most policies are purchased on an annual (or more frequent) payment basis. An annuity calculation is used to convert the NSP to a NLP. Appendix B illustrates this process for a five-year term policy and a whole life policy.

The gross premium

The discussion of premium computation has for simplicity omitted operating costs. The expense of carrying on the business is estimated on the basis of past experience; this amount is added to the net premium and is known as the *loading*. The *net premium plus* the *loading* is the *gross premium*.

Nature and purposes. The loading added to the net premium for known expenses and unknown contingencies is not uniform among companies. Among mutual insurers the loading is frequently heavier than among stock insurers. The additional premium strengthens the financial position of mutual insurers, and inequity is avoided through a return of any excess beyond needs for growth in the form of dividends to the policyholders.

The element of loading provides, first, for operating expenses and, second, for contingencies unforeseen in the calculations. The expense element includes such items as the cost of getting business and the cost of collecting premiums. Principal among these items are commissions on new business, subsequent commission payments for a term, and the state tax levied on premiums. Other expense items include the cost of settling claims and such general business expenses as salaries and the cost of keeping records.

Calculations. The loading is an amount per $1,000 of insurance, and it varies with the kind of policy and age at issue. To arrive at an equitable distribution of the loading requires complex actuarial calculations. These calculations involve the classification of expenses and a determination of the proportion of particular expense items to be charged to each class of policyholder.

Experience shows that expenses may be grouped into one of three broad categories: (a) those that vary with the size of the premium, (b) those that vary with the amount of the policy, and (c) those independent of both. Commissions that represent a proportion of the premium or premium taxes levied on the amount of the premium will vary as the amount of the premium varies. For example, the amount of tax and the amount of commission on an endowment policy for $1,000 will be higher than on a whole life policy issued at the same age. Home office expenses, including salaries, research, accounting, and the like, represent fixed costs that have no direct bearing upon either the premium or the policy amount but are to be distributed among all the policyholders. When all the variable and fixed factors are taken into consideration, a loading system determined to be equitable is worked out.

LIFE INSURANCE RESERVES

Insurance cost is computed to meet the death claims from year to year, plus the cost of carrying on the business. The natural premium increases from year to year. Up to this point in the computation of premiums, one side of the equation has consisted of benefits to be received and the other side of premiums to be paid. The aggregate of all premiums, increased by the assumed rate of interest, must produce a fund sufficient to pay all the benefits as policies mature.

Origin

The *level premium plan* introduced the element of *overpayment*. During the early policy years, a net premium considerably larger than is necessary to meet the mortality costs for these years is collected. As much of that premium as represents excess over calculated costs for each year is reserved for use in the later policy years when the net level premium payments are insufficient for meeting mortality costs. The reserve, then, does not represent a profit to the insurer but is held to meet the claims of policyholders.

A comparison of the natural with the level premium illustrates graphically the need for a reserve under the level premium plan. Figure 9–2 illustrates the trend of a *natural* premium. The vertical lines represent the premium charge of each succeeding year. *Level* premium payments for the same age are also shown.

Superimposing one curve upon the other, one sees at once the extent to which excess payments are made during the earlier years (Figure 9–2). The

Figure 9-2. Natural premium trend and level premium trend

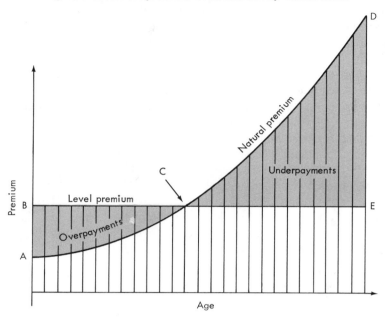

area *ABC* represents the excess premiums paid during the earlier years. The larger area *CDE* represents the deficiency during the later years of the amount actually collected from the current level premium. This, plus the interest derived from the investment of premiums, represents the reserve accumulated to carry the policy until paid. In computing the adequacy of a reserve, the insurer considers all the policyholders of a group. If an individual carries a policy a few years and dies, the insured pays more than the natural premiums (mortality costs). The excess is not a profit to the insurer since the reserve is necessary for the solvency of the group.

Definition

Very simply, the *reserve* is an amount which, augmented by premium payments required under outstanding contracts, will enable the life insurer to meet its policy obligations. The reserve is built up out of past premium payments and interest. More specifically, it is that portion of premiums paid on level premium life insurance policies which is held to pay future death benefits, policy loans, surrender values, and the like. It is represented by assets which the insurer invests, but it is, in fact, an insurer liability to be disbursed to meet the obligations of the policy contract.

For the purpose of computing the reserve, the basic equation used for the computation of premiums during the policy term is as follows: The present value of future premiums plus the reserve equals the present value of future benefits.[19] Transposing the equation, the reserve equals the present value of future benefits minus the present value of future premiums.

With reference to each policy, the reserve grows as the years pass. The difference between the reserve and the face of the policy at any given time represents an amount termed the "net amount at risk." As time runs, therefore, the net amount at risk decreases until it ultimately vanishes, unless death intervenes to mature a claim (see Figure 9–1).

The frequently made statement that the reserve accumulated against a life insurance policy should be paid to the beneficiary along with the face of the policy is the outgrowth of a misunderstanding. As a matter of fact, the reverse is not assigned to each particular policy.

The reserve account

The fundamental purpose of the reserve is to have assets available to meet the obligations of the insurer for the payment of claims in years to come. The premium calculations contemplate that the reserve will earn interest for the benefit of policyholders and beneficiaries, and it is accordingly invested in securities such as bonds, mortgages, stocks, and real estate. The financial statement of an insurer will show an amount under the heading "Admitted Assets." This represents investments and other credits approved by the state insurance department. The *legal reserve,* plus other liabilities and required capital or surplus, must not exceed the admitted assets if the insurer is to be permitted to continue business.

The ability of the insurer to meet all claims as they mature depends upon the adequacy of the reserve account. The legal reserve should never be regarded as an extra amount to meet contingencies or as a profit above mortality experience, for on the basis of the calculated experience the mortality costs will ultimately absorb the entire reserve. Only to the extent that actual experience is more favorable than the calculations will there be any excess over claims from the reserve account.

The mortality tables used as a basis for policy valuation in determining minimum legal reserves make no provision for contingencies other than reasonable margins against adverse mortality fluctuations. They do not provide for investment losses, changing expense ratios, or unfavorable mortality experience due to wars or epidemics. A satisfactory method for providing for

---

[19] The technicalities of the various methods used to determine the legal reserves required by the states are explained in chaps. 11 and 13 of Dan M. McGill, *Life Insurance,* rev. ed. (Homewood, Ill.: Richard D. Irwin, 1967). Also recommended for the student desiring further explanation of the arithmetic of life insurance, its contracts, and its legal aspects is S. S. Huebner and Kenneth Black, Jr., *Life Insurance* (New York: Appleton-Century-Crofts Co., 1976).

such contingencies is the accumulation of special *contingency reserves.* The account so accumulated is over and above policy legal reserve, and is actually part of the "surplus."

UNDERWRITING OF LIFE INSURANCE

Medical examinations

In computing premiums, life insurers use only tables based upon insured lives. Since life insurance premiums are computed on the basis of the expected mortality of such a group, the solvency of the insurer requires that the group of insureds be so selected that the actual mortality experience will be no greater than was anticipated when the rates were set.

The *medical examination* is one method that is used to avoid insuring applicants who know themselves to be suffering from a physical impairment that might shorten their lives. The purpose of the medical examination is not to find a perfect group for insurance. The examination undertakes, however, to eliminate from the group those who are suffering from ailments that tend to increase the mortality beyond that which the mortality table anticipates. It also helps classify the impaired risks into groups to which premiums adequate to the risk may be assigned, and it detects fraud such as that of an applicant who is aware of a very serious ailment.

When required, medical examinations are made by a physician appointed by the insurer. Exceptions to the practice of requiring a medical examination are usually made for group policies (see Chapter 14), for annuities (Chapter 12), and for industrial policies (Chapter 10), which are ordinarily sold for small amounts and are payable weekly. In other instances, policies are written that make use of a "nonmedical" plan which contemplates placing an increased burden on sources other than the medical examiner for required underwriting information. For much of the insurance that is written, however, the medical examination supplies information for determining whether or not, or on what basis, the applicant is acceptable for insurance.

The medical examiner usually takes less than an hour for the life insurance examination and filling out Part II of the application form. The physician also reports the applicant's physical characteristics; general condition; any abnormalities of primary systems such as the heart, the lungs, and the digestive and reproductive organs; and the result of blood pressure and urinalysis tests. X-rays or electrocardiograms are sometimes required for larger policy applications, or where the applicant's medical history indicates possible abnormal conditions.

If everyone in a community or country were insured, a medical examination would be unnecessary. Since, however, insurance is purely a matter of volition on the part of the individual, without medical examination there would be a tendency for the unhealthy to seek insurance and for others to neglect or postpone it. Where such a situation exists, there is said to be a condition of "adverse selection," or selection against the insurer.

Other factors and sources of information

Numerous other factors are considered by the insurer in the total underwriting process. *Personal health history* and *habits* are inquired about in the application; *family history* is also important; *occupation, morals, type of insurance, build* (relation of height and weight), and *residence* (U.S. or foreign) are among other information evaluated. *Aviation* interests as a private pilot may result in increases of $3 to $5 per $1,000 of insurance, but no increases are usually charged for any flying as a passenger (even crew members of scheduled commercial airliners receive standard rates). *Sex* is a major factor in the underwriting of life insurance contracts, as many insurers use special lower rates for females. The use of lower rates for *nonsmokers,* which a number of insurers have offered with good sales success during the past decade, may reduce premiums by about 2 percent.

The sources of information include several in addition to the *insured,* the *application,* the *agent,* and the *medical examination*: the *inspection report,* by an independent company (such as Equifax, Inc., or the American Service Bureau) check on the financial status, reputation, and habits of the applicant; and the *Medical Information Bureau* (MIB),[20] a central clearinghouse of all major health impairments noted for past applicants for life insurance.

Substandard or impaired risks

An impaired or *substandard risk* is a person in whom the hazard may be presumed to be increased because of the existence of unfavorable physical condition, family history, habits, or occupation. Through the development of the "extra-risk" type of policy, the benefits of life insurance have been extended to many persons who were formerly ineligible because of their classification as impaired risks. By means of actuarial studies, insurers were able to determine what extra premium should be charged to compensate for the extra risk. The result has been the reduction of declined applications for life insurance, to a point in 1977 where they amounted to only 3 percent of total applications,and extra-risk policies were 5 percent of ordinary contracts issued.[21] Liberalization of underwriting rules over the years means that today even cancer victims who have fully recovered may receive standard rates.

Impaired risks fall into two groups. In the first group, an extra premium

---

[20] For the interesting story of this important underwriting interchange among life insurers, see William B. Swarts, "A Decade of Change at MIB," *CLU Journal,* vol. 31, no. 2 (April 1977), p. 48.

[21] *Life Insurance Fact Book,* p. 99.

is charged to compensate for the hazards of *occupation*. About 1 in 11 extra-risk policies are of this type. The mortality range for occupational hazards varies from an additional charge of one third to three times normal mortality. Both accident and disease factors affecting potential mortality are considered. A window cleaner at the United Nations building has an obvious increased mortality risk. So do miners (lung disease and accidents), construction workers, and many other occupational groups. Even hobbies, such as skydiving or motorcycle racing, affect the decisions made by insurers, but not all sports affect the rate. Skin diving, for example, usually does not.

The second group of substandard risks includes those with *physical impairments*. Those of most frequent occurrence are heart disease (30 percent of all extra-risk policies), weight problems (19 percent), and other physical impairments (31 percent). Occupation and other reasons make up the remaining 20 percent.

A *numerical rating system* is used by most insurers to evaluate the total effects of physical condition, build, family history, occupation, habits, and other factors. Rating scales based upon debits and credits for these items are developed. A standard class may fall between 75 and 125, while numerous substandard classes (some as high as 500 to 1,000 percent of normal mortality) are identified. An example might be:

Average person's mortality	100%
Favorable family history	(−10)
Unfavorable occupation	+20
Unfavorable build and overweight	+15
Blood pressure	+35
Total	160%

Several methods of increasing premiums for substandard or impaired risks are used by life insurers. Most common are (1) adding an extra flat charge, such as $2 per $1,000 of insurance, and (2) increasing the insured's age, or "rating up" the policy by using the premiums charged to a person one or more years older than the insured.

Nonmedical life insurance

With a view to reducing acquisition expense, eliminating delay, and overcoming the sales resistance that sometimes presents itself in the form of an objection to a medical examination, the plan of writing life insurance without such an examination was instituted.

In Canada, where nonmedical life insurance made its first appearance, many life insurance applications were received in rural districts where the services of a physician were not always readily obtainable. This same factor—the unavailability of doctors for medical examinations—was an important contributing factor to the further extension of nonmedical life insurance business during and after World War II.

For the nonmedical application, agents must secure much of the information otherwise obtained by the medical examiner. They do not undertake anything in the nature of an actual physical examination but secure direct from the applicants specific replies to carefully drafted questions concerning the personal and family history and physical condition. The agent also determines as far as possible that the applicant is in sound health and able to work regularly. This information is carefully verified through an independent inspection report, which checks particularly such matters as intemperance and immoral habits. Infrequently the information obtained by this inspection may indicate the possibility of an impairment; in such circumstances a medical examination is required. However, the majority of nonmedical applications are decided on without an examination.

The objective of nonmedical life insurance is the same as that of contracts written following a medical examination, that is, to secure an average mortality for the group instead of an abnormally high mortality rate caused by adverse selection. The elimination of the medical examination cost permits a slightly higher mortality experience for the nonmedical life insurance contracts.

In nonmedical coverages, the insurer limits the amount of insurance and the age range. Many insurers make no differentiation between men and women. The trend is definitely toward liberalization of limits. Many life insurers today write $25,000 or more on a nonmedical basis at the younger ages. Some insurers have extended the nonmedical procedure to all applications through age 40 for amounts of $25,000 or less. For ages up to 50, the limit may be reduced to a maximum of $5,000 or $10,000. More and more insurers are writing individual plans, including term insurance and special contracts (except for preferred-risk policies available only to above-average risks), on a nonmedical basis. The practices seem to vary greatly by company, but increasing use of nonmedical life insurance is readily apparent.

A final example is the growing use of the *insurability option* in connection with many contracts (see Chapter 10). This permits the insured to purchase additional amounts of insurance at stated ages or future years without a medical examination. A $10,000 ordinary life policy taken out at age 22, for example, may include the right to buy six additional $10,000 contracts, one each at age 25, 28, 31, 34, 37, and 40. Standard contracts at regular rates would be issued, without any medical examination (no matter what the health condition was), if the insured chose to exercise the option to buy the additional insurance.

War clauses

Life insurance mortality tables do not reflect death rates to be expected from major military operations. Life insurers have usually attached the so-called war clause to policies issued at the younger ages during wartime. The most common type of war clause excludes death resulting from war.

War clauses cannot be attached to policies already in existence. Insurers follow different rules with respect to new business. It is generally the practice, however, to use the war clause for members of the armed forces. Sometimes insurers attach the clause to all policies issued to younger applicants who might enter military service. The protection provided by the group life insurance of $20,000 automatically provided to military personnel now relieves life insurers of some of the need to provide for the war risk.

FOR REVIEW AND DISCUSSION

1. In what ways does life insurance differ from other types of insurance? Why are these differences important to the insurer and to the insured?

2. Legally and technically, life insurance is not a contract of indemnity. Why not? Is there a relationship between life insurance and the *idea* of indemnity? Explain your answer.

3. Many situations give rise to an insurable interest in life insurance. Give an example of at least four different insurable interests.

4. The cost of life insurance is based upon three fundamental estimates that must be made by an insurer. What are they, and how accurately can they be predicted? Indicate any special problems, including trends which have been helpful or harmful.

5. How is the actuarial basis for the basic life insurance contracts (*a*) similar and (*b*) different?

6. What are the fallacies in the assessment plan when it is applied to life insurance? Can they be solved by a different premium-paying plan? (This concept can also be explored by having students assume that the class is forming an assessment company. Then have them discuss the likely problems as they become older.)

7. How would you explain the advantages and disadvantages of life insurance *as an investment* to a newly married couple? What factors would be important in determining your recommendations?

8. Tom and Joe are not related. Tom wishes to insure his life, naming Joe's children as beneficiaries, but is told he cannot do this. Do you agree or disagree? Why?

9. Jerry carries $50,000 life insurance with his wife Tina as beneficiary. Both perish in an aviation disaster. To whom will the insurance be paid? Could the problem be avoided by any special provisions in the insurance policy?

10. Mr. MacDonald disappears without any explanation. When will his wife receive payment as beneficiary under his life insurance policy?

11. What significant advantage do life insurance contract values have to the insured and his or her beneficiaries, if the insured has debts owed to a creditor?

12. Explain how a mortality table is constructed. Why are different mortality tables used rather than just one?

13. At the time the Commissioners Standard Ordinary (CSO) 1958 Mortality Table was adopted to replace the 1941 CSO Table, the latter table overestimated mortality rates. Did this have the effect of overcharging policyholders for their life insurance protection?

14. Why is it not possible to use the same mortality table to compute a life insurance premium and the purchase price of an annuity? How are annuity tables used in connection with the life contract?

15. Where does the life insurance reserve come from? How would you describe the purpose of the reserve? To what is it equal?

16. What are the sources of surplus to a life insurer from which it may return a dividend to its policyholders? Should the entire surplus be returned?

17. Name two classes of extra-risk hazards that may result in the classification of an applicant for insurance as substandard. Give examples.

18. Are medical examinations always required before life insurance is issued? If your answer is *yes,* explain why they are necessary. If your answer is *no,* explain why they are not needed.

Chapter 10

Concepts considered in Chapter 10—Individual life insurance contracts

Individual life insurance contracts are part of the
Broader financial services needed and desired by consumers today.
Major classes: (1) *individual,* including industrial, and (2) *group,* including creditor life.
Basic types of life insurance contracts are:
Whole life insurance policies: permanent contracts paid by (1) *single-premium payment,* (2) *limited-payment* period, (3) premium payments throughout life (the popular *straight life* or *ordinary life* contract), (4) *modified life* contract, smaller initial premiums.
Term insurance policies have increased in popularity.
Nature: temporary protection for a stated term or duration.
Uses: mortgages, business obligations, families with dependents.
Misuses may rely on low short-run costs and "buying term and investing the difference" *without careful long-run analysis.*
Conversion privileges to permanent contracts are important.
Endowment insurance policies emphasize the savings element.
Normal type combines term insurance (pays if you die) with a *pure endowment* (pays if you live).
Uses and misuses depend upon one's goals and protection needs.
Other types include the *retirement income* policy.
Cost comparisons: net cost and interest-adjusted methods help the buyer compare contract costs.
Special riders and policy combinations are plentiful, such as:
Guaranteed purchase option, permitting young policyholders to purchase additional standard insurance at stated ages;
Other combinations, such as double protection and joint life contracts.
Special life insurance markets include:
Family insurance plans:
Family income policy, combining term and whole life insurance;
Family maintenance policy, with decreasing term; and the
Family policy, a popular policy insuring the entire family.
Juvenile insurance plans, including the "jumping juvenile" policy.
Larger plans: minimum amounts, preferred risks, graded sizes.
Split-dollar plans, mostly for employer-employees.
Split-life insurance, an innovation of separate annuity and term-life contracts, with some tax advantages for buyers.
Variable life insurance, an equity-based product with wide market potential, in which the face value is not fixed, but changes.
Adjustable life insurance, permitting both premium and insurance amount changes to meet "life cycle" needs.

Individual life insurance contracts

Both men and women are life insurance consumers, in about a 3-to-1 ratio for policies purchased, and a 4-to-1 ratio for amounts of insurance bought. Both groups are becoming better buyers. Some say that our times are beginning to emerge as the age of the "professional consumer."[1] With knowledge, education levels, and communication media expanding rapidly, the consumer *should* be better. Yet how often he or she fails to be the informed prudent buyer that such advances in society make possible! Purchasers can and should ask for more varied and more effective services from sellers, and sellers must pay attention to the requests of buyers. The consumer, however, needs to know *who* and *what* to ask, and for life insurance one of the most important areas for questions concerns the types of life insurance contracts and services that are available. The related question of "How much life insurance should I own?" is treated in Chapter 16, after the student has learned about the many forms in which life insurance is available.

BROADER FINANCIAL SERVICES

Among life insurers a definite trend toward broader financial services has evolved. The basic question now is not whether such services should be broadened, but how far the typical life insurer can go in extending in an *efficient* manner its range of consumer products and services.

Many life insurers have already changed greatly from a decade ago. Others have not, and perhaps will not—feeling that their purpose is the specialized one of distributing life insurance contracts only. Most life insurers, however, have added *health* insurance, *group* insurance, and/or *annuities* to their business. The benefits of coordinating these contracts with basic individual life insurance policies, the sales and record-keeping advantages of the combination, and other advantages have made such diversification of product lines successful for most life insurers.

Within recent years the trend has extended to many other financial services. Numerous insurers are not prepared to offer a full range of financial services

---

[1] Credit for this term goes to Patrick Doyle, CLU, CPCU, who has often been able to "coin a phrase" of merit.

to their clients. *Mutual funds, variable annuities,* and *variable life* policies are the most talked-about additions, but some insurers are reorganizing (oftentimes through a holding-company corporate organization) in order to provide *banking, credit, trust,* and *investment* services of many kinds.

Although it appears that this trend will continue and probably accelerate, it is worthwhile and necessary to study life insurance as a separate subject. The life insurance contract as a distinct, unique, and one of the most widely used of all legal documents deserves such separate treatment. More than two out of three persons in the United States have life insurance—more than an astounding 140 million of the total population. There is an *additional* need today for proper coordination with the alternative and supplementary choices that are increasingly available in the total financial market for meeting consumer needs. However, the significance of life insurance as a basic part of financial protection and investment remains high.

THE MAJOR CLASSES OF LIFE INSURANCE

The life insurance business has developed two basic methods of distributing life insurance contracts: (1) *individual* insurance and (2) *group* insurance. The purpose of utilizing more than one system of marketing life insurance is to reach the largest possible number of insureds. No one technique has proved best in selling the idea of life insurance to all markets. The two basic methods are called the major classes of life insurance.

Four categories have been identified for many years: (*a*) *ordinary* life insurance, (*b*) *industrial* life insurance, (*c*) *group* life insurance, and (*d*) *credit* life insurance. The first two categories involve a separate policy contract for each purchaser and are therefore discussed in this chapter on *individual* life insurance contracts. The third category, *group* life insurance, concentrates its sales efforts by combining many individuals, usually in one group contract for employers. The group technique for providing life and health insurance protection is studied in Chapter 14, and group annuities are studied in Chapter 12. The fourth category, *credit life* insurance, is included in the group insurance totals because almost 85 percent of these contracts, sold through banks and finance companies (often in connection with installment loans), are sold on a group basis.

Table 10–1 shows the growth of the two major classes of life insurance. Today the individual class includes $1,328 *billion,* or 51 percent of the total, and the group class accounts for 1,255 *billion,* or 49 percent of the total life insurance in force in the United States. Group insurance increased its percentage of the total from 9 percent in 1930, to 22 percent in 1950, and to 49 percent at the beginning of 1978. In total, life insurance in force has grown from $41 billion in 1920, to $234 billion in 1950, and to $2,583 billion at the beginning of 1978.

Table 10–1. Growth of the major classes of life insurance in the United States (by life insurance in force; in billions of dollars and percentages)

End of year	Individual*		Group†		Total	
	Amount	Percent	Amount	Percent	Amount	Percent
1920	38.9	96.0	1.6	4.0	40.5	100.0
1930	96.6	90.7	9.9	9.3	106.5	100.0
1940	100.2	86.8	15.3	13.2	115.5	100.0
1950	182.8	77.9	51.7	22.1	234.2	100.0
1960	379.8	64.8	206.6	35.2	586.4	100.0
1970	769.1	54.9	633.0	45.1	1,402.1	100.0
1977‡	1,328.3	51.4	1,254.5	48.6	2,582.8	100.0

* Individual insurance includes industrial life insurance, which in 1978 was only 3 percent of individual insurance.
† Group insurance includes credit life insurance, of which almost 85 percent was group.
‡ Credit life figures added to group include only loans on life insurance of ten years' duration or less.
Source: *Life Insurance Fact Book* (Washington, D.C.: American Council of Life Insurance, 1978), p. 18.

Individual life insurance

Ordinary life insurance. The life insurance business has to a large degree emphasized the sale of *ordinary life* insurance. The protection is issued on the basis of individual applications through life insurance agents, and may be adapted to almost every insurance need. Today it accounts for about 50 percent of all life insurance in force. It is usually written in units of $1,000, and the average new policy is for over $18,000, having doubled in the past ten years. Premiums are computed on an annual basis, but may be paid monthly, quarterly, semiannually, or annually. Premiums are due and collectible at the home office or the branch office of the insurer. The emphasis of this chapter is placed on this type.

Industrial life insurance. In contrast to ordinary life insurance, *industrial life* insurance is written in small face amounts, usually less than $1,000. Premiums are normally payable weekly or monthly and are collected by company representatives at the home of the policyholder.

Industrial life insurance has historically been of substantial importance. It introduced the uses of life insurance and the habit of thrift to many millions of policyholders. To meet the requirements of the industrial classes, insurers were asked by the early 1900s to provide insurance with premium payments adjusted to the needs of workers, such as a small weekly payment of $0.10, $0.25, or more.

Although industrial life insurance in force has leveled off in recent years at about $40 billion and now represents less than 2 percent of life insurance outstanding as opposed to 10 percent 20 years ago, it remains the sole vital source of protection for many families. Some 66 million policies are still in force, averaging about $600 per policy.[2] Industrial life insurance (or "debit" insurance as it is sometimes called because of the method of accounting for the weekly collections) has declined in relative importance because of: the increased affluence of most families, which now can purchase much larger amounts of insurance than $1,000; the family policy (see later section); the availability of group insurance to most employees; and the death benefits paid under the federal social security plan. Also, many of the larger insurers that once sold primarily industrial life insurance have changed to issuing regular ordinary policies on a monthly premium basis. This form is called "home service" life insurance, and it is included in the ordinary life figures.

Most industrial insurance is issued without a medical examination, the insurer relying upon statements in the application by the applicant and the agent. Many policies are written on entire families, including each of the children. The method of collecting the premium and the expense of handling small sums add materially to the cost, and cause the rate for industrial life insurance to be higher than the rate for ordinary life insurance. However, for many insureds the collection service is just as real a benefit as the insurance itself, enabling many persons who otherwise could or would carry no insurance to have some protection. There are now few differences between the provisions in an industrial life insurance policy and those in most ordinary policies. The industrial life policy contains many of the nonforfeiture provisions and double indemnity provisions without extra premium. Industrial life insurance is in the strict sense not a different form of insurance protection, but rather a plan adapted to a particular market.[3] The first several hundred dollars of any life insurance is usually provided for last expenses and burial. Industrial life insurance provides for these immediate needs of low-income families.

Group life insurance

Group life insurance. *Group life* insurance is the most recent and most rapidly growing major class of life insurance, accounting for 49 percent (including credit life) of life insurance in 1978. It differs from ordinary life insurance in that the unit of selection is the group rather than the individual. Most group plans are sold to employers for their employees, but others are also sold to creditors, unions, trusts, and associations. Almost all of the insurance is term insurance. Usually, no medical examination is required. Consideration of annuities and insurance contracts involving groups will be given special treatment in Chapters 12 and 14.

Credit life insurance. The basic purpose of credit life insurance is to repay a debt if the borrower dies. Only one seventh of this category of life

---

[2] *Life Insurance Fact Book* (Washington, D.C.: American Council of Life Insurance, 1978), p. 31.

[3] Robert A. Marshall and Eli Zubay, *The Debit System of Marketing Life and Health Insurance* (Englewood Cliffs, N.J.: Prentice-Hall, 1975).

insurance is based on individual contracts; thus credit life insurance is essentially a method using group life policies. Relatively unimportant until 25 years ago, it has grown steadily since then from about $6 billion to almost $140 billion of life insurance in force, or more than 5 percent of all life insurance. Master contracts cover 80 million persons.[4]

Credit life is term insurance, usually decreasing in amount in conjuntion with the loan, which is paid off with the life insurance when the borrower dies. Life insurers issue the contracts through banks, finance companies, credit unions, and retailers. Credit life insurance has grown to be a significant part of our credit economy. Group creditor life insurance is discussed further in Chapter 14.

BASIC TYPES OF LIFE INSURANCE CONTRACTS

A great many different life insurance policies are offered to meet the varying needs of individuals. All are either whole life, term, or endowment policies or a combination of one or more of these. Such combinations may include the annuity principle, since annuities are a part of the life insurance business. This being the case, there are four contracts basic to the life insurance business: (1) *whole life* insurance, (2) *term* insurance, (3) *endowment* insurance, and (4) *annuities.*

Whole life insurance includes those forms in which the face amount is paid on the death of the insured whenever death occurs. This is a permanent form of insurance and covers the insured for life. *Term* insurance pays on the death of the insured only if the insured dies during the term covered. If the insured outlives the period, there is no obligation on the part of the insurer with respect to benefits of any kind. *Endowments* provide insurance coverage during a stated period and emphasize the savings element. The face of the policy is payable at the end of the endowment period to the insured if living *or* to the beneficiary if the insured dies during the period. *Annuity* contracts provide for periodic income payments to be made for a fixed period or as long as the annuitant or annuitants live. Annuities are separately treated in Chapter 12.

These four basic contracts form the foundation of the many life insurance coverages offered in the market. No matter how complex a coverage may seem or how many benefits or options are available, the policy effects its objectives by incorporating in a single contract the features of one or more of the basic contracts.

Summary comparison

A summary comparison of the basic and common life insurance contracts, not including annuities, is given in Table 10–2. Note that the cost comparisons emphasize the extreme differences in cost which may be chosen by an

---

[4] *Life Insurance Fact Book,* p. 33.

insured, from $30 to $430 or more for a $10,000 contract. The differences
are the result of the period for which protection is provided, when the benefits are payable, and the length of the premium-paying period. The uses depend upon the goals of the insured in regard to savings, protection, or a combination of savings and protection.

Also note that "cost" is used here to mean the same thing as "premiums"
paid for the various contracts. "Net cost" is a more technical concept. Net
cost is calculated by subtracting cash surrender values (and dividends paid
on participating policies) from the premiums paid over a period of time. This
concept is discussed at the end of the section on endowment contracts.

In forms of insurance other than life, the contingency insured against may
or may not happen. The policies are issued for a term and may run to expiration with no claim made. Some life policies are written for a term; many are
not. Many life insurance contracts are written on a permanent or whole life
basis; if such contracts are kept in force, the benefits provided must ultimately
be paid. Life insurance policies thus are classified as (a) permanent and
(b) temporary. Temporary, or term, life insurance provides protection only
for the number of years designated in the contract. It is more like the usual
insurance contract covering property. Permanent, or whole, life insurance
forms the basis of many insurance programs, while term insurance provides
temporary protection.

Whole life insurance policies

Whole life insurance may be written (a) on a straight life basis, (b) on a
limited-payment basis, or (c) on a single-premium basis. The whole life
contract known as the straight life policy is also known as the *ordinary life
policy.*[5] This has been termed the "bread-and-butter" policy of the industry.
It provides for periodic payment of premiums as long as the insured lives.
Benefits are payable at the death of the insured, though a policyholder may
stop paying premiums and take the accumulated equity in the form of cash[6]
or a reduced paid-up policy.

A whole life form known as the *limited-payment policy* provides for premium payments for a designated term or until the prior death of the insured.
At the end of the premium-payment term, the insurance is paid up for the life
of the insured. Under the *single-premium life policy,* the premium is paid at
the outset of the policy term in a lump sum, but most contracts are paid by

---

[5] The ordinary life policy is the straight life contract with premiums payable throughout life. Efforts have been made to limit the use of the term *ordinary life insurance*
to the straight life policy of the ordinary group and to use the term *ordinary insurance*
to apply to all of the contracts in the ordinary group. As a matter of actual practice,
this line of demarcation is not well maintained. Straight life insurance is an equally
important form in the industrial life insurance category.

[6] Gain of cash value received over aggregate premiums paid in is taxable as ordinary
income when amounts are received for reasons other than death.

Table 10–2. Comparison of basic and common life insurance contracts

Basic type	Protection period	When benefits are payable	Approximate costs for $10,000 at age 25*	How long premiums are paid	Uses
1. Whole life	Permanent	At death, any time	—	—	Combination of moderate savings and protection
a. Straight or ordinary life	"	"	$135	Throughout life	"
b. 20-payment life	"	"	$220	For 20 years	Paying up premiums during working life
c. Life paid up at 65	"	"	$150	To age 65	"
2. Term	Temporary	At death, only during term	—	—	Protection only
a. Yearly renewable term	"	"	$30, increasing each year	Varies—can be to age 65 or 70	Maximum protection
b. Five-year level term (renewable)	"	"	$55	5 years	Very high protection for limited period
3. Endowment	Permanent	At death, or if living, at end of endowment period	—	—	Combination of higher savings and protection
a. 20-year endowment	"	"	$430	20 years	"

* Costs are necessarily approximate for such general comparisons. Participating policies would be slightly higher, with net costs reduced by annual dividends. Nonparticipating policies would be somewhat lower. Smaller policies under $10,000 will be slightly higher; those over this amount may have a lower rate per $1,000. Those insuring women will also be somewhat lower in cost. Extra policy features such as waiver of premium, accidental death benefits, and so on, would increase these estimates. See Jerome B. Cohen, "Decade of Decision" (Washington, D.C.: American Council of Life Insurance, 1976), p. 14.

periodic installments. When no more premiums are payable on a contract, it is called a *paid-up* policy.

On the assumption that the payment of a single premium is a limited-payment policy with payments limited to a period of a year, it may be stated that whole life forms may be reduced to two classes: (1) straight life and (2) limited-payment life. When two or more lives are covered in one policy, the term *joint life* is applied to the contract.

In all of these forms, the policy matures only on the death of the person whose life is the subject of the insurance; termination of the policy prior to death through nonforfeiture or surrender values precludes, of course, a death settlement. The primary objective of the whole life form is the payment of its face to the beneficiary at the death of the policyholder. In contrast, term insurance pays on the death of the insured *if* the insured dies during the term covered.

The ordinary life insurance policy. The ordinary, or straight, life contract is the most widely sold whole life insurance policy. Not including group or industrial life insurance, the popularity of the various types of contracts, as measured by life insurance amounts in force, is shown in Table 10–3.

About 62 percent of ordinary individual contracts, as measured by amounts in force, are whole life contracts. Three fourths of these are straight life. Term insurance accounts for 32 percent of all life insurance in force, and endowment types account for about 6 percent.

During the past decade the use of the various types of contracts has changed. As a total, the ordinary insurance types have slightly more than doubled, while total group insurance in force increased more than three times in the same period. Within the ordinary class, the limited-payment life, paid-up life, and endowment contracts are decreasing in popularity, while the popularity of term life insurance has increased substantially.

The ordinary life policy is used not only for protection but as a means for savings. The policy values are available to the policyholder when the need for insurance protection has been outlived. Even on contracts calling for continu-

Table 10–3. Life insurance in force by individual basic types of contracts, 1977

	*Amount**	*Percent*
1. Whole life:		
a. Straight life	617	48
b. Limited-payment life	123	10
c. Paid-up life	45	4
2. Term life	430	32
3. Endowment and retirement income	74	6
Total	1,289	100

* Figures for amounts are in billions of dollars.
Source: *Life Insurance Fact Book* (Washington, D.C.: American Council of Life Insurance, 1978), p. 22.

ous premium payments to death, the insured may stop payments at any time. On retirement the policyholder may elect to discontinue premium payments on permanent insurance and take cash or keep a substantial amount of insurance in force; or if preferred, the cash value may be used to augment retirement income by electing an annuity settlement instead of cash.

The flexibility of the whole life form accounts for its appeal. Basic in the whole consideration, the contract is permanent unless the premium is not paid. Although the net protection element decreases (face value less cash value) as the older ages are reached, the insured has very long-term protection for such purposes as last expenses, income to beneficiaries, or estate liquidity. Future uninsurability, the attainment of advanced age, or other contingencies cannot terminate the protection. There is no necessity for conversion or for redrawing the plan to keep the insurance in force for life.

The ordinary life policy affords the lowest cost permanent protection plan available. The policy is issued on a level-payment premium basis, and the premiums continue throughout the lifetime of the insured. Many object to the requirement of the ordinary life policy that premiums be paid until death. In the declining years of a life productive capacity diminishes, so it is sometimes considered desirable that premium changes cease after old age is reached. To meet this need, a limited-payment life policy is offered.

Limited-payment policies. The limited-payment whole life contract provides for the payment of the face of the policy upon the death of the insured. It differs from the ordinary life policy in that premium payments are charged for a limited number of years only. After the stipulated number of annual premiums have been paid, the more usual number being for 10, 20, or 30, the policy then becomes a fully paid-up policy. Some are paid up at a specified age, such as age 65 or later.

Frequently, policyholders confuse the limited-payment life policy with an endowment form, and after making the stipulated payments, they expect to receive the face of the policy from the insurer. The face of the policy is not paid until the death of the insured, although the cash and loan values are higher than under an ordinary life form, the difference depending upon the number of payments called for in the contract. Obviously, the fewer the payments, the faster the reserve will accumulate during the premium-payment period. Therefore, a greater reserve will be found under a limited-payment life than under an ordinary life form.

Under the limited-payment form, a policyholder who dies during the early policy years will have paid more than for an ordinary life policy. On the other hand, the policyholder may find sufficient compensation for the extra outlay in the knowledge that at a later age, when income will be curtailed, the burden of paying life insurance premiums will also be eliminated.

Comparisons. In arranging the life insurance program, the question of the relative merits of the ordinary life policies and the limited-payment life policies is inevitable. There is no arbitrary advantage of one over the other.

As a general rule, when funds available for insurance premiums are scarce, the ordinary life form will prove preferable, since more insurance may be obtained for the amount available for premiums. Moreover, if the economic status of the insured improves, the insurance may be rearranged to a limited-payment plan. In the case of participating policies, an insured may elect to utilize dividends by applying them to premium payments to convert the policy into a paid-up form.

If cost is not a determining factor in the arrangement of the life insurance program, the insured may wish to eliminate further life insurance premium payments upon retirement through the limited-payment life policy. If some change of situation causes the insured to use the nonforfeiture (cancellation) provisions of the limited-payment policy, the nonforfeiture values are greater. The increased cash values will carry the policy fully paid for a longer period than would have been the case otherwise.

The single-premium policy is the extreme of the limited-payment contract. The premium under this contract is paid in a single sum. Because such premiums represent substantial amounts of money, most insureds are unwilling to take the risk of the large single payment. The policies do meet a need, however, in that they provide wealthy persons with an opportunity to provide for some future purpose in a manner that requires no further annual premium payments. Gifts or charitable bequests of life insurance are examples.

Modified life policies. To offset the advantages of the ordinary life policy (moderate cost, level premium, and the savings element), there are certain shortcomings. There is a tendency for those influenced primarily by cost and for those with large protection needs, such as young families, to be attracted from the ordinary life policy to the term policy. This may unduly delay the inauguration of a permanent program. To supply an immediate permanent policy with an initial premium that is lower than the ordinary life premium, a *modified life policy* is offered by many companies. For a three- or five-year period the cost is lower than that of the ordinary life policy; thereafter it is slightly higher. Such policies are particularly attractive to young professional persons as they start their careers or while they are in school prior to beginning fairly high-income jobs. Modified life policies have become quite popular, and account for about 4 percent of the amount of new contracts purchased today.

Term insurance policies

The earliest form[7] of life insurance contract on record provided insurance only for a stated period, or term. Today term insurance is one of the popular

---

[7] One of the earliest policy forms was written by the London Assurance in 1720. This policy provided insurance for one Thomas Baldwin on the life of Nicholas Browne for a term of 12 months.

forms, and its proportion of the individual life insurance purchased annually increased from 40 percent to 50 percent during the past decade.

Nature.   Term insurance is precisely what the name would imply, insurance for a term, or temporary period. This may be contrasted to whole life insurance, which is permanent insurance and covers as long as the insured lives. If term insurance is written for a year, it provides protection equal to the face of the policy for one year, no longer. If it is written for five years, the insurance covers for five years. At the end of the term, whether for one year, five years, or any other period, coverage terminates, and the policy has no value whatever. If the contingency insured against happens, the policy pays in accordance with its terms. If the contingency fails to happen, the premium paid is fully earned and at the end of the term the insurer is under no obligation to the insured.

Uses.   When protection for a limited period is the element sought in the purchase of a policy, then the term insurance contract meets the requirements of the lowest possible immediate cash outlay. Because the proportion of loading expense to premium is highest, this form of insurance is not the least expensive. The low premium charge on term insurance reflects the limited time covered by the policy. In particular, it reflects the fact that the higher percentage of deaths occurring in the higher age brackets are not covered by the temporary protection of term insurance.

In light of the low cash outlay required for immediate protection, particularly in the younger age groups, term insurance is recommended for two major uses: (*a*) to provide temporary insurance where the need for large amounts of protection is created by special situations[8] and (*b*) to obtain an option a permanent program. Sometimes term insurance is the only contract alternative that will provide sufficient amounts of life insurance to meet the consumer's large needs.

One of the principal uses of term insurance is to provide protection during a period of unusual financial strain. An individual may assume heavy obligations as part of a *business* venture. An untimely death and forced liquidation might seriously cripple the business. The prudent businessperson will frequently buy a term policy to cover the amount of the unusual liabilities for the length of time that is required for their liquidation.

Term insurance is also used to provide a fund for the liquidation of some particular *debt*. Frequently a term policy is carried in connection with a mortgage loan upon the home, with the insurance amount decreasing as the

---

[8] The student with small current income but large potential future needs for life insurance is one of these situations. Beware of the life agent who advocates only permanent insurance, or advises taking out loans or notes to pay the early premiums on such contracts. High cost for unneeded coverage, with harsh penalties for discontinuing the contract (the full loan becoming payable immediately), may be the result of some typical campus life insurance sales. See "Campus Life Insurance," *Consumer Reports,* March 1977, p. 168.

loan decreases. In order to see that dependents have a home without encumbrances in the event of the untimely death of the wage earner, a term policy is carried to provide the necessary funds for liquidation. With the growing number of two-income families, new policies are now available so that both wage earners can be included in joint mortgage redemption life insurance contracts.

Term insurance finds an important use in supplying adequate insurance at a low cost during a period when a large amount of insurance is most needed but when funds for meeting its cost are not available. A young man with *family dependents* who was recently graduated from college wishes the maximum insurance that money will buy, with the privilege of converting it to another form at a later date. In this instance, the term policy is in effect an option upon a later permanent insurance program. In the meantime, dependents are provided with a maximum of protection.

Misuses.   Much has been said about term insurance and its relative merits as compared with a whole life plan written on a level-premium basis. Advocates of term insurance may suggest several different forms of term insurance, from the smallest premium form of one-year term insurance to a much larger premium form of long-term insurance, such as term to age 65 or 70. In comparison with that of a level-premium plan, the cost of one-year term insurance (often with a renewable feature to certain ages) is low in the younger age brackets. As the years go on, it becomes increasingly higher, until in the later years of life it is for all practical purposes prohibitive.

Level-term plans illustrate the importance of the *duration of the term* protection to its cost. At ages 20–30, for example, a "term to 65" policy will cost approximately double that of a "five-year-term." Term protection beyond age 70 is seldom available because of the sharply increasing cost at the advanced ages. Cost comparisons must also be careful to denote whether a policy is *level* (same face value throughout the contract) or *decreasing* (lower face value each month as the contract continues). For example, a 30-year decreasing term policy for $10,000 would pay only approximately $5,300 if death occurred during the 15th year. Other features that must be compared are the *convertibility* and *renewability* of the contract. Most term contracts are convertible to permanent contracts, without a medical examination, for all or most of their term. Renewability of the contract, which is at a higher premium, is often a needed feature to guarantee continued insurability, especially for the shorter term contracts of 1 to 15 years. It does add to the cost of the contract, however.

Because of the apparently low premium in the earlier years, the attraction of term insurance is entirely forgotten in the later years of life. In the earlier years the insured is in a better income position to pay the premiums, but the premiums are low because the probability of death during these years is slight. As the insured reaches the age when earnings have a downward trend, the premium charges for term insurance are rising very rapidly. This has always caused policyholders to become resentful of the increasing premium payments. No matter how painstaking the explanation, policyholders tend to discount the high premiums of later years as too remote to be of importance when, in their younger years, they are attracted to term insurance by the comparatively low premium charges. There is a tendency toward wholesale abandonment of the term insurance plan when premiums reach a level that the insured cannot or will not pay.

We sometimes hear it stated that term insurance is an inferior type of coverage, and that a "cheap" coverage cannot be the better product that a higher premium will buy. The reasoning is not sound. The term contract is as safe, as adequate, and in every sense as satisfactory *for the purposes for which it is devised* as any one of the many types of contracts offered by life insurance companies.

It is also wrong to say that everyone should automatically *"buy term and invest the difference."* For policyholders such a system rests on several fallacies, primarily: (1) term insurance cannot always be purchased, for poor health or older age makes it either difficult or impossible to buy; and (2) the "difference" (between permanent and temporary protection cost) cannot always bring greater returns at comparable safety, for this depends on size, diversification, costs, mandatory nature, taxes, timing, types, and many other features of the alternative investment program.

The above disadvantages of buying term insurance and having a growing investment portfolio may be lessened. A long-term policy, to age 65 or 70, may accomplish the protection needs and objectives of a person up to retirement age. Some of the protection may be converted before the end of the term. The disadvantage of not continuing to "invest the difference" may be overcome by a resolute and knowledgeable investor with long-run perseverance and ability to resist the temptation to spend the difference currently. The two objectives for a good investment program must also be balanced—the delicate objective of achieving high safety of principal must be balanced with the objective of greater returns (after expenses and taxes) over a long period. (See section in Chapter 9 on the investment functions of life insurance.)

No life insurance company or agent should have the slightest objection to the use of the term policy in those situations where its use is indicated. It is not the term policy to which opposition is expressed, but its misuse. The most important point to consider is that term insurance was not designed to be permanent insurance. For temporary protection to cover temporary needs, the policy is admirable. For careful use in connection with moderate-length investment programs, it may be beneficial. To augment a permanent life insurance plan during a period when the need for coverage is greatest, term insurance is indicated. A number of combination policies (see later section of this chapter for special riders and policy combinations) have been worked out by life insurers making judicious and generous use of term coverage.

Conversion privileges. Life insurance companies have extended certain privileges in connection with the writing of term insurance with a view to encouraging insureds under this form to convert their coverage to a more permanent form. The one-year term policy may ordinarily be renewed for a given number of years without medical examination. The policy may likewise be converted into a permanent-type policy within a given number of years without medical examination. The particular disadvantage of term insurance is to be found in the possibility of allowing the policy to run to a point where another medical examination is required, and of being rejected or rated as an impaired risk upon application for further insurance.

When issued for a term of five years, for example, the policy may often include the privilege (at any time during the term) of converting the insurance without medical examination to a permanent form. Renewal rates increase at each five-year renewal: when taken out at age 25, the costs are about $5 per $1,000; when renewed at age 30, $6; at 40, $8; at 50, $15; at 60, $33; and at 65, $48. Longer term policies of 10 or 20 years may permit the policy to be converted at any time except during the last several years of the term. Under the longer term policies, unlike the yearly renewal form, a level premium is charged instead of a premium that increases annually, following the natural rate. This type of term insurance finds particular favor with those who intend to make the coverage a part of a permanent program but require low-cost protection for their immediate needs. The conversion is done as of the attained age of the insured, at the regular rates for that age.

Term insurance finds a primary use in providing a means whereby applicants may secure an option on the amount of permanent insurance necessary, before they are in a position to pay for it. For example, most young persons can afford to purchase *decreasing* or *level* term insurance to age 65 in adequate amounts (perhaps $100,000 for about $700 or $1,100, respectively, per year). There are, however, a number of other situations for which term insurance is admirably adapted, and numerous special policies have been devised to fit these needs.

When a term policy is converted, there are two options. The new policy may carry the date of the conversion, in which case the premium is charged on the basis of the then *attained age* of the insured; or the policy may be dated back to the original date of the term policy on the basis of the *original age,* with the insured, however, making up the difference between the term premium and the premium charge for the new policy, plus interest, from the date of issue of the term policy until the date of conversion.

Endowment insurance policies

The ordinary life policy provides for the payment of the amount of the insurance to a designated beneficiary upon the death of the insured. The *pure endowment* reverses the process and pays the amount of the insurance only in the event that the insured lives a specified term. The amount of the insurance is paid to the insured, if the insured is living at the end of the period; otherwise, the insurer pays nothing. There are few uses for pure endowments. Sometimes they are written for a child's education or for other specific purposes. Under the form, nothing is paid if the insured dies before the end of the period.

Most endowment policies offered by insurers incorporate the features of a term life insurance policy. When so written, if the insured dies during the term, the amount of the insurance is payable to a designated beneficiary. If living at the end of the period, the insured receives the amount.

Normal types.   The usual endowment policy is thus a combination of pure endowment and term insurance. For example, in the case of a ten-year endowment policy, if the insured lives to the end of the term, the face of the policy is paid under the pure endowment feature. On the other hand, if the insured dies during the endowment term, the term feature of the contract pays the face of the policy and the pure endowment feature pays nothing. The two features are combined in a single plan.

Endowment insurance is written under a number of different forms, each designed to meet particular needs. The terms for which they are written may vary from 5 to 40 years, or they may be written to mature at a designated age, such as 60 or 65 years. There are also limited-payment endowments. For example, an endowment payable at death or at the end of 40 years may be written so that premium payments stop at the end of 20 years.

Uses.   The investment feature of endowment insurance makes the premium charge substantially higher than that for ordinary life insurance. Obviously, the shorter the term, the higher the premium. Persons carrying ten-year endowments for $20,000 who die during the term, say at the end of the ninth year, leave no more insurance to their beneficiaries than if they had taken out ordinary life policies or ten-year term life policies for the same amount. Their annual insurance premiums, however, are substantially higher. (See examples of comparative costs in the early part of this chapter.) To express it differently, for the same premiums that insureds pay for endowment policies they could secure much greater protection under ordinary life forms. Because of this, it is important to recognize the uses of endowment insurance and to buy it when *saving* for a particular purpose is to be coupled with insurance.

The first use of an endowment policy is to provide for the *old age* of the insured. There are many who because of their nature or habits find saving money irksome and difficult. On the other hand, such people may find it easy to meet obligations. They regard an insurance premium as an obligation and pay it regularly at fixed periods. Thus, these insureds may accumulate a fund that they might not be able to accumulate in any other way.

Endowment insurance is also used to accumulate funds for other specific purposes. Notable in this class are policies designed to provide funds for the education of *children,* or to enable an insured to make a substantial *gift* to a college, church, or some charity. Through an endowment policy the fund may be accumulated gradually over a period of years and at the same time be guaranteed in the event of an untimely death.

Misuses. Of all the policies offered by the life insurers, perhaps none has caused greater misunderstanding than the endowment contract. Much of the criticism that is leveled at endowment insurance is based upon the high premium charge. If the endowment policy is purchased for protection, there may be a misuse of the contract and the insured may be paying more for the protection than is necessary. The situation is particularly serious if the resources that the insured can apply to insurance premiums are limited and the need for protection is great. However, in the situations for which the endowment contract is designed, there is no other contract that will serve as well.

Insurance agents sometimes point out the advantage of long-term endowments as compared with those offered by short-term endowments. Endowments maturing at the age of 60 or 65 can provide insurance for dependents until the insured reaches retirement age. Through the use of the settlement options of the policy, the matured endowment may then be used to provide an income for the policyholder. As with all forms of insurance, short-term endowments and long-term endowments render their maximum service when they are employed for the purposes for which they have been designed.

Other types. Almost all life insurers offer a popular endowment contract, usually called a *retirement income policy*. A certain monthly income is provided to the insured, the income to begin at an age selected by the insured when the policy is written. The point at which the income begins varies from 50 to 70. The premium charge varies with the age of the applicant and with the age at which the policy matures.

Policies of this class guarantee a certain income for a definite number of months. Thus, a policy with a principal amount might guarantee to pay at the age of 65 the sum of $10 a month for each $1,000 of insurance for a period of 100 months, and for as many months thereafter as the insured shall live. Under the terms of such a contract, if the insured dies after the age of 65 but before payment has been made for 100 months, payments will be continued to a beneficiary until the full 100 payments have been made. If the insured dies before the installment payments become due, the face amount of the policy, or the cash value if larger, is payable to the beneficiary in a lump sum.

COST COMPARISONS: NET COST AND INTEREST-ADJUSTED METHODS

One of the most perplexing problems for life insurance consumers is that choosing the type of contract, as has been discussed in the preceding section of this chapter, is only part of the necessary comparison. When purchasing life insurance, the buyer should also want to know how much the same contract will cost from one insurer as compared with others. Contrary to normal public opinion, life insurance prices do vary considerably, so consumer efforts in cost comparison are worthwhile.[9]

For nonparticipating term insurance, the problem is relatively simple. The premium cost paid each year by the policyholder can be directly compared, being sure to compare exactly the same type of term contract, that is, one-year contracts with one-year contracts, five-year with five-year, term to 65 with term to 65, and so on. Care must be taken to see that the contracts compared contain similar convertibility and renewability features.

For participating term insurance, the comparison must include consideration of the dividends paid annually to the policyholder. This can be done only on the basis of past dividends actually declared and paid, but usually the buyer is attempting to calculate what the future cost will be. This requires *estimates* of prospective dividends which are likely to be paid, but are not guaranteed, over a future period of time. Premiums paid less dividends equal "net payment."

For whole life and endowment insurance, there is the further complication of cash surrender values to consider. (Term policies usually do not have these guaranteed amounts payable to the policyholder if the contract is not continued.) These amounts must also be subtracted from the premiums paid, along with dividends if it is a participating contract, in order to know the "net cost" of the contract. Therefore, the *traditional method* of comparing the costs to policy holders of permanent contracts has been (for a 20-year comparison, $1,000 participation contract).[10]

1. Premiums paid for 20 years, at $24 per year		$480
2. Less dividends* estimated for 20 years	$130	
3. Less cash surrender value in 20th year	342	472
4. Net cost (total for 20 years)		$ 8
5. Annual net cost ($8 divided by 20)		$ 0.40

    * Omit this figure if contract is nonparticipating.

Basically, this calculation shows the average amount of each premium not returned if the policy is surrendered for its cash value. (Many contracts will show a net gain rather than a net cost, particularly if the time is longer than 20 years.)

But is this the real cost of life insurance for the policyholder? No, for the time value of the money paid to the insurer and the time that elapses before the insurer pays back the dividends and the cash surrender value (assuming that the contract is canceled after 20 years) are not considered in this method. Thus the comparison can be misleading.

---

[9] Differences of 10–20 percent are not uncommon, and the ranges may be much greater.

[10] *The Interest-Adjusted Method* (New York: Institute of Life Insurance, 1976), p. 4.

How can the comparison be improved? A special committee representing most of the life insurers reported in 1970 that a better method should be used. It is called the *interest-adjusted method,* and it is generally recognized as a fairer cost comparison because it does take into account the time value of the money received and paid out by the insurer. Many life insurance agents now use this method to show prospective buyers how their contract costs compare with those of other companies. In a few states such a comparison is mandatory in life insurance sales, but in most states it is authorized but only furnished to the consumer on request.[11] An example of the interest-adjusted method, for a situation similar to the one shown above, is:[12]

1. Premiums paid for 20 years, at $24 per year,
   accumulated at 4 percent $743.30
2. Less dividends* estimated for 20 years,
   accumulated at 4 percent $180.70
3. Less cash surrender in the 20th year 342.00   522.70
4. Interest-adjusted cost (total for 20 years) $220.60
5. Annual interest-adjusted cost index ($220.60 divided by
   30.969, which is the result of the accumulation of
   $1 per year at 4 percent for 20 years) .... $ 7.12

   * Omit this figure if contract is nonparticipating.

Several comments about the resulting interest-adjusted figure are pertinent. First, it is not what the consumer actually pays for the contract, which would be merely the premiums paid in each year less the annual dividends (if taken in cash). Second, it is an *index* and therefore useful only in comparing similar contracts at a fixed time under specified assumptions. Third, if you wanted to calculate your actual total outlay for the contract, this would depend upon whether you keep the policy as long as you live (or when it is surrendered for cash value), when the policy ends (by death or surrender), and what the actual dividends are. Finally, this method of cost comparison has the disadvantage of increased complexity for the average consumer.

The interest-adjusted cost index of $7.12 per $1,000 in the preceding example is a truer cost figure than the traditional net cost of $0.40. It does consider the time value of money. However, it is not a perfect comparison, and several other measures have been recommended. Belth[13] suggests a "level price method," and more recently a "retention method," to make still more accurate comparisons. These refinements consider additional factors such as the decreasing amount of protection (as cash values increase), the

---

[11] *Life Rates and Data* (Cincinnati: National Underwriter Co., 1977), p. xii.

[12] *The Interest-Adjusted Method,* p. 5. (Note the interest assumption of 4 percent, which for average persons is a relatively low assumption of aftertax secure savings return. Five percent or more is sometimes used in other comparisons today.)

[13] Joseph Belth, *Life Insurance: A Consumer's Handbook* (Bloomington: Indiana University Press, 1973).

probabilities of survival and lapse during the period of time studied, and the insurer's retention out of the expected value of premiums to be paid.

At present a consensus as to the one best cost comparison measure is lacking. The National Association of Insurance Commissioners (NAIC) has recommended a model bill for adoption by the states. This changes the term *interest-adjusted cost* to the "surrender cost index" and the term *net cost* to "net payment index," uses a 5 percent interest assumption, and would require agents to provide 10- and 20-year cost comparisons. (The possibility of insurer manipulations of dividends and cash values to make specific periods of comparison more favorable to their contracts would still exist.) Several federal price disclosure bills have been proposed[14] for enforcement by the Federal Trade Commission.

The consumer's dilemma is still real, even for the relatively few consumers who can, and would, use all the available data. The best general advice seems to be that the policyholder should use the interest-adjusted cost index[15] to at least determine whether a specific insurer has a reasonable price which is among the lower cost index categories. The time-consuming quest for the absolute lowest cost may be fruitless. It is perhaps much more important for consumers to be sure that they have selected the best type of contract to meet their own needs. Also, consumers might well concentrate on selecting insurers of proven financial strength, with an established reputation and well-trained agents. After all, the ultimate goal should be to obtain the best combination of reasonable cost *and* security and services provided by life insurance.

SPECIAL RIDERS AND POLICY COMBINATIONS

Guaranteed purchase option

The *guaranteed purchase option* can be attached to ordinary life and endowment (but not term) contracts. Under this "rider," which is an endorsement or added part to the basic contract, the policyholder is guaranteed the right *without medical examination,* to increase the amount of his or her life insurance of standard rates at specified times or ages.

Some people find optioning permanent insurance more satisfactory than convertible term insurance. The cost is low, and the additional amounts of permanent insurance are added gradually over a number of years. For example, an insured taking a $10,000 ordinary life policy at age 25 may be given five separate options (an added total of $50,000) to purchase an additional $10,000 contract at ages 28, 31, 34, 37, and 40. Some insurers permit

---

[14] Particularly by the late Senator Hart. These have been labeled "truth-in-life insurance" bills.

[15] Available annually for each insurer in *Interest-Adjusted Index* (Cincinnati: National Underwriter Co.).

six options or have four-year option intervals. Others permit the options to be exercised upon the marriage of the insured and at the birth of each child. One disadvantage of the purchase option is its relative inflexibility as compared with comparable term insurance amounts. The options can only be exercised at the stated ages or events, in the specified amount, and in the form of a whole life contract.

The time ultimately comes when many persons become partially or totally uninsurable, because of a deterioration of physical condition or other changes. The applicant may obtain some insurance as an impaired risk for a cost higher than the standard rates, but total uninsurability prevents the further purchase of any life insurance. The guaranteed purchase option provides protection against the possibility of being forced to pay more than the standard rates and guarantees the availability of insurance regardless of impairment. The popularity of this feature has increased rapidly during the past generation. It is often a desirable option for younger persons to add to their life insurance. The cost is relatively low—about $2 per $1,000 of the basic contract amount.

Other combinations

Another form of permanent insurance that incorporates the term idea is known as the *double protection policy*. This policy provides for the payment at death of the sum insured and for doubling the amount of insurance payable if death occurs within a period specified when the policy is taken out. The usual periods are 10, 15, and 20 years. The policy doubles the face value, combining a level amount of term insurance with the basic permanent insurance coverage. The double protection is to supply extra insurance when the need to provide for dependents is the heaviest. At the end of the period of double protection, the basic amount remains in full force to the end of life for the person covered. Premiums may be leveled throughout the lifetime of the insured, or when the double protection feature expires, they may be reduced substantially.

There are numerous other life insurance contracts. Many of them are infrequently used but available from insurers if the insured has a special need or desire for them.[16] Two such policies aim at overcoming a common policyholder objection that death causes the policyholder to forfeit the cash values or the premiums that have been paid on the policy up to that time. Such a comment indicates a misunderstanding of the level-premium plan, which does take the cash values accumulated and the premiums paid into consideration. However, if the insured wants more than the face value paid at death, a combination of ordinary life plus increasing term insurance for the cash

---

[16] See chap. 8 of Davis W. Gregg and Vane B. Lucas, eds., *Life and Health Insurance Handbook,* 3d ed. (Homewood, Ill.: Richard D. Irwin, 1973).

values or paid premiums may be written in what is called a *return of premium policy* and a *face amount plus cash value policy.*

Life income policies are sometimes issued to provide the beneficiary with a stated income amount, beginning at the insured's death. A guaranteed number of payments may be included, such as 20 years. The beneficiary named may not be changed, except for the guaranteed portion, which is based on an amount of whole life insurance. The rest of the contract, the life annuity to the beneficiary, is a deferred life annuity, such as is discussed in Chapter 12.

A contract called the *principal and income policy* pays at the death of the insured an income for the life of one beneficiary and then a principal amount to a second beneficiary. A man with children, for example, may provide for a life income to his wife and then distribution of the principal to his children.

Joint life policies are sometimes written for whole life or endowment forms of life insurance. The face value is payable upon the death of any one of the lives insured. Such a policy may be used by husband and wife or by partners in a business. Less flexibility for the individuals involved (for conversions, cash values, and so on) is a potential disadvantage. Joint life contracts have recently also become popular for paying off mortgages upon the death of a spouse. These are a form of decreasing term insurance. Sometimes these are called "contingent life" contracts, and they may be adapted to either family or business situations covering two or more lives. The concept is based upon coverage for "next death," or paying for each death as it occurs, with automatic continuance of life insurance on each survivor. Premium savings of one fourth to one half can be obtained by this form, although the contract has the disadvantage of somewhat increased complexity to the buyers.[17]

SPECIAL LIFE INSURANCE MARKETS

Many life insurance contracts are designed mostly in order to appeal to certain markets. They are combinations of the whole life, term, and endowment contracts, and they often offer special features which make them more attractive to specific kinds of policyholders. Examples of the contracts aimed at special markets are the family plans, juvenile plans, larger policy plans, split-dollar employer-ee plans, split-life insurance, variable life and adjustable life insurance.

Family insurance plans

There are three family plans: (*a*) the *family income policy,* (*b*) the *family maintenance policy,* and (*c*) the *family policy.* These plans are a

---

[17] "An Alternative to Multi-Life Selling," *Insurance Marketing,* September 1977, p. 58.

combination of ordinary life and term insurance. The first two are alike in principle but differ with respect to the term feature of the contract. There are a number of varieties of the third plan which provide in a single policy level-premium insurance for the entire family.

Family income policy. This is a combination of ordinary life and decreasing term insurance in a single contract. The contract provides that if the insured dies within an agreed period from the date of the policy, an income (usually $10 per month for each $1,000 of face value) will be paid the beneficiary for the balance of the term and that the face amount of the policy will then be paid. It is thus a combination of *decreasing* term insurance (for the income benefit) and ordinary life insurance (for the face value). A policy, for example, may be written to provide the income feature if the insured dies within 10, 15, or 20 years from the date of the policy. If the insured died 5 years after the contract was taken out, a $20,000 20-year family income policy would pay the family $200 per month for 15 years and then pay $20,000 in a lump sum. If the insured outlived the period indicated, the beneficiary would receive only the face amount of the insurance immediately upon the insured's death.

This policy finds popular use in protecting a wife and children. Realizing that the proceeds of his insurance might soon be exhausted in caring for and educating his children, a young man with a wife and small children provides his wife with an income during the period that the children are dependent. The period of the income is so arranged that when the children become self-supporting, the income terminates and the face amount of the policy is paid to the wife. A similar use could be made of this contract if the wife instead of the husband is the wage earner of the family.

Family maintenance policy. This policy has much in common with the the family income contract. It differs in that the term during which income payments are to be made is a fixed period which commences with the death of the insured. Policies may provide the income feature for a selected period, usually 10, 15, or 20 years from the death of the insured. Regardless of the date of death, if the insured dies within the selected period, income will be paid for the number of years specified. Unless otherwise provided, the face amount of the contract is then payable at the end of the period selected for income payments.

Like the family income policy, the family maintenance policy is a combination of ordinary life insurance and term insurance. Since the income feature continues for a period certain, the term insurance is not decreasing but is for a *level* amount. Since the face of the policy is not payable until the end of the income period, as in the family income form, the interest on the face amount of the basic policy enters into the premium calculations. Term insurance is provided for an amount equal to the monthly payments less the monthly interest which would be earned on the basic policy amount.

Family policy. This is a package form providing life insurance coverage for the entire family. It covers the father, the mother, and all living children. It is a condition of the policy that it will automatically cover children yet to be born at no additional cost.

Coverage on the father is usually ordinary life insurance. Protection on the mother and the children is for a lesser amount than for the coverage on the father and is usually term life insurance. Such a package might provide $5,000 ordinary life on the father with term coverage of $1,000 on the mother and each of the children. Coverage on the father may be increased in units of $2,500, with insurance on other members of the family increasing proportionally.

Insurance attaches to newborn children when they become 15 days old, and the insurance extends to cover stepchildren and adopted children. Under this plan, if the father dies, the family receives the insurance on his life and the premiums on their insurance cease. When the children reach a designated age, usually 21, their insurance terminates, but they have the privilege of buying up to five times that amount of permanent insurance at their attained ages without medical examination. The wife's insurance is often term insurance to the husband's age 65, but some forms insure the wife with permanent ordinary life insurance. A waiver-of-premium benefit is usually included in the family policy. Premiums are waived if the husband dies or is totally disabled. Accidental death benefits are sometimes included automatically, but this is often optional coverage.

The family policy has proved very popular since its introduction in the 1950s. Today about one out of six new policies are of the family policy type. Some authorities would point out that sometimes the premium cost which goes toward purchasing the insurance on the lives of the wife and children would be better used in purchasing larger protection on the "breadwinners" (the husband or the wife, if working) of the family if they are inadequately insured. However, the small difference in cost (about $10 a year for the basic $5,000 amount), as compared with the cost of insurance on the breadwinner alone, makes the family policy convenient and salable.

Juvenile insurance plans

The insurance of children from the age of one day upward is an important branch of the life insurance business. On the basis of experience, there seems to be no special hazard involved in insuring juveniles (usually identified as under age 15), and such insurance offers American families an opportunity to start a thrift program for their children at an early age.

Juvenile insurance is not in the strict sense a separate type of policy. It is rather a form modified to meet the needs of young children. The forms most usually written are: (a) 20-year endowment and (b) educational endowment at age 18. Ordinary life policies may, of course, be written; but at the early ages the premium differential between these and the limited payment or endowments is relatively small, and the higher priced policies have a considerable appeal.

Juvenile policies may now be written, subject to some differing laws of the states, to pay the full face amount of the policy on the death of the insured child. The former practice and laws scaled cash benefits to the child's age. Underwriting practice may still provide a graded coverage from the rated age zero. Insurers may require that the child be at least one month old. No medical examination is required for nominal amounts of insurance. Insurers are now willing to write very substantial amounts on juvenile lives, however, and many of these contracts require regular medical examinations before the policies are written. Ownership of the contract usually remains with the applicant (the parents, in the typical case) until the insured child reaches age 18 or 21. Some insurers and state statutes permit life insurance to be purchased by the children themselves if they are over age 15.

A feature peculiar to juvenile insurance may provide for the continuance of the insurance in the event of the death of the adult who applies for the policy and who assumes the responsibility for the payment of the premiums. The clause covering this provision, sometimes referred to as the "payor clause," provides for a *waiver of premiums* in the event of the death or the total and permanent disability of the adult applicant. If a payor benefit is desired, a medical examination covering the applicant is sometimes required.

A popular form of juvenile insurance has come to be known as *jumping juvenile* and derives its name from the fact that the face amount of the policy jumps to five times its original value at no added premium or medical examination when the insured child becomes 21 years of age. The policy is made available in units of $1,000. The more usual forms of permanent life insurance are available, and a common limit on the amount of initial protection is $10,000 or $15,000. The advantage of this insurance is that it guarantees standard life insurance of a child at the age of 21. Poor health before age 21 cannot prevent that child from purchasing any insurance at all, or increase the cost because of substandard classification. The premium paid per $1,000 at the age of issue remains constant throughout the life of the policy and does not increase when the child attains the age of 21. Finally, the policy builds up reserves rapidly, providing attractive cash or loan values. Instead of buying an educational policy, some parents purchase this form of coverage with the thought that the loan values will be available for education if needed; otherwise the coverage will serve as a start to a permanent life insurance estate for the young person.

As a comparison, the cost of "jumping juvenile" insurance at age 1 is about $40 for $1,000 (for life paid up at age 65), while a comparable policy without the jumping feature at age 21 would be about one fourth as much. After age 21, however, the cost remains at $40 per $1,000, while a comparable policy at that age will cost approximately twice as much.

Larger policy plans

A comparatively recent development, the outgrowth of competition, is the group of policies known as "specials." A distinguishing feature of the specials is that they are for larger than normal amounts and are issued at lower premium rates than the similar basic type of contract. In effect, these contracts use the idea of a quantity discount.

The specials generally follow one of three patterns and are known as (*a*) *minimum amount* policies, (*b*) *preferred risk* policies, and (*c*) *graded* policies with premiums based on size. At the outset, special policies were limited to whole life policies. However, many insurers now have special policies available in almost every basic insurance plan.

Minimum amount policies. As the name indicates, this form requires a policy written in an amount equal to or in excess of a minimum established by the company. This could be $5,000, $10,000, $25,000, or any other such minimum amount. A part of the premium reduction may flow from a lower commission rate paid the agent; the balance is derived from a distribution of certain of the expense items that are fixed on a policy basis. Costs that are often the same regardless of policy size include the cost of medical examination, factual data reports, bookkeeping, premium notices, and the like. The cost of such fixed expenses is lower for each $1,000 of insurance as the size of the policy increases.

Preferred risk policies. Policies in this category justify a lower premium charge on the basis of rigid selection. Certain classes may be selected, such as businesspersons and professionals, whose mortality experience is expected to be better than average. Usually, the contracts are also larger in size than the normal contract. A policy designed as an "executive policy," for example, would usually be for amounts in excess of $25,000.

While there may be some justification for a differentiation based upon flat expense items for the larger policies, cutting the preferred risks out of an ordinarily standard group must ultimately result in higher costs for those who are left. If the better-than-average experience is written as a special class at a lower-than-standard rate, it must follow in the long run that the experience of the remainder of the group will inevitably reflect this loss.

Graded policies, with premiums based on size. This plan of pricing is a logical consequence of the minimum amount policy plan. The same argument is advanced that certain fixed costs do not vary with policy size. This plan usually provides for size groups, or "bands," and as the amount of insurance moves from one group to another, the larger the amount of insurance reflected in the particular group, the less is the cost of each $1,000 of insurance.

The price variation differs among insurers; but, for example, one well-known insurer varies the price of a participating straight life policy issued at age 25, for $18 per $1,000 for a policy under $5,000, to $17 for a $5,000 to $25,000 policy, to $16 for a policy over $50,000. The rate reduction for an over-$50,000 policy as compared with an under-$5,000 policy is approximately 10 percent. A further premium reduction is allowed on many policies issued on the lives of females.[18]

Split-dollar employer-employee plans

The split-dollar plan involves an agreement between an employer and an employee[19] under which the employer purchases a single life insurance contract on the life of the employee. The employer agrees to contribute to the premium payments to the extent of the increase in the cash value each year or the net premium, whichever is lesser. The first-year premium is paid in its entirety by the insured employee, since there is no reserve or dividend credit.

The plan finds its acceptance in providing life insurance for the young executive "at a time when the need is most likely and at the lowest possible cost."[20] Any form of life insurance contract may be utilized. The plan is made effective by attaching the split-dollar endorsement to the life insurance contract of which it becomes a part. This endorsement reads: "In the event of the maturity of this policy by the death of the insured . . . there shall be paid from the policy proceeds to the X Corporation, . . . an amount equal to the cash value of this policy immediately prior to the insured's death, and the rights of any beneficiary designated by the insured shall be limited to the excess of the policy proceeds over such cash value."

By use of the plan employers can provide junior executives with a substantial amount of financial security at reasonable prices. The person whose life is insured pays each year the amount of the premium reduced by any dividends declared and by the amount of cash value of the policy is increased. In other words, dividends are credited on the premium and the employer pays each year an amount equivalent to the increase in cash value. The payment made by employers, however, is more of an investment than an expense since the cash value of the policy is returned to them when benefits are paid or the policy is surrendered for any reason. The plan provides low, net cost life insurance to an employee. The employer provides an incentive benefit that

---

[18] Some participating companies attain the object of coordinating net cost with size of policy by dividend adjustment rather than by a decrease in gross premiums. Graded dividends are distributed on the basis of size groups. To reflect the better mortality experience of female lives in the case of policies over a given minimum, an additional dividend is sometimes provided over and above that paid on male lives.

[19] The same type of plan is available and is sometimes useful in family situations. A father, grandfather, or other relative may purchase insurance on and for a young man, for example, helping him to buy whole life insurance on a split-dollar basis. The insured young man pays the net cost of protection, while the older person pays the increase in cash value (which is an investment, returned to him when the policy matures or is discontinued).

[20] Iskandar S. Hamwi, "The Split-Dollar Plan," *CLU Journal*, vol. 27, no. 3 (July 1973), p. 43.

will tend to encourage the continued employment of a valued employee simply by advancing funds that will in due course be returned without interest.

From the point of view of employers, the split-dollar consists of allocating a portion of their cash to insurance policy cash values. These values at all times and under all circumstances revert to the employer, though sometimes employers elect to use these values at the time insured employees retire to augment their retirement income.

Split-life insurance

Not to be confused with the split-dollar plans just discussed for employer-ee situations, which use a single contract to divide cash values and term protection, is a new life insurance product called *split-life insurance*. Less than ten years old,[21] the concept has been approved by most states and many companies are now writing such policies.

Basically, the idea is to obtain tax benefits through the use of *two separate contracts* of life insurance. One is an annual *deferred annuity* (see Chapter 12) to be held by an organization, such as a business corporation, an HR-10 (Keogh) Plan for self-employeds, or a nonprofit charitable institution, permitting premium payments to be made with tax-free dollars. The second contract is a *yearly renewable level term* insurance policy which can be purchased in the amount of $1,000 of insurance for each $10 of annuity payment by the purchaser. The very low term cost[22] (about $3 per 1,000 at age 45) is only available in connection with the annuity purchase.

Split-life contracts make it possible to use the cash value portion of the two policies, from the annuity, after it has been in force for 10 years and the insured is at least 60 years old. Contrary to a whole life contract, where taking the cash value would discontinue the life insurance protection, the term life protection of the split-life contracts can be maintained by continuing payment of the yearly renewable term premium or by conversion to a whole life policy.

The annuity and term life can be written on the same lives, or on different insureds. The market possibilities for split-life are considerable: Three common situations in which it might be used are for helping fund children's education, for providing estate liquidity and reducing estate taxes (by gifts of the annuity contract), and for purchasing key-person life insurance on their important employees of business firms. It can also be used with beneficial results in pension and profit sharing situations, and in cases of charitable giv-

---

[21] The originator was Con G. Demmas, an agent for Louisiana and Southern Life Insurance Company.

[22] Joseph M. Belth, "A Note on the Price of Split-Life Insurance," *Journal of Risk and Insurance,* vol. 39, no. 3 (September 1972), p. 501. The author concludes that there are some cost benefits, but not as many as some split-life advocates sometimes claim. The price structure is not greatly different from that of reasonably competitive straight life policies. However, the net cost *after* taxes can be an important factor in the purchase of split-life insurance.

ing.[23] Estate taxes in the family situation might also be reduced, for example, by having the ownership (of the term life contract) irrevocably transferred from the insured spouse to the other spouse.

Several of the tax issues have not yet been completely decided, but thus far the decisions have been favorable. In the key-person situation, the indirect use of the employer's annuity values to purchase the low-cost term coverage may be considered an "economic benefit" reportable to the employee, but the valuation of that benefit is still undecided. In the family situation, the face value of the term contract could be includable (early decisions have said no) in the estate of the insured on the basis that an "incident of ownership" exists in that the annuitant-insured's right to continue the term policy depends upon the continued existence of the annuity contract.[24]

The split-life concept has caused substantial emotional reaction within the life insurance business, on the part of both insurer executives and agents. Thus far it appears to be feasible and worthwhile in those situations where it is beneficial to the consumer. It is unlikely to be a panacea for life insurance needs or to become a complete substitute for the permanent cash-value insurance contract.

Variable life insurance

Another innovation in life insurance in recent years, with potentially broader market applications, is the *variable life insurance* contract. Early progress was blocked by legal complications, but in late 1976 the Securities and Exchange Commission ruled that life insurance contracts with an *equity base* would be subject to the Securities Acts of 1933–34 and the Investment Company Act of 1940. This ruling complicate the marketing of such contracts, for agents must also be licensed as security salespersons, and a prospectus with much detailed information must be given to the prospective buyer. This has slowed the impetus for the development of such contracts.

The fundamental idea is to change traditional· (fixed-dollar-value) whole life insurance, in which the insurer pays a stated face value. The problem is that this specified face value does not attempt to guarantee any particular purchasing power for the consumer. In an era of continuing inflation, this is a real disadvantage to the life insurance beneficiary.

To offset this disadvantage, the variable life contract bases its reserves and policy amount payable on investments that are devoted primarily to common stocks. The theory is that as inflation raises common stock values and dividends in a "separate account" maintained for the variable life policies, the

---

[23] Allan Kent, "Split Life: A New Alternative to Term and Permanent," *American Agent and Broker,* October 1972, p. 54. See also "Buying Life Insurance at Lower Rates while Aiding Charities," *Insurance Magazine,* January 1977, p. 55.

[24] "Advanced Underwriting Letter," Northwestern Mutual Life Insurance Company, March 28, 1973, pp. 1–2.

dollar values paid under the contract will also increase. Hopefully, the increases will counterbalance decreases in the purchasing power of the dollar. The death payments are guaranteed not to fall below a minimum face value, but could increase if the equity values increased. Cash values are *not* guaranteed, however, and loan values are usually only 75 percent of the cash values instead of the full amount.

How well will the variable life contract work? Details of the early plans vary considerably, but the early groundwork in such countries as the Netherlands, Canada, and Great Britain indicate that the concept is workable. In the United States, for example, if you had bought a $10,000 contract in 1950, the benefits might have increased to about $18,000 in 1967, dropped to $14,000 in 1970, and then risen to $20,000 in 1977. The individual experience of insurers will probably vary greatly, and this is why each contract will require careful study by the insured of the prospectus required by law.

The stimulus for variable life insurance appears to have been based on two conditions: inflationary pressures which have eroded the real value of fixed-benefit contracts, and a shift in consumer preference away from secure investments such as cash-value life insurance to more speculative investments.[25] The Equitable Life Assurance Society was the first major insurer to offer individual variable life insurance contracts, in 1976. Other insurers had sold a similar product earlier, but only on a group basis.

The potential disadvantages of variable life insurance should not be minimized. The fixed guarantees of traditional life insurance have been of significant value to the reputation of the business for security. Consumer misunderstanding as to how much the variable life values might decrease (or not be as large as expected) if equity returns are not favorable, could endanger this reputation. Expected policy loan values may not be available to policyholders. The increasing complexity of the contracts, with several different systems for systematically adjusting the face value,[26] could increase consumer perplexity about life insurance. Start-up costs for these new contracts in terms of insurer research and agent retraining will be high. It appears, however, that the trend is definitely in the direction of making variable life insurance available to the public. Most, but not all, of the states have authorized its sale, and many of the major life insurers are planning contracts for distribution in the next few years. Many of the arguments pro and con are similar to those discussed further in Chapter 12 in connection with variable annuities.[27]

---

[25] Douglas G. Olson and Howard E. Winklevoss, "Equity-Based Variable Life Insurance," *Wharton Quarterly* (Philadelphia: University of Pennsylvania) Summer 1971, p. 26.

[26] Ibid., pp. 31–32. Several systems have already been advocated: "constant ratio" design (by New York Life Insurance Company), a "constant face value" design, and a "unit variable" design (with variable premiums as well as face).

[27] For a review of both products, see Bernard G. Werbel ed., *Variable Annuities and Variable Life Insurance Primer* (Smithtown, N.Y.: Werbel Publishing Co., 1977).

The variable life product will probably include most of the features of fixed-benefit life insurance (except fixed cash values), and most observers predict that variable life insurance in time "may comprise a significant portion of the life insurance business sold in the U.S."[28]

Adjustable life insurance

Perhaps one of the major breakthroughs in the need of the consumer for modifying life insurance amounts to accommodate "life cycle" changes has been occurring in the late 1970s. This is the introduction by several insurers (Bankers Life and Minnesota Life are early examples) of the *adjustable life* insurance contract. The idea is somewhat like variable life insurance, in that a policy is sold that you can change as your needs change. However, instead of having the life insurance amount vary with the prospective increased earnings of an equity-based account, the policyholder makes the choices on changing the policy amount, upward or downward.

The usual whole life and term types of life insurance are combined, with a wide flexibility as to when and how changes can be made. Most important, the *premiums* can be changed as well as the insured values. This is accomplished by increasing or decreasing the length of the term coverage, or by reducing or lengthening the premium-paying period of the whole life coverage.

In addition, the policy amounts can be increased by several methods. Two of them are traditional methods already used in many other life insurance contracts ("guaranteed purchase options," as explained earlier in this chapter, and "dividend options," as discussed in Chapter 11). The new feature is "cost-of-living" increases, by which the insured up to age 55 is permitted to buy additional life insurance every three years, without a medical examination. The increases are limited to about 20 percent of the face value and a maximum of $20,000, and are reduced by life insurance amounts purchased through other contracts. during the given three-year period.[29]

The prospects appear bright for the adjustable life contract. It can help solve the problems of (1) meeting the changing needs of consumers, (2) the effect of inflation on fixed-dollar life insurance values, and (3) the long-raging dispute over term versus whole life insurance.[30] It may have some of its own problems, too, as the premium is up to 10 percent higher than that of traditional life insurance. On the other hand, it may enable the consumer to

---

[28] Harry Walker and Jerome I. Golden, "Variable Life Insurance," *Life and Health Insurance Handbook* (1973), p. 238. See also John R. Kerr and J. Finley Lee, "Variable Products and the Consumer," and Robert C. Klemkosky, David R. Klock, and David F. Scott, "The Changing Equity Market: Implications for Variable Life Insurance," *CLU Journal*, vol. 26, no. 2 (April 1972), p. 26, and vol. 27, no. 3 (July 1973), p. 28, respectively.

[29] "Adjustable Life Insurance," *Changing Times*, October 1977, pp. 17–19.

[30] "Flexible New Life Insurance Permits Buyer to Raise or Lower Premiums and Payoffs," *Wall Street Journal*, February 27, 1978.

save some of the time and costs of buying new policies or dropping old, separate policies.

The most difficult problem is probably the increased difficulty of selling a more complicated product. However, adjustable life insurance avoids the dual-regulation (SEC *and* state insurance departments) problem of variable life insurance. Because of this, the application of the concept may be one of the most significant changes for life insurance in the 1980s. "Its imaginative design and advanced technology will not in themselves make adjustable life an instant success, unless life agents and the insuring public like what they see. As with other products, the ultimate test will take place within the marketplace."[31]

FOR REVIEW AND DISCUSSION

1. Indicate which of the following statements are false. *Explain* your reasoning.
   a. Individual life insurance is larger than group life insurance in terms of life insurance amounts in force.
   b. Life insurance premiums can be reduced by buying "modified life" or "limited-payment life" instead of "ordinary life" insurance contracts.
   c. The usual kind of "20-year endowment" pays the face value only if the insured lives for 20 years.
   d. Joint life insurance contracts pay the beneficiary if both of the insureds die in the same accident.

2. The whole life policy is said to be the most important of all life insurance contracts. Explain *why* this statement may be considered accurate. What qualifications might you attach to this statement?

3. Term, whole life, and endowment life insurance are sometimes misused. Give an example of (*a*) a proper use and (*b*) an improper use of each of the basic types of life insurance contracts.

4. Evaluate the concept of "buy term and invest the difference," indicating what "difference" is referred to and what the primary strengths and fallacies of the technique are for the average life insurance policyholder.

5. If Betty purchased a 20-year endowment, a 20-payment life, a whole life, or a term policy, she would pay a different premium for each contract. If she dies while any of the contracts are in force, each contract pays the same amount of insurance. Thus it has been said, that life insurers charge different prices for the same thing. Show why this is not true.

6. Today's society might be characterized as one of (*a*) affluence, (*b*) inflation, and (*c*) consumer orientation. What effect on the types of individual life insurance contracts sold by insurers would you expect each of these factors to have in the next ten years?

7. Some life insurance agents sell very little term life insurance, while others

---

[31] Charles L. Trowbridge, "Adjustable Life—A New Solution to an Old Problem," *CLU Journal,* vol. 31, no. 4 (October 1977), p. 20.

sell this type of contract almost exclusively (and become known as "termites!"). Can you justify this wide difference?

8. Joe was recently graduated from law college. He has a wife and child and is at present earning approximately $17,000 annually. He is able to save, above his living expenses, $3,000 annually. He contemplates buying a home but has been advised that he should spend the major part of his savings on life insurance. What would you recommend?

9. Endowment insurance is said to be a combination of two forms of life insurance coverage. Can you explain what is meant by this statement?

10. Don is a young man, aged 24, earning an exceptionally good salary. He is unmarried and has no dependents. Don contends that he has no need for life insurance. Why would you agree or disagree?

11. Pat Nelson has purchased a house valued at $30,000. The monthly payment covers principal, interest, taxes, and property insurance. Assume Pat to be 25 years of age and married, and her loan to be for $22,000. What kind of life insurance might Pat consider to strengthen her position?

12. Differentiate between *split-dollar* and *split-life* contracts.

13. What are the purposes of the guaranteed purchase option? What alternatives are there in achieving these purposes?

14. Differentiate among the three primary life insurance contracts designed for families. Explain at least one advantage and one disadvantage of each.

15. Life insurance agents usually find less sales resistance to juvenile life insurance than to any other contract form. Is there a danger in this natural tendency to care more about one's children than about oneself?

16. How are large-amount life insurance policies issued, and what are the advantages to the policyholder?

17. Divide the class into two groups: one to justify the traditional fixed-benefit life insurance contract, and the other to explain the potential merits of the new variable life insurance policies.

18. How has the trend toward broader financial services by life insurers occurred, and what advantages do you see for the insurer and for the consumer?

19. Why is the "interest-adjusted" index method of comparing life insurance costs better than the traditional "net cost" method? What disadvantages may it still have?

Chapter 11

Concepts considered in Chapter 11—Life insurance contract features

Life insurance contract features include many provisions for *flexibility.*
  General form of the policy is adaptable to many needs.
  Insuring agreement and face of policy contain basic agreements.
  Application usually includes *medical examination* report in the contract.
  Standard provisions provide some uniformity of major clauses:
    Payment of premiums sets *inception* of coverage and *grace period.*
    The beneficiary, *primary* and *contingent,* should be carefully designated; usually they are *revocable* for flexibility.
    Ownership of policy and changes differ in contracts.
    Assignment is permitted, effective when in *writing* at home office.
    Dividends are distinguishing feature between
      Participating and nonparticipating policies.
      Dividend options: *cash, premium reduction, paid-up additions, interest deposits, one-year additional term insurance.*
    Policy form changes to other contracts are permitted.
    Lapse and reinstatement (within five years) requires *insurability.*
    Misstatement of age requires *adjusted face value* amount.
    Suicide within two years results in *return of premiums* only.
    Indebtedness reduces *settlement* amounts.
    Incontestability for *fraud* or other reasons is usually after two years.
  Cash, loan, and nonforfeiture benefits include:
    Cash values, which are *basic amount* available, or
    Policy loans at stated *6 (sometimes 5 or 8) percent* interest.
    Automatic premium loan option to prevent mistaken lapse.
    Extended term insurance for *full face value.*
    Reduced paid-up insurance of *permanent* insurance.
  Optional methods of settlement in *supplementary contracts:*
    Types permit a choice, in place of a lump sum, of:
      Specified amount installments.
      Specified period of installments.
      Life income payments (unique to life insurance).
      Interest payments.
    Uses are many, with proper planning and recognition of benefits.
  Disability and accidental death benefit extensions:
    Waiver-of-premium benefit for total and permanent disability.
    Double indemnity benefits.
    Total disability income benefits.

Life insurance contract features

Nine out of ten U.S. families, or two out of three Americans, have some life insurance today—but how many do a good job in purchasing life insurance contracts by knowing what features it includes?

A family spending $150 per month on staple groceries at a favorite market devotes countless hours every year to the process of shopping. Much time is used in reading labels and asking questions in order to determine the quality, cost, and potential uses of the products purchased. Yet what happens when the same family purchases a life insurance contract? Probably a part of only one or two evenings is set aside to permit a life insurance agent to visit their home. The agent tries desperately in a limited time to understand their needs and explain how life insurance can provide a solution to the basic family problems of savings and protection. Frequently the wife is not included in the conversations, and if she is, it is often the final decision only—made on the basis of "Well, if you think it's best, George, then we'd better have it."

A logical purchasing system for a major item in the family budget? Hardly, but then the typical method could be rationalized in terms of the many other hasty and uninformed decisions that consumers make. But wait, shouldn't at least the most important uses of family income be approached with at least some knowledge of the fundamental parts of what is being purchased? Not many persons buy an automobile without knowing at least its size, style, kind of engine, and color. Yet people often spend (or worse yet, don't!) an equal amount[1] of income on life insurance without really knowing what the basic features of the contract are.

This chapter introduces[2] the more important provisions of a life insurance contract. Every potential and actual policyholder should know about the features discussed here, for these rights and benefits are what the contract provides in return for its cost.

The analysis centers on the provisions found in the usual, individual whole life, or permanent life, insurance contract. Some of the features treated may

---

[1] In approximate figures, a $4,000 automobile purchased once every five years costs an average, after salvage, of $600 a year, or $50 a month. At about age 23, $50,000 of ordinary life insurance would cost about $60 per month.

[2] For further information, the student is referred to Janice E. Greider and William T. Beadles, *Law and the Life Insurance Contract* (Homewood, Ill.: Richard D. Irwin, 1974).

not be found in policies issued as industrial or group life insurance; for example, under such policies, limited or no cash and loan values may be present, or the settlement options may be limited to fewer choices.

GENERAL FORM OF THE POLICY

Basically, the life insurance policy is a promise by the insurer to pay a stated amount of money to the policyholder (or the beneficiary). The conditions under which the benefits are paid are significant. These conditions may include death, some types of disability, and in the case of endowments, a certain maturity date set in the contract.

In connection with the fundamental benefits, many important options and privileges are granted to the policyholder. These features combine to make the life insurance contract one of the most flexible agreements ever designed. The owner of the contract, or sometimes the beneficiary, has the right to: (1) stop or change premium payments, (2) change the recipient of the benefits, (3) assign the contract rights, (4) change the use of the dividends, (5) change to a different policy, (6) reinstate coverage, (7) take cash or loan values, (8) cancel the policy and receive accumulated benefits in a variety of ways, and (9) use the policy proceeds by receiving lump-sum or installment payments.

The parts of the life insurance contract discussed in this chapter include its: (1) *declarations* (found on the "policy face" and in the "application") and *insuring agreement;* (2) mandatory *standard provisions;* (3) mandatory *cash, loan, and nonforfeiture benefits;* (4) *optional methods of settlement; and* (5) optional *disability and accidental death benefit extensions of coverage.*

INSURING AGREEMENT AND FACE OF POLICY

On the first page of the policy appear the name of the life insurer, the name of the insured, the amount of the policy (termed the "face amount"), and the names of the beneficiary or beneficiaries. In the insuring agreement the insurer agrees to insure the life of the person named as the insured and to pay to the beneficiary the face amount of the policy upon the notice and proof of death of the insured while the policy is in force.

The type of policy purchased, the policy number, the age of the insured at the time the policy is issued, and the date of issue appear on its face. The face of an endowment policy will indicate that the policy proceeds are payable to the insured if he or she is living a given number of years from the date the policy is issued. The requirements for premium payments are stated, primarily the date when premiums are due and whether they are payable annually, semiannually, quarterly, or monthly. Any special features of the contract are mentioned, and a statement is made that provisions on subsequent pages form part of the contract. The New York insurance law requires a summary description of the contract at the bottom of the face and on the outside of the folded policy. The signatures of the officers authorized to issue the policy appear at the bottom of the first page.

APPLICATION

As a basis for accepting or rejecting an applicant for insurance, life insurers require certain information. This is contained in an *application,* which becomes a part of the contract. Insurers wish to know, for example, the name, residence, age, and occupation of the applicant as well as the plan of insurance applied for, when premiums are to be paid, the beneficiary and the contingent beneficiary, and other insurance in force. In addition, they wish to know the family record as to longevity and to have evidence of the physical fitness of the applicant. All of this appears in the application. Legally the application constitutes an offer for the purchase of insurance which the insurer may accept or reject.

If a medical examination is required, there are two parts to the application. The first is a questionnaire completed and signed by the applicant. The second consists of a report of the physical examination of the applicant made by the examining physician.

The representations by applicants in the part of the application which they sign and to the examining physician should be accurate and carefully considered. Except for fraud, the information supplied need only be substantially true and not literally so.[3] Persons who have no records and cannot recall all pertinent facts—for example, concerning past physical conditions—meet the requirements if their answers are conscientious and reveal all the information at their command.

Statutes controlling life insurance require that the insured be furnished with the entire contract. Policies now make the application a part of the contract, and a photostatic copy is attached. The policy ordinarily provides that no statement shall void the policy or be used in defense of a claim under it unless it is contained in the written application and a copy of the application is endorsed, or attached, to the policy when issued. The insurance buyer should beware of the practice of having the agent ask questions and fill out the application for the buyer—or at least should carefully check the application before signing.[4]

---

[3] The law in most jurisdictions now requires, in the absence of fraud, that statements in the application be considered representations, which must be "material" (or important), and not warranties. If not technically correct, representations made in good faith and without intent to defraud do not afford the insurer grounds for canceling the policy or refusing to pay a claim.

[4] But for an exception to the rule, where a false statement appears in the application attached to the policy, consider: "When an insured, in making application for a contract of insurance, reveals to the agent the correct answers to questions contained in the application, and the agent, who, acting within the scope of his authority, fills out the application blank, and, unknown to the insured; inserts in the application incorrect

STANDARD PROVISIONS

There is no standard policy form required by statute for life insurance contracts, but instead all newly issued life insurance policies must include the *standard provisions* (sometimes called "general provisions" in the policy) prescribed by the state statutes. New forms of policies are issued only when these have been approved by the state insurance department. It was early felt that a standard form of policy resulted in too much uniformity of available coverages. To provide more leeway with respect to coverages and at the same time adequately safeguard the interests of the policyholders, laws were enacted making certain standard provisions mandatory.[5]

Indicative of the nature of the standard provisions now universally required is the following summary of the ordinary life provisions of the New York law: (1) that there shall be a grace period of either 30 days or one month; (2) that the policy shall be incontestable after it has been in force during the lifetime of the insured for two years from the date of issue; (3) that the policy shall constitute the entire contract between the parties; (4) that if the age of the insured has been misstated, the amount payable under the policy shall be such as the premium would have purchased at the correct age; (5) that participation must be on an annual dividend basis; (6) that options shall be specified to which the insured is entitled in the event of default of premium after the payment of three annual premiums; and (7) that loan values shall be stated.

Since the standard provisions establish minimum requirements only and an insurer may file policies with more liberal provisions, the legislation permits more flexibility in life insurance contracts than would be permitted under a standard policy requirement. At the same time, a considerable degree of uniformity has developed in the contracts offered by most insurers.

The contract and payment of premiums

Taken together, (1) the face of the policy with the insuring clause, (2) the application, and (3) the subsequent pages containing options, privileges, extensions, or limitations constitute the complete contract of life insurance.

Since premium payments are of vital importance to the validity of life insurance, the policy carefully states how and when premiums are payable. Pol-

---

answers to the questions, the knowledge of the agent is imputed to the insurance company. If such company thereafter collects premiums on such contract, it is estopped from asserting as a defense that the answers contained in the written application were incorrect" (*National Aid Life Association* v. *Clinton,* 176 Okl. 372, 55 P [2d] 781. See also *Atlas Life Insurance Company* v. *Chastin,* 12 CCH Life Cases 5).

[5] Through the activities of committees of the National Association of Insurance Commissioners, as well as the work of such groups as the Committee on Insurance Law of the American Bar Association, most of the important laws governing the business of life insurance are to be found in the statutes of all jurisdictions.

icies require the payment of the first premium in advance, while the applicant is in good health. Premiums after the first are also payable in advance. Ordinary insurance premiums are computed on an annual basis, though they may be paid semiannually, quarterly, or monthly. Many policies will for comparative purposes include in the contract the premium amount if it is paid on these various bases.

The first premium paid satisfies the requirement for a consideration essential to the validity of the contract, and makes the insurance effective. There is no obligation by the insured to pay subsequent premiums, but the payment of such premiums is a condition before the insurer must fulfill its part of the contract.

Premiums are required to be paid either at the home office of the insurer or to an agent authorized to receive payment. The scope of an ordinary agent's authority will extend to the collection of the first premium, but the authority of the delivering agent to collect extends no further. (Industrial insurance is an obvious exception.)

Life insurers allow a *grace period* following the due date of a premium during which the insurance remains in force. The grace period is now usually expressed in days, and 31 days are most often allowed. If the insurance policy becomes payable by the death of the insured during the period of grace, any overdue premiums are deducted from the amount payable. If the premium is not paid before the end of the grace period, the policy becomes void, unless the automatic premium loan provision (see later section) applies.

The beneficiary

The *beneficiary* is the person or interest designated in the contract to receive the proceeds. Oftentimes this is simply done by naming the beneficiary on the face of the policy. If the designation is a complicated one, or if a change is made after the policy is first written, a beneficiary clause may be used, attached in the form of a rider or endorsement to the contract. There are many variations in the beneficiary clause. The final form depends upon the objective of the insured. While the life insurance agent will cooperate and advise, in the end the arrangement of beneficiary designations is the responsibility of the applicant. A beneficiary may be (*a*) primary or (*b*) contingent. The *primary* beneficiary is the beneficiary that is first entitled to the benefits of the policy following the death of the insured. A *contingent* beneficiary is entitled to the benefits only after the death of the primary beneficiary, and is often included in contracts.

Designation of beneficiary. The beneficiary designation is, in effect, a will making disposition of life values. The owner should give it as careful consideration as is given to the disposition of physical property by will.

The beneficiary may be designated as (*a*) the *insured or his or her estate,* (*b*) a *specifically named person* or persons, (*c*) a *class* or classes of persons, (*d*) a *business or other organization,* and (*e*) a *trustee.* Because each has its advantages, the form used is important. A careless or thoughtless selection may defeat the whole objective of the insurance.

If a policy is made payable to the executors, administrators, or assignees of an insured, the proceeds of the policy are subject to the claims of creditors upon the death of the insured. If no beneficiary is sufficiently designated, the policy becomes payable to the estate of the insured. If the estate is designated as beneficiary, the distribution of the insurance may be made by the insured's will or if there is no will, in accordance with the inheritance laws of the state.

When a wife[6] is designated a beneficiary without indicating her name, in the case of the death of the first wife, a second wife succeeds as beneficiary. In order to avoid any possible question, it is customary not only to designate the relationship as wife but also to state her name. The insurer in making payment is under no obligation to investigate the validity of the marriage. When "children" are designated as class beneficiaries and when it is apparently the intent of the insured, the term *children* will extend to include an adopted child. An insurance policy made payable to children includes all children, whether by the wife designated as beneficiary or by a former wife. If it is intended that only the children by the wife designated as beneficiary shall participate, the words "our children" or "children born of this marriage" should be used. Most companies limit the use of class designations and permit only a few types. Carelessly worded clauses create a strong possibility that certain individuals may unintentionally be excluded or included.

A business organization such as a partnership or a corporation may be named as a beneficiary. The settlement options may be limited in such cases, for obviously a life income provision is impossible for a corporate beneficiary. A trustee may be designated as a beneficiary, when discretionary power is desired in the distribution of the insurance proceeds.

Change of beneficiary.   With reference to the beneficiary, life insurance policies are written under two forms. Under the first, the beneficiary is named without right of change on the part of the insured, and the insurance designation in such cases is said to be *irrevocable.* A second method of designating the beneficiary (used by all but a few percent of the contracts) retain the right of change for the insured. Here the beneficiary is said to be *revocable.*

If the right to change the designation of beneficiary is reserved, the interest of the beneficiary is limited to an expectancy during the lifetime of the insured. The revocable beneficiary has no right to the proceeds until the death of the insured. The irrevocable beneficiary has a fixed or vested right in the contract.[7]

---

[6] About 60 percent of named beneficiaries are wives, 10 percent are husbands, 20 percent are children, and 10 percent are other relatives of the insured.

[7] This represents the general rule, but it is an oversimplification of the situation. A revocable beneficiary may have a vested interest if the beneficiary acquires an equitable interest. Such an interest may follow from (*a*) a contract or (*b*) a gift. Equitable in-

If the insured wishes to have flexible use of the policy and wishes to be under no obligation to secure the consent of a beneficiary, the revocable form is the proper form to use. The policy amount is then included in the insured's estate for federal estate tax purposes. This is the usual situation.

Policies as written now usually provide that if the beneficiary dies before the insured, even if the beneficiary is originally designed as irrevocable, the insured may proceed to name a new beneficiary.

Most policies provide a simple procedure for effecting a change. The beneficiary may be changed as often as desired by *filing a written request* for endorsement accompanied by the policy at the home office of the insurer. Upon endorsement on the policy the change becomes effective as of the date of the request.

Ownership of policy and changes

Some policies indicate a life owner. A policy naming a life owner offers the applicant the option of retaining control of the policy or of placing this control with another. A clause is used providing that during the lifetime of the insured the right to receive all cash values, loans, and other benefits accruing under the policy and the rights to exercise all options, changes, or amendments to the policy shall vest in the life owner alone. Ownership may usually be changed by following a procedure stated in the policy. Such a change is the best way to make a gift of a policy, divesting the owner of all "incidents of ownership" in order to exclude the policy values from the estate of the owner.

Assignment

A life policy may be freely assigned, and the consent of the insurer is not required. Thus the contract rights may be transferred to others in a sale, gift, or loan. It is usually provided under the terms of the policy, however, that no assignment shall be effective until the insurer has been notified in writing. The assignment relieves the company of any responsibility arising out of the assignment before the receipt of written notice.

It is not required that the assignee have an insurable interest in the life of the insured, though it is essential that the policy be so written at its inception that it is not invalidated for want of an insurable interest. A valid life insurance policy is assignable like any personal property. The U.S. Supreme Court has specifically stated that to deny the right to assign a life insurance policy or to restrict it to a person having an insurable interest, is to diminish

---

terest, for example, may arise between partners who agree to maintain policies each for the benefit of the other (*Smith* v. *Schoelkopf,* 68 S.W. [2d] 346). Completed gifts of policies have been upheld in the courts against beneficiaries named after the time of the gift (*McEwen* v. *New York Life Insurance Company,* 183 Pac. 373; 42 Cal. App. 133).

the value of the contract appreciably. However, transferring a policy to an assignee without an insurable interest, with the intent of providing a wager contract, has been held to be objectionable by the courts.

An assignment is to be distinguished from a change in the designated beneficiary. The power to change the beneficiary is a contractual power to appoint.[8] The right of assignment grows out of the nature of life insurance as property.[9] Depending on the purpose for which it is made, an assignment may take one of two forms: (*a*) conditional or (*b*) absolute.

The *conditional* assignment, sometimes known as a "collateral assignment," is used in connection with loans or other forms of indebtedness when a policy is used to provide security. Such assignments may be fixed at an amount sufficient to liquidate the indebtedness. They may also cover the extent of the creditor's interest and follow the amount of the debt as it increases or decreases. As a result of cooperation between banking and life insurance interests, a standard form has been devised. The form, sometimes known as the "ABA Form," is widely used and is as equitable as could be devised. Its general use has introduced a needed degree of uniformity in setting forth the rights reserved and transferred by the assignment.

An *absolute* assignment conveys to the assignee all right, title, and interest that the insured or policy holder may hold. The assignee is placed in the position of the original assignor and has the right to exercise all the powers and privileges of the contract.

After the death of the insured, the interests of the beneficiary can be assigned without the consent of the insurer and without regard to the conditions in the assignment clause of the policy.

Dividends

The importance of the dividends available to many life insurance policyholders is obvious from the fact that about two thirds of life insurance is written on a *participating* basis. Dividends often reduce the original purchase price of a life insurance contract by as much as 20 percent or more over the life of the policy. The original cost is usually higher, but the use of dividends provides the *chance* of lowering "net cost" if the insurer does well.

Participating and nonparticipating policies. Not only mutual insurers issue policyholder dividends, but many stock companies also give their insureds a choice between purchasing participating and nonparticipating contracts. The policies are alike in their essentials. The difference lies in the fact that the excess earnings of a participating contract are returned to the insured, whereas the earnings of a nonparticipating contract are retained by the insurer as profit for distribution to the stockholders.

---

[8] *Mutual Benefit Life Insurance Company* v. *Swett*, 222 Fed. 200.

[9] *City National Bank* v. *Lewis*, 74 Okla. 1; 76 Pac. 237.

Participating policies make provision for the distribution of dividends. The dividends represent a return of a part of the premium collected after *mortality* losses, *interest* earnings, and *expenses* have been determined. Dividends are distributed annually and are payable after the policy has been in force for a given period, usually one or two years.

Dividend options. Policies provide several options with reference to the use of dividends. The options are not the same in all policies, but they follow a general pattern. They may provide for (1) cash; (2) reduction of the current premium; (3) paid-up additional whole life insurance, increasing the face of the policy; or (4) accumulated deposits with the insurer, at a current rate of interest of 5 percent or more; and in many policies, (5) additional one-year term insurance amounts (the so-called fifth-dividend option). The amount of additional insurance that dividends will buy (in options 3 and 5) depends upon the attained age of the insured and upon the size of the dividends. Some policies also provide for conversion of the basic policy to a paid-up basis, or for maturing the policy as an endowment, at the request of the policyholder, if the accumulated dividends and the policy reserve are sufficient to do so. The accumulation of the normal dividends currently issued by most insurers will permit many policies to become paid up after about 25 years.

Policyholders may withdraw dividend accumulations at any time to take the cash value of any paid-up dividend additions that their policies have purchased. The initial choice on the way in which dividends are to be used is made on the policy application form. Many insurers permit a change from one option to another, although a change to the additional insurance options may require a medical examination to determine insurability. There is no one "best" answer on how to use your dividends. Much depends on the various needs of policyholders for cash (or reduced premiums) as opposed to their health condition and their need for additional insurance protection.

In recent years life insurance policyholders have used dividend options involving approximately $6 billion annually, as shown in Table 11–1.

Table 11–1. Use of various methods of dividend options

Type of option	*Percent of total dividend dollars*
1. Cash	19
2. Reduction of premiums	21
3. Purchase of additional life insurance protection (whole life or term)	32
4. Left as deposit	28
Total	100

Source: *Life Insurance Fact Book* (Washington, D.C.: American Council of Life Insurance, 1978), p. 44.

Policy form changes

Prior to an indicated age, usually 55 years, the insured may exchange his or her policy without medical examination for any *higher* premium-paying policy issued by the insurer. This may be advantageous if there has been a change in the insurer's needs, or in the insurer's ability to pay premiums.

To make an exchange to a higher premium plan, the insured is required to surrender the policy for rewriting and to pay the difference between the premiums on the new policy and premiums on the policy being surrendered, together with accumulated interest. Premiums would be as required for the original age of the insured. A change of this character betters the position of the insurer in that the reserve on the policy is increased and the amount at risk accordingly lessened. Thus, no medical examination or other evidence of insurability is required.

If a change is made from a higher to a *lower* premium form, not only are future premium payments lessened, but frequently the insurer is required to make a cash payment representing the reduction in the cash value and thereby increasing the actual amount at risk. The policyholder has no contractual right to insist on such a change. Before approving the change, the insurer will require the insured to furnish satisfactory evidence of insurability. The evidence required may be a full or short-form medical examination, or the change may be granted on the same nonmedical basis as some new business, requiring only a current statement by the insured.

Lapse and reinstatement

Insurance companies are ordinarily willing to revive a lapsed policy and usually stipulate in the contract that unless the policy has been surrendered for cash, it may be reinstated at any time within *five years* after default.

Payment of premium and of all overdue premiums, with interest, is required. Evidence of insurability satisfactory to the insurer must be submitted at the time the request for reinstatement is made. The older clauses required evidence of "good health," and the change of terminology to "insurability" indicates a requirement somewhat broader than evidence of good health. For example, a criminal condemned to death might be in perfectly good health, yet be determined to be uninsurable.[10]

Misstatement of age

Since the annual premium on a policy written with a level premium is based upon the attained age at the inception of the policy, applicants have sometimes

---

[10] *Kallman* v. *Equitable Life Assurance Society,* 248 App. Div. 146; 288 N.Y.S. 1032; 272 N.Y. 648; 5 N.E. [2d] 375.

deliberately misstated their age. In other instances, the misstatement has been the outgrowth of a mistake.

Life policies contain a special clause covering the subject that is equitable to both the insured and the insurer. The clause provides that if the age of the insured has been misstated, the amount payable under the policy shall be such at the premium paid would have purchased at the correct age. This is determined by the application of simple proportion. If an applicant states his or her age to be such that the premium for $1,000 insurance at that age is $20 and at the time of the insured's death it turns out that the correct premium should have been $25, the amount of proceeds payable (x) is determined as follows:

$$\$25:\$20 = \$1,000:x$$
$$\text{Hence, } \$25x = \$20,000$$
$$x = \$800$$

Since age misrepresentation is covered by a special clause, it cannot fall within the scope of the incontestable clause. Age discrepancies are most frequently discovered when proofs of death are being filed. Regardless of the time of discovery, the amount due under the policy is adjusted to coincide with the amount that the premium would have purchased had the age been correctly stated. If the applicant's age is uncertain or if verification may be difficult, arrangements may be made with the insurer when the policy is issued to accept the age given in the application. The insurer is said to "admit" the age and by so doing agrees not to raise the question at the time of settlement.[11] If any difficulties in proving age are anticipated, it is logical for the insured to do this, for after his or her death the beneficiary may have considerable difficulty in locating the necessary proof.

Suicide

Suicide is covered by the life insurance policy. In some of the older policies, suicide claims were paid only when the suicide was the result of insanity, but the dividing line between a sane and an insane suicide was extremely difficult to establish. Also, from a social point of view, the dependents of a suicide, sane or insane, are in as great need of the proceeds of life insurance as they would be if the insured had died as the result of an accident or illness.

Suicide today does not have any effect upon the life insurance proceeds except that to forestall premeditated suicides for the purpose of defrauding life

---

[11] An insured may take steps to do this at any time. Sometimes buildings containing public records are destroyed by fire or the records are otherwise lost. The following sources are listed in the order of preference: (a) a certificate of birth, (b) a certificate of baptism, (c) a legally certified copy of the entire page of the family Bible, (d) a school record, (e) a confirmation record, (f) a certificate of marriage, (g) a naturalization record, (h) a passport, and (i) an Army or Navy discharge paper. If none of the foregoing is available, other available evidence should be submitted.

insurers, the policy provides that it shall be in effect for a designated period of time before the full policy benefits become payable. The purpose is thus twofold: (1) to provide payment, regardless of suicide, after the stated period; and (2) to limit the payments for suicide within the stated period. A typical clause is expressed thus: "In the event of suicide of the insured, while sane or insane, within two years from the Date of Issue of this policy, the insurance under this policy will be a sum equal to the premiums paid to the Company."

Sometimes the stated period is one year, but the effect is the same—return of premiums is made rather than payment of the full face value.

Indebtedness and settlement

These provisions simply state that any indebtedness to the insurer will be deducted when the insurer makes a settlement with the insured. Outstanding policy *loans* will be subtracted from the face value or other benefits payable. *Settlement* includes payments (1) when a policy has become payable due to the death of the insured, (2) when an endowment has reached its maturity date, or (3) when a policy has been surrendered for cash value. The policy is given to the insurer in exchange for the settlement.

Incontestability

After the death of the insured, which may occur many years after the policy was issued, it may not be easy for a beneficiary to justify statements made by the insured when the policy was issued. For this reason, a denial of liability by the insurer on the grounds of fraud could complicate and delay settlements, and possibly deprive a beneficiary of payment.

To put an end to the possibility of involving the beneficiary in expensive litigation in life insurance settlements, life insurance contracts provide that the policy shall be *incontestable* after a certain designated period. The incontestable clause is a statutory requirement. Two years is the period more frequently used, though some policies are incontestable after one year.

Courts have usually held that *if* a stated period has been reserved in the policy within which the contract may be contested, fraud must be discovered within that time. A policy procured through fraud is not void but is voidable at the option of the insurer. Under the incontestable clause, the insurer is held to have abandoned voluntarily after one or two years its option to contest the contract.

To become incontestable, the period must elapse during the lifetime of the insured. If the insured dies during this period, the policy is always contestable. The clause protects both insureds and beneficiaries because after the period has expired technical defenses may not be advanced as a ground for denying payment. If the insurer has a defense, it must present that defense within a reasonable time, presumably when the insured is still alive and can answer it.[12]

Some policies exclude double indemnity benefits (see later section of this chapter) from the incontestable clause. Thus the insurer may still contest the extra benefits for accidental death, even after the stated one- or two-year period.

CASH, LOAN, AND NONFORFEITURE BENEFITS

Among the most important provisions in a life insurance contract are those which state the rights that the policyholder has in case the premiums are not paid. The insured does not lose the values accrued in the contract. The statutory standard provisions require that *nonforfeiture benefits* be provided for in the policy. Thus the policyholder whose premiums are not paid does not forfeit all of his or her benefits, but may exercise certain options at the time the contract is surrendered to the insurer: (1) *cash values*, (2) *extended term insurance*, and (3) *paid-up insurance*. Also, *loan values* are available, even without surrendering the policy.

Cash values

The amount of cash available to a policyholder on the surrender of the policy is called its *cash value*. Insureds who surrender their policies cannot receive back the full amount of the premiums they have paid in. During the years that their insurance has been in force, there has been deducted from their premium payments the cost of making good the claims of insureds whose policies matured. They have also contributed their share to the cost of the insurer's operations.

Some cash values are usually available after the first year of a permanent-type life insurance contract. In the early years of the policy the cash values are small, but as the policy becomes older, they increase more rapidly. A table of the cash values at the end of various years is included in the contract so that the insured will know the values at any point if the policy is discontinued. The cash value forms the basis for the determination of all the nonforfeiture values. Each is the mathematical equivalent of the other. Table 11–2 in the summary at the end of this section provides a comparison of the cash, loan, and other nonforfeiture benefits available in a typical contract.

Policy loans

Under insurance contracts with cash values, the insured may borrow from the insurer at a specified rate of interest. The table of cash values also shows

---

[12] Some companies have modified the clause: "This policy shall be incontestable after one year from its date of issue unless the insured dies in such year, in which event it shall be incontestable after two years from its date of issue."

the *loan value*. From it the insured may learn the amount which may be borrowed from year to year. (See examples in Table 11–2.)

Policies do not have a loan value until a sufficient period of time has elapsed to permit the building up of an appreciable policy value. Most contracts have a loan value after premiums for two full years have been paid, although many policies have some cash and loan values after one year.

The interest rate is provided in the policy. A rate of 8 percent is usual today, although 5 percent will be found in some older policies and 6 percent in some other policies. The interest charge is added to the premium payments after the loan has been made, or is sometimes paid in advance when the loan is made.

The loan does not have to be repaid by the insured but will be deducted from the policy proceeds when they are paid to the beneficiary. In this respect, the policy loan is unlike most other loans which require periodic repayment or renewal. Failure to repay the loan or to pay interest does not void the policy unless the total indebtedness, including accrued interests, equals or exceeds the cash value of the policy.

The policy-loan feature of permanent life insurance contracts has become a very valuable right in the current state of our high-interest economy. The specified interest rate in the contract cannot be changed by the insurer. Many insureds fail to recognize that they have built up these loan values gradually and now are entitled to loans of perhaps several thousand dollars at the very favorable annual interest rates of 5 to 8 percent. With mortgage loans at 10 percent or more, automobile loans at 12 percent or more, and personal loans at 24 percent (2 percent a month) or more, the right is indeed one which should be considered when necessary. That some persons are using this benefit is apparent from the growth of policy loans:[13]

Policy loans

	At beginning of			
	1962	1967	1972	1977
Dollars (in billions) of policy loans held as assets by U.S. life insurers	$5.7	$9.1	$17.1	$25.8
Policy loans as a percentage of all assets of U.S. life insurers	4.5	5.5	7.7	8.0

The growth of policy loans is of some concern to insurers. To accommodate immediate loans, (usually only a few days), insurers must maintain more liquid investments and also forgo other investments with greater returns. Tight money markets, with general interest rates on other loans at a high level, will

---

[13] *Life Insurance Fact Book* (Washington, D.C.: American Council of Life Insurance, 1978), p. 69.

encourage more policy loans. During the past dozen years, loans by life insurers to policy holders have more than tripled, although a slight decrease to 7.8 percent of assets (from a record recent high of 8.7 percent in 1974) occurred by 1978.

Automatic premium loan option

With the *automatic premium loan* provision, overdue premiums (beyond the grace period) are treated as a loan. The policy remains in force for its full amount until the total loans, plus interest against the policy, equal the cash surrender value. Not all policies contain this feature, but it is generally available on request without any additional charge in the premium until the option is used.

This feature is generally a desirable one for the insured to choose when application for the insurance is made. Usually all that is needed is for the applicant to check a box in the application which indicates that this feature is to be included. It prevents unintentional or unavoidable lapsing of the contract should the premiums not be paid during the stated grace period.

Extended term insurance

The *extended term* insurance option provides continued life insurance protection, after premium payments have been stopped, for the *full face amount of the policy* less any existing indebtedness. It will provide, for such a time as the net cash value of the policy will purchase (with a single premium payment), term insurance at the attained age of the insured. See Table 11–2 for examples of the number of years for which protection is provided under this option.

Usually, extended term insurance goes into effect upon lapse *automatically if no other option is selected*. The special mortality table to be used because mortality is higher than usual, and the rate of interest for the computations, are stated in the policy for this option and the one following. This option provides the maximum amount of continued protection for the insured.

Reduced paid-up insurance

If insureds elect to have their insurance continue in force for life or to the end of an endowment period, they may use their cash value for that purpose. In a whole life, a *reduced amount* of insurance is continued and paid to the designated beneficiary upon the death of the insured. In an endowment form, protection in the reduced amount is continued to the maturity date of the original policy, and then the insured receives the reduced amount in cash.

The distinction between the entended term insurance option and the reduced paid-up insurance option should be clear. In extended term insurance, the face value of the contract is continued in force but the protection is temporary. In reduced paid-up insurance, the protection is permanent but the amount is for a reduced face value policy. See Table 11–2 for examples of the reduced paid-up insurance amounts provided by this option.

The delay clause

Life insurance policies written today usually provide that the insurer may defer the payment of surrender or loan values for a definite period, usually six months. The clause affords the insurer protection against a "run" and is virtually identical with the protection afforded mutual savings banks by state legislation. Neither type of institution, except in the face of a drastic run, would ever need the delay privilege. It has been used rarely, if ever, by insurers.

Summary of cash, loan, and nonforfeiture benefits

The major choices that an insured has if the life insurance contract is lapsed (not continued) are three: (1) the *cash value,* (2) the *extended term insurance option,* or (3) the *reduced paid-up insurance option.* All of these options are based upon the cash values indicated in the contract by a table similar to Table 11–2. The *loan* option is also directly related to the cash values, but when the policyholder chooses to borrow against the cash values, the life insurance contract is *not* surrendered to the to the insurer, but continues in force. (Technically, this is not one of the nonforfeiture values, but is closely related to them.) Interest is paid on the loan, and if the loan is not repaid before the policy matures by death or by reaching the endowment age, it is subtracted from the policy payment. The best choice for the policyholder depends upon a careful appraisal of his or her age, health status, and need for the continued protection of the contract. If cash is needed, a policy loan would probably be the first choice, or perhaps canceling the contract and taking the cash value. If insurance is still needed, the choices are to take a loan and leave the policy in effect, or to cancel the policy and take the extended term insurance (for the full face value) or the reduced paid-up amount for a specified time period. Table 11–2 is a typical table of *guaranteed* nonforfeiture values for a whole life policy *issued at age 35.*

OPTIONAL METHODS OF SETTLEMENT

The values that accumulate or mature in life insurance contracts are called *proceeds* when they are paid out. Of all life insurance proceeds (death, matured endowments, and surrender value payments), about 8 percent are used each year to purchase *supplementary contracts* from insurers.[14] The pro-

---

[14] Ibid., p. 47.

**Table 11–2. Cash, loan, and other nonforfeiture values
(for each $1,000 of face value in the contract)**

Years the policy has been in effect	Cash, or loan, value	Extended term insurance*	Reduced paid-up insurance
5	$68	13	$164
10	172	19	369
15	269	20	514
20	372	19	639
30 (age 65)	550	16	786

* Rounded to full years.
Source: Sample life insurance policy, American Council of Life Insurance, 1978.

ceeds are exchanged for a new contract with the insurer which provides regular income or interest payments to the owner. The available alternatives to taking the proceeds as a lump sum are also called *optional methods of settlement* or *settlement options or modes.* Approximately $10 billion of accumulated policy proceeds have been left with life insurers and are now set aside under these supplementary contracts.

If a policy has proceeds available in the amount of $1,000 or more,[15] insurance contracts usually have options giving the insured the right to have the insurance made payable in installments. During his or her lifetime, the insured may elect to have the proceeds of the insurance paid under one of the optional plans instead of as a lump sum. However, usually the beneficiary makes this choice among the settlement options after the insured has died.

Types

Four basic plans have developed from which are derived the clauses of the life insurance policy providing optional modes of settlement.[16] The specific wording in the contracts and the company practices do vary, however. The basic plans are: (1) specified amount installments, (2) specified period installments, (3) life income payments, and (4) interest payments. Examples of the use of these benefits are included in Chapter 16, where life insurance programming and estate planning are discussed.

Specified amount installments.   Under this plan, periodic installments are paid to the beneficiary in *amounts specified* in the election, as long as the proceeds last. The policy benefits are distributed periodically to the beneficiary in

---

[15] Because of the expense factor, many policies restrict the right of the insured to ask for installments of less than $10 a payment.

[16] Newer policies sometimes make available as many as seven options—dividing the life income option into several types. The insurers offering these options on their newer policies ordinarily permit the same choices under all older policies. The right to utilize settlement options may be the outgrowth of either (a) a contract provision or (b) company practice.

a fixed amount until the principal and interest are exhausted. The guaranteed minimum interest rate is usually 3 percent or more, and additional amounts may be paid by many insurers if interest earnings justify a higher rate.

Specific period of installments. Under this option specified installments are paid to the beneficiary for a *specified number of years.* Payment is made in periodic installments for the number of years elected. Installments are increased by participation in excess interest earned by the insurer over the guaranteed rate. The payments are in such an amount that the proceeds of the insurance, together with interest, are entirely distributed over a stated period. This becomes a useful option in planning life insurance programs when the time for which an income is needed is definitely established. For example, $10,000 of proceeds will provide about $100 a month for 10 years, or $60 a month for 20 years.

Life income payments. Instead of receiving a fixed amount (or being paid for a fixed period) so long as the money lasts, the beneficiary may receive installments under a *life income option.* The objective is the distribution of income for the entire lifetime of the beneficiary. This gives beneficiaries protection against outliving their financial resources. The option is made available in the following forms: (1) the life annuity, (2) the refund annuity, (3) life income with period certain, and (4) joint and survival life income.

The *life annuity* pays installments only while the beneficiary lives, and no return of principal is guaranteed. The *refund annuity* provides for the payment of installments so long as the beneficiary lives. If the beneficiary dies before the sum of the installments received equals the principal sum of the insurance, the difference will be paid in a lump sum or installments to another beneficiary. The *life income with a period certain* pays annuity installments so long as the beneficiary lives. If the beneficiary dies before all of the certain payments have been received, the installments are continued to another beneficiary for the balance of the certain period (or the remaining payments are paid in a lump sum). In the *joint and survivorship life income* option, installments are not only payable over the life of one person but may be continued over the remaining lifetime of a second person. This option appeals to married couples with the idea that payments will continue during the lifetimes of both.

Annuity payments may be made annually, semiannually, quarterly, or monthly. If an annuity option is selected, it is not required that the entire proceeds of the insurance be used for that purpose, nor the beneficiary limited to the use of a single option. Annuity plans may be combined with other optional methods of settlement to the end of working out a tailor-made settlement plan that fits the requirements of any beneficiary.

Interest payments. Under this plan, the proceeds of the insurance are left with the insurer. A guaranteed rate of *interest* (3 percent or more) is paid to the beneficiaries, plus any excess interest earned under participating contracts. The interest is payable periodically during the lifetime of the payee, usually from the date of the insured to death. This option is like leaving the funds in a savings bank account, and the interest received is taxable in both cases.

The person entitled to the proceeds of the insurance may, therefore, leave the money on deposit with the life insurer, at interest, until it is needed. If that person dies, then the face value or other proceeds of the policy (accumulated dividends, for example, less any loans outstanding) become payable to the designated beneficiary of the payee. Oftentimes this option is named as automatic as of the date of the insured's death, pending later choice of another settlement option. This assures immediate interest earnings on the principal. The primary beneficiary is often given flexibility to meet emergencies or changing needs by being granted limited or full *rights of withdrawal* of part or all of the proceeds. For example, a limited withdrawal right might be specified as "up to $5,000 per year."

Uses

The optional methods of settlement are available whether the proceeds are payable as a death claim, or upon maturity as an endowment, or upon surrender on the policy for its cash value. Settlement options assume an important place in determining the type and amount of insurance to be purchased when the insurance program is being set up. The life insurance program is frequently correlated with social security benefits.

If substantial amounts of life insurance proceeds are available beyond the immediate needs of the payee for lump-sum amounts, settlement options can serve a real purpose in providing for *systematic liquidation* of capital. When a breadwinner of a family, for example, leaves the family with life insurance benefits, the insured may urge (or partially require) that the beneficiary choose some form of installment or life income payments in order to assure continued income to the family. Not all of the proceeds have to be committed to settlement options, but in many cases it is logical to use part of the total available as a basis for future income. If this procedure is followed, then the beneficiary can, for example, supplement the guaranteed income from the settlement options with higher yielding investments of other types.

The *life income option* is one of the most important benefits of a life insurance contract, for no other investment can assure an income for a period which will exactly equal an uncertain lifetime. Any other investment asset must either use its income only or use up some principal as well; and then one cannot know whether the principal will be used up before life ends. A life income option chosen by a female at age 65, with ten years certain, will pay the beneficiary about $6 per month for each $1,000 of life insurance.

Valuable rights to life income may exist in many older life insurance contracts, for these benefits may have been calculated on the older mortality tables, which assume higher death rates than actually exist today. The life income options available under such older contracts may be very liberal, and therefore favorable choices for the insured or the beneficiary.

DISABILITY AND ACCIDENTAL DEATH BENEFIT EXTENSIONS OF COVERAGE

Three major types of health insurance benefits are included in many life insurance contracts. The most common are (1) the *waiver-of-premium* benefit for total and permanent disability and (2) *double indemnity* for accidental death. The third type, *disability income*, is less frequently included. It is, however, a very important and much-needed coverage, and recent years have brought added attention to this optional feature of many life insurance policies.

The waiver-of-premium benefit

Under the terms of the waiver-of-premium benefit, if the insured becomes totally and permanently disabled by bodily injuries or disease (not self-inflicted or occurring before the insurance took effect), the payment of subsequent premiums is waived by the insurer. Virtually all insurers today write the waiver-of-premium coverage with many policies.

For the insured to qualify for the waiver-of-premium benefit, the usual policy requires that the disability: (1) be permanent, (2) be total, and (3) commence before a stated age. *Disability* is usually defined or interpreted as inability to perform activities in any gainful occupation for which the insured is reasonably fitted by education, training, or experience.

Permanent disability is presumed after the insured has been totally disabled *continuously* for a period of at least *six months*. Later recovery may be evidence that the disability did not continue as a permanent handicap. Premium payments due during the period of disability are waived.

Total disability under such a clause requires that the insured be so disabled as to be prevented from "performing *any* work or conducting any business for compensation or profit." The courts have given reasonable and not strict interpretation to this phrase. The irrecoverable loss of the entire sight of both eyes or the total and permanent loss of use of both hands, of both feet, or of one hand and one foot are automatically considered to be total disability. Many other disabilities may be shown to be total in their effect.

Total and permanent disability must commence before the anniversary date of the policy nearest the *60th* birthday. This requirement is necessary because nearly everyone would become disabled and eligible for these benefits at some point in old age were an age limit not specified. Some contracts provide limited waiver benefits (to age 65, or for two years) if a disability occurs between age 60 and age 65.

Premiums waived on account of this clause are not deducted from settlements made under the policy. The benefits and values—such as the sum insured, the loan and cash surrender values, and in the case of participating policies, the dividends–all remain the same as if the premiums had actually been paid in cash. Under the waiver-of-premium provision, the insurer in effect pays premiums due from the insured during the period of total disability. Indirectly the benefit represents a payment to the disabled insured.

It is an important benefit to add to most life insurance contracts, for it enables the protection to be maintained at a time when it is perhaps most needed. A lengthy disability often reduces one's income substantially, to a point where life insurance premiums could not be paid otherwise. The cost is relatively small, usually under $1 per $1,000 when added to the policy before age 45.

Double indemnity benefits

A popular feature of life insurance is the provision for the payment of *double indemnity* in the event of *accidental death*. Not all accidental deaths are covered by this clause, which supplies a seemingly endless variety of plots for television dramas.

Specifically, the double indemnity (sometimes triple or more) is payable in the usual policy if death occurs *"before the anniversary date of the policy following the insured's 70th birthday;*[17] *directly and independently* of all other causes, as a result of *accidental bodily injuries,* and occurs within 90 days from the date of such accident." *Excluded risks* usually listed are death from *suicide* while sane or insane; *military or naval service* in time of war; the taking of *poison* or the inhaling of *gas,* whether voluntary or otherwise; sensitivity to or overdose of *drugs*; or directly or indirectly from *disease* in any form; or occurring while *outside the Earth's atmosphere,* or in any kind of *aircraft or spacecraft except as a passenger* (thus most aviation deaths are covered).

On the basis of the needs of the beneficiary, it is hard to justify a greater payment if insureds die as the result of an accident than if they die of disease or other natural death. In fact, the cost of a sudden death may actually be less than that of a lingering one with extensive medical costs. Some insurers now offer triple benefits for specified accidental deaths in public conveyances, and a few will pay up to five times the face value of the life insurance contract.

The double indemnity benefit appeals particularly to individuals who feel their insurance program to be inadequate, or to those who feel a need for high-limit accident protection. There may be some justification for some extra

---

[17] Many variations in the wording, exceptions, and limits of this clause are used by different companies. In prior years many insurers used age 65 as the limit for accidental death benefits.

coverage on the basis that accidental deaths occur suddenly, when insureds are less likely to have provided adequately for their families. The premium is comparatively small, often under $1 per $1,000, on whole life policies begun before age 45. Thus, the insured may, for a relatively small additional premium, get extra protection in the event of accidental death. Although double indemnity is payable only in a small proportion of all deaths, life agents often point out that under the age of 40 accidents are the cause of death in more than 50 percent of the cases. Because people are becoming more and more accident-conscious, the double indemnity feature of life insurance has a wide appeal.

This coverage affords a double insurance protection on a limited basis but *not* double *life* insurance protection. When considering the double indemnity benefits for accidental death as a part of a life insurance program, one should remember (1) that cause of death usually has nothing to do with the needs of dependents and (2) that the double indemnity provision oftentimes gives a false sense of security. Persons may feel that they have, for example, $20,000 face value of life insurance in force whereas (except in the case of death caused by accident) they have only $10,000. There is no objection to including the coverage so long as its extent and nature are understood. Of the total death benefits of more than $10 billion paid by U.S. life insurers last year, it is estimated that less than 2.2 percent were extra payments for accidental death.[18]

The double indemnity feature is not included in the paid-up or extended term insurance provision of the life insurance policy in the event of premium default. The coverage may be discontinued upon the written request of the insured, and the extra premium charge discontinued.

Double indemnity for accidental death, like waiver-of-premium coverage, is widely written. Health and occupational hazards are determining factors in both disability and double indemnity coverages. For example, persons in certain occupations are in every sense acceptable for life insurance at standard rates, but the accidental death rate is considerably higher than normal. In this group are to be found farmers, carpenters, machinists, and many others. Then there are persons suffering from a medical impairment who may be accepted for life insurance, but whose defect may make an accident more likely and give rise to a claim for double indemnity.

If there is a loss of vision in one eye or an amputation that does not seriously handicap the applicant, then double indemnity may be written at an advance in premium. Insurers tend to reject risks when the hazard is unusual,

---

[18] *Life Insurance Fact Book,* p. 41. On page 96 the deaths by natural causes are shown as 91.4 percent of all insured deaths. Deaths by external causes, many of which may *not* meet the specific criteria of the double indemnity clause, included motor vehicle accidents (3.1 percent), other accidents (2.9 percent), and suicide and homicide (2.6 percent).

as in violent sports. Foreign travel is not now regarded as an increased hazard but may make investigation of the claim difficult or expensive.

Total disability income benefits

Some policies provide for monthly *disability income* payable in case of total *disability*. The types of disability coverage vary widely. There has been a tendency at times to restrict the scope of disability coverage under life insurance policies, and some insurers do not write this form of coverage. [19]

Under the more recent policies, insurers providing a monthly income benefit for total and permanent disability pay to the insured an amount equal to $10 for each $1,000 of life insurance upon receipt of proof that the insured is *totally* and presumably *permanently* disabled *before the age of 55 or 60.*

Evidence is required that the insured has become totally disabled[20] "by bodily injury or disease so that he or she is and will be thereby wholly prevented from performing any work following any occupation or engaging in any business for remuneration or profit, and that such disability has already continued uninterruptedly for a period of at least six months." The policy does not cover if the disability arises from bodily injury or disease occurring before the insurance took effect, if known to the policyholder and not disclosed in the application.

Income benefits are not written in connection with term insurance policies. When the insured has reached the age of 55 or 60 and the income disability provision of the policy no longer applies, future premiums on the policy are reduced by the amount of the premium charge for the disability benefits.

Disablity income is not written by all insurers, and the insurers which write the coverage have established underwriting rules that tend to restrict its availability to carefully selected applicants, men or women, who are employed. Some insurers may also insure housewives for smaller disability income coverage. Policies now written with the $10 per month clause may provide for the termination of the disability payments at the age of 65.

Life insurance disability protection may be used to augment other forms of

---

[19] Life insurance income benefits for disability were introduced in 1916. The early policies provided an annual income of $100 for each $1,000 of insurance, but the benefit was soon changed to $10 monthly. During the period following 1925 the disability business expanded rapidly and policy provisions were liberalized. The period of depression brought with it economic pressure, and dishonest claimants used the disability clause as a source of income. The life insurance business found itself facing grave difficulty. Generally speaking, benefits were sharply curtailed and premiums were advanced.

[20] Generally, "disability" is much more difficult to define than "death." However, interesting legal problems are beginning to arise with state laws, such as in Kansas and Maryland, where "brain death" is accepted as a definition of death. In other states both the heart *and* the brain must cease to function. A recent American Bar Association-recommended definition of death is: "For all legal purposes, a human body with irreversible cessation of total brain function, according to usual and customary standards of medical practice, should be considered dead."

health coverage. It is expensive in relation to the other health benefits in life contracts. As an example, disability income (including the waiver-of-premium benefit) may cost about $5 per $1,000 at age 30, but the cost increases as age advances to over $15 per $1,000 at age 50. Life insurance underwriters carefully watch disability income limits in relation to income earned by the applicant. Aside from this, life insurers usually establish an arbitrary upper limit of disability income for anyone insured. For example, the limit might be set at $2,000 per month, not exceeding 75 percent of earned income.

FOR REVIEW AND DISCUSSION

1. Indicate the *number* of the phrase in column B which is most closely related to the term in column A:

Column A	*Column B*
a. Beneficiaries	1. Face value of policy corrected
b. Dividend option	2. Life income
c. Nonforfeiture option	3. Up to cash value, at about 6 to 8 percent interest
d. Unique settlement option	4. Accidental death before age 70
e. Misstatement of age	5. Paid-up additions
f. Policy loans	6. Becomes part of the contract
g. Waiver-of-premium benefit	7. May be primary or contingent
h. Double indemnity	8. Conditional or absolute
i. Assignment	9. Only for permanent, total disability
j. Application	10. Extended term insurance

2. Indicate whether the following statements are true or false (with reasons, if false):
   a. Life insurance contracts are not very flexible, because they must be in writing and because they are important legal documents.
   b. Suicide results in full payment of the face value of a life insurance contract during the first (or sometimes the first two) years of the policy.
   c. Beneficiaries are usually revocable, rather than irrevocable, in life insurance contracts.
   d. Policyholders who cancel their life insurance contracts can obtain reduced paid-up insurance, or even insurance for the full face value, under the extended term insurance option.
   e. Disability income benefits are more common in life insurance contracts than are disability waiver-of-premium benefits.

3. What reasons can you give for the lack of a standard life insurance policy? In what sense is there such a contract today?

4. Identify the following found in most life insurance contracts: (a) *dividend* options, (b) *nonforfeiture* options, and (c) *settlement* options.

5. Describe a specific instance in which each of the usual settlement options would be appropriate. Do the same for the normal nonforfeiture options.

6. To what extent are the rights of a beneficiary of a life insurance contract affected by an assignment of the contract to a bank?

7. Explain why each of the three types of disability or accident insurance coverages added to many life insurance contracts is valuable to the life insurance buyer. Do these coverages provide permanent protection? Which type is most common? most important? most neglected?

8. A friend of Mrs. Harnack tells her: "The *settlement options* and *policy loan option* of life insurance contracts are almost worthless in today's economy of high investment returns." How would you *disagree?*

9. Y insures his life for the benefit of his wife and children. Upon his death, will only the children living at the time the policy was issued participate? Or children born after the policy was written? Or children by a former marriage of Y?

10. X insures his life for the benefit of B and later borrows on his policy from the insurer. X dies, and B contends that he is entitled to the full face of the policy and that the insurer should collect the loan from the estate of X. Is B correct?

11. What is the *suicide clause?* In your opinion, should the usual period of two years be lengthened or shortened?

12. Mrs. King is the beneficiary of Mr. King's policy, written for a face of $10,000 with a double indemnity benefit. He dies due to an accidental drug overdose. How much will be paid, and why?

13. Few contracts (if any) are more flexible than the typical life insurance contract. Explain at least seven features of the life insurance contract which make it adaptable to future changes in the needs or abilities of the policyholder.

14. Mr. and Mrs. Erwin have decided to cancel some life insurance, but they are afraid that they will forfeit all of their contract benefits if they do. How would you advise them?

15. "The problems of defining 'disability' are greater than those of defining 'death.' " Why would you agree, or disagree?

Chapter 12

Concepts considered in Chapter 12—Annuities and pensions

Annuities are a part of the life insurance business.

Compared with other life insurance contracts, however, they emphasize *liquidation* rather than creation of assets.

Importance and growth include persons, costs, and assets of *public* and *private, individual* and *group,* and *insured* and *noninsured* pensions.

Definition is that of a promise of a *periodic payment* to an *annuitant.*

Purposes and uses include *settlement options* and *pension* plans.

Cost factors include age, sex, special mortality tables, and interest.

Types of individual annuities are classified:

By plan of distribution—*straight (pure),* or *guaranteed refund life.*

By parties in the contract—*single,* or *joint and survivorship* life.

By time when distribution commences— *immediate,* or *deferred.*

By method of purchase—*single,* or *installment* payment.

By amount of payment—*fixed,* or the newer *variable* annuities.

Contract conditions of individual annuities include:

General provisions, much like other life insurance contracts.

No medical examination, as poor health favors the insurer.

Participation in dividends in many annuity contracts.

Group annuities (under pension plans) are very important:

Types and growth include *social* and *private, insured* and *noninsured* plans involving a significant $450 billion of assets.

Nature and purposes center on the guarantee of benefits to employees.

Eligibility usually requires a waiting period.

Retirement may be on either *normal* or *optional retirement date.*

Benefits are determined by: *basic plans* (fixed benefit or money purchase), *past service credits, variable annuity plans* (based on stock equity earnings, or cost-of-living indexes), *death benefits, vesting clause* (right to employer's contributions), *change or discontinuance.*

Financing sources, a choice of *contributory* and *noncontributory* plans.

Funding methods determine *how* benefits are financed:

Noninsured pension plans: *pay-as-you-go trust fund* (or "trusteed").

Insured pension plans: *individual policy, group permanent life, deferred group annuity, deposit administration.*

Combination of methods, also used frequently.

The Pension Reform Act (1974), or ERISA, is bringing tremendous changes, and opportunities, to the pension field.

IRAs, Keogh Plans, and TSAs have tax-deferred annuities as one of the choices for individual pension plans.

Annuities and pensions

It is easy for many persons to lack interest in annuities and pensions—after all, most of us are not ready to retire. But that's the reason everyone should be interested, because even when we are *old* enough to be ready to retire, few of us are *financially* prepared to do so. In reply to a question asking how he liked old age, the French actor Maurice Chevalier once said: "It's pretty good, considering the alternative!" Retired persons everywhere would probably agree, but they might add that it could be a lot better with a little more money.

Living too long (that is beyond the income-producing years,) may be as great an economic problem as not living long enough (premature death while still working). It also involves more persons, for at the age of 25 more than two out of three persons can expect to live to age 65 or beyond. The significance of this chapter on annuities is apparent.

Annuities and pensions are periodic income payments that can help make retirement financially possible. This chapter emphasizes *insurance* annuities, those insured by life insurance companies, of two basic types: (1) *individual* annuities, based on separate individually owned annuity contracts, and (2) *group annuities*, an important part of the pension field. Not all group pensions (usually purchased through employers) are insured, but all pensions use the annuity concept. Many private pension plans use insured group annuities to guarantee the payment of pensions. Other private plans are not insured. Also a part of the total pension field are government or social insurance pensions, which are discussed in Chapter 15.

Definition

An *annuity* may be defined as a periodic payment.[1] It may commence at a stated or contingent date, and it may be continued to a designated person for a fixed period or for the life or lives of the person or persons entitled to receive payment.[2] The person entitled to receive payment of an annuity from an insurer is the *annuitant*.

---

[1] Sometimes it is also defined to be a *regular* or *fixed* amount of payment.

[2] Annuities antedate by many centuries the contract of life insurance. In ancient Rome in the year 40 B.C., legislation gave rise to the development by Roman jurists of the first-known life annuity values graduated with reference to age. Loans in the Middle Ages were repaid in the form of annuities.

In this brief description, several preliminary observations are implicit. An annuity may be paid as an annual payment, but it often involves a more frequent periodic payment, such as each month. It may start at a fixed future date, or it may start on an unknown future date depending upon a death. Once payments have begun, they may be continued for a limited number of years; but in the more usual form, the duration of the payments is conditional upon the continued life of the annuitant. This is known as a *life annuity*.

Compared with other life insurance contracts

Annuities are a part of life insurance. They are based upon many of the concepts discussed in Chapters 9–11 in connection with life insurance contracts. Annuities use the ideas and techniques of, for example, mortality tables, present value discounting, dividends, reserves, and beneficiary designations. Life insurers write annuities (1) as *separate contracts,* on an *individual* or *group* basis; and (2) as *supplementary contracts*, using the proceeds of a life insurance contract to purchase an annuity benefit. The relative importance and growth of the general types of private annuities are seen in Table 12–1. There were approximately 18 million insured annuities in force at the beginning of 1978.

The purposes and some of the methods of annuities are different from those of other life insurance contracts. Annuities emphasize the systematic *liquidation* of assets rather than the creation of an estate, although some annuities help accumulate funds for later use. Many annuity contracts are designed to *stop* payment when death occurs, whereas most other life insurance contracts begin payment when death occurs. Most annuities require *no medical* examination before purchase, whereas many life insurance contracts do.

Importance and growth

The place of private annuities in today's financial picture reflects a combination of factors, of which some have caused growth in annuities and others have limited the use of annuities. Several basic growth factors are: the increased emphasis on individual retirement needs; the growth of group pension plans through employer and union help and interest; the fundamental growth of life insurance contracts; general economic trends, such as higher incomes and affluence; and favorable tax treatment of annuities permitting employers a business deduction for their costs and individual employees postponement of income tax on their annuity returns.

Some of the limiting factors include: increasing social insurance coverage for retirement, a prime purpose of annuities;[3] effective competition from

---

[3] As compared with more than 18 million persons covered by private insured annuities (see Table 12–1), government pensions (railroad, U.S. civil service, state, and

Table 12–1. Number* of private annuities in force, U.S. life insurers, 1950–77

	Individual annuities	Group annuities	Supplementary contracts	Total†
1950	1,235,000	2,210,000	217,000	3,662,000
1960	1,159,000	4,533,000	428,000	6,120,000
1970	1,708,000	7,260,000	607,000	9,575,000
1977	3,681,000	13,825,000	587,000	18,093,000

* Numbers of persons covered (for group annuities), at year-end.

† Does not include variable annuities, covering over 2 million persons, whose returns are not guaranteed amounts.

Source: *Life Insurance Fact Book* (Washington, D.C.: American Council of Life Insurance, 1978), p. 37 and p. 54.

private noninsured pension plans;[4] continued inflation, which favors the variable-type annuity that insurers are just beginning to market; the psychological emphasis of our younger generations on *now* as opposed to the *future*; and the Pension Reform Act of 1974, which increased the federal regulation of group pensions considerably.

The growth of private insured annuities shown in Table 12–1 is impressive except when compared with alternative media used for savings, and especially retirement, goals. The 18 million persons covered and nearly $8 billion income from private insured annuities represent an approximate doubling in each of the past two decades, yet many other media have also increased rapidly. Examples include the growth of mutual funds, savings and loan associations, and stock market investments. The greatest growth of private insured annuities has occurred in the group pension area (see later section of this chapter), while individual insured annuities have only recently shown a reversal of a declining trend. Tax-sheltered annuities for employees of nonprofit organizations and self-employed persons (the Keogh Act) have given impetus to the sale of individual annuities in the past decade.

Purpose and uses

In their basic use of liquidating assets, annuities occupy an important place in estate planning and insurance programming. The settlement options of life contracts (see Chapter 11) are examples of one of the most important uses of annuities. The various forms of annuities written by life insurers constitute an important sector of the business through which an essential service is rendered to insureds. For those whose emphasis is on retirement needs, the

---

local plans) cover 18 million persons, while OASDHI includes 117 million persons with wage credit coverage or benefits. *Life Insurance Fact Book* (Washington, D.C.: American Institute of Life Insurance, 1978), p. 50.

[4] Ibid. Private noninsured pension plans covered 7.5 million persons in 1950 and 32 million by 1978.

annuity is said to be the most certain, convenient, and complete protection against old age that can be arranged through voluntary action. It substitutes for speculative income a sound and secure return for one's own old age or that of another. The security of a sound life insurer, fortified by legally prescribed supervision, relieves the annuitant of the uncertainties of management and investment.

A second important function of the annuity is to use the capital of annuitants so that it will last them throughout their lives. Given a substantial fortune coupled with investment skill, some persons prefer to handle their own investments and are able to obtain an adequate income for living without drawing upon principal. However, many persons find it necessary to use at least a part of their capital upon retirement. The annuity provides a means by which this capital distribution can be spread over a lifetime.

The matter of capital distribution assumes grave importance for individuals who are in modest circumstances but have accumulated some capital. Persons 65 years old with $50,000 have somewhat of a problem in securing the maximum benefits of the fund for themselves during their lifetimes. Invested at a net of 6 percent, their income will amount to only $3,000 a year, or $250 per month. If they apportion a certain amount of their principal to be spent each year, they may reach a point at which income and principal are depleted and they find themselves dependent and in need. Even if this point is never reached, it is psychologically distressing to know that one's resources are constantly decreasing and that unless death comes soon, need will follow.

Where the bare income from capital is insufficient to meet its owner's needs, the investment of the capital in a life annuity will yield, particularly at advanced ages, a sum substantially in excess of the interest yield, and in addition the income is paid for life, regardless of how long the annuitant lives. The purchase price of a single-premium life annuity for a male, age 65, is about $1,200 for $10 monthly. On this basis an annuitant may obtain an income of about $420 per month for life for the payment of $50,000. (The comparable cost would be $1,400 for females, and the monthly income about $360.) Thus, the annuitant has the confidence of an assured income for life, leading to a serene mental attitude. It is contended that freedom from financial worry tends to prolong the life of the annuitant, and this has given rise to the insurance adage "Annuitants never die." A paraphrase of the same idea states: "Annuitants live longer than people!"

Cost factors

Interest earnings are not the only cost factor that determines the amount charged for annuity benefits. The cost is not ordinarily called the "premium," but rather the "purchase price." Of a given group of annuitants, some of the contract holders will die in a short time and others will live for a long time, but the number dying each year will follow closely the predictions of the mortality table. The cost of an annuity is based upon the mortality rates of annuitants, just as life insurance is based upon the mortality rates of insureds.

To determine the cost of an annuity by a mortality table based upon *insured* lives would dangerously underestimate the risk. Individuals who know they have serious health impairments rarely, if ever, purchase annuities. In life insurance groups there will be many impaired lives at retirement age. At that point in life, only persons who feel in good health would willingly make a substantial payment of principal in return for a life annuity. Thus, a smaller number of deaths than is expected under other life insurance contracts would be experienced. Annuity payments would continue longer than anticipated, and the annuity insurer would soon be in financial trouble. Annuitants, therefore, represent a selected group, and *special mortality tables* must be used in predicting their deaths. The Annuity Table for 1949 is the basic table used by most insurers and pension consultants. This table is modified in several different versions in order to reflect the improving longevity trend that has already occurred and the anticipated continuance of decreasing mortality.

It has been noted that in computing the life insurance premium, the younger the *age* of the insured when the policy is written, the lower the annual premium. In the case of an annuity, the reverse is true. The younger the annuitant, the greater must be the purchase price for the annuity to pay a designated sum for life. Obviously $10,000 will purchase a greater income for life for a person of 70 than it will for a person of 50. Annuities have a particular appeal to elderly people without dependents[5] who are concerned with providing a maximum income for life on the basis of available resources.

The *sex* of the annuitant is also important. Females have greater longevity than males and thus receive annuity payments of about the same amounts as males who are three to five years younger.

In this chapter annuities are divided into two basic types for discussion: *individual* and *group*. Major sections treat the types of individual annuities, their conditions, and the annuity as used today in many large group pensions plans.

TYPES OF INDIVIDUAL ANNUITIES

There are several approaches to the classification of annuities. The method used will depend upon the purpose of the classification. Basically, all annuities may be classified (*a*) as to the *plan of distribution* of proceeds, (*b*) as to the *parties in the contract*, (*c*) as to the *time distribution commences*, (*d*) as to the *method of purchase*, and (*e*) as to the *amount of the annuity payment*. Under each of these categories, the annuity is divisible into two or more subclasses as shown in Figure 12–1, which summarizes the classification of the types of individual annuities discussed in the following sections of this chapter.

---

[5] Various *refund* or *guaranteed* benefits are included in many annuities so that dependents or other beneficiaries can have some of the benefits of an annuity.

Figure 12–1. Classification of types of individual annuities

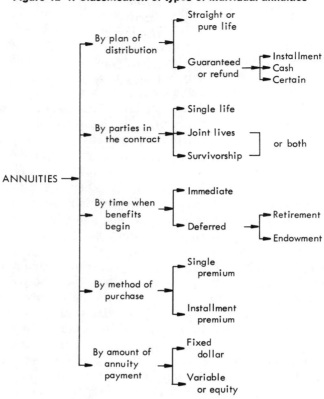

By plan of distribution

The *straight or pure life* annuity provides an income to the annuitant for life, without any guarantee of a minimum amount or number of income payments to the annuitant or a beneficiary. In contrast to the straight life annuity, most annuity plans provide payments either for a guaranteed amount, period, or cash refund.

Straight or pure life annuity. This agreement provides payments to the annuitant which continue throughout the life of the annuitant but terminate with his or her death, regardless of how soon that death occurs. Payments are made to the annuitant annually, semiannualy, quarterly, or monthly. Under this type of contract there is no guarantee of a definite number of payments, no cash value, and no provision for refund of any sort upon the death of the annuitant. The form is not popular, but under it annuitants are able to receive the largest possible payments and continue to receive those payments for life. The straight life annuity appeals particularly to persons of advancing age without dependents and of limited means who wish to secure the maximum benefit from their accumulations for their remaining days.

Guaranteed refund life annuities. Most annuities are issued with some guaranteed features which assure the annuitant (or the beneficiaries) a part or all of the cost of the annuity.

In the *installment refund life annuity*, if the annuitant dies before the aggregate of payments equals the purchase price, payments will continue to a designated beneficiary until an amount equal to the full sum of the single payment has been returned. The annuitant, or the designated beneficiary, is certain to receive an amount equal to the purchase price without interest. The annuitant, on the other hand, may live long enough to receive payments that will aggregate a sum substantially in excess of the purchase price. The annual payments under this form are somewhat less than the annual payments under the straight life annuity.

Another form, the life annuity with *number of payments guaranteed*, is similar to the installment refund life annuity. The payments continue during the life of the annuitant, with a guaranteed minimum number of years of payment. The form is thus called an *annuity certain*. For example, if payment is guaranteed for 20 years and the annuitant dies at the end of 5 years, payment will be made for a period of 15 years more to a designated beneficiary. If the annuitant, however, outlives the number of years guaranteed, payments are made until the death of the annuitant occurs, but nothing is paid to the beneficiary.

It sometimes happens that the purchaser of an annuity wishes to make provision for final expenses, such as funeral costs. Special contracts provide an annuity for life, with the additional provision of a lump-sum *cash refund* guaranteed to a designated beneficiary.

The reluctance to risk securing a return in annuity payments that is less than the cost of the annuity may operate to the disadvantage of annuitants. Knowing that the straight life annuity provides the maximum lifetime income for each dollar paid for an annuity, annuitants must decide (*a*) whether they need to leave funds for dependents or (*b*) whether their lifetime needs require their entire capital. Annuitants who have no need to provide for dependents can augment their income by electing an annuity without a refund.

By parties in the contract

Annuities are usually written on the *single* life of one person. They can, however, be written on several, or *joint*, lives. Both kinds of contracts are considered individual annuities because there is just one contract even when more than one life is included as the contingency for payments. Group annuities, written for many employees of a common employer, could be identified as another major division of annuities, as regards the number of parties in the contract. However, these annuities are given separate treatment in the final major section of this chapter.

Single life annuity. The typical annuity is based only on the *single* life of one person. The payments under the annuity are contingent on the continued life of the individual identified as the annuitant.

Joint life and survivorship annuity. Sometimes the need of an income involves more than one person, such as when spouses wish to make provision for the old age of both. The contract provides an annuity for the *joint* duration of more than one life. In a contract that is not often used, payments stop at the death of the first person. A contract widely used guarantees an income for two persons during the lifetime of both, and upon the death of one of them, it continues without reduction until the death of the *survivor*. After the first death, some policies reduce the survivor's annuity payments to two thirds. The contract may also be written to involve more than two persons; and when so written, the income is payable without reduction until the death of the last survivor of the group.

By time when distribution commences

Annuities classified as to when the first payment is made to the annuitant are either *immediate* or *deferred*.

Immediate annuity. Although the title is sometimes confusing, an *immediate* annuity provides its first payment at the end of the initial payment period after purchase. If the payments are annual, the first annuity payment would be due the annuitant one year after the contract began. If the payments are monthly, the first payment would fall one month after purchase.

Deferred annuities. Under most annuity contracts, probably four out of five, income to the annuitant does not commence until after a certain number of years or until the happening of some event. A *deferred* annuity may be written to provide an income at a certain age, or it may be written to provide an income to a beneficiary upon the death of the insured. A deferred *pure life* annuity can be written, but it is rare because no payment at all is made if the annuitant dies before the first payment comes due.

The *deferred refund* annuity, which is the usual type, includes the stipulation that the aggregate of the amount payable by the company to the annuitant shall equal the aggregate of the payments made for the annuity. Payments may be made annually, semiannually, quarterly, or monthly, or a single payment may be made.

The *retirement* annuity is a deferred annuity which enables an individual to provide an income for retirement by making convenient payments during the productive period of life. The annuitant selects a date for the commencement of payments. The amount of the income is based on the purchase price and the date selected. Retirement income contracts are written with the following provisions for optional settlements: life annuity, a cash refund annuity, or a life income, with payments guaranteed for a number of years certain.

This contract usually provides for a cash surrender value if the contract is surrendered before the payments to the annuitant commence. Some contracts provide for loans during this same period. An automatic paid-up annuity becomes effective upon default in the payment of premiums.

The *endowment* annuity, also known as the "retirement endowment," provides for a payment to the named beneficiary if the insured dies prior to the maturity date. If the insured lives to the maturity date, the insured may elect either a monthly income for life or a lump-sum settlement. The contract is, in fact, a retirement annuity coupled with decreasing term insurance running to maturity. The amount of the term insurance each year is the difference between the face amount of the policy and the cash value.

By method of purchase

Single payment annuity. The annuitant can pay a lump sum in return for a regular income for life or for a term. The contract is known as a *single payment* annuity. No further payments by the purchaser are necessary after the first is paid.

Installment payment annuity. However, the single payment is not always convenient, nor will the single payment annuity always meet the needs of the applicant. Life insurers, therefore, often sell the *installment payment* annuity. Arrangements may be made to make the payment annually, semiannually, quarterly, or monthly.

Obviously, only deferred annuities may be purchased on the installment basis. Immediate annuities, it follows from the definition, must be single payment annuities, and they require the deposit of a substantial sum at once. A deferred annuity may be a single payment annuity or an installment payment annuity.

By amount of payment—fixed and variable annuities

An annuity was defined as a periodic payment for a fixed period or for life. Although annuities sold by life insurers are usually for a *fixed* number of dollars, actually nothing[6] in the term *annuity* requires that each of the payments be equal.

One of the principal criticisms of annuities has been that fixed amount payments do not adjust themselves to inflation. To meet this situation, in part at least, a strong movement has been started in the life insurance business to write what has been termed *variable annuities*.

---

[6] Nothing in theory, at least. In practice, however, the term is thought by many persons to convey the impression of a *fixed* payment. This idea bothers some life insurers. These insurers feel strongly that to promise a *variable* payment will undermine an important basis of the life insurance business. If this is the true understanding of the layperson about an annuity, then a perplexing situation arises when one calls a payment (understood to be fixed in amount) a "variable annuity."

The variable annuity contemplates that part or all of the funds of the life insurer set aside to meet annuity payments shall be invested in *equities* instead of bonds and mortgages. The payments will be dependent upon the income that the equity investments produce. The variable income of the annuity would be similar to that of a diversified mutual investment fund.

Variable annuities are often written as deferred annuities. This means that payments for the annuity take place over an extended period. Investment in common stocks over such a period would tend to minimize losses that might otherwise occur if all the equities were purchased at any one time.

The idea of the variable annuity is, of course, to make it possible for the purchaser of the annuity to obtain the benefit of a diversified equity investment as a basis for higher retirement income without losing the benefit of the annuity principle that guarantees income for life. The purpose is to try to offset the decrease in purchasing powers of the dollar, which has dwindled from $1 in 1940 to $0.58 in 1950, to $0.47 in 1960, to $0.36 in 1970, and to less than $0.25 today.

Variable annuities are written both as *individual* and *group* annuities (see later section of this chapter). Most plans so far have been group plans, but the individual variable contract is now becoming more widely available. Most of the principles apply to either type.

One of the pioneers in the field of variable annuities is the College Retirement Equities Fund, a subsidiary of the Teachers Insurance and Annuity Association of America.[7] The CREF was established by a special act of the New York State legislature in 1952. The variable annuities provided by CREF are only a part of a retirement annuity system for teachers. An individual participant may elect 0, 25, 50, 75, or 100 percent of premiums to be applied to the purchase of a variable annuity in CREF. The remainder is used to purchase an annuity in TIAA. About half of the participants choose to have 50 percent of their premiums go to CREF. The fixed annuity part provides a guaranteed monthly income, while the CREF portion is not guaranteed, varying with the investment experience. TIAA–CREF has had success in marketing variable annuities on a group basis to educational and research institutions. A recent annual report shows a growth of assets and reserves to approximately $10 billion from more than 3,000 institutions that have benefit plans. The annuity unit value more than doubled during the period 1958–72, from $17 to $36, fell to $22 in 1975, and then rose to about $25 in 1977. Long-range participation over many years is emphasized as a necessity for success in the use of variable annuities.[8]

Other consumers have access in most states to many group and some individual variable annuities. The legal and other adjustments required by insurers

[7] See William C. Greenough and Francis P. King. *Retirement and Insurance Plans in American Colleges* (New York: Columbia University Press, 1959); and *TIAA–CREF Annual Report,* 1978.

[8] Roger R. Conant, "Inflation and the Variable Annuity—Revisited," *CLU Journal,* vol. 30, no. 4 (October 1976), p. 12.

slowed the trend in the 60s. However, by 1978 the number of persons covered by group variable annuities was more than 1.4 million and the number covered by individual variable annuities was 0.7 million. Reserves for the variable funds totaled $3.5 billion for group contracts and $1.5 billion for individual contracts. Most of the plans were based on the performance of equity funds, but about 250,000 persons were covered by plans which based the variable results on other indexes, such as the consumer price index.[9]

Early companies entering the variable annuity market were the General American Life Group with the Variable Annuity Life Insurance Company (VALIC), and the Aetna Life and Casualty Group with the Participating Annuity Life Insurance Company. The Prudential Life Insurance Company, too, led the battle for court and SEC approval. Several hundred other life insurers now have the new product for sale, and many others are planning to offer these contracts to consumers soon. Tax-deferred variable annuities are being offered through many nonprofit organizations under Section 403(*b*) of the Internal Revenue Code, and HR-10 plans under the Keogh Act are also making them available to more persons each year.[10]

Some life insurers do not wish to offer such contracts in connection with life insurance. They say, in effect, that any future *reduced* annuity payment will be difficult if not impossible for the insured to understand. They offer the solution of *additional* life insurance purchases as the method by which to hedge against the decreased purchasing power of the dollar.

A special problem faces those life insurers that write individual variable annuities. Although they can legally do so, a dilemma of legal jurisdiction arises. The decision has been rendered that the life insurer must meet state laws as well as the organization and prospectus requirements of the Securities and Exchange Commission.[11] An exception has been made in the case of *group* variable annuities sold under the provisions of the Investment Company Act of 1940. Such plans are exempt from the SEC jurisdiction, and regulation is provided by the life insurance laws of the states.

Undoubtedly the movement toward variable annuities will continue to be one of the most closely watched developments in the field of life insurance. The opportunities that variable annuities offer are great, and if inflationary tendencies continue in the U.S. economy, the growth of variable annuity plans is likely.

The consumer has a widening choice of purchase decisions to make. Mutual funds, whose assets grew more than tenfold during the last 20 years, now have strong competition from variable annuity plans. Both mutual funds and vari-

---

[9] *Life Insurance Fact Book*, p. 38.

[10] Paul A. Campbell, "Variable Annuities—Principles and Practice," in chap. 18 of Davis W. Gregg and Vane B. Lucas, eds., *Life and Health Insurance Handbook*, 3d ed. (Homewood, Ill.: Richard D. Irwin, 1973). See also *Variable Annuities and Separate Accounts: An Annotated Bibliography* (Bryn Mawr, Pa.: McCahan Foundation, American College of Life Underwriters, 1970).

[11] *Prudential Insurance Company* v. *S.E.C.*, 377 U.S. 953 (1964).

able annuities will have to be evaluated carefully by life insurance consumers in relation to fixed-dollar annuities. Many factors will need to be considered for the proper choice and coordination of these plans.

CONTRACT CONDITIONS OF INDIVIDUAL ANNUITIES

The conditions of annuity agreements vary with companies and with types of annuity. There are certain clauses, however, that either are legally required standard provisions or have been adopted by most companies. The insuring clause sets forth the promises of the insurer and outlines the types and conditions of payment.

General provisions

Most of the usual provisions are quite similar to those found in life insurance contracts. All companies reserve the right to require evidence that the annuitant is living before any annuity payment is made. They make every effort to save the annuitant from annoyance and usually accept the personal endorsement of the annuitant on the company's check or draft as satisfactory evidence. If because of misstatement of age an excess amount has been paid the annuitant, it is charged against current or subsequent payments. It is customary to issue annuity contracts providing for incontestability after one year from issue. The policy and application constitute the entire contract. The reserve basis is stipulated by indicating the annuity table used together with the interest assumption. The contract may be assigned, but the insurer assumes no obligations unless the assignment is filed at the home office. Nonforfeiture values are usually limited to a paid-up annuity for such an amount as the accumulated payments will buy as set forth in the contract.

No medical examination

No medical examination is required for the purchase of the usual annuity. In the case of life insurance, the medical examination serves to forestall unfavorable selection through the insurance of an undue proportion of impaired risks. Since in the case of an annuity, impairment can in no way adversely affect the interests of the insurer, a medical examination can serve no purpose. The risk lies in the annuitant's living an unusually long life. Consequently, contrary to the situation in the life insurance contract, insurance companies do not need to require a medical examination to determine any physical impairment that may tend to shorten life.

Participation

Both participating and nonparticipating annuities are written by life insurers. The lengthening of the average life of annuitants has made necessary an upward revision of annuity rates. Partly because it offsets this change, the principle of the participating annuity has become more popular. The idea is to guarantee payments based upon more conservative interest and mortality rates, with a view to returning to annuitants any extra savings over the calculations in the form of a dividend. Retirement income plans written by participating companies usually provide for the payment of dividends during the purchase price payment period. These plans also provide that the holder of the annuity contract may elect to receive the dividends in cash, apply them to payments due, or deposit them with the insurer at interest, to be withdrawn on demand.

GROUP ANNUITIES (UNDER PENSION PLANS)

Types and growth

The concept of annuities has been explained in terms of individual annuity contracts. The major application of the annuity principle, however, has been in the area of *group annuities* issued under *pension* plans for employees.

Table 12–1 showed the relative importance of annuities written by *private* insurers in the form of individual, group, and supplementary life insurance contracts. More than three fourths of the number of annuity contracts is provided by group annuities.

Both *social* insurance and *private* plans use annuities to provide retirement benefits. The private annuity plans may be *insured* or *noninsured*. The larger employee groups tend to operate their own pension funds, while the smaller ones often use insurers to guarantee their benefit payments and provide investment, payment, and advisory services.

The comparison in Table 12–2 shows the relative position and growth of these parts of the total pension field between 1960 and 1977, in terms of the number of persons covered. It shows growth between 1960 and 1976 of 76 percent in the number of persons covered by the various pension plans, including private, public, and OASDHI systems. The $500 billion in assets represented in these plans in 1978 is a potent force in the investment and capital markets of the United States. Rapid as the growth in the public and OASDHI plans has been, the private pension area has exceeded the percentage growth of the government plans in terms of people covered. Assets, too, have soared for the private pension plans, tripling in about a decade. Nearly one half of all private employees and close to three fourths of government civilian workers, have some retirement plan benefits in addition to OASDHI.[12]

The original purposes of pension plans were to improve morale and de-

---

[12] The relationship between the private and social insurance parts of the total pension field is thoroughly explored in Dan M. McGill, *Social Security and Private Pension Plans: Competitive or Complementary?* (Homewood, Ill.: Richard D. Irwin, 1977).

**Table 12–2. Major pension and retirement plans in the United States
(by number of persons covered, in millions)**

| | *Private* | | | | | *Grand* |
	Insured	*Noninsured*	*Total*	*Public**	*OASDHI†*	*totals*
1960	5.5	17.5	23.0	9.5	73.8	106.3
1965	7.0	21.1	28.1	11.6	87.3	127.0
1970	10.6	25.5	36.1	13.9	98.9	148.9
1975	15.2	30.3	45.5	16.9	110.1	172.5
1977	19.2	32.5	51.7	18.4	117.5	187.6

* Includes railroad, federal civilian, and state and local employees.
† Includes persons employed with coverage in effect at year end (including self-employeds), workers retired for age or disability, and their dependents receiving periodic benefits.
Source: *Life Insurance Fact Book* (Washington, D.C.: American Council of Life Insurance, 1978), p. 50.

crease labor turnover by offering faithful employees the prospect of security in old age. Other factors, such as tax inducements, pressure from organized labor, and increasing social and political pressures, became influential forces in the rapid growth of pensions plans.[13]

Nature and purposes

Group annuities are an important type of insurance contract used in order to guarantee the retirement benefits of employer-employee private pension plans. Private pension plans are not all insured; in fact, only about one third of the total private pension plan assets of more than $250 billion in 1978 were protected by insurance. As a matter of theory, there is no reason why any business institution might not set up its own pension plan and administer the fund itself. As a matter of actual practice, many difficulties have been encountered. Privately administered pension plans have in many instances been wrecked by unsound management. Considerable dissatisfaction has resulted because of the uncertainty of employees concerning the solvency of the plans and the rights they have in their pensions. The Pension Reform Act of 1974 was passed in order to correct these deficiencies. (See section at end of this chapter.)

It is natural for many businesses to turn the entire problem over to life insurers. Life insurers are equipped to make investments and have the statistical information that is needed to determine payments adequate to meet future problems. When employers lack adequate actuarial or investment facilities, it is regarded as good business to turn the administration of a pension fund over to an insurer. Uninsured pension plans have become an important factor in the field. In many instances they have become so large and so important as

---

[13] For a concise explanation of the underlying forces and factors, see Dan M. McGill, *Fundamentals of Private Pensions* (Homewood, Ill.: Richard D. Irwin, Inc., for the Pension Research Council, 1975), chap. 1.

to be able to command actuarial and management facilities that are in all respects adequate. However, employees have no guarantee of their pension other than the fund unless the plan is underwriten by a life insurance company.

The real purpose of a group annuity as used in a private pension plan is the third-party guarantee it provides for both employer and employee that the benefits will be paid. The administrative and investment services are important auxiliary purposes. The appeal of the insured pension plan is particularly strong for small and medium-sized companies, and for many business institutions it affords the only sound basis for the establishment of a pension plan.

When a retirement income plan is put into effect, a master contract is issued to the employer by the insurer. As with other group contracts, it is usual to give insured employees a membership *certificate* that outlines the benefits in detail. Circulars and booklets describing the benefits of the plan are usually distributed to employees. These are for convenience only, and always refer employees to the master group annuity contract for full details.

Eligibility

Employers are primarily interested in providing for employees who reach retirement age while in their employ. They are, therefore, not particularly interested in including temporary labor. This being the case, many private pension plans provide a *waiting period*, such as one year, for eligibility. Other plans require not only a waiting period but a minimum salary or an attained age. The waiting period must be adjusted to fit the individual business. Some employers have little difficulty with labor turnover, and their retirement plan can be made effective immediately, with all employees eligible. In some cases, the waiting period has been extended considerably beyond one year. The elimination of high turnover groups from the coverage simplifies administration and reduces costs.

Retirement dates

Two basic types of retirement dates are included in most group annuities, the normal retirement date and the optional retirement date.

Normal retirement date. "Normal retirement date" means the first day of the month nearest to the attainment of the established retirement age, which is usually 65. Employees are ordinarily expected to retire and begin receiving annuity payments at the normal retirement age. Factors that affect the selection of the normal retirement age are: (*a*) the age at which social security benefits are available, (*b*) the age at which superannuation occurs in relation to the employee's occupation, and (*c*) the relative cost of providing retirement at different ages. A majority of plans follow the social security program and provide normal retirement for males at 65 and females at 62, even though reduced OASDHI benefits are now available at 62 for males and at 60 for females. Pension plans must recognize other situations, but to provide a maximum annuity from the available funds, the normal retirement age should remain as near 65 as possible.

Optional retirement date. Pension plans ordinarily also provide for (*a*) an *early* annuity date or (*b*) a *postponed* annuity date.

It may sometimes be advisable, or desirable, for an employee to retire before the normal annuity date. Some plans allow the employee to retire within the ten-year period preceding the normal annuity date, or at stated ages such as 60 or earlier. Virtually all plans make some provision for early retirement. An employee who retires early receives a reduced income. This is so because the period for the accrual of benefits is shortened and the period of annuity income payments is lengthened. Some plans require the employer's approval for early retirement, but others do not.

Arrangements may also be made to have annuity payments commence at a date later than the normal annuity date, known as a "postponed annuity date." Some plans provide the same rate of annuity payments as would have been payable on the normal annuity date, in order to encourage retirement at the normal annuity date. In all cases, a postponed annuity date requires the consent of both the employee and the employer.

Types of annuities used

When a plan is established, an employer has to choose a particular form of annuity. The normal form may be (*a*) a *refund* annuity or (*b*) a *pure life* annuity. (See earlier discussion on types of individual annuities.) Most insurers writing group annuity contracts also provide optional retirement benefits, such as the joint and last-survivor type.

Benefits

The benefits under group annuities are determined by (1) the basic kind of plan, (2) the treatment of past service credits, and by such other important conditions as (3) the inclusion of variable annuity provisions, (4) death benefits, (5) vesting clauses, and (6) change or discontinuance provisions.

Basic plans. There are two basic benefit plans: (*a*) the *fixed benefit plan* and (*b*) the *money purchase plan*. Under the fixed benefit plan, the benefit is determined in advance and variables, such as age and sex, determine the cost. The situation is reversed under the money purchase plan; here the cost is fixed and the variables determine the benefit.

The fixed benefit (also called "defined benefit") plan receives the widest acceptance and is regarded as equitable in its application. Under the plan, benefits are based upon a formula.[14] An example of a formula might be a

---

[14] The benefit formula must give consideration to the tax status of the plan. Certain forms of apparent discrimination are permitted, such as limitation to salaried employees. A benefit formula is not considered discriminatory if benefits are integrated with social

monthly retirement income of 1½ percent of the monthly income times the number of years of service. Thus a 30-year employee earning $1,000 a month would receive a $450 monthly annuity.

Under the money purchase (also called "defined contribution") plan, both the employee and the employer contribute a fixed percentage of the employee's earnings. Usually their contributions are equal. The joint contributions are applied to purchase whatever annuity credits they will buy for the individual employee at the time of purchase and at the rates then in effect.

Under a fixed benefit plan based on earnings, retirement income is more readily estimated than under a money purchase plan. The fixed benefit plan appeals to employees because under it they can more readily determine in advance the amount of their retirement income.

Past service credits. Many employees with long service will receive little in the way of a retirement annuity if their only benefits are those that accrue for services from the beginning of a plan. Therefore, most retirement plans provide annuity credit not only for future service rendered following the inauguration of the plan but also for past service. *Past service credits* will depend largely upon the relative ages of the group. In some instances, a maximum period of past service is set as well as a maximum salary for the computation of past service annuities. For example, a plan may provide that the maximum period of past service to be recognized will be the most recently completed 25 years and that the maximum salary to be considered will be $10,000.

One of the most perplexing problems in instituting a retirement plan involves the handling of the *accrued liability* of the employer for past service. Employees nearing the retirement age will remain with the employer only a short period before reaching retirement status; and during this time the employer must build up from some source, capital sums sufficient to meet the accrued liability. The accrued liability is usually so large that for most organizations, a single payment to the trustee or the insurer is out of the question. Quite as important today is the fact that ordinarily only 10 percent of the accrued liability for past services is deductible by the employer for income tax purposes in a single year. For these reasons, installment funding is the common method. The plan to be adopted depends upon the immediate needs of the older employees and the financial position of the employer.

Variable annuity plans. In the field of pension planning, where both employer and employee are conscious of changing living costs, it is to be expected that the variable annuity will be given full attention. Employers from time to time have voluntarily adjusted their pension plans so as to raise benefits, but the variable annuity undertakes to accomplish revisions automatically by means of the investment portfolio.

security benefits. Higher paid employees should not receive benefits proportionately greater than those of the lower paid employees. Such rules determine whether the plan is "qualified," so that the employer can deduct pension costs as a normal business expense.

In the group field there are two approaches: (*a*) variables reflecting *stock market trends* and (*b*) variables reflecting changes in the *cost-of-living index*. The first of these follows the pattern already noticed in the discussion of individual variable annuities; the second is not dependent upon market movements in determining pension amounts.

Variables that reflect stock market trends are sometimes known as "equity unit plans." A part of the money available for employees' pensions is invested in equities. As the market value of the equity portfolio rises or falls, the income of the retired employee follows. Underlying this type of investment is the conviction that with the continued growth of the country, share values will continue to increase in value and thereby offset simultaneous increases in living costs.

The weakness in the plan is to be found in the fact that there is often no correlation between stock values and the cost of living. For example, the cost of living continued to rise during the 1974–75 recession, when the stock market plunged by 30 percent or more. To eliminate a downward revision of pensions in times of a declining stock market without an accompanying lowering of living costs, the variable annuity geared to the cost of living was devised. The benefits are directly related to the cost of living. A part of the employer's allocation to purchase retirement income is used to provide adjustments linked to the cost-of-living index.

Pensioners receiving retirement income based upon a variable annuity are freed to at least some degree from cost-of-living worries that may haunt others retired upon a conventional plan. It is interesting to note the increasing popularity of cost-of-living adjustments in pension plans. In 1963 a major impetus was given to the idea by legislation which provided cost-of-living changes in the pensions paid to federal employees and to retired members of the armed forces. Many public employee retirement systems, including the New York State system and the Canada Pension Plan, use the cost-of-living approach. Even some life insurers, such as Aetna Life, have adopted such plans for their own employees. A cost-of-living plan was adopted in 1972, effective in 1975, for the OASDHI benefits. The possible inflationary effect of such changes is one disadvantage of the broader use of this idea.

Death benefits. If employees die before retirement and they have contributed to a pension plan, a sum equal to their contributions is paid to their beneficiaries, oftentimes with interest. The accumulations under any annuity plan are substantial, and the death benefit may be a sizable amount. If the death of the annuitant occurs shortly after retirement, the heirs may react unfavorably if they learn that there are no annuity benefits payable to survivors. For this reason, insurers recommend a refund annuity as the normal form. If death occurs before the retired employee has received payments totaling his or her contributions, the balance is paid to a named beneficiary.

Vesting clause. If the pension plan contains a *vesting* clause, employees withdrawing from the plan prior to retirement are entitled to the benefits of the *employer's contributions* during the period of actual service. If the plan contains no vesting clause, the employee is entitled only to a cash refund of his or her own contributions with or without interest.

Not all pension plans today contain a vesting clause, but many do. Through it, the employee secures full title to whatever annuity has been accumulated by both the employee's and the employer's contributions. The clause has proved valuable to employers because it encourages employees to carry a greater part of the cost than they might under a plan without such a clause. On the other hand, employers no longer consider payments made for withdrawing employees as losses but as additional salary paid during years of actual service. The Pension Reform Act of 1974 (see later section), requires minimum vesting under several alternatives, such as partial vesting for 5 to 10 years and full vesting after 15 years.

Change or discontinuance. Few employers would be willing to enter upon a pension plan that would bind them irrevocably to its continuation. Yet, pension plans are designed to be permanent. Employers usually point out their intention to continue the retirement plan indefinitely but reserve the right to change or discontinue it at any time. It is usual to protect the employee by providing that discontinuance will not adversely affect the total retirement income credits earned, including the part contributed by the employer. Contracts ordinarily prohibit any cash return to the employer after a plan has terminated. Since the insurer, however, obligates itself only for the amount of annuity for which payment is received, if the past service benefit has not been fully purchased when the plan terminates, the paid-up annuity will not reflect these benefits.

Financing sources

In retirement annuities, the employer may pay the entire cost in a *noncontributory* plan or employees may pay part of the cost in a *contributory* plan. In recent years more than 80 percent of the total cost of all private pension plans has been paid by employers.

The premise that human effort is a production cost has led to the inference that the employer should bear the entire responsibility for providing pensions. Some feel, however, that the cost of pensions should derive in part from the employee. Those who favor a *contributory* form contend that wages are sufficiently high to warrant employee contributions. Such contributions, added to employer contributions, substantially increase the amount of the annuity. The contributory plan follows the pattern set by social security legislation. It invites employee interest, removes pensions from the category of paternalism, and gives the employee a sense of independence. Finally, employee participation creates a price consciousness. The employee who asks for increased benefits will be more conscious of their cost if part of that cost shows up as a wage deduction. The controlling argument for a contributory plan is that it usually provides more liberal retirement.

The advocates of a *noncontributory* plan contend that a pension represents a reward for service and is a form of deferred compensation which should be an obligation. Employee contributions are made from income after taxes, and net income is thereby reduced by the amount of the contributions. Employer contributions are usually deductible, and the actual reduction of net profits is less than the actual amount of the contribution. The noncontributory plan provides coverage for younger employees who might not participate in a contributory plan. In addition, it gives the employer more freedom in determining the nature of the plan, its benefits, and the method of operation. The early trend toward contributory plans was reversed in favor of the noncontributory plan by the impact of the federal income tax law, which provides that in a qualified plan the contributions of the employer are currently deductible without imposing a current tax burden on the employee. Unions have generally preferred noninsured plans because such plans afford them greater administration and control and because noninsured plans are usually on a noncontributory basis.

Funding methods

A final major characteristic[15] of pension plans is the method by which benefits are financed. Methods of funding retirement plans include: (a) a pay-as-you-go plan, (b) a trust fund plan, (c) an individual policy plan, (d) a group permanent plan, and (e) a group annuity plan. The first two methods are *uninsured*; the others are *insured* plans. The group annuity plan may be under (1) a deferred annuity contract or (2) a deposit administration contract.

Noninsured pension plans. A *pay-as-you-go* plan has no pension fund established and makes payments to employees out of current income. The plan may be formal or informal. An informal pay-as-you-go plan could be quite unsatisfactory. Since there is no predetermined plan, there is always the pressure to reduce retirement payments if the employer is in an adverse financial position, and some employees may be unfairly treated. A formal pay-as-you-go plan is only slightly better. Although there may be no discrimination as to payments, there is, however, no assurance that the plan will be in effect at retirement or throughout the lifetime of the employee. Continuation of the

---

[15] A thorough analysis of the contract provisions and cost factors is available in chaps. 33–41 of Davis W. Gregg and Vane B .Lucas, eds., *Life and Health Insurance Handbook,* 3d ed. (Homewood, Ill.: Richard D. Irwin, 1973); and Everett T. Allen, Jr., Joseph J. Melone, and Jerry S. Rosenbloom, *Pension Planning* (Homewood, Ill.: Richard D. Irwin, 1976).

plan is at the employer's discretion, and retirement costs may become a burden impossible to carry. A pay-as-you-go plan offers the least assurance to the employee of retirement security and by the same token affords the employer a minimum of benefits and satisfaction for funds expended. The trend is definitely away from pay-as-you-go plans and toward adequate funding through insurance or other means.

A *trust fund plan* may be established for the advance financing of a pension plan. Definite rules govern the fund. Funds are paid to the trustee, such as a bank or a trust company, that invests and administers them. For the fund to be sound, payments must be based on mortality, severance, and disability experience. Actuarial advice is essential, and a consulting actuary is usually retained to make the original estimates and periodic examinations of the fund.

Two major categories of trust fund plans are used: (1) a *pattern* plan, providing a flat dollar benefit at retirement which often varies with length of service, and (2) a *conventional* plan, providing benefits which vary according to both length of service and rate of compensation. The trust fund method of financing has become the most common type for retirement plans. Seventy percent of private pension assets, and two thirds of covered employees, are in noninsured, or trust fund, plans.[16] More than 32 million active workers are covered.

Trust fund plans are usually called "self-administered plans" because the employer retains responsibility, directly or indirectly, for their operation. The investment of the fund is governed by the trust agreement. Investment decisions are usually made by a committee composed of company executives or representatives of both employees and management. As an alternative, investment decisions may be left to a trustee alone or to a pension committee and a trustee.

The trust agreement outlines the administration of the plan. Payments may be made directly to retired employees from the trust fund, or the trustee may be authorized to purchase annuities for them. The appeal of the plan lies in the hope that the investment experience of the particular employer will be more favorable than the averages used by insurers. If investments are limited to U.S. government bonds and securities legal for trust funds or life insurers, the margin in favor of the trust tends to disappear. The agreement, however, may include preferred and common stocks. A trust plan is flexible, and the benefits may be revised from time to time as the needs of employees change or, more significantly, as changing conditions dictate.

Generally, the trusteed plans have been successful in their objective of securing somewhat higher investment returns. Their flexibility and their leeway to invest in stocks during a rising period of the stock market have been advantageous, for overall pension costs are reduced if investments bring greater returns. Private noninsured plans, for example, have had 60 percent or more of

---

[16] Allen, Melone, and Rosenbloom, *Pension Planning*, p. 185.

their assets in corporate stocks during recent years, whereas insured plans have generally had less than 20 percent. The life insurers have improved the competitive position of insured pension plans against the trusteed plans in recent years. Legislation in many states since the early 1960s has permitted life insurers to keep *separate accounts* for some part of the total assets of the insured pension plans. Common stock investments are made, averaging about 75 percent of the account, and usually for at least the amount of the employer's contributions prior to the retirement of the employee.

   Insured pension plans.   In contrast to the uninsured pension plans (pay-as-you-go and trusteed) are the *insured* pension plans. The major types include (1) the *individual policy* plan, (2) the *group permanent* life plan, and two types of group annuities, (3) the *deferred annuity* plan and (4) the *deposit administration* plan. The relative position of these insured plans is summarized in Table 12–3.

Table 12–3. Insured pension plans (beginning of 1977)

	Number of plans (in thousands)	Persons covered (in millions)	In billions of dollars*		Pension payments
			Payments into plans	Reserves, end of year	
Individual policy pension trusts†	187.5	2.0	$ 1.1	$ 6.0	$0.2
Group annuities‡	63.8	11.8	10.2	67.3	2.3
HR-10 (Keogh) plans	na	0.5	0.4	1.7	—
Tax-sheltered plans	na	1.1	0.9	4.3	—
Individual retirement accounts	na	0.7	0.8	1.0	—
Other plans	na	0.9	1.3	8.1	0.2
Totals	—	17.0	$14.7	$88.4	$2.7

  * Dash means-less than $50 million.
  † Includes group permanent plans, which are less than 5 percent of total.
  ‡ Includes immediate participation guarantee and deposit administrative plans.
  Source: *Life Insurance Fact Book* (Washington, D.C.: American Council of Life Insurance, 1977), p. 40.

   The importance of the group annuity plans (including the deposit administration type) is apparent: these plans comprise about 70 percent of the persons covered, account for over two thirds of the payments into plans, hold three fourths of the reserves, and make about 85 percent of the pension payments currently paid to annuitants.

   Under the *individual policy plan,* a trustee arranges for an individual policy for each eligible employee but retains control of it by means of an assignment. Note that this is not the same purpose for which a trustee is used in the "trusteed" plans discussed above, where the trustee exercises broad administrative and investment powers. A retirement annuity contract may be utilized; but if the employer wishes to provide a more sizable death benefit, whole life or other policies may be purchased. The individual policy pension trust plan is most useful in providing pensions for groups too small to be eligible under a group plan. Table 12–3 shows that individual policy pension trusts account for a large proportion of all insured plans but for only about 12 percent of the persons covered. The annuities are based upon the earnings of the employee. Each year the trustee purchases additional contracts. The normal form of the individual annuities purchased under this plan provides payments for ten years certain and life thereafter. Many insurers which write individual policy plans offer a "guaranteed issue" plan, which generally means that each covered employee is issued life insurance in connection with the pension plan up to a specified amount, such as $10,000.

Aside from providing permanent life insurance protection, *group permanent life insurance plans* have come to be used in connection with retirement plans. When so used, they may provide retirement income insurance or life insurance that can be converted to retirement income. The life insurance protection is available, up to certain limits, without a physical examination. Insurers writing group permanent life insurance require a minimum number of lives to be covered with a minimum amount of insurance on each life.

The most important type of insured pension plan is the *group annuity plan*. By contractual agreement with a life insurer, the benefits of the pension plan are guaranteed to the employee. Two types are used.

The *deferred group annuity* involves the purchase for each employee, *each year*, of a paid-up deferred annuity. At retirement the employee receives the income from the sum of all these annuities. The yearly contribution of the employer consists of both future service contributions and past service contributions. Under this plan, the employer can take no credit for anticipated termination due to employee turnover. The life insurer calculates the contributions of the employer, considering the expected mortality. The employer future service contributions each year, with employee contributions, if any, must be sufficient to purchase all future service benefits that accrue in the year. If the plan is terminated, the insurer administers all benefits previously purchased. Future service benefits are fully guaranteed as they accrue. Past service benefits are guaranteed as purchased and are based on past service contributions. These guarantees appeal to employees.

The *deposit administration group annuity* plan uses an unallocated fund of contributions from the employer to purchase each retiring employee an annuity *as the employee retires*. Certain types of businesses have a very large labor turnover, and most of the workers withdraw before retirement age. The deposit administration group annuity plan was devised to provide a method that would not call for the payment into the fund of sums to provide annuities for employees who would inevitably withdraw. Under this plan, the employer makes monthly deposits into a life insurance fund which accumulates at a guaranteed interest rate in an undivided employer fund. Employee contributions, if any, accumulate in individual employee accounts. As an employee is retired, the accumulation in the individual account is used to purchase a part of the employee's retirement income, and the balance of the employee's retirement income is purchased by a transfer from the employer fund. At retirement a single-premium retirement annuity is provided for the retiring employee.

The insurer makes no guarantee to the employee that the full amount of the annuity outlined in the original plan will be forthcoming. The employer may fail to provide sufficient funds. The insurer can pay only such annuity as the funds it has actually received will permit. On the other hand, the plan saves the employer the necessity of advancing payments for members of the group who almost surely will leave before retirement. The employer may build up the fund during periods of favorable business and may make smaller contributions during periods of business recession. The deposit administration plans are especially popular with larger firms (several hundred employees or more) that desire a flexible plan, with insurance guarantees as of retirement age for their employees.

Combination of methods. It is entirely feasible to use more than one method of providing annuity coverages. A usual combination is a group annuity contract and individual annuity contracts. A group annuity contract may be used to provide benefits based on salary up to a given amount, such as $5,000 or $10,000, for all employees. Benefits for employees earning more than the established limit could be provided through individual annuity contracts.

The distinction between insured and noninsured plans is not always definite. The deposit administration plans use noninsured accumulations prior to retirement and insured annuities thereafter. A trust is often used for noninsured plans (most of which are called "trusteed" plans) as well as insured plans. Some trusteed plans insure part of their total pension obligations.

Another trend of importance to the topic of combining pension methods is the growth of *multiemployer* pension plans.[17] Most prominent are the negotiated plans involving the larger national unions of construction workers, teamsters, longshoremen, miners, clothing workers, and others. The potential benefits of pooling experience and costs and the problems of coordinating numerous plans are illustrative of the gigantic decisions that must be made today in connection with pension plans such as these.

The Pension Reform Act (1974)

One of the most important federal decisions related to insurance in the past decade occurred in 1974, with the passage of the *Employee Retirement Income Security Act* (ERISA). This has become commonly known as the *Pen-*

---

[17] See Joseph J. Melone, *Collectively Bargained Multi-Employer Pension Plans* (Homewood, Ill.: Richard D. Irwin, published for Pension Research Council, University of Pennsylvania, 1963). Any researcher in the pension field should find good use for the nearly 20 books published by the council.

sion Reform Act, because it was aimed at correcting well-publicized failures of some pension plans to pay expected benefits to retired employees. A broad and complex set of regulations for private[18] pension plans has emerged.

The general purposes of the act are to strengthen the guarantees and the contractual nature of pension agreements with employers, and to raise the fiduciary responsibilities and conduct of pension plan managers. Minimum standards of vesting (nonforfeitable rights to the employer's contributions), prohibition of investment and loan transactions involving potential conflicts of interest by pension fund managers, and a government plan to insure pension plan terminations are among the important provisions of this 208-page act.

Problems.   The problems of adjusting to the provisions of the law have been troublesome and costly. Regulations to implement the law have been issued gradually during the past several years, and they have sometimes been in conflict with one another. The Department of Labor and the Treasury Department (IRS) have both been involved in setting these detailed rules. The *dual administration* of the law has created duplication and excessive paperwork for many employers, but gradually the rules for fuller disclosure and reporting requirements are being clarified and simplified. Temporary rules set in 1976 were eased somewhat, especially for smaller pension funds, by rules in final form that were issued in 1978.

In brief, ERISA applies to both insured and noninsured pension plans. It does not require employers to set up pension plans. It has undoubtedly been of value in strengthening existing pension plans for employees. However, its added rules and costs appear to have slowed the adoption of new pension plans considerably. Average pension plan costs are estimated to have increased 15 percent as a result of ERISA, but for some plans the increase may be much greater. Pension plan starts in 1976 were less than 6,000, less than one fifth of the number begun just two years earlier. In addition, pension plan terminations have been occurring at a rate of about one third more than was expected.

Major provisions.   The *major provisions*[19] of ERISA cover a number of important areas. *Participation* rules broaden coverage by prohibiting plans from excluding certain employees (age 25 or over, or after one–three years

---

[18] ERISA basically exempts government (public) pension plans. However, the provisions of ERISA which amend Internal Revenue Service codes (such as reporting requirements, maximum contributions and benefits, and tax benefits for qualified plans) are applicable to all plans, according to IRS officials (Alvin D. Lurie, in statements at the National Symposium of Public Employee Retirement Systems, September 14, 1977). Bills to enact ERISA-type laws for the public pension plans (PERISA) have been proposed but not passed for several years. A House Pension Task Force Report in 1978 called for sweeping reforms in the standards of public pensions for federal, state, and local employees.

[19] See *Pension Facts* (Washington, D.C.: American Council of Life Insurance, published annually).

of employment). *Vesting* requirements must be included in the pension plans, meeting one of three alternative guarantees: (1) 100 percent vesting after 10 years of employment; (2) 25 percent after 5 years of employment, increasing by 5 percent each year for 5 years and 10 percent for the next 5 years, so that there is 100 percent vested by 15 years; or (3) 50 percent vesting when age and length of service total 45 years (with a minimum of 5 years of service), plus 10 percent a year thereafter. Many pension plans have adopted the first ten-year vesting alternative minimum standard because it is the easiest to administer and explain to employees. Spouses must be given an option of choosing a continuing pension of at least half the employee's pension, if the retired employee dies before his or her spouse.

The *funding standards* of ERISA require certain minimums, such as being sufficient to meet current costs and amortize past service liabilities over 30–40 years. The *portability* of pension benefits is encouraged, if workers change jobs, by the tax deferment of vested accumulations put in individual annuities or the new employer's plan. *Plan termination insurance* is provided for in a new federal Pension Benefit Guaranty Corporation. Defined benefit plans (but not other types) are guaranteed by an assessment plan paid by employers, plus a potential liability of up to 30 percent of the net assets of the employer terminating a plan.

Fiduciary standards are enforced by the DOL and the IRS by making pension trustees, investment advisors, and anyone else with discretionary authority over a pension plan or its assets, personally responsible for carrying out their duties according to the "prudent man" rule. Conflicts of interest with the plan participants, and certain types of transactions and conduct, are prohibited, unless specifically exempted. The pension funds must be held in trust, or fully insured, to provide the plan's benefits and costs. Extensive *reporting and disclosure requirements* must be followed, both in reports to the IRS and the PBGC and in booklets of explanation given regularly to the employees. *Maximum pensions* for qualified plans are currently set by the law at 100 percent of final average compensation or, if less, at about $87,000 a year.

The future.   The massive amending process which private pensions are undergoing in order to meet ERISA requirements is still continuing. In fact, it is just getting under way. More then 50 percent of the regulations required by ERISA have not been issued in proposed or final form, and only 10 percent are now in final form.[20] The detailed regulations have been slow in forthcoming, but each causes many thousands of changes. Definitions of "prohibited transactions" and of the "parties-at-interest" in pension funds are examples of the difficulties. A whole new field of pension experts is emerging, suggesting that the tongue-in-check description of ERISA as "The Accountants, Actuaries, and Attorneys Relief Act of 1974" is not too much of an ex-

---

[20] George J. Pantos, "ERISA Update: What Lies Ahead?" *Risk Management,* September 1977, p. 34.

aggeration. In addition, employee benefit and risk managers for many firms are evaluating the need for pension fund liability insurance. In many ways ERISA should be an impetus to *insured* pension plans by the life insurance business, particularly among smaller companies that must now meet higher fiduciary standards for their pension plans.

The Pension Benefit Guaranty Corporation has had a busy start, with requests for plan determinations (to see whether assets are inadequate and whether it is necessary to appoint a trustee) running into the thousands each year. The employer's assessed cost is expected to be much more than the $1 per worker per year originally set. Failures by multiemployer plans, usually through unions, are likely to be high if some of the delayed requirements for them are not changed before application after a two-year moratorium.

In all, many parts of ERISA may become crucial to the continuation of pension plans in the 1980s. At the same time, the life insurance business should benefit from the stimulus provided by a law which mandates the prudent and careful actuarial funding of pension plans.[21]

IRAs, Keogh Plans, and TSAs

One provision of the Pension Reform Act has tremendously expanded the incentive for individuals to use individual annuities in their own pension plans. *Individual Retirement Accounts (IRAs)* were permitted by ERISA, starting in 1975, for workers who are not covered by a private pension plan where they are employed. The individual may make annual contributions of 15 percent of salary or wages up to a maximum of $1,500 (with nonemployed spouse, $1,750). The contributions paid in are currently tax deductible, and accrued earnings and capital gains on the funds held also escape taxes, until withdrawn at age 59½ or after. Life insurance companies are competing with other financial institutions to enroll participants in IRAs. Annuities, mutual funds, stocks, special IRA government bonds, and even savings accounts can be purchased for investment in IRA accounts. In effect, the IRA is a do-it-yourself pension plan, but the rules for purchasing, reporting, and withdrawing must be carefully followed to avoid tax penalties.

For self-employed persons, *Keogh (also called HR-10) plans* have been available since 1963. The maximum amounts deductible were sharply increased by ERISA in 1974, and they are now up to $7,500 a year or 15 percent of earned income, if less. Tax benefits and investment choices similar to those of the IRAs are available. Mutual funds and life insurance annuities (fixed or variable) have been the popular investment choices. The Tax Reform Act of 1976 introduced changes that also permit estate tax savings if the proceeds of Keogh plans are distributed to a beneficiary over more than one

---

[21] Charles C. Hinckley, "ERISA and the Life Insurance Industry," *CLU Journal,* vol. 30, no. 1 (January 1976), p. 44.

year. Figure 12–3 shows that several million persons have Keogh or IRA pension plans today, with several billion dollars invested. However, the potential market for these two types of individual pensions is estimated at 40 to 50 million persons, so considerable growth is predicted for the 1980s.

A third form of tax-deferred annuities, limited to academic employees and employees of nonprofit organizations, is available under Internal Revenue Code Section 401(c)3. These are called *tax-sheltered annuities, or TSAs*. A payroll deduction method of collecting the contributions through the employer must be used. Maximum limits for the annual tax-deductible contributions are determined by special formulas. Many life insurance companies are now selling both fixed and variable annuity contracts to this market.

The appeal of IRAs, Keogh plans, and TSAs lies in the *tax incentives* for individuals to build their own pension plans for retirement. Conversely, it has been said that the Pension Reform Act of 1974 "denoted a shift in public policy regarding private pensions from a tax-based orientation to one fundamentally related to *employee security*."[22] Annuities as discussed in this chapter can be used to achieve the benefits of both these objectives.

FOR REVIEW AND DISCUSSION

1. How important are annuities, and in what parts of the life insurance business are they used?

2. How are annuities (a) like and (b) unlike other life insurance contracts?

3. Are annuities an important savings medium today? Illustrate your answer with comparisons with other savings media and with reference to any general trends that are observable.

4. What classifications of annuities are important to an understanding of the various uses to which annuities may be put?

5. A fairly common type of individual annuity is a *deferred, installment payment, refund, single life* annuity. Explain the italicized terms, and note why the use of these features might be expected in an annuity.

6. Annuities and life insurance both involve life contingencies. Why is the usual medical examination dispensed with in writing annuities?

7. The 1958 CSO Table of Mortality is conservative for use in computing life insurance premiums. The use of this table for the purpose of computing the cost of an annuity would, therefore, be disastrous. Why?

8. Mr. Julian claims that a sound bond is a better type of investment than an annuity since it provides income and the principal remains intact. Is this statement correct? Explain why or why not.

9. Frank says: "I'm not worried about income for my old age because other things will take care of that. I won't need a private pension." Explain what

---

[22] William C. Greenough and Francis P. King, *Pension Plans and Public Policy* (New York: Columbia University Press, 1976), p. 67.

"other things" Frank may be thinking about, and state why you agree or disagree with his conclusion about a private pension.

10. If you were an employee, what factors would you stress in explaining to a co-worker why you were in favor of (*a*) an insured pension plan or (*b*) a noninsured pension plan?

11. An insurance executive states: "Our advocacy of variable annuities stems from the dilemma of many persons now retired on pension plans and annuity incomes that often fail to meet the buyer's needs, primarily because of the impact of inflation on the purchasing power of the dollar." How does the variable annuity remedy this situation? How successfully?

12. From the standpoint of the business of insurance, indicate why the variable annuity should or should not be written by a life insurer.

13. Explain briefly the basic methods by which benefits are (*a*) determined and (*b*) funded under pension plans.

14. Why are various retirement dates used in pension plans?

15. What advantages and disadvantages do group annuities have for pension plans as opposed to such alternatives as (*a*) trusteed plans and (*b*) individual policy plans?

16. "The Pension Reform Act of 1974 (ERISA) has brought many problems to pension plans, but it has also provided new opportunities for the life insurance business." Explain.

Chapter 13

Concepts considered in Chapter 13—Individual health insurance

Individual health insurance is rapidly growing, perplexing in variety.

Significance is its needed coverage for many insureds, by many insurers.

Classification and purpose are important to its understanding.

Definitions must distinguish accident, sickness, and disability.

Purpose is benefit payments for *medical expenses* and *loss of income*.

Classes of health insurance include:

Method of underwriting, *individual* and *group* health insurance.

Health perils, accident insurance for *injuries*, and sickness insurance for *illness*.

Health insuring organizations include choice among many private insurers, Blue Cross–Blue Shield associations, and other plans.

Health policies: commercial, industrial, mail-order, special-purpose.

Health losses and protection are included in *three basic contracts*:

Hospital, surgical, and regular medical expenses;

Major medical expenses; and

Loss of income protection.

Relationship to life insurance is close, for life insurers write more health insurance than casualty or specialized health insurers.

Provisions in a typical health policy are the—

Application and policy face, including the "accident insuring" clause.

Cancelabiity and renewability, a basic policy feature:

Cancelable, and renewable at option of insurer, or

Noncancelable and guaranteed renewable, an increasingly popular choice of the consumer.

Benefit provisions are the heart of the contract, and may include benefits for *dismemberment or loss of sight, total disability, partial disability, elective indemnity, double indemnity, medical expense,* and *waiver of premium.*

Exclusions and limitations on benefits are often necessary through:

Exceptions, for particular perils or losses;

Reductions, limiting benefits for some injuries or diseases; and

Riders for substandard health risks, excluding preexisting conditions.

The standard provisions help provide at least minimum uniformity.

Underwriting problems and special contracts:

Overinsurance requires the evaluation of potential moral hazard.

Factors affecting premiums are *benefits, occupation, sex,* and *age.*

Special health contracts: *professional, homeowner's disability.*

Individual health insurance

What do you want most in life? Well and poor persons tend to say *wealth,* but sick and rich persons invariably say *health.* Many of us in between probably choose "happiness"[1] as a general goal, hoping that it means some of both. This chapter concerns both goals, too, for the effect of ill health is increased expenses and loss of income, which result in less wealth—*unless* you have proper *health insurance.* If you don't, then some of that happiness may be lost, too.

SIGNIFICANCE OF PRIVATE HEALTH INSURANCE

If one were asked to name the major type of voluntary insurance which is a faster-growing type of protection, covering more persons, through more insurers, in more contract forms than *life* insurance, the only answer would be *health* insurance. The vast scope of this field of insurance is evident in its nearly 2,000 insuring organizations that cover 180 million (more than eight out of ten) Americans in thousands of different policy contracts.[2] Premiums for health insurance have quadrupled in the past ten years to more than $50 billion a year.

The above comments relate to the *private* health insurance business. The Social Security Amendments of 1965, which included the Medicare program of health insurance for the elderly, were a significant landmark in the expansion by government into insuring against health losses. Some observers predicted that this legislation would mean the continual erosion of the health insurance market. However, today six out of ten persons age 65 or older have private insurance policies to supplement Medicare benefits. This chapter and the next relate only to the private health insurance field. Chapter 15 discusses the developments in social health insurance. National health insurance proposals are treated there, though the student should realize that enactment of such a government insurance system would profoundly affect the private health insurance field.

---

[1] The statesman Disraeli appropriately said 100 years ago that "the *health* of a people is really the foundation upon which all their *happiness* and all their powers . . . depend." (In 1877 speech, italics added.)

[2] *Source Book of Health Insurance Data* (New York: Health Insurance Institute, 1976–77), p. 21.

CLASSIFICATION AND PURPOSE

Definitions

The term *health insurance* applies to those forms of insurance that provide protection against the financial impact of illness or injury. Originally a casualty insurance line, the earliest health protection offered was known as "accident insurance." Later, when sickness coverages were added, it was natural to extend the name of the coverage to "accident and sickness insurance" or "accident and health insurance." The term *disability insurance* has also been used. The older names have by no means been entirely replaced as a part of insurance terminology. However, taken as part of a personal insurance program with life insurance covering life contingencies, *health* insurance is the logical term to apply to health contingencies.

Purpose

Health insurance has as its purpose the payment of benefits for loss of *income* and *expenses* arising from illness and injury. Not only is the loss of time from productive enterprise the source of loss to the insured, but the cost of the care and necessary medical attention adds to the amount of the loss. Health insurance provides protection against (*a*) the loss of time or earning power and (*b*) the added expense of medical care.

Since most persons are dependent on the current income derived from their own efforts, time is their most valuable asset. Health insurance protects this asset as it is reflected in earning power, and in so doing protects the independence and welfare of the persons depending upon it. The function of health insurance for the family has been compared to that of business interruption insurance in business operations. It provides income when potential earnings are lost through disability.

Incapacity from illness or injury may also draw heavily upon savings to meet the costs of medical, nursing, or surgical care. Health insurance serves to preserve savings, paying for current expenses and making unnecessary the liquidation or mortgaging of the car or the home in order to pay heavy medical or surgical expenses. In this respect health insurance provides property protection.

Classes

Health insurance includes such a wide variety of insurers, contracts, underwriting methods, perils, and losses that the student should pay particular attention to the classes into which the total field is divided. As a summary, Figure 13–1 shows the organization of all health insurance into separate categories according to the different criteria used in the following sections of this chapter. Frequent reference to this breakdown of the field should be helpful

Figure 13–1. The types of health insurance

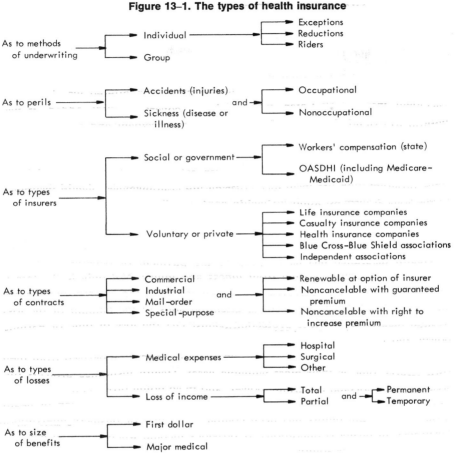

in reading the chapter and in understanding the relationships within the whole field of health insurance.

Method of underwriting. Health insurance is written in one of two ways: (*a*) policies covering the *individual* insured and in certain instances his or her family and (*b*) policies covering *groups* of persons. *Group* forms of health insurance are discussed in Chapter 14 in this text.

Health perils. In regard to the causes of losses or perils, health insurance may be divided into (*a*) *accident* insurance, for sudden and unexpected injuries; and (*b*) *sickness* insurance, for illness or diseases. This division was the basis for the traditional description of the fields. The terms have been supplanted to a large extent by the newer term *health* insurance, describing in one word both of the major perils.

Another way of dividing the perils of good health is to describe the source of the injury or illness as being (*a*) *occupational* or (*b*) *nonoccupational*. The distinction is useful in several forms of insurance, especially in social insurance plans established by government. Here the classification centers on describing the danger of poor health as one resulting from the work situation (covered under workers' compensation insurance in many cases) and all other situations. The outside-of-work causes would usually be provided for by the individual's own voluntary insurance, but in five states they might be compensated under "nonoccupational" or "temporary" disability laws (see Chapter 15).

Health insuring organizations.   The policyholder has a wide choice among types of voluntary insuring organizations. Totaling almost 2,000, there are 1,000 insurance companies, 150 Blue Cross or Blue Shield plans, and nearly 800 independent plans available. The independent plans include those sponsored by communities, unions, employers, colleges, private health clinics, and the health maintenance organizations (HMOs).

It is not to minimize the importance of the many other types of insuring organizations that this chapter analyzes only the policy forms of the insurance companies. The sheer scope of the complete discussion that would be required in order to discuss all the Blue Cross, Blue Shield, and independent plans necessitates confining the emphasis in this chapter to insurance contracts issued by licensed health insurance companies.[3]

The major differences between Blue Cross–Blue Shield and insurance companies are:

1. *Formation and sponsorship.* Blue Cross plans are community-sponsored, *nonprofit* associations organized under special state *enabling legislative acts* that exempt them from many of the insurance laws. The impetus for Blue Cross plans has usually come from the *hospitals.* Blue Shield plans are basically sponsored by *physicians* through the medical societies and formed in a similar manner.

2. *Operation.* The Blue Cross–Blue Shield plans usually make direct payments to *the participating hospitals or doctors* for the *services* rendered in, contrast to the insurance companies, which pay specified dollar amounts (*indemnity*) to the insureds for their medical expenses. Sometimes Blue Cross–Blue Shield rating procedures vary from those of the insurers, which emphasize "class" rating as opposed to "community" rating plans.

Blue Cross–Blue Shield plans, and other hospital-medical plans, are a significant part of the health insurance field. In 1977 more than $25 billion in "subscriptions" (or premiums) was received by these plans, or about half of the total health insurance premiums of more than $50 billion in that year. In the hospital-surgical-medical expense area alone, Blue Cross and Blue Shield are even more important that the indicated proportion. For major medical

---

[3] Those students desiring further information about health insurance are referred to: O. D. Dickerson, *Health Insurance* (Homewood, Ill.: Richard D. Irwin, 1968); and Davis W. Gregg and Vane B. Lucas, eds., *Life and Health Insurance Handbook,* 3d ed. (Homewood, Ill.: Richard D. Irwin, 1973).

expenses they are less important, and they do not write health insurance for loss of income.

The "Blues" have come into their share of criticism in recent years during the rapid escalation of health care costs, which have risen from $68 a year for each American in 1950 to an estimated $634 for 1977.[4] The Federal Trade Commission has resisted attempts by Blue Cross and Blue Shield to merge, citing possible monopoly consequences. Blue Cross and Blue Shield have also been criticized, along with other insurers, for a failure to help control and contain health cost increases. Their boards of directors are under increasing pressure to broaden their representation of the public, as most associations are now heavily controlled by doctors and hospital representatives, who thus can assert too much control over the prices charged for the services they provide. The Blues are also prime contractors for much of the Medicare program, and the need for tighter cost controls is also evident there.

Health insurance policies. Individual or family health insurance policies include: (1) commercial policies, (2) industrial policies, (3) mail-order policies, and (4) special-purpose policies. The *commercial policies* are written on selected risks with large medical expense indemnity limits, and they provide three fourths of the total income protection. The premiums are usually payable annually, semiannually, quarterly, or monthly. Because of their much broader coverage, commercial policies deserve the primary attention in this text. Except for the brief summary of the following three other types, this chapter discusses the usual commercial policies.

Industrial policies are quite similar to commercial policies, but more restricted in the amount and variety of their coverage. They are designed for the low-income groups, and premiums are collected at the home, as with industrial life insurance.

Mail-order policies are quite common, though the tremendous number of these forms and their great variability prevent their detailed discussion here. Since these policies are often very limited in the scope of their protection, consumers should be very careful in purchasing them. Most of them cover only a small part of the health coverage needed. They may cover only accidents, or only income while in the hospital, which provides very short-term protection. They are sold only through the mail or by extensive advertising, without the use of agents.

The *special-purpose policies* should be mentioned more fully here, as examples of the wide variety of coverages. Many special policies are written to cover travel. Some cover only one form of travel, such as travel by airplane, and others cover all travel accidents. Aircraft accident insurance is purchased through vending machines located in airports. Much broader travel accident policies on an annual basis are available through many insurance agents. Many of the major oil companies have made such travel accident insurance available

---

[4] "New Compresses for Health Care Costs," *Money,* January 1978, p. 71.

for purchase through their credit cards and monthly billing. American Express and other credit card companies have done likewise.

Another type of special-purpose policy, the so-called dread disease policy, covers medical expenses in connection with one or a number of specific diseases, such as poliomyelitis and cancer, that involve large amounts for medical expenses but occur infrequently.[5] Special-purpose policies are also written to cover injuries sustained while participating in sports, while on vacation, while in summer camps, or while on duty as a volunteer fire fighter. Policies are also written providing insurance for students.[6] Limited policies are offered to many newspaper subscribers, with the coverage usually restricted to very small amounts for accident injuries only. Generally, special-purpose policies are not recommended, because they are so limited in coverage and because they are not needed if the broader commercial forms are used.

Health losses and protection. A final method of classifying the various parts of health insurance is by reference to the kinds of losses caused by the interruption of good health.

Health insurance losses fall into one of two major categories: insurance against (1) the cost of *medical care* and (2) the *loss of income.* Three important types of insurance protection have emerged. These are (*a*) *hospital, surgical,* and *regular medical* expense protection; (*b*) *major medical* expense protection; and (*c*) *income* protection. The first two of these types help pay the cost of health care. The third type helps replace earnings lost as the result of illness or injury. Income protection policies are written on one person, while policies covering the cost of medical care are written on an individual or a family basis.

Hospital, surgical, and regular medical expense protection. There are two objectives of *hospital expense* insurance: (*a*) to help pay for the costs of room and board and (*b*) to help pay charges for extra hospital services. The policy limits the amount to be paid each day of hospital confinement, and there is a limit with respect to the number of days that coverage applies. Today policies providing $50–$150 or more per day for 70–365 days are common, and needed. Average room and board charges in the United States in 1977 were approximately $90 per day, and in some areas were as high as $200 per day, for semiprivate accommodations. Other specified miscellaneous benefits, up to $300–$1,000, are included, such as operating room fees and payment for X rays, laboratory tests, drugs, anesthetics, and the like. Broader contracts include maternity benefits, usually limited to a maximum of $100–$800. Many policies include the whole family in one contract.

---

[5] Dread disease policies and many of these special-purpose contracts are sometimes referred to as "limited policies," which may provide either benefits restricted in amount or duration or broad coverage limited to a specified hazard.

[6] Many university students have group health policies (see Chapter 14) available to them while in school. Now is a good time to look at your coverage. Some of these group health policies are quite limited, but many provide more coverage at less cost than do individual policies.

The costs of specified operations are covered under the *surgical expense form*. The protection includes surgery in a hospital, and it may include surgical procedures performed in the office or home. Policies generally list the operations for which benefits are provided together with a maximum amount payable for each, from $20–$1,000, perhaps. The schedule of operations generally includes all but the most unusual, and many insurers provide an equitable payment toward the cost of surgical procedures not specifically listed in the contracts. Not all policies covering hospitalization expenses include surgical benefits, but many do.

The *regular medical expense* form is designed to help pay for doctors' fees for nonsurgical care in a hospital, at home, or at the physician's office. It is usually written as an optional coverage in conjunction with the basic hospital and surgical benefits. Some policies may provide preventive services, home nursing, X-ray treatment, laboratory and other diagnostic tests, and ambulance service, among other benefits.

Major medical expense protection. Catastrophe coverage against medical care costs is the purpose of *major medical expense* insurance. Instead of providing so-called first-dollar coverage, major medical insurance aims at paying only quite large medical losses. The usual hospital and surgical contracts provide for normal medical expenses. There are, however, illnesses and injuries that are a catastrophe. The serious operation, such illnesses as cancer, multiple sclerosis, and the like, and injuries resulting in total and permanent disability may involve a person or a family in expenses running to thousands of dollars.

Because it is designed to meet health losses of this type, the major medical form has grown rapidly in popularity in the past two decades. Even as compared with other fast-growing health insurance fields, major medical policy growth has been phenomenal during the past 20 years:[7] (1) major medical plans, from 5 million to 90 million persons protected; (2) hospital expense plans, from 101 million to 178 million; (3) surgical expense plans, from 86 million to 169 million; and (4) regular medical expense plans, from 53 million to 162 million persons.

One example of a recent loss which illustrates the need for major medical insurance is:

```
Insured—husband, age 42, lung cancer
Expenses:
  Hospital room and board 40 days @ $90   =   $3.600
  Hospital miscellaneous expenses, 30 days =    1,800
  Hospital—special nursing, 10 days @ $100 =    1,000
  Surgery, removal of one lung             =    2,500
  Home nursing care, 100 days @ $40        =    4,000
  Miscellaneous—doctor, medicines at home  =    1,100
      Total  .........................         $14,000
```

---

[7] *Source Book of Health Insurance Data*, p. 22.

There are four identifying characteristics of major medical insurance: (*a*) the *deductible*, (*b*) *participation* or *coinsurance*, and (*c*) *high maximum limits*, for (*d*) *blanket medical expenses*.

The *deductible* feature obligates the insured person to pay the initial part of the expenses, which is called the deductible amount. Under individual and family major medical policies the common range of the deductible is between $100 and $1,000, and sometimes it goes as high as $2,000. The purpose is to avoid frequent small loss payments (usually covered by hospital insurance) and thus to keep the cost of the insurance low.

When expenses exceed the deductible amount, the policy benefits begin. Under a *coinsurance* feature (or "participation agreement"), the insurer then pays its share. For example, if the insurer is obligated to pay 80 percent of all hospital, doctor, and other medical bills in excess of the deductible sum, the remaining percentage, or 20 percent, is paid by the policyholder. The purpose of the coinsurance feature is to prevent overuse or excessive costs of medical facilities and treatment.

Policy benefits are payable up to a *high maximum* specified amount. This amount may be $10,000 or $25,000 and amounts of $50,000 or more are common today; $250,000 or unlimited amounts have also been written. The maximum benefit may be written to apply to each illness or injury, or the benefit may limit the aggregate expenses for several injuries. Today's rapidly rising medical costs suggest frequent reevaluation of the limit carried.

All types of medical expenses are covered, on a *blanket* basis, including hospital, surgical, doctor, nursing, and miscellaneous medical costs. There are no individual limits that apply for the various types of expense.

The deductible and the coinsurance features operate together as follows: With a policy carrying a $500 deductible, in the event of a medical expense of $5,500 the insured pays the first $500 of expenses. With an 80 percent coinsurance feature, the insurer pays 80 percent of the balance ($5,000), or $4,000, and the insured pays $1,000. The total cost to the patient would be $1,500, and much of this may be covered by other basic hospital-surgical policies which most insureds have.

Many variations of the deductible and coinsurance features are used. The policy may provide that the deductible operate on a family basis and not on the basis of each individual illness. For example, in the case of a common accident or a contagious disease, the policy may provide for a common deductible. Some companies write a *calendar* deductible, which applies the deductible only once during the policy year. In the case of the per illness or per injury deductible, the cutoff is a maximum benefit limit or usually for a period of two or three years.

Loss of income protection. Income loss is often the most important result of injury or illness, in many cases exceeding the cost of medical care. *Loss of income* protection becomes an essential part of any good health insurance program. This form, sometimes known as "disability income" protection, is designed to help replace loss of income or earning power because of illness or injury.

It is a major peril. For a person aged 22 the probability of a serious disability (90 days or more) is more than *seven* times as great as the probability of death; at age 42 it is more than four times as great; and at age 62 it is more than twice as great. Disability income loss payments by insurers are more than $3 billion a year.

Income benefits are usually expressed as a weekly or monthly sum. The definition of "disability" used in the contract is extremely important, as this determines the extent of benefits payable under the contract. The differences between "total" and "partial" disability, and other features, are discussed later in this chapter.

Contracts offered by the various insurers vary greatly. Because there are many different forms of coverage and many differences among insurers, there tends to be much competition with respect to selling. Sometimes, emphasis is placed upon the protection afforded rather than upon the premium charged. If emphasis is placed upon a particularly low premium, the coverage under the contract may be expected to be limited. In this field, as in others, it is unreasonable to expect to get more than what is paid for. The policyholder should give careful attention to the details of the contract because failure to understand the limitations of the policy may lead to disappointment.

Relationship to life insurance

More life insurance insurers write health insurance than casualty insurers or insurers that specialize in health insurance only. Also, even though health insurance is a major kind of insurance written by casualty insurers, (over $2 billion in premiums a year) life insurance insurers write more than four fifths of the total health insurance in the United States, excluding Blue Cross–Blue Shield coverage.

For a considerable time there was some reluctance on the part of life insurers to write health insurance coverages. Limited protection in the form of total and permanent disability income and a waiver-of-premium benefit during total disability represented the first attempts on the part of life insurers to recognize health impairments as a part of the life insurance business. However, in the course of analyzing the personal insurance needs of families it became readily apparent that loss of time and income attributable to injury or illness could disrupt family finances, as could expensive medical care. Health insurance appeared to be the answer.

Thus most life insurers today offer health insurance as an endorsement or "rider" to the life insurance contract, as in total disability waiver-of-premium and disability income benefits, and in extra payments for accidental death. (See Chapter 11.) Also, many life insurers write, under regular forms of individual or group health insurance, benefits for (*a*) hospital, surgical, and medical expense; (b) major medical expense; and (c) loss of income due to disability.

The close relationship of life insurance, health insurance, and social security benefits suggests that many of the features of these plans should be analyzed together. A complete estate planning program for the family necessitates a coordination of these voluntary and governmental insurance fields to provide the policyholder with an integrated arrangement for meeting personal insurance risks. Chapter 16 discusses this need further.

PROVISIONS IN A TYPICAL HEALTH POLICY

Although a "typical" health contract is as hard to find as the hypothetical "average" person of the U.S. Census Bureau statistics, this section endeavors to describe some of the more important provisions of such a policy. No one specific contract is used as a model; health contracts vary too much among companies and kinds of policies. The best advice that can be given to health insurance policy holders is to read *their* contract, for only then can they tell exactly what their rights and obligations are—and they will probably need the help and advice of good insurance agents to do that.

Many of the provisions discussed in this section are those of the usual commercial health insurance contract for medical expenses and loss of income (which the student should now recognize as having many variations in the health insurance field). For most individuals or families it is a contract purchased in addition to (1) a hospital-surgical policy and (2) a major medical expense policy. The loss of income becomes the predominant feature of the contract. Oftentimes, the contract may still be titled as an "accident and health" or "accident and sickness" policy. Normally, the provisions discussed here are those found in the conditionally renewable type of contract, that is, the kind which may be renewed at the option of the insurer. The provisions, except for the renewability feature, may be quite similar in most of their details to the noncancelable and guaranteed renewable contracts discussed later.

The general form and content of the health insurance policy may be divided into four principal divisions: (a) the *application and policy face*, (b) *cancelability and renewability*, (c) the *benefit provisions*, and (d) the *standard provisions*.

Application and policy face

Briefly, the policy face contains the essential elements of an insuring agreement between the insurer and the insured. A summary of the coverage and benefits, a statement of the renewability features, and a reference to the application are usually found here.

The application. The *application* is required as a basis for the contract, and the insurer relies upon the statements made therein for much of its underwriting information. All states require that the application be attached to the policy form; and both together constitute the contract. There is no standard form of application for a health insurance contract, although the applications of most companies follow a general pattern. They supply the underwriter information that will (*a*) identify the applicant, (*b*) give adequate information to determine the occupational exposure, (*c*) list health insurance benefits from all other sources and indicate whether insurance will exceed earnings, and (*d*) show the applicant's past and present physical condition. The insured acknowledges that false answers in the application may be used to bar recovery in the event that the answers are material to the acceptance of the risk assumed by the insurer.

The policy face. The printed *policy face* contains the name of the insurer, and it should state the times when the insurance takes effect and terminates. The entire consideration for which the policy is issued should appear in the contract. A summary of the benefit provisions (discussed in next section) usually appears on this first page. As an example of one clause which is normally found on the policy face, because of its extreme importance, the accident insuring clause deserves special attention.

Differences in wording in the *accident insuring clause* that may seem inconsequential to the layperson may have the effect of limiting the scope of the coverage. The clause may provide benefits for "bodily injury sustained through accidental means," or the clause may read "accidental bodily injuries," thus covering only unintended injuries that are accidental. The importance of the difference is that nearly half of all injuries are the consequence of an intended act and therefore not attributable to accidental means. The "accidental bodily injuries" coverage is the broader and preferable form.

The popular notion of an "accident" as anything unexpected is not enough to qualify for loss payment in some contracts. This difference is illustrated by the following example. A man piling wood strains his back and as a result is unable to work for two weeks. In piling the wood, he did exactly what he intended to do, though the injury to his back was a consequence. There was no accident; therefore, the injury would not fall within the insuring clause covering losses attributable to accidental means. If while piling the wood, the man had slipped and injured himself or had dropped a piece of wood with a resulting injury, there would have been an accident. The loss, therefore, would have been the outgrowth of an injury effected through accidental means.

The policy does cover losses attributable to disease or losses to which disease contributed. The phrase "independently of all other causes" that appears in the insuring clauses of many accident policies is very broad, and if interpreted literally it might nullify the intent of the contract. For this reason court interpretations have tended to favor the insured. If an infection is a natural or inevitable consequence of an accident, the accident is regarded as the cause of the infection or death. The courts have held that an injury that might naturally produce death in a person in a poor state of health is the cause of death even if the person would not have died had his or her previous health been different.[8]

Finally, there is the situation in which there is little evidence of the cause of a death except that it involved violence. For example, when an insured dies from injuries received at the hands of another, the legal doctrine of presumptions operates to hold that the injuries were accidental rather than intentionally inflicted.[9]

Cancelability and renewability

Except for the benefit provisions discussed in the next section, in which health insurance contracts differ so widely, probably no feature of health insurance policies is more important than their renewability. Many policies are sold today on a yearly basis with a right to cancel at any time during the policy term, or at least a right of the insurer not to renew. A demand arose for permanent health insurance policies, with the right to keep the policies in force by the timely payment of premiums, just as in the case of life insurance. These policies were said to be "noncancelable" and "guaranteed renewable." Policies written today fall into one of two broad patterns: (a) cancelable forms, and forms conditionally renewable at the option of the insurer, (b) noncancelable and guaranteed renewable forms.

Cancelable, and renewable at option of insurer, contracts. In this category are two classifications of health insurance policies: (a) cancelable at any time; (b) not cancelable but renewable at the option of the insuring company, which usually are "conditionally renewable," with the insurer's right to refuse to renew restricted.

Policies that are *cancelable at any time* afford the insurer not only the right to refuse to renew whenever any renewal premium is due but also the right to cancel the policy at any time on five or more days' written notice to the insured. Although such policies are not uncommon, for most contracts the feature that is more likely to be of importance is their renewability.

Policies that are *renewable at the option of the insurer* usually may not be canceled during the policy term, but they do not have to be renewed by the insurer. Most regulations prohibit a policy of this type from being called a noncancelable contract. A noncancelable contract in the true sense is one that is renewable for a term, or to a given age, at the option of the insured and without any right of the insurer to terminate coverage.

---

[8] Justice Cardozo, in the now often-quoted case of *Silverstein* v. *Metropolitan Life Insurance Company* (254 N.Y. 81; 171 N.E. 914), stated: "A policy of insurance is not accepted with the thought that its coverage is to be restricted to an Apollo or a Hercules."

[9] *Sheppard* v. *Midland Mutual Life Insurance Company*, 13 CCH Life Cases 1001; 152 Ohio 6; 87 N.E. (2d) 156. The court stated: "One of the well-recognized presumptions of the law is that, where it is shown that death resulted from bodily injury caused by violent and external means without showing as to how the injury was in fact sustained, there is a presumption that death did not result from suicide."

Most policies that are renewable at the insurer's option are *conditionally renewable*. It is usual to specify in the contract the restricted reasons for which renewal may be refused, such as nonpayment of premiums, attainment of age 65, or entitlement to full old-age medical benefits under the Social Security Act.

Where the insurer reserves the right to renew, that is, to discontinue coverage at the end of each yearly period, the insurer is not only able to give a broader coverage for lower premiums but can also experiment with new forms of coverage with greater freedom. Many contracts are currently written on the basis of conditionally optional renewal by the insurer. The practice is not as bad for the insured as it might seem. The premium cost is much lower, and among most reputable insurers the cases of nonrenewal are infrequent (often a fraction of 1 percent a year). For the insured who loses his or her coverage during failing health, however, the effect is serious. Consequently, there is an increasing interest in *noncancelable and guaranteed renewable* contracts of the types next discussed.

Noncancelable and guaranteed renewable contracts.   For truly permanent coverage a policy must not only be noncancelable but must also be guaranteed renewable for a given period at an agreed-on premium plan. No injury or illness will bring about a termination of coverage within the period fixed at the time the insurance is written. The National Association of Insurance Commissioners has defined the minimum requirements for a "noncancelable" health policy as renewability at the option of the *insured* to a given age, usually 60 or 65. The premium rate is guaranteed for the life of the policy. If premiums are paid when due, the insurer cannot refuse to renew the policy. If the policy is issued before or at age 44, it must be continued to age 50. A noncancelable policy issued after the age of 44 must be renewable for at least five years and provide maximum benefits for a period of ten years or to the age of 65.

A "guaranteed renewable" policy must meet these same requirements, but the *premiums may be changed by classes*. Policies providing hospital and medical expense benefits involve not only the contingency of sickness but also the uncertainty of the increasing cost of medical care. For this reason, many policies which may be renewed at the sole option of the insured contain the provision that the insurer may have the right to increase premiums at renewal for each individual policy, though most insurers can do this only for an entire class of policies. An increasing number of insurers guarantee renewal for life up to age 65. The objective is to enable the insureds to have coverage until they are eligible for the federal Medicare plan.

The premium rates for policies in this category are considerably higher (two, three, or more times) than those for policies in which the insurer has the option of refusing renewal. Disability increases rapidly with age. Premiums will be higher than is necessary to meet claims in the early years, and lower in the later years. This being the case, exactly the same kind of reserve is required for guaranteed renewable health policies as is required for level-premium life insurance. Usually, however, there is no refund of excess premium upon cancellation of health contracts, though some "cash value" health insurance policies have appeared recently.

The benefit provisions

The benefit provisions are the heart of the health insurance contract. These provisions indicate the amount and nature of the benefits for which the insurer is liable for stated disabilities. Benefits payable under a health insurance policy are payable directly to the named insured, except that in the case of death benefits payment is made to a beneficiary designated in the contract. It is through the benefits that the policy attains its objective of protecting incomes and reimbursing insureds for medical expenses. Some of the various available benefits will be treated individually. The more important of these are found in disability policies under the classifications: (*a*) *death* benefits, (*b*) *dismemberment,* (*c*) *total disabiliy,* (*d*) *partial disability,* (*e*) *elective indemnities,* (*f*) *double indemnities,* (*g*) *medical expense benefits,* and (*h*) *waiver-of-premium* benefit. Since the first benefit, for death, is similar to the accidental death benefits already discussed in Chapter 11, no further mention of it will be made here.

Dismemberment or loss of sight benefits.   Many health insurance policies contain a provision for the payment of lump sums for loss of sight or limbs instead of the weekly or monthly income benefits, but only if the disability is caused by an accident. It is customary to express the lump sums so provided in a multiple of the weekly or monthly benefit. Column 1 in Table 13–1 gives an example. If no weekly indemnity is provided, it is customary to indicate the indemnity for dismemberment and loss of sight in terms of the principal sum (or death benefit), as shown in column 2 of Table 13–1.

Table 13–1. Dismemberment and loss of sight benefits

	Column 1	*Column 2*
For loss of	*Sum equal to indemnity for:*	*Sum equal to:*
Both hands, both feet, or sight of both eyes	200 weeks	Principal sum
Hand and foot	200 weeks	Principal sum
Hand or foot and eye	200 weeks	Principal sum
Hand or foot	100 weeks	½ principal sum
Sight of one eye	65 weeks	⅓ principal sum
Thumb and index finger	50 weeks	¼ principal sum

Blindness and dismemberment benefits are often given prominence in the policy and may be mistakenly regarded as an added and attractive feature. As a matter of fact, if the policy gives the insurer the right to substitute a lump-sum payment for continued income payments, it may not be as broad as a policy providing long-term income payments for sickness as well as accident.

Total disability benefits. There is a wide range in the coverages afforded by the various health policies in the market. The definition of "total disability" under one policy may differ entirely from that under a second. For example, a few contracts may require house confinement for total disability, while most contracts define the condition as "inability on the part of the insured to perform any of the duties of *his or her* occupation." A third policy may define total disability as the "inability to perform the duties of *any* occupation whatsoever."

Over the years judicial decisions have broadened the more limited definitions. The courts have tended to interpret the "any gainful occupation" clause to mean something more than selling lead pencils on the street corner. If insureds were unable to engage in occupations for which they were reasonably fitted by education and experience and which would yield them a reasonable livelihood, then the policy was held to cover.

Largely as a result of these court decisions, the common statement of total disability appearing in modern health policies is: (1) a period of one or two years in which the insured is "unable to perform any and every duty pertaining to his or her own occupation"; (2) after which period it is "complete inability to engage in any and every gainful occupation for which reasonably fitted."

It is customary to further classify health loss-of-income policies as those requiring an elimination, or "waiting," period, and those without an elimination period. The elimination period is that period at the begining of a disability for which no benefits are paid. A policy may provide that benefits are not payable for the first several days, weeks, or months of disability.

Some policies, including mail-order ones, base benefits upon the first visit of a physician; others to the time when insureds are in a hospital. The highly restricted nature of such benefits is obvious when one knows, for example, that the average hospital stay is only about one week.

Partial disability benefits. Certain policies may make payments of income at a reduced rate if disability is determined to be partial. Accident policies often recognize partial disability. A policy that requires disability to be continuous and total from the time of the accident is too limited, since frequently real disabilities evidence themselves sometime after the accident. For partial disability a percentage of the weekly or monthly benefit is provided. Fifty percent of the benefit is usual, though sometimes the percentage is lower.

Insurers cover partial disability attributable to sickness much less frequently. The dividing line between no disability and partial disability is difficult to define. The test of partial disability rests upon the inability of the insured to perform a part of his or her work. The policy usually sets a limit to the period for which the insured is entitled to partial disability, such as a number of weeks, months, or years.

Elective indemnity benefits. In some instances the insured may be offered

Table 13–2. Accident policy schedule

For complete dislocation of joints:		For complete fracture of bones:	
Hip	$800	Skull	$900
Knee (patella excepted)	400	Thigh	800
Ankle	400	Arm, between elbow and shoulder	800
Wrist	350	Pelvis	650
Elbow	300	Shoulder blade	500
Shoulder	250	Leg (shaft), or kneecap	500
One or more fingers or toes	100	Collarbone, or forearm	400

an elective indemnity in the form of a lump sum instead of income payments during disability. Table 13–2 gives a schedule indicating the nature of the options offered under this clause.

Double indemnity benefits. Accident policies frequently provide for double indemnity in the event that injuries are sustained under specified circumstances, such as (a) while the insured is a passenger in or upon a public conveyance provided by a common carrier for passenger service; (b) while the insured is a passenger in an elevator car provided for passenger service only; (c) while the insured is in a building whose outer walls collapse or in a building that burns; and (d) if injuries are received by the explosion of a steam boiler, by a hurricane or tornado, or by a stroke of lightning.

As with the double indemnity feature in the life insurance contract, this benefit is devoid of logic. Dependents of a deceased insured have the same needs whether the accident that causes death is lightning, providing double indemnity, or a fall down a flight of stairs, where only the principal sum is paid. Or to cite another example, an accidental death in one's own car provides only single indemnity. Some of these benefits take on the characteristic of "window dressing." The chance of securing the additional benefit is often extremely remote, yet it is frequently held out as an attractive feature to encourage purchase of the particular contract.

Medical expense benefits. Medical expense benefits are included in many health policies. Some contracts cover only medical expenses, while others cover loss of income too. Many contracts of insurers cover only certain types of medical expenses, such as hospital-surgical expenses similar to those in Blue Cross–Blue Shield contracts. The contract usually provides hospital coverage as a per diem allowance for daily room and board with extra allowances for miscellaneous purposes for a maximum number of days.

When surgical benefits are found in the policy, an additional indemnity is provided. A schedule of amounts is ordinarily provided in the policy, and the amounts indicated are payable in addition to other indemnities. Table 13–3 gives a partial list indicating the nature of a schedule of indemnities for operations.

Waiver-of-premium benefits. Policies are written containing a clause which waives the requirement of premium payments after total disability has

Table 13–3. Schedule of indemnities for operations

Abdomen	$800	Eye—removal of	$500
Amputation of:		Goiter	600
Thigh	650	Inflammation of joint	350
Arm, leg, or entire foot	500	Mastoiditis—cutting operation ..	450
Forearm or entire hand	400	Paracentesis—tapping of:	
Chest—cutting into thoracic cavity ..	500	Abdomen	250
Ear, nose, or throat	200	Bladder	200

run for a given time during the indemnity paying period, such as 90 days. If premiums are paid up to that time, the policy cannot thereafter lapse during the total disability period. This provision is valuable because during a period of disability the needs of insureds may call for all their resources and they are not required to divert any of them to premium payments.

Exclusions and limitations on benefits

Contracts are often issued on insureds who for one reason or another are expected to have a greater chance or amount of loss than usual. Many contracts contain exceptions, reductions, or riders that limit benefits in either frequency or amount.

Exceptions. An *exception* in a health policy is a provision whereby coverage for a specified hazard is entirely eliminated. It is a statement of a risk not assumed. For example, the policy may not cover hernia. Some policies provide that losses caused by sunstroke, freezing, or injuries where there are no visible wounds are to be considered only under the sickness provisions of the policy. Other policies except coverage while the insured is in, or if the loss results from, military or naval service. Some policies specifically limit coverage to the United States and Canada or Europe. Because of the protection that workers' compensation and occupational disease statutes afford to most people actively employed, some insurers issue policies excluding occupational injuries and disease. These policies are known as "nonoccupational."

It is customary for individual health insurance policies to provide that benefits will be payable for disabilities occurring after the policy becomes effective. The intent is to exclude from coverage *preexisting conditions*— conditions that have their origin prior to the commencement of coverage under the policy. Since it is not always easy to determine the exact time of onset of sickness, and usual policy says that no benefits will be paid for sickness contracted and commencing from 15–30 days or more following the policy date. This is known as the *probationary period* or the "qualification period." The provision safeguards the insurer against applicants who fail to disclose fully their knowledge of an existing disease or impairment.

Not to be confused with the probationary period is the so-called *deductible period,* which runs from the inception of the disability and not the policy.

The deductible period is used to eliminate from coverage periods of disability during which the insured will be on sick leave and receive full wages. Or, perhaps it is used in recognition that savings of the insured could take care of a short disability of several weeks or months. The advantage of the deductible period to the policyholder is that it permits very substantial rate reductions. The deductible period may be regarded not only as an exception for shorter disability periods but also as a reduction in benefits.

Reductions. A *reduction* is a provision which takes away some portion, but not all, of the coverage of the policy under certain specific conditions. For example, the statement that disability income for hernia is limited to one month where the policy provides indemnity for longer than a month for other conditions is a reduction. Policies sometime provide for payment of only a percentage of the full benefits after the insured reaches a designated age. For particular sicknesses or specified conditions, there can be extra waiting periods, such as 9 or 12 months for maternity benefits.

Riders for substandard health risks. Normal health is usually a condition of coverage for a standard risk. However, policies are being issued today to people with impaired health, the specific condition being ridered out or otherwise qualified under the coverage. A recent development provides for full coverage with an increased premium. Where an unrestricted policy cannot be issued, the *impairment rider* or endorsement attached to the policy provides protection against all disability hazards, excluding only the causes of disability which exist at the time the policy is issued. The rider is an important factor in providing disability insurance. Without its use many more applications would be rejected. When a rider has been attached to a policy (for example, following an operation), the rider may be removed, after a period to be determined by the insurer, if no ill effects of the condition covered by the rider have evidenced themselves. Insurance for impaired risks is now available for many types of cardiac conditions, cancer, diabetes, epilepsy, and the like.

Sometimes, instead of issuing a policy with a rider, the underwriter finds it necessary to ask the applicant for a *postponement* of the application for a period of time following recovery from a disease or an operation. If the applicant shows continued recovery over a period of six months or a year, then he or she may be accepted for insurance with or without a rider.

The standard provisions

There is no standard health policy; competition has brought scores of contracts to the market. The nearest approach to a standard policy is to be found in the requirements laid down in the *standard provisions* acts adopted by the various states. Although there are some deviations in the laws as enacted, these laws are substantially in accord with the Uniform Individual

Accident and Sickness Policy Provisions Law, approved by the National Association of Insurance Commissioners in 1950. Sometimes these clauses are called "general provisions" in the contract. They may include some 11 optional provisions in addition to the 12 mandatory "standard provisions" adopted by almost all states.

The standard provisions are concerned with operating conditions and are to be distinguished from the benefit provisions of the policy. Policies must be approved by the insurance department of the state of issue, and exceptions in the policy must be given the same prominence as the benefits. Although each policy must contain the required provisions or approved corresponding provisions of different wording, the law is sufficiently flexibile to permit the insurer to experiment with more liberal policies and claim procedures. The purpose of the standard provisions is to effect a reasonable degree of uniformity in policies and to phrase important conditions in such a way as to make them understandable. The provisions serve to eliminate confusion and misunderstanding. As has been noted, there is no requirement with respect to a literal wording of the provisions.

The more important standard provisions concern rights of the policyholder to: (1) policy changes, (2) incontestability (after two or three years, usually), (3) a grace period for premium payments, (4) reinstatement, and (5) change of beneficiary. The insurer is given the following rights in the standard provisions: (1) written notice of loss (usually within 20 or 30 days), (2) proofs of loss, and (3) right to examine the insured and to autopsy. An example of an optional provision that is sometimes included is a clause which reduces benefits to conform with the proper rating classification if the insured misstates his or her age or changes to a more hazardous occupation. Other common optional provisions used today are: "other insurance" clauses, which reduce payments if there are other contracts of which the insurer has not been notified; "average earnings" clauses, which reduce or prorate loss-of-income benefits if all such benefits exceed the insured's recent earnings (see section on "overinsurance"); and "coordination of benefits" clauses, which determine the order of payment (up to 100 percent of expenses) among several medical expenses contracts that may apply.

UNDERWRITING PROBLEMS AND SPECIAL CONTRACTS

For the insurer, the disability risk involves considerable difficulty. Malingering and fraudulent claims have tended to swell the cost of benefits far beyond the expectations upon which premiums were predicted. Overinsurance has aroused the temptation to extend periods of disability that would unquestionably be shorter without insurance. In periods of unemployment unwarranted claims have increased sharply. Careful selection and rating, and the strict elimination of overinsurance, have been suggested as solutions to underwriting difficulties. These measures, together with a realistic attitude toward claim adjustment, will unquestionably help, but have proved difficult in application.

This section discusses the problem of overinsurance, the basic factors affecting the premium cost, and several special health insurance contracts.

Overinsurance

Many insurance contracts limit the payment to an amount that will indemnify the insured for his or her loss. In property insurance, the face amount of the policy limits the liability of the company; but if the actual loss to the insured is less than the face of the policy, the liability of the insurer is limited to the actual loss. Generally speaking, there is no way of fixing a definite indemnity for the loss of life. As for health insurance, its intent is to make good to the insured (1) the cost of medical care and (2) the loss of earnings directly attributable to the disability. Thus, it is necessary to measure medical care costs and to estimate reasonably the amount of income lost by the insured.

Life insurance underwriters limit disability income coverage on an indemnity basis. Because neither the number of insurance contracts that an insured may obtain nor the total amount payable under several contracts is limited, control of overinsurance is primarily the underwriter's job. In terms of adequate insurance coverage, there is nothing to be said for overinsurance. In the light of its dangers, there is much to be said against it. Since the contract itself is not usually limited to indemnity (that is, the insured does not have to prove the loss of a specified amount of income, and even an unemployed disabled person is entitled to collect under disability income contracts), the proper underwriting limits assume major importance in preventing overinsurance.

Overinsurance creates a continuing moral hazard in the health insurance field. There is overinsurance when the aggregate benefits exceed the loss which the insured suffers. The solution of the problem of overinsurance is not as simple as would appear at first glance. To be sure, human nature being what it is, there are situations in which the temptation to prolong a disability is strong if it proves profitable to the insured to do this. However, too drastic a reduction in benefits defeats the purpose of insurance. In an attempt to provide adequate insurance and at the same time protect the insurer against overinsurance, several clauses have been devised for use in the contracts providing disability income benefits. The first establishes the maximum amount which the insurer will issue for one person. The second establishes the maximum amount in force in all insurers in which the policy in question will participate.

The optional provisions of the Uniform Law often help prevent overpayment. In the case of "other insurance," one provision reduces the benefit payments proportionally if other unreported health insurance is found to be in force when a claim is presented. A provision particularly important for the long-term noncancelable and guaranteed renewable policy is the "average earnings" clause. The amount of benefit payable at any time is reduced if the insurance in force in all insurers exceeds the earned income of the claimant (or a specified percentage thereof, such as 80 percent) at the time of the commencement of disability, or his or her average monthly earnings for the two-year period preceding disability, whichever is the greater. The reduction is proportionate, and a minimum monthly benefit may be included.

One important consideration is that of establishing benefits as a percentage of net income instead of gross income. Not only are certain deductions made from a worker's pay, such as social security taxes, group insurance premiums, and contributions to a pension plan, but there are other expenses incidental to employment, such as transportation to and from work, union dues, working clothes or uniforms, and lunch money. Added to these are withholding taxes, since disability income is usually (up to $100 a week) free of income tax. A disability income may be substantially less in dollars than the total income and yet be the equivalent of take-home pay.

Factors affecting premiums

Benefits. A factor having an important bearing upon the cost of health insurance is the amount and the nature of benefits. The scope of some policies is limited to certain kinds of injuries, whereas other policies cover both injury and sickness for almost every conceivable disability. Obviously the cost must of necessity vary with the nature and the extent of benefits. Among the factors that have a bearing upon the cost of benefits are: (a) frequency of occurrence, (b) cost of benefit, and (c) duration. In determining the effect of accidental death benefits on costs, only knowledge of the rate of death by accident is required. In the case of surgical benefits, both the claim frequency and the amount of the average claim have a bearing. Disability income benefits involve the frequency of the disability and its average duration. The premium may vary from as little as $1 a year for a limited accident policy, such as those issued to newspaper subscribers or airplane travelers, to as much as several hundred dollars a year for a broad medical expense and loss-of-income contract for almost all injuries and diseases.

In addition to the amount and nature of the benefits, at least three other factors enter into the computation of the premium of a health policy: (1) occupation, (2) sex, and (3) age.

Occupation. Health insurance manuals have an elaborate system of classification of occupations. Basic rates are computed that reflect the average experience of all occupational classes. A reduction from this average is allowed for the less hazardous occupations, and increased premiums are charged where the loss experience is expected to be above the average. Occupations are grouped into classes which are given alphabetical designations. Evaluating occupational hazards and assigning each hazard to a class are tasks of no little magnitude.[10] The premium charge for a policy advances sharply from the lower rated classes to the higher, and some of the more liberal policies are not issued at all to those employed in the more hazardous occupations. Some of these "special risks" may obtain coverage from Lloyd's underwriters or specialty insurers. Some risks are usually classed as prohibited for occupational reasons, while others are written only after extra careful underwriting.[11]

Sex. The cost for health insurance benefits is considerably higher for women than for men, and when male and female risks are accepted for insurance, differing rating tables are provided for men and women or premiums for women are quoted as a multiple of those quoted for men. The cost of benefits for females may exceed the cost of similar benefits for males by at least 50 to 200 percent. Much of the increased cost of benefits for women is due to the fact that the claims of women are not only more frequent than those of men but last for a longer period. This results not only in longer disability income payments but in additional costs for hospital, surgical, and medical care. There are in addition costs attributable to maternity benefits. All of these factors tend to increase disability costs, with the exception of accidental death and dismemberment benefits, for women over comparable charges for men.

Age. The factor of age, while important, does not have the impact in health insurance that might be expected. Particularly under cancelable or optional renewable policies in the 50-year-and-under class, premiums do not usually vary with each age. However, age very definitely is a factor of increase under noncancelable and guaranteed renewable policies; there premium charges range upward year by year or by age groups. All premiums are raised for the senior years, this being justified by the morbidity (sickness) experience tables. For accident insurance the rates are often the same for a given manual classification between the ages of 18 and 60. Many insurers increase medical expense insurance premiums above age 50.

Special health insurance contracts

Several health insurance contracts have been designed for special situations which fall outside the normal underwriting practices of most insurers. Some

---

[10] The Health Insurance Association of America has four manual groupings, designated AAA, AA, A, and B, and is constantly evaluating occupations and adjusting rates to reflect experience. Some insurers use as many as 30 classes.

[11] Included in the typical prohibited groups are workers who use such substances as lead, acids, poisonous gases, or chemicals, and those engaged in dusty trades, such as woodworkers or granite workers. The carefully underwritten category includes actors, artists, musicians, and others who are self-employed but have no regular working hours or schedule.

insurers issue health insurance coverages under professional overhead, professional accident, and homeowners' disability plans.

Professional overhead policies. There is a *professional overhead policy* that covers expenses incurred during disabilities, usually with a waiting period of 30 days or more. This is a form of loss-of-time protection with benefit payments monthly. The insured is indemnified in an amount equal to actual business expenses for rent, taxes, public utility services, wages of employees, and other expenses normally incurred in the operation of the insured's office. The policy is of particular interest to architects, consulting engineers, dentists, doctors, lawyers, and public accountants, to mention but a few. It does not provide complete disability income protection for the insured, for it covers only business operating expenses.

Professional accident policies. Special *professional accident policies* provide sizable benefits for those whose professional activities would be seriously impaired as the result of an accidental injury. Members of the dental and surgical profession, for example, could suffer a much more serious loss than those engaged in other business operations through the loss of the use of fingers or a hand. Policies are written providing coverage from $5,000 upward for accidental injuries. Following is an example of such protection afforded by a policy written with a $100,000 limit: accidental death, total disability, or loss of a single leg, arm, or both eyes, $100,000; loss of use of one hand, foot, or eye, $50,000; loss of use of two or more fingers on one hand, $25,000.

Homeowners' disability policies. Term life insurance is sometimes written on a decreasing basis in connection with the mortgage on the dwelling of the insured. The *homeowner's disability policy* is planned so that if the insured dies before the mortgage is paid off, insurance will be available to liquidate the loan in full. Some homeowners' policies also cover mortgage payments in case the insured is disabled due to either injury or illness. The policy provides an inexpensive assurance that given a temporary disability involving considerable expense, the mortgage payments will be met. The benefits are payable for a limited period, usually about two years. This innovation is one of the first examples of a true "all-lines" insurance contract (see Chapter 27) combining fire, casualty, life, and health insurance in a single combination policy. The coverages are usually included without a medical examination, based upon statements about prior and present health condition made by the applicant.

FOR REVIEW AND DISCUSSION

1. A popular magazine recently included an article on the "most misunderstood facts about health insurance." For each of the following explain *why* you do *not* agree with the statement:

   a. All health contracts are about the same.

     b. You can't get health insurance if you have a history of illness.

     c. If you become sick or injured, you lose your policy.

     d. Major medical policies pay for all catastrophic medical expenses.

     e. The best way is to buy many health insurance contracts.

2. How would you outline the various classes of health insurance? Compare the different ways in which the whole health insurance field can be classified.

3. Health insurance contracts are noted for the extreme variability in the scope of the benefits they provide the policyholder. Briefly describe several examples illustrating (*a*) the narrowest and (*b*) the broadest types of contracts.

4. Describe the characteristic features of major medical insurance, and explain how each benefits the insurer and the insured.

5. Health policies for loss of income are written with waiting periods of one (or several) weeks or months. What reasons can there be for buying a policy with a waiting period as long as three or six months, or longer?

6. Explain which is the more important health insurance protection: (*a*) indemnity for loss of time or (*b*) medical, hospital, and surgical benefits?

7. Mary Perry says to Jane Plain: "My husband is 25 years old and healthy, I want him to have all the life insurance we can afford, rather than spend money for the unlikely chance of losing income by being disabled." If you were Jane, explain why you would agree or disagree.

8. What types of health insurance are most closely related to life insurance? Why might disability income *health* insurance still be needed?

9. Explain briefly the renewability feature, and four other important provisions, in a typical health insurance contract.

10. Is "noncancelable" health insurance really permanent? Explain, and indicate why this feature is important to the health insurance policyholder.

11. Are health insurance policies standardized? If so, discuss how; if not, discuss why they are not.

12. Explain the significance of the difference between the insuring clause of an accident policy which provides coverage against injury through "accidental means" and one which reads "accidental injuries."

13. Joe's policy provides for income if he is disabled so as to be prevented from engaging in *any* work or *any* business for compensation. He becomes deaf, and because of the nature of his business he is obliged to close it out. Is the insurer liable?

14. Mr. Skip A. Beatty has a heart impairment and is told that it is useless to apply for a health policy. To what extent, if any, are persons with heart impairments eligible for health insurance?

15. Explain the difference between an "exception," a "reduction," and a "rider." Discuss the impact of each on the cost of a health policy.

16. Is overinsurance in the field of health insurance a serious problem? Explain how it can occur, its relationship to the concept of indemnity, and what the insurer can do to prevent it.

17. Choose several important factors which affect the cost of health insurance contracts, and briefly show how the prices charged by insurers may vary according to each factor.

18. What factors would you discuss in analyzing the possible (a) growth and (b) decline of private health insurance in the future?

Chapter 14

Concepts considered in Chapter 14—Group life and health insurance

Group insurance techniques have been applied in life-health insurance to insure persons in group instead of individual contracts.

Group life insurance is one of the major classes of life insurance.

Nature and development: *master group policy, individual certificates.*

Unique features include: *legal limitations* on size and type of group (ten or more), and *group selection* with *no medical examination.*

The employer group life insurance contract is analyzed primarily as low-cost *yearly renewable term* insurance, in limited amounts.

Employee certificate provisions concern individual *amounts* set *automatically,* often based on one or two times annual *earnings,* and *beneficiary* and *conversion* provisions.

Financing employer group life insurance involves employer (*noncontributory)* or employer-employee *(contributory) premiums,* and *net costs* based on *group experience.*

Group creditor life insurance has many reasons for its *growing* use.

Franchise, or wholesale, and **salary savings plans** insure *small* groups.

Group health insurance is one of the most remarkable developments.

Nature and importance: about *three fourths of all* health insurance.

Fundamental characteristics include:

General types, for *medical expense* or *loss-of-income payments:* in *six basic plans:* (1) *hospital-surgical-medical,* (2) *dental and vision,* (3) *major medical,* (4) *disability income,* (5) *accidental death and dismemberment, and* (6) *HMOs.*

Eligibility provisions: *minimum number* of persons.

Costs, based on *contributory* or *noncontributory* plans.

Group hospital-surgical-medical expense insurance is usually *first-dollar coverage* for *hospital* charges and *surgeons'* and *physicians'* fees.

Group dental and vision care insurance are the newest and fastest-growing coverages.

Group major medical expense insurance is *catastrophe coverage.*

Basic features: *high maximum "blanket" benefits* ($25,000 to $100,000 or more), *deductibles* (sizable amounts such as $100 to $1,000), and *coinsurance,* the insured paying 20 percent of losses.

Primary types of plans are called: *supplemental* and *comprehensive.*

Group disability income insurance is nonoccupational coverage.

Group accidental death and dismemberment insurance is common.

Health maintenance organizations (HMOs) are a new alternative.

Impact of broadening social security programs is increasing with growth of *Medicare* and *Medicaid,* and *disability income benefits.*

Few, if any, developments in life and health insurance compare with the profound effect which the system of *group* insurance has had in the past several decades. The system of providing basic coverages through employers (and other groups) has been one of the most revolutionary and successful changes in insurance during the 20th century. This chapter explores the purposes and methods of group insurance, divided primarily into *group life* and *group health* insurance systems. Many of the same ideas apply in both these fields, but the differences are sufficient to recommend separate consideration.

Not all employee "fringe benefits," which often exceed 35 percent of wages, are group insurance benefits. Paid vacations, lunches, parking, and other extra benefits are provided by many employers without using insurance. But group insurance is "a major component of employee benefit plans and . . . an insurance technique of considerable economic, social, and political significance."[1] Its far-reaching effects include not only the basis and competition it provides for individual policy contracts and agents working under that system, but also its function as a deterrent to further encroachment into voluntary life-health insurance by the social insurance plans of the United States.

The general term, *group insurance* includes several kinds of insurance. The common principle of group selection has been used extensively for group *annuities* and pensions (discussed in Chapter 12). To a minor but growing extent the concept is being tried in the *property-liability* insurance field, providing automobile or homeowners' insurance for employees, for example (see Chapter 5). The present chapter concentrates on group *life* insurance, including credit life insurance, and group *health* insurance.

Approximately 52 percent of the total voluntary life and health insurance premiums of $66 *billion in* 1976 were written by the group method. Table 14–1 shows the rapid growth of group insurance from $5.5 billion in 1960 to $34.2 billion in 1976, a 485 percent increase. Group annuities insurance grew the fastest in this period, 842 percent, representing 30 percent of all group insurance premiums by 1977. Group life and group health insurance accounted for 22 and 48 percent, respectively. Within each type of insurance,

---

[1] Davis W. Gregg, "Fundamental Characteristics of the Group Technique," in Davis W. Gregg and Vane B. Lucas, eds., *Life and Health Insurance Handbook,* 3d ed. (Homewood, Ill.: Richard D. Irwin, 1973), p. 351.

Table 14–1. The growth of group insurance premiums written by U.S. insurance companies, 1960–1976

Type of group insurance	Premiums received (in millions of dollars)					Premium increase (in millions of dollars) 1960–76	Percent increase 1960–76	Percent of group insurance premiums* 1976	Percent of total life and health premiums† 1976
	1960	1964	1968	1972	1976				
Group health‡	$2,559	$3,777	$ 6,081	$10,591	$16,422	$13,863	542	48	25
Group life‡	1,850	2,645	3,929	5,634	7,511	5,661	306	22	11
Group annuities	1,088	1,467	2,217	4,044	10,249	9,161	842	30	16
Total	$5,497	$7,889	$12,227	$20,269	$34,182	$28,685	485	100	52

* Another significant observation is the percentage for each of these three major insurance types which is written by the individual and group methods. In 1976 the group technique accounted for 78 percent of health, 24 percent of life, and 73 percent of annuity insurance premiums of the above insurance companies.

† Of a total of $66,000 million total life and health insurance premiums in 1976 by U.S. life insurers (Blue Cross–Blue Shield health insurance figures not included in any of these figures).

‡ Credit life and health insurance is included in the group figures, because almost all credit insurance is written in group contracts.

Source: *Life Insurance Fact Book* (Washington, D.C.: American Council of Life Insurance, 1961, 1965, 1969, 1973, and 1977), pp. 52, 53, 55, 60, and 55, respectively.

group premiums were 78 percent of health, 24 percent of life, and 73 percent of annuity premiums.

GROUP LIFE INSURANCE

Group life insurance provides coverage on the lives of a group of persons in one contract. As a primary class of life insurance, it is in contrast to the ordinary and industrial life insurance classes, which use individual contracts and individual selection techniques.

Nature and development

More than 48 percent of the total life insurance in force at the beginning of 1977[2] in the United States, involving $1,126 billion, 178 million insureds, and more than 400,000 master contracts, was *group life insurance* protection. Approximately each six years since 1941 the amount of group life insurance has doubled, and in the past two decades alone it has grown more than tenfold.[3] In terms of sales dollars rather than insurance amounts, group life insurance premium receipts were also significant—more than 24 percent of all life insurance premiums, or over $7.5 billion. Group life insurance has maintained a record of remarkable growth to become one of the giants of the insurance business.

The reasons for its growth are many, but predominant among the factors have been the industrialization of the population, the desire of both employers and organized labor to develop employee benefit programs, and the tax advantages that are included in group life insurance.

As the group life contract was originally written, the members of the group were employees of a single employer.[4] The group concept has been expanded, and policies may now be issued to cover other groups for creditors, unions, associations, and trusts. Underwriting rules differ with the insurers, but the underlying concept is the same for all groups.

In the broad sense, the form is based upon the same fundamentals as any life insurance; but it is unique in the *group selection* of risks and the method of *mass distribution*. It differs from other life insurance in that selection based on the group is substituted for individual selection. Mass distribution and mass administration supersede contact with individual insureds. Hence, group

---

[2] The figures include credit life insurance, which accounts for about 9 percent. Credit life insurance is discussed later in this chapter, following treatment of the group life insurance written for employers. More than four fifths of credit life insurance is written as group coverage.

[3] *Life Insurance Fact Book* (Washington, D.C.: American Council of Life Insurance 1977), p. 18.

[4] The attention of the business world was first attracted to group insurance when the Equitable Life Assurance Society of the United States issued a policy effective July 1, 1912, covering the employees of Montgomery Ward & Company.

insurance may be termed "low-cost, wholesale protection." By considering groups of individuals, it has been possible to eliminate medical examinations and most other selection factors. Although there may be impaired lives in a group, adverse selection through an undue proportion of impaired lives is reduced to a minimum by the legal and underwriting regulations. The essence of group insurance is the substitution of group selection for individual selection.

Under the plan, a *master contract* is issued to the employer, creditor, union, or other person representing the group to be covered. Each person covered in the group receives a *certificate* detailing the protection afforded, such as the amount of insurance, the name of the beneficiary, and the privilege of converting to a standard form of whole life insurance (without evidence of insurability) upon termination of employment. Premiums are paid by the employer or other party that is the policyholder. A portion of the cost may be paid by the persons insured, or the cost may be paid entirely by the policyholder. Group insurance has found a receptive market in our economy.

Group life insurance is not to be regarded as a substitute for a program of individual life insurance. It does, however, furnish the bare requirements in the simplest and most economical form. The formula under which most plans are written provides insurance equivalent to about 1 or 1½ years' earnings, and the average amount per certificate is more than $15,000. Although not in any sense adequate, this does give the family of the deceased a small fund to meet current expenses and bills while an adjustment is in process. For some employees who are otherwise uninsurable under individual contracts, it provides minimum protection and thus achieves an objective that is desirable from a social viewpoint.

Group life insurance has several disadvantages. One is that the individual employees (or members of the group) do not receive advice about their total life insurance needs. Group insurance usually provides only minimal and "average" benefits for the entire group and not individual analysis of needs and their solutions. The contract is usually temporary, too, and primarily designed to provide basic benefits only while the person continues as a member of the group and only while the *group* continues the insurance contract. This may give some insureds a false sense of security unless they recognize that most group life insurance is fundamentally different in cost and duration from other forms of permanent individual contracts. Because most group life insurance is term insurance, no cash or loan values are ordinarily a part of the plan.

Unique features of selection and distribution

The distinguishing features of group life insurance include (1) restrictive legislation which defines and limits its scope and (2) the impact which group selection has on the insurers and insureds that are a part of the plans.

Legal limitations. Over 50 years ago the National Convention of Insurance Commissioners adopted the following definition of group life insurance:

> Group life insurance is the form of life insurance covering not fewer than fifty employees, with or without medical examination, written under a policy issued to the employer, the premium on which is to be paid by the employer or by the employer and employees jointly, and insuring all of any class of employees, determined by conditions pertaining to all employment, for amounts of insurance based upon some plan which will preclude individual selection, for the benefit of persons other than the employer.

The definition was recommended to the several states and was adopted by most of them and by large insurers as a basis for writing this class of business. Over the years, the state legislatures have enlarged the meaning of the terms *employer* and *group*.

To encourage uniformity among the states and to control expansion of the group idea, which some thought was getting out of hand, the NAIC in 1946 adopted a model group life insurance law and proposed it for enactment in the states. The *minimum size of the group* was reduced from 50 to 25 members for employer or labor union groups, and a $20,000 limit was placed on the amount of group life coverage for an individual life. In 1956 another model bill was suggested by the NAIC, lowering the minimum group size to *ten* and increasing the maximum individual coverage to $40,000, provided that any insurance between $20,000 and $40,000 did not exceed 150 percent of annual compensation. Some states have adopted these 20/40 limits, though many states (including New York) have higher limits or no statutory limit.

Classified by the *nature of the group* the Model Bill provides for: (*a*) *employer* group life insurance, (*b*) *creditor* group life insurance, (*c*) *labor union* group life insurance, and (*d*) *trustee* group life insurance. In the first category, the contracting parties are an employer and an insurance company. Employees are insured for the benefit of beneficiaries designated by the employee but not for the benefit of the employer. Credit or group life insurance covers the lives of debtors to the extent of their indebtedness to the creditor, and the creditor is the beneficiary. (See later section of this chapter.) Labor union group life insurance follows the pattern of employer group life insurance, except that the members of a union rather than the employees of an individual firm constitute the group. Trustee group life insurance enables two or more employers or two or more labor unions to provide insurance under a single contract through a trustee that acts for the employers or the labor unions.[5] The last two types are not discussed separately here, for their plans are identical in almost all respects with the normal employer group life insurance contract.

---

[5] Group insurance, including group life insurance, has been determined to be a proper subject for collective bargaining between employers and labor unions. The landmark case was the Inland Steel Company case in 1949.

In recent years group life insurance has been expanded in many states to other groups than the four types classified above. There is, however, great variety in the kinds of additional groups permitted to have this type of insursance. Some of the additional groups permitted by statute in a number of states are: members of professional organizations (doctors, lawyers, accountants, and others), depositors of a bank, student association members, agents of a common principal, and dependents of insured employees.

The insurance laws of each state customarily provide that no group insurance policy shall be issued until a copy of the contract has been filed with and approved by the insurance commissioner. The National Association of Insurance Commissioners has adopted *standard provisions* for group life insurance. Wherever the recommended law is enacted, the provisions are required as minimum protection. More liberal provisions may be substituted for the standard provisions if the insurance commissioner having jurisdiction approves.

The standard group life provisions provide for such items as: (1) a grace period, (2) incontestability, (3) the application being made part of the policy, (4) the conditions under which evidence of individual insurability may be required, (5) equitable adjustment of premium or benefits in case of misstatement of age, (6) designation of the beneficiary, (7) the issuance of individual certificates, and (8) conversion of insurance on termination of employment or of the group policy.

Selection of insureds. In providing that a *minimum of 25 employees* was required in order to constitute a group, it was the intent of those who drew the Model Bill to make the minimum number sufficiently large to assure the functioning of the law of averages. In those states where groups smaller than 25 are permitted or where no minimum number is specified, the underlying theory is not changed, but the responsibility for determining an acceptable group is shifted from the legislature or the state regulatory authority to the company underwriters.

At one extreme, a few states define a group as any number in excess of two. At the other extreme, very large group contracts have been written. The Travelers Insurance Company provides coverage for more than one-half million railroad employees and their families in one group contract. This contract is said to be "the largest single private group policy in America." This group is exceeded by the group insurance plan for federal government employees which covers more than 5 million persons. Servicemen's Group Life Insurance, under which each person in the uniformed services of the United States is insured for $20,000 on a voluntary basis with private insurers, is also a very large plan.

In *group selection* without medical examination, it would be unwise to allow any practice that would permit personal selection against the insurer. To avoid the element of unfavorable selection, all members of the group must be included, or at least a sufficient number to constitute a fairly representative risk. The group need not include all classes of employees. A policy may be issued covering the clerical force and the officials of a business; it may insure only employees with a number of years of service; or it may cover the workers in a given department. Any arbitrary grouping is permissible so long as all within the group are offered the insurance.

When the premium is paid entirely by the employer, the group is said to be *noncontributory* and the insurance extends automatically to all the members of the group. The group is *contributory* when the premium is to be paid jointly by the employer and the employee, and to warrant the insurance such a group must include a minimum of 75 percent of the employees in the class.

There is *no medical examination, usually,* of the individuals insured. A sometimes overlooked advantage of group life insurance is that some persons can obtain protection under the group plan when they could not obtain life insurance at standad rates, or possibly could not obtain life insurance at all. Because of the size of the groups it is assumed that the element of individual selection is removed, or at least reduced to an inconsequential minimum. This justifies the elimination of a medical examination. Another fact is that each of the insureds under a group policy is healthy enough to be in regular attendance of his or her work. Also, many of the larger employers now require at least some preliminary physical examination before hiring new employees. If an occasional poor risk is included, the law of averages tends to offset such a risk with the favorable cases.[6]

There are, however, some instances in which evidences of insurability may be required of individuals in group plans. Some examples are: (*a*) an employee who does not take insurance within a definite period (usually 31 days) after becoming eligible; (*b*) a person who rejoins the insured group after having been dropped for nonpayment of contributions; and (*c*) members of the group who have converted insurance to an individual policy.

The employer group life insurance contract

This section and the two immediately following discuss employer group life insurance in regard to (1) the employer's contract, (2) the provisions of the employee's certificate, and (3) financing.

Types of contracts. Group life insurance provides for protection (*a*) on a *term* basis and (*b*) on *permanent* plans. The first group life insurance contracts were written on the renewable term plan, and this practice has generally been followed through the years. A comparatively recent demand has created a market for group life policies with permanent values, like those offered, for example, by individual level-premium policies. The level-pre-

---

[6] Industrial life insurance and some ordinary life policies are also issued to individuals without the requirement of a medical examination. In these instances, however, each person submits an application which includes some statements as to present and past health.

mium insurance may be on a whole life, limited-payment, or endowment basis. Some contracts combine group term and paid-up life insurance. A number of companies that offer group life insurance on a level-premium basis distinguish it by the term *group permanent insurance.*

Many of the group life contracts include some of the group health insurance coverages analyzed later in this chapter, such as group accident and sickness, accidental death or dismemberment, hospital and surgical, or medical expense.

Group term. It is surprising to some persons to learn that almost all (97 percent or more) of employer group life insurance is written on a *yearly renewable term* insurance basis. Knowing the disadvantage which this type of contract has when it is used as an individual policy (see Chapter 10), the student may wonder how it has served so well for the vast majority of group plans. The answer lies in the contribution of the employer to the cost. Thus the increasing cost problem is not fatal to the plan should the average age of the group increase or the mortality experience of the plan grow worse. Group term also offers many advantages in simplicity, flexibility, administration, and full tax benefits to the employer and the employees.

Group term insurance is temporary rather than permanent protection for the employee. The policy could end any year at the renewal date if the employer does not continue it. It also stops when the worker leaves employment for any reason, such as retirement, disability, or resignation, unless the policy is converted to a permanent form of coverage (see the later section which explains the provisions for conversion in the employee's certificate).

The advantages of group term life insurance to the *employer* are summarized as follows: (1) the employer gains a low-cost, impartial method for furnishing death benefits to the family survivors of deceased employees; (2) public and employer-ee relations are improved; (3) competitive hiring and retaining good employees are aided; (4) the employer's cost is tax deductible to the corporation; (5) employee morale and productivity are enhanced; and (6) some government intervention into private insurance has perhaps been delayed. To the *employee,* these are some advantages of group term life insurance: (1) a layer of death insurance protection is added to social and other insurance benefits; (2) it may be the only life insurance of some otherwise uninsurable employees; (3) automatic payroll deduction from the employee or full payment by the employer makes lapses unlikely; (4) the lowest possible cost is attainable through expense reductions; (5) death benefits and the employer's contributions to the cost are not taxable to the employee as ordinary income; and (6) a conversion privilege permits conversion to a permanent individual contract without a medical examination of the terminated employee.[7]

Group permanent. With the growing appeal of group term life insurance,

---

[7] William G. Williams, chap. 26 in Davis W. Gregg and Vane B. Lucas, eds., *Life and Health Insurance Handbook,* 3d ed. (Homewood, Ill.: Richard D. Irwin, 1973), pp. 377–78.

those protected began to inquire into the possibility of securing the benefits of the permanent plans under group policies. In particular, they desired: values available to employees on termination of employment in addition to the right of conversion, and paid-up insurance before retirement and while the employee was engaged in active employment. If an employee stops working at an advanced age, the conversion privilege may be of little value if the employee is unable to keep the insurance in force on the basis of attained age premiums. At retirement most plans only continue the term insurance for a reduced amount. Accumulated values under a whole life premium would considerably lighten the burden of conversion.

As a proportion of the total group life insurance, however, group permanent insurance is still very small—probably less than 2 or 3 percent in 1978. The reasons include the increased cost, taxes, and administrative complexity. Some employers and employees provide for fully paid-up insurance prior to retirement. To attain the objective, the whole life policy or a whole life form paid up at 65 is used. Sometimes the plan extends whole life insurance only to long-term employees.

An alternative to *level premium* plans of group insurance is a combination of *group paid-up* life insurance. Under the plan the employee's contributions are applied each year to the purchase of single-premium paid-up life insurance at the attained age premium. As these amounts of group paid-up insurance build up, the amounts of group term insurance paid for by the employer decrease in such a way that the sum always equals the total death benefit called for by the plan of insurance.

Policy and certificate limits of insurance. Most life insurers fix the *minimum* amount for any one life at $1,000. A minimum of $50,000 is usually established for a group.

The *maximum* amount available to an individual employee generally depends on the statutory limits mentioned previously and on the total amount of insurance in force for the entire group. The schedule of maximum individual amounts may show, for example, a $20,000 limit in the case of a group with $1 million total insurance and $75,000 under a plan with a total of $50 million on all employees. Company practices vary considerably from the indicated limits. In addition to the total insurance in force on all employees, the maximums may be varied by such other factors as (1) the annual earnings of the employee, (2) the number of persons in the plan, (3) special classes for lower income groups, and many others.

With respect to the tax situation, large amounts of group life insurance paid for by an employer in a high tax bracket and payable to the employee's family without income taxes have resulted in a powerful appeal for this type of insurance in substantial individual amounts. Tax legislation changes under the 1964 Revenue Act limited the tax-free amount of group life insurance on each individual to $50,000. Above this amount the employee is required to pay income taxes on the cost contributed to the plan by the employer.

The purpose of requiring minimum limits and setting the maximum insurance per person is to attain a reasonably uniform distribution of insurance within the group. A maximum limitation precludes a concentration of risks in a few lives.

Probationary period. In order not to build up an undue expense for the insurance of temporary employees, the group contract may provide that the insurance is not to become effective for new employees until after they have been in continuous service for a designated period. The probationary period usually varies between 1 month and 12. An eligibility period of 31 days is normal after the probationary period, and during this time the employee may apply for inclusion in the group life plan without undergoing a medical examination.

Inception and termination of coverage. When group insurance is desired, a form is prepared supplying sufficient information to provide a tentative rate. If the result of the preliminary survey is satisfactory to the employer, an application for the insurance is filed. Upon the insurer's approval of the plan of insurance selected by the employer and upon the payment of the first premium or an agreed portion thereof, the insurance becomes effective. If, however, the policy is to be issued on a contributory form, with the employee sharing the cost, the insurance does not become effective until the required minimum number of employees have authorized their payroll deduction.

Since the policy is usually written on a yearly term basis, the master policy expires, unless renewed, at the end of the policy year. A severance of employment terminates the employee's insurance under the group policy, subject to the conversion privilege. In the case of the employee's temporary absence from the service of the employer because of physical disability or leave of absence, if the premium is paid by the employer, the insurance may be kept in force.

Employee certificate provisions

The employer group life master contract is supplemented by a certificate which is given to each insured employee. This briefly summarizes the contract amount, beneficiary provisions, and conversion privileges available to each individual.

Individual certificate amounts. A schedule of insurance amounts is set up in the contract for the different classes of employees. The individual employee has no choice of insurance amount. Automatic determination of individual coverage is effected in one of several ways: (a) a *flat amount* for all employees, (b) an amount based on *position*, (c) an amount based on *length of service*, and (d) an amount based on *earnings*.

By far the simplest determination is a *flat* amount of insurance for each employee. This plan has several shortcomings, not the least of which is a failure to recognize the needs, ability to pay, worth to the business, and period of service of the employee. Group insurance allocated on a *position* basis separates personnel into classes, such as officers, supervisors, clerical employees, salespersons, and the like. The amount of insurance is the same for all employees of one class, but it differs among the classes. This plan recognizes, within limits, both worth and length of service, but it introduces some administrative difficulties in establishing categories. Scheduling the amount of insurance on the basis of length of *service* rewards employees for long service. It fails, however, to consider differing income levels and provides lower coverage in the younger age groups, where the needs are frequently greatest.

The most widely used base for determining the amount of insurance is employee *earnings*. Payroll brackets are established, and all who fall within a given bracket automatically receive a predetermined amount of insurance; or, very commonly, the amount is set at a figure such as *one or two times annual salary*. This plan recognizes not only ability to pay but also the worth of the employee to the business. It fails to recognize fully the employee's need for protection, however, such as the number of dependents.

Basically, all plans should consider as fully as possible the employee's (*a*) need and (*b*) ability to pay. It may be, and frequently is, necessary to use more than one plan to accomplish these objectives.

Beneficiary provisions. A beneficiary (other than the employer) must be designated. Each employee may designate his or her own beneficiary. Policies may provide for the payment of the benefits to certain persons if the beneficiary dies before the employee or if no beneficiary has been named. For example, the policy may contain a *facility of payment* provision permitting the insurer to pay the insurance to the wife or husband, if living, or to the surviving children, to the father or the mother, or to the insured's executor or administrators. In some states, the right of relatives to receive if no beneficiary is named is governed by statute.

The policy indicates the steps required to change the beneficiary. Ordinarily, all that is required is the filing with the employer of a written notice on a form provided by the insurer. The employee may change the beneficiary from time to time.

Conversion privilege. Each employee insured under a group policy is usually given the right to continue the insurance as an individual *without medical examination* in the event that work with the employer is terminated. The employee has the right to convert to any of the permanent (not term) policies issued by the insurer for a face amount equal to that of the employee's group certificate. In most states this right of conversion extends for *31 days* after the termination of employment.

When the conversion privilege is exercised, the premium charged for the new policy is based upon current rates for the attained age of the employee at the time of conversion. If the master group policy is terminated for any reason, an employee who has been insured for five years may convert to an individual policy, without medical examination, in an amount of at least $2,000.

Policies provide that the employee shall be automatically covered without application, during 31 days following termination of employment, for the amount of his or her group coverage.

Knowing that the purpose of the conversion privilege is to protect the employee's right to maintain life insurance protection, it is incongruous to find that very little (probably less than 2 percent of the potential) group life insurance is actually converted. The prime reason may be ignorance of the important value of the conversion right to uninsurable or substandard applicants. Many employees do obtain new group life insurance from their new employer. The higher premium cost, in relation to group term coverage, which the insured must pay for a converted whole life individual contract discourages many. Still, for many substandard insureds the conversion privilege is a valuable right which should not be overlooked, as evidenced by the extra assessments levied against the employer for converted policies. Adverse selection is quite high, as the most unhealthy persons are most likely to convert their contracts. The extra cost to employers is sometimes as high as $170 per $1,000 of converted life insurance, so most employers do little more than notify employees of their right to convert the group coverage.

Financing employer group life insurance

Premiums.   Premiums on the group life policy, whether under a contributory or a noncontributory form, are forwarded to the insurer by the employer. When the employees are to share in the cost of the insurance in the *contributory* plan, their contribution is collected by payroll deductions. Under the *noncontributory* plan, the employee pays nothing and the entire cost is assumed by the employer. Employers usually make premium payments to the insurer monthly.

The basic rate for group insurance depends upon the industry in which the employees are engaged. The survey made following the filing of an application for insurance gives attention to the occupation of the various employees, sanitary and health conditions, the condition of the property, and many other employment hazards. The premium for a particular group is based upon the amount of insurance carried by, and the age of, each employee.

Experience has shown that because of the retirement of a certain number of older employees each year, with replacement in the younger brackets, the age of the group changes little from year to year, and hence the premium is practically stationary for the normal large-employee group.

In the beginning, the *noncontributory* plan was the general practice, as a gift or additional compensation to employees. The noncontributory form is considerably simpler in that all employees of a group are automatically covered. Also, the problem of apportioning costs among the classes of employees is avoided, and goodwill is engendered by an outright gift. Advocates of the *contributory* plan contend that group insurance is appreciated more if the employee contributes. It may be used to provide higher benefits than could be included in a noncontributory plan. Employee contributions in most contributory plans are limited by state laws as well as by practice to 60 cents (or less) per month per $1,000 of insurance. (See also Chapter 12 for more discussion comparing contributory and noncontributory financing.)

Net costs. The mortality experience under group life insurance plans has generally been favorable. Insurance actuaries have attributed the favorable mortality experience to the fact that numerous employees drop out of the group with advancing years and to the fact that the entire group must be working when the insurance is effected. The physically unfit and the weaker lives are eliminated, and those who remain are physically fit to carry on their work. Furthermore, favorable selection is found in the care exercised by the insurer in studying the nature of the hazards involved in the industry when the risk is rated.

Certain specific savings are available under group life insurance. Usually no medical examination is required. Also, commissions paid on this class of business are substantially lower than those for other classes, thereby reducing the acquisition cost of the business. Finally, the expense in issuing and handling a group life policy is less than that of handling a large number of individual policies. Hence, the premium for group life insurance is substantially lower than that for individual policies for most persons.

Dividends and rate adjustments based on the actual experience of the group are an important factor in the net cost of the plan. In an average industry the insurance cost will be less than one percent of the total amount of insurance in force. When the employee contributes even a small amount, and after dividends have been credited, the burden of a group plan upon the employer is relatively light. That burden has, however, been increasing in recent years as more benefits have been provided and as employers have borne the entire cost of many of the plans.

Group creditor life insurance

What kind of life insurance (a) has tripled in volume in the past 15 years? (b) has over 80 million insureds in the United States, although it still accounts for only about 5 percent of all life insurance in force? (c) is the only type of group life insurance in which the master contract policyholder is permitted to be the beneficiary? (d) has the *maximum* price for the coverage rigidly controlled in many states? (e) has achieved all its growth despite the fact that most states restrict the insurance amount per insured to under $5,000 or $10,000? The answer is *group creditor life insurance*.

The definition of group life insurance in the statutes provides for issuing a policy to a creditor to insure the lives of debtors. It covers that group of debtors who borrow on an installment basis, and the creditor is named as beneficiary.

Reasons for use. The policy appeals to lending institutions in that they are guaranteed repayment of the loan even though the borrower does not live to complete the transaction. Regardless of the ability of the borrower, there is a real danger of not collecting the loan if he or she dies. In any event, the lending institution is relieved of the difficulty of pressing an unsecured claim against an estate of limited means. From a second point of view, the coverage serves to increase business. Credit life insurance is used to repay the debt in case the borrower dies. No obligation is left behind for someone else to meet. Thus, credit life is attractive to both the borrower and the lender.

Types of loans and insurance provided. Policies are written to cover debtors making installment loans of the following types (*a*) unsecured personal loans and (*b*) indebtedness secured by (1) conditional sales contracts and (2) lease sales contracts. Although used at first to secure only limited types of smaller loans, group credit life insurance soon became very popular for many automobile loans and then for general personal loans and even credit card charges. While the tendency is to use individual term policies to cover mortgage loans on homes, the group plan has sometimes been extended to include this class of debtors.[8]

The limitation for each loan set forth in the laws of most states for group credit life insurance is $5,000 or $10,000; but the amount of insurance is limited in each instance to the unpaid balance of the debt, subject to the stated maximum. Ordinarily, as with employer group life insurance, no medical examination is required. Group creditor life insurance is usually written on a reducing term basis so that the amount of life insurance is limited to the amount necessary to pay off the debt.

Costs. The creditor is responsible for the payment of premiums, which are usually based upon the aggregate debts outstanding each month. The premium is relatively small since the amount of insurance in force with respect to any one debt decreases as repayments are made. Lending institutions charge the customer; absorb the cost by increasing the discount rate or service charges, which is the most common method, or absorb the cost as an operating expense. Due to the expense of maintaining age records, the premium charge is based upon the volume of loans rather than the ages of debtors. The age factor is reflected in the experience rate developed by the losses of the group.

Provisions. Individual certificates are not issued unless this is required by law. Individual insurance on the life of any particular debtor terminates if the group policy terminates or if the indebtedness is discharged or transferred to another creditor. The insurance also terminates when the loan has become

---

[8] The *Life Insurance Fact Book* credit life insurance figures now include mortgage protection of ten years' or less duration issued through lenders.

overdue a specified period of time, usually from one to six months. If during any policy year the number of insured debtors falls below the group underwriting requirements of the insurer (100 is usual), it may decline to insure new debtors. The policy covering debtor groups has no conversion provision.

Growth and problems.   Credit life insurance is a phenomenon of the credit economy in which we now live. It has eased the task of borrowing by reducing the risk of loss to lending institutions that would suffer by the death of debtors. There is more than $123 billion of credit life insurance in force, and it has been growing faster than any other type. Most of it is issued through group policies, although some 17 percent results from individual credit policies. About 80 million certificates under 90,000 master policies were in force in 1977, with an average individual coverage of approximately $1,500.[9] For a business that was only starting in the late 1920s, credit life has come a long way.

As might be expected, its rapid growth has been accompanied by some problems. One of the most difficult has been a tendency toward great competition in rates, while rates that were too high (with dividends going to the lending institution) were not recognized by the insureds. States such as New York and New Jersey have set recommended scales for the rates charged under group credit life insurance, with the lowest prices permitted for the largest groups. Other states have not legislated the rates to be charged. They have set maximum rates, however, and have exercised close scrutiny over the business. The insurance commissioner watches the relationship of premiums to losses, but in many states the losses paid are not much more than 50 percent, which may indicate excessive profits to insurers and lenders.

A model bill of the NAIC has helped curb the possible rate and contract abuses in about half the states. With such progress, the future of credit life insurance should remain bright in the credit economy of the United Sates.

Franchise, or wholesale, and salary savings insurance

Although not technically group insurance, since individual contracts are used, several types of distribution through groups have been developed in life insurance. These methods include franchise (or wholesale) insurance and salary deduction plans, for groups of fewer than 25 persons which are not sufficiently large to meet the requirement for the normal group policy. The size of the groups eligible for the coverage is usually five or more employees of one employer, or ten or more members of a trade, labor, or professional association.

Franchise insurance is a plan for the mass selling of *individual policies.*

[9] *Life Insurance Fact Book,* p. 22. For cost evaluation, see Joseph M. Belth, "Credit Life Insurance Prices," *Journal of Risk and Insurance,* vol. 40, no. 1 (March 1973), p. 115.

The contracting parties are the employee and the insurer, and a policy is issued to each individual included in the plan. The premium may be paid in full by the employee or by the employer and the employee on a cooperative basis. There is usually no medical examination, but evidence of the physical condition of the applicant is obtained from the questions answered in the application. The insurer has the right to deny an application for any reason, so in small groups adverse selection is avoided.

Salary deduction life insurance, also referred to as "payroll deduction" and "salary savings" insurance, is a plan for the sale of the regular forms of life insurance by personal solicitation of individual employees. The employer deducts the amounts agreed upon from the salary of the employees and makes monthly premium payments. Each participant selects the type and the amount of the policy. The premiums are usually paid entirely by the employee. Rather than being a different life insurance product, salary deduction life insurance is primarily a convenient method by which the employer encourages the employees to purchase regular individual contracts of protection.

GROUP HEALTH INSURANCE

Is U.S. Steel, Goodyear Tire and Rubber, or Pittsburgh Plate Glass the largest supplier of General Motors Corporation? Surprisingly, none of these is, for the largest GM supplier sells group health insurance to GM for its employees—more than $840 million worth each year![10] Other employers may also find themselves in a similar situation, a situation which puts group insurance at or near the top of the cost list for all the products and services that business firms purchase.

The group technique of insuring includes not only group life and group annuities,[11] but also group *health* insurance. The amazing growth of group health insurance in the United States is unique in the sense that no other country in the world has developed such a broad private system of protecting its population against the increased medical expense and the loss of income resulting from poor health.

Nature and importance

As with the other group plans, master contracts are issued to employers, unions, associations, or trustees for the benefit of individuals and their families. The basic characteristics are summarized as: (1) *three parties,* that is, the insurer, the employer (or other "policyholder"), and the individual members

---

[10] William F. Hamilton and Samuel P. Martin, "Benefits Fever," *Wharton Magazine,* Winter 1977, p. 19. Blue Cross–Blue Shield was the largest supplier, Metropolitan Life second, and U.S. Steel third.

[11] Group annuities were discussed in Chapter 12.

of the group; (2) insurance based on *group underwriting* rather than individual selection; (3) adverse selection reduced by *minimum size* group requirements and by restrictions on the freedom to choose the insurance, amounts, types and benefits; and (4) simplicity and *economy* of administration achieved by employer cooperation and employer contributions to the cost of plans.

By 1977 the health insurance receipts of all private insuring organizations were estimated at $52 *billion*, which represented nearly 4 percent of disposable personal income.[12] The premiums received by insurance companies made up about one half the total, and the premiums received by Blue Cross–Blue Shield plans made up the other half. *Group* health insurance accounted for more than 75 percent of the total. Group health insurance quadrupled in each of the past two decades. The largest dollar increases have occurred in group hospital and surgical plans as the result of the growth of employee groups having these health coverages.

Table 14–1 at the beginning of this chapter summarizes the relative growth of the group insurance technique in the fields of health, life, and annuities. Group health premiums written by U.S. life insurance companies (not including Blue Cross–Blue Shield or casualty insurers) are 48 percent of the total group insurance business. The group technique represents more than a $34 billion business today, or 52 percent of all life and health insurance premiums. The growth of group health was 542 percent between 1960 and 1976, exceeding the percentage increase of group life but not that of group annuities.

Factors in the rapid growth have included collective bargaining and union requests for more fringe benefits, favorable tax treatment (the premiums are usually deductible to the employer and not taxed as income to the employee), and the skyrocketing costs of medical care.

Health insurance for groups follows the pattern generally established for life insurance. There are three contract forms: (*a*) group, (*b*) franchise, and (*c*) salary deduction plans. Most persons are covered on a group basis. The other two types were discussed at the end of the group life section in this chapter. This section will concentrate on the group health contract forms.

Group health insurance may and often does cover dependents. In many instances an individual is covered by both a group policy and an individual policy. If the group policy does not provide all the coverage required, it may be supplemented by an individual policy. For many, however, the group policy may provide the only form of health protection.

Because of the greater opportunities for industrial employment, urban residents are more frequently covered under group health insurance policies than are rural residents. By 1977 more than 180 million persons had group hospital-surgical insurance coverage, over 92 million had group major medical, and more than 80 million had group disability income insurance.

---

[12] *Source Book of Health Insurance Data* (New York: Health Insurance Institute, 1976–77), p. 49.

Fundamental characteristics of group health insurance

Following generally the pattern of individual health insurance plans (Chapter 13), the principal kinds of group health insurance may be noted as: (1) *medical expense reimbursement* insurance and (2) *income reimbursement* insurance. The first type provides benefits for all forms of medical care costs; the second pays for temporary or longer term loss of income due to disability and accidental death and dismemberment benefits.

General types of group health insurance contracts.   For discussion in this chapter, the above coverages are divided into six classifications of contracts: (1) *group hospital-surgical-medical* insurance, (2) *group dental and vision care insurance,* (3) *group major medical expense* insurance, (4) *group disability income* insurance, (5) *group accidental death or dismemberment* insurance, and (6) the new *health maintenance organizations* (HMOs), which are beginning to provide a broad type of health care expense insurance.

Eligibility provisions.   Insurers have their own underwriting requirements with reference to group size. In some instances no minimum member participation is required by the insurer, but there must be compliance with the statutes of the state in which the employer is located. Where there is no minimum number of insureds, it is sometimes required that the total number be sufficient to meet the minimum annual premium, for example, $500.

The first Model Group Accident and Health Insurance Bill suggested that the group include at least 25 certificate holders. Subsequent revisions of the model bill since 1940 reduced the number to ten, and the latest bill mentions no minimum size. The setting of minimums for the size of the group would thus be left up to the underwriting practices of the insurers. Some states do have group health laws or rulings which define group health insurance; some states prescribe minimum percentage participation requirements (usually 75 percent); and many states set the minimum group size from two to ten members. These minimums do not apply to HMO plans, which from a practical standpoint usually start with at least several thousand subscribers.

All employees may constitute a group, or the employer may select a particular "eligibility group" based on: (*a*) the length of time the employee has been with the company, (*b*) a certain salary range, (*c*) occupation, or (*d*) a combination of these bases. In addition to policies purchased by employers to provide insurance for employees, policies are issued to such groups as members of labor unions or professional associations. A number of policies issued to associations or trusteeships have been the outgrowth of collective bargaining with a union in an industry or an area.

Group health coverages for medical expenses may in many instances be extended to cover the dependents of the insured employee. Dependents' coverage, usually including children up to age 19 (or 23 if in school), may include hospital, surgical, some forms of medical, and major medical expense. Stepchildren, adopted children, and foster children are included in the dependent category if they are actually dependent upon the employee for support and maintenance.

Costs. Many group health insurance plans, probably about 60 percent, are written on a "contributing" basis, with the individuals paying a share of the cost. In an employer group this means that both the employees and the employer (policyholder) pay part of the cost of the plan. Other plans may be "noncontributory," with the employer paying the entire cost. The individual plan participants pay the whole cost of their protection in a few cases.

The premium charges for group health plans are based on rates developed for the standard group for the type, size, and duration of benefits; sex; age; geographic variations; and other factors. The charges for the initial year are normally adjusted thereafter on the basis of the actual experience of the group, except for very small groups. Dividends may be used in participating contracts in order to vary the charges made each year according to the actual loss experience of the group.

Generally, group health insurance costs are lower than the costs of comparable coverage purchased under individual contracts. The difference may come from several sources: (1) the employer paying part of the premium, which reduces employee cost; (2) the favorable loss experience of a working group of employees; and (3) administrative savings, as compared with issuing individual contracts and collecting many separate premiums.

Group hospital-surgical-medical expense insurance

The group health plans which provide protection for medical care expenses do so on the basis of two different philosophies. Some plans cover essentially all the specified kinds of expenses "from the first dollar on" and are called *"first-dollar"* coverages. Certain maximums are usually set in terms of days of medical care or of maximum dollar limits. These limits may be set high enough to cover the costs of most normal losses, but often do not aim at providing protection for the very large losses. These are the types of contracts discussed in this section as subdivided into group (1) *hospital,* (2) *surgical,* and (3) *regular medical expenses* policies.

An annual survey[13] of group health insurance plans shows: (1) more than 92 percent of the persons covered in group hospital plans are also insured for surgical benefits, and (2) more than 82 percent have some regular medical coverage.

The second philosophy in covering medical expenses under group plans assumes that it is not of prime importance to the insured what kinds of medical care costs are involved. Instead, the plans aim at providing very high ($10,000 to $100,000, for example) maximum limits for *all* medical care expenses. These contracts are called *major medical* (or *catastrophe medical*)

---

[13] *Source Book of Health Insurance Data,* p. 22.

policies. Oftentimes, a deductible of several hundred dollars applies and expenses above the deductible are paid to the insureds on a "coinsurance" or participation basis with the insurer. These contracts are treated in the next major section of this chapter.

Group hospital expense insurance.   This coverage is designed to provide benefits to an employee (or other members of the group plan) who is confined to a hospital because of injury or sickness. The coverage is ordinarily written on a *reimbursement*[14] basis; that is, benefits are payable to the employee for charges actually made. This is usually written as a nonoccupational coverage to avoid duplication of workers' compensation benefits.

The benefits are classified as (1) other than maternity and (2) maternity. The other-than-maternity benefits are subdivided into (*a*) room-and-board benefits and (*b*) other miscellaneous benefits. Hospital expense benefits are often extended to cover dependents of the certificate holders under the group plan.

Benefits other than maternity.   For *room-and-board* benefits the policy provides a daily limit. This limit is usually not in excess of the charge made for semiprivate accommodations in the area in which the insured employee resides. Generally, the range is between $50 and $100 per day. The employee is reimbursed for the amount of the charges actually made by the hospital. Room-and-board benefits are payable until the limits for any one period of confinement have been reached. The maximum limits may vary from 31 to 365 days, and the most common limits are more than 120 days. Most contracts include treatment for alcoholism, drug addition, and mental disorders, although special maximum limits may apply.

Other benefits provide for the payment of miscellaneous *hospital charges* (other than those for room and board). The patient is reimbursed on the basis of charges actually made by the hospital for medical care and treatment. Professional services other than the services of an anesthetist and professional ambulance service are not covered. The limit placed in the policy for these hospital charges is usually a multiple of the daily limit for other hospital charges. This may be a multiple of 10, 15, or 20 times, and sometimes the limit may be much higher. For many of these plans the limit is $300 but it may be $1,000 or more for these costs.

Maternity benefits.   Room and board and other benefits are provided on much the same basis as other-than-maternity benefits. A limit is established for room-and-board and other hospital charges that is a multiple of the daily limit specified in the plan. A flat limit such as $200 to $600 is sometimes used instead of the multiple limit. The newborn child is normally included in the coverage during the first week or two.

---

[14] By insurance companies, that is. The Blue Cross plans differ in that they promise to provide certain *services,* such as semiprivate room accommodations, rather than reimbursement for the hospital charges for such services. The group hospital plans are said to have begun with service benefits provided to teachers of Baylor University, Texas, in 1929.

Employees and their dependents are eligible. The normal practice is to make employees insured on the policy date or within 31 days thereafter immediately eligible for maternity benefits. Otherwise the employees or dependents are eligible for benefits only if pregnancy begins while insured. Although one may question the "insurability" of such losses as maternity expenses, the coverage is popular for most groups. With the cost of maternity expenses (hospital and physician) now often exceeding $1,000, the need for including maternity coverage is also clear.

Group surgical expense insurance. Almost all group hospital insurance plans include *surgical* benefits. Like group hospital expense insurance, group surgical expense insurance is a nonoccupational form of protection. Benefits are payable whether or not the surgical operation is performed in a hospital, and the payments are made on a reimbursement basis. The insurer is liable only for the fees actually charged by the surgeon. This liability is limited by a schedule of maximum surgical benefits that appears in the policy. For serious operations the maximum often goes to $1,000 or more. (See Table 13–3.)

Obstetric benefits may be provided, but policies are written either with or without them. When such benefits are provided, they may extend to both employees and dependents. Benefits are scheduled in maximum fixed amounts for the usual obstetric services.

Group regular medical expense insurance. About four fifths of all the group hospital insurance plans include at least some coverage for *regular medical expenses,* especially physicians' fees for nonsurgical care. Some of the plans provide such insurance only for in-hospital visits by doctors. The payment is limited to $5 or more per visit for 31 days or more. Home and office visits to the doctor are sometimes included, with limits on the number of calls paid for by the coverage.

Diagnostic X-ray and laboratory expenses may be included in these group contracts. Today such coverage often applies whether the expenses are incurred in connection with a hospital confinement or at separate offices, laboratories, or diagnostic centers. Scheduled amounts of $25 to $50 for each examination or nonscheduled coverage of actual charges up to a maximum are included in these plans.

Group dental and vision care insurance

The special problems of extending medical care insurance to provide benefits for dental care and vision care expenses are other areas in which group health insurance plans are meeting significant challenges.

Dental insurance. One of the newest fields of rapid expansion in group health insurance is *dental insurance.* Although less than 2 million persons had such insurance coverage in 1965, group dental coverage is now available to more than 35 million persons. Coverage is provided through 35 dental service plans (nonprofit associations sponsored by dental societies and much like Blue Shield plans) and some 60 or more insurers. Many of the dental service plans are affiliated nationally in the Delta Dental Plans, which write about one third of the coverage. Insurers have about one half of the persons covered, and Blue Coss–Blue Shield and other prepaid group practice clinics have the remainder.[15]

Unions are stimulating wide interest in the field. Dental insurance coverage is broadening, too, to include most dental services. Diagnostic, preventive, restorative, and even orthodontic care are often all included. Limits do apply, however, such as per person annual, or lifetime maximums; coinsurance participation by the insured of 20–50 percent; and $25–$50 deductibles. Most plans are based upon paying the "usual, customary, and reasonable fees" for regular cleaning, oral exams, and fluoride treatments. Usually, 80 percent or more of expenses for X rays, fillings, extractions, and surgery is paid, and 50 percent or more for bridges, crowns, and orthodontic work. The annual limit per person is often set at $750–$1,000. An interesting feature is the emphasis on preventive care as well as payment for other dental expenses. The cost is usually a sizable addition to group health insurance expenses, often adding more than $100 per person or $400 per family to annual health insurance costs. The developments will be worth watching, for it has been estimated that more than 70 million persons will be covered by the early 1980s.

Vision care insurance.   The latest development is group *vision care insurance*. Larger employers and unions have been actively promoting the inclusion of such expenses in group health contracts. Many variations exist in this new field, but the preventive and corrective aspects are similar to those of dental insurance plans. Service contracts with optometrists, opticians, and physicians are sometimes used to help control costs. The typical plan includes examinations, fitting, frames, and lenses, but maximum payments for each category of expenses are common. For example, a maximum of $75–$100 for glasses every two years may be included. Such plans offer another interesting example of the trend toward including "prepayment" of fairly regular medical expenses with group insurance coverage for the larger medical costs.

Group major medical expense insurance

Development.   The fast growth of group *major medical expense* insurance is seen in its coverage of 25 million persons in 1960 and nearly 100 million today.[16] That growth is derived from (1) the rapid expansion in the use of the group insuring technique and (2) the increased recognition of the essential need for protection against the burden of large medical expenses as a result of serious injury or illness. Since both group insurance and major medical expense insurance are primarily innovations of the past several decades, group major medical insurance is truly a modern type of health insurance.

---

[15] "Insurance That Covers the Dentist Bills," *Changing Times,* May 1977, p. 43.
[16] *Source Book of Health Insurance Data,* p. 22. Some of the Blue Cross–Blue Shield plans also have major medical coverage.

The salient features of major medical insurance have already been noted in Chapter 13. In the field of group insurance the appeal for this coverage has been tremendous. Employers and employees alike have come to realize that the financial protection afforded by the usual hospital and surgical coverages is far from adequate if the illness is serious and prolonged. More than 90 percent of the persons who have major medical insurance are insured under group forms and less than 10 percent under individual forms.

The group policies differ greatly in their provisions. They are divided into two primary types, however: *supplemental* forms added to a basic group hospital-surgical-medical contract and *comprehensive* forms in which the basic and catastrophe medical expense coverages are combined in one policy.

Basic features. The methods by which group major medical plans express their basic features may be used to differentiate some of the plans. Special attention is given to provisions that were not discussed in Chapter 13 in regard to the individual major medical policies.

High maximum benefits. The most significant purpose of group major medical insurance is to extend medical care benefits to include payments for *catastrophe-type* injuries or for illnesses on a *"blanket" basis*. Contrary to most group hospital-surgical-medical plans, which are limited as to type and amount of medical expense, the goal is to provide protection for *all* types of medical expenses for the *larger* losses. This is accomplished by using deductibles of several hundred dollars or more while setting the maximum limits payable at high amounts, such as $25,000 or more. More than two thirds of covered employees have limits of $50,000 or more, and almost 40 percent have benefits of $250,000 or more.[17]

Maximum limits are usually set for each individual as a lifetime maximum, and as a calendar or benefit year maximum. A popular approach is to call for the satisfaction of a deductible every 12-month benefit year. When the maximum amount has been paid on behalf of any one person, coverage with respect to that person automatically terminates. Since payments on behalf of an individual tend to reduce the amount of effective insurance, it may be desirable that the insured submit evidence of insurability, and upon its approval the policy is reinstated to the full maximum amount.

Benefits are paid for "a bodily disorder, mental infirmity, or bodily injury." It is normal to include coverage for preexisting conditions which cause disabilities during the term of the policy. All types of medical expenses are included in the comprehensive "blanket" coverage, with a few exceptions. The more important types for which protection is provided are: (1) hospital room and board; (2) doctors' care and surgery; (3) professional nursing services; (4) prescription drugs and medicines; (5) anesthesia, oxygen, and X-ray examination and treatment; (6) blood, plasma, and surgical dressings; (7) rental of wheelchair, hospital bed, crutches, or other therapeutic equipment;

---

[17] Ibid., p. 27.

and (8) artificial limbs or eyes. The eligible charges are usually limited only by the maximum amount and by a general provision which requires that the services, treatments, and supplies be reasonably necessary for the care of the insured. Limits of $70 or more per day for the daily hospital room-and-board charges have been added frequently in recent years.

Included in most current contracts are medical expenses for *mental and nervous disorders* (90 percent include this) and *nursing home expenses* (more than half). Special limits often apply.

A few charges are excluded in order to prevent duplicate or unnecessary coverage: (1) charges which are paid for under workers' compensation or state nonoccupational disability laws; (2) confinement in a government-owned hospital (where the insured would not be obligated to pay in the absence of insurance); (3) war injuries; (4) eye, ear, and general health examinations; (5) normal pregnancy expenses; (6) dental treatment or cosmetic surgery, unless necessitated by an accidental bodily injury; and (7) self-inflicted injuries.

Deductibles. Different companies approach the deductible in different ways. There are (*a*) the *each illness* plan, (*b*) the *each individual* plan, and (*c*) the *family budget* plan. Group plans also use "corridor" and "integrated" forms of deductibles (see next section on "primary types").

Under the *"each illness"* plan, the deductible applies to each separate disability. Under the *"each individual"* plan, all expenditures incurred within a definite period of time, usually a year, are subject to but one deductible, regardless of how many different disabilities are involved. The *"family budget"* deductible applies one deductible for all covered members of a particular family with respect to all eligible expenses incurred within a given benefit year. This last plan may be the best protection, but in order to keep the costs within reasonable bounds a higher deductible is necessary.

The deductible varies greatly among the different group major medical contracts. It may be as low as $50 or as high as $1,000. Most plans use a deductible of about $200–$500. The deductible is designed to eliminate small claims from coverage. Payment of these small medical expenses should impose no serious burden upon the average family.

Coinsurance. After the deductible amount has been reached, a "coinsurance" or participation factor is applied to all eligible charges. Under this provision the insured pays a stipulated percentage of all charges over the deductible amount, such as 20 percent. The insurer pays the remaining percentage, such as 80 percent. The 80–20 plan is most common, although the 75–25 plan and some other variations are in use. The purpose is quite obvious: to prevent overuse of the medical services provided for in the contract. Requiring the insured to participate in a portion of the cost curbs excessive use.

Primary types. Group major medical insurance plans generally fall into one or two primary types: (*a*) *supplemental* major medical plans and (*b*) *comprehensive* major medical plans.

Supplemental major medical plans, sometimes termed "integrated," are written where there is already some group protection for hospital, surgical, or medical benefits. *Comprehensive* major medical plans, sometimes termed "basic," are written on groups which have no hospital, surgical, or medical benefits in force on a group basis or may be written to replace all other group health coverages (for medical expenses) already in force.

Supplemental plans. These plans are designed to coordinate major medical insurance with such other group health coverages as are written concurrently. The intent is to eliminate double coverage. About two thirds of persons having group major medical have this type. The deductible feature is retained. A plan in wide use is known as the *corridor deductible*. The plan excludes from eligible expenses covered by the major medical expense insurance all payments under the hospital-surgical-medical plan. Then a deductible known as the "corridor" of uncovered expenses is established. A usual figure is $100 or $200. In the case of an illness calling for an outlay of $3,600, for example, with the hospital-surgical-medical plan covering up to $1,000 and a $100 "corridor" deductible with a 20 percent coinsurance feature, the insurer would pay $2,000. The total out-of-pocket expense to the individual employee is $600, representing $500 coinsurance and the $100 corridor deductible.

Comprehensive plans. There is no underlying group hospital-surgical-medical coverage in these plans. Although the amounts and benefits vary, a typical plan provides an initial deductible of $100 for all claims on a calendar year basis. As a concession to expedite admission to hospitals, full coverage for hospital charges is allowed. All other covered expenses are reimbursed on an 80–20 percent coinsurance basis. There is a lifetime maximum for all claims.

Group disability income insurance

In addition to covering medical expenses, group health plans often provide *disability loss of income*. These forms are sometimes known as "accident and sickness" insurance, although care should be taken to recognize them as income plans rather than medical expense reimbursement plans.

Of a total of more than 80 million persons having disability income protection by 1977, group insurance policies covered about one half, individual policies about one fourth, and one fourth had other noninsured plans such as formal paid sick leave plans.[18]

Definition of disability. Disability income plans are designed primarily as supplemental coverage to workers' compensation insurance. The insurer agrees to pay the designated benefits "if the employee shall become wholly and continuously disabled as a result of nonoccupational accidental bodily injuries or nonoccupational sickness, and thereby be prevented from performing any and every duty pertaining to his or her employment."

---

[18] Ibid., p. 30.

It is usual in case of disability due to injury to have benefits begin with the first day of disability. In the case of sickness, in order to reduce administrative expense attributable to claims originating from minor illnesses, a waiting period is the standard practice. A period of seven days is the most common waiting period for sickness. Substantial reduction in the premium results from the use of such a waiting period.

Disability income benefits are usually payable only when the employee is under the care of a physician, and there is no provision for partial disability. The test of disability set forth in the policy is whether or not the covered employee can perform the duties of *his or her* occupation. Two weeks between successive periods of disability is usually required in order that the two periods be regarded as attributable to separate disabilities.

Group disability income insurance is usually written on a *nonoccupational* basis. The coverage is similar to plans required by five states under "temporary disability laws" (see Chapter 15). There are no conversion rights to continue disability income coverage on an individual policy basis after leaving employment.

Benefit levels and duration. Efforts are made to establish benefits at a level sufficiently high to relieve financial distress. About 80 percent of benefits are for *short-term or temporary* disability of less than two years. Benefit levels are generally set at some amount less than the full amount of take-home pay to discourage malingering.

There are a number of plans for determining the benefit *amount*. Under the *flat* plan, the weekly benefit is the same for all employees. Under the *earnings* plan, benefits are graded on the basis of earnings and are designed to replace a substantial part of the employee's earnings, such as two thirds or three fourths. The *position* plan calls for the allocation of a flat amount of benefit to a person occupying a particular position such as company officer, supervisor, or salesperson.

The policy then establishes a maximum *duration* for the payment of benefits in any one period of disability. A widely used plan provides first-day coverage for nonoccupational accidents, eight-day coverage for sickness (that is, a waiting period of one week), and 26 or 52 weeks as the maximum duration of disability income payments. Long-term disability, for periods of two, five, or more years, is becoming increasingly popular. However, only about one fourth of employees having group disability income coverage have the long-term type.

Group accidental death and dismemberment insurance

Another form of group health insurance aimed at replacing lost income is group *accidental death and dismemberment* insurance. This form provides for payment in the event of loss of life, sight, or limb through external, violent, and accidental means. The coverage may be written on either a 24-hour basis or a nonoccupational basis. The insurance is usually written in conjunction with one of the other forms of group insurance.

As an underwriting practice, insurers establish maximum and minimum amounts of insurance. A minimum of $1,000 and a maximum of $10,000 to $100,000 is common. Many plans provide the same amount of insurance for group accidental death and dismemberment insurance as for group life insurance. Typically, one half of the principal sum (payable for death) is paid for the loss of one hand or foot, or the sight of one eye. The insurer is liable for payment under this form only when loss covered by the policy occurs within 90 days after the injuries are sustained. There is no liability for suicide or war.

Health Maintenance Organizations (HMOs)

With personal health care expenditures rising tenfold during the past ten years, and now exceeding $140 billion a year, it is no wonder that tremendous pressure for new cost control measures has been put on the health care delivery system in the United States. One of the most important developments has been the emergence of *health maintenance organizations* (HMOs). Encouraged by the HMO Act of 1973, and amendments in 1976, a whole new approach to group health insurance has arisen.

Basically HMOs are designed as a new alternative to traditional fee-for-service group health insurance. Historically they derive from prepaid group medical practice plans that have had success in limited areas during the past several decades, such as the Kaiser Permanente, the Health Insurance Plan (New York), the Group Health Cooperative (Seattle), and several dozen others.

An impetus to the growth of HMOs occurred following 1973. Federal laws provided up to $325 million to aid in the planning and formation of such plans, and required employers of more than 25 employees to offer a federally certified HMO (if available in the area) as an option to any employee health fringe benefit. Today there are several hundred HMOs with combined enrollments of about 7 million persons, although most of these are not yet approved as "qualified" under standards set by the Department of Health, Education, and Welfare.

Many variations of health maintenance organizations exist, but all may be defined as a comprehensive set of health benefits and services guaranteed to an enrolled population for a fixed, prepaid fee. The HMO sells an agreement to its subscribers to provide, not just pay for, a stated range of health services, at fees ranging from perhaps $40 to $100 a month per family.

The subscriber buys, in advance, access to a team of doctors who are employees of the plan. The services both of general practitioners and specialists are provided in one-stop comprehensive medical care at a single location. Diagnostic, laboratory, outpatient, and hospital services are all included. Special emphasis is placed upon preventive care through regular examinations.

One goal of the HMOs is to reduce hospitalization costs, and some HMOs have dramatically reduced the number of surgical operations, for example, by as much as one half.[19] However, the overall costs of HMOs tend to run 5–10 percent higher than traditional health insurance premiums because of the broad services the HMOs provide. Early studies indicate that this results in better health for enrollees of HMO plans.

Not all HMOs have been successful, as some have undergone considerable financial and other problems in starting up. Success requires good medical management as well as good business management. Some HMOs have had to increase fees significantly, and several have failed. In general, the development of HMOs has not been as rapid as many observers predicted. The relatively small average size of new HMOs (about 5,000 subscribers) appears to be a handicap for efficient comprehensive service. The medical profession is still widely divided on the issue of whether medical services by salaried physicians can provide quality care, if built-in financial incentives divide profits among the employees of the HMO when costs are held down. Members sometimes dislike being restricted to physicians participating in the HMO and the difficulty of obtaining out-of-the-area services, or complain about impersonal institutionalized care.

Insurance compaines were active participants in establishing some of the earlier HMOs and are currently involved in more than 50 of them. Blue Cross plans have also been involved in HMOs and have invested about $57 million in about a hundred of them.[20] Some of the cost control methods emphasized by HMOs, such as encouraging doctors to regularly review one another's work through professional service review organizations (PSROs) and paying for "second opinions" before surgery is done, are being adopted by many group health insurers. Growing labor support of HMOs through unions and very strong federal government pressure for the continued growth of HMOs are present today. Most national health insurance proposals also feature the HMO concept.

Thus, it is reasonable to predict that the HMO movement will continue to expand. The relatively rapid growth of health maintenance organizations, with emphasis on preventive care as a good approach to reducing high health care costs, suggests that the HMOs may prove to be a significant alternative in health care delivery through the group insurance technique.

The impact of broadening social security programs

The entire area of private health insurance, including group health insurance, has been profoundly affected by the advent of recent governmental pro-

---

[19] "Too Much Surgery," *Newsweek,* April 10, 1978, p. 65. A FTC report in late 1977 emphasizes the indirect competitive pressure on other health insurers, hospitals, and doctors in helping to hold down costs.

[20] *HMO Update, No. 3* (Washington, D.C.: Health Services Administration, U.S. Department of Health, Education, and Welfare, 1976).

grams. In particular, the plans inaugurated by the federal government with the enactment of the Social Security Amendments of 1965 have been the basis for a new era best described as a combined private-public health insurance system.

The problem of medical care for the aged and disabled has been growing for the past two decades. Spurred by the ancillary problem of rapidly rising medical costs and by the idea that everyone has a "right" to adequate health care, social (and perhaps political) pressure has impelled the government to finance a substantial part of the medical costs of this part of the U.S. population.

Medicare. *Medicare,* as the primary amendment is called, now provides for much (estimated at about 40 percent) of the medical care costs of persons aged 65 and over and others covered by the plan. Nearly 30 million persons are covered. A compulsory (part A) *hospitalization* insurance system (HI) is the basic part, financed by a separate increase in the tax contributions under the social security (OASDHI) system. Ninety days of coverage applies for an illness, with another 60 days as a life-time reserve. A second part (B) is a voluntary, supplementary medical insurance system (SMI) for *physician and other medical services,* paid by monthly payments of $8.20 each (in 1979) from the insured and by the federal government. After a deductible amount of $60, part B pays 80 percent of the medical costs. It is administered by about 13 selected insurance companies that serve as the fiscal agents of the government for paying claims under the plan. See Chapter 15 for more information.[21]

Some of the more immediate effects of Medicare or private health insurance were: (1) revision of private contracts to provide coverage guaranteed renewable to age 65 instead of for life and (2) introduction of new insurance forms that provide coverage for those over age 65 only as a supplement to the Medicare benefits, which now cover more than one half of this age group.

Medicaid. *Medicaid,* as Title 19 of the amendments is called, began an expanded program of health care for "needy" persons under state public assistance programs. It is not an insurance program but really a federal-state matching grant system. That Medicaid is the "giant sleeper" of the Social Security Amendments of 1965 is suggested by the doubling of the federal appropriation for this plan, to $13 billion, between 1971 and 1977.

Social security disability income. A third expansion of social security health benefits occurred with the broadening of the definition of disability to include temporary disability (over 5 months and expected to last more than 12 months) rather than the former requirement for total and permanent disability. You must be unable to do "any substantial gainful work" in order to qualify for these disability benefits. This coverage is discussed further in the following chapter.

The need for coordination of the public-private insurance and welfare plans

---

[21] Robert J. Myers, *Medicare* (Homewood, Ill.: Richard D. Irwin, 1970) is also recommended.

for health care costs will be an important area to watch in years ahead. In particular, the increased support for a broader system of national health insurance (see end of next chapter) for all persons in the United States may bring tremendous changes to the health insurance field.

FOR REVIEW AND DISCUSSION

1. "The group insurance method is very important today as a means by which employers provide fringe benefits in employee benefit plans." Explain.

2. What features help prevent adverse selection against the insurer in the group life and health insurance contract? Explain each briefly.

3. What characteristics make group insurance different from other insurance plans? Explain the importance of at least three such characteristics.

4. Several different types of minimums and maximums are used in connection with group life insurance. Evaluate the need for such limits.

5. Group life insurance is necessarily designed to meet basic and average needs of the whole group. Explain how three features of the usual group life contract help in achieving these needs.

6. How can term insurance be the normal type used in group life policies when the increasing cost during the older ages makes term insurance (especially the yearly renewable type) unsuitable for many individual life insurance policyholders? Why is this type used instead of others?

7. To what extent do group life insurance plans (a) have standard provisions, (b) finance costs through employee contributions, and (c) have conversion rights (to permanent life insurance) that are actually used?

8. In terms of its advantages to employers and employees, why has group life insurance grown so rapidly in the last 20 years? (b) What disadvantages and what possible limitations do you foresee in the continued growth of this insurance during the next 20 years?

9. What factors have encouraged, and slowed, the tremendous growth of group health insurance coverages by insurance companies?

10. As an employee of I. B. Human Company, what group health insurance "fringe benefits" would you want the personnel manager to explain to you and your family? Briefly list six pertinent questions that you might ask.

11. What makes group health insurance cost the employee less than comparable individual insurance?

12. What major types of health insurance *losses* may be covered in typical group health insurance contracts? What basic *perils* besides injuries and sickness may be provided for by group insurance?

13. Two opposing philosophies in group health insurance are (a) covering all losses on a "first-dollar" basis and (b) covering only the larger losses on a "catastrophe" or "major medical" basis. With which philosophy do you agree most? Can the two ideas be used rationally together?

14. Why can't a policyholder usually be paid for all of his or her medical ex-

penses and loss of income due to health losses? Does this question have particular relevance to group health insurance? Explain why or why not.

15. Group health policies for loss of income frequently provide no waiting period for disability due to accident but provide one for disability due to sickness. Explain the logic of this situation.

16. Today many hospitals participate in group insurance *service* benefits. How does the loss payment differ from that of the plans offered by insurance companies?

17. What is meant by "blanket" protection in major medical expense insurance? How does it compare with other types of group insurance for medical expense?

18. Group major medical has been a fast-growing part of health insurance. Identify three of its primary features, and explain its rapid growth.

19. What has been the effect of rising medical costs on Medicare-Medicaid and on private health insurance plans?

20. Why is group disability income insurance a nonoccupational cover?

21. Some predictions say that dental insurance coverage will grow from the present 35 million persons to more than 70 million by the early 1980s. Divide the class into two groups (all those without any cavities in one group!), and discuss whether or not such a prediction is realistic.

22. How do health maintenance organizations (HMOs) differ from other group health insurance plans? What advantages and disadvantages do they have?

Chapter 15

**Concepts considered in Chapter 15—Government
life and health insurance**

Government provides or requires some insurance for large segments of
society.

Description and objectives center on *basic economic security* ideas:

The expanding role of government insurance (over $140 *billion* a year)
includes **"social insurance," "social security," public assistance** based
on *welfare* (proven "need"), and **increasing criticism**.

Background in the United States has been *relatively brief*.

The social insurance programs are extensive, but four major ones treat
the old-age, death, disability, and unemployment perils.

Old-age, survivors, disability, and health insurance (OASDHI) is by far the
largest of all the government insurance programs in the United States.

Eligibility is determined by—*covered employment* (more than nine out
of ten workers today), and *insured status* ("fully," "currently," or "disability").

Benefits are analyzed by *type* (including Medicare), *size* (related to
average monthly earnings), and *special earnings* and *disability requirements.*

Administration is by the *federal* government, with *tax collection* by IRS,
individual employee accounts recorded, and *approval and application*
for benefits required.

Financing involves:

Tax on employer and employee, of 6.13 percent *each* in 1979.

Need for understanding and fewer misconceptions.

Pay-as-you-go assessment plan with contingency trust funds.

Income shift among generations, from young to old.

A current recipient bargain, with only partial "earned" right.

Future self-supporting cost estimates, and **needed research.**

Unemployment compensation is analyzed in terms of:

Eligibility, in covered employment, willing and able to work.

Benefits, aimed at one-half normal wages for about 39 weeks.

Administration, basically by the *states,* with some federal standards.

Financing, a wage tax on *employers* (varies by experience).

Workers' compensation for *occupational* injuries and diseases.

Temporary disability (nonoccupational) insurance, in six jurisdictions.

Summary of four major social insurance programs.

Other social insurance programs briefly described are: the *Railroad Acts,
government employee* systems, and *veterans' benefit* programs.

Proposed National Health Insurance plans are discussed as to need and
objectives, and current proposals are compared.

Government life and health insurance

Reasonable *security* is a natural objective in a world of uncertainty. Providing, helping, or requiring systems aimed at assuring basic human needs has long been a function of society.[1] The concept is as old as humanity, and probably even predates the beginning of human life. The movie *Space Odyssey—2001* opens with vivid scenes of apelike creatures banding together in a world of insecurity. The tribe's purpose was collectively to obtain food, protection against predators, and other threatening mysteries of the universe. The more recent *Star Wars* and *Close Encounters of the Third Kind* suggest that the future may even increase our uncertainties.

DESCRIPTION AND OBJECTIVES

In modern times, the role of society has increased in terms of intent and methods. Its place is to help the individual achieve a minimum *money* income in spite of some perils of loss, thus securing the ability to purchase food, shelter, clothing, good health, education, and other necessities of life. Economic security has increasingly become a governmental rather than an individual function, and government or social insurance is one method by which this change has occurred.

The expanding role of government in economic security

Government's role in this process has expanded tremendously during the 1960s and 1970s. In the United States, the expansion has been particularly rapid in the past 40 years, from a relatively modest few billion dollars a year to **expenditures of more than \$260** *billion* for health, education, welfare, housing, and social insurance by the federal government alone.[2] With state

---

[1] David L. Bickelhaupt, "The Role of Government in Economic Security—Insurer, Initiator, and Regulator" (Columbus: Ohio State University, College of Administrative Science, Division of Research Reprint Series, 1970).

[2] See *Budget of the U.S. Government* (Washington, D.C.: U.S. Government Printing Office, 1979), p. 43. The estimated figures for 1979 are a total of more than \$260 billion: social insurance, \$100 billion; education, \$34 billion; public aid, \$49 billion; health and medical, \$53 billion; veterans' programs, \$19 billion; housing and other, \$7 billion. Projected estimates to 1983 increase the total of these items to almost \$400 billion.

and local government expenditures included, the figures practically double.

The government insurance systems in some other nations preceded those in the United States by many years. Health insurance, for example, has been available in government programs in Germany, Austria, Sweden, and Denmark since before 1900.[3] In this sense, the U.S. programs are relatively new.

The reasons for accelerated change

Acknowledging the inevitability of change, and the increase in government's role with regard to economic security, is merely a first step. One must also comprehend the *accelerating rate* of change, and the reasons *why* this change is occurring. To do so is to recognize that change is the natural condition of our environment today. Planning for adjustment to change replaces resistance to change.

Why has economic security become more and more the province of government rather than private enterprise? Some of the answers may be found in studying the background in which changes have taken place. History may help, but as Will and Ariel Durant have said: "Most history is guessing; the rest is prejudice. . . . We must operate with partial knowledge, and be content with probabilities."[4] Thus, insurance people should appreciate this approach.

The newer field of environmentalism should also help provide a foundation for an answer. *Explaining* the relationships between the culture of a society and its observed characteristics is the basis of this approach. It has proved valuable in such emerging fields as the study of comparative marketing systems and international cross-cultural investigations. Description of differences is supplemented by the analysis of differences and similarities among the many social, educational, political, and economic factors involved.

A better understanding of the role of government in economic security will be achieved by comparable study. A few examples of some of the factors (with a few possible effects on the government's role, noted in parentheses) are:

1. Social
   a. The decline in the agrarian society and the trend toward urbanization (increases dependence on regular money income).
   b. The improvements in communication (aiding information dissemination.
   c. The changing roles of the family, the church, and other institutions.
   d. Changes in individual initiative and reliance on the group.

---

[3] J. F. Follman, Jr., "Government Health Programs in Other Nations," *CLU Journal,* vol. 27, no. 3 (July 1973) p. 32.

[4] Introduction to Will and Ariel Durant, *The Lessons of History* (New York: Simon & Schuster, 1968).

2. Educational
   a. The rise in literacy and educational levels (understanding needs).
   b. Increased concern for the future (changing savings attitudes).
   c. Understanding the values of education in implementing other goals.
3. Political
   a. The growth of a more legalistic society (changing liability).
   b. The increase in federal power as opposed to state-local power.
   c. Changing goals of society: full employment, internationalism, economic stability, and so on.
4. Economic
   a. The trend toward industrialization (changing work hazards).
   b. Affluence and the rise of the middle-income group.
   c. The continuance of inflation for a sustained period.
   d. The effect of increasing longevity (influencing retirement needs).
   e. Decreased savings because of taxation and other factors.

Better understanding of environmental changes will result in a more meaningful appreciation of the present and probable future role of government in economic security.

Social insurance

Regulation of private enterprise is only one of the functions of government in a free enterprise economy. Insurance regulation is discussed in Chapter 8. In addition, government serves quite frequently as an *insurer* or as an instigator of private insurance systems. Sometimes government participation takes on characteristics of a partnership with private insurers, while at other times it appears to be competing with them in the quest for economic security. Societies, as well as individuals, families, and businesses, logically have goals which the technique of insurance helps achieve.

Social insurance is the term which collectively describes these efforts by government. Sometimes the term is defined very broadly to include all insurance plans in which the government acts as insurer, subsidizes the plan, or requires insureds to purchase the protection. Other more limited but useful definitions state specific characteristics that are generally required if plans are to be called social insurance: (1) *compulsory program*; (2) *minimum floor* of income; (3) *social adequacy,* rather than individual equity; (4) *benefits* loosely related to earnings; (5) right to benefits *with no needs test,* based on *presumed need*; (6) *benefits prescribed by law*; (7) *self-supporting contributory principle;* (8) *no full funding;* and (9) plan *not* established solely for *government employees.*[5]

---

[5] George E. Rejda, *Social Insurance and Economic Security* (Englewood Cliffs, N.J.: Prentice-Hall, 1976), pp. 18–26.

This text concentrates on several major programs of social insurance. Rather than try to include all the programs which might fit only some parts of a broad definition, the primary social systems for providing security against *old age, disability, death,* and *unemployment* are stressed.

The student should be aware that there are other social insurance programs, however, and that the concept of what is or is not social insurance may undergo change over time. Workers' compensation, for example, has become known as largely a type of social insurance during the last 50 years, even though private insurers are still important in the insuring of workers' compensation perils. Similarly, the automobile compensation plans discussed in Chapter 23 may change the basically private nature of automobile liability insurance systems. It will be helpful if the reader reviews the description of the fields of insurance in Chapter 2 and keeps in mind the changing concept of social insurance. This chapter concentrates on government *life and health* insurance, while Chapter 28 treats the newer role of government in property and liability insurance.

"Social security"

In general, the idea of society providing or requiring systems for obtaining economic security is popularly expressed as "social security." Oftentimes the specific nature of this term is clouded by misconceptions and misunderstandings. To many persons "social security" means a particular program, most frequently that of Old-Age, Survivors, Disability, and Health Insurance (OASDHI). Other persons often use the term in referring to the broad range of programs by which our federal, state, and local governments help bring economic security to individuals. In this broader sense, "social security" could include almost all government activities, from federal employment offices and minimum wage laws to municipal efforts to bring new industry to a certain city or area.

"Social security" is thus not used with precision in our everyday language. However, it ordinarily refers to those *assistance* and *insurance* programs which are required, subsidized, or actually provided by government. The primary objective of "social security" is simply stated as continued financial income, in spite of some perils, for the members of a society. It is *basic* economic certainty which is the goal.

Although there are few persons who would quarrel with this statement of the overall goal, many observers will differ in defining the more specific nature of the objective, and particularly in designing the method by which the goal should be accomplished. For example, should the objective be certainty in regard to *all* possible causes of financial adversity? Probably not, but society can pick out the major kinds of unpredictable losses—such as old age, unemployment, or industrial injury—which affect a major part of the population. What is a *major* kind of loss and part of the population? Does it include *all* of the old-age population, the disabled, migrant workers, and so on? How can such widespread social risks be differentiated from causes of the same losses which may be essentially individual[6] in their origin? And what about the *method* of providing a social solution to what have been identified as essentially social problems, that is, those in which the community as a whole will have to bear the costs if nothing is done to meet the economic losses they bring? (The next section on public assistance versus social insurance tackles this question.)

A final example of the difficulty in defining the goals of "social security" is the question of just what constitutes a minimum level of well-being. In our industrialized and urbanized society, the minimum "floor of protection" must be translated into a specific income (or certain services) to enable each person to obtain the necessities of life. Obviously the needs include food, shelter, and clothing, and most of the early social security programs aimed at these essentials. It is no easy task to reach agreement on the quality and quantity of these basic needs. Should the food minimum include steak at least once in a while instead of hamburger? Should nutrition and calories be the only criteria, or should reasonable variety be included in the goal? Is housing only a roof and four walls, or should the neighborhood and other factors be considered? In addition, how is allowance made in a broad national program for different costs in various areas of the country? There is no universal agreement, either, on many of the components of a minimum level of protection. Does it today, for example, include education, a television set, an automobile, and travel?

Public assistance and social insurance

The distinction between "assistance" and "insurance" is important. A *public assistance* program is based on the concept of proven "need." Benefits are available to its recipients only after they have shown (by lacking sufficient assets or income, or both) that society should help them in meeting basic minimum standards of food, shelter, and clothing. *Social insurance* programs are those systems in which (1) the elements of the insurance technique[7] are present and (2) the plans are required, and often also conceived, financed, and administered, by government with the objective of meeting certain economic security standards for a society.

---

[6] Such as, for example, injuries that are nonoccupational or unemployment that results from quitting work for personal reasons.

[7] This is where many definitions differ. Some authorities suggest that the only requirement is the combination ("pooling") of independent fortuitous risks in sufficient number to provide reasonable predictability. Other persons state that it is also necessary to have such characteristics as (1) transfer of risk, (2) a fund or other means on which to base the future solvency of the plan, and (3) equity of costs in relation to potential benefit payments.

Examples of programs generally held to have the characteristics of *public assistance* are: (1) the Old-Age Assistance (OAA) program and (2) federal-state aid to dependent children (ADC), the blind, and permanently and totally disabled persons. Examples of plans usually included as *social insurance* are: (1) the Federal Old-Age, Survivors, Disability, and Health Insurance program (OASDHI); (2) the state unemployment compensation systems; (3) the state workers' compensation plans; and (4) the state temporary disability (nonoccupational) insurance plans in five states. Other programs such as the railroad retirement and unemployment systems, federal government civil service and veterans' benefit programs, and state retirement systems are sometimes included, and these are discussed briefly at the end of this chapter. Within the total social security system, the distinctions between welfare and insurance are often imprecise and changing. One example is the program begun in 1974, under which aged, blind, and disabled adults become eligible for "supplemental security income" (SSI) in guaranteed minimum monthly amounts.

Increasing criticism

The U.S. insurance-welfare system designed for meeting economic security goals has attracted increasing and outspoken criticism in recent years. The general public, the press, politicians, liberals and conservatives, recipients and taxpayers, young and old, men and women, and blacks and whites—all appear to be dissatisfied with the present state of welfare programs. The increasing attitude of questioning has also affected the U.S. social insurance system. The reasons are plentiful: (1) a larger young population, (2) sharply rising taxes, (3) discrimination and inequities, (4) fiscal effects, (5) frauds, (6) worry about the system's financial soundness, (7) competition with private insurance systems, and others. This situation emphasizes the problems of coordination among social insurance and welfare systems, and of coordinating these systems with the private insurance business.

BACKGROUND

Social insurance in the United States is largely a product of the 20th century, and particularly of the last 40 years. Workers' compensation insurance appeared in the second decade of the century, but the real impetus toward extensive social insurance systems came in the 1930s with the passage of the federal Social Security Act of 1935. In addition to providing support for public assistance programs such as Old-Age Assistance, the act was the direct means by which the Old-Age Insurance system (now OASDHI, including survivors, disability, and health benefits) and the state unemployment compensation plans began. Temporary disability (nonoccupational) laws created another major division of social insurance in some states during the 1940s.

The Social Security Act was by far the most outstanding landmark in the development of social insurance. The depression of the 1930s was undoubtedly a factor in this legislation, but the reasons for the recognition of the needs and the choice of a gigantic social insurance program for the solution were more deep rooted. The United States had changed rapidly from an agricultural and family-oriented society to an urban and industrial one. The result was to create an increasing interdependence among all wage earners. Instead of depending upon individual and family initiative, ingenuity, and thrift to provide support in hard times, individuals turned to the government and to society as a whole to help them through economic hardships. The Great Depression focused attention on the plight of the aged and the unemployed, and from this grew the Social Security Act. The growth of social insurance from this beginning has been made possible by an unparalleled economic upswing in recent decades, enabling a high standard of living in the United States to support the continuing interest in alleviating the problems of industrial injury and disease, old age, unemployment, and disability. The concern is still evident today, with the federal administration pledged to major efforts in reducing unemployment and the undesirable economic effects of inflation.

The amendments to the OASDHI program have been steady during the past 40 years. Survivorship benefits were added for widows and children up to age 18 in 1939, even before the first retirement benefits for old age began. Liberalization has proceeded in many sessions of Congress, including 1946, 1950, 1952, 1954, 1956 (when disability benefits were introduced), 1958, 1960, 1961, 1965 (Medicare), and almost every year since then. The benefits of the program cover almost everyone, and its costs are paid by taxpayers to the extent of about one third of the total federal budget.

THE SOCIAL INSURANCE PROGRAMS

In a textbook of this scope, only a limited summary of the major provisions of the basic social insurance programs can be offered. The student desiring additional detail and further information about each of the social insurance systems is referred to comprehensive publications[8] which concentrate on social insurance against economic insecurity.

The remainder of this chapter will aim at establishing a familiarity with the four most important types of social insurance today: (1) Old-Age, Survivors, Disability, and Health Insurance; (2) unemployment compensation; (3) workers' compensation; and (4) temporary disability (nonoccupational) insurance. The section on workers' compensation will be abbreviated since

---

[8] John G. Turnbull, C. Arthur Williams, Jr., and Earl F. Cheit, *Economic and Social Security,* (New York: Ronald Press Co., 1973); Robert J. Myers, *Social Security* and *Medicare* (Homewood, Ill.: Richard D. Irwin, 1975 and 1970 respectively); Rejda, *Social Insurance and Economic Security* and others.

Chapter 22 on employers' liability and workers' compensation will discuss many of its aspects.

The general significance of the four primary social insurance programs is seen in the size of the yearly taxes (or, in the smaller part of the programs, insurance premiums) which now support them. As noted in Figure 2–3 of Chapter 2, the total taxes and premiums are nearly $150 *billion* a year, or 45 percent of the combined private and social insurance fields. About three fourths of the annual cost of social insurance today goes for the OASDHI program, for which taxes of more than $100 billion were paid in 1978.

Each of the social insurance plans has basic features with which the student of insurance should be familiar. The programs are analyzed in the following sections of the chapter on the basis of (1) eligibility, (2) benefits, (3) administration, and (4) financing.

OLD-AGE, SURVIVORS, DISABILITY, AND HEALTH INSURANCE

The largest and best-known social insurance system in the United States, OASDHI, is often mistakenly believed to be the only part of the 1935 Social Security Act, which actually also provided for nine other separate programs.[9] Title II of the act created the trust funds and requirements for the OASDHI program. Today more than 33 million persons are receiving social security benefits, including 21 million retired workers and dependents, more than 7 million survivors of workers, and nearly 5 million disabled workers and their dependents.

Eligibility

Covered employment. More than nine out of ten employed persons are now covered by the plan. The only major types of workers not covered by OASDHI are (1) some civilian government employees, (2) some agricultural workers, and (3) some employees of nonprofit organizations (those whose employers elected not to become part of the system). Many federal government employees and railroad workers are covered under other retirement systems, and many state and local government workers are included in OASDHI as a result of federal-state agreements with these employers. Thus, very few working persons are not now a part of the program. Both wage earners and self-employed persons are included.

---

[9] These include one other type of social insurance, unemployment compensation insurance, five public assistance programs, and three child welfare services. Portions of the following sections have been adapted from the *Social Security Handbook* (Washington, D.C.: Social Security Administration, U.S. Department of Health, Education, and Welfare). This is reprinted about every three years. Current laws and regulations of the Social Security Act should be checked in the two-volume series entitled *Compilation of the Social Security Laws* (Washington, D.C.: U.S. Government Printing Office).

Insured status. To be entitled to benefits it is necessary that a person be engaged in employment covered by the Social Security Act for at least a prescribed minimum number of quarters. Before 1978, one quarter of coverage is generally earned for each quarter in which at least $50 in covered nonfarm wages (and for each full $100 of covered farm wages) is paid in a year, or four quarters of coverage are earned for at least $400 of creditable self-employment earnings in a year. For 1978, one quarter of coverage for each full $250 of earnings will apply, with a maximum of four quarters of coverage in a year. After 1978, the $250 amount will be adjusted on the basis of tables, and after 1981 on the basis of average annual national wages.

Workers become eligible for benefits by achieving (1) "fully," (2) "currently," and (3) "disability" insured status. *Fully insured status* gives eligibility for all benefits except disability benefits. It is usually attained by having 40 quarters, or ten years, of coverage. However, the requirements may also be met by having worked a shorter period, including at least one quarter of coverage for each calendar year after 1950 (or after the year in which age 21 is attained, if later) prior to death or disability, or at or after age 62. A minimum of six quarters is required. *Currently insured status* alone gains eligibility only for the child's, mother's, and lump-sum survivorship benefits, and the worker must have been in covered employment during at least 6 of the last 13 quarters. *Disability insured status,* which is required for diability benefits, takes fully insured status *and* 20 quarters of coverage in the 40-quarter period ending with the quarter in which disability began. (Special rules apply for persons disabled before age 31.)

Benefits

Types of benefits. There are four basic types of benefits available to those persons who achieve eligibility under the OASDHI program. These are: (1) payments for *death,* including a small lump-sum payment and important survivors' income payments to widows with dependent children; (2) income payments for *disability* if it is total and is expected to last at least 12 months; (3) income payments after *retirement* age to either or both husband and wife (or to a child under 18, or 18–21 if in school, or any age if disabled); and (4) *hospital and medical* payments for fully insured persons aged 65 or over, or 65 before 1968,[10] under the Medicare program. Thus, in essence, OASDHI pays in cases of dying too soon (before the economic lifetime is completed), being disabled to a point which prevents earning an income, living too long (beyond the normal working lifetime), and incurring hospital-medical expenses at age 65 or older.

---

[10] Now also includes disabled beneficiaries (workers under 65, widows and widowers aged 50–64, and children aged 18 and over disabled before age 22) who have been on the benefit rolls for at least two years, and persons with chronic kidney diseases requiring dialysis or renal transplant.

In reference to the insured status of the worker, the following *types* of benefits are paid:

1. If the worker is *currently* insured:
   a. Lump-sum death payment:
      (1) To widow, widower, or anyone paying burial expenses.
   b. Survivorship income payments:
      (1) To a widow[11] with one or more dependent children under age 18 (or disabled before 22).
      (2) To an unmarried child prior to age 18 (or 18–21 if in school), or if the child is disabled before age 22.
2. If the worker is *fully* insured:
   a. Lump-sum death payment as in 1(*a*).
   b. Survivorship income payments as in 1(*b*), and also:
      (1) To widow or dependent widower at age 65 (or reduced amounts at age 60, or at age 50 if disabled).
      (2) To dependent parents at age 62.
   c. Retirement income payments:
      (1) To retired worker at age 65[12] (or reduced amounts at 62).
      (2) To wife or dependent widower or retired worker at age 65 or more, or reduced amounts at 62–64.[13]
      (3) To child of retired worker, prior to age 18, or if the child is disabled before then, or at 18–21 in school.
   d. Disability income payments:
      (1) To disabled worker under age 65.
      (2) To wife or dependent widower of disabled worker at her age 62, or when child under 18 or disabled before 22 is present (also to disabled widow at age 50).
      (3) To child of disabled worker prior to age 18, or if the child is disabled before 22, or if 18–21 and in school.

Generally, the worker's major benefit in being "currently" insured is that this enables the widow and dependent children to receive substantial *survivorship* income. If the worker is "fully" insured, these benefits and important other benefits are available: *retirement* income, and *disability* income (if special 20 or 40 quarters requirement is met, too). The lump-sum death payment ($225) is payable in the case of either a fully *or* currently insured worker. Medicare hospital benefits are available to nearly all persons over age 65 and to certain disabled persons.

---

[11] Income benefits to a widow will stop if she remarries; payments to a wife or a dependent husband will stop if a divorce is granted.

[12] Special transitional benefits are payable to certain persons who attained age 72 before 1972 (1970 for women).

[13] Or full amount at any age if eligible child is present (under 18, or disabled before 22).

One of the most significant programs was added to the provisions of the Social Security Act in 1965. Popularly known as *Medicare*, the program is in two separate parts: (1) compulsory basic hospital insurance (HI) and (2) voluntary supplemental medical insurance (SMI). Benefits began in 1966, and coverage applies to practically everyone 65 or older.[14] Eligibility has been expanded to include persons under age 65, including (1) totally disabled insured workers for at least 24 months, (2) disabled widows (over age 50) and children on the disability benefit rolls for 24 months, and (3) certain chronic kidney cases. Persons over 65 who are not on social security can purchase coverage for $63 or more a month. The sizable nature of the program is seen in the estimated benefits for 1979 of approximately $29 billion. *Medicaid*, a separate program of federal grants to the states for paying medical bills of "needy" persons, is not an insurance plan. Although begun at the same time as Medicare, under Title XIX of the Social Security Act, the plan is a federal-state *welfare* program. It grew rapidly to a cost of approximately $12 billion a year.

The basic benefits payable are (1) in-hospital services of up to 90 days in each spell of illness with a $144 basic deductible and coinsurance of $36 a day[15] after 60 days paid by the patient; (2) posthospital care in a qualified extended care facility for 100 days with $20 a day after 20 days paid by the patient; and (3) posthospital part-time home nursing or therapy care for 100 visits. Retirement is not necessary in order to have these benefits.

The supplementary medical benefits are optional but have been purchased by almost all persons 65 or over. The current charge of $8.20 a month is matched by general revenue (federal). Benefits include (1) physicians' services anywhere, (2) home health services for up to 100 visits a year, (3) outpatient hospital and physical therapy services anywhere, (4) limited ambulance services, and (5) miscellaneous dressings and medical equipment. An annual deductible of $60 applies, after which 80 percent of reasonable charges are paid. Special limitations apply for costs of mental care.

Size of benefits. As to the *size* of the benefits payable under the OASDHI program, two calculations are important. One is the *primary insurance amount* (PIA),[16] which is the amount of monthly income payable to the insured worker at retirement at age 65, or for disability. The benefit rates for all other types of benefits are calculated as percentages of the PIA. Reduced

---

[14] Minor exceptions apply to some aliens and government employees otherwise covered.

[15] These deductibles and coinsurance amounts are to be adjusted automatically each year after 1978 to reflect changes in hospital costs. A lifetime reserve of 60 days with coinsurance is available, in addition to the basic 90-day coverage. Psychiatric hospital care has a 190-day lifetime maximum.

[16] The mathematical complexities of the necessary calculations are compounded by new formulas which were developed with each of the OASDHI amendments. Tables of benefits later simplified the process.

benefits based on the PIA are available, if chosen, to retirees at age 62, wives at age 62, and widows at age 60.

The tables of benefits are related to the *average monthly earnings* (AME),[17] with indicated minimum and maximum amounts payable. A person's AME is figured (under the 1950 new-start method) by counting all the years of earnings after 1950, or age 21 if later, then subtracting the five years of lowest earnings and any years of total disability, and dividing the person's total remaining earnings. The earnings are subject to a specified maximum taxable earnings base in each year, which has changed from $3,600 in 1951, to $4,200 in 1955, to $4,800 in 1959, to $6,600 in 1966, to $7,800 in 1968, and by gradual amounts each year since 1971 to its 1979 amount of $22,900. It is scheduled for annual increases which make it $31,800 by 1981, and the scheduled base will then be subject to automatic changes according to the level of earnings in covered employment. Earnings for active duty in the uniformed services of the Unites States since 1956 are included, and prior military service may earn wage credits of $160 per month.

The benefit formulas and tables are heavily weighted in favor of the low-income worker. For example, the primary insurance amount is figured on a basis which in 1978 takes about 46 percent of the first $110 of average monthly earnings, only about 53 percent of the next $290 of average monthly earnings, and so on. With $400 per month AME, the PIA is $232, but with $800 AME it is $360. The minimum monthly primary benefit is $114.30,[18] and special maximum family benefits apply. The average primary benefit in 1979 was more than $250 per month for all retired workers.

Percentages of the PIA are applied in the following manner for the various types of OASDHI payments:

1. Lump-sum death payments—$255.
2. Suvivorship income payments—100 percent of the PIA to widow or dependent widower at age 65 (reduced if age 60–64) or 82.5 percent to a dependent child and to the child's surviving parent.
3. Retirement and disability income payments—100 percent of the PIA to the retired at age 65 (reduced if ages 62–64) or to the disabled worker; 50 percent of the PIA to the elderly spouse at age 65 (reduced if age 62–64) or child of the retired or disabled worker.

Table 15–1 shows the amount of monthly benefits payable under OASDHI provisions, at selected average monthly earnings, for the more common types of benefits. Over 21 million retired beneficiaries (or their dependents) are now receiving OASDHI benefits, as well as more than 7 million survivors and

---

[17] A new system of calculating "average *indexed* monthly earnings" (AIME) begins in 1979. Using national average wages to modify actual earnings, it will change the PIA benefit tables for many persons.

[18] Amendments provide for a higher special minimum PIA up to $180 for employment of 20–30 years or more.

Table 15–1. Examples of OASDHI monthly benefits*
at selected average monthly earnings

Types of benefits	Average monthly earnings†			
	$400	$800	$1,200†	$1,400†
Retirement and disability benefits:				
Retired worker—65 or older ⎱	$315	$494	$595	$638
Disabled worker—under 65 ⎰				
Wife at 65‡ or older	158	247	297	319
Combined retired worker at 65,				
and wife at 65	473	741	892	957
Survivorship payments:				
Widow at 60§	226	353	425	456
Widow and one child ‖	473	741	892	957
Maximum family payment	575	864	1,041	1,116

* Automatic cost-of-living adjustment now increases benefit amounts shown.

† *Total* earnings are *not* averaged; only those earnings are averaged upon which OASDHI taxes have been paid (excluding the five lowest years). Maximum creditable earnings are $22,900 in 1979, and further increases are scheduled for later years, but this amount has changed upward from $3,600 in 1954. Thus, most persons will *not* have maximum average earnings and therefore will not obtain maximum benefits for some years ahead.

‡ As an option, the retired worker and/or wife can obtain proportionally reduced benefits at age 62.

§ As an option, the widow can obtain these proportionally reduced benefits at age 60 or more at 62. At 65, benefits are the same as those of the retired worker at 65.

‖ Unmarried child under 18 or 18–21 if full-time student.

5 million disabled persons. Total benefit amounts exceed $100 billion a year. Medicare benefit limits have been discussed in the previous section.

Special earnings and disability requirements.   Some special provisions apply for determining retirement status and amounts payable. Under an annual earnings test,[19] retired persons may have deductions made from OASDHI benefits. Persons under age 72 are not considered fully "retired" if they earn wages or self-employment earnings of over certain amounts. If annual earnings exceed $4,500 (in 1979 tax year), monthly benefits are reduced on the basis of the excess earnings: $1 for each $2 of annual earnings over $4,500. In applying the earnings test, income is counted only if it results from continuing work, that is, it does not include income from investments, other pensions, or other sources not requiring active employment. After a person reaches age 72 (70, beginning in 1982), the earnings test does not apply and the person may earn unlimited income without reducing OASDHI benefits.

The requirements for disability income payments also deserve special note. These are cash benefits,[20] not medical care services, for severe, long-lasting

---

[19] The test also applies to all other OASDHI recipients under age 72, including widows, except disabled persons. The allowable earnings for beneficiaries other than those aged 65 or over are $3,240 a year. Automatic adjustments in these limits, in addition to scheduled increases to 1982, will also apply.

[20] Another type of disability benefit under OASDHI is the "disability freeze" provision, which permits a totally disabled worker to eliminate periods of at least five months' disability in the calculation of insured status and average monthly earnings.

disability which prevents a person from earning a living. The benefits are for total disability (inability to engage in any substantial gainful work) which can be expected to result in death or which has lasted or can be expected to last for a continuous period of not less than 12 months. A "waiting period" of five months applies. The disability may be a physical or a mental impairment based upon medical evidence. Examples include the loss of two or more limbs, vision, hearing, or speech, and disease such as multiple sclerosis and severe cancer. A separate wage tax and trust fund was established in 1956 to provide the disability benefits under OASDHI. The monthly disability benefits for an insured worker are the same as at retirement age 65, or the primary insurance amount. Payments stop if the insured person dies, becomes no longer disabled according to the definitions in the law, or reaches age 65.

Administration

The Old-Age, Survivors, Disability, and Health Insurance system is administered by the federal government. More than 150 million individual account records are maintained by the Social Security Administration in Baltimore, Maryland. The commissioner of social security supervises ten divisions of management, actuarial services, claims, planning, research, hearings and appeals, accounting, and other functions. Regional and field services are performed through district offices located in more than 600 major cities.[21] These offices inform the public about its rights and obligations in connection with OASDHI.

Medicare administration involves several other intermediaries, as the Social Security Administration has entered into contracts with Blue Cross–Blue Shield and some insurance companies for processing claims payments.

Tax collection. The taxes for the program are collected by the Internal Revenue Service. Employers deduct the required amounts from the wages of their employees and forward these amounts, plus the employer tax to the district director of internal revenue. Self-employed persons pay their OASDHI taxes directly to the IRS with their income tax statements. All the taxes are credited to three trust funds; the Federal Old-Age and Survivors Insurance Trust Fund, the Federal Disability Insurance Trust Fund, and the Federal Hospital Insurance Trust Fund. These funds are used only for the administration and benefit payments of the OASDHI program. They are held until needed by investment in securities of the U.S. government.

Individual accounts. As soon as workers first perform work covered by the Social Security Act, they must apply for a card which identifies each individual by name and number. The assigned account number is used for the

---

[21] The position of the Social Security Administration in the federal government is explained in the annual report of the Department of Health, Education, and Welfare.

worker's entire lifetime of credited earnings. Reports from workers and their employers each year are the source of the earnings credits.

Workers may check at any time on the status and record of their earnings under OASDHI. In fact, they should check regularly to see that their earnings have been reported and recorded properly by writing to the Social Security Administration, Baltimore, Maryland 21235. Forms for this purpose are available through local district offices and many banks and insurance companies. Unless this is done at least once every three years, it may be impossible under the law to make corrections if mistakes have occurred. Valuable rights to earnings credits may be lost if the individual does not do this.

Approval of benefits. It is also important for each worker and beneficiary to understand that OASDHI benefits must be applied for, as they are not paid automatically. When application is made for benefits, at death, disability, or retirement, certain proofs must be presented to the district offices. Marriage and birth certificates, proof of support for dependents, and medical proof of disability are required before the various benefit payments can be made. Since certain time limits apply, it is important that these proofs be rendered promptly. Usually the applications must be completed within two years after eligibility, but back payments may be limited to one year. Thus delay can be costly to the OASDHI recipients who neglect or postpone proper application and proofs for benefits.

A system for hearings before one of seven regional representatives and an appeals council in Washington are maintained for reconsideration of any decision in regard to eligibility or amount of OASDHI benefit claims.

Financing

Tax on employer and employee. The OASDHI program is paid for by taxes levied under the Social Security Act on the earnings of workers. In the case of wage earners in covered employment, both the *employer and employee* each pay an equal tax on the earnings; self-employed persons pay a tax which is slightly less than 1½ times the tax which a wage earner pays.

Originally the tax began in 1937 at 1 percent on both employer and employee. The schedule of taxes was set up to be increased periodically as the program got under way and the number of OASDHI beneficiaries increased. Revisions in the schedule[22] have occurred many times, and the recent tax rates and scheduled increases including Medicare tax are:

---

[22] The tax on each employer and employee changed from 2 percent in 1956 to 2¼ percent in 1957, to 2½ percent in 1959, to 3 percent in 1960, to 3⅛ percent in 1962, to 3⅝ percent in 1963, to 4.2 percent in 1966, to 4.4 percent in 1968, to 4.8 percent in 1969, to 5.2 percent in 1971, to 5.85 percent in 1973, to 6.05 percent in 1978, and to 6.13 percent in 1979. Further increases are scheduled to 1990, when the tax will be 7.65 percent.

Year	Employee	Employer	Combined employer-ee	Self-employed
1969–70	4.8 %	4.8 %	9.6%	6.9 %
1971–72	5.2	5.2	10.4	7.5
1973–77	5.85	5.85	11.7	8.0
1978	6.05	6.05	12.1	8.1
1979–80	6.13	6.13	12.26	8.1
1981	6.65	6.65	13.3	9.3
1982–84	6.7	6.7	13.4	9.35
1985	7.05	7.05	14.1	9.9
1986–89	7.15	7.15	14.3	10.0
1990 and after	7.65	7.65	15.3	10.75

The tax is applied against only the first $22,900 of annual earnings.[23] Thus the maximum current tax in 1979 is 6.13 percent each from employer and employee on a maximum earnings amount of $22,900, or $1404 a year. The combined employer-ee maximum tax is $2,808 and in 1985 it will be $5,372 under the present anticipated tax schedule. Self-employed persons now pay a maximum of $1,855, and in 1985 they will pay $3,772 a year. The increase of over 100 percent between 1966 and 1974 was very sharp, and the 1972–74 increase was almost 60 percent. The 1974–79 increase was even larger—nearly 250 percent!

Need for understanding.   Many of the misconceptions about the OASDHI program are related to its financing. Even though the Social Security Act is so complex as to discourage effort by most people to understand it, it seems imperative that more persons *should* try to learn how the program works. The person who misunderstands the program (or does not attempt to understand it) is certainly not fulfilling an important obligation. Many booklets are available without cost by calling or writing your local Social Security office. Examples include: *Social Security Information for Young Families, A Woman's Guide to Social Security,* and many others.

Pay-as-you-go assessment plan with contingency trust funds.   One popular misconception concerns the basic purpose and method of the financing system. OASDHI is not based on an actuarially funded plan, as are individual life insurance contracts and annuities issued by the private insurance business. The solvency of the plan rests on the right of the federal government to levy taxes and to change benefits or taxes in the future, if necessary. The financing of OASDHI is nearly a *pay-as-you-go*[24] plan, as is seen in the fact that

---

[23] The maximum tax base began in 1937 at $3,000 a year, was increased to $3,600 in 1951, $4,200 in 1955, $4,800 in 1959, $6,600 in 1966, $7,800 in 1968, $10,800 in 1973, $13,200 in 1974, $14,100 in 1975, $15,300 in 1976, $16,500 in 1977, $17,700 in 1978, and $22,900 in 1979. Further increases are scheduled for 1980–87. The maximum tax base will be $42,600 in 1987, and the base is subject to automatic adjustment after 1981 based on wage trends.

[24] In theory there is perhaps nothing wrong with a plan whereby current costs are paid by current contributions as long as it is recognized as such. A fully funded plan,

current annual contributions (taxes) just about equal current beneficiary payments. The trust funds of about $35 billion in 1978 are merely a partial reserve against the much larger amounts that will be paid under the system in future years.

The nature of the financing method is thus comparable to an *assessment* system in which the assessments levied on the future working populations will sharply increase as payments from the system expand. The trust funds are similar to a *contingency fund* rather than a full reserve from which to pay future benefits.

Income shift among generations. A most important effect of OASDHI is the shifting of income from one generation of workers to another. Today's taxes on workers are not, as is popularly believed, being set aside in order to prepay the current contributors their future benefits at death, retirement, or disability. Current taxes are used to pay current recipients, which means generally that the working generation today is paying now for the retired (or disabled or dying) generation. The retirement benefits of persons aged 30 today will be paid not from their own taxes for the next 35 years but from the taxes levied on their working children in the year 2014 and thereafter.

A current recipient "bargain." If a recipient of OASDHI retirement payments believes that he or she has fully "earned" the right to benefits (by the taxes paid up to age 62 or 65), the extent of actual contributions should be considered. On the average, the current beneficiary of retirement income has paid for not much more than 5 percent of the value of his or her benefits. Even at maximum tax rates since 1937, total taxes for the last 40 years would be only about $17,000 combined for employer and employee. Accumulated in a savings account, these taxes paid would have grown to about $28,000 today, which at the prevailing private annuity rates would provide roughly $230 a month. A retired worker at age 65 under current schedules of social security benefits would receive in this case about $460 a month, or double the value of what the taxes paid in and accumulated would provide. (In addition, if the retired worker is married, the spouse over 65 would receive 50 percent more in benefits.) Sound like a bargain? It is—for those currently retiring. In other words, it would cost many times the taxes that have been paid to purchase retirement annuity similar to the OASDHI benefit, and that comparison does not include any of the other survivorship, disability or Medicare benefits to which retired workers may be entitled.

The "bargain" that recipients of social security payments are now receiving is being paid for by the current working generation. Young entrants to the system today will pay for 1½ times the benefits that they will receive on the average at current benefits schedules. The low-cost bargain look of OASDHI benefits will disappear as the scheduled tax increases take effect and as the

---

involving $700 billion or more of assets, could have undesirable political and economic effects.

average insured workers have paid into the program for a longer period before they or their survivors begin to collect benefits.

The sizable benefits in relation to normal contributions are today a function of the fact that the program has not yet reached the mature stage when the number of new beneficiaries each year will be relatively stable. Now, many recipients qualify for benefits with perhaps only a few years of taxes paid. The expansion of the number of OASDHI recipients will continue during the next several decades.

Future self-supporting cost estimates. The financing of the OASDHI program is designed to be self-supporting, although the benefits paid out have exceeded the yearly income since 1975. Projected receipts under the 1977 amendments will again exceed the expenditures after 1980.[25] As long as the system continues indefinitely, future estimates of expenditures and receipts (and changes in the law, if necessary) can be made to assure the solvency of the plan. The long-range estimates are difficult to evaluate. The combination of assumptions which must be made in such estimates are fantastically complex. Even simplified recent estimates are based upon at least a quadruple set of factors, including predictions that the inflation rate will be down to 4 percent by 1982, that the unemployment rate will be down to 5 percent, that real wages will be up by 16 percent by 1984, and that birthrates will level out to 2.1 children per woman.[26] The projected deficits using these short-term assumptions are considerable; the longer run assumptions to the year 2030 result in a need for expenditures of 20 percent or more of payroll, with a deficit over scheduled income of more than 8 percent of taxable payroll. The Advisory Council on Social Security Financing and actuaries of the Social Security Administration review and revise these estimates periodically.

High-cost estimates and low-cost estimates for the future vary by billions of dollars. The differences in the estimates stem from the complexity and the relative unpredictability of the assumptions that must be made. Future mortality, birth,[27] marriage, divorce, remarriage, immigration, and disability rates all have to be included in the estimates, as well as basic employment data, interest earnings, and many other factors. Rapidly rising hospital and medical costs make the Medicare cost estimates very difficult.

Needed research on effects. The effects of OASDHI financing have reached a significance which suggests that much more economic and sociological research in this area is warranted. The results on income redistribution, labor force participation and productivity, consumption, savings, investment,

---

[25] A. Haeworth Robertson, "The Financial Status of Social Security after the Social Security Amendments of 1977," CLU Journal, vol. 32, no. 2 (April 1978), p. 14.

[26] Financing Social Security: Issues for the Short and Long Term (Washington, D.C.: U.S. Government Printing Office, July 1977).

[27] Just this one factor alone will have a tremendous effect on the cost burden to a shrinking base of active workers, and may require future funding from general tax revenues. See George E. Rejda and Richard J. Shepler, "The Impact of Zero Population Growth on the OASDHI Program," Journal of Risk and Insurance, vol. 40, no. 3 (September 1973), p. 313.

and economic growth should all be considered as major questions for analysis. The coordination of social security benefits and costs with private pension and other insurance is a mounting task for insurers and employers.

UNEMPLOYMENT COMPENSATION

The impetus for the states to establish unemployment compensation systems was established in the Social Security Act of 1935. A tax-offset device was used in which most employers were required to pay a 3 percent federal payroll tax *unless* the state created a state unemployment plan that met certain standards. As a result, all states within a few years passed unemployment statutes, permitting employers a 90 percent credit on the federal tax. This left a 0.3 percent federal tax to provide general administration for the state systems.

The primary *objectives* of unemployment compensation insurance are to help unemployed workers, by providing them with cash payments during involuntary unemployment, maintaining their standard of living, providing them with time to locate or regain employment, and helping them find jobs. Secondary objectives aim at promoting economic efficiency and stability, by achieving desirable countercyclical effects, improved social allocation of costs, and improved utilization of the labor force, and by encouraging employers to stabilize employment.[28]

Eligibility

In order to be eligible for unemployment compensation, an employee must have been working under covered employment and must also meet certain individual requirements.

Covered employment.   Not all workers are covered by the unemployment compensation laws of the states. More than three out of five workers are covered, however. The main exceptions are (1) self-employed persons, (2) agricultural workers and domestic servants, (3) employees of some smaller nonprofit organizations and some state and local governments, and (4) maritime and railroad workers. Separate federal legislation covers the last category, and many states have unemployment compensation laws that require (or permit, on an elective basis by the employer) coverage for some domestic servants, employees of nonprofit organization, and state and local government workers.[29]

Individual requirements.   In order to collect unemployment compensation benefits, workers in covered employment must meet several important requirements. They must be unemployed through no fault of their own, which

---

[28] Rejda, *Social Insurance and Economic Security,* pp. 373–76.

[29] *Social Security Programs in the U.S.* (Washington, D.C.: U.S. Government Printing Office, annual). Most states now cover state and local government employees in varying degrees. Five million workers were added by federal laws effective in 1972.

ordinarily disqualifies for benefits any worker who has voluntarily quit, has been discharged for misconduct, is involved in a labor dispute, or refuses suitable employment. The states vary considerably in these definitions for disqualification, and some permit unemployment benefits to workers unemployed because of an employer lockout or even a strike by the employees.

Unemployed workers must be *willing and able to work*. As proof of this, they must register for work at a public employment office, file a claim for benefits, not be sick or disabled, and be actively seeking work and available to take a suitable job if it is offered to them.

A third major requirement for benefits is that workers must have a prescribed minimum amount of recent work before the unemployment occurred. State laws vary considerably here, also, ranging from those which prescribe minimum earnings standards in a base period to those which require a minimum number of weeks of previous employment.[30] The purpose is to show some substantial recent attachment to the active labor force and contributions by the employer to the unemployment system.

Benefits

The laws of each state must be consulted in order to determine the amount and duration of unemployment benefits. Normally, the purpose is to provide a *temporary* replacement of a *part* of the worker's full-time weekly earnings.

Amount. Within stated minimum and maximum limits, the size of the weekly benefits is usually aimed at about one half of normal wages. Because of rising wages in recent years, the maximum limits are most important, and over half of the new claimants have been eligible for maximum payments in many states. The maximums vary from approximately $60 to $120 weekly, with the average payment falling in between these two figures. About a dozen states provide additional dependents' benefits, which increase the range of the above maximums. Increasingly, "flexible" maximums related to 50 percent of the statewide average weekly wage are being used.

Duration. The state unemployment compensation systems do not aim at a solution to long-term or permanent technological unemployment problems. Typically, most states provide benefits for only 26 weeks. Supplementary benefits for periods of high unemployment have become required since 1972 under 1970 federal employment security amendments, which extended benefits by 50 percent. This means a usual total maximum duration of 39 weeks. Since 1974, federal law has provided that an additional 13 weeks can be paid during periods of unusually high unemployment, so a total duration of one year's payments is possible. Current laws are phasing out this extension.

Special provisions in most of the states provide (1) some proportional pay-

---

[30] Ibid. About a dozen states require flat amounts of $300–$1,200, and about the same number specify a multiple, such as 30 times the weekly benefit, or require a multiple, such as 1.5 times the claimant's high-quarter average. Other figures quoted in this section also come from this source.

ments for partially unemployed persons who may replace some of their wages with odd jobs, (2) a waiting period of one week before unemployment payments can begin, and (3) payments to claimants attending approved training courses.

Administration

The direct administration of unemployment compensation systems is performed by the state governments, with the federal government participating indirectly through the standards it sets for meeting the requirements of the tax-offset law.

Federal standards. Since all or a portion of the state unemployment administrative expenses (as well as the approximate 90 percent tax offset) depends on the state's conforming to the federal standards, the requirements are usually met. These include provisions that (1) all state unemployment taxes be deposited in an account with the U.S. Treasury from which only benefits can be paid, (2) benefits be paid only through public or federally approved employment agencies, (3) full payments be made promptly when due, (4) workers have the right to appeal decisions of the state agencies, (5) permit workers to refuse unsuitable jobs under prescribed standards, and (6) administrative personnel be employed on a merit basis.

The Manpower Administration's Unemployment Insurance Service in the U.S. Department of Labor has the responsibility of determining whether the states have complied with the federal requirements.

State administration. The area of state administration is still quite broad, for each state must actually carry out the federal requirements as well as make many of its own decisions in regard to the unemployment compensation program. For example, the state decides the major questions of (1) eligibility (what workers are covered and how they qualify for benefits), (2) benefits (how much and for how long), and (3) financing (how much employers will be charged as a tax on payrolls).

The actual administrative work implementing the unemployment compensation law in each state is performed by the *state employment security agency*. Most of the states use independent departments of the state government or independent boards or commissions. In some states these agencies are under the state department of labor. Benefit claims are handled in about 2,100 local offices of the employment agencies of the states.

Financing

The basic source of funds for the state unemployment systems is a payroll tax levied on employers.[31] The standard tax rate on employers is 3.2 percent

---

[31] Ibid. Three states, Alabama, Alaska, and New Jersey, also require a small contribution (less than 0.5 percent) from employees.

of the wages up to $6,000 for each worker, of which 0.5 percent goes to the federal government and the remainder (up to 2.7 percent) goes to the state government under the tax-offset plan mentioned earlier. Administrative expenses are apportioned from the federal share by Congress. The actual tax rates vary by state and employer from 0.3 to more than 3.0 percent of the taxable payroll, which may be as high as $10,000 (Alaska).

The most significant variation in the employer's cost in the various states is found in the *experience rating* systems used in most states. Under these plans the tax rate on employers is changed according to the individual experience of each employer. Alternative higher taxes may apply in many states if the reserve funds fall below specified points. The various experience rating plans differ substantially, but most result in the individual employer paying (according to the employer's past unemployment record) rates which vary between perhaps 1 percent and the maximum standard percentage required. Experience rates aim at stabilizing employment, at better cost allocation, and at greater employer interest.

It is the pronounced social, political, and economic effects of unemployment which have necessitated that it be cared for under a social insurance system rather than a private insurance system. In addition to the complexity of defining who really is an "unemployed" person, the sizable funds necessary and the cyclical changes in unemployment are problems of a substantial nature. The many economic effects of the state unemployment compensation systems include countercyclical contributions, benefits adequacy or inadequacy, the impact of unemployment taxes, and interstate competition in unemployment compensation.

For perspective on the importance of unemployment insurance, the economic effects of the taxes collected and the benefits paid out in a given year should be noted. In the 1970s several recession years have resulted in several billion dollars more in payments than in taxes collected, while other years have brought the reverse situation.

WORKERS' COMPENSATION

In an unusual combination of social and private insurance, workers' compensation laws in all the states require[32] employers to provide certain benefits for *occupational* injuries and diseases. In about six states, only those diseases specifically listed in the law are covered. Workers' compensation was the first kind of social insurance to develop widely in the United States, many of the laws being enacted before 1920. Today there are 54 different programs

---

[32] Note that about three states have an "elective" rather than "compulsory" law. However, the loss of common-law liability defenses to the employer usually provides strong encouragement for the employer in the elective states to choose workers' compensation.

in operation in the states and Puerto Rico, as well as three federal employee plans.

The statutory requirement in most states can be fulfilled by the employer purchasing workers' compensation insurance from a private insurer or by qualifying as a "self-insurer." Eighteen jurisdictions have also established workers' compensation state funds for insuring employers, and six of these require that the benefits of the law be insured (unless a qualified "self-insurance" plan for larger employers is maintained) only with such state insurance funds. Self-insurance is permitted in 47 states, if certain size and bond requirements are met.

Further details of workers' compensation insurance and the derivation of state workers' compensation laws from the former system of employers' liability are presented in Chapter 22. The discussion here will be limited to a brief description of the major features of the programs. Several social issues concerning broader eligibility, higher and more uniform benefits, and the proposed federalization of workers' compensation laws are discussed in the final chapter of this book.

Eligibility

Benefits under workers' compensation laws are payable to many but not all workers. From a very restricted list of hazardous occupations 50 years ago, the laws have been extended to apply to most employers. Although not all jobs are covered, nearly 62 million, or four fifths, of the employees do have coverage under workers' compensation, with the following typical exceptions: (1) employees of firms with less than a minimum number of workers, the minimum ranging from 2 to 15; (2) farm workers' (3) domestic servants; (4) casual labor; and (5) employees of nonprofit charitable organizations or religious organizations.

In order to qualify a death, injury, or disease as covered by workers' compensation, the employee or beneficiary must show that it arose *out of and in the course of employment.* In other words, it must be a work-connected loss. Many states exclude losses that are the result of an employee's intoxication, gross negligence, or willful misconduct.

Benefits

Workers' compensation laws provide definite *schedules* of benefits for deaths and disabling injuries or illnesses. The variations among the states are wide, but most statutes require four basic types of benefits: (1) *medical care* costs, (2) *income* payments for disability or death to the worker or the worker's family, (3) *death* benefits, and (4) *rehabilitation* services, providing retraining, education, job guidance and placement, vocational rehabilitation facilities, or other services.

Medical care benefits are quite complete under the laws of most states. Classification of the extent of medical care under the various state laws shows that 46 jurisdictions have no arbitary limits, or unlimited authority to extend the limits, on the duration or the amount of medical benefits payable.[33] The remaining jurisdictions have some arbitrary limits on the extent of medical care provided.

Income benefits under workers' compensation laws are usually based upon the worker's wages at the time of death, injury, or sickness. Weekly payments are made to either workers or their survivors. Some states limit death payments to the widow or children to specific maximums ranging from about $16,000 to $65,000. Disabilities may be either partial or total, and either permanent or temporary. Lifetime payments are available in most states, but some states set a specific maximum duration of payments, such as four to ten years. Both minimum and maximum weekly benefit amounts are also usually set in the laws. To discourage malingering a maximum benefit amount of about two thirds of the normal weekly wage is established. Some laws provide lump-sum benefits in place of income payments for certain disabilities. A waiting period of from two days to one week sometimes applies before weekly benefits begin.

Administration

State governments are the administrators of the workers' compensation laws. In most states, this function is carried out through special *state commissions* appointed for this purpose. These commissions work closely with the employers and their insurers in performing the necessary administrative duties. Oftentimes, the work of the commissions takes on an advisory and quasi-judicial nature. The rules and procedures for filing, reviewing, and investigating claims for benefits are set forth in the laws. Decisions are reached, subject to the approval of the commissions, through various methods of direct settlement, formal agreements, or hearings. The usual criticisms express a desire for prompter or more accurate evaluation of claims, with better court administration. The periodic reappraisal of state systems is recommended.

Financing

The direct responsibility for financing workers' compensation benefits is placed upon the *employer*. Through the purchase of a private insurance contract, through self-insurance, or through insurance in a state fund, the employer must pay for the benefits as provided in the state laws.

The cost of workers' compensation insurance varies widely from state to

[33] This is for accidental injuries; only 45 states have unlimited coverage for occupational disease. See *Analysis of Workers' Compensation Laws* (Washington, D.C.: Chamber of Commerce of the United States, published annually), Comparison Chart III.

state, among the various occupations, and for each individual employer. The liability or restrictiveness of the benefits in the state law is an obvious cost factor. More hazardous occupations may have workers' compensation costs which exceed 20 percent of payroll, whereas clerical occupations with minimum industrial injury and disease perils may have costs of well under 1 percent of payroll. From year to year, the average premium cost approximates 1 to 2 percent of payroll for all occupations combined. Individual employers are given incentive to reduce losses through the many loss-prevention techniques of various experience rating plans, which adjust the insurance costs according to the losses and expenses of each business firm.

One of the issues of concern about workers' compensation is whether the expansion of the disability provisions of the Social Security Act (see earlier section of this chapter) causes unnecessary duplication of some of the income payments for longer term disabilities. Some disabled workers qualify for workers' compensation death benefits, although amendments to the Social Security Act now provide for an offset where total income benefits would exceed 80 percent of a worker's former earnings.

TEMPORARY-DISABILITY (NONOCCUPATIONAL) INSURANCE LAWS

In addition to disability income for occupational injuries or sickness, five states and Puerto Rico have compulsory temporary-disability laws which provide income payments for nonwork-connected disabilities. These states are New York, New Jersey, California, Rhode Island, and Hawaii.

The need for these laws stems from the fact that most state unemployment compensation systems require that the recipient of unemployment benefits be willing *and able* to work. Only a few states permit payments to disabled unemployed workers.

The fact that most states have not adopted such plans since the first four states named above began to do so in 1942–49 is largely explained by the rapid growth of other methods of paying such benefits. Employers have formalized many paid sick-leave plans, and private insurers have written an increased volume of group disability insurance for nonoccupational short-term disability. In total, about two thirds of wage and salary workers in private empolyment have some such protection, either through government or private plans. About one fourth of the private labor force is covered by the six temporary-disability laws.

Eligibility

The coverage of most workers is similar to that found under the usual unemployment compensation system, and a few categories of employment are excluded. The individual worker is required to show that the regular duties of his or her job cannot be performed, due to illness or injury. Certain disabilities, such as pregnancy or intentional self-inflicted injuries, may be excluded. In order to qualify for temporary-disability benefits, the worker must also have had specified minimum earnings for a required time before becoming disabled.

Benefits

The weekly benefit rates have the purpose of replacing one half or more of the wages lost due to disability. The minimum benefits vary from $10 to $25 weekly, and the maximum benefits vary from about $80 to $140.

The duration of benefits is also limited. Payments are made for a maximum of 26 weeks. A waiting period of one week (seven consecutive days) generally applies.

Administration

Four of the six programs administer the temporary-disability laws under the supervision of the state unemployment compensation board, commission, or department. New York uses the workers' compensation board to administer the disability payments, and Hawaii uses its Department of Labor and Industrial Relations.

Rhode Island is the only state which requires that the employer must provide the benefits through an exclusive, or monopolistic, state fund. The other programs permit the employer to choose among private insurers providing a group accident and health insurance contract, a state fund, and a self-insurance plan. The alternatives to a state fund must meet the requirements of the law as to the eligibility of workers for benefits and the amounts and duration of the payments.

Overall the proportion of covered workers insured with private insurers is approximately 50 percent, but the proportion varies from more than 90 percent in New York to less than 10 percent in California, where legislation designed to help prevent insolvency of the state fund has restricted the use of private insurers.

Financing

The *employee* is required to pay all or a portion of the costs of the temporary-disability benefits in each of the six plans. The tax is based on payroll, and it varies from 0.50 percent of wages in New Jersey (up to $4,800) and New York (up to a maximum of $0.30 per week), to 1.0 percent in California and 1.5 percent in Rhode Island.

In four jurisdictions, *employers* also bear part of the costs. In New Jersey, the employer pays 0.5 percent of covered wages (modified by the experience rating), and in New York and Hawaii the employer pays all additional costs of the program beyond the stated employee contribution.

Although many other states have considered temporary-disability bills, only Puerto Rico (1968) and Hawaii (1969) have passed such laws in the past 25 years. It appears that the private insurance business has expanded its efforts for coverage of the nonoccupational disability income peril and has successfully provided the needed coverage in this area of insurance in many states. Temporary disability is thus covered by both social insurance systems in six jurisdictions and as private insurance in the remaining jurisdictions.

SUMMARY OF FOUR MAJOR SOCIAL INSURANCE PROGRAMS

The fundamental characteristics of the four most significant types of social insurance in the United States are summarized in Table 15–2 as to eligibility provisions, benefits, administration, and financing.

Table 15–2. Summary of features of four major social insurance programs

Type of program	Eligibility provisions	Types of benefits	Who administers it?	Who and what finances it?
OASDHI	Covered employment* with certain time and earnings to become insured	Income for retirement, for total and permanent disability, and to survivors; and medical care for aged	Federal government	Earnings tax on employer and employee, and on self-employed persons
Unemployment compensation	Covered employment with specified individual qualification requirements	Temporary income to willing and able unemployed workers	State government	Payroll tax (mostly state) on employer
Workers' compensation	Covered employment and injury or disease arising out of and in the course of employment	Medical care costs, death, disability income, and rehabilitation; for *work* illness or injury	State government	Insurance purchased by employer
Temporary disability benefit laws	Covered employment with specified time and earnings requirements	Temporary income for *nonwork* disability from illness or injury	State government	Payroll tax on employee or on employee-employer

* Covered employment is work to which the laws apply, which varies among these programs.

OTHER SOCIAL INSURANCE PROGRAMS

Although the four social insurance programs that have been discussed in this chapter are the most important and widespread, other social insurance systems have developed some significance. Among these are the railroad retirement and unemployment plans, the government employee retirement plans, and veterans' administration benefit programs.[34]

The Railroad Retirement and Unemployment Acts

For several reasons, including strong early unionization of employees, the railroads established a pension system before the Social Security Act of 1935. Therefore, the railroad industry was excluded from the 1935 act, although later provisions have correlated the two systems by permitting combined credits for survivors' benefits under either OASDHI or the Railroad Retirement Act and by providing Medicare benefits since 1966. Retiring workers can qualify for retirement benefits under both programs if they have been employed long enough under both railroad and other covered employment of OASDHI.

Railroad workers have one of the most extensive social insurance benefit programs in the United States. Retirement benefits are paid at age 65 (or reduced benefits at 62) to workers who have 10 years of railroad service, or at age 60 if they have 30 years of service. The amounts are always higher than OASDHI payments and are calculated on a formula which takes into account both average monthly earnings and years of service. Survivors' benefits to widow and children are payable in lump-sum and monthly payments. Permanent disability payments are payable under liberal definitions after 10–20 years of service. Unemployment and sickness benefits are payable under the separate Railroad Unemployment Insurance Act.

The federal government administers the railroad social insurance program through a separate Railroad Retirement Board. The systems are financed by current taxes (shared equally by employer and employee, for the Retirement Act benefits), which are higher than OASDHI and other state programs of social insurance.

Government employee retirement systems

Federal employees, state employees, and some local government employees have separate social insurance programs which provide retirement, disability, and survivorship benefits.

Almost 4 million federal government employees, excluding members of the armed services, are most often covered under the provisions of the Civil Service Retirement Act. Special programs are used for some groups, such as

---

[34] *Social Security Programs in the U.S.*

foreign service officers and members of Congress. Such federal employees as are not included in these plans are generally included under the OASDHI program.

The Civil Service Commission administers benefits for federal civil service employees who are eligible for (1) retirement and disability annuities (generally much higher than OASDHI benefits in most cases and based on earnings and length of service) and (2) survivorship benefits to widows and children of employees. In contrast to OASDHI, employees who leave government service before retirement, after five years of service, are entitled to withdraw their contributions or to leave them with the program until an annuity is payable at retirement. The system is financed by a combined tax of about 15 percent on the employees' base pay and on the employing federal agency.

The Federal Employees' Group Life Insurance Act in 1954 and the Servicemen's Group Life Insurance Act of 1965 inaugurated group life insurance coverage for federal employees who are covered unless they choose not to be included. In addition, earlier veterans' life insurance programs such as National Service Life Insurance have more than $34 billion of life insurance in force for persons who served in the armed forces. Private insurers underwrite the current coverage in FEGLI and SGLI in very sizable group life insurance contracts. Health insurance benefits are also available to federal employees, with an optional choice among Blue Cross–Blue Shield, a group private insurer plan, and other alternatives. The benefits differ widely. The federal government pays a portion of the costs.

More than one half of the 12 million state and local government employees are covered by retirement systems which provide old-age and disability payments. The plans vary widely, but in general they have increased benefits considerably in recent years. The employee contributions, which most systems require, may be taken by the employee after a minimum number of years of service if the employee retires early or leaves government service. Some of the plans do not include survivors' benefits beyond a return of the worker's contributions, although increasing evidence of the extension of benefits in this area is found in such plans as those for police officers, fire fighters, and others. Most but not all state and local government employees are entitled to OASDHI benefits if the political subdivision has entered into a voluntary agreement with the federal government to have them included.

Veterans' benefit programs

More than 40 different benefits and services[35] are available to veterans of service in the U.S. armed forces. The Veterans Administration administers many of the benefits. These are primarily available to the veteran, but many

---

[35] A summary of these benefits and services is available from the Superintendent of Documents (Washington, D.C.: U.S. Government Printing Office) in a booklet titled *Veterans' Administration Fact Sheet, IS–1.*

of them are also paid or available to survivors or members of the veteran's family. A partial list includes: (1) compensation for service-connected deaths or disabilities, (2) pensions for non-service-connected deaths or disabilities, (3) benefits payable under U.S. Government Life Insurance or National Service Life Insurance, (4) veterans' burial expense payments, and (5) medical services of many kinds through Veterans Administration hospitals. Supplemental and special payments to those payable under the Social Security Act are made to widows of veterans who died of service-connected causes.

Some examples of veterans' benefits administered by other agencies are: (1) retirement pay from the individual branches of the armed services, (2) social security (OASDHI) wage credits for earnings while in the service, (3) burial space in national cemeteries, (4) farm and home loan benefits, (5) special unemployment benefits, (6) educational readjustment assistance, and (7) reemployment rights under the U.S. Department of Labor, the Civil Service Commission, and state employment offices. In all, the veterans' benefit programs entail a broad and important range of benefits and services for a large segment of the population.

The future

The future of these social insurance programs is apparently well established. It would be hard to conceive of abandonment of any of the major social insurance programs that have been discussed. The typical trend seems to be in the direction of expanding existing programs. Each has developed by increasing its coverage and the application of its requirements to new and wider groups of persons. Benefits have rarely been reduced but often extended as to kind, amount, and duration. The ultimate development in this area, as in all social insurance programs, will be determined by legislation governed by economic, social, and political considerations.

PROPOSED NATIONAL HEALTH INSURANCE PLANS

One of the favorite subjects of high school and college debates in the United States for more than a decade has been the topic of *national health insurance*. Based on the general philosophy that everyone should have access to high-quality medical care, most advanced nations except for the United States have adopted some form of universal compulsory health insurance. However, most United States citizens remain skeptical about such programs, including the National Health Service, which has been in effect for Great Britain since 1946, and the Canadian provincial plans of the 1960s, which became a complete national program in 1971.[36]

The proposals advanced in the United States have been frequent and

---

[36] Selected foreign plans are reviewed in U.S. House Committee on Ways and Means, *National Health Insurance Resources Book* (Washington, D.C.: U.S. Government Printing Office, August 1976).

varied, sometimes including as many as 20 bills within a period of a few years. Before several of the current proposals are examined, an evaluation of the need for a national health insurance plan and of the objectives of such a plan is in order.

The need

The usual rationale for a system of national health insurance for the entire United States population begins with analysis of the need. Most of the public opinion in this regard centers on the concern of most consumers with the high costs of medical care. This concern is to be expected in an era which has seen these costs more than double in ten years, even though the prices of cars, housing, and groceries have also had increases of nearly similar proportions.

One difference between medical care costs and such other costs is that medical care costs are not as evenly distributed among individuals and families on a year-to-year basis as are expenses which affect everyone. Although the average costs of medical care per person now exceed $550, the more than $150 billion spent for this purpose falls much more heavily on those who need medical care in any given year as opposed to the many who do not. The overall burden increased sharply, from about $90 billion in 1972 to more than $150 billion in 1978. The health care expenditures in the United States exceed those of any other nation in the world.

Private health insurance has helped spread the losses among many—and more than 90 percent of Americans have some health insurance, and about three fourths have some protection against catastrophic health losses. Critics emphasize the negative aspects of these figures, pointing out that 10 percent have no health insurance and that one fourth lack major medical coverage. Some people, of course, have physical deficiencies or lack the financial ability or the desire to purchase needed health insurance. Yet the proportion of persons protected by the private health insurance system in the United States is higher than the proportion protected by voluntary insurance anywhere else.

Nevertheless, a gap exists between the generally accepted idea that everyone should have access to quality medical care regardless of personal circumstances, and the present extensive (but not complete) coverage of voluntary health insurance to help meet this need.

The objectives

In addition to the general need for and "right" to medical care, the rationale for national health insurance seems to rest either on the appraisal of the present voluntary insurance system as inadequate or on the expectation that a compulsory system would be better.[37] The inadequacies stressed are

[37] Rejda stresses (1) the basic right, (2) the reform of present systems, (3) the inferior medical care for the poor, and (4) the need for greater redistribution of income. See chap. 11 in *Social Insurance and Economic Security*.

the previously mentioned incomplete coverage and such others as ineffi-
ciencies of marketing and lack of cost control. Many of the criticisms emphasize the inadequacies of the *health care system,* rather than merely the
faults of paying for health care services through *insurance.*[38] Regardless, the
quest for improvement is present in our current economy of high health care
costs.

The use of national health insurance to improve the delivery of medical
care services is the underlying objective. If this is to be used as the means
for accomplishing certain goals, the first step is agreement upon the suggested criteria under which such a system should be evaluated.[39] These include: (1) consumer participation and control; (2) universal eligibility for
all (without age, residence, race, income, physical, or other limitations); (3)
comprehensive and continuous medical services, both preventive and cura-
tive; (4) accessible and available services to all; (5) no cost barriers to
needed services; (6) quality controls to assure the best possible care, without
waste of funds; and (7) research, for new methods and review of the system.
Ideal goals such as these are not easy to put into practice, for many of the
subcriteria needed to implement specific parts of a broad plan meeting these
objectives are subject to much debate.

The proposals

The United States already has a partial system of national health insurance
in operation—the Medicare-Medicaid plans which cover a substantial portion
of the medical expenses of the elderly and some disabled persons (see Chapter 14). In effect, any of the current proposals for NHI would replace or
extend these plans on at least a partially mandatory basis to all citizens of the
United States.

The differences among the proposed plans, however, are significant. Some
provide for a very broad system of comprehensive "cradle-to-grave" medical
services, whereas others would institute only an insurance plan for meeting
catastrophic health losses. Some plans would give a predominant place to
existing private insurance, whereas others would substitute a completely mandatory program administered entirely by the federal government. The costs
in some plans would be borne entirely by taxpayers, whereas other plans
would distribute the costs among employers, employees, and taxpayers.

Three proposals of 1978 deserve special attention, although a fourth likely
contender will be the as yet unformulated plan to be proposed in 1979 by the
Carter administration, which is unlikely to be exactly the same as any of the

---

[38] Morrison H. Beach, "The National Health Care Issue: It's More than Financing
Treatment," *Protection,* September 1977, p. 6.

[39] Robert D. Eilers and Sue S. Moyerman, *National Health Insurance: Conference
Proceedings* (Homewood, Ill.: Richard D. Irwin, 1971), chap. 1.

other three. Any NHI bill which may be posed by Congress will probably involve substantial compromises among all of the major alternatives.

The Burleson-McIntyre National Health Act. If NHI is inevitable, as many feel, this bill is the choice of the private health insurance business. It would maintain free enterprise and the competitive health insurance field by financing the costs of a minimum level of comprehensive benefits (including catastrophic losses). Insureds would pay only an initial deductible of about $100 per family, and 20 percent of medical care costs up to a maximum of $1,000. Employers and employees would pay premiums for basic coverages; other individuals could purchase voluntary coverages; and premiums for all of these coverages would be tax deductible. The poor and near poor would be supported from general tax revenues, and Medicaid would be phased out. State pools of private insurers would provide benefits to all persons whose physical impairments make them generally uninsurable. The estimated additional cost would be at least $10 billion a year, but there are special provisions for reducing health care costs through increased ambulatory services and health care facilities planning.

The Kennedy-Corman Health Security Act. The broadest plan advocated, this bill would eliminate private health insurance and substitute a nationalized system of health insurance administered entirely by the federal government. Basically a "Let (Uncle) Sam do it" approach, the bill would be financed through an increased social security tax on employers, employees, and the self-employed, and about one half of the costs would be paid by general tax revenues. The coverage would be very extensive, including almost all medical care costs without limitations or deductibles. Health personnel and facilities would come under strict government regulation to promote better distribution and cost controls. Medicare and Medicaid programs would be absorbed in the new system. This plan would cost more than any of the other proposed plans, probably two or three times as much as the Burleson-McIntyre plan. Organized labor has supported this type of NHI.

The Long-Ribicoff Catastrophic Health Insurance Act. This third approach to NHI concentrates only on catastrophic medical losses. The plan is the least comprehensive in terms of benefits, and it would cost less to institute in the United States than any of the others. Everyone would be covered for hospital expenses after 60 days' confinement in a year, and for 80 percent of other medical expenses above a $2,000 deductible. Payroll taxes under social security would finance much of the costs, but general revenue taxes would pay for a Medical Assistance Plan for the poor, and others could purchase their own policies under a voluntary certification program meeting federal standards for basic health insurance benefits. Inadequate coverage is the basic objection that many have to this plan.

Other NHI proposals. In recent years many other plans have been proposed, but these have not gained much support beyond that of the group or groups making the proposal. The American Medical Association (AMA) has supported a Medicredit plan of tax deduction for most voluntary purchases of health insurance. The National Association of Insurance Commissioners has passed a model bill for adoption by each state, including comprehensive (basic and catastrophic) benefits and a pool of insurers to provide health insurance for persons who are normally uninsurable. A bill proposed by Senator Jacob Javits would fundamentally extend Medicare to the whole population. Many other NHI plans have been proposed.

One of the basic considerations today is the economic effect of increasing government costs during a period when inflation could be escalated or a recession triggered by the considerable expenses of most NHI plans. The political ramifications are readily apparent, too, and will undoubtedly play a large part in whether, when, or in what form national health insurance is legislated.

FOR REVIEW AND DISCUSSION

1. Social and private (voluntary) insurance in the United States have both grown rapidly in the past 40 years. How has the *purpose* of each of these major areas of insurance affected its growth pattern? How are social and private insurance alike? How are they different?

2. The government plays several roles in regard to insurance. Identify and illustrate each of these roles. *Why* have the government roles in regard to insurance increased, and which branches of government have taken the leadership in this expansion?

3. Paul Samuelson has said that "social security is, by all odds, the most successful program of the modern welfare state." Why do you think he said that? Do you agree or disagree, and why?

4. What specific criticisms are aimed at social insurance, and how do you evaluate the justification for each? (Discuss at least three.)

5. How do the objective and method of "social insurance" differ from those of "public assistance"? Give several examples. How does the Social Security Act of 1935 relate to these two terms?

6. Rapidly rising OASDHI taxes during the late 1970s are an issue of great economic and political concern. Discuss the needs and effects of these increases.

7. If more than nine out of ten workers are now covered by the OASDHI program, why shouldn't or can't everyone be included in this compulsory law?

8. What is the distinction between "fully," "currently," and "disability" insured status under the OASDHI program? What difference does it make?

9. What is the basis for determining the size of the OASDHI benefits payable? What other factors are considered, and how do these help carry out the social objectives of the program?

10. What disability benefits are included in OASDHI? What new benefits did Medicare add?

11. *Explain* the following comments about the OASDHI program:
    a. It is a pay-as-you-go plan, with a contingency trust fund.
    b. It is, basically, a social and economic program which results in a significant shift in income among different generations.
    c. It is a current recipient "bargain."
    d. It now includes four basic perils, but originally only covered one.
    e. Relatively, low-income groups receive higher benefit amounts; but they also pay more, relatively, in taxes.

12. The economist Milton Friedman has said that "OASDHI is a very good buy for people in the older age group, and a very lousy buy for people in lower age groups." Why do you agree or disagree?

13. Briefly explain two common misconceptions about the OASDHI program, pointing out why they exist and why they are fallacious.

14. Compare and contrast unemployment compensation and workers' compensation as to (*a*) eligibility, (*b*) benefits, and (*c*) administration.

15. A state enacts an unemployment insurance law that is best suited to its individual needs. What is the necessity for minimum federal standards?

16. Who pays for (*a*) OASDHI, (*b*) unemployment compensation, (*c*) workers' compensation, and (*d*) temporary-disability (nonoccupational) benefits?

17. Medicare has been a popular addition to the social security program. In what ways is it (*a*) consistent and (*b*) inconsistent with the purposes and methods of the other parts of the OASDHI program? How does Medicaid differ from Medicare?

18. What is the relationship among the goals of the OASDHI system, *group* life and health insurance provided by employers, and *individual* life and health insurance contracts? Diagram this relationship.

19. Divide the class into three "buzz groups." After 20 minutes, have a spokesperson for the first group evaluate the need for a national health insurance plan, a spokesperson for the second present the objectives of NHI, and a spokesperson for the third describe the proposal that the group would recommend for adoption by Congress.

Chapter 16

Concepts considered in Chapter 16—Coordinating life and health insurance

Coordinating life and health insurance is the essential element in planning for buying these types of insurance.

Life and health risk management involves avoidance, loss-prevention, insurance, and programming techniques of *money* management.

Personal life and health insurance planning is a significant part of individual or family financial planning and budgeting.

Personal life insurance programming involves analysis of:

The needs for lump-sum and income requirements and wants.

The method of fact-finding about all assets and income sources.

Integration with social security benefits in a diagram of goals and income needs met by *group* and *individual* life insurance.

A case study example of family life insurance needs and cost shows the process of estimating needs and providing means for achieving family goals for capital and income.

Personal health insurance programming uses a similar technique to plan for future medical expense and disability income losses.

A case study example of family health insurance needs and costs illustrates the significance of group insurance and OASDHI benefits.

Personal estate planning combines the *creation* and *liquidation* of assets in a beneficial plan.

Estate impairment results from substantial (30 percent or more) estate shrinkage from estate transfer costs, taxes, and other factors.

The estate planning process involves detailed fact-finding, and legal procedures to obtain maximum benefits at minimum costs.

The will is an essential key to achieving desired estate objectives.

The marital deduction, permitting one half of the estate to go to the spouse, and reducing the taxable estate, is an important benefit of estate planning.

The estate is often larger than expected.

The unified gift and estate tax is an important result of the Federal Tax Reform Act of 1976.

Trusts are one method for coordinating estates and minimizing taxes.

The estate planning team uses four types of professional persons.

Business life and health insurance planning requires facts, analysis, and the choice of useful tools, such as:

Buy-and-sell agreements, funded by insurance, and

Key person life and health insurance, for important employees.

Coordinating life and health insurance

Insurance is *money,* and for insurance to be useful the money must be provided in the right amounts at the right times. Budgeting for spending and saving can help, but for large or unexpected losses due to death, old age, and poor health the logic of life and health insurance is clearly apparent. How does a person, family, or business plan to meet these unusual needs for money? The answer to that question is the focus of this final chapter of Part III on coordinating life and health insurance.

LIFE AND HEALTH RISK MANAGEMENT

It is far easier to talk about one need or a single type of contract than it is to discuss a whole plan. *Risk management* does involve, necessarily, a good plan. In the early chapters, the technique is emphasized as one of *coordinated* risk analysis and treatment. The objective is to take care of risk in the best possible way, and much of that objective, except for some psychological and sociological effects, may be reduced to taking care of economic or *financial* needs. Money becomes the means to this end.

Insurance is an important part of most life and health risk-management plans. These plans should also be coordinated, both with each other and with the other methods for treating risk. For example, social security benefits should be considered in connection with group and individual life and health insurance programs. Also, the use of insurance should often be seen as an action to supplement *loss prevention* or purposeful *risk retention.* Annual medical checkups and good health habits are a fundamental step in maintaining a family's health condition. Losses that are frequent, small, and regular in their occurrence should be intentionally retained as part of health risk management. Proper family financial planning should coordinate retention, avoidance, savings, and insurance to meet the goals of treating life and health risks.

Persons or businesses as consumers have choices in selecting the various insurance markets and alternatives for treating life and health risks. The buying phase is often preceded by or combined with the planning of insurance purchases. Good planning is an essential step in good insurance buying and, in the broader sense, risk management, for both personal and business situations. In life and health insurance, the technique of good planning is called *programming;* in all other lines of insurance, the process is usually referred to as a *risk and insurance survey,* as treated in Chapter 3.

PERSONAL LIFE AND HEALTH INSURANCE PLANNING

Life and health insurance planning may serve (*a*) the individual and the family or (*b*) a business establishment. The first category is "personal insurance," and the second is "business insurance," which protects business organizations or associates against losses occasioned by the death or disability of members of the firm or key employees. This is a term applied to a specialized use for regular life and health insurance facilities—it is not a special form of policy developed for business purposes. Business life and health insurance will be discussed in a later section of this chapter.

Personal life insurance programming

Life insurance programming[1] for the individual or the family consists of a study of the need for capital resources and income. The study includes: (*a*) present and future needs and obligations, and (*b*) present and future resources, including life insurance, arranged to meet the needs and obligations at the least possible cost.

When life insurance programming made its appearance, many felt that it was primarily for persons of substantial means. For those who inherit or acquire great wealth, the problems of taxation, as well as the liquidation of assets for distribution, indicate life insurance as a means for conserving values. However, experience has shown that the individual of modest means, and more particularly the wage earner with dependents, also needs to make plans for the future and to integrate those plans with life insurance protection. One could argue, in fact, that proper planning is even *more* essential for modest estates, because these can least afford to be wasteful in the use of their limited assets. The principal item in many estates is life insurance. Many would die without resources, or even go bankrupt, but for the life estate created immediately with the purchase of life insurance.

The needs.   For any given family, needs may be divided into (*a*) necessities and (*b*) amenities. Through a conference or a series of conferences, the life insurance agent develops an outline of all the needs of the individual or family. The initial step in programming is to establish a priority of needs that must be met to satisfy minimum requirements. The necessities for living, food, shelter, and clothing, of course, come first; the amenities or luxuries next.

For necessities, the logical priority is: (*a*) last expenses; (*b*) emergency

---

[1] Life insurance programming may also include the broader aspects of estate programming, which includes consideration of all assets available to the estate. Cash, investments, and other valuable rights are coordinated with life insurance proceeds. Also to be considered are the problems of recommending legal advice for the drawing of appropriate wills and for establishing trusts to carry out estate objectives. See later section of this chapter on personal estate planning.

funds; (c) dependency income during the family-raising period; (d) life income for surviving spouse; and (e) mortgage payment. Next in the order of priority come: (f) educational funds; (g) special funds, such as charitable bequests, or for a dowry, or to set up a child in business; and (h) retirement income if the husband or wife live to retirement age. If the estate is large and resources are available, consideration may next be given to such items as life income for children, postgraduate work in college, and other special bequests or gifts.

The method. Two steps must be taken before recommending any program: (1) gathering all necessary factual data and (2) analyzing the data as they apply to the applicant's estate objectives. Information required will include: (a) the names and the relationship of all who are to benefit from the estate, (b) all the assets and inheritances of beneficiaries from other sources, (c) property held jointly, (d) life insurance protection, (e) all pertinent information touching upon business interests and plans, and (f) the amount and nature of all debts or other obligations. In short, the intelligent program requires a complete picture of all the personal and business resources of the person whose estate is being planned.

The trained insurance agent will require complete information on: the sex and age of the individual; his or her health; the age, sex, and number of dependents; personal and present wealth; loan or tax obligations; the applicant's and spouse's income; present insurance owned; and assets other than life insurance. Requiring special consideration will be such items as social security benefits, group insurance with employer, veteran's benefits, and retirement pensions. With insurance programming the problem is largely one of dovetailing any present insurance into the needs of the insured and supplementing where additional protection is needed.

After the data have been assembled and carefully analyzed, the prospect is then invited to estimate the minimum family *needs* if death should occur immediately. When the needs have been established, it is essential to determine the amount of *capital and income* required to accomplish the objective, and the *methods* for providing the amount at the time it is needed. The problem then resolves itself into (a) whether the needs indicated are feasible; (b) to what extent existing resources will supply the necessary capital to satisfy the requirements; (c) additional insurance required, if any; and (d) the most effective manner of distributing existing and new insurance between cash payments and income.

Many insurers today are using computers to simplify this process for many standard situations. "Electronic life insurance programming" can oftentimes be accomplished in less than an hour by the agent in the first interview. Immediate estimates of the life insurance amounts needed to meet selected family goals are obtainable on brief one-page forms, which the agent completes by telephoning a centralized computer hookup[2] to get the information

----

[2] An example of such computer service used by many insurers is Keypact, by Compu-tone of Atlanta, Georgia.

required. The computer answers, of course, are only valuable if the assumptions on which the calculations are based have been carefully made.

Assets other than life insurance are studied to determine (*a*) their money value and (*b*) the monthly income that these assets will produce. Mutual funds, stocks, savings, and assets of every sort are integrated into the program. An individual without capital has no assurance that he or she will live to accumulate investments to provide an income for minimum requirements. This being the case, life insurance, particularly where means are limited, forms the basis of the estate program. Investments and other resources may be utilized to build from the foundation established by the life insurance program.

Insurance policies are studied with a view to determining the maximum policy-paying power. Using the various settlement options to the maximum advantage may increase the potential paying power of the insurance as much as 50 percent. The summation value of periodic payments represents a substantial increase over the total face value of the insurance. Since *income* is one of the major requirements of any program, it is important to determine the paying power of the available insurance rather than simply list the face amount of the various policies. After the social security, pension and veterans' income have been utilized to their maximum effectiveness, it becomes necessary to determine the amount of new insurance essential to meet the objectives established in the statement of minimum needs. The living values of life insurance contracts, that is, the retirement benefits, may be taken partly in cash, partly in paid-up insurance, and partly in income if desired.

Integration with social security benefits. The original Social Security Act in 1935 provided old-age insurance for wage earners only; but the 1939 amendment extended old-age insurance to include survivorship benefits to the wage earner's family. In 1956 disability income benefits for total and permanent disability were added, and in 1966 the Medicare-Medicaid benefits began. Thus, social security benefits are of four types: (*a*) retirement benefits to elderly covered workers and their families, (*b*) death benefits to survivors of deceased covered workers, (*c*) disability income benefits, and (*d*) medical expense benefits.

It is essential that the full impact of these benefits receive consideration in the life and health insurance program as part of the planned estate. The process of integrating life insurance with other assets and sources of income is apparent, too, but the universality and size of OASDHI benefits is such that special attention is justified here. More than nine out of ten persons in the working population are now included. The substantial size of the benefits, often equivalent to more than $200,000 of life insurance and over $100,000 of retirement benefits for some families, is indicated in further detail in Chapter 15 on government life and health insurance and in Figure 16–1.

Figure 16–1 shows the substantial contribution of OASDHI benefits to the needs of a family. The diagram illustrates the income which the family (based on assumptions of age, income, and property owned, as shown) would receive from OASDHI if the husband died at the widow's age 25. Benefits would be $1,000 a month[3] for the widow until her son reached age 18. No further OASDHI benefits would be recieved until her age 60[4], when $400 per month becomes payable.

A similar procedure is just as useful for single persons, or for women instead of families. Lump-sum and income goals, and OASDHI benefits, of course, will be much different and generally less complicated. Income for dependent parents may be considered, as for dependent children in the family example. Given the possibility of future marriage and children, understanding the goals and methods of planning for the family life insurance needs and costs is important for all young persons.

A case study example of family life insurance needs and costs

As an illustration of how life insurance is used to help meet the needs of a typical family, Table 16–1 and Figure 16–1 show the procedure which might be followed in estimating gross needs, subtracting OASDHI and other benefits, and arriving at net capital and income needs. Five individual life insurance policies are used to provide for the net needs calculated in this example.

The total insurance recommended is $207,000, of which $10,000 for last expenses and $80,000 for retirement are ordinary life insurance to meet permanent needs and the balance is various types of term insurance to meet temporary needs. The total cost of the suggested program is $1,790 a year, or about 10 percent of the husband's assumed annual income of $18,000. Note that this program includes more ordinary life insurance than would be necessary to accomplish the same benefits with term insurance if the husband dies at an early age. The cash values of the ordinary life contracts would be available at retirement age even if early death did not occur, so this program will help accomplish substantial retirement objectives as well as survivorship protection objectives.

In the earlier years, such a program could be assured for the family (regardless of the husband's health) by purchasing part of the ordinary life insurance amount as term insurance, and planning to convert portions of the coverage during the first 15 years. Term insurance for this period would cost only about one third of the indicated costs for permanent insurance ($5 ver-

---

[3] Technically, income might be $1,116 for $1,400 monthly income or more but the $1,000 is based on an assumed average monthly earnings (AME) under social security of $1,200. Few qualify for the higher maximums because the taxable wage base (for lifetime) has been much smaller in the past. It is more realistic to assume a little less than the maximum, as has been done in the example given.

[4] Age 60 is the earliest age at which benefits can be received for widow's (unless disabled) retirement. Maximum amounts are 100 percent of the husband's PIA; reduced benefits at age 60 are 71.5 percent of this amount.

Table 16–1. Family life insurance program*

	Needs		
	Lump sum		
	Last expenses *Permanent*	*Mortgage repayment (declining balance)* *Ages 25–44*	*Education (for 2 children)* *At age 40*
I. Estimated gross needs (based on immediate death of husband)	$10,000 (funeral, taxes, pay off loans, etc.)	$40,000 (could be repaid but would not have to be)	$30,000 ($15,000 each as basic projected need)
II. OASDHI, group life, part-time work, and wife's private pension	$255 (maximum OASDHI death payment— omitted in other figures because so small)	—	—
III. Net needs (I less II)	$10,000	$40,000	$27,000
IV. How individual life insurance might meet these needs	$10,000 Ordinary Life Insurance Contract	$40,000 Decreasing Term Contract	$27,000 Group Life Insurance Contract, at 1½ times annual salary, would be nearly enough for this purpose.
Earnings (interest) from policies, if death occurs before age 60	—	—	—
V. Approximate annual costs of contracts‡	$150 ($15 per $1,000)	$200 ($5 per $1,000)	Assume employer pays this cost
VI. Life insurance contracts	Policy A	Policy B	Policy C (certificate)

* The following assumptions are the basis for this table.

      Family ages: Husband (28); wife (25); one child (3).

      Income: $18,000/year or $1,500/month.

      Property: $50,000 home, with $40,000 20-year mortgage; $1,000 cash savings, $4,000 stocks and mutual funds (hold this $5,000 for emergency needs); two cars valued at $8,000, with $4,000 bank loan outstanding.

      Employment: Husband, business management junior executive.
      Wife was secretary, could go back to work part-time after children are 18.

      OASDHI benefits: Although slightly higher maximum benefits might be available, for AME of $1,400 a month or more, the estimates here are based on the benefits shown for $1,200 a month in Chapter 15's Table 15–1.

sus $13 per $1,000), but the contracts, if converted to ordinary life insurance, would be at the attained age of the husband. At age 35 they would cost about

	Needs		
	Income		
Family dependency period (for 15 years) Ages 25–39	Widow support period (for 20 years) Ages 40–59	Widow retirement period (for 20 years) Ages 60–80	Total
$270,000 (full salary, or $18,000 a year, or $1,500 a month)	$288,000 (80 percent of salary, or $14,400 a year, or $1,200 a month)	$240,000 (two-thirds of salary, or $12,000 a year, or $1,000 a month)	$878,000 (total gross needs)
$180,000 (OASDHI— $12,000 a year, or $1,000 a month)	$144,000 (no OASDHI during this "blackout" period; this income is from wife's part-time work)	$144,000 (OASDHI— $4,800 a year, or $400 a month; wife's pension— $2,400 a year, or $200 a month)	
$90,000 ($500 a month)	$144,000 ($600 a month)	$96,000 ($400 a month)	$407,000 (total net needs)
No more insurance needed here	$50,000† Level Term to Age 60 Contract	$80,000† Ordinary Life Insurance Contract	$207,000 (total Life Insurance Contracts)
From Policy E and Pol. D ($130,000 × .05 = $6,500 a year or $540 a month)	From Policy E ($80,000 × .05 = $4,000 a year, or $330 a month)		
	$400 ($8 per $1,000)	$1,040 ($13 per $1,000)	$1,790
	Policy D	Policy E	

† Policy E—at $5.00 per month *for life* at age 60, per $1,000, $80,000 will provide needed $400 a month income.

Policy D—at $5.40 per month *for 20 years* at age 40, per $1,000, $50,000 will provide needed $270 a month income (other $330 a month comes from Policy E face value held at interest of 5 percent until age 60, if death occurs at ages 40–59).

‡ The costs for all of these contracts may vary considerably according to the particular insurers and the contract features chosen. Participating contracts would be about 15 percent higher than the costs shown, and some nonparticipating quotations could be lower.

$20 per $1,000, or at age 40 about $24 per $1,000. A "guaranteed purchase option" could also be used to assure the purchase of ordinary life insurance equal in amount to the base policy (at standard rates without a medical examination) at five or six stated ages between 25 and 40. The cost of this

Figure 16-1. Family life insurance program

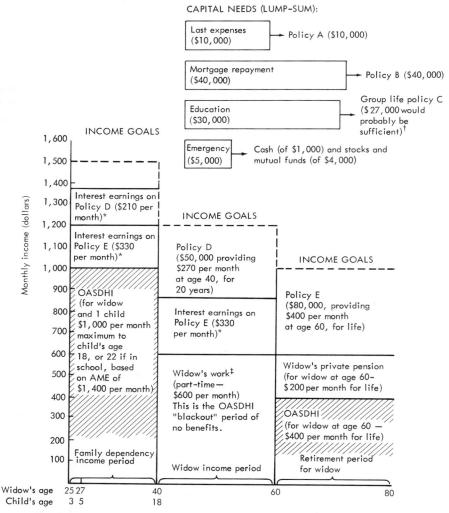

Dotted line shows income goals or objectives; shaded section shows social security (OASDHI) benefits, rounded to nearest $100.

* Interest earnings of about 5 percent, or $4.16 per month, for each $1,000 of proceeds would be available under a participating interest option, for the face values payable at the death of the husband by held until later years in the program.

† With interest earnings on $30,000, for death of the husband during wife's age 25–40.

‡ Under present "excess earnings" test, could disqualify wife for OASDHI benefits if more than about $3,240 a year was earned before *age 40,* which is one of the reasons that work prior to that time is not assumed in this example.

feature is very low, about $2 per $1,000, so most persons can guarantee at an early age the eventual purchase of adequate amounts of life insurance for their families. Flexibility in meeting the changing needs of young families is aided by these options.

The life insurance program must be fitted to the particular family goals chosen. Considerably more insurance would be needed if the income *goals* after age 40 were raised. In the example, 100 percent of normal income is assumed as the goal during the family dependency period, when help for the widow would be most necessary. About 80 percent of the normal family income is assumed as the goal for the widow period after the child or children are age 18 and two thirds of normal income for the retirement period. Not all families would make these choices, and the results of the indicated needs could increase considerably if higher goals were selected. Each $100 per month of income desired at age 40 for life, for example, requires over $25,000 more of life insurance in order to provide a settlement option with 20 years of guaranteed payments.

Note that the possibility of the widow *remarrying* is not assumed in the example. This is a personal choice. At a young age, particularly without several children, the widow's remarriage is a realistic assumption. After age 30 or 35, given the financial burdens of raising children, her remarriage is unlikely. Regardless, it is desirable not to leave the widow in the position of feeling an *obligation* to remarry in order to help the financial position of the family. Also, consideration must be given to the *loss* of all or part of the OASDHI mother's benefit if she remarries.

Work by the widow is also subject to much variation in the usual family situation. Many husbands would prefer not to force the widow to seek employment during the family dependency period or at least until the children are well along in school. She would also lose the OASDHI mother's benefit if she earned more than about $3,240 a year during this period. The outright assumption that the widow will take on full-time work during or after that period is oftentimes unrealistic. Her employability then depends on several factors: her work career experience, her educational background, job availability, the retraining or reeducation necessary (probably essential if she seeks work at age 40, after no work experience or after not working for 10–15 years), and her health (what if she is disabled?). The example takes a compromise position, assuming only part-time work with relatively minimal income of $600 a month during the ages 40–60.

Group life insurance, usually available in amounts of about 1½ to 2 times annual salary or $27,000 in the illustration, is suggested for use in meeting educational needs of the children, *if* the father dies prior to the wife's age 40. The father's death would be a serious financial blow to the continuation of education for the children. If the father is still living at age 40, other alternatives may help take care of college education costs: normal salary increases by middle age; the use of cash or loan values of the permanent life insurance contracts; other savings or investments; part-time work by the children or wife; or educational loans secured through federal grants or through using the life insurance as collateral for other personal loans. Although most employed persons will have some group life insurance in effect, particularly at the younger, more employable ages, consideration should be given to the fact that this protection is not the same as having individual life insurance contracts. The employer may stop the plan, or the employee may be fired or change jobs and lose the benefits of group life insurance, which is usually yearly renewable term protection only.

Particularly important in the illustration is the use of *interest earnings* on contract amounts payable because of the early death of the husband before retirement. The earnings shown are minimums partially guaranteed under the settlement option leaving the proceeds at interest. Additional interest is often paid if the settlement option is participating. Thus the relatively conservative total assumption of 5 percent is used in the example. Higher returns could probably be secured by taking the lump-sum face value and reinvesting it in bonds, stocks, or other media. However, note that the interest earnings estimated in the explanation at the bottom of Figure 16–1 are still several hundred dollars per month for each of Policies D and E. If the death of the husband does not occur before retirement, these amounts would not be available, nor would they be needed to meet the goals outlined.

The *retirement* assumptions of the illustration consider only the *widow's* situation. Further assumptions could be incorporated into the example to consider the position of the husband and wife, if both are living after age 65. Social security benefits would be about $600 a month (with an assumed AME of $1,200) for the husband, and about $300 a month for the wife, or a total of $900 a month. In addition, the husband may have a retirement income of several hundred dollars a month available from his own private pension. The cash values of the suggested $80,000 of permanent whole life insurance could also be used, if necessary, to supplement retirement income. At age 65, cash values of about $790 per $1,000 of life insurance would be available, or a total of over $63,000. Under a joint and survivor benefit settlement option, about $5.10 per $1,000, or approximately $320 per month, would be payable.

A warning is appropriate in regard to the *changing* needs of the typical family in regard to its life insurance program. Additional children, divorce, changing income, death or disability, job stability, increasing social security benefits, inflation trends, and many other factors should each be reconsidered in a regular and *frequent review* (perhaps even annually on a specific date) of the life insurance program. The goal, too, should encompass a full evaluation of life insurance in coordination with other financial resources, such as investments. Otherwise, the anticipated benefits are unlikely to meet actual needs. The life insurance estate, as the foundation[5] of the family's

---

[5] Life insurance accounts for almost 70 percent of *all* lump-sum payments to widows from *all* sources! Loran Powell and Paul W. Thayer, *The Widow's Study* (Hartford, Conn.: Life Insurance Agency Management Association, 1970).

economic position at the death of the breadwinner(s), is an essential part of any sound financial planning.

The place of the total insurance costs in the *family budget* should be considered. The above example might include the following approximate breakdown of family financial goals:

		Percent of total income of $18,000
1.	Housing	25
2.	Food	20
3.	Clothing, entertainment, and miscellaneous	12
4.	Insurance (life and health)	11
5.	Automobile and transportation	12
6.	Taxes (including OASDHI)	15
7.	Savings	5
		100

Personal health insurance programming

The same technique of planning as used in life estate programming is useful for choosing health insurance coverages. In fact, it is becoming more and more recognized by life and health agents and brokers that both life and health insurance plans must be integrated for successful long-range protection for the policyholder or the family. Social insurance, particularly Medicare and disability income under OASDHI, serve as a foundation but are only part of the total needs of a good health insurance program.

Unless proper health insurance is purchased, the life insurance program is threatened by inability to carry out estate objectives. Without adequate health insurance, a serious injury or illness may cause (1) extra expenses (or a drain on assets) for medical treatment or (2) loss of income which may prevent the policyholder from keeping life insurance in force.

Medical care coverages should have the following priority: (1) provision for hospital bills, (2) provision for surgical fees, (3) provision for medical care not requiring surgery, (4) provision for X-ray fees and the like, and (5) provision for ordinary home and office medical care. Where the amount available for premiums is limited, as it almost always is, some such ranking of importance to the buyer of various health insurance coverages is essential. For middle- or upper-income families, the major or catastrophe medical expenses may assume a priority position, with smaller normal losses of up to a few thousand dollars being taken care of out of savings or other assets.

The most important income losses to be provided for are those of total and permanent disability of the family's "breadwinners." Partial income losses, and temporary loss of income up to about a year, are considered of lesser importance.

Equally significant for most policyholders is *major* medical coverage on a "blanket" medical care basis. Many insureds, if they have other assets with which to take care of relatively normal medical costs (up to several hundred dollars, perhaps), may need a major medical contract more than they do a hospital-surgical policy for the more frequent kinds of losses. Medical expenses of several thousand dollars can be a crippling blow to most family budgets, and these catastropic types of health losses should be insured.

One example of the need for coordinating life and health insurance programs is seen in the provision in estate plans for "last expenses." Sometimes these expenses include, in addition to taxes and funeral and cemetery costs, the costs of prolonged and expensive medical care preceding death. If these costs are covered by a permanent life insurance contract, it is unnecessary to duplicate the coverage in health insurance planning, and vice versa.

The loss of income due to injury or illness is a major area of need for coordination between life and health insurance. Part of the loss-of-income problem can be alleviated by waiver-of-premium or disability income "riders" (see Chapter 11) to life insurance contracts. However, it must be remembered that these features are optional and not included in all such contracts. Also very important is the fact that they provide benefits only for *total and permanent* (normally, over six months) disability and not for partial or temporary inability to earn an income due to injury or sickness. There remains a pronounced but oftentimes neglected need for more complete protection against loss of income by having an "accident and health" policy (see Chapter 13) for permanent-partial or temporary-total disabilities. These income benefits should be related to the normal earnings of the insured (perhaps between 50 and 75 percent) rather than to the amount of life insurance in force, as the disability income in life insurance riders must be.

The income benefits of individual and group insurance and the rights under the federal OASDHI program should be coordinated in a diagram similar to Figure 16–1. With objectives set in terms of the monthly or yearly income necessary to support the family when the breadwinner is disabled, the social security benefits (for total and long-term disability only) provide a minimum base. Then the group and individual health policies for loss of income should supplement the program to reach toward the established goals throughout the years following a disability. For the sake of clarity, health insurance needs and possible solutions are presented separately in Table 16–2 and Figure 16–2.

A case study example of family health insurance needs and costs

The health insurance program shown in Table 16–2 and Figure 16–2 assumes about the same income goals as are assumed in the life insurance program illustration. The needed hospital-surgical expenses, as well as part of the major medical expense needs (up to $50,000 per illness or injury), are taken

Table 16–2. Family health insurance program*

	Needs (medical expenses and loss of income for disability)		
	Family dependency period: Ages 25–39	Wife support period: Ages 40–65	Retirement period: Age 65 and over
I. Estimate of needs			
A. Medical expenses			
1. Hospital-surgical expenses	Up to $90 per day, for 365 days, with up to $1,000 for miscellaneous charges and $8 per doctor visit up to 50	Same as ages 25–39	Assumes that Medicare benefits will be nearly sufficient, for most of hospital-surgical expenses (HI—Part A) and 80 percent of all other expenses above deductibles (SMI—Part B)
2. Surgical	Scheduled benefits to $1,000 maximum (maternity: hospital, plus $500)	Same as ages 25–39	
3. Major, or catastrophe, expenses	Up to $50,000 of "blanket" expenses‡ per illness or injury	Same as ages 25–39	
B. Loss of income			
1. Total and permanent	$1,500 per month	$1,200 per month	$1,000 per month
2. Partial and temporary	$800 per month, up to 39 weeks	Same as ages 25–39	
II. OASDHI benefits,† or part-time work, and wife's pension	IB(1): $1,000 per month to child's age 18	None from OASDHI; $600 per month from part-time work	Medicare expense benefits plus $600 per month from OASDHI and $200 per month from wife's pension
III. Group health insurance	IA(1), IA(2), and IA(3): full benefits as above; IB(2): full benefits as above	Same as ages 25–39	
IV. Net needs	IB(1): $500 per month	$100 per month	$200 per month
V. How individual health insurance might meet these needs	IB(1): Loss of income§ for sickness to age 65, lifetime for accident, or $500 per month (Policy A)	Same as ages 25–39	Cash values of permanent life insurance contracts could be used, if needed, to fill in $200 a month gap here
VI. Approximate annual costs of contracts	Policy A: $250 a year; Total $250 a year	Same as ages 25–39	

* Assumptions are same as for Table 16–1.
† These are approximate amounts. Reduced benefits could be obtained at age 60, or after age 50 if the wife is disabled.
‡ Assumes $200 deductible, and 20 percent coinsurance paid by insured, noncancelable and renewable to age 65, with premium increases by class.
§ Assumes this is for total and permanent disability only; noncancelable and guaranteed renewable, with premium changes, by class, to age 65 and waiting period of one month. Full salary replacement is assumed, although tax benefits and underwriting restrictions probably would make 80 percent of salary, technically, a more precise goal.

Figure 16–2. Family health insurance program

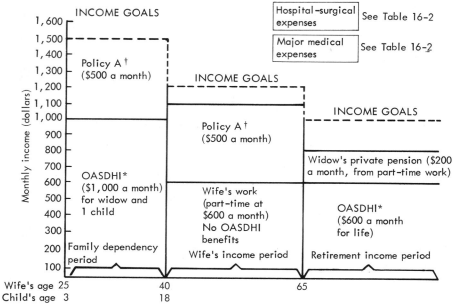

* Approximate rounded maximum benefits. Reduced widow benefits possible at age 60, or age 62, or at age 50 for disabled widow, not shown. Total and permanent disability of husband.
† For total and permanent disability of husband, to age 65 for sickness. If because of accident, benefits would be payable for life. Minor deficiency of $100–$200 a month income during widow and retirement periods are disregarded in this program.

care of by a *group* policy available through the husband's place of employment, with the employer paying the cost of these plans.[6] Income goals of $1,500 a month before age 40, and $1,200 between ages 40 and 65, are achieved by supplementing assumed OASDHI family benefits between ages 25 and 39, and part-time work by the widow between ages 40 and 65, with $600 a month. Policy A, an accident and health contract, provides $500 a month for total and permanent disability on a noncancelable and guaranteed renewable (with rate increases by class permitted) basis. This nearly fills in the "blackout period" with no dependent children, during which no OASDHI disability benefits are available to the wife for her husband's disability. Disability income benefits in life insurance contracts could also help meet this need, but here it is assumed that a separate health insurance contract is purchased.

[6] A reasonable assumption, since more than half of employed persons have approximately such coverage and two thirds or more of those having this coverage also have major medical coverage for limits of $50,000 or more. More than half of these plans are paid in full by the employer, with about 80 percent of total costs being paid by the employer. *See Source Book of Health Insurance Data* (New York: Health Insurance Institute, 1976–77), p. 38.

After age 65, Medicare benefits will take care of most medical expenses, although some advisers would suggest an individual contract at special rates for the over-65 age group, to supplement these coverages. Income from OASDHI of $600 monthly for the husband's disability and an assumed private pension based on the widow's part-time work ($200 a month) nearly meet the goal of $1,000 lifetime income per month at the older ages in the illustration. Life insurance cash values could be used to provide the $200 per month deficiency.

Total costs for individual Policy A would be about $250 a year, or a little over 1 percent of the annual salary of $18,000. Together with suggested life individual insurance of $1,790 a year, or 10 percent of income, insurance in the family budget shown earlier totals about 11 percent. This does not include OASDHI taxes, which will approximate $1,100 a year, or 6 percent at current rates.

Naturally, these estimates would be subject to many individual differences. The greatest variation in the insurance costs as a percent of total income would be in the life insurance section. Here the total might be substantially less, depending on how much is budgeted for other savings media. The permanent life insurance contracts are a combination, it should be noted, of both insurance protection and savings.

The personal insurance review examples are an illustration of *insurance programming* on a family basis. The next section of this chapter analyzes total estate planning. While the risks with which the individual is personally concerned are limited, they vary with occupation or profession, income, ownership of other assets, and family needs and personal goals. Again, while cost is of importance in every insurance program, its distribution may be of special interest to the individual. It sometimes happens that heavy premium payments fall due about the same time that taxes, notes, or other extraordinary expenses are payable. If the insured is operating on a budget system, the readjustment of premium payments to fit the financial plan may be necessary. If budgeting is not followed, insurance may be rearranged so that the heaviest premium payments fall due at a time when some particular income is received or in any other manner that will prove most convenient to the insured.

Personal estate planning

The preceding illustrations of life and health insurance programming are but part of the typical family's long-range financial planning. Total *estate planning* is a much broader process which concerns all aspects of the *creation* and *liquidation* of a family's assets. Insurance is one of the most important parts of estate planning, but the total process extends to many other significant factors, particularly the effect of taxes on the whole estate. The estate includes all assets owned or controlled by a person who dies.

The typical sad situation following a death is increased by the survivors' lack of knowledge about the assets of the estate—what they are, where the ownership documents are kept, and what can and should be done with them. Information on the debts and obligations, too, is usually lacking, as well as information on what procedures must be followed in order to "probate," or have the court approve, any estate settlement. Much is to be recommended in the advice that you should "teach your wife to be a widow (or husband a widower)."

The connotations of the term *estate planning* are often misleading. It is more than mere tax planning, and it is more than the mere liquidation or disposition of assets after death because it should include the "wisest and most prudent use of . . . assets during . . . lifetime as well as after death."[7] It is also wrong to assume that only the larger estates require estate planning. The smaller estates are those that can least afford to miss the potential benefits of proper estate planning techniques.

Estate impairment. It is often said that "it is not what you have but what you have left that counts." A recent example of estate shrinkage is that of actress Jayne Mansfield's estate of one-half million dollars, in which several final beneficiaries received less than $2,000 each. This rather extreme example emphasizes that not all the assets of an estate pass to the beneficiaries when a person dies. Another much-publicized example is the estate of Howard Hughes, which was originally estimated at several billion dollars. With lengthy court battles continuing in regard to validity of his will, corrections in property appraisals, and tax complications, the estate value had dwindled to less than one tenth of the original amounts within 2 years after his death.

Primary among the reasons for estate planning are the factors which oftentimes shrink the total estate values, or those which result in estate values going to the wrong persons or in values being used inefficiently.

Estate settlement costs often reduce the values going to beneficiaries by 30 percent or more. The substantial cost of estate transfer is one of these factors, but many others exist in the normal situation: inflation erosion of the purchasing power of the dollar, unstable and fluctuating asset values, lack of liquidity to pay immediate estate needs within a few months or estate taxes within nine months of death, and improper use of settlement systems under life insurance contracts. Lack of provision for long-term and costly disability losses due to poor health, too, can cause expected estate values to shrink drastically.

The estate planning process. In achieving the objective of transmitting property values from one generation to successive generations with minimum tax burden and maximum effectiveness, five basic principles are significant.

---

[7] Lawrence J. Ackerman, "Estate Planning Principles," in Davis W. Gregg and Vane B. Lucas, eds., *Life and Health Insurance Handbook,* 3d ed. (Homewood, Ill.: Richard D. Irwin, 1973), p. 844.

These recommend the use of (1) lifetime gifts, (2) successive life estates, (3) trusts, (4) gift tax privileges, and (5) the marital deduction.[8]

Before these techniques are used, the first step in estate planning involves obtaining facts about the client in regard to domicile (the effect of state laws on the estate vary greatly here), family and dependents, property owned and income rights, wills, and the objectives of the total estate plan.[9] Detailed questionnaires are the method by which these facts are obtained, ranging from checklists of a few items to many pages. Analysis of the prospective factors tending to impair the estate values and the design of a coordinated estate plan are the next steps in estate planning.

A survey book for the beginning student cannot hope to include all the legal and tax complications of estate planning. However, a few of the more important aspects will be sufficient to explain the major factors to emphasize the critical nature of estate planning. A major message is that good estate plans result only from necessary careful *planning*. This applies both to the *creation* of assets, in which life insurance is almost essential for most families, and to the *disposition* of assets, in which life insurance can be very effective as a secure foundation for the estate plan.

The will.   A key role is played in the process by having a legally qualified *will* for both the husband and the wife. Amazingly, thousands of persons die every year without valid wills. The result in these cases is that the state law decides for the family how and when the estate values are to be distributed. The court must must appoint an *administrator,* who may not be the *executor* you would have chosen to care for your estate. Many state inheritance laws do not provide for the needs of beneficiaries as one might expect. The typical state inheritance law, for example, allots one third of the estate to the wife, and two thirds to the children (assuming two or more children). This requires a guardianship to be established under the law if the children are under age 18 or 21, and distribution of the *income only* until they reach the age of majority. Other use of the principal is severely restricted and subject to court approval if proven necessary for their essential support and education. The basic question is summarized as: "Would you want the law to specify such uses, or would you rather have your will indicate how much and when your executor (or a trustee) should provide for the children?" It is possible to use estate values according to the deceased's instructions, but only if a valid will is executed in order to carry out these instructions.

The marital deduction.   From a tax standpoint, the key purpose of a will is to qualify the wife's estate for maximum use of the *marital deduction.* One

---

[8] William J. Bowe, *Estate Planning and Taxation,* 3d ed. (Homewood, Ill.: Richard D. Irwin, 1972), pp. 3–4. Also recommended in this area is Gilbert T. Stephenson, *Estates and Trusts,* 5th ed. (New York: Appleton-Century-Crofts Co., 1973).

[9] Ackerman, "Estate Planning Principles," pp. 846–49.

half of the total property values, no matter how large, can be given to the spouse outright, and be deducted from the taxable estate. The Tax Reform Act of 1976 also provided that a minimum marital deduction of $250,000 may apply, so that relatively little or no tax is necessary on any adjusted gross estate values of $500,000 or less. (See examples in Table 16–3.) As seen above, the intestate (no will) laws will not take advantage of the maximum deduction. It is important to consider both the potential estate tax applying to the spouse's estate, as well as the successive future estate taxes which may apply to the estates of the surviving spouse and the children.

Most tax goals of estate planning, and the examples in this text, concern the *federal estate* tax. The additional *inheritance taxes of the states,* which are much smaller, may also be involved in estate planning, with similar benefits. Income taxes are of lesser importance, although separating principal amounts to have the income separately taxed to children or trusts can also be a wise objective in some of the larger estates.

The estate. Although estates valued at several hundred thousand dollars or more seem large to many persons, the total values accumulated by middle- and upper-class families are often substantial. Invariably they are larger than expected, because all of the items that will be included have never been added up. A recommended procedure is to estimate the total estate values at periodic intervals during one's lifetime, in a "mock" or assumed estate situation, in order to see what approximate tax consequences would be likely. *All* assets owned at the time of death are included, and many other assets over which the deceased has control (such as powers of appointment and revocable gifts) may be considered part of the estate by the tax authorities. Real estate, automobiles, personal property, savings accounts, pension plans, group and individual life insurance (unless there are no "incidents of ownership," such as rights to change the beneficiary, use cash values, and so on), stocks, bonds, mutual funds, business interests, and many other items must all be included. Joint ownership of the home or savings and investment accounts are usually included at the *full* values. Fair market value is the normal amount for federal tax purposes, and many family-type businesses may represent much larger values than anticipated. Inflation has pushed many values higher than is realized.

The unified gift and estate tax. The Federal Tax Reform Act of 1976 changed estate planning considerably. Formerly, there was separate taxation of gift and estate values. Now a *unified tax and tax credit* applies to both cumulative lifetime gifts and deathtime transfers of assets. The combined tax ranges from 18 to 70 percent of the *taxable estate* value. The taxable estate excludes assets qualifying for the marital deduction, which is why this is so important. A unified tax credit (for both gifts and estate values) of $47,000 is subtracted from the calculated tax.[10] In determining the total taxable es-

---

[10] A separate schedule of tax credits applies for 1978 ($34,000), 1979 ($38,000), and 1980 ($42,000).

tate, the gross estate value is also reduced by the administration expenses, debts, and funeral expenses.

In spite of the fact that gifts of assets made while the deceased was alive are no longer completely excluded from estate values, *living gifts* can still be planned to help reduce the taxes payable. Individual gifts of up to $3,000 annually per donee, or $6,000 if the spouse joins in the gift, can be made without having any gift or estate tax apply to the transfer. Thus a considerable amount can be transferred gradually to the family or others during a lifetime. Other, larger living gifts can also aid in reducing the unified tax at the time of death, for the value of the gift at the time of the transfer (instead of possible much larger later values) is the amount which will be included in the unified estate value at death, and the amount of the gift taxes already paid and of the income earned on the gift values will also be excluded. Such larger gifts made within three years of the time of death are included in the unified taxable estate, so again advance planning of gifts becomes important.

Life insurance can be effectively used as gifts in order to reduce estate taxes. Donors can make gifts of life insurance to the spouse, children, or grandchildren, and if such gifts are made more than three years before the donor's death, the proceeds of the policies would not be included in the donor's estate. If the donor continues to pay the premiums after making the gift, the premiums would be a taxable gift, but could qualify for the annual $3,000–$6,000 gift tax exclusion. The donor should not retain any incidents of ownership, such as the right to change the beneficiary, use cash values, and so on.

Examples of how the combined gift and estate tax might apply to two hypothetical estates are shown in Table 16–3. In these examples, the relatively small tax applicable to a $460,000 estate is apparent, as are the rapid increases in the tax for larger estates. Estate No. 2's approximate doubling of taxable estate results in a net tax of $85,000, which is almost eight times the $11,000 tax payable on Estate No. 1.

While it is true that under the Federal Tax Reform Act of 1976 estates of up to $500,000 will pay relatively little or no tax with the unified tax credit, the importance of using the marital deduction to maximum advantage is emphasized. Leaving the surviving spouse outright by will at least one half of the adjusted gross estate reduces the taxable estate and the resulting tax considerably.[11] The sharp increases in tax for larger estates are illustrated: on a $500,000 taxable estate, the tax is $155,800; on $750,000, it is $248,300, on $1 million, $345,800; on $3 million, $1,290,800. (The $47,000 tax credit would be subtracted from each of these tax figures.) Also, these examples

---

[11] Careful use is also recommended if the spouse already has substantial assets, in which case it may *not* be advisable from a tax standpoint to utilize the deduction because the unified credit will exempt a larger estate than was exempted before the 1976 act. See Nahum L. Gordon, "The Impact of the Tax Reform Act of 1976 on Estate Planning," *CLU Journal,* vol. 31, no. 2 (April 1977), p. 11.

Table 16–3. Unified gift and estate tax examples

	Estate No. 1		Estate No. 2	
Estate at the time of death*.......		$450,000		$900,000
Gifts made within three				
years of death*		50,000		50,000
Gross estate		$500,000		$950,000
Less: Administrative expenses	$20,000		$40,000	
Debts	15,000		40,000	
Funeral expenses	5,000	40,000	10,000	90,000
Adjusted gross estate		$460,000†		$860,000
Less: Marital deduction‡		250,000		430,000
Taxable estate		$210,000		$430,000
Tentative tax		$ 58,000		$132,000
Less: Unified tax credit§		47,000		47,000
Tax		$ 11,000		$ 85,000

* This assumes that other gifts have been made to use up the $3,000–$6,000 annual gift exclusive that year. No gift tax is paid when the $50,000 gift is made because the later available unified tax credit is more than the gift tax which would be payable in this amount.

† It is noted that adjusted gross estates of $425,625, using the full marital deduction, would have no estate taxes to pay. The figures in Estate No. 1 were chosen in order to show how the net tax results on estates above this amount.

‡ Note that the $250,000 minimum marital deduction applies in Estate No. 1 and that one half of the adjusted gross estate applies in Estate No. 2.

§ Smaller credits apply until 1981 (see footnote 10).

concern only the federal gift and estate tax, and *state inheritance* taxes would apply in addition.

Estate planning is not a job for a do-it-yourselfer. The advice of attorneys specializing in estate planning is strongly recommended, particularly for larger estates. New rules apply under the 1976 Reform Act—a new "carry-over basis" for valuing estate property on the recipient's tax basis (or on fair market value as of December 31, 1976, which becomes very important), new rules applying taxes to "generation-skipping transfers" in trusts and life estates, and many others.[12]

Trusts. The substantial advantages of *trusts,* to which all or most of the assets are transferred at death, should be of primary concern in many estates. In addition to possible tax savings (often many thousands of dollars), the wife and children can receive the benefit of professional investment advice and service. A bank trust department is generally used. The advantage of having trustees make or aid in making decisions in regard to use of principal and income is also of real benefit to many wives unfamiliar with investments and asset conservation.

The goal is easily reached by drawing up a *trust agreement,* for which at-

---

[12] See Roger J. Stalowicz, "The Tax Reform Act of 1976—A Primer," and Alban Salaman, "The Tax Reform Act of 1976: Estate and Gift Tax Provisions," *CLU Journal,* vol. 31, no. 1 (January 1977), p. 13 and 24, respectively.

torney's fees would usually be only a few hundred dollars. In one common use of trusts, all of the wife's trust income is usually paid to the wife during her lifetime, and she may be given full powers to use the principal as well. Oftentimes, partial powers to invade the principal of the trust are given, restricting her use to a specified dollar amount or percentage of the trust each year. The income of a trust for the children may also be payable to the wife for her life. She may give this to the children (or leave it in the trust at the lower income tax rates applicable there), but according to specifications in the trust she may use the principal only for the direct and essential support and the medical or educational needs of the children. The husband may divide the estate assets between the two trusts as he see fit. He may wish to have the most liquid assets go to the wife's trust, while the assets with substanial market appreciation may be put in the children's trust.

Many options are available in setting up trusts, and these require professional legal advice. *Revocable* trusts, in which the creator reserves the right to reacquire the property in the trust, are most common. These create transfer taxes at the time of death and do not reduce estate taxes then, but they may be set up to reduce administrative costs and taxes in the estate of the beneficiary and to obtain income tax benefits for the trust income. *Irrevocable* trusts reduce estate taxes by removing the trust property from the taxable estate, but gift taxes are applicable when such trusts are set up, unless the tax is less than the unified gift and estate tax credit.

Life insurance may be a majority of the estate values, and it may be used beneficially to provide liquid assets (without losses if it is sold in a temporarily depressed market). Settlement options such as the life income option can be used to provide a foundation of secure income for the wife as long as she lives, and may also save on probate and administration costs. A "pour-over" testamentary (at death) trust can be used to consolidate life insurance and other assets in an *inter vivos* (living) trust, with several legal and administrative benefits.

Executor and legal fees total substantial amounts in estate settlements, often each amounting to 3 to 5 percent of the estate values. In Table 16–3, total estate expenses (other than federal estate taxes) and debts are conservatively estimated at about 7 to 8 percent, but they can be higher. In trust arrangements, the transfer is accomplished largely through the trusts, so debts and legal fees are of smaller importance.

The trust agreement specifies how the trust assets are to be used and invested. If the trustee is a bank trust officer, the assets may be invested in a common portfolio of the bank's trust assets, which are conservatively invested in a wide range of stocks and bonds. *Trust services* are not free; banks will charge about 5 percent (often graduated downward for assets over some figure such as $25,000) of the trust income plus about 0.2 percent of the principal, annually.

The pros and cons of trusts versus other estate settlement methods must be analyzed carefully by comparing costs, the safety of and return on investments, and the restrictions and flexibility of the total plan to meet estate objectives. A balance must usually be struck among estate costs; estate, gift, and income tax savings; freedom from financial management worries; and flexibility.

The estate planning team. One of the most valuable concepts of estate planning is that with proper forethought the family can have the coordinated services of a whole group of professional experts to help with the complexities of estate creation and liquidation. The *attorney* is, in effect, the captain of the team which has the goal of building up and using estate values in the best possible manner. The importance of legal documents and procedures makes the attorney's services essential. The accounting and tax aspects may also require the services of an *accountant.* If trusts are used in the estate plan, a bank *trust officer* provides valuable conservation and investment of the estate values. The fourth member of the team, the *life insurance agent,* may be considered one of the most critical choices for the family. Most likely, the agent is the only person who will motivate the family to take the necessary steps to purchase the life insurance that will create much of the estate values and to seek the services of the other estate team members to put the estate plan into effect. As such, the professional agent is indispensable in the usual estate planning process. The agent should not, and cannot, give legal advice or prepare legal documents. However, the life insurance agent should, and can, encourage families to seek the legal help needed to accomplish a sound personal estate plan, using life insurance in many of the ways which have been discussed.

BUSINESS LIFE AND HEALTH INSURANCE PLANNING

Good insurance planning is useful not only in personal estate programming but in many business situations as well. The objective of business life and health insurance is either to maintain a business as a going concern or to retain the values of the business interest for the benefit of an estate following the death or disability of the owner. Insurance is also used to protect the surviving members of a business where the loss or disability of a partner, stockholder, or key employee could (1) adversely affect control, (2) dissolve the business, or (3) adversely affect its value.

In a closely held business enterprise, numerous relationships must be considered in the event of death and disability. The death or disability of the owner in an individual proprietorship, of one of the owners in a partnership or a small corporation, or of a key employee calls for major financial adjustments. Without adequate funds the disabled person or the deceased owner's estate or the position of survivors, or both, may be adversely affected. Careful planning, combined with the skillful use of life and health insurance, may preserve for all members of a concern substantial values that might be lost otherwise. Two uses of life and health insurance are illustrated by buy-and-sell agreements and key person insurance contracts.

Buy-and-sell agreements

Business life and health insurance, to protect the interest of a deceased or disabled member and at the same time to protect the interest of surviving members, may be arranged in connection with a *buy-and-sell agreement.* This contract provides a sure market for the interest of the deceased or disabled person and a guarantee to survivors of its purchase at a reasonable price with the funds available for payment. It is a form of "business continuation" contract.

The details of the *buy-and-sell agreement,* also known as a purchase-and-sale agreement, must fit the needs of the parties, and will vary with the type of business organization. Certain characteristics of all such agreements fall, within limits, into a broad pattern.

The names of the parties appear in the agreement, and the purpose is detailed. The agreement will also include either the purchase price or a formula by which it may be determined. All parties commit themselves to the plan for the purchase of the interest of the deceased or disabled associate. The method of financing by the use of life or disability income insurance is set forth; and provision is made for changing the amounts of insurance, if necessary, from time to time. To establish a guaranteed minimum, it is usual to provide that the sale price will never be less than the insurance for this purpose. If a valuation formula is used and the amount of insurance proves inadequate, a time payment plan is set up for the balance.

Beneficiary arrangements determine whether the proceeds are to be payable to a trustee who will carry out the transfer or payable directly to the person who under the agreement must acquire the business interest of the deceased. There are numerous other details, such as the debts and the rights of termination, withdrawal, or amendment. The agreement, properly drawn, is binding and enforceable at law upon heirs, successors, or assigns. It also has important benefits for estate tax purposes, for the established values will usually be effective in setting the taxable values at the business interest for the estate.

A schedule of the life and health insurance policies is set forth, and the policies are filed with the agreement. Details are given as to the disposition of the insurance on the life of the surviving associates. The premium payment plan is covered, as are the conditions upon which rights and privileges under the policies may be exercised during the lifetime of the insured. The ownership of the contracts may be by the business firm, by the individual partners, or by a trust, depending on the particular business situation.

The carefully drawn buy-and-sell agreement, implemented with life insurance, precludes misunderstanding, and provides that the interest of a deceased or disabled associate will be purchased at a fair price. Life and health insurance can be used to make this financially possible at the time of need.

Key person life and health insurance

The principles underlying *key person life and health insurance* for one or more individuals held to be of particular value to a business are essentially the same, regardless of the form under which a business is organized. The objective of key person insurance is to insure the loss of services caused by the death or disability of a vital employee and to provide resources with which to secure the services of a successor in a competitive market. The insurable value may be determined by estimating the portion of the profits for which the key person is responsible, the cost of replacing and retraining the key person, or the investment that might be lost by the firm. The life and health insurance purchased to cover these costs may be payable to, and be paid by, the business itself.

Who can be insured as key persons? There can be little doubt of the right of a business organization to insure its president or manager. Other key employees can likewise be covered: an experienced sales manager; a leading salesperson with many personal clients; a specialist such as an engineer, a chemist, or a researcher; or a person whose management inspires the confidence of financial sources in the business. The list could be expanded to include many other such persons.

In addition to using key person insurance to reimburse the business for the loss of the services of a particular individual, insurance of this kind has been used as a means for attracting and holding such personnel. Because of the income tax, an increase in salary may be much less attractive than a plan to provide a continuation of salary for a number of years following an employee's death or disability. Key person insurance may work into the program of any business establishment as a means for stabilizing employment at the higher levels. Frequently, a combination of coverages is provided: indemnity to the business for the loss of the employee and salary continuation for the employee's dependents. Key person insurance is a valuable and frequently overlooked use of life insurance in the business field. Estimates place key person and other business life insurance at more than 12 percent of new business written.[13]

Key person *health* insurance is often neglected. Not only death, but disability as well, can disrupt the operations of a business. Key person disability income insurance can replace the economic loss of an employee's valuable services.

Other life and health insurance which might be considered part of the busi-

---

[13] *Life Insurance Fact Book* (Washington, D.C.: American Council of Life Insurance, 1978), p. 28.

ness field are all the *employee benefit plans* that use insurance as a financing mechanism. These include the *group* coverages for life, health, and annuity insurance, as discussed in Chapters 12 and 14. Also, *split-dollar* (see Chapter 10) and *deferred compensation plans* (nonqualified) are potential methods of using life and health insurance beneficially in connection with business interests.[14]

FOR REVIEW AND DISCUSSION

1. Insurance programming, as applied to life and health insurance, is part of risk management. Explain this relationship.

2. "Coordination with social security benefits is one of the most important tasks to be accomplished by good life and health insurance programming." Why do you agree with this statement?

3. In planning a life insurance program, explain the extent to which you think the husband should rely upon (*a*) investments other than life insurance, (*b*) work by his wife, (*c*) his wife's remarriage possibilities in case of his death, and (*d*) group life insurance coverages?

4. "Health insurance programming is just like life insurance programming." Why would you agree *and* disagree with this comment?

5. Life and health insurance costs for a typical family may average between 5 and 20 percent of annual earnings. Why is there such a substantial difference in the average estimates of cost?

6. "Estate planning is more than merely buying insurance," says a leading estate planning expert. How is this so?

7. Explain how a *will,* the *marital deduction, trusts,* and *gifts* may be used to obtain substantial tax benefits in a family's estate planning.

8. Who are the important members of the "estate planning team," and what part does each play in the estate planning process?

9. A friend of yours comes to you for advice, knowing that you have just completed a course in risk and insurance. He is very confused by the many life and health insurance contracts that are available. Making whatever assumptions are necessary, what recommendations would you give him in regard to the following questions?

   a. How should he estimate his life insurance needs, and how much life insurance does he need? Show your method of explanation to him as well as the approximate amounts calculated.

   b. What *riders* to the contracts would you suggest or not suggest? *Justify* your recommendations for (or against) at least three riders which are commonly available with life insurance.

   c. Explain the basic health insurance needs he must consider for his family and how you recommend that they be met by insurance.

---

[14] See chaps. 43 and 44 of Gregg and Lucas, *Life and Health Insurance Handbook.*

d. How might group insurance provide part of the solution to his requirements for life and health protection?

10. Suppose your parents are both approaching age 65 and have asked you for advice about social security. What would you tell them about their OASDHI benefits and costs?

11. Mr. Hoenie is 28 years old and has been working for six years since graduating from college. He has a wife and two small children, and is employed at an annual salary of $24,000. He has just purchased a home and a new car. The only life insurance he owns is $36,000 of group life through his employer and a $25,000 20-payment life policy that he took out ten years ago. Making whatever assumptions you consider realistic, discuss the following with reasons for your opinions:

   a. His needs and the types of contracts he should consider so that his family will have proper life and health insurance (outline form).

   b. The relationship of "social security" to his insurance program.

12. You have just had an estate program completed by a qualified chartered life underwriter (CLU) who has made a number of suggestions for the improvement of your life and health insurance program.

   a. Assuming that you have about $100,000 of life insurance, what uses would probably be made of the settlement options in your life insurance contracts? Why?

   b. How could he suggest coordinating your life and health insurance with your savings and investment objectives?

   c. Diagram the relationship of social security (OASDHI) benefits to you and your family as he probably would do in explaining a typical family life and health insurance estate program.

13. What programming benefits can you summarize to a new father, Mr. Z, who has just asked about his basic *health* insurance needs? What insurance contracts would you recommend? Do you think the "risk manager" at the plant where Mr. Z works could suggest any part of the solutions to his health protection needs?

14. Explain briefly how *business* life and health insurance can be a valuable part of planning by business firms.

15. The Federal Tax Reform Act of 1976 is said to "have made much advice about estate planning that was right suddenly wrong." Cite several examples of why this is true.

PART V

THE FUTURE OF INSURANCE

Most persons insure their homes, automobiles, and other property, even before insuring their life and health. Many also make sure that they protect themselves through insurance against the liability they may incur for injuries to other persons or damage to the property of others. Part IV presents the many and varied kinds of *property-liability* insurance which individuals, families, and businesses purchase for protection against these risks.

First, the standard *fire* insurance contract and its related forms of *allied lines* are discussed. Next, the forms of *indirect-loss* insurance, which are oftentimes neglected, are presented. *Transportation* (marine) insurance exhibits wide variety. The significant and changing area of *liability* insurance follows. The growing concept of automobile *no-fault* insurance and the *automobile* insurance contract, which everyone needs in our present-day automobile economy, merit treatment in separate chapters. *Crime* insurance and *suretyship,* and *miscellaneous* property and liability insurance, are then discussed, before the popular forms of *multiple-line* personal (homeowner's) and business coverages are treated.

This major section of the text ends with a new presentation of the plans of shared private-government protection available through *government*-encouraged insurance for riot, flood, and other perils. In all, a broad package of needed security of the modern consumer of insurance is included for the student to digest and understand.

Chapter 17

Concepts considered in Chapter 17—Fire insurance

The standard fire insurance contract is a useful example of one of the most common and relatively uniform insurance coverages. State laws are the most important *method* of achieving the *benefits* of *standardization.*

The basic parts of the New York standard fire policy are presented:

The declarations—statements as to the parties, period, property, perils, and premium of the contract.

The insuring agreement—the heart of the contract as to its: *inception and termination, property and location, personal nature, actual cash value, perils insured against (proximate* losses caused by *hostile fires* and *lightning),* and *assignment.*

The conditions and exclusions explain the contract terms as to: *concealment or fraud, excluded property and perils, suspension, added provisions, cancellation,* and *loss provisions* (including *mortgagee* interests, the *pro rata liability* clause, *notice* and *proof* of loss, *appraisal, repair,* and *subrogation* rights).

Fire insurance forms complete the basic fire insurance contract by attachments to the standard policy. These many different forms are illustrated as to their *purpose* (to complete the contract), *preparation and use,* and *types* (specific, blanket, floating, automatic, or schedule).

Clauses, sections of the forms or endorsements, are discussed: *purpose* (to extend, limit, or change the contract); *nuclear, water exclusion, liberalization,* and the *standard mortgage clause;* and the important *coinsurance clause,* discussed as to: *purpose* (to encourage a reasonable relationship of "insurance to value" in order to provide equity among policyholders), *formula and examples* (showing the potential severe penalties), *justification* in the rates, and *valuation problems;* and the *pro rata distribution clause* apportioning coverage among locations.

Endorsements add to the basic contract, for the purpose of modifying it by clarifications, extensions, or limitations, such as *extended coverage* (in most fire insurance contracts, adding such perils as windstorm, riot, explosion, and smoke), *broad form* (broadening and adding new perils), and *special form* endorsements (changing to an "all-risks" basis).

A review of the fire insurance contract shows how, in chart form, the basic parts may be summarized and analyzed.

Special and allied fire lines are: sprinkler leakage, crop, and builder's risk.

Concurrency, the desirable coordination of several insurance contracts through the use of similar wording, is explained in the final section.

One wonders whether modern society has shown sufficient progress in controlling one of humanity's greatest discoveries—the ability to use fire. Unfortunately, fire is also a formidable enemy. In the United States, more than 3 million fires each year destroy or damage property valued at nearly $4 *billion*. Such losses attest to the cost of carelessness or incomplete control of fire. Examples of current increases in the fire-loss potential permeate our everyday life: high-rise buildings, electricity for modern appliances, billions of cigarettes, arson, and inflammable products of the "plastic age."

Fire insurance is one of the most familiar kinds of insurance. Few persons owning property want to be without its protection. Fire insurance is generally known to its many policyholders, and it is one of the most standardized of all insurance contracts. For many insureds today it is the basis for their homeowner's contract, which is discussed in Chapter 27. Fundamental parts of the basic fire insurance contract, its forms and endorsements, and some "allied lines" are analyzed in this chapter.

The reader is also referred to several previous discussions, on fire insurance rating (in Chapter 6) and on claims procedures (in Chapter 7).

THE STANDARD FIRE INSURANCE CONTRACT

The purpose of fire insurance is to indemnify a named insured in the event that certain described properties are destroyed or damaged by the peril of fire. Without insurance, many fire losses could have disastrous financial results for families or businesses. In a contract easily understood by the insurer and the insured, it would appear simple to repay a person for a loss by fire. However, it has taken many years to accomplish today's advantageous uniformity.

The need for standardization

For many years, no standard contract was used by the fire insurers in issuing their contracts, and each home office and sometimes agents were entrusted with this responsibility. Extreme variability appeared, and the contracts became long and complicated. A shorter document, explicit in its pro-

467

visions and fair to both the insured and the insurer, was vitally necessary to the continued success of the business. Out of the recognition of this need developed the contract which is now referred to as the "standard policy."

Methods

In any field of insurance two basic methods of creating standard insurance contracts are available: voluntary or compulsory. The first is to have insurers by *custom or agreement* use uniform language in the contracts. Many insurance contracts today are standardized to some degree by this method. Even if some of the details of the contract are different, the basic provisions may become quite similar in this way.

The second method is standardization by *legislation*. In Chapter 8 it was noted that one kind of insurance regulation was to require certain contracts or part of contracts to be used by all insurers. In life and health insurance some "standard provisions" are required, although this makes only a small part of such contracts uniform. In property and liability insurance one of the most completely standardized contracts is found in fire insurance. The slow and gradual development of this contract is evidence of the difficulties involved in standardizing a product such as insurance.

Development

An early step toward standardization of the fire insurance contract was undertaken by some insurers, but its adoption was not compulsory. It became evident that in order to be effective, any decided reform must come through legislation. Massachusetts was the first state to adopt a standard policy form (1873), followed by New York (1877), and this form remained unchanged until an amended form was adopted in 1918 and again in 1943. When reference is made to the "standard fire policy" in this text, the "1943 New York form" is indicated. Forty-seven states now make the use of this form mandatory. Massachusetts, Minnesota, and Texas use a somewhat different form, although most of its provisions are similar to those discussed in the following pages.

Benefits

The new form is much simpler and considerably shorter than any of the older standard forms. The standard fire contract benefits the policyholder as follows:

1. Because the basic part of the policy is the same for all contracts, it is unnecessary for the insured to compare every sentence of each contract.
2. A uniform continuity of basic coverage is provided over time and among different insurers.

3. Economy in printing contracts results, because uniform printing of forms is possible for many different insurers.
4. With a standardized form, discrepancies among policies are reduced to a minimum and loss payments can be made more quickly and easily.
5. The meanings of the terms used in the standard contract are clarified and fixed under a uniform policy as court decisions establish a body of insurance law. Better understanding reduces litigation in regard to policy terms.

Standardization does not extend to all parts of what insureds finally see in their total policy contracts. Parts of the final and complete contract may vary among insureds and insurers. For example, the *declarations* (statements by the insured, rates, property description, etc.) part on the first page will vary in its style and wording. Also, the *forms* and *endorsements* attached to the basic parts of the policy contract may be partially uniform by custom but may be quite different in extending or restricting the coverage to certain perils, places, or properties.

Standardization by law pertains to two essential parts of the contract, the *insuring agreement* and the *conditions and exclusions.* Figures 17–1 and 17–2 in this chapter show the verbatim required language of the 1943 New York standard fire contract. The insuring agreement usually appears on the first page of the policy with the declarations. The conditions (often called stipulations) and exclusions are generally found on the back of the first page of the policy. Together, these two parts are the basis for the standard contract. This chapter discusses in detail the basic parts of the 1943 New York fire contract: first, the declarations; next, the insuring agreement; and then the conditions and exclusions. The forms, clauses, and endorsements used in connection with the standard contract are introduced in a later section of the chapter. Indirect loss insurance is treated in Chapter 18.

THE DECLARATIONS

About two thirds of the first page in the New York standard fire policy are devoted to information identifying the insurer and the insured, the duration of the contract, the property and the amounts insured, and the cost for the perils included in the coverage. The section is called the *declarations* because most of the data comes from statements or choices of coverage made by the insured.

Some of the usual information in the declarations section is:

1. The insurer, its address, and the policy number.
2. The insured's name and address.
3. The agent's name and address.
4. A warning that all policies covering the same property must be uniform.
5. A list of the insurance amounts and the rates and premium for each peril which is to be included.

6. The description and location of the property covered.
7. The forms and endorsements attached to the contract.
8. The name of the mortgagee, if there is one, to whom loss will be payable.
9. The date and the signature of the agent writing the contract.

The information in the declarations section may briefly be stated as the *parties, period, property, perils, and premium* of the contract. This classification is often meaningful for analyzing any insurance contract. However, the chronological sequence of the basic parts of the contract is followed here in order to avoid confusion. Under "perils," for example, the discussion would necessarily include part of the declarations, the insuring agreement, the conditions and exclusions, and the forms and endorsements. Toward the end of this chapter, the student may profitably review the whole contract in this type of framework, as shown in Figure 17–3.

THE INSURING AGREEMENT

The fundamental part of any insurance contract is its *insuring agreement,* in which the insurer basically states what it will do and what it will not do. This section of the fire insurance contract is not identified as such, but it is readily discerned as the central part of the agreement. In its paragraphs the insurer obligates itself to indemnify the insured for loss or damage to the described property within a stated period by the specific perils of fire and lightning. The brevity of the insuring agreement as shown in Figure 17–1 should not mislead the student into thinking that it is unimportant. It is the core of the legal agreement between the parties, and each part of the insuring agreement is discussed in the following analysis.

Inception and termination

A contract of insurance need not be in writing. Every day literally thousands of property insurance contracts are made without so much as a scratch of a pen. A policy is ordered by the insured, and the insurance agent agrees that it shall become effective immediately or at a designated time. When insurance coverage of this sort is effected, it is ordinarily for a short period, pending the drawing up and delivery of the formal contract or policy. Insurance in such an instance is said to be "bound." Upon receiving an order for insurance, the agent will record the name of the insured, the date on which the insurance is to become effective, the property to be covered, all pertinent information and conditions to be incorporated into the policy, and the amount of insurance (perhaps apportioned among several insurers, with the amount for each indicated). The insurer's liability begins then, unless a future time is stated.

Where written evidence of the agreement is desired, a form called a *binder*

Figure 17–1. Insuring agreement from first page of 1943 New York standard fire policy

In Consideration of the Provisions and Stipulations herein or added hereto and

of . . . . **Dollars Premium**

this Company, for the ⎱ from the. . . . . . . day of. . . . . . , 19. . . ⎰ at noon*, Standard Time, at
term of. . . . . ⎰ to the. . . . . day of. . . . . . , 19. . . ⎱ location of property involved,

to an amount not exceeding . . . . Dollars

does insure . . . .
and legal representatives, to the extent of the actual cash value of the property at the time of
loss, but not exceeding the amount which it would cost to repair or replace the property with
material of like kind and quality within a reasonable time after such loss, without allowance
for any increased cost of repair or reconstruction by reason of any ordinance or law regulating
construction or repair, and without compensation for loss resulting from interruption of business or manufacture, nor in any event for more than the interest of the insured, against all
DIRECT LOSS BY FIRE, LIGHTNING AND BY REMOVAL FROM PREMISES EN-
DANGERED BY THE PERILS INSURED AGAINST IN THIS POLICY, EXCEPT AS
HEREINAFTER PROVIDED, to the property described hereinafter while located or contained as described in this policy, or pro rata for five days at each proper place to which any
of the property shall necessarily be removed for preservation from the perils insured against
in this policy, but not elsewhere.

Assignment of this policy shall not be valid except with the written consent of this Company.

This policy is made and accepted subject to the foregoing provisions and stipulations and
those hereinafter stated, which are hereby made a part of this policy, together with such other
provisions, stipulations and agreements as may be added hereto, as provided in this policy.

* See text for explanation of 1977 change to 12:01 A.M. in many states for new contracts.

is used. Pending delivery of the policy, the binder would ordinarily be given to the insured for a large contract or for one which is to be in effect for a number of days. Fifteen days is a normal maximum of coverage under a binder. When a policy is issued following a binder, it is the custom to date the policy back to the inception date indicated in the original binder.

Under the standard policy, the insurance used to become effective at *noon standard time* (at the place of the property insured) on a given day and was written for a term that expired at noon on a specified day. In 1977 the Insurance Services Office announced revision of most new property insurance contracts to change the inception of coverage to *12:01* A.M. This has been done in most states by statute to conform with liability policies, and the statutes apply to both fire and many package contracts. A few states may still have the old requirement in their contracts for at least some of the commercial-line packages, but this requirement will gradually disappear for all property-liability contracts.

What happens if a fire has already started before the contract becomes effective? The loss is covered as long as the fire reaches the insured property sometime during the term of the policy, regardless of when the fire was originally ignited. An exception might apply if an applicant knew a fire was in progress and concealed this knowledge, for in such case the contract would be voidable by the insurer on the basis of concealment or fraud.

At the time indicated for termination of the policy, the coverage automatically ends—with one exception. If a fire causing damage breaks out before the policy expires, the insurer is liable for all the damage (subject to the maximum policy amount) even though part of the damage is caused by the fire continuing after the normal expiration time.

Most fire insurance contracts are written for one or three years. A discount is not allowed for the longer contracts, and a possible disadvantage of these contracts is that they may increase the likelihood of forgetting to increase the policy amounts to insure changing property values over a period of years.

Fire policies are usually endorsed with a full *reinstatement* of loss clause. The clause is not part of the insuring agreement but is found in added pages of the contract. It provides that any reduction in the amount of the policy because of a loss shall be automatically reinstated to the extent of, and concurrently with, the repair or replacement of the property damaged or destroyed.

Another provision of importance to the determination of the time during which the coverage is in effect is the permission for *cancellation* of the contract. The methods by which cancellation can be accomplished are set forth starting on line 56 of the conditions discussed below.

Property and location

The coverage of *property* is also limited to the listed and described property in the contract. This is usually done in the "declarations" section of the contract, explained previously.

Buildings, machinery, merchandise, household contents, and personal property are all examples of property commonly included in the policy. Both real and personal property may be included in the same contract, but no coverage applies unless the property is named and described.

The contract is also basically a *named location* coverage. It applies only at the location described in the policy, and it would not protect (except with written permission from the insurer) against loss elsewhere if the property were moved. It will be noted later that some of the forms attached to the basic policy do make the coverage applicable automatically to locations other than those specifically named.

Personal nature

The standard fire policy aims at indemnifying the owner of an interest for loss actually sustained to the property insured through the perils insured against. There is no agreement to pay a stated sum. The amount which appears on the face of the policy expresses the limit of the insurer's liability; the amount payable in any situation is determined by measuring the actual loss or damage. This amount is payable, however, not to anyone who may own the property damaged or destroyed but only to the party or parties named in the policy as insured. Property is not insured (as is sometimes stated), but the *person named* in the policy is insured if loss results from the perils covered. The insurance policy is of value primarily to the named insured. Other interests in the property covered by the contract have no interest in the policy or rights under it unless their rights are specifically incorporated into the agreement. Legal representatives, such as heirs or executors of the named insured, are included in the wording of the insuring agreement. Other interests, such as mortgagees, are included only if they are referred to by name in the declarations.

Actual cash value

Fire insurance indemnifies the insured "to the extent of the *actual cash value* of the property at the time of loss. . . ." Regardless of the policy amount, the loss payable is limited to the actual cash value of the property insured. The objective is repayment for the real loss sustained. The amount *may* be "market value" or "book value," but often it is not. For many types of property, especially real estate, the actual cash value is equal to the replacement cost less depreciation. From the cost of replacing the property new is subtracted a reasonable estimate of actual depreciation due to age, use, and other factors which have reduced the value of the property up to the time of loss. The depreciation amount subtracted is often much less than the book or tax depreciation figures.

Exceptions to the goal of paying actual cash value are the "valued policy" and "valued policy laws" in a few states, as discussed in Chapter 4. Another exception is the *replacement value coverage* sometimes written to insure business buildings, and frequently to insure dwellings, for the full replacement cost (without deduction for depreciation) at the time of the loss. Under the policy terms, replacement value coverage is payable only if the property is rebuilt. Many homeowners' contracts today include this feature if the policyholder has at least 80 percent of the property values insured. (see Chapter 27).

However, the basic contract does not undertake to supply "new for old." To do so could create a situation in which the insured might desire to have a loss in order to have new property in place of older property. Such a "profit" could increase the moral hazard of fire insurance and the possibility of arson or fraud.

As used in connection with fire insurance, depreciation includes the element of economic obsolescence. Thus, a property whose value is lessened by changing business conditions, neighborhood changes, and the like, is subject to depreciation when its value is computed for the purpose of loss adjustments. Actual cash value, which represents the actual value of the property destroyed expressed in terms of money, cannot be determined without giving consideration to depreciation of the physical property plus obsolescence.[1]

Repair or replacement costs.   Time and other factors frequently become an element in valuation. The policy adds the additional restriction: ". . . but *not exceeding* the amount which it would *cost to repair or replace* the property with material of like kind and quality within a reasonable time after such loss, without allowance for any increased cost of repair or reconstruction by reason of any ordinance or law regulating construction or repair."

When the value exceeds the cost of repairing or replacing, the replacement cost becomes a limit on the amount recoverable. For example, a family moving to a rapidly growing community that is suffering from a housing shortage might be willing to pay considerably more than replacement cost for immediate occupancy. However, this additional cost would not represent insurable value.

The clause limiting the loss to the "cost to repair or replace" is not an option to the insured; rather it expresses a privilege granted *to the insurer*. It places as an upper limit upon the cost, less depreciation, of repairing or replacing the materials that were damaged. The insurer only seldom uses its option to repair or replace, because it is much easier to pay a cash amount than it is to replace or repair property.

The liability of the insurer is not increased if a building law or other factor causes the cost of reconstruction to be more than the normal cost to repair or replace. It sometimes happens that insured property within a municipality fails to meet the requirements of the *local building code* adopted after the building in question was constructed. Fire policies do not cover such increased cost of repairs. For example, rebuilding a frame building in a downtown area may be prohibited. The policy would not pay the increased cost required to rebuild the property with fire-resistive materials such as brick or steel. Frequently, an ordinance also makes mandatory the demolition of a building when a substantial part of it is destroyed by fire. The New York form thus definitely settles these questions and does not pay for demolition costs or other increased costs incurred because of building codes. A special additional endorsement to the contract is necessary to cover such losses.

Indirect losses.   The insuring clause of the standard fire contract states that it covers "direct loss," and "without compensation for loss resulting from interruption of business." Unless the liability for *indirect* or *consequential* loss is specifically assumed under the contract, such a loss is not covered. Included in the category of indirect losses, which are discussed in Chapter 18, are those arising out of business interruption, such as loss of profit on goods destroyed that might otherwise have been profitably sold. Also, a building rendered unfit for use will deprive its owner of income and its occupant of the use value of the property. Sometimes leases are drawn with a fire clause per-

---

[1] *McCarney* v. *Newark Fire Insurance Co.* et al., 159 N.E. 902.

mitting cancellation by one or both parties in the event of a serious fire. Such a cancellation may deprive an owner or tenant of a valuable long-term lease. Indirect losses may form an important part of any fire loss, but they are not covered in the basic contract unless they are added to the coverage by endorsement.

Insurable interest. It is the element of insurable interest that takes insurance out of the wagering classification and makes it a contract of indemnity. When the nature of an interest or liability in regard to property is such that the insured would lose financially if a loss occurs, an *insurable interest* exists.

The insuring clause limits the amount that may be recovered to the "interest of the insured." Thus, insureds may not collect unless their interests in the property are such that the damage is actual loss to them. It is the intent of the policy to provide indemnity for loss sustained. A loss payment should not be made to persons who cannot show that they had a financial loss. For example, your neighbors cannot take out insurance on your home and collect for your loss.

Many different persons have insurable interests. Owners of property, mortgagees, bailees, leaseholders, and some creditors are among the more common examples of persons having an insurable interest. Illustrations of the types of losses which can be insured, covering various insurable interests, are: (a) loss to buildings, whether the insured has a legal title, an equitable title, or beneficial ownership; (b) damage to, or loss of use of, personal property; (c) loss of income in the forms of rents; (d) the interest of a bailee in the use of property or the bailee's liability for its destruction; (e) the interest of a person having a specific lien; (f) the interest of a partner in partnership property; (g) the liability of a transportation carrier to an owner; (h) the interest of a leaseholder if the lease is terminated by fire damage; (i) improvements on leased property made by tenants; (j) the interest of a mortgagee; and (k) the interest of a large majority stockholder in corporate property.

A mere expectancy without a definite legal basis is generally not insurable. A general creditor, therefore, has no insurable interest in the debtor's property unless a secured or specific lien such as a judgment lien has been acquired. A person named in a will as a legatee of property or a relative who may be an heir to an estate has no insurable interest prior to the death. To constitute insurable interest the element of financial loss must be present. If the interest in a property is limited to a hope or an expectancy, there is no insurable interest.

There may be several insurable interests in the same property. Sometimes the loss check is payable to several parties, or "as their interests may appear." The sum of the insurable interests may exceed the total value of the property. Many of the interests described above can be concurrent. Also, insurable interests based on indirect loss to property or on liability are not limited to the value of the property. In order to make the extent of coverage clear, the insurable interest should be definitely stated in the policy contract.

Originally the requirement of an insurable interest was satisfied only if the interest in the property existed both at the time the policy was issued and at the time of the loss. Except in a few states the doctrine has now been modified to recognize as valid a policy issued upon property in which an insurable interest did not exist at the time the policy was issued, but was acquired later and was retained at the time the loss occurred. This rule validates a policy upon a stock of goods that is being increased or changed from time to time. Requiring an insurable interest only at the time of loss also permits coverage on goods in transportation where the insurable interest may not be present now but may come into being as title or responsibility for the goods changes.

Executors, trustees, and heirs are frequently concerned with the validity of the insurance covering the property of the deceased. To make the coverage continuous, the standard contract states in the insuring agreement that the coverage remains effective for the insured's legal representatives in the event of the insured's death.

Perils insured against

The standard fire contract is a *named perils* or *specified* perils contract. This means that it covers only the listed perils described in the contract. In the basic part of the contract, these perils are "*fire, lightning,* and by *removal* from premises endangered by the perils insured against in this policy.*" Other perils are not covered, unless they are added in the forms or endorsements. The "extended coverage" perils of wind, explosion, smoke, riot, and others are a common addition.

Fire defined. The standard fire policy provides insurance primarily "against all direct loss by fire." The word *fire* is not defined in the contract but has been explained in detail as the courts have interpreted its full meaning. A frequently cited court definition serves as a basis for resolving doubtful cases. The case concerned spontaneous combustion in wet wool. Defining "fire," the court said; "Spontaneous combustion is usually a rapid oxidation. Fire is oxidation which is so rapid as to produce either flame or a glow. Fire is always caused by combustion, but combustion does not always cause fire. The word 'spontaneous' refers to the origin of the combustion. It means the internal development of heat without the action of an external agent. Combustion or spontaneous combustion may be so rapid as to produce fire, but until it does so, combustion cannot be said to be fire."[2]

The presence of heat, steam, or even smoke is evidence of fire, but taken by itself it will not prove the existence of fire. Unless accompanied by ignition, heat sufficient to cause charring or scorching does not constitute fire. To constitute fire, combustion must proceed at a rate sufficiently fast to produce a flame, a glow, or incandescence. Regardless of the amount of heat, there can

---

[2] *Western Woolen Mills Company* v. *Northern Assurance Co.,* 139 Fed. 637.

be no fire until ignition takes place. The loss resulting from a sizable hole burned in a couch would probably be covered even though no one was there to see the fire. A small scorch on a table, caused by a cigarette, would not meet the definition of a fire.

Friendly and unfriendly fires.   The insurance contract promises indemnity for loss arising from the happening of an unfavorable contingency. The element of accident in the cause is essential. Hence, a fire deliberately kindled and remaining within the limits intended for it is termed a *friendly fire,* and any damage that it may do is not covered by the fire policy. However, when a fire spreads beyond the confines intended for it and beyond the control of its custodian, it becomes an *unfriendly fire,* and the damage it causes is an insured loss.

The flame of a fire in a stove, a fireplace, or a furnace is regarded as a friendly fire. Damage from such fires in the form of smoke, soot, or heat is not covered by the fire policy. Thus, a cooking fire or an oil stove left burning in a room may smoke and send soot throughout the premises, but the loss is not covered by the basic fire policy. On the other hand, if the fire escapes from the confines in which it is intended that it remain, the fire becomes unfriendly (hostile), and the fire policy covers whatever damage is thus done. Consequently, if a breeze blows a curtain against the flame in a fireplace and the curtain burns, the property thus destroyed is covered.

Direct loss.   The insuring agreement specifies that to be covered under the policy a loss must be a *direct* loss. This has been construed by the courts to mean that fire must be the immediate or *proximate* cause of the loss as distinguished from the remote cause. Examples of losses included in the term *direct* or *proximate* are: loss or damage caused by smoke or heat from a hostile fire; damage by water or other materials used to extinguish the fire; damage caused by the fire fighters; and unavoidable exposure at or following the fire.

The proximate cause is held to be the efficient cause; that is, the cause which sets intervening agencies in motion. A proximate cause of loss need not be the nearest in time or in the sequence of events if it is the superior or controlling agency. A fire may be the direct cause of a loss or damage even though some intervening agency may form part of the chain of circumstances set in motion by the fire. For example, it was held that a fire in the tower of a building where it was confined with but slight damage was the proximate cause of a large machinery loss in a part of the building remote from the fire. The fire in the tower burned electric wires that caused a short circuit which in turn caused a general breakdown of the machinery. The entire loss was held to be by fire. In another case a ship caught fire and sank following a collision before the goods on board, which had been insured against loss by fire, had burned. Because the fire prevented the use of the available means for saving the boat, fire was held to be the proximate cause of the loss.

There are numerous examples of cases in which fire has been held to be the direct cause of the damage growing out of the collapse of walls which formed a part of ruins. When a building was destroyed by fire and part of the ruined walls fell two days later, damaging a neighboring property, the insurer covering the second property was held liable for a fire loss. If the walls fall two weeks after a fire, however, fire would not typically be considered the proximate cause of loss.

There are limits to the interpretation of the term *proximate*. If a fire truck on the way to a fire accidentally strikes and damages a store, the fire is not held to be the controlling agency and the fire insurers of the store owner are not responsible for the loss. The cause of the accident and the cause of the fire are held to be independent. Damage to the store by the fire truck is attributable to the accident or its cause (such as speed, slippery streets, or other factors) and not to the fire to which the fire fighters were going.

It has been held that where fire spreads to an insured building and there causes an explosion, the insurer is liable for all the damage. On the other hand, in the case of an explosion caused by a fire, concussion damage to neighboring properties is not covered by their basic fire policies. (Those contracts including explosion in the extended coverage endorsement, discussed later, would cover such a loss.)

Whether or not the policy covers in a given situation resolves itself into a determination of the intent of the contracting parties. In what is now held to be a leading case on proximate cause, Justice Cardozo says: "Our guide is the reasonable expectation and purpose when making an ordinary contract."[3] Fire must reach the thing insured or come within such proximity to it that the damage is within the compass of reasonable probability. Then, fire is the proximate cause because it was within the contemplation of the contract.

These examples pertain only to property insurance. The basic idea of proximate cause is also applied in liability insurance, but its application to specific examples of how far the responsibility for loss by the wrongdoer or the insurer extends may differ.

Lightning. The 1943 New York standard policy includes loss by *lightning* as well as by fire in the insuring clause of the policy. Lightning is frequently the cause of serious loss, either directly or by setting property on fire. In earlier contracts (which did not cover lightning), the difficulty of determining at what point the lightning damage ended and the fire loss began was eliminated by including both perils specifically in the contract.

Lightning is the natural discharge of electricity from the atmosphere. It does not include artificial electrical energy which sometimes causes damage to television sets, appliances, or other property.

Loss by removal. The loss incurred by removing property endangered by the perils insured against has been definitely assumed under the terms of the New York standard policy. The insured is obligated to do everything reason-

---

[3] *Bird* v. *St. Paul Fire & Marine Insurance Company*, 224 N.Y. 47, 120 N.E. 86.

able to save threatened property. When damage is sustained in the *removal*, the fire would normally be considered the direct and proximate cause, and the insurer, therefore, is liable. To avoid any doubt the contract specifically lists removal as a covered peril.

The removal must be deemed reasonably necessary, and the threatened danger must be of a nature that would prompt careful and prudent uninsured persons to take like actions in their own interests. Losses caused by breakage and exposure to weather during the process of removal are cause for proper claims. Losses by theft are specifically excluded later in the contract (line 24).[4] However, most courts have allowed coverage for theft in circumstances in which the losses were immediate and the insured acted prudently. A common example is theft by bystanders taking property at or near the scene of the fire.

The insurance follows the property to whatever point it is removed and continues in effect in the new location. The values are covered pro rata, or proportionally, on the old location and on each new location for a period of five days after the fire. When the five-day period has elapsed, insureds will be without insurance as to the new locations, unless they obtain new coverage.

Assignment

The transfer of the legal right or interest in an insurance contract to another person is called an *assignment*. Under the terms of the fire insurance contract, an assignment is valid only with the written consent of the insurer. An exception is the case of an assignment of rights to a claim after a loss has occurred. In many other contracts, assignment may be done without the consent of the other party, unless a statute or a contract provision restricts it.

It sometimes happens that with the sale of an insured property, it is desired to transfer insurance to the new owner. This can be accomplished by having the policy endorsed with the insurer's consent as well as the insured's assignment of interest. This can be potentially dangerous, as the new owner cannot take over any more rights than the seller had under the policy. (The seller may have violated some conditions of the policy, for example.) Another method is to have the policy delivered to the insurer or its agent with the request that the insured under the policy be changed and the coverage transferred from the insured named in the policy to the newly designated insured. An endorsement is used, stating that the interest of the named insured has on that date terminated and that the insurance shall continue in effect for the benefit of the new insured. The relationship between the two original parties is terminated, and a new contractual relationship established. Probably the best method of protecting the new owner's interest in the property is to have

---

[4] The following references to lines are to the numbered 165 lines of the back page of the 1943 New York standard fire policy reproduced in Figure 17–2 on the next page.

a new insurance contract effective when the property is sold, and to have the former owner's policy canceled.

THE CONDITIONS AND EXCLUSIONS

Concealment or fraud

It is provided on lines 1–6 (see Figure 17–2) that the entire policy shall be void if, whether before or after a loss, the insured willfully conceals or misrepresents any material facts or circumstances concerning the fire insurance, the property insured, or its interests, or in case of any fraud by the insured. The courts have held that the word *void* should be interpreted as *voidable* (at the option of the insurer).

An example of *misrepresentation* is a false statement in the declarations, such as stating that the building is "brick, with noncombustible roof, used as a single-family dwelling." It might be considered a *material* (important) misrepresentation if the building was actually a frame one, or had a combustible roof, or was occupied by several families.

Fraud frequently occurs in connection with the adjustment of claims. Examples include incorrect loss statements, concealment of salvage, falsification of records, false testimony given under oath, and false written proofs of loss. It has sometimes been offered as a defense that the false statements made in connection with the claim were for some purpose other than to defraud the insurers, such as to substantiate statements previously made to a credit company. The courts have held, however, that such a false statement is still fraud. Another example of fraud is *arson,* in which the insured intentionally sets fire, or has another person set fire, to the insured property for the purpose of collecting a loss payment. Unfortunately, such losses have increased greatly in recent years, with nearly one half of the larger fires estimated to have been set deliberately.[5] The insurer is not liable for such losses, if arson is proved. However, arson by a stranger, not acting under the direction of the insured, is covered.

Excluded property

Certain types of property are excepted from the coverage of the policy, while other types are uninsurable in any case. On lines 7–10, the policy reads: "This policy shall not cover accounts, bills, currency, deeds, evidences of debt, money, or securities; nor, unless specifically named hereon in writing, bullion or manuscripts." If bullion or manuscripts are to be included in the coverage, they must be specifically mentioned. With the exception of these articles, personal property in which an insurable interest exists may be covered.

---

[5] "Business Battles the Arsonist," *Business Week,* February 27, 1977, p. 64.

Figure 17–2. Conditions and exclusions from back of first page of 1943 New York standard fire policy

1 **Concealment,** This entire policy shall be void if, whether
2 **fraud.** before or after a loss, the insured has wil-
3 fully concealed or misrepresented any ma-
4 terial fact or circumstance concerning this insurance or the
5 subject thereof, or the interest of the insured therein, or in case
6 of any fraud or false swearing by the insured relating thereto.
7 **Uninsurable** This policy shall not cover accounts, bills,
8 **and** currency, deeds, evidences of debt, money or
9 **excepted property.** securities; nor, unless specifically named
10 hereon in writing, bullion or manuscripts.
11 **Perils not** This Company shall not be liable for loss by
12 **included.** fire or other perils insured against in this
13 policy caused, directly or indirectly, by: (a)
14 enemy attack by armed forces, including action taken by mili-
15 tary, naval or air forces in resisting an actual or an immediately
16 impending enemy attack; (b) invasion; (c) insurrection; (d)
17 rebellion; (e) revolution; (f) civil war; (g) usurped power; (h)
18 order of any civil authority except acts of destruction at the time
19 of and for the purpose of preventing the spread of fire, provided
20 that such fire did not originate from any of the perils excluded
21 by this policy; (i) neglect of the insured to use all reasonable
22 means to save and preserve the property at and after a loss, or
23 when the property is endangered by fire in neighboring prem-
24 ises; (j) nor shall this Company be liable for loss by theft.
25 **Other Insurance.** Other insurance may be prohibited or the
26 amount of insurance may be limited by en-
27 dorsement attached hereto.
28 **Conditions suspending or restricting insurance. Unless other-**
29 **wise provided in writing added hereto this Company shall not**
30 **be liable for loss occurring**
31 (a) while the hazard is increased by any means within the con-
32 trol or knowledge of the insured; or
33 (b) while a described building, whether intended for occupancy
34 by owner or tenant, is vacant or unoccupied beyond a period of
35 sixty consecutive days; or
36 (c) as a result of explosion or riot, unless fire ensue, and in
37 that event for loss by fire only.
38 **Other perils** Any other peril to be insured against or sub-
39 **or subjects.** ject of insurance to be covered in this policy
40 shall be by endorsement in writing hereon or
41 added hereto. ·
42 **Added provisions.** The extent of the application of insurance
43 under this policy and of the contribution to
44 be made by this Company in case of loss, and any other pro-
45 vision or agreement not inconsistent with the provisions of this
46 policy, may be provided for in writing added hereto, but no pro-
47 vision may be waived except such as by the terms of this policy
48 is subject to change.
49 **Waiver** No permission affecting this insurance shall
50 **provisions.** exist, or waiver of any provision be valid,
51 unless granted herein or expressed in writing
52 added hereto. No provision, stipulation or forfeiture shall be
53 held to be waived by any requirement or proceeding on the part
54 of this Company relating to appraisal or to any examination
55 provided for herein.
56 **Cancellation** This policy shall be cancelled at any time
57 **of policy.** at the request of the insured, in which case
58 this Company shall, upon demand and sur-
59 render of this policy, refund the excess of paid premium above
60 the customary short rates for the expired time. This pol-
61 icy may be cancelled at any time by this Company by giving
62 to the insured a five days' written notice of cancellation with
63 or without tender of the excess of paid premium above the pro
64 rata premium for the expired time, which excess, if not ten-
65 dered, shall be refunded on demand. Notice of cancellation shall
66 state that said excess premium (if not tendered) will be re-
67 funded on demand.
68 **Mortgagee** If loss hereunder is made payable, in whole
69 **interests and** or in part, to a designated mortgagee not
70 **obligations.** named herein as the insured, such interest in
71 this policy may be cancelled by giving to such
72 mortgagee a ten days' written notice of can-
73 cellation.
74 If the insured fails to render proof of loss such mortgagee, upon
75 notice, shall render proof of loss in the form herein specified
76 within sixty (60) days thereafter and shall be subject to the pro-
77 visions hereof relating to appraisal and time of payment and of
78 bringing suit. If this Company shall claim that no liability ex-
79 isted as to the mortgagor or owner, it shall, to the extent of pay-
80 ment of loss to the mortgagee, be subrogated to all the mort-
81 gagee's rights of recovery, but without impairing mortgagee's
82 right to sue; or it may pay off the mortgage debt and require
83 an assignment thereof and of the mortgage. Other provisions

84 relating to the interests and obligations of such mortgagee may
85 be added hereto by agreement in writing.
86 **Pro rata liability.** This Company shall not be liable for a greater
87 proportion of any loss than the amount
88 hereby insured shall bear to the whole insurance covering the
89 property against the peril involved, whether collectible or not.
90 **Requirements in** The insured shall give immediate written
91 **case loss occurs.** notice to this Company of any loss, protect
92 the property from further damage, forthwith
93 separate the damaged and undamaged personal property, put
94 it in the best possible order, furnish a complete inventory of
95 the destroyed, damaged and undamaged property, showing in
96 detail quantities, costs, actual cash value and amount of loss
97 claimed; **and within sixty days after the loss, unless such time**
98 **is extended in writing by this Company, the insured shall render**
99 **to this Company a proof of loss,** signed and sworn to by the
100 insured, stating the knowledge and belief of the insured as to
101 the following: the time and origin of the loss, the interest of the
102 insured and of all others in the property, the actual cash value of
103 each item thereof and the amount of loss thereto, all encum-
104 brances thereon, all other contracts of insurance, whether valid
105 or not, covering any of said property, any changes in the title,
106 use, occupation, location, possession or exposures of said prop-
107 erty since the issuing of this policy, by whom and for what
108 purpose any building herein described and the several parts
109 thereof were occupied at the time of loss and whether or not it
110 then stood on leased ground, and shall furnish a copy of all the
111 descriptions and schedules in all policies and, if required, verified
112 plans and specifications of any building, fixtures or machinery
113 destroyed or damaged. The insured, as often as may be reason-
114 ably required, shall exhibit to any person designated by this
115 Company all that remains of any property herein described, and
116 submit to examinations under oath by any person named by this
117 Company, and subscribe the same; and, as often as may be
118 reasonably required, shall produce for examination all books of
119 account, bills, invoices and other vouchers, or certified copies
120 thereof if originals be lost, at such reasonable time and place as
121 may be designated by this Company or its representative, and
122 shall permit extracts and copies thereof to be made.
123 **Appraisal.** In case the insured and this Company shall
124 fail to agree as to the actual cash value or
125 the amount of loss, then, on the written demand of either, each
126 shall select a competent and disinterested appraiser and notify
127 the other of the appraiser selected within twenty days of such
128 demand. The appraisers shall first select a competent and dis-
129 interested umpire; and failing for fifteen days to agree upon
130 such umpire, then, on request of the insured or this Company,
131 such umpire shall be selected by a judge of a court of record in
132 the state in which the property covered is located. The ap-
133 praisers shall then appraise the loss, stating separately actual
134 cash value and loss to each item, and, failing to agree, shall
135 submit their differences, only, to the umpire. An award in writ-
136 ing, so itemized, of any two when filed with this Company shall
137 determine the amount of actual cash value and loss. Each
138 appraiser shall be paid by the party selecting him and the ex-
139 penses of appraisal and umpire shall be paid by the parties
140 equally.
141 **Company's** It shall be optional with this Company to
142 **options.** take all, or any part, of the property at the
143 agreed or appraised value, and also to re-
144 pair, rebuild or replace the property destroyed or damaged with
145 other of like kind and quality within a reasonable time, on giv-
146 ing notice of its intention so to do within thirty days after the
147 receipt of the proof of loss herein required.
148 **Abandonment.** There can be no abandonment to this Com-
149 pany of any property.
150 **When loss** The amount of loss for which this Company
151 **payable.** may be liable shall be payable sixty days
152 after proof of loss, as herein provided, is
153 received by this Company and ascertainment of the loss is made
154 either by agreement between the insured and this Company ex-
155 pressed in writing or by the filing with this Company of an
156 award as herein provided.
157 **Suit.** No suit or action on this policy for the recov-
158 ery of any claim shall be sustainable in any
159 court of law or equity unless all the requirements of this policy
160 shall have been complied with, and unless commenced within
161 twelve months next after inception of the loss.
162 **Subrogation.** This Company may require from the insured
163 an assignment of all right of recovery against
164 any party for loss to the extent that payment therefor is made
165 by this Company.

The forms added to the contract must also be read carefully for excepted property such as automobiles, which are often excluded. Some contracts specifically include coverage on money or other of the above items which are excluded in the standard fire policy. For example, the homeowners' contracts often cover up to $100 on money and $500 on securities. Commercial risks can use the broad form money and securities policy, or accounts receivable or valuable papers contracts to insure such items.

Excluded perils

Lines 11–24 name several perils which are excluded from the standard contract, including *war* (in its various forms), some orders for destruction by *civil authorities, neglect* by the insured to prevent further damage, and *theft.*

In order to eliminate catastrophic war risks, all fire policies also specifically exclude loss caused by: (1) *Hostile or warlike action*[6] in time of peace or war, including action in defending against an actual, impending, or expected attack by an actual or proclaimed government or sovereign power; or by military, naval, or air forces; or by an agent of any such government or forces; or by any use by such a government of a weapon of war employing nuclear fission or fusion. (2) *Insurrection,* rebellion, revolution, civil war, usurped power, or action taken by governmental authority in hindering, combating, or defending against such an occurrence. The difficulties of defining a term such as war are obvious in the lengthy description of the actions associated with the term.

The importance of the exclusion for insurrection increased following the Los Angeles, Detroit, Newark, Chicago, and other riots of the 1960s and 1970s. An "insurrection" has usually been defined by the courts as including the attempt to overthrow the government, while losses from "riots" are often limited to injury to, damage to, or theft of specific persons or property. Public officials have generally avoided calling any disturbance, however widespread or illegal, an insurrection, for fear of permitting insurers to decline coverage.

The danger of assuming unpredictable risks which are not accidental in nature leads to the exclusion of property *destruction by civil authorities.* The exclusion does not apply to orders for destruction made to prevent the spread of a fire, such as the dynamiting of a block of houses to stop a conflagration. These losses would be covered, but others, such as the condemnation of a building by health authorities, are excluded.

The insured must be reasonably prudent in doing all that can be done at

---

[6] This phrase was tested in the courts in connection with the 1970 hijacking of a $25 million 747 airplane which was flown to Cairo and blown up by several Palestinians. The courts decided that this action was not "war" because it was not performed by governmental groups, but by a small political activist group. See "What Is a War?" *Time,* October 1, 1973, p. 112.

and after a loss to prevent as much damage as possible. The insured cannot *neglect to prevent further damage,* although this does not require unwise exposure to personal danger in a loss. Neither does this require the insured to act with perfect wisdom in the face of an emergency situation. Examples of unreasonable actions which might deny coverage are (1) not attempting to obtain nearby available help in removing endangered property from a building; (2) failing to turn in a fire alarm as soon as possible; or (3) not arranging to have property, such as machinery, dried off after a fire to prevent rust damage. The cost of removal or protection to prevent further damage after a fire would be includable in the insured's claim for loss.

Theft is specifically excluded as a peril covered in the fire insurance contract. Occasionally such losses may be covered as proximately (closely) related to other covered perils such as fire or riot, but the intent is to exclude all other normal theft losses.

Suspension

In order to protect the insurer with respect to changes in the risk, the coverage is suspended in certain situations. These policy conditions, on lines 28–37, are for the most part concerned with an increase in the hazard. They do not have the effect of voiding the policy permanently but rather act to suspend or restrict the insurance coverage temporarily. When the conditions that suspend the coverage no longer prevail, the insurance reverts to full force and effect.

When the risk is written and the rate fixed, it is assumed that the risk will remain constant during the life of the policy. If there is any important change, the insurer should have the opportunity to either cancel the policy or secure a higher premium. In every case what does constitute an *increase in the hazard* is a matter of fact, and hence in litigated cases it is a matter for the jury to decide. A change in occupancy, for example, having a business such as a dry cleaning shop in a dwelling, would probably be considered sufficient to suspend the insurance. Storage of five gallons of gasoline in the garage of a dwelling would not be called an important increase in hazard, but a thousand gallons might be.

The standard policy definitely incorporates a few special situations which increase the risk to a degree that warrants a suspension of the coverage. *Vacancy* for more than 60 days is one such increased hazard. However, many policies include coverage for some usual or incidental vacancy or unoccupancy in the wording of an attached form.

In the event of *riot* and *explosion,* the policy is not technically suspended but loss is restricted to damage by fire only. The basic policy does not cover sabotage, vandalism, and other like damage that might originate from a riot. In the case of both riot and explosion, if a property is partly demolished and a fire follows, the fire policy is not responsible for the wreckage caused before the fire but only for the loss caused by the fire to the property in its wrecked condition. Today, the difficulty of differentiating such losses is avoided in most contracts because they *include* explosion and riot perils specifically in commonly used endorsements to the fire policy. The best known of these is the "extended coverage" endorsement which is a part of about nine out of ten fire insurance contracts.

Added perils and provisions

The standard contract is adaptable to include additional perils, properties, and provisions. Emphasis is placed in lines 38–55 on the fact that such additions must be made in writing and attached to the basic policy. Since the basic policy is designed for use in connection with all classes of property and nearly every known insurable interest, it is impossible to have one complete contract that meets all needs. The policy thus permits covering perils other than fire, lightning, and removal and refers in the insuring clause to "the perils insured against in this policy." To allow for the inclusion of further perils, lines 38–41 provide: "Any other peril to be insured against or subject of insurance to be covered in this policy shall be by endorsement in writing hereon or added hereto."

Insurers have found that it is often necessary to clarify further the extent of the coverage. On lines 42–48 they have incorporated a further clause permitting endorsements. The policy is arranged with a blank page for the attachment of these additions. In this space is attached first of all an addition known as a *form*. It contains a description of the property to be insured and includes as well a number of *clauses* pertinent to the particular contract and the risk to be insured. *Endorsements* may also be added extending the coverage to include such perils as windstorm or explosion, or to include other extensions or restrictions on the policy coverage.

The standard policy, on lines 49–55, requires that *waivers* be in writing to be effective. The courts have held, however, that just as other provisions of the policy may be waived by anyone with authority to do so, so may the one that requires waivers to be in writing. Thus, in spite of the antiwaiver provision, the insured may occasionally prove that an oral waiver contradicts or modifies the written terms of the policy.

Cancellation

The *insured* may at any time have the policy canceled. No advance notice is required but the policy must be surrendered on demand. A penalty is applied, for the premium to be returned by the insurer represents the balance after charging for the expired term on the *short-rate* basis. For example, a one-year contract canceled after 180 days would cost 55 percent rather than one half of the premium. If the policy has been canceled as a convenience to both parties and is being renewed with the same insurer for the same or a greater amount, it is the custom to charge the earned premium on the *pro rata* rather than the short-rate basis. An example of this distinction follows: Suppose a three-year contract for $300 is canceled after 6 months. Because proportionally one sixth of the coverage duration has been used up, the pro rata return premium would be $300 less $50, or $250. If the insured requests the cancellation, the short-rate return premium would be $300 less $45, or $255. The smaller return to the insured is justified by expense and adverse selection against the insurer, as the insureds more likely to cancel are those that are less apt to have losses.

When cancellation is ordered by the *insurer*, five days' notice must be given every named insured or interest. In the case of a mortgagee, the policy provides on lines 68–73 that the policy may be canceled by giving such mortgagee a ten days' written notice of cancellation. When the insurer cancels, only a pro rata premium, as illustrated previously, may be charged.

The New York standard form makes cancellation effective without the insurer actually paying the return permium, provided that the insured is told that a return premium is payable upon request. The cancellation does not become effective until five days after its actual receipt by the insured. The day on which the notice is received is excluded; the days are counted beginning with the next midnight, running from midnight to midnight. The insured may be given the notice personally, or it may be sent by mail. Registered mail and return receipts are often used. Some forms fold into envelopes, thereby avoiding the possibility of the insured's claiming to have received an empty envelope.

Loss provisions

All of the remaining conditions and exclusions pertain to rights of and conditions on the parties to the contract after a loss has occurred. The importance of these sections of the required 165 lines in the standard policy is indicated by the fact that more than one half of the lines enumerate provisions which apply following a loss.

Mortgagee conditions after a loss are discussed on lines 74–85. The mortgagee should file proof of loss if the owner does not. If the loss is partial, the insurer may pay the whole mortgage to the mortgagee and take over any rights against the mortgagor. The same subrogation right applies if the insurer pays the mortgagee when the mortgagor is not entitled to payment of the loss, such as in the case of a policy violation. Other mortgage provisions are often included in the forms attached to the basic part of the contract. (See a later section of this chapter for discussion of the standard mortgage clause in the dwelling building and contents form.)

An important limitation on the payment made by the insurer for a loss appears on lines 86–89. The *pro rata liability clause* limits the liability of the insurer by stating that "this Company shall not be liable for a greater proportion of any loss than the amount hereby insured shall bear to the whole insurance covering the property against the peril involved, whether collectible or not." Thus, if insurer A had $10,000 fire insurance on a building and insurer B had $5,000 on the same building, each insurer would pay a proportionate share of any loss. If the loss were $9,000, insurer A would pay two thirds, or $6,000, and insurer B would pay one third, or $3,000, of the loss. The purpose of the pro rata liability clause is to prevent double payment of a loss to the insured, which would be a violation of the indemnity principle. Since more than one policy contract is a common occurrence in fire insurance, it is necessary that insurers specify by the wording that they will pay only their proportionate share of a loss.

Lines 90–122 list certain actions which should be taken following a loss. The acts are conditions which should be met as specified, or the insured may not be able to collect any claim against the insurer. The insured should do the following (or see that they are done by someone else):

1. Give immediate written *notice* of the loss. (Oral notification to the agent is usually held sufficient.)
2. *Protect* the property from further damage.
3. *Separate* the damaged and undamaged property.
4. Furnish an *inventory* of the damaged property, its costs, values, and losses sustained.
5. Render a written *proof of loss* within 60 days,[7] including detailed information about the loss (its time, origin, insurable interests, occupancies, insurance contracts in force, and so on).
6. Exhibit to the insurer the property and books of account.

Although seldom used, *appraisal* proceedings are provided for on lines 123–40. Either insurer or insured may ask for an appraisal if they do not agree on the loss amount. Each selects an appraiser, and the two appraisers choose an umpire who settles any differences in the two appraisals of loss. The method sometimes avoids resorting to the courts for determination of a difficult loss settlement.

The following section (lines 141–47) states again the optional right of the insurer to *repair, rebuild, or replace* the property destroyed or damaged with like kind and quality of materials. As noted earlier, this right is rarely exercised. It does act as a ceiling on payment, however, in case an insured refuses to accept a reasonable loss payment. The insured *may not abandon* damaged property to the insurer and claim a total loss (lines 148–49). The *loss is payable* by the insurer *within 60 days after proof of loss* is received (lines 150–56), though most losses are paid well in advance of that required time. According to lines 157–61, the insured *may not sue* the insurer until all the policy requirements have been complied with or *after one year* following the loss.

---

[7] In New York State, by statute the companies must request the proof of loss from the insured.

The final section of the New York standard policy incorporates the doctrine of *subrogation* into the policy with this clause: "This Company may require from the insured an assignment of all right of recovery against any party for loss to the extent that payment therefore is made by this Company." Though the right of subrogation exists without being expressly stated, the insurer is thus protected from having this right destroyed by action of the insured. The insured should be extremely careful that after a loss no rights of recovery against another party are waived, for such action by the insured might void the policy.

Although subrogation cases are much rarer in fire insurance than in automobile or liability insurance, there are some situations in which the insured's right of action against a negligent third party is extremely valuable to the insurer. For example, a careless neighbor may cause fire damage to your garage by burning leaves too close to your property. Your fire insurer would pay your loss but would expect to take over your rights to sue the neighbor. Another example frequently arises when repair or renovation work is done. Suppose the electrician in negligent and sets fire to your property. Again, your insurer will pay your loss but will expect to have the opportunity to bring action against the electrician or the contractor for recovery of its loss payment. The result is fair: the wrongdoer is ultimately held responsible for the loss, and fire insurance cost is kept lower by reducing the loss to the insurer.

FIRE INSURANCE FORMS

Fire insurance contracts are not completely standardized, but state laws make the insuring agreement, conditions, and exclusions uniform in the basic part of the policy. In the total contract, substantial differences appear in the forms, clauses, and endorsements which are attached to and become a part of the fire insurance contract. By these additions the contract is completed, clarified, and extended or restricted to meet the needs of the many different policyholders that purchase fire insurance.

Some of these additional parts of the contract are uniform and used with many policies. Rating bureaus and insurer customs help provide considerable standardization of some forms and endorsements. Most states require the insurance commissioner to approve these additions, and uniformity and fair wording are encouraged. Many other forms and endorsements are highly individualistic, varying among different insurers or insureds to meet specific purposes. This section reviews the more common ones.

Purpose

The statutory fire contract has been seen to include the insuring agreement and the conditions and exclusions. The declarations section precedes the statutory wording. A *form* is necessary to complete the contract. It contains information essential to clarifying the terms of the policy, including a description of the property to be insured and a number of clauses pertinent to the particular contract. The insuring agreement and the stipulations and conditions are general in their application. By means of the form, the contract is tailored to the specific risks and the particular needs of the insured.

Preparation and use

Standard forms are prepared by rating organizations, each form designed for a particular class of risk. Many rating bureaus prepare 50 or more such forms for different groups or classifications of property. There are forms for dwellings, stores, farms, apartments, manufacturing or mercantile properties, and many others.

The wording of the form is not prescribed by statute. Spaces are often left for typing details, such as the name and address of the insured, the amount of insurance, and special definitions of the property insured. Where this satisfies the needs of an individual insured, the form may be mineographed, typed, or even handwritten, but for the usual type of risk it is the general practice to use the printed standard forms.

Forms take precedence over the basic standard fire policy, but printed endorsements (see later section for examples of these) override forms. Also, any typewritten or handwritten wording, either in a printed document or its margin, would override printed matter. The wording which is most specific, or which most clearly reflects the intent of the contracting parties, is effective.

If there is no standard form available to meet special needs, it is quite customary in the case of sizable business risks to prepare and print such a form. Where this is done, the approval of the rating authority must be obtained before the form can be used. This approval serves two purposes. The form must afford the benefits of various liberalizing clauses and the protection expected by the insured. On the other hand, the form must also be checked to prevent discrimination against other insureds through an extension of the coverage not provided for in the rating structure.

It is easy to confuse the modifications permitted in the form with the terms and conditions of the basic policy itself. Certain coverages and privileges, as well as certain restrictions and conditions, originate in the form attached to the policy. It is therefore essential where coverage includes a number of policies on the same property to have all the policies carefully checked and to see that the forms are identical.

Types

Although dozens of forms are used in connection with the fire contract, the form will fall into one of the following five categories: *specific, blanket, floater, automatic or reporting,* and *schedule.* The individual of family purchaser of insurance will usually be concerned only with the first type, the specific form. The other four types are used mostly for insuring business properties.

Specific coverage. The *specific form* is the most common type in use. It covers primarily one kind of property in one definite location. When the building and contents are insured with definite amounts covered on each, the policy is specific. An example of this type of form is the *dwelling building and contents form,* which has several variations. Sample policy kits containing current editions of these forms are available, as noted in the Preface of this book.

The dwelling building and contents forms are good examples of the purposes of forms; completion and clarification of the contract. In addition, they provide some important extensions of coverage. The term *dwelling* as used in the declarations is defined to include the building and outdoor equipment and fixtures. *Contents* includes all household and family personal property, with a few exceptions such as animals, automobiles, and some boats. Without these definitions, there would be many problems in determining what is covered by these items in the standard fire contract.

The extensions of coverage are four: (1) the insured may apply up to 10 percent (of the amount of insurance on the building) for *related private structures* such as a detached garage or a toolshed; (2) the insured may also apply up to 10 percent (of the building insurance amount) for the loss of *rental value* of the dwelling or *additional living expense* (for either or both) while it is untenantable due to the perils insured against, with a maximum limit of one twelfth of the 10 percent each month; (3) *off-premises contents* are covered up to 10 percent (of the amount of insurance on the contents) for losses of family personal property while it is away from the premises, including losses that occur in hotels, college dormitories, summer residences, and so on; and (4) for *improvements, alterations, or additions* by an insured tenant, 10 percent (of the contents insurance amount) may be used. The extensions of coverage noted, in items (1) and (2) only, are an additional amount of insurance beyond the amount stated in the declarations of the standard contract. The cost of *debris removal* is separately noted in this section of the form as covered following a loss.

Blanket coverage. A *blanket form* covers by a single amount of insurance the same kind of property in different locations or different kinds of property at a single location. Thus, several buildings in different locations may be insured under a blanket policy, as may stocks of goods or merchandise located in different warehouses or stores, or building and machinery at a single location.

Floating coverage. A *floating form,* termed "a floater" in the insurance business, is used to cover goods in different locations when it is difficult or impossible to furnish an accurate description of the location. One form of floater covers certain specific goods wherever they may be, usually within certain prescribed limits as to territory. For example, the equipment of a traveling theatrical company is located in different hotels, theaters, or storage rooms or in transportation vehicles. A floater would cover this equipment wherever it might be so long as it remained within the limits prescribed. Such limits might be a single state, the continental limits of the United States, or worldwide.

Automatic or reporting coverage. *Automatic forms* are written with *reporting* requirements for changing values. They are used when it is difficult, if not impossible, to provide the insurer with an accurate statement of values because of changes or fluctuations, even though full insurance coverage is desired. The amounts are automatically adjusted without action on the part of the insured as the insurable values increase or decrease. The multiple-location contracts utilized by chain stores fall within this category. So long as the required reports are accurately made, the insurance adjusts itself to inventory changes within the limits of the policy. The automatic builder's risk form has the same effect. A building in the process of construction adds value day by day. Monthly reports are required, but a loss at a point between two reports will be protected by full insurance as the values of that day show. See Appendix C for more details on these forms.

Schedule coverage. *Schedule forms* are an example of specific coverage and are often used by certain large risks. All the buildings and their contents belonging to an insured may be grouped on a single form covering for several specific amounts instead of being written as blanket coverage in a single amount, as previously discussed. Separate policies with specific coverage on each item are thus unnecessary. While amounts of insurance are listed for each unit of the property, the policy covers each in proportion to the total values in the schedule. For full coverage the insured must have policies aggregating the total set forth in the schedule. An organization with widely scattered property, such as a state, a municipality, a church, or a university, frequently finds this form to be desirable.

CLAUSES

Purpose and use

Following the descriptive matter in the form, there are a number of *clauses* modifying the policy conditions. Some of these clauses are also found in the "endorsements" discussed in the next section of this chapter. The endorsements also help explain or modify the basic policy to which they are attached. Clauses are presented at this point in the text because they may be part of the forms just mentioned or a part of the endorsements treated later.

These clauses differ with the character of the risk, being sometimes permissive, sometimes liberal, yet often restrictive in their nature. Clauses have the effect (*a*) of extending or limiting the coverage provided by the statutory wording of the standard policy and (*b*) modifying the statutory provisions to meet the insured's requirements with respect to the perils covered. Clauses are usually printed in standard forms as separate sections. The first few words of each clause are printed in boldface, and these boldface words are usually the name by which the clause is known. Sample policy kits (or IIA Course Guides) may be referred to for the exact wording of most of the following clauses contained in the dwelling building and contents form and many other forms.

Several of the many important clauses are discussed separately. The *nuclear clause* and the *water exclusion clause* are significant restrictions on the coverage in many forms. The *liberalization clause* may provide an important extension of coverage to the insured if changes occur in the forms during the policy period. The *standard mortgage clause* is essential whenever the insured property is subject to a mortgage loan. The *coinsurance clause* is used in many property insurance contracts, and it is imperative that insureds understand its purposes and its limiting effect on loss payments. The *pro rata distribution clause* divides coverage under some blanket policies for business properties.

Nuclear clause

A mandatory *nuclear clause* which must be attached to all fire policies provides that the word *fire* does not embrace nuclear or radioactive contamination. The exclusion applies to any such loss, whether it be direct or indirect, proximate or remote, or whether it be caused by, contributed to, or aggravated by fire or any of the other perils insured by the policy. Whether controlled or uncontrolled, a radioactive contamination is covered. The intent of the clause is to exclude radioactive contamination but not to limit coverage with respect to other perils enumerated in the policy.[8]

Insurers provide special facilities for both nuclear energy liability and physical damage coverages. These risks are handled by an insurance pool of several hundred insurers that have combined to write up to nearly $400 million limits for property and liability protection per location. The experience of this group, now called the American Nuclear Insurers, has been good, with less than $1 million paid in claims during the past two decades. The 1957 Price-Anderson Act supplements private insurance by authorizing a U.S. government agency (now the Nuclear Regulatory Commission) to sell coverage to nuclear reactor operators, to the extent not available by private

---

[8] Indicative of the disastrous consequences of radiation is the $350,000 cost of cleaning up what was termed a "minor atomic mishap." Solvent exploded at Oak Ridge, scattering about one fiftieth of an ounce of plutonium into the air. All persons within a four-acre area turned in laboratory clothes to be decontaminated. They were checked physically. Buildings were washed with detergents and repainted, roofs were resurfaced, sod was removed and buried, and the surface of asphalt roads was chiseled.

insurance up to the required $560 million coverage per nuclear incident. It has been an example of effective private-government cooperation in insurance.

Water exclusion clause

Since the fire policy is commonly extended to include perils other than fire and lightning, to clarify the situation with respect to water damages the *water exclusion clause* disclaims liability with respect to water loss resulting from, contributed to, or aggravated by any of the following: (1) flood, surface water, waves, tidal water or tidal wave, overflow of streams or other bodies of water, or spray from any of the foregoing, all whether driven by wind or not; (2) water which backs up through sewers or drains; and (3) water below the surface of the ground, including that which exerts pressure on or leaks through sidewalks, driveways, foundations, walls, basement or other floors, or through doors, windows, or any other openings in such properties. If fire ensues, the insurer is liable only for the damage caused by the fire. If the policy covers other perils, the same rule applies.

In coastal areas, this clause assumes major importance. Hurricanes in Texas, Louisiana, Florida, New Jersey, and other states have brought public criticism for this exclusion. However, the concentrated and catastrophic nature of water damage by flood and hurricane in low-lying areas makes it nearly impossible in include such coverage in the regular fire insurance contract. (See Appendix C.) Loss prevention through construction techniques designed to meet such special perils is also a reasonable answer to these problems.

Flood damage of millions of dollars in many states during the last decade has focused public attention on the need for some form of insurance to alleviate the disastrous effects of floods. The Department of Housing and Urban Development (HUD) and private insurance companies provide a private-government plan in selected areas for flood insurance. The federal government issues the contracts, and establishes rates and limits for coverage marketed by the private insurers. Proper land use and flood control are emphasized. Further discussion is found in Chapter 28.

Liberalization clause

From time to time rating agencies or insurers extend coverage to include features previously not available. To save the cost of endorsing policies every time a change is made that would benefit the insured, a *liberalization clause* is a part of most of the commonly used forms. Its purpose is to give the insured the benefit of any advantageous change that develops. This is an example of such a clause (from the dwelling building and contents form):

If within 45 days prior to the inception of this policy, or during the term hereof, this Company adopts any forms or endorsements made part of this policy which would broaden coverage presently granted hereunder without additional premium charge, such broadened coverage will automatically apply to this policy.

If the liberalization clause is attached, all of these benefits automatically accrue to the insured without specific mention of each in the contract or by subsequent endorsement. This means that in the event of loss, the insured will get the benefit of any privilege or extension of coverage that has been adopted by the insurer.

Standard mortgage clause

This clause is often found as part of standard forms. It is completed by inserting the name of the mortgagee if there are loans on the property and the interest of the mortgagee is to be insured. The *standard mortgage clause* may also be added to the policy at any time in the form of an endorsement. The clause constitutes a separate and distinct contract between the insurer and the mortgagee. It applies only to the building items insured, not the contents.

The basic purpose of the mortgage clause is to protect the interests of the mortgagee or creditor. The clause gives the mortgagee legal rights as a party in the insurance contract taken out and paid for by the mortgagor or owner of the insured property. The clause avoids the necessity for a separate policy by the mortgagee, or for an assignment which is far less certain to protect the creditor. In effect, the mortgagee-creditor rather than the mortgagor-debtor receives the primary benefit from the mortgage clause. To protect the interests of the mortgagee, provision is made that if the owner defaults in premium payment, the mortgagee shall pay on demand for future protection if the insurance is desired to remain in effect. The mortgagee is not liable for payment of premium earned previous to such request.

The most important liberalizing feature of the clause is that which provides that the policy shall not be invalidated by any act or neglect of the mortgagor or owner of the property, or by any foreclosure relating to the property, or by change in ownership or increase in hazard. The mortgagee, which is often a bank or other financial institution that could not keep track of possible violations by many mortgagors, obtains certainty of insurance coverage for the property used as collateral for the loan. The duties imposed upon the mortgagee by the clause are concerned only with changes in ownership, occupation, or hazard when such changes are known by the mortgagee. If the hazard is thus increased, the insurer may request an increased premium.

Coinsurance clause

The *coinsurance clause* aims at an equitable control of the amount of insurance that the insured shall carry. Ordinarily it is used in property insurance for most *business* properties, and in some states (such as New York, for dwelling properties. The need for coinsurance requirements is less for many dwellings because the premium differences due to rates and values are less than those for business properties, where both rates and the larger values insured vary greatly. It limits the liability of the insurer to that proportion of the loss which the insurance amount bears to a given percentage of the value of the property at the time of the loss.

A number of clauses with different names are used to accomplish the same purpose. In fire insurance, with a common requirement of insurance equal to 80 percent of the value, the clause is referred to as the "80 percent coinsurance clause." Because the insured receives a lower rate when this clause is a part of the policy, the coinsurance clause is sometimes termed the "reduced-rate contribution clause." The following coinsurance clause is one now used:

> This Company shall not be liable for a greater proportion of any loss to the property covered than the amount of the insurance under this policy bears to the amount produced by mutilplying the actual cash value of such property at the time of the loss by the coinsurance percentage applicable (specified on the first page of this policy, or by endorsement).

The above coinsurance clause is found in many of the printed forms attached to the standard fire contract, such as in the general property form. The clause may also be added to some contracts as a specific additional endorsement if such wording is not already included.

Purpose. The purpose of the coinsurance clause is to provide equity among policyholders by encouraging them to carry a reasonable amount of insurance (usually 80 percent or more) in relation to the full value of their property. The policyholder receives the benefit of a reduced rate as compared with the "flat"[9] rate for fire insurance in return for a promise to the insurer that insurance at least up to the stated coinsurance percentage will be carried. Although the coinsurance clause does not make mandatory the carrying of insurance up to a specified percentage of value, losses are adjusted as if insurance in such an amount were carried. Where there is a deficiency, the insured is said to be carrying that amount of risk and is, therefore, a *coinsurer* to the extent of the deficiency. The coinsurance clause is the simplest and fairest method devised to adjust charges and loss payments on the assumption that reasonable insurance amounts in relation to property values are carried. The insured should carry at least the percentage of insurance specified in the contract. Otherwise the insurer pays only part of the loss.

Adequacy of fire insurance rates (see later section on justification of the

---

[9] A "flat" insurance rate, which is the alternative to the coinsurance rate, is not based on any assumed amount of insurance in relation to the value of the property. Losses are paid in full up to the amount of the insurance, regardless of whether the insurance amount is close to full value or only a small part of it. The rate is often 50 percent, or more, higher than the coinsurance rate.

ance clause is inoperative. The clause is operative in every loss. However, coinsurance clause) is another method of explaining the purpose of coinsurance.

Formula and examples. The application of the coinsurance clause may be expressed in the following formula based on the wording of the clause.

Let

$I.C.$ = Insurance carried (the amount of insurance),

$I.R.$ = Insurance required (the coinsurance percentage × the value of the property at the time of loss),

L = Amount of the loss.

Then

$$\frac{I.C.}{I.R.} \times L = \text{Amount the insurer pays.}$$

Suppose an insured purchased $60,000 of insurance from company **X** on a building valued at $100,000. If an 80 percent coinsurance clause were made a part of the contract and a loss of $40,000 occurred, the amount company **X** would be obligated to pay would be:

$$\frac{\$60,000}{\$80,000} \times \$40,000, \text{ or } \times \frac{3}{4} \$40,000 = \$30,000.$$

The insured would be a coinsurer to the extent of $10,000 since the property was not insured to 80 percent of the value as promised. If the property was insured for $80,000, the loss would be paid in full by the insurer:

$$\frac{\$80,000}{\$80,000} \times \$40,000, \text{ or } 100\% \times \$40,000 = \$40,000.$$

The second case, where the insured carried the $80,000 as required by the coinsurance clause, illustrates the important principle that the insured is *not just paid 80 percent of the loss*[10] when coinsurance is involved. The insured is paid the *full* loss amount (up to the amount of the policy) *if* at least the minimum required insurance amount is carried. The penalty applies *only* if the insured does not have at least the required amount. In the operation of the foregoing formula, the insurer is never liable for an amount in excess of the policies[11] and hence if the insurance was for $80,000 and the loss was $90,000, the insurer would be liable only for the $80,000 policy amount.

It is sometimes incorrectly stated that when the loss is total, the coinsur-

---

[10] This is a common mistake made by students who assume that this is how the coinsurance clause works.

[11] Nor an amount in excess of the *loss*. If the insurance amount in the example were $90,000, the insurer would pay 100 percent, not 90/80 times the loss, up to the $90,000 insurance amount. Insureds often carry more than the 80 percent required, in order to have enough coverage for serious losses (where the building values are destroyable to that extent), and also in order to be sure to meet the 80 percent requirement if property values are increasing.

ance clause is inoperative. The clause is operative in every loss. However, when the loss is total, the percentage of the loss that limits the amount the insurer pays will exceed the face of the policies. Because the full amount of the policies is payable in the event of a total loss, the impression follows that the clause is inoperative. Suppose, for example, that the loss was total in our previous case (instead of only $40,000) when the insurance carried was $60,000. Then the insurer would pay according to the coinsurance clause:

$$\frac{\$60,000}{\$80,000} \times \$100,000, \text{ or } \times \frac{3}{4} \$100,000 = \$75,000.$$

But since the indicated loss payment of $75,000 exceeds the policy amount of $60,000, the policy amount becomes the maximum payment, and $60,000 is paid.

A different example might involve several insurers insuring the same property. Assume:

Company X has $20,000 of insurance, with an *80%* coinsurance clause.
Company Y has $40,000 of insurance, with an *80%* coinsurance clause.
Company Z has $60,000 of insurance, with a *90%* coinsurance clause.
Value of property is $200,000. Total insurance is $120,000.
Loss of $96,000 occurs.

Only the lesser limit of liability amount indicated by (1) the coinsurance clause, and (2) the pro rata liability clause (discussed previously and found on line 86 of the standard fire policy) would apply. In the case of each of the companies in this example, the coinsurance amount would be the lesser amount, because the insurance required is more than the insurance carried:

$$\text{Co. X would pay } \frac{\$\ 20,000}{\$160,000}, \text{ or } \tfrac{1}{8} \times \$96,000 = \$12,000$$

$$\text{Co. Y would pay } \frac{\$\ 40,000}{\$160,000}, \text{ or } \tfrac{1}{4} \times \$96,000 = \$24,000$$

$$\text{Co. Z would pay } \frac{\$\ 60,000}{\$180,000}, \text{ or } \tfrac{1}{3} \times \$96,000 = \$32,000$$

Total payment $68,000

Justification. To understand the reason for coinsurance, one must consider the function of the insurance *rate*, or the cost per $100 of insurance. Insurance shifts the burden of risk from the individual to many persons. Since a fire in a property need not destroy it totally and since fire losses vary in degree—there being a great many small losses as compared with the number of total losses—unless each insured carries an adequate percentage of insurance to value, the burden of risk will not be equitably distributed.

Insurance premiums have been compared to a tax rate. In every community, taxes to defray community expenses are raised by an assessment levied upon property valued by assessors for that purpose. If each individual were permitted to choose a value upon which to be taxed, the burden would be unfairly distributed. So in fire insurance, if one insured insures in the amount of 50 percent of the property value, another 20 percent, and a third 80 per cent, and if each receives a loss payment in full up to the policy amount, those carrying the smaller amounts of insurance to value pay less than their share of the average premiums. To create an equitable situation, the amount of insurance to value carried by each insured should be uniform. The coinsurance clause requires that the insured carry insurance to a certain stipulated percentage of value or, failing to do so, bear a percentage of the loss.

Statistics from the Chamber of Commerce of the United States (Bulletin No. 6) show most fire losses to be small in relation to the values of the properties:

Ratio of loss to value	Percent of building fires
Between 0 and 20 percent of value	86
Between 20 and 40 percent of value	8
Over 40 percent of value	6
Total	100

These data show that if the coinsurance clause were not required, an insured could carry a small amount of insurance and yet be paid for almost all losses. The conclusion is that the insured should be encouraged to carry high amounts of insurance in relation to value (1) in fairness to other policyholders who would otherwise be paying more than their fair share of total premiums and (2) in order to have insurance in adequate amounts for one of its most important purposes, paying for large losses.

Coinsurance valuation problems and solutions. Since the amount for which the insurer is liable is dependent upon a percentage of the actual cash value of the insured property at the time of the loss or damage, the question of *valuation* is of the utmost importance. Moreover, so far as values are concerned, the entire burden is placed squarely upon the insured. The ways by which values are estimated differ, depending on the type of property. Problems in this area were discussed in connection with loss payments in Chapter 7.

With *stocks* of merchandise, the value of an inventory can be ascertained within reasonable limits through the record of purchases and sales. Large shifting values of some commodities require close watch, for the coinsurance requirement must be met on the basis of value at the time of loss. Seasonal inventory increases, such as in retail stores before the Christmas holiday season, necessitate insurance increases. In the case of *machinery and fixtures,* values are reduced each year through charge-offs made for depreciation and obsolescence. Tax rules encourage a rapid depreciation program, with the result that fixtures and machinery are carried on the books below their actual cash value. Insurance should be based on actual cash value, not book value.

Real estate affords the most difficult problem in valuation. Because of changing wage scales, material prices, and other market factors, building values are constantly fluctuating. A ten-year-old building that cost $100,000 may have a depreciated new replacement value far in excess of the original cost. Appreciation of value due to increased construction costs often more than offsets the actual depreciation of well-maintained property. Thus, an insurance program based upon the original cost, less depreciation, might be nothing less than disastrous. Another difficult problem is presented when market value and replacement value differ widely. Economic changes in communities sometimes result in properties being offered for sale at a market value very much below the replacement value. If a building would cost $40,000 to rebuild, yet sold for $10,000, how much insurance should be carried to avoid becoming a coinsurer? The answer is that because of economic obsolescence, depreciation,[12] and changing neighborhood conditions, the building has lost 75 percent of its real value. If the sales price is realistic, the building's insurable value is probably $10,000. It is, therefore, wise to eliminate the question of values for coinsurance purposes and to write such a risk flat. Because of the difficulty of agreeing on value and depreciation amounts, insurers are often reluctant to insure buildings on a coinsurance basis where depreciation exceeds 50 percent.

The difficulty of valuation is somewhat eased by a *property exclusions clause* which excludes certain types or parts of property from the valuation for coinsurance purposes. By the use of this clause in many forms, or by endorsements, such items as concrete foundations and the cost of excavations or grading and underground piping are excluded from the total valuation. This reduces the amount of insurance required by the coinsurance clause.

Properties equipped with approved automatic sprinklers and complying with inspection requirements may use a special form containing provision for a *guaranteed amount of insurance clause* as an alternative to the 90 percent coinsurance clause normally available to sprinklered risks. It is usual to require that the guaranteed amount be the full value of the property, and that a new statement of values be filed every year. The operation of this clause is identical with that of the coinsurance clause, with the one exception that the amount of insurance to be carried is agreed upon in advance.

The so-called *5 percent waiver clause* usually follows immediately after the coinsurance clause quoted earlier:

> In the event that the aggregate claim for any loss is both less than $10,000 and less than 5 percent of the total amount of insurance applicable to the property involved at the time such loss occurs, no special inventory or appraisement of the undamaged property shall be required.

---

[12] Suggested annual rates of depreciation depend upon the care of the particular building, and causes of depreciation must in each case be considered. A type of building whose life is estimated at 50 years might well be considered at the end of 20 years to be 40 percent depreciated. When repairs are neglected, or when some economic change in demand occurs, the building may be almost useless. On the other hand, the element of economic obsolescence and the element of depreciation may be very small.

The purpose of the waiver clause is to relieve the insured of the necessity of taking an actual physical inventory of the undamaged property in the event of small losses. The clause in no way suspends the operation of the coinsurance feature of the contract.

The greatest *disadvantage* of the coinsurance clause is the possibility of *misunderstanding* by the insured. Insurance agents who recognize the value of coinsurance are sometimes reluctant to advise an insured to adopt it. Insureds who believe they understand the operation of the coinsurance clause frequently forget to keep insurance amounts up to date. If the clause is to be used because of substantial rate savings to the insured, proper education and explanation to the insured are essential. The insured should understand his or her responsibility and possible penalty.

While an insured may secure a reduced *rate* by incorporating the coinsurance clause in the form, it does not always follow that a change from a flat-rate coverage to a coinsurance coverage will result in a lower *total cost*. The requirements of the clause as to the amount of insurance necessary may result in a lower rate per thousand, but because of the necessity of adding additional insurance the total premium charge may be higher. A careful comparison is recommended.

Pro rata distribution clause

Another clause used for some business situations but much less common than the coinsurance clause is the *pro rata distribution clause*. It divides the total coverage under a blanket policy (see previous section on types of forms) to apply specifically upon each separate location in the proportion that the value at each location bears to the sum of the values at all the locations. In connection with this clause, insurers usually require the use of a 90 percent coinsurance clause. The result is a distribution of the coverage that is fair to both the insurer and the insured. The clause is a great convenience in insuring *contents*. Frequently inventories are constantly shifting from one location to another but total value is more or less steady. When the contents may often be shifted from building to building, or when shipments in and out are involved, it is difficult to change specific insurance coverages to follow values. A blanket policy with the pro rata distribution clause automatically shifts the coverage as the relative values shift.

ENDORSEMENTS

Purpose

An *endorsement* is a provision added to the insurance contract by which the scope of its coverage is clarified, restricted, or enlarged. Certain endorsements, such as those that extend the perils covered, may be as long as the form and may be attached when the policy is issued. Other endorsements may be brief additions that are added to the contract after the contract goes into effect. A written contract may be completed without an endorsement, but not without a form being attached. Clauses are sections of either forms or endorsements.

General use

Many endorsements are merely typewritten additions to the contract, changing its amount, rate, or term. Errors may be corrected in the same manner. If a property is sold, the insurance may be continued for the benefit of the new owner by means of an endorsement. Some endorsements are in the nature of permits. For example, a permit may be added to the policy authorizing removal of the insured property and providing for coverage in another location. The policy provides for permission to add endorsements in those parts of the conditions found on lines 38–48.

One of the most common and important uses of endorsements with the fire insurance contract is the addition of *other perils*. Discussed in the next sections of this chapter are the popular endorsements: "extended coverage," "dwelling building and contents—broad form," and "dwelling building and contents—special form."

The extended coverage endorsement

This packaged endorsement, known when it was first introduced in the 1930s as the "supplemental contract," provides in a single addition *extended coverage* protection against the perils of windstorm, explosion, hail, riot, smoke, and several other perils. The endorsement is not, in fact, an additional contract but is rather an extension of the protection of the fire insurance contract to cover other perils without at the same time increasing the face amount of the policy.

There are several varieties of the *extended coverage endorsement,* including one for coastal areas which includes loss by waves. One of the most common wordings is that found in a separate section headed "extended coverage" at the end of the dwelling building and contents form. The coverage is in force if a premium for extended coverage is indicated on the first page of the policy.

Seven perils are included in a policy extended in this manner: (*a*) *windstorm;* (*b*) *hail;* (*c*) *explosion;* (*d*) *riot,* riot attending a strike, and civil commotion; (*e*) *aircraft* damage; (*f*) *vehicle* damage; and (*g*) *smoke* damage. There is no choice on the part of the insured as to which of these seven perils are included: all are automatically included in the package-type endorsement.

The coverage of the extended coverage endorsement is effected by a clause that substitutes the new perils to be covered for the word *fire* as it appears in the insuring clause of the statutory contract. All of the policy provisions are applied with respect to losses by the extended coverage perils exactly as they would be applied to a fire loss.

The $50 deductible clause of the dwelling building and contents form applies to losses caused by extended coverage perils, or sometimes only to losses caused by the wind and hail perils. In some jurisdictions full coverage is available for an additional premium, but the $50 deductible is the more usual. The deductible applies to each occurrence of loss, and to each dwelling if more than one are insured in the same policy. In some jurisdictions the deductible applies to both a building and its contents. Outdoor radio and television antennas and aerials, including their wiring and towers, are excluded from the windstorm coverage but can be specifically added for an additional premium.

Most of the wording of the extended coverage endorsement pertains to explanation of the perils, defining what is intended to be covered and what is not intended to be covered in the contract. For example, the *windstorm or hail* perils do not include coverage for frost, snow, or sleet, whether driven by wind or not. Windstorm or hail damage to the interior of a building or its contents is not covered unless the roof or walls are damaged first. *Explosions* are defined so that the following losses are not covered: steam explosions from property of the insured and sonic booms from aircraft. *Riot* coverage includes damage by striking employees and "pillage and looting occurring during and at the immediate place of the riot," but it does not include indirect losses such as interruption of business. *Vehicle* coverage excludes damage by any vehicle owned or operated by the insured or a tenant, and damage by any vehicle to fences, driveways, walks, lawns, trees, shrubs, or plants. *Aircraft* damage includes objects falling from aircraft but requires actual physical contact of the aircraft or its parts with the property insured (thus excluding sonic boom). *Smoke* coverage includes sudden, unusual, and faulty operation of any heating or cooking unit which is connected to a chimney or a smoke pipe, but not smoke from fireplaces.

An "apportionment clause" included in the extended coverage endorsement makes it important for the insured to have the extended coverage included in all fire policies covering the same property. If this is not done, the insurer pays proportionately: for example, if extended coverage is on two thirds of the property, only two thirds of the extended coverage loss would be paid.

The broad form endorsement

Another very common endorsement, the *dwelling building and contents—broad form,* is used to insure buildings (other than farm property) designed for occupancy by not more than four families or apartments and their contents. The current use of all the dwelling forms has been limited by the popularity of homeowners' contracts (see Chapter 27), which include coverages similar to forms discussed here. The forms are also used where homeowners' policies are not applicable, such as rental properties, unoccupied new or for-sale homes, and homes of smaller value.

The broad form endorsement includes all of the perils just discussed in connection with the extended coverage endorsement. In addition, it broadens the coverage of 4 of those perils and adds 11 new perils to the scope of the fire insurance contract. The result is a very comprehensive coverage for the dwelling owner or tenant. Although it is a "named perils" type of endorsement, including only those perils specifically named or listed in the wording used, the broad form endorsement provides adequate protection for most insureds.

A $50 deductible for any one occurrence applies to property covered by the broad form endorsement in the form used by many states. The deductible can be waived for an additional premium, but it seldom is because of the higher cost. A special deductible applies for the perils of vandalism and malicious mischief: 2 percent of the insurance amount, but not less than $100 nor more than $250.

The four extended coverage perils which are somewhat broadened are:

1. *Explosion.* This does cover *steam* boiler and some other explosion losses because there are no specific exclusions.

2. *Damage by aircraft.* This includes *sonic boom* because there is no definition requiring actual physical contact with the aircraft.

3. *Damage by vehicles.* This includes damage to insured property done *by any vehicle owned or occupied by any occupant of the premises,* except for damage to driveways, walks, lawns, trees, shrubs, or plants.

4. *Smoke damage.* This only requires that the damage be "sudden and accidental, other than smoke from agricultural or industrial operations," and thus could include unexpected smoke losses from *fireplaces* or units not connected to a chimney or a smoke pipe.

The 11 perils added by the broad form endorsement are:

1. *Bursting of heating systems.* This covers "sudden and accidental tearing asunder, cracking, burning or bulging" of a steam or hot water heating system or of appliances for heating water. Included would be boiler explosion, freezing, and other causes.

2. *Freezing of plumbing, heating and air conditioning systems and domestic appliances.* Freezing is also limited here in case the building is vacant or while all occupants are absent more than four consecutive days, unless due diligence has been used to maintain heat in the building or the water has been drained and shut off.

3. *Vandalism and malicious mischief.* This covers willful or intentional damage or destruction of the property insured. It does not cover glass breakage, which is separately covered (see item 9 below), damage from theft or pilferage, or losses if the building is vacant more than 30 consecutive days immediately preceding the loss. Note the special deductible mentioned pre-

viously. This peril can also be included in the extended coverage endorsement as one added peril, if an additional premium charge is made.

4. *Burglars.* Damage done in breaking into the property for burglary is covered, but this is not intended to include the property taken by the burglars. A 30-day vacancy exclusion also applies for this peril.

5. *Falling objects.* This includes damage by falling trees. The windstorm peril would cover most of such losses, but occasionally trees do fall without any wind being involved. Damage to the contents or the building interior is covered when the roof or walls first sustain damage from the outside. Outdoor radio and television antennas and aerials, masts and towers, outdoor equipment, awnings, fences, lawns, trees, shrubs, and plants are not covered.

6. *Weight of ice, snow, or sleet.* This includes physical injury to the building due to the weight of such elements. As above, most outdoor property is excluded, and patios, swimming pools, walls, and docks are additional specific exceptions. Many of these types of losses were covered in the unusually harsh winter of 1977–78.

7. *Collapse.* The actual collapse of a building or any part of it is covered here, but "settling, cracking, shrinkage, bulging or expansion" is not intended to be covered. Earthquake, flood, and landslide are excluded in this coverage and in all other perils of the broad form endorsement.

8. *Water or steam leakage or overflow.* Accidental discharge or leakage from plumbing, heating, air conditioning, or domestic appliances is covered. Rain leaking through a roof is not included in this coverage. For example, a faucet leaking or unintentionally left running for a few hours can cause considerable damage to floors, walls, and contents. Water damage from freezing of water pipes under some conditions of vacancy is not covered, nor are losses during vacancy of over 30 days. The damage to the system or appliance itself is not covered, but tearing out and replacing part of the building to effect repairs to the system is covered.

9. *Breakage of glass.* All glass which is part of the building, including storm doors and windows, is covered for loss by almost any cause except after 30 days' vacancy. The $50 deductible usually applied to all broad form perils is an important limitation.

10. *Electric current damage.* Sudden and accidental injury to property from artificially generated (thus not lightning) electric currents to electrical appliances, fixtures, and wiring is covered here. Tubes, transistors, and similar items are excluded.

11. *Removal.* Direct loss by removal of the property covered is included for 30 days on a pro rata basis, when such removal is from premises endangered by or for repair of damage caused by insured perils.

Other features of the broad form endorsement are explained later as the homeowners' policy, which is often written to include the broad form perils, is discussed in the chapter on multiple-line insurance. The broad form endorsement includes such other 10 percent features as: 10 percent off-premises coverage, replacement cost coverage for buildings, loss of rental value, and additional living expense coverage.

The special form endorsement

The *dwelling buildings and contents—special form* is used to insure the same types of dwelling properties as those discussed for the broad form endorsement.

One important distinction of this endorsement as compared with most others used with the fire insurance contract is that the special form is an "all-risks" coverage. It does not list or name the perils that are covered but merely states that "this policy is extended to insure against all risks of direct physical loss, except as hereinafter provided."

The result is among the broadest types of coverage available, even though some exclusions are necessary. The debate as to whether an "all-risks" coverage is much more comprehensive than a "named-perils" coverage is not important. An all-risks form with few exceptions may be broader than a named-perils form with few perils named or many exceptions noted. The reverse may also be true: an extensive listing in a named-perils form may provide better coverage than an all-risks form with many exceptions. In this case, the special form provides somewhat broader protection for most insureds. The difference is not too great, however, as can be surmised from the fact that in most territories the special form only costs a few cents more per $100 of insurance than the broad form.

Because an all-risks policy automatically *includes* all perils that it does *not* exclude, one advantage is that unusual losses and those that could not be reasonably anticipated are covered. A few illustrations for buildings insured under the special form are: spillage of a liquid stain on walls or floors; wind-driven rain that seeps in or comes through doors, windows, or bad roofs, to damage interior paint or wallpaper; and squirrels or other animals that chew the front porch woodwork. Similar damage to contents would also be covered.

Most of the exclusions are similar to those discussed in connection with the broad form endorsement, such as earthquake, landslide, flood,[13] freezing under certain conditions, vandalism during long-term vacancy, and some limitations on trees, plants, and other outside properties.

An example of an additional type of exclusion particularly needed by all-risks coverage is the exclusion for *wear-and-tear* losses. Because the intention is to cover accidental and sudden losses rather than the gradual accumulation of losses that might normally be expected, the wear-and-tear exclusion includes: deterioration; rust; mold; smog or industrial smoke; damage by birds,

---

[13] The exclusions for flood and water are the same for broad form and special form endorsements: damage from flood, surface water, waves, below-ground-level water, and back-up of sewers and drains.

vermin, or domestic animals; and the settling, cracking, bulging, or expansion of such properties as pavements, patios, or structural parts of the building.

A $50 deductible is almost always used in connection with the perils insured by the special form endorsement. The same type of all-risks coverage found in the special form is included in Forms 3 and 5 of the homeowner's policy, discussed in the later chapter on multiple-line insurance.

A REVIEW OF THE FIRE INSURANCE CONTRACT

Now that the forms, clauses, and endorsements to the basic fire insurance contract have been presented, it will be helpful to review these together with the preceding major parts of the contract around which this chapter has been organized. The entire typical contract (for dwelling building and contents), including its declarations, insuring agreement, conditions, and exclusions, is summarized from a different viewpoint in Figure 17–3. These parts of the whole contract are related to coverage in terms of *persons, property, perils and losses, premiums, locations, amounts, term, suspensions,* and *loss provisions.* Such an analysis is useful for any kind of insurance contract.

SPECIAL AND ALLIED FIRE LINES

As can be seen by the endorsements studied in the previous section, the field of fire insurance includes more than just the peril of fire. Windstorms, explosions, riots, water damage, smoke, and many other perils are often included in the fire insurance contract. A number of other miscellaneous perils are associated with fire insurance and included in the general term of *special and allied fire lines* of insurance. Some of these perils are written by endorsements on the fire contract; others are written predominantly by the fire insurance companies in separate contracts.

Appendix C, "Special and Allied Fire Lines," can be referred to for details of these many coverages. They are sometimes of importance to particular insureds, but their relatively infrequent use makes it unnecessary to include full discussion of their characteristics in this chapter. One of the most common is *sprinkler leakage insurance* for damage done by the accidental discharge of water from automatic sprinklers in a building. Legal liability for such sprinkler leakage damage is also an important type of coverage for those insureds who are responsible for sprinkler equipment. *Builder's risk insurance* is a special contract available for the changing values and ownership interest during construction. *Crop insurance* is written for specified types of crops for damage by weather, insects, and disease. *Flood insurance* is available in many areas with the federal government through private insurance agents (see Chapter 28). *Multiple-location contracts* are very important for larger businesses that need the flexible and automatic coverage of reporting forms. Other

Figure 17-3. Analysis of the fire insurance contract

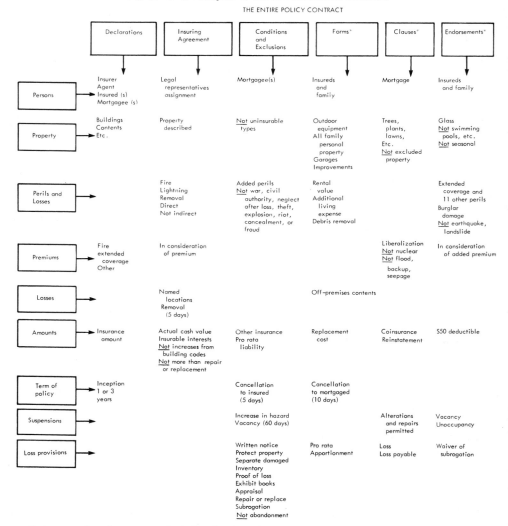

THE ENTIRE POLICY CONTRACT

	Declarations	Insuring Agreement	Conditions and Exclusions	Forms*	Clauses*	Endorsements*
Persons	Insurer Agent Insured (s) Mortgagee (s)	Legal representatives assignment	Mortgagee(s)	Insureds and family	Mortgage	Insureds and family
Property	Buildings Contents Etc.	Property described	Not uninsurable types	Outdoor equipment All family personal property Garages Improvements	Trees, plants, lawns, Etc. Not excluded property	Glass Not swimming pools, etc. Not seasonal
Perils and Losses		Fire Lightning Removal Direct Not indirect	Added perils Not war, civil authority, neglect after loss, theft, explosion, riot, concealment, or fraud	Rental value Additional living expense Debris removal		Extended coverage and 11 other perils Burglar damage Not earthquake, landslide
Premiums	Fire extended coverage Other	In consideration of premium			Liberalization Not nuclear Not flood, backup, seepage	In consideration of added premium
Losses		Named locations Removal (5 days)		Off-premises contents		
Amounts	Insurance amount	Actual cash value Insurable interests Not increases from building codes Not more than repair or replacement	Other insurance Pro rata liability	Replacement cost	Coinsurance Reinstatement	$50 deductible
Term of policy	Inception 1 or 3 years		Cancellation to insured (5 days)	Cancellation to mortgaged (10 days)		
Suspensions			Increase in hazard Vacancy (60 days)		Alterations and repairs permitted	Vacancy Unoccupancy
Loss provisions			Written notice Protect property Separate damaged Inventory Proof of loss Exhibit books Appraisal Repair or replace Subrogation Not abandonment	Pro rata Apportionment	Loss Loss payable	Waiver of subrogation

* Assume that the contract includes the "dwelling building and contents—broad form" and the clauses and endorsements it contains. Where an item is found in one of these, it is not repeated in the lists for the others.

special and allied lines discussed in Appendix C are water damage liability and tenants' improvements and betterments.

CONCURRENCY

Policies designed to cover identical properties should be written as nearly alike as possible with the same terms and conditions. When there are discrepancies, the insurance is said to be "nonconcurrent," and this may have the effect of complicating the problem of loss adjustment or providing inadequate coverage. Very minor differences in details may not cause problems, but major ones often do so.

Nonconcurrency occurs most frequently in a combination of specific and blanket policies. The owner of several buildings forming part of one establishment may take out specific insurance on certain of the buildings and blanket insurance covering several or all of the buildings. Another form of nonconcurrency is to be found when several policies cover on a given risk, but some are written with coinsurance and others without it. A special "limit of liability" rule apportions the coverages among the several contracts in these cases.

There are many examples of nonconcurrent contracts in fire, inland marine, and casualty insurance. Most of the problems are solved by inter-insurer cooperation under what is known as the 1963 *Agreement of Guiding Principles*. It is agreed in advance by almost all major insurers how any disputes in regard to overlapping coverages will be settled. These rules of priority and apportionment specify which type of contract is to be primary coverage for stipulated losses and which is to be excess coverage. Generally, the policy that is more specific as to described property or location is the first to pay for a loss.

For example, coverage on a limited-purpose basis is paid before any other insurance, such as a "blanket" policy affording a broader scope of coverage. Also, coverage specific as to location applies before "floater"-type contracts, except where the floater policy is issued to a transportation carrier or bailee. In a loss of a fur coat insured under both the furrier's (bailee customers) insurance and under the off-premises coverage of homeowner's insurance, the bailee's policy would apply first and any excess of loss over that payment would be paid by the homeowner's policy. Thus the participation of several different insurance contracts in a loss is settled in an orderly and consistent manner, and the loss payment is made without unnecessary delay.

FOR REVIEW AND DISCUSSION

1. *Why and how* are insurance contracts standardized? Give examples from several different types of insurance contracts.
2. Compare the basic *purposes* of the three main sections in the standard fire contract.
3. What *significance* do the following terms have in fire insurance: (*a*) standard policy? (*b*) insurable interest? (*c*) proximate loss? (*d*) actual cash value? (*e*) friendly fire? and (*f*) pro rata liability clause?
4. Johnny can't read well, but he is sure that fire insurance is written to cover losses of more than just the property value of the owner. Illustrate why you believe Johnny to be correct.

5. What has the phrase *"direct* loss by *fire"* in the New York standard fire contract been interpreted to mean? Explain fully.

6. Is the *actual cash value* paid under a fire policy based upon (*a*) assessed property valuation? (*b*) policyholder cost? (*c*) full replacement value? and (*d*) an amount for which the insured had offered it for sale?

7. Explain whether or not the fire insurer is liable in each of these cases:
    a. A roast cooking in the oven becomes badly burned, and smoke damages the dwelling and furniture.
    b. Some Kleenex on a mantelpiece accidentally catches fire. A person gathers up the tissue and throws it into a fireplace, not knowing that a diamond ring was in the burning Kleenex.
    c. Jewelry is thrown into a furnace with rubbish and destroyed.
    d. Mr. Gepeto negligently throws a match into a pile of shavings and destroys his woodworking plant.

8. The extended coverage endorsement is a widely used insurance endorsement. What is extended, and how is it accomplished?

9. Riot coverage is now considered much more important in property insurance contracts than ever before. How are the direct riot damage and the resulting fire loss covered by the usual fire insurance contract? Is this fair to insureds in rural areas?

10. What requirements does the insured have to meet after a fire loss? Is subrogation important in the fire insurance contract? Is your answer based on potential or actual benefits to the insurer or the insured?

11. Why may so many different forms and endorsements be added to what is supposed to be a *standard* fire contract?

12. Why would you agree that the dwelling building and contents forms add greatly to the coverage of the standard fire insurance contract?

13. Identify and contrast the purposes of the standard mortgage clause, the coinsurance clause, and the pro rata distribution clause.

14. Some clauses are restrictive, while others extend the coverage of the insurance contract. Give an example of each type, with explanation.

15. Why is the standard mortgage clause very favorable to the mortgagee?

16. Which of the following perils would probably be covered by a standard fire insurance contract with the broad form endorsement:
    a. Sonic boom damage?
    b. Steam boiler explosion?
    c. Vandalism not associated with a riot?
    d. Landscape or subsidence other than that caused by earthquake?
    e. Water leakage due to freezing of plumbing system?

17. Criticize the following statements about the fire coinsurance clause:
    a. "The insurance company merely pays 80 percent of the fire loss.'
    b. "The purpose of the clause is to make more profit for the insurer."
    c. "The 80 percent coinsurance requirement is not important, because in a large loss it does not matter."
    d. "Changing values for real estate or inventories do not affect the policyholder who insures with the coinsurance clause."

18. Barbara owns a building and carries insurance equal to 100 percent of its value, with an 80 percent coinsurance clause. Is she permitted to do this? What change would you make in her coverage?

19. Mr. I. M. Insecure has the following fire insurance on his business property, which is valued today at $200,000: $120,000 of insurance, with an 80 percent coinsurance clause included in the policy contract.

    a. Is his friend Mr. B. A. Success correct in telling him that he is not carrying enough insurance to meet serious losses and the coinsurance requirement? Explain.

    b. What would be paid in case of a $72,000 loss? Show your method.

    c. A $180,000 loss? Show your method.

    d. How would you explain to Mr. Insecure the reasons why he should carry more insurance in relation to his property values, and how the coinsurance clause does this in an equitable manner?

20. Would you, as an insured, prefer to have a "named-perils" or an "all risks" contract? Explain. Can you relate your answer to fire "allied lines"?

21. Why do most insureds need either the broad form endorsement or the special form endorsement for protection of their dwellings?

22. Show how the entire fire insurance contract may be easily summarized as to its coverage of persons, property, perils, and amounts of insurance.

23. What is "nonconcurrency," and how are some of its problems solved?

Chapter 18

Concepts considered in Chapter 18—Indirect loss insurance

The nature and classification of insurance for indirect losses divides this area into two basic types: *time element* and *no time element* losses.

Time element losses include the most common type of indirect loss insurance, business interruption, as well as contingent business interruption, rents and rental value, extra-expense, and tuition fees insurance.

Business interruption insurance is discussed in terms of its:

Importance, because of severe losses, but very often overlooked.

Purpose, which is to pay for income loss, including future profits and expenses, from such perils as fire, wind, riot, and others.

Difference from profits insurance, which covers only the profit lost because of damage to inventories of manufacturers.

Insurance amount values, estimated from gross earnings.

Loss illustrations of calculating profits and continuing expenses.

Forms, which today are based upon the use of a *gross earnings form* and for smaller businesses a *no coinsurance earnings* form.

Contingent business interruption insurance applies where direct damage to the *property of others* may cause income loss. *Off-premises power* and *selling agents' commissions* are also examples.

Rents and rental value insurance protects owners or tenants from loss of rental income or use of property following a loss such as fire.

Extra-expense insurance is significant for businesses where customer service must be continued at high additional costs after a direct loss.

Tuition fees insurance is a specialized need of colleges and schools.

No time element losses are those indirect losses in which the length of time required for restoration of property is not a determining factor:

Profits insurance on goods sold but not yet delivered.

Leasehold interest insurance, to cover the loss of long-term favorable leases canceled after a serious fire or other direct damage.

Temperature damage insurance, for loss to perishable property.

Matched set or parts insurance, for jewelry or clothing.

Errors and omissions insurance for financial institutions as mortgagees.

Depreciation insurance for replacement costs over actual cash values.

Valuable papers insurance for expensive or important records.

Accounts receivable insurance for collection loss due to record damage, for "all risks."

Rain insurance for loss of profits due to unfavorable weather.

Indirect loss insurance

The potential direct losses to property from fire, wind, water, and many other perils are well known and respected. Most property owners usually insure the values which may be lost by the immediate damage done to their property by these perils. Much less recognized and understood are the oftentimes equally significant losses which may result from indirect losses.

For example, what happens when a business has a fire loss? Suppose a bowling alley burns and it will take eight months to rebuild it. Can the owners complacently rely upon their fire insurance contracts to meet all their losses? Many insureds do, but they find that although the building and its contents are fully insured against direct losses, the *income* they have been producing is not insured. Probably fewer than one in three businesses insure the very purpose of their business—to create income and profits. This is one example of the many kinds of indirect loss insurance which are discussed in this chapter. In effect, the topic is "business survival insurance."

NATURE AND CLASSIFICATION

As opposed to direct loss coverages, which apply to physical loss or damage to the subject of the insurance, indirect loss coverages provide indemnity for losses that occur as a consequence of damage to property. Thus, such losses are sometimes called "consequential losses." For example, if an accidental fire destroys a store and its merchandise, the loss of the value of the building and its contents is a direct loss covered by the fire insurance contract. However, the owner of the store will also lose *income* because of the business interruption. This is an indirect loss of fixed expenses and profits over and above the actual physical damage to building and merchandise. Another example of an indirect loss is the loss of rental income due to fire causing property to be unusable. Such losses may be covered by *indirect loss insurance,* which may also include other perils such as windstorm, explosion, water, or riot. Indirect loss insurance is a form of after-the-loss insurance.

Indirect loss that is attributable to the time element required in order to restore damaged property to normal use is known as a *time element loss.* The coverages to provide insurance are known as time element coverages. Among the major time element losses are: (1) losses due to the *interruption of business* by damage to the insured's property; (2) *contingent* losses due to business interruptions; (3) loss of income from *rents,* or loss of *rental value,* caused by damage to the property; and (4) *extra expense* incurred to conduct business or maintain a home on a temporary basis following loss. Loss of *tuition fees* by educational institutions is an example of a special type of time element loss.

In contrast to indirect losses involving a time element, there are many indirect losses that have no relationship to the time required to restore property to normal use.[1] Among the major types are: (1) loss of *profits* on *manufactured goods* and (2) loss of *leasehold,* or excess rental value interest, due to the cancellation of a lease following damage to the property subject to the lease. Miscellaneous types include: loss of perishables due to *temperature change;* loss due to damage to *parts of matched sets*; losses growing out of *errors or omissions* for financial institutions as mortgagees; losses that are the difference between actual value and *replacement cost* new (depreciation); loss or damage to *valuable papers;* loss due to damage to *accounts receivable* records; and loss of profits and expenses due to *rain.*

Most of the major types of indirect loss are written by adding a form to the standard fire contract. For each type of indirect loss insurance, a good understanding of the contract can be achieved by considering the following in analyzing the coverage: What *perils, losses, properties, locations, persons or interests,* and *amounts* are covered? Also, any conditions excluding or suspending coverage should be noted, and the insured's duties and insurer's options after a loss should be reviewed.

TIME ELEMENT LOSSES

Losses that are dependent upon the time necessary to restore the property to normal operations are among the best-known kinds of indirect losses. The amount of the loss is largely determined by the element of time after the loss which is required to repair, rebuild, or restore property to normal use. The losses include lost profits, lost income, lost use of property, contingent losses to other parties, and increased expenses.

Business interruption insurance

Importance.   Although more than 90 percent of owners carry insurance to protect the physical properties used for their businesses, probably not more than 30 percent of these owners carry *business interruption insurance* to protect the earnings of their businesses. In many cases this is like a sea captain watching out for icebergs on top of the water but forgetting that most of the danger lies underneath.

---

[1] This chapter divides all indirect losses into "time element" and "no time element" losses. Another useful division could be between (1) losses which result in *decreases in income* and (2) losses which result in *increases in expenses.*

There is no fixed relationship between property damage loss or value and business interruption loss or value. The importance of business interruption insurance becomes apparent when it is recognized that a small property loss in a vital section of any business may cause a total suspension of operations with a resulting loss far in excess of the actual property damage loss. Consider, for example, the disastrous effects possible as the result of the destruction of an essential elevator or escalator in a department store. Damage of $5,000 to the elevator might result in the loss of $100,000 of earnings during a major sale. On the other hand, it is conceivable that very substantial property damage might occur without serious interruption of operations if the property could be quickly restored to provide normal business operations.

The great need[2] for business interruption insurance for mercantile risks is shown by the relationship between gross earnings (sales less cost of goods sold) and average inventory. Illustrations of this comparison include grocery stores with gross earnings of four times the dollar value of average inventory, drugstores with twice as much gross earnings as inventory, and gasoline stations with six times greater gross earnings than average inventory.

Purpose. *Business interruption insurance,* also known as *prospective earnings insurance* and *use and occupancy insurance,* protects against the *loss of income* because of the interruption of business *by fire or other perils.* Sizable business interrruption losses are caused not only by fires but also by *windstorms* and *explosions.*

The *riot* peril, too, is one which today should receive much greater attention in the insured's choice of perils to be included in the "BI" contract. New forms in recent years have clarified the interruption by a civil authority clause in these contracts. They cover loss of earnings due to a specific order denying access when there has been damage (such as by riot or civil commotion) adjacent to the insured's property. The damage must be within a few doors, or city blocks at the most. Loss due to a general citywide curfew is not covered, however. In essence, the insured *peril* must damage *property,* thus interrupting for a *period* of time the *production* capacity to create *profits.*

The contract is one of indemnity for the net profits not realized, plus such fixed charges and expenses as necessarily continue during the interruption, but only to the extent that such fixed charges and expenses would have been earned had no interruption due to an insured peril occurred. Business interruption insurance keeps the business in the position that it could have maintained for itself had there been no interruption. In a sense, its function for an employer is quite similar to the function of unemployment insurance

---

[2] John D. Phelan, *Business Interruption Primer* (Indianapolis Rough Notes Co., 1970). The importance of business interruption insurance is also apparent in the statement that "43% of all businesses suffering a serious fire loss never reopened—despite the fact that most carried insurance on building and contents" (p. 8). Later studies continue to verify this comment.

for an employee. It has also been called "living insurance" or "disability insurance" for businesses.[3]

Distinguished from profits insurance. Business interruption insurance is to be distinguished from *profits insurance* in that profits insurance looks to the past whereas business interruption indemnity looks to the future. As will presently be noted, profits insurance protects the insured against the loss of potential net profits on finished stock in the hands of a manufacturer or held in storage. When this stock is damaged or destroyed, the direct loss insurance will cover only an amount necessary to repair or replace the damaged property, not potential profits. Hence, profits insurance is necessary for complete indemnity. Time is not a crucial factor in determining the profits insurance loss. In the case of business interruption insurance, on the other hand, time is the essence of the contract. The contract looks to the future and protects the insured against the loss of future earnings during the time required to restore normal business operations after a physical damage loss.

The difference between the two forms of insurance is emphasized when it is realized that profits insurance on a mercantile stock will cover only the profit prevented on the stock on hand which is damaged or destroyed. For example, if a mercantile stock turns over ten times each year, this would mean that an interruption of six months in the business would result in a loss of five turnovers of the stock. Business interruption insurance would cover this loss, but profits insurance would cover only the loss of profits on the inventory actually on hand and damaged at the time of the loss.

Business interruption insurance amount. The first step in determining the business interruption insurance needed by, for example, the owner of a mercantile store, is to estimate the total values exposed to loss. Usually, these are the *gross earnings* of the firm. In the case of an interruption of business, the store owner would not lose the entire gross sales income, for the net cost of the merchandise in the store would be covered by direct property insurance against fire and other perils. (Other items such as discounts and bad debts would not be lost, either, in an interruption.) Thus, the store owner first calculates gross sales *less* the net cost of merchandise and these other items in order to arrive at estimated gross earnings.

The estimate of the *insurance* amount necessary to cover a business interruption *value,* or gross earnings, involves several other considerations. First, in a serious loss, would the store be able to get back in business, at least partially (perhaps at a temporary location), sooner than one year after the loss? Any factors such as the type of building construction and the availability of facilities for reestablishing the business are important in determining the percentage of business interruption value to be covered. Second, would the earnings of the store be subject to substantial fluctuation during the year, as for weddings in June or Christmas in December? If so, the estimate of lost

---

[3] Joseph R. Pierpont, "Business Interruption Insurance—What It Covers," *Risk Management,* December 1976, p. 34.

earnings must consider the peak periods of the year rather than only the average per diem loss.

This suggests that the coinsurance requirements of the particular contract form to be used in writing the business interruption insurance may vary considerably. The forms permit the choice of coinsurance to be 50, 60, 70, or 80 percent of the gross earnings determined as the insurable value. These coinsurance requirements give the insured a wide latitude in the event of fluctuating earnings. For the average mercantile business, 50 percent of the business interruption value is ordinarily adequate. Losses for minor peak periods are automatically covered so long as adequate insurance to value is carried, but where the business is heavily seasonal, larger amounts are indicated. Thus, perhaps 70 percent of the estimated business interruption value might be chosen as the insurance amount. Such a choice would be made on the assumption that it would rarely take longer than about eight months to get back in business in full. If the loss occurred during peak seasonal sales periods, the insured would have coverage for the larger losses that might result from the ill-timed shorter period.

One of the contentions about estimating business interruption values has been the supposed difficulty of predicting the amount of continuing expenses, whether full or partial. Under the popular gross earnings form (see later section), however, this is largely unnecessary,[4] because almost all expenses continue during the most likely interruption, one of short duration. In this case there are relatively few expenses which can be deducted from gross earnings (see later example of a business interruption *loss*) in calculating the BI *value*. The major item by far is usually ordinary payroll expense,[5] which can be deducted when the insurance contract is on an 80 percent or higher coinsurance form. Aside from this, probably only a small amount of power, heat, and refrigeration expenses not under contract, could be deducted (an extra premium is charged for this coverage).

Thus, in the later illustration, the business interruption value could be quickly estimated by merely subtracting $250,000 of ordinary payroll from the estimated gross earnings (or "net sales," as this is sometimes called) of $495,000, and a BI value of $245,000 established. This could be larger in a more serious loss, but again it is mostly the discontinuable ordinary payroll item which would increase the deductions substantially, as unskilled workers are laid off. Much of this payroll would not be a discontinuable expense unless the interruption lasted for several months or longer.

---

[4] This reasonable observation is credited to correspondence from Richard B. (Ben) Masters, CPCU, retired, Executive Manager of the Insurance Educational Association, San Francisco.

[5] Sometimes the payroll item is very large, and the insured wants coverage. A recent loss by Warner-Lambert Co., for example, included a claim for explosion direct property damage of $1 million, $2 million of lost profits, and $45 million of continuing payroll expenses, as reported in the *Wall Street Journal,* November 22, 1977.

The reasoning is similar to that in fire insurance, where in estimating values for the purpose of calculating the insurance amount needed in order to meet coinsurance requirements, some values are often excluded because they would not be damaged in a fire. (These deductions include the cost of excavation, the foundation, and underground piping.) In business interruption insurance, expenses are excluded that will not exist when there are no sales. These include such items as bad debts, discounts, sales tax, returns and allowances, prepaid outgoing freight, rent (when based on sales), commissions on sales, and a few other items deducted from gross income or sales in estimating gross earnings or net sales. The ordinary payroll realistically becomes deductible only in interruptions of longer duration. As the shutdown continues, more expenses begin to drop off, but the insurance amount stays in effect until it is used up in loss payments. That is why a 50 percent gross earnings form for an insured with fairly regular earnings may often cover a loss for eight months or longer, if some expenses discontinue but many remain.

In addition to providing indemnity to the insured for loss of profits and continuing expenses as a result of fire or other perils insured against, the policy agrees to pay *expenses incurred for reducing the loss* under the policy. This element is not computed in arriving at the business interruption insurable value, for it adds nothing to the risk. The operation of this clause is illustrated by the following example. Assume that a seasonal business suffers a fire just as it is about to fill a number of large orders. The loss of profits and continuing expenses is estimated to be $80,000, and work will probably be totally suspended for 90 days. As the business does not wish its customers to go to another concern, it rents a neighboring property, sets up machinery, and is operating at full capacity in 45 days. Although this involves working night and day shifts at increased labor costs of $20,000, the business considers it worthwhile since it is thereby able to maintain its contact with valuable customers. If by the expenditure of $20,000 the insured is able to reduce the loss to $40,000, for example, the insurance company is obligated to pay the $40,000 loss of profits and continuing expenses, plus the expediting expense item of $20,000. This makes the total loss payment $60,000 instead of the $80,000 that it would have been had the expediting expense not been incurred.

Business interruption loss.   A business establishment is operated for its *earnings*. Every going business at any given time finds itself in one of three situations: it is being operated at a profit, at cost, or at a loss. While business interruption insurance aims primarily to indemnify the insured for loss of *profits* because of an enforced cessation or limitation of operations, it does not follow that an insured has no loss if the business is not making a profit. When a plant is shut down, certain fixed charges must go on if the business is to continue to function. The policy, therefore, not only covers the loss of net profits on business prevented from being carried on but also includes the payment of such *fixed expenses* as must continue during the business interruption. Fixed expenses are covered to the extent that they would have been earned had there been no loss. Finally, the coverage pays for *expenses for reducing loss,* to the extent that they do reduce loss.

The *duration* of the loss continues only until the insured property is restored to the condition it was in before the loss, not until production or sales are returned to the same level as before.

If a business is operating at a profit and a fire causes suspension, the loss includes both the profit item and the fixed-charge item, plus any costs incurred in order to minimize the loss. If the business is operating at cost and a fire occurs, the loss is the same, less the profit item. If the business is operating at a loss, it may still be earning part of its fixed charges, and these represent a loss if business is suspended.

Comprehensive work sheets have been prepared for business establishments in order to estimate their potential business interruption loss. As an example, the year's loss of a business may be illustrated as follows:

1.	Estimated *Gross Business Income* from sales or services for 12 months following	$1,000,000
2.	Discounts allowed .... $ 2,000	
3.	Allowances for returns, etc. .... $ 1,000	
4.	Charge-offs for bad accounts .... $ 2,000	
5.	Net cost of merchandise or raw stock (whichever applies)* $500,000	
6.	Total 2 through 5. Deduct from 1	$ 505,000
7.	*Estimated Gross Earnings*	$ 495,000
8.	Salaries, commissions, and wages that may not be paid if operations cease $250,000	
9.	Delivery service, power, heat, refrigeration, telephone, insurance and tax rebates, and other operating expenses that may be discountinued $100,000	
10.	Total of 8 and 9. Deduct from 7	$ 350,000
	Balance represents *Estimated Business Interruption Loss*	$ 145,000

* This includes anything, such as packaging, that goes out the door with the product and is used up and consumed in the manufacture of the product, or any services contracted outside, such as delivery service.

Business interruption *loss* is thus estimated by calculating *gross earnings* and subtracting *expenses* which would *not continue* after damage to the physical property has occurred. The remainder is an estimate of the future profits and continuing expenses which would be lost as a result of the interruption of business.

For the average small mercantile establishment, business interruption loss can be determined with the knowledge of (*a*) turnover and (*b*) markup. Averages for a large number of classes of business have been determined by and are available from Dun & Bradstreet and other such financial services. For example, a jewelry store has a low turnover with a high markup and seasonal peaks. On the other hand a meat market has a relatively low markup with a high turnover. In the case of a jewelry store with a stock valued at $40,000 with a 75 percent markup, the gross earnings on one turnover would be $30,000. If the turnover is twice each year, then the annual gross earnings would be approximately $60,000, or an average of $200 a day for 300 working days. The business interruption loss for a year would be $60,000, less the discontinuable expenses. On the assumption that these expenses were estimated at $10,000, for example, the business interruption loss would be $50,000 if the business was stopped completely for one year.

Business interruption forms. Business interruption contracts are usually created by adding a form to the basic part of the standard fire policy. There are only two basic forms: one for *mercantile* and nonmanufacturing risks and one for *manufacturing* risks. The forms make no daily or weekly limitation of payment but require coinsurance based upon the annual business interruption value of the business. These forms have an advantage over the older per diem[6] and weekly forms in that they automatically adjust to fluctuating earnings. The insurer is liable for any loss during the period of coverage, whatever the amount, provided that the face of the policy is equal to or exceeds the coinsurance percentage of the business interruption value.

Seasonal or daily fluctuations in earnings are automatically taken care of, and the actual loss sustained is paid. In the case of a department store, for example, this would mean a high amount of indemnity for Saturdays, with lower amounts for the less active days, as well as higher sums for the periods of greatest activity, such as during the Christmas shopping season, and lesser sums for the dull periods between seasons. Department stores, in order to keep their organization intact during short periods of suspension, usually continue most of their employees and for this reason should include in the coverage the item of ordinary payroll.[7] On the other hand, a manufacturing plant may exclude such payroll from its insurable value or may insure it for a limited period or for the entire policy period, whichever coverage best meets its needs.

The *gross earnings form* is most widely used today for most businesses. The business interruption loss is estimated as discussed previously, and a choice made as to the coinsurance percentage desired. The rate decreases as a higher coinsurance requirement is used. The insured's *ordinary payroll* is covered,

---

[6] Per diem valued forms of business interruption insurance are still written. Some tax and loss settlement advantages, such as for a new business where gross earnings are difficult to predict, offset in some cases the disadvantages of a per day limitation. No coinsurance is required, and the loss payments are usually not taxed as ordinary income as in the other forms. A disadvantage is that the rates are normally higher. Power plant coverages may still be written on a valued basis, and in this field the term *use and occupancy* still prevails.

[7] Mercantile establishments in particular have the need to retain the entire staff during a period of shutdown. The need, however, is not limited to mercantile establishments. Competitive labor conditions create the necessity of retaining employees of all categories to be available when the business reopens rather than rely on the recruiting of a new staff.

though if payroll coverage is not desired it may be excluded by endorsement. Forms are written in some jurisdictions with an *agreed amount* instead of a percentage of coinsurance (if the insured files an annual statement of income and expenses), which has the advantage of eliminating the danger that the insured may become a coinsurer because of a deficiency in insurance.

A relatively new and promising solution to the difficulty of estimating coinsurance needs accurately is the *"no coinsurance" earnings forms* available in most states. These forms are designed for small and medium-sized business and provide a simple method of determining the amount of insurance. The business estimates its need for income for one month after a loss, and the policy is written for four times that amount.[8] The policy pays for loss of earnings, defined as net profit plus payroll and other continuing expenses, less any noncontinuing operating expenses. Many smaller firms needing several thousand dollars of coverage per month find this form increasingly attractive because of its simplicity. Its disadvantages are that it is not permitted for manufacturers and that it may be higher in cost for larger firms than the gross earnings form.

The business interruption forms contain a number of special exclusions, and the nature of these depends upon whether or not the policy is designed for a mercantile or a manufacturing risk. The policy may provide that there shall be no liability for (*a*) the destruction of any finished stock; (*b*) any increase of loss which may be occasioned by any ordinance or law regulating the construction or repair of buildings; (*c*) the suspension, lapse, or cancellation of any lease or license, contract, or order; (*d*) increase of loss due to interference with rebuilding by strikers; and (*e*) consequential or remote loss.

Contingent business interruption insurance

This type of indirect loss policy pays the insured for loss due to damage or destruction of property *not* owned or operated by the insured, but upon which the business is dependent for continued operation. Major suppliers and major customers need this insurance coverage whenever they are heavily dependent on one or a few sales outlets or sources of supply.

General forms. There are two forms of contingent business interruption insurance: (*a*) *contributing properties* coverage and (*b*) *recipient properties* coverage. The first form provides indemnity in the event that the insured business suffers an interruption loss due to the destruction of or damage to facilities of prime suppliers that provide materials, parts, or services to the

---

[8] The four times one month's loss of gross earnings is the result of assuming a maximum restoration period of four months, and of a common limitation in the contract of no more than 25 percent of the insurance being available during the first 30 days after loss. In many Western states the requirement is 33⅓ percent, so the insurance amount is commonly set at three times the first month's estimated loss.

insured. An example of the need for such insurance was a disastrous fire at Livonia, Michigan. A $50 million fire destroyed an essential transmission plant which supplied many General Motors automobile manufacturers. The vast business interruption suffered as a consequence by the automobile manufacturers was a contingent business interruption loss to them, resulting from the destruction of the properties of the prime supplier of transmission parts.

The second form, recipient properties coverage, insures against loss caused by damage to or destruction of facilities of prime customers of the insured. The subcontractor who supplies materials or parts to a prime contractor or customer might benefit from such coverage. In the event that the business place of the prime customer, termed in the policy the "recipient property," is damaged or destroyed so that the prime customer is no longer able to take the product of the insured, the subcontractor is covered for business interruption losses under recipient properties coverage. Such insurance is most important when a single large buyer purchases most of the total production, and when the product has limited possibilities in other markets.

Another example of the second form of contingent BI coverage is the loss which a smaller store would suffer as a result of destruction or damage to a major department or food chain store in a shopping center. The loss of income caused by the decrease in customers of the smaller store could be insured as a contingent business interruption coverage.

Off-premises power plant insurance. Another type of contingent business interruption coverage, which should become more popular as a result of the recent energy crisis, is a specialized contingent form covering the continued flow of utilities. Insurance is written to cover loss attributable to the interruption of the supply of electricity, heat, gas, water, or other energy. The source may be a public or a private utility. Since the coverage applies with respect to utilities received from plants *outside* the premises of the insured, the coverage is, in fact, a form of contributing properties business interruption insurance. It protects the insured against interruption of power, light, or other utilities due to fire damage at the source of supply. It may also be written to cover against windstorm, explosion, vehicle damage, and all the other perils insurable under the fire extended coverage endorsement. Interruption due to damage to transmission lines may be covered, as well as property damage at the generating plant.

Selling agents' commissions insurance. The selling agent who handles large quantities of the output of one or a few manufacturing establishments may suffer a severe loss of income if a continuous flow of the sales product is interrupted. The loss may be covered under a *selling agents' commission form* of contingent business interruption insurance.

The selling agents' commission form has a particular appeal when a substantial volume of sales is derived from the output of a single plant. It also appeals to the agent or salesperson who spends the entire year taking orders for a future seasonable delivery. Orders for calendars and advertising novelties, for example, are taken the year around, but deliveries are made in early December. If the plant were destroyed before delivery of the goods, the agent might suffer a severe loss. The goods need not have been completed, since it is sufficient to support a claim if the selling concern is unable to make deliveries because of a peril covered by the policy. The rate charged is the rate for business interruption insurance at the location where the goods sold by the agent are manufactured.

Rents and rental value insurance

If a property is rendered untenantable by fire, there is in addition to the direct loss or damage, a loss of rental income (if occupied by a tenant) or a loss of use (if occupied by the owner). Losses from this source are insurable under a rents or rental value form of business interruption insurance.

Rents insurance indemnifies the owner of a property if the owner's rental *income* is cut off or interrupted by fire or other peril included in the coverage. Rents insurance is a particularly important coverage for estates or trusts if the beneficiaries depend largely upon income from real estate holdings. *Rental value* insurance covers the occupant and indemnifies the occupant for the *loss of use* of the premises. The occupant may be the owner, in which case the indemnity is based upon what it costs the owner to secure premises similar to those destroyed or damaged. If the occupant is a tenant under a lease drawn so that rent continues during the unusable period, the tenant can be paid on the same basis.

Rent insurance forms in common use are written with coinsurance requirements varying from 60 percent to 100 percent. The rate is less as the ratio of insurance to value required by the coinsurance clause increases. The amount of insurance necessary for full coverage is the amount of income received during the estimated period required to rebuild the property if it is totally destroyed. In seasonal risks, the policy is written to limit its liability for loss of rent only during the months of customary occupancy.

The period for which a loss may be collected begins with the happening of the fire, or other contingency insured against, and runs for the period required with the exercise of reasonable diligence to restore the property. The loss must originate during the term of the policy, though the liability may continue beyond its termination.

In order to compare rents and rental value insurance with extra-expense insurance (discussed next), Table 18–1 summarizes who needs these indirect loss coverages, the exposed values, the basis for the loss amount, and some restrictions on the loss payments.

The student should avoid confusion with leasehold interest (for tenants) and excess rental value (for owners) insurance, discussed in the later section of "no time element losses." These types of indirect loss insurance pertain only to *increased* rental costs or values based upon *long-term leases*.

Table 18-1. Comparison of rents, rental value, and extra-expense insurance

Type of insurance	Who needs coverage	Exposed values*	Basis for loss amount	Restrictions on loss payments
Rents insurance	Owners (including estates)	Loss of *income* from tenants having to discontinue occupying premises	Loss of rents for the insured premises	Period required to restore property with reasonable diligence
Rental value insurance	Owners *or* tenants occupying the premises	Loss of *use value* due to having to discontinue occupying premises	Cost of renting similar other premises	Same as for rents insurance
Extra-expense insurance†	Owners *or* tenants	Additional expenses in order to continue use of premises	Expenses beyond normal, and expenses to reduce the loss	Often sets limits on basis of insurance amount for one month (40%), two months (80%), or longer (100%)

* These losses must be caused by the perils insured against, such as fire, wind, explosion, and other allied fire perils.
† Called "additional living expense" insurance for residences as opposed to businesses.

Extra-expense insurance

Business forms. Subject to the policy limits, *extra-expense insurance* covers all extra-expense or additional charges incurred by the insured *in order to continue* normal business following damage or destruction of buildings or contents by an insured peril. This may cover the cost of doing business at a location other than the usual permises of the insured. Business interruption insurance covers loss when the business is *discontinued*. Extra-expense insurance covers the additional cost of *continuing* a business following a loss. For example, if one location of a company with several production facilities were damaged, the company might incur additional expenses to put on an extra shift of employees at the undamaged locations.

The business interruption policy does cover some expenses incurred in order to continue part of a business or to get a business back into operation, limited to the extent that loss under the policy is reduced. Extra-expense insurance sets no such limitation and provides for any extraordinary outlay that is needed to keep a business in operation. It provides for the extra expense over and above normal operating costs that enables the insured to continue as nearly as practicable normal business operations immediately following damage or destruction to buildings or contents by the perils insured against. The policy does not cover loss of income in any respect.

The amount paid for extra expenses is limited by (1) the basic policy insurance amount and (2) a percentage of the total insurance amount which is set as the maximum that may be used each month following the beginning of indemnity. For example, a common requirement is a limitation of 40 percent during the first month of restoration, 80 percent during the first two months, and 100 percent for periods in excess of two months.[9] The period of indemnity continues during whatever time is necessary to restore the property to normal use.

Some types of businesses have a special need for protection against extra-expense losses. Such firms as banks, milk distributors, newspapers, laundries, and many others must provide at all costs *continuous service* to their customers. Otherwise, their clients are immediately lost to competitors. These businesses need somehow to continue daily service, and extra-expense insurance is an important means by which this can be accomplished. Extra help, services available at temporary locations, airfreight costs to replace needed equipment, and many other costs are typical of the extra expenses of these firms.

Some businesses need *both* business interruption and extra-expense insurance. *Combined* BI–EE *insurance* is available in some rating territories. Al-

---

[9] Coinsurance is not used in connection with extra-expense insurance, although the above monthly limitations serve a similar purpose in encouraging the insured to purchase an adequate amount of insurance.

though many retail stores may find business interruption insurance sufficient to repay them for the loss of fixed expenses and profits, other stores may decide that they could not be out of business very long before permanently losing a substantial number of customers to competitors. Only extra-expense insurance would help reduce these losses, by paying the additional costs of keeping the business in operation. Examples of the need include: unfortunate timing of a loss, perhaps when business is falling and a new store is opening up nearby; and a branch suburban store which needs to continue to operate in spite of a fire destroying the main downtown store.

The extra-expense coverage of this form is based upon 4 to 50 percent of the business interruption insurance amount, as selected by the insured. Separate percentage limits apply for shutdowns less than 30 days, 30 to 60 days, and more than 60 days. The protection is not an additional limit beyond that payable for a business interruption loss, but a part of it. The business interruption rate is increased from 20 to 100 percent, depending on the extra-expense limits chosen, for this type of combined BI–EE coverage.

Residential forms. Extra-expense coverage known as *additional living expense* is available for residents of dwellings and is written in connection with rental value insurance. This form bears the same relationship to rental value insurance that extra-expense insurance bears to business interruption insurance. Rental value coverage indemnifies the insured for the rental value of the home during the period that it is unfit for occupancy because of a loss caused by a peril covered by the insurance. The additional living expense form reimburses the insured for excess expenses necessitated by living elsewhere during the period that the property is not habitable.[10] This coverage is included in the homeowners' contracts discussed in Chapter 27.

The additional living expense contract covers reasonable and *necessary* living expenses. To establish a claim the expenses must be *incurred*. Thus, insureds may not create excessive charges to provide more luxurious quarters. Conversely, they may not move in with relatives or occupy less desirable quarters on a temporary basis and collect on the ground that they *could have* obligated the insurer for the better quarters under the terms of their policy.

Additional living expense insurance is not written with a coinsurance requirement, but the payment in any one month under the contract is limited to 25 percent of the face of the policy. This means that with excess costs of $100 monthly and an interruption of use of the premises of one month, $400 insurance would be required. The insurance should be at least four times the first monthly anticipated claim and should be in an amount sufficient to last for the time the family may be expected to occupy substitute quarters.

Additional living expense insurance does not pay the full cost of substitute

---

[10] Some cynical soul has coined the term "mother-in-law insurance" for extra living-expense cover, presumably because it obviates the need for going to live with in-laws while repairs to a dwelling are being made.

quarters but only the *excess* cost of the new quarters above the usual costs of living in the uninhabitable damaged property. Includable expenses in a typical claim for additional living expenses might be the *extra* costs of a hotel or motel for several weeks (perhaps followed by further rental of an apartment or house), eating meals out, laundry costs, extra travel expenses, and many other items.

Tuition fees insurance

Many educational institutions are dependent upon the income derived from tuition fees. A fire or other peril that destroys any substantial part of a school might require a temporary suspension of operations, with a consequent obligation to refund tuition collected or to cancel charges already made. After the work of reconstruction and repair is completed, some students formerly enrolled may not return.

Tuition fees insurance pays for loss occasioned by the necessity to return, or the failure to receive, tuition fees as the outgrowth of an insured peril. Recovery is not limited to the time required to restore the damaged property. If a school building is destroyed or damaged during a school term, the resulting transfers may not be determined until the opening of the next school year. If the reconstruction period runs to a date within 30 days of the opening of the next school year, the loss of tuition includes the loss from transfers that occurred because of the students' uncertainty regarding the completion date. The insured is expected to make use of other available property that will reduce the amount of the loss.

NO TIME ELEMENT LOSSES

Indirect losses in which the time required for the restoration of the physical property is *not* the determining factor in the payment of an insurance loss are of several types. Insurance of these losses is not as important as insurance of the time element losses previously discussed, but the consequences of not considering insurance protection for such losses can be serious in specialized situations.

Profits insurance

Profits insurance indemnifies the insured for loss of profits on finished goods. It is written by attaching a special form to the fire, windstorm, explosion, or other peril insurance contract. Under the fire or other direct loss contract, the measure of the damage to the insured is the cost to repair or replace. In the case of manufactured goods, this is limited to the manufacturing costs. If a warehouse is filled with completed goods not yet delivered, their destruction will result in a substantial loss of profits to the insured. Direct damage loss will be settled on the basis of the manufacturer's cost, rather than on the basis of the selling price for the goods.

In the case of seasonable goods, the profits of an entire year may be lost if fire occurs just before it is time to deliver the finished product. Christmas toys, for example, are ordinarily delivered during the month of October, but the manufacturing process takes place during the entire year. If the year's stock of toys of a manufacturing establishment is destroyed late in September, the loss of profits will be serious. Any business that has substantial amounts of finished stock in storage, regardless of their seasonable nature, can need profits insurance.

The distinction between profits insurance which covers profit loss on only one turnover of goods and business interruption insurance covering perhaps many business turnovers has already been made earlier in the chapter.

Two forms of profits insurance are written. One limits the liability of the insurer for loss of profits to the percentage of loss ascertained and adjusted under the direct property loss policies. A second form, known as the "unlimited form," adjusts the profits item without regard to the percentage of loss on the manufactured goods. The unlimited form is regarded as the most satisfactory protection.

Profits insurance is usually written only for a manufacturer. Loss of profits for a retailer is covered in business interruption insurance. It is expected that the retail merchant can replace at cost much of the damaged stock and would collect only the profits that were not earned during the restoration period. On the other hand, the manufacturer's finished goods cannot be replaced at cost for delivery according to the contract. The time needed for restoration is not a factor in the loss of the profit.

Contingent profits insurance is a special form used by insurance agencies whose commissions are contingent upon their loss experience. Many contracts between the agent and the insurer provide for an agreed commission, plus a contingent commission if the loss experience does not exceed a certain percentage of premiums. As the year's end approaches and the contingent commission is earned, there is the possibility that a serious loss might wipe out the contingent earnings of the agency. An insurance agency may purchase insurance against the loss of these anticipated contingent earnings.

Leasehold interest and excess rental value insurance

Leases often contain a cancellation clause which provides that either party to the lease may terminate it if a designated percentage of the property is destroyed. If a tenant possesses a particularly advantageous *long-term* lease, the lease will in all probability not be continued if the owner can terminate it. In that case, the tenant will lose a valuable interest in the lease. (Refer to Table 18–1 to help you understand how the types of insurance discussed in this section compare with rent, rental value, and extra-expense insurance.)

Leasehold value represents the increased rental value of premises to a tenant in excess of the actual rental agreement. Thus, it is quite possible that a property for which a 20-year lease calling for a $1,500 monthly rental was executed ten years ago might bring $2,000 a month today. If this is so, the holder of the lease has a leasehold interest in the property valued at $500 a month for the remaining 120 months. The insurable value is the discounted value of $60,000, or the present value of $500 a month for 120 months. The increased income value of the lease must be discounted at an assumed rate of normal interest, such as 5 percent, because it represents a value over a future time period. Leasehold insurance does not cover in the event of cancellation of the lease for any reason other than the happening of a loss due to one of the perils insured against.

In addition to the situation in which a tenant is paying less than the current market rental value of a property, there are other situations that create an insurable interest in a lease. Where good locations are scarce and are held under long-term leases, a concern might find it profitable to pay a substantial lump-sum *bonus* to secure a present tenant's location. This sum would be lost entirely if the premises were destroyed and the tenant's lease canceled. The policy is written for a face amount equal to the bonus, with the amount of insurance decreasing monthly to reflect the amortization of the bonus. A tenant's *improvements and betterments* may be insured for direct physical loss or damage during the unexpired term of the tenant's lease. In some situations a property owner may agree to make certain renovations for a prospective tenant and require the payment of *advance rent* for a year or more. The cancellation of such a lease would cause the tenant to lose a proportional share of the advance rent for the unexpired term of the lease. Like the bonus and the improvements, this form of advance rent may be covered, with the amount of insurance decreasing over the term of the lease.

In a leasehold interest policy, the lease furnishes the key to the entire underwriting problem. Oftentimes a copy of the lease is attached to the policy. A satisfactory form will require that the property be over 50 percent destroyed by fire (or other specified perils) before the lease may be canceled. Statutes in the state where the property is located govern in case there is no cancellation clause in the lease itself.

Rates for leasehold interest insurance are governed by the building rate. Since a leasehold interest decreases in value from month to month as the term of the lease runs toward expiration, the form provides for a continued reduction in the amount payable. So that it may be equitable, the premium is based upon an average of the amount the insurer has at risk during the policy term. Leasehold interest policies may be written on an annual basis or for a term. If a change in the leasehold value takes place, the insurance may be adjusted to cover accordingly.

A converse of the leasehold interest contract is found in the *excess rental value policy,* which protects the *owner* of buildings who has an advantageous lease that if canceled could not be renewed on equally favorable terms.

Temperature damage insurance

If a temperature change follows a fire loss originating in the insured premises, any loss to merchandise caused by the change is generally held to be covered by the fire insurance contract. If the merchandise is located in a building that secures its heat or refrigeration from a plant located some distance away, the policy issued on cold storage warehouses, packing plants, greenhouses, and other such risks (where there is a liability for loss or damage by interruption of power or change of temperature) usually exempts the insurer from such indirect liability. Where temperature change may cause such liability, policies may be endorsed to provide *temperature damage insurance* for loss caused by failure of heat or refrigeration.

Matched set or parts insurance

Another source of indirect loss is the loss or damage of one part of a matched set. The risk is especially important in the clothing business, where different parts of a garment are often sent to several locations for processing. Indirect loss or damage by the insured perils due to the reduction in value of remaining parts of clothing or suits is covered by an endorsement, whether the loss or damage is caused at the insured's location or elsewhere. Jewelers also find a need for *matched set insurance* on such articles as earrings, bracelets, and necklaces where the value of the set may be more than proportionally lost by damage or loss of one part.

Errors and omissions insurance

Financial institutions that lend money with real estate as security are always faced with the possibility that through some neglect on the part of the property owner, insurance in force when the loan was made will not be renewed. Painstaking care in checking expirations still leaves a loophole—error on the part of the employees to whom this responsibility has been assigned.

The *errors and omissions policy* for lending institutions protects against losses arising out of failure to have in force proper insurance to protect the mortgaged property as a result of error or omissions. The policy protects only the mortgagee, and it applies only when through error and omission, specific insurance is invalid or insufficient or has not been provided. Errors and omissions insurance protects the property interest of the lending institution; it is not for the benefit of the property owner.

Failure to record changes in ownership, insufficient insurance to meet coinsurance requirements, incorrect description, failure to report change of occupancy or increase of hazard when known, errors in ordering or renewing coverage, incorrect statements of ownership—these and scores of other errors are examples of the protection provided by this policy. (See also Chapter 20, which discusses the use of errors and omissions insurance as a *liability* rather than an indirect property loss coverage.)

Depreciation insurance

The fire insurance contract covers the insured for loss or damage to the extent of the actual cash value of the insured property at the time of the loss, determined by giving consideration to depreciation. An insured building whose value is lessened by age and use, changing business conditions, neighborhood changes, and the like, may be covered under a fire insurance contract, and yet the insurance may be less than the amount necessary to replace the loss or the damaged property.

Depreciation insurance, sometimes called *replacement cost*[11] insurance, pays for full replacement cost new of the insured property without deduction for depreciation. It provides indemnity for the expenditures that the insured is obliged to make in order to restore the property to its full usefulness as before the loss or damage. Depreciation insurance substitutes a figure representing the cost of replacement new for the term *actual cash value.* Only seldom would the replacement cost figure cause a smaller loss payment, which could happen if underinsurance caused a coinsurance penalty to be applied.

Depreciation insurance through replacement cost endorsements or clauses has become increasingly important in the past decade. Homeowners' contracts for residential risks and business multiple-line package policies both often include such protection now. Depreciation insurance is ordinarily written to cover buildings only, including machinery and equipment incidental to building service. A few insurers have in recent years begun to offer such replacement cost insurance on *contents,* too. Coinsurance is usually required for 80 percent or more of the full replacement cost. Some insurers specify a time limit, such as 12 months, within which repair or replacement must be completed with due diligence. The possible increased moral hazard, because the contract pays on the basis of replacement cost (new for old), is carefully watched.

---

[11] Formerly the term *depreciation insurance* was applied to separate policies covering this risk, while *replacement* cost referred to endorsements to the fire policy. Note that in the former case only the difference between replacement cost and actual value is covered.

The next three types of insurance discussed (depreciation, valuable papers, and accounts receivable) are sometimes classified as types of direct loss insurance. However, they are included in this text as further examples of indirect loss insurance because of the peculiar characteristics of the contracts. They cover principally the additional indirect losses which occur as a consequence of direct loss to these special kinds of tangible property.

Valuable papers insurance

Many persons and businesses have a great need for *valuable papers insurance*. Lawyers, doctors, authors, architects, photographers, banks, insurance companies and agencies, and the like, suffer extensive losses when their records are damaged. Indeed, protection for the expenses of replacement (or irreplaceable values) is needed to some extent in almost every business.

The valuable papers and records forms provide insurance under two headings: (*a*) specified articles and (*b*) all others. Specified articles are listed and valued, and the amount per article is the agreed value for the purposes of loss adjustment. All other papers and records are covered in a blanket amount, not separately valued. It is often required that the insured papers and records be maintained in a fireproof safe or receptacle, named and described in the policy, at all times except when they are in actual use. Good risk management may also be used to reduce valuable papers exposures, by having duplicate papers made and kept off the premises.

Accounts receivable insurance

Another type of insurance based upon losses resulting from damage to or destruction of records is *accounts receivable insurance*. This insurance may be writing on a reporting form or for a lump sum on a nonreporting form. For the reporting form monthly reports of values are submitted, providing greater flexibility where there is a considerable fluctuation in values. The nonreporting form appeals to smaller insureds who do not wish to be faced with the responsibilities entailed in monthly reports.

The policy covers as follows: (*a*) all sums due the insured from customers, including interest, provided that the insured is unable to collect credit payments as the direct result of loss of or damage to records or accounts receivable; (*b*) collection expense in excess of normal collection cost and made necessary because of such loss or damage; and (*c*) other expenses, when reasonably incurred by the insured in reestablishing records of accounts receivable following such loss or damage. A department store using many charge accounts for its sales is a good example of need for this policy. Were its records destroyed, many accounts would be uncollected. Even when duplicate records are maintained, they are seldom completely current and foolproof as an alternative method of treating this risk.

Notes are not covered by accounts receivable insurance. Losses due to electronic or magnetic injury, disturbance, or erasure of electronic recordings are not covered unless caused by lightning. Fidelity losses attributable to fraudulent or criminal acts of any insured are also excluded. The usual war damage and nuclear radiation or radioactive contamination exclusion apply, but the exclusions are few in comparison with the broad all-risks coverage of these policies.

Rain insurance

It would seem to be a far cry from covering direct loss or damage to property by fire to covering insurance for loss of profits due to rainfall. However, windstorm and earthquake losses became covered as extensions of fire insurance, for both direct and indirect losses. A logical further step was to provide indemnity for losses due to the interruption of a business activity when weather is the cause of the loss. *Rain insurance* pays for such loss incurred as a result of rain, hail, snow, or sleet, for (1) loss of funds advanced for expenses and (2) loss of income.

Typical situations in which rain insurance can be helpful in providing needed protection are graduation exercises, fairs, races, baseball and other sports events, and many charity benefit performances.

An application for the policy must be made at least seven days before the rain insurance policy attaches. Local agents are not authorized to bind the insurance without authorization from the home office of the insurer, and the business is not accepted until the premium has been paid in advance. It is an unusual type of insurance in comparison with more common insurance contracts, but nevertheless an indirect loss coverage of importance to some insureds. As someone has said, there's nothing dry about rain insurance!

Unlike other forms of insurance, rain insurance attaches for a very brief period, usually for only a few hours in a single day. The policy provides payment if rainfall occurs within certain specified hours. Two types of coverage are available. One provides for the measurement of the amount of precipitation, and the findings of an established weather station are usually relied upon for these readings. The nonmeasurement contract provides that payment shall be made under the policy if rain in any amount falls during the specified hours.

There are three common forms of rain insurance coverage. All of them are strict contracts of indemnity and pay only for the amount of loss that the rain actually caused. This is determined in different ways for different types of events. Some are based on income expectancy of previous years, some on fixed expenses incurred before the event, and some on the necessary refund of advance ticket sales.

FOR REVIEW AND DISCUSSION

1. What basic types of insurance are there against indirect losses? Give two examples of each, and mention for whom the insurance might be advisable.

2. Why is insurance for indirect losses an important form of insurance protection to the insurance consumer?

3. Barbara occupies loft space as a tenant in a two-story building which is destroyed by fire. What is the liability of the business interruption policy in the event that (*a*) the owner decides not to rebuild (*b*) the owner decides to

rebuild a four-story structure, and (c) the owner will rebuild but takes several months to determine what to do?

4. Sarah claims that the gross earnings business interruption contract with 50 percent coinsurance should be purchased only where a relatively short period of business interruption appears likely, such as a total cessation of business for six months. Explain the error in this statement.

5. For the purposes of determining business interruption insurable *value,* distinguish between gross earnings for a mercantile risk and gross earnings for a manufacturing risk. What factor is the cause of the major difference?

6. Mr. Harnack says that since he is not the owner of his own business building he does not need indirect loss insurance. If a fire occurs, he claims that he would move to a new location. Advise him.

7. A store carries a "no-coinsurance earnings" insurance policy for $10,000. Assuming a loss of $5,000 monthly for three months, what will the insurer pay? Why may this policy be better than the gross earnings form?

8. Show the amount of insurance required under a gross earnings BI form with 50 percent coinsurance, based on the following data: (a) net sales $310,000; (b) merchandise at beginning of year, $40,000; (c) merchandise purchased during year, $150,000; and (d) merchandise at end of year, $20,000. Assume a 10 percent increase in business for the year ahead over the year to which the above data apply.

9. Is BI coverage limited to the fire peril, or may it include other perils?

10. The Solar Manufacturing Company is operating at a loss and cancels its BI policy on the ground that there will be no interruption of profits if the plant is shut down. Is the reasoning correct?

11. A retail store owner says that he cannot imagine why he might ever need both business interruption *and* extra-expense insurance. How would you advise him, and what contract would you recommend?

12. Extra-expense insurance is written for businesses as well as other risks. What *other risks,* and *how*?

13. Give several examples of the need for (a) *contingent* business interruption insurance, (b) *profits* insurance, and (c) *rent* insurance.

14. Describe a *unique* feature of the following "no time element" coverages for indirect losses: (a) *rain* insurance, (b) *accounts receivable* insurance, (c) *valuable papers* insurance, (d) *errors and omissions* insurance, and (e) *depreciation* insurance.

Chapter 19

Concepts considered in Chapter 19—Transportation insurance

Major divisions of transportation insurance are *ocean marine* insurance and *inland marine* insurance.

Ocean marine insurance covers primarily sea perils of ships and cargoes, which can be protected from "warehouse to warehouse".

Development was as one of the earliest of all forms of insurance.

The basic contract and perils follow the old Lloyd's of London contract wording, and the contract is a 100 percent coinsurance, *valued* form covering perils of the sea, fire, enemies, jettisons, barratry, and "other like perils." (War and negligence of the crew are perils often added.)

The insurance interests include the *hull* (vessel), *cargo, freight,* and *liability* ("protection and indemnity"). Contracts can be written on *fleets* or *single* vessels, for *voyage* or *time*, and on *single-risk* or *open-cargo* forms.

Special ocean marine insurance concepts are important, some being the use of *implied warranties, average and loss clauses, coinsurance, sue and labor clause,* and *assignment.*

Marine insurance adjustments require special marine adjusters and involve unique terms such as *presumed lost, salvage,* and *abandonment.*

Rates are based on judgment of the ship's classification and many other factors; international competition is important.

Pleasure craft insurance has developed special contracts for yachts, cruisers, and outboard and inboard motorboats in recent years.

Inland marine insurance covers primarily the land or over the land (but sometimes water) transportation perils of property shipped by railroads, motortrucks, and other means of transport.

Needed is broad protection in many situations, in flexible contracts.

Development, based on changing needs of property owners, shippers, and the carriers, has been encouraged by the Nationwide Definition of marine risks.

Classes of inland marine insurance are basically four, with many varied contracts within each group:

Property in transit, in *trip transit, annual,* and *open* forms.

Bailee liability, for *legal liability* of the bailees, or for the customers.

Fixed transportation property, for bridges, tunnels, and others.

Floaters, both *personal* and *commercial,* in many different forms, including such diverse policies as those for valuable personal articles, mobile equipment, installations, conditional sales, and jewelers' "block" contracts.

If there were no transportation insurance, what individual or corporation could, or would, own or finance a new $40 million "supertanker"? Or a shipment of $80 million of gold bullion from one location to another? Or an art collection worth $30 million on exhibition throughout the world? Or a new $20 million bridge handling thousands of cars and trucks every day? The probable answer—no one; and our mobile, intercoordinated society of today might come to a screeching halt. But *with* transportation insurance, all of this is possible.

Take one major ocean marine loss—the sinking of the *Amoco Cadiz*[1] in 1978—and what do we see? A concentration of values exposed to many perils in an ocean voyage, in which the one loss "which never could happen" did. The result was over $12 million in insurance paid for the ship and its machinery, more than that figure for the 220,000 tons of crude oil spilled from its mammoth tanks into the sea, and multimillion dollars of liability damage yet to be settled. The problems of oil slick on nearly 120 miles of French tourist and fishing coastline involved the French and Liberian government (under whose flag the ship was operating), an Italian crew, U.S. shipowners, Dutch cargo owners, the British charterer of the ship, and many others. Obviously, this loss was a challenge to the future ingenuity of insurers around the world.

The previous two chapters have discussed the basic fire and allied insurance contracts and insurance for indirect losses. Another important part of property insurance is the very broad field of *transportation insurance*, which is concerned with the perils of property in (or incidental to) transit as opposed to property perils at a generally fixed location. The term does not include normal automobile insurance, which merits separate treatment in Chapters 23 and 24, and aviation insurance, which is presented in Chapter 26.

MAJOR DIVISIONS

Transportation insurance, usually known in the insurance business as *marine* insurance, has two major divisions. The first of these, *ocean marine*

---

[1] "Turbulent Wake of the Cadiz," *National Underwriter* (P. and C. ed.), April 7, 1978, p. 1. Another loss, which occurred in late 1978, became the largest single marine loss ever suffered, with $60 million of insurance on the German vessel München and $20 million on its cargo (*Business Week,* January 28, 1979, p. 24).

insurance, is one of the oldest written forms of insurance and has to do primarily with the insurance of sea perils.[2] It makes credit for international trade possible.

The second division, of comparatively recent origin, is *inland marine* insurance, which is primarily for land perils such as railroad and motor truck transportation, and for lake, river, or other inland waterway transportation risks. An inland marine policy now includes a wide range of policy forms that embrace every conceivable method of transportation outside of those risks that fall definitely within the ocean marine category.

OCEAN MARINE INSURANCE

Scope and development

Insurance historians tell us that the insurance of ocean marine perils preceded almost all other types of insurance. (See Chapter 2 for an account of the beginnings of such insurance several thousand years B.C.) The first ocean marine policies insured against the loss of the vessel or the cargo. Shippers found that even though they covered their goods while these were waterborne, damage such as total destruction by fire while the goods were on the docks at one end of the voyage or the other could be quite as disastrous as a total loss of the vessel at sea. The first extension of ocean marine coverages, then, was to provide insurance on the cargo while it was on docks or quays. From this, it was but a step to make the coverage effective at the warehouse of the shipper and to terminate the coverage at the warehouse of destination, by the so-called warehouse-to-warehouse clause. Thus was ocean marine insurance brought ashore.

The ocean marine business is highly specialized in its operation and is carried on primarily by large insurers. Most of the American marine risks are insured through the American Hull Insurance Syndicate, through which some 50 insurers cover several thousand ships for amounts up to $40 million per ship. Worldwide, Lloyd's of London is one of the famous insurers of ocean marine perils, and these perils account for nearly one half of its total insurance and reinsurance business. Ocean marine insurance provides protection for (*a*) ships or *hulls*; (*b*) goods or *cargoes*; (*c*) earnings such as *freight*, passage money, commissions, or profit; and (*d*) *liability* (known as *protection and indemnity*) incurred by the owner, or any party interested in or responsible for insurable property by reason of maritime perils.

Ocean marine contracts protect merchandise while it is in transit and in-

---

[2] Those with a nautical bent will enjoy such insurance books as Thomas Chubb, *If There Were No Losses* (New York: John B. Watkins Co., 1957); and William Bronson, *Still Flying and Nailed to the Mast* (Garden City, N.Y.: Doubleday and Co., 1963).

clude the perils of land and water conveyances and warehouses. Forms have been developed for special commodities. For example, flour products shipped to Europe may be covered against "all hazards and dangers of transportation" from the time these products leave the mills in America until they have been safely delivered. Cotton is insured under ocean marine contracts during processing; while it is being shipped by land by either trucks or railroads; and in ships until it is delivered abroad. This inclusion of land perils in the ocean marine contract focused attention upon the land transportation hazards where ocean perils were not a factor.[3]

The basic contract and perils covered

The modern ocean marine policies take their point of departure from the Lloyd's contract adopted in 1779. The perils clause in Lloyd's marine policy form[4] as it is used today follows the original pattern and reads as follows:

> TOUCHING The adventures and Perils which we the assurers are contented to bear and do take upon us in this Voyage, they are, of the Seas, Men-of-War, Fire, Enemies, Pirates, Rovers, Thieves, Jettisons, Letters of Mart and Countermart, Surprisals, Takings at Sea, Arrests, Restraints and Detainments of all Kings, Princes and People, of what Nation, Condition, or Quality soever, Barratry of the Master and Mariners, and of all the other like Perils, Losses and Misfortunes that have or shall come to the Hurt, Detriment or Damage of the said Goods and Merchandises and Ship, etc., or any Part thereof.

In the United States, the Lloyd's policy serves as the general core around which the various contracts offered by the insurance companies have been built. The value of the ancient phraseology and the reason for its retention lie in the fact that in the long period of its use, meanings have been definitely settled through the process of litigation.

Because of the international nature of marine insurance competition, coverages have considerable uniformity. In the United States the American Institute of Marine Underwriers standard clauses reflect the generally accepted practice in the American market. These clauses have met with considerable approval, but the fact remains that in the field of marine insurance there are no standard forms made mandatory by law.

Perils of the sea.   Looking more closely at the perils listed in the Lloyd's

---

[3] The development of insurance for land perils resulted in the establishment of that branch of the business to which is applied the seemingly contradictory term *inland marine*.

[4] For history buffs who enjoy a sense of humor, a delightful booklet, *Shipping and Insurance Sketches, 1867*, was published in 1967 (Insurance Institute of London, 20 Aldermanbury, London EC 2, 92 pages). A picture of marine insurance is recreated, even to the careful observation that secretaries in miniskirts were not a part of the London office scene in 1867. (They wore trousers and beards!)

marine policy, several are significant. *Perils of the seas* are mentioned first, and these include winds, waves, collisions, strandings, sinkings, and other such accidents. Not all perils *on* the seas are covered, however, for this would have a broader interpretation.

War.   The older perils clause mentions *war,* but most policies used now do not list war in the basic policy. In order to include war, an endorsement is attached to the policy. This additional printed form includes a clause known as the *free-of-capture-and-seizure clause* (FC and S). The war perils covered are specified in a paragraph which more clearly identifies the actions considered as war, many of which are also listed in the original perils clause: actions of "capture, seizure, destruction or damage by men-of-war, piracy, takings at sea, arrests, restraints and detainments, and other warlike operations." These include such actions before or after declaration of war, and also civil wars, rebellions, or revolutions. For more modern war perils, aerial bombardment, mines, torpedoes, and atomic or nuclear weapons are specifically included. A common alternative for insuring all of these war perils is to issue a separate policy covering them.

Fire.   One of the important covered perils *on* the sea is *fire,* and it is therefore named as a separate covered peril in the perils clause of the basic policy. Both direct and consequential losses are insured, including damage done by water or other materials used to contain or extinguish fire.

Enemies.   The listed peril of *enemies* is peculiar to marine insurance contracts, and this would generally include all types of taking the insured property by force, including pilferage. However, some contracts exclude pilferage by using the term *assailing thieves.* The pilferage peril is difficult to insure—pilferage is often the result of the shipper's negligence through improper packaging, and it leads to argument as to whether the carrier or the shipper had possession of the property at the time of loss. Thus, the pilferage peril is often excluded from the contract of the carrier, and if coverage is desired, it is insured by the shipper.

Jettisons and barratry.   Two unusual marine perils are *jettisons and barratry.* The *jettisons* covered are those that involve voluntarily throwing overboard parts of the ship or cargo in order to save the vessel from sinking or other damage. (See also later discussion under "general average" losses.) *Barratry* is also insured by the perils clause, and this generally means all kinds of fraud by the master or the crew with the intention of reaping gains at the expense of the owners. Examples include abandoning or setting fire to the ship, running the ship ashore or diverting it from its course, and embezzlement of the cargo.

All other like perils and losses.   The final phrase in the perils clause covers *all other like perils, losses, and misfortunes,* which might seem to imply that the ocean marine policy is an all-risks contract. This is not the case. The coverage only applies to perils that are of the same nature as the perils previously enumerated, and losses that are the outgrowth of those perils.

Negligence of the captain or crew.   A decision having a lasting influence upon the policy of marine insurance was rendered in the case of the steamer *Inchmaree*. The crew's negligence caused a check valve to close with salt, with the result that a pump was damaged. The loss was held not to be covered under the "and all other perils, losses, and misfortunes" clause of the marine policy. To counteract the effect of this decision and to provide indemnity for machinery damage resulting from the negligence of the master or crew, the *Inchmaree clause* was introduced into hull policies. This clause includes *negligence of the crew* in the list of perils insured against. If, for example, insufficient fuel is placed aboard a ship and the master is obliged to burn furniture to bring it into port, this is not a fire loss. Negligence in providing the proper fuel is the proximate cause of the loss, and negligence of this nature is covered. Another example might involve an explosion caused by negligence of the captain or crew. Other explosions are usually included by adding an "explosion clause" to cover bursting boilers and other losses due to latent (undiscovered) defects in equipment.

The insurable interests

As with fire insurance, the insured must have a financial interest in the subject of insurance in order to have an enforceable contract. An *insurable interest* is present when the insured has a relationship to the property or interests protected, such that a real value is lost, if a loss occurs. The interest need not exist when the insurance is effected, but it is absolutely essential that it exist at the time of the loss.

Valued form and 100 percent coinsurance. In contrast to the situation in fire insurance, in ocean marine insurance the policy is usually written on a *valued* form, making the agreed valuation binding upon both parties at the time the insurance is placed. This is a measure of the *amount* of insurable interest or full value. Ocean ships often have values of many millions of dollars, with cargoes of equal or larger value.

In the settlement of a loss under a marine policy, the liability of the insurer is similar to that of an insurer under a fire policy with the *100 percent coinsurance* clause. The principle is so thoroughly understood that it is recognized as established in law and need not be inserted in the policy in the form of a coinsurance clause. When rates are made, it is understood that the amount designated in the policy represents the full value of the risk. Failure to designate full value has no effect upon the insurance in case of total loss, and the full amount of the insurance is paid. In the event of partial loss, however, the insurer is obligated to pay only that portion of the partial loss that the amount of insurance bore to the value of the risk. To illustrate: If a cargo valued at $50,000 is insured for $25,000 and there is a loss of $10,000, even with $25,000 insurance the full amount of the loss cannot be collected. Since the amount of insurance to value is one half, the amount for which the insurer is liable is likewise one half.

Time and voyage policies. Another method of describing the interests insured in ocean marine insurance is in relation to the *duration* of the coverage. The policy is either a *time policy*, providing coverage for a fixed period of time (usually one year), or a *voyage* policy, insuring the subject matter only for the specific voyage described in the contract.

Hulls, cargo, freight, and liability interests. One of the most important classifications in ocean marine insurance divides contracts into four groups based upon the *type of interest* covered: (1) *hulls*, (2) *cargo*, (3) *freight*, and (4) *liability*. Each of these major types is next discussed in a separate section.

Hull. Hull policies cover various types of vessels. These policies are adapted to ocean ships, sailing vessels, builder's risks, port risk policies, fleet policies, and the like. A hull policy may cover the liability risk by incorporating a collision or running-down clause into the form.

In the interest of a lower premium, hull policies are written that provide for either a deductible average or a minimum franchise form. When the *deductible average* form is used, any sum agreeable to the parties may be written into the contract. It may range from a few hundred dollars to hundreds of thousands, depending upon the risk and the amount of loss that the insured is willing to carry. Under deductible average, the deduction is made from any loss. Under the *minimum franchise* form, no claim is paid unless the loss reaches a certain limit, but if the loss reaches or exceeds the designated limit, it is paid in full. This is the most frequently used form of deductible. Ordinarily 3 percent is used, but the designated limit is sometimes as high as 10 percent.

The *builders' risk form* covers the perils peculiar to ship construction. The policy attaches from the laying of the keel, and it covers not only the hull itself but also tackle, engines, boilers, machinery, and all furniture and fixtures as well as all material used in construction. The policy covers against fire and other named perils, and risks of launching may be included. Excluded are claims originating from loss of life and personal injury, workers' compensation and employers' liability, strikes, riot, civil commotion, earthquake, and war risks.

With the development of large companies to operate fleets of vessels, it was found that insuring the *fleet* under a single coverage had certain advantages. The most important of these was the inclusion of the less desirable and older risks in the policy at an average rate. If the vessels in the fleet were insured individually, the poorer vessels might be rejected altogether by the underwriters or accepted only at a very high rate. Ships operated as fleets are today frequently separately owned as a matter of law through a corporation formed to own each ship in the fleet. Another corporation is formed to operate it. This legal device has the effect of limiting liability claims in cases of accident, and calls for the *single vessel* coverage.

Even when navigation is *seasonal*, as in the case of the northern lakes, the vessel policies are written for a year, since fire and other perils are matters of concern whether or not the ship is in use. The insurer is interested in the location and conditions surrounding the ship during the winter months and incorporates a winter-mooring clause into the policy, requiring satisfactory conditions. If the vessel is laid up in port, a return premium is allowed.

Cargo. Anyone shipping or receiving goods by sea may have need for *cargo* insurance. Cargo policies may be written under a *single-risk form* providing insurance for a particular ship, or they may be written under *floating or open forms* which provide coverage for goods of a certain class up to a certain limit, their values to be declared subsequently. Freight coverage may be included in such policies. Many shipments are usually covered under an open-cargo form, automatically covering all of the insured's shipments on and after an effective date.

Open-cargo forms are designed to accommodate exporters or importers who are shipping goods throughout the entire year. Goods consigned to them are often aboard and under way before notice is in the hands of the owner. Under the export form, the insured issues certificates of insurance without delay as evidence of the fact that insurance is in effect. The import policy is sufficiently broad to attach automatic coverage even before the insured or the insurer know that the cargo is shipped. All shipments are covered from the time the interest of the insured attaches.

Freight. Policies issued to cover freight interests are usually designed to cover hull or cargo interests as well. The freight interest is usually included in the valuation. If a ship undertakes a voyage and the freight to be earned is not payable until the cargo is delivered, the total loss of the ship will also involve the loss of the freight to be earned on the cargo. It is thus normal in insuring the hull to include the income expected from freight for the voyage. In the case of a cargo shipment, the shipping charges will represent part of the value at the port of destination, and it is customary to add shipping costs (freight) to the value at the port of embarkation. This form of insurance bears a close resemblance of the purposes of business interruption insurance discussed in Chapter 18.

Liability. Damage to an insured ship as a result of collision constitutes one of the perils covered under the marine policy. The policy without special provision does not cover the liability of the shipowner for damage caused to other ships. To cover this liability, the *collision* or *running-down clause* (RDC) is made a part of the hull policy. If the insured vessel is at fault in an accident, the RDC pays for the damages to the other ship. In case both vessels in a collision are found to be responsible, the liability of each vessel is fixed in proportion to the degree in which each vessel is at fault. The collision clause is limited to provide indemnity only in the case of liability for physical damage to another vessel and its freight and cargo, including loss of use of the damaged vessel. The clause does not assume liability for damage to cargo in the custody of the insured vessel, or damage to persons, or damage to docks, piers, and the like.

If collision insurance is provided for fleets under a common ownership, there would be no payment under the ordinary collision clause in the case of a collision of two ships in the same fleet.[5] The situation is covered by the so-called sister-ship clause. The insured would be paid under the policy as if the vessels were owned or managed separately.

The collision liability provided in the RDC is often broadened by *protection and indemnity* (P&I) *insurance* in a separate policy, though sometimes this is added by an endorsement. The coverage is a highly specialized form of marine legal liability insurance with respect to vessel operations. The policy "protects" and "indemnifies" the owner and operator of the insured vessel with respect to (*a*) crew members, (*b*) persons other than employees, (*c*) cargo, (*d*) fixed objects, and (*e*) miscellaneous claims, including liability for customs or other fines or penalties. Protection and indemnity insurance is much broader than the coverage provided in the running-down clause, which covers only damage to other *vessels* (and loss of use) and their freight or cargo interests.

Coverage for liability of the insured for personal injury to and death of *crew members* is the source of a large number of claims. Negligence is not necessarily a condition precedent for liability. A crew member who is injured or becomes ill while in the service of a vessel is entitled to wages to the end of the voyage, maintenance, return passage, and medical care. If negligence of the vessel is a factor, a liability suit may be filed against the shipowner. Liability of the vessel to *persons other than employees* for bodily injury and death is covered, including claims of passengers, stevedores, and any other persons who may be working on the vessel or be on board. Any responsibility of the vessel owner for damage to *cargo* carried by the vessel is covered. If damage is attributable to negligence, the cargo owner may proceed against the ship for losses resulting from improper stowage, contamination, the unseaworthiness of the vessel, and shortages. Damage to *fixed objects* such as piers, docks, bridges, marine cables, and aids to navigation may run to very sizable sums. Unlike the usual liability policy, the coverage will pay damages if property belonging to the insured, such as docks and wharves, is damaged. Also covered are liability for *customs, quarantine,* immigration, or other *fines,* or *penalties* for legal violations for which the owner, master, or agents of the vessel are liable. The P&I policy is written on a deductible basis, with deductibles ranging from $250 to as high as $15,000 or more a claim.

Under the terms of the Longshoremen's and Harbor Workers' Compensation Act (1927) and its amendments, every employer with one or more employees covered by the act is obliged to secure the payment of compensation either by insurance or by qualifying as a self-insurer. The coverage includes "disability or death, of an employee resulting from an injury occurring upon the navigable waters of the United States (including any dry dock), if recovery

---

[5] One of the largest recent losses of this kind involved two mammoth supertankers, each nearly four football fields long, belonging to Bethlehem Steel Corporation. The collision occurred off the coast of South Africa, and damage claims of $35 million were estimated (*Wall Street Journal,* January 16, 1978, p. 25).

for the liability or death through Workers' Compensation proceedings may not be validly provided for by state law." This requirement does not extend to include the master or crew of any vessel. The insured's liability for compensation may be endorsed upon the marine policy that has been extended to cover P&I risks.

Special ocean marine insurance concepts

Ocean marine contracts are important for several concepts contained in additional clauses and features. The "implied warranties" of ocean marine contracts are unique in comparison with other insurance contracts. Other principles are found in many insurance contracts but were derived from the ocean marine field. These include the "average" and "memorandum" deductibles, coinsurance, the "sue and labor" clause, and assignment provisions.

Implied warranties. *Implied warranties* are seldom incorporated into the policy, for by law, they are made a part of the agreement without any expression on the part of the parties. Strict compliance is necessary since they form a condition precedent before an obligation exists on the part of the insurer. If the condition be broken at the inception of the risk, there is no contract whatever and the policy is void. In most other types of insurance, warranties (often interpreted as representations) can be breached without terminating coverage, although loss payment may then become voidable at the option of the insurer.

Among the more important of the implied warranties are those that have to do with (a) seaworthiness, (b) deviation, and (c) legality. The insurer has a right to expect that the vessel insured is *seaworthy*. Generally speaking, the ship must be tight; properly equipped with cargo properly stowed and not in excess of safe carrying capacity; with necessary food, fuel, water, and other stores; and with a competent master, officers, and crew and with a pilot when one is required by law or usage. The *deviation* warranty provides that the insured vessel must not deviate from the proper course of the voyage. (Exceptions are those deviations necessary for the safety or success of the voyage, such as to avoid an iceberg or a hurricane.) To comply with the warranty of *legality,* the venture must be lawful, and so far as it is within the control of the insured, it must be carried out in a lawful manner. Smuggling is an example of an illegal purpose.

Average and loss clauses. The term *average* appears frequently in connection with maritime insurance losses. The etymology of the term is not altogether certain, though the contention that it is derived from the French word *avarie* and means "loss" or "damage" is in line with its present-day use. For example, *general average losses* and *particular average losses* are discussed next.

General average losses. When the cargo, or a part thereof, is thrown overboard, or when a part of the vessel is sacrificed for the purpose of preventing the vessel from sinking or other damage, the property sacrificed is said to have been "jettisoned." Property jettisoned to save other property, by law, must be contributed for by all of the owners of the property saved. They each share proportionally, in relation to their values, in the loss. The contribution is termed a *general average loss*. There are three essentials, each of which must be present, in order to establish a claim for general average. The sacrifice must be (1) voluntary, (2) necessary, and (3) successful. If a mast is carried away in a storm, even though the ship rides more easily thereafter, there can be no claim for general average because of the act was not voluntary. The loss is covered, however, if the captain necessarily orders the mast cut away. If the property for which the sacrifice is made is not saved, obviously the owners derived no benefit from the sacrifice, and accordingly they are under no obligation to contribute to a general claim. The rules for settling general average losses vary in different countries.[6]

Particular average losses. A *particular average loss* differs from a general average loss in that it does not require contribution from other parties. It differs from a total loss in that the item of property insured is not destroyed or lost in its entirety. Thus, it is a partial loss to individual interests, such as that caused by a fire which damages the cargo of a particular person.

The rules for ascertaining the amount of a particular average loss differ with the interest involved. When a vessel's *hull* is damaged, the measure of indemnity is predicated upon the cost of repairs, less the customary depreciation deduction, depending upon the age, type, and condition of the vessel and the character of the repair. When certain items of a *cargo* are totally destroyed, the loss is determined by the proportion that the part lost bears to the value of the whole. Thus, if 5,000 barrels of potatoes are insured for full value at $50,000 and 1,000 barrels are totally destroyed, the loss is 20 percent of the insurance. If the goods are delivered at their destination in a damaged state, the difference between the sound and the damaged values at the port of arrival is determined. A partial loss of *freight* interest for the value of the shipping charges may be the result of a partial loss to either the ship or the cargo, or both. The measure of indemnity is determined by finding the proportion that the lost freight charges bears to the total freight charges.

Memorandum and FPA clauses. Under the broad coverage of the marine contract, insurers would be continually harassed by claims for trifling losses whenever shipments of certain susceptible types of merchandise were covered. To help solve the problem, a "memorandum clause" was added designating certain goods upon which the underwriter was relieved of all partial loss. On other goods less susceptible to damage, no loss was to be paid unless the damage amounted to a certain percentage of the value, known as the "average limitation." This was a "franchise" type of deductible, the claim being paid in full if the loss exceeded the deductible amount.

---

[6]Many nations follow the "York-Antwerp Rules" which cover disputable points such as the cost of repairing different ships, jettison of open deck cargo, and temporary repairs.

In modern cargo policies, the objectives of the memorandum clause is attained by the use of the *free of particular average (FPA) clauses*. A FPA clause may be issued with the intention that a loss shall usually be paid only if it is *total*. An example is the "free of particular average American conditions" (FPAAC) clause: "Free of particular average unless caused by the vessel being stranded, sunk, burned, or in collision but including jettison and/or washing overboard irrespective of percentage." This clause is used particularly for cargo shipped on deck, and partial losses are covered only for the specified perils. In the case of underdeck shipments, approved merchandise is ordinarily covered under the FPAEC (English conditions) clause: "Free of particular average under 3 percent unless the vessel be stranded, sunk, burned or in collision, each package separately insured." This clause relieves the insurer of paying petty claims, but if the loss to any package equals 3 percent it is paid in full. The insurer is liable if one of the casualties enumerated happens during the voyage, whether it is or is not actually the cause of the loss.

Sue and labor clause. A section of the perils clause provides that in case of loss or misfortune the insureds or their representatives are both permitted and obligated to take certain designated steps to prevent, limit, or reduce loss. This clause, known as the *sue and labor* clause, is a collateral agreement separate and apart from the provision to indemnify for loss or damage from the named perils. Payments made to an insured for expenses incurred under the sue and labor clause are not regarded as a partial loss and therefore are not subject to percentage restrictions that may apply to particular average claims. In the case of a total loss, compensation under the sue and labor clause might sometimes be payable over and above the face of the policy.

To establish a claim under the sue and labor clause, the expenditure must be the act of the insureds or their agents, and must definitely be made in order to save the ship or goods insured from damage by the perils insured against in the policy. Salvage charges are paid if the salvors act under contract with the insured.

Assignment clauses. Marine policies are usually assignable, but an insurable interest is required. The assignment may be invalid if the interests of the assignee materially change the character of the risk. After a loss covered by the policy, the policyholders may assign their rights of action to another. Cargo insurance policies have clauses to permit assignment before a loss and without the consent of the insurer by writing the insurance "on account of whom it may concern." In the case of hull policies, insurers, foreseeing the importance of moral hazard, incorporate in the policy a clause making the policy void if it is assigned without their consent.

Marine loss adjustments. The adjustment of marine losses involves a considerable degree of technical knowledge and, accordingly, is usually entrusted to experts. Marine adjusters represent all parties in the loss, and in effect act as arbitrators in the settlement.

In order to establish a claim under the policy, it is necessary to present certain information which is obtainable from marine documents. As a source of proof that the loss was caused by one of the perils insured against, reference may be made to the *log* of the vessel. When incorporated into a document made by the master under oath, the same information is termed the *master's protest*. In the case of a claim on a cargo, the *bill of lading* is presented to show that the goods on which the loss is claimed were actually aboard the ship in question. The *invoice* of the goods serves as a basis for arriving at the value of the shipment and for determining whether or not the insurance is adequate. The insurance policy or *certificate* is necessary in order to determine to whom the loss is payable, and in the case of a hull loss, the certificate showing ownership is essential. Having established a loss caused by a peril insured against and having furnished evidence of interest in the subject of the insurance, the claimant is then entitled to payment within 30 days.

An unusual circumstance prevails in ocean marine insurance if the ship has not been heard from after a reasonable time. It is then *presumed to have been lost*, and a claim for an actual total loss may be made. There is no time fixed by law after which a missing vessel should be presumed to be lost, as this depends upon the circumstances in each case. In England, a notice of missing vessels is posted at Lloyd's, and ten days thereafter claim may be made upon the insurers for total loss. In this country, 30 days may run before the payment for loss is due.

When used in connection with insurance and maritime law, the term *salvage* has two distinct meanings: (1) the property which is saved and (2) the compensation due to those who voluntarily assist in saving a ship or cargo in peril. Salvors have a legal interest in the property saved, and if they and the owners of the property are unable to agree upon an amount for a reward, the amount is fixed by an admiralty court. A vessel deserted by its crew without the intention of return is said to be a "derelict." In such cases an old rule awarded the salvors one half of the property saved, which is now held to be an upper limit for salvage. The actual amount depends upon the danger, risk, time expended, and skill necessary to save the threatened property. The work of salvors benefits the marine insurers, and the marine policy pays for the cost of salvage.

When the subject of insurance is wholly destroyed, irreparably damaged, or taken from the insured without hope of recovery, the loss is total and *actual*. Ships and cargoes, however, can suffer other types of losses. They may, for example, be stranded or sunk beyond recovery, or captured and taken from the insured's control. When the loss becomes total only because the subject matter of the insurance is abandoned, and the entire property is not actually destroyed, the loss is termed *constructive*. There is a constructive total loss when the cost of salvaging the ship or its cargo exceeds the values that can be saved. So far as the insured is concerned, the loss is total, though there may be some salvage to the insurer. In England, when the cost of repairing or recovering the ship or goods will exceed their value when restored, abandonment is permitted. In this country, claim for a total loss is permitted if the cost of repairs or expenditures will be in excess of 50 percent of the value of the property when restored.

In these cases, because the ocean marine contract is a valued policy unlike most other property insurance, there may be an *abandonment* (at the insured's option only) of the property. The insured gives up the property to the insurers, and the full insurance amount is paid. The insured must prove that a constructive total loss has occurred, and make the decision to abandon promptly so that the insurers can salvage as much of the property as possible, if they choose to do so.

Rates

Ocean marine insurance has long been written on the basis of judgment rates quoted by underwriters after an appraisal of the entire risk. As in other fields, statistical data are accumulated. However, because the perils covered for each particular voyage tend to differ in so many respects, it is not easy to determine a rate that may be generally applied. Even in the case of ships that are nearly identical, differences in management and policies of operation could easily have the effect of requiring entirely different rates. Ships sailing over an identical course present risks in summer that are different from those in winter. In some areas hurricanes may create a seasonal hazard, and in other areas a seasonal hazard is created by icebergs and fogs. Shoals, tides and currents, inadequate anchorages, and dangerous approaches affect navigation of the owners, the conditions of the coverage, and the effect of trade customs are also considered. In no other branch of the insurance business is judgment so important.

Marine insurance syndicates, such as the American Institute of Marine Underwriters, suggest advisory rates for certain types of cargo shipments made upon approved ships. Recent increased use of "containerization" (large sealed units and pallets) has decreased rates for theft and handling damages. In the case of a policy producing a sizable volume of business, the insurer would probably quote lower rates than those suggested. Conversely, a policy on susceptible merchandise might require rates higher than those quoted. The reputation of the shippers, their experience record, and the classification of the ship would modify the rates.

Vessel construction is an important factor in ocean marine rate making. Data bearing upon the construction and type of a vessel are assembled by *classification societies* and made available to insurance underwriters through periodic publications known as *registers*. Two of the most widely known are *The Record,* published by the American Bureau of Shipping, and *Lloyd's Register of British and Foreign Shipping.* The registers contain data on nationality; the number of decks; the condition of the rigging, engine, boiler, and equipment; and the date of the last survey.

The ocean marine insurance market tends to be international in its scope.

The growth of world trade in recent decades has created new and challenging insurance problems, such as the giant "supertankers" whose future costs have been predicted as $100 million or more per ship. American insurers have been permitted exemptions from antitrust legislation that permit them to combine in order to develop rates and share risks. American businesses tend to insure with U.S. firms, but in some years approximately 50 percent of American marine business is insured abroad. The large size of each risk and the international market make ocean marine insurance a highly competitive field.

Pleasure craft insurance

More than 10 million motorboats and yachts are owned and used privately for pleasure purposes in the United States. Many of the smaller pleasure boats are provided limited insurance through the homeowner's contract, which automatically includes fire and theft coverage up to $500 on boats and equipment and liability protection for boats up to certain sizes (sailboats, 26 feet; outboards, 25 horsepower; inboards, 50 horsepower). Some larger boats can be added to the homeowner's contract by endorsement.

Special contracts have been designed to cover the particular problems of motorboats and the millions of outboard motors in use today. These *outboard policies* provide physical damage insurance for the motors, boats, trailers, and equipment. Although called "comprehensive" policies, they are usually named-perils coverage, typically including such perils as fire, theft, collision, wind, and loss of motor overboard. Bodily injury liability insurance is not provided in these contracts, but limited (usually to $500, or the hull value) coverage for property damage liability to other boats is included under the "collision or running-down clause." In order to secure more adequate liability protection, the owner should also purchase protection and indemnity coverage which covers liability for loss of life and personal injury, and for property damage. Larger amounts of insurance than a limit set by the hull value are often advisable for owners of pleasure craft. Medical payments may be included, too.

Special *yacht policies* have been developed to meet the insurance needs of the owners of the larger boats, such as cabin cruisers, inboard motorboats, and sailing ships. Most such marine contracts are for a term of one year, covering the hull, sails, fittings, furniture, provisions, machinery, and equipment. If new, boats are valued at their purchase price; if secondhand, at cost plus improvements. The policy is valued, and full insurance to value is required.

The package policies usualy include (1) the hull, (2) protection and indemnity, (3) federal compensation, and (4) medical payments insurance. The insured vessel is insured for perils of the sea and other waters described, fire, theft, barratry (employee fraud causing ship damage), general average and salvage charges, latent defects and negligence, jettison, and "other like perils." Exclusions often include wear and tear, pilferage, war risks, strikes, riots and civil commotions, and damage sustained while racing. Partial losses are covered in full if these are equal to the deductible franchise expressed in the policy, which ranges from $25 to $500 and is usually about 1 percent of the value of the ship.

Certain geographical limits are designated in the policy, and the coverage applies only within the territory of intended use specified in the contract. Leaving these limits without the consent of the insurer constitutes a deviation and suspends the policy until the insured vessel returns to the cruising limits undamaged. Liability during water-skiing is often excluded, or coverage amounts are restricted to basic limits. The rates vary considerably, and discounts are frequently given to accident-free boaters and boaters who have passed accredited Coast Guard safety courses.

INLAND MARINE INSURANCE

Inland marine insurance is much more recent in its origins than ocean marine contracts. The impetus for inland marine insurance coverages appeared in the railroad age, and it grew rapidly during the automobile and airplane eras. In our mobile society, many families and most businesses need to know about the different exposures to loss covered by the varied field of inland marine insurance. The related field of aviation insurance is discussed in Chapter 26.

The need

For many years shippers looked to the gigantic *railroads* for reimbursement in the event of loss or damage to the goods shipped. Much litigation and delay stemmed from the failure of shippers to understand thoroughly the effect of liability limitations that were incorporated into the bills of lading. A growing tendency to seek private transportation insurance was crystallized during World War I when the government took over the transportation systems of the country.

About the same time, *automobiles and trucks* were becoming an increasingly important factor in the transportation system. The shipper had little or no assurance of the ability of the trucking concern to meet promptly a heavy claim for loss or damage. If the shipper owned the trucks, the contents needed to be separately insured. The *airplane* also exerted its influence. Shippers were apprehensive lest this method of transportation prove particularly hazardous.

Another important basis for inland marine insurance is the fact that the common carrier is *not* always liable for loss or damage to the goods owned by the shipper. The common-law liability of the carrier has been thus expressed:

"The law charges this person thus entrusted to carry goods against all events, but Acts of God, and of the enemies of the King."[7] The early common law has been modified in but few respects. A carrier is still not responsible for a loss occasioned by an "act of God" (such as a tornado, lightning, or a flood), by an order of the public authority, by a public enemy, by faults of the shipper, or by the inherent vice or nature of the goods. Although the carrier remains responsible for its own negligence, developments in recent years have tended not to curtail the principle of liability but to limit the amount for which the carrier may be held under "released" bills of lading.

When goods in the hands of a common carrier have reached their destination and have been placed in reasonable safety, the status of the carrier changes (usually in 48 hours) to that of a warehouser. The difference in status is that insurance against losses by fire, burglary, or other perils which involve no negligence would not protect the shipper's goods in the hands of a warehouser. When the carrier becomes a warehouser and is liable only for losses growing out of negligence, the protection which the shipper may expect from the carrier can change automatically. Failure to provide adequate protection to meet such situations may entail a serious loss to the shipper.

With the use of motortrucks as carriers, the owners of the trucks viewed their liability as a very serious risk indeed, often far in excess of the value of the truck upon which it was being transported. This led to a demand for insurance covering the legal liability of the carrier, and other bailees who had temporary custody of goods for owners. Not all persons operating transportation facilities come within the legal classification of common carriers. Some truckers who do not operate regularly established routes or who work primarily for one or two customers accept goods as bailees; in this instance, they are liable for negligence and are not insurers of the goods, as are common carriers.

Development of inland marine insurance

Inland marine insurance does not refer only to the insurance of transportation risks on inland waterways. It developed out of the need for inland transportation insurance involving land risks or waterborne risks, or both. It was natural that appeal for the coverage should first be made to marine insurers that were conversant with the problems of transportation risks and were authorized to write the business under the terms of their charters. Because of the flexibility of the transportation policy, much broader coverages were available under inland marine contracts than could be obtained under the old fire or casualty contracts. The inland marine contracts were particularly desirable when there were concentrated values. In the case of furs, jewelry, art treasures, and the like, a single policy covering all risks had a tremendous appeal as compared with insuring the risks against burglary, fire, and other

---

[7] *Coggs* v. *Bernard,* 2 Lord Raymond 909; 1 Smith's Leading Cases 369.

specific perils. When as was usually the case, the all-risks policy could be obtained for a cost much less than was required for an accumulation of separate policies, the appeal of the marine policy to the buyer of insurance was natural. This new form carried with it an adaptability that was not to be found in the older fire field. The fire insurance business had little flexibility with respect to policies and forms, and business for the most part was written at rates established by the bureaus. Thus competition flared between the fire and marine insurers.

The fire insurers made the initial efforts to bring order to the confusion that developed. They provided broader forms and worked out a definition of marine insurance which in 1933 was approved by the National Association of Insurance Commissioners. This became known as the "Nation-Wide Definition and Interpretation of the Insuring Powers of Marine and Transportation Underwriters." In 1953, the definition was considerably broadened and modified by the NAIC. The title was shortened to *The Nationwide Definition,* and it is divided into two parts. The first part states the conditions under which marine and transportation policies may cover (*a*) imports; (*b*) exports; (*c*) domestic shipments; (*d*) bridges, tunnels and other instrumentalities of transportation and communication; (*e*) personal property floater risks. The second part of the definition, known as the "restrictive section," specifies about six prohibited risks where the element of transportation is ordinarily lacking. A 1976 revision has been adopted in about one third of the states, providing greater flexibility and dividing the floater risk category into two separate divisions, personal and commercial floaters. Electronic data processing policies are a significant commercial class that has become eligible under the definition of marine insurance.

Another step in putting an end to unregulated competition was the development of uniform rates and forms. The Inland Marine Insurance Bureau is now part of the Insurance Services Offices as a rating body, and IMIB rates and forms set the pattern for much of inland marine insurance. However, many of the contracts in the transportation field are still unregulated. Pipelines, radio and television towers, salespersons' samples, store and equipment floaters, installment risks, and fine arts policies are still in the unregulated areas.

Classes of inland marine insurance

Basically a risk must involve an element of transportation to be eligible for an inland marine contract. Either the property is actually in transit, is held by persons (bailees) who are not its owners, is at a fixed location which is an important instrument of transportation, or is a movable type of goods which is often at different locations. There are four divisions or classes of inland marine insurance: (1) property in transit, (2) bailee liability, (3) fixed transportation property, and (4) personal and commercial floaters.

Inland marine policies are written on an all-risks or a named-perils basis.

When a policy is written on an *all-risks basis,* it provides broad automatic coverage of all risks without naming each peril in the contract. The only risks not included are those named in the listed exclusions of the policy. All-risks coverage does not necessarily include all losses, however, for some losses are certainties and do not involve risk. A loss must be attributable to some unpredictability that could not have been foreseen. Thus losses due to innate tendencies to deterioration or wear and tear are not covered. Policies written on a *named-perils basis* may provide a coverage limited to a few perils, or one that is virtually but not actually all risks.[8] The extent of the coverage will depend upon the number of perils which are specifically listed as being included in the policy coverage. Another name for such a contract is a "specified perils" policy.

The wide variety of inland marine insurance contracts will be apparent as the classes of coverage are discussed. Appendix D offers a detailed list of the prospects for marine and all-risks contracts, indicating for a number of common businesses and situations the types of insurance property and the form of the policies recommended. For example, manufacturers are shown as prospects for the following inland marine contracts: trip transit; motortruck cargo; parcel post; and floater policies for neon signs, exhibitions, installations, installment sales, salespersons' samples, patterns, garment contractors, and many others.

Exclusions vary with the type of contract. All contracts follow a general pattern, with the addition of exclusions necessary to delineate properly the extent of the coverage. In a named-perils policy it is customary to exclude loss by leakage, breakage, marring, scratching, and wet or dampness, and losses attributable to wear and tear or gradual deterioration.

All policies exclude losses caused by the risks of war, nuclear or radioactive force, and confiscation of goods in illegal transportation or trade by any government or public authority. Even in an all-risks contract, certain losses such as breakage of statuary, glassware, porcelains, and similar fragile articles are excluded. Losses caused by strikes, riots, or civil commotion may be excluded. Finally, it is customary to exclude loss or damage by any process while the property is actually being worked upon. Reference in every instance should be made to the particular contract to determine the exclusions which apply.

A valuable aid to the student of insurance is the understanding that all insurance contracts must have some exclusions. (See section in Chapter 17 for fire insurance excluded property perils.) In analyzing any policy, particularly in those of the inland marine all-risks type, it is most helpful to keep in mind

---

[8] For example, a policy written by one insurer on the George Washington Memorial Bridge spanning the Hudson River at New York covered against the perils of fire; explosion; collision; lightning, flood, floating ice, tornado, hurricane, windstorm, tidal wave, rainstorm, falling meteor, earthquake, or other acts of God; malicious mischief, banditry, sabotage, or other acts of violence; strikes, labor disturbances, riots, or other civil commotion; collapse or failure; and seizure or detention.

the *general types of exclusions* which may normally be expected. These include losses that are: (1) *uninsurable* or *catastrophic;* (2) usually *separately insured* in other contracts; (3) *excessive or unusual,* thus requiring special information, endorsements, and premium charges; (4) *normally expected,* thus not really risks; and (5) *not accidental* in nature.

Property in transit. The first major class of inland marine insurance is protection for property frequently exposed to loss while it is in transit from one location to another. Several different contracts are available for these risks, including the basic inland transit floater, the trip transit policy, the processing floater, the department store floater, and special forms which insure only one type of transportation, such as express, motortruck, parcel post, registered mail, first-class mail, or armored car and messenger shipments.

The insuring clause of the *basic inland transit policy* states briefly that the policy covers for an amount not exceeding the limit(s) of liability as stipulated in the attached form or endorsement(s). This is followed by a space on the face of the policy for the attachment of the proper form or endorsement. The policy is designed so that it may be modified to fit the particular needs of the insured. There are standardized forms to cover goods and merchandise shipped by common carrier. Policies may be issued to cover a single shipment, or as in the case of the open-cargo form, merchants, manufacturers, or others who ship and receive goods continuously may cover all shipments. There are two forms of policy in use, differing only in the manner of computing the premium. An *annual form* requires a deposit premium based on an estimated valuation of shipments to be covered during the policy period. An annual audit is made of the total value of all the actual shipments, and an additional premium is charged or a return premium paid to the insured. The *open policy* requires not a deposit premium but a monthly report, with premiums due and payable when the report is made.

The form attached to the basic policy lists the perils covered as well as the exclusions. The more important clauses in the basic policy follow the pattern already noticed in connection with ocean marine insurance, including a sue and labor clause and an average clause. Territorial limits for the coverage are established. Certain other clauses parallel to a considerable degree clauses already noticed in connection with fire insurance contracts. Adjusted claims are paid within 60 days, but no loss is paid if the insured has collected for the loss from others. Provision is made for the usual appraisal, court suit, and cancellation procedures when these are necessary.

Trip transit policies are available for single shipments of merchandise, household furniture, livestock, and heavy machinery while in transit by freight, express, motortruck, and inland or coastwise steamers. The insurer is usually not liable for loss caused by theft, robbery, civil commotion, strikes, riots, war, and like perils, except by special endorsement. Contracts are issued covering unique, unusual, or extremely rare properties. Exhibits, films, paintings, valuable stamp collections, and many strange and unusual risks involving transportation hazards have been covered. It would be difficult to draw a line beyond which marine insurers are unwilling to go in insuring special transportation risks.[9]

Inland marine insurance sometimes requires other special forms adapted both to the nature of the perils to be covered and to the means of shipment. Certain of these forms have, within limits, become reasonably standardized:

a. Express shipments policy, which covers all risks of fire, lightning, windstorm, flood, earthquake, landslide, theft, pilferage, nondelivery, transportation, and navigation.

b. Parcel post policy, which insures safe arrival of merchandise shipped by parcel post, first-class mail, or registered mail. This is an alternative to insurance available through the government postal system.

c. Registered mail policy, which covers shipments by registered mail and by express for business institutions having large values at risk. Such values are usually concentrated in currency shipments or shipments of securities.

d. Armored car and messenger policy, which provides insurance for shipments of money, securities, and other valuables made by armored motorcars and messengers.

e. Processing floater policy, for goods and merchandise sent from the premises of the owner to various locations for processing. This policy covers on a named-perils basis property such as cloth, metals, plastics, leather, and foods, (*a*) when the property is owned by the insured and is being processed by others and (*b*) while the property is in transit.

f. Department store floater policy, which is a special form of transit policy designed to meet the needs of department stores or other retail merchants that ship and receive merchandise. It covers all risks of loss or damage to the property insured subject to the usual inland marine exclusions.

Bailee liability.   Insurance to meet the needs of persons who have intentionally received temporary custody of the goods or property of others has resulted in the inland marine field in the development of *bailee liability* coverages. The term *bailment* pertains solely to personal property which passes temporarily into the possession of a person or persons other than the owner. The "bailor" gives up possession of the property to the "bailee."

Common law classifies bailees into three categories, based upon whether bailment is (1) for the sole benefit of the *bailor,* with no compensation for the care of the property; (2) for the benefit of the *bailee,* such as in borrowing property without compensation; and (3) for the mutual benefit of the *bailor and the bailee,* such as in cases where the bailee is repairing, transporting, or storing property for some compensation.

---

[9] Would you believe a barrel of monkeys? Well, an airplane full of them was shipped from South America to a zoo in the United States and insured. Other examples are numerous: a copy of the Gutenberg Bible that covered while the book was on display; an amount of $48,000 covering on a one-cent stamp of an early British Guiana issue; and four million cryptolaemus bugs imported to kill the mealybug which was destroying citrus fruit in this country.

The degree of care required differs in these situations. The bailee in the first category would be expected to exercise only *minimal* care of the property; in the second category, *exceptional* care; and in the third category, *ordinary* care, or that care reasonably taken by average persons caring for their own property.[10] In the absence of special agreements or statutes, most ordinary business transactions involving bailments fall into this last classification.

The type of property in the bailment also affects the degree of care required. An innkeeper would be expected to handle money in quite a different manner from the way in which a trucker would be expected to handle a load of cement. What constitutes ordinary diligence in one set of circumstances would be construed as gross negligence in another.

Various statutory liabilities apply to carriers, warehousers, and public garagekeepers, among others. Bailees are invariably liable for negligence or "failure to exercise the care that the circumstances justly demand."[11] The negligent performance of a required duty or failure to perform the duty will create a legal liability for damages on the part of the bailee. This is a liability imposed by law and not a liability which is the outgrowth of contract.

Insurance may be purchased to cover the bailee's *legal liability* for loss. In order to establish a loss, there must be (1) legal liability on the part of the bailee and (2) loss or damage due to a peril covered by the policy. Many losses involve no legal liability, yet the bailee because of the desire to maintain customer goodwill wishes to make good losses of property that occur while it is in the bailee's custody. Three forms of bailee policies are written: (*a*) for the sole benefit of the bailor, (*b*) for the sole benefit of the bailee, and (*c*) for the benefit of both. It is more usual today and more satisfactory to provide direct damage insurance which pays for damage to the property in the hands of the bailee whether or not there is any element of legal liability.

Many forms of insurance are written that have a bailee interest. Fire insurance contracts include coverage, for example, on property held in trust or on commission but not sold. There are also three such major inland marine forms: (1) motortruck carriers, (2) bailees' customers, and (3) furriers' customers. Statutory laws compel licensed public truckers to purchase a prescribed minimum coverage for *truckers' legal liability* for their shipments. Their legal liability as carriers may be written under a blanket form or under a gross receipts form on a named-perils basis. Under the blanket form, a list is made of the trucks operated by the insured and a limit of liability is set for each truck. Under the gross receipts form, a rate is applied to the total receipts of the business. This form has an advantage in that a percentage of every charge goes for insurance and thus no insurance costs accrue when the trucks

---

[10] *Levine* v. *Wolff,* 78 N.J.L. 306; 73 Atl., 73; *Mortimer* v. *Otto,* 206 N.Y. 89; 99 N.E. 189.

[11] A public carrier is not liable for loss or damage to goods due to an act of God. The negligence rule, however, makes such a carrier liable if through the negligence of the carrier the lost or damaged goods were brought within the operation of the destructive forces of the act of God (*Schwartz* v. *Adsit,* 91 Ill. App. 576).

are idle or empty. *Bailees' customers policies* are written on a named-perils basis and cover direct damage without regard to legal liability to goods in the custody or control of the insured for services such as cleaning, repairing, laundering, and the like. While the policy may be adapted to the needs of any business institution, three forms have attained wide acceptance: laundries, dyers and cleaners, and rug and carpet cleaners. Furriers and department stores accepting furs for storage offer as part of their service *furriers' customers insurance* all-risks protection on the stored items. The policy is written on a special inland marine form, and the dealer is furnished insurance certificates to issue to customers. The policy provides not only legal liability coverage up to the valuation on the receipt issued to the owners of the furs but also direct loss or damage without regard to legal liability. The policy may be endorsed with the excess legal liability endorsement which covers any legal liability in excess of the receipt valuations.

Fixed transportation property.   Bridges, tunnels, and other instrumentalities of transportation and communication are insurable under inland marine forms, although as a matter of fact they are fixed property. They are so insured because they are held to be an essential part of the transportation system.

Bridges are owned not only by various governmental units such as states and their political subdivisions but also by railroads and by companies that operate them for profit from the tolls. Enormous values are concentrated in a single structure, and oftentimes a bridge represents a major asset or substantial income. Auxiliary facilities (toll booths, for example) and equipment may not be included, but policies must exclude buildings, their contents, and supplies held in storage. The policies usually extend to cover more perils than those included in the fire policy, such as the marine perils of collapse, collision, or flood. The bridge policy is written to cover either (*a*) direct damage or (*b*) indirect losses of use and occupancy.

Bridge insurance covers direct loss or damage to the bridge and its approaches "however caused" with a limited number of exceptions. Included are such losses as fire, flood, ice, and explosion. The policy does not usually cover losses caused by or resulting from strikes, lockouts, labor disturbances, riots, civil commotions, sabotage, vandalism, or malicious mischief; from the violation of law; or from war risks. Losses occasioned by failure of the insured to maintain the structure properly are excluded. Examples of actual losses show that serious losses are possible and that insured amounts should be substantial.[12]

---

[12] The collapse of the $6,400,000 Narrows Bridge over Puget Sound, four months after its completion, demonstrated the very real possibility of heavy losses. The bridge was insured for $5 million under an all-risks inland marine form. Insurance on the Tappan Zee Bridge over the Hudson River was for $62 million direct damage and $6 million business interruption, underwritten 50 percent by 46 American companies and 50 percent by underwriters at Lloyd's. Other losses of sizable proportions were a large South American bridge whose supports were hit by a freighter in 1964; the "Silver

Next to bridges and tunnels in terms of insurable values come piers, wharves, and docks. The perils of fire, windstorm, and other perils ordinarily included in the fire contract may not be covered. Flood risks, collision, or collapse are insurable under the marine contract. Marine railways and dry docks, however, are insurable against all risks. Water pipelines are insurable, as are oil pipelines and power transmission lines. Radio towers are covered, and here the principal peril is collapse. Airway beacons and floodlights are insurable. Stop-and-go traffic signals often cost thousands of dollars. Dams may be insured, and the peril here is collapse or damage from ice or debris.

Floaters. In inland marine insurance, the term *floater* is used in the sense that insurance is provided to follow mobile insured property wherever it may be located, subject always to territorial limits of the contract. Floater policies are classified under the 1976 Nationwide Definition as (*a*) personal and (*b*) commercial. In the personal floater category are policies covering such items as jewelry, furs, silverware, and works of art. In the commercial floater category are policies covering contractors,' physicians', and farm equipment; theatrical property; salespersons' samples; consignment, installation, and installment sales floaters; and many others.[13]

The basic contract for all floaters is the *scheduled property floater policy*. It is a very simple policy that states on its face the usual insuring clause indicating that the policy covers "on property described below or in schedule attached." The property to be covered may be listed, and forms with additional clauses and stipulations attached. The standard clauses that appear in the basic property floater are in many cases repetitions of clauses that appear in policies already noticed.

Personal floaters. At some time or another everyone has personal property at a nonpermenanent location. The baggage of a traveler is a pertinent example, as is clothing at a laundry, an overcoat in a checkroom, or equipment used for sports. A number of personal property floaters are available that provide broad protection or insure articles of higher value.

Several floater policies covering personal effects are prefixed by the term *personal.* The policies are so different and their names are so similar that it is important to distinguish the different forms. Those most likely to be confused are: (*a*) the personal property floater, (*b*) the personal effects floater, and (*c*) the personal articles floater. Closely akin to the foregoing is the tourist's baggage form.

The *personal property floater* provides all-risks coverage not only away from the insured's residence but in the residence as well. The policy covers "personal property owned, used or worn by the person in whose name this

---

Bridge" over the Ohio River, which failed in 1967 with a tragic loss of almost 50 lives, and the collapse of a bridge over the Yadkin River in North Carolina in 1975.

[13] The most complete text available for further reference on ocean marine insurance and the many inland marine floater policies is William H. Rodda, *Marine Insurance: Ocean and Inland,* 3d ed. (Englewood Cliffs, N.J.: Prentice-Hall, 1970).

policy is issued and members of assured's family of the same household, while in all situations, except as hereinafter provided." The policy thus insures virtually every piece of personal property, with only a few exceptions such as boats, automobiles, and business property. Unforeseen and unexpected perils are automatically included in the all-risks protection, and only a few perils are excluded, such as the breakage of fragile articles, war, and wear and tear. The importance of this former classic example of all-risks insurance has decreased in recent years with the availability of similar broad coverage in the homeowners' policies (see Chapter 27).

The *personal effects floater* provides all-risks protection for the insured on personal property away from his or her residence. It does not specifically list the personal effects to be covered, but it includes all property usually carried by tourists and travelers.

The *personal articles floater* provides all-risks protection for the insured on furs, jewelry, cameras, silverware, fine arts, golfer's equipment, musical instruments, and stamp and coin collections. Formerly insured under separate contracts, these types of property, if two or more are insured, are now usually combined in the personal articles floater policy.

Depending upon the nature of the risk, inland marine floaters utilize one of three forms. These are (*a*) blanket, (*b*) scheduled, and (*c*) blanket and scheduled. There are many classes of personal property that involve in the aggregate substantial values but include no single item or items sufficiently valuable or distinctive to require scheduling. Such properties are insured under the *blanket* form. For example, the golfer's equipment floater is an all-risks blanket policy.

Scheduled property floaters are used to cover properties involving a number of separate items, each of substantial value. Such policies may be written on a very broad all-risks basis with the few exclusions that are typical of all inland marine policies. Cameras and musical instruments are examples of property that is insured in this way. Snowmobiles are a new type of risk covered by a scheduled policy. To be covered under a scheduled policy, and property must be carefully described to indicate clearly the item to be covered, and when more than one item is insured, each must be separately valued.

Furs and jewelry are often scheduled for coverage by individuals and their families. The policy covers worldwide against all risks. When new, the cost price is acceptable as a valuation; otherwise, an appraisal by a reliable furrier or jeweler is preferable. It is an underwriting practice not to insure furs for an amount greater than their cost. Insuring both furs and jewelry under a single policy is advantageous because as aggregate values exceed designated limits, the rate on the excess drops. A further reduction in the premium may be obtained if a $50-deductible clause is made a part of the policy.

There are certain types of personal property that lend themselves to a combination *blanket and scheduled* form of coverage. Items that have an unusual value may be scheduled, and other items may be covered on a blanket basis.

The personal property floater, already noticed, is an example of a scheduled and blanket personal property form. Another example is the *fine arts floater*. The policy is used in insuring private or public collections of pictures, tapestries, valuable rugs, statuary, antique furniture, rare porcelains, books, and other valuable items. Special forms are available for museums, art galleries, dealers, or other commercial enterprises. A final example is the *wedding presents floater*. In order to protect wedding presents, wherever they may be and until they are permanently located, the wedding presents floater provides a worldwide coverage against all risks. The policy must be written to expire not over 90 days after the wedding.

Commercial floaters. Property that is frequently moved about in connection with a business or profession may be insured under a business or commercial floater. Some of the more widely used commercial forms will be described.

The *physicians' and surgeons' equipment floater* is designed to cover professional instruments and equipment used by the insured in the practice of medicine or dentistry. It is an all-risk policy covering instruments and equipment carried by the insured from place to place, and instruments not customarily carried are excluded from the protection. If there are any unusually valuable instruments they may be scheduled, though for most physicians or surgeons blanket insurance is adequate.

The *salespersons' floater* policies insure samples transported from place to place for display to prospective customers. There are as many classes of samples as there are types of business. Obviously, a case of shoe samples, with 'only one shoe of a kind, is less of an attraction to thieves than is a case of jewelry. Some samples are shipped by railroad or air, while others are transported in the automobile of the salesperson.

The *radium floater* policy protects one of the most peculiar types of property that has ever been made the subject of insurance. Radium is a rare substance, now widely used by the medical profession, particularly in the treatment of cancer. Infinitesimal amounts have a very high value. In spite of the great care exercised in handling so valuable a substance, losses frequently occur. To indemnify the owner of radium in the event of its loss from any cause, war risks and gradual deterioration excepted, the all-risks radium floater is written by describing the individual items covered.

Installation floaters are written for a number of concerns whose business requires the complete installation of their product in working order in the premises of the customer before delivery is completed. For example, business firms specializing in store fixtures contract to remodel a given location, which may require anything from a new front to interior decoration. Machinery is often delivered installed, as are many other items. The business at any time will have goods partially installed in numerous locations and in transit. Such risks may be insured against fire and transportation perils, and against perils on the premises to which they have been consigned until installation is complete.

The *conditional sales approval floaters* may be written covering department stores and other businesses against the loss of goods sold on the installment plan, loaned, leased, or sent on approval. The development of merchandising has made it a usual practice to send out to prospective customers on approval or for trial such commodities as rugs, refrigerators, television sets, furniture, washers and dryers, and the like. Sales frequently involve installment payments. The floater covers goods in transit against many named perils, and in buildings, excluding premises owned, rented, leased, or used by the insured.

There are several forms of *agricultural machinery equipment and farm animals floaters.* Some companies also write livestock mortality insurance on valuable farm animals, poultry, and dogs or other pets on a named-perils basis. The business floaters here noted serve only as examples of the many parts of inland marine insurance. Policies are also written on neon signs, theatrical equipment, rolling stock, contractor's equipment, patents, and scientific instruments. An inland marine floater policy may be adapted to almost any conceivable type of risk involving property that is moving from place to place. Leased electronic data processing equipment is a modern example of risks newly eligible for floater coverage.

A final example of inland marine insurance adaptation in the business area is provided by the *inland marine block policies.* Originally written for jewelers and said to have originated with the underwriters at Lloyd's of London, block policies are written for jewelers, furriers, camera or musical instrument dealers, construction equipment and agricultural equipment dealers, and others. The policies are written on an all-risks basis, with the list of exclusions tailored to meet the particular class of business to be covered. The property is covered without limitation as to time on the insured's own premises, in contrast to the usual marine contract. In addition, the block policy provides in a single package coverage for: (*a*) goods on the premises of others; (*b*) goods in transit, including salespersons' samples; and (*c*) goods of others in the custody of the insured. With the exception of the jewelers' block policy, whose form has been standardized, there are variations in the terms of the other forms just noted. Because the jewelers' form is the oldest and has become standardized, it will serve as an example of a block policy.

The *jewelers' block policy* is written to provide comprehensive coverage for pawnbrokers, silverware dealers, and diamond wholesalers. The policy provides an all-risk cover against loss or damage "arising from any cause whatsoever," subject to a few exclusions such as inherent vice or insufficient or defective packing. There are five specific limitations in the amount of coverage: (1) to property at the named premises; (2) to property shipped by first-class registered mail, railway express, or armored-car service; (3) to registered airmail or express shipments in a given day to one recipient at the same address; (4) to property handled by parcel transportation services; and (5) to property in the custody of insured's personnel away from the premises. In addition to property of the insured, the policy provides protection against loss of property owned by customers of the jewelers or by dealers who may entrust property to them. Policies generally cover "in or upon any place or premises whatsoever" in the United States and Canada, and while being carried in transit. Particular emphasis is given to a number of conditions and warranties that appear. The insured is required to keep an accurate inventory so that the exact amount of loss can be determined. The insured also warrants that the protective devices and security guard service described in the proposal will be maintained. In all, the jewelers' block policy illustrates the specialized need of many busineses for the broad coverage of business floater contracts.

FOR REVIEW AND DISCUSSION

1. Explain *why* the need for transportation (marine) insurance has grown so rapidly in the past 50 years. In what parts of marine insurance has the development been most rapid?

2. Of what importance to a midwestern business is knowledge about ocean marine insurance? Is there any reason for an individual homeowner to understand ocean marine insurance, too?

3. Is the ocean marine policy a *standard* contract? Explain your answer.

4. Briefly explain the importance of the following principles in ocean marine insurance: (*a*) *warranties,* (*b*) *protection and indemnity insurance,* (*c*) *deductibles,* (*d*) *assignment,* and (*e*) *coinsurance.*

5. Any vessel used for pleasure purposes may be insured by yacht and motorboat insurance. What additional protection is afforded under the marine form that the fire policy cannot give?

6. Choose three terms of unique significance in ocean marine insurance losses, and explain why each is important.

7. "Marine insurance rates are judgmental ones, and international in character." Explain why you agree, or disagree, with this statement.

8. Why did most states adopt *The Nationwide Definition,* and what were its important effects in the insurance business?

9. Identify the basic *classes* of inland marine insurance, and give an example of each type.

10. What *general* types of exclusions should you expect to find in insurance contracts (even in "all-risks" inland marine policies)? Illustrate each general type with a specific exclusion found in some inland marine contract.

11. Why does a business need to know about bailments, and how does insurance relate to these situations? What difference does it make whether the bailee is a warehouser or a common carrier?

12. Mr. X, an employee of Mrs. B's hotel, allowed a trunk being transported from the airport to become wet, destroying $500 worth of clothing. Mrs. B denies liability on the ground that the trucker was negligent. Is Mrs. B liable? If so, is the risk insurable?

13. Credit sales are growing so tremendously in volume that insurance of the risk is necessary. Many customers feel that they should not pay for something that

is not fully theirs at the time the loss occurred. What form of coverage will provide adequate insurance, and what type of businesses need it most?

14. In a recently reported fire more than 200 clothing items at a dry cleaner were destroyed. Assuming that the cleaner was entirely free of neglect, what form of inland marine insurance would cover such losses, and why is it needed?

15. Gilbert Stuart's portrait of George Washington has been appraised at $250,000. Would the fine arts floater policy cover loss to this picture occasioned by the malicious throwing of acids upon it? Explain.

16. *a.* What types of *personal* "floater" contracts might an individual or a family consider? Which are blanket coverage, and which are scheduled coverage?

    b. What types of *commercial* "floater" contracts might be considered in the insurance program for a department store? for a jewelry store?

Chapter 20

Concepts considered in Chapter 20—The liability risk

The scope and magnitude of the liability risk involve every modern family or organization with increasing legal responsibility.

The legal basis for liability is *legal wrongs,* invading the rights of others. Legal wrongs may be *criminal* or *civil*. Criminal wrongs involve the public at large and are punishable by government action. Civil (or private) wrongs are based on (1) *contracts* or (2) *torts.*

Liability under contract law occurs only as a result of the invasion of another's rights under a contract, by:

Breach of contract, or not fulfilling promises in an agreement;

Bailee liability, which has been discussed in Chapter 19; and

Implied warranties, which often extend liability well beyond the specific written obligations of a contract.

Liability under tort law involves all civil wrongs not based on contracts:

Intentional acts or omissions, such as battery, assault, and trespass;

Strict or absolute liability, which applies even if there is no fault present; and

Negligence liability, which requires:

A legal duty to act or not act, under the circumstances;

A voluntary unintentional wrong, as determined by a prudent person's conduct;

A proximate relationship between the wrong, and

An injury, a death, or property damage as the result.

Modifications of the usual negligence liability rules sometimes occur by court cases or statutes:

Comparative negligence, where each party causing losses pays in the proportion that he or she is held liable;

Presumed negligence, which under certain circumstances may create a "prima facie" case of liability; and

Imputed negligence, which may extend the liability of some persons or organizations (such as employers, parents, automobile owners, and others) to injuries or damages caused by *others.*

Specific kinds of liability situations illustrate wide variety based upon: *real property ownership, attractive nuisance hazards* (injuries to children), *employees and agents, animals, government* units and *charitable* institutions, *nonownership liability* (automobiles), and *libel* and other related types of liability.

The liability risk

"To sue or not to sue"—that is the question! The answer is increasingly in the affirmative—or at least the answer is a rhetorical "Why not!" Situations involving injuries or damages that a generation ago would invariably have been assumed by the injured person are now regularly the basis for lawsuits by one person against another person or an organization.

What has changed in our society to create such great uncertainty in this area? Many factors are involved, including changing personal or moral[1] values and attitudes toward such institutions as the family, government, business, and the church. The social environment, too, has changed with such trends as urbanization, geographic mobility, nondiscriminization, the "automobile economy," professionalism, and the affluent society. Our ideas of individual, corporate, and social responsibility have undergone many changes, and these changes have been reflected in a pronounced reliance upon law to determine the extent of the liability risk.

What emerges is a world which places heavy emphasis on legal requirements and rights. Whether one likes it or not, rarely can important decisions ever be made for family or business without considering their legal implications. A birth, a death, a marriage, a divorce, the purchase of a home, a new job, a new car, a sales contract, or the formation of a business enterprise—all of these have significant legal consequences. The liability risks which accompany these and many other everyday events of our lifetime are the subject of this chapter. How liability insurance can help meet these escalating risks is discussed in Chapter 21.

SCOPE AND MAGNITUDE OF THE LIABILITY RISK

Sources

Because of the prevalence of claims, almost everyone is aware of the liability risk in operating an automobile. However, every form of personal, business,

---

[1] In a provocative look at the future, Dr. John D. Long evaluates the "public moral hazard" as it is influenced by such trends in our society as (1) population, (2) inflation, and (3) relaxed theological pressures. Further ideas on achievement, property ownership, waste, apprehension, honesty, responsibility and other "ethical pillars" of insurance are presented in his book *Ethics, Morality, and Insurance* (Bloomington: Bureau of Business Research, Indiana University, 1971).

or professional activity is also to some degree exposed to loss because of liability claims based on negligence. If a negligent act or omission interferes with the rights of any individual, the party responsible for the negligence is liable for damages to the injured party. There is also always the danger of alleged negligence which may result in expensive litigation. There may also be the breach of liability assumed under a contract or the breach of an implied warranty, such as the implied warranty of a seller that goods are fit for the purpose for which they are sold. To meet the legal consequences of all these exposures, liability insurance has become essential in our legalistic society.

Size of losses

The owner of a property knows that the limit of direct loss is the value of the property. Thus, if a building worth $50,000 is completely destroyed, it will result in a loss to the owner of $50,000. If an automobile worth $5,000 is stolen and never recovered, it represents a loss of no more than $5,000. In the case of liability claims, the limit may not be fixed with any reasonable certainty. This characteristic is in contrast to the situation in direct property insurance, where the direct maximum possible loss can be readily determined as the total property value.

Liability claims, therefore, may far exceed the capital invested in an enterprise. More than this, it requires a substantial sum of money to prove that there is no liability when a groundless claim is made. If there is liability and the injury is serious, such as one involving the permanent disability or disfigurement of an individual, in the absence of adequate insurance the verdict can bring financial ruin to an individual or business. The former limits for which liability policies were written are no longer regarded as adequate. Courts are taking judicial notice of dollar depreciation, and verdicts that would have been considered excessive in the past[2] are no longer regarded as sufficient to compensate an injured person for loss sustained as the result of an injury. The annual size of liability payments today in the United States has caused William E. Knepper, a past president of the International Association of Insurance Counsel, to refer to this multibillion-dollar cost as "the injury industry."

Liability verdicts today are not only high, and thus potentially ruinous to financial condition, but they are also extremely variable and unpredictable for an individual or business. Ten years ago losses were considered large if they exceeded $50,000 or $100,000. Today numerous examples of awards

---

[2] For example, in 1902 an award of $4,000 was held to be excessive for the loss of a right leg (*Chicago Railroad Company* v. *Jackson,* 55 Ill. 492; 8 Am. Rep. 661); and in 1911 a verdict of $10,000 was reduced to $5,000 in a case where both legs had been amputated (*St. Louis Railroad Company* v. *Hesterly,* 98 Ark. 240; 135 S.W. 874). Practically all settlements came within the usual $5,000 insurance limit, which today is sadly inadequate.

of more than $1 million for *one* person's injuries have appeared.[3] Contrary to popular notion, it is not only the urban states that have had large verdicts handed down by juries, for in many states the single-person awards have approached or exceeded $1 million. In 1978, $128 million, the largest judgment in U.S. history, was awarded to a 13-year-old boy against Ford Motor Company for burns resulting from a defective gas tank. This much-publicized award was later reduced to $6.3 million. For a single accident involving a number of persons, the claims and verdicts can skyrocket to many millions of dollars. High verdicts are by no means limited to those resulting from automobile accidents. Fires, explosions, building collapses, falls, poisonings, airplane crashes, and many other situations may create liability lawsuits. A Southgate Kentucky night club fire in which 165 persons died in 1977 has suits of more than $2.9 billion pending.

Although it is true that the majority of liability claims are settled or receive verdicts for far less than the original amounts asked in a court suit, this is poor consolation for the individual or business faced with a claim which may spell financial ruin after several years of uncertainty. The trend is significant, too, for the defendant may often be required to pay an award far beyond any expectation of maximum loss at the time insurance was purchased.

The large claims for liability are not always against big corporations, either. A California housewife was sued for over $800,000 of damages to residential homes on the basis that she was negligent in starting a backyard fire without a fire permit! The variability of liability claims, even for similar accidents, is self-evident in the following recent contradictory headlines: "Failure to Yell 'Fore' Costs Golfer $25,140" and "Golfer Must Accept Risk of Being Hit."[4]

Results of losses

Direct loss or damage to property destroys values already acquired, but a liability claim may destroy more by obligating the party held responsible for the loss or injury to make payments for years in the *future*. Legal obligations for serious negligence are not excused by bankruptcy. Individuals who believed themselves to be judgment proof are sometimes obliged to make weekly payments out of their incomes until judgments are satisfied. A court judgment may reach out to take bank deposits, securities, real estate, and a part of one's earnings for years to come.

Bankruptcy has sometimes been suggested as a way out for a person with-

---

[3] "$1 Million Judgments Continue to Increase," *Business Insurance,* February 20, 1978, p. 6. More than 100 such jury verdicts in the past four years are noted by Jury Verdict Research, Inc., in this article. Most were for paraplegic, quadriplegic, or brain damage cases.

[4] The first headline is from a Columbus, Ohio, newspaper; the second from Atlanta, Georgia.

out assets, and it is said to be judgment proof. This is not a simple procedure, and the consequences in the way of injury to business reputation and credit standing amount to a lasting injury. In many states failure to satisfy a judgment up to a given amount will result in the loss of a car owner's right to drive, and in some jurisdictions a jail sentence. Travelers do not realize that they are subject to the laws of the place where an accident occurs, and reciprocal agreements in another state may cost motorists the right to drive.

Fraudulent claims

During recent years, great loss and annoyance have resulted from *fraudulent* claims for alleged injuries. A number of individuals and gangs have been apprehended, but the menace has grown to such proportions that insurers have organized central index bureaus in different sections of the country for the filing and tabulating of claims. This system brings to light duplication of claims for the same alleged injury, and the frequency with which the names of doctors and lawyers appear in connection with doubtful claims "spots" them for observation.[5]

Aside from the professional fakers of claims, there are the amateurs who in any accident, however slight, go to bed immediately and experience all kinds of symptoms. Every claimant knows that it is expensive to contest a suit and that the defendant, disliking the attendant publicity, prefers a quick settlement. Insurers use their professional loss adjustment services to minimize the harmful effects of fraudulent claims.

The above is not intended to accuse all injured persons of being dishonest. Most claimants are honest, but some are not, and these persons can cost insureds (and uninsureds) and insurers a considerable sum. The cost of property defense is high—for fraudulent as well as valid claims. The typical plaintiff's attorney receives from one fourth to one third of the settlement. Defense attorneys are paid on the basis of minimum or fixed fees, or on a time basis, instead of a percentage of the settlement. For many defense proceedings, several thousand dollars of expense for court costs and legal expenses are involved.

THE LEGAL BASIS FOR LIABILITY—LEGAL WRONGS

A claim based upon liability imposed by law develops as the result of the invasion of the rights of others. A legal right is more than a mere moral

---

[5] Faked claims are sometimes made in such a manner as to prompt a quick adjustment to avoid unfavorable publicity. One man, after eating part of a chicken pie in a restaurant, would slip a dead mouse under the pastry and then "discover" the mouse presumably cooked in it. Another case is that of a man who would swallow a nail or a tack in a restaurant and allege that it had been in the food. X-ray pictures would be presented, and damages paid. His fraud was brought to light by careful investigation and comparison of claims among several insurers.

obligation of one person to another, for it has the backing of the law to enforce the right. Legal rights impose many specific responsibilities and obligations, such as not invading privacy or property, or not creating an unreasonable risk or actual harm to others.

The invasion of such legal rights is a *legal wrong.* The wrong may be (*a*) criminal (public) or (*b*) civil (private). A *criminal wrong* is an injury involving the public at large and is punishable by the government. The action on the part of government to effect a conviction and impose fines or imprisonment is termed a "criminal action."

Civil wrongs are based upon: (1) torts and (2) contracts. *Torts* are wrongs independent of contract (for example, false imprisonment, assault, fraud, libel, slander, and negligence). *Contracts* may involve legal wrong when implied warranties are violated, bailee responsibilities are not fulfilled, or contract obligations are breached. Although the government takes action with respect to crimes, civil injuries are remedied by court action instituted by the injured party in a "civil action." The remedy is usually the award of monetary damages. The liability consequences of a crime are not usually insurable, but the liability for damages growing out of a civil wrong may, and often should be, insured.

Figure 20–1 illustrates the *legal basis for liability.* Although liabilities include criminal wrongs, for liability insurance the emphasis is on *civil wrongs* and particularly on the many legal wrongs based upon *torts.* Of greatest importance are torts resulting from *negligence* (unintentional acts or omissions), which are said to encompass more than nine out of ten claims for personal injury or property damage to others.

Liability under contract law

Liability under contract law is based on the invasion of another's rights under a contract. It occurs only as a result of a *contract* between one party and another. In contrast, liability under tort law is based on the breach of one's duty to respect the rights of the general public. It may result from either common law or statute law.

In insurance terminology, the convenient but inaccurate term *legal liability* is sometimes used. All liability which is imposed by tort *and* contract law is "legal," since the rights of the injured party to damages are enforceable in courts of law.

Breach of contract. Not fulfilling promises made in an agreement, or *breach of contract,* is the most obvious type of civil wrong based on contracts. Contractual responsibilities often extend well beyond the specific written obligations of a contract, and insurance sometimes covers these civil wrongs based on contracts. Contract default in connection with surety bonds will be discussed in Chapter 25.

Bailee liability. *Bailee liability,* which results from bailment contracts, has

Figure 20–1. The legal basis for liability

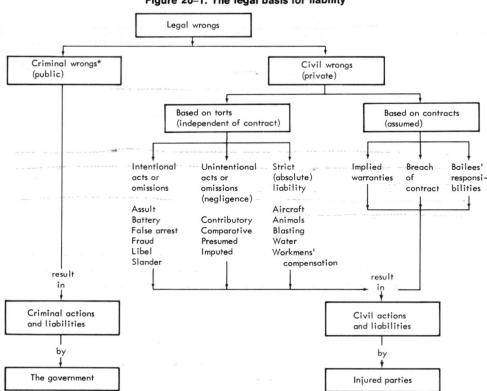

* The basis of criminal wrongs is always dependent upon specific governmental *statutes* or rulings. Civil wrongs *may* be based not only on statute law, but are most frequently the result of *common-law* (court) decisions.

been noted in Chapter 19. The responsibilities created in these special types of contract are important enough to be listed as a separate category of liability under contract law, although the previous discussion is not repeated here.

Implied warranties. One of the most common extensions of liability under contract law concerns manufacturers and distributors of products. In connection with sales or a contract to sell, the law imposes certain obligations termed *implied warranties*. Where a buyer reasonably relies on the skill or judgment of the seller, there is an implied warranty that the goods are reasonably fit for the purpose for which they were sold.

A seller may also be held liable if products are supplied to a user without giving proper notice of their dangerous qualities. The dividing line between negligence and liability growing out of implied warranty is not always clear. The point to be emphasized is that the seller may be held liable for injuries which the product may cause after it leaves the seller. The Consumer Products Safety Act of 1972 has recently increased the potential liability of many producers and sellers in this area. Products liability insurance is discussed in a separate section of Chapter 21.

Liability under tort law

Torts include all civil wrongs not based on contracts. As such, they are a broad residual classification of many private wrongs against another person or organization. They occur independently of contractual obligations, and may result (1) from intentional acts or omissions, (2) from strict liability imposed by statute law, or (3) from negligence. The requirements for tort liability are enumerated in the later section on negligence liability, the most important type of tort liability.

Intentional acts or omissions. Lawsuits sometimes occur because of injuries or damage caused by intentional acts or omissions. One example is *battery,* which is the offensive or harmful touching of another without his or her express or implied consent. *Assault* is a second example, and this involves threatened battery. Other examples include *trespass* (entry on land of another without permission) and *false imprisonment,* which results from the intentional unprivileged restriction of another's freedom of movement. This may cause harm to another by damage to reputation or mental distress. *Fraud* involves intent to cause loss to another, too, and is such a broad category as to be separately treated in many discussions of this subject. *Libel* (written) and *slander* (oral) involve false statements made about someone else, which cause damage to character or invasion of privacy (see later section of this chapter on insuring such liability). All of these acts are based upon planned or premeditated acts or omissions, although the harmful results may not have been anticipated.

Strict or absolute liability. The seriousness of the liability exposure is seen in a trend which in particular situations holds persons responsible for injuries or damages no matter how careful they may have been in trying to avoid losses to others. Under what is called *strict liability* or "absolute liability" certain persons are held liable for damages, regardless of whether or not fault or negligence can be proved against them. Although this doctrine is applied only in particular circumstances, the courts and statutes have been applying it with increasing frequency. Examples include: injury from blasting operations by contractors; injury caused by any type of wild animal kept in captivity (see also later section of this chapter about domesticated animals); and damage done by a release of pressure or weight of water, such as a weak dam bursting.

Other illustrations of this trend are the absolute liability, up to certain amounts, which airlines have for the safety of their passengers, and the broadest application of the "liability regardless of fault" idea, workers' compensation laws, which hold the employer liable for most employee work injuries and many diseases.

In food cases, too, the doctrine is often applied when foreign objects cause injury to or sickness of the consumer. Automobile manufacturers are increasingly being sued for defects which cause automobile accidents. Different state laws may apply, but some are broadening to permit strict liability suits for serious car faults leading to damages. In such cases, the plaintiff would not have to prove that the manufacturer knew, or should have known, of the defect.

In a modern application, a recent case held a merchant accountable under strict liability for sale of glue to a 13-year-old who died as a result of "glue sniffing." In spite of a state law which made it illegal for anyone under age 19 to possess the glue, the court held that violation of the law barring such sale created strict liability on the seller's part.[6]

Negligence liability. _Negligence_ is a tort, a civil wrong not based upon a contract. Most of the liability imposed by law stems from accidents attributable to negligence. If negligence can be shown to be the proximate cause of an injury to another, the negligent party is liable to the injured party for damages. Negligence is the _failure to exercise the proper degree of care_ required by circumstances. It may consist of not doing what was required under the circumstances, or of doing something that ought not to have been done. Behavior in any circumstances that fails to measure up to that expected of a careful _prudent_ person in like circumstances constitutes negligence. Faulty judgment may result in liability for negligence, even thought the motive behind the act was the best.[7]

Requirements for negligence liability. Four _requirements_ must exist before _negligence liability_ is present: (1) a _legal duty_, (2) a _wrong_, (3) a _proximate relationship_ between the wrong and an injury or damage, and (4) an _injury or damage_.

A _legal duty_ to act, or not to act, depends on the circumstances and the persons involved. A bystander has no legal duty to try to prevent a mugging, but a police officer does. Lifeguards have a legal duty to attempt to save a drowning victim, but others usually do not. Whether or not a legal duty is owed to someone else is decided by the courts, and many factors may determine the degree of care required. Examples include the duty of one person to respect another's right to bodily safety, or his or her right to the use of another person's property.

The previous sections have described various kinds of wrongs, indicating that negligence is one of the most common and important wrongs. A _wrong_ is a breach of legal duty, based upon a standard of conduct that is determined

---

[6] "Sale of Glue to Minnesota Minor Imposes Strict Liability on Seller," _Weekly Underwriter_, November 24, 1973, p. 30 (_Zerby_ v. _Warren_, 210 N.W. 2d 58), By 1977, the strict liability doctrine had been accepted in most states, but it often applies only in limited cases with special circumstances present.

[7] Even in these cases, the degree of care necessary to escape the charge of negligence varies. For example, a surgeon setting a fractured limb must exercise an entirely different degree of care from that exacted of a nonmedical person helping in an emergency.

by what a prudent person would have done or not done in similar circumstances. Criminal wrongs and the other kinds of civil wrongs (breach of contract or warranty) are not as pertinent as negligence is in this description of the word *liability*. To do a wrong, the act or omission must be *voluntary*. Thus, if a person in the course of avoiding great danger injures another person without intent, there is held to be no voluntary act and hence no liability. Negligence usually involves injury that is *unintentional*. On the other hand, it is no defense if the act which injures a party was done without intent to do an injury or if the motive behind the act was good and praiseworthy.

A third requisite for the fixing of liability is found in the rule that the voluntary act of the wrongdoer must have been the *proximate cause* of the injury. For the act to be held a proximate cause, there must have been a continuous succession of events from the act to the final event causing the injury. If there was an independent and intervening cause, the continuous succession of events was broken. Thus, a fire negligently ignited and spread by the winds is one continuous succession of events. If, however, a third party were deliberately pushed into the flames by someone else and injured, there would not have been a continuous sequence. No liability for the injury would attach to the party responsible for the fire.

The fourth requirement for negligence liability is that there be *injury* or *damage*. The guilty person must pay an amount that reasonably compensates the injured party for (a) bodily and other personal injuries and (b) loss of income due to disability, (c) pain and suffering, (d) disfigurement, and (e) any other losses for which the negligence is the proximate cause.

Loss of income due to inability to work often comprises a large proportion of liability cases. As an example of other losses, a husband may collect for the value of his wife's services as well as for "consortium," the term which the law applies to the companionship of the wife.[8] A parent may also collect for the loss of the services of an injured child and for the expenses attendant upon the injury. In the case of death, the heirs or next of kin may collect damages for the loss of the life. Some states fix a statutory limit for an instantaneous "wrongful" death; but if the party retains or regains consciousness after the injury and ultimately dies, the damage for conscious suffering is added to the damage for the death. Sometimes bodily injury is extended to include cases where no actual physical injury is suffered, but mental anxiety results from near accidents.

Compensation for *property damage* is measured by the difference in the

---

[8] At common law the right to maintain a suit for loss of consortium was limited to the husband (*Koscialak* v. *Portland Railway, Light & Power Company*, 126 S.E. 307; 189 N.C. 120). However, a change grew out of a suit filed by a wife who was injured in the District of Columbia in 1947. The court of appeals declared that it recognized that a husband is entitled to recover for the loss of his wife's consortium, said that the reverse was also true, and authorized the wife to file suit. Many similar decisions have followed.

value of the property before and after injury. Although the cost of repair and replacement may serve as a measure of damage, this does not always reflect the actual amount of the damage. If the cost to repair the damaged property is in excess of its value, then the measure of damage would be the value of the property immediately before the accident, less its salvage value immediately following the accident. Indirect losses resulting from the loss of use of the property may also be a part of property damage liability.

Modifications of the usual negligence liability rules.   Several modifications, by court cases or statutes, sometimes change the usual rules pertaining to negligence liability. These include *comparative* negligence laws and the doctrines of *presumed* and *imputed* negligence.

Contributory and comparative negligence.   Except where statutory enactments have modified the common-law rule, anyone who is so negligent as to contribute to his or her own injuries or damage cannot recover from another for these injuries. Such a person is said to be *contributorily negligent*.

The claimant frequently advances the plea that the alleged contributory negligence did not contribute to the injury, and that if the defendant had exercised reasonable care, the accident could have been avoided. There has developed a rule known as the "doctrine of last clear chance," which holds that although the claimant is negligent, there is liability if the defendant had a last clear chance to avoid the accident.[9] Today the rule is followed by statute in only a few states. It is, however, a concept that is often used in defense proceedings, sometimes successfully.

In its strict application, the old common-law doctrine of contributory negligence does not always produce equitable results. A very slight degree of negligence on the part of an injured person would bar recovery. Some thirty states have enacted statutes which provide that contributory negligence shall not bar recovery for damages. Such statutes apply the idea of *comparative negligence* and provide that damages shall be diminished by the jury in proportion to the amount of negligence attributable to the person injured or to the owner or person in control of the property damaged.[10]

At first glance there seems to be substantial merit to the idea of having 80 percent of the damages to others paid in an accident if a person has been held 80 percent negligent. In the same example, however, under comparative negligence if both parties suffer losses, the person who was primarily responsible for the accident would also receive 20 percent of his or her damages. The critics of the comparative negligence law used in some states

---

[9] The doctrine is said to derive from what attorneys refer to as the "Hobbled-Ass Case" (*Davies* v. *Mann*, 19 Eng. Rul. Cas. 189), decided in England in 1842. The defendant in the case drove his carriage against a donkey tied in the street and pleaded that the owner of the donkey was contributorily negligent in leaving it so tied. The court held: "Although the ass may have been wrongfully there, still the defendant was bound to go along the road at such a pace as would be likely to prevent mischief."

[10] A handy reference to these statutes is *Statutes Affecting Liability Insurance* (New York: American Insurance Association, 1977).

point out this drawback. Legal authorities also stress other faults in the law: the extreme difficulty or the impossibility of charging a jury to define liability with a precise percentage measuring stick and the noted tendency to increased litigation.[11] For these reasons the contributory negligence rule as reasonably applied in many states remains an important rule of negligence. Slight negligence tends to be disregarded, and suit against the party primarily responsible is permitted.

Presumed negligence. In order to establish a case, the claimant in ordinary circumstances must show a failure to exercise reasonable care. The burden of the proof, therefore, is on the claimant. In certain cases, however, *presumed negligence* may be assumed from the facts. The legal doctrine which applies— *res ipsa loquitur*, "the thing speaks for itself"—establishes a prima facie case of negligence. If the injury was caused by an inanimate object within the control of the defendant, and common experience has proved that such objects cause injury only if there is negligence, presumed negligence may apply. The burden of proof is shifted to the defendant, an exception to the common-law rule that a plaintiff must prove the defendant's fault.

The doctrine operates when an accident causes an injury; (*a*) if the instrumentality would not normally cause injury without negligence, (*b*) if inspection and use of the instrumentality is within exclusive control of the party to be held liable, and (*c*) if the party to be held liable has superior knowledge of the cause of the accident and the injured party is unable to prove negligence.[12] There must be no contributory negligence, and the accident must be of such nature that injury would not ordinarily occur without negligence.[13] The inference of negligence is to be deduced from the attending circumstances, and must be the only one that can reasonably be drawn. The rule does not apply if a definite cause for the injury can be established or if it can be shown that the injury probably resulted from an unavoidable cause, an act of a third person, or from causes due to other than a human agency.[14]

Modern situations to which this doctrine has been applied include automo-

---

[11] Anyone with serious injuries would almost always file a countersuit in a comparative negligence state. Even if the jury decided that one person was really 99 percent responsible for the accident, 1 percent of a large amount might be enough incentive for such a suit by the guilty party.

[12] *McCloskey* v. *Kopler et al.*, 329 Mo. 527; 46 S.W. (2d) 557.

[13] The doctrine arose in old English cases where all theories of the cause of an accident, other than that of negligence, were logically excluded by the facts themselves. In 1809 a sailor sued and proved a broken axle as well as his injuries by being thrown from a stagecoach. The court held that the evidence established a prima facie case and inquired. "What other evidence can the plaintiff give?" (*Christian* v. *Griggs,* 170 Eng. Rep. 1088). Speaking for the court, Chief Justice Mansfield stated: "In many cases of this sort, it must be equally impossible for the plaintiff to give the evidence required. But when the breaking down or overturning of a coach is proved, negligence on the part of the owner is implied. He always has the means to rebut this presumption, if it be unfounded."

[14] *Francy* v. *Rutland Railroad Company,* 119 N.E. 86; 22 N.Y. 482; and *Corpus Juris Secundum,* Carriers, Sec. 764 (e); 10 *American Jurisprudence,* Carriers, Sec. 1625.

bile injuries (in cases where no witnesses are available), railroad or aviation injuries, medical malpractice claims, and many damages caused by defective products.

Imputed negligence. Not only is a negligent person liable for *his* or *her* acts or omissions which cause injuries or damage to others, but sometimes the responsibility extends to negligence of *other* persons. Courts and statutes have extended the rules of negligence to apply to employers, landlords, parents, automobile owners, and many other parties.

If the negligent party acts in the capacity of employee or agent of another, the wrongdoer *and* the owner or operator of a property are sometimes liable. Employers are often personally liable for the torts of those they employ. If the tort is committed while the employee is acting within the apparent scope of the employer's authority or business, both parties[15] can be held liable. (See also later section in this chapter on liability for employees and agents.) Even in the case of employers hiring "independent contractors," whose actions are not in most cases directly under the control of the employer, liability may be imputed to the employer if the employee is given faulty equipment or directions for the work. Imputed liability is also important in property rentals, where landlords may be held responsible for the actions of their tenants.

Parents, too, although generally not liable for negligent actions of their children, may be held liable by some state statutes. These usually impose limited liability of several hundred dollars ($2,000 in Ohio) on the parents for damages caused by their children, but may extend further for specific types of dangerous instruments (guns, for example) used by minors. A child may also be legally liable for his or her own wrongful acts, but is seldom able to pay substantial damages.

Under statutes called "vicarious liability" laws, liability is often imputed to automobile owners even though they are not driving or riding in their cars. Also, under the "family purpose doctrine" such liability applies particularly to the car owner whose family members negligently use the car, either under the idea of agency (when the car is used for family purposes) or on the basis of using a dangerous instrumentality.

Several dozen states have passed "dram shop" or liquor liability laws which make all businesses dispensing liquor liable for injuries that may be caused by their intoxicated patrons, such as in an automobile accident.

SPECIFIC KINDS OF LIABILITY SITUATIONS

Many kinds of special liability situations exist. The following discussion of some of these important aspects of liability is not complete but merely illustrative of the wide scope and variety of the liability risk. The solutions to

---

[15] See 'Liability Exposures and Insurance for the Individual" (Northwest Ohio Chapter, Society of CPCU), *CPCU Annals,* vol. 26, no. 1 (March 1973), p. 5.

these problems often involve insurance coverages contained in various liability insurance contracts, but the significance of overall risk-management techniques should not be forgotten. (See beginning on next major section, on liability risk management.) Many other examples will be found in the discussion of general liability insurance in Chapter 21 and in the important chapters on employers' liability and automobile insurance which follow.

Real property ownership

A dangerous or defective condition maintained on a property is termed in law a "nuisance." Owners of property are responsible for injuries attributable to dangerous conditions. Tenants are responsible for nuisances created by themselves, or created by the landlords if the tenants do not effect corrections.

In the case of property owners, the prudence and diligence required differ with respect to the positions occupied by persons entering upon the property. The law divides such persons into two major classes: (1) trespassers and (2) invitees. One who goes without any right upon the lands of another is a *trespasser*. One who is expressly invited to enter, or who comes in the interest of the occupier of the property and for the occupant's benefit is an *invitee*. Milk truck drivers, letter carriers, and many salespeople fall into this class.[16]

It is held that trespassers take the risk of defects in the premises whether these defects be hidden or open, but that trespassers cannot be intentionally injured by a trap or other very dangerous situations.[17] The invitee, on the other hand, may hold the occupier of the premises liable for any loss or damage caused by a defect which though unknown to the occupier is of such a nature that a reasonable and prudent man would have discovered it by exercising reasonable diligence. The standard of care owed an invitee is to inspect, to correct, or to warn of dangerous conditions of all kinds which make the premises unsafe.

Snow and ice on public sidewalks may be the occasion of a liability claim, although not all jurisdictions have the same laws. The general rule holds that the owner of a property is not responsible for injury or damage caused by snow or ice that falls and forms naturally on sidewalks. A duty to correct the situation may arise if the sidewalks are used by the owner's customers or tenants. Municipal codes may require the removal of snow or ice within specified time periods after its accumulation. If some act of the tenant results

---

[16] A third category, a *licensee,* is sometimes noted in law as a person who has the owner's consent to be there, but is not there for any benefit to the owner. Usually, the duties of the owner to such a person are quite similar to the owner's duties to trespassers —that is, using reasonable care only to avoid intentionally injuries by warning the licensee of concealed and dangerous conditions.

[17] In a well-publicized case in Iowa, the state Supreme Court in 1971 awarded $30,000 to a *burglar* who was booby-trapped by a gun set up by the owners to protect their property. The trap was held to be an unreasonable and malicious means of doing this.

in collections of snow or ice in a form other than that which collects naturally, and thereby creates a dangerous situation, liability for injury may follow. An overflow from a defective gutter or a drain will create liability, for example.

When private property is open to the public, the public by implication is invited to use all the facilities generally made available. The owner or tenant is obligated to exercise reasonable care to maintain the property so that it is reasonably safe, and is expected to use reasonable foresight to anticipate any injury that might occur. If the design is such that it creates a dangerous condition, the owner or tenant may be held liable for injuries. With respect to stairways, entrances, ramps, and the like, there should be no dangerous conditions such as an unusual slippery condition or the absence of standard lighting and handrails. However, when persons have knowledge of the existence of any danger and deliberately expose themselves to it, they may not be able to collect damages for their injuries.

Attractive nuisance hazards

An important exception to the usual liability for injuries to trespassers is in cases of injuries to children because of an *attractive* nuisance. A line of decisions known as "Turntable Cases" held that a boy injured by a railroad turntable was not in the position of a trespasser.[18] It was held that the turntable attracted young children so strongly that they were enticed to play upon it, and this fact being known to the railroad, it was bound to use ordinary care to protect them from harm, even if they were trespassing.

The laws of some states do not apply the doctrine at all, although juries may be sympathetic toward children anyway. Other states vary considerably as to how they apply the concept against owners or tenants of property, and as to the age of the children (often "under ten") to whom it pertains. Usually the nuisance is an artificial or uncommon object or condition which attracts children, and is a threat to them because they do not realize the possible dangers.

The attractive nuisance doctrine is one of which both businesspersons and homeowners should be constantly aware in order to avoid or prevent such losses. Objects or situations that might become attractive nuisances are ladders, swimming or decorative pools, trampolines, bonfires, construction sites, gasoline, power lawn mowers, unlocked automobiles, motorbikes, elevators, and machinery and other properties of many kinds. All of these may give rise to liability claims on the attractive nuisance theory. This is an area in which loss prevention as a part of good risk management should be emphasized: building fences, using warning signs, hiring security guards, and not leaving keys in motor vehicles or machinery are examples of possible precautions.

---

[18] *Keep* v. *Milwaukee and St. Paul Railroad Company,* 21 Minn. Rep. 207. This was an 1875 case, and for the modern generation it should be mentioned that the turntable was a common railroad device at the end of the tracks upon which the railroad cars could be turned around.

Liability for employees and agents

Aside from the responsibility that attaches to the individual wrongdoer when acting in the capacity of agent or employee, responsibility may also attach to the principal or employer. This is predicated upon the legal doctrine of *respondeat superior,* which holds a principal or employer liable to third parties for damage caused by the negligence of an agent or employee. The severity of the rule is recognized when it is found to fix liability upon the employer for a wrongful act contrary to express instructions that is committed in the course of employment. For example, if a bank messenger uses a car contrary to orders and accidentally kills a person, the bank may be held liable for the tort of its employee. The employer cannot escape responsibility by showing that the employee acted contrary to orders or by showing that the work being done was not the work that the employee had been instructed to do.[19] The employer in such cases may have recourse against the employee for disobeying instructions (or the employee may be fired), but the employer still must pay the injured third party.

Liability for acts of animals

The keeping of a mischievous animal with knowledge of its propensities to injure or damage is a basis for absolute liability. In this group are to be found pets and other domestic animals, even sometimes animals ordinarily held to be harmless. Some states also have passed special statutes with respect to dogs, and in such states the owner is liable for injury notwithstanding a lack of knowledge of vicious propensities. To fix liability upon the owner of a domestic animal, the beast need be neither vicious[20] nor ordinarily classed as dangerous.[21] Wild animals are kept at the owner's peril; and the liability is absolute, regardless of diligence or absence of fault.

Liability of government and charitable institutions

Stemming from the feudal belief in the divine right of kings, the *doctrine of sovereign immunity* was borrowed in this country from England. In effect,

---

[19] When the injured party seeks to hold the employer or principal for the wrongful act of an employee or agent, there are three points to be determined: (1) that a tort was in fact committed, (2) that the wrongdoer was actually an employee or agent, and (3) that the act was within the apparent scope of authority of the employee or agent and in the furtherance of the principal's business when the wrong was committed.

[20] In a case decided in the Supreme Court of Vermont, a young mastiff ran to meet a visitor, and jumping up put his paws on the man's shoulders. The visitor fell and broke his leg. Suit for damages was defended on the ground that the dog was only playful and that the owner could not be liable unless the dog was vicious and the owner had knowledge of that fact. The court held that it was sufficient to fix liability if the owner knew that the dog was rough at play and might reasonably commit the injury.

[21] A California woman asked $25,000 damages from a neighbor for being kicked by a "giant" and "vicious" rabbit in her backyard.

this doctrine said that "the King can do no wrong," and thus could not be liable to anyone. Federal and state governments and political subdivisions of the states adopted this immunity from liability and could not be sued without their consent for the torts of their officers and agents.

Over the years, the courts developed a distinction between governmental and proprietary activities. Injury to an individual caused by a government officer engaged in a proprietary (profit-making) function was held not to be within the immunity that goes with governmental functions. Among the activities regarded as proprietary are the operation and maintenance of utilities such as waterworks, rental property, sewer systems, electric plants, airports, and the like. The line of demarcation between governmental and proprietary functions is extremely nebulous. In the case of proprietary functions, the tendency is to hold the governmental unit to the same degree of liability as attaches to private enterprise.

There has also been a strong trend to curtail the scope of immunity to governmental functions through legislation. For example, many states allow individuals to bring suit as the result of special legislation. In other instances states have set up administrative boards to investigate claims and, following the ordinary rules of liability, recommend legislative action. Other states have passed laws curtailing governmental immunity or eliminating it entirely.[22] The Federal Tort Claims Act makes the federal government liable for injuries to individuals in the same manner and to the same extent as a private individual. The tendency to hold more governmental units responsible for liability is clear, but the differences among various states and other units are still extremely large.

The question also presents itself as to the personal liability of individuals whose negligence gave rise to the loss or damage. Some courts have held that public policy should in any case prevent a diversion of public funds from public uses to settle private damages.[23] Such a holding does not preclude suit against a government officer, trustee, or employee individually. Generally speaking, the liability of public employees for private suit for negligence depends upon the positions and upon the nature of the act giving rise to the suit. Judges are held to have absolute immunity. For others, distinctions based on the nature of the wrong have been drawn.[24]

---

[22] For example, New York law provides: "The State hereby waives its immunity from liability and action and hereby assumes liability and consents to have the same determined in accordance with the rules of law as applied to actions in the Supreme Court against individuals or corporations, provided the claimant complies with the limitations of this Article" (113 N.Y. Laws 1929, ch. 467).

[23] *Devers* v. *Scranton,* 308 Pa. 13; 161 Atl. 540; *Taylor* v. *Westerfield,* 233 Ky. 619; 26 S.W. (2d) 557.

[24] For example, the personal liability of members of a school board with respect to *school bus* accidents is unsettled. Because of this uncertainty, automobile liability policies are purchased to cover municipalities or districts and are endorsed to cover the legal liability of individual board members, bus owners, and bus drivers. Although it is

Sometimes *charitable institutions,* including churches, hospitals, and like institutions, are immune from liability. The theory that charitable organizations, like governmental units, are fully immune from the responsibility for the negligence of employees or agents is far from safe. Early English law held that *respondeat superior* did not apply in the case of injuries occasioned by the negligence of the agents or employees of a charitable organization. The doctrine has been perpetuated by decisions in a number of states.[25]

However, the situation is not as simple as this. First of all, the question arises as to whether the institutions actually wish to avoid a moral responsibility. Many institutions carry liability insurance on the ground that there is a moral obligation to reimburse persons injured through the negligence of their employees. Entirely aside from the element of moral obligation, there is a wide diversity of opinion with respect to the doctrine of immunity, and most courts tend to hold charitable institutions responsible for negligence. The decisions range from full immunity to general responsibility.[26]

More important, the changing conditions of charitable institutions with respect to operations, income, property, and ability to meet damage claims have gradually set a trend from immunity to liability.[27] More recent decisions are tending to reject the immunity doctrine completely. Because of the erosion that has taken place with respect to the doctrine, it is extremely unwise for any charitable institution to assume that it is immune from liability for the negligence of its agents or employees.

Nonownership liability

Some perplexing questions of liability occur in connection with the ownership and operation of automobiles. Although many specific state statutes provide otherwise, it is the rule that when an automobile is borrowed (in good

---

accepted that a municipality cannot be sued for damages resulting from accidents caused by *fire apparatus,* the Supreme Court of Vermont has held that the drivers must answer for damages when they are at fault. In other cases in which the state could not be held liable, state officials have been held individually liable.

[25] In *Fire Insurance Patrol* v. *Boyd* (120 Pa. 624; 15A, 553), the court stated: "This doctrine (that a public charity is bound to apply its funds in furtherance of the charity and not otherwise) is hoary with antiquity."

[26] *McDonald* v. *Massachusetts Gen. Hosp.,* 120 Mass. 432 (1876), the first American decision to adopt the immunity doctrine, relied on an English case without realizing that the English decision had been overruled ten years earlier. The early decision has long since ceased as a binding precedent in most jurisdictions.

[27] Charities are now held to be in a much different position than when they were largely small institutions—many connected with churches—and of limited means. As has been stated: "Today they have become, in many instances, big business, handling large funds, managing and owning large properties and set up by large trusts or foundations. It is idle to argue that donations from them will dry up if the charity is held to respond for its torts the same as other institutions" (*Foster* v. *Roman Catholic Dioceses of Vermont,* 17 C.C.H., Negligence Cases 858; see also *Administrator* v. *Hospital of St. Vincent de Paul,* 107 S.E. 785).

mechanical condition), the car owner is not usually called upon to pay for damages arising out of its operation. On the other hand, if the operator of a car doing damage occupies the position of employee or agent of the car owner, the owner may be held liable.

The liability is based upon the doctrine of *respondeat superior,* and it applies not only to chauffeurs driving cars owned by their employers but also to salespersons, agents, or other employees who in the course of their employment use *their own cars* in transacting business for their employers. Employers may always have liability when a car (or boat or plane) is *owned, leased,* or *hired* by them. In addition, other *nonowned vehicles* may impose responsibility on employers. For instance, an employee of a laundry or grocery store delivering a package on the way from work, an employee of a contractor going from one job to another, a salesperson, a collector, or scores of others acting in their employer's interest and driving their own automobiles may involve their employers in huge accident claims. The danger is particularly acute in that the employee may have very few resources, while the employer is a logical target at which to aim heavy damage suits.

Libel and other related types of liability

A special liability risk, which is usually covered only by specific endorsement or in a separate contract, is faced by authors, publishers, and others. The exposure is that of libel and several other related perils.

Libel is something more than the liability due to negligence. A publisher or other person who holds someone up to scorn, contempt, or ridicule may be liable for heavy damages when an untrue and malicious statement is published. The law recognizes two classes of malice. When there is a deliberate desire to injure, there is malice in fact. A careless disregard for another's rights which results in errors constitutes malice in law. Absence of intent to libel does not constitute a defense. Publication of a retraction is not a complete defense and serves only to mitigate damages.

The exposure and losses are notable. For example, a much-publicized suit by a football coach at a Southern university resulted in a $3 million judgment against *The Saturday Evening Post,* for a libelous story which claimed that the coach had given a rival team its football plays. The case was settled before retrial for less than one sixth the original verdict. The biography of Howard Hughes was the basis for a large and complicated libel lawsuit. The late mayor of San Francisco was awarded $350,000, plus more than that in legal costs, for a malicious magazine article that linked him with the Mafia.[28]

Claims may be made for *slander* as well as libel. Libel is written defamation, and slander is spoken defamation of character. Radio and television

---

[28] "Alioto Is Awarded $350,000 plus Costs in *Look* Libel Case," *Wall Street Journal,* May 4, 1977.

stations may be sued, as may credit bureaus that make verbal reports to subscribers by telephone or otherwise. An insured may also become involved in claims for damages for *invasion of privacy*. The right of privacy concerns the peace of mind of the individual. Every person has some rights that private personal matters, such as adultery, should not be commented upon or scrutinized in public without his or her consent. (Public figures have fewer such rights.) Truth is not a defense to an action for the infringement of the right of privacy. Claims based upon *plagiarism* and *violation of copyright* against writers and publishers are further examples of the wide scope of these special cases of the liability risk in its many forms.

Other special situations

There are many special situations. The operator of a drugstore may incur liability claims that are an outgrowth of compounding prescriptions (a form of malpractice liability) or may incur products liability that may result from dispensing food. In fact, any person who sells foods may be subject to a liability claim based upon alleged injury from their use. Products and professional liability situations are discussed further in Chapter 21.

Property damage liability and personal injury may result from explosions, elevators, boats, and airplanes. Schools and colleges may be held responsible for injuries on their properties, particularly with reference to gymnasiums, swimming pools, grandstands, crowded auditoriums, and the like. In some instances the school itself may be liable for accident or injury, and in others liability may attach directly to a teacher[29] or trustee. Injury to others may grow out of participation in sports. In fact, a person may incur liability while simply walking along the street, as in the case of a man who is smoking and accidentally burns another person with a lighted cigar. In every instance the party concerned must exercise such care as a reasonably prudent person would use in the circumstances; and failure to do this, whether deliberate or unintentional, creates a liability for injury and damages if a person or property is injured as a result.

FOR REVIEW AND DISCUSSION

1. Describe the legal basis for liability, and explain why this is important to insurance consumers.
2. Why are liability risks sometimes considered more important than property risks? Cite several examples, including at least one illustration of the possible effect of an "attractive nuisance" on your property.

---

[29] Fortunately, for teachers and colleges the liability is not without some limit. The New Jersey Supreme Court ruled against a Columbia University student who had sued for $8,065 damages, claiming that the college had "failed to teach him wisdom." The judge sagely observed that "wisdom cannot be taught, if in fact it can be defined"!

3. What is the relationship among "legal wrongs," "torts," "negligence," and liability insurance? (Include the requirements for "negligence.")

4. What is the difference between liability under *contract* law and liability under *tort* law? (Illustrate your answer with examples of each.)

5. "Torts are not always based on unintentional acts, nor on fault." Explain both parts of this statement.

6. "Comparative," "presumed," and "imputed" negligence may each modify the usual negligence rules. Give an example of each of these rules, showing its results to the claimant.

7. How does the concept of strict or absolute liability change the usual negligence situation? When does this concept apply?

8. Jerry is an employee of the federal government and drives a postal truck. May the federal government or this employee be sued?

9. Mrs. Swank, a Sunday school teacher, is injured when a piano leg collapses. Is the church liable in the event that suit is filed?

10. Explain how real estate property ownership may create liability risk to trespassers and invitees.

11. What legal liability rule may make a business responsible for actions of employees or agents who cause injuries to others or damages to the property of others? Illustrate your answer with several examples.

12. Discuss how persons or organizations can become liable for losses caused by property they do *not* own.

13. Explain how libel and other related types of liability may create liability risks.

Chapter 21

Concepts considered in Chapter 21—General liability insurance

Liability risk management coordinates other methods with insurance.

Types of liability insurance losses are classified into major types as *bodily injury* and *property damage;* and *direct* and *contingent.*

The scope of major liability insurance contracts includes (1) *employers*, (2) *automobile*, and (3) *"general,"* which is further subdivided into: (1) *personal*, (2) *business*, (3) *professional contracts;* or (1) *primary* and (2) *excess contracts;* and *medical payments.*

The general liability insurance program is discussed:

Nature of and rationale for the revisions,

The basic policy format, with the three following parts:

Declarations, including statements by the insured about the coverage,

The policy jacket, with supplementary payments, definitions, and conditions applying to all general liability contracts of this type, and

The coverage parts, which contain the insuring agreements and exclusions.

Personal liability insurance contracts, the *comprehensive personal liability* policy and farmers' CPL, cover individual and family interests.

Business liability insurance contracts are numerous. Most common are:

Owners', landlords', and tenants' liability policy (OLT).

Manufacturers' and contractors' liability policy (M&C).

Comprehensive general liability policy (CGL).

Other business liability coverages: *storekeepers', contractual, products and completed operations, protective,* and *automobile.*

Professional or malpractice liability insurance contracts differ greatly and are important to medical and many other professional persons.

Excess insurance is broad, high-limit coverage of catastrophe losses of individuals and businesses. This is contrasted with "primary" coverages which pay losses first (or are the only protection), before the excess contracts apply:

Excess and surplus lines, often insuring risks difficult to place in normal markets,

Differences in conditions coverage, for all-risks physical damage and worldwide protection,

The umbrella liability policy, a popular form for businesses needing broader, higher limit insurance, and

Excess personal liability policies, for million-dollar or higher limit personal coverages.

Medical payments coverage pays medical expenses, regardless of liability, and is often included in general liability contracts.

General liability insurance

After recognizing negligence and other liability situations which create "the liability risk" in so many different ways, what next? Applying the risk-management technique may be of help to businesses or individuals as the risks are analyzed and the methods of risk treatment considered. Various types of general liability insurance are often important in treating liability risks, and these contracts are emphasized in this chapter.

LIABILITY RISK MANAGEMENT

Perhaps some liability situations can be *controlled*, through avoiding expenses such as by not owning real estate or by leasing automobiles or other equipment instead of owning it. Other risks might be controlled by minimizing losses with combination (and separation or diversification), loss prevention and reduction, or other noninsurance transfers, as discussed in Chapters 1 and 3.

Perhaps some potential liability losses can be *financed* through risk-*retention* methods such as by setting up a sound savings, reserve, or "self-insurance" plan. Perhaps some liability can be *transferred* to others, such as by "hold-harmless" agreements or other written contracts which make other persons responsible for part or all of liability losses.

However, several factors work against the exclusive reliance on these methods or risk treatment for liability situations. One is the complexity of the risk, based upon its legal nature, changing laws and interpretations, and the involvement of third parties (the claimant or injured person) in the legal liability process. Another is the large size of potential losses and the relative infrequency of loss as compared with most forms of property insurance. These characteristics make difficult the calculation of probabilities and variance of future losses, and they suggest the inability of many persons or firms to use risk retention as a sole method of liability risk management, without the danger of serious financial trouble from the larger losses.

Admittedly, some liability risks should be controlled by being avoided, or losses prevented, or risks transferred by special contracts—but by far the likeliest choice of individuals and businesses for financing most of the liability losses is to transfer the risk by purchasing *liability insurance.*

One thought for discussion is whether or not liability insurance may sometimes increase losses because of recklessness or carelessness. Although the author knows of no studies to document such an effect, it is possible that that such a tendency may exist when the financial losses caused by wrongdoers will be paid for by their insurers. Also, it may be argued that liability insurance has increased liability exposure because juries assume that defendants are adequately insured, and thus award larger verdicts. Appeals courts, too, may liberally expand the legal bases for making workers' compensation awards from insurance-generated funds.

TYPES OF LIABILITY INSURANCE LOSSES

Liability insurance is *not accident insurance,* or automatic payment for all accidents which cause damage. Rather, it defends the insureds when claims are made against them and settles with the claimants on reasonable terms *if* the insureds are legally liable for the loss or damage. The liability insurance policy makes such payments as the insureds would themselves have been obligated to pay because of the liability imposed by law. If there is no negligence on the part of the insureds and hence no legal liability, there is no obligation on the part of the insurer to make any payment to a claimant. The insurer, however, is obligated to defend the insureds against groundless claims, to bear the expenses thereof, and to make settlements subject to the limits of the policy in the event of unfavorable verdicts. In cases in which the question of liability is not clear, the insurer has the option to (and frequently does) make a settlement. By so doing, the insurer saves the expense of litigation, and the insureds are spared the inconvenience of a trial.

In the direct damage insurance contract there are two parties to the agreement—the insurer and the insured; the insured receives payment from the insurer for a property loss. In the case of liability insurance, the third party who is injured or suffers a loss is not the insured. Because of this, liability insurance has sometimes been termed *third-party insurance.* The term is entirely in order, but in using it one should remember that the third party is not an insured and usually has no right of action against the insurer. (Louisiana is an exception, for direct suits against the insurer are permitted there.)

In writing liability coverage, insurers frequently separate the property damage from the bodily injury covers. Hence, the liability insurance field is divided into two major classifications: (1) *bodily injury liability insurance* and (2) *property damage liability insurance.* Bodily injury liability policies are sometimes written setting forth a limit applicable to *each person* and a limit applicable to *each occurence.* Thus, an automobile liability contract may have limits of $10/20,000. This means that in any one occurrence not more than $10,000 will be paid for the claim of the given individual and not more than $20,000 as the aggregate of all claims for bodily injuries growing out of a single occurrence. In the case of property damage liability, a limit of liability is set that is applicable to any one occurrence. Exceptions to this practice are found, including some auto policies and the new general liability forms, which specify only an occurrence limit of liability for bodily injury. In other contracts, an "aggregate limit" for the policy term is established. Thus, in the *Nurses* case of malpractice and products liability coverages, a limit per claim, with another aggregate limit for the entire policy term, is the practice. Product liability policies are written with a limit for each person, for each occurrence, and for the policy term.

Insureds frequently cause injuries to persons under circumstances in which negligence cannot be proven or imputed. In these circumstances, the liability insurance company is obligated to make no payment to the injured party. In connection with the ownership of an automobile, for example, the owner may feel morally obligated to make payments to injured passengers, in cases where there is actually no negligence. The insured, for such losses, can provide *medical payments coverage.* The protection is not technically liability insurance, but it is often an important part of the liability insurance contract. (See later section of this chapter.)

As in the property insurance field, liability insurance may also be divided into direct and indirect types. One type is written to cover the primary or *direct* liability of the insured, and a second type of contract is written on *contingent* liability. Contingent liability insurance (often called "protective" liability insurance) covers the insured in cases where the insured might still be held indirectly liable. For example, such a situation might arise in the relationship of contractor and subcontractor. A subcontractor might be liable for an accident, but having no knowledge of the relationship, the injured party would in such case sue, and perhaps collect from the general contractor.

THE SCOPE OF MAJOR LIABILITY INSURANCE CONTRACTS

The types of liability insurance contracts for the many negligence and other liability situations are of great variety. As a consequence, no simple or logically inclusive classification is recognized. In this text, three major areas of liability insurance contracts are treated in separate chapters:

1. *Employers'* liability insurance contracts (and workers' compensation) in Chapter 22;
2. *Automobile* liability insurance contracts (and other types of automobile insurance) in Chapters 23 and 24; and
3. *General* liability insurance contracts in this chapter, including "excess" liability insurance policies.

The first two major areas deserve separate treatment, based upon either their importance within other significant insurance contracts or on their special purpose of taking care of a particular kind of liability loss. The third area, *general liability insurance contracts,* includes all forms of liability insurance except for employers' and automobile liability insurance.

A simple division of *all* liability insurance contracts into "business" and "nonbusiness" categories is not a better classification. Although it is important to make this distinction within each of the indicated major areas, the distinction does not separate the usual liability insurance contracts meaningfully. For example, employers' liability insurance is almost always a business responsibility, yet some individuals need it for nonbusiness situations such as covering household or domestic employees. Automobile liability insurance is a major concern of individuals and families, but it may also be of great importance to business, nonprofit, or governmental organizations. Thus, general liability insurance is the best available term to describe the "all-other" area of liability insurance. Within the liability insurance business, the category is well known.

The field of general liability insurance may be divided into three distinct types of contracts according to the nature of the activity creating liability: those providing protection against (1) *personal* or individual liability perils, (2) *business* liability perils, and (3) *professional* or malpractice liability perils. According to the size of the loss to which the coverage applies, liability contracts may also be classified as those which provide protection against (1) *primary*, and (2) *excess* or catastrophe perils. These classifications are used in the following major sections of this chapter which discuss general liability insurance contracts. Since *medical payments* coverage is technically not insurance against liability but is often included in liability contracts, a separate section at the end of this chapter is devoted to this important type of insurance.

THE 1973 GENERAL LIABILITY INSURANCE PROGRAM

Nature of and rationale for the revisions

Extensive changes in liability contracts were set forth in 1973. Although not required by law, as in fire insurance, the standard provisions of the new general liability forms brought a commendable updating and uniformity to this field of insurance, both for members of the Insurance Services Office and for most independent insurers.

The changes were among the most sweeping of all revisions of insurance contracts during the past decade. Many years of work were devoted to designing a contract that is now adaptable to many of the varied liability fields. Most important in these revisions was a reflection of the need for greater clarity and understanding in this very important segment of insurance. Changing liability exposures in our modern society, more liberal court interpretations, and changing needs of policyholders were all significant factors in making these revisions necessary.

The basic policy format

The new contracts are based upon three parts: (1) a *declaration sheet;* (2) a *policy jacket* which contains all the supplementary payments, definitions, and conditions common to all general liability contracts; and (3) *coverage parts* which include the insuring agreements and exclusions. These three parts are put together to form a complete policy. The more common types of coverage parts added are comprehensive personal liability; owners', landlords', and tenants' liability; manufacturers' and contractors' liability; comprehensive general liability; and several types of medical malpractice liability contracts.

The policies contain the equivalent of the usual four sections of insurance contracts, that is, declarations, insuring agreements, conditions, and exclusions. However, standard definitions and conditions for all liability contracts are contained in the jacket of the policy, while the coverage part purposefully requires the insuring agreements to be immediately followed by the exclusions pertaining to that coverage. Clarity of intent and ease of understanding are the rewarding results of this format.

Declarations

The *declarations* include statements which identify both the insured and the insurer. Important data about the contract terms are typed in on the form to show who, what, where, and when the insurance covers. The declarations provide that by accepting the policy the named insured agrees with the representations made and that the policy is issued in reliance upon the truth of these statements.

The policy jacket

The provisions common to all general liability insurance contracts are contained in the standard policy jacket. Three sections are identified as "supplementary payments," "definitions," and "conditions." The reading and analysis are eased by centralizing these in the policy jacket, and the length of the various "coverage parts" added is correspondingly reduced.

Supplementary payments. The first section of the policy jacket, which is applicable to all of the coverage parts that may be used with it, mentions several extra costs which are payable by the insurer in addition to the policy liability limit. These include: (1) premiums on bonds to release attachments relating to lawsuits defended by the insurer; (2) bail bond cost up to $250 per bond required for traffic law violations arising out of vehicles to which the contract applies; (3) reimbursement to the insured for reasonable expenses incurred at the insurer's request in assisting the company in the investigation or defense of any claim or suit, including actual loss of earnings not to exceed $25 per day.

Definitions. More than the usual number of definitions appear in the policy jacket, but some are more important than others for particular types of general liability contracts.

Whenever the word *insured* is used in the contract without qualification, it is defined to include any director, executive officer, stockholder, or partner of the insured if the named insured is a corporation or partnership. The coverage to directors, executive officers, stockholders, or partners applies only while they are acting within the scope of their duties in connection with the furthering of the interests of the business. When the named insured is an individual, the spouse is also included.

Coverage is provided on the basis of *occurrence,* rather than on the basis of accident. Older policies covered liability imposed by law for injury or damage caused by "accident," which was defined as "a sudden and unforeseeable event." This required that the event happen at a definite time and place and that it be unexpected and unintended. The new wording covers injury or damage caused by an "occurrence" defined as "an accident, including continuous or repeated exposure to conditions, which results in bodily injury or property damage neither expected nor intended from the standpoint of the insured." It is not required that the event be a sudden one. The word *accident* is used in this definition in order to clarify the time of coverage as being from the time of injury rather than from the time of exposure. It also makes the policy limits applicable only once for each occurrence instead of having multiple limits apply on the basis of a series of events due to the same factor (for example, a contractor's equipment hitting four automobiles in a collision is considered one occurrence).

Examples of the broadened coverage for liability losses based on an "occurrence" that would probably not be covered as an "accident" are:

1. Skin injury as a result of repeated use of a lotion.
2. Crops killed by fumes escaping continuously from a manufacturing plant.
3. Paint damage to homes by repeated exposure to dust and chemicals from trucks going to and from a construction site.
4. Sickness or disease caused by exposure to unsanitary conditions.
5. Injury resulting from assault and battery by an employee.

Another important definition helps clarify the difference between *product liability* and *completed operations coverages,* for some court decisions had held that these two kinds of liability were not separate. Contractors often had difficulty in determining whether or not installations in which defects later caused injuries were covered by products liability (usually) or completed operations. The new policy jacket contains a detailed definition of "products liability" hazard as injury occurring after the relinquishment of possession and away from premises owned by or rented to the insured. "Completed operations" is defined as injury or damage (not the negligent act or accident) arising out of operations or out of reliance upon a representation or warranty occurring *after* the operations are completed. This time is at the earliest of the following: (1) when all of the operations by or on behalf of the insured are done, (2) when such operations at the site are done, or (3) when the portion of the work out of which the injury arises has been put to its intended use. The importance of such definition is that completed operations coverage must be purchased to cover many contracting situations which may cause losses after the events specified have occurred.

Bodily injury means "bodily injury, sickness or disease sustained by any person which occurs during the policy period, including death at any time resulting therefrom." A coverage of increasing recent interest is the *personal injury hazard* which involves third-party claims for damages that are other than physical. The general liability program permits adding this coverage to the basic policies or writing it as a separate policy. Three groups of claims alleging the following offenses are covered by this liability insurance: (1) false arrest, detention, or imprisonment, and malicious prosecution; (2) libel or slander; and (3) wrongful entry or eviction, and invasion of privacy. All businesses may have some exposure to these claims. The handling of shoplifting suspects by retail stores is an example of a serious and quite common exposure.

Property damage is defined to include "physical injury to or destruction of tangible property which occurs during the policy period, including loss of use thereof at any time resulting therefrom." This excludes such violations of intangible property rights as unfair competition or patent infringement. The new definition, separated into a second part of the 1973 revision, does not require physical injury before a loss is covered, which broadens the coverage to include loss of use in cases where no prior physical damage to property has occurred (for example, store owners suing for loss of profits when a contractor's equipment breaks down and blocks access to the stores).

The 1973 changes also eliminate the former per person limit of liability, with only a per occurrence limit now applying for bodily injury coverage (except for products and completed operations, where a per year aggregate limit applies). The changes also added an exclusion for pollution damage (which used to be commonly added by endorsement), except when the pollution is sudden and accidental.

Other definitions are included in the policy jacket, such as automobiles, mobile equipment (racing and snowmobiles are excluded), and policy territory. For the precise differences in wording and meaning, several charts comparing the older and newer policies are available.[1] Although most analysts conclude that the coverage is broadened by the new wording of the revisions, some doubts have been expressed by authors who point out a number of new limitations which definitely or possibly may apply as the courts interpret the new wording.[2]

Conditions. The policy jacket also contains several important conditions upon which the obligations of the insurer and the insured are based.

---

[1] *General Liability Revisions,* Underwriters Adjusting Company, 1973; "What You Should Know about the Changes in the 1973 General Liability Policies," General Adjustment Bureau, 1973; and others.

[2] Charles H. Harry, "The 1973 General Liability Insurance Changes," *Risk Management,* June–July 1973, p. 8.

The *insured's duties in the event of occurrence, claim, or suit* are a combination of three former requirements for notice of accident (in writing, as soon as practicable, explaining the circumstances), claim or suit (immediately), and assistance and cooperation of the insured (for settlement in hearings and trials, etc.). These are reasonable requirements that enable the insurer to provide proper defense and obtain a fair settlement or judgment for the claim. The insured may provide "first aid" at the scene of the accident, but should not jeopardize the insurer's position by trying to make payments or to arrange a settlement. Such actions may be held as a breach of this condition.

Clarification of the insurer's right to *inspect and audit* the insured's property and operations is an important change in the new general liability contracts. Some court decisions under the old wording had held this to be not only a right but also an obligation of the insurer, with possible negligence if the insurer did not do so. The new wording specifically states this as a right, without any warranty by the insurer "that such property or operations are safe or healthful, or are in compliance with any law, rule, or regulation."

The *other insurance* condition determine what happens when there is more than one insurer. Instead of merely prorating or apportioning with other applicable insurance, this condition states that when the insurance is intended to be primary coverage, it shall pay before excess or contingent liability contracts contribute to the loss. If it happens that two or more contracts are both primary coverage on this basis (regardless of differences which may exist as to the policy limits), then each insurer shall pay on an "equal shares" basis. Each insurer would pay equal amounts of the loss up to the point at which the lower of the policy limits is exhausted, after which the higher limit policy would apply alone. For example, assume that for the same insured, insurer A has an applicable limit of $10,000 and insurer B has a $100,000 limit. If a liability judgment for $45,000 is rendered against the insured, insurers A and B will each pay $10,000, and then insurer B will also pay the balance of the judgment, or $25,000 more.

Conditions of less importance are those pertaining to financial responsibility laws, premium bases, and assignment. Other conditions which have remained essentially the same in the new general liability contracts are those permitting policy changes in writing, cancellation (by insured: anytime; by insurer: with five days' notice), the right of subgrogation by the insurer, and action against the insurer by the insured only after the insured has complied with all policy provisions and the final judgment of settlement of the claim has been determined.

The coverage parts

Two basic parts of the general liability insurance program have been explained above, the declarations and the policy jacket. The addition of a *coverage part,* containing the *insuring agreement and exclusions* pertaining to the insurance, completes the contract. Many different coverage parts can be used, to develop completed general liability insurance contracts knowns as:

1. *Personal liability:*
   a. The comprehensive personal liability policy.
   b. The farmers' comprehensive personal liability policy.
2. *Business liability:*
   a. The owners', landlords,' and tenants' liability policy.
   b. The manufacturers' and contractors' liability policy.
   c. The comprehensive general liability policy.
3. *Professional liability:*
   a. Professional or malpractice liability policies.

Other policies are more briefly mentioned. Some other policies permitted within this program include both general and automobile liability exposures, such as the comprehensive automobile liability policy, the comprehensive automobile and garage liability policy, and others. A total of more than 20 separate coverage parts may be used to create specific general liability insurance contracts.

The following discussion of specific contracts of the general liability insurance program is divided, as above, into three major groups: (1) *personal,* (2) *business,* and (3) *professional or malpractice* liability insurance contracts.

PERSONAL LIABILITY INSURANCE CONTRACTS

Two basic personal policies are the comprehensive personal liability policy and the farmers' comprehensive personal liability policy. The individual and the family need liability protection for numerous personal or individual situations. The ownership of residential property, participation in sports activities, the keeping of pets or animals, and many normal everyday activities all place a responsibility upon individuals not to cause injury or damage to other persons or their property.

Several other separate policies were used many years ago—a residence liability, a sports liability, and a dog liability policy—but now these coverages are almost always insured by the comprehensive personal forms instead.

Excess or catastrophe liability policies are discussed later in this chapter. Some of these provide coverages for individuals.

In the liability insuring clause, the comprehensive personal liability policies, unlike most liability policies, cover under a *single limit* the liability of the insured for damage on account of bodily injury to members of the public and to employees, and for damage to the property of others caused by an occurrence. The minimum single limit is $10,000, but as in the case of other liability coverages, policies are frequently written for larger limits, such as $25,000 or $50,000 or more. The single limit represents the maximum liability of the insurer, regardless of the number of persons injured or the extent of property damage attributable to a single occurrence.

The comprehensive personal liability policy and the farmers' personal comprehensive liability policy are both designed to provide comprehensive liability protection for a named insured and the members of his or her household. However, certain perils in the farm risk are not found in the usual household, and the farmers' comprehensive form is adapted to them. Although based primarily upon the personal liability exposures, the farmers' form does include some business liability perils.

Today the CPL and the farmers' CPL are typically included, along with fire, theft, and other insurance, in the homeowners' or farmowners' multiple-line contracts. The student should refer to Chapter 27 for further information.

BUSINESS LIABILITY INSURANCE CONTRACTS

About 20 different business liability policies can be developed by adding a coverage part to the basic general liability insurance program. The three best known are the owners', landlords,' and tenants' policy (OLT); the manufacturers' and contractors' policy (M&C); and the comprehensive general liability policy (CGL). Many businesses now include protection similar to these contracts within the various business multiple-line contracts (see Chapter 27).

Several other coverage parts are either commonly added to, or at least should be considered with, the above policies, or they are designed to fit special liability needs of certain businesses. Storekeepers', contractual, completed operations and products, protective, and automobile liability coverage parts are briefly presented as "other" business liability.

For each of these coverage parts the basic addition to the declarations and policy jacket is the *insuring agreement*. The insurer promises to pay *on behalf of the insured* all sums which the insured shall become obligated to pay as damages because of (1) *bodily injury* or (2) *property damage*. The insurer agrees to defend any suit against the insured for these damages, even if the suit is groundless, false, or fraudulent. These costs may be considerable, and they are paid in addition to the policy limits. One exception is that the insurer is not obligated to defend any new suit after the applicable limit of the policy has been exhausted by payment of judgments or settlements.

Exclusions in the new policies are required to follow immediately after the insuring agreement. These exclusions are, in general, considerably more understandable because of this location. The specific exclusions vary according to the coverage part. In many coverage parts a separate section defines in further detail the persons insured, the limits of liability, and the policy period and territory.

Owners', landlords', and tenants' liability policy

The *owners', landlords' and tenants' (OLT) liability policy* covers loss or expense, or both, resulting from claims upon the insured on account of bodily injuries or property damage to any person or persons not employed by the insured. The occurrence must be alleged to have been caused by reason of the ownership, maintenance, or use of the premises occupied by the insured. There is no restriction with respect to the use of the premises. The OLT policy covers liability insurance for *premises, operations in progress,* and *elevators.* For coverage of the full scope of business liability, including products and completed operations, the CGL is recommended.

The coverage is twofold as to location. For many types of businesses the principal exposure is within the place of business, while in other businesses the outside peril constitutes a substantial part of the exposure. The *on-the-premises* hazards include claims from falling on stairs, slippery floors, and the like, and also extends to elevators or sidewalks and passages adjacent. Examples of claims also include blood poisoning as a result of scratching a wrist while fitting a glove and injuries resulting from the collapse of a chair on which a customer was seated. The outside or *off-premises* hazards are important where accidents during the demonstration or installation of appliances in the customer's home may involve the employer of the salesperson in a claim for damages.

Two basic types of liability insurance are invariably included together in the OLT policy, although separate limits of liability apply to each: (1) *bodily injury*[3] liability coverage and (2) *property damage* liability coverage. Under the *bodily injury* protection, the insurer agrees to pay all sums which the insured becomes legally obligated to pay because of bodily injury, sickness, or disease (including death) suffered by members of the public for operations carried on at and from the premises of the insured. Automatic coverage is provided if the insurer is notified within 30 days after acquisition of new locations or undertakings, unless the insured is covered by other valid and collectible insurance.

Protection is afforded under *property damage* liability coverage for injury to or destruction of property of others, including loss of use. Usually included now is water damage liability coverage, such as damage to buildings or contents caused by discharge, leakage, or overflow from plumbing, heating, refrigerating, air conditioning, or automatic sprinkler systems.

The standard limits for the owners', landlords,' and tenants' liability policy are $25,000 per occurrence, with a limit of $5,000 for property damage liability coverage. Many types of businesses require much higher limits. Limits may be increased above the standard amounts for an additional premium. The rate of such increased amounts of coverage decreases per thousand dollars of protection as the policy limits are raised.

The OLT policy may be used in connection with the operation or ownership of any type of real estate, as well as many types of business establishments.

---

[3] Usually this requires physical harm, but some cases have involved mental or non-physical injury. A Michigan truck driver received a $150,000 award for psychotic results of an accident in which no physical injury was involved. The case caused *Time* (February 16, 1964, p. 75) to define "emotional trauma" as "a state of mind precipitated by an accident, stimulated by an attorney, perpetrated by avarice, and cured by a verdict"!

Owners of apartment houses, stores, and offices, for example, need liability insurance against claims of injuries or damage from falling plaster or signs, protruding pipes, dark stairways, slippery floors, torn carpets, defective railings, and many other hazards.

Manufacturers' and contractors' liability policy

The manufacturers' and contractors' M&C liability policy provides protection for the manufacturer or contractor similar in nature to that afforded under the OLT policy. Coverage is adapted, however, to insure against claims from members of the public at all premises and for all operations of the insured, which for these types of businesses often include scattered and changing locations. Applicants for employment, visitors, salespersons, deliverypersons, employees of contractors, children, and trespassers—all form a part of the public.

Contractors engaged in construction are protected in the operation of the machinery and equipment used in their work, both while it is at the work location and while it is being taken to and from the work location. Coverage for elevator liability is included, and the use of hoists and elevators for handling materials is one of the serious hazards of many manufacturers and contractors. Inspections and recommendations for loss-prevention techniques can be a particularly valuable service of insurers for such exposures.

As with the OLT policy (the student should also review the previous section in order to understand the M&C policy), only incidental coverages for contractual (assumed) liability are included. These are: (1) leases of premises, (2) easements, (3) municipal ordinance indemnification agreements (for example, such as for signs), (4) railroad sidetrack agreements, and (5) elevator maintenance agreements. All other contractual liability requires the addition of a separate coverage part for this exposure, as is explained in a later section of this chapter.

Manufacturers or contractors also need to analyze carefully their products and completed operations liability exposure, for which coverage is oftentimes needed. Such coverage can be obtained through the use of the comprehensive general liability policy or as a separate coverage part if only those hazards are to be covered.

Comprehensive general liability policy

The most important of all business liability policies is the comprehensive general liability (CGL) policy. It is the best method by which most businesses (except small ones) can obtain the full scope of coverage for noncontractual general liability hazards. For some the OLT or M&C policy may be adequate, but for many the CGL policy is the best alternative.

Many of the comments in the two previous sections apply to the CGL coverage part. It includes the basic liability protection of the OLT and M&C policies for premises, operations, elevators, and incidental contractual exposures (such as for leases of premises and some easements). However, it is broader in that it automatically includes coverage for completed operations, products, and independent contractor (or protective) liability exposures. It is designed to include in a single contract insurance protection against all these liability perils.

The policy also provides full automatic coverage for claims arising because of the acquisition of some property subsequent to the writing of the policy, and for the so-called unknown perils, about which the insured knows nothing, or which would usually not be covered by any named-perils policy.

Exclusions under the policy have been reduced to a minimum. The following also apply to the OLT and M&C policies: (1) assumed or contractual liability, except the named incidental types (see M&C policy section); (2) automobile or aircraft liability; (3) off-premises watercraft liability; (4) liability for war; (5) liability for injury or sickness of employees;[4] and (6) property damage to property owned by, occupied by, rented to, used by, or in the care, custody, or control of the insured. For specified types of insureds a few other exclusions apply, such as liquor liability and property damage liability for explosions, collapse, or underground damage.

Other business liability coverages

Several other coverages are or can be included in the three most common business liability policies just discussed.

Storekeepers' liability coverage. One coverage part, the *storekeepers' liability policy,* is an alternative to these three policies designed for small retail shops. A single insuring limit is used for both bodily injury and property damage liability coverages, and coverage for limited contractual and products liability hazards is included.

Coverage for the contractual liability hazard. In many cases of liability assumed by contract, specific insurance is necessary if adequate protection is to be provided. It has been noted above that only limited and incidental contractual exposures are covered in the basic general liability policies. The addition to these policies of a separate coverage for *contratual liability* exposures is frequently needed. Occasionally a separate policy is written for just this purpose.

The insurer provides liability insurance for bodily injuries or property damage liability that the insured has agreed to assume under a written contract. The agreement under which liability is assumed is usually identified in

---

[4] It is to be noted that workers' compensation and employers' liability protection are not included in the basic policy or by endorsement. The peril regarding employees is covered *only* under the workers' compensation policy.

the policy by reference, but in some instances a copy of the indemnity provisions of the contract is attached to the policy.

This policy finds frequent use in providing protection for contractors who are required to assume the responsibility for all liability of a municipality before they are issued a permit to store material on city streets, to bridge sidewalks, or to use public facilities in other ways. Other examples of the need for coverage of contractual liability hazards are written equipment leases, work or supply contracts, and hold-harmless[5] agreements. In hold-harmless agreements, which have increased in use in recent years, one party agrees to assume the liability of another party. Thus, the first party is "held harmless" (or not held liable) for some or all of the claims which may result. Leases and construction contracts often include such provisions.

Coverage for the products and completed operations hazard. One of the most rapidly growing fields of liability insurance is that of protection for *products and completed operations liability hazards.* The expansion of the manufacturer's responsibility, as well as that of all dealers and handlers of goods, has been mentioned in connection with implied warranties. Few areas of insurance challenge the insight and the professional advising capacity of the insurance agent or risk manager more than this changing field. The type, frequency, and severity of losses have skyrocketed in the past decade.[6] About two thirds of the products liability claims payments (averaging $14,000) are for bodily injury, while property damage claims average less than $4,000. Most of the payments are under $1,000, but less than 1 percent of the payments account for more than 50 percent of the payment dollars.[7] Large *claims* are more frequent than payments made, and often more unusual, too. For example, a department store was sued in 1979 by a woman for $2.8 million because they failed to correct a busted zipper on a pair of blue jeans.

Retailers, wholesalers, and manufacturers may be held liable for injury arising out of the use or consumption of merchandise *away from the premises* of the vendor. A well-known manufacturer, Bon Vivant, went bankrupt because of claims for contaminated soups. The liability for injury frequently arises with respect to food products, but almost every manufacturer or distributor has some products liability exposure. In some cases, the risk is exceptionally high, as for example in the case of the manufacturer of an essential

---

[5] For a review of the purposes, legal principles, evaluation, and controls in this area, see *The Hold-Harmless Agreement* (Cincinnati: National Underwriter Co., 1973).

[6] Think, for example, of the heart pacemaker! See "Pacemaker Failure Presents Exotic Products Liability Case in New York," *Weekly Underwriter,* October 27, 1973 (*Friedman* v. *Metronic, Inc.,* 345 N.Y.S. 2d 637). The widening problems of products liability are well discussed in a special section of the *CPCU Annals,* vol. 27, no. 1 (March 1974), pp. 5–45, and in "The Devils in the Product Liability Laws," *Business Week,* February 12, 1979.

[7] "Products Liability: The Facts and the Figures," *Journal of Insurance,* November–December 1977, p. 13. This article was based on a study by the Insurance Services Office of 25,000 claims in 1976–77.

part of airplanes. An improperly constructed electronic system, or even a simple nut or bolt, could be held responsible for the loss of a jet aircraft worth millions of dollars. Sometimes the insured is held liable for accidents caused by products used many years after their sale, and even by successive purchasers of the product.

Other cases illustrate the widespread nature of the products liability risk. One case involved a suit against a fire alarm company for $25,000 when the fire whistle stuck while a home burned! Smoke detectors, now sold by the millions, may cause similar claims if they are defective. Another case involved a lawsuit filed because a 375-pound body fell through the bottom of a casket at a funeral. Many liability cases have been against drug and chemical firms, such as the Salk polio vaccine personal injury losses and a Texas case of over $11 million damages which resulted when a wrong chemical was negligently put into cattle feed. The broadening of products liability risks is apparent in cases involving everything from a defective automobile to a football helmet, which was the cause of one $600,000 award in 1978. Soaps, deodorants, hair lotion, and cigarettes have been claimed to cause injuries and sicknesses ranging from allergies to fatal diseases such as cancer. The swine flu immunization program in 1977 resulted in nearly 3,000 claims against the U.S. government, including one death claim for $1 billion!

Recent large products liability awards include $150,000 to a child injured by a defective power lawn mower; $250,000 because an injury resulted from a forklift designed without a safety device; $2 million because of improper stabilizers on the 720 jet; $500,000 because a drug was not properly tested before marketing; $140,000 to a boy whose T-shirt was held to be dangerously flammable; and, in 1978, $6.8 million to a man injured by a rifle when its safety catch malfunctioned.

Major increases in the products liability hazard have occurred for a number of reasons: (1) "privity" (direct contractual relationship) is no longer needed in most states, so that an injured person may sue the negligent manufacturer or other parties as well as the retailer who sells the goods; (2) the doctrine of warranty has been extended, especially the sales warranty under the Uniform Sales Act and the Uniform Commercial Code;[8] (3) government commissions and private ombudsmen such as Ralph Nader have displayed a renewed interest in the consumer; and (4) the Consumer Product Safety Act of 1972, a federal law for testing, researching, and investigating standards of products, has had far-reaching effects on potential consumer products liability hazards.

The seriousness of the products liability risk has been called a "crises" by many in recent years. Some of the states have passed tort reform acts which attempt to limit products liability, and many others have such legislation under

---

[8] Frank E. Gibson, "The Law of Products Liability," *Bulletin of Business Research* (Ohio State University), vol 43, no. 1 (January 1968), p. 4.

consideration. These statutes may (1) set a time limit during which lawsuits can be filed after the manufacture or purchase of a product, or the discovery of a loss (2–12 years); (2) permit a "state of the art" defense based on new advances in technical knowledge, or the defense that the producer has properly warned the user about possible dangers; (3) restrict noneconomic damages for intangibles such as pain and suffering; (4) regulate contingency fees to attorneys; (5) eliminate claims based upon changes in the product by the user; or (6) reduce payments by the amount of collateral insurance and other sources.[9]

In 1977 a federal task force report concluded that although manufacturers of a few of the riskier products (aircraft parts and pharmaceuticals, for example, were having difficulty in obtaining coverage or were paying "unaffordable" rates, there was no widespread problem in most product liability lines.

Product liability insurance pays claims for damage caused by mistakes, imperfect ingredients, or foreign substances, as well as improper handling, labeling, packing, or delivering. The policy does not cover products consumed on the premises of the insured or any liability for injury to employees. Goods manufactured, sold, or distributed in violation of law are never covered. It is not necesary that the product actually be sold, since injury attributable to samples or souvenirs is covered.

The policy covers only for amounts for which the insured shall become legally obligated to pay as damages if the occurrence causing the loss occurs (a) away from the insured's premises and (b) after the insured has relinquished possession of the product to others. The policy is written with two limits: (a) a limit per occurrence, and (b) an aggregate limit. The per occurrence limit fixes a total liability for claims from one common cause, such as from one prepared or acquired lot of goods. The aggregate limit is the total liability for all damages under the policy for one year. Basic limits are $25,000 and $50,000. Higher limits may be purchased, and often should be, for adequate protection.

Purchase order agreements are sometimes written with a "hold-harmless" clause under the terms of which the manufacturer agrees to hold the retailer harmless for liability claims. The hold-harmless agreement is an assumed liability that is excluded under the products liability policy but may be covered by endorsement.

Coverage for the protective liability hazard. Several types of *protective liability* insurance may be important to certain policyholders. (See previous section on types of liability insurance.) The *owners' and contractors'* protective liability policy is designed to provide owners of property with protection for the *contingent* liability that may develop as the result of an accident caused by the negligence of a contractor. Contractors purchase the coverage to provide themselves with the same protection for claims that develop as the

---

[9] See "Product Liability Score Card," *Business Insurance,* February 6, 1978.

result of the alleged negligence of subcontractors. Members of the public fre-
qently file their suit for damages against the general contractor, or they file a
joint suit.

The protective policy provides direct liability protection in those situations
in which the law holds the owner or the principal contractor liable in spite of
the negligence of an independent contractor. These situations develop in connection with (*a*) unlawful work, (*b*) responsibility that cannot be delegated,
and (*c*) inherently dangerous work. An accident resulting from the violation
of a municipal ordinance would fall into the first category. The principal contractor cannot delegate to others duty to the public, such as the maintenance
of a safe sidewalk condition. Where an extremely hazardous operation, such
as blasting, is a part of an operation, the principal contractor may not escape
responsibility for injury to the public on the ground that the dangerous work
was let to a subcontractor.

Another form of contingent liability insurance that is occasionally needed
is the *principal's* protective liability policy. Newspaper, milk, baked goods
distributors, for example, hire persons who may be called either employees or
independent contractors. The policy provides protection under two insuring
clauses: (*a*) liability *to* independent contractors and (*b*) liability *for* independent contractors. Thus, if the insured is held liable for injury or damages
to a person described in the policy as an independent contractor, the insurance
covers. On the other hand, if the insured is held liable for injuries by independent contractors to members of the public, protection is also afforded.

Coverage for automobile liability hazards. Many *automobile liability*
coverages may now be combined in the new general liability program. Coverage parts for automobile physical damage, medical payments, garage, and
comprehensive automobile liability are available. Single contracts can be developed for a comprehensive CGL and automobile policy, or an OLT and
automobile policy, to provide packages of combined liability coverage.

$\widehat{614}$

PROFESSIONAL OR MALPRACTICE LIABILITY
INSURANCE CONTRACTS

The treatment of a patient by a medical practitioner (such as a surgeon,
physician, or dentist) with lack of care or professional skill and with injurious
results, constitutes malpractice. Liability for personal injury in such instances
is known as *professional* or *malpractice* liability.

Professional liability insurance was first written to indemnify medical professionals for loss or expense resulting from claims on account of *bodily
injuries*. Any malpractice, error, or mistake committed, or alleged to have
been committed, in performing medical services is covered.

Today, many other professional persons in addition to those in the medical
fields find themselves defendants in heavy damage suits. Professional liability
insurance has been extended into fields to cover losses where *monetary* dam-

ages (as opposed to bodily injury) are a consequence of the negligent professional services of the insured. Accountants, architects, advertisers, attorneys,
insurance brokers or agents, real estate agents, stockbrokers, consultants, data
processors, and many others may all be held liable for their professional errors
or mistakes. Failure to meet a standard of skill and care generally accepted
for any of these professions or occupations, with resulting injury to the client,
may obligate the responsible parties to defend themselves against claims for
damages.

Professional malpractice liability for the medical fields

The medical forms are presented here first because of their many unusual
liability features. The growing importance of professional liability insurance
for many nonmedical professional groups is emphasized in succeeding sections.

Physicians', surgeons', and dentists' liability policy. This form (which can
be attached to the general liability policy jacket) provides coverage for liability
arising out of professional acts or omissions committed by the insured or by
any person for whom the insured is legally responsible. Negligence is not required, as many medical acts are performed *intentionally*, and these are covered because the injury does not have to result from an accident.

The insuring clause providing indemnity to the insured for damages on
account of malpractice or mistake is very broad. Any claim whatever arising
from injuries either real or alleged comes within the scope of the policy. The
policy covers such claims as errors in recommending treatment or in prescribing or dispensing drugs or medicines, and claims arising through the performance of surgery or autopsies. It also defends counterclaims in suits brought
for the collection of fees. Physicians and other professional practitioners have
frequently been victimized by claims based upon alleged moral turpitude while
engaged in professional practice. Such claims are covered by this contract, as
are claims based upon undue familiarity, assault, slander, libel, and malicious
persecution. The policy covers claims for bodily injury, for property damage,
for care and loss of services, and losses of an intangible nature, in one major
insuring clause.

The policy does not cover the personal liability of the insured for claims
that cannot be traced to the professional practice of the insured. The policy
excludes claims arising by reason of the liability of the insured as proprietor,
superintendent, or executive officer in any hospital, sanatorium, clinic, laboratory, or other business enterprise.

In the case of professional persons, defense is an important factor. While
in other damage cases a settlement to avoid suit where liability is not clear or
is even denied may be the most inexpensive and expedient way to handle a
claim, professionals cannot afford to jeopardize their reputations in this manner. They therefore often need the right to refuse to allow payment for an
alleged injury. A feature peculiar to this policy is the requirement that the

insurer secure the written *consent of the insured* before settling any claim. When insureds feel that their profesional reputations are at stake, they may require the company to resist the case to the court of last resort, even though the claimant offers to compromise on a basis satisfactory to the insurers. The insurer obligates itself to defend the insured's reputation and to pay, subject to the policy limits, such award as may be made against the insured. Some new forms are limiting this risk by prescribing arbitration for certain conditions.

Policies are written on an occurrence basis with a limit per claim and an aggregate limit of liability for the policy period. The per claim limit is in contrast to the per person limit to be found in certain of the other liability policies, and the aggregate limit has no reference to a single accident. Obviously, most insureds should purchase much higher limits than the basic ones.[10] In addition to the policy written for an individual, many policies are written through groups such as medical societies and partnerships.

The *distinguishing features* of the medical forms of professional liability insurance (most of which also apply to the nonmedical forms), as compared with other liability insurance, in summary include: (1) importance of *defense* factor for maintaining professional reputation, (2) *consent* of the insured *before settling claims,* (3) very broad coverage of *negligence and even intentional acts* on an occurrence basis, (4) *per claim* and *per occurrence limits,* (5) one insuring clause for all damage claims, and (6) *high-coverage limits needed,* but high cost and limited market for some professional specialties.

In many areas and in a number of medical specialties, such as surgery, radiology, and anesthesia, a crisis of market availability has occurred in malpractice insurance. Beginning about the mid-1970s, the costs for malpractice coverage climbed rapidly as claims and awards increased substantially. Several insurers dominant in the malpractice field restricted or eliminated the writing of these contracts. The result was a severe shortage of markets for buying malpractice coverages, even with total premiums increasing from less than $100 million a year to more than $1 billion a year in the past decade.

The solutions have been varied. In many states special legislation has been passed to permit the use of joint underwriting associations (JUAs), in which all insurers writing liability insurance are required to participate in providing malpractice coverage for hospitals and medical professionals. Risk-management techniques have been encouraged in several of these states. In Florida and Ohio, for example, substantial credits of 15 percent or more are granted for the implementation of written risk-management policies by hospitals, the hiring of risk managers, and the formation of committees, including medical practitioners, to review losses and recommend loss-prevention practices. Other

---

[10] For examples of this need, see Bernard J. Daenzer, "Risk Management of the Professional Liability Exposures," *Weekly Underwriter,* November 10, 1973, p. 10, and November 24, 1973, p. 10. Also indicative of the escalating needs of professionals to keep current in this area is a new monthly publication available in 1978, the *Professional Liability Reporter* (San Francisco).

states have passed or are considering legislation which (1) requires that attorney's fees be on a declining sliding-scale basis for larger awards; (2)
mandates arbitration panels; (3) reduces payments by the amount collected
from collateral medical insurance contracts (hospital, surgical, and major
medical coverage); (4) eliminates the "Ad Damnum" provision in liability
suits, in which specific dollar amounts of claims are used in jury trials; or
(5) shortens the statute of limitations on lawsuits, thus reducing the "long
tail" or coverage from some claims that were delayed for many years, particularly in the case of minors filing suit after age 21.

Insurers have reacted by more restrictive underwriting requirements, and
by writing coverage on a "claims made" basis instead of the usual "occurrence"
basis. Only claims made or reported during the current contract are covered,
making pricing of the protection easier for the insurer by eliminating the
need to estimate claims that may occur long after an alleged malpractice incident happened.[11] A number of medical societies have also formed their own
insurers, often on a reciprocal basis, in order to provide malpractice insurance
to their own medical practitioners.

The crisis of coverage availability is not over, but it has been alleviated by
these legislative and market adjustments. The costs for malpractice insurance
will undoubtedly remain high, and medical professionals will probably continue to pay increasing costs, sometimes many thousands of dollars a year, for
adequate coverage of this current problem in the liability field.

Druggists' liability policy.   This is a malpractice coverage which also extends to provide product liability insurance protection.

The contract provides insurance against loss and expense arising from
claims for damages on account of bodily injury or death that results from
actual or alleged error on the part of drugstores or their employees in preparing, compounding, dispensing, selling, or delivering drugs, medicine, or
merchandise. Coverage is also provided for claims arising out of the consumption or use of beverages, food, or other products, including merchandise
of every character. This extends to losses caused by errors in labeling or delivering. Hence, a claim originating because two correctly compounded prescriptions were accidentally exchanged in delivery is covered. Also covered
are errors in reading or interpreting the physician's prescriptions and in referring to the number of a refill.

An exclusion with respect to claims attributable to illegality assumes some
significance in connection with this coverage. For example, the illegal employment of clerks, sales of prohibited drugs or of drugs that are contrary
to statutory regulation, or the compounding of a prescription by a person

---

[11] Robert C. Witt and George M. McCabe, "The Medical Malpractice Insurance
Pricing Problem: An Economic View," *CPCU Annals,* vol. 30, no. 2 (June 1977), p.
140. For the controversial statutory limitation of malpractice claims to a specified dollar
amount, see Richard B. Corbett, "The Medical Malpractice Problem: Are Limitations on
the Amount of Recovery a Viable Solution?" in the same issue, p. 151.

who is not legally qualified (except by an assistant present and under the phar-
macist's direction) will void the coverage so far as these acts give rise to
claims. Violation of the Medical Practice Act by prescribing treatment or
violation of the Harrison Narcotic Act or of laws governing the sale of alco-
holic liquors has the same effect. However, if the insured or the manager
does not intentionally violate the law, the policy protects the drugstore from
the illegal actions of employees who may knowingly commit an illegal act.

Hospital liability policy. Like the druggists' policy, this form is a combination coverage for malpractice and product liability. It is designed for use
by hospitals, clinics, homes for the aged, and mental-psychopathic and other
health institutions. Special forms have been developed recently for nursing
homes.

Coverage is provided for liability arising out of malpractice, error, or mistake
made in rendering or failing to render medical or nursing treatment, including
the furnishing of food or beverages. Product liability insurance is included,
both on and off the premises, for drugs or medical supplies or appliances
furnished or dispensed by the insured.

The need of hospitals for such insurance protection has escalated with the
malpractice problems of recent years. Some of the potential solutions provided
by statutory limitations and new JUAs and other insurers have been discussed
in the physicians', surgeons', and dentists liability section. Large losses are
illustrated by one 1978 settlement for a woman who had oxygen instead of
anesthesia administered to her, resulting in a $2 million payment based on
an estimate of more than $128,000 a year in future medical expenses.

Miscellaneous medical liability policy. This coverage is provided by endorsing one of the other professional liability policies. The policy to be used
depends upon the professional classification of the applicant for insurance.
The form is used to cover chiropodists, chiropractors, nurses, optometrists,
opticians, veterinarians, dental hygienists, and other technicians.

Other professional liability insurance

Many *nonmedical* professions also have a great need for professional liability insurance contracts. Special contracts have been developed for attorneys,
architects, and many other persons. The basic reason for these contracts is the
expanding legal liability for the specialized professions, the law requiring a
higher standard of care to be exercised by professionals in the performance
of their duties. Few real professional persons should be without such insurance.

Errors and omissions insurance. Usually, professional liability insurance
is called *errors and omissions insurance* when it applies to such office exposures as insurance agents or investment advisers. These forms often use
deductibles of $1,000 or more. They ordinarily do not require the consent of
the insured to settle claims. A limit of liability per claim and in the aggregate
for the policy period applies.

Many service businesses also have available to them specialized contracts closely related to professional liability insurance. Examples include advertising agencies, television stations, management consultants, travel agents, real estate agents, banks (which may also need the first-party indirect property type of E and O insurance for mortgagees, as discussed in Chapter 18), and data processing companies. Symptomatic of the vulnerable position of many professionals today is the general public attitude of dissatisfaction toward them—even toward attorneys in our legalistic, "sue syndrome" society.[12]

Directors' and officers' liability insurance. As a specialized type of professional liability coverage, one of the most talked about examples of recent years has been *directors' and officers' liability insurance* paying on behalf of the executives (or also to reimburse their corporation if the executives receive indemnification) for claims arising out of wrongful acts such as error, neglect, breach of duty, or misleading statements.[13]

Some policies of this kind have been written for more than $20 million limits. Lloyd's of London and a dozen or more U.S. insurers specialize in this market. Recent Securities and Exchange Commission rulings have greatly increased the potential liability of officers and directors for the improper use of inside information for investment decisions.

Early forms of this important coverage were written only for the very large corporations,[14] but today the market has expanded to include firms with assets of several million dollars or more. Increasing lawsuits by stockholders or even competitors (for antitrust or unfair competition, etc.) reinforce the need for D & O liability protection, in spite of yearly premium costs which often reach $10,000 or more. Deductibles of $5,000 to $20,000 are common, and a participation of 5 percent or more by the insured in loss payments is frequent. The intent is to cover negligence of directors and officers, and defense of such claims, but not active and deliberate fraud.

Many new liability exposures related to directors and officers are appearing. Alleged discrimination suits under the Equal Employment Act of 1972 or equivalent state or local laws are one example, and only a few insurers write this coverage. Another problem concerns "punitive damages," court awards in liability cases which go beyond ordinary compensatory payments to the injured party. The sizable nature of these increasing awards was brought dramatically to public attention with a $125 million award in 1977 to a young burn victim (later reduced to less than $3 million) against an auto manufac-

---

[12] Such as was expressed in "The Troubled Professions," *Business Week,* August 16, 1976, p. 126; and in "Those #☆×¿!!! Lawyers," *Time,* April 10, 1978, p. 56.

[13] See William E. Knepper, *Liability of Corporate Officers and Directors,* 2d ed. (Indianapolis: Allen Smith Co., 1973).

[14] Based on a survey by the Wyatt Company (Chicago) of nearly 2,000 organizations, more than 85 percent of which had assets exceeding $25 million, about three fourths had D & O contracts (averaging almost $10 million liability limits), and the average claim award, including defense costs, was $750,000. See Warren G. Brockmeier, "Status of D & O Liability Coverage," *Risk Management,* January 1977, p. 20.

turer for a faulty gas tank Although this was in connection with a products liability claim, punitive damage awards could also involve corporate officers or directors. Whether or not punitive damages[15] should be included in any liability insurance was hotly debated in 1977, with the Insurance Services Office excluding in its CGL forms, but then deciding to leave such protection in the standard forms. Many D & O policies exclude this coverage unless it is specifically endorsed on the contract.

EXCESS INSURANCE

Liability contracts, in addition to being classified as covering personal, business, and professional liability exposures, may also be divided into (1) *primary,* and (2) *excess* liability coverages. All of the contracts discussed on the previous pages are essentially primary, that is, they provide first (and often only) basic coverage for the perils insured. Deductibles may be used, but these are usually limited to a few hundred or thousand dollars. These primary contracts will not be treated further here.

In contrast to primary coverages, *excess* insurance is designed as catastrophe protection to provide very large limits of coverage (millions of dollars) for at least some unusual and larger exposures or perils which are not covered by any other insurance. Perils which are also covered first under primary contracts are often included, too, as additional insurance amounts—thus the term *excess insurance.*

If Rip Van Winkle were an insurance agent who woke up today after 20 years of sleep, he would have a difficult job in recognizing many of the titles used today in the business to describe insurance contracts. One of the most confusing areas would be the *excess insurance* field. Although some types of excess insurance have been available for more than 30 years, the popularity of these contracts has recently increased tremendously. The professional insurance man has a new vocabulary to learn, with "umbrella," "difference in conditions," "bumbershoot," "comprehensive ceiling," "surplus line," and many other terms important to agents and clients.

The *liability* area is very active in adapting the concept of excess insurance to its needs. It is here that most of the best-known excess contracts of recent years have evolved. Although the London and surplus lines insurers first developed these contracts, today there are dozens of U.S. insurers that write many of the types of excess liability insurance mentioned below. Sometimes they have "special risks" departments for this purpose. The coordination of excess coverages with primary coverages is an increasing problem.[16]

Some excess liability insurance is written for special situations requiring

---

[15] John D. Long, "Should Punitive Damages Be Insured?" *Journal of Risk and Insurance,* vol. 44, no. 1 (March 1977), p. 1.

[16] Arthur E. Parry, "The Primary-Excess Insurance Policy Tangle," *Risk Management,* September 1977, p. 21.

much higher limits of coverage than are normal for a particular single kind of liability insurance. Truck liability, products liability of manufacturers, and aircraft liability are examples of this type. The underlying prime contract determines the type of coverage, and the excess contract provides the same coverage and only adds an extra limit of insurance.

Excess and surplus lines

Excess insurance is taken here to mean insurance of high limits which is used to supplement basic policies of a substantial risk-retention program. Contracts of $1 million to $10 million or more, with a $1,000 to $10,000 deductible or more, would be typical. *Surplus line insurance* is often associated with excess insurance, for many such policies are designed for excess coverages. However, as it is defined in the state insurance codes, surplus line insurance usually refers to a difficulty in placement of the insurance in the normal markets. It does not necessarily involve very large policies, and it is *not* extra in the sense of not being needed, as the term implies. In addition to excess insurance, surplus lines are (1) substandard exposures, (2) unique or unusual perils, or (3) very broad coverages. Examples of each group are (1) tenements, bowling alleys, and supermarkets; (2) twin insurance, financial institution mortgage protection, and nonappearance of performers; and (3) "all risks" on buildings, valued use and occupancy, and builders' risk coverages. A current listing of all types of nonstandard and specialty contracts available would number more than 150.[17] Only a few of the more important contracts can be mentioned here.

Difference in conditions coverage

In the *physical damage* insurance area, *difference in conditions* (DIC) insurance has created strong interest in the merits of all-risks coverage. Essentially, this form converts named-perils insurance into all-risks insurance. It covers perils such as flood, water damage, collapse, and earthquake, as well as unusual and unknown losses. It can be endorsed on other contracts. Because of the many differences in insurance contracts issued for large corporations doing business on a worldwide basis, this form is an important one for *international* businesses to consider. Its advantage is in providing similar coverage everywhere by insuring the differences which often exist in the usual contracts issued for properties insured in foreign countries.

DIC coverage is catastrophe protection, often written with limits of $5 million to $10 million or more (separate limits may apply for the flood or earthquake perils) and deductibles of $5,000–$25,000 per loss or per claim.

---

[17] See *The Insurance Market Place* (Indianapolis: Rough Notes Co.), and *Excess-Surplus Lines* (New York: *Weekly Underwriter*), both published annually.

Lloyd's, Factory Mutuals, Industrial Risk Insurers, and several other major U.S. insurers provide a somewhat restricted but growing market for this unusually broad type of insurance.

Umbrella liability policy

One of the most popular forms of excess liability insurance is the _umbrella liability_ contract. The last 25 years have seen many variations of this policy appear. Many are nonstandard, and even those that follow a standard pattern have many important differences. The development has been from an extremely broad all-risks liability contract obtained through Lloyd's of London in the 1950s to a more restricted yet still very broad contract that is now available from many insurers.

The umbrella liability contract is "excess" in two respects: (1) it provides _extra limits_ with a combined blanket _single limit over other existing liability coverages,_ usually the required basic auto policy (BAP) limits of $500,000 (as an example), a general liability contract for $100,000/$300,000/ $100,000 limits, and employer's liability for $100,000; and (2) it is _extra coverage_ for other liability exposures not covered by the underlying liability contracts, above a self-retention limit of about $25,000. The maximum limit is high—at least $1 million, and often $5 million, $10 million, $20 million, or more. The retention deductible for smaller business firms is sometimes lowered from $25,000 to $10,000, or less.

The contract is an indemnity one, repaying the insured for a wide variety of liability losses. Although the contract forms vary, Figure 21–1 indicates the types of liability that are often included and the way in which the limits of coverages are applied. Note that the top of the "umbrella" (at the top of Figure 21–1) is uneven, providing $1 million limits _over_ the basic amounts available and over the deductible amount. Some insurers also sell these contracts on an "up to $1 million," or other amount, basis.

Figure 21–1 shows the broad protection of the umbrella liability contract. It adds many coverages that the business does not usually have in its underlying insurance, such as advertisers' legal liability, worldwide operations liability, personal injury liability, and many others. These are only insured above the insured's retention limit (or deductible) of $25,000. The result is that important catastrophe liability protection is achieved. The deductible does not apply to auto, general liability, and employers' liability losses, which are covered for the additional single limit of $1 million (or more, if the umbrella policy is larger) as soon as they exceed the basic underlying limits. Excess fidelity coverage is also included in some of these policies.

Examples of loss potential for the business insured are many: A salesperson leases an airplane, a company officer makes a business trip to Europe, an employee's automobile is driven to Mexico on business, or a security guard makes a false arrest. Large losses which indicate the need for catastrophe pro-

Figure 21-1. Umbrella liability policy illustration ($1 million)*

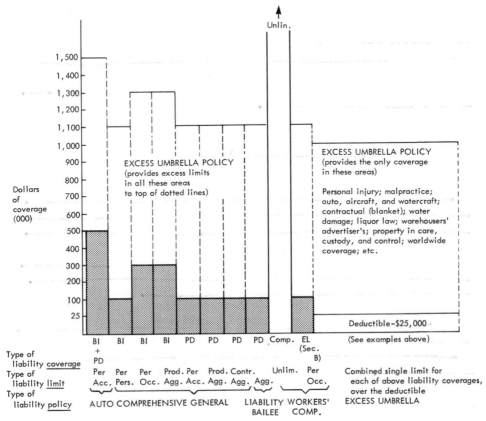

Abbreviations: BI (bodily injury); PD (property damage); Comp. (compensation); EL (employer's liability); Acc. (accident); Pers. (person); Occ. (occurrence); Agg. (aggregate, per year); Unlim. (unlimited).

* Many umbrella liability policies would have higher limits, such as $5 million or $10 million or more. A $1 million limit policy is used in order to show more clearly the relationship to a deductible of $25,000 and primary coverages (darkened space) of $100,000 to $500,000.

tection of the type that umbrella liability provides are: dams breaking and causing floods; thalidomide used that caused children to be malformed at birth; airplane crashes; rape and assault injuries to hotel or motel guests not provided with sufficient security; pollution damage by manufacturers; and many others.

The cost of the umbrella contract varies. Premiums, which must be partially based on judgment factors, decreased for several years, but rose again with the increasing losses and appreciation of the loss potential of liability situations. Smaller insureds may pay less than $500 for their umbrella contract; larger firms may pay many thousands of dollars.

Other excess business policies

A variation of the umbrella contract is used in the marine field, where it is called the *bumbershoot*. The purpose is to provide excess limits coverage above the primary marine protection and indemnity coverage. The problems of admiralty liability law and maritime workers' compensation are unique in this field, and careful coordination with, or inclusion within the umbrella liability policy is necessary.

One of the innovations from Lloyd's of London is the combination of all-risks *property* and all-risks third-party *liability* in a single excess contract known as the *comprehensive ceiling coverage*. This contract is very flexible and broad in its coverage. It serves as real catastrophe protection ($1 million, $5 million, $10 million, or more) over the basic fire, business interruption, crime, and liability contracts of the insured. It may be excess over such basic contracts as the SMP policy, the 3-D policy, and the comprehensive general liability policy.

Excess personal liability policies

Not all excess insurance is for business risks. The *excess personal liability* area is one of substantial interest, concern, and sales potential. Based on the fact that business and professional persons are often the target for large liability claims, these contracts provide important defense and catastrophe liability coverage for persons with higher income and assets to protect.

Many U.S. insurers have developed contracts of this type. Most are for limits of $1 million to $10 million above basic automobile liability coverage with $100,000/$300,000/$10,000 limits (or the new combined single limit PAP limit of $300,000—see Chapter 24), and comprehensive personal liability coverage for $50,000. A deductible is chosen by the insured to apply to losses *other than* those covered by the basic coverages. Usually, this is about $1,000, but it may be as low as $250 or as high as $10,000.

These policies usually apply to the entire family and include residence, personal injury, automobile, employer's, aircraft, sports, snowmobile, and watercraft liability (over basic, if insured owns a larger than a 26-foot boat). Sometimes excess major medical coverage of $50,000 or more is included. The usual exclusions include business pursuits or professional malpractice liability (both of which may be added by endorsement), property damage to aircraft, and nuclear energy liability. The cost for a $1 million personal excess liability contract with a $1,000 deductible is $50 or more a year. It is a recommended purchase for many business and professional persons because it helps meet the constantly changing large exposures to liability loss.

MEDICAL PAYMENTS COVERAGE

A very important supplement to many general liability contracts is *medical payments* insurance. It is optional with most of the business liability policies but is automatically included in the comprehensive personal liability policies. It is not written as a separate policy but as a part of liability and some other insurance contracts.

Medical payments insurance pays for all necessary and reasonable medical, surgical, ambulance, hospital, professional nursing, and funeral expenses for a person injured or killed in an accident arising out of the premises or operations of the insured, *regardless of negligence or liability.* In modern terms, it is a form of "no-fault" insurance (see Chapter 23).

The importance of medical payments coverage is that it avoids delay, difficulty, and costs involved in proving legal liability. It is most helpful for smaller losses, where a customer or a member of the public can be provided with rapid payment for such common injuries as sprains, cuts, bruises, or simple fractures. In many cases, the goodwill of a business can be enhanced greatly by medical payments coverage because the injured person does not have to prove liability or bring lawsuit against the business.

Payments made under the medical payments coverage do not prevent the injured person from later deciding that further payment is warranted, by proving the legal liability of the insured.

Medical payments coverage is often written in connection with the OLT policy and the CGL policy. It is rarely written with the M&C policy because the type of premises and the changing nature of locations is an exposure much different from that of the usual owner, tenant, or business firm dealing with customers from fixed locations used regularly by the public. Medical payments may not be written with coverage of the products liability hazard at all. The reasons include the possibility of many small claims from poisonings or faulty products, the potential cost of multiple injuries from one accident, and the probable encouragement of carelessness by the insured.

The usual limit for medical payments coverage is $500 per person. Quite frequently this limit is increased to $1,000 per person, and more is written with some policies. A second limit also applies, in the business liability contracts, per accident—usually $25,000 but occasionally more. The expenses paid for must be incurred within one year after the accident.

There is no medical payments coverage for injury to the named insured, any partner of the insured, or any employee while engaged in the insured's employment. Thus it is *not* accident insurance for a whole family or other person residing regularly on the premises covered by the liability policy, or for an employee of the tenant or resident. In this respect, medical payments coverage under general liability policies differs from automobile medical payments coverage (see Chapter 24), where injuries to the insured and to the insured's family are among those covered by the insurance.

Some business establishments have a first-aid station with a nurse, often a physician, and with other first-aid assistance as part of their regular organizations. Where this is the case, a discount is allowed from the medical payments premium.

In summary, the medical payments coverage is an easy and worthwhile addition to many liability policies covering many small injuries for which the insured would normally feel obligated, morally or legally, to the injured person.

CG-~~46/49~~ P 48

FOR REVIEW AND DISCUSSION

1. Risk management can be applied to some liability situations. Give three illustrations of this statement, other than insurance. Also explain why insurance is a commonly accepted technique for meeting liability risks.

2. What are the basic kinds of liability insurance losses, and how do these differ from accident insurance?

3. Illustrate three major types of general liability insurance contracts with an example of a specific policy of each type.

4. What changes have revisions brought to the field of general liability insurance contracts? Include several examples of the benefits to (a) the insured and (b) the insurer.

5. Why is liability insurance coverage on an "occurrence" basis, as it is usually written now, generally considered broader than coverage for an "accident"?

6. The owners' landlords', and tenants' policy covers both *premises and off-premises* liability. It may also include protection for *protective, contractual,* and *products* liability. Explain the need for each of these types of liability insurance by a property owner.

7. Mr. Hubbard is the owner of a building leased in its entirety to a tenant who has assumed all liability in the event that anyone is injured on the premises. Is the owner relieved of all risks?

8. A general contractor repairing a bridge failed to provide either a barricade or lights, and an automobile accident injured the driver. Suit was filed and damages were awarded. How could the contractor have been insured? Would your answer change if subcontractors were hired by the general contractor?

9. X is covered by a comprehensive general liability policy. As a result of an error, he caused the arrest of B. B brought action against him for false arrest and alleged mental anguish. Does the policy cover?

10. Beth became ill in a restaurant as a result of eating spinach in which pieces of glass were later found. Is this risk insurable? Could a fake claim also be insured? Do other businesses (besides restaurants) have such liability? Explain.

11. "Malpractice liability contracts" insure physicians, hospitals, druggists, and other like practitioners. Discuss the extension of professional liability to include other professional groups, such as lawyers, and directors and officers of business firms.

12. Mr. Fisher says: "Why should I pay for adding medical payments coverage

to my business liability policy? If I'm legally liable for someone's injuries, the policy will pay. If I'm not, I don't want to pay." *Explain* whether or not you agree with Mr. Fisher.

13. *Why* does a business need to consider *excess* insurance? Does the same situation exist for individuals?

14. Are the products and malpractice liability fields really in a "crisis" today? What statutory and other changes have been instituted in order to alleviate the problems of these fields?

Chapter 22

Concepts considered in Chapter 22—Employers' liability and workers' compensation

Employers' liability is a special part of liability law. The common-law employers' liability doctrines and statutes were largely replaced by:
Workers' compensation laws, making employers' "liability *without* fault for work injuries or diseases of their employees".

Constitutionality was tested in early court cases, but almost all states now have *compulsory* laws (a few are *elective*).

Scope and benefits of the laws include broad coverage of more than two-thirds of all employees (almost all public employees, and most private employees). The basic benefits are (1) *medical expenses,* (2) *income,* (3) *death,* and (4) *rehabilitation* expenses. Occupational *injuries* and *diseases* are covered by benefits which vary widely by state.

Administration of the laws is usually by a state commission.

Financing of the benefits is by *employers,* through insurance plans.

Workers' compensation insurers: Alternatives include *private insurers, state funds* (in some states), or an approved *self-insurance plan* (permitted in many states).

The standard workers' compensation and employers' liability policy is standardized not by law but by custom of the insurers, but it is nevertheless very uniformly accepted. Its basic parts include:

Declarations, providing basic underwriting data;

Insuring agreements, four in number, which identify workers' compensation and employers' liability coverages, definitions, and duration;

Exclusions, which are few; and

Conditions, which specify rights of insurer, insured, and employees.

Special rating plans are significant in workers' compensation because the basic or average rates are frequently modified by:

Experience rating plans, based on an individual employer's *past* loss experience, which is a direct incentive to the employer to reduce losses.

The premium discount plan, for decreasing *expenses* of larger insureds.

Retrospective rating plans, for *current* loss experience.

Second-injury funds encourage hiring partially disabled employees.

Workers' compensation losses differ from many other kinds of insurance because they are not based on fault and because the amounts are set forth in the state laws.

Other policy benefits are those which help *prevent* losses rather than pay for losses that have occurred. *Inspection services* are increasing.

Occupational Safety and Health Act (OSHA) and other federal laws are increasing federal involvement in workers' compensation.

Employers' liability and workers' compensation

Occupational disability because of *work injury* or *disease* is a peril of great importance to business and to society. The solution to the financial burden of disability because of employment is also a dual one: many of the state government requirements for workers' compensation insurance are met by insurance contracts purchased from private insurers.

An unusual blend of social and private insurance results, which explains the inclusion of this type of insurance in Chapter 15 on government life and health insurance as well as in this chapter. Employers finance the social-private system of insurance, which costs many billion dollars annually to provide the employee with compensation for work injuries and diseases.

The origin of workers' compensation laws is employers' liability law. Why and how employers' liability has been supplanted in the United States by the workers' compensation laws is evident in a brief review of the relationship between employer and employee in our changing industrial society. The development has been one progressing from *common-law liability* which defined an employer's responsibility for work injuries and diseases, to *employers' liability statutes,* and finally to the *workers' compensation laws* of the 20th century.

EMPLOYERS' LIABILITY

Common-law liability of employers

At common law an employer is liable to employees for damages due to injury when the negligence of the employer is the cause of the injury. However, the burden of proof in the case of accidental injuries rests squarely upon the employee to show that there was employer negligence and that this negligence was the cause of the injury or sickness. The word *negligence,* as used in this chapter, includes by implication all other common-law liability by the employer. This could involve, for example, intentional torts or breaches of contract by the employer arising in the employer-employee relationship. (See discussion in Chapter 20 which distinguishes these types of contract and tort liability under common law.)

The employer has three strong *defenses* against employee claims under *common-law liability.* Under the *contributory negligence rule,* the employee must also show that he or she did not contribute to the negligence. Further, when an employee has knowledge of the ordinary risks involved, he or she is paid for assuming those risks and, therefore, cannot recover for injuries caused thereby. The doctrine has been extended to apply in cases in which the employee continues to work without complaint after the discovery of failure on the part of his or her employer to afford proper protection. The employer's defense against such claims is referred to as the *assumption-of-risk rule*. Finally, the common law relieved the employer of responsibility when the cause of the injury was the willful wrongdoing or negligence of a fellow servant (employee). This defense is known as the *fellow-servant* (or *common employment*) *rule*. When two employees are working together, for example, one employee might negligently drop a heavy tool, causing injury to the other employee.

Modifications of the common law

The difficulty of an injured employee's establishing a case of liability can readily be understood. Through statutory enactment and a tendency on the part of the courts to interpret the rules favorably to employees, the position of the worker was somewhat bettered. The class of fellow-servant employees was narrowed to include only those who worked with the injured person, not the supervisor or manager. Other laws followed but were to a degree nullified by employers who required workers to sign contracts releasing them from liability.

A number of states adopted *employers' liability acts* about the turn of the century, by which the position of the employee was immeasurably improved. These were modeled after employers' liability legislation in the late 1800s in England, which held the employer responsible for defective machinery when it was the cause of an accident, as well as for the negligence of supervisors and others in authority. Employers' liability acts were initially rejected by the courts. The federal Employers' Liability Act of 1906 was held unconstitutional, but upon its reenactment in a new form it was upheld by the U.S. Supreme Court. This law abrogated the fellow-servant rule and modified the operation of the contributory negligence and assumption-of-risk rules. Finally, the law provided that contracts or other devices intended to exempt the employer from liability created by the act should be void.

Negligence on the part of the employer still had to be proved. Many accidents occurred where negligence could not be shown. Great expense and delay were suffered by both employers and employees in litigation, and the award of a jury in any case was often unpredictable. The disadvantageous position of the employee was still severe, for the immediate result of filing a suit or making a claim against the employer was twofold: the employee lost his or her job, and expenses were incurred which the employee could usually ill afford.

WORKERS' COMPENSATION LAWS

Even though the liability acts were designed to improve the position of the employee, they were, nevertheless, far from satisfactory. Employers' liability acts in all jurisdictions in the United States have now been superseded by workers' compensation laws.

The theory behind workers' compensation legislation completely disregards the old idea of liability based upon negligence. Rather, the theory is based upon the idea that the cost of occupational injuries and many diseases is to be charged to the *employer, regardless of liability,* and then passed on to the the consumer as a part of the cost of production.

Compensation laws make the employer responsible for indemnity to the disabled employee without regard to the matter of fault or negligence. The amount of indemnity to apply in particular cases is predetermined by the law, although it does not equal the full income received while employed. The laws relate payments to injuries or sicknesses; and if these are fatal, *death* benefits are provided for the employee's dependents. *Medical expenses, income,* and *rehabilitation benefits* are included.

Constitutionality

Just as employers resisted the trend toward liberalization under the employers' liability acts, so they questioned the constitutionality of the first attempts toward compensation laws. In 1910, courts held that the first statute that sought to impose a liability upon an employer "who has omitted no legal duty and has committed no wrong" was unconstitutional in New York, but a new compensation law was enacted in 1914. A number of states evolved a new plan to overcome the constitutional difficulties, giving employers a choice as to whether or not they would be governed by the workers' compensation act. Wisconsin had the first effective workers' compensation law in 1911. If they wished, the employer and the employee might retain their rights at common law, or they might elect to accept the compensation law. As an incentive to employers, the elective laws provide that if an employer fails to accept the compensation law, the employer loses the defenses of contributory negligence, negligence of a fellow employee, and assumption-of-risk by an employee. With the loss of the common-law defenses and the uncertainty as to jury awards, plus litigation costs, the compensation alternative offers a choice that employers find desirable.

Scope of the laws

In the beginning, workers' compensation laws were enacted only to protect employees engaged in certain industries regarded as hazardous, such as coal mining, blasting operations, and explosive manufacturing. The tendency in compensation legislation has been to enlarge the application of the laws. No state at present brings all occupations within the operation of the law, but most occupations are covered, regardless of the extent of danger in the work. Most states cover all public employments and most private employments. The result is that more than two thirds of all employees (and 85 percent of wage and salary employees) are now under workers' compensation laws. Agricultural, domestic, and casual labor are ordinary exempted, and some states exempt firms employing less than about three employees.

Compulsory and elective laws

Thus, based upon the *employer's* rights, there are two types of workers' compensation laws: (1) compulsory and (2) elective. Almost all of the state laws are *compulsory,* which means that all employers to whom the laws apply are required to pay for work injuries or diseases as specified under the compensation statutes. Only three states[1] still have the *elective* type of law (see above section on constitutionality), permitting the employer to accept or reject the workers' compensation act. If the employer rejects it, the common-law defenses discussed earlier are lost to the employer. As a result, such a choice is very unusual.

Employees also usually come under workers' compensation laws on a compulsory basis. Some states still permit employees to reject the applicable compensation law in writing, but normally this must be done *before* a loss occurs. This is also rarely done, because the employer then retains the common-law defenses and a liability suit against the employer by the worker would be difficult to sustain. In some cases, the employee may elect not to come under workers' compensation after a loss has occurred, but this applies only in certain circumstances, such as when a minor has been illegally employed or when the employer has willfully injured the employee.

Perils covered in the laws

Compensation is provided for all *injuries,* and many *diseases, arising out of and occurring in the course of employment.* No benefits under compensation acts are allowed when it is proved that the injury was occasioned by the willful intention of the employees or by their intoxication while on duty. An execption to the regulation covering intoxication is sometimes made if employers knew that the employees were intoxicated or that they were in the habit of being intoxicated while on duty.

Occupational disability includes both *injury* and *disease.* Occupational diseases are defined as diseases peculiar to the occupation in which the employee is engaged and due to causes in excess of the ordinary hazards of employment. In recent years, suits claiming compensation for such diseases as

---

[1] New Jersey, South Carolina, and Texas.

those developing from exposure to chemical fumes and dust, radioactivity, prolonged industrial noise, and even "cumulative trauma" on the job have come increasingly to the attention of employers.

Liability for occupational disease is based upon the common-law doctrine requiring the employer to use all reasonable precautions to safeguard employees from injury and to warn them of the existence of any particular danger. By statute in one form or another, occupational diseases have been covered in many jurisdictions—in some by the workers' compensation laws, in others by separate occupational diseases acts. Almost all of the states now provide compensation for all diseases resulting from employment. The schedule method is used in less than ten states, listing from 10 to 50 well-recognized occupational diseases. The trend has been away from the schedule type, and most observers agree that all occupational diseases should be included in all the state laws.[2]

Not all diseases contracted in the course of an occupation may be attributed to the work or its nature. In the case of an occupational disease there must be a cause-and-effect relationship between the occupation and the disease as well as a frequency and regularity of the occurrence of the disease in the particular occupation.[3]

The problem created by the inclusion of occupational diseases within the scope of workers' compensation is a serious one both to insurers and to employers. Insurers and insureds alike have raised two questions: First, since occupational diseases in general are progressive and recurring, at what point of time does liability for compensation begin? And second, in the event that there are more than one employer, which employer is liable? The trend of court decisions indicates the answers. When inability to work or earn because of certain express conditions occurs, the case is compensable. In other words, compensation starts from the time of actual disability. It has been held that employees are insured "in their then condition," and if their employment causes a disease to continue until they are incapacitated, the insurer at the time of the incapacity is liable.

Employees may be suffering over a long period from occupational diseases, such as silicosis or radiation,[4] that are progressive in nature. They may have

---

[2] "Workmen's Compensation: The States Are in Motion," *Journal of American Insurance,* Spring 1973, p. 16.

[3] An occupational disease has been defined as "one which arises from causes incident to the profession or labor of the party's occupation or calling. It has its origin in the inherent nature or mode of work of the profession or industry, and is the usual result or concomitant" (*Victory Sparker & Spec. Co.* v. *Franks,* 147 Md. 368; 128 A. 635).

[4] One of the most famous occupational disease cases in compensation insurance history diagnosed cancer as attributable to radon gas latent for 33 years. Workers swallowed particles of radium when they wet with their lips the tips of brushes used in painting numerals on watch and clock dials. The lethal nature of the process was unknown until death occurred. Such delayed effects of new materials or processes cause considerable concern for insurers. Other cancer victims have also been held to be covered for compensation payments (see *Utter* v. *Austin Hill Mfg. Co.,* 309 A, 2d 583, reported in *Weekly Underwriter,* January 12, 1974, p. 58).

changed their employment, yet the employers for whom they are working at the time their disease reaches a stage resulting in incapacity must bear the entire brunt of the compensation.[5] The tendency of many large employers to require preemployment physical examinations may discourage the hiring of partially incapacitated workers.

Types of benefits under the laws

The basic types of benefits include (1) *medical expenses,* (2) *income* benefits, (3) *death* benefits, and (4) *rehabilitation* benefits, which almost all of the states now provide.

Medical benefits. *Medical expenses* are a primary benefit, and all states now provide for *unlimited* or full coverage by law or administrative action. About one third of all benefits are for medical expenses. In previous years, in some states dollar limitations on total medical expenses applied, but these limits have been removed in all states except Georgia ($5,000) and New Mexico ($40,000).

Income benefits. Although the benefits for loss of *income* often differ by state, there are points of similarity in all the acts. Definite schedules of benefits are provided for different types of disability. While in certain cases lump-sum settlements may be made, it is usual to provide for the payment of benefits on a weekly basis. When used, the lump-sum benefits are in lieu of weekly benefits. For example, perhaps $25,000 might be paid for the loss of a leg or an arm, or $15,000 for an eye. The states vary greatly in terms of the size of the lump-sum settlement. Illustrative of the extremes are: for a hand, $9,200 in New Jersey, but $58,000 in Illinois; for a foot, $6,000 in North Dakota, but $38,000 in Hawaii; for loss of hearing of both ears, $17,000 in Maryland, but $60,000 in Massachusetts. Variations result from such factors as the types of industries in the state, average incomes, and many other political, social, and economic differences.

To discourage malingering, the more common weekly benefit is set at a fraction of the injured employee's weekly wage. This ranges from 55 to 90 percent of the average weekly wage,[6] subject to a sum set as a maximum and another set as a minimum. Thus, a typical state might allow 66⅔ percent of the injured employee's weekly wage but would in no case allow a sum in excess of $150 or below a minimum of $30. When the law provides a minimum, this does not mean that an injured employee whose average wage is less than the minimum will receive the minimum amount as compensation.

A maximum total payment is usually set in terms of amount, or as a multi-

---

[5] An exception exists in those states with "second-injury funds" (see later section of this chapter).

[6] Typically, the proportion is about 75 percent of *take-home* pay, having increased quite rapidly from 54 percent in 1972 ("State Worker's Compensation Now Replaces 75% of Injured Worker's 'Spendable Earnings,'" *Journal of American Insurance,* Winter 1975–76, p. 16).

ple of the weekly benefit, or in terms of both. Normally the duration is life or the period of disability, but about a half dozen states limit the duration to six to ten years of payments.

In order to eliminate the excessive expense of handling small losses and to prevent malingering when the injury is of no serious consequence, some laws provide a period of from a few days to one week during which no compensation is paid. This interval is called a "waiting period," and it acts as a kind of deductible. This period is now decreasing in most states to about three days, and often full retroactive payment is provided for losses of more than two weeks.

An important feature of compensation legislation is fixing with as much detail as possible the exact benefit due in each specific type of injury. Substantial variations appear in the provisions of the acts of the various states, but the following injuries or disabilities are usually specifically provided for: (*a*) fatal injury, (*b*) temporary total disability, (*c*) permanent total disability, (*d*) temporary partial disability, and (*e*) permanent partial disability. Some laws provide benefits in the case of such disfigurements as might be a handicap in securing employment.

The trend in the level of income benefits has been upward. Maximum weekly benefits, for example, have gone up, and time and amount limits have also increased. The size of the increases has not been as rapid as the general wage level rises, but other factors are also present. One is the fact that the federal OASDHI program also provides benefits for serious disabilities (total and permanent). In some cases disabled workers can collect from both workers' compensation and OASDHI a total benefit of up to 80 percent of their wages before they were disabled. The limitation (since 1966) is appropriate because these disability income payments are tax-free, making them as much as or somtimes even more than net normal earnings.

Death benefits. Some of the states with lifetime benefits, for total and permanent disabilities or death, have some amount limit in their law. Different limits are often set for maximums applicable to workers, as opposed to widows and dependents. *Death benefits* for survivors, for example, vary from $16,000 (Massachusetts) to $250,000 (Illinois).

Rehabilitation benefits. The value of *rehabilitation services* has been recognized by many insurers in recent years. The employee benefits by being rehabilitated or by being permitted to return to work at the earliest possible date. The cost of the claim to the insurer is reduced. The employer gets the worker back on the job sooner, and this ultimately reduces the cost of the insurance to the employer. In spinal cord injuries, for example, the average hospital stay can be reduced to four months at a rehabilitation center.[7] Nearly all of the state laws now provide for rehabilitation benefits as a logical and important part of workers' compensation.

---

[7] "Workers' Compensation: The Claims Dollar under Pressure," *Journal of American Insurance,* Summer 1977, p. 8.

Administration of the laws

While in some five[8] jurisdictions the administration of compensation law is left with the courts, the more usual method is to leave it with a special *state commission* (or administrator) appointed for the purpose. When the courts have jurisdiction, cases are heard by a judge or by a referee appointed by the judge.

In the interests of simplification and to expedite the settlement of disputed points, legislatures have preferred the appointment of a commission. These commissions have been invested with varying powers to make rules and regulations for the purpose of carrying out the provision of the compensation act. The state compensation administration is quasi-judicial, but much more supervisory and administrative. Commissions are given authority to appoint investigators to hear the evidence and make decisions. Most states use an agreement method in which employer and employee agree on the benefit amounts, subject to approval by the state authority. In the absence of fraud, the decision of the commission upon all questions of fact is usually final, but questions of law may always be appealed to the courts.

Financing of the benefits under the laws

It is the employer who has the direct responsibility for paying benefits to qualified workers in accordance with the workers' compensation laws. Indirectly, the consumer may be paying these costs if the product is one of relatively inelastic demand (where price increases do not decrease sales).

To guarantee that the benefits will be paid to the worker, employers are required in all states to have some form of insurance. In many states they are given a choice among private insurers, state funds, and self-insurance. The next section of this chapter explains these alternatives available to the employer.

Regardless of the insurance method chosen, the cost of workers' compensation benefits are substantial. Nationally, the cost of workers' compensation is over $10 billion a year. The costs vary considerably by state, type of occupation, and individual business firm. The general level of benefits is determined by the state laws which set forth the medical and income percentage, the duration, and the minimum and maximum payments. Different classifications have extremely different costs, as the rates may vary from a few cents per $100 of payroll for such classes as office workers to over $30 per $100 for hazardous occupations such as sawmill operators and steeplejacks.

Workers' compensation is obviously a major cost factor for many businesses. Humanitarian objectives, too, are significant, for many occupational injuries or diseases may be prevented. The financial incentive which employers have

---

[8] *Analysis of Workers' Compensation Laws* (Washington, D.C.: Chamber of Commerce of the United States, published annually) lists Alabama, Louisiana, New Mexico, Tennessee, and Wyoming.

under the workers' compensation laws which make them responsible and under the rating plans for insurance (see later section) has been the cause of industrial loss prevention with commendable results. Accident frequency and severity have been reduced by about one half during the past 40 years. Still, the overall costs of workers' compensation to business and industry are important, as these costs normally range from 1 to 2 percent of payroll from year to year.

WORKERS' COMPENSATION INSURERS

Employers are usually offered options as to how they shall guarantee the payment of workers' compensation claims. Insurance may be provided either through a *state fund* or by *private insurers* (stock, mutual, or reciprocal) authorized by the particular state to transact the business of workers' compensation. The exact requirements of the various states differ. Table 22–1 summarizes the number of states (1) in which the state fund has a monopoly[9]

Table 22–1. How insurance requirements of the state workers' compensation laws can be met in various states*

Type of insurer	Number of states
1. Private insurer	32
2. Competitive state fund	12
3. Monopolistic state fund	6

* In addition to the use of private insurers or state funds (of indicated two types), 47 states permit larger employers to qualify as self-insurers if they meet certain requirements.
Source: *Analysis of Workers' Compensation Laws* (Washington, D.C.: Chamber of Commerce of the United States, published annually).

of the compensation business, (2) the state funds are in competition with private insurers, and (3) the business of compensation insurance is entrusted to private insurers. As an alternative in each of the three groups, in 47 states employers who can provide satisfactory proof of financial ability may carry their own risk; that is, they may *self-insure*.[10]

[9] The "monopolistic state fund" means that the state is the *only* source of workers' compensation insurance and that private insurers may not write any workers' compensation insurance for risks in these states. The six states are: Ohio, West Virginia, Nevada, North Dakota, Wyoming, and Washington. The first two and the last named permit self-insurance as an alternative.

[10] Self-insurance is not permitted in Nevada, North Dakota, Texas, and Wyoming, although in Texas some risks are in effect self-insured by using a "fronting" policy. The 12 states that use "competitive state funds" include the large industrial states of New York, Pennsylvania, Michigan, and California.

From time to time the question of whether or not a state shall establish or abolish a *state fund* becomes a political question. Advocates of the state fund contend (1) that since workers' compensation insurance is virtually compulsory, it should be the duty of the state to provide a means for buying the insurance; (2) that with respect to a compulsory coverage it is inappropriate that it be a source of profit to private insurance; and (3) that since the cost of workers' compensation insurance is a cost of production, to allow a profit reflects an unnecessary charge to the consumer. State funds currently pay about one fourth of all workers' compensation benefits.

In answer to this, those who favor private insurance (1) raise the question as to whether a state fund does, in fact, provide protection at the lowest possible cost, because in the absence of competition inefficiency in management may evidence itself; (2) point out that competition affords a superior service[11] to policyholders, providing insurance on an interstate basis and that private insurers provide employers' liability protection, medical expense coverage, and other forms of protection not available through a state fund; (3) argue that under private insurance the cost is definitely established, whereas under a state fund an unseen cost may develop if the taxpayer is called upon to subsidize the fund to maintain its solvency; and finally (4) emphasize that in a system of private enterprise any activity that may be carried on to advantage by private business establishments should not be delegated to the government. Private insurers pay about 60 percent of all workers' compensation benefits paid each year.

The pros and cons of private insurers versus state funds are difficult to remove from political considerations. All of the six states with monopolistic funds have had the funds in existence for many years, and these states are very reluctant to give up or change a system that has been in operation for so long a time. The only major change from a monopolistic to a competitive state fund occurred in Oregon in 1965. One investigation of that state fund, which compared it with private insurers in Massachusetts, concluded that the private insurers provided superior marketing and administrative services and higher benefits at a somewhat increased cost.[12] The factors are complex; and the influence of unions, employers (large versus small, sometimes), insurers, and other interest groups is crucial in assessing the chances for a change to a competitive system.[13]

The question of whether or not to *self-insure* the risk of workers' compensation is another important decision for most of the larger employers. The

---

[11] "State Funds for Workers' Compensation: A False Economy," *Journal of American Insurance,* Winter 1977–78, p. 28.

[12] Mark R. Greene, "Marketing Efficiency and Workmen's Compensation—A Case Study," *Journal of Insurance,* vol. 24, no. 4 (December 1962), pp. 467–502.

[13] T. L. Gerlacher, "Should Private Insurance Companies Be Permitted to Write Workmen's Compensation Insurance in Ohio?" (M.B.A. thesis, Ohio State University, 1967).

general arguments in favor of self-insurance are the alleged lower administrative costs, minimization of litigation and quicker delivery of benefits, encouragement of rehabilitation, improved cash flow in claims payments, increased managerial benefits of direct contact between employer and employee, and increased incentives for accident prevention.[14] The choice is not a simple one, for it involves careful consideration of the *particular* employer in a particular occupational group in a particular state or states at the present time. Critics of self-insurance point out the increased administrative and claims payment burden on a self-insured employer, the loss of a third-party guarantor of benefits and buffer between employer and employee, difficulties of obtaining excess insurance, and the decrease in valuable loss prevention and loss-analysis services by the insurer.[15]

Self-insurance is quite common for large employers. With high loss frequency and sufficient spread of risk[16] the workers' compensation peril becomes one of the best examples of the use of self-insurance plans. Estimates of the total coverage of this type indicate that about 15 percent of workers' compensation losses are paid by self-insurers.

THE STANDARD WORKERS' COMPENSATION AND EMPLOYERS' LIABILITY POLICY

There is no standard workers' compensation policy in the sense that a standard form is required by statutory enactment. Because of the diversity of the compensation laws as enacted in the various states, insurers developed a standard form sufficiently broad to meet the requirements of insureds and at the same time meet the legal demands in each jurisdiction. The form is known as the "standard workers' compensation and employers' liability policy."

That the policy has served well is evidenced by the fact that only one major revision, in 1954, has occurred since its introduction more than 50 years ago. The revision reduced to a minimum the number of endorsements necessary, and the majority of policies are issued to the average risk without endorsements. There are a few situations, due to statutory requirements, manual rules, or underwriting practices, in which endorsements are still required.[17]

---

[14] Ralph R. Adams, "Advantages to Self-Insuring Workers' Compensation," *Risk Management*, December 1977, p. 10.

[15] C. Paul Kipp, "Evaluating the Feasibility of Self-Insuring Workers' Compensation," *Risk Management*, December 1977, p. 15. See also James S. Trieschmann and E. J. Leverett, Jr., "Self-Insurance of Workers' Compensation Losses," *Journal of Risk and Insurance*, vol. 44, no. 4 (December 1978), p. 635.

[16] For one method of analyzing this, see Larry D. Grant and Maurice E. McDonald, *Examining Employers' Financial Capacity to Self-Insure under Workers' Compensation* (Atlanta: Georgia State University, 1977).

[17] See Albert J. Millus and Willard J. Gentile, *Workers' Compensation Law and Insurance* (New York: Roberts Publishing Co., 1976). The new form is approved for use in 43 states and the District of Columbia, but it does not apply in Arizona or the 6 states which have monopolistic state funds.

The standard provisions for workers' compensation and employers' liability policies follow the pattern of liability policies with four main divisions: (1) declarations, (2) insuring agreements, (3) exclusions, and (4) conditions. Efforts have been made to follow the language of comparable provisions in liability policies. This rule makes for consistency and contributes to the understanding of both forms of insurance.

Declarations

The declarations consist of five items and cover such pertinent information as the name of the insured, the policy period, the states in which operations are carried on, and liability limits for employers' liability. The premium basis, rates, and classification of operations required by the insurer appear here. Basically the declarations provide the underwriting data relied upon by the insurer for the issuance of the policy.

Item 1 calls for the name of the insured, the address, the form of business organization, and all of the usual permanent workplaces of the insured.

Item 2 states the policy period. The policy runs from 12:01 A.M. standard time at the address of the insured. This reference is very important in the case of a risk that extends to a number of states and includes more than one time zone.

Item 3 is perhaps one of the most important of all the declarations. It states that coverage A of the policy applies to the workers' compensation law and any occupational disease law of the state or states listed, thus providing insurance for the entire liability of the insured under those laws. The policy covers all operations of the insured in the state or states listed. In the case of a concern operating on a nationwide basis, item 3 may list the states to be covered by inserting "all states except . . ." The excepted states are then listed. When this practice is followed, states with monopolistic state funds, states in which the insurer is not qualified to write compensation insurance, and states in which the insured is not within the provisions of the workers' compensation law must be listed as exceptions. An alternative method of obtaining wide geographic coverage is to use an "all-states" endorsement, which many insurers recommend.

Item 4 classifies the operations of the insured. The estimated total annual remuneration of all employees is given as a premium basis. The rates per $100 of payroll are listed together with the minimum premium, the total estimated annual premium, and the deposit premium. If premium adjustments are to be made on a semiannual, quarterly, or monthly basis, this is indicated.

Item 5 supplies a single limit to apply to the employers' liability feature of the coverage. Sometimes provision is made for a different limit of liability for certain operations, and in some states there are special requirements clarified by endorsement. This limit applies only to employers' liability coverage and not to workers' compensation. Compensation benefits are all fixed by the law.

Insuring agreements

There are four sections to the insuring agreements, designated by roman numerals. Insuring agreement I concerns coverage A for the insured's liability under the *workers' compensation* laws, and coverage B provides an *employers' liability* coverage with respect to injuries and sicknesses arising out of and in the course of employment. Insuring agreement II covers the matters of defense, settlement, and supplementary payments. Insuring agreement III provides for definitions. Insuring agreement IV is concerned with limiting liability to disease or injury that originates within the policy term.

Basic coverages. The standard workers' compensation and employers' liability policy basically affords the insured a twofold coverage in *insuring agreement I*:

> Coverage A—Workers' Compensation
> To pay promptly when due all compensation and other benefits required of the insured by the workers' compensation law.
> Coverage B—Employers' Liability
> To pay on behalf of the insured all sums which the insured shall become legally obligated to pay as damages because of bodily injury by accident or disease, including death at any time resulting therefrom, sustained in the United States of America, its territories or possessions, or Canada[18] by any employee of the insured arising out of and in the course of employment by the insured either in operations in a state designated in Item 3 of the declaration or in operations necessary or incidental thereto.

Coverage A takes notice of the definition of "workers' compensation law." This is defined in insuring agreement III and applies with respect to the state or states indicated in the declarations. If a state has a separate occupational disease law, coverage A of the policy covers the liability of the insured under that law, unless it is specifically excluded from the policy by endorsement.

Coverage B provides protection for the employer who is faced with a common-law or employers' liability claim. It is quite possible that such a claim be filed, particularly in those states providing employees with the option of coming within the operation of the compensation act. In most but not all states the workers' compensation acts have the effect of repealing employers' liability laws and terminating common-law liability. In addition to liability coverage for injury, a broad common-law disease coverage is afforded. It is to be noticed that the word *disease* appears in coverage B, and not the words *occupational disease*. Thus, coverage is afforded with respect to a liability claim attributable to any disease to which the employment may be alleged as a contributing cause.

Coverage B has the effect of including liability claims for injuries not covered by the compensation laws. Even though groundless, these claims will

---

[18] Worldwide coverage is provided, if exposures are temporary.

be defended by the insurer. Coverage B affords protection only with respect to injuries "arising out of and in the course of employment." This means that a claim for coverage must be traceable to the operations of the insured in a state specified in the declarations. Other claims would be covered by one of the standard liability policies. To avoid duplication in coverage there is usually an exclusion in liability policies with respect to employers' liability.

Since compensation benefits are fixed by law, there is no limitation with respect to them in the policy. A policy limit for coverage B is established in the declarations. A widely used limitation is $100,000, although for many business institutions this limit is not considered adequate and the insured may elect higher limits of $500,000 or $1 million.

Defense and settlement. *Insuring agreement II* is similar in effect to like clauses in liability insurance coverages. The clause obligates the insurer to defend the insured and places the matter of negotiation and settlement with the insurer alone. There is the usual requirement to pay bond premiums and expenses in effecting a settlement and to reimburse the insured for reasonable expenses incurred at the insurer's request. Such expenses incurred are all in excess of the limit of liability with respect to liability coverages and in addition to the amounts required to be paid under a compensation law.

Definitions. *Insuring agreement III* concerns definitions, closely coordinated with the coverages provided under insuring agreement I, which uses such broad terms as *the workers' compensation, states* and *bodily injury by accident or disease.*

Definition (*a*) ties the term *workers' compensation laws* as found in coverage A to the state or states indicated in item 3 of the declaration. If the state has a separate occupational disease law, coverage A provides occupational disease coverage. In a state having separate laws for compensation and occupational disease, if it is the intent of the insured to provide coverage for accidental injuries only and not for occupational disease, the coverage not to be provided must be specifically excluded from the policy endorsement. The definition of "workers' compensation law" does not include the U.S. Longshoremen's and Harbor Workers' Compensation Act.[19] Finally, the definition states that it "does not include those provisions of any such law which provide nonoccupational disability benefits."[20]

Definition (*b*) makes the word *state* mean any state or territory of the United States and the District of Columbia, if listed in the declarations.

Definition (*c*) clarifies the meaning of "bodily injury by accident" and "bodily injury by disease" in such a way that it would be impossible for an

---

[19] Because of the wide difference in longshoremen's risks, they are only included in the definition by endorsement. The insurer is thus afforded an opportunity to underwrite maritime risks apart from other lines.

[20] By virtue of an extension of the New York Compensation Law, nonoccupational disability benefits are brought within that law. The clause is incorporated in the policy to exclude coverage for nonoccupational disabilities.

injured employee to claim an accidental injury and then to hold the insurer liable for an occupational disease disability if a disease followed as a result of the injury. Under the terms of the definition, any given injury may be one or the other, but it cannot be both.

Definition (*d*) is usual to liability policies and provides that with respect to coverage B, assault and battery shall be deemed an accident unless committed by or at the direction of the insured.[21]

Time of losses. *Insuring agreement IV* has two parts. The first part of the agreement states that the policy applies only to an injury occurring during the policy period. The second part makes the insurer liable for an occupational disease that has developed over a long period of time. In the case of silicosis, for example, an employee may be exposed over a period of years during which the workers' lungs are gradually becoming affected. If the worker has been working in granite quarries and is now found to be disabled, even though several insurers provided coverage over the years, the one covering when the last injurious exposure developed assumes the liability.[22]

[handwritten: → Exception – 2nd Injury fund]

Exclusions

There are six exclusions. Other workers' compensation insurance, including coverage as a qualified self-insurer, is excluded in order to avoid duplicate coverage. Domestic or farm employment is excluded unless it is covered by the compensation law or described in the declarations. The remaining exclusions apply only under coverage B, the employers' liability coverage. The policy does not apply to assumed liability in a contract, to punitive damages for employees hired in violation of law or to any such employees hired in violation of law with the knowledge of the insured, to suits filed after 36 months after the end of the policy, or to obligations under unemployment or disability benefits laws of the states. The last exclusion also excludes employers' liability coverage for any obligations under workers' compensation or occupational disease laws of the states designated in the declarations section of the policy.

Conditions

The conditions follow closely those in policies making use of the national standard provisions program for liability policies. Most pertain either to calculation and payment of the premium, or to the settlement of losses.

---

[21] As in the case of all other accidents, an assault to be compensable must be one "arising out of and in the course of employment" (*Heiz* v. *Ruppert*, 218 N.Y. 148). If the assault is not compensable and suit is brought against the insured for the purpose of coverage B, the assault is held to be an accident and the insurer will provide defense.

[22] A few states require contributions from successive insurers of the same employee. In these states the policy is endorsed amending insuring agreement **IV** so that this policy condition complies with the state law.

Conditions relating to the premium. *Condition 1* of the policy deals with the manner of premium computation. Compensation premiums are computed as a percentage of the payroll of the insured. The premium that an employer must pay depends on (*a*) type of business (*b*) number of employees, and (*c*) total amount of remuneration that is paid to them. This information is found in the declarations.

The first paragraph of condition 1 incorporates by reference "the manuals in use by the company." By virtue of this clause the preparation of the policy is enormously simplified. If an employer should carry on operations not mentioned in the declarations, the premium will be computed for those operations by the use of manual rates. The insured, moreover, agrees that any change in classifications, rates, or rating plans or any changes in benefits provided by the workers' compensation law all become a part of the policy by the issuance of an endorsement by the insurer.

The second paragraph describes what is meant by "remuneration," and that the remuneration of all employees engaged in operations covered by the policy, whether executive officers or not, shall be included. The payroll submitted for determining the compensation premium includes all other persons performing work "which may render the company liable under this policy for injury to or death of such persons." This means, for example, that if employers sublet work, they must include the payroll of subcontractors in their compensation premium unless those subcontractors already carry their own compensation insurance.

The third paragraph explains that since workers' premiums are based on the actual payroll for the period covered, they cannot be computed until the end of the policy term. The policy is written with an estimated payroll. At the end of the policy term an audit is made; and if the estimated premium is in excess of the actual premium developed by the audit, the difference is returned to the insured. On the other hand, if the estimated premium is less than the premium developed by the audit, the insured is billed for the difference. If the risk is a particularly large one, arrangements may be made to determine the premium due on a periodic basis shorter than a year.

The fourth paragraph places an obligation on the insured to maintain all the necessary records for the purpose of computing the premium. The insurer may elect to ask the insured to forward those records for the purpose of computation of premium. However, except for small employers, it is the practice of the insurer to send an auditor to the office of the insured and there check payrolls and records. The right of the insurer is limited to "the information necessary for premium computation" and not to any other records or files.

The fifth paragraph of condition 1 precludes any misunderstanding by clearly stating that the premium is an estimated one.

Condition 2 covers the matter of policies written for a period longer than one year. It makes all the provisions of the policy, including premiums and coverage amounts, apply separately to each consecutive 12-month period.

Conditions relating to loss settlement. Most of the remaining conditions in the standard workers' compensation and employers' liability policy have already been noticed in connection with previous insurance contracts. Several of the clauses specify rights of the *insurer* to (1) inspection and audit of the insured's books; (2) written notice of injuries, claims, or lawsuits, as soon as practicable; (3) assistance and cooperation of the insured in hearings, trials, obtaining witnesses, and the like; (4) proportional contribution from other insurance payable for covered losses; (5) subrogation for payments made under the contract; and (6) assignment of the contract only when the insurer consents to it in an endorsement.

Rights of the *insured* are also explained in several of the conditions. The insured who has complied with the policy terms has the right of action against the insurer if the employers' liability benefits are not paid as provided. Changes in the policy may be made by endorsement, and all terms in conflict with the compensation law are made to conform to it. The insured may cancel the contract at any time, and the insured also has the right to ten days' notice in case the insurer cancels.

One condition (8) introduces a feature not usually found in liability coverages. In addition to protecting the named insured, the policy states that the provisions of the insuring clause relating to workers' compensation or employers' liability are the *direct obligation* of the insuring company *to any insured employee* (or, in the case of death, to dependents). Since the contract is made primarily for the benefit of employees and their dependents, they have a direct right of action against the insurer. Only recently have some auto and other liability contracts included such a right.

The policy further provides that the obligations of the insurer to the employee shall not be affected by the failure of the employer in any way to comply with the policy requirements. Examples are default by the employer in the payment of the premium after an accident, failure to give the insurer the notice required by the policy, and death, insolvency, bankruptcy, legal incapacity, or inability of the employer. A notice to the employer of an injury is presumed to be notice to the insurer.

SPECIAL RATING PLANS

In addition to the classifications and rates referred to in the declarations, which provide the basis for workers' compensation premium costs, the insured may have several opportunities to benefit from individual risk rating plans. These features include (1) experience rating plans, (2) premium discount plans, (3) retrospective rating plans.

These plans are the basic rating modifications applied to average rates that are derived first from total industry group statistics. These data are subdivided into industry groups such as "manufacturing," contracting," and so on, and then into more than 700 classifications of industrial products or processes, for each of which a "manual" rate is set.

Experience rating plans

Experience rating plans are based upon the *past loss experience* of the *particular risk* under consideration. All states permit experience rating. If the loss history shows a cost below normal for the class, a credit in the rate is allowed, while an unfavorable experience results in a debit. The credit is applied to the manual rate to find the new or adjusted rate. When the risk is very large, with a "credibility factor" of 1.00, the risk is said to be self-rated. To qualify for experience rating, the risk must produce a designated annual average premium figure at manual rates. In most states, the insured whose premium exceeds $750 per year must use the experience rating plan. For the purpose of determining experience, the plan requires a period of not less than one year and can usually include a maximum of three years.

The term *standard premium* is used to designate that premium determined by applying manual rates to the employer's payroll modified by experience rating. When the annual standard premium exceeds $1,000, two additional types of plans may further modify the premium charge. These include (*a*) the premium discount plan and (*b*) five retrospective rating plans.

The premium discount plan

Workers' compensation rating plans recognize that certain factors that enter into the premium charge do not increase proportionately as the premium increases. The principal factors considered are (*a*) losses, (*b*) claim expense, (*c*) engineering and accident prevention, (*d*) administration and payroll audit expenses, (*e*) acquisition costs, and (*f*) taxes. Under the premium discount plan a definite portion of the first $1,000 of premium is allocated for insurer expenses and acquisition costs. As the premium increases, it is the purpose of the plan to give credit for those expenses that do not increase proportionately. It is a mandatory device to reflect expense savings for larger risks. Premium in excess of $1,000 is grouped in brackets and a discount applied. The discount is greater in the higher brackets. The net effect of this plan is to provide a reduction from the standard premium as the premium increases in amount. The theory upon which these premiums are computed is sometimes referred to as the "principle of graded expense."

Retrospective rating plans

Retrospective rating plans differ from the experience rating plans mentioned above. Modification for |current loss| experience is the distinguishing feature of the retrospective plans. These plans are not separate and apart from experience rating but are, in effect, supplementary to it. While experience rating looks definitely to the past to determine the rate for the future, retrospective rating permits the insured to change the premium based upon losses of the current year. It is an optional arrangement for eligible risks whereby a premium will be computed based upon the losses which actually occurred during the policy period.

At the inception date of the policy the actual anticipated experience can only be estimated. Under the retrospective plan, if the experience is particularly good, a credit is reflected in the premium charge. If the experience is unsatisfactory, the cost to the insured is reflected in an increased premium. For the protection of the insured, upper limits to the cost are established; and for the protection of the insurance company, lower limits are established. Individual claims included in the loss experience are often limited beforehand to stipulated maximum amounts, such as $10,000. The term *cost plus* has sometimes been applied to this rating plan.

In actual operation the plan provides for three premiums: (1) the minimum retrospective premium, (2) the maximum retrospective premium, and (3) the retrospective premium. The plan provides that the insured shall pay in any case the premium known as the minimum retrospective premium. On the other hand, the insured can never be called upon to pay more than the maximum retrospective premium. The premium that the insured will actually pay will probably fall somewhere between the two; this is known as the "retrospective premium." It is determined by adding to the basic premium the losses incurred, modified to provide for taxes and claim adjustment expenses.

The retrospective rating plan gives the insured the same credit for decreasing administration and acquisition expenses as does the premium discount plan. In addition, however, the retrospective rating plan reflects current losses in the current premium charge. This is, in fact, a protected profit-sharing plan. With a good experience, the insured shares the profits. With an unfavorable experience, the amount of loss in any year is subject to a definite limit. This is particularly attractive because the insured gets immediate credit for lower loss experience. From the point of view of the insurer, the plan is equally attractive because anything that will stimulate loss-reduction activity on the part of the insured will in the long run reflect to the benefit of the insurer. Overall, one of the most important effects of the compensation rating plans is the direct incentive that they provide to all parties to use the best loss-prevention and loss-reduction techniques.

There are five forms of retrospective rating: plans A, B, C, and J, which apply to workers' compensation only, and plan D, which may also apply to liability, automobile, burglary, and glass insurance. These plans are alike in principle but vary in detail, principally with reference to the fixing of the maximum and minimum premiums. In addition, several states have adopted retrospective plans of their own. All of the plans, however, are alike in that they aim to have the current premium based upon the loss experience of the current year.

As rating plans and electronic data processing capabilities have broadened in availability and application, the retrospective plans have increased in popularity. Techniques and costs have been refined so that the use of such plans is spreading to more types of insurance (with high loss frequencies) and more insureds.

SECOND-INJURY FUNDS

With the increasing use of experience and retrospective rating, attention has been focused on all of the factors that may increase or reduce loss experience and hence workers' compensation cost. Great emphasis has been placed upon accident-prevention service, and it has been natural to consider physical factors. This has directed attention to employees so incapacitated that a second injury would result in total disability.

The term *second injury* in compensation parlance refers to an injury that taken in connection with a previous injury will result in an incapacity greater than would have resulted had there been no previous injury. For example, persons who have lost an eye or a hand could become totally incapacitated as a result of losing the remaining eye or hand. Unless the statutes provide specifically to the contrary, the cost of disability arising out of the second injury reflects upon the employer in whose employ the second injury is sustained. The result of this situation is to place an undue burden upon the employer who employs the already seriously injured person.

To counteract this situation and to encourage employers to hire already handicapped workers, most states[23] have by statute limited the liability of the current employer to the disability resulting from the second injury. The statutes in such circumstances provide that after having received all of their regular compensation benefits from their employers, such injured workers will be entitled to additional weekly benefits during the continuance of incapacity out of the *second-injury fund* administered by the state. It is usual to provide that the fund be financed by contributions from insurers writing compensation insurance. Payments for the second-injury disabilities are made out of this fund. If the injury is total, special compensation is provided. It is also provided that if the injured worker is able to secure employment but not at the level of previous employment, the worker may receive compensation based upon the difference between present and past weekly earnings, before the second injury occurred.

---

[23] *Analysis of Workers' Compensation Laws.*

WORKERS' COMPENSATION INSURANCE LOSSES

More than 2 million persons a year are hurt at work in the United States, according to the National Safety Council, which estimates the annual compensation payments and production losses at $16 billion, including 245 million workdays in time lost annually. No wonder employers are concerned about rising workers' compensation costs!

Claims for injury or disease made by workers against employers are (a) compensation claims or (b) liability claims. The adjustment of compensation claims follows a different pattern from the adjustment of liability claims based on negligence. The compensation claim investigation concerns itself with coverage and with the nature and extent of the injury without the necessity of determining negligence. The liability feature of the policy provides liability protection when for some reason the injury or the injured employee is not within the protection of the compensation act and negligence by the employer must be shown.

Compensation claims are based upon the provisions of a workers' compensation act or an occupational disease act. All liabilities with which the employer might be charged under the acts are assumed by the insurer. Benefits are prescribed in the acts. Workers' compensation insurance is, in fact, group accident and sickness insurance limited to occupational disabilities. Not only do the acts relieve the injured workers of the necessity of proving negligence, but they also usually deny them the right to sue under the common law.

Common-law *liability* may be brought, however, by employees against employers for disability that does not come within the scope of the compensation acts, such as, for example, occupational diseases that are not compensable. To hold the employer liable, the employee must be able to show that the contraction or aggravation of the disease was caused by the negligence of the employer. There is no statutory limit to such common-law suits. Insurance covers for a specific limit of employers' liability.

Compensation acts are "liability without fault" statutes and establish a uniform payment for the injured employee that is measured by the nature and the extent of the injury. The standard of recovery varies from state to state but is in every instance fixed by the legislature. The amount of the award for any compensable injury is not a problem for the insurer, except that it must follow the employer-employee agreement procedure specified by the particular state. In establishing arbitrary awards for compensation claims, which are in many instances less than could be anticipated in negligence cases, the legislatures have based the amount of these awards on the assumption that prompt payment without delays, costs, and litigation is better for all parties than fuller compensation subject to such contingencies.[24]

Compensation laws require that an injured employee give *notice* of an

---

[24] *Ruso* v. *Omaha & Council Bluffs Street Railway*, 98 Neb. 436; 153 N.W. 510.

accident or injury within a specified period, usually 30 days. The time limit for diseases is longer. Upon receiving notice of the injury of an employee, the employer proceeds immediately to notify the insurer and the industrial commission. As in all insurance investigations, the adjuster first determines the coverage. The first step following a loss notice is to determine that the injury reported was one "arising out of and in the course of employment." The injured person is interviewed, and usually a signed statement is taken. Signed statements are also taken from any available witness to the accident as a part of the routine investigation. A death case may require a postmortem examination in order to determine compensability. If an autopsy is required, steps must be taken to secure the consent of relatives. The death certificate, coroner's reports, newspaper reports, and the like are all sources of information.

The adjuster incorporates all pertinent data in a *report* to the insured. The effect of the injury on the particular individual, a written report of the attending physician, any suggestions with respect to treatment, and any subrogation possibilites are included. When a final appraisal of the disability has been made, a complete breakdown of benefits due by weeks and amounts is determined.

The report will also cover payments for *medical benefits* as provided in the compensation act or any expected payments that are anticipated. The adjuster is particularly interested in seeing that the disabled person receives proper medical care. At present in most jurisdictions there is no limit on the amount or on the period of time for which the employer is obligated to provide medical care. This is considered good business from the point of view of the injured employee, the employer, and the insurer. The best medical care will operate to reduce the period for which indemnity payments are required.

At the conclusion of the investigation, the adjuster undertakes to reach an *agreement* with the employee with respect to compensation under the provisions of the act. When such an agreement is reached, a memorandum concerning the details, signed by all parties, is filed in the office of the compensation commission. If upon review the commission finds the agreement to be in conformity with the provisions of the compensation act, it is approved. If the insurance adjuster and the employee fail to reach an agreement in regard to the compensation, appeal for an award must be made to the commission. A petition for an award may be made; and after proper notice and hearings, a final decision is rendered by the commission.

OTHER POLICY BENEFITS

One of the most important benefits of workers' compensation insurance is the impetus to *loss-prevention* efforts that it provides to both insurer and insured. The individual risk rating plans have been shown to be of direct benefit to employers who lower their insurance costs by good loss experience. With rising costs, loss prevention and better employee motivation and understanding can be among the most effective controls of employers.

Loss prevention in industrial injuries and disease has also been achieved by considerable activities of the insurers, even though the workers' compensation contract does not legally oblige them to engage in such activities. The insurers inspect the workplaces covered and suggest to the insured such changes or improvements as may operate to reduce the number and severity of accidents. A high accident frequency may be attributable to poor management and indifference. Management sometimes overlooks hazards attributable to poor housekeeping, such as obstruction in passageways and aisles, slippery floors, lack of adequate handrails or guards, and the like. Improvements in housekeeping may be effected at modest cost. Safety meetings for the education of management and employees require some time and effort. If management is sincerely interested in reducing costs by improving its loss ratio and will cooperate with the inspection and engineering service of the insurer, improvement can frequently result.

Insureds realize that industrial injuries and diseases are a direct source of monetary loss. Work is interrupted; superintendents and others lose time from productive effort; machinery is broken and goods are spoiled because of the mental upset of witnesses to the accident. These and other factors tend to make the "hidden costs" of industrial accidents a serious drain, even though the employer's obligation to the injured worker is covered by insurance. These indirect costs, including such items as loss of time by other employees, the costs of replacement or rehiring, decreased productivity and morale, are estimated at four times the direct cost of workers' compensation insurance.[25]

Inspection service is becoming an increasingly important factor in the placing of compensation insurance. An unfavorable loss experience coupled with poor or indifferent management would place a business in the category of an undesirable risk from the insurer standpoint. On the other hand, hazardous occupations are insurable if management evidences an interest in loss-prevention activities. Some insurers have organized highly specialized engineering and research services for the purpose of investigating and studying extra-hazardous working conditions and of devising, if possible, safer methods and conditions. In new manufacturing processes where there is no previous industrial experience, the expert knowledge of experienced research engineers proves of great assistance in discovering safe methods. If a favorable experience is reflected in the premium, the direct saving is often substantial. Accident-prevention services provided by insurers include the following: (1) engineering consultation service, (2) periodic inspection service,

[25] H. W. Heinrich, *Industrial Accident Prevention* (New York: McGraw-Hill Book Co., 1950), pp. 50–61. This book is a classic pioneering effort in the field of loss prevention. See also Daniel C. Peterson, *Techniques of Safety Management* (New York: McGraw-Hill Co., 1971); and J. A. Grimaldi and R. H. Simons, *Safety Management* (Homewood, Ill.: Richard D. Irwin, 1975).

(3) employee and supervisor training programs, (4) distribution of informative materials, (5) claims services, (6) employee safety meetings, and (7) advisory committees to work with supervising officials.

OCCUPATIONAL SAFETY AND HEALTH ACT AND OTHER FEDERAL LAWS

Job safety for employees escalated to the top of the major workers' compensation issues with the passage of the *Occupational Safety and Health Act (OSHA) of 1970*. This federal law usurped from the state considerable control of work-safety regulations, and a state must put into effect rules at least as stringent as the federal standards if it wishes to maintain jurisdiction for work-safety conditions of employees within its borders. The penal (fines of $10,000 or more) and investigative rules of OSHA are extensive and far-reaching, with many employers feeling the effects of inspections across the nation by 1,400 federal compliance officers who are enforcing the safety regulations under the act. Although the long-range effects will be beneficial in creating a safer working environment and in preventing losses, employers must pay the costs, including the fines for OSHA violations. Insurers are facing potential increased liability if the laws are not met.

One pronounced effect of the Occupational Safety and Health Act of 1970 was the establishment of the National Commission on State Workers' Compensation Laws. Charged with the responsibility of "evaluating current state laws to determine if such laws provide an adequate, prompt, and equitable system of compensation," the commission published a comprehensive treatment of current state laws in 1973.[26] It specified 21 substantive minimum standards recommended to the state compensation systems, including unlimited medical care and rehabilitation benefits, higher income benefits, compulsory coverage of all employers and employees, and other changes. Many, but not all, of the states have improved their compensation laws to meet these standards.

The progress of OSHA has not been without difficulties. The Department of Labor, through the Occupational Safety and Health Administration, is responsible for setting the rules for legally permitted exposures to hazards in the workplace. Another organization, the National Institute for Occupational Safety and Health (NIOSH), works under the Department of Health, Education, and Welfare (HEW) in conducting occupational health research, and recommends standards for safe exposures to hazardous substances.

The scope of the immense task is illustrated by the fact that in 1977 the Labor Department rewrote the general industry standards in a 250-page document which *revoked* more than 1,100 regulations that were classified as

---

[26] National Commission on State Workmen's Compensation Laws, *Compendium on Workers' Compensation* (Washington, D.C.: U.S. Government Printing Office, 1973).

outdated or "nitpicking" job safety rules. Complaints from employers, unions, and even employees themselves mounted during the mid-1970s to encourage the revisions. Much detailed work remains to be done, especially as OSHA changes its regulatory focus from minor safety regulations and extends into the more ambitious health standards for such exposures as cancer-causing chemicals.[27] As OSHA tried to concentrate on major safety violations, the largest fines in OSHA history were levied in 1978 on several employers following citations for serious and willful violations in grain elevators (Farmers Export Company explosion, $116,000) and steel companies (U.S. Steel, $216,000).

One setback to OSHA authority occurred in early 1978. The U.S. Supreme Court ruled unconstitutional the unannounced inspections of workplaces. OSHA inspectors now may first have to obtain a search warrant from a judge, who may require proof that there is "probable cause" to believe that safety hazards or violations are present in a workplace. In actual practice, few employers are requiring federal OSHA inspectors to obtain search warrants, in spite of the fact that employers can do so under the present law.[28]

In recent years there has been increased pressure for *federalization* of the state workers' compensation acts to require minimum standards for workers' compensation laws in all the states. Such proposals have the desirable objectives of achieving greater uniformity among the states and of raising the coverage and benefit levels specified by some of the more limited states laws now in existence. However, the details and problems of applying workers' compensation standards on a national basis after more than 50 years of state jurisdiction are considerable. State rights versus federal rights are involved in this issue; increased costs may result for many employers; and reaching agreement upon the exact standards to be applied will not be easy.

FOR REVIEW AND DISCUSSION

1. Is the peril of occupational disability taken care of by "social" or "private" insurance in the United States? Explain your answer.

2. State workers' compensation laws are almost all *compulsory* laws. They are also either (a) *monopolistic* or (b) *competitive*. What do these terms mean?

3. Why have workers' compensation laws been adopted in all of the states? Shouldn't injured employees be able to show negligence on the part of the employer before the employer is held liable?

4. What kinds of benefits are provided by the workers' compensation laws? How are the amounts determined?

---

[27] Estimates made in 1978 were as high as $88 billion for the future costs of manufacturers and consumers in meeting standards for more than 2,000 toxic substances suspected of causing cancer.

[28] "Job-Safety Inspectors Seldom Required to Get Warrants Despite Justices' Ruling," *Wall Street Journal*, July 17, 1978, p. 10.

5. The workers' compensation policy provides (*a*) *liability* and (*b*) *compensation* coverage. What is the extent of the protection afforded?

6. Do workers' compensation laws cover all, or just some, employees? Explain, including reference to the changes that have occurred in this respect since the early workers' compensation laws.

7. Give an example of these types of disability: (*a*) temporary, (*b*) permanent partial, (*c*) permanent total, and (*d*) occupational disease.

8. There are a few monopolistic workers' compensation state funds, while some states offer state funds as an alternative to private insurance. Why, in your opinion, has not the state monopoly idea been more widely adopted?

9. Mrs. X is a salad maker in a restaurant and contracts a skin infection caused by handling vegetables. Is this an occupational disease? Would this be covered by the standard workers' compensation policy without endorsement? Illustrate why this peril is important.

10. Discuss the advantages and disadvantages which employers may have by "self-insuring" their workers' compensation responsibilities, as is possible in most states for larger employers.

11. It has been stated that insurers make it difficult for physically handicapped employees to secure employment because of increased costs under the experience-rated compensation plans. If you were an employer operating a large industrial plant, would you feel financially safe in employing persons already injured in industrial accidents or disabled veterans?

12. A.B. filed suit against his employer, claiming that he had contracted silicosis because the paint plant in which he worked was not properly ventilated. He was awarded $30,000, and a flood of suits from other employees followed. How would the position of the employer be better if the disease were covered by the compensation act?

13. What characteristics make the workers' compensation policy (*a*) simpler than other insurance contracts and (*b*) sometimes more difficult to write than other insurance contracts?

14. What special rating plans are used in workers' compensation insurance? Briefly explain their primary purposes.

15. Explain the importance of the following in workers' compensations insurance: (*a*) loss-prevention work, (*b*) "second-injury funds," (*c*) "self-insurance," and (*d*) rehabilitation.

16. What *types* of insurance do employers use to comply with the financial requirements of workers' compensation laws? Which of these types predominate?

17. How do workers' compensation contracts vary from other insurance contracts in their (*a*) loss provisions and (*b*) loss procedures for claims?

18. How is the *federal* government becoming more involved in (*a*) occupational disabilities and (*b*) workers' compensation plans?

19. One of the most significant laws concerning workers' compensation in the 1970s was the Occupational Safety and Health Act. Discuss its effects and difficulties.

Chapter 23

Concepts considered in Chapter 23—Automobile insurance—fault and no-fault

Automobile insurance is part of our "automobile economy" today, in which the car is both friend and foe. Problems for consideration include the needs for, the costs of, and the solutions provided by fault and no-fault insurance.

The need for automobile insurance is observed from:

Three viewpoints: society, the motorists, and the injured victims.

Growing concern of customers, insurers, agents, and government.

The cost of automobile insurance is a primary factor:

Increasing costs are substantial, particularly rising *liability losses.*

Rate regulation has aimed at maintaining—

Price competition among rating bureaus and independent insurers.

Nonprice competition, services by insurer and agent, also important.

State regulation uses three approaches: *prior approval, file and use,* and *open competition* rating laws.

Solutions to the need for automobile insurance are evolving.

Basic current and changing solutions have created changes in the tort liability system, and various proposals of a social insurance nature have been adopted to meet the problems.

Financial responsibility laws are the basic answer in most states to the need to encourage the purchase of automobile liability insurance.

Compulsory liability insurance is used in about half of the states; evidence of insurance must be shown before license plates are issued.

Automobile insurance (assigned risk) plans in all states assure almost everyone that liability insurance can be purchased.

Other "residual market" mechanisms include *reinsurance facilities, joint underwriting associations,* and, in one state, an automobile *state fund* insurer.

Unsatisfied judgment funds are used in five states; an innocent victim is paid for losses caused by financially irresponsible motorists.

Uninsured motorists coverage is available to insureds in all states, as one of the most successful methods devised for paying innocent victims.

Automobile no-fault insurance plans of several types may help alleviate the liability system problems of automobiles. Insurers and states are experimenting with many "true," "modified," and "pseudo" no-fault plans, and with expanded first-party "add-on" coverages.

Another crucial solution is *automobile safety and loss prevention,* through the continued efforts of government and private insurance.

Automobile insurance—fault and no-fault

Every textbook author is a gambler to some degree, even (and perhaps especially) when insurance is the topic, because terminology and ideas fade so fast into history. Recording the past and present is *not* enough. In the quest for knowledge whose value is not for its own sake, the *real* value is knowledge for helping to shape the understanding and decisions of the future.

Take automobile insurance as an example, and note the title of this chapter. Probably no topic currently on the insurance scene is of greater importance, or in a state of greater change and uncertainty. Certainly no chapter that desires to have up-to-date relevance could be titled "tort" liability (fault) automobile insurance, yet it is not a reasonable prediction that the title should be only "no-fault" (not based on negligence). The title fault and no-fault implicitly carries the author's prediction, for the late 1970s and early 1980s at least, that the solutions for the future will contain both systems of automobile insurance. It is not expected that a simple choice will be made between fault and no-fault, but rather that the complex changes now in the making will adjust to a combination of both concepts.

For essential background, this chapter first discusses the *need* for automobile insurance today; then one of the basic factors, *cost*; and finally the current and changing *solutions,* including no-fault, which are being adopted by law and the insurance business to meet the needs of modern society.

THE NEED FOR AUTOMOBILE INSURANCE

One of the most obvious signs of affluence in the United States today is the number of automobiles—bulging over on the roads, the shopping centers, the parking lots, and even the eyesore auto graveyards. In suburbia a major problem is how to get two cars in a one-car garage, or three into a two-car garage!

Automobile—friend and foe

The "automobile economy" of the United States today is an amazing world of mobility, responsibility, and danger. It has provided many opportunities and advantages for work and recreation, yet at the same time it has created substantial risk and insurance problems. Could anyone really have imagined a generation or so ago that more than 140 *million* motor vehicles would be traveling today over our highways? Or could the awesome effects of this era in terms of death, injuries, and monetary costs have been predicted?

The annual toll has reached alarming proportions: about 50,000 persons killed, over 5 million persons injured, 26 million accidents, and at least $47 billion in lost wages, property damage, and legal medical, and insurance costs.[1] Almost 2 million American deaths have been due to highway accidents during the 20th century. Annual fatalities from automobiles are double the number caused by accidents in the home, 4 times the number caused by work accidents, 8 times the number resulting from fires, and 20 times the number resulting from aircraft and boating accidents.[2]

Automobile liability insurance

With such obvious needs for insurance protection, it is little wonder that the automobile insurance field has grown to a gigantic size, exceeding $30 billion in annual premiums. More than 60 percent of the premiums are for *liability* and related insurance, with the remainder for physical damage coverage on the automobile of the insured. Thus, many of the ideas discussed in previous chapters about employers' and general liability insurance also apply to automobile insurance. Automobile liability insurance deserves separate treatment, however, and this chapter presents some of the major issues and proposed solutions to its current problems. Chapter 24 will present the automobile coverages, especially the common "personal automobile policy" by which most private automobiles are insured today.

Viewpoints on the need

Three viewpoints are pertinent in appraising the need for automobile insurance, that of (1) the society, (2) the automobile motorist, and (3) the injured victims of automobile accidents. More than any other kind of voluntary insurance, automobile insurance must be looked at not only as an individual solution to an individual problem of risk but also in its *social* or public aspects. Among the responsible-thinking citizens in the United States, there is almost universal acceptance of the idea that everyone owning or using an automobile should purchase liability insurance. The uncertainty of financial disaster due to an automobile accident is so widespread a risk today that few persons are exempt from its possibility.

The losses are dramatic, and they are more often attributable to causes of human origin than most other losses. More than 87 percent of *all* traffic accidents are reported to involve *improper driving*, and in *fatal* accidents

---

[1] *Insurance Facts* (New York: Insurance Information Institute, 1978), p. 35–36.
[2] Ibid., pp. 36–37.

speeding is a factor in one third of the accidents and drinking drivers in about one half.[3] Automobile injuries of one person are often caused by, and traceable to, another person, but in many cases the multiple factors involved render it difficult to place responsibility for such accidents solely on one person.

The compromise method of treatment for the risk becomes partially individual and partially social in its methods and objectives. Some accidents are perhaps primarily the result of *social negligence.* For example, consider the effects of such underlying causes as the number of automobiles manufactured; the lack of adequate roads; improper engineering of highway grades, curves, and traffic signals; and weak driver-licensing laws and tests. The immediate cause of automobile accidents may *usually* be the "nut behind the wheel"—but perhaps the "freewheeling society" in which we live must shoulder its share of the blame, too.

The *individual* who owns or uses an automobile (or other motor vehicle) has some of the familiar risks which all property owners face. Part or all of the value of the automobile may be lost through a variety of perils, such as fire, theft, or collision. In addition, owners or drivers have an enormous risk in not knowing whether their automobiles will cause damage to the property of other persons, or injury to other persons, for which they may be held liable. Individuals or families may also suffer death or disability losses due to medical care expense and lost income as a result of an automobile accident. In summary, the individual risks require protection from all the important fields of insurance: (1) property, (2) liability, (3) life, and (4) health.

Another viewpoint from which automobile insurance should be considered is that of the victims. If they are *innocent victims,* certain legal rights accrue to them against the parties responsible for their property damage or personal injury loss. To obtain payment, they must usually prove the other party liable. Time and costs may be involved in carrying out the legal right, and even then the negligent parties may not be able to pay for the results of their irresponsibility. The result is that some innocent victims of automobile accidents remain uncompensated.

From *society's* viewpoint, the effects may be similar regardless of who was the cause of the accident. The victims and their families may become burdens of the government through various public welfare or social insurance programs.

The need to consider all of the three viewpoints in reaching a conclusion about how to treat the automobile risks suggests that some governmental action encouraging or requiring insurance is necessary. Each of the solutions discussed later in this chapter shows that this is true, although the method and extent of the requirements differ greatly in the various types of state laws designed to cope with the problem.

---

[3] Ibid., p. 36.

Growing concerns for the "automobile problem"

Somehow, in the ferment of the 1970s, automobile insurance has emerged as a prime target for criticism. For insurers it has become a major source of complaints. Everyone seems concerned about the "automobile problem." Customers are disturbed by rising costs, delays, and seeming inequities of coverage and claims payment. Insurers are trying to find answers in industry proposals and experimental plans, while complaining of rising losses and low profit margins. Agents have increasing difficulty in placing automobile insurance for many insureds—the young, the old, the accident repeater, and others.

Government bodies, including federal and state bodies, are also vitally concerned. A two-year, $2 million investigation by the Department of Transportation of the entire broad field of compensation of auto accident victims and the regulation of automobile insurance was published earlier in the decade.[4] Numerous U.S. Senate inquiries have been conducted on rating systems, monopoly tendencies, market shortages, insolvencies, repair costs, "air bags" and other safety features, and many other topics related to automobile insurance. Most criticism has been implicitly directed against the insurers, but the major explicit criticism has been against the liability system as a whole. Still, one could easily conclude that nothing is right about automobile insurance, and that the automobile insurers are the logical ones to blame for the whole mess. No such oversimplification of "the problem" is fair, however, because *the automobile problem* is really a complex group of related problems.

Some aspects of the problem may be the same basic problem as seen from different viewpoints. If one problem had to be singled out, perhaps the choice might be to identify it as the problem of the *unpaid automobile accident victim*.[5] The presumption is that the victim is innocent, and that someone else, or everyone else, is responsible for the accident and/or for the lack of payment for the injuries and damages that the victim has suffered.

Stating the problem in this way is also an "innocent" way of expressing it. It reminds one of the leading question "When did you stop beating your wife?" Any answer is incriminating. The same is true for the automobile problem as stated—any answer presupposes a favorable result for the "victim." The only difference in the answers is *how* and *how much* is to be paid, and *by whom*.

Professor Hall analyzed the components of the automobile problem some years ago into five areas, and the evaluation remains pertinent:
1. The *automobile as a necessity* in terms of both transportation and psychological status needs.

---

[4] *Automobile Insurance and Compensation Study* (Washington, D.C.: U.S. Government Printing Office). Twenty-four reports in 26 volumes were made in 1970 and 1971 on different parts of this federal study.

[5] Sometimes this problem is stated as that of the "uninsured motorist," but the result rather than the cause of the problem appears to be a better way of stating the difficulty today.

2. The *great size of the automobile hazard* in terms of injuries, damages, and the uncertainties of the tort liability system.
3. Automobile *liability insurance is a necessity* to safeguard assets and meet state government requirements.
4. Automobile insurance has become a *form of social insurance* because it is compulsory or quasi-compulsory.
5. The automobile and all factors in its use, such as safety, insurance, tort law, and so on, have *great political appeal.*

Each of these components of the total problem is discussed thoroughly, and the critical inquiry which this author brings to the subject is not only recommended reading but essential reading for any serious student in this area.[6]

Cost appears to be one of the primary factors in regard to each of the "problems" which most writers on this topic mention. For this reason, the cost of automobile insurance is discussed separately in the next section. Remember, however, that the concern over cost is related to a second major aspect of the problem—that of determining how the costs to the injured *victim* of automobile accidents can be met through insurer and government action. That is the major topic of this chapter—the section on current solutions.

THE COST OF AUTOMOBILE INSURANCE

"When a fellow says it hain't the money, but the principle o' the thing—it's th' money!"[7] So goes an old joke, but today in automobile insurance the joke is nothing to laugh at. With the annual cost of automobile accidents approaching $50 *billion* in 1979 and the cost increasing 10 percent or more a year, the money and the principles become undeniably significant. Some of the principles have been introduced in the preceding section. This section treats the cost aspects of the problem.

It is important for policyholders and students of insurance to know as much as possible about automobile insurance prices. They should at least be familiar with the reasons why the costs for automobile insurance are high and with how automobile insurance rates are regulated. What factors determine the cost for the many different classifications of insureds is also important to the individual consumer. That topic is discussed in Chapter 24.

Increasing costs

Automobile insurance is one of the important costs of operating an automobile. The costs are estimated as follows:[8]

---

[6] C. A. Kulp and John W. Hall, *Casualty Insurance* (New York: Ronald Press Co., 1968). See pp. 418–23, as well as the remainder of chaps. xi, xii, and xiii.

[7] F. McKinney Hubbard, *Hoss Sense and Nonsense,* 1926.

[8] The analysis of such costs differs somewhat with the assumptions made. This is based on a Federal Highway Administration survey using a standard-size car driven

Depreciation	4.9 cents per mile
Maintenance	4.2
Garages, parking tolls	2.2
Gas and oil	3.3*
Insurance	1.7
Taxes	1.6
Total	17.9 cents per mile

* Since this study, cost of this item undoubtedly has risen somewhat.

Some policyholders pay more for their automobile insurance than they do for gas or for maintenance. This comes as a shock. A greater shock comes to those automobile owners, especially young persons, who find that their annual cost for insurance may exceed the total value of their older-model car!

Automobile insurance costs have increased rapidly, approximately doubling in many areas during the last ten years; yet in the past decade automobile insurers have lost more than $1 billion writing the protection they provide for policyholders.[9] The reasons are many: the lag of rate increases behind the rising costs, changing marketing methods (see Chapter 5), the reluctance of state authorities to approve higher rates, the difficulty of predicting losses and expenses in a rapidly expanding field, and many other factors.

The fundamental reason for the increase in automobile insurance costs is traceable to the *loss* portion of the premium dollar paid for automobile insurance. During the last decade the average costs for bodily injury and property damage liability claims each increased about 100 percent.[10] The expense portion of automobile insurance premiums has actually decreased (by about 10 percent during the last ten years), in spite of the general tendency toward the higher cost of doing business today as compared with several years ago.

Thus, in analyzing the losses paid by automobile insurers, the reasons for much greater insurance costs are spotlighted. What, for example, would cause *bodily injury liability* payments and medical payments to increase? These factors emerge: (1) more cars, more drivers, more mileage driven, more accidents; (2) sharply rising hospital and medical costs for treating accidents; (3) more loss of income, based on rising wages, when injuries do occur; and (4) a sharp upward trend in the size and number of claims made, the settlements paid, and the verdicts granted by juries in personal injury cases.

100,000 miles over ten years in suburban Baltimore. Compact-size cars showed 1.6 cents insurance costs of a total cost of 14.6 cents, and subcompacts 1.2 cents of 12.6 cents. *Insurance Facts,* 1978, p. 34.

[9] Losses and expenses have exceeded premiums received by all automobile insurers by this amount. Investment income, fortunately, has enabled the insurers to stay in business without destroying the financial strength of most companies. Some insurers have succeeded in making a profit; many others have suffered rather consistent underwriting losses.

[10] *Insurance Facts,* p. 51.

What about *property damage liability, collision, and physical damage* insurance costs? Here other factors are pertinent: (1) higher property values, for cars as well as the property which automobiles damage; and (2) higher repair costs, especially for automobile repairs, based on increased labor and materials costs. With labor costs at an average $13 per hour or more, the cost of replacing the same selected parts went up from about $600 in a 1972 car to more than $1,200 in a 1978 car.[11] A startling figure from industry studies shows that it would cost more than $21,000 to replace all the parts of a totally wrecked car with a factory price of less than $5,000![12]

Inflation is an underlying factor in many of the reasons for rising automobile insurance costs. Prices have gone up for most things. The prices of items important to insurance have increased very sharply, such as a more than 50 percent increase in hospital care costs in the last five years.

Ironically, many of the reasons for cost increases are well beyond the control of the insurers themselves. Certainly it must be recognized, for example, that the insurance industry does *not* control hospital costs, repair bills, inflation, car design, highway construction, driver licensing, and many other parts of the problem. It may be true that some of the increased payments under automobile insurance contracts are due to fraud or exaggerated claims, but it can also be readily seen that many basic factors are responsible for the increases in the prices of all kinds of automobile insurance during recent years.

Rate regulation

The prices charged for automobile insurance contracts do vary, not just for different contracts and different territories but also for essentially identical policies in the same areas. This is contrary to the belief of most persons, consistently revealed by many consumer research surveys, that all insurers charge about the same price.

Price competition. How can the contradiction be explained? It is obviously based upon lack of information and understanding by the buying public. As to the reasons for that lack of information and understanding, two factors loom as most significant. First, the many pricing mechanisms for automobile insurance are not simple. They include many variations in both regulation and practice. The regulatory provisions of the 50 states differ greatly, both as to the objectives and wording of the laws and as to the extent to which the laws are applied. These differences appear in sharp focus when one analyzes the num-

---

[11] Ibid., p. 50. See also, on pp. 52–53, the Insurance Institute for Highway Safety low-speed crash test results for 1978 cars. Federal requirements are shown as reducing costs substantially for five-mile-an-hour front and rear accidents, but these are only part of the total cost problem. New 1979 standards continue to require better bumpers and design aimed at small damage to vehicles in low-speed collisions.

[12] "What's Driving Up Auto Insurance Costs?" *Journal of American Insurance,* Spring 1977, p. 9.

erous automobile insurance markets and the actual practices of the competing
insurers. Second, insurance consumers are after all, no more sophisticated in
their approach to buying insurance than in their approach to buying most other
goods and services. Decisions are not always carefully calculated, and they are
made with tremendous differences in education, ability, initiative, and interest.
Indeed, like most other products, automobile insurance is probably purchased
as often on the basis of emotional factors and partial information as on the
basis of rational decision making with all the factors at hand.

Nonprice competition.   Another point is most significant. Why shouldn't
the prices for automobile insurance vary considerably? Contracts do differ in
their terms, and even in identical contracts the product is largely a bundle of
services, not limited merely to indemnification for loss. It also includes many
hard-to-measure benefits. Just as important to most buyers of automobile insurance as its price (though price is certainly a dominant factor in many decisions, perhaps too many) are such needs as (1) the opportunity to learn
about their requirements, and how insurance can provide the best solutions;
(2) the advice and counsel of the insurer and agent in making the decision as
to proper coverage; (3) the promptness, efficiency, and fairness of the loss
payments; and (4) the careful protection of the insured's right to own and
drive an automobile by meeting the various vehicle regulations of the states.
Nonprice competition is very important to the automobile insurance buyer.

State regulation.   The background for the main issue of state regulation of
rates is set with the above observations. The problem is essentially one of the
extent to which there should be price *competition* as opposed to price *cooperation* in automobile insurance, or put another way, the proper extent of public
control of price competition[13] in this field. (The topic was also discussed
briefly in Chapter 8.)

A summary of the current methods of control is warranted. Three major
legislative methods may be identified: (1) "prior approval," (2) "file and
use," and (3) "open competition" laws.

Most of the states still use a *prior approval* law which permits rate changes
only after the state has approved them. As a result of the McCarran Act
(Public Law 15, 1945), these states adopted within a few years laws modeled
after bills approved by the National Association of Insurance Commissioners.
These are known as "all-industry laws," because many states adopted them,
but this does not mean that all of the states did so. The laws apply to many
forms of property-liability insurance in addition to automobile insurance.
They permit insurers to choose among several alternatives: (1) filing their own
rates, (2) adopting the rates filed by a rating organization, or (3) using deviated rates based upon their own experience. The rates must be filed with the

[13] C. Arthur Williams, Jr., and Andrew F. Whitman, "Open Competition Rating
Laws and Price Competition," *Journal of Risk and Insurance,* vol. 40, no. 4 (December
1973), p. 483.

state insurance department, and the insurance commissioner or superintendent must approve them before they are used by the insurers. The laws basically permit competition through independent, bureau, and deviated rates, and they provide for regulated cooperation through the rating bureau approach to rate making. The standards used by the states to evaluate compliance with the objectives of these rate regulation laws vary considerably, as does the application of those standards. Competition is encouraged but somewhat controlled. The result in most states is that automobile insurance consumers find, if they look for it, a reasonable degree of price competition.

About ten states use the *file and use* approach to automobile insurance rating. The law in these states does not mandate approval of the rates by the insurance commissioner. Contracts and rates are filed, but can be used by the insurers immediately. The commissioner can disapprove the filings at a later time if such a decision is made.

The *open competition* approach is based upon the idea that competition is the best regulator of insurance prices. About 16 states follow this practice, with laws which provide minimum regulation as long as the general objective of maintaining competition in order to achieve rate adequacy, reasonableness, and fair discrimination are met. Essentially these are nonfiling systems, and the commissioner does not review forms or rates. The Senate Antitrust and Monopoly Committee encouraged this type of law. Other regulators, and an increasing number of insurer executives, are advocating state law changes to adopt the open competition approach to rate regulation.

A review of the rationale and development of the various rating laws shows the complexity of the current situation in regard to government and consumer criticism of higher rates, cancellations, and underwriting practices. The competitive-type laws are gaining favor, but the revision of the prior approval laws may take many years in some states. The trend toward the open competition approach is encouraged by (1) independent insurers that desire more freedom in setting rates, (2) many stock and mutual bureau insurers that want to achieve more adequate rate increases, and (3) the desire of state regulators to squelch criticism from the federal government of the inadequacy of state regulation in maintaining price competition in automobile insurance.

SOLUTIONS TO THE NEED FOR AUTOMOBILE INSURANCE

The key to the family automobile(s?) is truly the sign of one of the highest standards of living that any nation has ever enjoyed. Yet, with the key goes a frightening responsibility for the control of the costs, both physical and financial, which are associated with it. To the individual, these costs create the need for automobile insurance.

The need, as shown in the "automobile problem," and the costs of automobile insurance have been discussed in the two preceding sections. These sections point out some of the reasons why the interest of the public is now centered upon automobile insurance. The growth of competition and costs, financial losses of unparalleled proportions in some years, changing government regulations, and consumer mistrust combine to create continued expectation of change to achieve improvements in automobile insurance.

Basic current and changing solutions

The need is easily overdramatized in some of the types of "growing concern" noted in the early part of this chapter. However, the concern *is* there, and the public appeal *is* strong. News articles often sensationalize automobile accidents to obtain the reader's attention. Dramatic pictures of multivehicle crashes leave the public with the impression that automobile accidents are caused not by individuals but by a horrible series of unfortunate circumstances. For example, gasoline tankers explode, and smog or snow cause chain reaction accidents on crowded superhighways, involving many deaths, injuries, and property damage claims in seconds. The implication of these rather isolated cases is apparently (extrapolating the examples to *all* automobile accidents): "Who can possibly be blamed for automobile accidents?" Although the answer "no one" may be appropriate for some such accidents, the answer today may still be an identifiable "someone" for the more usual two-car and less complex accidents.

The conclusion reached by this author is born of necessity as well as conviction and agrees with that of a former colleague.[14] The assumption is that the tort liability system is so basic a part of our society in the United States that its application to the automobile field will continue. Changes *will* occur, but much more slowly than predicted, and they are likely to occur in an evolutionary manner rather than a revolutionary one. Some parts of the automobile liability risk may be determined as social in nature, requiring a social insurance plan as a solution. However, it is assumed here that for at least the span of this text edition, *individual* responsibility for many automobile accidents will continue to be the basis for much of the usual automobile insurance contract.

As of 1979, the trend is clearly toward change. To try to predict the exact outcome of the many new state laws and experimental plans, however, would be impossible. Apparently some form of *no-fault* plan will be used in connection with *some* part of *some* of the automobile contracts for *some* insureds. Whether this no-fault trend will be for all on a compulsory basis or for some on an optional basis will be determined *sometime* in the 1980s.

This section aims first at understanding the *past* and *current* solutions to the need for automobile insurance. A later section will review briefly the newer no-fault programs, especially those that have appeared in the last few years, which

---

[14] John W. Hall, at Georgia State University. See Kulp and Hall, *Casualty Insurance,* p. 479.

seem to characterize the changing and questioning attitudes of today's consumers, insurers, and regulators.

Aside from the practical need for protection against potentially severe losses, automobile insurance is *needed* because it is *required by government*. Thus, the current solutions are all fundamentally connected with *legislation* which requires some type of *insurance* plan.

In certain fields of business, the federal government and a number of states have enacted legislation making adequate vehicle coverage a condition which must be met before a license to operate is issued. Common carriers such as trucking concerns and taxicab or bus operators fall into this category. The Interstate Commerce Act requires all interstate common carriers to furnish evidence of liability insurance to the Interstate Commerce Commission. In addition to the state laws that apply only to common carriers, some jurisdictions require that a certificate of insurance be on file with the state authority in the case of private transit carriers. A few states also require insurance before issuing an automobile registration or license to certain individuals, such as minors under the age of 21 or 18.

The most important types of automobile insurance legislation and plans, however, apply to *all* or *nearly all* automobile owners or drivers. Table 23–1 summarizes the scope and general characteristics of these laws and plans. As to *purpose,* they can be divided into groups which attempt to (1) increase the universality of third-party liability insurance (nos. 1 and 2, *financial responsibility* and *compulsory liability laws*); (2) provide a pool or fund in which private insurers participate (nos. 3–5, *assigned risk, other residual market,* and *unsatisfied judgment* plans); (3) encourage the purchase of first-party coverage for the insureds own losses (nos. 6 and 7, *uninsured motorists* and *no-fault* plans); or (4) reduce losses (no. 8, *safety and loss-prevention* plans).

Each of these areas is discussed separately in the following sections of this chapter.

Financial responsibility laws

In connection with the operation of an automobile, about half of the states only *encourage* the purchase of liability insurance by means of financial responsibility legislation but do not require everyone to buy it. These laws are designed to make it impossible for reckless and *financially irresponsible motorists* (those who have *become involved in an accident*) to secure a license to drive a car unless there is a guarantee that they are able to pay and will pay, within the limits established by the statutes, damages for which they become liable.

Early laws. The earliest financial responsibility laws differed in detail from state to state but were alike in principle. Instead of requiring motorists to purchase insurance before they are licensed, the laws operate on the principle that once motorists demonstrate themselves to be careless drivers by

Table 23-1. Summary of automobile insurance legislation and plans

Type of legislation or plan	Purpose	Scope of use	General characteristics
1. Financial responsibility laws	To increase purchase of third-party liability insurance	About one half of the states	Typical law requires purchase of 10/20/5 (or higher) liability limits, *after* being involved in an accident, for future liability claims by others
2. Compulsory liability laws	To increase purchase of third-party liability insurance	About one half of the states	Require purchase of liability insurance *before* car license and plates are issued
3. Assigned risk (auto insurance) plans	To pool the higher-risk drivers	More than 40 states	If motorists have been refused regular insurance, they may obtain coverage through such a plan, which apportions these insureds among all private insurers doing business in the state
4. Other residual market mechanisms	To pool the higher-risk drivers	Eight states	Three types of laws pool loss experience of higher-risk drivers by a "reinsurance facility" (four states), a "joint underwriting association" (three states), or a "state fund" (one state)
5. Unsatisfied judgment funds	To pool payments to unpaid victims	Five states	Provide innocent victim with payment for losses caused by others who cannot be identified or by others who are unable to pay for judgments against them
6. Uninsured motorists coverage	To encourage insureds to purchase own coverage	All states	Adds coverage in insured's *own contract* for income and medical expense losses *caused* by uninsured motorists to any occupants of the insured's car
7. Automobile no-fault plans	To have insureds purchase *own coverage**	About one half of the states	Most plans (the "modified" type) abolish tort liability suits except for serious injuries and have insureds collect losses from their *own* insurer
8. Safety and loss prevention plans	To reduce automobile accidents or losses	Many states; federal and industry plans	Promote traffic safety and laws, better drivers' licensing laws, safer vehicle manufacture, and coordinated accident reporting and research

* Note that no-fault plans are *first-party* insurance contracts, for coverage with the insured's own insurance company, as opposed to the *third-party* coverage provided for *liability* of the insured to other persons in the other laws and plans of this table.

becoming involved in an accident for which they are *found liable,* they must prove their financial responsibility or lose their license to drive.[15]

To strengthen the financial responsibility legislation by eliminating the first victim's possibility of remaining unpaid under the so-called one-bite laws, a new type of law was enacted. Under this type of law motorists must immediately establish their ability to answer for damages if *involved in an accident.*[16] If motorists are not insured, they are required to furnish security that in the judgment of the state authorities will satisfy any judgment that may be recovered against them. In contrast to the earlier laws, which required motorists to establish their ability to answer for damages only after a judgment had been awarded, and then only with respect to future claims, the newer type of law requires motorists involved in an accident to provide security immediately to cover any possible judgments that may be expected to result from an accident that has already occurred.

Current laws. Most statutes require at least minimum bodily injury of $10,000 per person and $20,000 per occurrence and property damage limits of $5,000. Some states require higher limits, such as 15/30/5 or 25/50/10.[17] There is no waiting until the motorist is convicted of a traffic violation or a judgment is awarded for damages. The motorist must be prepared to respond to damages immediately upon the happening of an accident.

The law applies to the accident that has occurred as well as the accidents that may occur in the future. Such laws are known as "security-type laws" and are in contrast to the earlier laws in which only future accidents were considered. This type of law provides a powerful incentive to insure, since motorists understand that failure to satisfy the state authorities with respect to financial responsibility following an accident will result in the immediate suspension of license and registration. Financial responsibility must be evidenced at the time of any accident involving personal injuries, although many state do not apply the law to property damage accidents of under $100, or sometimes more.

The primary purpose of financial responsibility laws was to provide *en-*

---

[15] This type of plan generally fell short of the objective of the sponsors of financial responsibility legislation. One of the earliest such laws was passed in Connecticut in 1925. Financially irresponsible motorists continued to operate cars on the road without insurance because many who met with injuries were unwilling to incur the cost of a suit if it appeared that the judgment would be uncollectible. In such circumstances, the negligent persons were not "found liable," and they suffered no penalty. Even in the cases where licenses were revoked, the negligent parties could have their licenses restored by furnishing proof of financial responsibility for *future* accidents by the purchase of an insurance policy.

[16] This type of law appeared in New Hampshire in 1937. In many states the present legislation is based upon a model safety responsibility law that is applied not only after an accident but also in specified cases where the motorist has a number of serious motor vehicle violations, such as reckless driving or speeding.

[17] The states' financial responsibility laws differ substantially. For a summary of these differences, see *Insurance Facts,* p. 67. Seventeen states have higher, and only three states have lower, limits than 10/20/5.

couragement for all motorists to purchase liability insurance, *without compelling everyone* to do so. This goal the laws have reasonably achieved because most persons know that their driving privileges will be jeopardized if they have an accident while uninsured. The percentage of insured drivers has increased from 40 percent 35 years ago to over 85 percent in most of the states today. Many of the states with particularly effective financial responsibility law enforcement have increased the percentage to above 90 percent insured. Only a few states have less than 75 percent insured.

Compulsory liability insurance legislation

In contrast to the financial responsibility laws, approximately one half of the states have *compulsory laws* which make the demonstration of financial responsibility a condition precedent to obtaining registration. All owners of automobiles are required to produce an insurance policy[18] *before license and plates will be issued.* In essence, this makes financial responsibility mandatory in order to own and use a car. It was not until 30 years after Massachusetts adopted a compulsory law in 1927 that a second state, New York, passed such a law. North Carolina became the third state to do so, in 1958. About 25 states and territories adopted compulsory liability provisions in connection with no-fault laws effective by 1979.[19]

Pros and cons.   Advocates of compulsory insurance point to the danger of a serious accident when an uninsured and financially irresponsible driver is liable for damages and unable to pay. As a guarantee of protection to the public against financial loss, compulsory insurance is held by its advocates to be superior to the usual financial responsibility law, under which approximately 15 percent of registered vehicles remain uninsured in the U.S.

Opponents of compulsory insurance object to the compulsion forced upon all car owners, whether or not they are bad drivers. They contend that this tends to increase recklessness, thereby causing more accidents instead of lessening them. Insurers have little opportunity to select their risks, and the loss suits tend to increase abnormally, the courts are congested, and the rates are perhaps higher as a result of unfavorable experience.[20] There is also a belief that

---

[18] As an alternative, the laws also permit the filing of cash, bond, or collateral in amounts equivalent to the required insurance contract limits of liability. Practically speaking, the insurance policy is the only method used.

[19] These included Puerto Rico in 1970; Florida in 1972; Connecticut, Michigan, and New Jersey in 1973; and Colorado, Hawaii, Kansas, Nevada, and Utah in 1974; and since then, California, Delaware, Georgia, Idaho, Kentucky, Maryland, Minnesota, North Dakota, Oklahoma, Pennsylvania, South Carolina and Virgin Islands. The American Insurance Association publishes a current summary of these laws.

[20] Claims increased as much as 25 percent or more, for example, in the first few years following the enactment of a compulsory law in New York and North Carolina. New York and Massachusetts also have the two highest basic coverage rates in the country. However, these facts may not be proof that the compulsory laws are bad, for it may be that they have succeeded in their objective of paying more accident victims.

property damage claims are fraudulently converted into bodily injury claims since only bodily injury coverage is required by many of the laws.

The compulsory law does *not* mean that all motorists are insured.[21] Of motorists licensed in the compulsory states, probably about 5 percent are uninsured, such as: (1) hit-and-run drivers, (2) drivers of stolen cars, (3) motorists insured when plates were issued but for whom the insurance has lapsed, and (4) fradulently registered cars. Uninsured motorists may also include many (estimated at about 20 percent) out-or-state drivers. The cost of administering the compulsory law is high, involving millions of dollars.

Another criticism is leveled at the tendency of the compulsory laws to provide less protection, as many persons expect the required minimums to meet their full needs. This may create an "underinsured" problem of less-then-adequate policy limits. Policy coverage also tends to be restricted by political considerations, as promised lower rates are secured by limiting the policy coverage. In Massachusetts, for example, unless it is endorsed to do so, even the new no-fault (since 1971) policy does not cover (1) accidents occurring on private property, (2) accidents occurring out of state, or (3) guests in the car. A final objection raised is the possible threat to private enterprise that may result from the compulsory law, with a state insurance fund perhaps usurping a field of insurance which now accounts for 40 percent or more of the business of property-liability insurers.

The lack of unbiased data leaves many of the arguments for and against compulsory automobile liability insurance unsolved. It is an emotionally charged problem, yet one of extreme importance to both society and the private insurance business. The idea and objectives are reasonable in many respects, but they are often misunderstood as automatically bringing a full solution to the problem.

Neither the compulsory laws nor the financial responsibility laws do much to increase the prevention of accidents, which is perhaps the fundamental and most-needed goal. Better enforcement of existing motor vehicle and safety laws is essential and tackles the problem at its root. The increasing and unnecessary losses on the highways should not be condoned under any of the current or proposed solutions to the problem of the automobile accident victim.

The future will undoubtedly bring further action by the states in attempts to achieve better solutions. The compulsory law is apparently a growing but not popular choice. It has been defeated in many bills introduced regularly in the past three decades in many states, and support for it seems to have increased only when it has been adopted along with the new no-fault laws.

The current situation appears to cause less concern over compulsory automobile liability insurance among insurers and much more concern over

---

[21] Or that all auto accident injuries are covered. Those who are responsible for their own injuries, for example, as well as the victims injured by the several types of uninsured motorists mentioned in this paragraph, are not covered except under the no-fault laws.

changes which may usurp part or all of the tort liability system (see no-fault plans discussed later). Some of these plans are implicitly based upon compulsory features requiring insurance, so that compulsory insurance becomes less a separate decision and more a portion of a much greater and more complex change.

Automobile insurance (assigned risk) plans

As a corollary to either the basic financial responsibility law or the compulsory automobile liability insurance law, the *automobile insurance plans* (formerly called *assigned risk* plans) have been developed to meet the problem of rejected risks. Today, these plans assure almost all persons in more than 40 states that insurance is available. Every state has felt the necessity of making insurance available to all who are entitled to it. Since private insurers have the right to select risks, an applicant may sometimes have difficulty in securing adequate insurance. Provision has been made under the automobile insurance plans for taking care of this "residual market" of higher-risk drivers by equitably distributing individually rejected risks among all insurers.

How the plans work. The plans are not the same in all states, but they follow a similar pattern. Generally, if motorists have refused insurance by one or more private insurers, they may apply to the manager of the assigned risk plan. If upon investigation, the applicant is found to be eligible for insurance according to the standards of the plan, the manager of the plan assigns the risk to an insurer. Assigned risks are rotated among the different insurers in proportion to the business that each insurer writes in the state. All insurers are obligated[22] to accept risks as assigned unless absence of good faith can be shown. An applicant who can be shown to be engaged in operations such as gambling, dealing in narcotics, or other illegal enterprise, or who has been a habitual violator of the law, need not be accepted as an assigned risk. Insureds covered as assigned risks include not only persons with poor accident records,[23] but also the hard-to-underwrite classes of drivers such as very old, inexperienced, or very young drivers in some areas. Only about 2 percent of all registered vehicles are insured in these plans, but the sit-

---

[22]A decision of the U.S. Supreme Court held in 1951 that an insurer writing automobile liability insurance must assume its share of assigned risks. The constitutionality of the California law was questioned, and the answer given by the decision was that the police power of the state "extends to all the great public needs," including the compensation of innocent victims of highway accidents (*California State Automobile Association Inter-Insurance Bureau, Appellant,* v. *John R. Maloney, Insurance Commissioner,* 340 U.S. 105; 71 Sup. Ct. 601, 95 Law Ed. 788).

[23] Only extreme cases of many law violations or accidents result in being refused insurance coverage in the assigned risk plans. Less than 1 or 2 percent of applicants are denied coverage. In what must be a classic case, consider the problem of a 39-year-old Columbus, Ohio, driver who had had 50 accidents in a nine-year period, including 28 in the most recent three years. Surprisingly, in only two accidents was he found at fault, and in none were there any serious injuries!

uation differs greatly by state, with several states (including Delaware, New Jersey, and New York) having more than 6 percent.[24]

The policyholders who purchase their insurance protection through the automobile inusrance plans usually pay a higher rate than other insureds. A surcharge of 10 percent to as high as 200 percent is often applied, depending on the policyholder's accident record, motor vehicle violations, and other factors. More than three fourths of the plans make available liability limits higher than are required by state law, and also collision, comprehensive, and medical payments coverages.[25]

The latest figures available show that the higher charges do not offset the poorer loss experience for those classifications or automobile insureds. Cumulative losses, almost all of them in the past decade, have exceeded premiums by more than $1 billion—and that does not include administrative expenses. In order to operate successfully in the future, the automobile insurance plans must be helped by rate increases and by better driver-licensing procedures in all the states. Reexamination of all drivers every few years has been recommended by a National Traffic and Motor Vehicle Safety Act which has become effective in several states.

Other "residual market" mechanisms

In addition to the automobile insurance plans just discussed, several states have attempted to solve the "residual market" problem by using other methods to pool the loss experience of high-risk drivers. Eight states passed laws of three different types in the years 1973–75.

Four of the laws set up *reinsurance facilities.* Effective in Massachusetts, North and South Carolina, and New Hampshire, these mechanisms require insurers to accept all applicants for automobile insurance if they have valid driver's licenses. Then the insurer may decide to cede (reinsure) some of the highest risks to the reinsurance facility of its state, which operates a combined pool for all reinsured risks. Losses and expenses of the facility are shared among all insurers in proportion to the total automobile insurance they write in the state. Canada has used a reinsurance facility for more than ten years.

Three states established *joint underwriting associations,* which differ from the reinsurance facilities in that they identify a small number (about 8–14) of insurers as "servicing carriers" which issue contracts, collect premiums, and pay claims on behalf of the JUA. The JUA is proportionally owned and operated by all the insurers doing business in the state. Each agent or broker is

---

[24] *Automobile Insurance Plans Service Office Insurance Facts—1977* (New York: AIPSO, 1977), pp. 11–12. Variations by year are considerable, and in some cases the percentage has been as high as 20 percent.

[25] "Industry's Insurance Market for Drivers Who Can't Find One," *Journal of American Insurance,* Winter 1975–76, p. 19.

assigned a servicing carrier in order to provide all agents and brokers with access to a market in which to place the higher risk. Florida, Missouri, and Hawaii each has a JUA, which establishes rates and commission for high risks within the state. One difference is that Hawaii mandates that welfare recipients are entitled to free automobile insurance (up to the statutory minimum limits).

One state, Maryland, chose to insure canceled or rejected drivers in an automobile insurance *state fund.* The state-run company guarantees the availability of 100/300/100 liability and physical damage limits and other coverages written through all the regular agents and brokers in the state. Claims are handled by the fund's own personnel. Deficits were so large during the first three years that now the private insurers are assessed proportionally, which in effect causes the voluntary market insureds to subsidize the annual residual market deficits.

Although the three different residual (involuntary) market mechanisms were intended as improvements on the automobile insurance plans (AIPs), research to date does not seem to show much progress, nor to permit definitive conclusions as to which system is more costly.[26] In the seven states having reinsurance facilities and joint underwriting associations, operating losses through 1976 approached one-half billion dollars, almost half of which were Massachusetts' deficits. Thus many crucial questions remain unanswered. It would seem, however, that the alternative systems' lack of positive benefits (and the fact that no further states have adopted such plans since 1975) leaves most of the states with the AIPs as the major solution to the perplexing problems of the residual markets.

Unsatisfied judgment funds

In addition to the residual market availability of insurance and other problems, another area of concern is the innocent unpaid victims of automobile accidents. How should they be paid for losses caused by others who cannot be identified, are uninsured, or are otherwise unable to pay for their mistakes?

Five states have adopted legislation which provides the innocent victim of an automobile accident with a source of payment for losses caused by a financially irresponsible motorist. A separate *unsatisfied judgment fund* (UJF) is established with the purpose of paying bodily injury losses, and in addition (in three states) property damage losses, (1) if the victim proves liability by obtaining a judgment against another party who was negligent in causing the accident and (2) if the victim shows that the judgment cannot be recovered, that is, remains unsatisfied.

---

[26] J. Finley Lee, *Servicing the Shared Automobile Insurance Market* (New York: National Industry Committee on Automobile Insurance Plans, August 1977).

The states which have established this type of fund are North Dakota (1947), New Jersey (1952), Maryland (1957), New York (1958), and Michigan (1965). Nine provinces in Canada have such plans, too, the earliest having been established in 1945. New York's plan set up a Motor Vehicle Accident Indemnification Corporation. This plan differs from the others in using a nonprofit corporation (rather than a state fund) administered by the insurers to pay the claims.

Certain minimum limits or deductibles sometimes apply, and maximum amounts of coverage are also specified.[27] Negligent motorists are not relieved of liability for the damages or injuries they have caused; their driving privileges are revoked until the UJF has been reimbursed for the amount paid to the innocent victim.

The basic financing of these funds is by a levy, usually assessed against the *uninsured* motorists of the state. However, some states also charge insured motorists a fee at the time of registration. Several states charge the *insurers* writing automobile business about one half of 1 percent of their net premiums. The fee charged the uninsured motorist has risen sharply in recent years. This fee is for the right *not* to purchase automobile liability insurance and it does not provide any liability protection for the uninsured motorist.

An evaluation of the merits and disadvantages of unsatisfied judgment funds refers to the following benefits: (1) providing some recourse to innocent victims; (2) keeping more irresponsible motorists off the road; (3) a small reimbursement of the funds, about 5 percent, by the uninsured motorists; and to the following faults: (1) the financial inequity of the costs being paid by insured motorists; (2) the fund deficits that have resulted from inadequate levies; and (3) the complicated, expensive, and cumbersome procedures used by the funds.[28].

Uninsured motorists coverage

The most widely used method of providing payment to victims of automobile accidents caused by financially irresponsible motorists is *uninsured motorists coverage* (UMC). For a small cost, usually about $10 a year, insured motorists may include this coverage *in their own* automobile insurance contracts. It is basically protection for the entire *family* (and relatives in the household), as car occupants or pedestrians, against losses caused by un-

---

[27] G. Victor Hallman, *Unsatisfied Judgment Funds* (Homewood, Ill.: Richard D. Irwin, 1968), pp. 127–34. The maximums are $10,000 per person and $20,000 per accident, except for Maryland, which has 20/40 limits. Where property damage is covered, it is usually covered only up to $5,000 per accident, with deductibles of $100–$200.

[28] Sajjad A. Hashmi, "Unsatisfied Judgment Funds," *Journal of Risk and Insurance,* vol. 31, no. 1 (March 1964), p. 93. See also "The Problem of the Uninsured Motorist: A Proposed Solution," *Journal of Risk and Insurance,* vol. 24, no. 3 (September 1967), p. 363.

insured motorists. Loss payments include medical payments and loss of income. Other persons riding in the insured auto are covered, and the coverage extends to other cars driven by an insured. UMC also covers hit-and-run cases, whose victims usually cannot collect their damages because they have no one to ask for payment.

The standard form of this coverage is treated in further detail in the later discussion of the personal auto policy in Chapter 24. Different contracts may have somewhat different wording, so the insured should read the endorsement to determine the extent of protection.

The state laws are also important, as all states now require that uninsured motorists coverage be offered in automobile insurance contracts. In many states the insured may refuse in writing to have the coverage included. Many states make the coverage mandatory, and it must be included in all policies written for automobiles in those states. Details of the coverage vary considerably in some states. Most states require 10/20 limits, and higher limits must be made available. Property damage coverage is included in only a few states. Newer contracts may also include underinsured motorist coverage.

Uninsured motorists coverage accomplishes the objective of payment to innocent victims without a separate system such as the UJF. It is not necessary that the victim secure a judgment against the wrongdoer; however, the victim must show that the negligent party had no liability insurance. Delays and administrative costs are reduced by having the insurer pay the insured for injuries for which the uninsured motorist is liable. In many states an arbitration process is used when this is necessary in order to arrive at a fair payment figure.

Evaluation of UMC shows that it is a valuable and relatively simple solution to many of the problems of unpaid automobile accident victims. Criticism of UMC points out that it would be more equitable to have the uninsured (rather than the insured) motorist pay the costs. It is also sometimes difficult for an insurer to decide that an uninsured motorist is liable in an accident, because then the insurer must pay the insured under the UMC coverage. The potential conflict of interest is troublesome.

An interesting expansion of UMC in most states includes within the definition of an "uninsured automobile" a motor vehicle for which liability insurance is in effect at the time of an accident but is uncollectible because of the insolvency of the insurer. Government investigations have stressed the number of automobile insurer insolvencies in recent years. Actually these have been relatively few in number, and they have usually involved high-risk, substandard specialty insurers. It is appropriate, however, for the consumer of automobile insurance to have this additional protection within the UMC coverage.

Automobile no-fault insurance plans

One of the major problems with a new word or phrase is that great misunderstandings result because so many meanings become attached to it during its formative stage. Thus, there are many different interpretations of no-fault *automobile insurance* at its current stage of development.

The meaning of no-fault. The "fundamental basis for a no-fault system is the *abolishment of tort liability* in automobile accidents, with drivers or owners accepting responsibility for *some or all* losses sustained by pedestrians and by occupants of their own vehicles in return for immunity from liability for those losses."[29] The need for establishing fault[30] before loss payments are made is largely eliminated by such plans, and the insured motorist at least in most cases, has the right to collect directly from his or her *own insurer*. Thus, *no-fault* insurance is primarily *first-party* (the insured), rather than third-party (other persons) coverage. Tort liability actions are either eliminated, or, more usually, are restricted to the more serious losses. (See Chapter 20 for discussion of torts and negligence.)

The distinction between "true" no-fault plans, "modified" no-fault plans, and "pseudo" no-fault plans is important. *True* no-fault plans abolish all liability claims. Most no-fault plans are of the *modified* type, with tort liability suits only permitted in cases of serious injuries. Several states have adopted *pseudo* no-fault laws, which are called no-fault but do not restrict liability lawsuits. Delaware, Maryland, and Oregon are examples. These laws have been called "yes-fault" by the American Insurance Association which emphasizes that they involve *no* restriction on liability lawsuits, even though they do expand medical expense and income loss payments to the first-party injured insureds. Sometimes these are called "add-on" plans, because they are additional coverages included in the insured's policy.

The public dilemma is seen in surveys such as those conducted by the American Institute of Public Opinion in 1977. Although three fourths of U.S. adults indicated a familiarity with no-fault plans, only one in three of these persons can correctly describe how the plans work, and their opinions were almost equally divided between approval and disapproval of the plans. Public awareness of the no-fault concept has increased considerably in recent years, but much confusion still exists.

Before any decision is made for or against no-fault, then, it is necessary to ask: *"What* no-fault plan or law?" Succeeding sections discuss the many proposals, experimental plans, and state laws which must be distinguished.

Legislative action needed. The place of legislation in the picture is prominent. In each of the previously discussed "solutions" to the problem of the unpaid auto accident victim, some legislative action by the states was required—a financial responsibility law, a compulsory automobile liability insurance law, an assigned risk plan setting up a placement facility for poorer risks

---

[29] Willis P. Rokes, *No-Fault Insurance* (Santa Monica, Calif.: Insurors' Press, 1971), p. 3.

[30] The term *liability-without-fault,* used with workers' compensation laws where compensation is the *exclusive* remedy, is not technically correct. Most auto no-fault plans are really *payment-without-fault* to the injured person, but other remedies may still be available. Thus the plans are more properly looked upon as *automobile accident insurance* rather than as a complete departure from the concepts of fault and liability.

or an unsatisfied judgment law. Even in the relatively successful uninsured motorists coverage solution to the problem, the most rapid use and progress have occurred in states that have legislated the coverage into existing contracts—some on a required basis and others on an optional basis which permits the insured to refuse the coverage.

Most of the proposals advocating no-fault plans also rely heavily upon legislative approval and changes. For this reason, fortunately, the revolutionary aspects of the suggested reforms have been slowed. However, when the reforms do obtain legislative sanction, the situation can undergo broad and rapid change.

The ultimate solution, however, is far from settled yet. About one third of the *states* have passed laws which deserve to be called no-fault according to the concepts discussed previously. However, these laws vary considerably in scope and detail, as will be seen in a later section of this chapter.

In addition, a *federal no-fault law* that would set minimum standards for the states is under debate in the U.S. Senate. In early 1978 the Senate Commerce Committee, after a close 9–7 vote, recommended the passage of such a model bill (S. 1381). Whether the final bill will require or merely encourage action in the states, what limits will apply, when tort actions will be permitted, and other points will be under further debate in the Senate and the House. It is very difficult to predict whether a federal no-fault law will be passed, but there is little question that the possibility is there and that it continues to provide a strong impetus for debate and action on state no-fault laws.

A brief review of early no-fault plans will provide a better perspective for discussion of the no-fault laws that have been adopted in the states.

Early no-fault plans.   One might think that automobile no-fault plans are a product of the 1970s, but actually the basic concepts have been recommended in plans dating back several decades or more. One of the first, the *Columbia plan,* advocated a "true" no-fault plan in 1932, in which no-fault compensation benefits would replace liability payments as the only payment to injured parties. Two other no-fault plans were recommended in the 1950s, one a "full-aid" voluntary plan of scheduled benfits for all persons involved in automobile accidents and the other a compulsory plan that was based not on arbitrary schedules but on actual individual economic loss (not including pain and suffering).[31]

Since 1946 the Canadian province of *Saskatchewan* has applied the theory that automobile accidents are a social cost and responsibility rather than a negligent person's individual cost and responsibility. Accident insurance bene-

---

[31] *Report by the Committee to Study Compensation for Automobile Accidents* (Columbia University: Council for Research in the Social Sciences, 1932; Albert A. Ehrenzweig, *"Full Aid" Insurance for the Traffic Victim* (Los Angeles: University of California Press, 1954); and Leon Green, *Traffic Victims: Tort Law and Insurance* (Chicago: Northwestern University Press, 1958).

fits (of quite limited amounts for death or disability) are paid to all persons injured by or in automobiles, regardless of fault. Most medical expenses are covered by a government health insurance plan. Tort actions against negligent parties are permitted for claims in excess of the scheduled benefits provided by the law, and insurance for both compensation and liability benefits is purchased through a compulsory government insurance plan. Although the long existence of the Saskatchewan plan attests to its workability in an uncrowded area, it is emphasized that only part of injury losses is covered by the no-fault provisions. The no-fault provisions have the advantage of lessening delays in measuring and paying benefits, since the scale of benefits is set by law.

Another early no-fault plan was an experimental *family compensation plan* introduced by the Nationwide Companies in the 1950s, in which their policyholders had the option of purchasing limited alternative compensation benefits for all injured persons in an automobile accident. The coverage was discontinued in 1967 after studies showed that it did not discourage many claimants from filing tort claims and that it did not reduce loss payments. A different proposed plan of this era was the *Conard plan,* which was not adopted by any state, but would have integrated social security disability income payments and Medicare-Medicaid medical expense payments by deducting such payments from tort liability claims.

A pronounced impetus for bringing no-fault plans to the attention of the states was provided in 1965. The *Keeton-O'Connell plan,* proposed by two law school professors, was a modified no-fault plan called "basic protection insurance."[32] The plan sought to do away with most automobile tort liability lawsuits by having insureds paid by *their own insurers* for most out-of-pocket medical expenses and income losses (up to $10,000 per person). It permitted regular tort claims only for pain-and-suffering losses exceeding $5,000. The advantages were alleged to include less fraud, more equitable distribution of losses, reduced court congestion and delays, faster loss payments, and reduced automobile insurance costs. In the late 1960s numerous critics evaluated these benefits as unlikely and claimed that the plan also possessed other disadvantages, such as encouraging indifference to safety, doubtful constitutionality,[33] and rating problems (with better risks paying more and worse risks less). Nevertheless, the industry and public discussion engendered by the no-fault idea of the proposed Keeton-O'Connell plan resulted in several additional steps toward other automobile no-fault insurance plans.

---

[32] Robert E. Keeton and Jeffrey O'Connell, *Basic Protection for the Traffic Victim— A Blueprint for Reforming Automobile Insurance* (Boston: Little, Brown & Co., 1965). See also, by the same authors, *After Cars Crash—The Need for Legal and Insurance Reform* (Homewood, Ill.: Dow Jones-Irwin, 1967); and Jeffrey O'Connell, *The Injury Industry* (New York: Commerce Clearing House, 1971).

[33] An Illinois no-fault law was declared unconstitutional in 1972 on the basis that a medical expense threshold discriminated against low-income citizens. However, in many other states including Michigan's Supreme Court in 1978, the courts have upheld the constitutionality of no-fault laws.

Competing insurer organizations advocated voluntary approaches during the late 1960s. An experimental plan put forward by the American Mutual Alliance, called the *guaranteed benefits plan,* was tried in several states. This plan offered automobile accident victims a choice of (1) taking automatic payments for medical expenses and lost income (up to $12,500, plus 50 percent more for noneconomic losses, or (2) suing under normal tort liability law. In effect, the plan was an extension of the system of "advance payments" by insurers for automobile liability cases. Under the plan, no releases are required and payments are speeded to the injured person. The American Insurance Association proposed a system in which the insured's own insurer provided *complete personal protection* for automobile accident injury payments without regard to fault. It went farther than the Keeton-O'Connell plan by suggesting the abandonment of the fault concept completely, and substituting a compulsory automobile accident system for economic (medical expenses and wage) losses.

Two plans were legislated outside the mainland United States in these crucial years of change. In Puerto Rico a law termed the *social protection plan* became effective in 1969. Everyone in an auto accident there is paid unlimited medical benefits, death benefits up to $10,000, disability income of 50 percent of salary (for two years, with low weekly maximums), scheduled dismemberment benefits up to $5,000, and a $500 funeral benefit. The negligent party is relieved of liability up to $10,500 ($3,500 for pain and suffering, $7,000 for all other damages), with workers' compensation and other private insurance, other than life insurance, decreasing the benefit payments. The government administers the plan, which in an important difference from the Keeton-O'Connell proposal, is financed by an annual tax on each motor vehicle.

North of the border, most of the Canadian provinces adopted a law which inaugurated a limited-pay-without-fault plan in 1969. The *Canadian plan,* as it was called, has private insurers pay injuries on an optional no-fault basis up to $5,000. Through a nationwide pool of private insurers, poorer risks are reinsured in a reinsurance facility that is designed to reduce the alleged social stigma of being placed in an assigned risk or automobile insurance plan, as in most states in the United States. Evaluation of this plan indicates that it has not been very successful, with continual problems of underwriting losses and lack of confidence by the insurers resulting in proposals for modification.[34]

State no-fault laws, 1970–1978. With this background of many different proposals and limited legislation for automobile no-fault insurance, the decade of the 1970s began an era of legislative action in which various U.S. states passed no-fault laws. Although the debate regarding the pros and cons has been continuing on in many state legislatures, (see next section), no-fault plans are here in about 16, or one third, of the states. Most of these plans are

---

[34] Lee, *Servicing the Shared Automobile Insurance Market,* p. 66.

"modified" rather than "true" no-fault systems, for liability suits are still permitted if medical costs go above a certain level, or "threshold," usually $1,000 or less. Michigan's law is closest to a true no-fault plan, for it does not use a threshold figure and it severely restricts accident victims' lawsuits to those involving deaths or very serious injuries. About another half-dozen states add on medical expense and disability income no-fault coverage, without any restriction on tort liability claims, in a type of pseudo-no-fault law. Oregon, Texas, Virginia, and Wisconsin are examples.

Massachusetts was the first state to enact a no-fault law in 1970, and by the the mid-1970s 16 states[35] had legislated no-fault benefits. The state laws vary considerably, and comparative analysis becomes quite complex. For example, the *no-fault benefits* for medical expenses are limited to a figure such as $2,000 or $5,000 per person in some states, while in other states such expenses are unlimited except by a requirement that the expenses be reasonable. Loss-of-income payment is restricted in many states by definite weekly, monthly, or total maximums, and often by duration maximums (one year, etc.) Some states combine medical and income losses and set one maximum for a combination of both, such as $5,000–$50,000. In many of the state laws other limits apply in various combinations for funeral expenses, substitute household service for the injured person, percentage maximums for wages lost (75–100 percent), and death and survivors' benefits.

The important restrictions on *tort liability* lawsuits also vary considerably. The threshold of medical expenses above which tort claims are permitted is unreasonably low, such as $200 or $500, in many of the no-fault states. This means that the number of liability claims is not substantially reduced. However, the trend in recent years have been toward a new method of setting the limits for tort action. More of the no-fault laws are restricting the circumstances under which plaintiffs can sue for pain and suffering, anguish, or other "general damages" to serious injuries or deaths. The law, for example, may verbally describe and specify permanent loss of body members or functions, or permanent scarring and disfigurement, or 60 days or more of disability, as the only permitted basis for lawsuits involving noneconomic losses. Thus far, these changes seem to be an improvement, although it must be remembered the citizens of the states that use verbal definitions are giving up important liability rights to sue for such damages.

Vehicle damage liability does not come under most of the no-fault laws. Michigan provides property protection insurance for property other than the insured's as a part of its no-fault law, but in other states the no-fault benefits are limited to personal injuries. Research indicates that no-fault plans

---

[35] Colorado, Connecticut, Florida, Georgia, Hawaii, Kansas, Massachusetts, Michigan, Minnesota, Nevada, New Jersey, New York, North Dakota, Pennsylvania, Utah, and Kentucky. See *Analysis of Automobile No-Fault Statutes* (New York: General Adjustment Bureau, February 1977). See also Robert H. Barrett, "How to Analyze a No-Fault Automobile Insurance Law," *CPCU Annals*, vol. 25, no. 2 (June 1972), p. 101.

should not include property damage claims because the long delays and expensive attorney costs which characterize personal injury lawsuits are not present.[36]

Space does not permit an individual analysis of all the no-fault state laws. However, the relative success of the Michigan law suggests a more detailed description of this law to be advisable. In many ways this law is the broadest of the 16 no-fault laws. Every owner of a motor vehicle[37] must maintain 20/ 40/10 liability limits. Tort liability is abolished for covered motor vehicles *except* for: (1) intentional harm caused to persons or property; (2) noneconomic losses, unless the injured person has suffered death, serious impairment of body function, or permanent disfigurement; and (3) damages for expenses, work loss, and survivors' loss in excess of the maximum limits of the law. (Note that no dollar amount threshold for medical expenses applies; instead the threshold is called a "verbal" one.) Benefits for personal injuries, payable on a no-fault basis, include all reasonable and customary charges for unlimited medical expenses and rehabilitation, funeral expenses up to $1,000, work loss of income (and substitute services of $20 per day) for three years of 85 percent of earnings up to $1,000 per month (plus annual cost-of-living increases). The benefits are reduced by the amounts payable under workers' compensation and social security. Property protection of up to $1 million damage to tangible property other than vehicles or their contents is included, with an optional $300 deductible. (Properly parked cars are covered as an exception to this property protection part of the law.) Subrogation rights by insurers for collision losses are eliminated. The law also requires insurers in Michigan to offer their policyholders the option of designating their health insurance as primary coverage before the automobile coverage applies for medical expenses.[38]

Evaluation of the results of state no-fault laws. No simple conclusion has yet emerged as to whether the state no-fault laws have been really successful. The effects of the laws on the total costs of automobile liability insurance have been studied in some states, with savings as compared with tort liability calculated as considerable in Massachusetts (about 50 percent) but as much smaller in Florida (about 25 percent).[39] Critics question these and other stud-

---

[36] Robert I. Mehr and Gary W. Eldred, "Should the No-Fault Concept Be Applied to Automobile Property Damage?" *Journal of Risk and Insurance,* vol. 42, no. 1 (March 1975), p. 17.

[37] Designed for public highway use, if it has more than two wheels. Under most of the state no-fault laws, private passenger cars are the only vehicles included, with commercial cars, all trucks, and motorcycles not subject to the laws.

[38] Pennsylvania does this, too. Considerable debate has arisen as to whether health insurance should be primary coverage, or whether costs are reduced more by having auto insurance as primary (as in New York and New Jersey). See also B. P. Russell, "The Issue of Primary: Who Serves Best?" *Journal of Insurance,* January–February 1973, p. 2.

[39] Calvin H. Brainard, "Massachusetts: Loss Experience under No-Fault in 1971— Analysis and Implications"; and Calvin H. Brainard and John Fitzgerald, "First-Year

ies as being too limited and not current and as not including the increased costs of motor vehicle physical damage costs and other add-on costs of motor medical expense and disability income coverages. Other comparisons of how much rates have increased in the 16 no-fault states as compared with the other states indicate no significant total difference.[40] The savings on fewer liability claims and on reduced costs in settling directly with the insured for injuries often appear to be largely offset by payments to insureds who would not collect under tort liability.

Advocates of the no-fault laws emphasize other benefits besides costs. They claim that the purpose of no-fault laws is to pay more of the insurance premium dollar to automobile accident victims, and to do so quicker and more equitably. Research shows (1) that less than half of claimants are able to recover benefits under the liability system (which excludes the negligent victims, one-car crashes, and combined or undetermined fault cases), (2) that serious injuries are compensated for only 30 percent of their losses which minor injuries are overpaid, and (3) that the average time to final settlement is 16 months after an accident.[41] Although the overall effectiveness of no-fault laws has not been established, some studies show that the portion of the premium dollar received by victims for economic losses has increased in certain no-fault states, such as Michigan and Florida.[42] It has also been found that the frequency of bodily injury liability claims has been cut substantially in some no-fault states.[43]

Opponents of no-fault legislation include some insurers, trial lawyers and their professional associations, and others. Such opponents vigorously deny that no-fault can reduce automobile costs, and argue that legislation should not take away an individual's right to sue for pain and suffering. The effect of no-fault laws on personal responsibility for negligence, with possible increased carelessness as a result, is pointed out as a major defect. One of the greatest difficulties under no-fault is in changing rating systems which may inequitably allocate higher costs to persons involved in accidents who are in

---

Cost Results under No-Fault Automobile Insurance: A Comparison of the Florida and Massachusetts Experience," *Journal of Risk and Insurance*, vol. 40, no. 1 (March 1973), and vol. 41, no. 1 (March 1974), p. 95 and p. 29, respectively. See also Jerry D. Todd, "The Costing of Automobile No-Fault Insurance," *Journal of Risk and Insurance*, vol. 43, no. 3 (September 1976), p. 431.

[40] State Farm Insurance Company studies, in 1975.

[41] U. S. Department of Transportation, *Economic Consequences of Automobile Accident Injuries* (Washington, D.C.: U.S. Government Printing Office, 1970), vol. 1.

[42] *No-Fault Press Reference Manual* (Bloomington, Ill.: State Farm Insurance Companies, 1973 and continuously updated). This reference also refutes the idea that no-fault laws have caused heavy insurer losses in no-fault states, claiming that inflation pressures and some legislatively mandated premium reductions in a few states have been the major causes of these losses. See also U.S. Department of Transportation, *Survey of 16 No-Fault States* (Washington, D.C.: U.S. Government Printing Office, 1977).

[43] Michigan and Colorado, in a 1978 actuarial study sponsored by the U.S. Senate Commerce Committee.

no way responsible for them. Injured persons may suffer serious losses, be only partially compensated under the no-fault system, and then have their rates increased. At the same time, the negligent parties may merely say "We're sorry," and have no losses or rate increases. Departing from the traditional legal concept that the person at fault in automobile cases should pay is repugnant to many persons, whether or not their livelihood depends on the tort liability system. Although there is legal precedent for such change in the U.S. workers' compensation system, treating automobile accidents as a social rather than an individual responsibility is not the same as holding employers liable without fault.

Interrelated issues. In summary, the present situation remains chaotic. The emphasis seems to be shifting from the idea of having fault determine the liability of one person to another to the idea of no-fault compensation when someone is injured. Yet most of the state no-fault laws were passed before 1975, and progress in other states in recent years has been minimal. *Whether or not the laws should* change in this way is not fully researched, documented, or supported by the public, the insurers, the legal profession, or other parties involved in the changes.[44] Just *how* the laws should change is also debatable in many respects.

The complexity of the issues is not limited to the no-fault concept, as many other related issues are involved. One author points out that the automobile reforms are really three clashes of principles between (1) *public* and *private* insurance, (2) *federal* and *state* regulation, and (3) *fault* and *no-fault* systems. He concludes that in the long range the key issue still in doubt is the first, whether government-operated or privately operated systems will prevail.[45]

It is almost more difficult to think of *un*related issues than it is to name problem areas which are involved with the automobile and its insurance. (Pollution? Gas shortages? Discrimination? Safety? Products liability? Fraud?) Expanded health benefits for all under proposed federal *national health insurance* will also be crucial to the issue of who is going to pay for the medical costs of automobile accident victims. *Cost inflation* in medical costs, jury awards, and automobile repair costs are also a major part of the impetus toward solving the "automobile problem" which this chapter described in its beginning section.

Perhaps these are all part of *the* problem, but how can *the* solution be adopted until we really know? Research should help identify the problem or problems. When one considers that liability law has been applied to the auto-

---

[44] For research on no-fault systems in seven European countries (France, Great Britain, Germany, Italy, Netherlands, Sweden, and Switzerland, see Werner Pfennigstorf, *Compensation of Auto Accident Victims in Europe* (Chicago: American Mutual Insurance Alliance, 1972), which is also reported on by Everett T. Bartelbaugh, Jr., in the *CPCU Annals*, vol. 26, no. 2 (June 1973), p. 36, with the conclusion that the systems seem to be working well.

[45] Robert E. Keeton, "Beyond Current Reforms in Automobile Reparations," *Journal of Risk and Insurance*, vol. 40, no. 1 (March 1973), p. 31.

mobile situation for a half century or more, a few years' wait for a solution does not seem too long if better solutions can be formulated during that time. The problems are so serious, and so many alternatives have been considered, suggested, or partially adopted, that time appears to be one of the important ingredients required for the development of the successful answer.

Tort liability reform.   The need for time is stressed by those who advocate *correcting the existing liability systems*. Reforms that will alleviate the undesirable aspects make some good sense—*if* they can be achieved with reasonable rapidity by such things as better rating laws, fewer underwriting restrictions, noncancellation guarantees, contingency fee controls, rehabilitation, more complete uninsured motorists coverage, and insurer insolvency protection. However, from a practical view, there appears to be little chance that all of these changes will occur on a broad enough base to discourage existing or new state no-fault laws. Many of these improvements will be needed regardless of state-by-state adoption of limited no-fault laws.

The advocates of complete reform programs now mirror the attitude of the American population today—"freedom *now*," "black power *now*," "peace *now*," and so on. Perhaps no-fault systems will provide some of the needed answers to some of the problems. The fundamental issues, however, are not that easily swept aside, and will involve many changes in many directions to keep up with the social changes of the late 1970s and early 1980s.

The relationship of automobile liability reforms to *all* areas of liability law is stressed in one recent report[46] about the tort system. This summary of needed tort reforms is critical of the tendency in recent years to make most changes through the courts rather than through legislative action. Six recommendations are made that would affect the general applicability of the tort system to liability law: (1) the need for a conscious policy of statutory guidance in making necessary adjustments; (2) the use of arbitration for small cases, and on a compulsory basis for claims under $10,000; (3) the improvement of the legal process to eliminate unmeritorious cases and to hasten trials; (4) the stabilizing and tightning of key rules of law, such as by defining the "foreseeability" of injuries and by codifying comparative negligence laws; (5) the assurance of reasonable costs of legal counsel by limiting contingency fees (to 40 percent of awards up to $50,000 and 25 percent thereafter); and (6) the reformation of the court systems through careful study by state planning commissions. The question of auto-related liability is discussed separately, with the conclusion that true no-fault statutes must be prepared for, but adopted only if close monitoring of the experience of the best existing systems justifies their enactment. Recommendations for needed reforms in product, professional, and government liability and in workers' compensation systems are also included.

---

[46] "Righting the Liability Balance" (California Citizen's Commission on Tort Reform, Fall 1977), *Journal of Insurance*, January–February 1978.

Another crucial solution: Automobile safety and loss prevention

One final solution to the automobile problem(s) needs emphasis. *Traffic safety, or loss prevention* in regard to automobile accidents, should be a major objective of our society. The solutions discussed in this chapter are primarily *insurance* solutions. Few of these solutions include accident prevention among their goals, but nevertheless these solutions must be evaluated in terms of their potential correlation with the effect upon automobile accidents. Although insurance is blamed for rising automobile costs, how can it solve such a problem as the approximately 25,000 traffic deaths (about half of all traffic deaths) caused each year in the United States by the use of alcohol?

Efforts are being made, however, to coordinate the safety work of insurers, government, and independent researchers, such as those in universities. The Insurance Institute for Highway Safety promotes broad research studies and annual traffic safety conferences. On the government level, the National Highway Traffic Safety Administration is helping to formulate safety regulations for states and automobile manufacturers. A number of these regulations, requiring better bumpers, seat belt systems, air bags, and other safety designs and equipment, gradually are going into effect. More will undoubtedly be enforced in future years. The bureau also lists these as the top-priority areas: (1) driver licensing, (2) traffic records, (3) alcohol, (4) emergency medical services, (5) motor vehicle registration, (6) police traffic services, and (7) accident location and cause research.[47] How far the states have to go is indicated by the fact that only a few states had their long range *plans* approved by the Department of Transportation through this agency by 1979. The difficulties of applying safety standards are also noted: only 27 states now require periodic safety inspections of automobiles, after 8 states dropped such programs because of high costs and problems of enforcement.

It is also sad to note that cooperation by the public in auto accident prevention is woefully lacking. Although safety belts have been required for more than ten years on all passenger vehicles manufactured in the United States, studies show that fewer than one out of five drivers use them! Similar less-than-satisfactory results could be noted in the public's cooperation in complying with the national 55 miles per hour speed limit, which is also a proven means of saving lives on the highways of America.

To have the prettiest automobile rather than the safest one seems to be losing favor among automobile buyers, although beauty, style, and chrome are admittedly still much pleasanter to talk about than safety belts and harnesses, padded dashes, collapsible steering columns, double-lock doors, brake systems, and the hundreds of other features which determine just how safe an

---

[47] Examples of such research conducted under the Transportation Safety Act of 1974 are: *Societal Costs of Motor Vehicle Accidents* (Washington, D.C.: U.S. Department of Transportation, National Highway Traffic Safety Administration, December 1976); and *Analysis and Summary of Accident Investigations, 1973–76* (Washington, D.C.: U.S. Department of Transportation, Federal Highway Administration, 1977).

automobile is. With help from Ralph Nader's investigations of the automobile field and more support from an educated and concerned public, progress in automobile and traffic safety should improve. Research will be the basis for much of this work of the future. One example is the work being done under federal contracts to develop research safety vehicles (RSVs) that will produce safe, fuel-efficient, and reasonably priced automobiles for the 1980s.[48]

One hopes that the solutions are less drastic than the bill passed by the California Senate recently (it did not become a law) to outlaw all gasoline-powered automobiles. Although this was proposed as an antipollution bill, it might also serve to shock some complacent persons into action leading to real solutions for automobile insurance! Another extreme example of how much further loss-prevention efforts can go is the recent sentencing of a Moscow drunken driver to execution by a firing squad.[49] This deterrent to bad driving habits illustrates how mild current U.S. punishments of traffic safety violators are.

The active role of insurers, as well as government and the public, in every field affecting atuomobile insurance will be needed in the future in order to make progress in the crucial area of automobile loss prevention.

FOR REVIEW AND DISCUSSION

1. Why is automobile insurance needed? Whose viewpoints are pertinent, and how do those viewpoints differ?
2. Automobile liability insurance is unquestionably one of the great dilemmas of the insurance business today. It is oftentimes just referred to as "the automobile problem," but realistically it is a complex group of interrelated problems.
   a. What do you identify as *three* of the major problems?
   b. In your judgment, why has each of these problems arisen?
   c. What is being done about each of these problems by (1) the insurers and (2) the government?
   d. Show how the problems you have chosen are interrelated.
3. Is the increasing cost of automobile insurance due primarily to the *loss,* the *expense,* or the *profit* portion of insurance premiums? Explain why you did or did not choose each of these premium segments.
4. What factors have caused the rising costs of automobile bodily injury liability insurance? Automobile physical damage insurance?
5. How is state insurance regulation related to the problem of rising automobile insurance prices?

---

[48] "The Socially Responsible Car," *Journal of American Insurance,* Summer 1977, p. 23.

[49] This sentencing was reported in the *Columbus* (Ohio) *Citizens-Journal* on January 21, 1978, for truck driver Valentin Shimko, who killed seven people and injured eight others at a crowded subway-trolley-bus stop.

6. What approaches are used to regulate automobile insurance rates? Which approach is most widely used, and which is most effective?

7. Mr. Beane mentions that the rising toll of automobile accident deaths is outrageous, and he doesn't "see why the bad drivers should be allowed to purchase automobile insurance." Mrs. Beane doesn't agree with him, saying that "bad drivers are just the ones who most need to have the insurance and for the injured victims' sake should be required to have insurance." With whom do you agree, and why?

8. Which of the "automobile insurance solutions" are based upon *government* action? Which on *voluntary* action by insurers or insureds? Explain.

9. What are automobile (assigned risk) insurance plans? Explain their (*a*) purpose, (*b*) method of operation, and (*c*) success, or lack of it. What other systems have some states adopted to solve the problems of the automobile "residual market"?

10. Discuss (*a*) the merits and (*b*) the faults of the following solutions to the "problem of the unpaid innocent automobile accident victim":
    a. Compulsory automobile liability legislation.
    b. Financial responsibility laws.
    c. Unsatisfied judgment funds.
    d. Uninsured motorists coverage.
    e. Automobile (assigned risk) insurance plans.
    f. No-fault automobile insurance plans.

11. Differentiate among the state laws which you consider to be the *three major* types of legislation that are designed to cope with the problem of the unpaid automobile accident victim.

12. What are the (*a*) advantages and (*b*) disadvantages of uninsured motorists coverage as a solution to the automobile accident victim problem?

13. How do automobile *compensation* and automobile *accident insurance* differ? Which term applies best to the no-fault plans that have been adopted?

14. Divide the class into groups, and assign each group one of the automobile no-fault insurance solutions, such as the "true" no-fault, the "modified" no-fault, and the "pseudo" no-fault laws. Have each group prepare a statement explaining why its solution is the best possible answer to the automobile dilemma today.

15. Relate automobile safety and loss prevention to the solution you choose as the best one for meeting the automobile insurance problem today.

16. Explain how the "true" no-fault laws vary from others which have been called "yes-fault" or "add-on" laws. How do the individual state laws in each category differ?

17. How may the *long*-range problems of no-fault automobile insurance vary from the short-range ones?

18. Evaluate the success of state no-fault laws during the past decade. Will other legislation be needed to improve the situation?

Chapter 24

Concepts considered in Chapter 24—Automobile insurance coverages

Basic coverages for automobile insurance usually include *liability, medical payments, uninsured motorists,* and *physical damages* protection.

Basic policy forms are partially standardized for insuring *personal* (emphasized in this chapter) and *business* auto exposures (see Appendix E).

Underwriting is a major task of insurers trying to attain a profit by—

    Selection of insureds—restricted today by the *"right to buy"* concept, limited rights to *cancel,* and broader *renewal* guarantees.

    Rating, or pricing, for—

        Automobile classifications, *private passenger, commercial, public.*

        Private passenger auto liability premiums, which have 161 classifications (not counting territory) based on the age, sex, and marital status of the *operators;* the *use* of the auto; and *driver training, good student, multicar,* and *safe-driver* rules.

        Physical damage premiums, which also consider the *car's age and value,* and *deductibles.*

Basic parts of the personal policy (PAP), illustrating the *readable contract trend,* with *personalized and simplified format,* are:

    Declarations, containing basic data about insureds, autos, and coverages, and the **insuring agreement and definitions.**

    Part A—Liability is the most important coverage and includes:

        Bodily injury and property damage in a *single limit of liability.*

        Defense and supplementary payments for *defense, investigation, bonds.*

        Covered persons insured are carefully defined.

        Policy limits and **other insurance** are explained.

    Part B—Medical payments is small in cost but pays *regardless of fault* for insured, family, and other occupants in the insured's car.

    Part C—Uninsured motorists protection for the insured, family, and guests —for injuries caused by uninsured motorists.

    Part D—Damage to your auto is *physical damage* insurance for:

        Comprehensive (other than collision) coverage for "all risks."

        Collision coverage for damage by hitting other objects, even if the insured's own fault, usually on a $100 or more deductible basis.

    Part E—Conditions in order to collect under the contract after an accident or loss—what insureds should and should not do when filing claims.

    Part F—General provisions applies to the entire contract, explaining assignment, cancellation, no-fault coverage (if applicable), and other items.

    No-fault coverage in some states is a new type of contract coverage which does away with at least some tort liability, and provides for loss payment by the insured's *own* insurance company.

Automobile insurance coverages

More than 110 million automobiles and 30 million trucks and buses fill the roads of America. Each one is an *individual* problem for its owner or driver, as well as a collective source of the problems of costs, losses, and need for insurance protection discussed in Chapter 23. This chapter explains how individual motorists solve many of their problems through the purchase of adequate *automobile insurance coverages*.

The good news is that, with very few exceptions, motorists can buy automobile insurance today in a form that represents one of the broadest of all insurance contracts, covering many different cars, drivers, and coverages (liability, property, and medical) in one convenient policy. In doing so, motorists transfer almost all of their risks to the insurers. The bad news is that some problems remain.

What remains for the insureds to criticize? The *cost* of the contract is probably the basis of most complaints, with generalized comments of "it's too high" or "it's gone up too much" appearing most frequently. *Coverage, availability,* and particularly the *services* that go with the contract are other major sources of grumbling by policyholders. The speed and amount of loss payment, the defense of claims, the advice on coverages and losses, and the cancellation of protection are among the subjects of policyholder complaints. This chapter treats both automobile insurance coverages and their costs.

BASIC INSURANCE COVERAGES

Automobile insurance is the largest field of property-liability insurance, accounting for more than 40 percent of total premiums. There are two major divisions of the automobile insurance business. The first provides the *casualty* (mostly *liability*) coverages; and the second, the *physical damage* coverages. The casualty coverages are: (*a*) bodily injury liability, (*b*) property damage

681

liability, (c) medical payment, (d) uninsured motorists, and, in some states, (e) no-fault coverage. In the physical damage category are to be found those forms of automobile insurance that protect the insured from loss or damage to the car itself; these are (a) fire, (b) theft, (c) collision, and (d) a number of miscellaneous coverages such as windstorm, hail, earthquake, explosion, water damage, flood, riot and civil commotion, and vandalism and malicious mischief. All of the perils mentioned in (d) are often combined with fire and theft coverage in what is called "comprehensive physical damage" coverage.

The portions of the total automobile insurance premiums of $23 billion for the major coverages are:[1]

Casualty (liability, medical payments, and uninsured motorists) coverage	65%
Physical damage coverage	35%
	100%

Because automobile physical damage insurance is so intimately associated with the automobile liability business, it is logical to discuss the two classes of business together. Although separate contracts were formerly written for liability and physical damages, today almost all of the contracts issued combine both major coverages in a single policy.

BASIC POLICY FORMS

Automobile insurance is not a field in which all contracts are alike. There are some similarities among the most common automobile contracts, and many provisions have been standardized by the voluntary action of insurers who use forms developed by associations of insurers or rating bureaus.[2] However, in general the automobile insurance market is one with a relatively unstandardized product. More than 800 insurance companies sell automobile insurance, and the field is known both for price competition and for nonprice competition in the form of contract variations. Some contract differences are significant to the insurance buyer; others are sales "frills" and attention-getting features. Wise automobile owners read their automobile insurance contracts to determine exactly what has been purchased.

Different automobile contracts are used for different exposures to loss. The two general kinds of automobile exposures are those associated with *family* (personal) and *business* (commercial) use.

For more than the past 20 years, most family automobile owners and drivers have been insured by the "family automobile policy," with a small part of the

---

[1] *Insurance Facts* (New York: Insurance Information Institute, 1978), p. 12.

[2] The major ones are the Insurance Services Office and the National Association of Independent Insurers. Although some of the larger insurers have developed their own contracts, with minor differences from the bureau forms, this chapter analyzes the ISO contracts because of their wide use.

market protected by a somewhat more limited contract known as the "special automobile policy." Most business automobile exposures have been insured by the "basic automobile policy" or the very broad "comprehensive automobile policy," which has often been combined with general liability coverages. A specialized contract, the "garage liability policy," has also been available for automobile sales and service business firms.

As part of the trend toward more readable and understandable insurance contracts, major changes occurred during 1977–78. The Insurance Services Office introduced new automobile insurance contracts in order to reduce the number of contracts and simplify the language used in the policies. The result is that in most states family automobile exposures are now insured under a new contract known as the *personal auto policy* (PAP),[3] and business automobiles are insured in a policy called the *business auto policy* (BAP), which was just beginning to be used in late 1978. The analysis of the PAP contract is emphasized in this chapter, because of its widespread use for automobile insurance protection of individuals and families. The BAP contract coverage is summarized in Appendix E for the benefit of more advanced insurance students.

P691

UNDERWRITING

Basic parts and goals

Automobile underwriting is based upon the same purposes and principles as were discussed in Chapter 6. The functions of underwriting were described as the *selection* and *rating* of insurance for a group of insureds who will in total provide the insurer with a reasonable profit and maintain its financial strength.

In automobile insurance during recent years this has been a considerable task. The job has been made more difficult in the past decade by factors such as were mentioned in Chapter 23:

wants us to know?

1. The increasing costs of automobile accidents, for many underlying reasons such as rising medical and repair costs, income losses resulting from injuries, and jury verdicts.
2. The types of rate regulation applied by some states, which create a time lag between increasing costs and permitted rate increases.
3. Social considerations, in which insurance is required or encouraged by every state, cancellations are more restricted, and applications are harder to deny than ever before.

The underwriting process is usually performed through the combined efforts

---

[3] Another new contract, used by many insurers that are members of the National Association of Independent Insurers (NAII), is the *Family Car Policy*. This has been approved in many states, and it has the same purposes of easy-to-read understandability as the PAP policy. Some individual insurers still use contracts designed only for use by their own insureds.

of the insurer, its agents, and some organizations outside the insurance business. Insurers have the main responsibility for the selection and rating of insureds because they are accepting the risk of loss. The initial responsibility, however, often falls on the agents. They are the ones who solicit the prospects for insurance or accept applications. The application is ordinarily a signed *written statement* by the applicant, including basic information about the automobile, its location and use, its drivers, the amounts and types of insurance desired, and the insurance accident and traffic violation records. Oftentimes the agent may bind the coverage immediately, pending the writing of the actual contract at the insurer's home or branch office, or at the agency office. Agents strive to obtain a reasonable group of insureds for their insurers. If they do a poor job of selecting, with many insureds in the less desirable classifications or with high loss results, they may find that the insurer no longer wants them as representatives. Many agents are most interested in writing automobile insurance for persons or families that are (or are prospects for being) insured with their agencies for home, health, or other types of insurance as well as the automobile policy. Oftentimes, the underwriting decisions of the agent are supplemented by *credit investigations* (Equifax or others) and by motor vehicle department reports requested by the insurer. This is a common practice, especially for new applicants, younger drivers, and many other of the more difficult classifications. Insurers must use such information carefully to avoid lawsuits claiming inaccuracies under the Fair Credit Reporting Act.

The underwriting task requires a balancing of objectives. On the one hand, simplicity and economy of applying the rules, classifications, and rates are highly desired. On the other hand, a fair and equitable system, distinguishing by class and rate wherever a sizable difference can be determined accurately, is needed. The compromise is between the two extremes of (1) utmost simplicity (one rate to all) and (2) extreme but costly complexity (overrefinement into too many classifications). In essence, the goal is expressed but not precisely defined in the rating laws of many states as one which requires *fair* discrimination among insureds but prohibits rates that discriminate unfairly.

Selection

A growing public concept, summarized as the "right to buy insurance," has caused great concern to insurers in recent years. In automobile insurance, the idea manifests itself in an attitude that *everyone* ought to be able to buy insurance. Partially, this concept is derived from vague reference to inalienable rights under the Constitution, or rights to protect as well as own property. The growing social nature of automobile insurance (see Chapter 23), with the state requiring or highly encouraging its purchase, has probably been a major factor in the development of this attitude. The concept is contrary to one of the basic ideas of underwriting, that is, that the insurer should be able to *select* the insureds with whom it desires to do business.

How can these concepts be brought together? In practice, the theories must be applied on a less-than-absolute basis. The complete freedom of an insurer to select its insureds is impossible today, as all states have assigned risk plans through which almost all of the substandard, higher rated risks can obtain coverage. The complete right of an individual to buy insurance is tempered by several practical qualifications: except for a very small percentage of motorists (less than 1 percent is estimated, mostly alcohol or drug addicts and habitual traffic offenders), an individual can obtain insurance coverage. However, some applicants may not be able to specify the insurer, the coverages, or the limits they want, and such applicants may have to pay a premium much higher than the standard cost.

The common practice by which insurers have voluntarily curtailed their *right to cancel* the automobile insurance contract further illustrates the growing restrictions on the selection of insureds. Starting in the early 1960s, many insurers guaranteed that the policy would not be canceled by the insurer after an investigation period of about 60 days, except for a few stated commonsense reasons. The exceptions included nonpayment of premiums, fraudulent misrepresentation, and/or loss of the driver's license by the insured, and several serious motor vehicle offenses, such as driving while intoxicated, leaving the scene of an accident without reporting, and three moving traffic violations within 18 months. The noncancellation agreement has been broadened by most insurers to permit cancellation only for (1) nonpayment of premiums or (2) suspension or revocation of the driver's license or motor vehicle registration of the insureds who customarily drive the automobile. Almost all state laws also similarly restrict the right of the insurer to cancel today. Reasons for cancellation are to be given the insured in the case of cancellation, and most states specify 10–30 days' notice before cancellation. On new business, most states permit cancellation (without the restrictions) during an underwriting period of about 60 days.[4]

The problem is broader than just noncancellation, however, which only guarantees the insured protection during the policy period (not over one year). Some insurers, including several large independent insurers, have extended the noncancellation provision to include a *five-year renewal* guarantee. A few additional exceptions beyond the two basic ones stated above are specified, such as convictions for a hit-and-run accident, driving while intoxicated or drugged, and motor vehicle homicide.

---

[4] The state laws are far from uniform, however, as many add other permissible reasons for cancellation, such as physical or mental conditions, endangering public safety, fraudulent claims, habitual use of drugs or alcohol, and others. See *Fire, Casualty, and Surety Bulletins* (Cincinnati: National Underwriter Company, Casualty-Surety Section Cra.) for comparisons of the individual states.

The criticism of insurers also extends to *refusal to write* certain classes of insureds, by age, occupation, or other such characteristics. Arbitrary refusal on such bases is now condemned by the major automobile insurance associations, and by state laws which restrict the right of the insurer to refuse or to discontinue contracts indiscriminately.

Government needs to make real efforts to remove the irresponsible, unfit, and reckless drivers from the road. Then it is possible to apply the objective that everyone with a valid driver's license should be able to obtain automobile insurance. On behalf of the insurers it may be noted that (1) few, if any, drivers who really *deserve* to be driving are arbitrarily denied automobile insurance coverage; (2) cancellations and nonrenewals are a very small part of the total number of insureds; and (3) improvements in state laws, contract provisions, and insurer practices in automobile underwriting have been significant.

The dilemma of the insurer—and perhaps a reason why everyone should not have the "right to buy" automobile insurance—is shown in the following example from the State Farm Insurance Companies files. A 25-year-old applicant was turned down after admitting to two citations on his motor vehicle record in the past five years. He complained to the Department of Insurance and told it that he was getting a little disgusted with the way the so-called good agencies tried to take advantage of people. However, instead of two citations, he actually had 19, a total of 46 entries on his motor vehicle report, and he had been picked up 11 times for speeding. His car wasn't too hot either—six noisy muffler traffic tickets—and once he didn't even have any license plates for it.

Rating

If nearly all motorists are (or should be) insured, the practical emphasis of underwriting shifts from selection to *rating,* or pricing, of the automobile insurance contract.

Automobile classifications. Automobiles are classed as: (1) private passenger, (2) commercial, (3) public, (4) dealers', and (5) miscellaneous. These classifications are based to some degree upon the type of car and to a greater degree upon the use of the car. The class designations are for the purpose of differentiating among the various major types of automobile risks. The miscellaneous category includes a number of automobiles designed for special purposes, such as fire and police vehicles, ambulances, hearses, auto homes, motorcycles, snowmobiles, motor scooters, tractors (not of the truck type), and trailers or semitrailers. Automotive equipment not insurable under the automobile policy includes golf carts, lawn mowers, and power shovels. Risks of this type are normally insured under separate inland marine or other contracts.

Private passenger vehicles are the example chosen in this chapter for illustrating the classification and rating system of automobile insurance. (See the next several headings of this section.)

Commercial vehicles are classified in accordance with the size of the vehicle and the business use classification of the insured. In addition to factors of weight and use, some territories give consideration to a mileage-radius factor. Commercial trucks involving long-distance (more than 50 miles) operations are definitely more hazardous than those confined to a local territory. For rating purposes, *public* automobiles include private and public livery, taxicabs, and buses. Because public automobile rates are high and because there is no risk when the car is not in operation, a system of rating has been devised on an earnings basis per $100 of gross receipts or on a mileage basis. Garage, service station, and other automobile *dealers* are treated separately from other commercial insureds under special contracts designed for their particular needs.

When there are five or more commercial or public cars under a single ownership, a "fleet" policy is issued, based upon discounts and the estimated average future exposure. The advance premium charged is adjusted at the end of the policy term by determining the actual number of vehicles and their use during the policy term.

Private passenger automobile liability premiums. As insured in the personal automobile policy, the rating procedure for private passenger automobiles illustrates the process of determining automobile insurance premiums. Different factors are important in calculating the price charged by the insurer for the various basic coverages, as discussed later in this chapter. However, the major portion of the price of automobile insurance applies to the liability and physical damage coverages. The medical payments coverage and the uninsured motorists coverage are relatively small parts of the total premium and therefore are not included in this description of the rating system.

The classification and rating system for private passenger automobile insurance in most states since 1976 produces 161 classifications, not including differences in territory. This is the plan described in the following paragraphs. About four states use plans which result in 260 classes, and about a half dozen use the pre-1965 plan of nine classes.[5]

The *base premium* for bodily injury and property damage *liability* is determined by two factors, the *territory* and the *limits of liability* chosen for the contract. Tables showing the basic premiums for the minimum limits for bodily injury liability coverage and property damage liability coverage are developed for each territory. Higher limits are also available. The new personal auto policy uses tables with a single combined limit for all liability coverages (see later section).

---

[5] Some individual insurers also still use the nine-class system based upon the pre-1965 plan. Youthful male drivers under 25 are all put in one of two classes, married or unmarried, and no separate class for female drivers is used. Business use and driving to work are also factors.

The territorial designation is according to the state and territory in which the automobile is principally garaged and used. Some states have as many as 50 separate rating territories, while others have only a few. The differentiation is based upon both the usual rural-urban differences in exposure to loss and upon the loss experience in the territory for several years. Claims statistics in changing the rates are determined by accidents charged to the location where the car is principally garaged and used. Thus an accident caused by a person from a large city is not charged to a small city where the accident may have occurred. The rates vary considerably by territory. Even within the same state, the rate for the same coverage may be several times as high in one section as in another.

Primary rating factors. Next, two sets of *classification factors,* primary and secondary, are determined, and the total is applied to the base premium. The *primary classification factors* are:

1. *Age, sex,* and *marital status* of the automobile operators.
2. The *use* of the automobile.
3. *Driver training* and *good student* qualifications.

A growing controversy in recent years concerns the use of age and sex differentials in automobile insurance rating. Three states (Hawaii, North Carolina, and Massachusetts) by 1979 prohibited rate classifications based on age or sex, but other states maintained the system described here.

Age of the drivers and owners is an important factor, for many research studies have shown that the younger age groups are the cause of many more accidents, particularly fatal and serious ones, than their proportion of the total number of drivers would indicate. For example, the National Safety Council reports that drivers under age 25 are 22 percent of all drivers but are involved in 38 percent of all accidents. The current system used in most states reflects statistics which show that the youngest drivers are the most likely to have accidents, but that the accident rate goes down gradually from age 18 to age 29.

Older operators are divided into three groups (no youthful drivers):

1. Females, ages 30–64, only operator.
2. Age 65 or over, one or more operators.
3. All others.

The youthful operator classifications also reflect the fact that in general youthful *male* operators have more accidents[6] than youthful *female* operators and that youthful *unmarried* men have more accidents than youthful *married* men. The classes developed are in four groups, with further breakdowns for

---

[6] The age-old controversy over which sex drives better is not resolved by this fact alone. Where, when, and how much males and females drive may show otherwise. Let the argument continue, and *vive la différence!*

age 17 (or under), each age to 20, and combined age classes for ages 21-24 and 25–29. The number of classes developed total more than 100:

4. Females, unmarried, under age 25.
5. Males, married, under age 25.
6. Males, unmarried, under 25, and not owners or principal operators of the insured automobile.
7. Males, unmarried, under age 30, and owners or principal operators.

In approximate terms, the relationship among these groups is illustrated by the range of the factor applied, from less than 1.00 for the first group, 1.00 for the second and third, and a progressively large factor for groups 4–7, with group 7 males age 17 having a factor of more than 3.00 applied.

Operators affect the above classifications if they are residents of the same household as the insured or if they customarily operate the insured automobile. Unmarried females and males under age 25 who are absent from home while attending school over 100 miles away are rated as being married.

The above age-sex-marital factor is combined in tables with the *use* factor, based upon five classes.

1. Pleasure use.
2. Used to or from work less than 15 miles one way (10 miles, in some plans).
3. Used to or from work more than 15 miles one way (10 miles, in some plans).
4. Business use.
5. Farm use.

When the first group is rated as 1.00, the factor applied to groups 2–4 is higher and the factor applied to group 5 is lower.

Driver training is important for youthful drivers from age 17 through age 20. It saves lives, reduces accidents, *and* lowers insurance rates. The standards for qualified courses are usually set by the state education departments, often involving about 30 hours of classroom work and 6 hours of driving. Those with driver training receive a lower rating factor, about 5–10 percent less than that of drivers of the same age without driver training. This one factor can make a substantial dollar difference for many youthful drivers.

Good students also receive lower rates from some insurers by meeting certain qualifications (full-time students earning a B average, in the upper 20 percent of class, or on the honor roll or equivalent). The rates average about 20 percent less than those for other students. The theory is that the better students use automobiles less than other students.

Secondary rating factors. There are three types of *secondary classification factors.* The *multicar* exposure factor is based on the idea that if more than one private passenger car is owned by one person (or by relatives of the same household in joint names), the cars will not each be used as much as is the case where only one car is owned. This factor results in a combined premium that is at least 15 percent less than the total premium for single-car exposures would otherwise be.

For 1971 and later model cars, a secondary factor is applied to to classify authos by *type of vehicle* into standard, intermediate, and high performance cars and sports cars.

Another secondary factor is the *safe-driver rating plan* which is used by many insurers to distinguish among drivers on the basis of their accident record, traffic conviction record, and experience (for principal operator only). A "point system" is used to classify drivers into five groups. "Chargeable"[7] accidents during the past three years count one point each whenever they involve bodily injury, or property of more than $200. (The rates go up 30 percent for one accident, 70 percent for two, 120 percent for three, and higher!) Most plans vary somewhat, but 1–3 points are assigned against the insured for motor vehicle violations such as driving while intoxicated, hit and run accidents, and license suspension or revocation. Lack of experience (less than three years' license) by the principal operator of the insured automobile counts as one point against the insured. Although called a secondary factor (applied after the first factors), the importance of the safe-driver plan in increasing rates substantially is apparent in the indicated rate increases.

In review, the primary classification factors (age-sex-marital status, use, driver training, and good-student rules) and the secondary classification factors (multicar, type of vehicle, and safe-driver plans) are combined to be applied against the base premium for each car insured to determine the insurance premium.

Other rating factors.   Other systems have been used in the past. During World War II, mileage (based on gas ration cards) was a simple system. Use and age factors were subsequently determined to be a more accurate basis for predicting losses. For several years in the 1960s discounts were given for "compact" cars, but these, too, were determined to be unjustified by most insurers as better statistical experience was obtained. In fact, these cars have been recently determined to have personal injury risk 40 percent or more greater than that of full-size cars.[8] Undoubtedly, the future will bring other revisions in the system of rating, with some traditional factors being discarded and new ones accepted. One of the promising new systems in use by several insurers employs psychological tests as a method of classifying younger drivers.[9]

Private passenger automobile physical damage premiums.   Automobile

---

[7] These do not include accidents in which the insured was not at fault, such as those in which (1) the insured is reimbursed by or has a judgment against someone else and (2) the car was legally parked.

[8] "The Small Car—A Mixed Blessing," *Journal of American Insurance,* Spring 1977, p. 1.

[9] Grinnel Mutual Reinsurance Company has claimed good success with its system, adopted in the early 1960s, and broadened use is recommended. See C. F. Haner, "Pre-

physical damage[10] insurance premiums are also heavily dependent on the *territory* in which the motor vehicle is operated. The next elements for consideration are the *age and value of the car.* Four age groups are applicable to the comprehensive physical damage and collision coverages: for the current year model and for each preceding year up to three (or older). As the car becomes older, the premium decreases. Automobiles are grouped into different classes identified by the letters A–Z, according to their appropriate values. In anticipating collision and physical damage losses, it is recognized that a Cadillac owner should pay more than an owner of a lower priced car since damage and repair costs will differ substantially.

Collision insurance also uses premiums which vary by *use* of the car, and for the private passenger cars the classes are much the same as for liability insurance.

A final factor of importance is the use of *deductibles* in physical damage coverage. Most policyholders prefer to carry part of collision losses themselves, and the $100 deductible form is most often used. Deductibles of $200–$1,000 and higher are also now available. The insurance buyer should check on the difference between deductible coverages, for often a substantial saving is possible through the use of the higher deductibles. (See later section of this chapter on collision coverage.) For other physical damage losses, the "comprehensive" coverage used to be written without a deductible, but today many contracts have a $50 or a $100 deductible apply. Insureds should consider their ability to withstand smaller losses without strain on their financial budget. For many insureds, the use of a higher deductible with the premium saved going toward the purchase of higher liability limits or other coverages is a good risk-management decision.

THE PERSONAL AUTO POLICY (PAP)

The late 1970s may become known as the era of the major breakthrough toward better consumer understanding of insurance. Although the spirit of consumerism has prevailed for a decade or more (see Chapter 29 for further discussion of this issue), one of the most serious obstacles to real improvement in insurance has been the legal nature and form of insurance contracts themselves. Since these contracts are written by legal and underwriting departments of insurers and often conform to state laws formulated by committees of legal experts, it is not surprising that most insurance contracts contain heavy doses of what critics call "legalese."

---

diction of Automobile Claims by Psychological Methods," *Journal of Risk and Insurance,* vol. 31, no. 1 (March 1968), pp. 49–59. See also William D. Wells, "Psychographics: A Critical Review," *Journal of Marketing Research,* May 1975, p. 196.

[10] For damage to the insured's *own car,* by such perils as fire, theft, collision, and miscellaneous causes. The two most usual coverages are (1) collision and (2) "comprehensive" physical damage (all risks except collision). See later sections of this chapter.

The readable contract trend

The encouraging trend toward simplicity has not been abrupt, but two insurance contracts deserve credit for much of the improvement in personal lines of coverage—the Homeowner's '76 contract, explained in Chapter 27, and the *personal auto policy*,[11] introduced in 1977 and expected to be used in all states before 1980.

Contracts in plain English have also arrived in other fields. Sometimes this has happened because business firms have experimented with and voluntarily used new and more readable contracts. Banks have simplified consumer notes, mortgage loans, trust forms, and other documents. Widespread use, however, seems to require action by the lawmakers, too. An example is the New York law which in 1977 was the first one to require consumer contracts to be written in plain English. This has served as an impetus to relatively rapid changes, even in advance of the effective date in late 1978 for many requirements of the law.

Real progress in attaining more understandable language in insurance contracts will need cooperation among many insurers, their associations, and the legislatures. Not all insurers will join in these major changes willingly, and state-by-state laws will be gradual. The stage is set, however, for an escalation in the next several years which will undoubtedly champion easier-to-read insurance contracts for the consumer of the 1980s. Already the trend has spread to commercial lines, where the *businessowner policy* (see Chapter 27) appeared in 1976, and the *basic auto policy* (see Appendix E) was scheduled for widespread use beginning in late 1978.

The use of simpler language is not always advantageous to insurance consumers. From a legal standpoint, the changes may be a disadvantage sometimes (1) by reducing the value of legal precedents interpreting the language of older contracts and (2) by weakening the presumption that all ambiguities should be interpreted against the insurer.

Personalized and simplified format

One of the most noticeable changes in the readable contracts is the use of simplified language, particularly the references to "you" and "your" for the insureds, and "we" and "our" for the insurers writing the coverages. In the personal auto policy the results are a reduction of one half, from 9,000 to 4,500 words. Larger printing, shorter sentences, emphasis of key words, a glossary of more technical terms, and fewer endorsements (reduced from 45 to about a dozen) also aid considerably in making the contract more understandable to the average policyholder.

The PAP is essentially a combination of and replacement for two contracts

---

[11] Developed by the Insurance Services Offices (ISO) for use by its affiliated companies.

used for several decades to insure private passenger auto risks—the family automobile policy and the special package automobile policy. Many of the same basic coverages are included, but the general format of the contract is rearranged and some of the elements as to limits of coverage and conditions from both of the older policies are used. Definitions of some terms are changed and clarified to help simplify the contract coverage.

Declarations

In general appearance the PAP of different insurers may look quite different. The individual insurers following the Insurance Services Offices form may design their own cover and declarations page. The remaining parts are standardized, however, and these are discussed individually by sections in the following analysis.

Because sample policy kits[12] are available to most students, the entire automobile insurance contract is not reproduced here. Emphasis will be placed on evaluating the meaning of the major provisions of all the parts, but the student may occasionally benefit by referring to the actual contract wording in the policy itself as the PAP is explained.

The declarations page usually includes most of the basic information about the insurer, the insured, the policy period (usually one year, beginning at 12:01 A.M.), the automobile(s),[13] the premiums, and the limits of liability for each of the coverages. Several items give the insurer important data upon which the classification and premium for the insurance contract are based. These items include the description of the automobile or automobiles, their cost, their use, whether or not a mortgage or loan is in existence on them, the location at which they will be principally garaged, and whether or not within the past three years any insurer has canceled automobile insurance for the insured.

It is noted that the coverage parts listed in the declarations are identified as A through D. The contract is a "schedule" type of policy, as the policyholder chooses (by agreement with the insurer in the declarations) many of the coverages to be included by scheduling the limits of liability for each coverage and paying the appropriate premium charge. Part A (liability) and any of the coverages in Part D (damage to your auto) may be written alone or in conjunction with one another. Part B (medical payments) and Part C (uninsured motorists) can be written only with Part A. Medical payments coverage is optional, but uninsured motorists coverage is required by law in many states unless specifically excluded. The usual contract will include all four of these

---

[12] Such as those published by the Insurance Information Institute, 110 William St., New York, N.Y. 10038, or the American Mutual Insurance Alliance, 20 North Wacker Drive, Chicago, Ill. 60606.

[13] Space is provided for two or more cars, since many families insure more than one car in the same policy, with a reduction in cost of 15 percent or more.

coverages. In addition, the last two parts of the contract are included in all contracts, so the total six parts of the contract are:

Part A—Liability
Part B—Medical payments
Part C—Uninsured motorists
Part D—Damage to your auto
Part E—Duties after an accident or loss
Part F—General provisions

The valuation and territorial class, safe-driver plan points, and driver training and multicar rating factors are shown. The declarations page also refers by number to any endorsements which are attached to the later pages of the contract. On the bottom lines the contract is confirmed as a legal contract by signatures of authorized representatives of the insurer.

Automobiles eligible to be written under the PAP are those owned by an individual (or by a husband and wife residing together in the same household), not those owned by corporations. Vehicles with four-wheel drive, usually not including trucks, qualify for this coverage. Trucks which may be insured under this form include pickup, sedan delivery, or panel trucks not customarily used in the insured's business or occupation or used similarly by farmers, ranchers, or federal employees. The vehicles covered must be owned by the insured or leased from others under a contract of at least six months.

Insuring agreement and definitions

The front page of the policy includes a brief insuring agreement and a group of definitions applying to the entire contract.

The use of "you" and "your" is explained as referring to the named insured and spouse living in the same household. "We" and "us" and "our" mean the insurer.

"Covered auto" is any vehicle listed in the declarations, which includes any *owned* trailer of a type designed for use with a private passenger automobile. (Farm wagons or implements towed by such vehicles are also covered.) A *nonowned* auto or trailer used as a *temporary substitute* for an owned vehicle while it is being repaired is included. Full coverage also applies to *acquired vehicles in addition to* the ones described in the declarations if the insured asks that they be covered within 30 days after the acquisition. *Replacement vehicles* are also covered automatically except for physical damage coverage, and the insured may ask for Part D coverage within 30 days.

"Family members" are those persons related to the named insured or spouse by blood, marriage, or adoption, if they reside in the household of the named insured.

Part A—Liability

Bodily injury and property damage. The basic promise of the insurer in the liability portion of the PAP is to "pay for bodily injury or property damage for which any covered person becomes legally responsible because of an auto accident." Liability decisions aim at requiring those persons who are responsible for a loss to pay for it. Both injury to other persons, including death, and damage to the property of other persons are included. Gratuitous payments are not a part of liability coverage; a legal responsibility must exist before the insurer will pay the injured party under this provision of the contract. Note that the PAP uses the word *accident,* not the word *occurrence* which was used in the earlier auto contracts and other general liability policies. Although this word is usually considered to be more limited in coverage, the continuous or repeated exposure included in the occurrence coverage of general liability insurance is not significant in auto risks. The intent of the change to the word *accident* in this contract is to make the coverage more understandable to the policyholder, not to limit the protection of the policy.

Single-limit coverage. One of the most significant changes in the personal auto policy is the *single limit*[14] of coverage for both bodily injury and property damage. There were separate limits before in the family automobile policy, and bodily injury coverage had both a per person and a per occurrence limit. Now the single limit applies in any one auto accident, regardless of the number of covered persons, injured claimants, or property damage claims.

In the case of accident in another state which specifies higher financial responsibility limits than the single limit of the policy, the PAP will provide whatever coverage is required by the law. This also applies to compulsory insurance or no-fault laws in these other states.

Defense and supplementary payments. The insurer agrees to *settle or defend* any claim or suit asking for bodily injury or property damages because of an auto accident. This duty in the "defense clause" ends when the limit of liability has been exhausted. Settlement and defense costs include those of investigating claims, defense attorney fees, court costs, and other expenses of negotiation and defense.

In addition to the policy limit, there are several *supplementary payments* provided for: (1) up to $250 for bail bonds when these are required after an auto accident resulting in covered damages (not for other traffic violations); (2) premiums on appeal and release of attachment bonds in suits defended by the insurer; (3) accrued interest on judgments that the insurer must pay, up to the time that payment is offered; and (4) reasonable expenses, and up to $50 a day for loss of earnings, of an insured attending hearings or trials at the request of the insurer.

---

[14] If state laws require separate limits, the state single limit applies accordingly, but it will not increase the total limit of liability.

Note that first-aid expenses after an accident are included for covered persons under medical payments coverage. In previous auto policies, these expenses were included for everyone injured in an auto accident by being specifically mentioned in the coverage.

Covered persons.   One of the broadest features of the personal auto policy is that it protects more than just the named insured. The insurance applies to ownership, maintenance, or use of any auto or trailer (as defined earlier) by a *covered person*, defined in the contract to include, with respect to *owned* automobiles:

1.   The *named insured* and *spouse* and any *relative* (including wards or foster children) living in the same household. This includes persons temporarily away from the household, such as children boarding at college.
2.   *Any other person* driving the named insured's auto, if the driver can demonstrate that a reasonable belief that permission to use the auto exists (in previous policies, permission for use had to be given by the insured).
3.   *Any person or organization,* for liability arising out of any covered person's use of the covered auto on behalf of that person or organization (such as an employer).

With respect to *nonowned*[15] *automobiles* of the insured, the PAP provides liability coverage for:

4.   *Any person or organization,* for the *named insured's* or *family members'* (see earlier definition) use of any auto or trailer, other than the covered auto or one owned by the person or organization. A common example is the borrowing or driving of someone else's car by the insured or members of the insurer's family (with reasonable belief of the right to use it.) This coverage is often called "drive-other-car coverage." It also provides protection to employers or organizations, for other cars which may be used on their behalf by a covered person.

The extension of coverage under the automobile contract to these four categories of covered persons is seen as a very important part of the policy coverage. However, the coverage is limited by *exclusions*. Four exclusions pertain to the use of specific *types of vehicles*:

1.   Vehicles used in the auto business (selling, servicing, parking, etc.).
2.   Trucks used in any other business or occupation (except "covered autos," which may include pickup or panel trucks not customarily used in the insured's occupation, or such trucks used similarly by farmers, ranchers, or federal employees).
3.   Vehicles with less than four wheels.

---

[15] Don't let this word confuse you. Of course, all autos are owned by someone. As used in the auto contract and discussion here, a nonowned auto means one that is owned by *someone other than you,* the insured.

4. Any vehicles while they are used to haul property or persons for a fee (except in shared-expense car pools, which are covered).

Also excluded is bodily injury to *employees* of the insured (except domestic employees if workers' compensation is not required). Another exclusion is coverage for *property rented to, used by, or in the care of the insured* (except damage to a nonowned residence or garage or damage to nonowned automobiles not furnished or available for the regular use of the named insured or family members). This means that vehicle damage to nonowned autos which are furnished or available for regular use is *not* covered. Only *liability* coverage for the named insured and spouse is provided in such cases. A final exclusion refers to a certain kind of *wrongdoing* by any person, for *intentional* bodily injury or property damage.

Policy limits and other insurance. The importance of the single limit of liability under the PAP has been mentioned previously. Because all bodily injury and property damage claims come under the single limit, it is imperative for the policyholder to consider the purchase of as high a limit as is available and affordable. Although smaller standard limits (or those required by the state laws) are purchasable, few insureds should consider less than a $50,000 limit, and most should buy at least $100,000 or $300,000 liability limits. Most insurers will also quote the cost of even higher amounts, such as $500,000 or more, upon request.

The cost of the additional premium for higher limits is not as much as might be imagined. Most claims are small, so a premium increase of 20–40 percent over the $50,000 coverage will purchase the higher limits needed. The insurance contract can provide security and peace of mind to the insured only *if* proper limits are purchased. The insured who has a $50,000 policy but is sued for $250,000 (not an unlikely case today) has great uncertainty, perhaps for several years of uninsured worry during negotiations or trial. Thus the insurance will not do in this type of situation what it is intended to do—even if the actual payment eventually turns out to be much smaller than the amount originally claimed. Trying to save on the cost of automobile insurance by purchasing lower liability limits is generally unwise.

Illustrations of the potential need for high single-limit coverage under the PAP are plentiful, and follow the examples of the large liability lawsuits and judgments mentioned in other liability situations (see Chapters 20, 21). In the auto field, multiple-car crashes are common, sometimes involving many persons. Property damages, too, can involve several $10,000 autos, $20,000–$40,000 buses, mobilehomes or trucks (plus valuable cargoes), and other property damage.

Motor vehicle accidents often involve more than one auto insurance contract. If a covered person is using someone else's car, the driver's PAP applies only as *excess* insurance over any other insurance covering the loss (such as the owner's insurance). In such cases the owner's insurance policy pays the loss up to the full limits of its liability, and only then does the driver's insurance policy pay up to its maximum liability for the remaining amount of the loss. Each time you loan your car to someone else, you should remember that your insurance will apply first. Suppose that Lisa DeMaria borrow Tom White's car, with a reasonable belief in her right to use it, and that she has an accident. Tom White's insurance contract will provide the primary coverage for any liability claims, and Lisa DeMaria's insurance contract will provide excess coverage only if needed.

Only in a few cases will a car that the insured owns be covered by more than one automobile insurance contract, usually as the result of a mistake or a misunderstanding. If this does occur, then the PAP provides that it covers only "in the proportion that its limit of liability bears to the total of all applicable limits." Insurer A, for example, with a $50,000 limit, would pay only a one-third share of a liability loss if the insured also had a contract with a $100,000 limit on the same owned car through Insurer B. Insurer B would pay a proportional two thirds of the loss, up to its policy limit. The same prorating of duplicate coverage would apply if medical payments coverage in more than one contract were in existence on the same owned car.

Part B—Medical payments

The policyholder may include Part B—*medical payments* coverage in the personal automobile policy to cover the cost of *medical services* for the *named insured, relatives,* and *anyone else in the insured's car.* Part B does not apply to pedestrians, or to occupants of buildings or other vehicles into which an insured vehicle may crash. This is really automobile accident insurance for medical care costs, and the protection applies *without regard to whose fault* the accident was. In effect, this is one of the original no-fault coverages which has been available in auto insurance for many years.

The cost is small, usually varying from about $15 to $30 per year, depending on the basic charge in the policy for bodily injury liability and the limits of coverage chosen. Most policies have about a $2,000 limit *per person,* but that limit may be raised to the usual maximum $5,000 limit for approximately $10 per year more. The higher limits are recommended, and some insurers now offer up to $10,000 coverage.

The advantage of having automobile medical payments coverage in addition to liability insurance is that payment is made promptly, without a wait for the determination of liability. This coverage also avoids many embarrassing or difficult liability claims or lawsuits by friends injured in your car, and it provides compensation for you and for members of your family who are often unable to sustain a liability claim against you. Also, under the "guest laws"[16] in many states, the persons in your car must often prove "willful or wanton misconduct" by the owner or driver. This makes it unlikely that the liability

---

[16] See *Statutes Affecting Liability Insurance* (New York: American Insurance Association, December 1977).

portion of the contract will pay for the occupants of your car in these states. Medical payments coverage avoids these problems of establishing legal liability, and in addition it pays for many injuries which may be considered moral rather than legal responsibilities.

The coverage is quite broad, for *all reasonable medical expenses* (including surgical, dental, ambulance, hospital, and nursing) are paid, as well as funeral expenses, up to the policy limit. Injuries occurring "in, upon, entering or alighting from" the automobile are covered. The high cost of medical services today makes the need for such protection obvious. With six persons injured in your car, per person policy limits of $2,000 could provide $12,000 of needed coverage for family and friends.

A change in the PAP extends the coverage to medical expenses incurred within *three years* (rather than the former one year) from the date of an accident. The coverage is primary for auto accidents, with benefits payable even though the injured persons may collect benefits from other hospitalization, accident, or disability insurance. However, payments are now excluded under medical payments coverage if benefits are required or available under workers' compensation laws.

In the case of *nonowned* autos operated by the named insured or relatives, the coverage now applies only to the named insured or relatives. (Other occupants are covered by the policy on the nonowned vehicle or by their own policies.)

The coverage now applies to an insured struck as a pedestrian by any motor vehicle, including a motorcycle, but a new specific exclusion applies while any person is occupying a motorcycle. A few other exclusions prevent duplicate coverage, such as when persons are injured in public conveyances.

Part C—Uninsured motorists

The recognition of the need for insurance to pay the insured, family members, and their passengers for bodily injury caused by a negligent but uninsured motorist has led to the inclusion in the personal auto policy of coverage C—*protection against uninsured motorists*. Increasingly popular since the early 1960s, this coverage is now mandatory in some states for every automobile insurance contract issued; and in most states it is included in the contract unless the insured specifically rejects it in writing.

Coverage is usually now issued for a single limit of bodily injury[17] liability as stated in the policy declarations. A limit similar to that of the basic liability coverages normally applies. By definition, an uninsured automobile is one which is not covered by a bodily injury[18] liability policy or bond at the time of

---

[17] The reasons for this coverage and its relationship to the problem of the innocent unpaid automobile accident victim have been discussed in Chapter 23.

[18] *Property damage* (to the insured's car) is not included, except in a few states (with a $100 or more deductible).

an accident. The definition is extended to include a hit-and-run automobile when the owner or operator of the car cannot be determined. It also includes other cars for which no insurance applies, such as stolen or improperly registered automobiles.

Uninsured motorists coverage costs only a few dollars a year. The premium is usually a flat amount for one automobile of about $10–15. An additional automobile is included for a lesser amount.

The insurance applies whether or not the injury caused by the uninsured motorist results from the occupancy of an automobile. The named insured and relatives are protected with insurance against accidents caused by uninsured motorists which occur when they occupy the owned automobile, operate bicycles, or are pedestrians. In any nonowned automobile operated by the named insured, only the named insured and relatives are covered.

The insurance business approaches this coverage with some reluctance since the adjustment of a loss involves two interests that are essentially diverse. The insured must show (although a lawyer is not necessary) that the uninsured person was negligent and that the negligence caused the injury. Suppose Mr. A is injured in an accident caused by Mr. B, who is uninsured. In the case of a disputed claim the insurer finds itself in the unhappy position of working against its own interest if it presses the interest of Mr. A to the limit in an effort to establish liability on the part of Mr. B. The contract undertakes to work out an adjustment through an agreement between Mr. A and the insurer. If they fail to agree that Mr. A is legally entitled to recover damages against Mr. B, or if they fail to agree as to the amount thereof, the matter is settled by *arbitration* under the rules of the American Arbitration Association.

The purpose of the protection is to provide for the insured the amount that would have been collected from an uninsured driver. The negligent driver does not have to be insolvent; UM coverage applies if he or she is uninsured. It has been stated that the insured who carries liability insurance takes care of the "other person." In the case of uninsured motorists coverage, the insurance is comparable to the collision insurance on the insured's own car. Here, instead, it is bodily injury protection for the insured and others—as long as the "other person" is negligent and uninsured. The limit of payment is not now (previously it was) affected by the other available uninsured motorists limits.

Underinsured motorists coverage is also available, but only by an optional endorsement added to the PAP. It pays when the automobile bodily injury liability insurance carried by the negligent third party is exhausted.

Part D—Damage to your own auto

Physical damage coverage for your own automobile is provided in the PAP under Part D, if the declarations page indicates a premium charge and policy limit for the protection. This coverage should not be confused with property damage liability, which is the damage to the property of other persons for which you are held liable.

Part D may include *all physical damage* losses to your auto, or *collision losses may be excluded if the collision peril is not shown in the declarations as* covered and a premium charge is not indicated. *Other than collision* losses (similar to the "comprehensive" coverage of the older forms) are covered by a separate premium amount. Towing and labor costs may be included in this part of the PAP, for emergency road service up to $25 per disablement, with an endorsement costing only a few dollars. The collision and comprehensive (other perils) coverage will be discussed separately, as each has its own insuring agreement.

The importance of physical damage insurance is related to the value of the automobile and to the need and ability of the owner to replace or repair the vehicle if it is damaged. Since most newer automobiles today are items of large value in relation to the assets of a family, most owners do need this insurance protection. However, as the value of an older car decreases, a time may be reached when physical damage insurance is not necessary to cover a possible maximum loss of a few hundred dollars. It is unwise to go without this coverage, however, if the value of the automobile is such that your income or assets could not readily replace the car as required for your work or family.

Sometimes you have little choice as to whether or not you purchase physical damage insurance. Most installment contracts for the purchase of automobiles require that sufficient physical damage insurance be purchased to protect the value of the car used as collateral. Two warnings are important in these cases: (1) the insurance which the bank or other creditor suggests or requires is usually limited to coverage on the car itself and should not be misunderstood as including the very important liability or other automobile coverages; and (2) if the insurance cost is included in the finance plan, be sure to ask what coverages are included and to know the cost involved.

Collision coverage. *Collision* insurance reimburses you for damage to your automobile sustained by reason of a collision with another car or with any other object, movable or fixed. The policy also specifically includes loss to the automobile caused by upset.

As with medical payments insurance, even if you did not carry collision insurance, you *might* be able to recover damages from another person who caused the accident. However, you would be wise to consider purchasing collision insurance since (1) you or the driver of your automobile may be responsible for the loss, whether or not another car is involved in the accident; *and* (2) if another party is responsible for the damage, you must prove negligence; *and* (3) there may be delay and uncertainty in collecting from a negligent person (who may not have sufficient assets or insurance to pay the damages). If you carry collision insurance, *regardless of whose fault* the loss is, you will be paid for the damages to your car.

Collision losses are one of the most common situations in which *subrogation* may apply. If you collect the damages from your insurer, the insurer may then take over your rights to sue the responsible party and recover the payment made to you. Whether or not the insurer will actually do so depends on many factors, including the accident facts, who was liable, the size of the loss, and whether or not proof of negligence is readily available and recovery of claims is likely from the other person.

Collision insurance is also a common illustration of the use of the *deductible*. It is the basic purpose of the deductible to avoid the high cost and administrative expense of frequent small collision losses.

The normal collision deductible in the PAP, which also applies to the comprehensive (other than collision) perils, provides that there shall be no liability on the part of the insurer unless the loss exceeds a named amount. Then the amount of the loss payment is only so much of the loss as exceeds the deductible amount. For example, under a $100 deductible form, if the loss is $90, there is no payment by the insurer; if the loss is $300, the insurer pays the policyholder $200.

Although the $50 deductible is still used in auto insurance, deductibles of $100 or more are being used with increasing frequency. Some agents and insurers often advise a $250 deductible, and deductibles of up to $1,000 or more are available. The reduction in cost to you often justifies the decision to accept a larger portion of collision losses yourself. For example, if you can afford a $250 loss, and the reduction in premium for a $250 deductible as compared with a $100 deductible is $40, it may be unwise to have the smaller deductible. In effect, you may be paying a substantial premium for insurance you don't really need.

Some contracts used to waive the deductible (and some may still do so) if the loss was caused by a collision with another automobile insured by the same insurer. However, in the PAP there is no waiver of the deductible in such cases.

Ordinarily, you can expect to receive the deductible amount from the insurer if the insurer subrogates for the entire amount, including the deductible, and is successful in subrogation proceedings against another negligent party. The cost of the legal proceedings must be considered in a proportionate recovery. The insurer does not profit in subrogation cases and often recovers only a part of the payment it has made to you.

A most important fact is that the collision insurance applies not only while the named insured is operating the automobile but also while *other persons* are operating it with a reasonable belief that they have the right to do so.

One of the most significant changes in the PAP as compared with older contracts is that physical damage insurance applies only to *your* covered auto. *Nonowned or temporary substitute* cars which you or your relatives use are *not* covered. However, under the new provisions of the liability section of the PAP, you are protected for *legal liability* for damages to such cars in your custody. Family members are similarly covered when they borrow or use other cars. A possible advantage of the new wording is that a deductible does not apply in those cases in which you or your relatives are liable for the physical damage to nonowned or temporary substitute cars.

The insurer's limit of liability is usually for indemnity based upon the "actual cash value" of the automobile,[19] although some contracts, especially for business vehicles, use a stated value form. The actual cash value wording protects the policyholder for losses on the basis of value as of the time of the loss, not exceeding the cost of repair or replacement. Other valid and collectible physical damage insurance of the insured on the automobile applies on a pro rata basis.

Comprehensive (other than collision) coverage. With the exception of collision losses, *comprehensive physical damage* is virtually an *all-risk* physical damage coverage. It is now written in the PAP instead of the limited coverages that were formerly used for fire, theft, and other named perils. Protection is afforded for any direct and accidental loss of, or damage to, your automobile and its normal equipment.

Although the broad wording of the contract, "to pay for loss caused other than by collision to the owned automobile" (used by an insured), would automatically include losses on an "everything but" basis, the clause does give specific examples of the types of perils that are not considered to be collision losses and are therefore covered. Among these perils are the following: fire, theft or larcency, windstorm, earthquake, flood, vandalism or malicious mischief, riot or civil commotion, missiles, falling objects, contact with birds or animals, breakage of glass (except intentional breakage), and explosion.

Many strange and unexpected losses have been included in this coverage. Mention may be made of cases involving damage to a fender kicked by a horse, damage to the finish of an automobile caused by arsenic tree spray or paint, and damage by Fourth of July firecrackers, battery acid, and Halloween vandals. Damage by animals, such as running into a dog, deer, cow, or other animal, is specifically stated in the policy to be included under the comprehensive coverage.

To be covered, the damage must be accidental. It is not accidental damage if you break a window so that you can get into the car with the keys locked inside. The breakage of glass due to a collision is included as a covered comprehensive physical damage loss, but in a policy provision that applies only to glass breakage in a collision, the insured may choose to have it considered a collision loss. This avoids having a double deductible apply to glass breakage as both a collision and a comprehensive loss.

Another "supplementary payment" is provided in a clause which grants reimbursement for actual transportation expenses incurred following the theft

---

[19] The principle is the same as that used in the fire insurance policy. No dollar amount for payment is stated in the contract except the maximum limit. The replacement cost less reasonable depreciation is a basis, and this is often determined by market value.

of an automobile. This is a type of "loss of use" coverage that begins 48 hours after the theft and ends when the automobile has been returned to use or the loss has been paid. Coverage is limited to up to $10 per day to a maximum of $300. The amount paid is in addition to the loss payable for the damages caused by the theft.

Another change in the PAP is that personal effects in the auto are no longer covered. A very limited coverage had applied under previous policies.

Most of the other provisions of this section are applied to both comprehensive and collision coverages. Many are similar to the definitions, clauses, and exclusions already discussed in Part A of the personal automobile policy. The coverage applies to the owned automobile while it is being used either by the named insured or by anyone else using it with a reasonable belief of being entitled to do so. Nonowned automobiles are *not* covered. Newly acquired additional cars must be reported within 30 days of acquisition. A replacement automobile requires notification within 30 days after acquisition only if physical damage coverage is desired on the new vehicle.

Other exclusions are: (1) damage due to wear and tear, freezing, mechanical or electrical breakdown or failure (except that caused by theft); (2) damages to tires,[20] unless the damage is by fire, vandalism, malicious mischief, or theft, or is coincident with other losses covered by the policy; (3) loss caused by war or nuclear weapons; (4) camper bodies (unless specifically declared); (5) loss to CB radio, two-way radio, and telephone equipment (unless endorsed on the policy).

The comprehensive coverage in the PAP may be written for the amount of "actual cash value," and the several choices among deductibles that are used for the collision coverage discussed previously. Similar advice applies with regard to using the largest deductible possible in order to lower the premium cost for the comprehensive coverages.

Part E—Conditions in order to collect under the contract

The new and simplified wording of this part of the PAP specifies what any person seeking coverage under the policy should do following an accident or loss. Many of the provisions are promises that you as the insured must fulfill before you can expect the insurer to make payments under the contract. Note that these are "conditions," although called "duties" in the contract, that if you do not fulfill them, the insurer may not have to pay the loss. (Legally, a duty would permit the insurer to force you to meet the promises made.)

Some of the provisions are restrictions on the extent of liability of the insurer. Only automobile losses that occur in the *United States and Canada* (including U.S. territories or possessions) or while you are being transported between ports of these countries are covered. Residents of the Southern border

---

[20] Note that ordinary flat tire losses are not included. To be covered by physical damage, the loss must be due to a collision or another identifiable covered peril.

states and travelers who visit Mexico should note that separate protection must be purchased if they wish to be covered while driving in Mexico. Since Canada's required liability limits in some provinces exceed the financial responsibility laws of some states, care should be taken to check the insurance contract and laws before driving in Canada.

You promise to pay any *premium adjustment* necessary due to an acquisition of replacement or additional automobiles. When *two or more automobiles* are insured under the contract the liability and medical payments limits apply as if only one automobile were insured.

When an accident occurs, *written notice* should be given by you or on your behalf to the insurer or its agents *as soon as practicable*. Oftentimes this would involve a phone call to the agent, followed up within a few days with a written signed report which the agent may help you prepare. The notice should contain particulars to identify you as the insured, as well as reasonably obtainable information respecting the time, place, and circumstances of the accident, together with the names and addresses of the owner and all available witnesses and the license number of the car involved in the collision. If a claim is made or a suit is brought, you should immediately forward to the insurer every demand, notice, summons, or other process that you have received.

In the event of an accident that may involve a claim for damages, you should give the insured notice of whether you feel liable or not. Printed forms indicating the nature of the data desired by the insurer are often used. Where there is a bodily injury, an estimate of the extent of the injury is needed. Significant items are whether or not the injured persons receive first aid or medical attention, the name of the attending physician, and the name and location of the hospital. If the driver of your car is someone other than you, the driver's name, address, and license number form an essential part of the report. The exact location of the accident, together with the weather conditions and the condition of the highways, should be noted, and a detailed sketch should be made showing the relative positions of the cars just before and after the collison.

In complying with the state requirements for reporting accidents, you should make a duplicate copy of any written reports and forward a copy to the agent or insurer. If members of the police force were present at the accident scene, a notation should be made of their names or badge numbers. You should not make any admission as to the liability, and you should not make any efforts to negotiate a settlement of the claim. By virtue of the contract the insurer has exclusive control over the adjustment of the claim, and you should not make any attempt to effect a settlement without the consent of the insurance company. By doing so, you run a risk of placing yourself ouside the protection of the policy.

With respect to the liability and collision coverages you are not divested of all responsibility once you have turned the adjustment over to the insurer. In fact, by virtue of the *assistance and cooperation clause* you should render full assistance in the settlement or adjustment of a suit and you should not admit or assume liability. The clause is held to be a material condition, and if you fail to comply with its requirements you forfeit your right to indemnity under the contract.[21] To warrant forfeiture, the breach must be substantial and material.[22] Failure to comply to the letter in matters that are slight or inconsequential will not jeopardize the insurance. You only need to disclose as accurately as possible all information which you may have.

Where claims are made by relatives or friends, you may frequently feel in sympathy with their needs. However, admitting liability untruthfully or giving false information intentionally to build up the case of the claimant constitutes a breach of the cooperation clause.[23] You should give a full and truthful account of all the circumstances leading up to and attending an accident, and if the insurer requires it, you should attend court and testify to these facts as a witness.[24]

To indicate in a legal action that you are covered by insurance may result in a mistrial or may reverse a judgment for the plaintiff. The rule is based upon the assumption that if the jury knows that an insurer and not the individual defendant is to pay the damages, there will be a temptation to be generous with the insurer's money, so that in borderline cases sympathy rather than the facts at issue may be the determining factor.[25] Reference to "insurance" directly or by inference may jeopardize the case. The rule is not universally accepted in the light of the wide distribution of insurance and the use of some defense counsel that regularly represent insurers.[26] Where, however, the rule is in force, attorneys will be on the alert to turn it to their advantage whenever the opportunity presents itself.

In liability and collision claims, but not with respect to medical payments, the insurer is *subrogated* to all rights of recovery that you may have. You should do whatever else is necessary to secure the subrogation rights of the in-

---

[21] *Royal Indemnity Company* v. *Morris*, 37 F. (2d) 90, 281 U.S. 784.

[22] *George* v. *Employer's Liability Assurance Corporation, Ltd., et al.*, 291 Ala. 307, 122 So. 175.

[23] *Guerin* v. *Indemnity Company of North America*, 107 Conn. 649; *Bassi* v. *Bassi*, 165 Minn. 100; *Finkel* v. *Western Automobile Insurance Company*, 24 Mo. 285.

[24] *Frances* v. *London Guarantee & Accident Company, Ltd.*, 100 Vt. 425, 138 Atl. 780.

[25] The logic behind the rule has been expressed thus: "He must have appreciated the effect it would have made upon a jury trying a case between two citizens, when it was known that a corporation, and not the defendant, would have to discharge the judgment for damages. He must have known that the wavering balances would go down against the 'soul-less corporation.' No amount of admonition to the jury could remove the effects of the testimony, because it could not remove the knowledge that the suit was not one between citizens, but between a citizen and a corporation" (*Carter* v. *Walker*, 165 S.W. 483).

[26] For example: "and, in addition, we would say that the custom of carrying casualty insurance is now so universal and so generally recognized that a mere individual reference to the fact that defendant was thus protected should not constitute error in absence of a showing of injury." *Russell* v. *Bailey*, 290 S.W. 1108.

surer. It is important that you do nothing whatever after a loss to prejudice the subrogation rights of the insurer, either by relieving another of liability or by assuming responsibility yourself. You may feel that you are to blame for an accident, but you may be mistaken.

Some special conditions are outlined for the insured under *physical damage losses*. These include: (1) *protection* of the insured automobile *from further loss*, (2) a sworn *proof of loss* within 91 days, (3) rights to *appraisal*, (4) *no abandonment*, and (5) *no benefit to bailee*. These conditions are essentially the same as those that have been noticed in connection with other property insurance coverages.

A few special conditions apply only to the medical payments and uninsured motorists coverages. These provisions ask you to execute authorization for obtaining *medical reports* and to submit to *physical examinations* by physicians when and as often as reasonably requested.

Part F—General provisions

An *assignment* of the policy will not bind the insurer until it consents. To be valid, the assignment must be *in writing*, and must be signed by an authorized officer of the insurer. Because of the nature of automobile coverages, the insurer wishes to underwrite its insureds carefully. In the event of the named insured's death, the policy shall then cover the named insured's spouse, legal representatives in performing their duties, and anyone in temporary custody of the automobile.

Cancellation provisions require the insurer to give the policyholder ten days' notice in writing, with a proportional return (or offer to return) of unearned premium to the end of the policy period. If the insured cancels, the return of premium is calculated on the customary short-rate basis. The personal automobile policy and many other automobile insurance contracts have recently limited the right of the insurer to cancel the liability portion of the coverage. (See discussion of underwriting selection of risks earlier in this chapter.)

One provision in the policy *incorporates the declarations* into the agreement. The policy embraces all agreements relating to the insurance that exist between you and the insurer or any of its agents. Thus it is important that all material information called for appear in the declarations, as the contract is issued by the insurer in reliance upon their truth.

Several provisions of Part F have already been noted in connection with specific coverage parts of the PAP. You should report additional vehicles and replacement vehicles within 30 days of acquisition if you want physical damage coverage for the new vehicles. No coverage applies for a person using a vehicle unless that person reasonably believes that a right to do so exists. These are important differences between the PAP and other auto insurance contracts.

With today's increasing mobility of persons by automobile comes the increased risk of being held responsible for meeting financial responsibility laws in many states. Some of the required limits (see Chapter 23) may be higher than the law requires in the insured's own state. In such cases, most contracts now include, *automatically,* the higher limit coverage specified by any other state or by any Canadian province in connection with the insured's automobile insurance contract.

No-fault coverage

The emerging era of no-fault benefits also creates an expanding need for coverage that is adjusted to rapidly changing conditions. The PAP extends automatically (at no additional cost) coverages to pay no-fault benefits if covered persons drive into a state where they need no-fault protection. When applicable, the requirements of no-fault laws are available to the insureds.

If the insured lives in a state that has recently passed a no-fault law, it is necessary that the contracts be changed to include the no-fault provisions. For existing contracts this may be done by the law itself, while for new and renewal contracts the wording of the contracts will be changed or endorsed to modify the contract coverage.

The endorsement provisions vary considerably by state. As a *fairly typical example of "modified" no-fault insurance* (and in contrast to the more extensive Michigan no-fault insurance discussed in Chapter 23), *New Jersey* has added a "basic personal injury protection endorsement" to accomplish this change. The endorsement is two pages long, and it specifies and defines the coverage to include automobile accident benefits payable, regardless of fault, for:

1. Medical expenses (all reasonable medical expenses, unlimited).
2. Income continuation (not exceeding $100 per week, and total of $5,200).
3. Essential services (substitute cost of care and maintenance of insured and relatives, subject to daily limit of $12 with aggregate of $4,380 per person per accident).
4. Survivors (above benefits become payable to dependent surviving spouse or children).
5. Funeral expenses (not exceeding $1,000).

The no-fault benefits are available in private passenger automobile accidents in New Jersey for bodily injury to the named insured; relatives who are residents of the household; "other persons" occupying the automobile or using it with the named insured's permission; and pedestrians. If the accident occurs outside New Jersey, "other persons" are covered only for medical expense. Excluded are persons committing a felony or high misdemeanor or attempting to avoid arrest by a police officer, and persons acting with intent to cause injury or damage. The insurance is compulsory for all owners who register or principally garage their car in New Jersey, and it includes required liability limits of 15/30/5 in addition to the no-fault benefits.

The insureds are exempted from tort liability action for automobile accidents in the state. Injured persons can sue if the injury results in permanent disability, significant disfigurement, loss of a bodily function or bodily member, or death; or if medical expense exceeds $200, exclusive of hospital, X-ray, and other diagnostic medical expense. This is an extremely low "threshold," and many other states have been increasing their limit to $1,000 or more. The lower amounts do not reduce the number of tort liability claims and costs significantly.

This insurance does not apply to loss or expense to which any insured is entitled under any workers' compensation law, Medicare, or any other no-fault law; or under any other automobile medical payments insurance. Uninsured motorists coverage is reduced by any payments under the "personal injury protection endorsement."

The potential complexity and complications are apparent from this summary of the New Jersey no-fault endorsement. Automobile insurance consumers must be careful to understand their rights and obligations with these additions. (See earlier discussion of current no-fault laws in other states in Chapter 23.)

FOR REVIEW AND DISCUSSION

1. *Who* is protected by the personal auto policy (PAP), and *what* automobiles?

2. Suppose your friend Barbara asks your advice on proper protection she should have for her new automobile. What explanations would you offer her for the most important coverages, and what approximate limits would you suggest that she include in the personal auto policy?

3. Are automobile insurance costs similar (*a*) for all insureds and (*b*) for similar protection for all insurers? (*c*) Should they be? Explain.

4. John Sure says: "Everyone has a *right to buy* automobile insurance because it's needed today by families as much as groceries or a house are needed." Suzy Dubious replies: "But automobile insurers must *underwrite* their business, or they will go broke." Divide the class into two groups to discuss and report to the class on (*a*) how these two ideas conflict with each other; and (*b*) how these two ideas can, or are, brought together in the automobile insurance marketplace.

5. In determining the premium for automobile liability insurance, what factors are considered in addition to the territory in which the car is garaged?

6. Someone says to you: "Your private passenger automobile rate classification depends not upon *who* you are but upon *what* you do and have done, and upon your *car*." Would you agree or disagree? Explain.

7. Mr. Iiskee has just purchased a personal auto policy (PAP) with a $300,000

limit for bodily injury liability and property damage liability and a $5,000 limit for medical payments.

    a. What kind of property damage would such a contract cover? Give several examples.

    b. Does the medical payments coverage pay for losses even if Mr. **Riskee** is not liable for them? Explain. *Whose* injuries does it pay for?

    c. What additional coverages would you suggest that Mr. Riskee have on his *own* car? Explain each briefly.

    d. Would you recommend that the uninsured motorists coverage be included in this policy? Why or why not?

8. What are the "supplementary agreements" in the personal auto policy, and why may they be important to the policyholder?

9. Does a husband's personal auto policy cover his wife and children while they are driving the car of a friend? Explain. What difference does it make if the friend also has a similar policy?

10. A lends his automobile to B and rides with B to the railroad station. They are in a hurry to catch a train, and B negligently attempts to pass another car on a hill. There is a collision, and both passengers in the car are seriously injured. Can A, the owner of the car and the named insured, sue B? If so, will A's policy protect B?

11. Mary, the daughter of X, is injured while riding to a Girl Scout meeting in a friend's car. Does the father's medical payments coverage on his personal automobile afford any relief in this situation?

12. X carries Part-D—damage to your own auto (comprehensive physical damage) coverage. Explain why you think the following losses would, or would not, be covered:

    a. Because of a delay in putting antifreeze into the automobile radiator, there is a freeze-up with serious damage.

    b. Would it be the same if there were damage resulting from the freezing of parts due to lack of lubrication?

    c. Vandals rip the car radio antenna off and dump red paint over the car.

    d. The car is stolen, and the thieves collide with an oncoming car in an attempt to escape from the police.

    e. X carries both comprehensive physical damage and $100 deductible collision coverage. The car skids and strikes a light pole by the side of the road, damaging the windshield to the extent of $200.

13. Identify (by *letter*) the basic type of automobile insurance coverage from the list below which would provide protection for the following losses under the personal auto policy, and *explain briefly why*:

    Coverage A—liability
    Coverage B—medical payments
    Coverage C—uninsured motorists
    Coverage D—damage to your own car

Loss

    a. Damage to your own car by colliding with a tree.

b. Medical expenses of a pedestrian because of your your negligence.

c. A broken finger by a passenger shutting the car door.

d. Damage to your own car by a tornado.

e. Damage to another person's car caused by the negligent operation of your car.

f. Injury to your wife while she is riding in a friend's car, caused by another car driven by a person who has no insurance.

g. Loss of income of a person injured in another car caused by the negligent operation of your car.

h. Damage to a neighbor's front porch and lawn caused by the negligent operation of your car.

i. Cost to defend you against a lawsuit, involving your car, even though nothing was paid.

j. Hospital expenses for you from an automobile accident in which you were negligent and ran off the road.

14. *Whose* injuries does the uninsured motorists coverage (C) of the personal auto policy cover? *When?*

15. What *additional* rights, and *reduced* rights, will an insured have under the new no-fault laws in many states? How is the contract coverage of the insured *extended* to apply in other states in which the insured may be traveling, in regard to financial responsibility and no-fault laws?

16. How has the new personal auto policy (PAP) made the contract more understandable to the average automobile insurance consumer?. Explain fully.

Chapter 25

Concepts considered in Chapter 25—Crime insurance and suretyship

Crime insurance and suretyship both deal with the increasing peril of *dishonesty,* or *crimes against property.* Basic divisions are:

Burglary-theft insurance, which covers *nonemployee* dishonesty:

    Perils are *burglary, robbery,* and *larcency (theft* includes all three).

    Underwriting faces *moral hazard, adverse selection,* and *underinsurance.*

    Basic contract parts are the declarations, insuring agreements, exclusions, and conditions.

    Personal theft insurance is common today in homeowners' policies.

    Business burglary-theft insurance (often in *special multiperil policies*) includes contracts for:

        Mercantile open-stock burglary policy for merchandise.

        Safe burglary policy for money, securities, and other property.

        Mercantile robbery policy for inside or outside "holdup" coverage.

        Paymaster robbery policy for large amounts of money coverage.

        Forgery insurance, primarily for outgoing commercial paper.

        Storekeepers', and office, burglary and robbery for $1,000 or less.

        Money and securities policy (broad form) for *"all risks"* of loss.

        Comprehensive 3-D policy for the broadest *dishonesty* insurance.

        Blanket crime policy, with a single insurance amount.

Suretyship involves a *guarantee* that a person will perform an obligation.

    Nature and development from personal to corporate sureties are traced.

    Insurance and suretyship are compared and contrasted.

    General divisions (*fidelity* and *surety* bonds) and basic features are noted.

    Fidelity bonds insure the peril of *employee dishonesty,* for private and public employers, in *individual, schedule, blanket (commercial blanket* and *blanket position),* and *public official* bonds.

    Judicial bonds are of two types—*fiduciary* and *court* bonds.

    Contract bonds are *construction, supply, maintenance,* and other types.

Crime insurance and suretyship

One of the first impressions that students have about the total property-liability insurance field is the almost overwhelming variety of perils and coverages that it includes. Part IV has already introduced fire, indirect loss, transportation, liability, workers' compensation, and automobile insurance. The scope of the field does not stop there, but also encompasses crime perils discussed in this chapter, including the closely related suretyship guarantees. Appendix F also discusses less common coverages, including some crime insurance and bonds for financial institutions, and liability for crime losses available in some areas.

The relationship between the crime and surety fields may be seen by the size of their annual insurance premiums, as shown in Table 25–1.

Table 25–1. Crime insurance, suretyship and miscellaneous coverage

Kind of insurance		Net premiums written
Burglary-theft insurance		$ 130,000,000
Suretyship		
a. Surety bonds	$660,000,000	
b. Fidelity bonds	290,000,000	950,000,000
Total		$1,080,000,000

Source: *Insurance Facts* (New York: Insurance Information Institute, 1978), p. 10. Premium figures are for 1977.

Thus the total size of the crime and suretyship fields of insurance represents approximately a billion dollars of annual premium—hardly insignificant, but relatively small in relation to fire and allied lines ($4 billion), transportation ($2 billion), liability ($7 billion), workers' compensation ($9 billion), and automobile ($30 billion) insurance.[1]

Separate treatment of these areas is warranted for several other reasons. The previous figures do not include insurance and bond premiums when these miscellaneous perils are included in the newer and very popular multiple-line insurance coverages (see Chapter 27). Also, the insurance and risk-

---

[1] *Insurance Facts* (New York: Insurance Information Institute, 1978), p. 10.

management concepts and principles for these fields are sometimes quite different from those for the types of property-liability insurance discussed previously. Many of the basic ideas may be similar, but the specialized nature of these perils warrant a closer look at their problems and solutions, including the unusual features of the insurance coverages for them.

BASIC DIVISIONS OF CRIME INSURANCE, INCLUDING SURETYSHIP

Crime insurance, or as it is sometimes called, *dishonesty* insurance, pays owners for the loss of their property due to its being wrongfully taken by someone else. The related field of *suretyship* is partially based upon the dishonesty peril but also involves a broader guarantee of the satisfactory performance of duties by various persons.

Money is the type of property that is most commonly taken dishonestly. This area of crimes against property is likely to conjure up visions of "Bonnie and Clyde" bank holdups, but the field of crime insurance is much broader.

First, the types of property[2] insured include merchandise and many types of personal property other than money. Second, the criminals taking property are either (1) members of the *public* (the most notorious being labeled "public enemies") or (2) *employees*. Employee dishonesty is the basis of the *fidelity bond* business, an important part of suretyship.

The subject of the first major section of the chapter is *burglary-theft* insurance, which covers nonemployee dishonesty. Employee dishonesty, although obviously also a type of crime insurance as described above, is discussed in the second major section of this chapter, as a part of *suretyship*. Suretyship also includes some bonds, such as judicial and contract bonds, which cover losses due to neglect as well as dishonesty.

Many of these types of bonds and insurance are for coverage of *business* exposures, which probably involves three fourths or more of the total premiums. Some of the burglary-theft insurance, particularly the important theft coverage that is now included in the homeowners' policies, and some of the surety bonds are for *personal* exposures.

From a risk-management standpoint, crime coverages are important both because of the high concentration of certain types of property values exposed to loss and because of the frequency with which losses occur. Stolen property losses of more than $4.7 *billion* occur each year, not including property losses due to employee dishonesty, and more than 10 million robberies, burglaries,

---

[2] Crime insurance as discussed in this chapter is mostly property insurance. The term also includes a few forms of liability insurance, however, such as innkeepers' and warehousers' legal liability, and safe deposit box insurance (see Appendix F).

and larcenies were noted in a single recent year.[3] The total annual cost of crimes against property probably exceeds $25 billion,[4] of which perhaps one fourth goes toward private crime prevention efforts. Such efforts include those of individual property owners as well as collective plans, for example, the Insurance Crime Prevention Institute supported by many insurers, and the National Crime Protection Institute, which was set up at the University of Louisville to help train police officers in better crime protection techniques.[5] The need to coordinate private and public efforts is also important. Increases in suburban crimes and in fire losses due to arson are examples of troublesome crime areas today.

BURGLARY-THEFT INSURANCE

Most crimes against property, except those committed by employees, are included in what the insurance business calls *burglary-theft* insurance. The direct effect of such losses is borne by individuals and organizations, and increasing insurance costs are a part of the burden. One innovative judge recently decided that burglars should pay their share, too, and sentenced a burglar to pay a restaurant's insurance costs for three years! The need to coordinate risk control (especially loss prevention) techniques with risk financing through insurance is increasingly recognized. Crime prevention efforts through the cooperation of industry and government authorities are an essential part of maintaining market availability for burglary-theft insurance.[6]

Perils

Technically, the term *theft* is broad enough to include any act of stealing or taking another's property. This peril includes three parts: (1) burglary, (2) robbery, and (3) larceny. Theft by business employees is discussed separately under fidelity bonds.

---

[3] Ibid., pp. 62. Burglaries totaled more than 3 million; larcenies, approximately 6 million; auto thefts, almost 1 million; and robberies, almost ½ million. The comparison with fire losses for 1977 is $3.8 billion of loss in 3.1 million fires (pp. 35–37).

[4] *The Cost of Crimes against Business* (Washington, D.C.: U.S. Government Printing Office, 1976).

[5] William Rykert, "Crime Prevention: A New Strategy," *Journal of Insurance,* vol. 33, no. 6 (November–December 1972), p. 8. The entire issue is devoted to articles on crime prevention. An anti-car theft program is featured in the same journal, vol. 39, no. 6 (November–December 1978), in Warren L. MacKenzie, "Santa and the Christmas Summons", p. 28.

[6] An example of cooperative educational, statistical, and enforcement efforts is the new National Crime Prevention Association. Its programs are reviewed in the reports of its first meeting, in "Crime Prevention: a Common Cause," *Journal of Insurance,* vol. 38, no. 6 (September–October 1977), pp. 9–24.

Burglary, robbery, and larceny are not always defined identically in the statutes of different jurisdictions. To eliminate any element of uncertainty, policies covering theft losses provide a definition of the peril to be covered. Briefly, *burglary* is the taking of the property of another by the forcible breaking and entering of the premises. *Robbery* consists of the carrying away of the personal property of others in their presence by violence or by putting them in fear. *Larceny* is any theft except burglary or robbery. Larceny losses would include thefts by sneak thieves, shoplifters, mechanics, or others having access to the premises of the insured.

Other losses related to the above perils are included in some burglary-theft contracts. *Damage to the property* of the insured by burglary, robbery, vandalism, and malicious mischief is often included. A few contracts, such as the "package" crime insurance coverages discussed later, include *destruction* by almost any cause, and some contracts include *disappearance,* where no proof that the property was taken is required.

Underwriting

Burglary-theft insurance is quite different from most of the types of insurance discussed so far in this text. One of the most unusual characteristics of burglary-theft insurance is the high degree of *moral hazard,* the increased possibility of loss because of fraud or dishonesty by the insureds themselves. The basic act of stealing is often difficult to prove, and deciding whether the insured or others are responsible is not an easy task in many crime coverages. The generally broad definitions used in many of the contracts (such as "theft," "mysterious disappearance," etc.) and the high concentration of value in many of the types of property covered (such as money, jewelry, etc.) also add to the moral hazard.

Normally, only those insureds with substantial exposure to loss insure against the burglary-theft perils. It was noted earlier that only $130 million in annual premiums insure these perils. The estimated almost $5 billion annual loss would indicate that substantially less than 5 per cent of such losses are insured. The tendency for the best insureds not to insure and for the worst ones (from the standpoint of potential loss) to insure is pronounced. Fortunately, some progress in reducing the effects of such *adverse selection* against the insurer is being made as more insureds purchase these types of insurance. For example, the homeowner's program, which automatically includes theft coverage, has helped spread burglary-theft coverage to most homes and families. The special multiperil (SMP) program for businesses, too, is making such coverage much more readily available to insureds as an optional choice in the contracts. (See Chapter 27.)

The basic tendency to *underinsure* the potential burglary-theft exposure is also a serious problem. For most other types of insurance, the insureds buy coverage at or close to the value of the property, either because they realize the possibility of serious or total loss (fire insurance) or because they are forced to do so (automobile collision and physical damage on financed cars are bought on an actual cash-value basis). Most burglary-theft insureds purchase only a small amount of coverage, assuming that very large losses are unlikely. Two methods are used to encourage the insured to purchase insurance amounts in reasonable relationship to value. One method is the *coinsurance* clause, discussed later in connection with open-stock burglary insurance. This operates like the fire insurance coinsurance clause, but the percentage requirement is often permitted to be less than 80 percent of value, and a maximum loss potential limit is usually established in order to reduce the required amount when certain types of property are insured. A second method is the *rating system,* which is based upon a graded or sliding scale that reduces the cost of burglary-theft insurance per $1,000 as more insurance is purchased. For example, the first $1,000 of personal theft insurance might cost the insured $80 per year; the second $1,000, only $50; and the third or more, $30.

Burglary-theft insurance is carefully underwritten by most insurers. Inspection reports are commonly used in order to determine such things as the condition of the premises, the neighborhood, and the protective features of the property. Loss-prevention advice by agents and insurers can be of substantial value to insureds, both in preventing losses and in reducing rates. Actual and potential burglary alarm or security guard systems, locking devices, safes, inventory and cash systems, and many other features should be carefully evaluated as the process of risk management is followed in developing recommendations for the prospective insured. Increasing problems of availability of coverage in urban areas have also led the federal government to encourage loss prevention and the insuring of crime losses (see Chapter 28).

Basic contract parts

Policies in the burglary-theft category generally follow the pattern already noticed with respect to many other insurance contracts. There are four sections: (1) declarations, (2) insuring agreements, (3) exclusions, and (4) conditions. Most policies have about four pages. The printed policy is included in the first three pages, and the fourth, which is virtually blank, is reserved for endorsements.

Declarations. The first page of the policy contains for the most part the declarations, which are basically all the essential statements and specifications required for the particular risk. They contain the name, address, and business of the insured; the policy period and the coverage, together with the limits of insurance, the premium to be charged, and the premises to which the policy applies.

The declarations will state whether or not a burglar alarm or security guard system is maintained, or any other warranty with respect to special protective features that reflect in a reduction in premium. These protective measures are conditions which are usually interpreted as suspending the coverage while they are not maintained, or excluding the coverage of losses attributable to their absence. Finally, there is a statement with respect to a history of previous losses or cancellations during the past five years, and whether any such insurance has been declined by any insurer.

Insuring agreements.   The insuring agreements are preceded by a short paragraph in which the insurer agrees to indemnify the insured named in the declarations for certain losses. The insurer does so in consideration of the payment of the premium and in reliance upon the statements in the declarations. The insuring agreements then describe the perils (see above section) against which the insurance is written and the property covered.

The insuring agreement may consist of one or more parts. While the insuring agreement establishes in a broad way the nature of the perils to be covered, the extent of the protection can be determined only in connection with the exclusions, definitions, and conditions contained in the contract.

Exclusions.   The exclusions in theft coverages are designed primarily to save the insured from paying twice for the same coverage. For example, theft of an automobile is excluded since such vehicles are ordinarily specifically insured. Other exclusions deal with features that apply to the particular type of coverage. Most contracts exclude losses attributable to war.

Conditions.   The conditions follow the types already noticed with respect to other insurance contracts. They provide for notice and proof of loss, subrogation, assignment, cancellation, other insurance, action against the insurer, changes, special statutes, declarations, and a clause covering payment, replacement, and recovery. These clauses are to be found in one form or another in all theft policies. The notice of cancellation when the insurer elects to cancel, is ten days in most instances, but longer in some forms.

The conditions peculiar to an individual policy concern themselves primarily with (*a*) definitions and (*b*) ownership of the property covered. Because of the differences in statutory definitions of various forms of theft, the extent of the coverage is clarified by specific definitions of theft in the conditions. Other terms, such as *custodian, guard, messenger,* and *premises,* are carefully defined. Loss is defined to include damage. Other specific definitions appear where the coverage requires it. Following the definitions is a condition with respect to ownership of the property insured. Burglary policies usually provide coverage for both the property of the insureds and property for which they may be held liable.

Personal theft insurance

All theft insurance may be divided into (1) *personal* and (2) *business* types. The remainder of this section on burglary-theft insurance is separated in this manner.

Two forms for personal theft are: (*a*) the broad form personal theft policy and (*b*) the personal theft policy. These contracts are seldom written today as separate policies, but their coverage is similar to that available to the insured in the popular homeowners' policies.

The *broad form personal theft policy* provides two major types of coverage: (1) theft from the premises or a depository and (2) theft away from the premises. The coverage is very broad in that the word *theft* includes burglary, robbery, and larceny. It may be attributable to burglars, servants, occasional employees, or for that matter anyone except relatives permanently residing with the insured. The peril of *mysterious diappearance* is also named, but it is covered by interpretation rather than by being specifically defined in the contract. It applies to any insured property, except a precious or semiprecious stone removed from its setting in any watch or piece of jewelry. This means that if any piece of insured property is missing, with the exceptions noted, and there is no explanation for its disappearance, then the loss is covered by the policy. Suppose a watch worn by the insured disappears, but it is not known whether the watch was stolen, merely fell off, or was misplaced somewhere. Such loss would probably be covered as a mysterious disappearance.

Including the peril of "mysterious disappearance" affords an extremely liberal coverage. Some insurers hesitate to include the mysterious disappearance feature because they regard it as a "claim breeder." Frequently there is grave doubt as to whether the claims are actually the outgrowth of theft losses. The homeowners' program restricts its contracts to pay only for loss "from a known place under circumstances when a probability of theft exists."

Coverage includes the property of the insured, the insured's family, relatives, guests, residence employees, and other permanent members of the household. On-premises coverage applies automatically when the named insured moves to new premises. Off-premises coverage is worldwide and extends to provide coverage on property unattended in automobiles and property in charge of a carrier for hire. The policy also covers damage caused by burglars, robbers, and thieves to the insured property or to the premises occupied by the insured, and loss or damage caused by vandalism or malicious mischief.

For the purpose of insurance, property is classified into: (*a*) jewelry, sterling silver, and furs; (*b*) other property not specifically insured; and (*c*) specified articles described and insured for specific amounts. Specified limits of insurance are applied to the first two categories, and specified amounts are applied to each article in the third category. If a separate amount of insurance is set for the jewelry, silver, and furs group, and another for other property in the second category, this is called "divided coverage." It is not necessary, however, to separate jewelry, silver, and furs, although this is often done. Property not specifically insured is covered by "blanket coverage," the amount of insurance applying to any losses of general personal property, such as household furniture, clothing, rugs, musical instruments, cameras, money ($100 limit, usually), and securities. In addition, any particularly valuable items may be scheduled and insured for a separate amount, and this is called "specific coverage."

The insured may elect one or several combinations of divided, blanket, and specific coverage. The rates vary according to the choices of the insured, the occupancy of the premises, and the territorial classification.

Business burglary-theft insurance

Insurance against burglary-theft perils includes several basic types for most general businesses. Banks and other financial institutions have special forms (see Appendix F for some examples). Also very important today are the "package" crime coverages discussed at the end of this section. Many of these forms are now included in the SMP or other multiple-line insurance policies (see Chapter 27).

Mercantile open-stock burglary policy. Basically, this policy provides (a) burglary insurance and (b) insurance coverage for property damage attributable to burglary. The burglary peril is defined in the policy, and by means of specific endorsements in connection with certain carefully underwritten risks, the policy may be extended to cover the perils of theft, larceny, and robbery.

Unlike insurance coverages for money and securities that are written on all-risks or broad forms, all-risks policies are never written to cover mercantile open stock. The policy is a specified-perils contract covering (a) burglary, (b) property damage, (c) robbery by threat or violence to a security guard, and (d) in some instances theft.

The contract indemnifies the insured for loss of the insured property caused by *burglary* while the premises are not open for business. This includes breaking out (of someone hiding in the premises) as well as breaking in by actual force and violence as evidenced by visible marks made by tools, explosives, electricity, or chemicals. The policy covers all *merchandise* in the insured premises as well as furniture, fixtures, and equipment, but not money and securities.

The property insured must be on the "premises" described in the contract application, which means the interior of the building, excluding island showcases or outside show windows not opening directly into the interior of the premises. Specific types of property excluded are furs or fur articles taken from inside show windows by breaking glass from outside; any property over $100 taken from outside show windows that are inside the building line; jewelry in excess of $50 per article; manuscripts; and records. Several of these limitations can be removed by an endorsement for an additional premium. The property insured is basically merchandise, but it is also extended to include property that the insured holds as a bailee. Burglary losses caused or aided by the insured, an associate, or an employee are not covered.

As is usually the case in burglary insurance, *property damage* by a burglary or an attempted burglary is covered. Under this policy this includes not only merchandise but furniture, fixtures, and equipment in the premises. Damages to the premises are covered if the insured is the owner or is liable for the damage.

Theft coverage is only rarely provided in this policy, and insurance is practically never the answer for retail stores where shoplifting losses are an inevitable part of doing business. The importance of good risk-management practices to prevent employee theft is seen in the annual losses due to shoplifting: $4 billion in inventory shortages and 4 million shoplifters caught. The prevention of such losses through internal controls (audits, closed-circuit TV, sensormatic devices fixed to merchandise, security guards, and so on) is strongly advocated.[7]

All of the coverages apply only while the premises of the insured are closed to business. The contract is sometimes said to be a "nighttime, Saturdays, Sundays" policy. The other exclusions are few: (*a*) loss in excess of actual cash value or cost to repair or replace, (*b*) losses contributed to by a change in the condition of the risk or occurring while a protective system for which a premium reduction is allowed is not maintained; (*c*) losses due to war, vandalism, malicious mischief, and nuclear energy; (*d*) loss attributable to dishonesty of employees; (*e*) loss or damage that cannot be ascertained from the records of the insured; and (*f*) "mysterious disappearance" (unexplained) losses.

The merchantile open-stock burglary form introduces a feature peculiar to this type of policy. The rating manual provides for a classification of risks according to the type of business and establishes a limit known as the *coinsurance limit* for each classification. There is also a *coinsurance clause* requirement expressed as a percentage of the value of the stock and based upon location. The country is divided into territories, and the requirement varies from 40 percent to 80 percent because of the larger or more frequent losses in urban areas. New York City and Los Angeles are included in the highest percentage group.

The coinsurance limit expressed for a class of business is in a dollar amount. It represents a maximum probable loss for the type of goods in the class. For example, the coinsurance limit might be set at $10,000 for heavy goods such as pianos, but at $20,000 for smaller, more stealable goods such as clothing. To determine the amount of insurance to be carried for a given risk, and therefore to avoid a coinsurance penalty, it is necessary to know (*a*) the value of the stock, (*b*) the coinsurance limit, and (*c*) the coinsurance percentage as determined by the rating territory.

To avoid penalty the insured must carry an amount of insurance which equals or exceeds the *smaller* of either the coinsurance limit *or* the amount

---

[7] Al Frantz "Shoplifting—The $4 Billion 'Boost'," *Journal of Insurance,* vol. 39, no. 1 (January–February 1978), p. 24; and "Shoplifting—Is Prevention the Only Insurance?" *Insurance Marketing,* June 1978, p. 30.

determined by applying the coinsurance percentage to the value of merchandise at the time of loss. The operation of the coinsurance clause under the foregoing condition may be illustrated by the following example:

Value of inventory of a television store $60,000
Coinsurance percentage for specified territory, 60 percent 36,000
Coinsurance limit for specified territory 30,000

To comply with the coinsurance clause, the insured must carry 60 percent of the value of the inventory; but since the coinsurance limit is less than 60 percent of the value of the inventory, the coinsurance requirement is fully satisfied if $30,000 of insurance is carried.

Safe burglary policy. The insurance agreement of this policy provides indemnity to the insured for loss of the insured property from within the vault or safe by safe burglary. The term *safe burglary* is defined to mean the felonious abstraction of insured property from the covered safe when all doors of the safe are duly closed and locked.

The property insured includes (*a*) money, (*b*) securities, and (*c*) other property. The coverage is not limited to strictly mercantile risks but may be issued to any person or organization owning a safe or vault. Money is defined as "currency, coins, bank notes, bullion and traveler's checks, registered checks, and money orders held for sale to the public." Securities include all negotiable and nonnegotiable instruments representing either money or other property, such as stamps, checks, drafts, bonds, and stock certificates or contracts. The policy also covers other property of any kind kept by the insured in the safe, except manuscripts, records, and accounts.

In order to establish a loss under a mercantile safe policy, it must be shown that a *burglary* actually occurred or was attempted. Entry to the safe or vault must have been effected by the use of tools, explosives, electricity, or gas or other chemicals upon the exterior of the safe, at a time when it was properly closed and locked by at least one combination or time lock. Evidence of the force used must appear on the exterior of the safe. An adequate set of books must be maintained from which the value of the lost or damaged items can be determined.

Under the safe burglary policy, the insurer is not liable for losses occurring while a combination or time lock, burglary alarm, vault, or private security guard service warranted in the policy declarations is not maintained. These protective measures are considered conditions of the contract, which if unmet will suspend or exclude coverage for losses. Losses effected by opening the door of the safe, vault, or chest by manipulation of the lock are regarded as theft losses not in the burglary category. If the manipulation is performed by an employee of the insured, the protection is available through a fidelity bond coverage.

The contract extends to cover *property damage* caused by burglary of the insured's safe or any attempt at a burglary. Property damage coverage extends to the insured's safe or vault together with the insured's property within. It also covers property damage to furniture, equipment, and merchandise on the premises, if the insured is the owner or is liable for damages to the premises.

Rates for safe insurance are quoted per $1,000 of insurance carried and depend upon the following features: (1) the type of safe, (2) the territory, (3) the class of business, and (4) the property covered. Safes are classified into groups of fire-resistive and burglar-resistive safes. Discounts are allowed for features that tend to minimize the risk, such as a private security guard, safes equipped with an approved relocking system, premises protected with tear-gas systems. Discounts are allowed when there is more than one safe in a single location.

Mercantile robbery policy. Stores, offices, and other organizations are not immune from robbery during business hours; and messengers carrying money and valuables are held up and robbed. Messenger and robbery insurance coverages are: (*a*) inside holdup insurance, which covers robbery risks (and kidnapping, if included); and (*b*) outside holdup insurance, which covers the risk of messenger robbery. Either coverage is available separately in the *mercantile robbery policy.*

The inside holdup coverage covers loss or damage to the insured property through robbery or attempted robbery and loss or damage to furniture, fixtures, and other property. The coverage is effective on a 24-hour basis and furnishes protection only within the insured's premises. Loss or damage to merchandise stolen from a show window by a person who has broken the glass from the outside is covered while the premises are regularly open for business.

Kidnapping is sometimes resorted to by robbers who hold an owner or an employee, usually off the premises, later forcing the person detained to open the premises or supply information, keys, or other means of admission.

The outside holdup feature of the contract covers the insured for robbery losses if the robbery or attempted robbery takes place outside the premises of the insured. This feature of the contract covers not only messenger robbery but also damage to money, securities, merchandise, or the container in the possession of the messenger resulting from robbery or attempted robbery. The protection applies outside the insured's premises and provides 24-hour protection.

As with other robbery coverages, the premium for inside and outside robbery is dependent upon the territory in which the risk is located, the number of persons on duty within the insured's premises, the kind of business, the protective measures, and the kind of property. Credits on the rate under the messenger robbery form are allowed when certain designated precautions are taken. Examples are the use of a private conveyance, a locked messenger chest or satchel attached by a chain or a wire strap to the custodian or vehicle conveying the funds, and a route limited to the interior of the building. Burglary (and robbery and theft, if desired) coverage in the home of the custodian may be endorsed to the messenger or interior robbery policy.

Paymaster robbery policy. Many businesses and organizations need off-premises coverage only because they pay their employees in cash and transfer large sums of money from point to point. The *paymaster robbery policy* provides day and night protection for the insured from loss by robbery from a custodian *outside* the insured's premises of money or checks held solely for payroll purposes. It also covers an amount not exceeding 10 percent of the amount of the insurance, for money and securities not intended solely for payroll purposes.

Differing from the messenger robbery form, the policy covers *inside* the insured's premises for loss or damage of money or checks intended for payroll purposes. While on the premises of the employer, employees of the insured are protected against loss of money or checks which is the outgrowth of a robbery of the custodian or an attempt thereat. Payroll funds taken by a safe burglary do not come within the protection of the policy. Losses to payroll funds are covered if such losses are attributable to the kidnapping of a custodian.

Paymaster robbery, or all-risks, coverage is also available by endorsement under the money and securities broad form policy (see later section).

Forgery insurance policy. The *depositor's forgery policy,* sometimes referred to as a "forgery bond," is issued to individuals, firms, or corporations. It is not issued to banks and savings and loan associations. The policy is divided into two sections: (a) covering outgoing items and (b) covering incoming items. The policy usually protects the insured only for outgoing items, against forgery losses on commercial paper (checks, drafts, notes, etc.) issued or presumed to have been issued by the insured or an authorized agent. The incoming coverage is seldom written today, as most of these losses should be guarded against by ordinary business credit procedures.

Storekeepers', and office, burglary and robbery policies. A type of "package" crime insurance, including limited amounts of a number of types of burglary-theft insurance, is available to the small *storekeeper and merchant.* It provides at reasonable cost a convenient blanket burglary and robbery coverage.

The storekeepers' form in a single "all-or-none" policy covers the insured against loss of money, securities, and merchandise, together with damage to property. The coverage is provided under seven headings, with $250 insurance applying to each as follows: (1) inside robbery, (2) outside or messenger robbery, (3) kidnapping the custodian and forcing the custodian to open the premises, (4) safe burglary ($50 limit on money and securities), (5) theft from a bank depository or a custodian's home, (6) open-stock burglary, and (7) damage to the premises by burglary or robbery. The limit for each coverage may be increased in multiples of $250 to a maximum of $1,000. A broad form of this policy adds several other coverages, such as forgery, vandalism, and malicious mischief.

A policy similar to the storekeepers' policy is written to provide a burglary and robbery coverage for *offices*. It covers office equipment and other property but excludes merchandise. A $100 limit applies to money and securities. The class of risk for which the office form is designed includes accountants, architects, attorneys, auditors, insurance offices, brokers, contractors, dentists, doctors and the like. Policies similar to those for stores and offices are available to service stations and other risk.

Money and securities policy (broad form).   To provide a broader package of coverage for money and securities, an important special policy was developed. *The money and securities policy (broad form)* offers much more than only burglary and robbery coverage. It insures money and securities for *all risks* of disappearance, wrongful abstraction, and destruction (including fire). Other property is covered only for safe burglary, robbery, or theft from a messenger's home. Damage to property caused by burglary or robbery is included.

The policy does not provide employee dishonesty coverage or open-stock burglary coverage. Available to many businesses, this policy has two optional insuring clauses: (*a*) inside protection and (*b*) outside protection. The policy may be written to cover either or both.

The policy may be written to cover securities only. This form has a particular appeal to institutions and individuals that own large values in securities. Individuals in the capacity of trustees or treasurers of endowed institutions, investment trusts, holding companies, and brokers frequently have in their possession securities with a face value running into large sums of money. Even with the protection afforded by the safe-deposit box, the possibility of loss growing out of mysterious disappearances, entry to the box by misrepresentation or fraud, as well as burglary or robbery, constitutes a real peril. In addition, fire, theft, tornado, riot, explosion or other like perils might cause the destruction of the box and its contents. With the exception of certain bonds written for financial institutions, almost all other policies specifically exclude losses growing out of the destruction of money and securities.

Comprehensive dishonesty, disappearance, and destruction policy.   This contract, familiarly known as the 3-D *policy*,[8] was designed to provide the broadest possible crime coverage for business firms. Since it combines *fidelity and burglary* coverages, it is a convenient method of insuring all crime perils. It combines in a single document coverages that at one time were available only as separate policies.

The basic printed form, available in the 3-D policy or as an endorsement

---

[8] The student is referred to other sources for some policy details not included here. See Harold F. Gee, *Comprehensive 3-D Primer* (Indianapolis: Rough Notes Co., republished about every four years); and *Fire, Casualty,* and *Surety Bulletins* (Cincinnati: National Underwriter Co., loose-leaf).

under the special multiple-peril policy (SMP), contains five separate and optional insuring clauses, with a separate limit of insurance for each:

1. *Employee dishonesty coverage* (in either the commercial blanket *or* blanket position bond forms discussed in the next section). Covered are loss of money, securities, or other property through any fraudulent or dishonest act or acts committed by any *employees,* acting alone or in collusion with others. Embezzlement is a common example.

2. *Loss inside the premises coverage.* The actual destruction, disappearance, or wrongful abstraction of *money or securities within* the insured's premises (or banking or safe-deposit premises) is included. The *broad form* perils of burglary, robbery, or theft are covered, and *other property* is covered for safe (or locked cash drawer) burglary or robbery.

3. *Loss outside the premises coverage.* Loss of money or securities is covered *off* the insured's premises, for destruction, disappearance, or wrongful abstraction while being conveyed by a messenger or an armored car vehicle or while within the living quarters of the home of a messenger. Loss of other property is covered for off-premises robbery in these same circumstances.

4. *Money orders and counterfeit paper currency coverage.* Loss is covered due to the acceptance in good faith of (1) any post office or express money order, if not paid on presentation, or (2) any counterfeit U.S. or Canadian paper currency. Such bogus items are sometimes called "incoming" risks.

5. *Depositor's forgery coverage.* Covered is loss for the insured, or any bank in which the insured has an account, through forgery or alteration of checks, drafts, promissory notes, or similar written promises to pay money. Examples of such "outgoing" risks include checks made or drawn in the name of the insured to fictitious payers, by anyone impersonating another, or payroll checks endorsed by someone without proper authority. This coverage is not often purchased in the 3-D policy, because banks which cash such forgeries without proper identification of the payees would usually be responsible for such losses.

In addition to the five basic coverages, 13 other endorsements are available in order to include mercantile open-stock (burglary or theft), payroll, office equipment, credit card forgery, extortion, and other crime coverages.

Because of the breadth of the coverages provided by the 3-D policy, protection may be extended to virtually every conceivable type of crime loss. The insured is not required to carry protection under all of the insuring clauses but elects those coverages desired in the policy. The policy does not have a uniform limit applying to each of the insuring clauses; an optional amount may be elected to apply to each of the various clauses.

The broad protection of the 3-D policy and its advantage of convenience have made it one of the most popular methods for businesses to insure their crime and fidelity bond perils. Fidelity bonds, covering employee dishonesty, are closely related to the topic of crime insurance as described thus far in this chapter. They are also an important part of suretyship, and the reader's attention is called to the fidelity bond section in the later part of this chapter.

Blanket crime policy. This contract is very similar to the 3-D policy. However, a major difference is that it includes the first five basic coverages as a package; all are included *automatically*. Another basic difference is that the *blanket crime policy* provides a *single insuring limit* rather than separate limits for each of the coverages. The minimum amount must be at least $1,000, but other minimums, such as $10,000 for fidelity coverage, may also apply. For example, a $100,000 policy would provide a total of that amount as needed for any of the fidelity, money and securities, or forgery coverages included in the contract. Office equipment theft, payroll, extortion, and other coverages are optional.

SURETYSHIP

Nature and development

The contract of suretyship is a credit device that made its appearance with the earliest development of business obligations. Under the terms of a surety agreement, or *bond,* one party becomes answerable to a third party for the acts or neglect of a second party. The answerable party is the *surety,* and the one for whose debt or obligation the surety is responsible is the *principal debtor,* or more commonly referred to as the *principal* or *obligor.* The person protected by the agreement is called the *obligee.* For example, in a fidelity bond, the surety accepts the responsibility of the employee (the obligor) to the employer (the obligee) for faithful performance of the duties of employment. In a contract bond, the surety accepts responsibility of the contractor (the obligor) to the property owner (the obligee) for carrying out the construction or supply contract.

Before the writing of surety bonds became an established business, persons acting in a fiduciary capacity or occupying positions of trust requiring sureties were obliged to appeal to relatives or friends. More often than not, the *personal* surety signed a bond without remuneration and purely as a favor. This practice was the source of many difficulties, not to say loss and hard feelings.

Corporate surety bonds were first offered in England around 1720 to insure the honesty of servants, but it was not until 1840 that the corporate fidelity business for insuring employees became established. The first American company was organized in New York in 1853. Corporate suretyship, however, was slow in developing. There was considerable resistance to the substitution of the impersonal corporation for the locally known personal surety. As the idea of corporate sureties became better known, individuals became increasingly reluctant to assume obligations without remuneration. Also tending to stimulate the development of corporate suretyship were the permanence and stability of the surety corporations. These are subject to the regulations provided by the statutes; their chief function is to meet losses when they come. Individual sureties are unable to supply a bond with the same safety and stability that a surety company can. For this reason, those requiring bonds today insist upon satisfactory corporate sureties.

Insurance and suretyship

With the change to surety bonds issued by corporations, the courts began to adopt the insurance rule which applies to "contracts of adhesion." When the contract is drawn up primarily by one party, the benefit of the doubt goes to the other party (the insured, or obligee) in the case of an ambiguity.

Suretyship, especially fidelity bonding, is thus treated like insurance in some respects. The bonds look like insurance contracts, too, and they are often issued by agents who write both insurance contracts and surety bonds. The regulation of bonds usually falls under the state insurance departments. If the definition of insurance is limited to transfer of risk, bonds meet this criterion (although the pooling method and purpose do differ somewhat).

Although much the same as insurance, practically speaking, the surety bond differs in several ways. Bonds always have *three parties* to the contract (see previous section), whereas insurance contracts often have only two. *Individuals may* act as sureties, although they seldom do, and in such instances the agreement has little in common with the usual contract of insurance.

Also, a primary distinction is that in bonds there exists a *right of indemnity* between the surety and the principal debtor. If the surety is called upon to pay a loss under the bond, the surety may in turn proceed against the principal, who is primarily liable on the agreement. This is in contrast to the insurance contract, which obligates the insurer to pay losses in accordance with the policy terms without recourse to any other party to the contract. The liability of the principal is to be contrasted with the liability of third parties against whom an insurer may proceed under its rights of subrogation. In the case of subrogation, the third party is not a party to the contract.

Another basic difference is that most insurance contracts anticipate that there will be losses, the outgrowth of the happening of the contingency covered by the policy. In the surety contract, on the other hand, the promise of the surety is secondary, after the failure of the principal to perform a specific obligation. Failure may be occasioned by dishonesty, incompetence, or lack of resources. Surety bonds are usually written on the assumption that *losses* will be a *relatively small* part of the cost of the bond. They are written to strengthen the credit or provide a guarantee for the principal rather than with the primary purpose of paying losses.

In summary, the distinctions between suretyship and insurance are of some value but do not always hold true if all types of insurance are compared with all types of bonds. The differences are much more meaningful when specific types of insurance are contrasted with specific types of bonds (for example, crime insurance with contract bonds, etc.).

General divisions of suretyship

Bonding companies divide bonds into two classes: (a) *fidelity bonds* and (b) *surety bonds*. In the strict sense, all corporate bonds in which a surety agrees to answer for the nonperformance of a principal are surety bonds. The difference between a fidelity bond and a surety bond lies in the nature of the obligation. In the case of a fidelity bond, the obligation of employees to be honest with their employers is implied rather than contractual. The bond undertakes to reimburse an obligee (the employer) for loss of money or property growing out of dishonest acts of the principal (the employee). The surety bond, on the other hand, obligates the surety to be responsible for the performance of an expressed obligation of the principal. In the case of surety bonds, while a dishonest act may give rise to a loss, it is likewise true that negligence and lack of ability on the part of the principal may create a liability on the part of the surety.

The business of corporate suretyship has developed[9] into three major divisions. These are: (1) fidelity bonds, (2) judicial bonds, and (3) contract bonds. Three other classes are of lesser importance (see Appendix F): depository and miscellaneous, license and permit, and federal. A brief summary of each class follows. Figure 25–1 shows the relationship among the major classifications. Note that surety bonds are divided into three subtypes here.

Under *fidelity bonds* the surety company reimburses employers for dishonesty losses of employees. The employer may be an individual, a firm, a corporation, or the public.

Judicial bonds, sometimes referred to as "court bonds," are those required in court proceedings. There are two categories of judicial or court bonds. The *fiduciary* obligations are those filed in behalf of an executor, a guardian, or a trustee. In the second category, which comprises the type filed with the court for bail or when a case is appealed, are those involving a *financial guarantee*.

Contract bonds guarantee property owners who enter into contracts for construction that the work will be completed in accordance with the terms of the agreements. The surety company guarantees the performance of contracts and the credit of the person, such as contractors, who obligate themselves to build or to perform some specific service.

Miscellaneous bonds include depository bonds that guarantee bank deposits and a number of other miscellaneous forms, such as those filed in connection

---

[9] For the development and special problems of the field, see James S. Burkhart, "Fidelity and Surety Bonding in the 1970s," *CPCU Annals*, vol. 24, no. 4 (December 1971), p. 341.

Figure 25-1. Types of fidelity and surety bonds

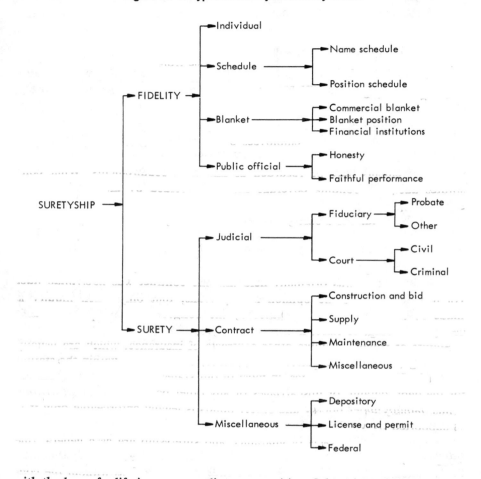

with the loss of a life insurance policy or securities. Others include *license and permit bonds* to pay the public authorities or third parties for violation of the terms of licenses or permits, and *federal bonds* required in connection with federal immigration laws or export and import duties (see Appendix F.)

Basic features of fidelity and surety bonds

There are certain features which are common to many fidelity and surety bonds. These characteristics will be discussed briefly before some of the more usual types of bonds are analyzed in reference to their specific provisions. Many of these features are concerned with identifying the limitations under which the surety promises to make payment for losses.

Penalty of the bond. When a designated sum is written into the bond as a limit of the liability of the surety, the amount is called the *penalty* and the bond is a *fixed-penalty bond*. The penalty corresponds to the face or insurance amount of an insurance policy. Some bonds, known as *open covenant bonds,* are written in which no amount of penalty is fixed. These guarantee that the surety will pay whatever damages arise from the nonperformance of the obligation assumed by the principal.

Obligation to bond. It is important for those who hold positions of trust to understand that losses to property in their care that are occasioned by their negligence carry with them a personal liability. Failure by the directors to provide fidelity coverage upon employees of a bank is negligence, for example, and the directors may be held personally liable for dishonesty losses. Statutory requirements may be regarded as minimum requirements. What constitutes adequate bonding coverage must be decided by the circumstances surrounding each particular case.

Effect of fraud. If a surety has been induced by fraud of the principal to become a party to the bond, this fraud will not constitute a defense against an innocent obligee who has acted in reliance upon the bond.

As to the obligation of the obligee to inform the surety of all the facts affecting the risk, it was originally held that the contract was *uberrimae fidei* (of utmost faith). Some opinion now prevails, that only when inquiry is made by the surety and disclosures by the obligee are incomplete, insufficient, misleading, or false, is the contract jeopardized.

Statute of frauds. Unlike other contracts of insurance, which are usually in writing (but are not required to be), surety contracts fall within the statute of frauds. Under these statutes, in most of our states, an agreement to answer for the debt, default, or miscarriages of any other person must be *in writing.* Thus, liability under fidelity and surety bonds is legally enforceable only if it is supported by written evidence of the agreement.

Assignment. Contracts of guarantee and suretyship are as a general rule assignable, even before a breach, unless by their terms assignment is limited or restricted. Fidelity bonds are not assignable before a loss without the consent of the surety because a definite principal is contemplated by the insurer and another may not be substituted.

Subrogation. In contracts of suretyship, upon the payment by the surety of a debt of the principal, the surety is subrogated to all the rights of the cerditor against the principal whose debt has been paid. This includes all securities, funds, liens, priorities, or equities held by the creditor as security.

Acts discharging surety. When a surety is liable for the honesty of an employee, upon the discovery of any dishonesty in connection with the duties for which the employee is bonded, the employer is obligated to dismiss the dishonest employee at once or to secure the consent of the surety for continued employment. Failure to follow this procedure will release the surety from any liability for loss occasioned by further dishonest acts of the employee.

Unless provided in the bond, no particular supervision over the bonded employee is required. It is usual, however, in the case of corporate fidelity bonds to require a warranty that periodic examinations or audits of the principal's accounts will be made. Failure to comply affords grounds for releasing the surety.

Contractor's bonds as a rule contain a clause permitting changes, alterations, or additions without the consent of the surety. Even with this clause, if a change is such that the work becomes essentially different from that originally contemplated, the nonconsenting surety may be released.

Cosureties. Bonds issued in very large amounts are sometimes signed by more than one surety. Each company obligated on such a bond is known as a *cosurety*. When the individual limits of liability for the cosureties are set, it becomes necessary to do this through an agreement between the sureties that is known as a "side agreement."

Reinsurance. The laws of the various jurisdictions in this country fix a limit to the liability that is to be assumed by a surety company on a single risk. When attractive business is offered, but the limit of liability is in excess of that which the company may legally assume, or is willing to assume, it may write the bond and reinsure the excess liability with other surety companies, just as insurance companies reinsure their excess lines.

Indemnitors. An indemnity agreement is occasionally used when a contract bond is required by an applicant whose financial position or experience falls just short of meeting the surety's standards. The *indemnitors* are individuals who assume much the same responsibility as that assumed by an accommodation endorser of commercial paper. In the event of a default by the principal, the indemnitors assume the obligation. If called upon, the surety may in turn seek reimbursement from the indemnitors. Upon what grounds can a surety company justify asking for indemnitors if it is in the business of surety underwriting and is paid a premium for assuming the risk? The answer is the same as that which justifies a bank, which is in the business of lending money, in requiring endorsers before lending upon an unsecured note. The credit of the applicant is otherwise insufficient.

Legal capacity. To be bound on a contract of surety, the principal must have legal capacity since the rules that apply in other forms of contract also apply here. For example, the agreement of an infant or an insane son is voidable. In the case of suretyship, the incapacity of the principal does not affect the liability of the surety. The surety is still liable even when the surety becomes a party to the agreement without knowledge of the incapacity of the principal, unless induced to do so through fraudulent concealment or misrepresentation.

Fidelity bonds

General classes. A fidelity bond pays an employer for loss growing out of *dishonest acts of employees*. Fidelity bonds are classified as to the extent of the protection they afford against (1) larceny and embezzlement and (2) dishonesty. For the purposes of underwriting, bonds are classified as: (1) bonds required by private employers to cover loss through dishonesty of employees and (2) bonds required of public officers for the faithful performance of their duties.

As to form, bonds are written as follows: (1) *individual* bonds, (2) *schedule* bonds, and (3) *blanket* bonds. Schedule bonds are written as (*a*) *name* schedule and (*b*) *position* schedule. Blanket bonds are subdivided into (*a*) *commercial blanket* and (*b*) *blanket position.* Since these classes represent some of the most important fidelity coverages, each will be discussed briefly in separate sections.

In addition to the foregoing, a large number of blanket bonds are written for banks and other financial institutions. The fidelity coverage often forms only a portion of the protection afforded. The specialized nature of these bonds causes them to be used less frequently by general business, so their discussion is reserved for more complete analysis in Appendix F.

A few bonds are restricted to the perils of larceny or embezzlement and hold that court convictions for these crimes are necessary before the company is liable. Most fidelity bonds today, however, cover the broader peril of dishonesty, which includes all forms of theft, fraud, and misappropriation of an employer's property, regardless of whether or not it is technically a crime.

Importance. Dramatic robberies with guns blazing and police sirens screaming are popular fare for television and movies, but it is the much less obvious "white-collar crime" that costs corporations an estimated $40 billion every year. The notorious bank robber's haul only averages $10,000 according to FBI statistics, while the real growth industry for dishonesty is computer fraud, which exceeds $400,000 per loss. (See the Equity Funding scandal discussed in Chapter 8.)

A substantial part of the losses caused by criminals in gray flannel suits instead of stocking masks are caused by employees. The above figure for white-collar crime also includes general frauds against consumers, but these are not directly related to the fidelity bond field, which is the subject of this section. The multibillion-dollar annual loss in the United States because of employee dishonesty is one example of the significance of fidelity bonds. Even more startling is the fact that only a very small part (probably less than 10 percent) of the total losses are recovered under dishonesty bonds, either due to lack of insurance or to substantial underinsurance.

Another reason for the importance of fidelity bonds is the use of these contracts in business *risk management*. Losses occur in fantastic amounts under the most unusual and unexpected circumstances. Many of the losses occur gradually over long periods of time, and only ultimate discovery shocks employers with the realization that thousands of dollars have been lost. Trusted bookkeepers steal money, but much more is lost through other employees who take tools, merchandise, raw materials, and other property. Purchasing agents, salespersons, clerks, supervisors, and executives all cause many losses, of the more obvious cash and financial assets as well as mundane by-product wastes that practically no one would expect to be stolen. For example, one employee in collusion with suppliers provided fraudulent samples of metal scrap to raise the price of purchased materials, and another sold broken glass to a competing bottle manufacturing plant.[10]

The only answer is for employers to exercise constant vigilance to reduce the probability and the extent of such losses, and to purchase fidelity bond coverage. Many business firms have elaborate security systems involving many security guards, police dogs, and electronic devices. Others hire professional firms, such as Pinkerton's and the William J. Burns International Detective Agency, to design and maintain safeguarding systems, to perform the very important employee investigations, and to do other loss-prevention work. When it is learned that less than 10 to 15 percent of businesses insure against employee dishonesty, the scope of the risk retained and the parallel need for loss prevention are emphasized. The techniques of embezzlement, for example, require close scrutiny of *every* employee because no clear-cut description of the typical embezzler is possible. The analysis of the causes of embezzlement, which include (1) need or desire, (2) rationalization, and (3) opportunity, furnishes the employer with many prospective methods by which management can control some employee dishonesty.[11]

Contract term and restoration clauses. Both individual and schedule fidelity bonds may be written on either a *term basis* or a *continuous basis*. If written for a term, the period is usually a year and the bond expires at the end of the term, as does an ordinary insurance policy, unless a continuation "certificate" is added. With the continuous form, which is the most common form for fidelity bonds, if premiums are paid when due, the bond remains in force until a party to the agreement takes steps to effect termination.

Fidelity bonds of all types may be canceled at any time by the employer or the bonding company. If the company wishes to cancel, notice is required and the conditions governing the notice are incorporated into the bond. As the conditions apply to an individual employee, they terminate in accordance with the terms of the bond on his or her death, resignation, or discharge.

Fidelity bonds provide coverage only if loss is sustained while the coverage is in effect or is discovered within a certain designated time. The cutoff period is usually one or two years. If a bond is terminated and a new one is purchased, the new surety usually agrees to pay for losses (up to the old limit) that occurred under the old bond but were not discovered until after the new bond became effective. This coverage formerly required special coverage called a "superseded suretyship rider."

---

[10] *Honesty Insurance,* booklet published by Insurance Company of North America, 1977.

[11] A good survey of such controls, analyzed in flowcharts and with checklist questions to help evaluate present systems, is contained in *How to Reduce Embezzlement Losses* (New York: Royal Globe Insurance Companies).

There are two types of *restoration clauses,* and it is important to recognize the difference between them. Under a simple restoration clause, a fidelity bond is automatically reinstated to its full amount after a loss. However, the amount reinstated is effective only for *future* losses. The most common and comprehensive restoration form is known as the "retroactive restoration clause," and it is used for most blanket bonds. The retroactive restoration clause automatically restores the full face of the bond as to *prior* losses following the discovery of a dishonest or fraudulent act. If a loss antedating the first loss is discovered later, that loss, as well as future losses, is covered in the full amount of the bond.

Individual bonds. The simplest bonds for private employers are *individual* bonds, which are written to guarantee against dishonest acts of a named individual. On the basis of an application from the employee, an investigation is made by the surety company. If the risk is acceptable, the surety company signs the bond, and this is delivered to the employer. Signature of the principal (employee) is the practice still followed, but it is not essential, because the employee is liable for any dishonest act without regard to the bond itself. In the beginning, fidelity bonds were all individual. Separate bonds were written for each employee, with the result that considerable confusion was experienced in keeping all employees covered and in renewing bonds as they expired. To overcome this difficulty, the schedule bond was devised.

Schedule fidelity bonds. The *name schedule bond* lists the names of all the employees to be covered and provides surety protection in a single document. The insuring clause indicates the acts of dishonesty to be covered. The name and a bond limit for each bonded employee is listed in the schedule. This permits flexibility in the amount of coverages. For example, the treasurer of a concern may be bonded on a name schedule bond for $50,000, while outside salespersons may be provided with satisfactory coverage in the amount of $10,000. As new employees are added to the staff, their names may be included in the coverage by endorsement; and if employees leave, they may be removed from the schedule. The persons named in the schedule are not required to sign the bond. Employees are required, however, to sign an application in which each agrees to indemnify the surety against any covered loss that he or she causes.

The principal difference between the name schedule bond and the *position schedule bond* is to be found in the method of preparing the schedule. In the name schedule bond, defaults of persons designated by name are covered. Instead of naming the persons to be covered, the position form contains a list of positions in the schedule, and the persons holding those positions are covered by the bond.

This bond appeals particularly to business concerns having a considerable turnover in personnel. In the schedule, every position to be covered is listed; and if two or more persons occupy the same position, the number in that position must be listed. For example, it would be logical for a schedule to show one person in the position of treasurer, but it might show 20 persons as outside salespersons. If two or more persons concurrently occupy a position, each must be bonded for the same amount. If the number of employees concurrently occupying a position is not correctly stated in the schedule, the employer is obliged to contribute to the loss only to the extent that the bond does not cover every employee.

Under the position schedule bond, an automatic coverage for 60 days is provided which protects the employer in the event that additional persons are added to the same covered position. New positions of a class not already designated in the schedule may also be added automatically, but in this case it is usual to set a limit for the liability of the company, such as $5,000. The automatic coverage continues for 60 days, and it is terminated at the end of that period unless a written request for continuation is filed by the employer and the coverage is accepted by the surety.

Blanket fidelity bonds. Individual and schedule bonds involve considerable detail and care where there are frequent changes in personnel. In addition, losses frequently develop that are traceable to unbonded or inadequately bonded personnel. *Blanket fidelity bonds* cover *all employees.* There are two forms: *(a) commercial blanket bonds* and *(b) blanket position bonds.* Banks and other financial institutions have special blanket forms which are not available to general business firms (see Appendix F).

The commercial blanket bond is written for a stated limit *per loss,* with the aggregate lump sum applied collectively to all employees. The blanket position bond follows the pattern of the commercial bond in that it covers all the employees of the insured. However, it differs in that the blanket position bond applies the loss limit to *each employee.* In the case of the blanket position bond, the company is theoretically liable for the penalty of the bond multiplied by the number of employees, but only if the employees are in collusion.

The minimum limit sold is $2,500 per employee for the blanket position bond and $10,000 for the commercial blanket bond. The maximum limit is usually $100,000 for the blanket position bond, but no maximum limit is set, except by company practice, for the commercial blanket bond. Amounts such as $100,000 or more are quite common, and the cost of such a bond for a medium-sized retail store, for example, might be several hundred dollars per year. The rates vary with the number and type of the employees.

The Surety Association of America publishes an "exposure index" which estimates the needed bond limits on the basis of the sum of current assets (5 percent of goods and 20 percent of other current assets) and gross sales or income (10 percent).

The definition of employees covered by the commercial blanket bond and the blanket position bond is identical. Both bonds cover all natural persons (except directors of the insured, if a corporation, who are not also officers of the corporation) who are in the regular service of the insured. They must be compensated by salary, wages, or commission, and they must be under the direction of the insured in the performance of their duties. The bonds do not cover factors, brokers, commission merchants, consignees, or other like representatives or agents. Territorial coverage includes all of the United States and Canada; and if desired, coverage may be extended to include approved employees in foreign countries. Executive officers of a corporation owning a majority of stock may be excluded from the coverage. Others excluded are canvassers, chauffeurs, collectors, demonstrators, drivers, driver's helpers, and outside salespersons of companies in certain designated lines of business. These employees are known as "Class A special employees," and they are sometimes excluded from the blanket bond and covered for a limited amount under a schedule bond. This plan results in a substantial saving in premium.

The commercial blanket bond provides that the payment of a loss shall not reduce the amount payable for any other loss whether it is sustained before or after the shortage under consideration. In other words, there is no reduction in liability for a loss, though the limit with respect to any one employee is the penalty of the bond. This provision is unnecessary in the blanket position bond since the full penalty of the bond applies to each employee and a loss payable with respect to one employee in no way affects the coverage on the others.

There is also a difference in the discovery period after the termination of the entire bond. The commercial blanket bond allows 12 months, whereas the blanket position bond allows 24 months. Both forms provide group coverage in that fraudulence or dishonesty losses are paid if these are attributable to one or more employees even though the guilty party may not be designated.

Public official fidelity bonds. The law requires that certain public officials be bonded, but losses frequently occur that are attributable to the acts of minor employees not covered by the statute. It is possible to provide a blanket bond for public employees that extends protection against all dishonesty or against all losses resulting from failure to perform the duties of their positions as required by law.

There are four forms of blanket bond written for public officials. These are (a) the honesty blanket bond, (b) the honesty blanket position bond, (c) the faithful performance blanket bond, and (d) the faithful performance blanket position bond.

Coverage under the faithful performance form provides protection against loss from the failure of employees to perform faithfully the duties of the office as required by law or to keep accurate accounts of all properties and monies in their control. In contrast, coverage under the honesty forms is limited to loss from dishonest or fraudulent acts committed by employees.

The blanket bond covers all officers and subordinates (except treasurers and tax collectors) who are not required by law to furnish an individual bond to qualify for office. All such employees of a municipal subdivision may be covered on a single bond; or a separate bond may be executed for the different divisions or departments of any state, county, city, town, village, or other political subdivision.

Judicial bonds

All bonds filed in judicial proceedings are included within the category of judicial bonds. Judicial bonds are sometimes referred to as "court bonds," but this term is more commonly used to designate a particular class of judicial bonds.

The field is divided into two groups. *Fiduciary bonds* constitute the first group and include those bonds which guarantee the faithful performance of a trust administered under the supervision and jurisdiction of a court. The second group includes all those bonds required of litigants in a court action. This is the group to which the term *court bond* is usually applied.

The coverage afforded by each subdivision is quite different. Fiduciary bonds provide a guarantee that principals will discharge their trust honestly and in accordance with the law. The coverage is broader than one strictly against dishonesty since it also covers losses occasioned by negligence or lack of ability. Court bonds are given in connection with litigation, and the obligation is the payment of money. Honesty, integrity, high standing, or ability have no effect in determining the obligation if the litigation is in the end decided against the principal. Examples include injunction, appeal, and bail bonds.

Fiduciary bonds.   One of the most common types of fiduciary bonds is the *probate bond.* The guarantee of a probate bond that fiduciaries will fulfill their trust in accordance with law involves numerous specific obligations, such as the filing of inventories, taking prompt steps to conserve assets, properly investing funds, and properly making distributions where so directed. The surety company is interested not only in the honesty of the bonded persons but also in their knowledge of the fiduciary's responsibilities and their ability to fulfill the requirements of the trust. Among the more frequently used probate bonds are those required by administrators, executors, guardians, conservators, and testamentary trustees.

Because of the nature of the guarantee under a probate bond, surety companies are not always willing to assume the risk without retaining some control over the direction and management of the estate. This has given rise to the writing of bonds under a special *joint-control agreement* executed at the time application for the bond is made. When the principal and the surety agree to joint control, the principal is required to deposit all funds belonging to the estate in a bank under the name of the estate. Checks may then be drawn on this account by the fiduciary, but they must be countersigned by a representative of the bonding company.

Applicants for fidelity bonds frequently resent the request of surety companies for joint control, feeling that such a request reflects upon their honesty.

However, the obligations placed by law upon fiduciaries are not always simple matters to those unacquainted with the duties of the position to which they have been appointed. Fiduciaries, by some improper act, though committed with the best intentions, or by the failure to act through carelessness or inadvertence, many bring huge personal losses upon themselves. The fiduciary has nothing whatever to lose through cooperating with a surety company and permitting the exercise of joint control, and stands in a position to gain from the experience and wide knowledge of surety company representatives.

Fiduciary bonds *other than probate* are of several kinds. Into this classification fall fiduciaries appointed in the district, county, circuit, and state courts other than probate. Such fiduciaries are appointed to handle an estate or to manage property or a business when there are a number of conflicting interests; and when an impartial person in charge is needed to safeguard the interests of all and ultimately effect an equitable distribution of assets. In this group are to be found conservators, trustees, custodians, receivers, liquidators, assignees of creditors, and referees.

Court bonds. This category includes all bonds filed in behalf of litigants in connection with judicial proceedings in the courts. The *court bond* finds its usefulness in permitting the principal to maintain an action when the court requires a surety to protect the other party from loss in the event that the action brought is unsuccessful. Liability under the bond, therefore, is not contingent upon the honesty or ability of the principal. The obligation assumed by the bonding company is the payment of money in the event that the action brought, for which the bond is given, comes to an unfavorable termination from the point of view of the principal. It is this feature that sometimes causes these to be called "monetary obligation" bonds.

A creditor who lives outside the state in which an action is brought against a debtor is required to file a bond guaranteeing the payment of the costs of the suit. If property of a defendant is held as a means for satisfying a claim if the action is successful, the plaintiff is required to file a bond guaranteeing the defendant against loss through having the property tied up. Again, if a plaintiff undertakes to compel a defendant to do or refrain from doing certain things, a bond is required to protect the defendant against loss if the plaintiff is unsuccessful. Bonds of this type are termed *plaintiff's bonds.*

It is often necessary or convenient for the defendant to file a bond. For example, when property has been tied up pending the outcome of an action, the defendant may release the property and secure its use by filing a bond. The use of bonds of the monetary obligation group is a matter of everyday routine in the courts. Some of the more widely used *defendant bonds* are called attachment, injunction, replevin, sheriff, appeal, and bail bonds.

Contract bonds

Contract bonds furnish a good example of the valuable services rendered by the surety bond business. Without such bonds, many contractors would not or could not perform their work. Contract bonds are basically credit guaran- tees. They encourage banks and suppliers to lend money or extend credit for needed working funds.

The value of contract bonds is apparent from the gigantic size of the con- struction industry. Public construction invariably requires a contract bond before bids and contracts are awarded. Such tremendous structures as Houston's Astrodome, civic centers, highways, bridges, and tunnels could not be attempted without adequate bonds.

Private construction of apartments and business buildings also requires millions of dollars of protection to guarantee that work will be successfully completed on schedule, in spite of weather delays, strikes, labor or material shortages, financial dishonesty, equipment failure, erroneous cost estimates, subcontractor defaults, and many other uncertainties.

The four main classes of contract bonds are as follows: (1) construction, (2) supply, (3) maintenance, and (4) miscellaneous. The *miscellaneous* group includes a wide variety of other bonds, such as a compensation bond of a self-insurer under a workers' compensation act.

Construction contract bonds. Contractors undertaking the construction of public works or public buildings are usually required by law to furnish a bond. The advantages of the surety bond in guaranteeing the faithful per- formance of the contract have also proved attractive to private construction projects.

The guarantee under a *construction contract* bond obligates the surety to indemnify the owner if the contractor fails to complete the undertaking. To make the owner whole in the event of default by the contractor, the surety is faced with the choice of finishing the work or of reimbursing the owner for the cost in excess of the original contract price. In addition to the foregoing, most contract bonds, particularly in public contracts, guarantee that the con- tractor will pay all labor and material bills incurred. The surety is also re- quired to indemnify the owners for losses occasioned by injury to employees or the public. This risk is usually insured by the contractor under the proper public liability and workers' compensation forms. Some element of mainte- nance may be incorporated into construction contracts as part of the bond. This is usually limited to a guarantee to the owner for a year against incompe- tent work or the use of defective materials. Surety underwriters scrutinize construction contracts carefully to determine the extent of the maintenance risk.

Bid bonds, sometimes termed "proposal bonds," form an important sub- division of the construction and supply contract group. Bid bonds are filed before the contract is awarded and usually accompany the bid. Their purpose is to guarantee that the bidding contractors, if awarded the contract, will sign the contract, supply such bond as is required, and carry on the work to a satisfactory conclusion. Bid bonds fall into three main types. Under the first type, if the contractor should fail to sign the contract and furnish a satisfactory *final bond,* the surety would be liable for an additional cost to the owner because of rebidding the contract. The second type of proposal obligation is known as a *bid letter,* a *surety's consent,* or a *surety's agreement.* This is a communication addressed to the owner in which the surety company agrees to execute the final contract bond if the named bidder is awarded the contract. The third type is known as an *automatic bid bond.* It operates as the final bond if the bidder is successful and is awarded the contract. Frequently owners offer bidders the option of filing either a bid bond or a certified check. The amount of the bond or check is usually placed at about 5 to 10 percent of the contract price. In the case of automatic bonds the face will equal that required for final bonds.

By the terms of the *mortgagors' completion bond,* the surety guarantees the lender of money that the owner will complete the building described in a contract in accordance with its terms and deliver it free of liens. Bonds of this class are, strictly speaking, not contract bonds; however, they are used in connection with the financing of construction projects. The construction contract bond guarantees that if the owner makes payments to the contractor as they become due, the contractor will faithfully complete the work. A failure to make payments when due relieves the contractor of the obligation to finish, and there is no obligation on the part of the bonding company on the contractor's construction bond to proceed with the work since there has been no default by the contractor. In such circumstances, a bank or other lender might find a partially completed building, heavily encumbered with liens, on its hands. The completion bond is given by the owner, not the contractor, to the lender of money. It guarantees that no act or default of the owner will give grounds for failure by the contractor to complete the building.

A brief illustration will indicate the *relationship of bid, construction, and completion bonds* mentioned in a construction operation. Assume a group of persons with a valuable piece of land and a sum of money. They decide to erect a hotel but need $1 million more to use their land profitably. They bring their plans to a group of investment bankers, together with an estimated operating statement. The bankers wish to be assured that the building costs will remain within estimates and that a completed and unencumbered building will be available as security for the mortgage. When they advertise for bids, the promoters will require a bid bond of all bidders. This will guarantee that the successful bidders will undertake the work or indemnify the owners for any loss occasioned by their failure to do so. When the job is let, the contractor will furnish the owners with a construction bond, which guarantees that the contractor will fulfill the terms and conditions of the agreement. The lenders of the money will require a completion bond from the owners of the property. This guarantees that the owners will administer the funds and advance their own share so that the building will be completed unencumbered by liens.

Supply contract bonds.   *Supply contract bonds* guarantee the faithful performance of contracts for furnishing supplies and material at an agreed price. The materials do not become part of the realty or attach thereto, at least until after the contracts in question have been completed. A newspaper publisher might use such a bond to guarantee its newsprint supply. Supply contract bonds are often required by governmental units. The surety is liable for any loss sustained by the obligee through failure to secure the supplies in accordance with the conditions of the contract. This includes any additional expense attendant upon securing substitute supplies, and it may include loss or damage occasioned by delay.

Maintenance bonds. *Maintenance bonds* are given to guarantee that the principal will maintain in good condition all or some part of a construction project. The bonds are also used in connection with supply contracts when the performance of the material sold is guaranteed by the seller. The maintenance bond finds frequent use in connection with highway construction work for various government jurisdictions. In connection with building contracts, the element of maintenance is most often found in the guarantee of a roof for a stated period of years. Maintenance guarantees against defective materials or work are sometimes also made in connection with materials such as waterproofing, insulation, and paint.

Miscellaneous surety bonds

A number of other *miscellaneous surety bonds* are briefly described in Appendix F. Included are those shown at the bottom of Figure 25–1, such as depository and related bonds, license and permit bonds, and federal bonds of various types. These bonds are used for specialized purposes, and are further examples of the wide scope and variety of the field of suretyship.

FOR REVIEW AND DISCUSSION

1. Dishonesty is the major peril for the fields of crime insurance and suretyship. Explain why you agree or disagree with this statement.
2. Money stolen in a blaze of gunfire is the stereotypical crime insurance loss. What parts of crime insurance does such an example *not* include?
3. What makes burglary-theft insurance difficult for insurers to underwrite?
4. "A business has very wide choices in deciding how it should take care of the peril of nonemployee dishonesty." Discuss this statement in terms of (a) insurance and (b) risk management.
5. How has the multiple-line trend affected the personal and the business fields of burglary-theft insurance?
6. Classify the basic parts of the field of crime insurance in outline form. Why is it important to understand such classification?
7. Identify several of the "package" crime insurance contracts, and explain their advantages to the insured.

8. What are the disadvantages of the storekeepers' burglary and robbery policy for a merchant's crime insurance needs, and what other contracts are available?

9. A fiction writer describes a masked man entering a store and taking cash at gunpoint. He remarks that the burglary policy had not been renewed, so the storekeeper was not paid for his loss. Why is this an incorrect inference?

10. A burglar's explosion of a safe damages a fine oil painting, but nothing is taken. Is the property damage loss covered under the burglary policy? Would destroyed paper money be covered?

11. What is the purpose of the fidelity bond? How does it differ from judicial and contract bonds?

12. A large manufacturer of color television sets reads about the tremendous losses resulting from employee dishonesty. What bond coverage should he purchase, and how else could he apply good risk management to this peril?

13. What are the similarities and the differences between "insurance" and "suretyship"?

14. The treasurer of a corporation is bonded in the sum of $25,000. A former bookkeeper, now deceased, and the treasurer are suspected of collusion, but the officers are unable to identify each employee's actual responsibility for a shortage. What is the position of the corporation if each of the employees concerned is specifically bonded? What type of bond should this business probably have?

15. Contrast the protection afforded by the blanket position bond with that afforded by the commercial blanket bond.

16. "The 3-D policy is a type of blanket crime insurance but is not the same as the blanket crime insurance policy." Explain.

17. Probate bonds are required when a person is appointed by the court to safeguard the estate of an incompetent. What other situations may require fiduciary bonds? What other types of judicial bonds are there?

Chapter 26

Concepts to consider in Chapter 26—Miscellaneous property and liability insurance

Miscellaneous property and liability insurance is a broad field:
  Aviation insurance has developed rapidly since the "jet age."
    Insurers include several large syndicates, or groups of insurers.
    Basic nature is like that of auto insurance, but with larger exposures.
    Aircraft classification: airline, private, industrial, commercial, special.
    Types of contracts include *hull, aircraft liability, admitted liability, medical payments,* and *comprehensive light plane.*
    Aviation rates are nonstandard, open market, and international.
  Boiler and machinery insurance combines property-liability insurance:
    Nature: *direct* and *indirect* losses to insured's property. Liability to others for their property or injury losses is included as direct loss.
    The basic contract is written separately, or with special multiperil policies.
    Direct losses are those by explosion, collapse, rupture, and other breakdowns of steam boilers, machinery, or electrical equipment.
    Indirect losses include *consequential, use and occupancy, outage,* and *power interruption.*
  Glass insurance is for expensive plate glass and other special types.
    Basic coverages are for "all risks" of breakage or damage by chemicals, with fast replacement of glass an important service.
  Credit insurance is catastrophe protection, for wholesalers primarily.
    Nature and development, a guarantee with insurance characteristics.
    Foreign or export credit insurance, helping to expand world trade.
    Underwriting the risk, based on credit ratings and coinsurance.
    The peril covered: insolvency of, or uncollectibility from, customers.
    Types of contract include general and extraordinary.
    Policy provisions define insolvency, normal loss, and other terms.
  Title insurance is important only in some geographic areas:
    The peril insured is undiscovered *past defects* in real estate title.
    The need arises from human errors in meeting legal requirements.
    The title insurer has extensive abstract research facilities.
    The basic policy is for indemnity to owners or mortgagees.
    Contract provisions include claim conditions and term (perpetual).
    Use of a group policy by mortgage companies is convenient.

Miscellaneous property and liability insurance

Few areas of business offer greater variety than the property-liability insurance field. A continual challenge is provided for anyone choosing a career in it.

Take property-liability agents, for example. Although much of their daily work may involve the automobile and basic fire insurance needs of their clients, the *usual* day will require their immediate attention to at least several other kinds of insurance exposures or losses. After writing a special "all-risks" policy for jewelry and furs, they may next consider a merchant's need for theft insurance or a bank's choice among several fidelity bonds. Before the day is finished, they will probably have at least one more unusual type of coverage or loss to analyze. Perhaps it will be a private yacht or airplane to insure, or a shopping center plate glass loss to settle.

All of these properties and perils are encompassed in the wide spectrum of property-liability insurance in Part IV of this text. Prior chapters have treated fire, indirect loss, transportation, liability, workers' compensation, automobile, and crime insurance. Chapter 26 takes up the remaining types of miscellaneous property and liability insurance, including *aviation, boiler and machinery, glass, credit,* and *title.* Each of these types of insurance has some unusual features which are not found in other insurance contracts.

The size of these miscellaneous markets is approximately $645 million of premiums each year: aviation insurance, $150 million; boiler and machinery insurance, $215 million; glass insurance, $35 million; credit insurance, $45 million; and title insurance, about $200 million.[1]

AVIATION INSURANCE

The jet age is almost 30 years old, and "flight has grown into an absolute essential for mobile modern man, yet the question 'Is flying really safe?' still troubles those who don't know that (1) scheduled air flying is more than six times safer than driving, based on miles traveled per fatality, (2) more people die by falling off ladders than by crashing in airliners, and (3) only 1 of 1,000 commercial pilots dies in a year in a plane."[2]

---

[1] *Insurance Facts* (New York: Insurance Information Institute, 1978), p. 10.

[2] "Safety in the Air," *Time,* April 8, 1966, p. 30. Boating accident fatalities are approximately 1,300, compared to the 1,800 annual aircraft deaths in the United States (*Insurance Facts,* pp. 60–61).

The dramatic impact of airplanes on life in the United States is seen in the nearly 7 *billion* miles flown every year. The shrinking size of the globe is a real thing for many persons, either in terms of their own travel or in terms of the goods that come to them from throughout the world.

With changing modes of transportation come changes in risk. Aircraft accidents are not as frequent as the Caspar Milquetoasts think but when crashes occur, they are serious and they are well publicized in the newspaper headlines. Actually, the accident and fatality rates per million aircraft miles flown have decreased substantially in the past decade. However, the rapid growth of the aircraft industry leaves sizable problems of direct effect on the insurance and accident problem: larger planes (supersonic aircraft carrying more than 400 passengers), more planes (tripled in the last ten years), crowded airport runways, pilot and traffic controller personnel requirements, and others.

Development

Aircraft insurance received little attention until after World War I. The first contracts that were issued made use of the fire or automobile forms. The early experience was far from successful, characterized by a considerable element of trial and error, high premiums, and large deductibles.

The civilian aircraft industry is now a giant in the transportation field. More than 140,000 active aircraft, including 3,000 owned by more than 50 commercial air carriers, are flying millions of passengers and billions of ton-miles of mail and freight. Some 5,000 aircraft and more than 3,000 helicopters are used by businesses. More than 600,000 active pilots are licensed.[3] The increased use of aircraft is sufficient to label this the aerospace age. New and recent examples include rental planes, crop spraying, advertising, cattle herding, pipeline patrols, fire fighting, hovercraft, and many others.

Insurers

Not all insurers write aircraft insurance, but several hundred U.S. insurers do. For many years almost all aircraft risks were written by insurers organized into underwriting groups (or syndicates). Two of the largest, the U.S. Aircraft Insurance Group and the Associated Aviation Underwriters, each has about 20 to 40 insurers or members. Such syndicates still account for a substantial part of the business, especially the protection for the large airline transportation and aircraft manufacturing companies. More than 20 syndicates at Lloyd's of London specialize in aviation insurance. International competition for aviation insurance is keen. Some of the larger individual in-

---

[3] Robert R. Piper, "A Guide to Light Aircraft Insurance," *CPCU Annals*, vol. 25, no. 3 (September 1972), p. 197.

surers now cover many planes and helicopters that are privately owned or are owned or used by business firms.

With the passage of federal regulatory legislation, the Civil Aeronautics Board and the Federal Aviation Administration have made mandatory safety measures that might otherwise be disregarded. Control is exercised with respect to the certification of pilots, and regulations cover aircraft flights in the United States.

Adequate insurance facilities exist in this country for handling most aviation risks. However, many special aviation problems for insurers are appearing, and adequate market capacity for aviation insurance often requires many insurers and reinsurers throughout the world. Single aircraft values of $5 million to $50 million and desired liability limits of $10 million to $300 million illustrate the large and increasing exposures in aviation insurance today.[4] The "superbird" of the skies, the Concorde, is valued at more than $40 million, almost double the cost of the Boeing 747 aircraft.

Basic nature

Aircraft coverages basically parallel the automobile coverages. They are divided into two classifications: direct loss and liability coverages. However, the perils in aircraft insurance differ so much from the perils in automobile insurance that aircraft coverages have been developed which vary widely from the automobile policies in many important features. Excluded from discussion here are the aviation accident insurance contracts issued to passengers, which are a type of health insurance treated in Chapter 13.

As compared with the automobile risk, aircraft insurance involves primarily a total loss business, and much larger sums. A modern jet airliner equipped to carry more than 400 people costs $25 million or more. In connection with aviation, direct loss insurance, depreciation, and obsolescence are factors of tremendous importance. Losses are in many instances much greater than and different from those attached to the automobile. One of the most important of the factors influencing aircraft losses is the physical condition, training, and experience of the pilot. Although it is true that inexperienced drivers of automobiles are responsible for many accidents, the incompetence of a pilot is disastrous. The adage has developed: "Good pilots die in bed." Automatic warning systems in modern aircraft aim to reduce pilot error of many kinds.[5]

The liability peril stems from the same source as that of automobile liability and is also based upon the accepted common-law rules of negligence. How-

---

[4] Henry V. White-Smith, "Aviation Insurance—Past, Present, and Future," *Lloyd's Log,* November 1977, p. 18.

[5] For example, radar and "ground proximity warning systems." See "Topical Problems in Air Safety," *Sigma* (North American Reinsurance Corp.), September 1976.

ever, the decisions tend to hold the operators of aircraft absolutely liable without the common-law defense of contributory negligence; in addition, the trend of legislation is in the direction of absolute liability. An example is the 1978 settlement of more than $62 million paid to 1,100 relatives of victims in the 1974 crash of the Turkish DC-10 near Paris, with payments ranging from $10,000 to $900,000.[6]

Because of the large amounts involved and the peculiar nature of the risk, the underwriting problems are usually handled by agents or managers who are specialists in aviation coverages. In total, the aircraft insurance business has become an unusual blend of features—combining aspects of automobile, fire, liability, and inland marine insurance in a specialized insurance area which also has close dependence on reinsurance techniques.

Classification of aircraft

Planes are classified in accordance with the use to which they are put: (1) airline, (2) private business and pleasure, (3) industrial aid, (4) commercial, and (5) special uses.[7] The first classification applies to large scheduled and nonscheduled air carriers. The second applies to individually owned aircraft used for business or pleasure. Industrial aid applies to corporate-owned aircraft used to transport employees, executives, and guests. The commercial classification includes charter aircraft operated by a flying school, sales agencies, and taxi or similar operations of a fixed-base operator. Dealers or distributors fall into a special-uses group, as do a number of risks involving unusual conditions, such as flying clubs, crop dusting, photography, and law enforcement.

Types of contracts

The basic policy forms include: (1) *hull policies,* which cover the risks of loss or damage to the insured aircraft itself; (2) *aircraft liability coverages,* which are written to cover public and passenger liability and property damage liability; (3) *admitted aircraft liability coverage,* which provides for voluntary settlements to injured passengers; and (4) *medical payments coverage,* which provides medical expenses regardless of liability. These contracts and a *comprehensive light plane policy* which combines many of these coverages are each discussed separately in the following sections.

In addition, special forms are written for (a) *hangar keeper's liability,* which covers the bailee's liability with respect to aircraft stored for safekeep-

---

[6] *Columbus* (Ohio) *Dispatch,* May 12, 1978.

[7] W. W. Walter, "Aviation Insurance," in *Property and Liability Insurance Handbook,* ed. John D. Long and Davis W. Gregg (Homewood, Ill.: Richard D. Irwin, 1965), p. 322.

ing or repair; (*b*) *airport and air meet liability,* which provide protection similar to the owners', landlords', and tenants' forms generally written for property owners; (*c*) *products liability,* which covers manufacturers, sales or repair organizations, and the like, against liability claims attributable to defective products or work; (*d*) *aircraft workers' compensation and employers' liability;* (*e*) *aviation personal accident* insurance; and (*f*) *cargo liability,* covering legal liability for loss or damage to cargo or baggage.

Insurance against liability for damage to another's cargo is to be distinguished from property insurance covering the insured's own cargo. Cargo insurance is not classed as an aviation line but is written by fire companies in their inland marine departments. Cargo liability is written as a separate form and covers the liability of the aircraft owner to shippers for loss or damage to merchandise for which the airline may be legally liable. Passenger baggage liability covers aircraft owners' liability for loss or damage to passengers' baggage.

In aviation insurance, a distinction is made between *ground* coverages and *flying* coverages. Hangar fire, windstorm, and theft perils come within the scope of ground coverages, which cover while the aircraft is not in motion. Accidental damage or "crash insurance," public and passenger liability, and property damage are the more important flying coverages, during the aircraft's actual takeoff run and continuing until it has safely completed its landing run.

Only aircraft licensed by the U.S. Department of Commerce are regarded by insurers as risks eligible for insurance. Since the skill and experience of the pilot are said to constitute 90 percent of the insurer's risk, particular emphasis is centered on the qualifications and character of the pilots who will fly the insured planes.

Hull insurance. The hull policy provides insurance against direct loss or damage from the perils defined on the schedule of coverages attached to the policy. Policies are written on either a named-perils basis or an all-risks basis. When written on a *named-perils* basis, the policy may be arranged to include any or all of the following coverages: (1) fire, (2) crash insurance, (3) stationary land damage, (4) windstorm, and (5) theft. These perils are similar to coverages under other property insurance contracts, and "crash insurance" is merely a different name for the same type of protection afforded by automobile collision coverage.

When written on an *all-risks* basis, which is common today, the policy includes such perils as fire, crash damage, windstorm, earthquake, flood, and every other conceivable risk which may damage the plane.

The more usual all-risks hull coverages include: (*a*) all risks while the aircraft is not in motion, (*b*) all risks except while in flight (includes taxiing), and (*c*) all-risks ground coverage extended to include all risks while in flight. This last form is the most comprehensive obtainable. The usual exceptions are wear and tear, deterioration, conversion (taking without authority) by a person in possession of the aircraft, and loss due to mechanical breakage or structural failure.

Fire is essentially a ground hazard. The insured plane is covered against fire from any cause, as well as against explosion and lightning, while not in flight. The fire hazard in aviation is particularly great not only because of the construction of the plane itself but also because of the conditions usual to the hangars in which planes are stored. Causes of plane fires include backfiring engines, short circuits, and the development of static electricity. All airplane fire rates are "loaded" because of the conflagration hazard. A hangar fire, once started, burns furiously because of gasoline, and the chances of saving planes stored inside are negligible.

Windstorm is strictly a ground coverage and, therefore, covers no loss whatsoever occasioned by flight or descent, which is covered under crash insurance. The insured machine is covered while in the hangar or in the open for damage caused by hail, storm, rain, sleet, snow, earthquake, flood, or water. Windstorm insurance is an essential coverage for airplanes. Cases are recorded in which planes were carried into the air on a strong wind and completely wrecked. An airplane safely housed in its hangar may also be seriously damaged by collapse of the hangar.

Crash insurance covers loss or damage that may occur to the insured aircraft by collision with the ground or another object during flight or any attempt thereat.

The policy provides that the insurer will pay the insured value of the plane, including its equipment, in the event of total loss. The rates for hull insurance are based on the assumption that the aircraft is insured for *100 percent of value.* No coinsurance clause actually appears in the contract, but the practice of requiring insurance 100 percent to value is in line with that followed generally in inland marine business. In all hull policies, total loss payments are reduced by depreciation. In the case of partial loss, the liability of the insurer is limited to the cost of repairing the damaged property with material of like kind and quality.

Deductibles apply in a variety of ways and amounts. In the case of light planes, 5 percent of the insured value often applies as a deductible if the loss occurs while the aircraft is in motion. For other losses, a dollar amount, such as $100, usually applies. Larger aircraft often use 5 to 10 percent deductibles.

To provide participation of the insured in all losses and at the same time limit small claims, the *participation form* of policy is offered. Instead of reducing the loss by a flat amount, as is required where the policy is written with a deductible, the participation form requires the insured to bear a percentage of each claim, regardless of its size. The insured must determine whether it is more important to eliminate all partial losses up to a certain amount and to collect everything in excess of that, or to bear a percentage of all losses, which increases in dollar amount as the amount of the loss increases. With a $10,000 plane and a 10 percent deductible, in the case of a total loss the insured would collect $9,000. Insuring the same plane with a 25 percent participation would limit the amount of the claim to $7,500 in the event of a total loss. The use of deductibles and participation forms has the effect of modifying the rate in favor of the insured. The higher the deductible or the rate of the participation, the lower will be the premium charged the insured.

Aircraft liability. With the exceptions to be noted, public and property damage liability afford essentially the same insurance protection as similar coverages in automobile insurance. Although the automobile policy generally covers the passenger bodily injury liability hazard automatically, in aviation policies the insured chooses separate coverage (*a*) for bodily injury liability excluding passengers and (*b*) for passenger bodily injury.

The bodily injury liability coverage excluding passengers does not cover: (1) liability imposed upon or assumed by the insured under any workers' compensation act or plan, or (2) liability for injuries sustained by employees or pupils of the insured. In the case of property damage liability coverage the coverage excludes: (1) property belonging to, or in the custody of, the insured or the insured's employees or pupils; (2) property which is rented or leased and for which the insured is legally responsible; and (3) property carried in or upon the insured aircraft.

There is an "additional insured" clause similar to that found in the automobile liability policy, extending coverage to friends or members of the family while they are flying the plane of the insured. The policy also provides a fly-other-aircraft provision which protects the private owner insured while flying a borrowed plane. The policy excludes any liability in connection with racing, aerobatics, crop dusting, spraying, seeding, hunting, herding, or dropping objects from the aircraft.

Because of the values involved and the possibility of catastrophic accidents, typical limits for bodily injury other than passenger liability are $100/300,000. Property damage rates are quoted with a $100,000 limit. Passenger liability coverage is written with a standard limit of $5,000 per passenger seat (the pilot's seat is not counted). The CAB requirements for commercial aircraft are $75,000 per seat, and $100,000 is often carried to meet varying state laws.

The terrific damage that a crashing airplane can do to both the human body and property emphasizes the need for even higher limits than those mentioned. Single death or disability cases have been settled for amounts well over $1 million. Multiple death claims from one aircraft accident have exceeded $100 million. In the case of property damage the need for high limits, sometimes overlooked, is likewise essential.

Admitted liability coverage. *Admitted liability* coverage is closely akin in principle to medical payments in the automobile field. In the event of bodily injury to a passenger the insurer will offer a settlement on a definitely determined basis, regardless of whether the insured is legally liable. In consideration of the payment of these benefits, the claimant releases the insured from any further liability as a result of the accident. If the injured passenger refuses to release the insured from further liability, the policy will pay any legal claims for damages that may be established up to the amount of the benefits indicated. This form, used mostly by business aircraft owners, is now used only infrequently.

Medical payments. The similarity of medical payments to admitted liability coverage is found in the fact that medical payments are offered the injured passenger without the necessity of establishing liability. Under the admitted liability coverage, however, the policy limits are high enough to satisfy a liability claim in the ordinary course and a release is required from the injured party. Medical payments cover not only passengers but the pilot as well. Coverage is written only in connection with passenger liability insurance. The limits for each passenger and the pilot ordinarily begin at $500, but these may be increased to $2,000 or more, depending upon the underwriting practices of the insurer. As with automobile medical payments, payment is made for reasonable medical, surgical, ambulance, nursing, and funeral expenses.

Comprehensive light plane policy. A special hull policy has been provided for light planes—that is, planes weighing under 10,000 pounds fully loaded —to cover comprehensive risks, including crash. The perils are specifically named, but the policy covers a wide range of additional risks, such as earthquake, flood, denting, marring, and the like. Unlike the automobile comprehensive, this is usually not an all-risks cover. Moreover, the insured bears a portion of the crash loss in the form of participation and in return secures a considerably lower rate. A $50 or $100 deductible usually applies to all ground coverages except fire, theft, and transportation; and typically a deductible of $250 or more applies to in-motion coverages.

Aviation rates

In contrast to other property fields, aviation insurance provides no common rating schedule for insurers showing rates applicable to different classes of aviation risk. Rates, therefore, are not standard and are to a large degree based upon judgment. The final rate quotation is made only after the underwriter has been given an opportunity to appraise the physical condition, age, weight, flying characteristics, and depreciated value of the plane. If the plane is used in connection with a business operation, the operator with good equipment, a good reputation, and a good loss experience secures the most favorable rate consideration.

Rates are ordinarily quoted on an annual basis. Typical hull coverage rates may be 1.5 percent or more of the aircraft values. Dealers or business organizations that have an active turnover in the number of aircraft owned may secure a policy providing for periodic reporting of risks, with premiums computed from the reports of the number and nature of the planes at risk. In some instances crash insurance may be written based on the number of hours the insured plane is flown. Most of the coverages for scheduled airlines are written on a reporting basis.

p. 770

BOILER AND MACHINERY INSURANCE

Nature

Insurance policies issued to many businesses upon boilers, turbines, electrical machinery, and similar objects provide coverage for two classes of loss: (1) direct loss and (2) indirect loss. A single policy may cover boilers or machinery, or both. Other names for boiler and machinery insurance are engineering, breakdown, and power plant insurance.

Examples of loss causes include explosions, the cracking of pressure vessels, electrical short circuits (without fire), lack of proper lubrication, bursting flywheels, and many others. The size of loss is large, often $100,000 or more, and sometimes many millions of dollars. The exposures continue to grow, with some exposures valued at more than $100 million each.

Direct loss provides indemnity in the following cases: (a) damage to the insured's property, whether to the insured object or to other property; (b) damage to the property of others for which the insured may be liable; (c) liability for loss of life and injury to employees when the coverage is not provided by the compensation laws of the jurisdiction; and (d) liability for loss of life and injury to persons who are members of the public—that is, not employees. Note that the use of the words *direct loss* here is different from its use in other types of property insurance, because it includes several kinds of *liability* losses (property damage liability, b; employer's liability, c; and bodily injury liability, d).

Indirect loss is covered as follows: (a) consequential loss to perishable materials when caused by accident to the boiler or other object insured; (b) business interruption under a use and occupancy form; (c) indemnity for indirect losses caused by an accident when there is no business interruption under the outage form; and (d) power interruption due to loss of power from a source off the premises.

In addition to paying losses, boiler and machinery insurance is very important for the *loss-prevention and engineering* services of the insurer. About one third of the premium dollar is devoted to inspection costs, exposure analysis, repair suggestions, and other risk-management techniques.

The basic contract—types of direct loss perils insured

Boiler and machinery insurance is usually written in a separate contract. However, increasing use of the multiple-line contracts for businesses has rapidly expanded its inclusion (usually on an optional basis) in such contracts as the special multiperil policy, as discussed in Chapter 27.

The standard provisions of different insurers are not identical word for word. The basic policy is used for all power plant insurance, including the use and occupancy and the consequential loss forms as well as direct damage coverages.[8]

The basic policy is completed by attaching a number of schedules. Most of the newer contracts do not require the listing of separate objects, covering instead by "blanket" definitions groups of pressure equipment and machinery for the generation or use of power. A common definition for accident is used, applying to most objects insured.

The standard provisions allow for six forms of coverage in the *insuring agreements,* with *all but the bodily injury liability coverage* being *mandatory*:

1. The *property damage* section provides insurance for damage to the insured object, as well as damage to other property owned by the insured.

2. The *expediting charges* section reimburses the insured for reasonable costs incurred in effecting the speediest possible replacement of the damaged property. These charges include expenses incurred for temporary repairs, for overtime work, or for rushing the transportation of material by an agency more expensive than would ordinarily be used. The amount payable is limited to the amount for which the insurer would otherwise be liable as direct damage loss on the property, but with a limit for expediting charges, usually $1,000.

3. The *property damage liability* section defends the insured against claims and makes payment for liability for damage to the property of others caused by an insured accident.

4. The *bodily injury liability* section is the *only optional coverage,* but if included, it covers the insured against bodily injury to persons injured by an insured accident. The usual defense and settlement provisions are included, as is reimbursement for first-aid relief given at the time of the accident. Liability under any workers' compensation law is not covered, but there is no other exclusion with respect to liability to employees.

5. The *legal expenses* section covers the cost of defending liability claims as well as the usual defense costs of interest on unpaid judgments, premiums on attachment and appeal bonds, witness and attorney's fees, and other defense costs. These costs do not reduce the amounts available for claim payments.

6. The *automatic coverage* section provides protection for newly acquired objects similar to those described in the schedules. The clause requires written notice to the insurer within 90 days after a newly acquired object is put in operation, and the premium is computed accordingly.

Boiler and machinery insurance is primarily a material damage coverage.

---

[8] A special form for residences covers only the explosion of boilers and water heaters and furnace gas explosions. An off-premises form covers boilers not owned or operated by the insured. The boiler may be located in another building or in another part of the building that the insured occupies.

Bodily injury liability is provided where there is no public liability or workers' compensation coverage or where the coverage is deemed inadequate. The six coverages apply, *in sequence,* as needed. Bodily injury liability provided by the boiler and machinery policy is considered as excess and noncontributing insurance when there is other like insurance.

For example, suppose an insured has a $100,000 steam boiler contract, and a separate general liability contract with a $50,000 bodily injury limit per person. An explosion results in $25,000 damage to the boiler, $1,000 of expediting charges to repair the boiler, $10,000 of damages to the property of others, and an $80,000 bodily injury settlement with a member of the public. Payments would be made for each of these losses in the sequence mentioned. However, only $30,000 would apply to the bodily injury loss, because it applies only as excess coverage.

The policy defines the term *one accident* to include all resultant or concomitant accidents, regardless of the number of objects involved, as long as these accidents are the outgrowth of a single general occurrence. If two or more objects are involved, the highest limit applying to any one of the objects governs.

Large deductibles are commonly used, often $1,000 to $10,000. Separate deductibles may apply to direct and indirect losses, or a single one may be used for both coverages.

Direct losses—the types of property insured

Steam boilers and vessels. Coverage for steam boilers is written on the basic boiler and machinery contract and provides indemnity for loss or damage caused directly by the *explosion, collapse,* or *rupture* of the insured boilers or vessels.[9] An identifying schedule listing the objects[10] covered, the pressure approved by the insurer for each, the kind of boiler, and other essential data is made a part of the policy. The boiler policy does not cover explosions in the firebox or tubes of the boiler unless such explosions are optionally included in the schedules or the contract is endorsed to cover furnace explosion. Frequently, serious firebox or smoke pipe explosions occur because gases accumulate from unconsumed fuel or for other reasons.

The boiler coverage excludes loss or damage to property of the insured resulting from an explosion caused by the burning of the structure containing the boiler, or loss or damage to the insured's property by fire. Fire damage

---

[9] The boiler policy is not confined to the insuring of steam boilers but may provide insurance for numerous other vessels which are liable to explosions from internal pressure, such as air tanks, kettles, refrigerating and air conditioning systems, steam pipelines, separately fired superheaters, and water heaters.

[10] It is customary to apply the term *object* to the vessel covered, interpreted in accordance with the manual definitions for the specific types. Thus, a boiler includes its parts, such as gauges, safety valves, superheaters, and interconnecting pipes. Auxiliary piping of various types for many objects should be specifically scheduled.

to the property of the insured is covered by the fire policy insuring the property. The liability coverage, however, includes the insured's legal liability for damage to the property of others resulting from an explosion caused by fire or from a fire caused by an accident covered by the policy. The policy also excludes liability for loss or damage from the explosion[11] of a boiler while any safety valve limiting the pressure in it is with the insured's knowledge and consent removed, rendered inoperative, or set to blow off at a pressure in excess of that approved for it by the insurer as stated in the policy schedule. Finally, the policy excludes loss from stoppage of the plant or from any other indirect result of an explosion. Indirect loss may be covered under special forms.

Engines, electrical machinery, and turbines. Coverage may be written to insure *engines* that derive their power from steam, oil, or gas. Pumps, compressors, and refrigerating machines are objects insurable under the form. The policy covers damage caused by sudden and accidental breaking, deforming, burning out, or rupturing of the insured machine or any of its parts. Flywheel[12] insurance may be written on many types of revolving machinery, such as wheels, fans, blowers, centrifugal dryers, separators, and other rotating objects. The definition of "accident" in engine policies is broad enough to include every form of breakdown.

Insurance for *electrical machinery* provides protection against losses from "breakdown," defined as "the sudden, substantial, and accidental breaking or burning of the machine, or any part thereof which immediately stops the functions of the machine, and which necessitates repair or replacement." Motors, generators, and exciters are insurable, as are power and distribution transformers, switchboards, circuit breakers, and units of electrical control and starting for motors.

The protection afforded for *turbines*[13] is essentially the same as that provided for other power plant equipment. Direct and consequential loss to property may be covered, as well as liability for personal injury. Four kinds of

---

[11] The boiler policy defines an "explosion" as a sudden substantial tearing asunder of the boiler caused solely by steam pressure or by the internal pressure of air, gas, or liquid. Boiler insurance may be written to provide *limited* coverage (against explosion caused by internal pressure) or *broad* coverage (losses caused by the accidental burning, bulging, cracking, or collapse of the boiler).

[12] Sometimes a rapidly moving wheel disintegrates in a "flywheel explosion," which can wreck plant, machinery, or neighboring property and cause injury and loss of life. Wheels weighing ten tons have been thrown more than 1,000 feet! Engine losses, however, are not limited to flywheels. Cylinders explode, hurling fragments with terrific force. Moving parts become crystallized from "fatigue," or some part of the engine may give way as a result of improper lubrication, loosened parts or other causes.

[13] A turbine is a rotary engine which converts the energy of supplied water or steam into mechanical or electrical energy. A delicately balanced rotor enclosed in a heavy outer casing turns upon the impact of the steam or water. The centrifugal force so generated is capable of terrific destruction. Large units, such as are used by public utility companies to generate power, not infrequently cost millions of dollars, and repairs frequently involve large expenditures.

coverage are written, from very limited explosion to the broadest breakdown perils.

Indirect losses

There are four forms of boiler and machinery insurance covering indirect damage. These are (a) consequential loss, (b) use and occupancy, (c) outage, and (d) power interruption. The first three of these forms cover indirect loss caused by accident covered under the policy on the premises of the insured. Power interruption covers the insured for loss of power from a source off the premises.

Consequential loss. This form is designed to protect the insured against spoilage due to interruption of heat, burnout of motors, interruption of power, or failure of refrigeration caused by an accident to the insured object. In types of risk where there is danger of spoilage to perishable goods, the *consequential loss* may far exceed the direct damage caused by an accident.[14] Losses of this character, which are consequences of an accident to the object insured but are not directly caused by it, are not covered unless an additional premium is paid and the consequential loss endorsement is attached to the policy.

Use and occupancy. *Use and occupancy* insurance covering any of the objects insured under power plant forms is also usually added to the direct damage policies by endorsement. In principle the coverage is the same as that of other business interruption forms (see Chapter 18), having as its purpose the payment of continuing fixed charges and indemnification for loss of profits due to shutdown as a result of accident. It may be written on either a stated (or "valued") basis or an actual loss (or "nonvalued") basis.

The significance of use and occupancy insurance for power sources should be considered. The violence that attends explosions sometimes leads to an undue emphasis upon direct damage and liability coverages, and the neglect of the potential losses that may flow from business interruption. The heart of an industrial plant is its power equipment. Apartments, hotels, public utilities, theaters, and other business establishments are all dependent for income upon the operation of their heating and power plants. The cost may be thousands of dollars for each day that the plant or business cannot be operated.

Outage. Indirect loss for the period an insured object is out of use is called *outage*. Interruption of business is not a factor. Outage insurance differs from use and occupancy insurance, which provides only for loss caused by the

---

[14] A small motor furnishing power in a dairy might burn out, and even a few minutes' shutdown in pasteurizing might result in a large loss. A boiler out of commission in a greenhouse, or the refrigerating system in a cold-storage plant, may run a consequential loss to thousands of dollars while the direct damage loss is negligible. Contact of refrigerants with food products may also result in spoilage, and contamination damage is a direct power plant insurance loss and not a consequential loss.

interruption of business. Outage insurance provides for the payment of a stated hourly payment for each working hour that the insured object has been incapacitated because of an accident of the kind insured against for direct damage. The insurance is only written by attaching an outage endorsement to the direct damage policy.

Power interruption.   Power failure in New York City a few years ago focused public attention on the consequences of a widespread lack of electricity. Doris Day, too, in the movie *Where Were You When the Lights Went Out?* dramatized the possibility and effects of such interruption of services.

An accident in a power plant off the insured's premises, which causes loss to a user of the power through the interruption of the service, is not covered by the electrical machinery policy. *Power interruption* insurance provides indemnity against loss arising from the total or partial deprivation of usable service furnished by a public utility. The policy is written separately from other boiler and machinery coverages, and may include the service of electricity, steam, water, gas, or refrigeration. Two forms of coverage are available: (*a*) hourly indemnity for loss of use and (*b*) property loss due to spoilage, which is paid on the basis of the actual loss sustained. Business interruption is not a factor to the establishment of a claim under either form.

GLASS INSURANCE

The uses of glass for light, display, and ornamentation have reached such an extent that the investment in the glass used in a structure or in connection with the operation of a business represents the outlay of large sums. The growing use of large plates tends to concentrate substantial values, and glass is peculiarly subject to breakage.

Glass set in show windows is particularly susceptible to breakage. Riots, strikes, runaway automobiles, and accidental or deliberate breakage by people are some of the common hazards. Other hazards to which this and other glass are subject include breakage caused by burglars, defective settings, explosions, sudden temperature changes, hail, windstorms, the settling of buildings, and falling articles.

Basic coverages

The *comprehensive glass policy* provides a coverage that is an *all-risks* contract, with very few exceptions. Similar coverage is available in one of the special multiperil (SMP) forms (see Chapter 27). It pays the insured for all damages to glass, lettering, and ornamentation insured by the policy due to breakage of the glass or the accidental or malicious application of chemicals. The policy also provides three coverages for losses that may be incidental to glass damage: (1) damage to frames and bars, (2) installation of temporary plates, and (3) removal of obstructions. There are only three exclusions:

(*a*) fire; (*b*) war, including invasion, civil war, insurrection, rebellion, or revolution; and (*c*) nuclear or radioactive energy.

The multiple-line package contracts now insure many glass exposures. Residence glass breakage is covered in the homeowners' policies, and either automatically or optionally, limited glass breakage is included (usually with limits of $50 per plate or $250 per occurrence) in the SMP policies for many businesses.

Broken glass. The policy provides that the insurer will replace broken glass described in the schedule, and any lettering or ornamentation insured under the policy. Rapid and efficent *replacement service* is one of the prime benefits of glass insurance for many policyholders. Insurers can usually obtain service from glaziers more quickly, and at lower cost, than property owners can arrange for themselves.

Glass broken by windstorm, expansion cracks, flying substances, the settling of a building, earthquake, or other accident is covered by the policy. Protection is afforded for deliberate breaks, such as those prompted by malice or vandalism. As an alternative to replacing the glass, the insurer may pay for the replacement in cash. When a broken plate is replaced, the policy automatically covers the new plate and no additional premium is required.

Frames, temporary plates, and obstructions. The cost, not to exceed $75 each, is included for several incidental costs. Repairing or replacing window sashes contiguous to the insured glass with like material is covered if this is made necessary by damage to or breakage of the insured glass. Coverage is also provided for the cost of boarding up or installing temporary plates in openings in which damaged insured glass is located. The boarding up or the temporary installation must be made necessary by unavoidable delay in replacing the damaged glass. Removing or replacing fixtures or any other obstruction in order to replace the damaged glass is covered by the policy, except for the cost of removing show window displays.

Other contract features

The type of indirect loss insurance provided by the above three $75 insuring agreements may be increased for the payment of an additional premium in a situation where it appears that $75 will not cover the cost. Unless otherwise described in the schedule, each plate insured is covered as plain plate, flat glass set in frames. Liability of the insurer is limited to the actual cost (up to the amount insured) of the glass, lettering, or ornamentation and its replacement, at the time of the breakage.

Glass insurance is not limited to the protection of ordinary window or plate glass. The comprehensive glass policy may also cover many special types of glass bricks and blocks, Thermopane, safety glass, and other building glass. Stained glass set in leaded sections, such as the glass used in church and memorial windows, may be covered under a form that also includes marring, scarring, and scratches. Neon and glass signs are also insurable under a comprehensive glass policy. Such signs are written on either a deductible basis or a full-cover basis. The deductible varies from $10 to $100 for each insured object, with a corresponding reduction in premium as the deductible increases.

In the event of loss, immediate written notice must be given either to the insurer at its home office or to its authorized agent. The policyholder is further required to make all reasonable efforts to preserve the glass for salvage and to prevent further loss or damage. Immediate notice affords the insurer an opportunity for investigation as soon after the accident as possible, with a view to collecting damages from responsible parties if possible.

CREDIT INSURANCE

Nature and development

Most businesses insure their physical property assets against catastrophes caused by perils such as fire and windstorm. Surprisingly, most do not insure their assets against catastrophes caused by uncollectible accounts and bad debts, in spite of more than $3 billion of losses in the United States in each recent year due to business failure.[15]

Credit insurance[16] is a contract under which an insurer indemnifies the insured against *abnormal credit loss* occasioned by the insolvency of debtors. Most of the insureds purchasing this kind of insurance are *wholesalers,* but coverage is available for any manufacturer or distributor with annual sales of $500,000 or more.

The question was raised in the early days of credit insurance as to whether it was a contract of insurance or of surety. The courts have held that credit insurance agreements are in fact contracts of insurance and should be treated as such. The outstanding feature that distinguishes a strict guarantee from credit insurance is to be found in the fact that the credit risk is not based upon the individual standing of the primary debtor but rather upon the credit experience of a large group of debtors belonging to a certain class. A second distinguishing feature is that in a guaranty the agreement is made for the accommodation of the debtor, usually as a basis for securing credit. In credit insurance, the policy may be obtained without any knowledge or consent on the part of the debtor.

Credit insurance is by no means a major[17] branch of the insurance business, though the demand for the coverage is increasing and the coverage is

---

[15] *Insurance Facts,* p. 64.

[16] The distinction between the *commercial* credit insurance discussed here and *consumer* credit insurance such as credit life and health insurance is important. The term *credit insurance* has always been understood to mean the commercial type. For further details, see A. A. Dilworth, "Commercial Credit Insurance: Safety Belt for the Business Roller Coaster," *Journal of Insurance,* vol. 34, no. 5 (September–October 1973), p. 26.

[17] Annual premiums are only about $45 million. See *Insurance Facts,* p. 10.

appearing in new fields. For example, the area of *foreign* credit insurance has taken on increased significance.

Foreign or export credit insurance

Internationalism and the global concept have become bywords of the modern era. With improved transportation and communication, the exchange of goods and services throughout the world has increased to heights undreamed of, except perhaps by unusual men such as Wendell Willkie in his vision of "one world."

One of the world trade barriers which is gradually lessening is the availability of credit. Starting in the early 1960s the United States began to encourage the expansion of exports with the first large-scale U.S. *foreign* or *export credit insurance plan*. The Foreign Credit Insurance Association, now including more than 60 U.S. insurers, was established.

The plan differs in some ways from the credit insurance discussed above. Foreign credit is designed as a credit guarantee plan for *exporters* and often includes coverage for losses from nonpayment due to "political" as well as "commercial" risks. *Insolvency* and long-term *default* which result in the lack of payment for goods and services sold in foreign markets are the major perils insured against.

The FCIA is in effect a working partnership between the private insurance industry and the U.S. government–owned Export-Import Bank of Washington (Eximbank). Insurance companies bear the normal commercial credit risks of buyers' insolvency, while Eximbank covers such hazards as the inconvertibility to dollars of local currency, war, revolution, expropriation, and other political risks.

Short-term credit (up to six months) and medium-term credit (six months to five years) are insured up to 85 percent of losses due to commercial risks and up to 95 percent for political risks. The insurer wants the exporter to have a vested interest in potential losses. The exporter must furnish credit information to FICA on the purchasers. The normal approximate cost of the commercial risks is less than 1 percent of the value of the goods, depending on the (1) length of credit, (2) the type of risks insured, and (3) the country to which the goods are being sent. Political risks may be included for about three fourths of the cost of the commercial risks. The total cost thus varies from about 1 to 3 percent of the values insured.

The short-term credit policy is intended for exporters that ship consumer goods, but almost all products are eligible. The medium-term policy differs from the short-term policy by usually being available on a single-case basis rather than including all the shipments within a certain period. It also insures installment payments payable rather than accounts receivable, and it is used for larger transactions, such as shipments of heavy equipment and durable goods.

Two benefits to exporters that use these credit insurance policies are (1) the broader market they have because a major part of the risk is transferred to FCIA and (2) the greater ease with which financing can be obtained from banks when the exporters' foreign accounts are insured. The value of export credit insurance to a nation is also significant. Many other countries are more advanced in the use of credit insurance than the United States, and insure a higher percentage of their exports.

The future of this type of insurance is bright, even though obstacles are present. The need for such insurance is based upon the difficulties of credit sales in foreign countries whose language and customs vary from those of the shipper's country. Increased foreign commerce, the fact that export credit insurance is now available for most foreign buyers, and the trend toward liberalized contract terms and rates are favorable factors in this expanding field of insurance.

Underwriting the risk

It is not the function of credit insurance to replace credit investigations with the contract of indemnity. Rather, the insurance is a form of indemnity for unforeseen abnormal losses where credit investigations are made. The function of credit insurance is to protect the working capital and to strengthen the financial statements of businesses. It is not intended for retailers, because the cost of credit investigations to determine potential insolvency of consumers would be prohibitive for all but very large accounts.

Insurers place upon the liability they will assume a limitation based upon the *credit rating* of the customers of their insureds. Credit ratings are usually determined by references to the services of established mercantile agencies such as Dun & Bradstreet.[18] The cost of credit insurance varies, but it is usually less than $1 per $1,000 of shipments.

Since control of the extension of credit rests with the insured, policies are written with a *coinsurance* stipulation that the insured bear an agreed percentage of each loss. The coinsurance features of the contracts vary. Percentages of 10 and 20 are usual. The higher percentages are used when the risk is greater, or in the case of an inferior rating coverage with high limits. The condition is comparable to deductible coverage using a percentage of loss as the amount of the deductible. Unlike the user of coinsurance in the fire insurance contract, the insured never receives full recovery for a loss.

The peril covered

Credit insurance covers the peril of loss by the insured arising out of the *insolvency of customers* to whom credit has been extended. In the past the

---

[18] Dun & Bradstreet is the agency widely used as a basis for underwriting, although the ratings of other agencies operating in a specialized field have been accepted.

commercial credit insurance contract issued in this country by domestic insurers was available, as a rule, only to manufacturers and wholesalers; but it is now available and used by service organizations such as advertising agencies. The insured assumes credit losses as are normal. The policy pays for any *abnormal or excess loss* resulting from the insolvency of debtors to whom credit has been extended in the regular course of business.

There is a tendency to assume that careful credit analysis will preclude the necessity for credit insurance. Although it is true that many credit losses result from business incompetence, it is equally true that a large proportion of credit losses are the outgrowth of physical disasters such as fire, tornado, or earthquake. The accounts of a business operating over a widespread area may be threatened by a catastrophe which carries with it a trail of credit losses that extend their consequences to the far corners of the country. Accounts receivable are actually subject to every physical hazard that threatens the assets of the creditor.

Types of contract

Only a few companies write most of the credit insurance in the United States. The major difference in the contracts offered is that one type of contract, known as the "general coverage policy," is designed to cover all insurable accounts of the insured against credit losses in excess of normal. In contrast to this, "extraordinary coverage" provides insurance against credit losses on one or a few accounts. The rates vary substantially, but generally they are less than one tenth of 1 percent of the covered sales volume.

Policy provisions

Credit insurance policies are usually written for a *term* of one year. Two forms are written with reference to the coverage of losses that occur after the end of the policy term. Term policies cover losses that occur through insolvencies on *sales* during the term, while continuous policies cover losses that occur through *insolvencies* during the term. Credit insurance policies are terminated if the insured becomes insolvent during the policy term or if they are issued to a partnership and the partnership is dissolved.

Since the insolvency of debtors is the peril covered by a credit policy, it is essential to have a clear understanding of the meaning of the term as used in the contract. In the absence of words limiting the meaning of *insolvency* to a definition set forth in a policy, a debtor need not necessarily be adjudicated a bankrupt to be insolvent. Failure to meet obligations in the usual course of business is sufficient to hold the insurer liable for loss.

Most contracts set forth at some length the conditions which will warrant a claim on the ground of insolvency. The coverage is not restricted to the legal definition of insolvency. In addition to actual insolvency, the coverage extends to provide protection in situations where collection might prove difficult because of the impairment of assets due to the debtor's death or disappearance, or because of the filing of receivership or bankruptcy proceedings against the debtor.

In every business, year in and year out, bad accounts are to be expected and are absorbed as an annual charge-off. The recurring amount of such *normal loss* can be calculated for any business within reasonably close limits, usually expressed as a percentage of gross sales. In the credit insurance policy it is termed the *primary loss*. It is not the function of credit insurance to provide indemnity for the primary loss. Every credit policy indicates a primary loss for the business insured determined by previous experience, and there is no liability by the insuring company until the insured has absorbed the amount set up as the primary loss.

The policy sets forth the period within which the insured must file a *claim*. A usual period is 20 days after acquiring knowledge of the debtor's insolvency and within but not later than 20 days after the termination of the contract.

In filing a claim, the whole account against the debtor is placed with the insurer for attention and collection. This notice constitutes authority for the insurer to place the account for collection with any attorney it may select. The insurer undertakes to effect an adjustment within a period not to exceed 60 days. The policyholder is obligated to assign to the insurer the claim allowed in adjustment and is required to warrant the legal validity of the indebtedness for the amount of the claim.

Most credit insurance policies are now written with a provision affording the insured the right to file past-due accounts with the insurer for collection before these accounts shall have become more than 90 days past due under the original terms of sale. When a past-due account is filed with the insurer, it is treated as if the debtor were insolvent. After the collection charges and expenses are deducted, remittance is made to the insured.

Under general coverage policies there is no *cancellation* privilege. Under extraordinary coverage issued on individual debtors, the insurer or the insured is allowed the privilege of canceling coverage by written notice as to future shipments to any debtor.

TITLE INSURANCE

The peril insured

The peril covered by a title insurance contract is loss growing out of undiscovered defect in the title to an insured property.[19] The policy guarantees the title search to a purchaser, mortgagee, or other interested party, covering

---

[19] An alternative to title insurance appears in some dozen or more states that have passed Torrens acts. Under the Torrens system, the property owner applies to a court which, after suitable hearing of any claims by other parties, registers absolute title in the name of the owner. These are voluntary systems that are used extensively only in a few large areas, including New York, Boston, and Chicago.

the insured against loss arising out of *undiscovered defects in existence* at the time the policy was issued.

In contrast to other forms of insurance, title insurance looks backward for the source of a claim rather than forward. The usual insurance contract covers loss growing out of the happening of some unfavorable contingency subsequent to the issuance of the policy. Title defects which may arise following the issuance of a title policy are not within the scope of the coverage. To support a claim, the defect must have been in existence and undiscovered when the policy was issued.

The need for title insurance

The term *real property* refers to land and to rights issuing from the possession of land. Title to real property may be acquired in a number of ways, the more common being transfer with the consent of the owner, by will, and by descent regulated by statute. To secure title to the rightful owner, the law sets up certain formalities governing transfers which must be complied with in detail; otherwise, the transfers may be defective.

A transaction involving the sale of real estate usually involves substantial sums of money. The purchaser is interested in knowing that the seller has good title to the property being conveyed. A search is made at the record office covering all grants, conveyances, wills, liens, encumbrances, taxes, or other matters that might have the effect of clouding the title. A document called an "abstract" is prepared. It is referred to a lawyer who carefully examines it and gives an opinion as to the title. However, the most careful scrutiny of the records by a competent attorney will not in every case bring to light existing causes which may prove a title to be defective.[20]

The title insurance company

Title insurance companies are large corporations with resources that are ample to carry the risks assumed. Unlike other insurers, most of them tend to confine the scope of their activities to a limited territory. This is made necessary by the nature of this business.

There are between 100 and 200 title insurers, with total annual premiums of several hundred million dollars. Loss ratios are very small (less than 5 percent of earned premiums), as about one half of the premium is devoted to the title search and the abstract. The costs of defense also take up a substantial portion of the premium.[21]

Since the abstract of title is the basis of the contract, title companies have

---

[20] *The Title Industry: White Papers, vol. 1: The Nature and Need for Title Insurance Services* (Washington, D.C.: American Land Title Association, 1976).

[21] Jerry D. Todd and Richard W. McEnally, "Profitability and Risk in the Title Insurance Industry—The Texas Experience," *Journal of Risk and Insurance,* vol. 41 no. 3 (September 1974), p. 415.

built up and maintained up-to-date records for the real estate of the territory in which their operations are conducted. These records are referred to as an "abstract plan," and this eliminates the necessity of making a complete search of title every time a transfer is made. The writing of a new policy upon a property formerly insured involves only a reference to the records covering changes since the issuance of the last previous policy.

In urban communities where values are high and real estate turnover is rapid, title companies render an important service. In communities where values are low and transfer is infrequent, the volume of business will not support a title insurance company. In such communities the purchaser of real estate or the mortgagee must be content with a title opinion without the guarantee of an insurance contract. The availability, types, and distribution methods used in title insurance vary greatly in different parts of the United States.[22]

The basic policy

Title insurance contracts are not at all uniform, but the usual forms issued to owners and mortgagees are alike in certain essentials.

The insuring clause provides indemnity to the insured, heirs, and devisees, subject to an indicated limit: (1) by reason of any *defect of the title* of the insured to the estate or described interest; (2) by reason of the *unmarketability of the title* of the described insured; or (3) because of *liens or encumbrances* at the date of the policy, save for those specifically expected by the schedules or conditions of the policy.

The schedule describing the subject matter of the insurance sets forth: (1) the estate or interest of the insured, (2) a description of the property whose title is insured, and (3) the deed or other instrument by which the title or interest is vested in the insured. A second schedule sets forth discovered defects that are, therefore, not within the scope of the protection.

Contract provisions

A final section of the policy contains the conditions and limitations of the contract between the insurer and the insured. *Assignment* of a title policy is not usually permitted unless the policy is held by the owner of a mortgage or other encumbrances, in which case the contract may be transferred to an assignee of the insured. The insurer may by special agreement permit assignment in other cases, but the only safe method for obtaining adequate and full protection in the case of the transfer of equity is to secure a new policy or to have the current policy brought up to date.

---

[22] And special problems of tie-in sales with real estate producers exist in some areas, too. See Alfred E. Hofflander and David Shulman. "The Distribution of Title Insurance: The Unregulated Intermediary," *Journal of Risk and Insurance*, vol. 44, no. 3 (September 1977), p. 435.

Whenever a claim is settled by the insurer, the policy provides that the insurer shall be entitled to all *subrogation* rights and remedies which the insured would have had in respect to the claim. The insured is obligated to transfer these rights to the insurer and to permit the insurer to use the name of the insured in any necessary action in connection with recovery or defense. When payment does not cover in full the loss of the insured, the insurer's subrogation rights are limited to the proportion that the amount paid by the insurer bears to the entire loss.

The policy defends the insured against all actions or proceedings founded on a claim of title or an encumbrance prior to the policy date. The policy then sets forth in some detail the *conditions under which loss may arise,* such as actions of ejectment, dispossession, or eviction founded upon a claim of title, a lien, or an encumbrance. One common example would be the claim of a wife to her dower rights in real estate, which perhaps had not been properly satisfied and recorded by a prior purchaser.

When liability has been definitely fixed, the loss is payable within 30 days. The insurer is given the right to a valuation of the insured estate or interest by three *arbitrators* chosen thus: one by the insurer, one by the insured, and an umpire chosen by both. The valuation may be fixed by the agreement of any two.

In order to recover under a title contract, the insured must show that a loss has actually been sustained. When the insured is without title, in the absence of any unusual circumstance, the *measure of damages* under a title insurance contract would be the purchase price. When title actually passes but a lien is subsequently discovered, the measure of damage is the cost of discharging the lien. When the defect is in the form of an encumbrance, the measure of damage is the difference between the value of the property unencumbered and its value with the encumbrance.

The title insurance policy is personal and does not follow the property. It is usually perpetual, though sometimes the coverage is limited to 25 years. When the insured property is transferred, the insurance terminates, and if the new owner desires coverage, a new policy is issued. Premiums are paid in a single payment at the time the policies are written, and no further payments are required during the term. The cost varies by location, type of policy, amount of insurance, and other factors. A typical policy for the owner of a $50,000 home might cost several hundred dollars. Policies are sometimes written for a reduction in premium when they are reissued within five years from the date of the original insurance.

Use of a group policy

A group title insurance policy is used for the convenience of large users of title policies. Life insurers and mortgage companies, for example, are issued a master policy with certificates indicating each risk to be covered. The group policy has particular appeal for the mortgagee who wants to know the type of coverage on every risk but who does not want to examine a number of different forms or policies. The group form involves no difference in the underwriting procedure. It is simply the use of the uniform master policy with individual certificates that has found such general acceptance in other fields of insurance.

FOR REVIEW AND DISCUSSION

1. What do the types of miscellaneous property-liability insurance in this chapter have in common? How are they unlike?

2. Discuss aviation insurance (*a*) from the viewpoint of loss severity and insurer capacity to provide coverage and (*b*) in regard to hull coverage and the use of "deductibles," "participations," and "coinsurance."

3. What forms of aviation insurance are written to protect against (*a*) damage to the owner's aircraft? and (*b*) liability for damages and injuries to other persons or their property?

4. What important differences from the automobile policy are found in the aviation policy with respect to claims for bodily injury?

5. "The inspection feature of a boiler and machinery (power plant) policy is of greater value than the insurance feature." Explain.

6. What changes have the multiple-line package policies brought to boiler and machinery insurance and to glass insurance?

7. What is the peril insured against by power interruption insurance? Does such insurance cover power interruption attributable to equipment owned or operated by the insured? Explain.

8. What insuring agreements provide coverage under the usual boiler and machinery insurance policy? How are indirect losses covered?

9. What is meant by the statement that "the bodily injury liability coverage of the boiler and machinery contract is *excess* insurance"?

10. When *should* a business firm purchase glass insurance? When should it *not* purchase such insurance?

11. The comprehensive glass policy is an "all-risks" contract. Explain why the following losses would or would not be covered:
    a. Fire in adjoining premises causes the glass to crack.
    b. The surface of the glass is scratched with a diamond ring.
    c. Several plates of glass are broken during a strike at the insured's property.
    d. Chemicals thrown on the glass ruin its surface.

12. How does *foreign* credit insurance differ from regular credit insurance?

13. Fire, flood, windstorm, drought, crop failure, or other local catastrophes may unfavorably affect the ability of a debtor to meet obligations. Will credit insurance prevent loss from these sources?

14. Credit insurance is said to be (*a*) "a guarantee of working capital" and (*b*)

"an endorsement of the customer's promise to pay." Explain each of these statements.

15. For what, and to what extent, is the insurer liable under a title insurance policy? Would an assigned policy provide a new owner full protection?

16. In comparison with many other insurance contracts, what unusual features does a title insurance contract have? Explain three such features briefly.

Chapter 27

Concepts considered in Chapter 27—Multiple-line and all-lines insurance

Multiple-line and all-lines insurance trends in the U.S. are very important.

Product diversification trends "spread the risk" among various major *lines* of insurance; expansion to related *financial services* is emerging.

Multiple-line insurance characteristics include its—

Nature, a combination of traditional fire and casualty insurance.

Development, which has been strong since the multiple-line laws.

Significance, approximately $12 billion annual sales and many changes.

Purposes, which are summarized in its—

Policyholder advantages of *coverage, cost,* and *convenience.*

Insurer advantages of the same type, plus greater *stability.*

Disadvantages, restricting flexibility and causing misunderstanding.

Multiple-line insurance contracts are different from multiple-line *insurers or groups;* or from *multiple-peril, package,* or *all-risks contracts.*

Personal multiple-line contracts have been very popular.

Homeowners' policies analysis centers on—*who* (persons), *what* (property and perils), *when* (policy duration), *where* (places), and *how* coverage applies (package, perils, premiums, etc.).

Mobilehome policy is similar to the homeowners' contract.

Farmowner-ranchowner's policy combines business and personal exposures.

Other personal multiple-line contracts for valuable articles.

Business multiple-line insurance contracts have grown rapidly since the early *manufacturer's* and *block* policies, particularly with the popular:

Special multiperil (SMP) policies now available to almost all commercial risks, combining broad coverage for property-liability perils.

Businessowners' policies (BOP), in the new "readable" type package contract for smaller apartment, office, and retail store businesses.

All-lines insurance is a separate and more recent trend.

Nature and extent: writing *fire, casualty, life,* and *health* perils.

Property-liability insurers have often become all-lines groups by forming or purchasing life insurer affiliates, or through holding companies.

Life insurers are becoming all-lines groups, especially many of the largest life companies in the 1970s.

The future promises greater acceptance of this idea, including all-lines *contracts* insuring home, auto, life, and health perils in one *combination personal-lines package policy.*

Financial services conglomerates are also a significant trend to watch.

Mergers and growth of business take several forms.

The position of insurance in these changes is controversial, but increasing.

Multiple-line and all-lines insurance

Ever hear of a supermarket for insurance? That's what many insurance companies and agents are, because they offer an amazing variety of insurance products. The old "five-and-ten" is a piker compared with the "$5,000 to $100,000" coverage offered for sale to consumers of insurance.

The modern age not only offers the many "lines" of insurance in thousands of different individual contracts, as discussed in Parts III and IV of this text, but also in various combination packages of *multiple-line* and *all-line* insurance. The trend toward combination packages began in the 1950s, and it has picked up speed continuously since then. From "one-stop shopping" we seem to have moved into a new era of "one-contract buying" to meet the demands of the convenience-hungry consumer.

When one looks at the development of the total U.S. field of insurance and risk, it is amazing to find that the basic principle of *product diversification* went relatively unused until the second half of the 20th century.

PRODUCT DIVERSIFICATION TRENDS

The marketing concept of selling many products and services so that good results in one kind of business will help offset bad results in another is an application of the adage "Don't put all your eggs in one basket." Insurers have long applied this idea of "spreading risk" in many of their underwriting rules, for example, fire and windstorm catastrophe limits by geographic area, and retention limits above which large exposures are transferred to reinsurers. However, they have been much slower in applying the concept by doing business in many "lines" of insurance. The reasons have been partially financial and managerial but also historical and regulatory.

One of the most dynamic developments in insurance during the past 30 years has been a trend toward the combination of insurance and related coverages that have been treated for many years as separate and distinct parts of the business. Three examples of the trend are discussed in this chapter.

The first example, *multiple-line insurance*, which combines many of the kinds of property and liability insurance analyzed in Chapters 17–26, is an accomplished fact with numerous insurers and contracts today. Chapter 27 includes a concise but reasonably complete description of its nature, significance, purposes, development, and contracts. Since multiple-line insurance is a merging of types of insurance already separately presented in Part IV of this text, unnecessary duplication of the coverage details is avoided. The important homeowners' contracts, however, are discussed carefully, and briefer examples of other personal and business multiple-line insurance are included.

All-lines insurance, the second example, is a newer and less complete part of the general trend. Because it involves the combination of *life and health* insurance (discussed in Part III) with *property* and *liability* protection, a section near the end of this chapter concerns its progress and potential future development.

Financial services, the third example, is the most recent of the trends. Most of this development has occurred in the past decade, but the expansion in the area through mergers and holding companies has been very rapid. The "sizzling 70s" have seen much more of the broadening of insurers into related consumer services (and vice versa!), such as mutual funds, variable annuities, credit, and other savings media.

Figure 27–1 shows the relationship among product lines in insurance and risk and the potential development in related financial services.

MULTIPLE-LINE INSURANCE CHARACTERISTICS

Nature

Multiple-line insurance is the combination of the traditional "lines" or basic types of coverages known as *fire* and *casualty* insurance.[1] The most common illustration of multiple-line insurance combines fire perils with liability (and/or theft) protection. Individually these basic perils would be mono-line in character; in combination they become multiple-line insurance.

---

[1] One might be tempted here to replace the term *fire and casualty* with *property and liability*. Historically, under the legal definition by which the states have separated the fields of insurance, the term *fire and casualty* is necessary in describing the origin of multiple-line insurance. However, in theory, *property* insurance and *liability* insurance are properly contrasted as the two fundamental parts of multiple-line (nonlife) insurance. This is the more accepted use of the term today. *Casualty* insurance creates such difficulties of logical definition as almost to defy its use, but the term has longstanding legal and business acceptance as including the fields of liability, theft, workers' compensation, automobile, health, surety, and a wide variety of miscellaneous coverages. (See earlier discussion in Chapter 2.)

Figure 27–1. Product diversification trends

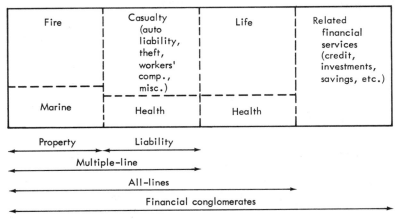

Note: Dotted lines represent past, or partial, barriers among product lines.

In discussing multiple-line insurance, it is necessary to recognize that the term includes many parts. For example, one might refer to or study separately such facets as multiple-line insurance *contracts* or multiple-line *insurers*. Another subdivision of the topic of multiple-line insurance is multiple-line *groups*. A multiple-line group involves fire and casualty insurers combined by common ownership, management, or reinsurance arrangement. It may have a history, legal organization, and operations that are substantially different from those of a multiple-line insurer which involves only a single company or corporate identity writing both fire and casualty lines of insurance. Many insurance groups or "fleets" are operated, even today, as closely affiliated enterprises with the same officers for several of the individual insurers within the group. Other insurer groups are loosely related, and the separate insurers may have complete autonomy within their activities and substantially different personnel and practices. However, a multiple-line insurer must by definition be a single insurer.

Furthermore, basic functions of insurer activities may be separately defined and discussed under such terms as multiple-line *sales* (or *agents*), multiple-line *underwriting,* multiple-line *rating,* and multiple-line *claims adjustment.*

It is difficult to review in one chapter the entire field of insurance from a multiple-line viewpoint. It becomes necessary to emphasize only a portion of what is collectively known as the multiple-line insurance trend.

Development

The multiple-line trend has not been a rapid nor a consistent change. Viewed the perspective of history, the trend appears as a long series of changes, including complete reversal of the trend at some points. Since the 1930s however, the major impetus to multiple-line insurance has been a relatively fast and continuous movement.

The experience of foreign insurers with broad charters suggested that early American insurers might have adopted similar multiple-line operations. However, mono-line insurers were accepted almost from the beginning of American insurance. For whatever reasons of limited capital or special interest in restricted areas of insurance, almost all American insurers through the 19th century did business within restricted lines of fire, marine, or other specialized areas.

The voluntary acceptance of what became known as the "American system" of mono-line insurance was encouraged and required by insurance department regulations and laws of the states throughout the century. One of the basic reasons for the compartmentization of insurance became, then, restrictive legislation. The states apparently concluded that it was easier and better to regulate insurance by licensing and limiting insurers to do business only in specific categories of insurance.

The first real adoption of the multiple-line principle began in the early 1900s with legislation in some states which permitted fire and marine insurers to combine, and later allowed fire insurers to have casualty subsidiaries and casualty insurers to own fire insurers. The success of the insurer group or "fleet" operations and the need for broader insurance coverages for automobiles, airplanes, and other valuable movable properties encouraged multiple-line operations. The trend slowed, however, with various restrictions on the expanding powers of marine insurance, which encouraged many insurers to continue mono-line practices in specified types of insurance.

The modern multiple-line trend began with a resurgence of the insurer groups that wrote both fire and casualty protection in separate but closely related enterprises. The advantages of broader insurance powers were recognized in the Diemand Committee Report to the National Association of Insurance Commissioners in 1944. In the next five years the states began to permit limited or partial multiple-line operations by passing "partial multiple-line laws." One insurer could then write both property and liability protection for specified items such as automobiles, aircraft, certain types of personal property, reinsurance, and insurance outside the United States.

"Full multiple-line laws" followed thereafter, giving a single insurer the legal power to write all forms of fire and casualty insurance. In effect, this legislation broke the legal barriers which had existed between fire and casualty insurance for a century or more. As long as the insurer met the capital and surplus requirements for the various lines, it could be licensed to write all types of insurance protection except life insurance. The major landmark in this development was New York State's passage in 1949, of such full multiple-line insurance legislation. By 1955 all of the states permitted, by specific legislation or departmental rulings, full multiple-line insurance operations.

The capital and surplus requirements for the formation of a multiple-line insurer vary among the states from $100,000 to more than $4 million. It is not to be inferred that all fire and casualty insurers today operate on a multiple-line basis. Insurance organizations doing business only within a single major line of insurance still exist. Almost all of the larger fire and casualty insurers today, however, operate as multiple-line organizations. They began as single-line insurers and broadened their licensing powers and insurance activities to include other lines of protection. Charter amendments permitting the broadened activities and mergers of fire and casualty insurers were the major techniques of change in the multiple-insurance trend.

Significance

Multiple-line insurance extends the concept of product diversification to insurance. Just as manufacturers have discovered that it is often better to produce several related products rather than rely only on one, so insurers now sell protection against many perils. This is

> hailed enthusiastically as the technique by which insurance can achieve modern economies and efficiency. It is also berated, just as vehemently, as the cause of many of today's major insurance problems, from changes in policy forms and rating to such dilemmas as how to obtain adequate capital, maintain uniform statistics, train new personnel, and revise company organizations.[2]

The increasing scope of the literature pertaining to multiple-line insurance is also evidence of its major significance during the past two decades. Revision of ideas, operations, articles, textbooks, and insurance courses all attest to the widespread effects of multiple-line insurance.

One of the clearest indications of the place and growth of multiple-line insurance is its sales figures. Thus, Table 27–1 shows the amazing growth record of homeowners' and commercial multiple-peril contracts. In 20 years the annual sales have increased from less than $200 million to almost $12 *billion,* or a sixty-fold increase! Commercial multiple-line policies, which had a later start, have grown to become nearly one half of the total multiple-line field.

Multiple-line insurer *groups* have grown steadily since the 1940s. About 220 stock and mutual insurer groups including more than 750 separate insurers, were in business by 1977.[3] These groups wrote more than 80 percent of the total property-liability insurance premiums of $60 billion.

Insurers classified as multiple-line *insurers* (single corporate identities

---

[2] David L. Bickelhaupt, *Transition to Multiple-Line Insurance Companies* (Homewood, Ill.: Richard D. Irwin, 1961), p. 3.

[3] *Best's Aggregates and Averages* (New York: A. M. Best Co., 1977), pp. 2–19.

**Table 27–1. Multiple-peril* contracts, selected years, 1956–76
(in millions of dollars of premiums written)**

Year	Homeowners' multiple-peril contracts	Commercial multiple-peril contracts	Total multiple-peril contracts
1956	178.9	17.7	196.6
1960	763.7	55.6	819.3
1964	1,333.1	371.3	1,704.4
1968	2,077.0	993.3	3,070.3
1972	3,300.0	2,100.0	5,400.0
1976	5,420.0	4,030.0	9,450.0

* This term rather than *multiple line* is used in order to conform to the statistical source, The contracts noted here are also properly classified as multiple line. (See footnote 7.)

Source: *Insurance Facts* (New York: Insurance Information Institute, 1977), p. 14. The 1978 issue of this publication (p. 13) revises some of these figures by excluding farmowners' multiple-peril contracts and reporting these separately. The 1977 figures are: homeowners', $6,800 million; commercial, $5,000 million; and total multiple-peril contracts, $11,800 million.

writing both fire and casualty insurance) wrote approximately $30 billion,[4] or 50 percent of the total premiums, by 1977.

Purposes

The amazing growth of mulitple-line insurance is explained by the advantages of the multiple-line technique, which may vary considerably, according to the viewpoint of the party involved.

Policyholder advantages. From the viewpoint of the *policyholders,* the advantages of multiple-line contracts may be summarized as improvements in (1) *coverage,* (2) *cost,* and (3) *convenience.* In effect, the results are better protection and service at lower costs, and a reduced number of contracts, companies, agents, and premiums for the insured. Cost economies are naturally uppermost in the minds of most policyholders, and these may be substantial. Oftentimes, the combination of coverages in a single multiple-line contract may bring savings of 20 to 40 percent as compared with the cost of protection in several separate property and liability contracts. The prime advantage of better coverage and service under a multiple-line contract should not be forgotten, however. The purchase of a multiple-line contract usually results in fewer gaps in protection than does the purchase of several individual policies covering separate perils. Also, overlapping coverages or overinsurance which may occur under separate policies are avoided through less confusion in regard to which policy covers which peril.

[4] Ibid., pp. 46 and 2–5B. Stock and mutual insurers so classified numbered more than 230.

Insurer advantages. In many ways the objectives of insurers entering into multiple-line operations are also those of the policyholder, although further goals may be reasons for the insurers' interest. Fundamental to all of the insurer motives is the general impact which multiple-line operations should have in *stabilizing, or maximizing, underwriting profits* by diversifying the company's business.[5] The "spread of loss principle" which is basic to all insurance is applied in the acceptance of many kinds of perils. For example, the averaging of fire losses with liability losses over a period of time should result in greater stability of operating results, and thus financial strength, for an insurer. A bad year of fire losses may be offset by some profits from theft, liability, or other kinds of insurance.

In addition to achieving stability of earnings and profits, the multiple-line insurer may achieve increased *profits, power*, and *prestige*. If multiple-line contracts increase total sales and lower costs through increasing the average size of contracts, then a multiple-line insurer may obtain greater influence, industry position, and prestige as an insurer. The benefits to policyholders mentioned above are also likely to bring success to the insurer, for satisfied insureds are of great importance to the continuing growth of insurers.

Disadvantages

Possible disadvantages that may accompany the adoption of multiple-line insurance should be mentioned. The policyholder usually does not have quite the freedom of choice that exists when separate contracts are selected. Certain minimum coverages must be included in most multiple-line contracts, and the insured may be paying for a few types of unwanted protection. The same idea applies to the insurer—for example, it may accept a good fire insurance policyholder at the expense of including some questionable burglary or liability business. Another basic problem is the general difficulty of readjusting to change, including the effort, time, and costs that change requires. There is also the uncertainty that arises from new contract wording, whose precise meaning often takes a number of years of legal interpretation to determine. A final problem is the unwarranted assumption that these broader multiple-line contracts provide automatic and complete coverage for *all* losses. They do not and cannot, and a false sense of security may be created from undue reliance upon them to accomplish the impossible.

MULTIPLE-LINE INSURANCE CONTRACTS

The summary here of multiple-line insurance contracts can only include some of the major multiple-line coverages. For accuracy in detail and

---

[5] Howard F. Blasch, J. D. Hammond, and Ned Schilling, "Planning Insurance Company Line Mix for Profit Maximization," *Risk Management,* September 1977, p. 41.

timeliness the reader must supplement this chapter with reference to the bureau and company forms, manuals, and rules applicable under the laws of his or her own state.[6]

Terminology once again becomes significant in clarifying discussion in this section on multiple-line insurance contracts. Caution must be exercised in using terms which may be confused with the expression "multiple line." For example, one might discuss *multiple-peril*[7] insurance contracts, but multiple-peril contracts are not necessarily *multiple-line* insurance policies. The two perils combined may be all within one insurance line, such as fire. The extended coverage endorsement is multiple peril but not multiple line in nature because it includes only fire and allied lines of insurance. Similarly, the store-keepers' burglary and robbery policy combines several perils in one contract, but since all are casualty coverages, it is not a multiple-line policy.

A *package policy* is always a multiple-peril contract, because it includes a number of separate perils in one contract. One additional characteristic, however, makes package policies a distinctive part of the development of multiple-line insurance. In package contracts the policyholder must accept substantially all of the perils combined in the package; multiple-line contracts merely involve combining fire and casualty perils, which may be done either by "packaging" (*all-or-none* choice by the insured) or by "scheduling" (permitting choices as to the coverages included). Most modern package policy contracts are also multiple line in nature, but the differentiation is necessary for a proper understanding of how these closely related types of contracts have grown.

Similarly, the terms *all risks* and *comprehensive* may also cause confusion to insurance students and consumers if they are not properly used. Both of these terms include the attribute of broader coverage in insurance policy contracts, but each term may have precise meanings that are widely dissimilar.

Many contracts are called *comprehensive* when they include only a few perils; other such contracts may include many perils. The term is not standardized in the insurance business, and it generally refers only to the fact that it is a combination form of comparatively liberal coverage. Examples include the comprehensive general-liability policy and the comprehensive automobile physical damage coverage.

---

[6] For up-to-date specific information on multiple-line contracts, the reader should consult such loose-leaf, continuing reference services as the *Fire, Casualty, and Surety Bulletins* (Cincinnati: National Underwriter Co.), the *General Insurance Guide* (Smithtown, N.Y.: Werbel Publishing Co.), or the *Policy, Form, and Manual Analysis Service* and other publications, such as *Homeowners Guide* and *Personal Insurance Guide* (Indianapolis: Rough Notes Co.).

[7] Note that the preceding statistics on multiple-line growth are technically referred to as multiple peril. The inconsistency is necessary because of the lack of other data. The figures do not include "extended coverage" premiums when written only with the fire insurance contract, but do include the premiums for this coverage when written in the "homeowners' and commercial multiple-peril" contracts.

All-risks contracts are distinguished by the type of insuring agreement used. If the policy lists each peril that it covers, it is a "named-perils" or "specified-perils" contract. If the contract says it covers, for example, "all-risks of physical loss except enumerated exclusions," then it is an all-risks type of contract. Note that "all-risks" should not be taken literally, for invariably a few exclusions are specifically identified. Examples of all-risks contracts are the personal property floater, the dwelling buildings and contents special form, and the glass insurance[8] policy.

For further discussion, the multiple-line insurance contracts are separated into two basic groups, those that are essentially *personal* (individual, family, or nonbusiness) and those that are designed primarily for *business* situations.

Personal multiple-line insurance contracts

The most popular and the best known of multiple-line insurance contracts today are the homeowners' policies. The use of these forms has been of the most significant and widely accepted of multiple-line techniques. Some other examples of personal mutiple-line insurance contracts are briefly mentioned at the end of this section.

Homeowners' policies.   During the past 25 years the homeowners' policies used by insurers and their bureau associations have been changed frequently. The major programs have had at least five extensive revisions. The situation in 1979 is that consumers in various states are not all using completely standardized forms. Some bureau policies, such as those of the Insurance Services Office (ISO), have been approved for use in most, but not all, states. A few of the larger insurers (such as State Farm, Nationwide, Allstate, and St. Paul) have developed and use their own contracts.

More than half of the states have approved the use of the "Homeowners '76" program,[9] introduced by the ISO in 1976 for experimental use in six states, and now adopted in many others. The positive response from insurers, agents, and consumers indicates that this will be in countrywide use soon, and the analysis in this chapter is thus based upon these popular homeowners' policies. Some differences from the 1968 program will be pointed out in the following sections, as the older forms may continue to be used in some states, and renewal contracts may not be changed to the Homeowners '76 program for several years.

Basically, the coverage changes (see later section) are relatively minor. However, the coverages are both broadened and narrowed. The appearance and format have been extensively revised. The new personalized and simplified

---

[8] The title of the glass policy is the *comprehensive* glass insurance policy, which is an example of how the terms discussed above are used in the insurance business without making the distinctions explained.

[9] This program and the forms are copyrighted by the Insurance Services Office, with permission for their use granted to its members, subscribers, and service purchasers.

language (reduces the number of words by 40 percent, from 12,000 to 7,000) is the most obvious of the changes, with "you" referring to the named insured (and spouse) and "we" meaning the insurance company. The policies are in booklet form, and use 25 percent larger type than the former contracts. All of these changes aid readability, as explained in the Chapter 24 discussion of the personal auto policy.

The major parts of the contract are also reorganized for understandability, and the traditional "165 lines" of the standard fire contract are eliminated. Their content is rewritten under five new section headings. "Definitions" (and boldface type for important words) precede the parts explaining "coverages," "perils insured against," "exclusions," and "conditions." Although contract analysis could follow these headings of the fundamental parts of the policies, the following evaluation is instead divided according to the contract's *purposes*. (This procedure was suggested to the reader as an alternative and meaningful method of contract analysis in Chapter 17 for the fire insurance contract.) Accordingly, the emphasis here is on *who* is covered, *what* is covered, *when* and *where* the protection applies, and *how* this protection is provided at a certain price. The old but effective outline of who, what, when, where, and how provides a convenient framework for analyzing homeowners' policies.[10]

Who is covered. As to *who* is covered by the homeowners' policies, the primary purpose of these contracts is to provide multiple-line coverage to *owners* who occupy their private residences.[11] These would be "the named insured" in the contract (or insureds, if joint owners), which includes the spouse if a resident of the same household. A rather important addition to the eligibility rules permits *tenants* to obtain the same combination of fire, theft, and liability perils in what is known as a tenant's homeowner's policy form. Homeowners' policies are oftentimes insurance for the personal property and personal liability of the whole family. "Insured" means you as the named insured in the declarations, as well as *residents of your household*, if they are either your relatives or any other persons under the age of 21 who are in your care.

What is covered. The homeowners' policies state *what is covered* by reference to the *property* and *perils* included in the coverage. The homeowners' policies are basically combinations of the perils in the standard fire policy (and allied perils forms), the residence burglary and theft policy, and the comprehensive personal liability policy.

Several *additional limits* of property coverage are included in the Homeowneres '76 program. Debris removal occasioned by an insured loss is

---

[10] Detailed analysis is also available in *Homeowners '76 Policy Program Guide* (Indianapolis: Rough Notes Co., 1978).

[11] The purpose is protection for essentially one- or two-family private and personal residential coverage, although the rules of some states permit insuring situations which include the owner-occupant of up to four-family houses and as many as two roomers or boarders.

covered (up to 5 percent of the property coverage). Trees, shrubs, plants, and lawns (up to 5 percent, or $500 each for the first three items mentioned) are covered for named perils only. These perils include fire, lightning, explosion, riot, aircraft, vehicles not owned or operated by a resident of the residence premises, vandalism, malicious mischief, and theft, but do not include windstorm or other unspecified perils.

The important *comprehensive personal liability* coverage was introduced earlier (in Chapter 21), but is reviewed briefly here as contained in Coverage E in Section II of the homeowners' policy forms. The premises liability protection applies to occurrences, defined as accidents including injurious exposures to conditions, which result in bodily injury or property damage on your premises. It includes your permanent residence, whether it is a dwelling owned by you or an apartment that you rent; a temporary residence of any insured, whether owned or rented; vacant land (except farmland); and even your cemetery lot. Secondary permanent residences may also be included in the declarations, or added to the policy. The policy extends to provide protection for losses attributable to an insured's (*a*) pets, bicycles, and small boats (owned watercraft with outboard motors not over 25 horsepower, or other rented ones; and owned or rented inboards or inboard-outboards with not over 50 horsepower, or sailboats not over 26 feet long); (*b*) sports, such as golfing, hunting, or fishing; and (*c*) any type of occurrence away from home for which an insured is held responsible.

The contract covers your liability and that of the other insureds for loss or damage that is the outgrowth of personal activites, except in an automobile accident or in business or professional acts. Aircraft and motorized land vehicles designed for public road use and subject to motor vehicle registration are not covered. Neither are *owned* motorized snowmobiles and other such recreational motor vehicles off the insured locations, but coverage does apply on the residence premises or off the premises if such vehicles are rented or borrowed. Golf carts while used for golfing purposes are covered, whether owned or operated by any insured and whether on or off the premises.

The business pursuits of any insured are not covered in the basic policy, but the policy may be extended to include some business activities if an insured is not the principal owner or partner (examples: teachers or salespersons). Incidental business pursuits on the premises, such as a doctor's office, an art or music studio, and the like, may also be covered by an endorsement.

The standard limits of liability coverage are $25,000 per occurrence, but higher limits of $50,000, $100,000, or $300,000 are recommended, for small additional premiums. For example, the $300,000 limit is only about $6 more a year than the $25,000 limit (in Ohio—it may be more elsewhere).

The contract excludes assumed liability, except liability assumed under a written contract relating to the premises. The wording of the insuring clause taken together with the exlusion provides protection to you if certain liabilities are assumed in a "hold-harmless" clause under a lease. Employers' liability to full-time residence employees (not more than two in some states) is covered without charge if they are not entitled to benefits under any workers' compensation law. Fire legal liability coverage for damage to nonowned premises and furnishings is included. This protection appeals to tenants, particularly those who rent valuable seasonal properties. It protects you as a tenant from damage suits growing out of injury to or destruction of a home which you have rented or its contents, if the loss is caused by one of the perils noted.

Medical payments (Coverage F of Section II—liability insurance) provides coverage of reasonable medical expense within three years for injuries to residence employees and to members of the public injured on or off the premises of the insured. It applies, regardless of legal liability, if the injuries are attributable to the activities of an insured or of your residence employees while they are engaged in your employment or of an animal owned by or in the care of any insured. The basic limit is $500 per person, but a few dollars increases this to $1,000 or $2,000. Injuries to regular residents of your household (except residence employees) are *not* covered. This is liability insurance and not accident coverage for everyone.

Theft coverage is now defined in the homeowners' contracts as "attempted theft and loss of property from a known location when it is likely that the property has been stolen." Thus, "mysterious disappearances" are sometimes but not usually covered. Theft from an unattended off-premises auto is not included unless there is forced entry. (Form 5 includes such losses, and the coverage for such unlocked-car losses can be added in other forms.) Any equipment for the recording or reproduction of sound (stereos, tape decks, CBs, etc.) is not covered for any perils, while in an automobile, except by endorsement.

Perils not included in homeowners' contracts are earthquake, landslide, flood, war, and the backing up of sewers.

When coverage applies.   The minimum duration of coverage is one or three years. Some insurers also issue continuous policies. Contracts can be paid for on an annual installment basis. The coverage begins at 12:01 A.M. at the location of the home. The insurance agent often has the power to bind coverage immediately for the insured while the policy is being prepared.

Where coverage applies.   The protection is basically at a fixed location—the home of the insured. However, coverages away from the home are also significant. For example, personal property or contents away from the home are covered on a worldwide basis. Personal property is also covered while in transit to a new residence, and for 30 days after you begin to move the property there. A 10 percent limit off premises under the old form no longer applies, except for property that is usually situated at another residence of an insured. The family liability and medical payments to other persons also apply both at home and away from the premises. Seasonal (secondary) dwellings in the same state may be added by endorsement in the minimum amount of $5,000.

How coverage applies.   *How* the homeowners' policies provide the coverage discussed in the preceding paragraphs can be explained in several ways. The policies are *multiple line* in character, combining fire, theft, and liability protection in one contract. The policies are also *package* contracts in the sense that they must include certain coverages. The insured is given some leeway in choosing the amounts of coverage on the home, personal property, liability, and medical payments. This characteristic of the insured having to accept basic perils, and to a certain extent amounts of insurance which are fixed by percentage formulas, makes the homeowners' policies essentially package rather than schedule type contracts. Coverages may be increased by endorsement, but the only exception to the prescribed minimums is that personal property at home may be decreased to 40 percent of the amount of coverage on the dwelling. The *all-risks* technique is also used in connection with homeowners' policies in forms 3 and 5, which cover "all risk of physical loss" to the insured property except for specified exclusions. Form 6 may be endorsed to provide all-risks coverage on the insured's alterations and additions.

Pricing, another part of how the homeowners' policies work, is accomplished by a so-called *indivisible premium*. This is one which has a combined charge for all basic perils to property included in the contract. Premium charts are used to show the cost of the various forms based upon varying amounts of coverage for the home and the related amounts on the garages, contents, and additional living expense perils. By this process no separate charge is made for each of the individual perils included in the contract. This is contrary to the traditional system in fire insurance, in which the premium is calculated by adding together separate charges for fire, windstorm, and miscellaneous perils. The homeowners' rate is a package premium for the minimum amounts of coverage in the package contract. Additional charges are calculated for the increases in insurance amounts permitted above the mandatory minimums. For example, the basic amount of insurance on the contents or personal property is automatically 50 percent of the dwelling home insurance amount, but the coverage on the contents or personal property can be increased. The basic required liability limit of $25,000 can also be increased. (See later summary in Table 27–2.)

Deductibles are used in connection with each form. A $100 deductible usually applies to all property losses including loss of use, except fire department service charges. Some of the state rules vary but larger deductibles of $250 or $500 (at 10 or 20 percent credit, respectively) are available, or a $50 deductible at a 10 percent increased cost can be purchased. All forms except form 5 can eliminate the deductible, or have a special theft deductible of $250 apply. A new feature applies the $100 deductible on a flat basis to each occurrence, instead of using the "disappearing" deductible of the older forms, which paid in full for losses over $500.

One other important feature of the homeowners' policies is that *replacement cost coverage* is provided on the home, the garages, and related private structures. This applies *if* the whole amount of the insurance on the buildings is 80

Table 27–2. Homeowners' policies, summary of coverages

	Policy Section I (property coverage)				Policy Section II (liability coverage)
	Coverage A	Coverage B	Coverage C	Coverage D	Coverages E and F
	Home	Garage or separate related structures	Contents or personal property	Additional living expenses	Comprehensive family liability and medical payments for others
Amounts	This amount is chosen as the basic contract coverage Minimum $15,000 for forms 1 and 2; $20,000 for form 3; and $30,000 for form 5	10% of home amount of insurance	50% of home (worldwide, but 10% of *contents amount* applies to property usually situated away from home) Minimum for forms 4 and 6, $6,000	20% of the home, or 10% under form 1; and under form 4, 20% of the contents amount; and under form 6, 40% of the contents amount	Basic amounts are: $25,000 (liability) and $500 (medical payments); Coverage E— liability can be increased up to $300,000, and Coverage F— medical payments up to $1,000 or $2,000, for small added premiums
Form: **Basic** (No. 1)*	Fire and lightning Extended coverage perils (wind, explosion, smoke, and so on) Theft, vandalism				All five forms include the above perils of (1) liability and (2) medical payments. (Additional coverage for "damage to property of others" (for insureds under age 13), up to $250, regardless of legal liability, is also a part of each form.)
Broad (No. 2)	All basic form perils as above, plus miscellaneous perils such as falling objects, collapse, water damage, rupture of heating systems, and freezing (essentially these are the broad form fire endorsement perils)				
Special (No. 3)	"All risks of physical loss" except those specifically excluded (such as flood, earthquake, landslide, war, backing up of sewers); broad form on contents				
Contents broad (No. 4)	Contents only covered—*not buildings* Covers same named perils as broad form 2 Can be used alone for tenants				
Comprehensive (No. 5)	Covers same all-risks perils as special form 3 but includes both *home and contents*				
Condominium unit owners (No. 6)	Covers personal property same as contents broad form 4, but adds: basic limit of $1,000 for additions and alterations to the building, and additional living expense up to 40 percent of the contents amount; endorsements permitted for theft when rented to others, and "loss assessments" by the condominium association				

* A new *Modified Coverage Form* (*No. 8*) became available in 1978. Designed for insureds who own older homes whose market value is much less than the replacement value, it provides that all losses be paid at *actual cash value* rather than have the replacement cost option (see text) apply. Basically, this contract is the same as form No. 1, with some reduced coverage for theft, off-premises personal property, and other items.

percent[12] *or more* of the replacement cost. Thus depreciation will not be subtracted in calculating the claim payable, and the policyholder will receive full repair or replacement cost on these items. When the full replacement cost is more than $1,000 or more than 5 percent of the insurance amount, the property must be actually repaired or replaced before this provision applies. Note that this provision is *not* the same as a "coinsurance" requirement (see Chapter 17), which is seldom used in homeowners' contracts except in a few states such as New York. Payment on a replacement cost basis is an extra *benefit* to the insured in these contracts, rather than a penalty to be applied for underinsurance.

A few insurers are experimenting with replacement cost coverage on *personal property,* paying fully for losses of items even if they cost more now than when you bought them. This may be an advantage to you, especially for major furniture and appliance losses, but there is an increased premium cost. Insurers must be careful of the moral hazard, which could increase losses under this coverage. However, early reports indicate reasonable success with such increased coverage, which may become more widely available in the future.

An *inflation guard endorsement* is available at a small additional cost. The policy amount on all the insured properties is automatically increased 1 percent every three months (or 12 percent over a three-year policy), helping to meet rising construction and replacement costs. This is a convenient way of avoiding underinsurance caused by inflating property values. The quarterly percentage increase can be increased by one-half percent increments beyond the basic 1 percent.

Additional living expenses are included when an insured peril causes the premises to be uninhabitable. The limit is 20 percent of the building insurance amount under most forms, except form 1, which has a limit of 10 percent. Form 4 and form 6 apply the percentage limit to the contents amount (20 and 40 percent, respectively). This covers the extra costs of living elsewhere while repairs are being made, and it is an important coverage in many serious losses. New wording often also includes fair rental value of that part of the residence rented or held for rental to others, by calling this "loss of use" coverage.

One final feature is the provision for an endorsement to the homeowners' policies of insurance for specifically named *scheduled personal property.* Very broad all-risks protection can be provided at low cost by scheduling valuable properties such as jewelry, cameras, furs, antiques, artistic objects, and collections. Endorsements may also add protection for earthquake damage and theft from unlocked automobiles.

A few *special limits* apply to specific articles as to the amount of coverage.

---

[12] 1978 revisions permit modification by endorsement permitting you to select 50, 60 or 70 percent, and retain this replacement cost feature of the contract. This may be advisable on older homes whose replacement value is high or difficult to determine.

An attempt is made to provide reasonable coverage for valuable or hard-to-value articles such as money ($100 limit); credit card, forgery, and counterfeit money ($500 limit); watercraft and their trailers ($500 limit); other trailers ($500 limit); grave markers ($500 limit); and accounts, securities, and manuscripts ($500 limit). Specific theft limits apply to unscheduled jewelry and furs ($500 per loss in the aggregate); to silverware, goldware, and pewter ($1,000 limit); and to guns ($1,000 limit). Several of these limits can be increased by endorsement: money to $1,000, jewelry and furs to $1,000, silverware to $3,000, and so on.

Comparison of coverages. A summary table may help to explain the homeowners' policy forms. Table 27–2 indicates the major property, perils, and amounts of coverage which the six basic homeowners' forms provide. The most significant result of all these forms is to combine the fire and allied perils, theft, and liability insurance for owners who occupy their homes, and to achieve this same combination of coverages for tenants who use form 4 and condominium-unit owners who use form 6. The major differences among the six forms are found in the scope of the *property perils* that are included in addition to the basic fire and lightning coverage: form 1 adds extended coverage perils; forms 2, 4, and 6 add broad form perils; form 3 adds all-risks perils to building coverage; and form 5 covers all-risks on both buildings and contents. (See Chapter 17 for further explanation of the perils).

The special form (No. 3) is currently purchased by about one half of all dwelling owners buying homeowners' policy contracts. Apartment renters need the contents form (No. 4), and the market for the condominium-unit owners' form (No. 6) is increasing. Perhaps one tenth of the policyholders use the limited protection of the basic form (No. 1), and about the same proportion purchase the all-risks coverage of the comprehensive form (No. 5).[13] The special form (No. 3) is attracting an increasing number of policyholders. This provides all-risks coverage on the buildings similar to that of the dwelling buildings special form endorsement and the broad form named-perils coverage on the contents. The result is very adequate coverage, only excluding a few known perils such as spillage of liquids or animal damage to contents, as compared with the broad form (No. 2).

The coverage as to property and perils is illustrated by an example showing the insurance provided by the special form (No. 3). (Page 787, top.)

Comparison of costs. A comparison of approximate costs in Table 27–3 illustrates how the basic forms vary for a homeowner or tenant in a class 1–6 rating territory in the Midwest.[14] Thus, the small increase in premium for

---

[13] In effect, form 5 provides all-risks coverage by combining the standard fire insurance policy (with the dwelling special form attached), the comprehensive liability policy, and the personal property floater policy. The higher cost relative to that of other forms and a mandatory deductible have discouraged its use.

[14] Rates vary considerably by territory, class of fire protection, type of building, and urban-rural differences in exposure, as well as among various insurers. For one detailed comparison, see *Homeowners' Insurance Price Comparisons in New York State* (New York: New York Insurance Department, 1973).

Property and perils coverage	Amounts of coverage
Section I (property)	
a. Home	$50,000
b. Separate garages or related private structures (total, not each)	5,000
c. Contents, or personal property at home, or away from home ($2,500 limit if usually situated at another residence)	25,000
d. Additional living expense	10,000
Section II (liability)	
e. Comprehensive personal liability	25,000
f. Medical payments	500
g. Damage to property of others	250

Table 27–3. Homeowners' policies, summary of costs

Form	Basic coverage amount*	Approximate annual cost†
Basic (No. 1)	$50,000 dwelling	$174
Broad (No. 2)	50,000 dwelling	186
Special (No. 3)	50,000 dwelling	194
Contents (No. 4)	15,000 contents	96
Comprehensive (No. 5)	50,000 dwelling	283
Condominium unit-owners (No. 6)	50,000 unit	221

* For frame dwelling in forms 1, 2, 3, 5, 6, and for contents in fire-resistive building in form 4; the usual flat deductible of $100 per loss is applicable.

† Annual, although most are written for three years with annual, quarterly, or monthly premiums.

form 3 can be seen as compared with forms 1 or 2 (less than $20 difference), and the rather substantial increase for form 5 ($90). The reduced cost of the homeowners' policies over separate fire, theft, and liability contracts is estimated at about 25 percent. At the above rates, the homeowner under form 3 is insuring more than $90,000 of assets ($50,000 dwelling, $25,000 contents, $5,000 for separate related private structures, $10,000 for additional living expense), plus the basic liability coverage, for approximately one fourth of 1 percent a year of the values protected. In a serious loss, the homeowner could collect up to the above limits under each of the separate coverages.

A special word of advice is needed in regard to contents coverage. The best way to be sure that you have enough coverage is to take, and keep up to date, a household inventory. Agents and companies have forms that are helpful in doing this. Photographs of each room also help considerably.

Summary of the major changes brought about by the Homeowners '76 program. With the anticipated adoption of Homeowners '76 contracts in most states and the gradual discontinuation of the older forms (specifically, the 1968 form), a brief summary of the major differences of coverage will be needed for several years. Form 2 is used in the comparison, although most of the items discussed are similar in all of the forms.

As to *who* is covered, the major change is the addition of form 6 for condominium-unit owners. A clarification has also been made to specifically include the personal property of a student who is an insured while the student is at a residence away from home, with theft coverage if the student has been there at any time during the 45 days immediately before the loss. (This also affects *where* coverage applies, as does the off-premises coverage noted in the next paragraph.)

As to *what* is covered,there has been a significant increase in the coverage for personal property used or owned (this formerly had to be "usual and incidental to the occupancy of the premises as a dwelling") by an insured to the *full* amount of the *personal property limit, while the insured is away from the insured premises* or in transit to a new residence. A 10 percent limit existed previously, and this now only applies to property usually situated at another residence. There is now no coverage for personal property of the insured in a portion of the residence premises which has been rented to others.

Additions in the *types of property* covered include grave markers, credit cards, (formerly covered only by endorsement), and safety glass replacement where safety glass is required by law. The changes in the *limits* of coverage for special classes of property include specific $1,000 theft limits for silverware and related items, and the same for guns. The limit of coverage for any one tree, shrub, or plant was doubled to $500 (this includes many named perils, but not windstorm or freezing).

The *perils* coverage has not changed significantly in the '76 program. Minor changes in definitions, largely to conform with most interpretations in previous forms, are found. Examples are vandalism *or* malicious mischief (formerly "and"); coverage of awnings, fences, and outdoor equipment for damage from falling objects; an exclusion for seepage through swimming pools; and an exclusion of damage from freezing in a vacant other structure while it is unoccupied (formerly said "vacant or unoccupied"). Debris removal after a covered loss (up to 5 percent of the dwelling amount) is an important additional coverage.

The *liability* coverages (Section II) contain only a few changes. Medical payments coverage is extended to three years (instead of one) from the date of an accident causing bodily injury. A new nuclear or radiation contamination exclusion applies for medical payments. This eliminates possible losses involving many persons; in prior forms catastrophic medical payments losses were subject to a $25,000 per accident limit. The obligation to defend any liability claim or suit is stated to be at the insurer's expense by counsel of its choice, as is the obligation to settle any loss that the insurer decides is covered. This obligation ends when the amount that the insurer pays for an occurrence (defined to include any one accident or to result from continuous or repeated exposure) equals the stated limit of liability in the policy. Formerly, this had been a supplementary coverage which could be paid beyond the policy limits. Reasonable expenses incurred by you at the insurer's request, including actual loss of earnings, are increased from $25 to $50 per day.

As to *how* the coverage applies, the Homeowners '76 program remains essentially a multiple-line, indivisible premium contract. Perhaps the most significant change is its use of a flat *deductible* (usually $100) that reduces most loss payments, instead of a disappearing deductible that affects larger losses. The ISO forms are clear in stating that the *liberalization clause,* extending the contract to include any broadening features that the insurer may adopt within 60 days prior to the policy period or during the policy period, does *not* apply the new coverages of the Homeowners '76 forms *to the older contracts.* However, the '76 contracts would automatically include revisions of the HO '76 program that broadened coverage without additional premium.

Mobilehome policy. With several million mobilehomes in the United States today, it is not surprising that a new policy for insuring them was developed in the early 1970s. The market for the *mobilehome policy* is expanding rapidly, as about half of all the new homes sold are mobilehomes. A package policy approach is used, similar to that of the regular homeowners' policies. The policy combines fire, windstorm (very important), and allied lines coverage on the mobilehome; personal property; additions to the mobilehome (on an optional basis); additional living expense; theft; and liability exposures. The eligible mobilehomes are those portable units that are built to be towed on their own chassis with frame and wheels and are designed for year-round living (the policy is not intended for small trailers). A minimum new-cost value of $4,000 is required (many mobilehomes cost $10,000 or more). Unscheduled personal property is insured for a minimum of $2,000, and additional living expense for $15 per day up to 45 days, but both of these limits may be increased. Many of the endorsements usual to homeowners' policies are available, such as deductibles higher than the usual $100 flat deductible, the earthquake peril, scheduled valuable personal property, and a secondary residence. A special endorsement for collision or upset coverage of the mobilehome is optional, with a $100 or $250 deductible.

Farmowner-ranchowner's policy. *The farmowner-ranchowner's policy* is an example of a multiple-line insurance contract which combines personal and business multiple-line insurance. The coverage is quite similar to that of the homeowners' forms. Fire, theft, and liability protection is provided on the dwelling ($12,000 minimum) and contents. Separate coverage amounts, in addition to those usually found in homeowners' policies, apply for other structures and for farm personal property. The coverage of property perils is either like that of the basic form (No. 1) or it includes more extensive named perils, as in the broad form (No. 2).

The liability insurance is the equivalent of the farmer's comprehensive personal liability policy now in use, covering liability, medical payments, and animal collision. The liability coverage includes the important product liability exposure. Liability for injuries to employees is not included in the farmers' CPL. The animal-collision cover is optional; it provides a limited form of livestock mortality insurance for the insured. The policy pays the insured for loss by death of cattle, horses, sheep, hogs, and the like, if death is caused by collision between an insured animal and a motor vehicle not owned or operated by the insured or the insured's employees. The animal collision applies only to insured animals killed on a public highway while not being transported.

Other personal multiple-line contracts.   A number of other insurance contracts may be classified as multiple-line coverages. Each of these contracts combines fire and casualty insurance perils; in fact, the development and use of these contracts preceded by many years the homeowners' policies which today are the most popular multiple-line contracts. The *personal property floater*, the *personal articles floater,* the *outboard motorboat policy,* and the *valuable papers policy* are examples which have been discussed in previous chapters. They are better known as inland marine insurance contracts because they were developed prior to the real impetus and legal sanction for multiple-line contracts.

These forerunners of full multiple-line legislation in the states were a significant part of the multiple-line trend. Fire, allied, and theft perils were combined in the all-risks, worldwide protection of the personal property floater in the early 1930s. The personal articles floater also appeared then. It was designed for articles of high value which were scheduled in a specific list of items, such as jewelry, furs, collections, and historical and artistic objects. The valuable papers policy, which may also be used by businesses, provides coverage for hard-to-value properties such as blueprints, plans, and manuscripts. The outboard motorboat policy reveals a strong heritage from the ocean marine field of insurance and combines fire, theft, and even limited liability protection in one policy.

Business multiple-line insurance contracts

The tremendous growth of commercial multiple-peril contracts has been noted in Table 27–1. From less than $100 million in premiums, the field has grown in little more than two decades to $5 *billion* in premiums a year!

General development.   Five contracts stand out in the development of multiple-line protection for business prior to the early 1960s. Since then many new contracts have appeared, with rapid changes in this volatile area.[15] The special multiperil (SMP) program of the Insurance Services Office (discussed in the next section) gradually replaced most of these contracts in the past decade to become most important to many insurers. A brief review of the earlier business multiple-line contracts shows how the SMP program developed.

One of the early experiments in multiple-line insurance for business was the *manufacturer's output policy*. It covered all personal property of the manu-

---

[15] Recommended for current and further details than are provided in this text are the form and manual loose-leaf services mentioned in footnote 6.

facturer on an all-risks basis while the property was away from the premises of the insured. It was originally a specialized policy for the automobile industry only, but later it became available to several hundred classes of manufacturers. Unlike most insurance contracts, the policy was continuous, remaining in effect until canceled. A minimum premium of $5,000 restricted the contract to large risks. A reporting form adjusted the premiums to the property values actually in existence during the year. Automobiles were covered at any location. This contract is available today, although its title has been changed to the "manufacturer's policy."

Block policy contracts were one of the first examples of business multiple-line coverage. The *jeweler's* block policy is still generally written. It is an inland marine policy covering the entire merchandise and contents of the jeweler's store on an all-risks basis. Several similar policies have been regarded as primarily inland marine insurance, even though they are also part of the multiple-line trend. These contracts include the *furrier's* block policy and a variety of *dealers'* block policies (equipment, appliances, cameras, instruments, and so on). Fire and theft coverages both on and off the premises are provided in all of these contracts; therefore they are multiple-line contracts, even though they are still written as part of the inland marine field.

All-risks *property* coverage was expanded in the 1960s to four other categories of business risks. The addition of liability coverages to make multiple-line contracts more complete occurred later, with the development of the SMP program. In recent years the SMP program has almost entirely eliminated the use of these separate forms, which were usually attached to the fire insurance contract to create broader coverage. The *commercial property form* for merchants provided retail and wholesale stores with all-risks property coverage on the stock, furniture, and fixtures, and on improvements and betterments of the insured. The *office contents form* was created to provide similar all-risks property coverage for most offices. The *industrial property form* provided smaller manufacturing businesses with all-risks coverage similar to that of the output policies for automobiles and other manufacturers. It included the business property of the insured, the personal property of others for which the insured might be liable, machinery and equipment, and even buildings. A *public and institutional property* program for schools, churches, hospitals, and government units provided broad property coverage for all real and personal property. An adaptation of these plans is now available under the special multiperil program (discussed next), which provides property and *liability* protection in many states.

Special multiperil (SMP) program. Package multiple-line coverages for business risks have been a rapidly changing part of insurance. Forms that have been adopted in some states have not been approved in others. Bureaus such as the Insurance Services Office have helped standardize many forms, but differences exist among the various states and also between bureau companies and independent insurers.

One of the early contracts that appeared as part of the special multiperil program was for mercantile properties, including retail and wholesale establishments. SMP contracts also became available for businesses whose primary function was to provide services rather than goods. The first of these to become available was a contract for *motel* (now *motel-hotel*) owners; then specialized policies emerged for *office* building owners, *apartment* building owners, and *processing or service risks,* such as cleaners, repair shops, barbershops, and many other classifications. After several years of experimentation with the development of these *separate* "programs," revised SMP rules were put into a single consolidated manual.

The outstanding characteristic of these policies was the provision of property *and liability* coverages in one policy. Usually, these coverages were mandatory, and included both real and personal property. The policies were a combination of the package and schedule approaches to insurance. The basic package included some fire and liability insurance, but the insured optionally selected other coverages, such as theft, business interruption, boiler and machinery, glass, valuable papers, and other miscellaneous perils. The policies included either named property or all-risks perils. The basic liability form was not comprehensive, but the limitation of coverage to specified premises and only incidental operations could be changed to comprehensive general liability coverage. Combined single limits (without a separate per person limit) applied on a per occurrence basis and on an aggregate basis for bodily injury and property damage liability, which included premises, protective, and products exposures (see Chapter 21).

As a hypothetical example of how the SMP benefits consumers, a retail clothing store might have the lower costs and broader coverage of an SMP contract as illustrated by Table 27–4. In the example, for about 10 percent less cost the mercantile policy adds protection against business interruption, burglary and theft, and vandalism and malicious mischief, and increases the liability coverage to more adequate limits. Other examples might, of course, add similar or greater increases in coverage that would cause the total cost to exceed the original cost of individual policies.

New simplified SMP package. In 1977 a new *simplified SMP package* was adopted to eliminate the duplicate coverage of the many separate policies that had been developed to provide all-risks coverage of business personal property. The SMP now uses a policy "jacket" in booklet form of the declarations, insuring agreements, and general provisions common to all policies, except for a few of the older forms for builders' risks, condominium associations, and risks to physicians' and surgeons' equipment. To this are added a form with basic conditions and definitions (Form MP-4) and a form to insure *buildings* on either a *named-perils* basis (Form MP-100) or an *all-risks* basis (Form MP-101). For *personal property* a similar choice is made by the insured, by using either Form MP-100-A or Form MP 101-A. Only one *liability* form (Form MP-200) is attached for all eligible risks, with one optional

**Table 27-4. Cost and coverage comparison—individual policies
and special multi-peril (SMP) policy**

		Three-year cost* of	
Individual policies	Amounts of coverage	Individual policies	Mercantile package
1. Standard fire policy with broad form coverage endorsement	$100,000 on building	$ 600	$ 400
2. Standard fire policy with broad form coverage endorsement	$150,000 on contents	1,000	700
3. Public liability	25/50/5 limits	150	200 (with single limit of $100,000)
4. Business interruption	$60,000 gross earnings	None carried	100
5. Burglary and theft	$20,000 merchandise	None carried	150
6. Vandalism and malicious mischief	Added to fire policies	None carried	50
Total three-year cost ..		$1,750	$1,600

* Costs are illustrative and not meant to be exact. They would vary in actual practice by substantial amounts according to many factors such as sprinkler systems, store area, territory, and protective features. Insurance rates also differ between bureau and nonbureau members. If similar coverages are compared, the package discounts under SMP contracts are usually approximately 15 percent.

endorsement form available to include employer's nonownership automobile liability protection.

The SMP can now be used for *almost any type of commercial or institutional operation*. The only exceptions are farms, motor vehicle businesses, bowling alleys, rooming houses, apartment dwellings with fewer than three units, and very large business properties which may qualify for a special plan for "highly protected risks." The most important addition is the eligibility of the SMP for contracting risks.

A revised manual of rules is divided into *five parts*: general policy rules, and rules for the four specific coverage areas of property, casualty, crime, and boiler and machinery. Policy terms of up to three years are provided for, instead of the older one- or three-year terms.

The *general conditions and definitions* in Form MP-4, together with the declarations page, replace the 165 lines of the old standard fire policy. The three parts are : (1) general conditions, stating the premium computation, time of inception (12:01 A.M.), cancellation, subrogation, and other items; (2) conditions applicable to Section I (property coverage), similar to much of the fire contract wording, but adding deductible (usually $100), coinsurance, and nuclear clauses; and (3) conditions applicable to Section II (general liability), including an explanation of supplementary payments, the insured's duties after a loss, and other terms.

Section I (*property coverage*) uses only the four previously mentioned forms to provide either named-perils or all-risks coverage on buildings (building Forms MP-100 or 101) and personal property (Personal Property Forms MP-100-A or 101-A). Usually both the building and its contents must be insured, but a tenant may cover only the contents, or a landlord only the building. Both of the named-perils forms include vandalism and malicious mischief. Reporting value coverage can be added by endorsement to provide for changing property values. Replacement cost coverage can also be purchased. Many optional forms are available for the addition of business interruption, extra expense, glass, water damage, earthquake, sprinkler leakage, and many other perils. These tailor the contract to meet the particular insured's needs. Automobiles are the major type of property not included in the SMP.

Section II (*general liability coverage*) provides standard liability coverage for a declared location and its incidental operations. Combined single limits (minimum of $25,000), on an occurrence and on an aggregate basis for bodily injury and property damage apply in the basic liability form (MP-200). If desired, dual limits (per person, per occurrence) are available. Products liability and completed operations liability are included, unless deleted. Separate optional medical payments coverage applies, with a minimum of $250 per person and per accident. Any of the standard general liability coverages that can be written in separate general liability contracts may now be provided in the SMP, including comprehensive general liability coverage (see Chapter 21). Automobile nonownership liability, and explosion, underground, and collapse (XCU) liability, can be added by endorsement. Workers' compensation is not included in the SMP.

Sections III and IV provide *crime* and *boiler and machinery coverage* on an optional basis. A wide range of choices permits the insured to choose among the types of perils discussed in Chapters 25–26—burglary, robbery, and theft (inside or outside the premises); blanket fidelity bonds (employee dishonesty); depositor's forgery; and boiler and machinery direct and indirect losses. The only significant related perils that cannot be included here are surety bonds, which must be written separately.

In all, the new simplified SMP package policy is a flexible multiple-line contract that enables many business risks to insure their total property and liability exposures, with the exceptions of workers' compensation, automobile, and surety bonds, as noted.

Another multiple-line policy, the businessowner's policy (BOP), has become increasingly popular for smaller businesses since the mid-1970s, and it deserves special attention.

Businessowner's policy program (BOP). An alternative to the SMP for many small and medium-sized businesses of the apartment, office, and retail store types is now also widely used. The *businessowner's policy (BOP)* which has been available since 1976, combines property and liability exposures.[16] It differs from the SMP by including: (1) more limited eligibility (specified types of businesses with a smaller building size and occupancy area); (2) a more fixed package of coverages, with somewhat less flexibility in choosing limits and coverages; (3) broader protection through the use of several automatic provisions for replacement cost coverage and the absence of coinsurance requirements; and (4) a more readable style of contract, replacing the 165 lines of the old standard fire contract with revised format and wording.

Eligible risks are described to include only buildings classified as *apartment* buildings (not more than six stories high and with no more than 60 dwelling units), *office* buildings (not higher than three stories or exceeding 100,000 square feet in area), and *mercantile* buildings (not over 7,500 square feet in area). Tenants may also purchase the BOP for offices of up to 10,000 square feet in one building, and for mercantile operations of up to 7,500 square feet. Many risks eligible for SMP contracts are specifically ineligible, such as condominiums, contractors, wholesalers, and banks. Retail stores are one of the largest eligible classes as a market for the BOP. Most of the BOP contracts have annual premiums of under $1,000.

The insured under the BOP contract makes *relatively few choices of coverage.* Two alternative forms are used for property coverages: a *standard* form (MLB-700) insuring named perils (fire, extended coverage, vandalism, and sprinkler leakage), and a *special* form (MLB-701) insuring all risks. The insured selects a full replacement value for insurance on the building and/or its contents, which, like the homeowners' policies, then automatically includes many additional coverages for a package of protection with an indivisible premium. Loss of income and rather high liability coverages are also built into the BOP. The insured may choose to add, for additional premium, optional coverages for employee dishonesty, boilers and machinery, glass, exterior signs, and earthquake exposures. Burglary and robbery are automatically included in the special (all-risks) form, and may be added to the standard (named-perils) form.

The *premium rates* for the BOP package are based on an indivisible premium for the basic coverages. As compared with the costs of individual contracts for fire, theft, liability and other perils, these rates provide savings similar to those illustrated for the SMP in Table 27–4. The annual premiums are stated as provisional amounts, subject to audit at expiration time for all of the exposures covered. For example, if other premises are acquired during the policy term, there would be an additional charge for liability.

Analysis of the BOP policy *property coverages* indicates that they contain

---

[16] The BOP contract discussed here was developed by the Insurance Services Office (ISO) after several independent insurers filed such contracts in the mid-1970s. For more detailed analysis, see the *Fire, Casualty, and Surety Bulletins* (Comm. Multi-peril pages Pb); and *Businessowner's Policy Program* (Indianapolis: Rough Notes Co., 1976).

several additional unusual features as compared with those of the standard fire contract and the SMP program. The standard named-perils (MLB-700), for example, includes an *automatic quarterly increase in the building coverage of 2 percent* (or higher, if so indicated in the declarations). Another automatic increase in the insurance amounts is a *25 percent increase in peak season fluctuations of business personal property*. It applies if the insured's average monthly values for the preceding 12 months are fully covered by declared insurance limits on this property. The SMP coverage for such fluctuations requires an endorsement. *Off-premises* property coverage is limited to $1,000 in the BOP, or to $10,000 for 30 days while the property is at newly acquired premises owned, leased, or operated by the insured. *No coinsurance* requirement applies in the BOP. Automatic coverage for *loss of income* with no stated limit is a part of the BOP contracts, to a maximum of 12 months of indemnity during the time that is required to resume normal operations. Other coverages included in the BOP, but not the SMP, are wind and hail protection for trees, shrubs, and plants (with limits of $250 per item, $1,000 per occurrence), and protection for collision and other damages to property in transit. The basic flat *deductible* is $100 per property loss in any one occurrence, applying separately to each building, its contents, and personal property in the open. The aggregate deductible applied in any one occurrence is $1,000.

The special form (MLB-701) property coverages are similar to those of the named-perils form, except that the perils included are on an *all-risks* basis. The special form property coverages include *theft* insurance for all business personal property, which is not covered in the named-perils form except by adding burglary and robbery coverage. Money and securities used in the insured's business are included in Coverage D automatically, but this is limited to $10,000 on premises and $2,000 off premises. A special deductible of $250 applies to theft and employee dishonesty losses.

The *liability coverages* in Section II of the BOP contracts, both the standard and special forms, are very extensive. The insured need only choose a *$300,000* or *$1 million* liability limit. Medical payments coverage of $1,000 per person and $10,000 per accident is included, with no options. The liability protection is comparable to that of comprehensive general liability coverage (see Chapter 21). It includes products and completed operations; fire legal liability to structures rented or occupied by the insured (special additional limit of $50,000); blanket contractual liability for written agreements; personal injury liability for false arrest, libel, slander, or invasion of privacy; nonowned automobile liability; and even host liquor liability at functions incidental to the insured's business. The "insured" is defined to include any employee of the named insured while acting within the scope of his or her duties, coverage which must be endorsed on most other general liability contracts. The liability coverage of the BOP illustrates vividly the broad coverage that this important multiple-line contract provides to businesses.

ALL-LINES INSURANCE

Nature and extent

All-lines insurance is a separate current trend, but one almost as apparent and significant as the multiple-line trend. The all-lines approach combines *property, liability, life, and health* insurance. Although this combination may be accomplished by a single contract or single insurer[17] only in a few examples and a few states, multiple-line insurers have created an all-lines trend in the past 25 years by purchasing or forming separate life insurers. More than 100 of the 220 larger property-liability insurer groups listed in *Best's Aggregates and Averages,* for example, have one or more life insurers in their group of insurers.[18] The early growth in the 1960s was startling. The groups now number more than several hundred, including life insurers that expanded by adding property-liability companies to their operations.[19] The result has been many all-lines insurer *groups,* although all-lines *contracts* and all-lines *insurers* are still rare except in limited cases

Property-liability insurers have become all-lines groups

The most frequent action in the formation of all-lines groups has been taken by property-liability insurers. Either by purchasing a life insurer or by forming a new life affiliate, multiple-line insurers have often become all-lines groups.

Some of the early *reasons* why this trend emerged have been concisely reviewed: (1) basically, it caters to the buyer's convenience by providing one-stop shopping; (2) volatile loss ratios in property and liability insurance have caused property-liability insurers to look to life insurance as a stabilizer for their operations; (3) the property-liability insurers have a ready-made sales force for selling life insurance; and (4) many property and liability insurance agents deal with business firms, which makes for a natural entry into the

---

[17] Emphasis is on the phrase "by a single contract or a single insurer." In contrast to the multiple-line trend, which started with (1) multiple-line *groups* and (2) extended to multiple-line *companies* and (3) then to the rapid growth of multiple-line *contracts* in the last decade, the all-lines trend is still largely centered on the first phase, that is, all-lines insurance company *groups.*

[18] *Best's Aggregates and Averages* (New York: A. M. Best Co., 1977), pp. 46 and 2–5B.

[19] Even prior to 1970, one source notes 253 groups of both life and nonlife companies with an average of more than four companies per group (Richard de R. Kip, "Insurance Company Groups," *CPCU Annals,* vol. 22, no. 3 [September 1969], pp. 197–202). This study does not differentiate between property-liability companies that added life companies or life companies that added property-liability insurers. Many groups include only two companies, but one group contained 5 life insurers and 27 nonlife companies.

group life insurance business of these firms.[20] The three C's—coverage, cost, and convenience—summarize many of the advantages.

Practically all of the larger property-liability insurers and many of the smaller ones now have life insurance affiliates. These groups emphasize the opportunities which property-liability insurers have in overcoming the most serious problem of life companies—finding life insurance prospects. Encouragement to the local agent to place more life insurance business along with the insureds' automobile, homeowner's, and other insurance has taken many forms. One of the most pointed methods was observed when one of the largest insurers offered agents higher commissions on property-liability business *if* certain quotas of life insurance production were met!

Exclusive agency companies have been very successful in building their life insurance operations to significant parts of their all-lines group operations. Examples are Allstate, Nationwide, and State Farm Life, which has become ranked as one of the top 20 life insurers.

Life insurers are becoming all-lines groups

Life insurers are expanding their operations by starting or purchasing property-liability insurers. In past years they have been held back by legal barriers that prevented a life insurer from owning substantial stock in other insurers. However, such prohibitions have been largely removed.[21] The entry of life insurers into all-lines operations will probably be a *gradual development,* for a number of reasons: (1) licensing laws in most states prevent a single insurer from doing business in both the life and property fields,[22] so the permitted insurer group technique of all-lines operations (which is sometimes more unwieldy) will have to be used; (2) about two thirds of life insurance is

---

[20] Benjamin N. Woodson, "All-Lines Underwriting: Five Years Later," *CLU Journal,* vol. 16, no. 3 (Summer 1962), pp. 239–42, reaches the interesting conclusion that the greatest change was the "applicability of life insurance methods to the underwriting and sale of personal-line and casualty coverages." Direct billing by the insurer, group insurance sales, and reduced commissions on renewals are examples of these methods that continued to increase during the 1970s.

[21] New York State's highest court reversed a former decision and stated that out-of-state life insurers might purchase fire and casualty companies. Although other legal barriers exist (such an antitrust and monopoly acts), this decision hastened the all-lines trend in the decade of the 1960s. The suit concerned the purchase of Aetna Insurance Company by the Connecticut General Life Insurance Company.

[22] Only 13 states permitted the early "inclusion of life, fire, and casualty writing powers in *single insurers.*" These were Alabama, Alaska, Connecticut, Delaware, Georgia, Maine, Mississippi. North Dakota, Oregon, Rhode Island, South Carolina, Tennessee, and Wisconsin. New York still does not permit this, and any insurer doing business in New York cannot under the application of the Appleton Rule to out-of-state insurers use such broad powers. See Hugh D. Harbison, "Legal Environment for All Lines Insurance" in Dan M. McGill (ed.), *All Lines Insurance* (Homewood, Ill.: Richard D. Irwin, 1960) chap. 2, p. 23. More states have changed their laws to allow this, but many still do not allow one corporation to be an all-lines insurer.

written by mutual insurers, and these are limited in expansion by the amount of their surplus; (3) profits in property-liability insurance in recent years have been volatile, especially in relation to those of the more stable life insurance field; and (4) the changes necessitated by all-lines operations are considerable, involving a major impact on management, product development losses and expenses, underwriting, marketing, education and training, regulation, and investments.[23] However, many observers feel that despite the problems of life insurers in entering all-lines insurance, the movement will continue to grow. The reasons for expecting growth are competition, economy, and the growing recognition of the mass market concept.

The legal problems have decreased with the advent of related trend—that of "holding companies" which own several corporate enterprises. If state laws prevent a life insurer from owning a property-liability insurer directly, both the life insurer and the property-liability insurer can be owned by a holding company and operated as an all-lines group. The last 20 years have seen many such reorganizations. It is a movement which has been reinforced by the increased interest in broader financial services and by the general corporate merger trend. An example is Phoenix Mutual Life's entry into the property-liability field in 1976.

In the 1960s, several large life companies acquired property-liability affiliates: Connecticut General Life—Aetna, Lincoln National Life—American States, State Mutual Life—Hanover, and others. In addition, several large life insurers, including Prudential, began to write reinsurance in the aviation field, which needed the increased capacity in order to insure rapidly expanding jumbo jet aircraft exposures.

The long-anticipated movement by the larger life insurers into the property-liability field began in earnest *during the 1970s.* Prudential, Metropolitan, Equitable, John Hancock, and National Life and Accident were among the largest to begin all-lines activities. Perhaps 100 other life insurers have initiated or acquired property-liability operations in order to become all-lines insurers. A decreasing proportion of life insurers remain convinced that specialization in life insurance only is the best answer for the future.

Farthest along in this development of the companies mentioned above are Prudential and Metropolitan both of which set up separate property-liability companies, causing shock and fear among the established property-liability insurers. The potential increased competition from their agents (Prudential has 25,000; Metropolitan has 19,000) was obvious. The *reasons* given by Prudential for becoming an all-line group include: (1) reaction to the competition from property-liability companies entering the life field, (2) the use of substantial life insurer surplus to increase the potential financial stability of total operations, (3) the opportunity to realize an investment re-

---

[23] See chaps. 4–11 on each of these impacts of all-lines insurance. This was the first book to use the title *All Lines Insurance.*

turn equal to or greater than investments in other ventures, and (4) the appeal of all-lines distribution to both the agent and the consumer.[24] Other reasons are the advantages of an integrated marketing and management system, better use of technical personnel, and the desire for a hedge against (1) loss of employee benefit markets to competition, (2) loss of health insurance markets to expanding social insurance plans, and (3) inflation factors, which increase premiums more for property-liability lines than for life insurance.

The Pru's research indicates a strong *consumer demand for all-lines* agents. More than three fifths of the consumers surveyed (particularly young ones, where the percentage was 75 percent) said that they "would prefer" to have one insurance agent for all their insurance needs rather than different agents for different types of insurance, and almost 30 percent were "very interested" in having one agent handle all insurance needs in order to obtain greater convenience and service.[25] In addition, other surveys showed that 22 percent of the respondents already had such an agent and that 60 percent of those greatly interested in having one agent already had one.

The consumer is attracted to the concept. The ability of the life insurance agent to stay in regular personal (not just telephone) contact with his or her clients is indicated as a strong reason for the long-range success of life agents in property-liability insurance. The probable gradual nature of expansion is stressed because of the need for underwriting selectivity, the reluctance of clients to change insurers in a tightening market, and the need to retrain agents so that they can serve as all-lines family insurance counselors. The cost of retraining is a big factor: many insurers of all types are devoting much more time to expanding their agents' capabilities in new fields.[26]

Marketing results thus far have been reasonably successful for the life insurers, although the underwriting results for property-liability business have not always been good, as might be expected for initial operations in a new field. The Prudential lost $90 million in underwriting property-liability insurance in one recent year, and Metropolitan lost $24 million, incurring start-up costs of more than $400 million and $200 million, respectively.[27]

The potential *benefits* of having life insurers sell in the property-liability areas cited are greater financial stability for the total insurance market, reaching difficult and broader markets, the introduction of new ideas, greater competition and thus less government intervention, increased total underwriting capacity, and a better long-range management viewpoint for insur-

---

[24] Leroy J. Simon, "Why the 'Rock' Moved into Property-Liability," *Journal of Insurance,* vol. 34, no. 4 (July–August 1973), p. 21.

[25] Martin Albaum, "From Life Insurance Agent to Family Insurance Counselor" (presentation at the American Risk and Insurance Association annual meeting, in Miami, Florida, on August 22, 1973).

[26] "Life and Casualty Insurers Meet Head-on," *Business Week,* August 29, 1977, p. 87. Nationwide devotes 30 percent of its training time to life insurance, for example, in contrast to only 10 percent a decade ago.

[27] Ibid., p. 86.

ance. Anticipated larger and steadier incomes for their agents are frequently mentioned by life insurers as expected benefits.

The future

Some executives predict that the division in the insurance industry will end in the next decade.[28] All-lines insurance has a long way to go before it earns its title fully, however. Perhaps in the future there will be many contracts that really deserve to be called *all-lines contracts*. At present only a few all-lines types of policies are written by a small number of insurers in a few states. An example is disability insurance and life insurance for a home mortgage, which is written along with a homeowner's contract (and automobile insurance, in some cases).

A *combination personal-lines package policy* is defined as a single policy with a specific premium computation plan with potential savings to the consumer over separate policies, offering at least one basic home and automobile coverage. A "true" personal-lines package policy is "one policy that encompasses all lines of insurance for a family and its possessions, meaning basic property, basic casualty, plus some form of life and health coverage."[29]

Early efforts at marketing these broad contracts were often limited and relatively unsuccessful. Burkhart notes the W. J. Perryman Co. (Alabama) in 1960 as the first insurer to include life coverage with home and auto, and the General America (Safeco) Companies in 1943 as the first insurer with a combined home-auto policy. The Founders Insurance Company was next, in 1951. The Cincinnati Insurance Company and the Midwestern Indemnity Company began writing a combination home-automobile contract in 1957 and have "the distinction of being the only known early pioneers in this unique field to still actively market their home and auto combination policy."[30] Other companies offering such contracts since about the early 1960s are Republic-Franklin, Indiana Farmers, Western Reserve, and Gulf American. More insurers adopted this practice in the 1970s.

Several other combination coverages are being marketed by various insurers on an account selling system, but are not packaged in one contract or policy jacket, or do not include automobile protection. Hanover, Nationwide, Atlantic, Continental-National-American, Meridian Mutual, American States, and Shelby Mutual are mentioned.

Three big insurers have broken into the field. First, the Insurance Company of North America (1969), then, in 1973, the Continental Insurance Com-

---

[28] *Ibid.* Edward J. Noha, chairman of the CNA companies.

[29] James S. Burkhart, "History, Development, and Future Potential of Combination Personal Lines Package Policies," *CPCU Annals,* vol. 26, no. 4 (December 1973), p. 129. Other specific references to companies in this section, unless otherwise noted, come from the same source.

[30] Ibid., p. 131. In 1978, this company also obtained approval in Ohio to add homeowner's reducing term life insurance (in $25,000 or $50,000 amounts) to its combination contract.

panies and the Travelers. INA's is almost a true personal-lines package, offering home and auto coverage, with optional "excess" personal liability (see Chapter 21) and accidental death and dismemberment. It uses a variable percentage savings discount and an indivisible premium. Continental's is a true all-lines "personal comprehensive protection" (PCP) policy, with combined home-auto property and liability, excess liability, hospital, and disability income and mortgage life insurance at unique premium modification rates. Extensive advertising in major magazine media featured the idea of covering "you, your home, and auto" all in one policy. A detailed 50-page comparison of the coverages with current homeowners' and auto contracts emphasizes the easier wording and broader coverage aspects of the comprehensive contract. The Travelers' "Com Pac" combines home and automobile insurance at a 10 percent discount, but does not include life or health protection.

The three major insurers mentioned above are sufficient evidence to suggest that the new era of true all-lines contracts for the personal field started in the 1970s. Although it is much too early to predict lasting effects, these efforts by well-recognized insurers are too broad geographically to go unnoticed by consumers or competitors. It will take other large insurers to make this a real trend for the insurance business, but the convenience and cost savings features may well combine with other trends, such as monthly billing, to make these innovations grow more rapidly in the next decade.

Undoubtedly, increased competition in all-lines selling will be an important part of tomorrow's insurance market. The advantages of survey selling and such other features as automatic monthly check payment plans are obvious to many policyholders. Many agents or agencies have been operating as all-lines sales forces for years. As a result of the rapid entry of property and liability insurers into all-lines operations by creating all-lines groups, many life insurers have also become all-lines organizations. Considering the advantages which accrue to the life insurers by doing so and the need to protect their markets, life insurers have sound reasons for evaluating the prospects of all-lines insurance.

The insurance product of tomorrow may be a direct outgrowth of the trend to multiple-line and all-lines insurance. It may well be a market dominated by "package" contracts of property, liability, life, and health insurance. It must be consumer-oriented (see Chapter 29) if it is to be successful. The progressive insurer is reanalyzing its organization structure, its financing and training system for agents, and its total marketing and underwriting plans in order to provide better all-lines insurance for the modern buyer.

FINANCIAL SERVICES CONGLOMERATES

Mergers and growth

One of the most pronounced characteristics of U.S. business during the last 20 years has been the "urge to merge." Sometimes this has involved only business firms that have competed directly in one product or service. The advantages of economies of larger scale and broader markets have been attractive in our increasingly mobile economy.

In many other cases, mergers have taken place in a different sphere—that of combining businesses offering different but related products or services. Both vertical (production and distribution) and horizontal (on the same level) integration have occurred. Pooled capital, production, and distribution facilities have helped combat rising material and labor costs. Product diversification has been desired for greater stability of operating results in a rapidly changing market.

The true "conglomerate" type of merger combining *un*related businesses, has appeared, too. Primarily during the past several years, this phenomenon has attracted much attention. It faces the restraints of some legislation and court action, particularly the antitrust provisions of the Sherman, Clayton, and other federal acts. However, many conglomerates have been successful in their operations.[31]

The position of insurance

At this point the insurance business is a part of all three of the above tendencies toward combination of business firms and growth in their size. Mergers of insurers doing business in the same type of insurance, such as two fire insurers combining, have occurred over several decades. Mergers and expansion to multiple-line insurers increased rapidly during the 1960s. All-lines insurer groups, particularly property-liability insurers purchasing or forming life insurer affiliates, became numerous throughout the late 1960s and the 1970s.[32]

The *financial services conglomerate* is one of the most significant trends of the 1970s. The "zaibatsu," which has long been a prominent form of business in Japan, uses the banking-financial base for its large-scale activities in many endeavors. Legislation by Congress and court interpretation may well determine the future of this method of business in the United States. Banks rushed to transform themselves into holding companies during the last dozen years, and several thousand were operating mutual funds, finance companies, and other related activities by 1979. They may be restricted from entering manufacturing and other industries, but their continued expansion beyond the traditional "banking" field to include other financial services such as insurance and travel services is to be expected in a computer economy. Several savings and loan associations have begun to market, in one payroll deduction, combinations of term life insurance, mutual fund shares, and savings programs.

---

[31] See Dan Cordtz, "What Does U.S.I. Do? Why, Almost Everything," *Fortune,* February 1973, p. 73, for what is called "the ultimate conglomerate."

[32] Alan L. King, "Conglomeration within the Property and Liability Insurance Industry," *CPCU Annals,* vol. 27, no. 4 (December 1974), p. 314.

The issue is controversial. There is widespread fear of concentration of power, lessening competition, and other disadvantages. Yet the advantages of convenient consumer services at lower costs are predicted. The expansion of life insurers into variable annuities and mutual funds (see Chapter 12) creates closer ties of insurance with investment and banking. So also does the increased emphasis of property-liability insurers on the results of their investment portfolios. One of the questions to be answered in the 1980s is whether bankers' and investment firms' expansion into insurance fields will be more rapid than insurers' expansion into banking and its related fields.

Management thinking, as well as state and federal regulation, will need to be reoriented toward the new problems of "financial supermarkets." The current trends to reduce the traditional separation of life and multiple-line operations in the United States could have some hidden, long-range benefits in spite of unsettled conditions for a while in the marketplace; for "perhaps insurance people will begin to think of the insurance industry as a single industry, and to face its problems with a more united front."[33] The advantages and potential benefits of all-lines operations—for insurers, agents, and consumers—seem ready to be reaped in the "exuberant 80s."

FOR REVIEW AND DISCUSSION

1. Product diversification is a trend that is seen in many types of businesses today. Compare and contrast product diversification in the past 20 years of insurance with that of other businesses.

2. Explain how the multiple-line and all-lines insurance trends are perhaps related to the risk-management concept (as discussed in Chapter 3).

3. If multiple-line insurance contracts provide greater coverage than comparable separate policies, how can the multiple-line contracts have a lower premium? Is this the only significant result of these contracts?

4. What is *multiple-line* insurance, and how does it compare with *all-lines* insurance? What separate parts can you identify in the multiple-line trend? Why are they significant?

5. Has the multiple-line trend been recent? Rapid? Continuous? Explain.

6. Are all insurers now multiple-line insurers? Why or why not?

7. What is the difference between multiple-line insurance and "package" policies? All-lines insurance? Multiple-peril contracts? All-risks policies?

8. What are the goals of multiple-line insurance for the insurers?

9. How have multiple-line insurers been formed? What legal problems exist? What other problems do multiple-line operations bring to an insurer?

10. Mr. Riskee has just been married and has purchased a new suburban home.

---

[33] Bernard L. Webb, "The Framework for Insurance Marketing Changes," *Journal of Risk and Insurance,* vol. 41, no. 2 (June 1974), p. 239.

Why would you recommend a homeowner's policy to him? What form would you suggest, and why?

11. What personal multiple-line insurance contracts were used before home-owners' policies? Why are they considered multiple line in nature?

12. Give a brief illustration of at least four kinds of liability exposures covered in the comprehensive personal liability section of the homeowner's policy, indicating for each whether or not tenants as well as property owners might incur such losses.

13. What implications might the multiple-line trend have for the "independent" and the "exclusive" agency systems of insurance marketing?

14. Some of the homeowners' policies use the "named-perils" approach in providing protection, while some use the "all-risks" approach. (a) Differentiate these two approaches, indicating the basic perils included in one homeowner's form which uses each approach. (b) State your recommendations, with reasons, for the homeowner's form and the limits of coverage to be used by a family owning a $50,000 home.

15. Why do you think the personal multiple-line contracts were developed on a large scale before the business contracts using the same technique?

16. What forms of business multiple-line policies existed before 1960? Where did they come from, and how could they be developed before the "full" multiple-line laws of the early 1950s?

17. What features characterize the popular special multiperil (SMP) contracts, including the new simplified SMP package policy, for businesses? How do these contracts compare with the new businessowners' policies (BOP)?

18. Explain (a) several factors which may hasten and (b) several factors which may slow down the all-lines insurance trend. What part of the development of all-lines *groups* is most evident now? All-lines *contracts?*

19. Divide the class into two groups: one to discuss the benefits which a well-established life insurer may achieve as a leader in the life insurance business only, the other to show why the life insurer should expand to all-lines insurance or even noninsurance financial enterprises.

20. If you were the president of a property-liability insurer, what would you suggest to your executive committee as methods by which your agency force could be encouraged to sell life insurance for a proposed life insurer affiliate?

21. What (a) advantages and (b) disadvantages does a financial services conglomerate have to offer in relation to each of the major functions of an insurer, that is, product development, underwriting and rating, marketing, claims payment, and miscellaneous activities?

22. What future do you predict in the 1980s for the financial services conglomerate? Carefully explain your reasoning and the factors involved.

Chapter 28

Concepts considered in Chapter 28—Government property and liability insurance

Government property and liability insurance, although not a new field of study, is nevertheless one of *increasing* scope and *changing* complexity.

General nature of the government's involvement is *more recent* and *less encompassing* than its involvement in the life and health insurance fields.

A new era for the 70s and beyond has evolved since the Housing and Urban Development Act, with the federal government helping to *maintain insurance availability* for some *high-risk perils and areas.*

Comparison with social insurance: many plans are *optional* rather than compulsory, thus not technically "social insurance."

An overview indicates the emphasis here on four recent programs.

FAIR plans in 28 states are now helping urban property owners obtain insurance against *riot and related perils.*

The problem is one of *serious civil disorders* since 1965.

The answer was *federal reinsurance of state* "fair access to insurance requirements" (FAIR) *plans* under the HUD department.

How the FAIR plans operate as insurer pools in the states is explained, with agents of private insurers servicing the business.

Flood insurance is now available under a *federally insured* plan, using agents of private insurers to sell and service the contract.

The problem was accentuated by mid-1960 uninsured flood losses.

National Flood Insurance Act of 1968 inaugurated the new plan.

Coverage limits and community qualification rules are set by HUD.

The result is much increased availability of limited flood coverage.

Impetus ahead is predicted in new rules for federal disaster relief.

1977-78 changes had the federal government assume the full flood insurance risk, and set higher available limits for covered properties (now more than 1 million policyholders for $43-billion coverage).

Crime insurance is the newest federally sponsored insurance program.

The concept is like that of the FAIR plans, but involves the federal government directly as an *insurer* in urban areas at "affordable" rates.

The contracts are for both residential and commercial properties.

The results have been slow, and involve substantial problems.

The future of federal insurance and reinsurance plans raises questions and may include the proposed National Catastrophe Insurance Act.

U.S. overseas political risks are insured in a unique government-private plan, encouraging direct U.S. private investments abroad.

Government-required liability insurance is a growing area, especially with *compulsory automobile insurance* under no-fault laws.

Government property and liability insurance

Until the 1970s this chapter was not needed in a basic insurance text. Today it is, for billions of dollars of property and liability exposures in the United States are now protected by government systems of insurance and reinsurance for floods, riots, crime and other property and liability perils. This chapter parallels Chapter 15, Government Life and Health Insurance, in Part III, where the gigantic federal OASDHI program of social security, state workers' compensation,[1] and unemployment and nonoccupational disability income plans are discussed.

GENERAL NATURE

In property and liability insurance the emergence of government involvment in insurance has been more recent and less encompassing than in life and health insurance. Until the last decade only scattered examples of direct government insurance of property-liability perils are found. The emphasis was on selected losses, such as damage to property values by war, nuclear energy property and liability damages, credit losses on exports, crop insurance disasters, and savings account losses in bank and savings and loan association accounts. Most of the areas were those in which the risks were so large that unless government provided the insurance system, the private insurance business could not do so, or at least had not done so.

A new era for the '70s and beyond?

However, in the years following the Housing and Urban Development Act of 1968 there emerged a new era in which government became actively involved in providing reinsurance in order to maintain *existing* private insurance systems for high-risk urban properties against riot and crime perils. In addition, the government decided that the neglected problem of floods and water damage in beach areas needed insurance not being provided by most private

---

[1] Note that the work injury and sickness perils could be included in this chapter, as a supplement to Chapter 22, Employers' Liability and Workers' Compensation. However, it is so closely related to the health peril, that it is logically included in Part III rather than Part IV.

insurance plans. Thus government insurance systems were inaugurated in these areas.

Comparison with social insurance

The student of insurance and risk should note than many of the government property and liability insurance plans have some similarities to the concept of *social insurance*, as developed in Chapter 2, but also differ in some essentials. Basically, the purpose is similar—helping to provide economic security against some specific perils for the well-being of large groups of persons in our society. In contrast to the life-health social insurance plans, however, the insurance developed in the property area oftentimes is *not compulsory* for the properties exposed to loss. (Nuclear energy liability already is, and automobile liability is becoming, an exception to this statement.) Social plans in life and health insurance are largely based upon laws which *require* that all eligible persons be a part of the program (OASDHI), or that employers *must* provide certain benefits (workers' and unemployment compensation, for example). The federal or state government taxing power over employers and employees is used to enforce the compulsory feature of these laws.

Upon analysis, most other government property insurance plans will be found to lack the compulsory nature which this text has included as a requisite for social insurance. Some plans may lack other characteristics which are important in describing social insurance, such as widespread application to meet reasonably universal problems of maintaining economic security in a society.

An overview

In describing the fields of insurance, Chapter 2 identified several insurance systems which were defined as "voluntary" government plans, where the government may provide the insurance but permits the coverage to be purchased on an optional basis. Included in this category are such programs as those of the Federal Crop Insurance Corporation, Federal Housing Administration insurance of mortgages, and title insurance under Torrens title laws in some states. The Federal Deposit Insurance Corporation and the Federal Savings and Loan Insurance Corporation, which insure deposits or shares up to $40,000 per account, are also sometimes[2] included in this classification of "voluntary" government insurance plans.

A few other plans might be included as government property-liability insurance. These include plans in some states and municipalities which have "self-insurance funds" for insuring government property against fire and other perils. Although some of these plans may qualify as true insurance systems, many lack some of the requirements for sound use of the insurance

---

[2] An exception should be made in the case of national and state banks which are required to carry this insurance and thus fall within our definition of social insurance.

technique. In connection with workers' compensation, many states have established a "second-injury fund" which encourages the hiring of handicapped workers. The employer is required to pay for a second disabling injury only to the extent that it separately causes loss of income and not for the combined results of both the first and second disability. The balance of payments comes from the state's second-injury fund.

Further details on all of these programs will not be included in this chapter. Several are mentioned elsewhere: foreign export credit insurance and state title insurance laws in Chapter 26, crop insurance in Appendix C, and nuclear energy property and liability insurance in Chapter 7. This chapter will concentrate on the *newer* federal *riot* and *crime* programs for urban properties, the *flood* insurance program of the Federal Insurance Administration, and on the *political risks* insurance program of the Overseas Private Investment Corporation (OPIC). A final section will look at the *future* potential for compulsory liability insurance (especially automobile) which could be classified as part of the government's increased interest in property-liability insurance.

FAIR PLANS

Fair Access to Insurance Requirements (FAIR) plans are now in operation in 28 states, the District of Columbia, and Puerto Rico, helping urban property owners to obtain riot and other insurance protection. In addition, property owners in high-risk areas along the Atlantic and Gulf Coasts in seven states have beach and windstorm plans available. Because the FAIR plans are so much larger, the following description concentrates on the FAIR plans for urban properties.

The problem

In response to the serious riots and civil disorders in many states during 1965–68, which caused restricted insurance availability in some urban areas, the federal government acted to bolster the private insurance business. The Urban Property Protection and Reinsurance Act of 1968 (Public Law 90–448) was the direct result of recommendations of the President's National Advisory Panel on Insurance in Riot-Affected Areas.[3]

The problem was severe. Civil disorders had caused losses of $38 million in 1965 (Watts and California), $68 million in 1967 (Newark, Detroit), $79 million in 1968 (in Washington, Baltimore, Chicago, and other locations following the assassination of Dr. Martin Luther King), and $31 million in 1969.[4] Others continued to occur in scattered locations in the 1970s. Many

---

[3] As part of the report of the National Advisory Commission on Civil Disorders, this commission's report was titled *Meeting the Insurance Crisis of Our Cities* (Washington, D.C.: U.S. Government Printing Office, 1968).

[4] *Insurance Facts* (New York: Insurance Information Institute, 1977), p. 43. The 1978 publication does not detail these losses, but does mention on page 46 the more recent riot losses of $28 million in July, 1977 in New York City.

homeowners and businesspersons in the urban areas of primary concern had increasing difficulty in obtaining proper riot insurance coverage in connection with their fire and extended coverage contracts.

The answer

The federal government's answer was to make available a new riot reinsurance program through a National Insurance Development Fund under the Department of Housing and Urban Development (HUD). Although all insurers are not required to purchase this reinsurance, the many hundreds of insurers that do must also participate in HUD-approved and state-supervised FAIR plans or voluntary pools which make basic property insurance more readily available in the high-risk urban areas.

A model plan has been developed by leading insurance associations to meet the HUD requirements for approval. This is called the Model Uniform Basic Property Insurance Inspection and Placement Program. It requires inspection procedures for homes and businesses, a plan for placing the business with insurers, and a joint reinsurance plan within each state for the participating insurers. Other states may use individually developed plans, but these, too, must meet the fundamental federal requirements.

This was not the first time the U.S. government acted as a reinsurer. In World War II (1942–47) the federal War Damage Insurance Corporation provided catastrophic loss coverage for U.S. properties, with private insurers sharing profits and losses up to $20 million. Nuclear energy property and liability insurance has been available since 1956 through private insurers and pools which now provide approximately $140 million in property coverage and $220 million in liability coverage. The Atomic Energy Commission guarantees further indemnity up to $560 million. The HUD plan was a major impetus for the further expansion of private insurer-federal resinsurer plans for riot and related perils. The motive of government in these plans was not to serve as the primary insurer of the perils, but to initiate action by private insurers in these fields by serving as the reinsurer.

The reinsurance plan involves several layers of payments in this order: (1) out of the individual insurer's retention and participation (up to 2.5 percent of the premiums written in the state), (2) out of the reinsurance premium held in the National Insurance Development fund for each state (the percentage of losses payable to the insurers varies from 90–98 percent, depending on the size of the losses incurred), (3) out of potential assessments against all insurers that purchase riot reinsurance in the state (up to 2 percent of all property premiums collected), (4) out of state backup layers (up to 5 percent of all property premiums paid), and (5) from the borrowing authority of HUD (up to $250 million for catastrophic losses).[5] The last item is a loan which must be

---

[5] John R. Lewis, "A Critical Review of the Federal Riot Reinsurance System," *Journal of Risk and Insurance*, vol. 38, no. 1 (March 1971), p. 32.

repaid from future reinsurance premiums charged the insurer. The premium rate charged to the insurer has varied from 1.25 percent on covered lines to 0.15 percent, following better-than-expected loss experience. The role of the federal government is clearly that of a backup for the private insurance system.

How the FAIR plans operate

Each state that has a FAIR plan has formed a pool or syndicate to make property insurance (principally riot, but also fire and allied lines[6] and theft insurance) available to property owners who cannot obtain coverage in the regular market. FAIR plan insurance is not intended to replace coverage normally available, but is for the purpose of providing "fair access to insurance" based on the physical characteristics of the property (rather than on rejection for its poor location). Agents of the insurers help the purchasers in making applications, obtaining the contracts, handling premiums, and filing claims as necessary. Insurers in each pool share in the losses and expenses of each plan in proportion to the property insurance premiums they write in the state. The insurers are required to reinsure losses for specified property insurance lines with the federal government plan.

The insured pays a standard rate unless the property insured fails to meet certain minimal requirements, as many properties do. The state plan sets the rates, and the states vary widely in the details of their rating plans. An application for coverage cannot be denied on the basis of location in a likely riot area or on the basis of other environmental hazards beyond the control of the property owner. When the property owner cannot obtain insurance in normal insurance markets, application is made through an agent for a free inspection of the property. If the property is acceptable under the usual underwriting requirements in regard to its structual condition (regardless of its location in an unacceptable neighborhood), a contract is issued. If the property requires structural improvements of a serious nature, the insurance may be denied until the changes are made. In many cases, the deficiencies will be less serious and the property found insurable, with a surcharge. The excess charges often run from 50 to 100 percent of the standard rates, under either the FAIR plan or other "schedule excess" plans used in many states.[7] The owner can remove these surcharges by making the necessary improvements.

Individual insurers are not required to write coverage without limit, but they notify the plan of the limits that they will accept on each class of business. The minimum amount of $5,000, but the FAIR plan facility may submit an appli-

---

[6] Vandalism and malicious mischief must also be offered, except in states where the normal market is adequate.

[7] Andrew F. Whitman and C. Arthur Williams, Jr., "FAIR Plan and Excess Rate Plan Rates in Minnesota," *Journal of Risk and Insurance,* vol. 38, no. 1 (March 1971), pp. 44–51. See also Michael L. Smith and C. Arthur Williams, Jr., "FAIR Plan Insureds: Occupancy and Location Characteristics and Experience," *Journal of Risk and Insurance,* vol. 42, no. 1 (March 1975), p. 156.

cation to not more than five insurers, so that the property owner can obtain at least $25,000 of insurance. Maximums also apply, with $100,000 on habitational property and $500,000 on commercial property at any one location (including contiguous buildings).

The results

Twenty-eight states have the FAIR plans, which by 1978 were issuing 902,000 contracts insuring property values in excess of $28 *billion*. In the early years after the inauguration of the HUD plan, these FAIR plans sustained losses of almost $83 million.[8] Only a few states have been able to make a profit on FAIR plan business to date. About two thirds of insured properties are commercial risks.

Special plans in operation in seven states offer *beach and windstorm coverage* along the Atlantic and Gulf Coast areas. The states are Alabama, Florida, Louisiana, Misissippi, North Carolina, and South Carolina, and Texas. (Louisiana and North Carolina also have the regular FAIR plan coverages for urban areas). More than 92,000 contracts were in force, with almost $3.5 billion of properties insured.

Although the adequacy and equity of FAIR plan rates have been criticized, the initial crude rating system has been modified to include some improvements; and in spite of the fumblings of a new program, "the FAIR plans have unquestionably provided a real service to the public."[9] Problems of "dumping" (by the insurers) of the poorest risks into the plans have occurred in some cases, but the lower commissions (usually 8–10 percent) allowable under the plans have encouraged agents to secure regular coverage in most cases where it is possible to do so. The use of FAIR plans by insureds varies greatly in the various states and cities in which these plans operate. Many states have less than 5 percent of the total fire and extended coverage premiums in the plans, while other may have more than 20 percent (Washington, D.C., for example).

The federal riot reinsurance program has been compared with commercial excess reinsurance, which also provides stability and catastrophe protection on an aggregate excess-of-loss basis (see Chapter 6); while the noteworthy differences include the federal riot insurance program's application on a state-by-state basis, its highly arbitrary rating system, its lack of a contractual commitment for future premium credits or refunds, and its general inflexibility.[10] The same author summarizes its implications, strengths (politically feasible and fiscally workable), and weaknesses (state-by-state application, the ultimate absorption by private insurers of a clearly social problem, the unwilling-

---

[8] *Insurance Facts,* p. 23.

[9] George K. Bernstein, "Critical Evaluation of FAIR Plans," *Journal of Risk and Insurance,* vol. 38, no. 2 (June 1971), p. 272.

[10] Lewis, "A Critical Review," p. 34.

ness of many states to expose general revenues to back up the FAIR plans, and vague definitions of the riots and losses covered). His conclusions stresses the open criticisms and high costs of the plans.

Although the total program offered substantial relief and stability for the private insurers during a very critical period, the long-range effects of the government's action on the urban property insurance market and private insurance business remain largely to be seen. By any measure, the FAIR plans are currently a significant factor in the insuring of urban property. One possible undesirable effect, pointed out by the Government Accounting Office in 1978, is that these plans may be creating incentives for arson where the property owners are not required to verify building values.

FLOOD INSURANCE

Another serious problem of insurance availability has surfaced in recent years. Until a decade ago, the flood peril for fixed-location property was usually considered to be "uninsurable" because of its catastrophic nature, high concentration or risk, and economic unfeasibility.

The problem

Sometimes associated with extensive hurricane losses, the many millions of uninsured losses by flood damages, such as those suffered in Alaska (1964) and in Hurricane Betsy (1965) and Beulah (1967), prompted action by the federal government in 1968. Fixed-property (real estate) owners, in particular were incapable of obtaining proper coverage except in Lloyd's markets at high rates and under many limitations.

The private insurers emphasized the difficulties of adverse selection, with the property owners in areas that were most likely to suffer sizable and frequent losses being the only applicants for flood insurance. In addition, the insurers stressed problems of equitable and marketable prices for the cost of coverage in such areas, as compared with other areas that had very infrequent but catastrophic losses. The result was that few persons had insurance available on a realistic basis, and many hardships were created by this uninsured peril. Government declarations of "disaster areas" following flood damage were primarily stopgap measures aimed at emergency aid and restoring properties with low, long-term loans after the losses had occurred. The use of general tax revenues to do this for the specific unfortunate property owners was questioned.

The National Flood Insurance Act of 1968

To alleviate the problem, the National Flood Insurance Act was passed to inaugurate a coordinated program of land-use and loss-prevention measures, with an attempt to make flood insurance coverage more widely available in the

United States. Before-the-loss funding was chosen as a much needed part of an insurance system to meet the flood peril.

Basically, the act set up a reinsurance program of the federal government in order to initiate action by private insurers at subsidized rates. A pool of about 100 insurers, the National Flood Insurers Association (NFIA), was formed in order to underwrite the coverage in selected areas which met the requirements of the Department of Housing and Urban Development. The insurers, through their regular agents, write the protection at rates and commissions (15 percent) set by the government in communities that have satisfied the program standards. The federal government subsidizes part of the cost of the insurance.

Coverage limits and community qualifications.   The limitations of coverage were extensive. In addition to being restricted only to communities which agreed to meet (over a period of years) extensive land-use and control requirements set up by HUD, the eligible dwelling and smaller business properties (with assets under $5 million) could obtain up to specified maximum limits of insurance. These limits were set at $17,500 per single-family dwellings, $5,000 on contents, and $30,000 on multiple-family dwellings, commercial, and nonprofit structures. A deductible of $200 or 2 percent of the insurance amount, if greater, applied. Rates varied from $0.25 to $0.45 per $100 of coverage. The limits were raised in 1974 by the Flood Disaster Protection Act of 1973. (See later section for current limits.)

HUD regulated the qualification procedure for communities that applied to participate in the program. The U.S. Corps of Engineers completed flood control and other studies of the area, and determined actuarial rates. (These requirements were mostly waived during an emergency period while the communities met qualification standards.)

Before flood insurance could be obtained in a community, the community must have applied to come under the program. Temporary approval was often obtained in a few weeks. The next step took the most time, as extensive delineation of flood-prone areas had to be conducted and could take up to three years or more for large communities. The implementation of the survey, which might cost up to $2,000–$3,000 per mile of stream or river surveyed, plus the numerous zoning and building code changes, took the flood insurance and flood control process out of the hands of the individual. Yet the individual could use the information that was available to determine whether a prospective property was exposed to the peril of flood and to see whether flood insurance was then advisable. Once the flood-prone areas were designated, the communty had six months to change their zoning and building codes in these areas. Building was prohibited unless special flood proofing was used in the construction of new buildings. Other areas were identified for open-space use, such as for parks or golf courses.

Contributing to the peril of flood resulting from rain, rivers, tidal waves, hurricanes, melting snow, and rising sewers, are the hazards of urbanization. Where forests and grasslands once stood, square miles of rooftops, streets, and parking lots quickly divert precipitation to storm sewers that are not designed to handle these sudden surges of large volumes of waters.

Considerable incentive was given to the participating insurers to begin the flood insurance program: The NFIA's share of losses was limited by a stop-loss reinsurance arrangement with HUD in which insurer losses in any one year could not exceed 125 percent of annual premiums; and HUD also agreed to reimburse the insurers for 90 percent of their losses during the emergency period prior to acceptable actuarial rate studies.

One insurer in each state was designated as the servicing company for flood insurance contracts. All agents sent applications to the insurer, which issued the policy and administered it for a small $15 service fee. The contract was a separate one, not an endorsement of existing fire and extended coverage policies. It covered flood and mudslide (a 1969 amendment) damage, including overflow of inland and tidal water or unusual and rapid accumulation or runoff of surface water in normally dry land areas. The backing up of sewers was not covered.

The coverage was not looked upon as a profit maker for either insurers or agents. Insurers normally offered their services largely for the public relations value of providing the coverage as a public service. Agents tended to accept applications, but were criticized for lack of promotion in regard to the availability of the protection. Exceptions to this were found, but it took several years before extensive efforts were made to publicize the flood insurance program in the individual states (such as were made in Ohio by the Ohio Insurance Institute). In fact, a $1 billion lawsuit was filed in Pennsylvania, claiming that the government and insurers failed to publicize the program widely enough before Hurricane Agnes caused extensive damage in 1972 floods in the Wilkes-Barre and Harrisburg areas.

The results.   For several years after the original act it was difficult to characterize the flood insurance program as even reasonably successful. By mid-1970, only 158 areas had qualified and only about 5,500 contracts had been issued, but the broadened provisions of the emergency program had begun to increase applications rapidly by the end of the year.[11]

Catastrophic and widely publicized flood damage in the Rapid City, South Dakota, area and much flood damage following Hurricane Agnes on the Eastern seaboard in 1972 sharply increased interest in the flood insurance program. During the next year the number of communities qualifying almost doubled, and the number of policies and the amount of the flood insurance more than doubled.

Flood insurance became available in every state under the program, ranging from 1 community in some states to more than 390 in Pennsylvania.

---

[11] Robert S. Felton, William K. Ghee, and John E. Stinton, "A Mid-1970 Report on the National Flood Insurance Program," *Journal of Risk and Insurance,* vol. 38 no. 1 (March 1971), p. 4.

Availability of coverage, even with federal subsidization of up to 50 percent or
more of actual estimated costs, was only part of the problem. Because of the
newness of the program and the unfamiliarity of consumers with the substantial benefits, may property owners exposed to flood losses did not act to purchase the coverage. An estimated 7,000 communities were in flood-prone
areas, yet only a third of these were eligible for the flood insurance program,
and in Hurricane Agnes less than 1 percent of $3 billion in damages was
covered by the federally subsidized insurance program.[12]

Impetus ahead? The Flood Disaster Protection Act, effective in 1974,
substantially increased the rather modest limits of coverage available under the
flood insurance program at the chargeable or subsidized rates. Much discussion also occurred in regard to achieving better "spread of risk" by including
more disaster-type perils, such as earthquake, landslide, and earth movement.
(See later section on the future.) The new statute also raised federal participation in the program from a $4 billion limit to $10 billion, and forbade federally
regulated banks and savings and loan associations to make property loans in
an identified flood hazard area, unless the property had minimum flood
insurance.

Another impetus to the program occurred in January 1974, when new rules
became effective in regard to eligibility for federal disaster relief. In areas
where federal flood insurance is available, unless property owners have purchased the insurance coverage within one year after its availability, their grants
and loans under the disaster relief program may be reduced by the amount of
flood insurance they could have purchased. The past extensive nature of these
benefits, such as long-term loans of 2 percent interest and "forgiveness"
clauses of $2,000 or more, has been pointed out by the federal insurance ad-
ministrator as a substantial reason why business leaders should encourage the
purchase of flood insurance. Why should taxpayers, including corporations,
pay for such benefits under the disaster relief programs, when flood insurance
is available to property owners to protect themselves against loss? He recommended much broader limits and eligibility under the flood insurance program
in order to reduce disaster relief costs, which were already taking an estimated
$1 billion of taxpayer money anyway.[13]

1977–1978 changes

After a year of problems and discussion, on January 1, 1978, HUD enacted
"Plan B" of the 1968 act, which *discontinued the participation of private insurers in accepting flood insurance risks.* The role of the insurers is now

[12] "A New Effort to Control Flood Loss," *Journal of American Insurance,* Winter
1972, p. 20.

[13] George K. Bernstein (remarks at the Risk and Insurance Management Society
annual meeting, Atlanta, Georgia, April 1973).

limited to serving as agents for the federal government, which now assumes the full insured amounts under the program instead of sharing the risk, as it did under the former partnership. The rates and commissions remain the same for agents of selected private insurers who sell and service the contracts. HUD has contracted with a private computer firm, EDS Federal Corporation, to act as the fiscal administrator under the Federal Insurance Administration.

In late 1977 *new insurance limits* were set. When a community first qualifies for the flood insurance program, emergency status permits insuring up to $35,000 coverage on a single-family dwelling at 25 cents per $100, and contents coverage up to $10,000 for 35 cents per $100. Multi-unit residences and small businesses are eligible for amounts of up to $100,000 on buildings and equal amounts on contents.

A second layer of coverage becomes available after HUD sets rates in an area: up to $185,000 on single-family dwellings, $250,000 on other residences and businesses, and $200,000 on other structures. Contents limits increase to $60,000 on all residential risks, $300,000 on businesses, and $200,00 on other risks.

More than 16,000 of 20,000 flood-prone communities in the United States now qualify for flood insurance. Insurance covers almost 1.2 million policyholders with $43 billion of property protection against floods.[14]

CRIME INSURANCE

The newest of the large federally sponsored insurance programs in cooperation with private insurers started in 1971 under the Housing and Urban Development Act of 1970. Paralleling the problems of riot insurance availability in many urban areas was the increasing difficulty of property owners in obtaining crime insurance coverage.

The concept

The program is similar in concept to the FAIR plans, but the coverage is different in that it has always been written *directly* by the *federal* insurance administrator rather than indirectly through reinsurance. The FIA has the authority to write such insurance in any state in which there is a "critical" shortage of crime insurance coverage at "affordable" rates. These rates are determined by the Federal Bureau of Investigation (FBI) and census studies, in which an affordable rate is one that a reasonably prudent person should be willing to pay for coverage, on the basis of costs and benefits under the policy in his or her territory.

---

[14] *Insurance Facts,* 1978, p. 28–29. An excellent summary of the development of federal flood insurance to its current sizable proportions, is found in Samuel H. Weese and J. Wesley Ooms, "The National Flood Insurance Program—Did the Industry Drop Out?" *CPCU Journal,* vol. 31, no. 4 (December 1978), p. 186.

States are given the opportunity to establish pools or assigned-risk-type plans to provide the coverage, but if they fail to act within a certain time, then the federal government can offer the protection. The insurance is now written in about 22 states, using selected private insurers (Aetna Casualty, INA, and American Universal were early selections in some areas) as servicing agents.

The contracts

Both residential and commercial contracts are sold to eligible property owners. They must meet federal standards of loss-prevention efforts, including such things as dead bolt locks on doors and locks on all windows. The requirements for commercial properties are more extensive, and may include alarm systems for certain high-risk classes of business. Free inspections are offered to determine protective device requirements.

The property owner has no choice but to accept or reject rather inflexible contracts offered by the FIA. The residential policy is a package of burglary and robbery coverage, with a maximum of $10,000 insurance. Deductibles of $75 to $100 apply, or 5 percent of the gross amount of the loss, if greater. Annual premiums for the residential contract vary from $40 to $80 for $10,000 insurance depending on the location of the property in lowest, average, or highest crime areas. The commercial policy rates vary more, and deductibles of $50 to $200 or 5 percent of the gross loss amount, apply. Coverage can be purchased up to a maximum of $15,000, and the insured is permitted to buy burglary (merchandise, safe, etc.) and/or robbery (inside, outside, messenger, etc.) coverages. The cost varies from $40 to $120 annually.

The results

Although early predictions for the rapid growth of the federal crime insurance program were made, the progress to date has been quite slow. Less than 10,000 contracts were in force by 1973, and the number of states in which coverage was deemed necessary by the FIA was not expanding appreciably. By 1977, 33,000 policies were in force, 45 percent of them in New York City.[15]

Numerous problems in acceptability of the program and its contracts have been encountered. Some lack of enthusiasm on the part of agents in selling the coverage is connected with the federal standards for protective devices, which are somewhat stringent and often unclear. Commissions up to 16 percent are looked upon as too low by many agents, as this may mean only $5 for the sale of a low-premium policy. Reductions in rates, clarification of the stan-

---

[15] 'HUD Crime-Insurance Program Is Slated to Be Renewed on Hill despite Little Use," *Wall Street Journal,* March 15, 1977. Some additional growth is noted in *Insurance Facts,* 1978 (p. 30), with 41,000 policies in force for a total of $285 million coverage.

dards, and increased publicity about the availability of coverage in the high-risk crime areas may increase interest in the program during the future. As an additional impetus to the use of crime insurance under the existing FAIR plans, it has been suggested that the federal insurance administrator disqualify states for riot reinsurance if the states do not help make the federal crime insurance program work.[16] This may be unlikely, but it is not impossible, and increased momentum for the broadening of crime insurance coverages by the private insurers is therefore indicated.

In early 1978, efforts were being made by the FIA to experiment with new sales methods for crime policies. He sought to encourage sales by using consumer groups and community organizations in the inner city areas to obtain applications for a "finder's fee." Losses on the program continue to be high —following early losses of about $20 million.[17]

THE FUTURE OF FEDERAL PROPERTY INSURANCE AND REINSURANCE PLANS

Numerous questions are raised by such plans as the federal riot, flood, and crime insurance plans. Does availability in some areas, or for some types of property, discriminate against other areas and other types of property? Can inequities be avoided in the charges made to insureds, insurers, and taxpayers? What limits should be availabe per item of property (building or contents)? How far in total capacity can the private insurers, and the government, go? Can real advantages in terms of better loss prevention be achieved through the federal standards? For what other perils should similar programs be considered? Does government participation as *reinsurer* of only very large losses contradict its other roles as *insurer* of crime and flood coverages and Medicare? The future involvement of the federal government in the riot, flood, and crime insurance programs is likely to increase, if for no other reason than their substantial public and political appeal.

One example of the possible future direction of federal property insurance and reinsurance is legislation before Congress in the form of a National Program of Catastrophe Insurance (Senate Bill S.4111), first proposed in 1972. Under this bill, a *National Catastrophe Insurance Act* would set up a Catastrophe Insurance Corporation to hold reserves built up from a *mandatory* inclusion of catastrophe perils in all fire insurance contracts. The perils included would be flood, plus any other catastrophe peril as specified by the board of directors of the corporation after public hearings. It could include, but would not be limited to, such other perils as earthquake, wavewash, mudslide, war damage, subsidence, and atomic accident. Claims would be payable

---

[16] Ibid.

[17] Frederic M. DuBois, "Where Do We Go from Here with FAIR Plans?" *CPCU Annals,* vol. 24, no. 4 (December 1971), p. 360.

only if the president of the United States declared losses as occurring in a major disaster area. Insurance amounts, deductibles, and eligibility requirements would be flexible, based upon recommendations of the corporation.

One author, in reviewing this proposal, urges congressional action (as opposed to the state-by-state approaches now in use) to implement such an act immediately.[18] He cites the advantages of an insurance program, rather than disaster relief,[19] as: (1) rates reflecting private equity, with social adequacy; (2) loss-prevention incentives; (3) discouraging high-risk construction in high-risk areas; (4) avoiding bureaucratic relief programs; (5) greater stability for federal and state budget planning; and (6) systematic and certain loss payments as a matter of right rather than charity.

His recommendations for amendment to the bill include: (1) consideration of other methods of defining coverage areas rather than the president's declaration of a disaster area and (2) a loading on most property-liability premiums (except those now providing catastrophe peril coverage) up to a maximum of 10 percent rather than 5 percent. A proposal by the National Association of Insurance Commissioners for similar catastrophe insurance (based on a tax-deductible reserve held by insurers instead of a federal corporation) is said to be inadequate, as are other alternatives such as federal reinsurance, expansion of the state FAIR plans, and other voluntary approaches.

Another author stresses the difficulties of establishing a proper rating system for a broad catastrophe insurance system.[20] The outcome of these proposals remains very much in doubt in the late 1970s, although their political appeal is strong.

U.S. OVERSEAS POLITICAL RISKS INSURANCE

The *Overseas Private Investment Corporation* is an important and interesting combination of government and private insurance.

Purposes and growth

This program has the basic purpose of encouraging direct U.S. private investments abroad, primarily by making available investment guarantees against three types of political risks: *inconvertibility of foreign currency*; (2)

---

[18] Andrew F. Whitman, "Proposed National Catastrophe Insurance Legislation," *CPCU Annals,* vol. 27, no. 3 (September 1973), p. 88.

[19] Which is itself called a disaster. See "It's A Disaster," *Fortune,* April 10, 1978. Cited are the inadequate definition of what constitutes a disaster, complicated regulations of the Federal Disaster Assistance Administration to determine when "temporary" housing aid should stop, and the fact that 100,000 families in 1977 received about $885 million in disaster aid.

[20] Dan R. Anderson, "All Risks Rating within a Catastrophe Insurance System," *Journal of Risk and Insurance,* vol. 43, no. 4 (December 1976), p. 629.

expropriation, nationalization, or confiscation by a foreign government; and
(3) *war, revolution, or insurrection.*

OPIC was created under the Foreign Assistance Act of 1961 and its 1969 amendments. OPIC's 1977 *Annual Report* shows an expansion of annual gross revenues from $33 million in 1972 to $55 million by the beginning of 1978. OPIC's efforts to cover U.S. private investments are centered on insuring new investments in more than 80 eligible "less developed friendly countries and areas." OPIC also finances the investigation and development of projects of U.S. investors in those countries and areas by coordinating the work of its Washington staff with that of U.S. embassy officers overseas.

Primary emphasis has been placed upon the needs of small and medium-sized U.S. companies and banks, and a special effort has been made to encourage mineral exploration in less developed countries. In fiscal year 1977, of 89 insured projects about 40 percent were for projects of $500,000 or less and almost two thirds were for projects of $1 million or less.

Total OPIC insurance coverage of $750 million written (in the most recent 15 months) on investments of more than $330 million was approximately equally divided among inconvertibility, expropriation, and war risks. During the past four years, more than 500 projects insured by OPIC involved an estimated net foreign exchange gain of almost $4 billion, and 170,000 new jobs in 35 countries. Two thirds of the countries, primarily in Latin America and Asia, had less than $1,000 per capita gross national product.

Insurance and reinsurance pool

OPIC is required by statute to maintain its operations on a self-sustaining basis through insurance and reinsurance arrangements, with due regard to the principles of risk management. It does this by combining private insurance and U.S. government guarantees through a unique pool called the Overseas Investment Reinsurance Group. In 1978, 14 U.S. and foreign private insurers participated to the extent of more than 13 percent (the remainder being OPIC's participation) in pool limits of $40 million per country and $80 million annual aggregate limits. Other pool limits apply to individual projects, such as $2 million for inconvertibility and $10 million for expropriation. The insured usually retains the risk of loss of at least 10 percent. A separate Lloyd's reinsurance agreement covers OPIC for maximum limits of nearly $25 million per country and a $75 million worldwide aggregate.

The OPIC program is guaranteed by the full faith and credit of the United States. Individual projects result from agreements with the approval of the host foreign government. The form of investment includes not only conventional equity and term loans, but also assets contributing to long-term projects, licensing and technical assistance agreements, production-sharing agreements, and joint ventures. Many of the insurance coverages run for long periods, and equity investments can be insured for up to 20 years.

The definitions of the three optional perils insured are generally quite broad. *Currency inconvertibility* includes measures taken by exchange authorities, denying access to foreign exchange, and the passive failure of authorities to act on applications for foreign exchange within a specified period, such as 60 days. *Expropriation* is defined to include not only classic nationalization, but creeping expropriatory action lasting more than three months on institutional loans or more than a year on other losses. *War* risks are for war, revolution, or insurrection losses within the country in which the project is located, and a formal declaration of war is not necessary. Physical damage losses on covered property are insured, as is default on scheduled payments on debt contracts for periods of three to six months or longer.

Future development

Congressional renewals of OPIC's authority to operate the combined government-private insurance of these risks have sometimes been reluctant, but in 1978 the program was renewed through September 1981. The objection to OPIC stems from the allegation that domestic jobs are transferred overseas as a result of its activities, although OPIC denies this charge. The expansion of exports through OPIC-assisted projects, the improvement of U.S. access to mineral and energy resources, and the protection of competitive market positions abroad are held to improve the U.S. economy and employment position and to offset by far any such job losses in the United States. The gradual growth of private insurance involvement is still a goal, but the need for OPIC in insuring expansion in developing countries is generally recognized for the near future. (See also Chapter 29 for discussion of international insurance as an issue for U.S. insurers.)

GOVERNMENT-REQUIRED LIABILITY INSURANCE

To achieve social objectives, some kinds of liability insurance are required by government. These requirements guarantee payment from a negligent person to an injured, innocent accident victim. The most widely discussed type of *compulsory liability* insurance is *automobile* liability insurance. It is not discussed here because the coverage is far from universal yet. Only 3 states (Massachusetts, New York, and North Carolina) adopted such legislation before the trend accelerated in the 1970s with the advent of no-fault automobile insurance laws in 20 or more states, which typically have included compulsory coverage as part of their plans.[21] The remaining states still prefer

[21] Note that the compulsory feature under no-fault laws is automobile insurance *coverage* (on a no-fault basis), but that the compulsory provision applies to both the first-party (the insured) *and* his or her third-party liability to others, where applicable. Mention should also be made of another government insurance innovation, in Maryland, that started a state automobile insurance company for some insureds in that state in 1973.

to encourage an automobile driver or owner to purchase such insurance as a result of "financial responsibility" laws, which do not make the insurance mandatory at the time a car is registered for a license.

The advantages and disadvantages of these alternative solutions to the problem of the unpaid automobile accident victim are discussed in Chapter 23. Separate evaluation in this chapter is not necessary, but the increasing importance of this trend should be carefully noted in connection with the expaning role of governement in liability insurance.

In addition, some states require liability insurance for selected situations. The owners of public vehicles, such as buses and taxicabs, must often meet state requirements by purchasing automobile liability insurance with specified limits of coverage. Young drivers under 21 years of age or less are required to carry automobile liability insurance in some states. The Interstate Commerce Commission requires motor vehicle common carriers to purchase liability insurance with prescribed minimum limits. Milk distributors in some states are required to carry products liability coverage. Nuclear reactor operators must furnish millions of dollars of public liability insurance, and this has affected the development of nuclear power in our energy-short nation whenever such protection is unavailable.[22]

Many other examples may be found, even outside the liability insurance field. For example, bonds are often required in state statutes for such situations as public construction contracts and for certain state officials (such as treasurers). The federal government requires bonds for trustees of union funds and aliens. Court bonds are required by many courts in many legal procedures. All of these are illustrations of government-required insurance contracts, but the limited nature of their application to special situations tends to cause them not be be included in the discussion here of more broadly applicable government insurance plans for property and liability insurance.

Other proposals and laws for government insurance are increasingly frequent. In 1976, Congress passed a bill to insure foreign art exhibits in the United States for up to $50 million. Public interest has also encouraged the House to pass a bill (not yet law) to compensate crime victims for their medical expenses. Twenty-four states already have limited plans for such losses.[23]

In all, this chapter, as one of the first in textbooks to separately discuss the increasing role of government in property and liability insurance, should warn the student of a major new viewpoint to consider in evaluating property-liability insurance as discussed in Chapters 17–27. It is unlikely that the government role in these fields of insurance will diminish. All indications are that the federal and state government positions will grow in sponsoring, in-

---

[22] Dan R. Anderson, "The Price-Anderson Act: Its Importance in the Development of Nuclear Power," *Journal of Risk and Insurance,* vol. 30, no. 4 (December 1977), p. 253.

[23] "Measure to Compensate Victims of Crime Narrowly Clears House for the First Time," *Wall Street Journal,* October 3, 1977.

itiating, requiring, insuring, and reinsuring property-liability insurance of the future.

FOR REVIEW AND DISCUSSION

1. Compare and contrast the area of government property-liability insurance with that of government life-health insurance.
2. What has happened since 1968 to escalate the involvement of the federal government in property and liability insurance?
3. How does the usual government involvement in property-liability insurance differ from the definition of "social insurance" developed in the early part of this text?
4. Describe the *problem* of "fair access to insurance requirements," and the *answer* which the FAIR plans help to provide property owners.
5. Can everyone obtain insurance coverage for his or her property exposures under the state FAIR plans? Explain why or why not.
6. Who assumes the major risk under the federal riot reinsurance plans? Explain.
7. How do you evaluate the success of the FAIR plans and the federal reinsurance program for urban properties?
8. Why were floods considered "uninsurable" for many years? How has this situation changed?
9. The federal flood insurance program is described as one that combines both loss prevention and insurance protection. Explain.
10. To what extent has flood insurance been a successful new program for the government, insurers, and property owners? Should the future bring further success? Why?
11. In what respects is the federal crime insurance program different from those for riot and flood insurance?
12. What contradictions do you see in the four most recent and important areas of federal insurance involvement in the property-liability field?
13. How is government *liability* insurance involvement different from the major types of government property insurance?
14. Do you think a proposal such as the National Catastrophe Insurance Act, or a similar voluntary plan, is the solution to the hardships which disasters cause? Why or why not?
15. What do the expanding automobile no-fault laws have to do with the role of government in liability insurance?
16. Explain (*a*) the purpose of the Overseas Private Investment Corporation and (*b*) the types of political risks insurance that are available through it.
17. Are private insurers doing all they can to slow the need for government (especially federal) plans for insuring property and liability risks? Explain what they are doing and also what you think they should or should not do to help the current situation.

PART V

THE FUTURE OF INSURANCE

No business will have much future unless it looks frequently and carefully ahead. One of the most common characteristics of successful private enterprises is their emphasis on increasing their ability to predict the future. Innovation and research to anticipate rather than merely react to inevitable changes are hallmarks of strong growth industries. Insurance should be no exception—in fact, insurance is inherently based on uncertainties in regard to *future* economic losses.

Thus, understanding insurance must include more than looking at the past and present. IBM's motto "Think!" could be paraphrased as "Think *ahead!*" to emphasize the need for long-range planning for future years. Studying today's problems, trends, and issues in order to prepare for tomorrow's solutions is the focus of the final part of this text.

Chapter 29 discusses issues—divided into (1) consumer, (2) business, and (3) social viewpoints—that are likely to be major developments in the decade of the 1980s and beyond. It is not intended as a crystal ball in which to see the entire future of insurance and risk. Its purpose, instead, is to serve as a partial mirror in which to take another look at some fields that have been studied, and to relate *selected* topics to the future changes that seem to be indicated. The topics, which realistically can only be a small portion of a comprehensive treatment for all areas, have been chosen on the basis of (1) their *significance* and timeliness of the subject, (2) their potential *interest* to the student of insurance, and (3) their *expected value* in reviewing some concepts and introducing several other valuable ones. In essence, they are topics which the student of tomorrow is likely to see emphasized in *change*—which will always be essential to the success of any dynamic field.

Chapter 29

**Concepts considered in Chapter 29—Consumer,
business, and social issues**

Consumer, business, and social issues cover areas of interest and importance to insurance *students of the future.*
Consumer issues emphasize consumer needs and viewpoints on insurance:
    Consumerist trends show the significance and *increased role* of better educated and more vocal purchasers.
    Potential effects on insurance are *widespread,* as the "marketing concept" in an affluent society pays more attention to consumer behavior.
    Current examples include *hot lines* to insurers or state departments, *consumer guides* to insurance knowledge, more *readable homeowners' and auto contracts,* and better *cost comparison information in life insurance.*
Business issues are many; only a few of major importance are selected.
    Internationalism represents a crucial issue for insurance management.
        Growth of world business is seen *everywhere* in its global aspects.
        Rationale for world insurance involves *spread-of-risk* principles and the motivating factors of *policyholders, profits, power, prestige.*
        Dimensions of international insurance show the *predominance of U.S. and European* marketing, and *great disparity in development.*
        U.S. insurers in the world market have progressed from *reinsurance* and *associations* of insurers to direct insurance sales abroad.
    Marketing philosophies in property-liability insurance will change traditional "exclusive" and "independent" agency systems.
    Arson problems are a major and growing dilemma for property insurance.
    An insurance exchange in New York is an exciting new market.
    New types of insurance include *kidnap-ransom* and *legal-expense.*
Social issues are influencing the insurance environment greatly.
    The ethical pillars of insurance are vital to the future, with adaptation to "social responsibility" and changing personal and social attitudes.
    Government regulation crosses many areas of discussion, including:
        No-fault automobile laws, in chaotic development in many states.
        Environmental control laws, increasing many federal standards.
        Consumer Products Safety Act, bringing increasing difficulties.
        Pension reform legislation on "vesting" and funding under the Pension Reform Act has increased federal regulation of private pensions.
        Group property-liability insurance legislation is being formuated by the states in a competitive battle among different types of insurers.
        Property-liability insurance rating and profitability is a complex area.
        Other social issues are many, including national health insurance and many federal-state jurisdictional problems in regulation.

Consumer, business, and social issues

Future areas of change and concern often grow out of today's controversies or issues. In insurance such topics are multi-sided, and one of the tactics of a good teacher seeking to have students analyze an issue is to suggest that the topic under discussion be scrutinized from several viewpoints.

THREE MAJOR VIEWPOINTS

The changes occurring, and those possible or likely to take place, include at least three major viewpoints: the *consumer,* the *insurance business,* and *social* (*government*). Each of these groups may be subdivided into more specific viewpoints, such as personal or business consumers, insurers or agents as part of the business, and federal or state governments.

In effect, this technique is used as a framework for this entire text; for Part I emphasizes the consumer viewpoint in regard to risk and insurance; most of Part II treats the functional aspects of insurance from the business viewpoint; and Chapters 8, 15, and 28 concentrate on the viewpoint of government insurance regulation and systems. (Parts III and IV adopt a "line" approach to the study of specific types of insurance, partially including the perspective of all three viewpoints.)

For the sake of organization, these three viewpoints are used in this chapter in order to classify the topics discussed. However, it is important to recognize that few, if any, of the subjects are issues which affect only one viewpoint. The *primary* effect may be characterized as most important from one viewpoint, but invariably each of the issues—no matter how classified—may also be considerably influenced by (and have great effect on) the other viewpoints. It is the *combined* result of thinking through each of these issues from all sides that will help most in a proper understanding of the selected topics.

The issues are chosen from among hundreds of others that might have been singled out for discussion.[1] They are representative of the many issues which often cut across all lines of insurance and encompass all viewpoints. Some of these topics are mounting "problems," the answers to which are unclear, and may remain unclear for many years. All are issues, however, which are projected as significant for the future of insurance.

Predictions are dangerous, but they *do* have value. They become warnings to planners and guidelines for decision makers. Even at their worst, they serve in retrospect as amusing and useful examples of cloudy crystal-ball gazing. Another valuable purpose is that looking to the future forces human thinking away from the channels of everyday concern to encompass broader perspectives than would ever be achieved otherwise. The present is rarely satisfying by itself; it is in the future that improvements and ideals reside. Thus insurance *should* look to the future, despite the perils of prediction, in order to find the best potential for development.

CONSUMER ISSUES

The consumer viewpoint on insurance and risk, which in many respects has been underemphasized in many business subjects in the past, has been popularized as part of the general trend toward "consumerism." The needs and position of the consumer are receiving much greater attention than ever before.

Significance of insurance to consumers

For example, observers of the insurance business frequently and justifiably applaud the significance of insurance as an essential part of our democratic society. The logic and statistics of this point are persuasive, picturing multi-billion dollars of sales, assets, and investments[2] by insurance, which serves as the cornerstone of an expanding free world. Forgotten sometimes is the fact that these dollars come from families and businesses that want a foundation of security in a rapidly changing, and often insecure, environment.

The importance of insurance to our society *and* its citizens is well illustrated in a pamphlet published by the Ohio Insurance Institute.[3] Statistics are presented in the form of what would happen if insurance ceased to be available for just one month in the state. The results are illustrated with figures on lost

---

[1] Dr. Walter Diehl, general manager of Swiss Reinsurance Company, has said that "anyone attempting to comment on the future of insurance finds ... an embarrassing situation on account of the many possible aspects to the topic," *Sigma* (North American Reinsurance Corp., July 1978, p. 1). This author agrees, but embarrassment is more desirable than neglecting to attempt to choose and discuss pertinent factors in the future of insurance.

[2] For examples, see Chapter 2.

[3] "Insurance ... It Touches Your Life Every Day" (Ohio Insurance Institute, 1978).

taxes ($10 million); increased unemployment; unstarted buildings and business firms; reimbursed losses to homes, automobiles, and other property; foreclosed mortgages; unmade bank loans; financial hardship for families whose breadwinners died or were disabled; and various other cutbacks in what are today taken for granted as normal business activities.

The message is clear—insurance *is* significant, influencing almost every facet of our society. An important corollary is that, more so than ever before, insurance has become a business *profoundly* affected with a *public* interest. Its position and influence are such that, like it or not, this new dimension demands increasing attention from all those persons and organizations that are concerned with insurance in the era of consumerism. Today, the rising voice of the consumer in the economic and societal arena is heard loud and clear. With prosperity, consumers have achieved an unparalleled status in the decision making of the marketplace and in governmental activities.

Everywhere one sees the accent on "the collision of consumerism and business" which has been upsetting marketing organizations in recent years. For a decade or more, articles have stressed the uncomfortable dissatisfaction of the consumer who is rightfully looking for new values and who voices new-muscled complaints against (1) deceptive promotion, (2) hidden charges, (3) sloppy service, and (4) unsafe or impure products.[4] With persons such as Ralph Nader spearheading the attack, the consumer protection trend[5] has gained momentum. Anyone who believes that the trend will fade away should appraise the account of its origins, causes, and probable future[6]. It is probably less true to call consumerism "a new wave" than to recognize it as an old idea with a new name. Basically it means honesty, information, and fair play for the buyer; but it *is* here to stay—and with it the need for business to adjust to the new relationships created by the more powerful voice and actions of the consuming public.

Potential effects on insurance

Closely related to consumerism is a relatively new approach to solving some of the problems of marketing. Called the *marketing concept* in the textbooks, the idea is based upon the income revolution which has happened in most family budgets. The rise of all incomes, and particularly the incomes of persons in the middle-income group, permits many more expenditures for

[4] "The Consumer Revolt," *Time*, December 12, 1969, pp. 89–98. See also *Consumerism at the Crossroads*, a national opinion poll conducted for Sentry Insurance Companies by Louis Harris and Associates, August 1977.

[5] Consumer deception and the laws needed to control those who perpetrate it are strongly reviewed by Senator Warren G. Magnuson (with Jean Carper) in *The Dark Side of the Marketplace: The Plight of the American Consumer* (Englewood Cliffs, N.J.: Prentice-Hall, 1968).

[6] Frederick D. Sturdivant, *The Future of Consumerism in Retailing* (College of Administrative Science, The Ohio State University, Reprint Series, March, 1978), p. 99.

discretionary items than ever before. Instead of food, shelter, and clothing, consumers contemplate choices among automobiles, household appliances, travel and vacations, sports equipment, and many new luxuries of today's society.

The result is a tremendous strengthening of the role of the consumer, providing a new focus for marketing effort. In general the transition has been one from an emphasis on selling what a company had, to *producing* the goods and services that are needed and wanted by the consumer. This new era of consumer-oriented marketing is the sphere within which changes in the insurance business are occurring today.

The increased role of the consumer is readily apparent in the United States today; in Europe and elsewhere around the world, economic advances are rapidly providing the same basis for continued change and pressure in this direction.

Take a careful look at insurance consumers today. That's fundamentally what all the new "surveys of buying habits" and "consumer behavior studies" are trying to do. Life-styles are changing, and with the new emerging attitudes toward instant gratification, the family, religion, leisure, sex, work, and other values, the consumer must be studied in adapting marketing stategies to a new era.[7] Consumers today are more highly educated, have the advantage of "instant communication" via television and other media, and have access to many more markets than ever before. They are a part of our "affluent society," so they have more assets and more income with which to purchase protection for those assets. Even so, they are apt to be more cost conscious than in years past, because they *know* they now have a wider choice of insurers, agents, contracts, services, and costs. They understand the need for insurance better than ever before, but would still like to find the best way to keep costs down in our society of rising inflation and taxes. The "best" way also involves, in their thinking, the simplest and most convenient way to obtain the most adequate insurance coverage. The advantages they are searching for in their role of making choices as consumers are: (1) the lowest *cost*, (2) the broadest *coverage*, and (3) the most *convenient* method.

Insurers are caught up in the consumer revolt in a number of ways. One is in the increasing emphasis on the cost of insurance, repeatedly seen in the growing reluctance of regulators to grant price increases for certain types of insurance coverages. The power of the press and the increased interest of unions in such rate increases are also readily apparent. More complete and explicable answers must be found to satisfy legislators and the public on the true profits in the property-liability insurance field. (See later section on this as a "social issue.") Insurers must strive to develop and explain pricing systems for all forms of insurance to consumers.

---

[7] Roger Blackwell and Wayne Talarzyk, "Changing Lifestyles: Input for Adaptive Strategies," *Bulletin of Business Research* (Ohio State University), vol. 53, no. 1 (January 1978), p. 1.

Another effect of consumerism on insurance may be an accelerated adoption of the risk-management concept—a maxi-viewpoint of insurance *and* loss prevention *and* other alternatives for handling risk.[8]

Inherent in the consumerist society is the need for a much broader and more sophisticated look at the entire research efforts[9] of the insurance business. New developments in computers, systems analysis, sociology, and many other fields[10] are beginning to be applied with increasing frequency to insurance.

Current examples of the consumer trend

Typical of the desire for more information, and of the willingness of business and government to provide it, are the *consumer hot lines* installed by many insurers and state insurance departments. An example is the opening of an "Office of Consumer Information" by the Travelers Insurance Companies in the early 1970s. Most of the 70,000 inquiries during the first 2½ years of operation came through toll-free telephone calls. The answers were given, often following immediate checks with department heads, by volunteer and retired employees rehired to staff and new effort at consumer contact. Surprisingly, almost two thirds of the calls were from noncustomers of the insurer. More than 60 percent of the calls were made in order to get information, facts, and explanations. Less than 20 percent were made to complain, urge action, or berate the insurer. The mood of the caller was characterized as "friendly" in more than 40 percent of the calls; 17 percent of the callers were "frustrated"; and less than one fourth were "hostile" or "had been offended." In follow-up research, more than 80 percent of the callers were found to be very satisfied with the first contact made in response to their inquiries. The questions that were most frequently asked centered on automobile rates, no-fault plans, and cancellations; readability of contracts; how to cut insurance costs; homeowner's contract value increases with inflation; rapidity of claims payment; differences among basic life insurance contracts; and health insurance and Medicare.[11] A similar hot line system installed a

---

[8] For examples, see James H. Killian, "The Insurance Role in Product Safety," *Journal of Insurance,* vol. 34, no. 6 (November–December 1973), p. 7; and Mary Finnell, "Should Safety Management Be Included in the Risk Management Function?" *Risk Management,* April 1978, p. 38.

[9] Examples include *Monitoring Attitudes of the Public* (New York: Institute of Life Insurance, 1975); and *Youth 1976: Attitudes of Young Americans* (New York: American Council of Life Insurance, 1976).

[10] Illustrative of such work are John Scanzoni, *Family Production Consumption, and Interpersonal Behavior,* Occasional Paper Series No. 2 (Bryn Mawr, Pa.: McCahan Foundation, July 1969); and James S. Burkhart, "Computer Underwriting," *CPCU Annals,* vol. 30, no. 1 (March 1977), p. 69.

[11] From correspondence with the Office of Consumer Information, Travelers Insurance Companies; and *Answers to Questions People Have Been Asking Us about Insurance* (Hartford, Conn.: Travelers Insurance Companies, 1973).

decade ago in handle emergency claims reports had received its one *millionth* call by 1979.

Ohio, Kansas, and other states have had similar experience with hot lines installed in their state insurance department offices. Inquiries have been encouraged by publicity in regard to this service. The highest percentage of calls (about 40 percent) concern auto insurance, and life and health each prompt about 20 percent of the calls.

Another example of worthwhile attempts by the state insurance departments to improve understanding is the publication of pamphlets concerning topics of interest and importance to the insurance consumer. The Pennsylvania department published a series of *shopper's guides* on topics ranging from hospital and surgery charges to comparative life and auto insurance costs to checklists on how to pick a good agent and insurer. Other states have printed booklets emphasizing contract coverages rather than costs.[12] The NAIC also approved a buyer's guide and policy *cost* summary for life insurance in 1977 which has been adopted by many insurers and is now required in 21 states. Although criticized as incomplete and unfair by some insurers, the information given to the public is generally commendable for having improved consumer education about insurance.

A broader look at consumerism might reflect on the responses which have come from the insurance business in meeting consumer needs during the past 20 years. One author emphasizes the contract changes, from the old "pick and choose" system of separate and limited property liability policies to the new era of broad, easy-package homeowners' contracts at lower prices, the refined automobile insurance rating system with its greater equity, and comprehensive liability contracts and high-limit umbrella liability policies.[13]

Also important to mention are the FAIR plans (see Chapter 28), expanding products liability insurance, mass merchandising plans through employers and associations, a $2 billion urban investment program in blighted areas of large cities by life insurers,[14] and the new "readable" homeowners' and auto insurance contracts discussed in previous chapters. In Chapter 10 the very current consumer topic of price disclosure in life insurance was explored, showing how policyholders have more "interest-adjusted" cost comparisons available than ever before.

Government has also responded with many consumer affairs bureaus and commission and study groups on both federal and state levels. Legislation of considerable importance to the consumer has been passed: the Occupational Safety and Health Act of 1970 (with more stringent rules for job safety, and

---

[12] Such as, for example, three booklets titled *Consumer Guides* on life, health, and auto insurance published by Ohio.

[13] John J. Savage, "Challenge and Consumerism: Response," *Journal of Insurance,* vol. 33, no. 1 (January–February 1972), p. 18.

[14] Life insurers now publish a regular report on their social investments, community projects, equal employment opportunities, company contributions, environmental concerns, and other activities. See *Response* (Washington, D.C.: Clearinghouse on Corporate Social Responsibility), and their annual report titled *Social Report.*

federal compliance officers to investigate employee complaints and work conditions); the Consumer Products Safety Act of 1972; and the riot, crime, and flood insurance initiated by the Housing and Urban Development acts. These actions have had and will continue to have far-reaching effects on consumers and on the insurance business.

BUSINESS ISSUES

The issues presented in this section are merely samples of the problem (and opportunity!) areas of insurance which directly affect the conduct of the insurance business. The international trend is emphasized because it will probably increase greatly in the future and therefore should be of particular interest to any student of insurance. Marketing philosophies, arson problems, an insurance exchange, and unusual new types of insurance are also mentioned.

Internationalism

More than a quarter of a century ago one of the most courageous and bestselling books of the modern era proclaimed that "our thinking in the future must be world-wide."[15] Few indeed are the topics or issues today which can be discussed merely on a national scale; the ramifications beyond national boundaries are too frequent and too important to omit. The broader aspects of international activities are crucial to today's work marketplace. Truly, it has been a "shrinking world" when in only two decades the time required for a trip across the Atlantic has decreased 65 percent, international mail has increased 120 percent, student exchange programs are up 240 percent, and overseas telephone calls have skyrocketed more than 3,000 percent![16] Increased communication continues this trend every year.

Growth of world business.   Everywhere one sees evidence of interest and activity in the global aspects of business—in new products for import and export, in new international organizations, firms, and departments. The revival of some foreign languages, the vast increases in foreign travel and contacts, and the new curricula developed in the colleges for international business studies are further examples of forces combining to make the "foreign" world not as foreign as it used to be.

International business (and particularly insurance) has aroused a degree of interest and achieved a potential which can reasonably be compared to the day in the 1400s when Columbus piqued the imagination of Queen Isabella and opened the doors of the New World, or the day in the 1800s U.S. envoy Townsend Harris negotiated the opening of doors for trade with

---

[15] Wendell L. Willkie, *One World* (New York: Simon & Schuster, 1943), p. 2. See also Edward Bates, "Impacts of Current Socio-Economic Forces," *International Insurance Seminars: Reports and Studies,* August 1977.

[16] It's a Shrinking World," *U.S. News & World Report,* June 11, 1973, p. 98.

Japan. With world trade at record levels, and U.S. investments abroad growing with foreign investment in the United States, the interrelationships of
world business are readily apparent. The insurance program of the Overseas
Private Investment Corporation (OPIC), discussed in Chapter 28, is an
example. The reopening of trade with Communist China in 1979 is another.

The Parker Pen Company 50 years ago advertised that its pen "wrote in
every language." Now look at any issue of *Time, Business Week, Fortune,*
or similar publications, and count the companies which feature their international marketing prowess! In the current generation the pace of international business has quickened until it permeates almost every aspect of modern
life. Gen Hirose, president of the Nippon Life Insurance Company, has
claimed that the *economic* basis of world friendship is making more progress
than the political basis, and international insurance may well be one of the
leaders in this trend.[17]

Rationale for world insurance.   "Thinking big," in a geographic sense, is
as valuable in insurance as in general business. The advantages of surveying
the world[18] insurance scene are many. The principle of free trade advocated
long ago by Adam Smith and other economists has an important application
in insurance, which involves a basic need for diversification and spread of risk.
What else motivates insurance companies to operate outside their home
country? These factors have been mentioned:

1. *Service* to U.S. clients now operating overseas in foreign markets, one of
   the earliest and most important reasons, as U.S. businesses (and their
   properties and people) need insurance protection in foreign countries.
2. *Profits,* with high potential in expanding economies.
3. *Competition,* an impetus for insurers to keep up with existing competitive developments.
4. *Magic and intrigue* of foreign operations, a generalized psychological
   motivation for such expansion.
5. *Communication and statistical information* improvements, which make
   possible the understanding and evaluation of foreign markets on a sounder
   basis than ever before.
6. *Prestige and public relations,* other important qualitative factors.[19]

A realignment of these motivating factors may summarize the goals of
foreign operations:

---

[17] At the International Insurance Seminar, Tokyo, Japan, 1970. The concept has been
repeatedly expressed at similar seminars held from 1972–79 in Mexico, Spain, Norway,
and the Philippines.

[18] In fact, one might argue that insurance, with the insuring of U.S. astronauts in
their trip to the moon, has already gone "out of this world." Losses have, too, as the
largest claim ever ($30 million) for a space test satellite explosion was paid in 1977.

[19] Mention should also be made of at least one deterrent to a truly international
community—nationalism, which sometimes needlessly restricts business with foreign
companies. See Edwin W. McCrae, "The International Business Environment," (Ohio
State University) *Bulletin of Business Research,* vol. 52, no. 4 (April 1977), p. 1.

1. *Policyholders.* The objective is more clients, retention of existing business relationships, and better-satisfied customers. Protecting or expanding markets is the description of this process.

2. *Profits.* This goal is a logical one for any private enterprise economy. It may take the form of *higher* immediate profits (short-run), higher long-run profits, or—separately or in combination with these goals—the desire for greater *stability* of profits through diversification and spread of risk among different countries.

3. *Power.* The objectives of growth, in terms of policyholders, contracts, or assets, may sometimes be for its own sake, rather than a method by which to achieve profits.

4. *Prestige.* This term may be used to describe the desire to improve a public image for the company or its executives. It can also be a legitimate and valuable tool by which the previous goals can be reached.

The four "p's"—policyholders, profits, power, and prestige—are an artificial but quite complete method of reviewing the goals and advantages of foreign market operations. Even though only hundreds of the many thousands of businesses and insurers now operate on a truly international scale, the stake is big and growing bigger.

Dimensions of international insurance. To appreciate the dimensions of international insurance, one should first look at the "big picture," the panorama of how insurance looks in the whole world. By continent, the contrasts in the importance of insurance are revealing. In Table 29–1, North America (with the United States accounting for about 90 percent of these totals) emerges as predominant. With a little less than 10 percent of the world population, North America has more than one half of world insurance sales (premiums). If Europe and North America are combined, the figures total 25 percent of the population and more than 80 percent of the insurance volume! The potential for expansion of the world insurance markets is startlingly obvious.

The growth of insurance outside North America is also evident in Table 29–1. In only a decade, the share of other continents in the total world premium volume grew from one third to almost one half. Insurance premiums grew more than sixfold in Asia, and more than fourfold in Latin America. In Europe, Africa, and Australasia, premiums more than tripled. Japan's remarkable progress from less than $3 billion in premiums to more than $20 billion accounted for 90 percent of Asia's rapid growth. In Europe the nine countries of the Common Market were a significant factor, premiums increasing from $18 to $65 billion with the considerable help of the harmonization of regulation and the reduction of legal restrictions within the Common Market's free trade area.[20]

---

[20] Werner Pfenningstorf, "The European Common Market for Insurance," *Risk Management,* October 1976, p. 22.

**Table 29-1. Growth of free world private insurance in terms of premiums (sales)
and in percent of totals, 1965 and 1975**

Continent*	1965 premiums† Billions of U.S. dollars	Percent	1975 premiums† Billions of U.S. dollars	Percent
North America	$46.1	66%	$113.4	53%
Europe	17.9	25	65.0	31
Asia	3.6	5	23.2	11
Australasia	1.3	2	4.6	2
Latin America	0.8	1	3.6	2
Africa	0.7	1	2.2	1
Totals	$70.4	100%	$212.0	100%

* Excludes the Eastern-bloc countries, for which figures are not available.
† Excludes social insurance premiums or taxes.
Source: *Sigma* (North American Reinsurance Corp., May 1977, pp. 3–4.

The world's largest insurance countries in terms of premium volume are the United States, with almost 50 percent of the total; Japan (almost 10 percent); West Germany (9 percent); France and Great Britain (5 percent each); Canada (4 percent); the Netherlands, Italy, and Australia (about 2 percent each); and Switzerland, Belgium, and Spain (about 1 percent each).[21]

The free world insurance market, not including the social insurance systems, totaled $212 billion in premiums during 1975, up from $70 billion in 1965. The U.S. part of this total was $108 billion, or approximately 50 percent, representing 7 percent of the nation's gross national product. More than a dozen other countries have a ratio of private insurance premiums to gross national product of 4 percent or higher. Such progress is not universal, however, as is shown in the per capita insurance premium figures, which exceed $490 per year in the United States but are less than $12 in such countries as Brazil, Mexico, and India. Another contrast shows the United States with $2.5 trillion of life insurance values in force, but only a few countries, such as Canada, the United States, New Zealand, Sweden, Japan, Australia, the Netherlands, and the United Kingdom, with life insurance nearly equal to or greater than one year's national income.[22] The conclusions are: (1) insurance is a big world business; (2) the United States is particularly important, and (3) there is great disparity in the development of insurance among individual areas and nations of the world.

The basic tenet of insurance—spread or diversification of risk—underscores the ideas that world business is dependent upon insurance, and that insurance is dependent upon the existence of an international market. That

[21] *Sigma* (North American Reinsurance Corp.), May 1978, p. 6.

[22] *Life Insurance Fact Book* (Washington, D.C.: American Council of Life Insurance, 1978), p. 104.

insurance is dependent upon an international market is illustrated by many points. Of particular significance is the mechanism of reinsurance, by which insurers spread their risks throughout the world. For many concentrated, high-value properties, such as ships, airplanes, refineries, and dams, and for certain perils with catastrophic potential, such as hurricane, flood, earthquake, and aviation crashes, the majority of insurance contracts just could not be written without the world reinsurance market capacity. Would you as an insurance company president want to take on, alone, a $200 million exposure for the damage and injury one 747 airplane could cause? Or a $100 million dam or utility exposure? Or a $50 million building?

In summary, it is probably true that more than one third of all the insurance written in the world is dependent upon the ability of insurers to write insurance or reinsurance outside their own country.

U.S. insurers in the world market. Insurers are meeting the challenge of international insurance needs in several ways. One method is by the established *reinsurance* market, which has for many years solved the bulk of problems in making insurance a global product. Some 70 U.S. insurers have entered the reinsurance market in the past 20 years, many on an international basis. Another way is through the use of *associations* in insurers, such as the American Foreign Insurance Association (AFIA) and the American International Underwriters (AIU), which have been active for more than 40 years. A third method, popular with U.S. insurers since the 1960s (an exception is the Insurance Company of North America, which earlier established direct branches of its company) is the *direct purchase or start of a foreign subsidiary insurer,* or *an international joint venture*[23] or *cooperative agreement* between foreign and U.S. insurers. Among these are: Aetna Life and Casualty (Assicurazioni Generali), Travelers (Guardian and Riunione Adriatica), Lincoln National Life (Union), Continental of New York (Phoenix), Occidental (Heiwa Life), Continental-National-American (Winterthur), and Nationwide (Neckura). Also operating overseas are the Atlantic Companies, Combined Group, Hartford Companies, Kemper Group, Globe, and others.[24]

Each year U.S. insurers operating abroad write more than $400 million in property-liability insurance and more than $100 million in life insurance premiums.[25] Their corporate structure, investment and reserve position, and marketing methods are oftentimes different abroad than in the United States,

---

[23] John D. Hogan, "Innovations in Insurance Marketing: The International Joint-Venture" (paper presented at the American Risk and Insurance Association annual meeting, Miami, Florida, August 1973).

[24] Henry G. Parker III, "The Global Scene: Operations and Opportunities Overseas," *Journal of Insurance,* vol. 34, no. 2 (March–April 1973), p. 24.

[25] *Position Paper on International Insurance and Reinsurance* (Washington, D.C.: Chamber of Commerce of the United States, 1972), p. 11. Other estimates, including reinsurance, are more than $750 million for 40 U.S. companies (see Parker, "The Global Scene," p. 24), with predictions for 1980 at $3 billion (p. 28).

but the conclusion is strong that "insurance is bound to become more and more international in character."[26]

International insurance, in addition to its consumer and social effects in various countries, also has a direct economic effect on the balance of payments. For example, U.S. insurers have traditionally purchased more insurance (particularly reinsurance) abroad than they have sold in foreign markets, while other countries (notably the United Kingdom and Switzerland) have sold more than they have bought. Losses paid under such contracts also affect the net inflow or outflow of capital.

Marketing philosophies in property-liability insurance

The continued competition between "exclusive" agency insurers and "independent" agency insurers (see Chapter 5) is not only expected in the future of property-liability insurance, but is probably a healthy situation for the consumer. The leading exclusive agency companies, such as State Farm, Allstate, and Nationwide, have made remarkable progress in competing with other well-established insurers. From the mid-1940s to the mid-1970s they increased their market share from about 5 percent to 26 percent.[27] Most of the progress has come in the automobile and personal-lines coverages, while independent agents continue to predominate in the commercial-lines area. The reasons are many, but the older distinctions between these marketing systems are changing with the increased use of direct billing, brokerage agreements with many insurers, and such other developments as mass merchandising plans (see later section of this chapter). Whether or not the systems will merge, the best qualities of both systems will be one of the interesting trends of the 1980s to watch.

Arson problems

One of the perplexing problems of property insurance during the last decade has been the rise of *arson,* the deliberate setting of fires for fraudulent purposes such as collecting insurance, which seems to have reached almost epidemic proportions. The National Fire Protection Association estimates that more than one third of all fires of unknown origin are related to arson and that more than $2 billion of property values are destroyed each year by this crime.[28] Buildings and their contents, and automobiles, are common targets.

---

[26] Michael J. Faulkner, "The Techniques and Problems of Multinational Insurance Operations," *CPCU Annals,* vol. 26, no. 3 (September 1973), p. 87.

[27] Bernard L. Webb, "The Framework for Insurance Marketing Changes" *Journal of Risk and Insurance,* vol. 41, no. 2 (June 1974), p. 239.

[28] "Target: Arson," *Journal of American Insurance,* vol. 53, no. 4 (Winter 1977–78), p. 12.

Although the immediate effect of arson falls on the insurers that suffer increased losses, there are also many indirect effects—displaced tenants, uninsured losses, increased claims expenses, lost lives and injuries, business insolvencies and increased unemployment, the straining of fire department facilities and risks to fire-fighting personnel, and many others. The results have been depicted in television reports, books,[29] and articles as disastrous for many of the persons involved.

Thus far the battle against arson has been relatively ineffective, and major new efforts and changes seem needed for the 1980s. In spite of high costs, possible liability suits for alleged arson, and the difficulty of legally proving arson, insurers must intensify their investigations and their resistance to paying suspected arson losses. Research indicates that insurers should (1) pay more attention to the financial position of the insured in the underwriting process, (2) use more scientific investigative techniques, and (3) support legislation to reclassify the seriousness of arson as a crime.[30] Rewards for arson information leading to conviction have been offered by some insurers, but it remains difficult to prove intent in arson cases and the penalties remain relatively light in most states.

The need is for *combined* efforts by government officials in combating the crime of arson, insurer cooperation in the investigations, and even consumer help through vigilante organizations and a better understanding of the severe impact of arson losses. Some cities, such as Boston and Cleveland have mobilized various interests in attempts to reduce widespread arson, but in many areas little is being done. In 1978 Senator John Glenn introduced legislation to reclassify arson as a Part I crime, requiring reports to the FBI (rather than relying on voluntary reports), and earmarking more than a million dollars for arson research. Other national efforts have included a model arson penal code proposed by insurer groups for adoption in the states and the levying of severe penalties for many arson cases which cause or threaten death or injury to firefighters or other persons. A number of states[31] have also already passed model reporting-immunity laws, protecting insurers against any potential liability arising from giving information on suspected arson to authorities.

The recommendations of experts[32] for solutions to the arson problem include a task force approach to fix responsibility for arson control, overcoming

---

[29] John Barracato and Peter Michelmore, *Arson!* (New York: W. W. Norton and Co., 1976).

[30] Robert A. Hershbarger and Ronald K. Miller, "The Impact of Economic Conditions on the Incidence of Arson," *Journal of Risk and Insurance,* vol. 45, no. 2 (June 1978), p. 275.

[31] Connecticut, Georgia, Illinois, New York, North Carolina, Ohio, and Texas. "Target: Arson," p. 15. Also see "Arson Lab Fights Fire With Facts", *Journal of American Insurance,* vol. 54, no. 1 (Spring 1978), p. 9.

[32] From a series of seminars held at Battelle Memorial Institute, Columbus, Ohio, in 1976.

apathy by a better public information program, improved training for arson investigators, national reporting of data, and stricter and more uniform state arson laws. Failure to heed such advice would be foolish indeed.

An insurance exchange

An exciting new proposal for an *insurance exchange* in the United States, similar to the underwriting syndicate marketplace of Lloyd's of London, appeared in 1978. The concept was approved for implementation in New York after April 1979, following submission of a constitution and bylaws to the state legislature.[33] Included in the proposal was another plan to have a "free trade zone" in New York for specially licensed insurers to write specified high-premium ($100,000 or more), unusual, and high-risk types of insurance without prior regulatory approval of rates and forms. Individuals who met certain means tests of experience, knowledge, and minimum investment (probably $100,000 or more) would be licensed as brokers for syndicate groups whose members would have limited liability as insurers. Required reinsurance would guarantee a syndicate's obligations under the insurance contracts that it issued. It was proposed that 20 such syndicates be established, with a total initial capacity for insuring up to $200 million. As a new and different insurance market, providing an entity such as the stock exchanges now provide for the securities business, the insurance exchange may create many new challenges for insurance in the United States.

New types of insurance

Did you ever hear of "antimonster insurance"? Believe is or not, that's one of the recent kinds of insurance developed for any attack against swimmers who compete in races in Scotland's Loch Ness. Such specialized innovations continue to appear every year in the insurance field, but of greater importance are newer insurance coverages that are developed for much broader use in many directions. The new and different ideas in insurance are limited only by the insurer's imagination, some legal regulations, and consumer acceptance.

Many new coverages for changing risk exposures have become available in the past decade. One example is *skyjacking* insurance, paying airline travelers as much as $100 a day for delays caused by airplane hijackers. This insurance was popularized by the numerous skyjackings of the early 1970s, but the need for it has been substantially lessened by government requirements for baggage inspections and increased security at airports.

Problems of insolvency in the investment field created the need for a government-industry insurance plan to protect clients against the *failure of*

---

[33] "Insurance Exchange Is Born," *Business Insurance,* July 10, 1978, p. 1.

securities brokers. In the early 1970s the securities industry cooperated with the federal government to bolster public confidence by forming the Securities Investor Protection Corporation (SIPC), insuring customers up to $20,000 in cash or $50,000 in securities for losses caused by the insolvency of securities broker-dealers. SPIC does not protect customers against losses due to fluctuating security prices.[34]

With restrictions by auto manufacturers on new-car warranties, which decreased typical warranties from five years or 50,000 miles to one year or 12,000 miles, new insurance contracts are now available for *mechanical breakdown.* These contracts extend the warranty for parts and labor costs by three to five years at prices of $175 to $225 for new cars; such contracts are also available in most states on some used cars.[35]

Other examples illustrate the breadth and variety of new insurance contracts. *Dental* and *vision care* insurance were discussed in Chapter 14 as the major growth coverages in the health insurance field during the 1970s. *Variable and adjustable life insurance* contracts to meet inflation needs were explained in Chapter 10, and future developments in these coverages may create substantial markets for these innovative contracts in the 1980s.

Two types of insurance, not discussed previously in this text, are next presented as current examples of how insurers must adapt to the changing needs of insurance consumers.

Kidnap and ransom insurance. Large businesses have become an increasing target for kidnappings of company executives or members of their families. After the widely publicized Lindbergh case in the 1930s, Lloyd's of London wrote some *kidnap/ransom insurance* contracts for relatively modest amounts up to $100,000 (it reportedly paid $50,000 for the Lindbergh's baby). However, it was not until the 1970s that numerous kidnappings in South America began to escalate interest in such protection, and the largest single ransom payment was more than $14 million.[36] Italy has become infamous for crimes involving corporate or political hostages, crimes that culminated with the world-shocking murder in 1978 of the former Christian Democratic premier Aldo Moro.[37] The 1970 Venezuela kidnapping of William Niehous, vice president, Owens-Illinois Corporation, which remains unsolved to date, brought the potential exposure to U.S. firms sharply into focus.

---

[34] Harold C. Krogh, "The Securities Investor Protection Corporation: Financial Stringency in Securities Forms," *CPCU Annals,* vol. 30, no. 1 (March 1977), p. 78. The limits of coverage were doubled in 1977 amendments.

[35] "Insuring Cars against Breakdown," *Money,* July 1978, p. 50.

[36] "The Growing Spectre of Executive Kidnapping," *TWA Ambassador,* August 1976, p. 22. In 1970–73, 250 kidnapped executives were reported freed by ransom payments totaling millions of dollars.

[37] "Striking at Italy's Heart," *Newsweek,* March 27, 1978. In 1975, 62 kidnappings were reported in Italy; in 1976, 48; and in 1977, 76.

Ransom insurance is written primarily by only a few insurers in the United States,[38] and by Lloyd's of London. Some persons criticize writing it at all as against public policy (for encouraging such crimes), but most people recognize the legitimate need for protection against the potentially catastrophic losses that may result from kidnapping. The contracts normally written have several unusual features: (1) insureds first have to pay ransom from their own resources (to avoid being in a position to pay larger or quicker ransom demands); (2) notification to and cooperation with the police is required; (3) a policy condition requires secrecy about the existence of the insurance; and (4) a survey of security systems and guards is made, with appropriate discounts in insurance costs allowed.[39]

The ransom insurance policy is usually issued for worldwide coverage, although certain countries can be excluded. The name, size, type of industry, and number and geographic distribution of covered employees for a company are important in determining the premium cost, which varies from a few thousand dollars for $500,000 coverage to $30,000 or more for $5 million limits. Per occurrence and aggregate limits are normal, with 10 percent of losses up to some figure such as $25,000 or more retained by the insured.[40] Threats to kill or injure an insured (extortion) as well as actual kidnapping and ransom demands are covered in some but not all contracts. In all, this coverage is an unusual example of the response of insurers to the changing needs of business for catastrophic protection against a real exposure in a society that seems to be increasingly lawless.

Legal-expense insurance. A new and large market for prepaid legal services in group insurance plans for employees is emerging for development in the 1980s. An outgrowth of group life and health insurance as a fringe benefit through your place of employment, *group legal insurance* is becoming a popular coverage for middle-income Americans. Although group legal insurance was somewhat reluctantly supported by bar associations and insurers in the formative years of the early 1970s, its development has been spurred by two legal changes. The Taft-Hartley amendments of 1973 allowed legal services to be a part of union negotiations, and the Tax Reform Act of 1976 stated that neither employer contributions nor the value of group legal services were taxable income to employees.

Thus far most of the group insurance coverage for "legal health" services has resulted from collective bargaining agreements, with several thousand contracts now in existence covering a total of less than 3 million workers. (Recent examples of large groups adding such benefits are new plans in 1977 that covered 150,000 Chrysler Corporation employees and 85,000

---

[38] Such as American Home, Chubb and Son, Nation Union Fire, First State, and Stewart-Smith.

[39] Anthony A. Cassidy, "Lloyd's Kidnap-Ransom Insurance," *Risk Management,* September 1976, p. 6. Loss prevention techniques are emphasized in Marsh and McLellan's *Kidnap or Hostage Situations* (1978).

[40] Ibid.

New York State public employees.) However, the potential market is estimated at 70 million persons and annual premiums of $3 billion.[41] This large market is beginning to attract insurers, and many new plans are being approved by the insurance departments of various states. Credit unions, bar associations, and even Blue Cross associations[42] are sponsoring legal-expense insurance plans. College students are covered by about 200 plans, too.

One of the earlier articles on this subject optimistically called legal-expense insurance "an idea whose time has come."[43] Although growth of the plans has been slow in the early 1970s, the changing attitude of bar associations and the need for such plans to help in budgeting and paying for rising legal costs are seen as creating mounting pressure for more widespread availability.[44]

The legal-expense insurance plans vary considerably in several respects. Some are "closed panel" types, with the insured choosing among a panel of attorneys employed to provide specified legal services to a group. Others are "open panel" plans, permitting individuals to choose their own attorneys. In regard to the scope of the legal services covered, some plans are very limited and others are comprehensive in nature, including preventive or consultative legal advice (wills, uncontested divorces, bankruptcies, etc.), defense in civil and criminal actions, and plaintiff actions in nontort situations not covered by other sources. The limits of coverage range from $500 to $5,000 a year, and the premiums range from $5 per month per insured to two or three times that amount.

One of the unanswered questions is whether these group insurance plans will lower legal costs, as is one of their prime objectives, or whether the existence of such insurance may create rising costs from the legal profession. The broader marketing possibilities, now that the Supreme Court has ruled that soliciting and advertising professional services is not prohibited by any bar association code of ethics, will be an important factor in determining the longer range costs of prepaid legal-expense insurance. The developments will be an interesting part of the insurance scene to watch in the decade ahead.

SOCIAL ISSUES

Fundamental issues pertinent to insurance have taken on an increasingly social outlook in recent years. The close relationship of insurance to the environment within which it operates is being examined more now than ever

[41] John S. Clayton, "Legal Insurance for the Middle Class," *Insurance Marketing,* October 1977, p. 10.

[42] "Insurance to Cover the Lawyer's Bill," *Business Week,* April 18, 1977, p. 46. Blue Cross of Western Pennsylvania has filed plans for marketing three plans, ranging from $60 to $140 per family cost for a year's coverage of $450 to $5,000 of various legal services.

[43] Lee R. Morris, "Prepaid Legal Service Insurance," *CPCU Annals,* vol. 26, no. 3 (September 1973), p. 98.

[44] Claude C. Lilly, *Legal Services for the Middle Market* (Cincinnati: National Underwriter Co., 1974).

before, and many of the answers for the future combine the efforts of the private insurance business with government legislation and insurance. Although some experts warn that the social insurance area is growing too fast in competition with the voluntary insurance system, most agree that the application of insurance techniques to individual, social, *and* combined individual-social problems will be of greater importance in the future than in the past.

The ethical pillars of insurance

One of the most revealing looks to the future has been taken by Dr. John Long of Indiana University.[45] In questioning the flexibility of insurance to meet expected changes in the environment, he analyzes the projected environment to the year 2000 to wonder whether or not insurance can thrive, or even exist, given the anticipated changes. Will the basic attitude toward achievement and acquisitiveness, for example, change so that the motivations to work will drastically affect the desire to earn and possess wealth (and insurance to protect such assets)?

The desires for a higher quality of working and leisure life[46] are already witnessed as undergoing much change. Will this affect insurance positively or adversely? The basic attitude toward the preservation of values and the distaste for waste are also examined in their relationship to insurance. Also, personal attitudes are rapidly changing; and with any decreases in apprehension for the future, in honesty, in obedience to laws, and in the desire to preserve stabilizing traditions of personal responsibility and charity, come fundamental changes in attitudes toward insurance.

The institution of insurance is seen as surrounded by these "pillars of strength," any one of which could drastically change the desire, need, and significance of future insurance systems. The ramifications of thoughtful consideration of such topics are sobering, if not frightening. The adaptability of insurance to meet whatever environmental changes occur should be one of the most important objectives of forward-thinking insurance management. Rarely and only partially can insurance change the environmental conditions under which it works. Most progress must occur by the insurance business adjusting in a responsive way, both before and as personal and social values change. Only in this manner can the industry remain healthy in our society of the future.

The era of increasing "social responsibility" is already upon the American business scene. Insurance companies will have to reshape their priorities in

---

[45] John D. Long, *Ethics, Morality, and Insurance: A Long-Range Outlook* (Bloomington: Bureau of Business Research, Indiana University, 1971). See also "The Ethical Pillars of Insurance," *CLU Journal,* vol. 26, no. 1 (January 1972), p. 61.

[46] *The Changing World of Work* (American Assembly, Columbia University, November 1973), p. 10.

order to accommodate many of the areas of social concern. For example, the tremendous life insurance investment departments will have to consider the pronounced effect of such popular causes as environmental pollution, racial equality, highway safety, and urban blight in their decisions.[47] They must balance the obligations for profit and stability which they hold to policy-holders and stockholders against increased responsibility to our society as a whole. This will be a challenging task and one which, if done poorly, could easily cause an adverse attitude of consumers toward the product of life insurance. In addition, life insurers must adapt to other economic and social trends, such as inflation, new family patterns, new income standards, and new consumer marketing habits (see Chapter 27 on all-lines insurance and financial conglomerates).

Government regulation

Another area of great concern for insurance is the legislative framework within which it operates. Anyone who believes that the future of insurance holds the prospect of diminishing legislative control of many phases of the business is thinking wishfully. The increasing quantity, variety, and extent of regulation have been clearly seen on the federal and state levels during recent years, and pending bills promise additional momentum for future legislation directed at insurance. The following are some examples of the kinds of issues at hand.

No-fault automobile laws. Chapter 23 shows the substantial impetus toward no-fault insurance which has been created by more than 20 states' no-fault plans by 1979. Although the issue has been treated by state laws thus far, the impending threat of a federal no-fault law is by no means merely idle conjecture. Congressional committees have only narrowly defeated federal proposals for minimum no-fault standards, and these proposals could obtain the necessary increase in support at any time. How rapidly most or all of the states act, and how well they act, in the 1980s will be determining factors, unless other legal, economic, or political factors intervene. The confusion of insurers, agents, and regulators on the many and varied no-fault plans has caused a chaotic situation for automobile insurance of the 1970s. Consumers are understandably confused, also, but in general the idea has gained accep-tance among them, even if that acceptance is based upon sketchy knowledge of the real effects of the laws on their tort liability rights and their potential cost savings. The situation could perhaps best be stated by saying that "the issue is yet in doubt," but there is no doubt that the issue will be an active one for business and government during the 1980s.

---

[47] Kenneth M. Wright, "Social Concerns, Public Policy, and Life Insurance Invest-ments," *CLU Journal,* vol. 26, no. 1 (January 1972), p. 32; and William G. Pritchard, "Social Responsibility in the Marketplace," *CPCU Annals,* vol. 27, no. 1 (March 1974), p. 46. See also Footnote 14.

One important, unresolved issue is the extent to which, if the no-fault concept is universally applied in the automobile insurance area, the idea might be useful in other areas. No-fault divorce laws are already operable in some states, but what about extension of the concept to medical malpractice lawsuits and the even larger area of products liability claims?

Environmental control laws.   A seeming myriad of federal laws are extending controls to many parts of manufacturing and business activities that were previously regulated only by the states. Examples in the early 1970s include the Clean Air Act, the Water Pollution Act, the Pesticide Control Act, the Occupational Safety and Health Act (see Chapter 22), and the Noise Act. In the latter part of the decade the emphasis shifted to national energy bills, including price and other controls which will be crucial factors in insurance developments of the 1980s. All of these laws have a great effect on the property and liability exposures of insureds, and thus are of direct concern to insurers and consumers.[48]

The Consumer Products Safety Act.   In a field burgeoning with problems of increasing multimillion-dollar lawsuits, products liability costs are now becoming a major factor in the pricing policies of many businesses. Insurers have difficulty in setting realistic insurance rates to cover the rapidly expanding products liability claims. The predictions are for even greater problems ahead. Although industry symposiums[49] and government bodies have frequently centered on the problems and proposals for reform in products liability, a consensus of the best solutions has not yet appeared.

The Consumer Products Safety Commission, which is a powerful new federal regulatory agency, requires notification by manufacturers, distributors, and retailers of any substantial product hazard of which they are aware. Failure to comply may result in civil penalties of up to $500,000 and one year in jail. The burden seems to have shifted from the consumer to the vendor; and this trend will have much effect on future liability lawsuits and insurance to cover the increasing liability caused by failures to meet the detailed requirements of the commission for design, management, record keeping, and other provisions (see also Chapter 22).

Pension reform legislation.   All during the 1970s there has been increasing concern about the major changes necessary in the control of pension plans. The classic case of a Studebaker plant in Indiana which closed with 4,000 workers receiving only about 15 percent of "vested" benefits was frequently cited as reason for the need for federal minimum standards. Vesting, which concerns the right of the employee to obtain contributions which the employer has made under pension plans, is a major issue. The Pension Reform

---

[48] Edward F. Seitzinger, "Federal Legislators Seek Premption of State Authority," *For the Defense* (Milwaukee: Defense Research Institute, vol. 14, no. 9 (November 1973), p. 110.

[49] For example, see most of the *CPCU Annals,* vol. 27, no. 1 (March 1974), pp. 5–43.

Act of 1974 (ERISA), discussed in Chapter 12, requires private pension plans to guarantee gradual nonforfeitable rights accumulating during the first 10 to 15 years of work to full rights to these proceeds (regardless of whether the pension plan stops or employees leave their jobs before retirement). The act also includes mandatory insurance to guarantee these benefits, strong fiduciary rules, and special tax incentives to those workers who are not in private pension plans, so that they can set up their own individual retirement programs. The combined efforts of consumers, employers, and government in regard to these extensive and expensive controls are readily seen as a continuing priority issue for the future.

Group property-liability insurance legislation. Many of the states already permit some forms of mass merchandising plans through employers and employees (see Chapter 5). Few, however, permit automobile, homeowners', and other personal insurance contracts on a "true group" basis, with full group rating and underwriting, as in life and health insurance. In order to permit this, the state insurance laws in regard to discrimination and marketing practices must be changed. The issue of what the benefits and problems of such plans really are to consumers, insurers, employers, and agents is still largely unresolved. Regulators are uncertain as to what additional legal controls are necessary, although pressure for permitting these plans has increased with the many "mass-marketed" plans (of individual contracts at regular or discounted individual rates) now in operation in many states.

Some large insurers are actively marketing such plans already, while others have not done so for their commercial clients. It appears that two key factors, in addition to employer and union interest, will be important in the future: the development of no-fault automobile insurance, and the possibility of extending tax deductions for employer contributions to the cost of personal insurance in these plans. Both could provide considerable support to the growth of group property-liability insurance in the coming decade. Another related, unsettled factor is the battle between automobile insurers and Blue Cross–Blue Shield associations as to whether auto insurance or health insurance will be the primary coverage for medical costs of automobile accidents under the new no-fault laws. Unions support the health insurers in this controversy, because they have already negotiated extensive benefits for health insurance paid for by employers. The outcome of this issue may determine the future of mass merchandising in the property-liability lines.

Property-liability insurance rating and profitability. Another area of special interest to consumers, but directly affecting insurers and government as well, is the question of how rates are set, and how profitable (or unprofitable) the property-liability business has been in recent years. The issue was raised to prominence by a study[50] which indicated that there have not been exces-

---

[50] *Studies on the Profitability, Industrial Structure, Finance, and Solvency of the Property and Liability Insurance Industry* (Boston: Arthur D. Little, Inc., 1970).

sive rates in this sector of the business, but the complexities of choosing the proper rate base and formulas have created much discussion and criticism.[51] The NAIC has developed a form of measuring profits which may become an authoritative standard that regulators can use in approving the rates of insurers, but wide acceptance has not yet been attained.

A broader area of discussion also promises to provide continued debate within the industry, and with regulators, during the years ahead. This is the analysis of competition in property-liability insurance, particularly in regard to the tremendous task which the insurance department has of administering rate regulation (laws for automobile and homeowners' lines, especially) in many of the states.[52] The issue is not limited only to this phase of the business, as life insurance, too, comes in for its share of the problem of maintaining reasonable competition in a business that also requires cooperative efforts to bring the consumer the best possible products at prices that are high enough (but not too high) and fair to different purchasers.[53]

The traditional methods of rating automobile insurance appeared as one of the hottest topics for debate in the late 1970s. Geographic territories, age, sex, and marital status as major pricing factors have been challenged in many states. Age and sex differences are now prohibited in several states, such as Hawaii (1974), North Carolina (1977), and Massachusetts (1978). These restrictions mostly benefit young male drivers, who in most plans now pay the highest automobile insurance premiums, by increasing rates for other groups, particularly older drivers. Even though accident statistics also clearly vary for urban and rural areas, basing premiums on geographic boundaries within a state has been claimed as unfair and social undesirable. (It may be unfair not to do so, too, as the opponents of this view point out.) Some states are trying to restrict the ways in which insurers classify risks by territory, by requiring the combination of urban and suburban (or rural) territories. The political appeal of lowering high auto insurance costs in urban areas by this method is a powerful factor in the clamor for challenging existing rating classifications, in spite of the years of accident data which indicate large differences in accident rates and costs in smaller territorial classes.

Surcharges on the rates charged inexperienced (mostly young) drivers are being tried in several states as an important new rating factor. Also, greater reliance on individual accident records seems indicated in the newer rating plans. The validity of such merit rating systems, with low rates for accident-

---

[51] George L. Head, "Synopsis of Measurement of Profitability and Treatment of Investment Income in Property-Liability Insurance," *CPCU Annals,* vol. 24, no. 4 (December 1971), p. 379; and Stephen W. Forbes, "Profitability in the Nonlife Insurance Industry, 1955–74", *CPCU Annals,* vol. 30, no. 2 (June 1977), p. 126.

[52] See "Competition in Property and Liability Insurance in New York State" (State of New York: Insurance Department, 1973).

[53] Mark S. Dorfman, "Workable Product Competition in Life Insurance Markets," *Journal of Risk and Insurance,* vol. 34, no. 4 (December 1972), p. 613.

free drivers and drivers with no traffic violations, is questioned, however, because of the unreliability of motor vehicle records in many states. The perfect rating system is probably unattainable, but there is no doubt that in the years ahead government, insurers, and consumers will be increasingly involved with many changes which treat auto insurance costs as a major social issue.

Another related issue in automobile insurance is alleged "redlining," or refusal to write insurance in certain territories, which may involve unfair discrimination against some ethnic, religious, or racial groups. A Federal Trade Commission investigation launched in 1978 is probing for evidence, beginning in California, to determine the validity and the extent of such practices.

Other social issues

This chapter could easily continue for many pages more to point out issues for discussion from a social viewpoint. Many of the other issues have been mentioned in preceding chapters. The student is encouraged to review some of the earlier chapters to locate further problems which will undoubtedly also be major issues for the future. For example, health insurance has a special and imminent issue in the proposals for *national health insurance,* as discussed in Chapter 15, which are bound to become well-publicized and hotly debated plans, particularly during national election years. The issues are expansive in scope and will affect everyone, including insurers, the medical profession, hospitals, health care consumers, and taxpayers. Many related topics are current: evaluation of the Medicare program, increasing concern for the social security (OASDHI) program (see Chapter 15), and the burgeoning influence of "the one institution . . . having the most impact on American life today"[54]—the Health, Education, and Welfare Department (HEW), with its nearly $200 billion budget. Another example of an excellent topic for student discussion is the *effects of inflation* on property and liability insurance values and losses, as related to Chapters 20, 24, and 27.[55]

Numerous social issues concern the eventual supremacy of *federal versus state control,* so the insurers and consumers are often in the middle of a jurisdictional battle that involves conflicting and complex problems which affect them tremendously, yet over which they have relatively little direct influence. One example of this is the federal government's recent challenge to the exemption of the insurance business from the antitrust laws. The McCarran-Ferguson Act (Public Law 15) has provided this special exemption (see Chapter 8) for nearly 35 years, but pending Supreme Court cases may broaden the application of federal jurisdiction to such areas as (1) joint

---

[54] "The Beneficent Monster," *Time,* June 12, 1978, p. 24.
[55] "Pacing Insurance With Inflation," *Business Week* (March 5, 1979), p. 102.

decisions by insurers on reasonable time charges for auto repairs; and (2) simultaneous changes in malpractice coverages to a claims-made basis, which are alleged to be a boycott and against antitrust laws. Another example is the growth of *insurer insolvency guaranty funds* in the states,[56] with federal bills for national insurance guaranty funds frequently proposed to replace them. The federal-state quest for control of insurance regulation goes on in many directions.

Insurance consumers and insurers must make their positions clear in the total environment of these regulatory and other social issues pertaining to insurance. The issues raised in this chapter, with their consumer, business, and social viewpoints, should leave the reader with much food for thought. A challenging future for insurance lies ahead in coordinating these many delicate and significant issues for the best interests of all.

FOR REVIEW AND DISCUSSION

1. Give an example of how the *consumer, business,* and *government* viewpoints may be related in discussing one major issue in insurance today.

2. How and why has *consumerism* occurred in the United States? Is it really a new idea? How is the recent increased role of the consumer different from the consumer's earlier role?

3. What examples of the *response* to consumerism can you cite from the fields of insurance?

4. What changes are foreseen for insurance for the next five years, as a result of the "consumer revolt"?

5. *Other than* the examples mentioned in this chapter, what are insurers doing to adapt to the era of consumerism?

6. Why is internationalism of special significance to the insurance business?

7. What rationale can an insurer develop for becoming international in scope?

8. Explain two important factors about the dimensions of international insurance today.

9. *How,* primarily, have insurers been international in the past? What new changes are appearing in the expansion to global insurance markets?

10. Does insurance help a nation's international balance-of-payments situation? Explain.

11. Marketing systems are changing in the property-liability field. How and why?

12. What can be done about the "arson epidemic" of recent years, and whose responsibility is it to provide the solution?

13. A new "insurance exchange" has been proposed in New York. What may be its potential benefits and problems?

14. Discuss the need for and the potential problems of (*a*) *kidnap-ransom* and

---

[56] Jean C. Hiestand, "The Insurance Guaranty Funds and Their Implications for the Insurance Business," *CPCU Annals,* vol. 30, no. 2 (June 1977), p. 112.

(b) *legal-expense* insurance as recently developing new types of insurance. What other new types of insurance have you read about lately?

15. Discuss some of the "ethical pillars" upon which the future of insurance will be based. Which ones may cause problems for insurance, and which may enhance its position?

16. What evidence can you give of the increasing "social responsibility" of insurance? What examples of the *lack* of it?

17. Which of the social issues in regard to government regulation of insurance are being solved primarily on (1) the state level, (2) the federal level, and (3) on both the state and federal levels?

18. Safety has grown in the past decade as an area for increased government regulation. Explain two such changes.

19. What other social issues not featured in this chapter would you choose as being of considerable importance to the future of insurance?

20. Explain how the traditional methods of auto insurance rating are being criticized today, and how this is becoming a major issue effecting consumers, insurers, and legislators.

APPENDIXES

Appendix A

Compound interest and present value tables

| | Column 1 | | | Column 2 | | | |
| | Amount of 1 at *compound interest* for selected interest rates, or $(1 + i)^n$ | | | *Present value* of 1 at compound interest for selected interest rates, or $v^n = (1 + i)^{-n}$ | | | |
n	2½%	3½%	5%	2½%	3½%	5%	n
1	1.02500	1.03500	1.05000	.97561	.96618	.95238	1
2	1.05062	1.07122	1.10250	.95181	.93351	.90703	2
3	1.07689	1.10872	1.15762	.92860	.90194	.86384	3
4	1.10381	1.14752	1.21551	.90595	.87144	.82270	4
5	1 13141	1.18769	1.27628	.88385	.84197	.78353	5
6	1.15969	1.22926	1.34010	.86230	.81350	.74622	6
7	1.18869	1.27228	1.40710	.84127	.78599	.71068	7
8	1.21840	1.31681	1.47746	.82075	.75941	.67684	8
9	1.24886	1.36290	1.55133	.80073	.73373	.64461	9
10	1.28008	1.41060	1.62889	.78120	.70892	.61291	10
11	1.31209	1.45997	1.71034	.76214	.68495	.58468	11
12	1.34489	1.51107	1.79586	.74356	.66178	.55684	12
13	1.37851	1.56396	1.88565	.72542	.63940	.53032	13
14	1.41297	1.61869	1.97993	.70773	.61778	.50507	14
15	1.44830	1.67535	2.07893	.69047	.59689	.48102	15
16	1.48451	1.73397	2.18287	.67362	.57671	.45811	16
17	1.52162	1.79468	2.29202	.65720	.55720	.43630	17
18	1.55966	1.85749	2.40662	.64117	.53836	.41552	18
19	1.59865	1.92250	2.52695	.62553	.52016	.39573	19
20	1.63862	1.98979	2.65330	.61027	.50257	.37689	20
21	1.67958	2.05943	2.78596	.59539	.48557	.35894	21
22	1.72157	2.13151	2.92526	.58086	.46915	.34185	22
23	1.76461	2.20611	3.07152	.56670	.45329	.32557	23
24	1.80873	2.28333	3.22510	.55288	.43796	.31007	24
25	1.85394	2.36324	3.38635	.53939	.42315	.29530	25
26	1.90029	2.44596	3.55567	.52623	.40884	.28124	26
27	1.94780	2.53157	3.73346	.51340	.39501	.26785	27
28	1.99650	2.62017	3.92013	.50088	.38165	.25509	28
29	2.04641	2.71188	4.11614	.48866	.36875	.24295	29
30	2.09757	2.80679	4.32194	.47674	.35628	.23138	30
40	2.68506	3.95926	7.03999	.37243	.25257	.14205	40
50	3.43711	5.58493	11.46740	.29094	.17905	.08720	50
60	4.39979	7.87809	18.67919	.22728	.12693	.05354	60
70	5.63210	11.11283	30.42643	.17755	.08999	.03287	70

n = number of years; v = value; i = interest rate.
Column 1 shows growth of $1 left at compound interest.
Column 2 shows what $1 due in future years is worth now.

Appendix B

Life insurance premium calculations

The net single premium

The "net natural premium" represents the amount that each insured must pay into the insurance fund at the beginning of a year so that the beneficiary of each insured who dies during that year may receive the amount of the insurance. This premium has sometimes been defined as "the cost to each individual of the death claims of the group." The net natural premium is computed by applying an interest credit to the natural premium computed from the mortality table. The natural premium on the age of 35 was noted in Chapter 9 as $2.51. Applying credit for interest on the basis of 2.5 percent, the net natural premium becomes $2.44.

It is possible to compute a lump sum that will pay in advance and in full the annual premiums on any type of insurance policy. This is accomplished by finding the sum which if paid when the policy is issued and augmented by interest earnings during the term will pay the benefit as it comes due. This sum is known as the *net single premium* (NSP).

For a five-year term policy. The computation may be simply illustrated for the five-year term policy. Assume entrants at the age of 35, each insured for $1,000. The mortality table indicates that during the first year there will be 23,528 deaths, and, accordingly, during that year $23,528,000 will be paid as death claims. To compute a five-year term premium, the process is repeated for each of the succeeding years through the five-year term. The rate computation is based upon the assumption that the death benefits are paid at the end of the year in which the deaths occur. To arrive at the basic equation expressing equality between the premiums and the benefits, it is necessary to reduce the benefits to the present value at the beginning of the policy term. The payments due at the end of the first year, therefore, are discounted for one year; those due at the end of the second year, for two years; and so on throughout the term. (See Appendix A for the discount factors.) The sum of the discounted benefits is then found and divided by the total number of entrants at the beginning of the term, and the result is the net single premium for the term.

This is illustrated for the five-year term policy at 35 years for $1,000 as follows:

1st year 23,528 claims = $23,528,000 due end of year
2d   "   24,685   "   =   24,685,000   "   "   "   "
3d   "   26,112   "   =   26,112,000   "   "   "   "
4th   "   27,991   "   =   27,991,000   "   "   "   "
5th   "   30,132   "   =   30,132,000   "   "   "   "

Applying the discount factor,

$23,528,000 × 0.975610 = $ 22,954,152.08
24,685,000 × 0.951814 =   23,495,528.59
26,112,000 × 0.928599 =   24,247,577.09
27,991,000 × 0.905951 =   25,358,474.44
30,132,000 × 0.883854 =   26,632,288.73
                           $122,688,020.93

$122,688,020.93 ÷ 9,373,807 = $13.09

The sum of $122,688,020.93 represents the present value of all estimated death claims during the five-year term. To find the net single premium for each insured, this sum is divided by 9,373,807 (the number of entrants), and the premium thereby determined is $13.09. Thus, if at the beginning of the term each entrant pays $13.09, the insurer will have sufficient funds to pay $1,000 to the beneficiary of each insured who dies during the term.

For a whole life policy.   The net single premium of a whole life policy is computed exactly like that for the term policy except that instead of finding the mortality costs for a definite number of years, the computation runs through the entire mortality table from the year of entrance. The result is the net single premium for a whole life policy at the age of 35. This works out as follows:

Year	Age	Number living	Deaths each year	Death claims payable	Discount factor	Present value of future death claims
1	35	9,373,807	23,528	$23,528,000 × 0.975610 = $		22,954,152.08
2	36	9,350,279	24,685	24,685,000 × 0.951814 =		23,495,528.59
3	37	9,325,594	26,112	26,112,000 × 0.928599 =		24,247,577.09
				[This process is continued throughout the table. In the interest of brevity, only the first three and the last calculations are shown.]		
65	99	6,415	6,415	$ 6,415,000 × 0.200886 =		1,288,683.69
						$3,938,192,458.72

$3,938,192,458.72 ÷ 9,373,807 = $420.13

The present value of the total payment of 9,373,807 entrants at the age of 35 from the above calculations is $3,938,192,458.72. This sum divided by the number of entrants gives the amount of $420.13, which is the net single premium for a whole life policy for $1,000 at the age of 35.

The term policy and whole life forms here noted illustrate the method of computing the net single premium. The method is the same for other policy forms.

Most insureds are reluctant to pay a lump sum for insurance coverage. In the case of an early death, the cost of the insurance would be very high under the single-premium plan as compared with the annual premium basis.

There is also the practical fact that most persons are not able to pay for life insurance on a single-premium basis.

The net level premium

The net single premium represents a full cash-in-advance payment for a life insurance contract. The usual requirement of the insured is a partial payment plan on an annual basis, or at less than annual intervals. To provide an installment premium plan that is mathematically equivlent to the net single premium, a premium may be charged that remains the same from year to year throughout the premium-paying period. This is known as the *net level premium plan* (NLP).

Utilizing the annuity principle. The net single premium takes into consideration the expected mortality experience in determining the amount of benefits to be paid each year. When the present value of the benefits is divided by the number of entrants, no further consideration of mortality expectation is required. Under the level premium plan, the time of death definitely determines the aggregate amount of premium paid by each insured. The annual premium is identical for each member of the group; but even though the member dies during the first policy year after the payment of a comparatively small first annual premium, the beneficiary will still receive the face of the policy with no obligation for further premium payments. The insured who pays premiums for many years receives identical treatment. This further spread of the premium risk is part of the insurance feature of the level premium plan.

Since the level premium plan calls for the annual payment of premiums during the premium payment period by living policyholders, it is necessary to examine the anticipated mortality experience to determine (*a*) the number of premiums that may be expected and (*b*) the year in which it may be expected that each premium will be paid.

Annuity plans are based on the payment of installment benefit amounts to all the members of the group that survive from year to year in return for a large annuity premium deposit made previously. The lump sum or cost of the annuity is the equivalent of all of the annual payments discounted and divided by the number of entrants. The problem of converting a net single premium to a net level annual premium is the reverse of determining the cost of an annuity. For the annuity, the payments are known and the cost is found by discounting the payments. To determine the level premium from the known single premium, the net single premium is converted to the equivalent annuity due.

Ordinarily, an annuity contract calls for the first annuity payment to be made at the end of one year and annually thereafter. If the annuity is payable at the first of each year, beginning with the first year, it is called an *annuity due*. In the case of an annuity due, all the entrants receive an annuity payment the first year, but each year thereafter a payment is made only to the survivors. Since every insured in a group pays a premium when the policy is issued, it is the annuity due that is comparable to the annual premiums paid on a level premium basis for a life insurance contract. To convert a net single premium to a net level premium, it becomes necessary to find the annuity due that is its mathematical equivalent.

Converting the NSP to an NLP. A net single premium is converted to the equivalent of an annuity due through the use of simple proportion. If an annuity due of $1 yearly may be purchased for $20, then to purchase the same annuity due in the amount of $5 will take $100. The amount is determined by dividing the cost of the annuity due of $1 into the amount available. To convert a net single premium into a net level premium, which amounts to the same thing as converting it to an annuity due, the amount of the net single premium is divided by the value of an annuity due of $1 for the premium-paying term of the policy.

The whole life annuity due. To determine the value of an annuity, the mortality table is used to determine the number of entrants at the required age. Contrary to life insurance, annuity payments are concerned with the number of survivors. For a life annuity due for $1 a year at age 35, since there are 9,373,807 entrants, there will be due immediately $9,373,807. At the end of the second year, since there are 9,350,279 survivors, there will be due $9,350,279; but to reduce this amount to its present value the one-year discount factor must be applied. This process is continued, applying the appropriate discount factor throughout the annuity term. The sum of all annuity payments discounted is found and divided by the number of entrants, and the result is the net cost of the annuity due in question. A temporary annuity due of $1 a year for five years at age 35 is illustrated as follows:

Age		Number living	Present value of $1 @ 2½%	Present value of annual payments
35	$1 due now	9,373,807	$1.00	$ 9,373,807.00
36	$1 due one year from now	9,350,279	0.975610	9,122,225.70
37	$1 due two years from now	9,325,594	0.951814	8,876,230.93
38	$1 due three years from now	9,299,482	0.928599	8,635,489.69
39	$1 due four years from now	9,271,491	0.905951	8,399,516.54
				$44,407,269.86

The present value of all annuity payments is $44,407,269.86. This sum divided by the number of entrants equals $4.74, the individual share of the present value of all annuity payments. This is the net cost for an annuity payment of $1 a year beginning immediately at the age of 35 and continuing for five years.

The five-year term is here used as a simple explanation of the principle. To determine the premium of an annuity due to continue for the whole life, the same procedure is followed to the end of the mortality table. Thus:

Age		Number living	Present value of $1 @ 2½%	Present value of annual payments
35	$1 due now	9,373,807	$1.00	$ 9,373,807.00
36	$1 due one year from now	9,350,279	0.975610	9,122,225.70
37	$1 due two years from now	9,325,594	0.951814	8,876,230.93

[As for the whole life policy, this procedure is carried out until there are no survivors. As before, only the first three and the last calculations are given.]

99	$1 due 64 years from now	6,415	0.205908	1,320.90
				$222,860,196.46

Individual share equals $222,860,196.46 ÷ 9,373,807 = $23.775 = $23.78

Summary of the NLP computation.   To consolidate what has thus far been stated, the computation of a net level premium involves four steps: (*a*) find the present value of the benefits; (*b*) divide by the number of entrants in the group to determine the net single premium; (*c*) find the present value of an annuity for $1 for the term premium payments are to be paid; and (*d*) divide the net single premium by the present value of the annuity due.

Let:

B = Discounted benefits
E = Entrants in a given group
A = Present value of annuity due of $1 for premium-paying period
NSP = Net single premium
NLP = Net level premium

We then have:

$$B \div E = NSP$$
$$NSP \div A = NLP$$

The value of an annuity due of $1 a year for a five-year term at age 35 has just been computed to be $4.74. The net single premium for a five-year policy of $1,000 at age 35 has also been found to be $13.09. The problem is to determine from these two figures the five-year net level annual premium. If $1 a year for five years has a present value at the age of 35 of $4.74, then it follows that the payment for five years that is equivalent to $13.09 is $13.09 divided by $4.74, or $2.76. This figure represents the net annual level premium of a five-year term policy at age 35. The solution is a matter of simple proportion: $4.74:$13.09 = $1:x$. The product of the means equals the product of the extremes. Hence, $4.74x = 13.09, and $x = 2.76.

Appendix C

Special and allied fire lines

Nature of special and allied fire coverages

There are a number of perils and losses that are so closely associated with the fire business that inclusion of the lines in the general field of fire insurance was logical. For example, the writing of sprinkler leakage insurance is a natural accompaniment of fire insurance.

Sprinkler leakage insurance

The automatic sprinkler system is a device designed to make fire, itself, a security guard. A building protected with a sprinkler system is piped throughout, and at given intervals, "heads" are set. These heads open if the temperature rises to a predetermined point. Thus, when a fire occurs in the vicinity of a sprinkler head, the head is opened and water released on the fire. Water damage caused by the opening of sprinkler heads to extinguish an accidental and unfriendly fire is covered under the fire policy.

It occasionally happens, however, that water is discharged from the sprinkler system when no fire is involved. The fire policies do not cover the damage. The *sprinkler leakage contract* provides indemnity against direct property loss or damage caused by the discharge or leakage of water or other substances from within an automatic sprinkler system, including valves, pumps, pipes, and tanks. The sprinkler policy may be written to cover buildings or their contents, or both. Damage caused by the collapse or fall of tanks which form a part of the sprinkler system is a very important coverage, since water tanks located on the roof of a building can cause terrific loss when the supports collapse. Damage to the sprinkler system itself is covered in some forms.

Not only may sprinkler leakage insurance be written to cover direct damage, but it may also cover all of the indirect losses for which fire insurance is written. (See Chapter 18.)

Sprinkler leakage policies usually require at least 25 percent coinsurance. The rates are reduced so sharply as the percentage in the coinsurance clause is increased that the insured will do well to consider carefully the advisability of a high amount of insurance with a high coinsurance clause.

A sprinkler system in a building may result in serious loss or damage to the property of others, and if any element of negligence can be shown, the owner may be held legally liable. One of the most frequent causes of *sprinkler leakage liability* loss is freezing. Other causes which may introduce the element of liability include not maintaining the system properly, faulty parts, and unsafe construction. In all sprinkler leakage policies covering contents items there is a limited legal liability protection for loss to property similar to the insured's and held in trust or storage or on commission. For claims of a tenant attributable to sprinkler leakage, a policy is needed that covers liability imposed by law. If there is any assumed liability, there is a special form by which that extra risk is included.

Water damage insurance

The sprinkler leakage policy excludes liability for water damage losses except for water leaking from inside the sprinkler system. To provide complete water damage insurance, the *water damage policy* is essential. The policy covers direct loss or damage caused by the accidental discharge, leakage, or overflow of water or steam from plumbing systems, tanks, heating systems, elevator tanks and cylinders, standpipes for fire hose, industrial and domestic appliances, and refrigerating and air conditioning systems. The policy also covers loss or damage caused by rain or snow admitted directly to the interior of the building through defective roofs, leaders, or downspouts, or by open or defective windows, transoms, ventilators, or skylights.

The coverage is fairly comprehensive. Except in special situations the policy does not cover seepage, leakage, or influx of water through building walls, foundations, lowest basement floors, sidewalks, and the like. Losses attributable to aircraft, fire, lightning, windstorm, earthquake, and explosions are not covered. Such losses are expected to be covered by the policies written to cover loss against these perils. Direct damage caused by the water leakage is covered, but there is no coverage for damage to the system, tank, or other source of the water damage loss.

As with sprinkler leakage, there are three forms of *water damage liability* protection: (*a*) limited protection under the property damage form, (*b*) liability imposed by law, and (*c*) assumed liability.

Tenant's improvements and betterments

It is customary for a business tenant to lease real estate in a condition requiring repairs or renovation involving substantial expenditure of money. To have an insurable interest in *improvements or betterments,* it is not necessary that the tenant have a written lease nor is it necessary that the improvements be installed during the term of the lease. It is required, however, that they be installed at the expense of the tenant who is the insured and that after installation the tenant have no legal right to remove them.

Insurable tenant's improvements, therefore, are of a nature that makes them a part of the building. They cease to be the property of the lessee and instead are the property of the owner of the building. Nevertheless, they are available for the tenant's use so long as the rental agreement remains effective. It is this loss-of-use interest in the improvements that the policy covers.

Insurance is now written frequently as an endorsement to the fire insurance contract to include improvements and betterments in the contents item of the fire insurance coverage. This permits recovery by the tenant entirely independently of and apart from recovery by the owner of the real estate. In the event that improvements and betterments are damaged or destroyed during the policy term by the perils insured against, there is coverage for two situations: (a) where the owner refuses to restore but the lease is not canceled and (b) where the lease is canceled.

If the owner pays for restoring the improvements, it is apparent that the tenant has suffered no loss. The owner secures title to the improvements once they become part of the real estate, and their value should be considered for valuation and coinsurance purposes. On the other hand, *if the owner refuses to replace* the betterments, *but the lease is not canceled,* and the tenant pays for them, then the tenant's insurance covers. Settlement is made on the basis of the actual cash value of the damaged improvements or betterments.

The improvements and betterments may be destroyed, or they may be partly damaged. If the premises, however, are sufficiently (often 50 percent is stated) damaged to warrant cancellation of the lease, then from the standpoint of the tenant the betterments are a total loss. *If the lease is canceled,* settlement is made by paying the insured pro rata for the unexpired term of the lease based on the original cost of the improvements. No consideration is given to either depreciation or increased costs.

Builder's risk

A building in the process of construction presents a situation in which values are constantly changing. If insurance is placed at infrequent intervals, there will be periods of overinsurance and periods in which the insurance is inadequate. To eliminate such a situation and at the same time provide an equitable insurance plan, three *builder's risk forms* have been devised. The first provides no automatic coverage as values increase, and is usually undesirable because of the frequent endorsements needed.

To provide automatic coverage and at the same time eliminate the necessity of monthly reports, a *completed value form* provides for placing insurance at the commencement of construction for the full projected value of the building when it will be completed. The rate charged is usually about 50 percent of the 100 percent coinsurance builder's risk rate, to allow for any overinsurance of values during construction.

All of the forms usually cover not only the building under construction but also fences, tool houses, builder's machinery, implements, supplies, and materials of every description used in connection with the construction if these are located on the insured or adjacent premises. The completed value form is the most popular method of insuring builder's risk exposures, because (assuming proper values) the insured is fully protected throughout the construction period and no further reports of values are required.

Another method of covering increasing values automatically is the *reporting form*. A policy is written as soon as there is any insurable property on the premises for a beginning provisional amount. The total limit of liability for the completed value of the building is also stated. The insured is required to furnish the insurer with a monthly statement of values. Upon receipt of the statement, an endorsement is attached to the policy showing the increase in the insurable value and premium. The policy protects the insured automatically as the value at risk increases, pending the attachment of the monthly endorsements. To illustrate its operation: If at the time of the last report the values were $50,000 and just before the time for the next report they had increased to $55,000 and a fire occurs, the policy covers for the full value of $55,000, even though this amount is not endorsed on the policy. The "full reporting" clause (like 100 percent coinsurance) is mandatory. The interest of the contractor or owner, or both, may be covered under the policy, and the usual fire, extended coverage and vandalism and malicious mischief perils may be included. All-risks coverage is also available by a special endorsement.

In some states a contractors' form automatically provides a binder to cover for 30 days any new projects started. A newer special builders' form is also available in some jurisdictions, insuring builders similarly for automatic coverage at new project locations without the need to issue separate new policies.

Flood insurance

Insurance against rising water is to be distinguished from insurance against leakage or rain. The term *flood insurance* is applied to forms covering against direct loss by flood, such as the overflow of a river or a tidal wave. Marine policies covering the perils of transportation include loss or damage from the rising of navigable waters, and flood losses are covered under the all-risks transportation floater. Policies covering bridges may include flood loss. Automobiles are covered by comprehensive physical damage coverage in personal and business auto contracts, and in auto dealers' forms.

Insurance against flood loss to buildings and contents is now frequently written in many areas, through a federal flood insurance program (see Chapter 28) which began a decade ago.

Crop insurance

Among the numerous perils that threaten the destruction of crops are unfavorable weather conditions, hail, floods, insects, and disease. The distress resulting from widespread crop failure has focused the attention of agricultural interests upon the necessity for *crop insurance*. Private insurers write several hundred million dollars in crop insurance premiums annually for this specialized risk.

Policies become effective at the date agreed upon when the application is filed, and the application ordinarily provides that the coverage will be effective provisionally 24 hours after the application has been received by the insurer, during which time the insurer has an opportunity to decline the business if it wishes to do so. The insurance coverage is reduced pro rata as harvesting progresses.

No liability is assumed for loss or damage resulting in injury to trees, vines, leaves, bushes, plants, blooms, or blossoms, when such products as fruits, beans, grapes, or strawberries are insured. There is liability only to the extent that the product itself has been affected. It is usual to provide a limit of liability per acre, and policies may include a clause that there shall be no liability on the part of the insurer unless the crop is damaged more than a certain designed percentage—5 percent is a figure frequently used. If the crop can be reset or reseeded, the insurer pays only the actual cost of these operations.

Underwriting insurance on growing crops presents numerous difficulties. At the planting season it is impossible to know what the market will be at the time of harvest. A solution that has seemed to be equitable provides that if there is a loss covered by the policy, the insurer will pay on the basis of the decreased yield. This plan provides indemnity to the insured for a partial loss, even though much of the crop may be salvaged and a profit shown for the year's operation.

Frost and freeze coverages are written for owners of orchards or growing citrus fruits or other crops that are particularly susceptible to frost damage. One of the major difficulties is the effect that serious frost losses have upon the market price of the balance of the crop. If the frost losses throughout a wide territory are severe enough to reduce the entire crop seriously, then part of the loss is regained by the increased value in the part of the crop that is marketable. This increased value is, of course, of no assistance to the orchard owner whose entire crop is destroyed. If, however, part of the crop is salvaged, the scarcity is beneficial. Providing for only a partial settlement at the time the damage occurs and a final settlement based upon income received when the salable crop has been marketed, is a normal procedure.

Crop-hail insurance is a popular form of crop coverage and usually provides indemnity for the percentage of physical damage resulting from hail or from wind accompanied by hail. To establish a loss it must be shown that the actual hail damage equaled or exceeded 5 percent of the loss. Crops are usually insured on a "specific amount per acre" basis. The amount of insurance usually represents the cost of production, though it may be increased to include a portion of the expected profit from the crops. Insurance may range from $10 per acre on grain to as high as several thousand dollars an acre on shade-grown tobacco.

Crop insurance is written by some private insurers on an *all-risks* basis to cover such perils as blight, insect pests, and drought. All-risks crop insurance differs from other forms of crop insurance in that it is virtually a crop guarantee. Instead of determining the amount of loss or damage attributable to an insured peril, the insurer is obligated to pay the insured any difference between the coverage and the amount of the crop actually produced. Efforts have been made to eliminate the moral hazard by reducing the amount of insurance to a part of the average yield, such as three fourths.

The insurance of crops has also been provided for many years by the *Federal Crop Insurance Corporation,* an agency of the U.S. Department of Agriculture. Federal crop insurance is not available in all counties, and in most of the counties where it is offered it is made available only on a few crops. This is a type of voluntary government insurance, as defined in Chapters 2 and 28. The Agricultural Consumer Protection Act of 1973 extended federal crop insurance on an all-risks basis for serious damage (of more than one third of the potential crop) without cost to farmers. Taxpayers paid more than $600 million in 1974, and various bills were proposed in 1977–78 to limit the expansion of this type of program.[1]

Multiple-location contracts

The trend of big business frequently results in the distribution of property values among many locations. To provide complete and adequate protection for insureds having contents at a number of locations and with fluctuating values over the year, the *multiple-location forms* have been prepared. All locations may be covered by a single policy, with automatic coverage for new locations. Property suitable for coverage under the multiple-location forms includes contents only. Among the insurable items are merchandise, machinery, supplies, furniture, fixtures, and the insured's interest in betterments.

Reporting forms eliminate the necessity of canceling and rewriting or endorsing policies where the values at various locations fluctuate. Savings are reported in commissions and administration, as it is less expensive to write one policy for 100 or more locations than it would be to write a separate policy for each location. Comparable economies are achieved in accounting, collection expense, credit reports, and underwriting. Multiple-location rate adjustments apply only to that portion of the basic annual premium which is in excess of $1,000. Both the reduced costs and the convenience of having a single contract cover all locations appeal to the insured.

The insurance is written under two general types of coverage: (1) reporting and (2) coinsurance. The forms differ with respect to the number of locations required, whether or not they are reporting forms, the rating plans, and the requirements for minimum premiums.

It is the intent of reporting forms to follow fluctuating values so that when-

---

[1] "Off the Record," *Mutual Insurance Bulletin,* May 1977, p. 4.

ever a loss occurs full insurance to value will be provided. The insurer obligates itself in this respect, but to make the contract effective the insured must meet certain obligations.

The *value-reporting requirement* obligates the insured to report in writing to the insurer not later than 30 days after the last day of each calendar month: (1) the exact location of all property covered, (2) the total actual cash value of insured property as each location, and (3) the specific insurance in force.

Failure on the part of the insured to make the required report causes *penalties for noncompliance.* The obligation of the insurer is limited to no more than the amounts included in the last report filed prior to a loss, less specific insurance. The form also contains an "honesty clause" which provides that if the last reported value prior to a loss is less than the actual cash value at the time the report is made, then the insurer is liable only in the proportion that the value reported bears to the actual value. If an insured reports a $50,000 value where there is $100,000 actual value and sustains a $10,000 loss, the insurer is liable only for $5,000, or 50 percent of the loss.

Since the full amount of insurance coverage that the policy will provide cannot be known at the outset, the forms are written with a *provisional amount of insurance.* A deposit premium is collected, and the premium is adjusted at the end of the policy term on the basis of actual values reported.

Reporting forms also provide a *maximum limit of liability* for the insurer which is to be distinguished from the provisional amount of insurance. Where two or more locations are involved, a separate limit is established for each location. If reports are made showing values in excess of liability limits, premiums are collected for the full values reported, but if the values exceed the liability limits established, the liability limits apply. If values are ever determined to be in excess of liability limits, steps should be taken immaitely to have the limits increased.

Where *specific insurance* is written and is considered in the computation of the final premium, the insured is obligated either to continue the specific insurance in force or to increase the limit of liability immediately under the reporting form if the specific insurance expires. Multiple-location coverages are usually excess over specific insurance payments. Limits of liability for multiple-location coverages are always determined by subtracting the specific insurance from peak values.

In effecting the final *premium adjustment,* an average of the total monthly values reported for the term of the policy is determined, and if the premium on this average at the applicable rate exceeds the provisional premium, the insured is required to pay for the excess. If the premium is less than the provisional premium, the insurer is obligated to return any excess paid, above any minimum premium that may apply.

Appendix D

Partial prospect list for marine, inland marine, and "all-risk" lines

Insurable property	Form of policy
Art collectors, dealers, and Galleries	
Paintings, works of art, antiques, and objects of art or historical value	Fine arts
Banks	
Customers' furs for storage	Furriers' customers
Electric signs	Neon sign
Financed installment accounts	Installment floater
Fine arts	Fine arts
Securities, currency	Armored car and messenger
	Registered mail
Floor plan accounts	Floor plan
Bridge owners and mortgagees	
Bridges	Bridge property damage
	Bridge use and occupancy
Broadcasting stations	
Radio towers	Individually drawn
Churches and chapels	
Paintings, works of art, and stained-glass windows	Fine arts
Projection machines	Camera
Religious articles and vestments	Special floater
Clubs	
Guns	Special floater
Horses and saddlery	Livestock floater
Paintings, works of art, and stained-glass windows	Fine arts
Paraphernalia	Special floater
Power lawn mowers	Special floater
Projection machines	Camera
Property on exhibition	Exhibition floater
Theatrical scenery, costumes, and "props"	Theatrical floater

Insurable property	Form of policy
Colleges and schools	
Athletic equipment	Special floater
Bandplayers' uniforms	Special floater
Guns	Special floater
Horses and saddlery	Livestock floater
Musical instruments	Musical instrument floater
Paintings, works of art, rare books, manuscripts, and art glass windows	Fine arts
Paraphernalia	Special floater
Projection machines	Camera
Property on exhibition	Exhibition floater
Scientific instruments	Special floater
Theatrical scenery, costumes, and "props"	Theatrical floater
Tickets (for athletic events sent by mail)	Individually drawn
Trophies (possessing quality of fine arts)	Fine arts
Contractors	
Equipment	Contractors' equipment floater
Machinery, tanks, etc.	Installation floater
Department stores	
Customers' furs for storage	Furriers' customers
Electric signs	Neon sign
Fur stock	Furriers' block
Jewelry stock	Jewelers' block
Paintings, pictures, etc.	Fine arts
Merchandise	Department store floater
	Exhibition floater
	Installation floater
	Installment floater
	Motortruck merchandise floater
	Marine cargo policy
	Parcel post
	Transportation
Doctors	
Medical lamps	Physicians' and surgeons' floater

---

* Reprinted by permission of the Royal Liverpool Insurance Corp.

Insurable property	Form of policy
Doctors (continued)	
Radium	Radium floater
Surgical and scientific instruments and apparatus	Physicians' and surgeons' floater
Dyers and cleaners	
Customers' furs for storage	Furriers' customers
Customers' goods	Dyers and cleaners
Exhibitors	
Property on exhibition	Exhibition floater
Works of art	Fine arts
Exporters or importers	
General merchandise	Marine cargo policy Transportation— location
Farmers	
Livestock	Livestock floater
Mobile agricultural machinery and equipment	Mobile agricultural machinery and equipment floater
Horses and wagons	Livestock floater
Governments (town, city, county, and state)	
Bridges	Bridge property damage Bridge use and occupancy
Musical instruments	Musical instrument floater
Power lawn mowers	Special floater
Road machinery and equipment	Contractors' equipment
Securities, etc.	Registered mail
Surveyors' instruments	Special floater
Tunnels (vehicular and rail)	Property damage Use and occupancy
Voting machines	Voting machine
Works of art	Fine arts
Individuals	
Cameras, furs, jewelry, and silverware	Personal articles floater
Coin collection	Coin collection
Golfers' equipment	Golfers' equipment
Guns	Special floater
Model railroads	Special floater
Musical instruments	Musical instrument floater
Outboard motorboats and motors	Outboard motorboat
Paintings, other objects of art, and antiques	Fine arts floater
Personal effects	Personal effects floater
Personal property	Personal property floater form Trip transit
Power lawn mowers	Special floater

Insurable property	Form of policy
Individuals (continued)	
Riding horses and equipment	Livestock floater
Stamp collections	Stamp collection floater
Trophies (with qualities of fine arts)	Fine arts
Wedding presents	Wedding presents
Yachts and motorboats	Yacht
Jewelers	
Electric signs	Neon sign
Jewelers' stock	Jewelers' block
Parcel post shipments	Parcel post
Street clocks	Neon sign
Libraries	
Books (while loaned, leased, or rented)	Transportation— location
Paintings, works of art	Fine arts
Property on exhibition	Exhibition floater
Rare books and manuscripts	Fine arts
Stained-glass windows	Fine arts
Manufacturers, distributors, wholesalers, and retailers	
Electric signs	Neon sign
Exhibitions	Exhibition floater
General merchandise	See policies listed for department stores
Ladies' and men's wear	Garment contractors' floater
Patterns	Transportation— location
Privately owned rolling stock and locomotives	Individually drawn
Musicians, bands, and orchestras	
Musical instruments and orchestrations	Musical instrument floater
Bandplayer's uniforms	Special floater
Photographers	
Cameras and equipment	Camera
Photographic supplies	Parcel post
Property of others	Bailees' customers
Publishers and printers	
Books, magazines, etc.	Parcel post (transportation— location)
Property out for processing	
Truckers	
General merchandise	Motortruck merchandise floater
Warehousers	
Customers' furs for storage	Furriers' customers
Household goods and general merchandise	Motortruck merchandise floater Transportation floater

This brief summary of changes occuring during 1978–79 in the field of _commercial auto coverages_ supplements Chapter 24 for the more advanced student of insurance. It should also be useful to the general business student who is making decisions as a consumer faced with the need for insuring commercial (business) auto exposures.

Generally, the changes appeared as part of the trend toward contract simplification, which was illustrated in Chapter 24's explanation of the personal auto policy (PAP). Many of the same objectives apply: reduction of the number of contracts and forms, personalized wording ("you," "we," etc.), single-limit liability coverage, and revised structure of the contracts and their provisions.

The business auto policy (BAP)[1] is the basis for these changes. Approval for its use in more than half of the states is expected by 1979, but a year or more will be needed before older forms are replaced as policies renew. Four older commercial auto contracts will no longer be used, including the comprehensive auto liability policy (CAL) and the basic automobile liability policy (BAL), which have insured most of these business auto exposures in preceding years. A new garage policy (GP) will be used for auto sales, service, and dealer risks, but it will not be discussed here.

The business auto policy (BAP)

Designed as a self-contained contract, the _business auto policy (BAP)_ will still provide an option for combination of coverage with the comprehensive general liability policy (CGL—see Chapter 21) by using a common declarations page. However, if this approach is used, both contracts should be insured with the same insurer to avoid any problems of overlapping or uninsured protection.

Following the declarations pages the BAP contract is divided into six parts, each of which will be separately discussed in the following sections. Liberalizations and limitations in the change to this new contract will be emphasized, rather than an item-by-item review of concepts already treated in the text

_____

[1] Filed for countrywide use by the Insurance Services Office (ISO), but adoption by the individual states is occurring gradually.

870

for the personal auto policy. Particular attention will be given to provisions which are different for business as compared with personal auto exposures.

Declarations. The declarations pages are much more extensive than in the personal auto policy. The seven items pertain to (1) the named insured, (2) the schedule of coverages chosen, (3) the description of ten covered auto "designation symbols," and schedules for (4) covered autos you own, (5) hired or borrowed autos, (6) employer's nonownership liability, and (7) gross receipts or mileage basis for public auto or leasing rental firms.

The major innovation is the use of the numbered designation symbols 1–10, which determine the choices made by you as to which autos are to be insured. Symbol 1 is the broadest designation, for *any* auto on a comprehensive basis. The others designate *owned* autos only (or are limited to private passenger autos, other than private passenger autos, or autos subject to no-fault or compulsory uninsured motorists laws); *specifically described* autos, *hired* autos, or *nonowned* autos only.

Item 2 in the declarations is very important, for this schedule of the coverages uses the designated symbols to indicate the liability, personal injury protection (no-fault), medical payments, uninsured motorists, and physical damage coverages which apply in the contract. Extreme care must be exercised by you and your agent to see that the appropriate designated symbol numbers are correctly inserted in this section of the declarations. Errors could mean lack of needed protection.

Part I—Words and phrases with special meanings. This section contains a half page of definitions important to the contract. "You" are the person or organization insured, and "we" means the company providing the insurance. "Accident" is used rather than "occurrence," as in the PAP contract, but the definition includes continuous or repeated exposures resulting in bodily injury or property damage that you neither expected nor intended. Of special significance to business auto risks is the fact that "auto" means a land motor vehicle, trailer, or semitrailer designed for travel on public roads, and that "mobile equipment" is separately defined to include such vehicles as bulldozers, graders, farm machinery, and those that are designed for use off public roads for use solely on your premises, or are not required to be licensed.

Part II—Which autos are covered autos. The numerical designated symbols in the declarations determine which autos are considered covered autos for each of your chosen coverages. Vehicles acquired during the policy period are usually automatically covered, but if the coverage is only for specifically described autos (symbol 7) the newly acquired vehicle must be reported within 30 days. Temporary substitute vehicles are covered automatically for liability coverage only if coverage is carried for hired and nonowned autos. Physical damage coverage for these autos must be endorsed on the contract. This is a change from the comprehensive auto liability policy formerly used in many of these situations. Covered autos include trailers with a load capacity of 2,000 pounds or less, and mobile equipment while it is being carried or towed by a covered auto.

Part III—Where and when this policy covers.   Accidents or losses are covered in (or while being transported between) the United States, its territories or possessions, Puerto Rico, and Canada.

Part IV—Liability insurance.   Most of the wording and interpretations for this section are similar to those of the personal auto policy discussed in Chapter 24. The single most important change is the *combined single limit* of liability for bodily injury and property damage. Insurers are developing conversion tables in order to advise policyholders of recommended amounts to assure adequate limits. For example, a policy formerly written for $100,000/$300,000/$50,000 limits should use a single limit of at least $350,000.

A new exclusion of special importance for business exposures is that "loading and unloading" limits coverage to the immediate operation of placing property on, or removing it from, a covered auto. This restricts coverage by applying the "coming to rest" rule rather than the broader "completed operations" rule, which has caused considerable problems in various court interpretations.[2]

Part V—Physical damage insurance.   Two options for coverage apply in this section: "comprehensive" and "specified perils" (fire, theft, etc.). The specified perils coverage is written as a package, although fire, or fire and theft, perils can be written by special endorsements. The definitions correspond to previously discussed explanations of these coverages. Collision, and towing charges, may also be included in the physical damage insurance protection.

Part VI—Conditions.   These conditions, which apply to the entire contract, are similar to the conditions of the personal auto policy. For businesses, the use of trailers is common and coverage for a trailer is clarified by stating that it applies only on an excess basis while it is used with a motor vehicle that you do not own.

---

[2] For examples, see *Fire, Casualty, and Surety Bulletins* (Cincinnati: National Underwriter Co.), F. and C. Sections Auto (Casualty) B–7.

Appendix F

Special crime insurance bonds

CRIME INSURANCE AND BONDS FOR FINANCIAL INSTITUTIONS

Bank burglary and robbery insurance

Since the greatest concentration of money and securities is in banks and other financial institutions, these institutions are targets for burglary and holdup. Institutions carrying blanket bond coverage are protected for burglary and robbery losses. The individual burglary and robbery policy is still used (*a*) for institutions that do not require the broad protection furnished by a blanket bond or do not elect to pay the premium for such a bond, and (*b*) as excess cover for large institutions that require more burglary and robbery insurance than the blanket bond provides.

The standard bank burglary and robbery policy provides four distinct coverages: (1) burglary, (2) robbery, (3) property damage caused by either burglary or robbery, and (4) property damage caused by vandalism or malicious mischief. The form now in use was developed in cooperation with the American Bankers Association. A separate limit of liability and a separate premium are designated in the policy for each peril.

The property damage feature provides indemnity for loss sustained as the result of damage to money and securities or to the premises, furniture, fixtures, vaults, safes, or the like, when caused by burglary or robbery or any attempt thereat. Providing protection for vandalism losses eliminates the possibility of a dispute as to whether the damage in a particular case is actually an attempted burglary. Fire damage to money and securities is covered. However, fire losses to premises and other contents are never covered under the bank burglary and robbery insurance policy, regardless of how the fire is caused.

There is no loss under a burglary policy if the vault is left unlocked or if it is opened through a manipulation of the combination. Bank burglary and robbery rates apply special discounts for approved alarm systems, locks, security guards, and other features.

Safe-deposit boxes insurance

In the absence of negligence there is usually no liability on the part of a bank for loss to the contents of rented safe-deposit boxes. However, the question of liability is sometimes uncertain, and the owners of securities or other valuables in rented boxes are also interested in insurance against loss of the contents.

Bank forms. Insurance written for the bank is the combination safe depository policy. It covers against the risks of loss of property in customers' safe-deposit boxes through burglary or robbery, damage or destruction caused by the hazards or attempts thereat and vandalism or malicious mischief. All property is covered, including money. Damage to the premises, safes, vaults, and other furnishings of the insured institution is covered. The measure of loss is the pecuniary loss, not sentimental value.

Damage to the premises, equipment, or furnishings of the lending institution is paid for first, and the balance of the insurance is prorated among the boxes. While this contract is not a legal liability form and the interest of box renters is covered regardless of the liability of the bank the protection afforded may be limited to legal liability by endorsement. There are no restrictions as to how the loss or damage must occur, nor is there any limitation as to the amount applicable to each box.

Lessee form. This form, issued to lessees of the safe-deposit boxes, indemnifies them for loss or damage to their own property or to property for which they are liable. The burglary coverage is effective while such property is contained in leased or rented boxes in a designated vault. The robbery feature provides coverage inside the premises of the bank while at least one officer or employee of the bank is on the premises. The most popular form is an all-risks securities safe-deposit form. The policy provides insurance against any form of theft or larceny and includes the unexplainable disappearance or misplacement of securities.

Blanket bonds for financial institutions

There are many blanket bonds that are designed to meet the fidelity and other theft protection needs of financial institutions. Several are in general use for commercial banks, savings and loan associations, stockbrokers, credit unions, and small loan companies.

The blanket bond idea was the outgrowth of a demand for a comprehensive protection designed to cover not only the fidelity risks but also other theft perils. Prior to the development of the blanket bond, lending institutions were obliged to buy separate policies covering the fidelity of employees, the risk of burglary and robbery, forgery coverages, and protection involving safe-deposit boxes. To meet the need of financial institutions for a complete and comprehensive coverage in a single contract, the blanket forms were developed.

The broadest and most widely used is the *bankers' blanket bond* (Form 24). It consists of three major divisions: (*a*) the insuring clauses which indicate the risks covered; (*b*) the exclusions indicating the risks not insured or to what degree the coverages are modified; and (c) the discovery period, which covers such features as the notice requirements in event of loss, the reinstatement provisions, and the like. It is the intent of the bond to provide as complete coverage as possible for property of the insured, or property of others held by the insured. It is insured against such acts as embezzlement, burglary, robbery, theft, larceny, and forgery. The bond is not in actual fact an all-risks cover in that it has not been found feasible to cover losses due to clerical errors, carelessness, and incompetence. In addition to the perils noted, the bond covers indemnity for loss of property through damage, destruction, misplacement, and mysterious disappearance.

A special *insurance company blanket bond* is written, similar to the blanket bond protection available for banks. The form for life insurance companies is extended to indemnify the insured against the dishonest acts of general agents, soliciting agents, and servicing agents. The bond contains six insuring clauses: (a) dishonesty of employees, (b) on-premises hazards, (c) in-transit hazards, (d) forgery or alteration, (e) securities coverage, and (f) counterfeit currency. The insuring clauses providing forgery and securities protection may be deleted by endorsement. Coverage may be extended by endorsement to cover loss of property while the property is within the premises of agents.

Liability insurance for crime losses

Policies covering the *liability* of the insured imposed by law upon custodians are included in the crime insurance category because burglary and robbery are among the principal sources of loss. Two specialized forms are: (a) innkeepers' liability and (b) warehousers' liability.

The *innkeepers' liability form* protects the innkeeper in the event of liability for the injury to, destruction of, or loss of property of guests. The policy provides no protection directly for the guests. The liability of an innkeeper is considerably greater than that of a bailee. Originally, innkeepers were held liable for all losses whether by reason of burglary, theft, fire, or negligence, unless the loss was occasioned by negligence or misconduct of the guest or by an act of God or the public enemy.[1] The common-law liability has been modified by statute in all jurisdictions in this country, but to provide protection against the various liabilities that may arise, the hotel and innkeeper's policy is needed. Contractual liability is excluded, with the exception that written agreements made with a guest before a loss do not fall within this exclusion. Losses caused by loss of or damage to automobiles or property in automobiles, as well as property in the insured's custody for laundering or cleaning, or merchandise for exhibition, sale, or delivery by guests, are not covered, except by endorsement.

---

[1] *Wilkins* v. *Earle,* 42 N.Y. 172.

The *warehousers' liability form* covers warehousers and other like bailees for their liability for loss of property in their custody. Burglary and robbery losses from any cause, subject to limited exclusions, are covered. The policy is usually written with a deductible which may be as little as $50 or as much as $10,000 or more. The deductible applies to each occurrence giving rise to one or more claims and not to each claim. The exclusions include war risks, money, securities, and perishable goods. Because of legal requirements, in some states fire and sprinkler leakage losses are not covered, and these risks are in such circumstances insured separately.

OTHER SURETY BONDS

Surety bonds other than contract

A number of miscellaneous surety bonds that involve financial guarantees are not included in the judicial or contract bond classification (see Figure 25–1): (1) depository and miscellaneous, (2) license and permit, and (3) federal. Many of these forms have become standardized to comply with statutory requirements or the needs of private enterprise.

Depository and miscellaneous bonds. *Depository* bonds guarantee that a bank in which funds (usually public) are deposited will pay the funds so deposited on demand. With the advent of the government Federal Deposit Insurance Corporation, such bonds are rarely required today.

In the miscellaneous category are to be found public *warehouse* and *grain elevator* bonds guaranteeing that merchandise described in a storage receipt shall be delivered on presentation of the receipt and in accordance with its terms. *Auctioneer* bonds guarantee to the owner of property entrusted to an auctioneer for sale that the auctioneer will faithfully account for the proceeds. *Lost securities* bonds guarantee that when a valuable instrument is lost, the person to whom a duplicate is issued will reimburse the issuing party for any loss or expense suffered should a claim subsequently be made under the original instrument. *Insurance companies* are required to make a deposit of securities or to file a bond in a sum prescribed by the statutes which guarantee the payment of any liability incurred under policies issued in the state. Statutes frequently require *investment companies,* or firms selling securities or their agents or representatives, to file a bond guaranteeing compliance with the statutory requirements.

State and municipal license and permit bonds. *License and permit* bonds are required by various political subdivisions to guarantee to the public authority that the licensee or permittee will comply with the terms of the license or permit. In some instances bonds are required to extend indemnity to third parties who may be injured. Examples of enterprise's for which license or permit bonds are sometimes required include: blasting operators, cigarette dealers, collection agencies, contractors, detectives, electricians, employment agencies, fumigators, funeral directors, garage and filling station operators, taxi drivers, loan companies, nursery operators, pawnbrokers, plumbers, public accountants, and travel bureau operators.

Federal bonds. The federal government requires the filing of bonds in a wide number of situations. Before a permit is granted to manufacture and distribute certain articles subject to an *internal revenue tax, a bond is filed with guarantees that the principal shall comply with the regulations of the government and pay all taxes in the manner required*. Such bonds are filed by manufacturers and distributors of intoxicating liquors to establish a bonded warehouse, or in connection with the manufacture of cigars and cigarettes.

Some articles destined for *export* may be shipped free of tax, but with the permit necessary to allow such shipments the government requires a bond guaranteeing the amount of the tax and providing for a penalty if the goods are not actually exported or if after export they fraudulently reenter the country.

Under the federal immigration laws, *aliens* not otherwise eligible for admission may be temporarily admitted for medical care or as students, tourists, or visitors. When so admitted, they assume an obligation to leave the country within an agreed period and file a bond guaranteeing departure or guaranteeing that the alien shall not become a public charge.

Customhouse bonds are required when permits are obtained for the temporary importation of dutiable items. These bonds are used particularly in connection with exhibits but are also used to cover works of art, models, and samples that are imported temporarily.

Author and case index

A

Ackerman, Lawrence J., 454 n, 455 n
Act Regulating Insurance upon Lives,
    etc., 224 n
Adams, Ralph R., 629 n
Administrator v. *Hospital of St. Vincent*
    de Paul, 581 n
Albaum, Martin, 800 n
Allen, Everett T., Jr., 334 n, 335 n
Anderson, Dan R., 820 n, 823 n
Andrews, Frederick, 216 n
Atlas Life Insurance Company v.
    Chastin, 292 n

B

Baglini, Norman A., 64 n, 145 n
Barnes, J. Richard, 72 n
Barracato, John, 839 n
Barrett, Robert H., 671 n
Bartelbaugh, Everett T., Jr., 674 n
Bates, Edward, 833 n
Beach, Morrison H., 434 n
Beadles, William T., 289 n
Belth, Joseph M., 120 n, 232 n, 272 n,
    281 n, 385 n
Bernstein, George K., 812 n, 816 n
Bickelhaupt, David L., 49 n, 131 n,
    135 n, 208 n, 403 n, 775 n
Bird v. *St. Paul Fire and Marine*
    Insurance Company, 478 n
Black, Kenneth, Jr., 247 n
Blackwell, Roger, 830 n
Blanchard, Ralph H., 60 n
Blasch, Howard F., 777 n
Bowe, William J., 455 n
Brainard, Calvin H., 672 n
Brocknmier, Warren G., 608 n
Bronson, William, 536 n
Brown, Stephen, 132 n
Brucker, Jack E., 68 n
Buley, R. Carlyle, 41 n
Burkhart, James S., 729 n, 801, 831 n

C

Cahn, William, 41 n
California State Automobile Association
    Inter-Insurance Bureau Appellant
    v. *John R. Maloney, Insurance*
    Commissioner, 662 n
Campbell, Paul A., 325 n
Cannon, Donald J., 41
Cardoza, Benjamin, 356 n
Carper, Jean, 829 n
Cassidy, Anthony A., 842 n
Cheit, Earl M., 409 n
Chicago Railroad Company v. *Jackson,*
    566 n
Chicago, St. Louis & New Orleans R.R.
    Co. v. *Pullman Southern Car Co.,*
    92 n
Christian v. *Griggs,* 575 n
Chubb, Thomas C., 41 n, 536 n
City National Bank v. *Lewis,* 296 n
Clayton, John S., 843 n
Coggs v. Bernard, 550 n
Conant, Roger R., 324 n
Cooper, Robert W., 170 n
Corbett, Richard B., 606 n
Cordtz, Dan, 803 n
Corpus Juris Secundum, 575 n
Crane, Frederick G., 210 n
Crisci v. *Security Insurance Co.,* 190 n
Cummins, J. David, 134 n, 170 n

D

Daenzer, Bernard, 65 n, 605 n
Daniel, Hawthorne, 41 n
Davies v. *Mann,* 574 n
Davis, James V., 68 n
Denari, Edward J., 74 n
Denenberg, Herbert S., 138 n, 218 n
Devers v. *Scranton,* 580 n
Dickerson, O. D., 348 n
Diehl, Walter, 828 n
Dilworth, A. A., 760 n

Subject index

A

Accidental death benefits, 308–11, 396–97
Acts of God, 7
Actuaries, 227–28
  mortality tables, 238
Adjustable life insurance, 284–85
Agency
  American system, 132–33
  versus direct selling, 130–31
  direct-writing system, 132–33
  exclusive, 132–35
  independent, 132
Agency law principles, 100–101
  agreement, 100
  apparent authority, 101
  estoppel, 100
  ratification, 100–101
  waiver, 100
Agent; *see* Insurance agent
Agreement of Guiding Principles (1963),
    507
Aid to dependent children, 408
Air transportation insurance, 141
All-lines insurance, 48, 50, 772, 797–801
  combination personal-lines package
      policy, 801
  life insurance, 798–801
  property-liability insurers, 797–98
All-risk policies, 778–79
American Agency System, 132
American Annuity Table, 241
American Association of University
    Teachers of Insurance, 125
American Bureau of Shipping, 547
American College of Life Underwriters,
    125
American Foreign Insurance Association,
    837
American Hull Insurance Syndicate, 536
American Institute of Marine
    Underwriters, 537
American Institute for Property and
    Liability Underwriters, 125
American Insurance Association, 148
American Risk and Insurance Association,
    125

American Society of Chartered Life
    Underwriters, 126
Annuity, 228, 259
  amount of payment, 323–26
  contract conditions, 326–27
  cost, 318–19
  deferred, 322
  definition, 315–16
  endowment, 323
  group; *see* Group annuities
  group variable, 325
  growth, 316–17
  guaranteed refund, 321
  immediate, 322
  installment refund, 321
  joint, 321–22
  life, 316
  method of purchase, 323
  mortality tables, 240–41
  retirement, 322
  single life, 322
  split-life insurance, 281–82
  straight or pure, 320–21
  tax sheltered, 342
  variable, 323–25
Annuity Table for 1949, 241
Appleton Rule, 204
Arson, 838–40
Associated Factory Mutual Insurance
    Companies, 112
Atomic Energy Commission, 810
Attractive nuisance, 577
Automatic sprinkler systems, 153, 498
  leakage insurance, 861–62
Automobile insurance, 141, 154–55
  accident prevention, 676
  age-sex-marital factor, 688–89
  assigned risk plans, 662–63
  basic coverages, 681–82
  basic policy forms, 682–83
  business auto policy (BAP), 683,
      691–708
  casualty coverages, 681–82
  classification of automobiles, 686–87
  collision coverage, 701–3
  compulsory liability legislation, 660–62
  costs, 651–53

*This book has been set in 10 and 9 point Times
Roman, leaded 2 points. Part numbers and
titles are 18 point Helvetica Bold and
chapter numbers and titles are 14 point
Helvetica Bold. The size of the type page is
28 by 46 picas.*